WTO Law and Policy

WTO Law and Policy presents an authoritative account of the emergence of the World Trade Organization (WTO) and the basic principles and institutional law of the WTO. It explores how political economy has shaped the WTO's legal philosophy and policies, and provides insights into how international trade law at the WTO has developed.

This textbook examines the legal obligations of the Member States of the WTO under the multilateral trade agreements, the legal remedies available under the rules-based dispute settlement system, and incorporates the most relevant case laws from the WTO's jurisprudence. It outlines several key contemporary issues which the WTO faces as well as areas that need reforming. Each chapter covers a specific topic in relation to the framework and functionality of the WTO, with particular focus on the legal aspects of the multilateral trade order. The book is guided by the legal pronouncements of the Dispute Settlement Body (Panels and Appellate Body), and the commentaries on the interpretation of the provisions of the covered agreements.

This book is ideal for all students studying international trade law, including those coming to international law, international trade law, and WTO law for the first time.

Jae Sundaram is a reader in international trade and maritime law at the University of Buckingham, UK.

WTO Law and Policy
A Political Economy Approach

Jae Sundaram

LONDON AND NEW YORK

Cover image: byheaven

First published 2022
by Routledge
2 Park Square, Milton Park, Abingdon, Oxon OX14 4RN

and by Routledge
605 Third Avenue, New York, NY 10158

Routledge is an imprint of the Taylor & Francis Group, an informa business

© 2022 Jae Sundaram

The right of Jae Sundaram to be identified as author of this work has been asserted in accordance with sections 77 and 78 of the Copyright, Designs and Patents Act 1988.

All rights reserved. No part of this book may be reprinted or reproduced or utilised in any form or by any electronic, mechanical, or other means, now known or hereafter invented, including photocopying and recording, or in any information storage or retrieval system, without permission in writing from the publishers.

Trademark notice: Product or corporate names may be trademarks or registered trademarks, and are used only for identification and explanation without intent to infringe.

British Library Cataloguing-in-Publication Data
A catalogue record for this book is available from the British Library

Library of Congress Cataloging-in-Publication Data
Names: Sundaram, Jae, author.
Title: WTO law and policy : a political economy approach / Jae Sundaram.
Description: Abingdon, Oxon ; New York, NY : Routledge, 2022. | Includes bibliographical references and index.
Identifiers: LCCN 2021050793 | ISBN 9780367028169 (hardback) | ISBN 9780367028176 (paperback) | ISBN 9780367028183 (ebook)
Subjects: LCSH: World Trade Organization. | Foreign trade regulation. | LCGFT: Textbooks.
Classification: LCC K4610 .S86 2022 | DDC 343.08/7—dc23/eng/20211206
LC record available at https://lccn.loc.gov/2021050793

ISBN: 978-0-367-02816-9 (hbk)
ISBN: 978-0-367-02817-6 (pbk)
ISBN: 978-0-367-02818-3 (ebk)

DOI: 10.4324/9780367028183

Typeset in Baskerville
by Apex CoVantage, LLC

Contents

Preface — xviii
List of abbreviations — xix
List of abbreviated cases — xxii

PART I
Trade Theory, Founding of the WTO, and Key Principles — 1

1 Trade Theory and the World Trade Organization — 3

Learning Objectives 3
1. *Introduction* 4
2. *International Trade Theories* 4
   2.1 *Mercantilism* 5
3. *Pre-Classical Theories* 7
   3.1 *Pre-Classical: Physiocrats* 7
4. *Classical Economics: Adam Smith* 9
   4.1 *Invisible Hand* 10
   4.2 *The Division of Labour* 10
   4.3 *Absolute Advantage and Factors of Production* 11
5. *Classical Economics: David Ricardo* 11
   5.1 *Gold Standard* 12
   5.2 *Theory of Diminishing Returns – The Corn Model* 13
   5.3 *Theory of Comparative Advantage and Foreign Trade* 14
6. *Classical Economics: Karl Marx* 16
   6.1 *Criticism of Classical Economics* 17
   6.2 *Historical Materialism and Economic Theory* 17
   6.3 *Labour Theory of Value* 19
   6.4 *Theory of Rent, Money, and Surplus Value* 19
7. *Liberalism* 21
8. *The Keynesian Economic Thought* 22
   8.1 *Historical Background and Writings* 22
   8.2 *Keynes and Classical Economic Thought* 22
   8.3 *The Theories* 23

8.4 Keynes's Legacy 25
9. Summary 26

2 The World Trade Organization 33

Learning Objectives 33
1. Introduction: Trade in the Pre- and Post-World War II Era 34
2. Origins of the GATT/WTO: Road out of Bretton Woods 35
3. Evolution: The GATT to the WTO 37
    3.1 Negotiating Rounds of the GATT 37
    3.2 The Uruguay Round of Negotiations 39
    3.3 The Marrakesh Agreement Establishing the WTO 41
4. The Law of the WTO 42
    4.1 Sources of WTO Law 43
    4.2 WTO Law and International Law 45
    4.3 WTO Law and General Principles of Law 46
        4.3.1 Due Process 47
        4.3.2 Good Faith (Bona Fide) 49
        4.3.3 Estoppel and Res Judicata 51
5. Mandate of the WTO 53
    5.1 Objectives of the WTO 53
    5.2 Functions of the WTO 55
        5.2.1 Implementation and Administration of Trade Agreements 55
        5.2.2 Providing a Forum for Trade Negotiations 56
        5.2.3 Dispute Settlement 56
        5.2.4 Trade Policy Review 57
    5.3 Ministerial Conference 57
    5.4 General Council and Meetings 58
6. Summary 59

3 Dispute Settlement at the WTO 69

Learning Objectives 70
1. Introduction 70
2. Dispute Settlement in the GATT 71
3. Dispute Settlement in the WTO 75
4. Theoretical/Legal Framework and Jurisdiction of the DSU 76
    4.1 Theoretical/Legal Framework 76
    4.2 Jurisdiction: Exclusive Forum for Adjudication 78
5. Recourse to WTO Dispute Settlement 80
    5.1 Legal Basis of Dispute 82
    5.2 Categories of Claims 83
        5.2.1 Violation Complaints 83
        5.2.2 Non-Violation Complaints 84
        5.2.3 Situation Complaints 85

6. The DSB and Stages of the Dispute Settlement Process 85
   6.1 Consultation 86
      6.1.1 Nature and General Features of the Consultation Phase 88
      6.1.2 Failure to Consult and Period of Consultation 89
      6.1.3 Plurilateral and Private Consultations 90
   6.2 Panel: Request, Terms of Reference, and Establishment 90
   6.3 Multiple Complaints and Joint Panels 93
      6.3.1 The Panel: Time Scales and Working Procedures 93
      6.3.2 Burden of Proof 95
      6.3.3 Panel Report 97
   6.4 The Appellate Body 98
      6.4.1 Historical Background 98
      6.4.2 Appellate Body: Nature and Composition 100
   6.5 Appellate Review 101
      6.5.1 Structure, Scope, and Timeframe 101
      6.5.2 Review of New Issues, and Receipt of New Evidence and Arguments 104
      6.5.3 Scope and Remit of the Appellate Review Process 105
7. Other Features of the WTO Dispute Settlement 106
   7.1 Amicus Curiae Briefs Before the Dispute Settlement 106
   7.2 Other Entities of the Dispute Settlement 109
8. Implementation and Compliance Review 109
   8.1 'Extension' Under Article 21.3 DSU 110
   8.2 Compliance Review Under Article 21.5 DSU 111
   8.3 Remedies Under Article 22 DSU 113
9. Developing Countries and the WTO Dispute Settlement 114
   9.1 Special and Differential Treatment 115
   9.2 Special Rules for Developing Country Member States 115
   9.3 Special Rules, Decision of 5 April 1966 116
   9.4 Special Rules for Least Developed Country Member States 116
   9.5 Legal Assistance for Developing Country Member States 116
10. Summary 117

4 Non-Discrimination: Most-Favoured Nation Treatment 138

Learning Objectives 138
1. Introduction 139
2. The Most-Favoured Nation Obligation Under GATT 139
   2.1 MFN Treatment Obligation: Origins 139
   2.2 Nature of MFN Treatment Obligation: Article I:1 141
   2.3 Interpretation of MFN Obligation: Likeness 144
      2.3.1 Likeness Under the GATT Era 145
      2.3.2 Likeness Under the WTO Era 146
   2.4 MFN Obligation and Special and Differential Treatment 147

        2.4.1 Special and Differential Treatment Under GATT 147
        2.4.2 Special and Differential Treatment Under GATT 1994 149
        2.4.3 Additional Preferential Treatment Vis-à-vis *Enabling Clause 151*
    2.5 Exception to MFN: Regional Integration, Quotas, and Waivers 152
        2.5.1 Regional Integration (GATT Article XXIV) 152
        2.5.2 Quotas 152
        2.5.3 Waivers 153
3. *The Most-Favoured Nation Obligation Under GATS 153*
    3.1 Nature of the MFN Treatment Obligation: Article II:1 of GATS 154
        3.1.1 Measures Covered Under Article II:1 155
    3.2 'Like' Service and 'Like' Service Suppliers 156
        3.2.1 Treatment 'No Less Favourable' 157
    3.3 Derogation From MFN Obligation Under GATS 159
4. *Summary 160*

5   Non-Discrimination: National Treatment   167

Learning Objectives 167
1. *Introduction 168*
2. *Origins and Rationale for National Treatment 168*
3. *National Treatment Provisions of GATT 170*
    3.1 Article III: Objectives 170
    3.2 Direct and Indirect; De Jure *and* De Facto *Discrimination 172*
    3.3 Article III:2, First Sentence: Fiscal Measures 172
        3.3.1 Article III:2 Like Products 173
        3.3.2 Article III:2 Taxed 'In Excess Of' 174
        3.3.3 The 'Aims and Effects' Test 174
    3.4 Article III:2, Second Sentence 175
        3.4.1 Directly Competitive or Substitutable 176
        3.4.2 Not Similarly Taxed 177
        3.4.3 Applied so as to Afford Protection 177
    3.5 Regulatory Measures – Article III:4 178
        3.5.1 Law, Regulation, or Requirement Affecting the Internal Sale . . . 178
        3.5.2 Domestic Product Needs to Be 'Like' . . . 180
        3.5.3 Afforded Less Favourable Treatment . . . 180
4. *National Treatment Obligation Under GATS 182*
    4.1 National Treatment Obligation – Article XVII:1 183
    4.2 Violation of National Treatment Obligation 185
        4.2.1 Undertaking of Specific Commitments 185
        4.2.2 Measures Affecting Trade in Services 186
        4.2.3 Like Services and Service Suppliers 186
        4.2.4 Treatment No Less Favourable 188
5. *Summary 191*

PART II
General Exceptions, Non-Tariff Barriers, Subsidies, CVDs, and AD Measures   197

6   General Exceptions Under GATT   199

Learning Objectives   199
1. Introduction   200
2. General Exceptions Under GATT 1994   200
   - 2.1 Drafting History and the Chapeau to Article XX   201
   - 2.2 Article XX of GATT: Remit, Nature, and Function   203
   - 2.3 Two-Tier Test Under Article XX and Burden of Proof   205
   - 2.4 Particular Exceptions Under Article XX: (a), (b), (d), (g)   206
     - 2.4.1 Exceptions Under Article XX(a): Public Morals   207
     - 2.4.2 Exceptions Under Article XX(b): Protection of Human, Animal, or Plant Life or Health   210
       - 2.4.2.1 The First Element: Design and Structure   211
       - 2.4.2.2 The Second Element: 'Necessity'   212
       - 2.4.2.3 Burden of Proof   214
     - 2.4.3 Exceptions Under Article XX(d): Secure Compliance With Laws or Regulations   215
       - 2.4.3.1 The First Element: Design   216
       - 2.4.3.2 The Second Element: Secure Compliance   217
       - 2.4.3.3 The Third Element: Necessity   219
     - 2.4.4 Exceptions Under Article XX(g): Conservation of Exhaustible Natural Resources   220
       - 2.4.4.1 The First Element: 'Conservation of Exhaustible Natural Resources'   221
       - 2.4.4.2 The Second Element: 'Relating To'   223
       - 2.4.4.3 The Third Element: 'Made Effective in Conjunction With'   225
     - 2.4.5 Exceptions Under Article XX(j): Acquisition or Distribution of Products in Short Supply   227
     - 2.4.6 Exceptions Under Article XX(e) and XX(f)   229
3. Summary   229

7   Tariff and Non-Tariff Barriers   236

Learning Objectives   236
1. Introduction   237
2. Tariffs and Customs Rules: The Political Economy   238
   - 2.1 GATT/WTO Tariff Negotiations   238
   - 2.2 Negotiations and Reduction of Customs Duties   238
     - 2.2.1 Tariff Negotiations and Article XXVIII bis   238
     - 2.2.2 Protection of Tariff Concessions: ODCs   240
   - 2.3 The Schedules of Concession and Classification of Goods   244

        2.4 Types of Customs Duties/Tariffs 245
            2.4.1 Ad Valorem and Non-Ad Valorem Tariffs 245
            2.4.2 Tariffs: Bound, Applied, and TRQ 246
        2.5 The DSB's Interpretation of Schedules of Commitments 247
    3. Customs Duties and Other Charges on Exports 250
        3.1 Export Duties: History and Political Economy 250
        3.2 Rules on Export Duties 251
        3.3 Debates and the Proposal for Change 253
    4. Non-Tariff Barriers/Measures: NTBs 254
        4.1 The Political Economy of NTBs: GATT and WTO 254
        4.2 Quantitative Restrictions: Rules and Types 255
            4.2.1 The Scope of 'Restriction' 257
            4.2.2 Quantifying the Limiting Effect of the Measure at Issue 259
            4.2.3 De Facto Prohibitions or Restrictions 259
        4.3 Exceptions to Article XI:1 260
    5. Customs-Related NTBs 261
        5.1 Agreement on Customs Valuation 261
        5.2 Agreement on Import Licensing Procedures 263
        5.3 Agreement on Pre-Shipment Inspection 264
        5.4 Agreement on Rules of Origin 265
    6. Summary 266

8 Economic Emergency Measures   275

Learning Objectives 275
1. Introduction 276
2. The Political Economy of Safeguards 277
3. The Safeguard Regime Under GATT/WTO 278
    3.1 Formation of Safeguard Measures in the GATT and WTO 278
    3.2 Uruguay Round and Beyond 279
4. Article XIX GATT and the Safeguard Agreement 280
    4.1 Safeguard Agreement 280
        4.1.1 Investigation and Provisional Application 282
        4.1.2 Increased Imports and 'Unforeseen Development' 283
        4.1.3 Determination of Injury 284
            4.1.3.1 Serious Injury and Threat of Serious
                     Injury 285
            4.1.3.2 Factors to Be Considered 286
            4.1.3.3 Identifying the Relevant Domestic Industry 287
            4.1.3.4 Causation and Non-Attribution 288
5. Special Safeguard Measures Under WTO Agreements 289
    5.1 Special Safeguard Measures Under Agreement on Agriculture 290
    5.2 Emergency Safeguard Measures Under GATS 291
6. Balance-of-Payments Measures 292

    6.1 Political Economy of BOP Measures and the GATT 292
    6.2 Balance-of-Payment Measures Under GATT 1994 294
        6.2.1 Nature and Scope of Balance-of-Payment Measures 294
    6.3 Balance-of-Payment Measures Under GATS 298
7. Summary 299

9 Subsidies and Countervailing Measures   305

Learning Objectives 306
1. Introduction 306
    1.1 Political Economy of Subsidies and Subsidised Trade 307
    1.2 The Concept of Subsidy 308
        1.2.1 Financial Contribution 309
            1.2.1.1 Direct Transfer of Funds 311
            1.2.1.2 Foregone or Not Collected Revenue 313
            1.2.1.3 Purchase of Goods or Provision of Goods and Services 316
        1.2.2 Benefit Conferred 317
        1.2.3 Specificity of the Subsidy 320
        1.2.4 'Government or Public Body' 323
2. Regulation of Specific Subsidies Under the SCM Agreement 325
    2.1 Prohibited Subsidies 325
        2.1.1 Export Subsidies 326
        2.1.2 Import Substitution Subsidies 330
    2.2 Actionable Subsidies 331
        2.2.1 Causing Injury to Domestic Industry 332
            2.2.1.1 Like Products 332
            2.2.1.2 Domestic Industry 333
            2.2.1.3 Injury 333
            2.2.1.4 Causation 337
        2.2.2 Subsidies Causing Nullification, Impairment, or Prejudice 337
        2.2.3 Market Definition 339
        2.2.4 Displacement and Impediment to Imports 341
        2.2.5 Causation and Article 6.3 342
            2.2.5.1 Causation, the 'But for' Approach 344
    2.3 Actionable Subsidies and Special Remedies 346
    2.4 Non-Actionable Subsidies 348
3. Imposition of Countervailing Duties 348
    3.1 Procedures for Investigation and Imposition of CVDs 349
    3.2 Conduct of CVD Investigation 351
        3.2.1 Concluding the Investigation 354
    3.3 Imposition and Collection of CVDs 355
        3.3.1 Duration and Review of CVDs 357
            3.3.1.1 Administrative Review 357
            3.3.1.2 Sunset Review 359

xii   Contents

        3.3.1.3 *Judicial Review* 360
    3.3.2 *Institutional and Procedural Provisions* 361
4. Special and Differential Treatment for Developing Country Member States 361
5. Subsidies Provisions in Other WTO Agreements 362
    5.1 *Agreement on Agriculture* 362
    5.2 *GATT* 365
    5.3 *TRIMs Agreement* 365
6. Summary 366

10 Dumping and Anti-Dumping Measures   377

Learning Objectives 378
1. Introduction 378
2. WTO Law on Dumping 379
    2.1 *History and Political Economy of Dumping* 379
    2.2 *Dumping: Types and Practice* 382
3. The Anti-Dumping Legal Framework of the WTO 382
    3.1 *Article VI of GATT* 383
    3.2 *The Anti-Dumping Agreement* 384
    3.3 *Investigation of Dumping* 385
        3.3.1 *Adequacy of Evidence* 386
        3.3.2 *Evidence and Due Process* 387
    3.4 *Determination of Dumping: Normal Value, Export Price* 388
        3.4.1 *Normal Value, Export Price, and 'Like Product'* 389
        3.4.2 *Zeroing* 393
        3.4.3 *Non-Market Economies* 397
    3.5 *Determination of Injury to Domestic Industry* 397
        3.5.1 *Domestic Industry* 398
        3.5.2 *Injury* 399
        3.5.3 *Material Injury* 400
        3.5.4 *Threat of Material Injury* 403
    3.6 *Causation* 405
4. Imposition of Dumping 406
    4.1 *Provisional AD Measures* 406
    4.2 *Price Undertakings* 407
    4.3 *Imposition and Collection of AD Duties* 407
    4.4 *Duration and Review of AD Duties* 409
    4.5 *Anti-Circumvention of AD Duties* 410
5. Institutional and Procedural Requirements of AD Agreement 411
    5.1 *Dispute Settlement and Review of AD Measures* 411
    5.2 *The Committee on Anti-Dumping Practices* 413
6. Special and Differential Treatment for Developing Country Members 413
7. Summary 414

PART III
GATS, TRIPS, TBT, and SPS Agreements   423

11 Trade in Services   425

Learning Objectives 426
1. Introduction 426
   1.1 Political Economy of GATS: The Uruguay Round of Negotiations 427
2. Objectives and Obligations of GATS 430
   2.1 Scope, Definition, and Services Covered 431
   2.2 Modes of Supply 433
   2.3 The Relationship Between GATT and GATS 435
3. General Obligations and Disciplines 436
   3.1 Most-Favoured Nation (MFN) Treatment Obligation 436
   3.2 Transparency Obligations 436
   3.3 Domestic Regulation 437
4. Specific Commitments 439
   4.1 Market Access Under GATS 440
   4.2 National Treatment Under GATS 443
      4.2.1 Establishing Violation of NT Under GATS 444
      4.2.2 Like Services or Service Suppliers 445
      4.2.3 Treatment No Less Favourable 447
   4.3 Market Access Vis-à-vis National Treatment 448
   4.4 Additional Commitments 449
   4.5 Withdrawal of Commitments 450
5. General Exceptions Under GATS 450
   5.1 Article XIV: The Two-Tier Analysis 452
      5.1.1 Article XIV: The Necessity Test 453
   5.2 Chapeau of Article XIV 454
   5.3 Economic Integration Exception (Article IV) 455
   5.4 Derogation From MFN Obligations 455
6. Specific Rules for Telecommunications and Financial Services 455
   6.1 Telecommunications 455
   6.2 Financial Services 458
      6.2.1 Prudential Carve-Out 459
      6.2.2 Understanding on Commitments in Financial Services 459
7. Security Exceptions Under GATS 460
   7.1 Article XIV bis of GATS 460
8. Summary 461

12 Intellectual Property Rights   468

Learning Objectives 469
1. Introduction 469
2. Political Economy of TRIPS 470

        2.1 Uruguay Round: Forum Shifting From WIPO to GATT 471
    3. Intellectual Property Rights: Historical Origins 472
        3.1 Economic Theories and Private Rights 472
        3.2 Economic Analysis of Intellectual Property Laws 475
    4. Objectives and Scope of the TRIPS Agreement 478
        4.1 Structure and Basic Principles of the TRIPS Agreement 480
            4.1.1 Intellectual Property 481
        4.2 TRIPS Agreement and WIPO Conventions 482
        4.3 The NT and MFN Treatment Obligations 483
        4.4 Exhaustion of Intellectual Property Rights 485
    5. Rights Protected Under the TRIPS Agreement 486
        5.1 Copyright and Related Rights 486
            5.1.1 TRIPS Agreement and the Berne Convention 1971 487
            5.1.2 Copyright Protection Under TRIPS 487
        5.2 Trademarks 490
        5.3 Geographical Indication 496
        5.4 Patents 499
            5.4.1 Compulsory Licencing 501
            5.4.2 TRIPS Flexibilities for Public Health Purposes 504
        5.5 Layout Designs of Integrated Circuits 505
    6. Enforcement of Intellectual Property Rights 506
        6.1 General Principles 506
        6.2 Civil and Administrative Procedures and Remedies 506
        6.3 Provisional Measures and Border Measures 508
        6.4 Criminal Procedures 508
        6.5 Acquisition and Maintenance of Intellectual Property Rights 508
    7. Institutional Provisions of the TRIPS Agreement 509
        7.1 Council for TRIPS 509
        7.2 Transparency and Dispute Settlement 509
    8. Special Rules for Developing Country and LDC Members 510
        8.1 Transitional Periods 510
        8.2 Technical Assistance and Transfer of Technology 511
    9. Summary 511

13 Technical Barriers to Trade: TBT Agreement   524

Learning Objectives 525
1. Introduction: The Role of TBT and SPS Agreements 525
2. Scope and Application of TBT Agreement 526
    2.1 Application of TBT Agreement 529
        2.1.1 Principal Actors Under the TBT Agreement 529
        2.1.2 Temporal Scope of the TBT Agreement 529
    2.2 TBT Agreement and Other WTO Agreements 530
        2.2.1 The GATT 1994 530

                2.2.2 The Agreement on Government Procurement and the SPS Agreement 532
        3. Substantive Provisions of the TBT Agreement 532
                3.1 MFN and NT Treatment Obligations 533
                        3.1.1 Technical Regulations 534
                        3.1.2 Like Products 537
                        3.1.3 Treatment No Less Favourable 538
                3.2 'Least Trade Restrictive' 542
                        3.2.1 'Legitimate Objective' 543
                        3.2.2 'Not More Trade Restrictive Than Necessary' 544
                3.3 The Obligation to Use International Standards 548
                        3.3.1 'Existence of Relevant International Standards' 549
                        3.3.2 International Standards 'As a Basis' for Domestic Standards 550
                        3.3.3 'Ineffective and Inappropriate International Standards' 551
        4. Other Substantive Provisions of the TBT Agreement 552
                4.1 Equivalence and Mutual Recognition 552
                4.2 Performance Requirements 553
                4.3 Transparency and Notification 553
                4.4 Special and Differential Treatment 555
        5. Institutional Provisions of the TBT Agreement 556
                5.1 TBT Committee 557
                5.2 Dispute Settlement and TBT Agreement 557
                5.3 Technical Assistance 558
        6. Summary 558

14 Technical Barriers to Trade: SPS Agreement   566

        Learning Objectives 567
        1. Introduction: The Role of SPS Agreements 567
        2. Scope and Application of the SPS Agreement 567
                2.1 Measures to Which SPS Agreement Applies 568
                2.2 The Temporal Scope of the SPS Agreement 571
                2.3 SPS Agreement and Other WTO Agreements 571
                        2.3.1 The GATT 1994 571
                        2.3.2 The TBT Agreement 572
        3. Substantive Provisions of the SPS Agreement 573
                3.1 Basic Principles 573
                        3.1.1 The Right to Take SPS Measures 573
                        3.1.2 'Only to the Extent Necessary' 574
                        3.1.3 Scientific Basis for SPS Measures 574
                        3.1.4 No Arbitrary or Unjustifiable Discrimination 578
                3.2 International Standards and Harmonisation 579
                3.3 Obligation to Assess Risk 581
                        3.3.1 Risk Assessment 581

xvi *Contents*

   3.3.2 Based on Risk Assessment 583
   3.3.3 Appropriate Level of Protection 584
   3.3.4 'Not More Trade Restrictive Than Required' 586
  3.4 The Precautionary Principle and SPS Agreement 587
   3.4.1 Where SPS Measures Are Adopted as a Precaution 588
   3.4.2 Maintaining Provisional SPM Measures Based on Article 5.7 590
 4. Other Substantive Provisions of the SPS Agreement 590
  4.1 Recognition of Foreign SPS Policy and Measures 591
  4.2 Adaptation of Regional Conditions 591
  4.3 Control Inspection and Approval Procedures 593
  4.4 Transparency and Notifications 594
  4.5 Special and Differential Treatment 595
 5. Institutional Provisions of the SPS Agreement 596
  5.1 SPS Committee 596
  5.2 Dispute Settlement 597
   5.2.1 Scientific Experts 597
   5.2.2 Standard of Review 598
  5.3 Technical Assistance 599
 6. Summary 600

PART IV
RTAs, Environment, Human Rights, and Reform of the WTO   607

15 Regional Trade Agreements   609

Learning Objectives 609
 1. Introduction 609
 2. History of RTAs: Regionalism 610
 3. Political Economy of RTAs 613
 4. Article XXIV of the GATT: Customs Unions and FTA Exceptions 614
  4.1 Customs Unions 615
   4.1.1 Conditions for the Formation of a Customs Union 618
  4.2 Free-Trade Areas 618
  4.3 Interim Agreements 619
 5. Special Rules for Developing Country Member States 620
 6. Obligation to Notify the CRTA 620
 7. RTAs and Dispute Settlement at the WTO 621
 8. Emergence of Mega-RTAs 624
 9. Summary 625

16 Environment, Human Rights, and Trade   629

Learning Objectives 629
 1. Introduction 629

2. GATT, the WTO, and the Environment 631
3. Sustainable Development and the WTO 633
4. Jurisprudence on Environmental Issues 635
    4.1 US – Tuna I (Mexico) 635
    4.2 US – Tuna II (Mexico) 636
    4.3 US – Shrimp 637
    4.4 EC – Approval and Marketing of Biotech Products 637
5. RTAs, MEAs, and the Multilateral Trading System 638
6. Trade, Human Rights, and the WTO 640
    6.1 Human Rights Obligations of Member States 642
    6.2 Human Rights Vis-à-vis WTO Law 643
    6.3 WTO Agreements and Human Rights 644
        6.3.1 TRIPS Agreement: Private Rights, Human Rights, and Access to Medicines 644
        6.3.2 GATS Agreement: Trade in Services and Right to Work 644
        6.3.3 Human Rights and the DSU 646
7. Summary 648

17 The Case for a Reform of the WTO   655

Learning Objectives 655
1. Introduction 655
2. The Doha Round: The Failure of Multilateral Negotiations 656
3. WTO Working Practice: Consensus-Driven Decision-Making, SDT 657
4. The Reform of the DSB 658
    4.1 Appointment of Appellate Body Members 659
    4.2 EU's Solution: The MPIA 659
5. The Pandemic and the WTO's Response 660
6. Summary 661

Index   664

Preface

While researching for my monograph, which was published in 2018, the thought of writing a book on GATT 1994 emerged. This idea was to gradually develop into a strong desire to pen a textbook on WTO laws. Writing a textbook, whatever the subject be, is daunting, due to the enormity of the task, and I felt it would never come to pass. This journey, right from the moment I submitted my proposal with the publishers (Taylor & Francis), the brief period of suspension of work due to the COVID-19 pandemic, and to the moment of finalising the first draft of the finished work, has been a true learning curve.

A big thanks to the WTO, as I benefitted enormously from the legal information available on its webpages, which includes the reports of the Panels, and Appellate Body, analytical index, and other official documentation. I would like to take this opportunity to express my gratitude to Prof Indira Carr for her words of encouragement when I set out on the journey, and my good friend Dr Francis Grimal, who was a great source of support throughout this period. I would also like to express my sincerest thanks to Taylor & Francis for all the support, and importantly for giving me the necessary extension when the pandemic hit, to enable me to complete the work to a revised deadline. Finally, if there are any errors and omissions in this book, they are entirely mine.

Jae Sundaram
Buckingham, UK
August 2021

Abbreviations

AB	Appellate Body
ACP	African, Caribbean, and Pacific
ACWL	Advisory Centre on WTO Law
AD	Anti-Dumping
AD	Agreement Anti-Dumping Agreement
AfCFTA	African Continental Free Trade Area
AFTA	Association of Southeast Asian Nations Free Trade Area
AG	Agreement on Agriculture
ANZCERTA	Australia – New Zealand Closer Economic Relations Agreement
ASEAN	Association of Southeast Asian Nations
ATC	Agreement on Textiles and Clothing
BOP	Balance of Payment
CARICOM	Common Market of the Caribbean
CJEU	Court of Justice of the European Union
COMESA	Common Market of the Eastern and Southern Africa
CPTPP	Comprehensive and Progressive Agreement for Trans-Pacific Partnership
CRTA	Committee on Regional Trade Agreements
CTD	Committee on Trade and Development
CTE	Committee on Trade and Environment
CTG	Council for Trade in Goods
CTS	Council for Trade in Services
CVD	Countervailing Duty
DDG	Deputy Director-General
DG	Director-General
DSB	Dispute Settlement Body
DSU	Understanding on Rules and Procedures Governing the Settlement of Disputes (also referred to as the Dispute Settlement Understanding)
EC	European Community
ECJ	European Court of Justice
ECOSOC	UN Economic and Social Council
ECOWAS	Economic Community of West African States
ECT	European Community Treaty
EEA	European Economic Area
EFTA	European Free Trade Association
EU	European Union
FTA	Free Trade Area

GATS	General Agreement on Trade in Services
GATT	General Agreement on Tariffs and Trade
GNP	Gross National Product
GPA	Government Procurement Agreement
GSP	Generalised System of Preferences
HS	Harmonised System [International Convention on the Harmonized Commodity Description and Coding System]
ICITO	Interim Commission for the International Trade Organization
ICJ	International Court of Justice
IMF	International Monitory Fund
IP	Intellectual Property
ITA	Agreement on Trade in Information Technology Products
ITO	International Trade Organization
LDC	Least Developed Country
LFN	Least Favoured Nation
MERCOSUR	Mercado del Sur (free-trade area between Argentina, Brazil, Paraguay, and Uruguay)
MFN	Most-Favoured Nation
NAFTA	North American Free Trade Agreement
NAMA	Non-Agricultural Market Access
NGO	Non-Governmental Organisation
NPR-PPMs	Non-Product Related Processes and Production Methods
NT	National Treatment
ODCs	Other Duties and Charges
OECD	Organisation for Economic Co-operation and Development
OIE	World Organization for Animal Health
PIL	Public International Law
PPM	Process and Production Method
PTAs	Preferential Trade Agreements
QRs	Quantitative Restrictions
RCEP	Regional Comprehensive Economic Partnership
RTAs	Regional Trade Agreements
SADC	South African Development Community
SCM	Subsidies and Countervailing Measures
SDGs	Sustainable Development Goals
SMEs	Small and Medium-Size Enterprises
SPS	Sanitary and Phytosanitary Measures
SPS Agreement	Agreement on the Application of Sanitary and Phytosanitary Measures
SSG	Special Safeguards
STDF	Standards and Trade Development Facility
TBT	Technical Barriers to Trade
TBT Agreement	Agreement on Technical Barriers to Trade
TFA	Agreement on Trade Facilitation
TNC	Trade Negotiations Committee
TPRB	Trade Policy Review Body
TPRM	Trade Policy Review Mechanism
TRIPS	Trade-Related Aspects of Intellectual Property Rights

TRIPS Agreement	Agreement on Trade-Related Aspects of Intellectual Property Rights
TRIPS Council	Council for Trade-Related Aspects of Intellectual Property Rights
TRQ	Tariff Rate Quota
TTIP	Transatlantic Trade and Investment Partnership
UN	United Nations
UNCTAD	United Nations Conference on Trade and Development
URAA	Uruguay Round Agreement on Agriculture
USMCA	United States-Mexico-Canada Agreement
VCLT	Vienna Convention on the Law of Treaties
VERs	Voluntary Export Restraints
WB	World Bank
WCO	World Customs Organization
WHO	World Health Organization
WIPO	World Intellectual Property Organization
WTO	World Trade Organization
WTO Agreement	Marrakesh Agreement Establishing the World Trade Organization

Abbreviated Cases

WTO: Panel and Appellate Body Reports

Short Title	Full Cause Title and Citation
Argentina – Ceramic Tiles	Panel Report, *Argentina – Definitive Anti-Dumping Measures on Imports of Ceramic Floor Tiles from Italy*, WT/DS189/R (28 September 2001) (adopted 5 November 2001).
Argentina – Financial Services	Appellate Body Report, *Argentina – Measures Relating to Trade in Goods and Services*, WT/DS453/AB/R (14 April 2016) (adopted 9 May 2016).
Argentina – Financial Services	Panel Report, *Argentina – Measures Relating to Trade in Goods and Services*, WT/DS453/R (30 September 2015) (adopted 9 May 2016, as modified by Appellate Body Report WT/DS453/AB/R).
Argentina – Footwear (EC)	Appellate Body Report, *Argentina – Safeguard Measures on Imports of Footwear*, WT/DS121/AB/R (14 December 1999) (adopted 12 January 2000).
Argentina – Footwear (EC)	Panel Report, *Argentina – Safeguard Measures on Imports of Footwear*, WT/DS121/R (25 June 1999) (adopted 12 January 2000, as modified by Appellate Body Report WT/DS121/AB/R).
Argentina – Hides and Leather	Panel Report, *Argentina – Measures Affecting the Export of Bovine Hides and Import of Finished Leather*, WT/DS155/R (19 December 2000) (adopted 16 February 2001).
Argentina – Hides and Leather (Article 21.3(c))	Article 21.3(c) Arbitration Report, *Argentina – Measures Affecting the Export of Bovine Hides and Import of Finished Leather*, WT/DS155/10 (31 August 2001).
Argentina – Import Measures	Appellate Body Report, *Argentina – Measures Affecting the Importation of Goods*, WT/DS438/AB/R; WT/DS444/AB/R; WT/DS445/AB/R (15 January 2015).
Argentina – Import Measures	Panel Report, *Argentina – Measures Affecting the Importation of Goods*, WT/DS438/R; WT/DS444/R; WT/DS445/R (22 August 2014) (adopted on 26 January 2015, as modified by Appellate Body Report 15 January 2015).
Argentina – Poultry Anti-Dumping Duties	Panel Report, *Argentina – Definitive Anti-Dumping Duties on Poultry from Brazil*, WT/DS241/R (22 April 2003) (adopted 19 May 2003).
Argentina – Preserved Peaches	Panel Report, *Argentina – Definitive Safeguard Measure on Imports of Preserved Peaches*, WT/DS238/R (14 February 2003) (adopted 15 April 2003).
Argentina – Textiles and Apparel	Appellate Body Report, *Argentina – Measures Affecting Imports of Footwear, Textiles, Apparel and Other Items*, WT/DS56/AB/R (27 March 1998) (adopted 22 April 1998).
Argentina – Textiles and Apparel	Panel Report, *Argentina – Measures Affecting Imports of Footwear, Textiles, Apparel and Other Items*, WT/DS56/R (adopted 22 April 1998, as modified by Appellate Body Report WT/DS56/AB/R).

List of abbreviated cases   xxiii

Short Title	Full Cause Title and Citation
Australia – Apples	Appellate Body Report, *Australia – Measures Affecting the Importation of Apples from New Zealand*, WT/DS367/AB/R (29 November 2010) (adopted 17 December 2010).
Australia – Apples	Panel Report, *Australia – Measures Affecting the Importation of Apples from New Zealand*, WT/DS367/R (9 August 2010) (adopted 17 December 2010, as modified by Appellate Body Report WT/DS367/AB/R).
Australia – Automotive Leather II	Panel Report, *Australia – Subsidies Provided to Producers and Exporters of Automotive Leather*, WT/DS126/R (25 May 1999) (adopted 16 June 1999).
Australia – Salmon	Appellate Body Report, *Australia – Measures Affecting Importation of Salmon*, WT/DS18/AB/R (20 October 1998) (adopted 6 November 1998).
Australia – Salmon	Panel Report, *Australia – Measures Affecting Importation of Salmon*, WT/DS18/R (12 June 1998) (adopted 6 November 1998, as modified by Appellate Body Report WT/DS18/AB/R).
Australia – Salmon (Article 21.5 – Canada)	Article 21.5 Panel Report, *Australia – Measures Affecting Importation of Salmon*, WT/DS18/RW (18 February 2000) (adopted 20 March 2000).
Australia – Tobacco Plain Packaging	Panel Report, *Australia – Certain Measures Concerning Trademarks, Geographical Indications and Other Plain Packaging Requirements Applicable to Tobacco Products and Packaging*, WT/DS435/R, WT/DS441/R, WT/DS458/R, WT/DS467/R (28 June 2018) (adopted 28 August 2018).
Brazil – Aircraft	Appellate Body Report, *Brazil – Export Financing Programme for Aircraft*, WT/DS46/AB/R (2 August 1999) (adopted 20 August 1999).
Brazil – Aircraft	Panel Report, *Brazil – Export Financing Programme for Aircraft*, WT/DS46/R (14 April 1999) (adopted 20 August 1999, as modified by Appellate Body Report WT/DS46/AB/R).
Brazil – Desiccated Coconut	Appellate Body Report, *Brazil – Measures Affecting Desiccated Coconut*, WT/DS22/AB/R (21 February 1997) (adopted 20 March 1997).
Brazil – Desiccated Coconut	Panel Report, *Brazil – Measures Affecting Desiccated Coconut*, WT/DS22/R (17 October 1996) (adopted 20 March 1997, upheld by Appellate Body Report WT/DS22/AB/R).
Brazil – Retreaded Tyres	Appellate Body Report, *Brazil – Measures Affecting Imports of Retreaded Tyres*, WT/DS332/AB/R (3 December 2007) (adopted 17 December 2007).
Brazil – Retreaded Tyres	Panel Report, *Brazil – Measures Affecting Imports of Retreaded Tyres*, WT/DS332/R (12 June 2007) (adopted 17 December 2007, as modified by Appellate Body Report WT/DS332/AB/R).
Brazil – Taxation	Appellate Body Report, *Brazil – Certain Measures Concerning Taxation and Charges*, WT/DS472/AB/R, WT/DS497/AB/R (13 December 2018) (adopted 11 January 2019).
Brazil – Taxation	Panel Report, *Brazil – Certain Measures Concerning Taxation and Charges*, WT/DS472/R, WT/DS497/R (30 August 2017) (adopted 11 January 2019, as modified by Appellate Body Report WT/DS472/AB/R).
Canada – Aircraft	Appellate Body Report, *Canada – Measures Affecting the Export of Civilian Aircraft*, WT/DS70/AB/R (2 August 1999) (adopted 20 August 1999).
Canada – Aircraft	Panel Report, *Canada – Measures Affecting the Export of Civilian Aircraft*, WT/DS70/R (14 April 1999) (adopted 20 August 1999, upheld by Appellate Body Report WT/DS70/AB/R).
Canada – Aircraft (Article 21.5 – Brazil)	Article 21.5 Appellate Body Report, *Canada – Measures Affecting the Export of Civilian Aircraft*, WT/DS70/AB/RW (21 July 2000) (adopted 4 August 2000).

(*Continued*)

(Continued)

Short Title	Full Cause Title and Citation
Canada – Aircraft (Article 21.5 – Brazil)	Article 21.5 Panel Report, *Canada – Measures Affecting the Export of Civilian Aircraft*, WT/DS70/RW (9 May 2000) (adopted 4 August 2000, as modified by Appellate Body Report WT/DS70/AB/RW).
Canada – Aircraft Credits and Guarantees	Panel Report, *Canada – Export Credits and Loan Guarantees for Regional Aircraft*, WT/DS222/R (28 January 2002) (adopted 19 February 2002).
Canada – Aircraft Credits and Guarantees (Article 22.6 – Canada)	Recourse to Article 22.6 Arbitration Report, *Canada – Export Credits and Loan Guarantees for Regional Aircraft*, WT/DS222/ARB (17 February 2003).
Canada – Autos	Appellate Body Report, *Canada – Certain Measures Affecting the Automotive Industry*, WT/DS139/AB/R, WT/DS142/AB/R (31 May 2000) (adopted 19 June 2000).
Canada – Autos	Panel Report, *Canada – Certain Measures Affecting the Automotive Industry*, WT/DS139/R, WT/DS142/R (11 February 2000) (adopted 19 June 2000, as modified by Appellate Body Report WT/DS139/AB/R, WT/DS142/AB/R).
Canada – Continued Suspension	Appellate Body Report, *Canada – Continued Suspension of Obligations in the EC – Hormones Dispute*, WT/DS321/AB/R (16 October 2008) (adopted 14 November 2008).
Canada – Continued Suspension	Panel Report, *Canada – Continued Suspension of Obligations in the EC – Hormones Dispute*, WT/DS321/R (31 March 2008) (adopted 14 November 2008, as modified by Appellate Body Report WT/DS321/AB/R).
Canada – Feed-in Tariff Program	Appellate Body Reports, *Canada – Measures Relating to the Feed-in Tariff Program*, WT/DS426/AB/R (6 May 2012) (adopted 24 May 2013).
Canada – Feed-in Tariff Program	Panel Reports, *Canada – Measures Relating to the Feed-in Tariff Program*, WT/DS426/R (19 December 2012) (adopted 24 May 2013, as modified by Appellate Body Reports WT/DS426/AB/R).
Canada – Periodicals	Appellate Body Report, *Canada – Certain Measures Concerning Periodicals*, WT/DS31/AB/R (30 June 1997) (adopted 30 July 1997).
Canada – Periodicals	Panel Report, *Canada – Certain Measures Concerning Periodicals*, WT/DS31/R (14 March 1997) (adopted 30 July 1997, as modified by Appellate Body Report WT/DS31/AB/R).
Canada – Pharmaceutical Patents	Panel Report, *Canada – Patent Protection of Pharmaceutical Products*, WT/DS114/R (17 March 2000) (adopted 7 April 2000).
Canada – Pharmaceutical Patents (Article 21.3(c))	Article 21.3(c) Arbitration Report, *Canada – Patent Protection of Pharmaceutical Products*, WT/DS114/13 (18 August 2000).
Canada – Renewable Energy	Appellate Body Report, *Canada – Certain Measures Affecting the Renewable Energy Generation Sector*, WT/DS412/AB/R (6 May 2012) (adopted 24 May 2013).
Canada – Renewable Energy	Panel Reports, *Canada – Certain Measures Affecting the Renewable Energy Generation Sector*, WT/DS412/R (19 December 2012) (adopted 24 May 2013, as modified by Appellate Body Reports WT/DS412/AB/R).
Canada – Wheat Exports and Grain Imports	Appellate Body Report, *Canada – Measures Relating to Exports of Wheat and Treatment of Imported Grain*, WT/DS276/AB/R (30 August 2004) (adopted 27 September 2004).
Canada – Wheat Exports and Grain Imports	Panel Report, *Canada – Measures Relating to Exports of Wheat and Treatment of Imported Grain*, WT/DS276/R (6 April 2004) (adopted 27 September 2004, as modified by Appellate Body Report WT/DS276/AB/R).

List of abbreviated cases   xxv

Short Title	Full Cause Title and Citation
Chile – Alcoholic Beverages	Appellate Body Report, *Chile – Taxes on Alcoholic Beverages*, WT/DS110/AB/R (13 December 1999) (adopted 12 January 2000).
Chile – Alcoholic Beverages	Panel Report, *Chile – Taxes on Alcoholic Beverages*, WT/DS110/R (15 June 1999) (adopted 12 January 2000, as modified by Appellate Body Report WT/DS110/AB/R).
Chile – Alcoholic Beverages (Article 21.3(c))	Article 21.3(c) Arbitration Award, *Chile – Taxes on Alcoholic Beverages*, WT/DS110/14 (23 May 2000).
Chile – Price Band System	Appellate Body Report, *Chile – Price Band System and Safeguard Measures Relating to Certain Agricultural Products*, WT/DS207/AB/R (23 September 2002) (adopted 23 October 2002).
Chile – Price Band System	Panel Report, *Chile – Price Band System and Safeguard Measures Relating to Certain Agricultural Products*, WT/DS207/R (3 May 2002) (adopted 23 October 2002, as modified by Appellate Body Report WT/DS207AB/R).
Chile – Price Band System (Article 21.3(c))	Article 21.3(c) Arbitration Report, *Chile – Price Band System and Safeguard Measures Relating to Certain Agricultural Products*, WT/DS207/13 (17 March 2003).
Chile – Price Band System (Article 21.5 – Argentina)	Article 21.5 Appellate Body Report, *Chile – Price Band (Article 21.3(c)) System and Safeguard Measures Relating to Certain Agricultural Products*, WT/DS207/AB/RW (7 May 2007) (adopted 22 May 2007).
Chile – Price Band System (Article 21.5 – Argentina)	Article 21.5 Panel Report, *Chile – Price Band (Article 21.3(c)) System and Safeguard Measures Relating to Certain Agricultural Products*, WT/DS207/RW (8 December 2006) (adopted 22 May 2007, upheld by Appellate Body Report WT/DS207/AB/RW).
China – Auto Parts	Appellate Body Reports, *China – Measures Affecting Imports of Automobile Parts*, WT/DS339/AB/R, WT/DS340/AB/R, WT/DS342/AB/R (15 December 2008) (adopted 12 January 2009).
China – Autos (US)	Panel Report, *China – Anti-Dumping and Countervailing Duties on Certain Automobiles from the United States*, WT/DS440/R (23 May 2014) (adopted 18 June 2014).
China – Broiler Products	Panel Report, *China – Anti-Dumping and Countervailing Duty Measures on Broiler Products from the United States*, WT/DS427/R (2 August 2013) (adopted 15 September 2013).
China – Electronic Payment Services	Panel Report, *China – Certain Measures Affecting Electronic Payment Services*, WT/DS413/R (16 July 2012) (adopted 31 August 2012).
China – GOES	Appellate Body Report, *China – Countervailing and Anti-Dumping Duties on Grain Oriented Flat-Rolled Electrical Steel from the United States*, WT/DS414/AB/R (18 October 2012) (adopted 16 November 2012).
China – GOES	Panel Report, *China – Countervailing and Anti-Dumping Duties on Grain Oriented Flat-Rolled Electrical Steel from the United States*, WT/DS414/R (15 June 2012) (adopted 16 November 2012, upheld by Appellate Body Report WT/DS414/AB/R).
China – HP-SSST (EU)/China – HP-SSST (Japan)	*Appellate Body Report, China – Measures Imposing Anti-Dumping Duties on High-Performance Stainless Steel Seamless Tubes (HP-SSST) from Japan/China – Measures Imposing Anti-Dumping Duties on High-Performance Stainless Steel Seamless Tubes (HP-SSST) from the European Union*, WT/DS454/AB/RAdd.1; WT/DS460/AB/R (14 October) (adopted on 28 October).

(*Continued*)

(Continued)

Short Title	Full Cause Title and Citation
China – HP-SSST (EU)/China – HP-SSST (Japan)	Panel Report, *China – Measures Imposing Anti-Dumping Duties on High-Performance Stainless Steel Seamless Tubes (HP-SSST) from Japan/China – Measures Imposing Anti-Dumping Duties on High-Performance Stainless Steel Seamless Tubes (HP-SSST) from the European Union*, WT/DS454 and Add.1/WT/DS460 (13 February 2015) (adopted 28 October 2015, as modified by Appellate Body Report WT/DS454/AB/RAdd.1; WT/DS460/AB/R).
China – Intellectual Property Rights	Panel Report, *China – Measures Affecting the Protection and Enforcement of Intellectual Property Rights*, WT/DS362/R (26 January 2009) (adopted 20 March 2009).
China – Publications and Audiovisual Products	Appellate Body Report, *China – Measures Affecting Trading Rights and Distribution Services for Certain Publications and Audiovisual Entertainment Products*, WT/DS363/AB/R (21 December 2009) (adopted 19 January 2010).
China – Publications and Audiovisual Products	Panel Report, *China – Measures Affecting Trading Rights and Distribution Services for Certain Publications and Audiovisual Entertainment Products*, WT/DS363/R (12 August 2009) (adopted 19 January 2010, as modified by Appellate Body Report WT/DS363/AB/R).
China – Rare Earths	Appellate Body Reports, *China – Measures Related to the Exportation of Rare Earths, Tungsten, and Molybdenum*, WT/DS431/AB/R/, WT/DS432/AB/R/, WT/DS433/AB/R (7 August 2014) (adopted 29 August 2014).
China – Rare Earths	Panel Reports, *China – Measures Related to the Exportation of Rare Earths, Tungsten, and Molybdenum*, WT/DS431/R/, WT/DS432/R/, WT/DS333/R (26 March 2014) (adopted 29 August 2014, as modified by Appellate Body Reports WT/DS431/AB/R, WT/DS432/AB/R, WT/DS433/AB/R).
China – Raw Materials	Appellate Body Reports, *China – Measures Related to the Exportation of Various Raw Materials*, WT/DS394/AB/R/, WT/DS395/AB/R/, WT/DS398/AB/R (30 January 2012) (adopted 22 February 2012).
China – Raw Materials	Panel Reports, *China – Measures Related to the Exportation of Various Raw Materials*, WT/DS394/R/, WT/DS395/R/, WT/DS398/R (5 July 2011) (adopted 22 February 2012, as modified by Appellate Body Reports WT/DS394/AB/R, WT/DS395/AB/R, WT/DS398/AB/R).
China – X-Ray Equipment	Panel Report, *China – Definitive Anti-Dumping Duties on X-Ray Security Inspection Equipment from the European Union*, WT/DS425/R (26 February 2013) (adopted 24 April 2013).
Colombia – Ports of Entry	Panel Report, *Colombia – Indicative Prices and Restrictions on Ports of Entry*, WT/DS366/R (27 April 2009) (adopted 20 May 2009).
Colombia – Ports of Entry (Article 21.3(c))	Article 21.3(c) Arbitration Award, *Colombia – Indicative Prices and Restrictions on Ports of Entry*, WT/DS366/13 (2 October 2009).
Colombia – Textiles	Appellate Body Reports, *Colombia – Measures Relating to the Importation of Textiles, Apparel and Footwear*, WT/DS461/AB/R (7 June 2016) (adopted 22 June 2016).
Colombia – Textiles	Panel Report, *Colombia – Measures Relating to the Importation of Textiles, Apparel and Footwear*, WT/DS461/R (27 November 2014) (adopted 22 June 2016, as modified by Appellate Body Report WT/DS461/AB/R).
Colombia – Textiles (Article 21.3(c))	Article 21.3(c) Arbitration Award, *Colombia – Measures Relating to the Importation of Textiles, Apparel and Footwear*, WT/DS461/13 (15 November 2016).
Colombia – Textiles (Article 21.5)	Panel Report, *Colombia – Measures Relating to the Importation of Textiles, Apparel and Footwear*, WT/DS461/RW (5 October 2018).

List of abbreviated cases   xxvii

Short Title	Full Cause Title and Citation
Dominican Republic – Import and Sale of Cigarettes	Appellate Body Report, *Dominican Republic – Measures Affecting the Importation and Internal Sale of Cigarettes*, WT/DS302/AB/R (25 April 2005) (adopted 19 May 2005).
Dominican Republic – Import and Sale of Cigarettes	Panel Report, *Dominican Republic – Measures Affecting the Importation and Internal Sale of Cigarettes*, WT/DS302/R (26 November 2004) (adopted 19 May 2005, as modified by Appellate Body Report WT/DS302/AB/R).
Dominican Republic – Safeguard Measures	Panel Report, *Dominican Republic – Safeguard Measures on Imports of Polypropylene Bags and Tubular Fabric*, WT/DS415/R, WT/DS416/R, WT/DS417/R, WT/DS418/R (Jan. 31, 2012) (adopted 22 February 2012).
EC – Approval and Marketing of Biotech Products	Panel Reports, *European Communities – Measures Affecting the Approval and Marketing of Biotech Products*, WT/DS291/R, WT/DS292/R, WT/DS293/R (29 September 2006) (adopted 21 November 2006).
EC – Asbestos	Appellate Body Report, *European Communities – Measures Affecting Asbestos and Asbestos-Containing Products*, WT/DS135/AB/R (12 March 2001) (adopted 5 April 2001).
EC – Asbestos	Panel Report, *European Communities – Measures Affecting Asbestos and Asbestos-Containing Products*, WT/DS135/R (18 September 2000) (adopted 5 April 2001, as modified by Appellate Body Report WT/DS135/AB/R).
EC – Bananas III	Appellate Body Report, *European Communities – Regime for the Importation, Sale and Distribution of Bananas*, WT/DS27/AB/R (9 September 1997) (adopted 25 September 1997).
EC – Bananas III (Ecuador)	Panel Report, *European Communities – Regime for the Importation, Sale and Distribution of Bananas*, WT/DS27/R/ECU (May 22, 1997) (adopted 25 September 1997, as modified by Appellate Body Report WT/DS27/AB/R).
EC – Bananas III (US)	Appellate Body Report, *European Communities – Regime for the Importation, Sale and Distribution of Bananas, Complaint by the United States*, WT/DS27/R/USA (22 May 1997) (adopted 25 September 1997, as modified by Appellate Body Report WT/DS27/AB/R).
EC – Bananas III (Article 21.5 – Ecuador II)	Appellate Body Report, *European Communities – Regime for the Importation, Sale and Distribution of Bananas*, WT/DS27/AB/RW2/ECU (26 November 2008) (adopted 11 December 2008).
EC – Bananas III (Ecuador) (Article 22.6 – EC)	Recourse to Article 22.6 Arbitration Report, *European Communities – Regime for the Importation, Sale and Distribution of Bananas*, WT/DS27/ARB/ECU (24 March 2000).
EC – Bananas III (Article 21.5 – US)	Appellate Body Report, *European Communities – Regime for the Importation, Sale and Distribution of Bananas*, WT/DS27/AB/RW/USA (26 November 2008) (adopted 22 December 2008).
EC – Bananas III (US) (Article 22.6 – EC)	Recourse to Article 22.6 Arbitration Report, *European Communities – Regime for the Importation, Sale and Distribution of Bananas*, WT/DS27/ARB (9 April 1999).
EC – Bed Linen	Appellate Body Report, *European Communities Anti-Dumping Duties on Imports of Cotton-Type Bed Linen from India*, WT/DS141/AB/R (1 March 2001) (adopted 12 March 2001).
EC – Bed Linen	Panel Report, *European Communities – Anti-Dumping Duties on Imports of Cotton-Type Bed Linen from India*, WT/DS141/R (30 October 2000) (adopted 12 March 2001, as modified by Appellate Body Report WT/DS141/AB/R).
EC – Bed Linen (Article 21.5 – India)	Article 21.5 Appellate Body Report, *European Communities – Anti-Dumping Duties on Imports of Cotton-Type Bed Linen from India*, WT/DS141/AB/RW (8 April 2003) (adopted 24 March 2003).

(*Continued*)

(Continued)

Short Title	Full Cause Title and Citation
EC – Bed Linen (Article 21.5 – India)	Article 21.5 Panel Report, *European Communities – Anti-Dumping Duties on Imports of Cotton-Type Bed Linen from India*, WT/DS141/AB/RW (29 November 2002) (adopted 24 March 2003), as modified by Appellate Body Report WT/DS141/AB/RW).
EC – Chicken Cuts	Appellate Body Report, *European Communities – Customs Classification of Frozen Boneless Chicken Cuts*, WT/DS269/AB/R, WT/DS286/AB/R (12 September 2005) (adopted 27 September 2005).
EC – Chicken Cuts (Brazil)	Panel Report, *European Communities – Customs Classification of Frozen Boneless Chicken Cuts, Complaint by Brazil*, WT/DS269/R (30 May 2005) (adopted 27 September 2005, as modified by Appellate Body Report WT/DS269/AB/R, WT/DS286/AB/R).
EC – Chicken Cuts (Thailand)	Panel Report, *European Communities – Customs Classification of Frozen Boneless Chicken Cuts, Complaint by Thailand*, WT/DS286/R (30 May 2005) (adopted 27 September 2005 as modified by Appellate Body Report WT/DS269/AB/R, WT/DS286/AB/R).
EC – Chicken Cuts (Article 21.3(c))	Article 21.3(c) Arbitration Report, *European Communities – Customs Classification of Frozen Boneless Chicken Cuts*, WT/DS269/13, WT/DS286/15 (20 February 2006).
EC – Commercial Vessels	Panel Report, *European Communities – Measures Affecting Trade in Commercial Vessels*, WT/DS301/R (22 April 2005) (adopted 22 June 2005).
EC – Computer Equipment	Appellate Body Report, *European Communities – Customs Classification of Certain Computer Equipment*, WT/DS62/AB/R; WT/DS67/AB/R; WT/DS68/AB/R (5 June 1998) (adopted 22 June 1998).
EC – Computer Equipment	Panel Report, *European Communities – Customs Classification of Certain Computer Equipment*, WT/DS62/R; WT/DS67/R; WT/DS68/R (5 February 1998) (adopted 22 June 1998, as modified by Appellate Body Report WT/DS62/AB/R; WT/DS67/AB/R; WT/DS68/AB/R).
EC – Countervailing Measures on DRAM Chips	Panel Report, *European Communities – Countervailing Measures on Dynamic Random Access Memory Chips from Korea*, WT/DS299/R (17 June 2005) (adopted 3 August 2005).
EC – Export Subsidies on Sugar	Appellate Body Report, *European Communities – Export Subsidies on Sugar*, WT/DS265/AB/R, WT/DS266/AB/R, WT/DS283/AB/R (April 28, 2005) (adopted May 19, 2005).
EC – Export Subsidies on Sugar (Australia)	Panel Report, *European Communities – Export Subsidies on Sugar, Complaint by Australia*, WT/DS265/R (15 October 2004) (adopted 19 May 2005, as modified by Appellate Body Report WT/DS265/AB/R, WT/DS266/AB/R, WT/DS283/AB/R).
EC – Export Subsidies on Sugar (Brazil)	Panel Report, *European Communities – Export Subsidies on Sugar, Complaint by Australia*, WT/DS266/R (15 October 2004) (adopted 19 May 2005, as modified by Appellate Body Report WT/DS265/AB/R, WT/DS266/AB/R, WT/DS283/AB/R).
EC – Export Subsidies on Sugar (Thailand)	Panel Report, *European Communities – Export Subsidies on Sugar, Complaint by Australia*, WT/DS283/R (15 October 2004) (adopted 19 May 2005, as modified by Appellate Body Report WT/DS265/AB/R, WT/DS266/AB/R, WT/DS283/AB/R).
EC – Fasteners (China)	Appellate Body Report, *European Communities – Definitive Anti-Dumping Measures on Certain Iron or Steel Fasteners from China*, WT/DS397/AB/R (15 July 2011) (adopted 28 July 2011).

Short Title	Full Cause Title and Citation
EC – Fasteners (China)	Panel Report, *European Communities – Definitive Anti-Dumping Measures on Certain Iron or Steel Fasteners from China*, WT/DS397/R (3 December 2010) (adopted 28 July 2011, as modified by Appellate Body Report WT/DS397/AB/R).
EC – Hormones	Appellate Body Report, *EC – Measures Concerning Meat and Meat Products (Hormones)*, WT/DS26/AB/R, WT/DS48/AB/R (16 January 1998) (adopted 13 February 1998).
EC – Hormones (Canada)	Panel Report, *EC – Measures Concerning Meat and Meat Products (Hormones), Complaint by Canada*, WT/DS48/R/CAN (18 August 1997) (adopted 13 February 1998, as modified by Appellate Body Report WT/DS26/AB/R, WT/DS48/AB/R).
EC – Hormones (US)	Panel Report, *EC – Measures Concerning Meat and Meat Products (Hormones), Complaint by the United States*, WT/DS26/R/USA (18 August 1997) (adopted 13 February 1998, as modified by Appellate Body Report WT/DS26/AB/R, WT/DS48/AB/R).
EC – Hormones (Article 21.3(c))	Article 21.3 (c) Arbitration Report, *EC Measures Concerning Meat and Meat Products (Hormones)*, WT/DS26/15, WT/DS48/13 (29 May 1998).
EC – Hormones (Canada) (Article 22.6 – EC)	Recourse to Article 22.6 Arbitration Report, *European Communities – Measures Concerning Meat and Meat Products (Hormones), Original Complaint by Canada*, WT/DS48/ARB (12 July 1999).
EC – Hormones (US) (Article 22.6 – EC)	Recourse to Article 22.6 Arbitration Report, *European Communities – Measures Concerning Meat and Meat Products (Hormones), Original Complaint by the United States*, WT/DS26/ARB (12 July 1999).
EC – IT Products	Panel Reports, *European Communities and its member States – Tariff Treatment of Certain Information Technology Products*, WT/DS375/R, WT/DS376/R, WT/DS377/R (16 August 2010) (adopted 21 September 2010).
EC – Poultry	Appellate Body Report, *European Communities – Measures Affecting the Importation of Certain Poultry Products*, WT/DS69/AB/R (13 July 1998) (adopted 23 July 1998).
EC – Poultry	Panel Report, *European Communities – Measures Affecting the Importation of Certain Poultry Products*, WT/DS69/R (12 March 1998) (adopted 23 July 1998, as modified by Appellate Body Report WT/DS69/AB/R).
EC – Sardines	Appellate Body Report, *European Communities – Trade Description of Sardines*, WT/DS231/AB/R (26 September 2002) (adopted 23 October 2002).
EC – Sardines	Panel Report, *European Communities – Trade Description of Sardines*, WT/DS231/R and Corr.1 (29 May 2002) (adopted 23 October 2002, as modified by Appellate Body Report WT/DS231/AB/R).
EC – Seal Products	Appellate Body Reports, *European Communities – Measures Prohibiting the Importation and Marketing of Seal Products*, WT/DS400/AB/R, WT/DS401/AB/R (22 May 2014) (adopted 18 June 2014).
EC – Seal Products	Panel Reports, *European Communities – Measures Prohibiting the Importation and Marketing of Seal Products*, WT/DS400/R, WT/DS401/R (25 November 2013) (adopted 18 June 2014, as modified by Appellate Body Reports WT/DS400/AB/R, WT/DS401/AB/R).
EC – Tariff Preferences	Appellate Body Report, *European Communities – Conditions for the Granting of Tariff Preferences to Developing Countries*, WT/DS246/AB/R (7 April 2004) (adopted 20 April 2004).
EC – Tariff Preferences	Panel Report, *European Communities – Conditions for the Granting of Tariff Preferences to Developing Countries*, WT/DS246/R (1 December 2003) (adopted 20 April 2004, as modified by Appellate Body Report WT/DS246/AB/R).

(Continued)

(Continued)

Short Title	Full Cause Title and Citation
EC – Tariff Preferences (Article 21.3(c))	Article 21.3(c) Arbitration Report, *European Communities – Conditions for the Granting of Tariff Preferences to Developing Countries*, WT/DS246/14 (20 September 2004).
EC – Trademarks and Geographical Indications (Australia)	Panel Report, *European Communities – Protection of Trademarks and Geographical Indications for Agricultural Products and Foodstuffs, Complaint by Australia*, WT/DS290/R (15 March 2005) (adopted 20 April 2005).
EC – Trademarks and Geographical Indications (US)	Panel Report, *European Communities – Protection of Trademarks and Geographical Indications for Agricultural Products and Foodstuffs, Complaint by the United States*, WT/DS174/R (15 March 2005) (adopted 20 April 2005).
EC – Tube or Pipe Fittings	Appellate Body Report, *European Communities – Anti-Dumping Duties on Malleable Cast Iron Tube or Pipe Fittings from Brazil*, WT/DS219/AB/R (22 July 2003) (adopted 18 August 2003).
EC – Tube or Pipe Fittings	Panel Report, *European Communities – Anti-Dumping Duties on Malleable Cast Iron Tube or Pipe Fittings from Brazil*, WT/DS219/R (7 March 2003) (adopted 18 August 2003, as modified by Appellate Body Report WT/DS219/AB/R).
EC and Certain Member States – Large Civil Aircraft	Appellate Body Report, *European Communities and Certain Member States – Measures Affecting Trade in Large Aircraft*, WT/DS316/AB/R (18 May 2011) (adopted 1 June 2011).
EC and Certain Member States – Large Civil Aircraft	Panel Report, *European Communities and Certain Member States – Measures Affecting Trade in Large Aircraft*, WT/DS316/R (30 June 2010) (adopted 1 June 2001, as modified by Appellate Body Report WT/DS316/AB/R).
Egypt – Steel Rebar	Panel Report, *Egypt – Definitive Anti-Dumping Measures on Steel Rebar from Turkey*, WT/DS211/R (8 August 2012) (adopted 1 October 2002).
EU – Biodiesel (Argentina)	Appellate Body Report, *European Union – Anti-Dumping Measures on Biodiesel from Argentina*, WT/DS473/AB/R (6 October 2016) (adopted 26 October 2016).
EU – Biodiesel	Panel Report, *European Union – Anti-Dumping Measures on Biodiesel from Argentina*, WT/DS473 (29 March 2016) (adopted 26 October 2016 as modified by Appellate Body Report WT/DS473/AB/R).
EU – Energy Package	Panel Report, *European Union and Its Member State – Certain Measures Relating to Energy Sector*, WT/DS476/R (10 August 2018).
Guatemala – Cement I	Appellate Body Report, *Guatemala – Anti-Dumping Investigation Regarding Portland Cement from Mexico*, WT/DS60/AB/R (2 November 1998) (adopted 25 November 1998).
Guatemala – Cement I	Panel Report, *Guatemala – Anti-Dumping Investigation Regarding Portland Cement from Mexico*, WT/DS60/R (19 June 1998) (adopted 25 November 1998, as reversed by Appellate Body Report WT/DS60/AB/R).
Guatemala – Cement II	Panel Report, *Guatemala – Definitive Anti-Dumping Measures on Grey Portland Cement from Mexico*, WT/DS156/R (24 October 2000) (adopted 17 November 200).
India – Additional Import Duties	Appellate Body Report, *India – Additional and Extra-Additional Duties on Imports from the United State*, WT/DS360/AB/R (30 October 2008) (adopted 17 November 2008).
India – Additional Import Duties	Panel Report, *India – Additional and Extra-Additional Duties on Imports from the United State*, WT/DS360/R (9 June 2008) (adopted 17 November 2008 as reversed by Appellate Body Report WT/DS360/AB/R).
India – Agricultural Products	Appellate Body Report, *India – Measures Concerning the Importation of Certain Agricultural Products*, WT/DS430/AB/R (4 June 2015) (adopted 19 June 2015).

Short Title	Full Cause Title and Citation
India – Agricultural Products	Panel Report, *India – Measures Concerning the Importation of Certain Agricultural Products*, WT/DS430/R (14 October 2014) (adopted 19 June 2015 as modified by Appellate Body Report WT/DS430/AB/R).
India – Autos	Appellate Body Report, *India – Measures Affecting the Automotive Sector*, WT/DS146/AB/R WT/DS175/AB/R (19 March 2002) (adopted 5 April 2002).
India – Autos	Panel Report, *India – Measures Affecting the Automotive Sector*, WT/DS146/R WT/DS175/R (21 December 2001) (adopted 5 April 2002).
India – Patents (EC)	Panel Report, *India – Patent Protection for Pharmaceutical and Agricultural Chemical Products, Complaint by the European Communities and Their Member States*, WT/DS79/R (24 August 1998) (adopted 22 September 1998).
India – Patents (US)	Appellate Body Report, *India – Patent Protection for Pharmaceutical and Agricultural Chemical Products*, WT/DS50/AB/R (19 December 1997) (adopted 16 January 1999).
India – Patents (US)	Panel Report, *India – Patent Protection for Pharmaceutical and Agricultural Chemical Products, Complaint by the United States*, WT/DS50/R (5 September 1997) (adopted 16 January 1999, as modified by Appellate Body Report WT/DS50/AB/R).
India – Quantitative Restrictions	Appellate Body Report, *India – Quantitative Restrictions on Imports of Agricultural, Textile and Industrial Products*, WT/DS90/AB/R (23 August 1999) (adopted 22 September 1999).
India – Quantitative Restrictions	Panel Report, *India – Quantitative Restrictions on Imports of Agricultural, Textile and Industrial Products*, WT/DS90/R (6 April 1999) (adopted 22 September 1999, upheld by Appellate Body Report WT/DS90/AB/R).
India – Solar Cells	Appellate Body Report, *India – Certain Measures Relating to Solar Cells and Solar Modules*, WT/DS456/AB/R (16 September 2016) (adopted 14 October 2016).
India – Solar Cells	Panel Report, *India – Certain Measures Relating to Solar Cells and Solar Modules*, WT/DS456/R (24 February 2016) (adopted 14 October 2016, as modified by Appellate Body Report WT/DS456/AB/R).
Indonesia – Autos	Panel Report, *Indonesia – Certain Measures Affecting the Automobile Industry*, WT/DS54/R, WT/DS55/R, WT/DS59/R, WT/DS64/R (2 July 1998) (adopted 23 July 1998).
Indonesia – Autos (Article 21.3(c))	Article 21.3 (c) Arbitration Report, *Indonesia – Certain Measures Affecting the Automobile Industry*, WT/DS54/15, WT/DS55/14, WT/DS59/13, WT/DS64/12 (7 December 1998).
Indonesia – Import Licensing Regime	Appellate Body Report, *Indonesia – Importation of Horticultural Products, Animal and Animal Products*, WT/DS477/AB/R, WT/DS478/AB/R (9 November 2017), (adopted 22 November 2017).
Indonesia – Import Licensing Regime	Panel Report, *Indonesia – Indonesia – Importation of Horticultural Products, Animal and Animal Products*, WT/DS477/R, WT/DS478/R (26 December 2016) (adopted 22 November 2017 as modified by Appellate Body Report WT/DS477/AB/R, WT/DS478/AB/R).
Japan – Agricultural Products II	Appellate Body Report, *Japan – Measures Affecting Agricultural Products*, WT/DS76/AB/R (22 February 1999) (adopted 19 March 1999).
Japan – Agricultural Products II	Panel Report, *Japan – Measures Affecting Agricultural Products*, WT/DS76/R (17 October 1998) (adopted 19 March 1999, as modified by Appellate Body Report WT/DS76/AB/R).
Japan – Alcoholic Beverages II	Appellate Body Report, *Japan – Taxes on Alcoholic Beverages*, WT/DS8/AB/R, WT/DS10/AB/R, WT/DS11/AB/R (Oct. 4, 1996) (adopted 1 November 1996).

(*Continued*)

(Continued)

Short Title	Full Cause Title and Citation
Japan – Alcoholic Beverages II	Panel Report, *Japan – Taxes on Alcoholic Beverages*, WT/DS8/R, WT/DS10/R, WT/DS11/R (11 July 1996) (adopted 1 November 1996, as modified by Appellate Body Report WT/DS8/AB/R, WT/DS10/AB/R, WT/DS11/AB/R).
Japan – Alcoholic Beverages II (Article 21.3(c))	Article 21.3(c) Arbitration Report, *Japan – Taxes on Alcoholic Beverages*, WT/DS8/15, WT/DS10/15, WT/DS11/13 (14 February 1997).
Japan – Apples	Appellate Body Report, *Japan – Measures Affecting the Importation of Apples*, WT/DS245/AB/R (26 November 2003) (adopted 10 December 2003).
Japan – Apples	Panel Report, *Japan – Measures Affecting the Importation of Apples*, WT/DS245/R (15 July 2003) (adopted 10 December 2003, upheld by Appellate Body Report WT/DS245/AB/R).
Japan – DRAMS (Korea)	Appellate Body Report, *Japan – Countervailing Duties on Dynamic Random Access Memories from Korea*, WT/DS336/AB/R (28 November 2007) (adopted 17 December 2007).
Japan – DRAMS (Korea)	Panel Report, *Japan – Countervailing Duties on Dynamic Random Access Memories from Korea*, WT/DS336/R (13 July 2007) (17 December 2007, as modified by Appellate Body Report WT/DS336/AB/R).
Japan – DRAMS (Korea) (Article 21.3(c))	Article 21.3(c) Arbitration Report, *Japan – Countervailing Duties on Dynamic Random Access Memories from Korea*, WT/DS336/16 (5 May 2008).
Japan – Film	Panel Report, *Japan – Measures Affecting Consumer Photographic Film and Paper*, WT/DS44/R (22 April 1998).
Korea – Alcoholic Beverages	Appellate Body Report, *Korea – Taxes on Alcoholic Beverages*, WT/DS75/AB/R, WT/DS84/AB/R (18 January 1999) (adopted 17 February 1999).
Korea – Alcoholic Beverages	Panel Report, *Korea – Taxes on Alcoholic Beverages*, WT/DS75/R, WT/DS84/R (17 September 1998) (adopted 17 February 1999, as modified by Appellate Body Report WT/DS75/AB/R, WT/DS84/AB/R).
Korea – Certain Paper	Panel Report, *Korea – Anti-Dumping Duties on Imports of Certain Paper from Indonesia*, WT/DS312/R (28 October 2005) (adopted 28 November 2005).
Korea – Certain Paper (Article 21.5 – Indonesia)	Article 21.5 Panel Report, *Korea – Anti-Dumping Duties on Imports of Certain Paper from Indonesia*, WT/DS312/RW (28 September 2007) (adopted 22 October 2007).
Korea – Commercial Vessels	Panel Report, *Korea – Measures Affecting Trade in Commercial Vessels*, WT/DS273/R (7 March 2005) (adopted April 11, 2005).
Korea – Dairy	Appellate Body Report, *Korea – Definitive Safeguard Measures on Imports of Certain Dairy Products*, WT/DS98/AB/R (14 December 1999) (adopted 12 January 2000).
Korea – Dairy	Panel Report, *Korea – Definitive Safeguard Measures on Imports of Certain Dairy Products*, WT/DS98/R (21 June 1999) (adopted 12 January 2000, as modified by Appellate Body Report WT/DS98/AB/R).
Korea – Procurement	Panel Report, *Korea – Measures Affecting Government Procurement*, WT/DS163/R (1 May 2000) (adopted 19 June 2000).
Korea – Radionuclides (Japan)	Appellate Body Report, *Korea – Import Bans, and Testing and Certification Requirements for Radionuclides*, WT/DS494/AB/R (11 April 2019) (adopted 26 April 2019).
Korea – Radionuclides (Japan)	Panel Report, *Korea – Import Bans, and Testing and Certification Requirements for Radionuclides*, WT/DS495/R (22 February 2018) (adopted 26 April 2019, as modified by Appellate Body Report WT/DS494/AB/R).

Short Title	Full Cause Title and Citation
Korea – Various Measures on Beef	Appellate Body Report, *Korea – Measures Affecting Imports of Fresh, Chilled and Frozen Beef*, WT/DS161/AB/R, WT/DS169/AB/R (11 December 2000) (adopted 10 January 2001).
Korea – Various Measures on Beef	Panel Report, *Korea – Measures Affecting Imports of Fresh, Chilled and Frozen Beef*, WT/DS161/R, WT/DS169/R (31 July 2000) (adopted 10 January 2001, as modified by Appellate Body Report WT/DS161/AB/R, WT/DS169/AB/R).
Mexico – Anti-Dumping Measures on Rice	Appellate Body Report, *Mexico – Definitive Anti-Dumping Measures on Beef and Rice, Complaint with Respect to Rice* WT/DS295/AB/R (29 November 2005) (adopted 20 December 2005).
Mexico – Anti-Dumping Measures on Rice	Panel Report, *Mexico – Definitive Anti-Dumping Measures on Beef and Rice, Complaint with Respect to Rice* WT/DS295/R (6 June 2005) (adopted 20 December 2005, as modified by Appellate Body Report WT/DS295/AB/R).
Mexico – Corn Syrup (Article 21.5 – US)	Article 21.5 Appellate Body Report, *Mexico – Anti-Dumping Investigation of High Fructose Corn Syrup (HFCS) from the United States*, WT/DS132/AB/RW (22 October 2001) (adopted 21 November 2001).
Mexico – Corn Syrup (Article 21.5 – US)	Article 21.5 Panel Report, *Mexico – Anti-Dumping Investigation of High Fructose Corn Syrup (HFCS) from the United States*, WT/DS132/RW (22 June 2001) (adopted 21 November 2001, upheld by Appellate Body Report WT/DS132/AB/RW).
Mexico – Taxes on Soft Drinks	Appellate Body Report, *Mexico – Tax Measures on Soft Drinks and Other Beverages*, WT/DS308/AB/R (6 March 2006) (adopted 24 March 2006).
Mexico – Taxes on Soft Drinks	Panel Report, *Mexico – Tax Measures on Soft Drinks and Other Beverages*, WT/DS308/R (7 October 2005) (adopted 24 March 2006, as modified by Appellate Body Report WT/DS308/AB/R).
Mexico – Telecoms	Panel Report, *Mexico – Measures Affecting Telecommunications Services*, WT/DS204/R (2 April 2004) (adopted June 1, 2004).
Morocco – Hot-Rolled Steel (Turkey)	Panel Report, *Morocco – Anti-Dumping Measures on Certain Hot-Rolled Steel from Turkey*, WT/DS513/R (31 October 2018) (adopted 8 January 2020).
Peru – Agricultural Products	Appellate Body Report, *Peru – Additional Duty on Imports of Certain Agricultural Products*, WT/DS457/AB/R (20 July 2015) (adopted on 31 July 2015).
Peru – Agricultural Products	Panel Report, *Peru – Additional Duty on Imports of Certain Agricultural Products*, WT/DS457/R (27 November 2014) (adopted on 31 July 2015, as modified by Appellate Body Report WT/DS457/AB/R).
Peru – Agricultural Products (Article 21.3 (c))	Article 21.3(c) Arbitration Award, *Peru – Additional Duty on Imports of Certain Agricultural Products*, WT/DS457/15 (16 December 2015) (adopted on 31 July 2015).
Philippines – Distilled Spirits	Appellate Body Reports, *Philippines – Taxes on Distilled Spirits*, WT/DS396/AB/R, WT/DS403/AB/R (21 December 2011) (adopted 20 January 2012).
Philippines – Distilled Spirits	Panel Reports, *Philippines – Taxes on Distilled Spirits*, WT/DS396/R, WT/DS403/R (15 August 2011) (adopted 20 January 2012, as modified by Appellate Body Reports WT/DS396/AB/R, WT/DS403/AB/R).
Russia – Commercial Vehicles	Appellate Body Reports, *Russia – Anti-Dumping Duties on Light Commercial Vehicles from Germany and Italy*, WT/DS479/AB/R (22 March 2018) (adopted 9 April 2018).
Russia – Commercial Vehicles	Panel Reports, *Russia – Anti-Dumping Duties on Light Commercial Vehicles from Germany and Italy*, WT/DS479/R (27 January 2017) (adopted 9 April 2018, as modified by Appellate Body Reports WT/DS396/AB/R, WT/DS403/AB/R).

xxxiv List of abbreviated cases

(Continued)

Short Title	Full Cause Title and Citation
Russia – Pigs (EU)	Appellate Body Report, *Russian Federation – Measures on the Importation of Live Pigs, Pork and Other Pig Products from the European Union*, WT/DS475/AB/R (24 February 2017) (21 March 2017).
Russia – Pigs (EU)	Panel Report, *Russian Federation – Measures on the Importation of Live Pigs, Pork and Other Pig Products from the European Union*, WT/DS475/R (19 August 2016) (adopted 21 March 2017, as modified by Appellate Body Report WT/DS475/AB/R).
Thailand – Cigarettes (Philippines)	Appellate Body Report, *Thailand – Customs and Fiscal Measures on Cigarettes from the Philippines*, WT/DS371/AB/R (17 June 2011) (adopted 15 July 2011).
Thailand – Cigarettes (Philippines)	Panel Report, *Thailand – Customs and Fiscal Measures on Cigarettes from the Philippines*, WT/DS371/R (15 November 2010) (adopted 15 July 2011, as modified by Appellate Body Report WT/DS371/AB/R).
Thailand – H-Beams	Appellate Body Report, *Thailand – Anti-Dumping Duties on Angles, Shapes and Sections of Iron or Non-Alloy Steel and H-Beams from Poland*, WT/DS122/AB/R (12 March 2001) (adopted 5 April 2001).
Thailand – H-Beams	Panel Report, *Thailand – Anti-Dumping Duties on Angles, Shapes and Sections of Iron or Non-Alloy Steel and H-Beams from Poland*, WT/DS122/R (28 September 2000) (adopted 5 April 2001, as modified by Appellate Body Report WT/DS122/AB/R).
Turkey – Rice	Panel Report, *Turkey – Measures Affecting the Importation of Rice*, WT/DS334/R (21 September 2007) (adopted 22 October 2007).
Turkey – Textiles	Appellate Body Report, *Turkey – Restrictions on Imports of Textile and Clothing Products*, WT/DS34/AB/R (22 October 1999) (adopted 19 November 1999).
Turkey – Textiles	Panel Report, *Turkey – Restrictions on Imports of Textile and Clothing Products*, WT/DS34/R (31 May 1999) (adopted 19 November 1999, as modified by Appellate Body Report WT/DS34/AB/R).
Ukraine – Passenger Cars	Panel Report, *Ukraine – Definitive Safeguard Measures on Certain Passenger Cars*, WT/DS468 and Add.1 (26 June 2015) (adopted 20 July 2015).
US – 1916 Act	Appellate Body Report, *United States – Anti-Dumping Act of 1916*, WT/DS136/AB/R, WT/DS162/AB/R (28 August 2000) (adopted 26 September 2000).
US – 1916 Act (EC)	Panel Report, *United States – Anti-Dumping Act of 1916, Complaint by the European Communities*, WT/DS136/R (31 May 2000) (adopted 26 September 2000, upheld by Appellate Body Report WT/DS136/AB/R, WT/DS162/AB/R).
US – 1916 Act (Japan)	Panel Report, *United States – Anti-Dumping Act of 1916, Complaint by Japan*, WT/DS162/R (29 May 2000) (adopted 26 September 2000, upheld by Appellate Body Report WT/DS136/AB/R, WT/DS162/AB/R).
US – 1916 Act (Article 21.3(c))	Article 21.3(c) Arbitration Report, *United States – Anti-Dumping Act of 1916*, WT/DS136/11, WT/DS162/14 (28 February 2001).
US – 1916 Act (EC) (Article 22.6 – US)	Recourse to Article 22.6 Arbitration Report, *United States – Anti-Dumping Act of 1916*, Original Complaint by the European Communities, WT/DS136/ARB (24 February 2004).
US – Animals	Panel Report, *United States – Measures Affecting the Importation of Animals, Meat and Other Animal Products from Argentina*, WT/DS447/R (24 July 2015) (adopted 31 August 2015).
US – Anti-Dumping Methodologies (China)	Appellate Body Report, *United States – Certain Methodologies and Their Application to Anti-Dumping Proceedings Involving China*, WT/DS471/AB/R (11 May 2017) (adopted 23 May 2017).

List of abbreviated cases   xxxv

Short Title	Full Cause Title and Citation
US – Anti-Dumping Methodologies (China)	Panel Report, *United States – Certain Methodologies and Their Application to Anti-Dumping Proceedings Involving China*, WT/DS471/R (19 October 2016) (adopted 23 May 2017, as modified by Appellate Body Report WT/DS471/AB/R).
US – Anti-Dumping and Countervailing Duties (China)	Appellate Body Report, *United States – Definitive Anti-Dumping and Countervailing Duties on Certain Products from China*, WT/DS379/AB/R (11 March 2011) (adopted 25 March 2011).
US – Anti-Dumping and Countervailing Duties (China)	Panel Report, *United States – Definitive Anti- Dumping and Countervailing Duties on Certain Products from China*, WT/DS379/R (22 October 2010) (adopted 25 March 2011, as modified by Appellate Body Report WT/DS379/AB/R).
US – Anti-Dumping Measures on Oil Country Tubular Goods	Appellate Body Report, *United States – Anti-Dumping Measures on Oil Country Tubular Goods (OCTG) from Mexico*, WT/DS282/AB/R (2 November 2005) (adopted 28 November 2005).
US – Anti-Dumping Measures on Oil Country Tubular Goods	Panel Report, *United States – Anti-Dumping Measures on Oil Country Tubular Goods (OCTG) from Mexico*, WT/DS282/R (20 June 2005) (adopted 28 November 2005, as modified by Appellate Body Report WT/DS282/AB/R).
US – Carbon Steel	Appellate Body Report, *United States – Countervailing Duties on Certain Corrosion-Resistant Carbon Steel Flat Products from Germany*, WT/DS213/AB/R (23 November 2002) (adopted 19 December 2002).
US – Carbon Steel	Panel Report, *United States – Countervailing Duties on Certain Corrosion-Resistant Carbon Steel Flat Products from Germany*, WT/DS213/R (3 July 2002) (adopted 19 December 2002, as modified by Appellate Body Report WT/DS213/AB/R).
US – Carbon Steel (India)	Appellate Body Report, *United States – Countervailing Duties on Certain Corrosion-Resistant Carbon Steel Flat Products from India*, WT/DS436/AB/R (8 December 2014) (adopted 19 December 2014).
US – Carbon Steel (India)	Panel Report, *United States – Countervailing Duties on Certain Corrosion-Resistant Carbon Steel Flat Products from India*, WT/DS436/R (14 July 2014) (adopted 19 December 2014, as modified by Appellate Body Report WT/DS436/AB/R.
US – Carbon Steel (India) (Article 21.5 – India)	Panel Report, *United States – Countervailing Duties on Certain Corrosion-Resistant Carbon Steel Flat Products from India*, WT/DS436/RW (15 November 2019).
US – Certain EC Products	Appellate Body Report, *United States – Import Measures on Certain Products from the European Communities*, WT/DS165/AB/R (11 December 2000) (adopted 10 January 2001).
US – Certain EC Products	Panel Report, *United States – Import Measures on Certain Products from the European Communities*, WT/DS165/R (17 July 2000) (adopted 10 January 2001, as modified by Appellate Body Report WT/DS165/AB/R).
US – Clove Cigarettes	Appellate Body Report, *United States – Measures Affecting the Production and Sale of Clove Cigarettes*, WT/DS406/AB/R (4 April 2012) (adopted 24 April 2012).
US – Clove Cigarettes	Panel Report, *United States – Measures Affecting the Production and Sale of Clove Cigarettes*, WT/DS406/R (2 September 2011) (adopted 24 April 2012, as modified by Appellate Body Report WT/DS406/AB/R).
US – Continued Suspension	Appellate Body Report, *United States – Continued Suspension of Obligations in the EC – Hormones Dispute*, WT/DS320/AB/R (16 October 2008) (adopted 14 November 2008).

(*Continued*)

(Continued)

Short Title	Full Cause Title and Citation
US – Continued Suspension	Panel Report, *United States – Continued Suspension of Obligations in the EC – Hormones Dispute*, WT/DS320/R (31 March 2008) (adopted 14 November 2008, as modified by Appellate Body Report WT/DS320/AB/R).
US – Continued Zeroing	Appellate Body Report, *United States – Continued Existence and Application of Zeroing Methodology*, WT/DS350/AB/R (4 February 2009) (adopted 19 February 2009).
US – Continued Zeroing	Panel Report, *United States – Continued Existence and Application of Zeroing Methodology*, WT/DS350/R (1 October 2008) (adopted 19 February 2009, as modified as Appellate Body Report WT/DS350/AB/R).
US – COOL	Appellate Body Reports, *United States – Certain Country of Origin Labelling (COOL) Requirements*, WT/DS384/AB/R, WT/DS386/AB/R (29 June 2012) (adopted 23 July 2012).
US – COOL	Panel Reports, *United States – Certain Country of Origin Labelling (COOL) Requirements*, WT/DS384/R, WT/DS386/R (18 November 2011) (adopted 23 July 2012, as modified by Appellate Body Reports WT/DS384/AB/R, WT/DS386/AB/R).
US – COOL (Article 21.5 – Canada)	Panel Reports, *United States – Certain Country of Origin Labelling (COOL) Requirements*, WT/DS384/RW, WT/DS386/RW (20 October 2014) (adopted 29 May 2015, as modified by Appellate Body Reports WT/DS384/AB/R, WT/DS386/AB/R).
US – COOL (Article 21.5 – Mexico)	Panel Reports, *United States – Certain Country of Origin Labelling (COOL) Requirements*, WT/DS384/RW, WT/DS386/RW (20 October 2014) (adopted 29 May 2015, as modified by Appellate Body Reports WT/DS384/AB/R, WT/DS386/AB/R).
US – Corrosion-Resistant Steel Sunset Review	Appellate Body Report, *United States – Sunset Review of Anti-Dumping Duties on Corrosion-Resistant Carbon Steel Flat Products from Japan*, WT/DS244/AB/R (15 December 2003) (adopted 9 January 2004).
US – Corrosion-Resistant Steel Sunset Review	Panel Report, *United States – Sunset Review of Anti-Dumping Duties on Corrosion-Resistant Carbon Steel Flat Products from Japan*, WT/DS244/R (14 August 2003) (adopted 9 January 2004, as modified by Appellate Body Report WT/DS244/AB/R).
US – Cotton Yarn	Appellate Body Report, *United States – Transitional Safeguard Measure on Combed Cotton Yarn from Pakistan*, WT/DS192/AB/R (8 October 2011) (adopted 5 November 2001).
US – Cotton Yarn	Panel Report, *United States – Transitional Safeguard Measure on Combed Cotton Yarn from Pakistan*, WT/DS192/R (31 May 2001) (adopted 5 November 2001, as modified by Appellate Body Report WT/DS192/AB/R).
US – Countervailing Duty Investigation on DRAMS	Appellate Body Report, *United States – Countervailing Duty Investigation on Dynamic Random Access Memory Semiconductors (DRAMS) from Korea*, WT/DS296/AB/R (27 June 2005) (adopted 20 July 2005).
US – Countervailing Duty Investigation on DRAMS	Panel Report, *United States – Countervailing Duty Investigation on Dynamic Random Access Memory Semiconductors (DRAMS) from Korea*, WT/DS296/R (21 February 2005) (adopted 20 July 2005, as modified by Appellate Body Report WT/DS296/AB/R).
US – Countervailing Measures (China)	Appellate Body Report, *United States – Countervailing and Anti-Dumping Measures on Certain Products from China*, WT/DS437/AB/R (18 December 2014) (adopted 16 January 2015).
US – Countervailing Measures (China)	Panel Report, *United States – Countervailing and Anti-Dumping Measures on Certain Products from China*, WT/DS437/R (14 July 2014) (adopted 16 January 2015, as modified by Appellate Body Report WT/DS437/AB/R).

Short Title	Full Cause Title and Citation
US – Countervailing Measures (China) (Article 21.5 – China)	Appellate Body Report, *United States – Countervailing and Anti-Dumping Measures on Certain Products from China*, WT/DS437/AB/RW (16 July 2019) (adopted 15 August 2019).
US – Countervailing Measures (China)	Panel Report, *United States – Countervailing and Anti-(Article 21.5 – China) Dumping Measures on Certain Products from China*, WT/DS437/RW (21 March 2018) (adopted 15 August 2019, as modified by Appellate Body Report WT/DS437/AB/RW).
US – Countervailing and Anti-Dumping Measures (China)	Appellate Body Report, *United States – Countervailing and Anti-Dumping Measures on Certain Products from China*, WT/DS449/AB/R (7 July 2014).
US – Countervailing and Anti-Dumping Measures (China)	Panel Report, *United States – Countervailing and Anti-Dumping Measures on Certain Products from China*, WT/DS449/R (27 March 2014).
US – Countervailing Measures on Certain EC Products	Appellate Body Report, *United States – Countervailing Measures Concerning Certain Products from the European Communities*, WT/DS212/AB/R (9 December 2002) (adopted 8 January 2003).
US – Countervailing Measures on Certain EC Products	Panel Report, *United States – Countervailing Measures Concerning Certain Products from the European Communities*, WT/DS212/R (31 July 2002) (adopted 8 January 2003, as modified by Appellate Body Report WT/DS212/AB/R).
US – Countervailing Measures on Certain EC Products (Article 21.5-EC)	Article 21.5 Panel Report, *United States – Countervailing Measures Concerning Certain Products from the European Communities*, WT/DS212/RW (17 August 2005) (adopted 27 September 2005).
US – DRAMS	Panel Report, *United States – Anti-Dumping Duty on Dynamic Random Access Memory Semiconductors (DRAMS) of One Megabit or Above from Korea*, WT/DS99/R (29 January 1999) (adopted 19 March 1999).
US – FSC	Appellate Body Report, *United States – Tax Treatment for 'Foreign Sales Corporations'*, WT/DS108/AB/R (24 February 2000) (adopted 20 March 2000).
US – FSC	Panel Report, *United States – Tax Treatment for 'Foreign Sales Corporations'*, WT/DS108/R (8 October 1999) (adopted 20 March 2000, as modified by Appellate Body Report WT/DS108/AB/R).
US – FSC (Article 21.5 – EC) Article 21.5	Appellate Body Report, *United States – Tax Treatment for 'Foreign Sales Corporations'*, WT/DS108/AB/RW (14 January 2002) (adopted 29 January 2002).
US – FSC (Article 21.5 – EC) Article 21.5	Panel Report, *United States – Tax Treatment for 'Foreign Sales Corporations'*, WT/DS108/RW (20 August 2001) (adopted 29 January 2002, as modified by Appellate Body Report WT/DS108/AB/RW).
US – FSC (Article 21.5 – EC II) Second Recourse to Article 21.5	Appellate Body Report, *United States – Tax Treatment for 'Foreign Sales Corporations'*, WT/DS108/AB/RW2 (13 February 2006) (adopted 14 March 2006).
US – FSC (Article 21.5 – EC II) Second Recourse to Article 21.5	Panel Report, *United States – Tax Treatment for 'Foreign Sales Corporations'*, WT/DS108/RW2 (adopted 14 March 2006, upheld by Appellate Body Report WT/DS108/AB/RW2).
US – FSC (Article 22.6 – US) Recourse to Article 22.6	Arbitration Report, *United States – Tax Treatment for 'Foreign Sales Corporations'*, WT/DS108/ARB (30 August 2002).

(*Continued*)

xxxviii List of abbreviated cases

(Continued)

Short Title	Full Cause Title and Citation
US – Export Restraints	Panel Report, *United States – Measures Treating Exports Restraints as Subsidies*, WT/DS194/R (29 June 2001) (adopted 23 August 2001).
US – Gambling	Appellate Body Report, *United States – Measures Affecting the Cross-Border Supply of Gambling and Betting Services*, WT/DS285/AB/R (7 April 2005) (adopted 20 April 2005).
US – Gambling	Panel Report, *United States – Measures Affecting the Cross-Border Supply of Gambling and Betting Services*, WT/DS285/R (10 November 2004) (adopted 20 April 2005, as modified by Appellate Body Report WT/DS285/AB/R).
US – Gambling (Article 21.3(c))	Article 21.3(c) Arbitration Report, *United States – Measures Affecting the Cross-Border Supply of Gambling and Betting Services*, WT/DS285/13 (19 August 2005).
US – Gambling (Article 21.5 – Antigua and Barbuda)	Article 21.5 Panel Report, *United States – Measures Affecting the Cross-Border Supply of Gambling and Betting Services*, WT/DS285/RW (30 March 2007) (adopted 22 May 2007).
US – Gambling (Article 22.6 – US)	Recourse to Article 22.6 Arbitration Report, *United States – Measures Affecting the Cross-Border Supply of Gambling and Betting Services*, WT/DS285/ARB (21 December 2007).
US – Gasoline	Appellate Body Report, *United States – Standards for Reformulated and Conventional Gasoline*, WT/DS2/AB/R (29 April 1996) (adopted 20 May 1996).
US – Gasoline	Panel Report, *United States – Standards for Reformulated and Conventional Gasoline*, WT/DS2/R (29 January 1996) (adopted 20 May 1996, as modified by Appellate Body Report WT/DS2/AB/R).
US – Hot-Rolled Steel	Appellate Body Report, *United States – Anti-Dumping Measures on Certain Hot-Rolled Steel Products from Japan*, WT/DS184/AB/R (24 July 2001) (adopted 23 August 2001).
US – Hot-Rolled Steel	Panel Report, *United States – Anti-Dumping Measures on Certain Hot-Rolled Steel Products from Japan*, WT/DS184/R (28 February 2001) (adopted 23 August 2001 modified by Appellate Body Report WT/DS184/AB/R).
US – Hot-Rolled Steel (Article 21.3(c))	Article 21.3(c) Arbitration Report, *United States – Anti-Dumping Measures on Certain Hot-Rolled Steel Products from Japan*, WT/DS184/13 (19 February 2002).
US – Lamb	Appellate Body Report, *United States – Safeguard Measures on Imports of Fresh, Chilled or Frozen Lamb Meat from New Zealand and Australia*, WT/DS177/AB/R, WT/DS178/AB/R (1 May 2001) (adopted 16 May 2001).
US – Lamb	Panel Report, *United States – Safeguard Measures on Imports of Fresh, Chilled or Frozen Lamb Meat from New Zealand and Australia*, WT/DS177/R, WT/DS178/R (21 December 2000) (adopted 16 May 2001, as modified by Appellate Body Report WT/DS177/AB/R, WT/DS178/AB/R).
US – Large Civil Aircraft (2nd Complaint)	Appellate Body Report, *United States – Measures Affecting Trade in Large Civil Aircraft (Second Complaint)*, WT/DS353/AB/R (12 March 2012) (adopted 23 March 2012).
US – Large Civil Aircraft (2nd Complaint)	Panel Report, *United States – Measures Affecting Trade in Large Civil Aircraft (Second Complaint)*, WT/DS353/R (21 March 2011) (adopted 23 March 2012, as modified by Appellate Body Report WT/DS353/AB/R).
US – Lead and Bismuth II	Appellate Body Report, *United States – Imposition of Countervailing Duties on Certain Hot-Rolled Lead and Bismuth Carbon Steel Products Originating in the United Kingdom*, WT/DS138/AB/R (10 May 2000) (adopted 7 June 2000).

Short Title	Full Cause Title and Citation
US – Lead and Bismuth II	Panel Report, *United States – Imposition of Countervailing Duties on Certain Hot-Rolled Lead and Bismuth Carbon Steel Products Originating in the United Kingdom*, WT/DS138/R (23 December 1999) (adopted 7 June 2000, upheld by Appellate Body Report WT/DS138/AB/R).
US – Line Pipe	Appellate Body Report, *United States – Definitive Safeguard Measures on Imports of Circular Welded Carbon Quality Line Pipe from Korea*, WT/DS202/AB/R (15 February 2002) (adopted 8 March 2002).
US – Line Pipe	Panel Report, *United States – Definitive Safeguard Measures on Imports of Circular Welded Carbon Quality Line Pipe from Korea*, WT/DS202/R (15 February 2002) (adopted 8 March 2002, as modified by Appellate Body Report WT/DS202/AB/).
US – Line Pipe (Article 21.3(c))	Article 21.3(c) Arbitration Report, *United States – Definitive Safeguard Measures on Imports of Circular Welded Carbon Quality Line Pipe from Korea* (26 July 2002).
US – Offset Act (Byrd Amendment)	Appellate Body Report, *United States – Continued Dumping and Subsidy Offset Act of 2000*, WT/DS217/AB/R, WT/DS234/AB/R (15 February 2002) (adopted 27 January 2003).
US – Offset Act (Byrd Amendment)	Panel Report, *United States – Continued Dumping and Subsidy Offset Act of 2000*, WT/DS217/R, WT/DS234/R (29 October 2001) (adopted 27 January 2003, as modified by Appellate Body Report WT/DS217/AB/R, WT/DS234/AB/R).
US – Oil Country Tubular Goods Sunset Reviews	Appellate Body Report, *United States – Sunset Reviews of Anti-Dumping Measures on Oil Country Tubular Goods from Argentina*, WT/DS268/AB/R (29 November 2004) (adopted 17 December 2004).
US – Oil Country Tubular Goods Sunset Reviews	Panel Report, *United States – Sunset Reviews of Anti-Dumping Measures on Oil Country Tubular Goods from Argentina*, WT/DS268/R (16 July 2004) (adopted 17 December 2004, as modified by Appellate Body Report WT/DS268/AB/R).
US – Oil Country Tubular Goods Sunset Reviews (Article 21.3(c))	Article 21.3(c) Arbitration Report, *United States – Sunset Reviews of Anti-Dumping Measures on Oil Country Tubular Goods from Argentina*, WT/DS268/12 (7 June 2005).
US – Oil Country Tubular Goods Sunset Reviews (Article 21.5 – Argentina)	Article 21.5 Appellate Body Report, *United States – Sunset Reviews of Anti-Dumping Measures on Oil Country Tubular Goods from Argentina*, WT/DS268/AB/RW (12 April 2007) (adopted 11 May 2007).
US – Oil Country Tubular Goods Sunset Reviews (Article 21.5 – Argentina)	Article 21.5 Panel Report, *United States – Sunset Reviews of Anti-Dumping Measures on Oil Country Tubular Goods from Argentina*, WT/DS268/RW (30 November 2006) (adopted 11 May 2007, as modified by Appellate Body Report WT/DS268/AB/RW).
US – Poultry (China)	Panel report *United States – Certain Measures Affecting Imports of Poultry from China*, WT/DS392/AB/R (29 September 2010) (adopted 25 October 2010).
US – Renewable Energy	Panel Report, *United States – Certain Measures Relating to the Renewable Energy Sector*, WT/DS510/R (27 June 2019).
US – Section 110(5) Copyright Act	Panel Report, *United States – Section 110(5) of the US Copyright Act*, WT/DS160/R (June 15, 2000) (adopted 27 July 2000).
US – Section 110(5) Copyright Act (Article 21.3(c))	Article 21.3(c) Arbitration Report, *United States – Section 110(5) of the US Copyright Act*, WT/DS160/12 (15 January 2001).

(*Continued*)

(Continued)

Short Title	Full Cause Title and Citation
US – Section 110(5) Copyright Act (Article 25)	Article 25 Arbitration Report, *United States – Section 110(5) of the US Copyright Act*, WT/DS160/ARB25/1 (9 November 2001).
US – Section 211 Appropriations Act	Appellate Body Report, *United States – Section 211 Omnibus Appropriations Act of 1998*, WT/DS176/AB/R (2 January 2002) (adopted 1 February 2002).
US – Section 211 Appropriations Act	Panel Report, *United States – Section 211 Omnibus Appropriations Act of 1998*, WT/DS176/R (6 August 2001) (adopted 1 February 2002, as modified by Appellate Body Report WT/DS176/AB/R).
US – Section 301 Trade Act	Panel Report, *United States – Sections 301–310 of the Trade Act of 1974*, WT/DS152/R (22 December 1999) (adopted 27 January 2000).
US – Shrimp	Appellate Body Report, *United States – Import Prohibition of Certain Shrimp and Shrimp Products*, WT/DS58/AB/R (12 October 1998) (adopted 6 November 1998).
US – Shrimp	Panel Report, *United States – Import Prohibition of Certain Shrimp and Shrimp Products*, WT/DS58/R (15 May 1998) (adopted 6 November 1998, as modified by Appellate Body Report WT/DS58/AB/R).
US – Shrimp (Thailand) / US – Customs Bond Directive	Appellate Body Report, *United States – Measures Relating to Shrimp from Thailand / United States – Customs Bond Directive for Merchandise Subject to Anti-Dumping/Countervailing Duties*, WT/DS343/AB/R; W2/DS345/AB/R (adopted 1 August 2008, DSR 2008:VII, p. 2385/DSR 2008:VIII, p. 2773).
US – Shrimp (Article 21.5 – Malaysia)	Appellate Body Report, *United States – Import Prohibition of Certain Shrimp and Shrimp Products – Recourse to Article 21.5 of the DSU by Malaysia*, WT/DS58/AB/RW (22 October 2001) (adopted 21 November 2001).
US – Shrimp (Article 21.5 – Malaysia)	Panel Report, *United States – Import Prohibition of Certain Shrimp and Shrimp Products – Recourse to Article 21.5 of the DSU by Malaysia*, WT/DS58/RW (15 June 2001) (adopted 21 November 2001, as modified by Appellate Body Report WT/DS58/AB/RW).
US – Softwood Lumber III	Panel Report, *United States – Preliminary Determinations with Respect to Certain Softwood Lumber from Canada*, WT/DS236/R (adopted 1 November 2002, DSR 2002:IX, p. 3597).
US – Softwood Lumber IV	Appellate Body Report, *United States – Final Countervailing Duty Determination with Respect to Certain Softwood Lumber from Canada*, WT/DS257/AB/R (19 January 2004) (adopted 17 February 2004, DSR 2004:II, p. 571).
US – Softwood Lumber IV	Panel Report, *United States – Final Countervailing Duty Determination with Respect to Certain Softwood Lumber from Canada*, WT/DS257/R and Corr.1 (adopted 17 February 2004, as modified by Appellate Body Report WT/DS257/AB/R, DSR 2004:II, p. 641).
US – Softwood Lumber IV (Article 21.5 – Canada)	Appellate Body Report, *United States – Final Countervailing Duty Determination with Respect to Certain Softwood Lumber from Canada – Recourse by Canada to Article 21.5 of the DSU*, WT/DS257/AB/RW (adopted 20 December 2005, DSR 2005:XXIII, p. 11357).
US – Softwood Lumber IV (Article 21.5 – Canada)	Panel Report, *United States – Final Countervailing Duty Determination with Respect to Certain Softwood Lumber from Canada – Recourse by Canada to Article 21.5 [of the DSU]*, WT/DS257/RW (adopted 20 December 2005, upheld by Appellate Body Report WT/DS257/AB/RW, DSR 2005:XXIII, p. 11401).
US – Softwood Lumber V	Appellate Body Report, *United States – Final Dumping Determination on Softwood Lumber from Canada*, WT/DS264/AB/R (adopted 31 August 2004, DSR 2004:V, p. 1875).

List of abbreviated cases   xli

Short Title	Full Cause Title and Citation
US – Softwood Lumber V	Panel Report, *United States – Final Dumping Determination on Softwood Lumber from Canada*, WT/DS264/R (adopted 31 August 2004, as modified by Appellate Body Report WT/DS264/AB/R, DSR 2004:V, p. 1937).
US – Softwood Lumber VI	Panel Report, *United States – Investigation of the International Trade Commission in Softwood Lumber from Canada*, WT/DS277/R (adopted 26 April 2004, DSR 2004:VI, p. 2485).
US – Softwood Lumber VI (Article 21.5 – Canada)	Appellate Body Report, *United States – Investigation of the International Trade Commission in Softwood Lumber from Canada – Recourse to Article 21.5 of the DSU by Canada*, WT/DS277/AB/RW (adopted 9 May 2006, and Corr.1, DSR 2006:XI, p. 4865).
US – Softwood Lumber VI (Article 21.5 – Canada)	Panel Report, *United States – Investigation of the International Trade Commission in Softwood Lumber from Canada – Recourse to Article 21.5 of the DSU by Canada*, WT/DS277/RW (adopted 9 May 2006, as modified by Appellate Body Report WT/DS277/AB/RW, DSR 2006:XI, p. 4935).
US – Stainless Steel (Mexico)	Appellate Body Report, *United States – Final Anti-Dumping Measures on Stainless Steel from Mexico*, WT/DS344/AB/R (adopted 20 May 2008, DSR 2008:II, p. 513).
US – Stainless Steel (Mexico)	Panel Report, *United States – Final Anti-Dumping Measures on Stainless Steel from Mexico*, WT/DS344/R (adopted 20 May 2008, as modified by Appellate Body Report WT/DS344/AB/R, DSR 2008:II, p. 599).
US – Stainless Steel (Mexico) (Article 21.3(c))	Award of the Arbitrator, *United States – Final Anti-Dumping Measures on Stainless Steel from Mexico – Arbitration under Article 21.3(c) of the DSU*, WT/DS344/15 (31 October 2008, DSR 2008:XX, p. 8619).
US – Stainless Steel (Mexico) (Article 21.3(c))	Panel Report, *United States – Final Anti-Dumping Measures on Stainless Steel from Mexico – Recourse to Article 21.5 of the DSU by Mexico*, WT/DS344/RW (6 May 2013, unadopted).
US – Steel Safeguards	Appellate Body Report, *United States – Definitive Safeguard Measures on Imports of Certain Steel Products*, WT/DS248/AB/R, WT/DS249/AB/R, WT/DS251/AB/R, WT/DS252/AB/R, WT/DS253/AB/R, WT/DS254/AB/R, WT/DS258/AB/R, WT/DS259/AB/R (adopted 10 December 2003, DSR 2003:VII, p. 3117).
US – Steel Safeguards	Panel Reports, *United States – Definitive Safeguard Measures on Imports of Certain Steel Products*, WT/DS248/R, WT/DS249/R, WT/DS251/R, WT/DS252/R, WT/DS253/R, WT/DS254/R, WT/DS258/R, WT/DS259/R, and Corr. 1 (adopted 10 December 2003, as modified by Appellate Body Report WT/DS248/AB/R, WT/DS249/AB/R, WT/DS251/AB/R, WT/DS252/AB/R, WT/DS253/AB/R, WT/DS254/AB/R, WT/DS258/AB/R, WT/DS259/AB/R, DSR 2003:VIII, p. 3273).
US – Supercalendered Paper	Appellate Body Report, *United States – Countervailing Measures on Supercalendered Paper from Canada*, WT/DS505/AB/R (6 February 2020) (adopted 5 March 2020).
US – Supercalendered Paper	Panel Report, *United States – Countervailing Measures on Supercalendered Paper from Canada*, WT/DS505/R (5 July 2018) (adopted 5 March 2020, as modified by Appellate Body Report WT/DS505/AB/R).
US – Tax Incentives	Appellate Body Report, *United States – Rules of Origin for Textiles and Apparel Products*, WT/DS487/AB/R (4 September 2017) (adopted on 22 September 2017).
US – Tax Incentives	Panel Report, *United States – Rules of Origin for Textiles and Apparel Products*, WT/DS487/R (28 November 2016) (adopted 22 September 2017, as modified by Appellate Body Report WT/DS487/AB/R).

(*Continued*)

(Continued)

Short Title	Full Cause Title and Citation
US – Textiles Rules of Origin	Panel Report, *United States – Rules of Origin for Textiles and Apparel Products*, WT/DS243/R and Corr.1 (adopted 23 July 2003, DSR 2003:VI, p. 2309).
US – Tuna II (Mexico)	Appellate Body Report, *United States – Measures Concerning the Importation, Marketing and Sale of Tuna and Tuna Products*, WT/DS381/AB/R (adopted June 13, 2012, DSR 2012:IV, p. 1837).
US – Tuna II (Mexico)	Panel Report, *United States – Measures Concerning the Importation, Marketing and Sale of Tuna and Tuna Products*, WT/DS381/R (adopted 13 June 2012, as modified by Appellate Body Report WT/DS381/AB/R, DSR 2012:IV, p. 2013).
US – Tyres (China)	Appellate Body Report, *United States – Measures Affecting Imports of Certain Passenger Vehicle and Light Truck Tyres from China*, WT/DS399/AB/R (adopted 5 October 2011, DSR 2011:IX, p. 4811).
US – Tyres (China)	Panel Report, *United States – Measures Affecting Imports of Certain Passenger Vehicle and Light Truck Tyres from China*, WT/DS399/R (adopted 5 October 2011, upheld by Appellate Body Report WT/DS399/AB/R, DSR 2011:IX, p. 4945).
US – Underwear	Appellate Body Report, *United States – Restrictions on Imports of Cotton and Man-made Fibre Underwear*, WT/DS24/AB/R (adopted 25 February 1997, DSR 1997:I, p. 11).
US – Underwear	Panel Report, *United States – Restrictions on Imports of Cotton and Man-made Fibre Underwear*, WT/DS24/R (adopted 25 February 1997, as modified by Appellate Body Report WT/DS24/AB/R, DSR 1997:I, p. 31).
US – Upland Cotton	Appellate Body Report, *United States – Subsidies on Upland Cotton*, WT/DS267/AB/R (3 March 2005) (adopted 21 March 2005, DSR 2005:I, p. 3).
US – Upland Cotton	Panel Report, *United States – Subsidies on Upland Cotton*, WT/DS267/R, Add.1 to Add.3 and Corr.1 (adopted 21 March 2005, as modified by Appellate Body Report WT/DS267/AB/R, DSR 2005:II, p. 299).
US – Upland Cotton (Article 21.5 – Brazil)	Appellate Body Report, *United States – Subsidies on Upland Cotton – Recourse to Article 21.5 of the DSU by Brazil*, WT/DS267/AB/RW (adopted 20 June 2008, DSR 2008:III, p. 809).
US – Upland Cotton (Article 21.5 – Brazil)	Panel Report, *United States – Subsidies on Upland Cotton – Recourse to Article 21.5 of the DSU by Brazil*, WT/DS267/RW and Corr.1 (adopted 20 June 2008, as modified by Appellate Body Report WT/DS267/AB/RW, DSR 2008:III, p. 997).
US – Upland Cotton (Article 22.6 – US I)	Decision by the Arbitrator, *United States – Subsidies on Upland Cotton – Recourse to Arbitration by the United States under Article 22.6 of the DSU and Article 4.11 of the SCM Agreement*, WT/DS267/ARB/1 (31 August 2009, DSR 2009:IX, p. 3871).
US – Upland Cotton (Article 22.6 – US II)	Decision by the Arbitrator, *United States – Subsidies on Upland Cotton – Recourse to Arbitration by the United States under Article 22.6 of the DSU and Article 7.10 of the SCM Agreement*, WT/DS267/ARB/2 and Corr.1 (31 August 2009, DSR 2009:IX, p. 4083).
US – Washing Machines	Appellate Body Report, *United States – Anti-Dumping and Countervailing Measures on Large Residential Washers from Korea*, WT/DS464/AB/R (7 September 2016) (26 September 2016).
US – Washing Machines	Panel Report, *United States – Anti-Dumping and Countervailing Measures on Large Residential Washers from Korea*, WT/DS464/R (11 March 2016) (adopted 26 September 2016, as modified by Appellate Body Report WT/DS464/AB/R)

List of abbreviated cases   xliii

Short Title	Full Cause Title and Citation
US – Wheat Gluten	Appellate Body Report, *United States – Definitive Safeguard Measures on Imports of Wheat Gluten from the European Communities*, WT/DS166/AB/R (adopted 19 January 2001, DSR 2001:II, p. 717).
US – Wheat Gluten	Panel Report, *United States – Definitive Safeguard Measures on Imports of Wheat Gluten from the European Communities*, WT/DS166/R (adopted 19 January 2001, as modified by Appellate Body Report WT/DS166/AB/R, DSR 2001:III, p. 779).
US – Wool Shirts and Blouses	Appellate Body Report, *United States – Measure Affecting Imports of Woven Wool Shirts and Blouses from India*, WT/DS33/AB/R (25 April 1997) (adopted 23 May 1997, and Corr.1, DSR 1997:I, p. 323).
US – Wool Shirts and Blouses	Panel Report, *United States – Measure Affecting Imports of Woven Wool Shirts and Blouses from India*, WT/DS33/R (6 January 1997) (adopted 23 May 1997, as upheld by Appellate Body Report WT/DS33/AB/R, DSR 1997:I, p. 343).
US – Zeroing (EC)	Appellate Body Report, *United States – Laws, Regulations and Methodology for Calculating Dumping Margins ('Zeroing')*, WT/DS294/AB/R (adopted 9 May 2006, and Corr.1, DSR 2006:II, p. 417).
US – Zeroing (EC)	Panel Report, *United States – Laws, Regulations and Methodology for Calculating Dumping Margins ('Zeroing')*, WT/DS294/R (adopted 9 May 2006, as modified by Appellate Body Report WT/DS294/AB/R, DSR 2006:II, p. 521).
US – Zeroing (EC) (Article 21.5 – EC)	Appellate Body Report, *United States – Laws, Regulations and Methodology for Calculating Dumping Margins ('Zeroing') – Recourse to Article 21.5 of the DSU by the European Communities*, WT/DS294/AB/RW and Corr.1 (adopted 11 June 2009, DSR 2009:VII, p. 2911).
US – Zeroing (EC) (Article 21.5 – EC)	Panel Report, *United States – Laws, Regulations and Methodology for Calculating Dumping Margins ('Zeroing') – Recourse to Article 21.5 of the DSU by the European Communities*, WT/DS294/RW (adopted 11 June 2009, as modified by Appellate Body Report WT/DS294/AB/RW, DSR 2009:VII, p. 3117).
US – Zeroing (Japan)	Appellate Body Report, *United States – Measures Relating to Zeroing and Sunset Reviews*, WT/DS322/AB/R (adopted 23 January 2007, DSR 2007:I, p. 3).
US – Zeroing (Japan)	Panel Report, *United States – Measures Relating to Zeroing and Sunset Reviews*, WT/DS322/R (adopted 23 January 2007, as modified by Appellate Body Report WT/DS322/AB/R, DSR 2007:I, p. 97).
US – Zeroing (Japan) (Article 21.3(c))	Report of the Arbitrator, *United States – Measures Relating to Zeroing and Sunset Reviews – Arbitration under Article 21.3(c) of the DSU*, WT/DS322/21 (11 May 2007, DSR 2007:X, p. 4160).
US – Zeroing (Japan) (Article 21.5 – Japan)	Appellate Body Report, *United States – Measures Relating to Zeroing and Sunset Reviews – Recourse to Article 21.5 of the DSU by Japan*, WT/DS322/AB/RW (adopted 31 August 2009, DSR 2009:VIII, p. 3441).
US – Zeroing (Japan) (Article 21.5 – Japan)	Panel Report, *United States – Measures Relating to Zeroing and Sunset Reviews – Recourse to Article 21.5 of the DSU by Japan*, WT/DS322/RW (adopted 31 August 2009, upheld by Appellate Body Report WT/DS322/AB/RW, DSR 2009:VIII, p. 3553).
US – Zeroing (Korea)	Panel Report, *United States – Use of Zeroing in Anti-Dumping Measures Involving Products from Korea*, WT/DS402/R (adopted 24 February 2011, DSR 2011:X, p. 5239).

xliv *List of abbreviated cases*

WTO: Request for Consultations

Short Title	Full Cause Title and Citation
India – Anti-Dumping Measures	Request for Consultations, *India – Anti-Dumping Measures on Batteries from Bangladesh*, WT/DS306/1 (20 February 2004).
Korea – Inspection of Agricultural Products	Request for Consultations, *Korea – Measures Concerning the Testing and Inspection of Agricultural Products*, WT/DS3/1 (1995).
Korea – Telecommunications Procurement	Request for Consultations, *Korea – Laws, Regulations and Practices in the Telecommunications Procurement Sector*, WT/DS40/1 (1996).
Peru Tax Treatment	Request for Consultations, *Peru – Tax Treatment on Certain Imported Products*, WT/DS255/1 (2002).
Turkey – Restrictions on Imports	Request for Consultations, *Turkey – Restrictions on Imports of Textiles and Clothing Procedures*, WT/DS40/1 (1996).
US – Softwood Lumber	Panel Report, *United States – Measures Affecting Imports of Softwood Lumber from Canada* (SCM/162) (19 February 1993) (adopted on 27 October 1993).
US – Anti-Dumping Investigation (Mexico)	Request for Consultations, *United States – Anti-Dumping Investigation Regarding Imports of Fresh or Chilled Tomatoes from Mexico*, WT/DS49/1 (1996).

GATT 1947 Panel Reports

1 *Australia – Ammonium Sulphate*, GATT Working Party Report, *The Australian Subsidy on Ammonium Sulphate*, GATT/CP.4/39 – II/188 (31 March 1950) (adopted 3 April 1950).
2 *Belgium – Family Allowances*, GATT Panel Report, *Belgian Family Allowances (Allocations Familiales)*, BISD 1S/59 (adopted 7 November 1952).
3 *Canada – FIRA*, Panel Report, *Canada Administration of the Foreign Investment Review Act*, L/5504–30S/140 (25 July 1983) (7 February 1984).
4 *Canada – Herring and Salmon*, Panel Report, *Canada – Measures Affecting Exports of Unprocessed Herring and Salmon*, L/6268–35S/98 (20 November 1987) (22 March 1988).
5 *Canada – Ice Cream Yoghurt*, Panel Report, *Canada – Import Restrictions on Ice Cream Yoghurt*, L/6568–36S/68 (27 September 1989) (5 December 1989).
6 *Canada – Provincial Liquor Boards (US)*, Panel Report, *Canada – Import, Distribution and Sale of Certain Alcoholic Drinks by Provincial Marketing Agencies*, DS17/R – 39S/27 (16 October 1991) (18 February 1992).
7 *EC – Oilseeds I*, Panel Report, *European Communities – Payments and Subsidies Paid to Processors and Producers of Oilseeds and Related Animal-Feed Proteins*, L/6627–37S/86 (14 December 1989) (adopted 25 January 1990).
8 *EEC – Animal Feed Proteins*, Panel Report, *EEC Measures on Animal Feed Proteins*, L/4599–25S/49 (2 December 1977) (14 March 1978).
9 *EEC – Imports of Beef*, Panel Report, *European Economic Community – Imports of Beef from Canada*, L/5099–28S/92 (23 January 1981) (adopted 10 March 1981).

10 *EEC – Minimum Import Prices* Panel Report, *European Community Programme of Minimum Import Prices, Licences and Surety Deposits for Certain Processed Fruits and Vegetables*, L/4687–25S/68 (4 October 1978) (18 October 1978).

11 *EEC – Parts and Components*, Panel Report, *EEC – Regulation on Imports of Parts and Components*, L/6657–37S/132 (22 March 1990) (adopted 16 May 1990).

12 *Germany – Sardines*, Panel Report, *Treatment by Germany of Imports of Sardines*, G/26–1S/53 (30 October 1952) (31 October 1952).

13 *India – Tax Rebates on Exports*, Application of Article I:1 to Rebates on Internal Taxes, Ruling by the Chairperson, II GATT BISD (24 August 1948).

14 *Italy – Agricultural Machinery*, Panel Report, *Italian Discrimination Against Imported Agricultural Machinery*, L/833–7S/60 (15 July 1958) (23 October 1958).

15 *Japan – Alcoholic Beverages I*, Panel Report, *Japan – Customs Duties, Taxes and Labelling Practices on Imported Wines and Alcoholic Beverages*, L/6216–34S/83 (13 October 1987) (10 November 1987).

16 *Japan – Semi-Conductors*, Panel Report, *Japan – Trade in Semi-Conductors*, L/6309–35S/116 (24 March 1988) (4 May 1988).

17 *Japan – SPF Dimension Lumber*, Panel Report, *Canada/Japan: Tariff on Imports of Spruce, Pine, Fir (SPF) Dimension Lumber*, L/6470–36S/167 (26 April 1989) (19 July 1989).

18 *Spain – Unroasted Coffee*, Panel Report, *Spain – Tariff Treatment of Unroasted Coffee*, L/5135–28S/102 (27 April 1981) (adopted 11 June 1981).

19 *Subsidy on Ammonium Sulphate*, 3 April 1950, GATT BISD (Vol II) at 188 (1952).

20 *Uruguayan Recourse to Article XXIII*, L/1923–11S/95 (15 November 1962) (adopted on 16 November 1962).

21 *US – Fur Felts Hat*, Working Party Report, *Report of the Withdrawal by the United States of a Tariff Concession Under Article XIX of the General Agreement on Tariffs and Trade*, CP/106 (27 March 1951).

22 *US – Imports of Spring Assemblies*, Panel Report, *US – Imports of Certain Automotive Spring Assemblies*, L/5333–30S/107 (11 June 1982) (26 May 1983).

23 *US – Malt Beverages*, Panel Report, *United States – Measures Affecting Alcoholic Beverages*, DS23/R – 39S/206 (16 March 1992) (19 June 1992).

24 *US – Manufacturing Clause*, Panel Report, *The United States Manufacturing Clause*, L/5609–31S/74 (1 March 1984) (15/16 May 1984).

25 *US – MFN Footwear*, Panel Report, *United States – Denial of Most-Favoured-Nation Treatment as to Non-Rubber Footwear from Brazil*, DS18/R – 39S/128 (10 January 1992) (adopted 19 June 1992).

26 *US – Restrictions on Imports of Tuna Products* (1982), Panel Report, *US – Prohibition of Imports of Tuna and Tuna Products from Canada*, L/5198–29S/91 (22 December 1981) (22 February 1982).

27 *US – Section 337*, Panel Report, *United States – Section 337 of the Tariff Act of 1930*, L/6439–36S/345 (16 January 1989) (7 November 1989).

28 *US – Superfund*, Panel Report, *United States – Taxes on Petroleum and Certain Imported Substances*, L6175–34S/136 (5 June 1987) (adopted 17 June 1987).

29 *US – Taxes on Automobiles*, Panel Report, *United States – Taxes on Automobiles*, DS31/R (11 October 1994) (not adopted).

30 The Decision of 5 April 1966 on *Procedures under Article XXIII applying to disputes between developing and developed contracting parties* (BISD 14S/18).

31 The Decision on *Dispute Settlement*, contained in the Ministerial Declaration of *29 November 1982* (BISD 29S/13).

32 The Decision on *Dispute Settlement of 30 November 1984* (BISD 31S/9).
33 The Decision of 12 April 1989 on *Improvements to the GATT Dispute Settlement Rules and Procedures* (BISD 36S/61;63) para. F(a).
34 The Understanding on *Notification, Consultation, Dispute Settlement and Surveillance*, adopted on 28 November 1979 (BISD 26S/210).
35 The Understanding Regarding Notification, Consultation, Dispute Settlement and Surveillance (28 November 1979), GATT (BISD 26S/210; 212).

Reported Cases: International Court of Justice (ICJ)

1 *Aegean Sea Continental Shelf (Greece v Turkey)* [1978] ICJ Rep., p. 3.
2 *Anglo-Iranian Oil Company, United Kingdom v Iran* [1952] ICJ Rep., p. 93.
3 *Barcelona Traction, Light and Power Company Ltd* [1970] ICJ Rep., p. 32.
4 *Delimitation of the Maritime Boundary in the Gulf of Maine Area (Canada/US)* [1984] ICJ Rep., p. 246.
5 *Fisheries Jurisdiction Case* [1974] ICJ Rep., p. 3.
6 *Gulf of Maine Case* [1984] ICJ Rep., p. 309.
7 *Kasikili/Sedudu Island* [1999] ICJ Rep., p. 1045.
8 *Maritime Dispute (Peru v Chile)* [2014] ICJ Rep., p. 3.
9 *Maritime Delimitation in the Indian Ocean (Somalia v Kenya)* (Preliminary Objections), 2 February 2017.
10 *Namibia (Legal Consequences) Advisory Opinion* [1971] ICJ Rep., p. 31.
11 *Nicaragua v United States of America* [1986] ICJ Rep., p. 114.
12 *North Sea Continental Shelf Cases* [1969] ICJ Rep., p. 3.
13 *Question of Delimitation of the Continental Shelf between Nicaragua and Colombia* (Preliminary Objections) [2016] ICJ Rep., p. 100.
14 *Temple of Preah Vihear* [1962] ICJ Rep., p. 143.
15 *WHO v Egypt* (ICJ Advisory Opinion, 25 March 1951).

Reported Cases: UK and Other Jurisdictions

1 *Chief Constable of North Wales Police v Evans* [1982] 3 All ER 141.
2 *Earth Island Institute v Hogarth*, United States Court of Appeals for the Ninth Circuit, 484 F.3d (9th Cir. 2007) 1123.

Part I
Trade Theory, Founding of the WTO, and Key Principles

1 Trade Theory and the World Trade Organization

Learning Objectives	3
1. Introduction	4
2. International Trade Theories	4
2.1 Mercantilism	5
3. Pre-Classical Theories	7
3.1 Pre-Classical: Physiocrats	7
4. Classical Economics: Adam Smith	9
4.1 Invisible Hand	10
4.2 The Division of Labour	10
4.3 Absolute Advantage and Factors of Production	11
5. Classical Economics: David Ricardo	11
5.1 Gold Standard	12
5.2 Theory of Diminishing Returns – The Corn Model	13
5.3 Theory of Comparative Advantage and Foreign Trade	14
6. Classical Economics: Karl Marx	16
6.1 Criticism of Classical Economics	17
6.2 Historical Materialism and Economic Theory	17
6.3 Labour Theory of Value	19
6.4 Theory of Rent, Money and Surplus Value	19
7. Liberalism	21
8. The Keynesian Economic Thought	22
8.1 Historical Background and Writings	22
8.2 Keynes and Classical Economic Thought	22
8.3 The Theories	23
8.4 Keynes's Legacy	25
9. Summary	26

Learning Objectives

This chapter aims to provide the students with

1. An introduction to international trade theories;
2. An introduction to the classical economic theories of Adam Smith, David Ricardo, and Karl Marx;
3. An introduction to liberalism, Keynesian economic thought, and Keynes's legacy; and
4. An introduction to the economic theories that underpin the WTO.

DOI: 10.4324/9780367028183-2

1. Introduction

A study of the World Trade Organization and its laws presuppose an understanding of the underlying economic principles that shaped international trade in the twentieth century and how they continue to do so in the twenty-first century. While an overview of the economic principles of the post-World War II era of international trade – from the 1940s, as well as during the GATT era before the founding of the WTO in 1995 – will shed light on the underlying economic principles that drive the multilateral trade organisation's objectives and operations, it may not suffice for the current discourse. As international trade has been an important feature of the world economy for centuries, it will serve our purposes to take a peek into the development of economic thoughts from the sixteenth century onwards, which coincided with the discovery of the 'New World'. This discovery brought unheard of wealth to European shores in the form of gold, silver, and more. It was also a time when 'mercantilist' thought was fast emerging in Europe, supporting the expansion of empires and the founding of nation states, besides the development of international trade. The aforementioned approach will allow us to gain a deeper understanding and appreciation of the underlying theories, principles, and justifications of the international economic order which we currently have in place.

The WTO's economic principles are based on the neoliberal model of capitalism, which is an extension of economic liberalism that emerged in the post-World War II era. The business-to-business (B2B) model of international trade is predicated on the economic principles driven largely by profits and the desire to earn foreign exchange. On the other hand, international trade as performed under the aegis of the WTO does not have the same narrow economic model, as the objectives of the multilateral trade body goes beyond mere profit making, as it has a much wider remit containing non-economic reasons.

2. International Trade Theories

Although international trade's origins can be traced back thousands of years in human history, it is not to be understood that it was performed on the back of a well-thought-out economic policy or even a business plan, for that matter. In the early millennia, there was scepticism about trading with 'foreigners', and the Greek and Roman writers took differing views on the use of the sea to pursue trade, with some being ambivalent about the advantages of being close to the sea. Writers like Plutarch, though, held the view that in the absence of the sea, man would be "savage and destitute", as it promoted exchange amongst different nationalities.[1] Plutarch's words highlight the interdependence of human cultures and how trade helps by not only being beneficial to the trader but also facilitating a more important function, *viz.*, exchange of resources, ideas, cultures, *etc*. The Greek philosopher Aristotle had his reservations about international trade, or trading overseas, and condemned the use of 'money' in trade (as opposed to barter), branding the same as 'justly discredited' – for it is not in accordance with nature, but involves men's taking things from one another.[2]

The theory of international trade concerns itself with the causes, the structure, and the volume of international trade and is essentially microeconomic in approach and outlook. The theory of international trade proceeds on the assumption that trade takes place in the form of barter, or money, and the international accounts of a country *vis-à-vis* all the others always balance, which means that no balance-of-payment problem exists. International trade theory is contained in three main models, which are (i) the classical theory (Torrens-Ricardo), which states that the determinants of trade are to be found in technological differences between countries; (ii) the Heckscher-Ohlin theory, which stresses the differences in factor endowments between different countries; and (iii) the neoclassical theory, according to which these determinants are to be found simultaneously in the differences between technologies, factor endowments, and tastes of different countries (Gandolfo, 2014).

2.1 Mercantilism

Mercantilism was a school of thought that emerged in sixteenth- to eighteenth-century England and amongst the key nation states of continental Europe. It is considered as a long chapter in the history of European economic thought that shaped national economic policies roughly between 1500 to 1800 (Allen, 1991) and is viewed as the precursor to the classical school of economic thought. The term *système mercantile* was first used in 1763 by French writer de Mirabeau in a passage in his work *Philosophie Rurale*, in which he overtly attacked the idea that a nation may profit from the importation of money (Magnusson, 2015). In the 1860s, German writers used the expression *Merkantilismus* to refer to this particular school of thought, and corresponding terms such as 'mercantilism' in English were used (Viner and Irwin, 1991).[3] It is also to be borne in mind that the word 'mercantilism' has been used in a number of ways and does not have a standard definition.

Although mercantilism was the major economic thought spanning over three centuries, no major theoretical treatises are to be found on the subject. It should be noted that the precepts of mercantilism were the economic components of state building, which provided much of the justification. Vaggi and Groenewegen note that the discovery of the New World and the establishment of colonies in the fifteenth century by European states witnessed a large flow of gold and silver into Europe from Mexico and Peru, which resulted in semi-barter exchanges in markets giving way to more widespread use of money.[4] Most of the gold from the New World was flowing into Spain, which applied bullionist restrictions over a lengthy period of time and imposed the death penalty for exporting gold and silver. Although prohibited from being exported, Spanish gold found its way all over Europe and to some extent was responsible for the long period of inflation.

The cornerstone of mercantilism was the notion that a nation's wealth was through the accumulation of gold and silver, and that nations without gold and silver mines could obtain them only by selling more goods than they bought from abroad. England did not have any gold or silver mines, and an export of goods and services to provide for an accumulation of bullion was seen as the way forward, with a unilateral gain in foreign trade and in specie inflow.[5] Hence, the earliest phase of mercantilism was referred to as 'bullionism'. Mercantilists measured national wealth as the amount of 'international reserves' at the disposal of a state, which in their view could be increased by bringing in more gold and silver within the jurisdiction of a state or preventing the 'outflow' of the same.[6] Under the doctrine, a great deal of emphasis was placed on maintaining an excess of exports of goods and services over imports, as the objective was to promote production and commerce, which in turn contributed to the prosperity and power of the nation state. Manufacturing activities were gradually brought within the nation state, which necessitated taking protectionist measures from foreign competitors, leading to the end of the age of 'bullionism' and the birth of new mercantilist thinking.[7] In short, mercantilism was to steadily grow into an economic theory and political movement which advocated utilising the state's military power to ensure internal markets and their supply sources were protected.

Only with the publication of *Wealth of Nations*, in which Adam Smith interpreted mercantilism as the opposite of the 'free trade system', was mercantilism constructed into a coherent system (Magnusson, 2015).[8] Later, mercantilism was also to be portrayed as 'protectionism'. The authors of mercantilism were businessmen or government officials on the Continent who were keen on self-promoting their policies, rather than being dispassionate scholars advocating for a sound economic policy based on principles. The works were often short and took the shape of pamphlets and were designed to convince the public and the government to implement the policies most favourable to their trading companies. The work of Thomas Mun, published in 1664, entitled *England's Treasure by Forraign Trade*, and referred to as the 'classic of English Mercantilism' by Schumpeter, presents a justification for adopting such an approach towards trade beyond the seas (Vaggi and Groenewegen, 2006).[9] Mercantilism can be considered as the earliest systematic theorizing in political economy.

Most strikingly, the classical mercantilists favoured national gains through the power of a centralised state, while abandoning the goals of universal good which were promoted earlier under transnational Christendom (Paul and Amawi, 2013). The doctrine elevated the commercial interests to the level of national policy, as it led to government intervention in the market, imposing higher tariffs on foreign goods to restrict import trade, and simultaneously improving export prospects for domestic goods through the grant of subsidies. These measures, according to mercantilists, would ensure more money came into the country, discourage wealth leaving the country, and help maintain a positive balance of trade with a surplus of exports. For the mercantilists, money and gold were the only source of riches – which was in limited quantity and to be shared amongst the countries. International trade could not benefit all countries simultaneously.

As international trade became more important, merchants allied themselves with the state to exploit the emerging possibilities of international commerce, culminating in the formation of big merchant trading companies, for example the Dutch East India Company and the English East India Company. These companies both went on to establish transcontinental trading corporations, and also along the way facilitated colonisation of parts of sub-Saharan Africa, the Indian subcontinent, the Caribbean, *etc*. Favours granted to those close to power were often defended with mercantilist reasoning. Implementation of mercantilist economic principles became a cause of frequent European wars and actively encouraged colonial expansion with a view to discover gold and silver. England was to emerge victorious in the trade wars that were to follow amongst the European nation states of Spain, Portugal, Holland, and France in the sixteenth, seventeenth, and eighteenth centuries. Nevertheless, historical economist Gustav Schmoller from the late nineteenth century perceived mercantilism as a doctrine of state building that was used to bolster a weak state to that of a nation state (Schmoller, 1987).

The mercantilists urged their governments to closely regulate international trade in order to maintain favourable balance of trade (arguing for aggressive export and restrictive import policies) and to promote manufacturing of raw materials at home, rather than importing manufactured goods (Trebilcock, Howse, and Eliason, 2013). However, the mercantilists never adequately explained how the foreigners were to pay for imports without the ability to export. Increasing the population, as a source of labour, and military manpower were favoured by the mercantilists, but on the other hand it was argued that wages were to be kept low to minimise production costs. The mercantilists considered the colonies as a potential source for the demands of the mother-country exports, tax revenues, raw materials, unusual products and gold, military bases, source of manpower, an outlet for unwanted population, *etc*. (Allen, 1991). One could see mercantilism was geared more towards geopolitics as well as economics, and the competitive struggle of the European nation states is part of the history of mercantilism. While not being recognised as a 'proper doctrine', mercantilism had received widespread criticism and condemnation in some quarters. Hunt and Lautzenheiser (2011) note that it is hard to determine how much of mercantilist thinking was driven by the desire to increase the power of the state and how much of it was to promote a policy which would protect the interests of the capitalists (2011).

According to Adam Smith, who devoted a chapter in his acclaimed work to discuss mercantilism as a doctrine,[10] the fundamental fallacy of mercantilism lay in the fact that it confused wealth with money. In Smith's view, those who gained through the system of mercantilism were the monopolistic merchants and manufacturers who increased their capital, and not the general public; and that the whole 'commercial system' at its core was a giant conspiracy led by powerful interest groups pursuing their own selfish interests. J. R. McCulloch, another critic of mercantilism,[11] who is credited with writing the preface to Smith's book, was of the opinion that the mercantilist notion of wealth was incorrect, as the wealth of individuals and that of states was not to be measured by the abundance of their products, but only by the value of the commodities through which they were able to procure the precious metals; and that to merely increase the amount of national wealth by imposing a ban on the export of bullion and encouraging the importation of bullion cannot be considered as a sound system. However, in 1752 David Hume was able to question the fundamental tenet of mercantilism by demonstrating that international trade was more likely to maintain an equilibrium in the balance of payments through the price-specie-flow mechanism.[12]

During the early nineteenth century, Smith's idea of a 'commercial system', which he espoused in his work published in 1766, was to find favour with the economists of his time and establish itself as a key doctrine. Mercantilism, which had endured for about three centuries as an economic thought, was to decline and fade away with the arrival of the physiocrats and the emergence of Scottish moral philosophers Adam Smith and David Ricardo.

3. Pre-Classical Theories

Capitalism as a dominant political economic thought and socio-economic system was to emerge in the aftermath of mercantilism. With the publication of Smith's and Ricardo's works, capitalism gained in significance and cemented its place as the single most important economic system in the world. As Samuels (1992) notes, important considerations are resident in the expositions of the physiocrats and the English/Scottish economists from the eighteenth and nineteenth centuries, as they are concerned with the institutions which make the economy what it is today. They also concern the power structure which helps form the economy and the economic role of both government and other, non-legal forces of social control.

3.1 Pre-Classical: Physiocrats

A group of French economic proponents known as physiocrats were to emerge in the 1750s, advocating economic freedom.[13] The leading figure amongst the physiocrats was François Quesnay, who served as royal physician to the king of France, Louis XV.[14] Quesnay was equally interested in the then prevailing social system in France, apart from his chosen avocation – medicine.[15] He proceeded to synthesise his knowledge of agriculture and his training as a medical doctor to put forward his 'economic' theories, which are well captured in his work from 1758 and entitled *Tableau Economique* (The Economic Table). In his work, which was originally prepared for Louise XV, Quesnay strongly advocated that the production from the land was the foundation of prosperity, and that the manufacturing and industrial crafts were only derivatives of wealth.[16] In other words, for Quesnay only agriculture was capable of yielding a surplus (*produit net*), and manufacturing did not create a net product, as it took up as much value as inputs into production as it created in output. Hence, the wealth of a nation was to be measured by the size of the net product and not in the stocks of gold or silver – which was clearly contrary to the mercantilist's position. It should be borne in mind that before the Industrial Revolution, industrial activity yielded extremely low returns, but farming on the other hand produced a far better yield despite the use of primitive methods of cultivation.

Quesnay's principles were premised on the grounds that there was a circular flow of economic coordination, which relied on the interdependency of the various specialised activities within the economic order. The physiocrats' conception of man and the social order is to be found in the work of Pierre-Paul Mercier de la Rivière entitled *The Natural and Essential Order of Political Societies* (1767). According to de la Rivière, man had the right to secure what was necessary for his survival, and that right would also include the right to acquire (by his own work) those things that are useful to his existence as well as the right to keep them after their acquisition. Quesnay was critical of the economic policy of the French kingdom, which according to him was too close to the commercial interests. In Quesnay's view France was an agricultural kingdom, a large country with rich soil and in need of an economic policy that would support a large agricultural production leading to prosperity. For Quesnay the farmers constituted the core of the productive class, and their level of production depended very much on the size of their capital, which could be aided by the implementation of the correct economic policy.

Quesnay strongly advocated a single tax on landed property – to be directly paid by the landlords – instead of a complicated scattered taxation. Under this system the farmers would pay the whole net product to the landlord, who in turn would pay all the taxes to the king and the Church, relieving the farmers of any threat from the taxman. The physiocrats demanded the abolition of the *corvée*,[17] the removal of restrictions on internal trade and labour migration, state-sponsored monopolies, and trading privileges, besides the dismantling of the guild system. Quesnay was against price fixing and held the strong view that only competition could regulate prices with equity and that there was no need for the government to regulate the prices at which goods were bought and sold. In other words, the best policy for the government to follow was *laissez passer et laissez faire* – meaning 'let be and let pass',[18] and in the context to be understood as 'let goods pass and leave men to take their decisions'. It can be seen that the physiocrats were opposed to all feudal, mercantilist, and government restrictions and favoured the freedom of business enterprise at home and free trade abroad. The physiocrats at their peak were influential in getting an act passed in 1764 concerning the freedom of the grain and flour trade.

Another name worth mentioning here is Anne-Robert-Jacques Turgot, who was acquainted with the physiocrats Gournay and Dupont. It is documented that Turgot met with Adam Smith during the latter's stay in Paris in 1765. Turgot penned essays on political economy, covering topics on taxes, grain trade, money, interest, *etc*. When appointed by Louis XVI as the contrôleur général, he swiftly re-established the freedom of the internal grain trade. Turgot endorsed Quesnay's view of free trade and argued that it would not raise the average price of corn in France, as it would rise only due to a change between supply and demand. Commentators note that he was directly in line with classical political economy, and not entirely in line with the physiocratic principles expounded by Quesnay (Steiner, 2003). Turgot also developed theories relating to value (based on utility), capital, profit, and interest. Turgot did not share the political ideas of the physiocrats with regards to legal despotism and preferred the simple principle of 'complete freedom' over that of 'enlightened monarch' as one of the pillars of the organisation of modern societies. Turgot also held the view that the physiocrats should elaborate more on the principle of competition and free trade.

It is evident that both Quesnay and Turgot contributed enormously to the foundations of French political economic thought, and it is only just to say that they offered the most important material on the subject prior to the work of Adam Smith. Hoselitz (1968, p. 637) notes that physiocrats were instrumental in developing a full-fledged theoretical system of capitalism at a period when "in all European countries capitalism as a dominant social system was yet non-existent". For Marx, and Engels the physiocrats were the first "systematic spokesmen of capital" (Marx and Engels 1979).[19] Their economic analysis exposed the weaknesses of mercantilism, and their ideologies proved favourable to the French Revolution of 1789, which in turn swept away the numerous obstacles to progress. While the physiocrats' examination of the society as a whole and the analysis of the laws surrounding the circulation of wealth and goods were a lasting contribution to economics, their views on industrial activity and trade as being sterile were wrong. In sum, through the promotion of *laissez faire* economy, the physiocrats paved the way for capitalistic economic development.

4. Classical Economics: Adam Smith

The Industrial Revolution, which was still in a nascent state in the mid-eighteenth century, was to make inroads into the political economic thinking of the time, paving the way for the emergence of classical economic thought. The steam engine, the spinning jenny, and the power loom were transforming the employment landscape, and real wages started to climb. During the mid and later part of the eighteenth century, Scotland produced a distinguished branch of the European Enlightenment. Some of the pre-eminent figures who were part of the movement included David Hume and Adam Smith and contributed much to the intellectual activity. Some of the important fields that the Scottish Enlightenment contributed to were the enquiry into 'the progress of society', touching upon history, moral and political philosophy and, importantly for discussions, political economy. The period of Enlightenment, which was embodied in unbounded faith in science, reason, and economic individualism as opposed to superstition, religious fanaticism, and aristocratic power, gained ground and spread fast. Enlightenment thinkers were optimists who generally believed that human thought and energy could produce virtually unlimited progress, and the philosophy was built on the individual's ability to reason and the concept of natural order.

Adam Smith, the Scottish economist, is perceived as the founder of modern economics[20] and leader of the Scottish Enlightenment. A pioneer of political economy, Smith's work *An Inquiry Into the Nature and Causes of the Wealth of Nations* is considered to be the first modern work on economics. Smith is credited with propounding the trade theory of absolute advantage and also a more sophisticated theoretical approach to international trade (Schumacher, 2013). Smith was elected professor of logic in Glasgow College in 1751, the following year he assumed the chair of moral philosophy, and in 1759 he was to publish his work *The Theory of Moral Sentiments*.[21] Smith spent over two years in France,[22] during which period he became friends with the physiocrats Quesnay and Turgot and also commenced work on his book *An Enquiry Into the Nature and Causes of the Wealth of Nations*. The book was published in 1776 in two volumes and was to have a colossal global impact, establishing Smith's reputation as the protagonist of modern economic thought.

The key influencing factors on Smith were the general intellectual climate of his time, *viz.*, the period of Scottish Enlightenment; the doctrines of the physiocrats – especially Quesnay[23] and Turgot;[24] his writer-philosopher friend David Hume; and above all Sir Isaac Newton, whose model of natural science he greatly admired as being universal and harmonious.[25] Smith in his book put forward a universal formula for prosperity and financial freedom that was to revolutionise economic thought for the centuries to come. Smith's sympathies lay with the average citizens, and he had little regard for the men of commercial power. Smith claimed that his model for economy would result in "universal opulence which extends itself to the lowest ranks of the people" (Smith and Cannan, 1976, Vol 1, Ch I, p. 15). He branded his model, which he espoused in his book, as the "system of natural liberty" (Smith and Cannan, 1976, Vol 2, Ch IX, p. 208), and sought to dismantle the conventional view of economy, which had allowed the mercantilists to take control of commercial interests and political powers of the day and replace them with his own view of the real source of wealth and economic growth (Skousen, 2007). In Smith's view mercantilist policies only benefitted the producers and the monopolists and merely imitated real prosperity. A proponent for limited government, Smith's economic theory is closely linked to classical political liberalism.

4.1 Invisible Hand

A distinguishing feature of Smith's work from his predecessors was the development of a complete model of nature, structure, and workings of the capitalist system. It was the first fully systematic 'quasi-natural-law treatment' of economics, which presented a unified concept of economic system with mutually interdependent parts (O'Brien, 2004). The famous phrase 'the invisible hand' was coined by Smith to explain the system of free enterprise that benefits society in general, even though it is not the aim of any particular economic agent to do so. The expression was a metaphor for describing the mutually beneficial aspect of trade in an exchange economy that emerged as the unintended consequence of individual human actions (Vaughn, 1989).[26] This notion helped Smith develop the first comprehensive theory of the economy as an interrelated social system. In Vaughn's analysis the metaphor is composed of three logical steps – that human action often led to unintended consequences by the actors, that such unintended consequences could result in an order that is understandable to the human mind, and that the overall order is beneficial to the participants in ways that they did not intend but nevertheless find desirable.

For Smith the players in the economy pursued their own personal goals and interests, *viz.*, the businessman pursued profit from his investments,[27] the consumer was on the lookout for a good deal on a commodity (lowest price and good quality), and the worker was to find the highest wages possible (Smith, 1977). The self-interested behaviour is channelled in such a way by the invisible hand that the social good emerges from the activity. Newton's vision of the universe is quite visible when Smith presents his argument that hidden beneath the apparent chaos of economic activity is a natural order. However, in a clear departure from the *laissez faire* doctrine, he warned that the operation of the invisible hand would likely fail in case of collusion amongst market actors who seek to manipulate prices and restrict supply.

4.2 The Division of Labour

Smith presented his major explanation for the growth of national wealth as the 'division of labour', an unfamiliar phrase during his time. According to Smith, both gross and net revenue of society depended upon the division of labour. For Smith, the division of labour increased the quantity of output produced as each worker goes on to develop increased skill in performing a single task repeatedly; that time will be saved if the worker were not to move from one type of work to another; and that machinery can be invented to increase productivity once tasks are simplified through the division of labour. To prove his point, Smith presented the example of a pin factory, where each worker was taxed with a particular task – the division of labour – leading to higher production and efficiency. In short, division of labour leads to both quantitative and qualitative production improvements, stimulation of technological development, and thereby a further enhancement to productivity. Smith also stressed that there was more scope for the application of the division of labour in the manufacturing process than in agriculture, and that the division of labour was limited by the extent of the market. With the prior arguments Smith was out to prove that his idea of wealth of nations was a clear break from traditional economic notions then in prevalence, which was based on mercantilism (Smith, 1977).

4.3 Absolute Advantage and Factors of Production

Smith, a strong proponent of free trade, viewed the theory of international trade being clearly founded on the division of labour, which contributed to the improvement in the productive powers of labour. Using labour as the sole input, Smith propounded his principle of absolute advantage, according to which a country will have an absolute if it can produce a particular commodity at a lower cost than another – this meant that fewer resources are allocated to provide the same amount of the commodity as compared to another country. According to Smith, this efficiency in the production of the commodity created 'an absolute advantage', which allows for beneficial trade. Absolute advantage was built on a country's intrinsic capability to produce more of a particular commodity than a competitor country could. When countries produce commodities of their absolute advantage, they would gain by exchanging part of its output with each other for the commodity of its absolute disadvantage.

Smith further argued that it was not possible for all nations to become simultaneously rich, as the export of one nation is the import of another, and strongly advocated free trade, whereby all nations engaged in trade will stand to gain, and absolute advantages in different commodities would help them gain simultaneously. Smith was able to see clearly the interconnection between the social classes and the sectors of production; the distributions of wealth and income; commerce; the circulation of money; the processes of price formation; and the process of economic growth (Hunt and Lautzenheiser, 2011). Not surprisingly, Smith's theory of absolute advantage included the three distinct factors of production – land, labour, and capital, and the three categories of return – rent, wages, and profit. Using the factors of production, he was able to demonstrate the flow of goods and services between the sectors involved, as well as amongst the different socio-economic groups, *viz.*, landlords, capitalists, and labourers.

5. Classical Economics: David Ricardo

David Ricardo, whose parents migrated from Holland to England, was trained from an early age by his father in stock broking. Ricardo was very successful in his stock broking business and became a wealthy man even before his 30th birthday. Ricardo is considered the most rigorous theoretician of the classical economic school, and it is generally agreed that he is the creator of the classical theory of international trade. Ricardo's contribution to trade theory is unique, in the sense it stands out as one of the masterpieces in the history of trade theory, and even today serves as a point of reference in the discipline. Jones and

Weder (2017) note that Ricardo created the first real system of political economy with a methodological approach with the use of mathematical and tabular expressions, thereby shaping the field itself. Ricardo was a businessman, political economist, and member of Parliament,[28] and he proved to be a success in each of the chosen activities. A strong advocate of free trade, Ricardo was to make several lasting contributions to the field of economic analysis, including through his theory of comparative advantage, presentation of the law of diminishing returns in agriculture, and the inclusion of the distribution of income in economic analysis.

He published his *Essay on the Influence of a Low Price of Corn on the Profits of Stock; Shewing the Inexpediency of Restrictions on the Importation of Foreign Corn* (known as *Essay on Profits*) at a time when the question of Corn Laws was brought before the Parliament for debate. James Mill, one of Ricardo's enduring friends, encouraged him to write an elaborated version of his *Essay on Profits* (*Essay*), while Ricardo was not convinced that he possessed the necessary qualities to embark on a project of that scale (Gerber, 2017).[29] Implored by Mill, Ricardo started work on the larger book soon thereafter, and went on to publish *On the Principles of Political Economy and Taxation* (*Principles*) on 19 April 1817.[30] Ricardo defined the principal problem in political economy as the determination of the laws/rules that regulate the natural course of rent, profit, and wages. He addressed the issues both in the *Essay* and in the *Principles*, which resulted in covering, on the one hand, the laws/rules governing rent, profit, and wages, and on the other hand developing the labour theory of value, a theory of international comparative advantage, monetary theory, and a detailed analysis devoted to "the influence of taxation on different classes of the community" (Ricardo and McCulloch, 1846).

5.1 Gold Standard

The Bank of England's gold reserves had dipped to dangerous levels following the almost two-decade-long warfare with France in the late eighteenth/early nineteenth century. According to Ricardo, the problem was not the low value of the pound sterling but the high price of gold. The situation prompted the Bank of England to suspend cash payments, and as a result, individuals holding paper currency were not able to redeem them for gold. In 1813, the price of gold rose steadily from its mint price of £3.17 per ounce to a market price of £5.10, which was also coupled with general price inflation. This witnessed gold being sold in the private domestic market or overseas market for a higher price. The situation prompted Ricardo, who had dealings with the Bank of England, to conclude that the bank was overissuing paper currency, as it was no longer checking the requirement to pay gold on demand. He concluded that by increasing the money supply, the Bank of England drove up prices of commodities, and in the process reduced the value of the currency (Brue and Grant, 2013).

Ricardo recommended a return to the gold standard, suggesting that if the price of gold in the market rose, currency could be redeemed for gold at the bank at the mint price, and that every overissue of bank notes would be automatically cancelled by the flow of paper to the bank (Brue and Grant, 2013). Ricardo proposed a gold bullion standard to eliminate the cost of coinage and to economize on gold, besides proposing that the bank bought and sold gold bullion rather than coin on demand, with at least 20 ounces as the minimum transaction (Brue and Grant, 2013). The UK Parliament was to adopt Ricardo's proposals in 1819, and the Bank of England was ordered to resume gold payments in ingots of 60 ounces. The proposal put forward by Ricardo and passed into law was to serve for more than a century.

5.2 Theory of Diminishing Returns – The Corn Model

Ricardo's work is the first successful example of economic model building, which is contained in the 'Corn Model' of aggregate economic relationships (O'Brien, 2004). England became a regular importer of corn and other grains from foreign countries from 1770 onward, and driven by the land-owning class had introduced a duty on the imported grain. The early eighteenth century witnessed a dramatic increase in the price of corn leading to an increase in the price of bread, wheat, and so on, with the hardest hit being the working class.[31] The Corn Laws developed thereafter prevented the importation of corn into England, thereby causing resort to the use of inferior land at home, witnessing a fall in the average and marginal products of labour and capital. Ricardo considered the Corn Laws as unworkable and counter-productive – possibly leading to a stationary state[32] – and went on to expound the corn model in his work.

The whole economic system was presented as a single-output model, producing corn by applying labour and capital to land. Under this model the inputs, outputs, and distributive shares were stated in corn, and at times the term 'corn' was used to mean all agricultural wage goods, with the underlying assumption that the commodities were in fixed proportions in the wage-good basket (O'Brien, 2004). Although the concept of diminishing returns in agriculture was first presented by Turgot and the physiocrats, it was Ricardo who reformulated the principle and applied to land rent. For Sraffa, Ricardo provided a rational foundation by stating that the profits of the farmer regulated the profits of all other trades (Sraffa, Vol I). In the model presented by Ricardo, the input factor, the output factor, and distributive shares were all presented in corn terms. Ricardo also used the term corn to mean all agricultural wage goods, with the underlying assumption that the commodities were in fixed proportions in the wage-good basket (O'Brien, 2004).

In the aforementioned model, when land that was less fertile (than that already cultivated) was brought into cultivation, it resulted in decreasing returns to scale, besides also witnessing a decline in the average and marginal product of the labour and capital. Also, the rate of profit was no longer determined by the ratio of corn produced to the corn used in the production, but by the ratio of the total labour of the nation to the labour required for producing the necessaries for that labour (Sraffa, Vol I). This led to the incorporation of the labour theory of value within the model, *i.e.*, the exchangeable value of a commodity that would entail as a prerequisite usefulness that can be fabricated and replicated by labour. According to the labour theory of value, the exchangeable value of commodities is determined by the quantities of labour expended on their production – where the relevant quantity of labour is the greatest quantity expended per unit of output sold. This labour theory would apply only when commodities exchange at their natural prices, defined by uniform wage and profit rates – *but rent is excluded as a component price*. Under this theory, all prices are expressed in terms of a domestically produced commodity – gold, which serves as the *numéraire* (Peach, 1993).

From the aforementioned, one can deduce that the value-in-exchange of a commodity depends almost exclusively on the comparative quantity of labour expended on each (Sraffa, Vol I: 12). Ricardo considered this principle as an important doctrine in political economy. From here, it follows that if innovation allows for a commodity to be produced more efficiently, the relative amount of labour falls comparatively to the other goods, and it thus becomes less expensive. Likewise, when production encounters difficulties, the commodity becomes more expensive and will cost relatively more compared to the other commodities. Concerning wages, Ricardo introduced a distinction between the market price of labour and the natural price. He defined natural price as "that price which is necessary to enable the labourers, one with another, to subsist and to perpetuate their race, without either increase or diminution" (Ricardo, Vol I: 93).

The corn model also incorporated the theory of rent, which was developed by Ricardo,[33] where rent was treated as an intramarginal surplus (O'Brien, 2004). This meant that the price of the product, *viz.*, corn, was determined by the supply price at the margin of cultivation, with the total rent being the sum of the differences between price and cost of production on all the intramarginal cultivation (O'Brien, 2004). The reality of English industry demonstrated that labour in its purest form was not sufficient and thus led to the idea of capital, which for Ricardo bestowed labour (Gerber, 2017). Ricardo further expanded this to include circulating and fixed capital. The circulating capital is used in fixed proportions to labour, and where the amount of labour required for production is known, the circulating capital is identified. Fixed capital, however, is not proportional to labour and could be substituted for labour. According to Ricardo, whenever there was only circulating capital in the production process, the price of the commodity increased (Gerber, 2017). However, the factor land is excluded in Ricardo's labour theory of value.

The Ricardian corn model can be illustrated with the use of the following symbols:

i   **w** is the wage – in terms of corn, per worker;
ii   **L** is the number of workers employed in the cultivation of corn;
iii   **Y** is agricultural output;
iv   Then, **wL** is the aggregate capital employed in agriculture;
v   **Y − wL** is net product, or surplus, also in corn.

The rate of profit can then be defined as follows:

$$r = (Y - wL) / wL = (Y / L) - w) / w = (\pi - w) / w \text{ or}$$
$$r = (1 - wl) / wl$$

Source: Vaggi and Groenewegen (2006).

In the prior definition of profit π is the productivity of labour in corn production, or corn product per unit of labour, and $l = L / Y$ is the labour necessary to produce one unit of corn. In the model, the rate of profit depends on the real wage rate **w** (the quantity of corn annually required for the subsistence of a worker), and the productivity of the labour employed in the cultivation of corn $\pi = 1 / l$. Accordingly, the rate of profit varied directly with changes in productivity and inversely with real wages (Vaggi and Groenewegen, 2006).

5.3 Theory of Comparative Advantage and Foreign Trade

The theory of comparative advantage, which is over 200 years old, is considered as one of the most important theories to be developed on international trade and has become an essential intellectual toolkit for the economist. Ricardo was the first economist to distinguish international trade from domestic trade through his theory of comparative advantage and also demonstrate that international trade followed different rules from domestic trade (Sraffa, Vol I: 132). The theory of comparative advantage underpins free trade, which economists around the world argue as being beneficial for all trading nations around the world. One can also state that the theory of comparative advantage lends support to the WTO process of trade liberalisation, which seeks to maximise global economic welfare through trade liberalisation. From a more modern perspective the theory of comparative advantage could be brought within the field of normative economics.

Chapter VII of Ricardo's *Principles*, entitled 'On Foreign Trade', contained some of his key arguments (Gerber, 2017).[34] Most surprisingly, Ricardo does not use the term 'comparative advantage' in Chapter VII, but goes on to present the concept of comparative advantage in an unambiguous manner. The comparative advantage theory developed by David Ricardo argues that a country doesn't have to have an absolute advantage for beneficial trade to occur. According to the theory every country – whether advanced or behind in terms of the productivity of its labour in comparison to other countries – will be able to engage in beneficial trade with others. A country possessing a productivity advantage will only export those goods in which it had a comparative advantage over others and will not be looking to export everything (Irwin, 2017). An advanced country – both economically and technologically – would be at an advantage to import goods even if it were to be in a position to produce them more efficiently domestically than in another country. Conversely, countries that are not technologically advanced, and not possessing absolute productivity advantage in anything, could still be in a position to export goods in which its comparative disadvantage was the least. Likewise, they could benefit from importing goods in which their comparative disadvantage was the greatest (Irwin, 2017). In simple terms the ability of a country to produce a particular good or service at a lower marginal and opportunity cost over another is referred to as comparative advantage.

To demonstrate the theory of comparative advantage, Ricardo used the now well-known example of Portugal and England exchanging wine and cloth. In Ricardo's example both countries initially produce cloth and wine, where (i) England needs 100 labourers and Portugal needs 90 labourers to produce the same quantify of cloth; and (ii) England needs 120 labourers to produce the same quantity of wine as produced by Portugal with only 80 labourers (Sraffa, I: 135). Obviously, the different labour requirement arises due to dissimilar circumstances prevailing in England and Portugal, *viz.*, climate and other natural or artificial advantage (Sraffa, I: 132). With the help of the 'four magic numbers',[35] – the figures identifying the number of labourers used in the theory – Ricardo was able to explain his theory and argue that it would be advantageous to both England and Portugal if they were to specialise according to their respective comparative advantage and trade with each other (Schumacher, 2013). Ricardo's illustration appears to reassure countries that no nation needs to fear free international trade as it can only be advantageous for both nations, only comparative production costs matter in international trade, and absolute production costs are insignificant (Schumacher, 2013). When production cost ratios are equal in both nations no gains can be made by specialisation, and trade cannot take place as there will be no incentive for it (Schumacher, 2013).

According to Ricardo, a state will benefit if it specialises in the production of goods whose manufacture is intensive in its abundant resources. From another perspective, *viz.*, labour value formulation, the value of a commodity is measured by the quantity of labour embodied in the production. Ricardo's assertion that international trade is different from domestic trade is based on the premise that labour and capital do not move between nations as they do inside a nation (Schumacher, 2013). According to Ricardo the reasons for the capital being immobile are

> the fancied or real insecurity of capital, when not under the immediate control of its owner, together with the natural disinclination which every man has to quit the country of his birth and connexions, and intrust himself with all his habits fixed, to a strange government and new laws.
>
> (Sraffa, Vol I: 136)

Likewise, labour is rendered immobile from the latter reason. As a result, comparative production advantage determines free international trade, unlike domestic trade. Writing about Ricardo's contribution, John Stuart Mill noted as follows, "It is not a difference in the absolute cost of production, which determines the interchange [between nations], but a difference in the comparative cost" (Mill, 1844).

6. Classical Economics: Karl Marx

The contributions of Karl Marx to modern economic thought is significant, in that it seeks to demonstrate through 'scientific socialism' that capitalism had internal contradictions that would eventually bring about its demise. Karl Marx was born on 5 May 1818 to a Jewish couple, Heinrich Marx and Henriette Pressburg. Heinrich Marx, a descendent from an old family of Jewish rabbis, was not religious and had converted to Protestantism before Karl Marx was born. The conversion to Protestantism was also to avoid restrictions placed on Jews in Prussia during that time. Karl Marx initially studied at the *Friedrich-Wilhelm Gymnasium* in Trier, and later at the universities of Bonn and Berlin. Two years after his doctoral thesis on natural philosophy was accepted at the University of Jena, Karl Marx (hereafter Marx) married Jenny von Westphalen in 1843. Marx took to journalism after his formal studies and was increasingly drawn to political and social issues.

Marx emigrated to Paris to escape the Prussian censorship and lived there between 1843 and 1845. During his time, he was to meet his lifelong friend, co-author, and collaborator Friedrich Engels, who had earlier sent Marx manuscripts for publication detailing the conditions of the working class in Manchester, England. In 1848, Marx and Engels published the *Manifesto of the Communist Party*, which was soon to become the rule book for the communist movement around the world. Between 1848 and 1849 Marx was expelled from France, Belgium, and Prussia, which saw him emigrate to London, where he was to spend the rest of his life.[36] When one refers to the writings and philosophical expositions of Marx, it is imperative that the discussions include the contributions of Engels. Marx and Engels had different characters and different temperaments – while Marx was more speculative, Engels was more impetuous (Mandel, 1971).

Mandel (1971) notes that although it was Marx who almost single-handedly developed the entire edifice of Marxist theory, it was Engels who urged him to take up the study of political economy.[37] While in London, Marx dedicated 15 years of his time for the study of economics. Three major philosophical strands that influenced Marx were (i) German idealism and the writings of Hegel, (ii) socialist ideas that were gaining ground in Europe at that time,[38] and most importantly (iii) 'classical political economy', as expounded by David Ricardo (Dobb, 1973).[39] The influence of Marx's ideas on political, economic, and social levels are sufficiently well known. As his philosophical expositions are concerned, Marx formulated a complete and integrated intellectual system, which contained elaborate conceptions of ontology and epistemology, of the nature of society and the individual's relationship to the society, and of the nature of the process of social history (Hunt and Lautzenheiser, 2011).[40] Marx's approach to the discipline was doubtlessly methodical in both its substance and its construction.

His work *Capital*, which was an analysis of capitalism, was contained in three volumes, of which only the first volume was published during his lifetime in 1867. For Marx, the objective behind writing *Capital* was to prove that capitalism was not everlasting, which he sought to demonstrate by presenting the inherent contradictions of capitalism. The substance of volumes 2 and 3 were written mostly during Marx's time, yet it remained unfinished. Friedrich Engels, his collaborator, took upon himself the task of editing and publishing the remaining two volumes of the work posthumously in 1885 and 1894. Marx, during his time, also wrote a series of seven notebooks, besides penning numerous pamphlets and articles. The notebooks were compiled and published in German under the title *Grundrisse der Kritik der Politischen Ökonomie* (Foundations of the Critique of Political Economy), and later were published in English as *Grundrisse*. Marx is considered the most important of all philosophers and theorists on socialism.

6.1 Criticism of Classical Economics

Marx was, first and foremost, profoundly influenced by the theories of value and profits as expounded by Adam Smith and David Ricardo. Marx, although quoted frequently from the writings of Thompson and Hodgskin, was highly critical of many of their ideas. Marx's chief criticism of classical thinkers (barring Smith) was that they did not have an historical perspective to their approach, and that if they had studied history and embraced such an approach it would have led them to discover that production was a social activity, which takes many forms and modes, "depending on the prevailing forms of social organization and their corresponding techniques of production" (Hunt and Lautzenheiser, 2011, p. 203). For Marx it was essential to understand history, as it showed that the European society had passed through several epochs, or modes of production, which included slave society, feudal society, and later on capitalism (McLellan, 1980).

For Marx the British classical economists confused the laws of development of the economy and societies with laws of nature, and by doing so failed to realise that such regularities were specific to a particular phase in the history of mankind (Vaggi and Groenewegen, 2006).[41] Marx sought to do exactly that through his theory of 'historical materialism', by studying the evolution of the societies in terms of their material economic bases. Marx strongly criticised the English economists for presenting as universal and timeless the laws of economic life, which were only merely the regularities of a particular, time-bound economic order found in the particular region. Here, Marx was critical of the false universalisation of the particular and the transitory, as it misrepresented the true working of the capitalist order (Unger, 2007).

In Marx's view the failure on the part of the classical school to differentiate between the key features of production (in all modes of production) and those that were specific to capitalism had led to confusions and distortions in the theories. Marx identified two particular areas that led to confusion, *viz.*, the belief that capital was universal in all production process, and that all economic activity could be reduced to a series of exchanges (McLellan, 1980). Marx took the view that capital was an instrument of production, and production was not possible without an instrument of production or without stored-up past labour. In Marx's view the power of capital yielded profits to a special class within the society. Marx through his enquiry sought to understand how this particular aspect of capital came into existence and how it was sustained by the capitalists. Marx was critical of the presuppositions present in capitalist economic theory. Marx considered all production an appropriation of nature, and that property appropriation was a precondition of production (McLellan, 1980). This was in sharp contrast to the position taken by earlier economists who considered property as sacrosanct and identified property in its existing form as capitalist private property.

6.2 Historical Materialism and Economic Theory

The theory of 'historical materialism' is Marx's main contribution to the social sciences, besides his contribution to economic theories.[42] Historical materialism presented Marx's theories on the evolution of society and the role individuals and the factors of production played therein. Marx attempted to explain the origin and development of society from a purely materialistic perspective by identifying the material forces that play a crucial role in the formation and the emergence of human society. Marx postulated the proposition that human beings cannot survive without social organisations, which are in turn based on social labour and social communication, and that it was social existence that determined social consciousness. For Marx materialism was the basis of the sociological structure, as material conditions (economic factors) directly affected the structure and progression of the society.

Historical materialism underscores the important role of production of material conditions in the progress of societies. The crucial role that social reality played was the way in which different classes of the society were related to the economic resources of the society and their relationship towards production. Relations of production are considered as stabilised structures that are capable of reproducing, and incapable of being changed gradually, but can only be changed qualitatively through social revolution or social upheaval. Marx also noted that quantitative change is incapable of bringing about structural modification but only occurs within the modes of production (Mandel, 2018). To view the relations of production at the point of production in isolation is not appropriate, as the relations of production are the sum total of social relations which is established by humans.

Marx sought to understand the society in its entirety, arguing that the society evolved from one epoch to the other before eventually arriving at a capitalist model. He presented his ideas through the lens of historical materialism, predicting the possible future of societies. Marx's general theory of society deals extensively with the contradictions found in capitalist societies. Marx's views on democracy were based, again, on a study of the events that marked a turning point in the histories of America, England, and France. This particular approach to history and the development of society was absent from the theoretical expositions of the political economists who preceded Marx and Engels. Through his writings Marx conceptualised a future 'proletarian democracy', which would eventually culminate in bringing about a communist state, where goods would be held in common.

Historical materialism, while not opposed to an individual's free will, states that an individual's choices are predetermined by the social framework, which is in turn influenced by education, prevailing moral values, *etc.*, and the outcome of the impact of a multitude of different interests and emotions – which is again sociological and not individual psychology (Mandel, 2018). Marx notes that class interests are predominant in societies, as a ruling class will always try to defend its position, and hence class struggle is a permanent feature of human society. Marx in his *Communist Manifesto* notes, "the history of all society hitherto is the history of class struggles" (Marx and Engels, 2004, p. 62). Likewise, historical materialism also recognises a specific history of science, art, philosophy, political and moral ideas, religion, *etc.*, which all, in Marx's view, follow their own logic. Under historical materialism the ruling ideology of each epoch was the ideology of the ruling class, and that when that ruling class disappears, its ideology continues to survive through customs and other social norms.

Under historical materialism an epoch of social crisis is brought about by growing conflict between the principal mode of production (*i.e.*, the prevailing social order) and the further development of the productive forces (Mandel, 2018). Further, such social crisis is bound to have an impact on all walks of social life, *viz.*, politics, ideology, morals, and law, as well as on the economic life of the individual. For Marx and Engels, the emergence of a classless society is closely intertwined with the process of a withering away of the state, leading to the dictatorship of the proletariat. In the scheme of things envisioned by Marx, socialism was only the transition phase when the capitalistic mode of production is challenged before leading to a communist state (Vaggi and Groenewegen, 2006). Under the communist state individuals received according to their needs as opposed to their efforts prevalent in a capitalist mode of production.

Marx did not consider himself as an economist, although his contribution to economic theory is unquestionable. Through his theory of historical material, Marx attempted to unify the major social sciences – sociology, anthropology, and economic analysis – into a single 'science of society' (Mandel, 2018). Interestingly, for Marx there are no eternal economic laws which would be valid for every epoch of human history. Although his economic analysis was not so popular, his political thoughts were more popular and influential, the key examples being the emergence of communist Russia, People's Republic of China (China), Cuba, *etc.*

6.3 Labour Theory of Value

As noted earlier Marx was influenced by the writings of both Smith and Ricardo. It is not an exaggeration to state that his work continued in the classical school of economics.[43] One can observe that Marx inherited the 'labour theory of value' from the classical school but yet made a radical break by considering labour as value.[44] In *Capital*, Marx analysed the laws that regulate the capitalist mode of production, positing the argument that commodities were a visible sign of wealth, but not necessarily the essence of wealth and value. He further explored the relationship between money, commodity, and capital in the production process, highlighting that under the 'simple commodity production', labour was free both in the sphere of circulation and in production.

Marx emphasised that production and exchange were dictated by the use of value of commodities, where money was an intermediary, and presented the exchange relationship as *commodity-money-commodity* (C-M-C). For Marx, value attached to labour was the total labour potential that exists at a given point in time in a society which is employed for producing a certain commodity. He also noted that the capitalist mode of production took place on the basis of exchange value and not according to its use value and formulated the relations as *money-commodity-money* (M-C-M), or more precisely as M-C-M' where M' > M (Vaggi and Groenewegen, 2006).[45]

In Marx's view value is social, as it is determined by the result of an individual producer; it is objective as it is presented when the production process is completed; and it is also historically relative because it changes with each important change of average productivity. Mandel (2018) notes that Marx's 'law of value' is but his version of Adam Smith's 'invisible hand', and that it is this 'law of value' that regulates the economy, determining what is produced and how it is produced.[46] The 'law of value' also regulates the exchange between commodities, which is dictated by the quantities of socially necessary abstract labour they embody. The same 'law of value' also regulates the distribution of society's labour potential through the regulation of exchange between commodities.

6.4 Theory of Rent, Money, and Surplus Value

Marx considered rent as an important element in the analysis of capitalism, and his theories are based on an analysis of agricultural production, as opposed to his theory of capitalism which is based on an analysis of industrial production.[47] Ricardo and Marx developed their theories of rent from the basis that land was owned by landowners who leased them out to capitalists, who in turn produced commodities (McKeown, 1987). Marx's rent theory differed from Ricardo's rent theory, in that it was founded on a different value theory and a different notion of margin. It is to be noted here that Marx developed his theory of rent through a criticism of Ricardo's rent theory. Marx's theory presented two different types of rent, *viz.*, absolute rent and differential rent, which is developed in volume III of *Capital*.

The principal objective behind Marx's theory is to demonstrate that capitalism carries out agriculture as a business, with the motive of profits, where ground rents appropriated for the landowners are a burden, as they imply an additional production-cost resulting in a higher price for the agricultural output (Mandel, 2018). Non-produced resources are not created by human labour. In capitalist commodity production, as in the case of agriculture and mining, there is a reliance on the use of non-produced resources, *i.e.*, land.[48] In agriculture and mining, less productive labour determines the market value of goods or minerals, and hence more efficient farms and mines make surplus profits, which Marx identified as differential rend (Mandel, 2018). Marx made the argument that in the capitalist mode of agriculture the surplus value produced will not enter the general process of redistribution of profit, as it will be appropriated by the landowners and capitalist farmers. Marx identified this as the absolute rent, which is over and above differential rent.[49]

Marx's theory of money was neglected by Marxist scholars in the twentieth century,[50] but in more recent times it has become a subject of debate. Marx devoted sufficient space for the discussion of money in his writings, which can be found in both *Grundrisse* and *Capital*. Marx's theory of money is integrated with the theory of capitalist form of production, and money's role is determined by its functions within the capitalist economic relations (Brunhoff, 2005). He derives this from the theory of commodity as a unity of use value and exchange value. He argued that value was the embodiment of socially necessary labour, and that commodities exchange with each other in proportion to the labour quanta they contain (Mandel, 2018). Marx sought to demonstrate how a produced commodity, like gold, could emerge as the conventional equivalent, to function as a universal medium of exchange for all other commodities, or as the dominant monetary form. Beginning from the twentieth century, the monetary system has developed away from a commodity money system and toward a system where the general equivalent is an abstract unit of account, *viz.*, the 'dollar', which does not have a definite equivalent of a produced commodity (Foley, 1986).

Marx posited the argument that money was a commodity, and commodity economies follow the labour theory of value, as it could also play the role of exchange. Contemporary authors, like Foley (1986), take the position that Marx's theory is compatible with non-commodity forms too. One could also say that money was viewed by Marx as a form of value. In *Grundrisse*, Marx identifies the properties of money as follows:

> The properties of money are: (1) a standard for the measurement of the exchange of commodities; (2) means of exchange; (3) representative of commodities (and thus the object of a contract); (4) as a universal commodity alongside special kinds of commodity. All these properties arise from the definition of money as the exchange value of commodities, severed from them and having its own objectified existence.
>
> (McLellan, 1980, p. 60)

Value, for Marx, was the exchangeability of commodities, which resides as a social substance in the commodity through the labour expended in their production (Foley, 1986). Money, the general equivalent of value, can be something other than a commodity – for instance, after having begun as a commodity, it can evolve into non-commodity forms (Foley, 1986). Interestingly, throughout his work Marx maintained his conception of money as a commodity and that of gold as its final evolutive form (Germer, 2005).

Through the theory of surplus value, Marx sought to place the capitalist mode of production in its historical context. Surplus value can take any form, including goods appropriated by the ruling class, *e.g.*, where feudal rent is paid as a certain quantity of the produce (produce rent), sharecropping, and money rent (Mandel, 2018). In simple terms, surplus value is the social surplus produced. Mandel (2018) notes that surplus value is a residual theory of the ruling classes' income, and that under Marx's theory of exploitation, the income of the ruling classes can be reduced to the product of unpaid labour. Of all his writings, Marx considered his theory of surplus value to be his most important contribution. Of all the nineteenth-century philosophers, it was Marx who was able to foresee clearly how capitalism would function, develop, and transform the word (Mandel, 2018).

7. Liberalism

Liberalism is not a set of scientific propositions about political theory and economic principles but an ever-changing body of political opinions and attitudes (Voegelin and Algozin, 1974). Liberalism is more a political movement in the context of the surrounding Western revolutionary movement. As regards social, political, and economic life, the classical liberals emphasised maximising individual freedom (Butler, 2015). Although classical liberals accepted that freedom can never be absolute, since one person's freedom may conflict with another's, they did not completely agree on where the limits to personal (and government) action should lie. The key principles of classical liberalism included the presumption of freedom; primacy of the individual over the collective; minimising coercion; rule of law; right to property, trade, and markets; civil society; *etc.* The ten principles of classical liberalism can be summarised as follows:

i The Presumption of Freedom – *classical liberals want to maximise freedom in our political, social, and economic life.*
ii The Primacy of Individual – *classical liberals see the individual as more important than the collective. This means they are not prepared to sacrifice individual freedom for collective benefits.*
iii Minimising Coercion – *classical liberals prefer to minimise coercion. They seek to achieve goals through peaceful agreement rather than threats or force.*
iv Toleration – *classical liberals believe that the main reason to interfere with people's freedom is to prevent them doing or threatening actual harm to others.*
v Limited and Representative Government – *classical liberals concede that some force may be needed to prevent people injuring others, which the authorities should possess.*
vi The Rule of Law – *classical liberals insist that law should apply equally to everyone, regardless of gender, race, religion, language, family, or any other irrelevant characteristics. In short, they advocate 'the rule of law', which was referred to by John Adams (1785–1836) as 'a government of laws, and not of men.' The rule of law also makes life more predictable, as it allows us to anticipate how people (including officials) will or will not behave.*
vii Spontaneous Order – *classical liberals dispute that a large and complex society needs a large and powerful government to run it. See, for instance, the Austrian social theorist F. A. Hayek (1899–1992), who called the result 'spontaneous order'.*
viii The Property, Trade, and Markets – *classical liberals believe that wealth is not created by governments, but by the mutual cooperation of individuals in the spontaneous order of the marketplace. This stems from the respect for private property and contract, which allows specialization and trade.*
ix Civil Society – *classical liberals believe that voluntary associations are better at providing individuals' needs than are governments. Yet, they recognize that people are not isolated, atomistic, self-centred beings, but are social animals and live in families and groups.*
x Common Human Value – *classical liberals wish to harness our common humanity for mutual benefit.*

8. The Keynesian Economic Thought

The Keynesian system of economic thought is one of the most momentous schools of economic thought to emerge in the twentieth century. Considered the central feature of twentieth-century macroeconomics, the Keynesian system takes its name from John Maynard Keynes, the twentieth-century economist, or more precisely macroeconomist. Keynes emerged as the most influential intellectual figure and is also credited with saving liberalism through the incorporation of elements of materialism and Marxism in his principles (Paul and Amawi, 2013). John Maynard Keynes was born on 5 June 1883 in Cambridge, England, to John Neville Keynes and Florence Ada Keynes.[51]

Keynes was educated in Eton, and later in King's College, Cambridge, where he majored in mathematics. Keynes, during his university days, was active in several societies, including the Discussion Society, where he met Bertrand Russell, McTaggart, and others. His first book on economics was *Indian Currency and Finance*, which was written based on his working experience at the India Office. During his time at the India Office, Keynes also worked on his theory of probability. World War I saw him take up a position at the Treasury and later as the principal representative of the British Treasury in the peace negotiations at Versailles. The experience of participating in the peace negotiations led Keynes to write two further books, entitled *Economic Consequences of the Peace* (1919) and *Revision of the Treaty* (1922). At 28, Keynes became editor of the *Economic Journal*, which position he held until 1945.

8.1 Historical Background and Writings

Keynes published his first major book, *The Treatise of Money*, in 1930, which was followed by *The General Theory of Employment, Interest and Money* (herein after *The General Theory*) in 1936. *The General Theory* to this day remains a major presence in economics. The theories that Keynes propounded form the foundations of the Keynesian school of economics. Unlike Keynesian economics, Keynes's economics was philosophically driven. His theories were founded on his vision of a civilised life and strongly influenced by his theory of probability. *The General Theory* was more a reaction to the principles associated with Alfred Marshall and A. C. Pigou.[52] Keynes's ideas found incentive by the economic crisis brought about by the Great Depression of the 1930s.

Keynes, with his background working at the India Office and involvement in the peace negotiations at Versailles, adopted a macroeconomic approach to his theories, which was in line with the approach taken by the economists from the National Bureau of Economic Research.[53] Post-World War I saw the growth of large-scale industrial production and trade, making the economy more susceptible to statistical measurements and controls. This, in turn, required the adoption of an overall view of the economy (Harcourt and Kerr, 2003). The changing landscape also led to persistent unemployment, and Keynes considered this as definite evidence that markets do not embody a natural tendency toward a socially beneficial equilibrium (Paul and Amawi, 2013). While working at the Treasury during the war, Keynes was responsible for managing the crisis in external finance of the military and civilian imports Britain needed at that time.[54] This experience was to come to his aid when he headed the British delegation to the Bretton Woods Conference, where the development of a post-war international payment system was finalised (Davidson, 2009).

8.2 Keynes and Classical Economic Thought

Keynes lived through the interwar period, which was blighted by financial instability and economic turbulence, and his philosophy was more a product of an atheistic generation.

Keynes and his contemporaries considered themselves as following a rational system of ethics and conduct to replace religious hocus-pocus (Skidelsky, 2010). Keynes offered a theoretical justification for the state regulation and ownership of markets in response to the early years of the Great Depression. Breaking away from liberal traditions, Keynes strongly advocated state management and participation in financial markets, and at one point even turned against free trade.[55] Under classical economic theory, interest rates and wage rates adjust 'automatically' in response to shock, which was referred to as the self-adjusting market economy. Keynes held the firm view that orthodox classical theory could not provide the guidelines for the development of a civilised system, which was borne out of his experience in British economics from the 1920s. For Keynes the classical economic theory failed when the unemployment rate appeared to be stuck near or above 10 percent for well over a decade.

Keynes's criticism of the classical economy focused on its weakest point, *viz.*, its conception of money. His premise was that classical economists had blindly accepted Adam Smith's proposition that the function of money is to serve as a means of exchange. Keynes argued, however, that money that is referred to in classical economics is but a form of exchange, or barter; that only when the value of goods/things come to be expressed in terms of money can we see the true development of a monetary system, where things acquire stable values (Clarke, 1988). Keynes put forth the argument that all developed economies viewed money as being state money, which meant that money was only a symbol of value, and an independent form of value. Being a monetary economist who was concerned with monetary policies, Keynes advocated exchange mechanisms based on currency management, where the central banks played a key role in maintaining parity for the currency.

Keynes considered both the theory of probability and economics as branches of logic, as opposed to mathematics. Keynes sought to reconstruct the classical economic theory, as in Keynes's view the classical system assumed that there was a dichotomy between the real and the monetary (Harcourt and Kerr, 2003). Keynes's first-hand experience with the British economy of the 1920s convinced him to conclude that orthodox classical theory could not provide the guidelines for a civilised system. Keynes felt the necessity of developing a new economic theory which would present a clearer understanding of the classical economics, which was perpetuating widespread unemployment, and once again set mankind on the road to a more civilised society (Davidson, 2009). It would be another decade before Keynes could come up with his revolutionary theories.

8.3 The Theories

Keynes's early writings focused primarily on the application of monetary theory to current practical policy. His work at the India Office gave him the opportunity to grasp the monetary developments in India, as India had just suspended its silver standard and adopted an innovative exchange policy. Needless to say, his first real outing on the theoretical front commenced on the theme of gold-exchange systems and currency management. Keynes, following World War I, advocated the restoration of a global monetary order, to resume normal business life. His views and arguments on the subject are to be found in his works *Economic Consequences of the Peace* (1919) and *Tract on Monetary Reform* (1923). Skidelsky notes that *Economic Consequences of the Peace* presented the theoretical core of Keynes's arguments, where he was able to use his theory of probability to support his argument to question Germany's ability to pay reparations (Skidelsky, 2010).[56] Keynes, who was part of the British delegation to Versailles during the treaty negotiations, was critical of the imposition of reparation cost on Germany. Keynes argued that it was the Allied governments that were foolish and ignorant to create such a dreadful economic situation, as he did not see the application of the principles of classical economic theory.[57]

Keynes commenced work on *The Treaties of Money* in 1925, which was eventually published in 1930. *The Treatise of Money* never achieved a unity of clearly expressed ideas, as it started with one set of ideas and concluded with yet another set, exhibiting the changing patterns of thinking in the author, which factor was noted in the preface to the book by Keynes. Debates carried out following the publication of the work amongst the Cambridge economists effectively led to the discussions gradually moving away from price levels and stability and towards the process of income generation. The prior discussions helped in the evolution of the principal ideas behind *The General Theory* which was published in 1936 (Vaggi and Groenewegen, 2006). *The General Theory* captured the gloominess of the 1930s, where Keynes offered several detailed analyses of the causes of the Great Depression and the lethargic nature of recovery, besides presenting macroeconomic solutions. *The General Theory* was a theoretical work touching upon some of the most important monetary issues prevailing at that time, but also in part a statement of the theoretical case for monetary reform. In short it was about the management of money across the world, and it had an immediate and immense influence on economic thoughts to emerge on both sides of the Atlantic. In *The General Theory*, Keynes presented his formula for national income determination, which is arrived at using total spending as a multiple of autonomous demand, which is to this day used as a standard in macroeconomics textbooks.

Keynes considered the gold standard as a flawed mechanism. He felt it should not be used for the management of monetary economies and instead advocated for the development of another system which would permit sufficient international liquidity for trade purposes, besides allowing for autonomy over domestic monetary and other economic policies (Tily, 2007). Keynes put forward exchange management and capital control policies to replace the gold standard. The mechanism advocated by Keynes came to be adopted around the world following the failure of the gold standard in the post-World War I era.[58]

Keynes strongly advocated for the need to develop a monetary theory of production, *i.e.*, a theory of production and value in a monetary economy (Keynes, 1933). His case was that the traditional understanding of a barter and monetary economy (as propounded by the traditional economists) needed to be recast as one between a real-exchange economy and the monetary economy (Hayes, 2013). According to Keynes, although money would be used by a real-exchange economy, the role of money was still neutral but more efficient than barter. For Keynes the volume of investment and the 'propensity to consume' determine between them a unique level of income and employment. Keynes's theory of underemployment equilibrium attempted to demonstrate that a free enterprise economy may sink into a condition of permanent mass unemployment unless stimulated through governmental policies (intervention). This is based on the premise that consumer expenditure was linked directly to national income and was unlikely to expand unless income expanded; and that investment opportunities were limited in a developed economy like the UK, where private investment may continue at a level that fell below full employment (Burns, 1946). Unless there was a significant increase in consumption, coupled with an expansion of private investment at home along with an increase in net exports, it follows that it would lead to an increase in unemployment.

Under the Keynesian model the extent of any change in output is determined by consumer consumption, which in turn is subjected to their income. Hence, when there is a fall in investment, the GDP (aggregate output) will fall and thereby reduce the savings proportionate to the fall in investment. This, according to Keynes, was the point of 'underemployment equilibrium', where the economy will come to a standstill in the absence of an external stimulus, and that in a closed economy the stimulus will have to come from the government, which Skidelsky classifies as the essence of hydraulic Keynesianism

(Skidelsky, 2010). Burns notes that there is a similarity of this theory to the Ricardian model, where it is postulated that in the production function in agriculture, the marginal product diminishes as the input of labour increases (Burns, 1946). Likewise, under Keynesian economics too, consumer expenditure increases with national income, but by less than the increment of income. It is clear from the aforementioned that Ricardian economics treats the production function as fixed, whereas Keynesian economics treats the consumption function as fixed.

Keynes, under the theory of national income determination, envisaged varying both government spending and taxation to affect the level of demand in the economy, advocating 'fiscal fine-tuning' by national governments to maintain demand at a high level to promote full employment, and in the event of high demand leading to inflation, governments could direct official control over wages and prices and determine an income policy. Keynesian economic theory is the total spending in the economy, *i.e.*, aggregate demand, and its effects on the output and inflation. Aggregate demand, which is one of the principle tenets of Keynesianism, is influenced by economic decisions, which at times is erratic. Keynes's 'theory of prices', which is contained in chapter 21 of *The General Theory*, was firmly based on the theoretical concepts of the conditions of supply and demand, changes in marginal cost, and the elasticity of short-period supply (Keynes, 2018). Then again, one of the objectives of *The General Theory* in Keynes's (2018, p. 262) own words was "to bring the theory of prices as a whole back to close contact with the theory of value". In Keynes's view, money prices as well as output tend to vary with changes in demand, and in the short term, at less than full employment.

Keynes developed various 'elasticity' concepts in *The General Theory*, such as the elasticity of output e_o, the elasticity of money prices e_p, and the elasticity of money wages e_w. These elasticity concepts represented proportionate changes in the different variables for a given proportionate change in effective demand (Davidson, 2009). Keynes presented the change in money prices for any given relative change in demand as $e_p = 1 - (1 - e_w)$, offering the argument that prices will show some change for any given change in demand, unless $e_o = 1$ and $e_w = 0$. Keynes (2018, p. 265) maintained in *The General Theory* that, at less than full employment, an "increase in effective demand will, generally speaking, spend itself partly in increasing the quantity of employment and partly in raising the level of prices". Keynes's intellectual involvement and response to the ever-changing economic and political developments were phenomenal. Against the backdrop of the Great Depression, Keynes developed most theories that we now come to associate with 'Keynesian' economics.

8.4 Keynes's Legacy

Doubtlessly one of the most influential economists of the twentieth century, Keynes stands out as someone who successfully challenged classical economic principles. It is not an exaggeration to say that leading Western economies embraced Keynes's economic policies before the outbreak of World War II. Keynes's theories formed the basis for the economic policies in Europe, the US, and other parts of the world during the period after the Great Depression to the early part of the 1970s. Considered the founder of modern economics, his theories form the basis for the Keynesian economics, which experienced a revival in 2008–2009. In the aftermath of the financial crisis of 2007–2008, several leading economists advocated the government intervention, which is a key Keynesian idea, to mitigate the financial crisis. It is well documented that several bailouts took place in the leading economies, *viz.*, the US and the UK, to offset the economic woes brought about by the financial crisis of 2007–2008.

9. Summary

Economic theories, akin to political thought, play an important role in the governance of both domestic and world economies. Numerous aspects have helped shape the evolution of trade theory over the past 500 years, with the important aspects being the vision espoused by powerful trading nations, discovery of the New World, political economy, and emergence of clear economic thought in the twentieth century. In the aftermath of World War II, significant changes were made to the international economic order to avert a repeat of the prevailing economic, social, and political environment that led to the two world wars. Key institutions, *viz*., the United Nations (UN),[59] the International Monetary Fund (IMF), the World Bank, and the GATT were created to facilitate international trade.[60] The international order witnessed the accession of China and Russia – whose economies are based on state enterprise – to the membership of the World Trade Organization, whose objectives are based on free market economy and trade liberalisation. A combination of capitalism and free market economy remains the principal economic theory that underpins international trade theory today.

Notes

1 "[W]e may say that if there were no sea, man would be the most savage and destitute of all creatures. But, as it is, the sea brought the Greeks the vine from India, from Greece transmitted the use of grain across the sea, from Phoenicia imported letters as a memorial against forgetfulness, thus preventing the greater part of mankind from being wineless, grainless, and unlettered." See Plutarch, 'Whether Fire or Water Is More Useful,' *Moralia, XII* (Harvard University Press, 1957) 299.
2 Aristotle was prejudiced against trade and had a dislike for 'coined money'. For Aristotle, exchange and barter of surplus goods were natural, but the use of coined money as a medium of exchange was contrary to nature. See Sinclair, T. A. and Trevor J. Saunders, *Aristotle: The Politics* (Penguin Books, 1992).
3 Magnusson argues that mercantilism can also be called the 'mercantile system' to depict some parts of the political practice and political economy during the said period. Magnusson also takes the position that mercantilism is both theory and practice. See Magnusson (2015).
4 The flow of precious metals from the American colonies of Spain during the sixteenth century was to produce a very high inflation in Europe. As precious metals guaranteed command over goods, the mercantilists considered them as the substance and the definition of both private and national wealth. The expression 'bullion' was used to refer to the precious metals. Not surprisingly, the power of the state depended on the amount of gold and silver it had in its coffers, and it further made it possible to build ships and to pay armies. See Vaggi and Groenewegen (2006).
5 Allen notes that the analysis of mutually advantageous exchange, based on the principle of comparative advantage, was not adequately formulated until the early nineteenth century. See Allen (1991).
6 Vaggi and Groenewegen divide the era of mercantilism into (i) the period of bullionism and (ii) the period of balance of trade. See Vaggi and Groenewegen (2006).
7 For instance, in seventeenth-century France, Colbert, the minister of finances of Louis XIV, introduced policies designed to protect French domestic manufactures from foreign competitors.
8 Some commentators opine that since Smith had the occasion to go through the *Philosophie Rurale*, it was likely that he picked up the expression from there.
9 Thomas Mun became the director of East India Company in 1615 and was the author of pamphlets in which he described the benefits from trade involving export of bullions in order to import goods. See Vaggi and Groenewegen (2006).
10 Smith published *An Inquiry Into the Nature and Causes of the Wealth of Nations* in 1776, which is considered his *magnum opus*.
11 John Ramsay McCulloch was a Scottish economist, who was influenced by Adam Smith and David Ricardo, is widely regarded as the leader of the Ricardian school of economists after the demise of Ricardo in 1823.

12 If a country were to have surplus currency, then the price of domestic commodities would tend to rise as against the price of foreign commodities, and money would flow out of the country. Likewise, if a country were to experience a shortage of currency, then the domestic commodities would decline, thereby attracting foreign currency until the shortage had disappeared.
13 The term physiocrats came from the Greek word 'physiocracy', which meant 'rule by nature'.
14 The other prominent physiocrats of the time included the Marquis de Mirabeau, Pierre-Paul Mercier de la Rivière, Dupont de Nemours, La Trosne, and the Abbé Baudeau.
15 Steiner (2003) notes that Quesnay was well established in his profession – a member of the Académie des sciences (Paris) and of the Royal Academy of Sciences (London) (also an author of several books on medical subjects), and it is still unclear why Quesnay left the practice of medicine to pursue economics.
16 Quesnay argued that there would be nothing left to be transformed into finished goods and other uses once the resources of the earth had not been exploited, and in the division of labour, it was the agricultural sector that was the foundation of society and its economic wellbeing. His work, *Tableau Economique*, outlined the interdependency of the various specialized activities within the economic order, underpinning his argument that production from land was the foundation of a society's prosperity.
17 *Corvée* was the forced labour a farmer owed to the state in lieu of taxes at that time in France.
18 The phrase *laissez passer et laissez faire* is credited to Vincent de Gournay and is widely thought the equivalent of the Chinese expression '*wu wei*' (a Daoist principle), which stands for non-action. It is thought that Gournay adopted the phrase from Quesnay's writings on China, *viz.*, *Le Despotisme de la Chine* from 1767.
19 See Marx and Engels (1979), p. 194.
20 The works of François Quesnay, David Hume, Ferdinando Galiani, and Anne-Robert-Jacques Turgot were instrumental in shaping the classical school of economic thought to come in the eighteenth century.
21 The book discusses the moral forces that restrain selfishness and bind people together in a workable society, and it should be viewed as representing Smith's earlier ideas, as it presents another facet of Smith's thinking.
22 Smith was charged with tutoring the stepson of Charles Townsend, chancellor of the Exchequer, which enabled him to retire with a handsome annual pension of £300.
23 Smith originally planned to dedicate his book *Wealth of Nations* to Quesnay, had the latter lived until the book went into print.
24 From the physiocratic thinkers, Smith drew the theme of wealth as 'the consumable goods annually reproduced by the labour of society' and the concept of the circular process of production and distribution. Edwin Cannan notes that Smith benefitted from his examination of the French system and that there was no trace of the theories of distribution and macroeconomic dimension in Smith's lectures before his travels to France (Cannan, 1896).
25 Newtonian scientific thinking established that order and harmony characterise the physical universe, and at its core it had the concept that through systematic reasoning, people could discover not only these physical laws but also those that govern the society.
26 Smith only used the term 'invisible hand' thrice in his writings – once in the *History of Astronomy*, once in the *Theory of Moral Sentiments*, and once in *The Wealth of Nations*. See Smith (1977), p. 30.
27 Adam Smith, in volume 1 of his treatise *An Inquiry Into the Nature and Causes of the Wealth of Nations*, noted as follows: "It is not from the benevolence of the butcher, the brewer, or the baker, that we expect our dinner, but from their regard to their own interest".
28 Although Ricardo's time in Parliament was short, four years, he was nevertheless a voice of reform. He supported the enquiry into the criminal justice system, supported the abolition of death penalty for forgery, and voted for criminal law reform. In terms of trade policy, he supported the implementation of free trade, voted against renewal of sugar duties, and opposed timber duties. He took every opportunity to educate the House of Parliament in the principles of political economy, which included the repeal of trade restrictions, minimal taxation, and return to convertible currency. Needless to say, he found himself mostly on the losing side.
29 Writing about James Mill's request, Ricardo notes in his letter of 18 August 2015 to JB as follows: "Mr. Mill wishes me to write it over again at large, I fear the undertaking exceeds my powers" (Sraffa, Vol VI, 249). At one point, Mill writes, "As I am accustomed to wield the authority of a schoolmaster, I therefore, in the genuine exercise of this honourable capacity, lay upon you my commands, to begin to the first of the three heads of your proposed work, rent, profit, wages – viz. *rent*, without an hours delay" (Sraffa, Vol VI, 321).

30 Commentators in the past had misinterpreted Ricardo's reluctance to undertake the work to mean that his book was written as a statement of opinions made for his own purposes, and the publication was only an afterthought (Dunbar, 1887). Sraffa argues that through its acceptance by other commentators this belief gained general currency. Nevertheless, the Ricardo-Mill correspondence, which has been analysed in detail by Sraffa (Vol VI), dispels this opinion and establishes the true position that from the very beginning the idea of publication was present in Ricardo's mind, although from time to time he had doubts about his ability to achieve his object.

31 This also coincided with an increase in population at that time. After 1780, the rate of population went up to nearly 10 percent per decade and reached a peak during Ricardo's active time as a political scientist. See Gerber (2017).

32 O'Brien notes that Smith had also envisaged a stationary state, but it was not imminent, and Ricardo on the other hand had provided a mechanical model to establish his case that it was imminent. See O'Brien (2004).

33 Some commentators take the position that the doctrine of rent was developed simultaneously by Ricardo, Thomas Malthus, Edward West, Robert Torrens, and John Rooke in 1814. O'Brien (2004) notes that Ricardo developed the theory of rent independently.

34 Gerber considers this chapter as 'grand-extraordinary' due to its contents and its value. Interestingly, Ricardo's central arguments are to be found, almost entirely, in three paragraphs.

35 The term 'four magic numbers' was used by the Nobel Laurette Paul A. Samuelson when referring to Ricardo's comparative advantage theory. See Samuelson (1969).

36 Engels was to support Marx financially throughout his life, and also left an estate in his will for the daughters of Marx.

37 Engels, who was born into a wealthy German family, was sent to England by his father to learn the conduct of business affairs. Engels was to encounter the appalling conditions of the labourers in the large-scale capitalist industry in Manchester, which was to change the course of his thinking for the rest of his life. While Marx was still criticising communism, Engels declared himself openly a communist.

38 It should be noted here that Marx lived in the era of industrial and social revolutions which was gradually entering the modern era.

39 Dobb notes that the expression 'classical political economy' was first used by Marx.

40 The authors argue that as Marx's system is an integrated whole, and no part of it can be understood fully except by putting it into proper context within the whole.

41 Marx branded the classical economists 'bourgeois'. This term was to later on be used by most communists to refer to capitalists and anyone who was critical of communist ideals and communism.

42 Marx thought it was Engels who conceived the idea of 'historical materialism', but Engels claimed it was Marx who first propounded it. Regardless, it is widely considered that 'historical materialism' is a contribution from Marx.

43 Hunt and Lautzenheiser (2011, p. 203) posit the argument that Marx's theories on the subject are "an extension, refinement, and elaboration" of Smith's and Ricardo's ideas.

44 In Ricardo's writings, labour is a *numéraire*, a tradable economic entity.

45 Marx noted that it "would be absurd and without meaning if the intention were to exchange by this means two equal sums of money" See Marx, (1887), p. 104.

46 Interestingly, Marx was not a great fan of the 'invisible hand'. He noted that the 'invisible hand' was not capable of leading to maximum economic growth or to optimum human wellbeing for the greatest number of individuals.

47 McKeown (1987) notes that for this particular reason, Marx's analysis of rent does not integrate well into the remainder of his analysis.

48 A similar position is to be found in mining, in which the mine shaft is the non-produced resource; in oil and gas extraction, the ground beneath which the oil or natural gas is located is the non-produced resource.

49 Mandel (2018) notes that historical evidence from the twentieth century has confirmed the validity of Marx's theory of land and mining rents. He also observes that Marx's prediction that mechanization will penetrate food and raw material production has been substantiated.

50 Marx's theory of money was overlooked by most scholars in the first two-thirds of the twentieth century. It was not until the 1970s, when Isaak Illich Rubin (1973), Suzanne De Brunhoff (1976), and Visser (1977) wrote about Marx's theory of money, that Marx's contribution to this aspect of economics came to light. Earlier writers had either discredited his contributions or had not

considered it worth the discussion. For instance, in 1962, Schumpeter had commented on Marx's propositions on money as being "distinctly weak", and that it "did not succeed in coming up to the Ricardian standard" See Schumpeter, (1997), p. 27.
51 John Neville Keynes was the registrar of the University of Cambridge where he also taught logic and political economy.
52 Interestingly, Alfred Marshall taught both Keynes and Pigou at Cambridge. Pigou was to later appoint Keynes to a lectureship at Cambridge University.
53 Working at the India Office gave Keynes the first-hand experience of how the government offices worked and helped him gain a good understanding of the role of money in the economy. Later in 1915, Keynes was appointed to the Treasury's No. 1 Division, which was concerned with the financial direction of the war. This was to educate him in the importance of controlling expectations if one wanted to control the exchange rate. See Davidson (2009).
54 Keynes's war experience marked the start of his career as a radical economist.
55 Writing in the *Irish Quarterly Review*, Keynes observed, "I sympathize, therefore, with those who would minimize, rather than with those who would maximize, economic entanglement among nations. Ideas, knowledge, science, hospitality, travel – these are the things which should of their nature be international. But let goods be homespun whenever it is reasonably and conveniently possible, and, above all, let finance be primarily national". See Keynes (1933).
56 Article 231 of the Treaty of Versailles (referred to as the War Guilt Clause) made Germany and her allies accept responsibility for the damage caused to the Allied and Associated Governments as a direct result of German aggression during World War I. The principal idea behind forcing Germany to accept responsibility for the war was that it enabled the Allies to impose on Germany a hefty reparation payment to France and Belgium, where the majority of military conflict took place. Interestingly, the French finance minister, Louis-Lucien Klotz, wanted to invoice Germany for £15 billion, which could be paid in 34 annual instalments of £1 billion a year.
57 Keynes, in his book *The Economic Consequences of the Peace*, noted, "But the fact that all things are possible is no excuse for talking foolishly. It is true that in 1870 no man could have predicted Germany's capacity in 1919. We cannot expect to legislate for a generation or more". See Keynes (1924), p. 189.
58 Tily notes that these proposals from Keynes were indeed the precursors of the proposal for an International Clearing Union that was the British Government's contribution to the Bretton Woods' deliberations. See Tily (2007). See also chapter 2 for a discussion on the Bretton Woods meeting.
59 The UN was formed months before World War II ended.
60 See chapter 2 for a detailed discussion of the creation of the GATT, and the WTO.

Select Bibliography

Allen, William R. 'Mercantilism,' in Eatwell, John, Murray Milgate, and Peter Newman (eds.) *The World of Economics* (Springer, 1991) 440–448.

Brennan, David M., David Kristjanson-Gural, Catherine P. Mulder and Erik K. Olsen (eds.). *Routledge Handbook of Marxian Econmomics* (Routledge, 2017).

Brue, Stanley L. and Randy R. Grant. *The Evolution of Economic Thought* (Cengage Learning, 2013).

Brunhoff, Suzanne de. 'Marx's Contribution to the Search for a Theory of Money,' in Moseley, Fred (ed.) *Marx's Theory of Money: Modern Appraisals* (Palgrave Macmillan Publishers, 2005) 209–221.

Burns, Arthur F. 'Economic Research and the Keynesian Thinking of Our Times,' in Burns, Arthur F. *Economic Research and the Keynesian Thinking of Our Times* (NBER, 1946) 3–38.

Buterbaugh, Kevin and Richard Fulton. *The WTO Primer: Tracing Trade's Visible Hand Through Case Studies* (Palgrave Macmillan, 2007).

Butler, Eamonn. *Classical Liberalism – A Primer* (The Institute for Economic Affairs, 2015).

Cannan, Edwin (ed.). *Adam Smith Lectures on Justice, Police, Revenue and Arms* (Oxford: The Clarendon Press, 1896).

Clarke, John J. *Oriental Enlightenment: The Encounter between Asian and Western Thought* (Routledge, 1997).

Clarke, Simon. *Keynesianism, Monetarism and the Crisis of the State* (Edward Elgar Publishing, 1988).

Dam, Kenneth W. *The GATT: Law and International Economic Organization* (University of Chicago Press, 1970).

Davidson, Paul. *John Maynard Keynes* (Palgrave Macmillan, 2009).

De Brunhoff, Suzanne. *Marx on Money* (Urize Books, 1976).

Dobb, Maurice Herbert. *Theories of Value and Distribution Since Adam Smith: Ideology and Economic Theory* (Cambridge University Press, 1973).

Duckenfield, Mark. (ed.). *The Battles Over Free Trade Volume 4: The Emergence of Multilateral Trade, 1940–2006* (Routledge, 2008).

Dunbar, Charles Franklin. 'Ricardo's Use of Facts,' *Quarterly Journal of Economics* Vol 1, No 4 (July 1887) 474–476, 475.

Eagly, Robert V. *The Structure of Classical Economic Theory* (Oxford University Press, 1974).

Ebling, Richard M. 'Economic Ideas: The French Physiocrats and the Case for Laissez-Faire,' *The Future of Freedom* (31 October 2016) <www.fff.org/explore-freedom/article/economic-ideas-french-physiocrats-case-laissez-faire/> (accessed 16 June 2018).

Foley, Duncan K. *Understanding Capital: Marx's Economic Theory* (Harvard University Press, 1986).

Gandolfo, Giancarlo. *International Trade Theory and Policy* (Springer, 2014).

Gerber, Thomas. 'David Ricardo: His Personality, His Times and His Principles,' in Jones, Ronald W. and Rolf Weder (eds.) *200 Years of Ricardian Trade Theory* (Springer International, 2017) 19–40.

Germer, Claus. 'The Commodity Nature of Money in Marx's Theory,' in Mosley, Fred (ed.) *Marx's Theory of Money: Modern Appraisals* (Palgrave Macmillan, 2005) 21–35.

Gilpin, Robert. *The Political Economy of International Relations* (Princeton University Press, 1987).

Gilpin, Robert. *Global Political Economy: Understanding the International Economic Order* (Princeton University Press, 2001).Haberler, Gottfried Von. *Theory of International Trade with Its Applications to Commercial Policy* (William Hodge & Company, 1936).

Harcourt, Geoffrey Colin and Prue Kerr. 'Keynes and the Cambridge School,' in Samuels, Warren J., Jeff E. Biddle and John B. Davis (eds.) *A Companion to the History of Economic Thought* (Blackwell Publishing, 2003) 343–359.

Hayes, M.G. 'Ingham and Keynes on the Nature of Money,' in Pixley, Jocelyn and Geoffrey Colin Harcourt (eds.) *Financial Crises and the Nature of Capitalist Money: Mutual Developments from the Work of Geoffrey Ingham* (Palgrave, 2013).

Hoekman, Bernard and Michael M. Kostecki. *The Political Economy of the World Trading System* (Oxford, 2009).

Hollander, Samuel. *Ricardo: The New View, Collected Essays I* (Routledge, 1995).

Hoselitz, Bert F. 'Agrarian Capitalism, the Natural Order of Things: François Quesnay,' *Kyklos* Vol 21, No 4 (1968) 637–664.

Hunt, E.K. and Mark Lautzenheiser. *History of Economic Thought: A Critical Perspective* (M.E. Sharpe, 2011).

Irwin, Douglas A. *Peddling Protectionism Smoot-Hawley and the Great Depression* (Princeton University Press, 2011).

Irwin, Douglas A. 'Ricardo and Comparative Advantage at 200,' in Evenett, Simon J. (ed.) *Cloth for Wine? The Relevance of Ricardo's Comparative Advantage in the 21st Century* (CEPR Press, 2017) 7–13.

Jones, Ronald W. and Rolf Weder (eds.). *200 Years of Ricardian Trade Theory: Challenges of Globalization* (Springer International, 2017).

Keynes, John Maynard. 'National Self-Sufficiency,' *Studies: An Irish Quarterly Review* Vol 22, No 86 (1933) 177–193.

Keynes, John Maynard. *The Economic Consequences of the Peace* (MacMillan and Co., 1924).

Keynes, John Maynard. *The General Theory of Employment, Interest, and Money* (Palgrave Macmillan Publishing, 2018).

Lee, Eun Sup. *World Trade Regulation: International Trade under the WTO Mechanism* (Springer International, 2012).

Magnusson, Lars. *The Political Economy of Mercantilism* (Springer, 2015).

Mandel, Ernest. *The Formation of the Economic Thought of Karl Marx: 1843 to Capital* (Monthly Review Press, 1971).

Mandel, Ernest. 'Marx, Karl Heinrich (1818–1883),' in *The New Palgrave Dictionary of Economics* (Palgrave Macmillan, 2018) 8394–8422.

Marx, Karl. *Communist Manifesto* (1848).
Marx, Karl. *Capital: A Critique of Political Economy Vol I* (Progress Publishers, 1887).
Marx, Karl and Friedrich Engels. *Pre-Capitalist Socio-Economic Formations* (Progress Publishers, 1979).
Marx, Karl and Friedrich Engels. *The Communist Manifesto* (Broadview Editions, 2004).
Matsushita, Mitsuo, Thomas J. Schoenbaum, Petros C. Mavroidis and Michael Hahn. *The World Trade Organization: Law, Practice, and Policy* (Oxford University Press, 2015).
McKeown, Kieran. *Marxist Political Economy and Marxist Urban Sociology* (Palgrave Macmillan, 1987).
McLellan, David. *Marx's Grundrisse* (MacMillan Press, 1980).
Meek, Ronald L. *The Economics of Physiocracy: Essays and Translations* (Routledge, 2003).
Mill, John Stuart. *Essays on Some Unsettled Questions of Political Economy* (Longmans, 1844).
O'Brian, Denis P. 'Classical Economics,' in Samuels, Warren J., Jeff E. Biddle and John B. Davis (eds.) *A Companion to the History of Economic Thought* (Blackwell Publishing, 2003) 112–129.
O'Brien, Denis P. *The Classical Economists Revisited* (Princeton University Press, 2004).
Paul, Darel E. and Abla Amawi (eds.). *The Theoretical Evolution of International Political Economy: A Reader* (Oxford University Press, 2013).
Peach, Terry. *Interpreting Ricardo* (Cambridge University Press, 1993).
Peach, Terry. 'Ricardo, David (1772–1823),' in *The New Palgrave Dictionary of Economics* (Palgrave Macmillan, 2018) 11686–11704.
Ricardo, David and John Ramsay McCulloch. *The Works of David Ricardo* (John Murray, 1846).
Saad-Filho, Alfredo and Deborah Johnston (eds.). *Neoliberalism: A Critical Reader* (Pluto Press, 2005).
Samuels, Warren J. 'The Physiocratic Theory of Economic Policy,' *The Quarterly Journal of Economics* Vol 76, No 1 (1962) 145–162.
Samuels, Warren J. *Essays in the History of Mainstream Political Economy* (Macmillan Press, 1992).
Samuelson, Paul A. 'Presidential Address: The Way of an Economist,' in Samuelson, Paul A. (ed.) *International Economic Relations* (Palgrave Macmillan, 1969) 1–11.
Schmoller, Gustov. *The Mercantile System and Its Historical Significance* (The Macmillar Company, 1987).
Schumacher, Reinhard. 'Deconstructing the Theory of Comparative Advantage,' *World Social and Economic Review* Vol 2013, No 2 (2013) 83–105.
Schumpeter, Joseph A. *Ten Great Economists: From Marx to Keynes* (Routledge Publishing, 1997).
Skidelsky, Robert. *Keynes: The Return of the Master* (PublicAffairs Books, 2010).
Skousen, Mark. *The Big Three in Economics: Adam Smith, Karl Marx, and John Maynard Keynes* (M.E. Sharpe, 2007).
Smith, Adam and Edwin Cannan. *An Inquiry in the Nature and Causes of The Wealth of Nations, Volume 1 and 2* (University of Chicago Press, 1976).
Sotiropoulos Dimitris P., John Milos and Spyros Lapatsioras (eds.). *A Political Economy of Contemporary Capitalism* (Routledge, 2013).
Sowell, Thomas. *Classical Economics Reconsidered* (Princeton University Press, 1974).
Sraffa, Piero. *The Works and Correspondence of David Ricardo, Vol I: On the Principles of Political Economy and Taxation* (Liberty Fund, 2004).
Sraffa, Piero. *The Works and Correspondence of David Ricardo, Vol VI: Letters 1810–1815* (Liberty Fund, 2004).
Steiner, Philippe. 'Physiocracy and French Pre-Classical Political Economy,' in Samuels, Warren J., Jeff E. Biddle and John B. Davis (eds.) *A Companion to the History of Economic* (Blackwell, 2003) 61–77.
Stoll, Peter Tobias and Frank Schorkopf. *WTO: World Economic Order, World Trade Law* (Martinus Nijhoff Publishers, 2006).
Tily, Geoff. *Keynes Betrayed: The General Theory, the Rate of Interest and 'Keynesian' Economics* (Palgrave Macmillan, 2007).
Trebilcock, Michael J., Robert Howse and Antonia Eliason. *The Regulation of International Trade* (Routledge, 2013).
Unger, Roberto Mangabeira. *Free Trade Reimagined: The World Division of Labor and the Method of Economics* (Princeton University Press, 2007).
Vaggi, Gianni and Peter Groenewegen. *A Concise History of Economic Thought: From Mercantilism to Monetarism* (Palgrave, 2006).

Van den Bossche, Peter and Werner Zdouc. *The Law and Policy of the World Trade Organization: Text, Cases and Material* (Cambridge University Press, 2017).

Vaughn, Karen I. 'Invisible Hand,' in Eatwell, John, Murray Milgate and Peter Newman (eds.) *The Invisible Hand* (The Macmillan Press, 1989) 168–172.

Viner, Jacob and Douglas A. Irwin. *Essays on the Intellectual History of Economics* (Princeton University Press, 1991).

Visser, Hans. 'Marx on Money,' *Kredit und Kapital* Vol 10, No 2 (1977) 266–287.

Voegelin, Eric and Keith Algozin. 'Liberalism and Its History,' *The Review of Politics* (1974) 504–520.

Winham, Gilbert R. 'The Evolution of the World Trading System: The Economic and Policy Context,' in Bethlehem, Daniel, Donal McRae, Rodney Neufeld and Isabelle Van Damme (eds.) *The Oxford Handbook of International Trade Law* (Oxford University Press, 2009) 5–29.

Zhang, Wei-Bin. *International Trade Theory: Capital, Knowledge, Economic Structure, Money, and Prices over Time* (Springer, 2008).

2 The World Trade Organization

Learning Objectives		33
1.	Introduction: Trade in the Pre- and Post-World War II Era	34
2.	Origins of the GATT/WTO: Road out of Bretton Woods	35
3.	Evolution: The GATT to the WTO	37
	3.1 Negotiating Rounds of the GATT	37
	3.2 The Uruguay Round of Negotiations	39
	3.3 The Marrakesh Agreement Establishing the WTO	41
4.	The Law of the WTO	42
	4.1 Sources of WTO Law	43
	4.2 WTO Law and International Law	45
	4.3 WTO Law and General Principles of Law	46
	4.3.1 Due Process	47
	4.3.2 Good Faith (*Bona Fide*)	49
	4.3.3 Estoppel and *Res Judicata*	51
5.	Mandate of the WTO	53
	5.1 Objectives of the WTO	53
	5.2 Functions of the WTO	55
	5.2.1 Implementation and Administration of Trade Agreements	55
	5.2.2 Providing a Forum for Trade Negotiations	56
	5.2.3 Dispute Settlement	56
	5.2.4 Trade Policy Review	57
	5.3 Ministerial Conference	57
	5.4 General Council and Meetings	58
6.	Summary	59

Learning Objectives

This chapter aims to help students understand:

1   The origins and the negotiating rounds of the GATT;
2   The Marrakesh Agreement and the creation of the WTO;
3   The laws that underpin the WTO and sources of the WTO law;
4   WTO law and international law, WTO law, and general principles of law; and
5   The mandate of the WTO and the objectives and functions of the WTO.

DOI: 10.4324/9780367028183-3

1. Introduction: Trade in the Pre- and Post-World War II Era

The period prior to World War I witnessed an expansion of world trade, which was down to moderate tariffs and a fully functional international monetary system. Also facilitating the expansion of international trade was the network of bilateral treaties amongst major trading nations. World War I witnessed the breakup of the workable equilibrium between economic policies, trade, and payment mechanisms developed in the nineteenth century. Post-World War I, the tariffs continued to remain high, with a number of countries continuing to hold on to wartime tariffs, an environment which did not assist in the promotion of international trade. The efforts by the League of Nations to revive the economy were not fruitful.[1] The 1920s and 1930s witnessed a political decline with the rise of fascism and Nazism in Europe and an economic decline in the form of the Great Depression (having its origins in the US), which was to last for over a decade. One of the key contributing factors for the Great Depression was the policy of both protectionism and trade restrictions practised by leading trading nations at that time.

In 1921, the US enacted the Forney-McCumber Act, which increased protectionism, and also vested the president with the powers to unilaterally retaliate against unfair trade practices. Attempts made in the 1920s, through the League of Nations, to discuss liberalised trade did not succeed. In the aftermath of the New York stock market crash in 1929, the US, under the Hoover administration, was to enact the Smoot-Hawley Tariff Act 1930,[2] against the backdrop of a legislative system that encouraged protectionist pressure groups (Winham, 2011, p. 141). The Act pushed import duties much higher, leading to retaliatory action from other trading nations, *viz.*, Canada, Spain, Italy, and Switzerland. This move by the US government was strongly opposed by US economists of the time. The international financial crisis of 1931 brought about the collapse of international capital markets and also the abandonment of the international gold standard.[3] The United Kingdom (UK), for its part, in 1932 entered into an arrangement with its dominions, *viz.*, Australia, Canada, New Zealand, and South Africa, to give preferential treatment to the goods originating in each other's territories (Irwin, Mavroidis, and Sykes, 2008).[4] Likewise, Germany under Nazi rule was to conclude a series of bilateral agreements with Central European countries, thereby creating a new trading bloc, to its own benefits. Such protectionist trade policies led to a decrease in world trade output – which fell by more than half. In short, the protectionist trade policies adopted by developed nations led to a slump in trade transactions and in the contraction of world trade.

Tariffs were to become an election issue in 1932, as the US public did not sympathise with the protectionist trade agenda forged by the Smoot-Hawley Tariff Act. With the election of Franklin Roosevelt as president, the US softened its stance on tariffs and passed the Reciprocal Trade Agreement Act (RTAA) in 1934, which authorised the president to reduce tariffs by up to 50 percent in bilateral trade.[5] Simply put, the RTAA transferred tariff-setting policy to the presidency and ushered in the trend of liberalism, which continued after an interruption during World War II. The delegation of powers to the president to negotiate tariffs, with no *ex post* congressional approval, marked a shift in the trade policy (Schnietz, 2000; Hiscox, 1999) and saw the US concluding over 20 trade agreements during the 1930s. It is also to be noted that the provisions contained in the trade agreements were to form the basis of future multilateral accords (Irwin, Mavroidis, and Sykes, 2008). The policies and practices wreaked havoc on global trade and also exacerbated the political tensions that erupted into war in 1939 (Gowa, 2015). Even during WWII, both US and UK policymakers sought to establish a post-war economic order which would avoid the pitfalls of depression and unemployment – a system that would allow addressing and repairing the economic problems, and at the same time allowing for a reconstruction and reengagement of the international community in trade (Duckenfield, 2008). Both the US and the UK feared a return to the days of trade protectionism, which was considered to be the major contributing factor for the failure of international trade.

Stoll and Schorkopf (2006) note that the experiences from the Great Depression of the 1930s was influential in the efforts to form an international economic order in the post-World War II era. In order to avoid a return to the 1920s and 1930s, a number of international agendas were promoted by developed nations even before the war drew to a close, which included the creation of international institutions with specific agendas and remits. The initiative was taken with a view to conduct international relations amongst the nation states in a regulated and orderly fashion in the post-world war era to foster economic growth. One of the key institutions to emerge in the aftermath of World War II was the United Nations (UN), in 1945.[6] Article 55 of the UN Charter commits Member States to cooperate on economic and social issues, which clearly encapsulates the awareness that peace cannot be perceived as merely the absence of violence but, most importantly, also involves an active engagement in economic and social aspects for the perpetuation of peace.[7] In the post-World War II era, countries were still emerging from the ravages of war, with some emerging from long colonial rule. Parts of Asia, sub-Saharan Africa, and South America were still under colonial rule with controls still resting with European powers. The US was to emerge as a leading political and economic power, while also being prepared to take on a leadership role in building a new international economic system. Between November 1947 and March 1948, the United Nations Conference on Trade and Employment was held in Havana, Cuba, which saw the adoption of the Havana Charter for International Trade Organization, referred to as the ITO.

2. Origins of the GATT/WTO: Road out of Bretton Woods

A discussion on the laws of the WTO will not be complete without an understanding of its origins in the GATT 1947, as the customs and procedures of the WTO are to be found in the GATT. The institutions that govern international trade have been shaped by the economic policies put in place by the leading trading nations, influenced by economic theories that offered to generate more wealth. The institutions of governance also transformed with the change in the philosophy and vision. The developed nations through negotiations sought to reduce tariffs and other barriers in pursuit of an expanded trade agenda. The post-World War II era witnessed the emergence of the GATT, which in effect was the precursor to the overarching multilateral trade organisation, the WTO. The GATT's origins are to be found in the Bretton Woods Conference, in New Hampshire, where the delegates of 44 nations led by the US and the UK proposed comprehensive plans for the post-World War II reconstruction of the world economy and development through the formation of institutions that would eliminate the economic causes of war. The proposals included the creation of economic and financial institutions, and the conference established the charters for the International Bank for Reconstruction and Development, *i.e.*, the World Bank (WB), and the International Monitory Fund (IMF). The Bretton Woods agreements were an unprecedented experiment in international rule-making and institution building and a decisive step in the historic reopening of the world economy (Ikenberry, 1993). The GATT, the predecessor to the WTO, began in 1947 with the membership of 23 countries.

While the US-led delegation envisioned a non-discriminatory, multilateral trading system, the UK's position was one of preferential economic groupings through imperial preferences and bilateral trading (Ikenberry, 1993). Despite divergent views held by the two key trading nations of the US and the UK, an agreement was reached in devising post-war arrangement for international trade.[8] The notable exception from the conference was the charter for an international trade body, which was later mooted by the US in 1945, under the 'Proposals for Expansion of World Trade and Employment', for the creation of the ITO. The UK, working alongside the US, took the proposal forward through the UN, to include specific provisions for trade, development, commodity agreements, *etc*. The proposal was to be given full shape in the Havana Charter in 1947. A comprehensive code, the Havana Charter contained general statements of principle and specific commitments of national policy, both dealing with national barriers to trade.

The GATT, which was largely based on parts of the Havana Charter, was built on 'commitments', or promises of nations that came together to trade with each other. The economic order proposed not only reflected the US interests and its strong economic position in the post-World War II era, but also set the broad limits on the shape of the post-war international economic order. In Ikenberry's view, the policy ideas inspired by Keynesianism, embraced by economists and policymakers from both the UK and the US, largely contributed to the acceptance of a middle ground forged by Keynesian ideas during the Bretton Woods Conference (Ikenberry, 1993). This Keynesian 'new thinking' helped overcome the political stalemate between the two trading nations.

If the UN were to be considered the response of the concerned world powers to military aggression brought about by Nazism and fascism, then the Bretton Woods Conference can be viewed as the response from developed trading nations led by the US and the UK to avoid a repeat of the economic environment that contributed to World War II. The vision for the ITO was the combined effort of US and UK bureaucracies and was backed by leading economists from both sides of the Atlantic.[9] The WB was established as an international financial institution to provide loans to countries for their capital programmes and has as its stated goal the reduction of poverty.[10] The IMF, another brainchild of the Bretton Woods Conference, was primarily intended to reconstruct the international payment system. The ITO, on the other hand, was to serve as the institutional foundation to administer the Havana Charter[11] on international trade and was referred to as the third leg of the Bretton Woods stool.[12] Although agreed upon in the 1947–48 Havana Conference, the ITO's origins predate both the founding of the UN as well as the Bretton Woods Conference. The Havana Charter vested the ITO with very broad powers, containing detailed guidelines and far-reaching international trade regulations for the conduct of trade amongst nations. Importantly, the Charter contained provisions committing Member States to economic development and the labour market, besides trade in natural resources.

The ITO unfortunately did not come to fruition, as it faced obstacles in the Member Countries where debates were held on the proposals, with many not being able to agree to the terms of the Charter. The proposal, when presented to the US Congress, faced stiff opposition, prompting the US president to withdraw the proposal from any further discussions in 1950. The GATT that was signed in 1947 was more in the form of a temporary agreement (Jackson, 2000), where the countries that came together only agreed to a 'set of rules' to govern trade amongst one another, with the undertaking of a reduction in import tariffs for other Contracting States with the support of an interim commission – Interim Commission for the International Trade Organization, or ICITO. The ITO did not have any institutional framework, but only a small secretariat with a limited 'institutional apparatus.'

As the GATT was negotiated at the same time as the ITO Charter was being drafted, tariffs were negotiated on GATT terms even in 1947.[13] Jackson notes that although completed in October 1947, the GATT technically never came into force and was being applied through a 'Protocol of Provisional Application'.[14] It was agreed amongst the signatories to continue to negotiate multilateral trade using the provisions of GATT, although the ITO was not realised as an international trade organisation.[15] In truth, the GATT did not involve a formal treaty, or even an international organisation for that matter. The reason that GATT was adopted through an executive order in the US, rather than by congressional ratification, provided the US exporters with reduced tariffs and the enhanced market access that they sought (Woolcock, 2012), which also prompted the US to remove some of the preferential trading arrangements finalised prior to World War II.

3. Evolution: The GATT to the WTO

Although the GATT was never intended to function as a trade organisation, the next four decades witnessed the growth in membership due to its success in reducing trade barriers amongst Member States with increased trade flow. Tariffs on manufactured goods fell from roughly 35 percent prior to 1947 to 6.4 percent in 1986, and the trade regime was to become deeper and wider in terms of its membership and the issues covered. As the GATT did not have a formal treaty, it evolved as a member-driven forum for trade negotiations. The GATT also embodied a number of codified and implicit principles, with the most important one being that of non-discrimination, to be found in the most-favoured-nation principle (MFN – Article I), and national treatment (NT – Article III). The MFN principle, which was earlier only used in bilateral trade agreements, was promoted by the US and introduced as a core principle of the GATT.[16] The other key principles were the prohibition of quantitative and other non-tariff restrictions contained in Article XI (Dam, 1970), which was designed to delegitimise the use of protectionist measures other than tariffs (Winham, 2011). The process that helped shape the GATT was reciprocity, or reciprocal market access, which stemmed from the political economy of trade liberalisation in the US.[17] The primary purpose of the GATT became the facilitation of trade in a liberalised environment, as opposed to being conducted in an environment beset with protectionism.

3.1 Negotiating Rounds of the GATT

Because the GATT was a member-driven forum instead of treaty based, the members were required to initiate and engage in negotiations to achieve tariff reductions. With the growth in membership, multilateral trade negotiation rounds followed, and the vision for further reduction in trade barriers became the primary objective, *i.e.*, reduction of tariffs on imports from other GATT members. The negotiating rounds were eight in all, with the first four focusing primarily on institutional matters and tariffs and taking place in Geneva (1947), Annecy (1949), Torquay (1951), and again in Geneva (1956). The fifth round – the Dillon Round (1960–1961) – was more devoted to negotiations on reduction of tariffs. The sixth round – the Kennedy Round (1963–1967) – took up for negotiation tariffs and anti-dumping measures, and the seventh round – the Tokyo Round (1973–1979) – primarily focused on tariffs, non-tariff measures, and 'framework' agreements. The Uruguay Round (1986–1994), the longest-lasting GATT round, focused on tariffs, non-tariff measures, trade in services, IP rights protection, dispute settlement, trade in textiles and agriculture, and most importantly the creation of the WTO. The eighth round of GATT negotiations culminated in the successful establishment of the WTO, with an expanded coverage to include trade in services and intellectual property (IP) rights protection.

One of the criticisms levelled at the developed countries-led GATT was that the countries who stood to gain the most from an open trading system also made the rules (Sell, 2012).[18] The developing countries, in response to the GATT, established the United Nations Conference on Trade and Development (UNCTAD). On the strength of the studies carried out by UNCTAD which reflected the developing country concerns, GATT signatories assented to some of the developing countries' requests (Sell, 2012). For instance, in 1971, the GATT established a Generalised System of Preferences (GSP) which offered non-reciprocal market access for developing countries' goods, where developing countries were not required to reciprocate. However, it did not work well in reality, as the GSP still exempted many goods where the developing countries were most competitive.[19] The role of UNCTAD receded over time, particularly after the oil price shocks and subsequent debt crises of the 1970s and 1980s. Eventually, with more developing countries embracing neoliberal economic policies, UNCTAD was overshadowed by GATT.

The tariff negotiating rounds, which took place between rounds one and five, were more reciprocal in nature, where tariff concessions were negotiated between trading partners and then automatically extended to all other states through the core principle of MFN. During the Geneva Round of negotiations in 1947, a total of 123 agreements, covering around 15,000 tariff items and affecting about 40 percent of world trade, were concluded. The tariff negotiations were conducted on a bilateral and product-by-product basis, requiring countries to establish lists of 'requests' for tariff concessions from each trading partner (WTO, 2007). As far as OECD countries were concerned, the bilateral and product-by-product tariff negotiations facilitated an improved access to the US market, and in return to buy US capital goods. The Annecy Round in 1949 witnessed the accession of 11 more countries to the GATT fold. As the binding agreements amongst the contracting parties were to expire in January 1951, a meeting was scheduled for the autumn of 1950 in Torquey, where the parties would leave the majority of commitments made in earlier rounds intact. Unlike in the first round, the original 23 countries negotiated tariff reductions only with the 11 acceding countries, concluding 147 bilateral agreements and delivering tariff reductions on 5,000 items (ICITO, 1950).

Well into the fifth round of negotiations, trade amongst the contracting states was not fully liberalized as envisaged, though progress was made. One of the identifiable reasons for not being able to achieve full liberalisation was the European countries' heavy reliance on non-tariff measures during the 1950s, which meant any tariff concessions given during the negotiations were not meaningful (Winham, 2011). In 1953, the cause of multilateralism was undermined due to the waiver granted for US agricultural support. This particular instance was to provide the precedent for the exclusion of agriculture from the GATT rules for the next 40 years (Woolcock, 2012). In the 1950s, there was an increased focus in Europe and Japan towards reconstruction. This meant Europe had very little to offer at the GATT tariff negotiations until their economies recovered, leading to a lack of forward movement in the GATT negotiations during the 1950s. Gradually, there was also a shift in focus from negotiation on tariff reductions to the negotiation of codes of behaviour, which were multilateral in nature and also more detailed. The next significant round of GATT negotiation was the Kennedy Round (1963–1967), initiated by the US, which was to result in more tariff reductions than achieved in any other GATT negotiations since 1947.

In the post-World War II era, the European Economic Community (EEC) had grown in stature and was fast emerging as a major trading block. The common external tariff (CET) and the common agricultural policy (CAP) established by the EEC was proving to be a challenge to US exporters to the EEC. In order to limit the effects of the CET and to establish GATT discipline over the CAP, the US proposed a more comprehensive negotiation, resulting in the Kennedy Round (1963–1967). Part IV of the GATT was drafted in during this round to facilitate entry of newly independent countries to become contracting parties, thereby effectively establishing a two-tier system, *i.e.*, one for OECD countries and one for developing countries (Woolcock, 2012).[20] The Kennedy Round witnessed the participation of the European Community (EC) as a single entity and the application of Article XXIV, with the EEC establishing a precedent by allowing customs union as an exception to the MFN principle. The important political achievement of the Kennedy Round was the triumph of the principles of trade liberalisation over protectionism. Success in this regard was brought about by the fear that a deadlock in the negotiations would be considered a failure that would go beyond the issues presented at the table (Winham, 2011), and needless to say the contracting nations were under pressure to avoid a breakdown. One of the important outcomes of the Kennedy Round was the establishment of the Anti-Dumping Code, which was an economic success for some of the developed countries led by the US.

Although trading nations were encouraged to extend liberalisation into the area of non-tariff barriers to trade, the early 1970s witnessed an increasing use of non-tariff barriers by trading nations in response to the surge of exports from Japan and the newly industrialised economies. In 1971, the US government suspended the convertibility of the US dollar into gold, prompting a breakdown of the fixed exchange system that was negotiated in 1944 under the Bretton Woods Agreement, leading to a period of uncertainty (Winham, 1986).[21] These developments rekindled fears in the minds of the major trading nations, prompting them to reject protectionism[22] and to call for a new round of GATT trade negotiations. The Tokyo Round of GATT negotiations (1973–1979) officially commenced in 1973 but was delayed for a number of reasons, including the need for the US to pass legislation authorising the president to negotiate and the US presidential election of 1976 (Winham, 2011). The negotiating round produced separate multilateral agreements, or legal codes,[23] covering government procurement; subsidies and countervailing duties; and a series of revisions of GATT Articles, besides also producing qualified MFN codes. It is also to be noted that US efforts to bring agriculture under GATT discipline met with failure. The 'club-model' of the international trade policy was consolidated with the US-led OECD countries assuming responsibility for shaping the rules. This also saw the emergence of the newly industrialised nations (NIEs) as an important group amongst the developing countries (Woolcock, 2012). In sum, the Tokyo Round of negotiations was successful in terms of rule-making exercise, as opposed to the earlier rounds of negotiations where the focus was on tariff reduction.

3.2 The Uruguay Round of Negotiations

The longest running negotiation round of the GATT was the Uruguay Round (1986–1994), which resulted in the formation of WTO as the principal rules-based organisation for the conduct of multilateral trade. Seen as the most comprehensive of the negotiating rounds, the Uruguay Round expanded the GATT disciplines to include IP rights protection, trade in services, and investment. The Uruguay Round also produced a range of international agreements between the contracting parties which was integrated under a common legal system. Six years after the conclusion of the Tokyo Round of negotiations, the GATT ministerial meeting of November 1982 initiated an elaborate work programme and took the decision to commence a fresh round of negotiations on a broader and more ambitious agenda. In fact, the next trade round was mooted at a time when trade cooperation was anything but possible, as the general economic conditions prevailing during the early 1980s were deteriorating with widespread inflation, unemployment, monetary instability, and also large payment imbalances (Croome, 1998). Despite the fact that the Tokyo Round of negotiations made good progress in reducing protectionism from non-tariff barriers, the sharply deteriorating international economic situation of the early 1980s intensified protectionist demands in the advanced/industrialised nations. There was also pressure from the US-led advanced industrialised nations to expand the GATT regime to include new issues, *viz.*, services, investment, and IP. The proposals were met with resistance from the developing countries led by India and Brazil, who argued that they were not sufficiently developed to negotiate on the issues identified on an equal footing with the developed nations, as a level playing field, and any outcomes produced could be lopsided. The US also made agricultural reform its top priority, as it was worried about the CAP of the EC, which involved the imposition of variable import levies (Rausser, 1995).[24] The Uruguay Round of negotiations also sought to reverse the pattern of protectionism with respect to textiles and clothing that had evolved under the MFA which emerged in the 1970s.[25] It should not be forgotten that in all the preceding rounds of negotiations the one stumbling block was agriculture, where no clear agreement was reached.

At the week-long special ministerial meeting that took place at Punta del Este prior to the actual Uruguay Round of negotiations in September 1986, it was agreed between the US and the Indian delegates that although the negotiations would cover a range of issues, a separate structure would be adopted for dealing with services (Winham, 1997). The developing countries led by India and Brazil had also raised similar concerns about the inclusion of IP rights protection in the agenda.[26] The smaller countries wanted to see the GATT rules implemented properly in the disputes, and some of the developed country players, like the European Community, was not particularly keen to propose or support any new initiatives in the GATT, barring the inclusion of IP in the discussions. In contrast, the US was interested in bringing new ideas to the table, spurred on by its free market policies under President Reagan. The US sought to liberalise world trade in agricultural products and also proposed a basis for relations between the developed and more advanced developing countries (Croome, 1998).

The negotiators at the Uruguay Round were clear from the beginning that it would be a 'single undertaking', which meant there were no 'opt out' options available and the participants had to accept the whole package. The proposal was significant, as it removed the option of being selective and thereby shrunk the scope of state autonomy. This approach also paved the way for private sector actors, who were already playing an unprecedented role in the negotiations, to push hard to include some of their pet issues – one of them being international IP rights protection (Sell, 2012).[27] In 1988, two years from the commencement of the negotiations, it was decided at the Montreal Ministerial Mid-Term Review Conference to introduce a trade policy review mechanism to improve the implementation of the GATT rules and also to create greater cooperation between GATT, IMF, and the World Bank. Midway through the negotiations, it was further agreed that the contracting parties would meet once every two years at the ministerial level.

The Uruguay Round witnessed a comprehensive institutional reform of the world trading system since the establishment of the GATT in 1947. The agenda for the Uruguay Round of negotiations contained reform of GATT rules; measures to strengthen the GATT institution; market access; and importantly the three new areas of services, investments, and IP. The Punta del Este Declaration also contained an agreement to discontinue the use of any trade restrictive measures inconsistent with GATT rules and to also scale back such measures that were not consistent with GATT rules before the completion of the Uruguay Round (UN DESA, 1996). The negotiating countries were divided into 15 separate groups,[28] with each focused on a particular agenda. The WTO's dispute settlement procedures were fully revamped, making them substantially stronger –in both form and substance – than in their previous edition under GATT.[29] The Declaration also removed several distortions from the GATT that had previously weakened the integrity of the trading system.

3.3 The Marrakesh Agreement Establishing the WTO

The notion of creating a global trade organisation emerged gradually during the course of the negotiations, as negotiations and observers realised the need for a better institutional structure and a mechanism to resolve disputes to oversee the implementation of the agreements (Matsushita, Shoenbaum, Mavroidis, and Hahn, 2015). The negotiators were concerned about how and when agreements would come into force and the modalities of the implementation of the agreements. These concerns went directly to the root of the issues, *i.e.*, the 'functioning of the GATT system'. The proposal for a trade organisation had originally come from Professor John H. Jackson, who urged the negotiators to use the Uruguay Round as a launchpad to found a new 'World Trade Organization' (Jackson, 1990).[30] In 1990 the initiative to establish an international organisation for trade was put forth at the Uruguay Round by the then Italian trade minister, Renato Ruggiero (later the second director-general of the WTO), and then by Canada which formally proposed the establishment of a 'World Trade Organization' (Van den Bossche and Zdouc, 2017). The proposal was to create an international organisation to administer the different multilateral agreements and other instruments related to international trade formalised through the GATT.

The proposal was not well received by the US and most developing countries for different reasons. The developing countries were hostile to the idea, as in their view support could only be offered if the international trade organisation was situated within the framework of the United Nations, *i.e.*, the UNCTAD. Another factor that was plaguing the minds of the developing countries was the fear of supranationalism and the possibility of reconstructing the GATT into an international organisation for trade (Jackson, 1991). The European Community supported the proposal for a multilateral trade organisation by submitting its own proposal, on the grounds that the GATT needed a sound institutional framework "to ensure the effective implementation of the results of the Uruguay Round" (GATT, 1990). The Uruguay Round negotiators were receptive to the proposal put forward by Professor Jackson (Matsushita, Shoenbaum, Mavroidis, and Hahn, 2015), which received further support in 1991 when the EC, Canada, and Mexico tabled a joint proposal for an international organisation for trade, which in turn paved the way for further negotiations resulting in the draft *Agreement Establishing the Multilateral Trade Organization* in December 1991, commonly referred to as the Dunkel Draft, after the then director-general of the GATT.[31] The US remained opposed to the establishment of a global multilateral trade organisation and even campaigned against the proposal. With growing support for the proposal from most participants – both developed and developing countries alike – the US found itself isolated. In 1993 the US under the new Clinton Administration dropped its outspoken opposition of the new international trade organisation. On 15 December 1993, the US formally agreed to the establishment of the new organisation, which paved the way for commencement of work on the creating of the multilateral trade organisation, or the World Trade Organization.

The draft Final Act contained agreements on transitional measures, the termination of the GATT 1947, and the Tokyo Round agreements, which were to be covered under the new WTO agreements. It was also agreed that the WTO would come into existence on 1 January 1995. The Marrakesh Agreement Establishing the World Trade Organization (WTO Agreement) consisted of multilateral trade agreements annexed to a single document.[32] The Final Act prescribes reduction of tariffs on industrial products by an average of more than one-third; the progressive liberalisation of trade in agricultural goods; and the establishment of the World Trade Organization to facilitate the implementation of multilateral trade agreements and to serve as a forum for future negotiations. By signing the Final Act, the participants in the Uruguay Round of negotiations certified that the annexed agreements, including the legal texts, the schedules of concessions and commitments in trade in goods, and the schedules of specific commitments in trade in services, were the result of their negotiations. The Agreement Establishing the World Trade Organization was signed in Marrakesh in April 1994 and entered into force on 1 January 1995.[33] After the establishment of the WTO on 1 January 1995, the WTO and the GATT 1947 existed side by side for one year, and the GATT 1947 was eventually terminated at the end of 1995 and replaced with the GATT 1994.[34]

The Sutherland Report on 'The Future of the WTO' noted as follows:

> The creation of the World Trade Organization (WTO) in 1995 was the most dramatic advance in multilateralism since the inspired period of institution building of the late 1940s.
>
> (Sutherland Report, 2004)

4. The Law of the WTO

WTO law is a complex body of law and has made a substantial contribution to international trade law since the formation of the GATT in the 1940s. The custodian of several multilateral agreements and the principal institution for international trade, the WTO is linked in profound ways to the international economic order. The WTO as the principal multilateral trade organisation has made a significant contribution to economic development in both developed and developing countries. The body of WTO law is complex and to be found in the agreements of the WTO, the Dispute Settlement Understanding (DSU) of the WTO, the GATT, *etc*. These are not on the same legal footing, as some identify specific legal rights and obligations of the Member States, while others clarify and elaborate on rights and obligations. It should be added that the jurisprudence of the WTO is still evolving, with growing membership of the WTO, increase in trade and disciplines of trade, with an ever-growing number of disputes that come to be referred to the DSB.

The GATT rules are to be found contained in 35 articles of the General Agreement (Jackson, 2000), the most important of which are Article I, covering the most-favoured nation principles, and Article III, covering the national treatment obligation. The two articles together form the foundation of the non-discrimination principle, which underpins the GATT regime. As all agreements are annexed to the agreement establishing the WTO, the expression 'the WTO Agreement' is understood to cover the totality of all the agreements. The Annexes of the WTO Agreement include Annex 1, which is divided into three parts, namely Annex 1A, Annex 1B, and Annex 1C, and Annexes 2, 3, and 4.

- Annex 1A consists of the Multilateral Trade in Goods; GATT 1994; and the Agreements on Agriculture; the Application of Sanitary and Phytosanitary Measures; Textiles and Clothing; Technical Barriers to Trade; Trade-Related Investment Measures; Implementation of Article VI of the General Agreement on Tariffs and Trade 1994 (Antidumping Agreement); Implementation of Article VII of the General Agreement on Tariffs and Trade 1994 (Customs Valuation Agreement); Pre-Shipment Inspection; Rules of Origin; Import Licensing Procedures; Subsidies and Countervailing Measures; and on Safeguards. For the purposes of clarity, Annex 1A includes a General Interpretive Note which provides that, in the event of a 'conflict' between provisions of the GATT 1994 and another Annex 1A Agreement, the provision of the latter to prevail.

- Annex 1B consists of the *General Agreement on Trade in Services* (GATS) and its annexes.
- Annex 1C consists of the *Agreement on Trade-Related Aspects of Intellectual Property Rights* (TRIPS Agreement).
- Annex 2 consists of the *Understanding on Rules and Procedures Governing Settlement of Disputes* (Dispute Settlement Understanding or DSU), which establishes the procedures for resolving trade disputes among WTO members.
- Annex 3 consists of the *Trade Policy Review Mechanism*, which establishes a periodic review of each WTO member's compliance with WTO agreements and commitments.
- Annex 4 consists of the plurilateral trade agreements[35] on *Trade in Civil Aircraft*; on *Government Procurement*; *International Dairy Agreement*; and *International Bovine Meat Agreement*.[36]

The governance of the WTO is with the Ministerial Conference which meets every two years to review the organisation's performance and set out policy. The task of day-to-day functioning is entrusted with the General Council and other subsidiary bodies, such as Councils for Goods, for Services, and TRIPS. Additionally, committees are also established under the 12 of the 13 multilateral goods agreements and the plurilateral agreements.[37]

4.1 Sources of WTO Law

In a domestic legal system, methodologies are found incorporated (depending on the legal system) to ascertain what the law is and to demonstrate how the law is created, *i.e.*, the legal process through which it was arrived at. A similar approach cannot be adopted in international law to arrive at the source of law, as there is no single body able to create laws internationally that is binding upon everyone (Shaw, 2017). The WTO laws naturally fall within the category of international law and does present one with the task of investigating its source, *i.e.*, a survey of the process whereby the rules emerge (McDougal and Reisman, 1980). This brings one to Article 38(1) of the Statute of International Court of Justice (ICJ), which is widely recognised as the most authoritative statement as to the sources of international law. Article 38(1) reads as follows:

> The Court, whose function is to decide in accordance with international law such disputes as are submitted to it, shall apply:
>
> a   international conventions, whether general or particular, establishing rules expressly recognized by the contesting states;
> b   international custom as evidence of a general practice accepted as law;
> c   the general principles of law recognized by civilized nations;
> d   subject to the provisions of Article 59, judicial decisions and the teachings of the most highly qualified publicists of the various nations, as subsidiary means for the determination of rules of law.

In a commercial sense, especially in international trade, the expression 'sources of law' would refer to the law that comes to govern the legal relations of the parties who have undertaken to perform according to the chosen law, which may also identify and include a judicial setting/ forum. Mavroidis (2008) posits the argument that with the exception of *jus cogens*,[38] the states have autonomy to determine the law that would govern their relations. This proposition gains in significance, as the WTO is a rules-based multilateral organisation comprising sovereign states and custom territories that have come together to negotiate trade policies to facilitate trade amongst nations. Also, as part of the agreement, the sovereign states have undertaken to abide by the rules of the WTO, which includes submitting any disputes that may arise in the course of their conduct of such trade to the Dispute Settlement Authority of the WTO. In other words, the substantive rights and obligations of the Member States of the WTO is governed by the Understanding on Rules and Procedures Governing the Settlement of Disputes (DSU). For the purposes of Article 38(1)(a), the rules of the DSU can be considered as 'rules expressly recognised by the contesting parties'. In short, the membership of the WTO presupposes adherence to the rules, the agreements of the WTO, and submission of any disputes to the DSU. Nevertheless, Articles 1, 2, and 3 of the DSU limits its jurisdiction to disputes concerning the 'covered agreements' as specified in Appendix 1.[39] Some of the other agreements mentioned in Appendix 1 of the DSU include the Havana Charter; agreements mentioned in the TRIPS Agreement;[40] agreements mentioned in the SCM Agreement; and other international agreements.

It is also argued that there are additional sources to WTO laws, *i.e.*, state practice, secondary laws, and implied powers of WTO adjudicating bodies (Mavroidis, 2008). As regards state practice, we are directed towards Article XXIX of GATT, which required that WTO Member States follow certain chapters of the Havana Charter, pending the establishment of the ITO.[41] With regards to secondary law, the covered agreements of the WTO establish legal authority to provide a suitable mechanism for the creation of rules. For instance, Article IX(2)[42] of the WTO Agreement vests the Ministerial Conference and the General Council with the authority to adopt interpretations of the WTO Agreement and of the multilateral trade agreements. Likewise, Article X of the WTO Agreement establishes a process to amend the WTO agreements. Mavroidis (2008) argues that WTO agreements do have in place the necessary mechanism for something akin to secondary law, and it cites the example of the changes made to Article 31 of the Agreement on Trade-Related Aspects of Intellectual Property Rights (TRIPS) following the procedure. Mavroidis also raises the issue that if the various WTO committees (Anti-dumping Committee, *etc*.) often adopt decisions and recommendations that are of general applicability, one could conclude that they have vested in them the powers to create law. Similarly, when the Appellate Body (AB) was charged with the authority under Article 17(9) of the DSU to establish its own *Working Procedures*, such powers are a reflection of primary laws (Mavroidis, 2008).

It is also reasoned that unless implied powers are recognised, where framers had not explicitly provided an organ with such powers to regulate issues, such organ may not fulfil its function (Mavroidis, 2008).[43] However, there is no explicit narrative in the WTO Agreement, defining the sources of WTO law in detail, as the sources are not often self-explanatory. Mavroidis (2008) opines that while it is the privilege of the WTO's framers to define the sources of law, it remains the privilege of the adjudicating bodies to identify the interpretive elements, and he cites the example of *amicus curiae* briefs and powers of the Appellate Body. It is also to be noted that reports of the Panels and Appellate Body are clear sources of law other than the texts of the WTO agreements, as they are to be viewed as 'judicial decisions' and 'subsidiary sources' of international law under Article 38(1)(d) of the Statute of the ICJ (Palmeter and Mavroidis, 1998). Panel reports would also include reports from prior Panels, *i.e.*, the ones established under GATT 1947.

4.2 WTO Law and International Law

The development of a comprehensive legal regime under the auspices of WTO has given rise to questions concerning whether WTO law is a part of international law or should be considered a separate species; the new international trading regime's relationship with traditional international law; and so on. It would be a good point to commence the enquiry with the Marrakesh Agreement Establishing the World Trade Organization. The Marrakesh Agreement could be considered a 'particular' international convention within the meaning of Article 38(1)(a) of the Statute of the ICJ, as well as a number of annexed agreements and legal instruments dealing with trade in goods and services, and IP rights (Palmeter and Mavroidis, 1998). The Vienna Convention on the Laws of Treaties 1969 (VCLT) relates only to the treaties[44] concluded between sovereign states that are parties to the VCLT, which came into force in 1980.[45] Nevertheless, the VCLT not only codifies existing norms of customary law but also seeks to achieve a progressive development of the law of treaties, which brings into focus its retroactivity (Dörr and Schmalenbach, 2018).[46] As Qureshi notes, the jurisprudence of the WTO is replete with references to Articles 31 and 32 of the VCLT (Qureshi, 2015). Article 3.2 of the DSU states that pronouncements of the DSB cannot come to add or diminish the rights and obligations contained in a covered agreement of the WTO.[47] The second sentence of the same provision states clearly that the dispute settlement system of the WTO is not only there to preserve the rights and obligations of Member States under the covered agreements, but also to clarify the provisions of the said agreements "in accordance with customary rules of interpretation of public international law".[48]

In *US – Gasoline*, the Appellate Body observed that the 'direction reflects a measure of recognition that the General Agreement is not to be read in clinical isolation from public international law'.[49] This observation of the Appellate Body clearly indicates that the WTO legal system forms part of the general international legal order and permits the Appellate Body to seek interpretive advice from sources of public international law. Article 3.2 also specifies that adjudicating bodies must reach their conclusions using customary rules of interpretation, which in Qureshi's view is founded on the need to ensure certainty and clarity in the process of interpretation of the WTO agreements (Qureshi, 2015). McLachlan notes that treaties are themselves creatures of international law and rely for their enforcement and operation on being part of the international legal system (McLachlan, 2005). As observed by McNair, treaties must be applied and interpreted against the backdrop of general principles of international law (McNair, 1961).

Pauwelyn (2001) takes the position that WTO is part of the corpus of international law and argues that, similar to international environmental law and human rights law, WTO law is yet another branch of International law.[50] In Pauwelyn's opinion, treaties are automatically born into the system of international law, in the same way that private contracts are automatically born into a system of domestic law. Pauwelyn goes on to postulate the argument that any new treaty is subsumed under general international law and hence created within the wider corpus of public international law, including pre-existing treaties. Marceau, on the other hand, takes the position that the very conclusion of the WTO Agreement as formal treaty, followed by the establishment of the WTO as an international organisation, are "developments that had the effect of subjecting the WTO fully to international law" (Marceau, 2001). McRae, on the other hand, describes the work of WTO as the 'new frontier' of international law (McRae, 2000). One can also add that international trade law, with the jurisprudence of the WTO, is to be considered as an integral part of international law. As noted by the former WTO director-general Pascal

Lamy, "WTO participates in the construction of international coherence and reinforces the international legal order" (Lamy, 2007, p. 977). Applying the prior arguments, it can be safely summarised that the WTO Agreement (including the annexes) falls within the tapestry of public international law and hence is subject to the general principles of public international law. A majority of commentators on the subject share this view (Jackson, 1997; McRae, 2000; Petersmann, 1999).

Customary international law plays a crucial role in the WTO's dispute settlement process. By definition, 'customary international law' concerns both the process through which certain rules of international law are formed and the rules formed through such a process (Treves, 2006).[51] In essence, customary rules are the result of a process through which elements of fact acquire a legal character, which in turn creates rights and obligations (Treves, 2006). Article 3.2 of the DSU specifies that the purpose of the dispute settlement is to clarify the provisions of the WTO agreements "in accordance with customary rules of interpretation of public international law".[52] Palmeter and Mavroidis (1998) note that in practice the Appellate Body had been guided by Articles 31 and 32 of the VCLT, which codify customary international law and had led to customary international law finding its way into the WTO dispute settlement. In *EC – Hormones*, the Panel was asked to decide if 'precautionary principles'[53] were part of customary international law. The Panel observed that even assuming that the precautionary principle was customary international law, it would not override explicit provisions of the covered agreements (SPS Agreement) that were intended to codify the principle, *i.e.*, Article 5.7 of the SPS Agreement.[54] The Appellate Body in *EC – Hormones*, while observing that "the precautionary principle indeed finds reflection in Article 5.7 of the SPS Agreement",[55] failed to take a position on whether the precautionary principle is a principle of customary international law, but instead noted that the status of the precautionary principle in international law is still very much the subject of debate.[56]

The issue arose once more in *EC – Biotech* before the Panel, which closely followed the views expressed by the Appellate Body in *EC – Hormones* and noted that the debate on the matter was still ongoing.[57] Customary international law rules are essentially default rules for treaty interpretation, which apply to treaties in the absence of the contracting states opting out of them (Mitchell, 2008). They to a greater degree assist in completing international contracts, *i.e.*, treaties, by filling in the gaps – this feature gains in significance in the case of the WTO, which is a multilateral trade organisation strongly grounded on 'agreements' entered into between sovereign states. It is also to be noted here that the WTO (like the GATT before it) is firmly grounded on agreements entered into between the Member States, and not on custom (Palmeter and Mavroidis, 1998). This means the questions of custom will rarely be raised before the Panel or the AB.

4.3 WTO Law and General Principles of Law

General principles of law are akin to customary international law in that they are considered part of general international law and are in principle binding on all state parties. The WTO adjudicating bodies have repeatedly referred to and used general principles of law as a basis of or to lend support to their decision-making process, wherever possible. One can identify the following legal principles as being part of the WTO legal order through usage.

a   Due Process;
b   Good Faith (*bona fides*);
c   Estoppel and *Res Judicata*.

4.3.1 Due Process

Due process is also referred to as 'fundamental fairness', 'natural justice', and 'procedural fairness'. Although the principles of due process can be understood to mean fairness/natural justice/procedural fairness, it is difficult to encapsulate it precisely in a definition. Some legal scholars trace the concept of 'due process' to the Magna Carta of 1215, where the phrase used is 'the law of the land'.[58] The expression 'due process' is now used in lieu of 'law of the land.' According to Lord Hailsham of St Marylebone, the expression in its present English form could be traced to the Petition of Rights of 1627 and the Habeas Corpus Act 1640 in England (Hailsham, 1983).[59] In 1791, the phrase 'due process' was incorporated into the Fifth Amendment of the US Constitution,[60] and hence some commentators hold the view it is predominantly an American concept (Gaffney, 1999). On the other hand, some commentators have observed that due process is the halting work of millennia, tracing the its origins to 450 BC to the *Lex Duodecim Tabularum* (Twelve Tablets) of Roman law (Kotuby and Sabota, 2017). Law VIII, Table I, narrates the right of parties as follows (Scott, 1932):

> If the plaintiff and defendant do not settle their dispute, as above mentioned, let them state their cases either in the Comitium or the Forum, by making a brief statement in the presence of the judge, between the rising of the sun and noon; and, both of them being present, let them speak so that each party may hear.

Under Law IX, Table I, the judge is to "render his decision in the in the presence of the plaintiff and the defendant", while under Law X, Table I, the judge is to make his decision before the sun sets on the day – referring to an extreme time limit. On the other hand, Law III, Table II, identifies the necessity of letting in evidence to support ones' case that had been brought before the judge.

> Where anyone is deprived of the evidence of a witness let him call him with a loud voice in front of his house, on three market-days.

The origins of due process date back to the civil law traditions found codified in the Twelve Tables. The *Livro de als Legies* (circa 1265) by King Alfonso X of Castilla, Leon, and Galicia was to influence the civil law concept of due process; it contained procedural, substantive, and organisational rules (Kotuby and Sabota, 2017). It is also to be noted that a similar charter in the lines of the Magna Carta were being issued on the Continent by monarchs in Hungary, the Roman emperor, and the king of Aragon (Judge, 2015).[61] In sum due process, which clearly has its origins in domestic law, forbids a state from depriving its citizen of their life, liberty, or property without recourse to law. The common law process of due process is defined by Walker as "the conduct of legal proceedings according to established principles and rules which safeguard the position of the individual charged" (Walker, 1980, p. 381). In essence, due process under common law involves two basic rules, *viz.*, the 'bias rule' and 'hearing rule' (Mitchell, 2008). The rules govern procedural due process, which is concerned with how the decision is made rather than its substance.[62]

Importantly, the scope of due process under common law is not limited to its application to criminal procedure and has expanded to include proceedings before civil courts and before tribunals and administrative bodies.[63] The principle of due process is also well recognised and applied in international tribunals. Mitchell notes that due process is an essential component of "any legal system seeking legitimacy and effectiveness" (Mitchell, 2005, p. 144), which implies not only due process before domestic courts and tribunals, but also legal systems found established through international organisations, including the WTO. Also, the doctrine of denial of justice under customary international law requires states to administer justice relating to aliens according to a minimum standard (Mitchell, 2008), which implies due process. A number of human rights treaties also impose due process obligations on the state. For instance, Articles 99, 104, and 105 of the Geneva Convention relative to the Treatment of Prisoners of War 1949, the International Covenant on Civil and Political Rights 1996 (ICCPR) 1966, Article 6 of the European Convention for the Protection of Human Rights and Fundamental Freedoms 1950, and the American Convention on Human Rights 1969 all require that due process is followed by sovereign states.

For our purposes, it is imperative to understand the nature of due process in the WTO dispute settlement system. Though the WTO does not possess the powers of a sovereign state and does not deal in matters relating to private rights, *etc.*, it is nevertheless an organisation which is engaged in the administration of multilateral trade amongst sovereign states who are its Members. WTO is viewed as an organisation embodying democratic principles in administrating trade, as well as in the adjudication process established under the rules-based Dispute Settlement System – all of which strengthens the proposition that the legal proceedings and the process of enforcement at the WTO are conducted following due process. Under the DSU, the parties to a dispute are subject to a set of rules, primarily designed to ensure due process and leading to unbiased decisions. WTO rules on dispute settlement protects fairness between the parties in legal proceedings, both before the panel and the AB. Article X:3(a) of the GATT 1994[64] extends the said principle to its Member States by requiring that all contracting parties administer the laws, regulations, decisions, and rulings as identified in Article X:1 in a uniform, impartial, and reasonable manner. It is to be borne in mind that the principle of due process has been long recognised and established in international law. As Professor Cheng notes in his seminal work on the matter, there are two cardinal characteristics of a judicial process, *viz.*, (i) the impartiality of the tribunal and (ii) the juridical equality between the parties in their capacity as litigants (Cheng, 2006).

In *US – FSC*,[65] the Appellate Body noted, the "procedural rules of WTO dispute settlement are designed to promote . . . the fair, prompt and effective resolution of trade disputes", which underpins the due process rule in the fair resolution of trade disputes and captures the spirit of the Dispute Settlement System of the WTO. Also, one can identify the key provisions of the WTO that emphasise the importance of the rule of law in most key agreements of the WTO. The DSU incorporates due process by imposing the bias rule – *e.g.*, the DSU makes clear that panellists should be free of any actual or perceived bias (Mitchell, 2005). In keeping with this rule, Article 8.2 of the DSU states, panellists "should be selected with a view to ensuring the independence of the members", and Article 8.3 of the DSU states that citizens of the governments involved in the dispute (as parties, or third parties) should not serve as panellists unless the parties agree otherwise. The bias rule, in similar lines, is extended at the appellate level. Article 17.3 states that the members of the Appellate Body "shall be unaffiliated with any government" and that they "shall not participate in the consideration of any disputes that would create a direct or indirect conflict of interest".[66]

The DSB also adopted rules for conduct to maintain the integrity of dispute settlement,[67] which reflect the bias rule and apply to panellists, Appellate Body members, arbitrators, experts, members of the Secretariat assisting panels or arbitrations, and members of the

Appellate Body Secretariat (Rule IV). At the hearing stage, the rules of the DSB requires that those parties who may come to be directly affected by the decision to be issued with prior notice of the case that they may be required to answer, with the notice also to contain the time and place of such hearing. The complainant is required to give sufficient notice to the respondent together with the legal basis of the claim. This requirement is met through Article 4.4 of the DSU – dealing with request for consultations; Article 6.2 – dealing with establishment of the panel; and Articles 12.6 and 15.1 – dealing with written submission to the panel (Mitchell, 2005).

As regards Article 6.2, the Appellate Body in *India – Patents (US)*[68] and *Korea – Dairy*[69] observed that a panel request must precisely identify the relevant WTO provisions. This proposition will also apply to panel requests, where specific measures at issue are clearly identified. The Appellate Body in *Brazil – Desiccated Coconut*[70] noted that the terms of reference played an important role by fulfilling the due process objective, as they presented the parties (including third parties) with "sufficient information concerning the claims at issue in the dispute in order to allow them an opportunity to respond to the complainant's case". The Appellate Body has repeatedly stressed the importance of the due process objective and observed on a number of occasions that it would proceed to dismiss claims that are not set out properly in the Notice of Appeal, on the basis that the respondent did not receive sufficient notice of the case it had to meet.[71] It is evident that the WTO, to ensure that due process is followed throughout the hearing, has in place the necessary provisions to be adhered to by all parties at various stages of the hearing. A more detailed discussion of the relevant provisions of the DSU on due process will be undertaken in chapter 3 of the book dealing with the DSU.

4.3.2 *Good Faith* (Bona Fide)

It is no exaggeration to state that the principle of good faith forms the basis of every legal system. The principle binds individuals, juridical persons, and sovereigns alike. In the words of Professor Cheng,

> *Pacta sunt servanda*, now an indisputable rule of international law, is but an expression of the principle of good faith which above all signifies the keeping of faith, the pledged faith of nations as well as that of individuals. Without this rule, International law as well as civil law would be a mere mockery.
>
> (Cheng, 2006)

Good faith requires that parties have a fair dealing in the exercise of their rights, and also at the same time prohibits them from benefitting from their own illegitimate action. For H.L.A. Hart, *pacta sunt servanda* was "the minimum content of Natural Law" (Hart, 1994, pp. 193–200).[72] Good faith, according to Lord Mustill, is viewed as "the fundamental principle of the entire system" (Mustill, 1988, p. 111). Good faith, which has its roots in both Eastern and Western legal systems, is now a strong fixture of the international legal order,[73] and is well codified in international law.[74] The VCLT codified the principle of good faith, which has now been widely accepted as setting forth the rules of customary international law. Article 26 of VCTL refers to the obligation to perform any treaty in good faith, and for our purposes, the WTO treaty and the relevant agreements. Although numerous reports of the WTO speak of performing the treaty in good faith, there are only a few instances in which the Appellate Body had explained what the obligation entails.[75] Article 3.10 of the DSU obligates the parties to settle disputes in good faith and reads as follows:

> It is understood that requests for conciliation and the use of the dispute settlement procedures should not be intended or considered as contentious acts and that, if a dispute arises, all Members will engage in these procedures in good faith in an effort to resolve the dispute. It is also understood that complaints and counter-complaints in regard to distinct matters should not be linked.

Article 4.3 of the DSU enjoins that the parties are to enter into consultation in good faith, with the relevant passage worded as follows:

> If a request for consultations is made pursuant to a covered agreement, the Member to which the request is made shall, unless otherwise mutually agreed, reply to the request within 10 days after the date of its receipt and shall enter into consultations in good faith within a period of no more than 30 days after the date of receipt of the request, with a view to reaching a mutually satisfactory solution.

With regard to the principle of good faith, the Appellate Body in *US – Shrimp* noted as follows:

> The *Chapeau* of Article XX is, in fact, but one expression of the principle of good faith. This principle, at once a general principle of law and a general principle of international law, controls the exercise of rights by states. One application of this general principle, the application widely known as the doctrine of *abus de droit*, prohibits the abusive exercise of a state's rights and enjoins that whenever the assertion of a right "impinges on the field covered by [a] treaty obligation, it must be exercised bona fide, that is to say, reasonably".[76]

This leads one to raise the question of whether the WTO possessed any normative autonomy with regard to the principle of good faith. The Appellate Body of the WTO has consistently rejected any normative autonomy of the principle of good faith in the absence of a clear manifestation in the WTO agreements. For instance the Appellate Body in *US – Offset Act (Byrd Amendment)* observed that there was sufficient basis to conclude that a dispute settlement panel could determine, in an appropriate case, if a Member State has not acted in good faith, and went on to reverse the panel's finding that the US acted in bad faith on the evidence, and noted as follows:

> Nothing . . . in the covered agreements supports the conclusion that simply because a WTO Member is found to have violated a substantive treaty provision, it has therefore not acted in good faith. In our view, it would be necessary to prove more than mere violation to support such a conclusion.[77]

Both the Panel and Appellate Body in their subsequent reports have been equally sceptical towards the recognition of an independent good faith obligation adding to a substantive obligation contained in the covered agreements (Ziegler and Baumgartner, 2015).[78] It is also noted that both the Panel and the Appellate Body have readily accepted and embraced the use of the principle of good faith to give shape to certain good faith obligations where they to be embodied in more concrete manifestations, such as article 26 of the VCLT, in particular if used the process of interpreting a WTO agreement (Ziegler and Baumgartner, 2015).[79] Article 3.2[80] of the DSU lays down, "[r]ecommendations and rulings of the DSB cannot add to or diminish the rights and obligations provided in the covered agreements", and Article 19.2 of the DSU[81] enjoins, "the Panel and Appellate Body cannot add to or diminish the rights and obligations provided in the covered agreements". In *Chile – Alcoholic Beverages*, Chile argued that contrary to Articles 3.2 and 19.2 of the DSU, the Panel through its findings had added to the rights and obligations of WTO Members under the WTO Agreement. The Appellate Body while rejecting the argument observed as follows:

> In this dispute, while we have rejected certain of the factors relied upon by the Panel, we have found that the Panel's legal conclusions are not tainted by any reversible error of law. In these circumstances, we do not consider that the Panel has added to the rights or obligations of any Member of the WTO. Moreover, we have difficulty in envisaging circumstances in which a panel could add to the rights and obligations of a Member of the WTO if its conclusions reflected a correct interpretation and application of provisions of the covered agreements.[82]

Likewise, in *Mexico – Taxes on Soft Drinks*, the primary argument of Mexico's brief was that the Panel should have declined to exercise jurisdiction on the matter. While addressing the issue, the Appellate Body observed that doing so would be contrary to Articles 3.2 and 19.2:

> A decision by a panel to decline to exercise validly established jurisdiction would seem to "diminish" the right of a complaining Member to "seek the redress of a violation of obligations" within the meaning of Article 23 of the DSU, and to bring a dispute pursuant to Article 3.3 of the DSU. This would not be consistent with a panel's obligations under Articles 3.2 and 19.2 of the DSU. We see no reason, therefore, to disagree with the Panel's statement that a WTO panel "would seem . . . not to be in a position to choose freely whether or not to exercise its jurisdiction."[83]

From the foregoing one can conclude that Articles 3.2 and 19.2 of the DSU, to a certain degree, limit the mandate of the DSB, which led some commentators to hold the opinion that establishing an independent good faith obligation would have several policy implications, including destroying the separation of violation and non-violation claims and the risk of judicial activism within the DSB (Zeitler, 2005). Substantive good faith, in the WTO context, seeks to fill in the gaps of treaty law. Panizzon notes that customary rule of *pacta sund servanda* on the one hand evokes good faith's formative function of gap-closing, and on the other implies that international legal system based on a treaty is complete, especially with the WTO (Panizzon, 2006).

4.3.3 *Estoppel and* Res Judicata

Estoppel is a general principle of law, originating in both civil and common law traditions. Estoppel stems from the obligation of good faith and is well recognised as a principle of customary international law and general principles of law (Mitchell, 2005). An example of estoppel in international law would be as follows: a representation made by State A that is relied on by State B and to its detriment may preclude State A from acting in a contrary fashion. Estoppel is shown where the other party, relying on the representation, changes its position to its detriment or suffers some prejudice.[84] A considerable body of reports from the ICJ supports the view that estoppel is a general principle of international law, which rests on the wider principles of good faith and consistency (Crawford, 2012).[85] The principle of estoppel is explicitly recognised in trade disputes, both domestic and international. Nevertheless, estoppel does not have any substantive content.

Estoppel's effect is to hold a party to a representation where another party has relied on that representation. Ensuring consistency in state relations (Member States of the WTO), especially given the fact that a sovereign state would look to act in a strategic manner to protect its interests at the WTO, it is only the doctrine of estoppel that could possibly "provid[e] security and predictability to the multilateral trading system" as laid out under Article 3.2 of the DSU (Mitchell and Heaton, 2010). Estoppel appears to be consistent with the covered agreements of the WTO. In *US – Softwood Lumber*, the GATT Panel for the first time carried out a comprehensive discussion of estoppel,[86] where the panel had the occasion to discuss to what extent the parties, by signing the MOU, had waived their rights under the GATT and were thus estopped from any further action. The report, although detailed, did not have a conclusive say on the issue, but nevertheless, due to the detailed discussion, it is only fair to infer that the panel viewed the principle of estoppel as having some relevance within the GATT legal framework. In *Guatemala – Cement II*, Mexico proceeded to introduce a fresh complaint against the same practice,[87] after the rejection of its initial complain by the Appellate Body. Guatemala took the position that Mexico was estopped from pursuing new complaint. Disagreeing with Guatemala, the panel held that the principle of estoppel is relevant only if the complaining party had clearly consented to the particular behaviour in question, which Mexico had not.

In *Argentina – Poultry Anti-Dumping Duties*, Argentina argued that Brazil was estopped from submitting the dispute on file before the panel, as the very same dispute had been adjudicated by a Mercosur panel. The WTO Panel, while accepting the parameters of the principles of estoppel as presented, dismissed Argentina's arguments holding that Article 3.2 did not require panels to rule in any particular way and thus to conform their own decisions to those of other adjudicating forums.[88] In *EC – Export Subsidies on Sugar*, the Appellate Body noted that it had never before applied the principle of estoppel and took the opportunity to discuss and present its views on the principle. The Appellate Body made the observation that the principle of estoppel had come to be narrowed down to Articles 3.7 and 3.10 of the DSU, and that the said Articles required Member States to exercise their "judgment as whether action under these procedures would be fruitful".[89] Mavroidis notes that the analysis by the Appellate Body in the case had nothing to do with the principle of estoppel as it is known in public international law, and that estoppel in the public international law context is "conceived as an obstacle to submitting a claim" (Mavroidis, 2008, p. 441). Some commentators opine that estoppel as understood in international law could in principle be relevant in the WTO legal regime, but has yet to be applied (Mavroidis, 2008; Matsushita, Shoenbaum, Mavroidis, and Hahn, 2015).

As regards the principle of *res judicata*, the panel in *India – Autos*, after a detailed discussion, held that the principle has its place in the WTO legal order, and that the same cannot be applied in the absence of satisfying the stringent conditions attached to the principle. The panel also proceeded to identify the conditions as follows:

i   The measures challenged in the original and the subsequent disputes must be identical;
ii The claims in the two disputes must be identical as well; and
iii The parties in the two disputes must be identical.

The discussion of the panel in relation to the principle of *res judicata* is largely in line with the wider understanding of the principle under international law.[90]

5. Mandate of the WTO

Through the mandate of the contracting sovereign states, the WTO Marrakesh Agreement created the WTO as a new international organisation with a legal personality and came into existence as an institution on 1 January 1995.[91] The WTO has a very broad mandate in relation to facilitating international trade amongst its Member States through its network of multilateral agreements. The WTO has a collective mandate, as it is an institution created through the collective endeavour of sovereign states, with the principles of non-discrimination and trade liberalisation at its heart. The explicit agreement of the parties is found contained in the Marrakesh Agreement, granting the authority to establish an international institution to pursue specific goals, as identified earlier. Importantly, the administration of the multilateral trade is entrusted to a collective institution. It is to be noted that the shared belief about the benefits of trade liberalisation, including efficiency gains, access to new markets, access to new technology, *etc.*, defines the scope of the institution's activities. The following section takes up for studying the major objectives, the key functions, and membership of the WTO.

5.1 Objectives of the WTO

The WTO's objectives and policy are set out in broadest terms in the Preamble to the WTO Agreement and reads as follows:

> Recognizing that their relations in the field of trade and economic endeavour should be conducted with a view to raising standards of living, ensuring full employment and a large and steadily growing volume of real income and effective demand, and expanding the production of and trade in goods and services, while allowing for the optimal use of the world's resources in accordance with the objective of sustainable development, seeking both to protect and preserve the environment and to enhance the means for doing so in a manner consistent with their respective needs and concerns at different levels of economic development,
>
> Recognizing further that there is need for positive efforts designed to ensure that developing countries, and especially the least developed among them, secure a share in the growth in international trade commensurate with the needs of their economic development.

The objectives set out in the first two paragraphs of the Preamble to the WT Agreement can be identified as

  i   Raising standards of living;
  ii Attainment of full employment;
  iii Growth of real income and an effective demand;
  iv Expansion of production of, and trade in, goods and services; and
  v   Protection and preservation of the environment.

The principal objectives of the WTO are mostly taken from the GATT, with the addition of three elements, and so is much of the language. Most noticeably the WTO Preamble refers to production of and trade in goods and services, whereas the GATT dealt only in goods; identifies the objective of sustainable development; and importantly recognises and stresses the need to integrate developing countries and least developed countries.

In *US – Shrimp*, the Appellate Body had the occasion to highlight the statement in the Preamble on the objective of 'sustainable development' in the following manner:

> the language of the Preamble to the WTO Agreement demonstrates a recognition by WTO negotiators that optimal use of the world's resources should be made in accordance with the objective of sustainable development. As this preambular language reflects the intentions of negotiators of the WTO Agreement, we believe it must add colour, texture and shading to our interpretation of the agreements annexed to the WTO Agreement, in this case, the GATT 1994. We have already observed that Article XX(g) of the GATT 1994 is appropriately read with the perspective embodied in the above preamble.[92]

In *US – Shrimp*, the Appellate Body also noted that there cannot be a restrictive interpretation of the Preamble in terms of the commitment to protect the environment in the following observation:

> Given the recent acknowledgement by the international community of the importance of concerted bilateral or multilateral action to protect living natural resources, and recalling the explicit recognition by WTO Members of the objective of sustainable development in the preamble of the WTO Agreement, we believe it is too late in the day to suppose that Article XX(g) of the GATT 1994 may be read as referring only to the conservation of exhaustible mineral or other non-living natural resources.[93]

Likewise, in *US – Gasoline*, the Appellate Body emphasised the importance of the Preamble in the context of environmental issues as follows:

> Indeed, in the preamble to the WTO Agreement and in the Decision on Trade and Environment, there is specific acknowledgement to be found about the importance of coordinating policies on trade and the environment. WTO Members have a large measure of autonomy to determine their own policies on the environment (including its relationship with trade), their environmental objectives and the environmental legislation they enact and implement. So far as concerns the WTO, that autonomy is circumscribed only by the need to respect the requirements of the General Agreement and the other covered agreements.[94]

The objectives of the WTO are sought to be achieved through the performance of trade in an environment of sustained trade liberalisation, as identified in the agreements of the WTO. The means to achieve the avowed objectives of the WTO are (a) the reduction of tariff barriers, and other non-tariff barriers to trade; and (b) the elimination of discriminatory treatment in international trade relations. In this regards the Preamble in para. 3 reads as follows:

> Being desirous of contributing to these objectives by entering into reciprocal and mutually advantageous arrangements directed to the substantial reduction of tariffs and other barriers to trade and to the elimination of discriminatory treatment in international trade relations.

5.2 Functions of the WTO

The key functions of the WTO as contained in Article III of the WTO Agreement can be summarized as

i   The implementation, administration, and operation of the covered agreements and multilateral agreements, besides providing the framework for the implementation process;
ii To provide the forum for negotiations amongst its Member States in respect of the multilateral trade relations;
iii To administer the Understanding on Rules and Procedures Governing the Settlement of Disputes – the DSU (provided in Annex 2 to the Agreement);
iv To administer the Trade Policy Review Mechanism (provided in Annex 3 to the Agreement); and
v   With a view to achieving greater coherence in global economic policymaking, the WTO is to cooperate, as appropriate, with the IMO and the World Bank.

A sixth function of the WTO that is worth mentioning here, in the light of the Doha Ministerial Declaration (WTO, 2001) is

vi To provide the necessary technical assistance to developing country and least developed country Member States, to allow them to integrate into the WTO's trading system.

The key functions of the WTO can be studied under the broad heads, as set out in the following sections.

5.2.1 Implementation and Administration of Trade Agreements

Article III of the WTO Agreement identifies the first function of the WTO as the facilitation of the implementation, administration, and operation of the WTO Agreement and the multilateral and plurilateral agreements annexed to it.[95] The WTO plays a central role in setting the necessary rules for the orderly implementation and administration of the agreements, and also provides a common institutional framework to realise the objectives of the goals set out in the WTO Agreement. There are two levels of implementing the WTO agreements, *viz.*, as an institution that enforces the implementation mechanisms and methods embedded in the WTO agreements and by each Member at its national level through legislation that entrenches the WTO agreements into the domestic legal system (Zhang, 2003). The implementation of the WTO agreements involves the interaction among WTO agreements, the WTO and its Members, with interrelated functions and modalities (Zhang, 2003).

It is to be observed here that there is no specific mechanism or procedure within the WTO for the implementation of the various multilateral trade agreements, as rules differ depending on the applicable agreement. It is open to the Member States to complain in response to non-compliance by other Member States with regards to any specific WTO agreements. Bohne notes the technical cooperation, the foundations of which are to be found in the Marrakesh Declaration (Bohne, 2010).[96] The guidelines adopted by the Committee of Trade and Development in 1996 (WTO, 1996) contain the general objectives of technical cooperation, which can be summarised as

i   The strengthening and enhancing of institutional and human capacities in the public sector for an appropriate participation in the multilateral trading system;

ii   The improvement of knowledge of multilateral trade rules and WTO *Working Procedures* and negotiations; and
iii The assistance in the implementation of commitments in the multilateral trading system and in the full use of its provisions, including the effective use of the dispute settlement mechanism.

The Doha Ministerial Conference has further emphasised the need for technical cooperation in the WTO. As part of technical cooperation,[97] the WTO Secretariat has concluded a Memorandum of Understanding with UNCTAD, where the parties have agreed to cooperate for the purposes of technical cooperation, capacity building, training, research, and analysis, through specific interagency programs or in other areas, or as mandated under the Doha Development Agenda (WTO-UNCTAD, 2003; Bohne, 2010).[98]

5.2.2 Providing a Forum for Trade Negotiations

The WTO is also to provide a forum for negotiation on new trade rules amongst members. The forum for negotiation is for matters dealt with under the annexed agreements and also for further agreements to be negotiated under the framework of the Marrakesh Agreement.[99] As discussed earlier, under the GATT trade negotiations were carried out since 1947 in Geneva, eventually culminating in the creation of the WTO in the Uruguay Round (1986–1994). The GATT rounds were primarily aimed at tariff reductions, which also led to the expansion of trade in sectors other than goods. Since the creation of the WTO, the Member States have negotiated and concluded the following agreements, to name a few:

i   Further market access commitments for specific services and service suppliers (on financial services,[100] on the movement of natural persons,[101] and on basic telecommunications services[102]);
ii   The liberalisation of trade in information technology products;[103]
iii The amendment of the TRIPS Agreement regarding the rules on compulsory licensing to ensure access for developing countries to pharmaceutical products;[104]
iv   The amendment of the Agreement on Government Procurement to set the basis for expanded coverage of and disciplines under this agreement;[105] and
v   The accession of 30 countries to the WTO.[106]

A new round of trade negotiations was opened in Doha in 2001 with specific objectives. The Doha agenda contains a negotiating agenda to bring about a "further major reduction in existing trade barriers" covering agriculture, services, and industrial goods. It is noted here that the Doha Round is still ongoing, and an agreement is yet to be arrived at.[107]

5.2.3 Dispute Settlement

One of the key functions of the WTO relates to the administration of the WTO dispute settlement system. Article 3.2 of the DSU states as follows:

> The dispute settlement system of the WTO is a central element in providing security and predictability to the multilateral trading system.

The WTO's dispute settlement system is compulsory and considered as one of the strengths of the WTO. It is arguably the most important international dispute settlement body. The DSU almost operates as an international court for trade law, by applying rules of law, handing down binding decisions on the parties, and imposing sanctions in the event of non-compliance of outcomes (Matsushita, Shoenbaum, Mavroidis, and Hahn, 2015). Article 3.3 of the DSU underscores the importance of the prompt settlement of disputes for the effective functioning of the WTO and for maintaining a proper balance between the rights and obligations of Members.[108] The DSU, which is referred to as the "jewel in the crown" by Van den Bossche and Zdouc (2017), helps preserve the rights and obligations of the Member States under the WTO agreements and clarify the provisions of the agreements. One of the stand-out features of the DSU is the timeframe that is prescribed for completing the adjudication process, and also the objective of endeavouring to find solutions to the trade disputes before the Panels and Appellate Body, as opposed to handing down judgements. It is noted here that the reports of the WTO Panel and Appellate Body are only binding as between the parties to the dispute, are not interpretations of the WTO agreements, and do not have any legal effect on other Member States (Matsushita, Shoenbaum, Mavroidis, and Hahn, 2015). Also, the recommendations and ruling of the DSB cannot add or diminish the rights and obligations provided in the WTO agreements.[109] See chapter 3 for a detailed analysis of the DSU.

5.2.4 Trade Policy Review

The administration of the Trade Policy Review Mechanism (TPRM) of the WTO is one of the most important function of the WTO and can be counted among the GATT/WTO's accomplishments. Annex 3 of the WTO Agreement provides for the TPRM, which requires a regular collective appreciation and evaluation of the individual Member States' trade policies and practices, and how they impact on the functioning of the multilateral trading system.[110] The TPRM qualifies as a peer review mechanism, and helps in improving policymaking, in the adoption of best practices and also in complying with established standards and principles. The TPRM helps to achieve greater transparency in and the understanding of trade policies and practices of other Member States and also to contribute to improved compliance by all Member States with their WTO obligations (Van den Bossche and Zdouc, 2017).

Annex 3 to the Marrakesh Agreement clearly excludes any linkages between the trade policy review and the dispute settlement mechanism. Annex 3 para. A(i) explicitly prohibits information from the trade policy review from being used in dispute settlement procedures or the trade policy review from being used to impose new policy commitments on Members.[111] The main objective behind the introduction of the TPRM, which was surveillance of the trade policies of members to ensure their conformity with WTO rules, was largely achieved (Matsushita, Shoenbaum, Mavroidis, and Hahn, 2015). It can also be asserted here that rule of law has been established through the WTO rules in conjunction with TPRM and through the mechanism of the DSU (Matsushita, Shoenbaum, Mavroidis, and Hahn, 2015).

5.3 Ministerial Conference

As discussed earlier, the WTO belongs to its members, who make their decisions through the various councils and committee. The highest decision-making organ of the WTO is the Ministerial Conference, and Article IV.1 of the Marrakesh Agreement states that there shall be a Ministerial Conference at least once every two years.[112] Being the highest decision-making body, the Ministerial Conference is authorised to take decisions on all matters under any of the multilateral trade agreements.[113] The Ministerial Conference is explicitly granted specific powers on

a   Adopting authoritative interpretations of the WTO agreements;[114]
b   Granting waivers;[115]
c   Adopting amendments;[116]
d   Decisions on accession;[117] and
e   Appointing the director-general and adopting staff regulations.[118]

So far, 11 Ministerial Conferences have been held since the formation of the WTO, which are

   i   Singapore (1996)
  ii   Geneva (1998)
 iii   Seattle (1999)
  iv   Doha (2001)
   v   Cancún (2003)
  vi   Hong Kong (2005)
 vii   Geneva (2009)
viii   Geneva (2011)
  ix   Bali (2013)
   x   Nairobi (2015)
  xi   Buenos Aires (2017)

It is to be noted that Ministerial Conferences are not always successful in reaching agreements among Member States. For instance, the Seattle Ministerial failed to reach a clear agreement amongst Member States on the opening of a new round, and the Cancún Ministerial Conference failed to reach an agreement on how negotiations of the Doha Round were to proceed.

5.4 *General Council and Meetings*

The authority, functions, and remit of the General Council are to be found in Article IV.2 of the Marrakesh Agreement, which is as follows:

> There shall be a General Council composed of representatives of all the Members, which shall meet as appropriate. In the intervals between meetings of the Ministerial Conference, its functions shall be conducted by the General Council. The General Council shall also carry out the functions assigned to it by this Agreement. The General Council shall establish its rules of procedure and approve the rules of procedure for the Committees provided for in paragraph 7.

The General Council, which meets every month, is composed of the representatives of the Member States – who are ambassador-level diplomats – and responsible for the management of the day-to-day affairs of the WTO. Importantly, in between sessions of the Ministerial Conference, the General Council is entrusted with their powers. The General Council is also charged with supervising the WTO's dispute settlement system and to convene the TPRB.

In short, both the DSB and the TPRB are the alter egos of the General Council (Van den Bossche and Zdouc, 2017). It also carries out specific functions such as adopting the annual budget and financial regulations and making necessary arrangements for effective cooperation with international organisations and NGOs. There are also subsidiary bodies which report to the General Council, *viz.*, (i) the Council for Trade in Goods, (ii) the Council for Trade in Services, and (iii) the Council for TRIPS.

6. Summary

The foundations of the WTO are predicated on the multilateral cooperation amongst sovereign nations and their participation in the multilateral trading system. Since the WTO is a forum for the exchange of liberalisation commitments, it strongly relies on multilateral trade negotiations where the Member States exchange market access and other policy commitments. In the absence of the covered agreements (which are discussed in the ensuing chapters), the plurilateral agreements together with a rules-based dispute settlement system under the DSB, the stated objectives of the WTO cannot be met. Learning from the shortcomings of the GATT, the rules-based dispute settlement system was incorporated into the WTO's legal framework with a compulsory mandate that all Member States submit their disputes before the DSB. What we note from the foregoing is that the law of the WTO is international in nature and strongly founded on the principles 'due process' and 'good faith', and the process of interpretation of the covered agreements falls on the DSB. The DSB has often resorted to customary rules of interpretation when interpreting WTO agreements and with the help of the VCLT. A detailed study of the DSB and its origins and functions are carried out in chapter 3 of the is book.

Notes

1. The World Economic Conference of 1927, organised by the League of Nations, only led to further discussions or produced talking points on tariffs, customs valuation, *etc.*, and did not produce the desired effects.
2. Buterbaugh and Fulton portray the Smoot-Hawley Act as the "enduring protectionist villain" that brought about the rise of fascism, as well as the radicalism in Japan that sowed the seeds of World War II. Winham notes that the Act raised duties to historic levels and represented "a new level in the long movement by nations toward closing off their economies to foreign imports". See Buterbaugh and Fulton (2007), p. 18.
3. Helleiner observes that as the 1930s saw an increased use of capital controls; it also marked the break with tradition in financial affairs. See Helleiner (1994).
4. Referred to as 'imperial preference', the scheme involved both higher duties on non-British Empire goods and lower duties on Dominion goods.
5. The architect behind the US trade policy and the RTAA is identified as Cordell Hull, a southern Democrat and strong advocate of international cooperation on trade matters who served as secretary of state under President Roosevelt. Hull is also credited with giving the State Department a lasting intellectual direction during the GATT negotiations of the 1940s.
6. The United Nations Conference on International Organization (UNCIO), also referred to as the San Francisco Conference, was a convention that took place between 25 April and 26 June 1945 and resulted in the creation of the UN. Hence, technically the UN was in place before World War II ended in September 1945.
7. One of the special organs created by the UN soon after its formation was the Economic and Social Council (ECOSOC).
8. Gardner describes the post-war settlement as a 'political miracle'. See Gardner (1986).
9. Economists John Maynard Keynes (UK) and Harry Dexter White (US) played a key role in putting forth the vision for a post-war economic resurgence. Buterbaugh and Fulton note that the

US, the UK, and other trading nations were seeking to establish a stable international marketplace through the establishment of 'embedded liberalism' in the international trading system. See Buterbaugh and Fulton (2007).
10 However, according to WB's Articles of Agreement, all its decisions are guided by a commitment to the promotion of foreign investment in international trade and the facilitation of capital investment.
11 The Havana Charter is referred to formally as the 'Final Act of the United Nations Conference on Trade and Employment', provided for the establishment of the ITO. Keynes proposed the establishment of the ITO and other financial institutions with a view to stabilise international trade. Keynes, unfortunately, did not live to see the birth of the GATT 1947, as he passed away in 1946.
12 The expression 'the third leg of the Bretton Woods stool' had been used by several commentators while referring to the ITO. For instance, see Diebold (1993), p. 335.
13 Jackson notes that much of GATT was taken verbatim from the draft of the ITO Charter, as it was expressly tied to the prospective ITO. For instance, Article XXIX of the GATT is entitled 'The Relation of the Agreement to the Havana Charter'. See Jackson (2000).
14 Article XXVI governs how governments may accept the Agreement, presenting a formula to ascertain when the requisite number of governments have accepted the Agreement, so that it may enter into force. However, with the exception of Haiti, there is no available record to demonstrate that any government has accepted the Agreement. See L/2375/Add. 1, 20 (5 March 1965), as cited by Jackson (2000).
15 Twenty-three countries signed what was called a Final Act authenticating the text of the GATT (55 UNTS 194; TIAS 1700). Also, the Protocol of Provisional Application of the General Agreement on Tariffs and Trade (30 October 1947, UNTS 55, 308) provided for the preliminary application of the rules from 1 January 1948.
16 The MFN principle was introduced into the GATT to counter the ill effects of the practice of bilateral tariff preferences, which was prevalent in the pre-World War II era amongst trading nations.
17 The principles of trade liberalisation were contained in the Reciprocal Trade Agreement Act 1933, which was passed in the US to offset the disastrous effects of the Smoot-Hawley Tariff Act 1930. Diebold (1952) notes that GATT simply multilateralised the bilateral negotiation process established under the RTAA. Winham notes that early GATT tariff negotiations were multilateral only in name and were actually bilateral as between principal supplier nation and principal consumer nation. See Winham (2011).
18 Sell also notes that the asymmetrical and self-serving circumstances of GATT's birth still lingers on today in the WTO and concludes by noting "inequality is baked into the cake". The issues highlighted will be discussed in the final chapters of this book. See Sell (2012), p. 144.
19 The exemptions included textiles, under the Multi Fibre Arrangement (MFA), and various agricultural products.
20 The two-tier system was later consolidated in the Tokyo Round in the 1970s.
21 Winham notes that the devaluation of the leading currency in 1971 was akin to the devolution of the British pound in 1931, which led to a monetary disequilibrium lasting for about five years.
22 At the end of the Downing Street Conference in London on 8–9 May 1977, the participating nations (Canada, France, Italy, Japan, West Germany, the UK, and the US) issued a declaration comprehensively rejecting protectionism as a remedy for the world's difficult economic and trade problems, further promising strong political leadership to expand opportunities for international trade and to strengthen the world trading system.
23 Croome notes that the codes were not self-executing and had to be brought into effect by the signatories. See Croome (1998).
24 The variable import levy acted on a sliding tariff that ensured that foreign goods were not imported below a certain price, which was clearly a protective measure.
25 The MFA governed the world trade in textiles and garments. Introduced as a short-term measure in 1974, the MFA imposed quotas on the quantity of textiles a developing country could export to developed countries, and was in force until 2004, lasting for a clear three decades.
26 The issues relating to inclusion of intellectual property will be dealt with in later chapters, covering the TRIPS Agreement.
27 This was the first instance where private sector actors were allowed to play any role in the GATT negotiations.
28 There was a total of 117 negotiating countries participating in the Uruguay Round of negotiations, with 113 having full member status of the GATT. Of the 117 participants, 88 were

developing countries. Earlier, under the Tokyo Round about 100 countries participated in the negotiations, of which 70 were full Member States.
29 The dispute settlement procedures of the GATT 1947 were flawed, in that a losing party to the dispute could block the adoption of a panel or the report of a panel, as enforceability of any panel was through 'consensus'.
30 Professor Jackson had advocated the formation of a world trade organisation in 1990, in his work entitled *Restructuring the GATT System*. Professor Jackson argued that it was time to cure the 'birth defects' of the GATT by creating an organisation that would be a UN specialised agency with an organisational structure and a dispute settlement mechanism.
31 'Draft Final Act Embodying the Results of the Uruguay Round of Multilateral Trade Negotiations', GATT Doc. MTN.TNC/W/FA, dated 20 December 1991.
32 Signed in Marrakesh, Morocco, on 15 April 1994, the Final Act was a formidable document, consisting of over 26,000 pages and detailing all the agreements and procedures in technical language.
33 Jackson notes that the birth of the WTO, depending on one's perspective, can be viewed as "either a modest enhancement of the General Agreement on Tariffs and Trade (GATT), which preceded it, or a watershed moment for the institutions of world economic relations embodied in the Bretton Woods system". See Jackson (1997), p. 399.
34 GATT 1994 consists of the GATT 1947, excluding the Protocol of Provisional Application, as amended by all legal instruments that entered into force under the GATT before 1 January 1995.
35 According to WTO Agreement Article II:3 the plurilateral agreements are binding only on the parties that have accepted them. The plurilateral agreements are the only *a la carte* aspect of the WTO.
36 However, with effect from 1 January 1998, the *International Dairy Agreement* and the *International Bovine Meat Agreement* were terminated. See WTO, 'Deletion of the International Dairy Agreement from Annex 4 of the WTO Agreement,' Decision of 10 December 1997 (WT/L/251), 17 December 1997; WTO, 'Deletion of the International Bovine Meat Agreement from Annex 4 of the WTO Agreement,' Decision of 10 December 1997 (WT/L/252), 16 December 1997.
37 There are several other committees established for dealing with trade and environment, trade and development, and Regional Trade Agreements (RTAs). Besides the aforementioned, the GATS Council has also established committees to deal with telecommunications, financial services, and maritime services. It is to be noted that no committee is provided for the Agreement on Pre-Shipment Inspection.
38 Rules of *jus cogens* by their very nature are part of general international law and prevail over all past and future treaty norms. See Vienna Convention on the Law of Treaties, *opened for signature* 23 May 1969 – hereafter VCLT. See also Pauwely (2001).
39 Covered agreements contained in Appendix 1 of the DSU also include provisions of other international agreements, which are to be regarded as sources of WTO law.
40 The Paris Convention 1967, the Berne Convention 1971, the Rome Convention, and the Treaty on Intellectual Property in Respect of Integrated Circuits.
41 It is common knowledge that the ITO never came into existence. Mavroidis (2008) notes that during the 1960s and 1970s many states that acceded to the GATT did not have a legislation on competition law, and were in fact in violation of Article V of the Havana Charter, which they were to observe under Article XXIX. Nevertheless, no known complaints were filed against such violations, and that in WTO state practice, the provision is legally inoperative.
42 Article IX(2) of the WTO Agreement reads as follows: "The Ministerial Conference and the General Council shall have the exclusive authority to adopt interpretations of this Agreement and of the Multilateral Trade Agreements. In the case of an interpretation of a Multilateral Trade Agreement in Annex 1, they shall exercise their authority on the basis of a recommendation by the Council overseeing the functioning of that Agreement. The decision to adopt an interpretation shall be taken by a three-fourths majority of the Members. This paragraph shall not be used in a manner that would undermine the amendment provisions in Article X."
43 The author warns that any gap-filling exercise is not to be considered a source of law.
44 Article 2(1)(a) VCLT reads as follows: "'Treaty' means an international agreement concluded between States in written form and governed by international law, whether embodied in a single instrument or in two or more related instruments and whatever its particular designation."
45 Article 4 of VCLT reads as follows: "Without prejudice to the application of any rules set forth in the present Convention to which treaties would be subject under international law independently

of the Convention, the Convention applies only to treaties which are concluded by States after the entry into force of present Convention with regard to such States."

46 It can be seen that Article 4 explicitly precludes the application of progressive rules to past treaties. But if the VCLT provisions reflect established customary law, then such provisions will be applicable to treaties concluded by sovereign states prior to the entry into force of VCLT on 29 January 1980. This position was confirmed by the ICJ in *Kasikili/Sedudu Island* [1999] ICJ Rep. 1045, at para. 18. The ICJ reasoned that Article 31 of the VCLT reflected customary international law, and as a result VCLT applied to the treaty in question (an Anglo-German Treaty from 1980), even though the parties – Botswana and Namibia – were not parties to the VCLT.

Also, if the rules laid down in Articles 31–33 of the VCLT reflect universal custom, they can be applied to treaties concluded before the VCLT entered into force and to treaties between states that are not all parties to the Convention. See also *Maritime Dispute (Peru v Chile)* [2014] ICJ Rep., p. 3, para. 57; *Question of Delimitation of the Continental Shelf between Nicaragua and Colombia* (Preliminary Objections) [2016] ICJ Rep., p. 100, para. 33; *Maritime Delimitation in the Indian Ocean (Somalia v Kenya)* (Preliminary Objections), 2 February 2017, para. 63.

47 Article 3.2 of the DSU reads as follows: "The dispute settlement system of the WTO is a central element in providing security and predictability to the multilateral trading system. The Members recognize that it serves to preserve the rights and obligations of Members under the covered agreements, and to clarify the existing provisions of those agreements in accordance with customary rules of interpretation of public international law. Recommendations and rulings of the DSB cannot add to or diminish the rights and obligations provided in the covered agreements."

48 *Ibid*.

49 See Appellate Body Report, *US – Gasoline*, p. 17, where the Appellate Body also observed that 'general rule of interpretation' set out in Article 31 of the VCLT has been relied upon by all parties (including third parties), and that the said rule of interpretation had i) attained the status of rule of customary or general international law, and (ii) it forms part of the customary rules of interpretation of public international law.

50 Pauwelyn also argues, the "increased inter-dependence between states and between issue-areas (*e.g.*, trade and environment, human rights, and economic development) made the strict separation between different fields of international law all the more artificial". See Pauwelyn (2004).

51 Treves also notes that all existing general rules of international law are customary.

52 Article 3.2 of the DSU reads as follows: "The dispute settlement system of the WTO is a central element in providing security and predictability to the multilateral trading system. The Members recognize that it serves to preserve the rights and obligations of Members under the covered agreements, and to clarify the existing provisions of those agreements in accordance with customary rules of interpretation of public international law. Recommendations and rulings of the DSB cannot add to or diminish the rights and obligations provided in the covered agreements."

53 The principle is used by policymakers to justify discretionary decisions in situations where there is the possibility of harm from making a certain decision – embarking on a particular course of action – when extensive scientific knowledge on the matter is lacking. The principle implies that there is a social responsibility to protect the public from exposure to harm when scientific investigation has found a plausible risk. For instance, Principle 15 of the Rio Declaration on Environment and Development 1992 reads as follows: "In order to protect the environment, the precautionary approach shall be widely applied by States according to their capabilities. Where there are threats of serious or irreversible damage, lack of full scientific certainty shall not be used as a reason for postponing cost-effective measures to prevent environmental degradation."

54 See Panel Report *EC – Hormones*, para. 8.157.

55 See Appellate Body Report *EC – Hormones*, para. 124.

56 *Ibid.*, para. 123.

57 See Panel Report *EC – Biotech*.

58 Clause 39 of the Magna Carta became the foundation of the idea that no freeman could be imprisoned without recourse to a fair trial. Clause 39 reads as follows: "No freeman shall be taken or imprisoned or disseised or exiled or in any way destroyed, nor will we go upon him nor send upon him, except by the lawful judgement of his peers or by the law of the land."

59 Lord Hailsham also notes that to ensure due process there should be an independent judiciary, a fair hearing in accordance with the rules of natural justice, access to the courts, public hearing, and the advice of and representation by an independent legal profession.

60 The Fourteenth Amendment from 1867 reinforces the doctrine by stating as follows: "[N]or shall any State deprive any person of life, liberty, or property, without due process of law."
61 Lord Judge notes that round about the time of the recording of the Magna Carta, equivalent charters were being issued on the Continent by other monarchs. In 1222 and 1231, the Golden Bull was issued in Hungary; in 1220 and 1231, charter concessions were made by the Holy Roman Emperor, and in 1283 and 1287 grants were made by the king of Aragon. Nevertheless, none of them had the long-term impact of the Magna Carta.
62 See *Chief Constable of North Wales Police v Evans* [1982] 3 All ER 141.
63 For an example at the domestic level, see S 33 of Arbitration Act 1996 (UK), which reads as follows: "(1) The tribunal shall – (a) act fairly and impartially as between the parties, giving each party a reasonable opportunity of putting his case and dealing with that of his opponent, and (b) adopt procedures suitable to the circumstances of the particular case, avoiding unnecessary delay or expense, so as to provide a fair means for the resolution of the matters falling to be determined. (2) The tribunal shall comply with that general duty in conducting the arbitral proceedings, in its decisions on matters of procedure and evidence and in the exercise of all other powers conferred on it."
64 Article X:3(a) of GATT 1994 reads as follows: "Each contracting party shall administer in a uniform, impartial and reasonable manner all its laws, regulations, decisions and rulings of the kind described in paragraph 1 of this Article."
65 See Appellate Body Report, *US – FSC*, para. 166.
66 Mitchell notes that the apprehension of bias may come to be diminished through the appointment of Appellate Body members for four-year terms (Article 17.2) and through the requirement that the Appellate Body membership be broadly representative of WTO membership (Article 17.3). See Mitchell (2005).
67 See 'Rules of Conduct for the Understanding on Rules and Procedures Governing the Settlement of Disputes'.
68 See Appellate Body Report, *India – Patents (US)*, para. 94.
69 See Appellate Body Report, *Korea – Dairy*, para. 120.
70 See Appellate Body Report, *Brazil – Desiccated Coconut*, para. 167.
71 See, for instance, Appellate Body Reports, *US – Upland Cotton*, *EC – Banana III*, and *US – Countervailing Measures on Certain EC Products*.
72 Hart in his seminal work 'The Concept of Law' discusses in detail the minimum content of natural law.
73 "All civilizations, from the earliest, have recognized the rule, and it has been handed down throughout the centuries . . . The oldest religions of Asia (Confucianism, Buddhism, Hinduism, and later Islam) paid special attention to the obligation of complying with agreements entered into." See *Pacta Sunda Servanda*, in 7 Encyclopedia of Public International Law (Rudolf Bernhard ed., 1984) 364.
74 For instance, Article 2(2) of the Charter of the United Nations codifies the duty to fulfil one's obligations in good faith; and Articles 33 of the Manila Declaration on the Peaceful Settlement of International Disputes 1982 codifies the duty to settle disputes in good faith.
75 See Panel Report, *EC – Tube or Pipe Fittings*, para. 7.307, where the Panel held that the defendant was acting in good faith even though some confidential information was not submitted to the Panel.
76 See Appellate Body Report, *US – Shrimp*, para. 158.
77 See Appellate Body Report, *US – Offset Act (Byrd Amendment)*, para. 298. For a discussion, see Mitchell (2005) at pp. 364–366.
78 See, for instance, Panel Reports, *EC – Bed Linen (Recourse to Art. 21.5 DSU)*, paras. 6.89–6.91; *Argentina – Poultry Anti-Dumping Duties*, paras. 7.34–7.36.
79 See, for instance, Panel Reports, *Korea – Procurement*, para. 7.101; *US – COOL*, para. 7.605.
80 Article 3.2 of the DSU reads as follows: "The dispute settlement system of the WTO is a central element in providing security and predictability to the multilateral trading system. The Members recognize that it serves to preserve the rights and obligations of Members under the covered agreements, and to clarify the existing provisions of those agreements in accordance with customary rules of interpretation of public international law. Recommendations and rulings of the DSB cannot add to or diminish the rights and obligations provided in the covered agreements."
81 Article 19. 2 of the DSU reads as follows: *In accordance with paragraph 2 of Article 3, in their findings and recommendations, the panel and Appellate Body cannot add to or diminish the rights and obligations provided in the covered agreements.*
82 See Appellate Body Report, *Chile – Alcoholic Beverages*, para. 79.

83 See Appellate Body Report, *Mexico – Taxes on Soft Drinks*, para. 53.
84 See *North Sea Cases* (1969) IC. Rep. 26, *Temple of Preah Vihear* (1962) ICJ Rep., p. 143, *Gulf of Maine Case* (1984) 309. Interestingly, claims based on acquiescence and estoppel were accepted in 1990 for an arbitration award (under GATT 1947) on Canada/EC Article XXVIII Rights, where Canada was ruled to have relinquished its rights under the GATT 1947, while remaining silent during the negotiation of a bilateral wheat agreement (GATT BISD 37S/80).
85 See, for instance, *Temple of Preah Vihear* (1962) ICJ Rep., pp. 6, 61–65 (Judge Fitzmaurice); *Delimitation of the Maritime Boundary in the Gulf of Maine Area (Canada/US)* (1984) ICJ Rep., pp. 246, 305.
86 See Panel Report, *US – Measures Affecting Imports of Softwood Lumber from Canada*, paras. 308–325.
87 See Panel Report, *Guatemala – Cement II*, paras. 8.23 and 8.24.
88 See Panel Report, *Argentina – Poultry Anti-Dumping Duties*, paras. 7.37 and 7.38.
89 See Appellate Body Report, *EC – Export Subsidies on Sugar*, para. 312. Article 3.2 also makes it clear that the aim of the dispute settlement mechanism is to secure a positive solution to a dispute and to arrive at a solution that is mutually acceptable to the parties, which is consistent with the covered agreements. The article also emphasises that in the absence of a mutually agreed solution the objective "is usually to secure the withdrawal of the measures concerned if these are found to be inconsistent with the provisions of any of the covered agreements".
90 See Panel Report, *India – Autos*, paras. 7.54 to 7.66.
91 Article VIII (1) Marrakesh Agreement.
92 See Appellate Body Report, *US – Shrimp*, para. 153.
93 *Ibid.*, para. 131.
94 See Appellate Body Report, *US – Gasoline*, p. 30.
95 Article III:1 of the WTO Agreement reads as follows: "The WTO shall facilitate the implementation, administration and operation, and further the objectives, of this Agreement and of the Multilateral Trade Agreements, and shall also provide the framework for the implementation, administration and operation of the Plurilateral Trade Agreements."
96 Article 5 of the Marrakesh Declaration of 15 April 1994 contains the following recital: "Ministers recognize the need for strengthening the capability of the GATT and the WTO to provide increased technical assistance in their areas of competence, and in particular to substantially expand its provision to the least-developed countries."
97 Funding for technical assistance is available at the WTO through the WTO Trust Fund. See WTO (1996).
98 See Article II of the Doha Development Agenda.
99 See Article III (2) of the Marrakesh Agreement.
100 Second Protocol to the General Agreement on Trade in Services, S/L/11, dated 24 July 1995; and Fifth Protocol to the General Agreement on Trade in Services, S/L/45, dated 3 December 1997.
101 Third Protocol to the General Agreement on Trade in Services, S/L/12, dated 24 July 1995.
102 Fourth Protocol to the General Agreement on Trade in Services, S/L/20, dated 30 April 1996.
103 Agreement on Trade in Information Technology Products (ITA), in Ministerial Declaration on Trade in Information Technology Products, adopted on 13 December 1996 and entered into force on 1 July 1997.
104 Protocol Amending the TRIPS Agreement, WT/L/641, dated 8 December 2005.
105 Protocol Amending the Agreement on Government Procurement, GPA/113, dated 2 April 2012.
106 See, for instance, Protocol on the Accession of the People's Republic of China.
107 The Doha Round of negotiations is part of the discussion in chapter 17 of this book.
108 Article 3.3 Understanding on Rules and Procedures Governing the Settlement of Disputes reads as follows: "The prompt settlement of situations in which a Member considers that any benefits accruing to it directly or indirectly under the covered agreements are being impaired by measures taken by another Member is essential to the effective functioning of the WTO and the maintenance of a proper balance between the rights and obligations of Members."
109 The third sentence of Article 3.2 Understanding on Rules and Procedures Governing the Settlement of Disputes reads as follows: "Recommendations and rulings of the DSB cannot add to or diminish the rights and obligations provided in the covered agreements."
110 See TPRM, para. A(i).
111 *Ibid.* The third sentence of para. A(i) reads as follows: "It is not, however, intended to serve as a basis for the enforcement of specific obligations under the Agreements or for dispute settlement procedures, or to impose new policy commitments on Members."

112 Article IV.1 of the Marrakesh Agreement reads as follows: "There shall be a Ministerial Conference composed of representatives of all the Members, which shall meet at least once every two years. The Ministerial Conference shall carry out the functions of the WTO and take actions necessary to this effect. The Ministerial Conference shall have the authority to take decisions on all matters under any of the Multilateral Trade Agreements, if so requested by a Member, in accordance with the specific requirements for decision-making in this Agreement and in the relevant Multilateral Trade Agreement."
113 *Ibid.*
114 Article IX:2 of the WTO Agreement.
115 Article IX:3 of the WTO Agreement.
116 Article X of the WTO Agreement.
117 Article XII of the WTO Agreement.
118 Article VI:2 and VI:3 of the WTO Agreement.

Select Bibliography

Benedek, Wolfgang. *Die Rechtsordnung des GATT aus völkerrechtlicher Sicht* (Springer, 1990).

Bhuiyan, Sharif. *National Law in the WTO Law: Effectiveness and Good Governance in the World Trading System* (Cambridge University Press, 2007).

Bohne, Edehard. *The World Trade Organization: Institutional Development and Reform* (Palgrave MacMillan, 2010).

Buterbaugh, Kevin and Richard Fulton. *The WTO Primer: Tracing Trade's Visible Hand Through Case Studies* (Palgrave Macmillan, 2007).

Cheng, Bin. *General Principles of Law as Applied by International Courts and Tribunals* (Cambridge University Press, 2006).

Crawford, James. *Browlie's Principles of Public International Law* (Oxford University Press, 2012).

Croome, John. *Reshaping the World Trading System: A History of the Uruguay Round* (WTO, 1998).

Dam, Kenneth W. *The GATT: Law and International Economic Organization* (University of Chicago Press, 1970).

Diebold, William. 'The End of the ITO,' *International Finance Section, Princeton University* Vol 16 (1952) 1–37.

Diebold, William. 'Reflections on the International Trade Organization,' *Northern Illinois University Law Review* Vol 14 (1993) 335–346.

Dörr, Oliver and Kirsten Schmalenbach. *Vienna Convention on the Law of Treaties: A Commentary* (Springer International, 2018).

Duckenfield, Mark. (ed.). *The Battles Over Free Trade Volume 4: The Emergence of Multilateral Trade, 1940–2006* (Routledge, 2008).

Gaffney, John P. 'Due Process in the World Trade Organization: The Need for Procedural Justice in the Dispute Settlement System,' *American University of International Law Review* Vol 14 (1999) 1173–1222.

Gardner, Richard N. 'Sterling-Dollar Diplomacy in Current Perspectives,' *The Royal Institute of International Affairs* Vol 62 (1986) 21–23.

GATT. 'Communication from the European Community,' (MTN.GNG/NG14/W/42) (9 July 1990).

Gowa, Joanne. 'Explaining the GATT/WTO: Origins and Effects,' in Martin, Lisa L. (ed.) *The Oxford Handbook of the Political Economy of International Trade* (Oxford, 2015).

Hailsham, Lord. *Hamlyn Revisited: The British Legal System Today* (Stevens & Sons, 1983).

Hart, H.L.A. *The Concept of Law* (Oxford University Press, 1994).

Helleiner, Eric. *States and the Reemergence of Global Finance: From Bretton Woods to the 1990s* (Cornell University Press, 1994).

Hiscox, Michael J. 'The Magic Bullet? The RTAA, Institutional Reform, and Trade Liberalization,' *International Organization* Vol 53, No 4 (1999) 669–698.

Ikenberry, John G. 'The Political Origins of Bretton Woods,' in Bordo, Michael D. and Barry Eichengreen (eds.) *A Retrospective on the Bretton Woods System: Lessons for International Monetary Reform* (Chicago University Press, 1993).

International Trade Organization (Interim Commission). 'Specialised Agencies,' *International Organization* Vol 4, No 1 (1950) 136–138.

Irwin, Douglas A., Petros C. Mavroidis and Alan O. Sykes. *The Genesis of the GATT* (Cambridge University Press, 2008).

Jackson, John H. *World Trade and the Law of GATT: A Legal Analysis of the General Agreement on Tariffs and Trade* (The Michie Company, 1969).

Jackson, John H. *Restructuring the GATT System* (Chatham House, 1990).

Jackson, John H. 'Strengthening the International Legal Framework of the GATT-MTN System: Reform Proposals for the New GATT Round 1991,' in Petersmann, Ernst-Ulrich and Meinhard Hilf (eds.) *The New GATT Round of Multilateral Trade Negotiations: Legal and Economic Problems* (Kluwer Law, 1991) 17, 21 and 22.

Jackson, John H. *The World Trading System: Law and Policy of International Economic Relations* (MIT Press, 1997).

Jackson, John H. *The Jurisprudence of GATT & the WTO: Insights on the Treaty Law and Economic Relations* (Cambridge University Press, 2000).

Jackson, John H. *Sovereignty, the WTO, and Changing Fundamentals of International Law* (Cambridge University Press, 2006).

Judge, Lord. 'Magna Carta: Destiny or Accident?,' *UNSW* (29 September 2015) <https://media.sclqld.org.au/documents/lectures-and-exhibitions/2015/20150929-Magna-Carta-Destiny-or-Accident.pdf> (accessed 14 May 2018).

Kolb, Robert. *The Law of Treaties: An Introduction* (Edward Elgar Publishing, 2016).

Kotuby Jr., Charles T. and Luke A. Sabota. *General Principles of Law and International Due Process: Principles and Norms Applicable in Transnational Disputes* (Oxford University Press, 2017).

Lamy, Pascal. 'The Place of the WTO and Its Law in the International Legal Order,' *European Journal of International Law* Vol 17 (2007) 969–984.

Lee, Eun Sup. *World Trade Regulation: International Trade under the WTO Mechanism* (Springer International, 2012).

Marceau, Gabrielle. 'Conflicts of Norms and Conflicts of Jurisdictions: The Relationship between the WTO Agreement and MEAs and Other Treaties,' *Journal of World Trade* Vol 35 (2001) 1081.

Matsushita, Mitsuo, Thomas J. Shoenbaum, Petros Mavroidis and Michael Hahn. *The World Trade Organization: Law, Practice, and Policy* (Oxford University Press, 2015).

Mavroidis, Petros C. 'No Outsourcing of Law? WTO Law as Practised by WTO Courts,' *American Journal of International Law* Vol 102 (2008) 421–474.

Mavroidis, Petros C. *Trade in Goods* (Oxford University Press, 2013).

McDougal, Myres S. and Michael Reisman. 'The Prescribing Function in World Constitutive Process: How International Law Is Made,' *Yale Studies in World Public Order* Vol 6 (1980) 249–284.

McLachlan, Campbell. 'The Principle of Systemic Integration and Article 31(3)(c) of the Vienna Convention,' *International and Comparative Law Quarterly* Vol 54 (2005) 279.

McNair, Arnold Duncan. *The Law of Treaties* (Clarendon Press, 1961).

McRae, Donald. 'The WTO in International Tradition: Continued or New Frontier?,' *Journal of International Economic Law* Vol 3 (2000) 27.

Mitchell, Andrew D. 'Due Process in WTO Disputes,' in Yerxa, Rufus and Bruce Wilson (eds.) *Key Issues in WTO Dispute Settlement: The First Ten Years* (Cambridge University Press, 2005) 144–160.

Mitchell, Andrew D. *Legal Principles in WTO Disputes* (Cambridge University Press, 2008).

Mitchell, Andrew D. and David Heaton. 'The Inherent Jurisdiction of WTO Tribunals: The Select Application of Public International Law Required by the Judicial Function,' *Michigan Journal of International Law* Vol 3 (2010) 559–619.

Moak, Ken. *Developed Nations and the Economic Impact of Globalization* (Palgrave MacMillan, 2017).

Mustill, Justice. 'The New *Lex Mercatoria*: The First Twenty-Five Years,' *Arbitration International* Vol 4, No 2 (1988) 86–119.

Palmeter, David and Petros C. Mavroidis. 'The WTO Legal System: Sources of Law,' *American Journal of International Law* Vol 92 (1998) 398–413.

Panizzon, Marion. *Good Faith in the Jurisdiction of the WTO: The Protection of Legitimate Expectation, Good Faith Interpretation and Fair Dispute Settlement* (Hart Publishing, 2006).

Pauwelyn, Joost. 'The Role of Public International Law in the WTO: How Far Can We Go?,' *American Journal of International Law* Vol 95 (2001) 535–552.

Pauwelyn, Joost. *Conflict of Norms in Public International Law: How WTO Law Relates to Other Rules of International Law* (Cambridge University Press, 2003).

Pauwelyn, Joost. 'Bridging Fragmentation and Unity: International Law as a Universe of Interconnected Islands,' *Michigan Journal of International Law* Vol 25 (2004) 903.

Petersmann, Ernst-Ulrich. 'Dispute Settlement in International Economic Law: Lessons for Strengthening International Dispute Settlement in Non-Economic Areas,' *Journal of International Economic Law* Vol 2 (1999) 189.

Qureshi, Asif H. *Interpreting WTO Agreements: Problems and Perspective* (Cambridge University Press, 2015).

Rausser, Gordon C. 'The Uruguay Round and the GATT Negotiations,' in Rausser, Gordon C. (ed.) *GATT Negotiations and the Political Economy of Policy Reform* (Springer, 1995) 1–33.

Schnietz, Karen E. 'The Institutional Foundations of U.S. Trade Policy: Revisiting Explanations for the 1934 Reciprocal Trade Agreements Act,' *Journal of Policy History* Vol 12, No 4 (2000) 417–444.

Scott, Samuel P. *The Civil Law I* (The Central Trust Company, 1932).

Sell, Susan K. 'GATT and the WTO,' in Pettman, Ralph (ed.) *Handbook on International Political Economy* (World Scientific, 2012) 141–155.

Shaw, Malcolm N. *International Law* (Cambridge University Press, 2017).

Stoll, Peter Tobias and Frank Schorkopf. *WTO: World Economic Order, World Trade Law* (Martinus Nijhoff Publishers, 2006).

Trachtman, Joel P. 'The Domain of WTO Dispute Resolution,' *Harvard International Law Journal* Vol 40, No 2 (1999).

Treves, Tullio. *Customary International Law* (Oxford University Press, 2006).

United Nations Department of Economic and Social Information & Policy Analysis (UN DESA). *World Trade after the Uruguay Round: Prospects and Policy Options for the Twenty-First Century*, Sander, Harold and András Inotai (eds.) (Routledge, 1996) 37–51.

Van den Bossche, Peter and Werner Zdouc. *The Law and Policy of the World Trade Organization: Text, Cases and Material* (Cambridge University Press, 2017).

VanGrasstek, Craig. *The History and Future of the World Trade Organization* (WTO, 2013).

Walker, David Maxwell. *The Oxford Companion to Law* (Oxford University Press, 1980).

Wilkinson, Rorden. *The WTO: Crisis and the Governance of Global Trade* (Routledge, 2006).

Winham, Gilbert R. *International Trade and the Tokyo Round Negotiations* (Princeton University Press, 1986).

Winham, Gilbert R. 'Explanations of Developing Country Behaviour in the GATT Uruguay Round Negotiation,' *World Competition* Vol 21, No 3 (1997) 349–368.

Winham, Gilbert R. 'The World Trade Organisation: Institution-Building in the Multilateral Trade System,' *World Economy* Vol 21, No 3 (1998) 349–368, 353.

Winham, Gilbert R. 'An Interpretive History of the Uruguay Round Negotiations,' in Macrory Patrick F.J., Arthur E. Appleton and Michael G. Plummer (eds.) *The WTO: Legal, Economic and Political Analysis* Vol 1 (Springer, 2005) 3–26.

Winham, Gilbert R. 'The Evolution of the World Trading System: The Economic and Policy Context,' in Bethlehem, Daniel, Donal McRae, Rodney Neufeld and Isabelle Van Damme (eds.) *The Oxford Handbook of International Trade Law* (Oxford University Press, 2009) 5–29.

Winham, Gilbert R. 'The Evolution of Global Trade Regime,' in Ravenhill, John (ed.) *Global Political Economy* (Oxford University Press, 2011) 137–172.

Woolcock, Stephen. 'A Multilateral System,' in Pettman, Ralph (ed.) *Handbook on International Political Economy* (World Scientific, 2012) 121–139.

WTO. Committee on Trade and Development, 'Guidelines for WTO Technical Cooperation,' (WT/COMTD/8) (16 October 1996).

WTO. 'Deletion of the International Dairy Agreement from Annex 4 of the WTO Agreement,' Decision of 10 December 1997 (WT/L/251) (17 December 1997).

WTO. 'Deletion of the International Bovine Meat Agreement from Annex 4 of the WTO Agreement,' Decision of 10 December 1997 (WT/L/252), (16 December 1997).

WTO. *The Legal Texts: The Results of the Uruguay Round of Multilateral Trade Negotiations* (Cambridge University Press, 1999).

WTO. *Doha Ministerial Declaration* (WT/MIN(01)/DEC/1) (20 November 2001).

WTO. Report by the Consultative Board to the Director-General Supachai Panitchpakdi, 'The Future of the WTO: Addressing Institutional Challenges in the New Millennium' (the 'Sutherland Report') (WTO, 2004).

WTO. *World Trade Report 2007: Six Decades of Multilateral Trade Cooperation: What Have We Learnt?* (WTO, 2007).

WTO-UNCTAD. 'Memorandum of Understanding between the World Trade Organization and the United Nations Conference on Trade and Development,' (16 April 2003).

Yearwood, Ronnie R.F. *The Interaction between World Trade Organisation (WTO) Law and External International Law: The Constrained Openness of WTO Law (A Prologue to a Theory)* (Routledge, 2012).

Zeitler, Helge Elisabeth. '"Good Faith" in the WTO Jurisprudence, Necessary Balancing Element or an Open Door to Judicial Activism?,' *Journal of International Economic Law* Vol 8, No 3 (2005) 721–758.

Zhang, Xin. 'Implementation of the WTO Agreements: Framework and Reform,' *Northwest Journal of International Law & Business* Vol 23 (2003) 383–431.

Ziegler, Andreas R. and Jorun Baumgartner. 'Good Faith as a General Principles of (International) Law,' in Mitchell, Andrew, Muthucumaraswamy Sornarajah and Tania Woon (eds.) *Good Faith and International Economic Law* (Oxford University Press, 2015) 9–36.

3 Dispute Settlement at the WTO

Learning Objectives	70
1. Introduction	70
2. Dispute Settlement in the GATT	71
3. Dispute Settlement in the WTO	75
4. Theoretical/Legal Framework and Jurisdiction of the DSU	76
4.1 Theoretical/Legal Framework	76
4.2 Jurisdiction: Exclusive Forum for Adjudication	78
5. Recourse to WTO Dispute Settlement	80
5.1 Legal Basis of Dispute	82
5.2 Categories of Claims	83
5.2.1 Violation Complaints	83
5.2.2 Non-Violation Complaints	84
5.2.3 Situation Complaints	85
6. The DSB and Stages of the Dispute Settlement Process	85
6.1 Consultation	86
6.1.1 Nature and General Features of the Consultation Phase	88
6.1.2 Failure to Consult and Period of Consultation	89
6.1.3 Plurilateral and Private Consultations	90
6.2 Panel: Request, Terms of Reference, and Establishment	90
6.3 Multiple Complaints and Joint Panels	93
6.3.1 The Panel: Time Scales and *Working Procedures*	93
6.3.2 Burden of Proof	95
6.3.3 Panel Report	97
6.4 The Appellate Body	98
6.4.1 Historical Background	98
6.4.2 Appellate Body: Nature and Composition	100
6.5 Appellate Review	101
6.5.1 Structure, Scope, and Timeframe	101
6.5.2 Review of New Issues, and Receipt of New Evidence and Arguments	104
6.5.3 Scope and Remit of the Appellate Review Process	105
7. Other Features of the WTO Dispute Settlement	106
7.1 *Amicus Curiae* Briefs Before the Dispute Settlement	106
7.2 Other Entities of the Dispute Settlement	109
8. Implementation and Compliance Review	109
8.1 'Extension' Under Article 21.3 DSU	110
8.2 Compliance Review Under Article 21.5 DSU	111

DOI: 10.4324/9780367028183-4

8.3 Remedies Under Article 22 DSU   113
9. Developing Countries and the WTO Dispute Settlement   114
  9.1 Special and Differential Treatment   115
  9.2 Special Rules for Developing Country Member States   115
  9.3 Special Rules, Decision of 5 April 1966   116
  9.4 Special Rules for Least Developed Country Member States   116
  9.5 Legal Assistance for Developing Country Member States   116
10. Summary   117

Learning Objectives

This chapter aims to help students understand:

1. The origins of the disputes settlement systems and the creation and establishment of the Disputes Settlement Body (DSB) under the WTO legal order;
2. The core principles of the DSB and key features of the DSB;
3. The two-tier mechanism of the DSB, the stages of the dispute settlement, and Panel and Appellate Body proceedings;
4. Implementation and compliance review; and
5. Developing countries and the WTO dispute settlement.

1. Introduction

International disputes are resolved in various ways, but it is highly desirable that they are resolved through peaceful means. History tells us that nations waged wars over trade and commercial policies.[1] When international trade agreements are entered into between countries, it is inevitable that dispute will arise in the course of their performance. The two key methods often used to resolve international disputes are (i) negotiations through diplomatic channels between the concerned state parties and (ii) submission of such disputes to an independent international body for arbitration, or adjudication. The UN Charter, recognising the need for maintaining order amongst the nation states, requires that all Member Countries endeavour to settle disputes through peaceful means.[2] The WTO, a multilateral trade organisation with state membership, boasts of a clear rules-based dispute settlement system, which was one of the key outcomes of the Uruguay Round of negotiations. Of all international dispute settlement mechanisms established in the post-WWII era, the WTO's dispute settlement system stands out as the most elaborate rules-based apparatus.[3] The GATT 1947 created an essential template of rules to facilitate trade amongst the contracting parties through the creation of ITO, which was intended to serve as one of the key international institutions in the post-WWII era. President Harry Truman, while delivering a speech at Baylor University, Texas, made the following observations about the ITO:

> [I]n order to avoid economic warfare, our Government has proposed, and others have agreed, that there be set up, within the United Nations, another agency to be concerned with problems and policies affecting world trade. This is the International Trade Organization. This organization would apply to commercial relationships the same principle of fair dealing that the United Nations is applying to political affairs. Instead of retaining unlimited freedom to commit acts of economic aggression, its members would adopt

a code of economic conduct and agree to live according to its rules. Instead of adopting measures that might be harmful to others . . . countries would sit down around the table and talk things out.

(Truman, 1947)

Unfortunately, as discussed earlier in chapter 1, the US Congress did not support the creation of the ITO, constraining the contracting parties to continue to trade under the framework of the GATT, but with no clear institutional structure. While the GATT 1947 provided for a legal platform and a framework to reduce tariffs and perform trade,[4] it only briefly referred to the rights of the Member States to raise a dispute in the event of a violation of the GATT rules and did not contain an elaborate set of rules for the settlement of disputes brought before it.[5] It encouraged a diplomatically negotiated settlement of disputes amongst the contracting parties to the GATT – in short, it was not a rules-based formal dispute settlement. Even in the absence of a clear mechanism for dispute resolution, the parties carried on with *ad hoc* arrangements put in place by the GATT Secretariat.

2. Dispute Settlement in the GATT

The Havana Charter 1948 set out the rules for international trade and for the establishment of the ITO. Most importantly, Chapter VIII of the Charter contained detailed procedures for 'settlement of differences' which included consultation, arbitration, *etc*.[6] The drafters of the Havana Charter[7] contemplated the entry into force of the ITO and a suspension of Part II of GATT, which contained the substantial part of the legal commitments, other than the MFN obligation and tariff guarantees. This aspect is captured in Article XXIX, which states that GATT was not intended to function on a permanent basis, and worded accordingly.[8] As history records, the Havana Charter never entered into force, but the provisions contained in GATT was utilised by the Contracting Parties as a default framework to carry on mutual trade activities and to negotiate the reduction of tariffs. It was expected that GATT would be subsumed under the umbrella of the ITO. Instead, GATT entered into force on 1 January 1948, as it was felt that to wait for the ITO to come into existence would be costly, as the GATT already consisted of thousands of reciprocally agreed tariff concessions (Footer, 1997).[9] The GATT served a dual purpose by encapsulating the rights and obligations of the contracting parties and serving as the *de facto* organisation to administer trade, and in that process emerging as the fountainhead of modern international trade law.[10] In the early days of the GATT 1947, trade disputes were decided by the chairperson of the GATT Council and later on by working parties composed of representatives chosen from all interested contracting parties (WTO, 2004).[11]

Dispute settlement under GATT evolved gradually through practice on the basis of the recitals contained in Articles XXII and XXIII. In particular, Article XXIII was the centrepiece of the dispute settlement in GATT. Although the words 'dispute settlement' are not mentioned anywhere in the aforementioned articles, they do provide for a two-tiered consultative process, *i.e.*, to engage in bilateral consultations and multilateral consultations,[12] for written representations, or proposals to the other contracting party for consideration for a satisfactory adjustment, with the provision of the CONTRACTING PARTIES giving a ruling on the matter.[13] Article XXIII dealt with the 'impairment or nullification' of benefits, and also authorised the CONTRACTING PARTIES to refer such matters to the Economic and Social Council of the United Nations and others.[14] The GATT did not have a clear mandate for a dispute settlement system within its framework,[15] referring such differences that arose between contracting parties to a UN body that had a dispute settlement system was justified, *viz*., the ICJ.[16] Article XXIII outlines how disputes are to be processed, without establishing any formal procedure for handling such disputes. Not surprisingly, in the early years, contracting parties proceeded to set up working parties to deal with disputes falling within the ambit of Article XXIII (2).

The key features of the process laid out under Articles XXII and XXIII can be summarised as follows:

i   Establish a measure of consultation prior to invocation of the process identified under the two articles;
ii Proceedings can be brought on grounds of 'nullification or impairment' of benefits expected under the Agreement – with such actions not being dependent on actual breach of legal obligation;
iii Such proceedings vested in the Contracting Parties the power to investigate, recommend actions, and to 'give a ruling on the matter'; and
iv Vested the Contracting Parties the power in certain cases to authorize 'a contracting party or parties' to suspend GATT obligations to other Contracting Parties.[17]

The working parties adopted reports through consensus decision-making, in the absence of a well-articulated formal dispute resolution mechanism setting out clear procedures.[18] These working parties (composed of all interested contracting parties, including the parties to the dispute!) were later on replaced by panels comprising independent experts unrelated to the parties in dispute (ITC Report, 1985; WTO, 2004). Beginning from 1952, panels were composed of five independent experts from the GATT contracting parties, and efforts were made by the GATT Secretariat to make the procedures more formal.[19] The panels were to prove both practical and popular, and eventually went on to replace the working party procedure. The panel process, primarily set up to assist the GATT Council in dealing with Article XXIII matters, was investigative and quasi-judicial in nature with the emphasis on diplomatically negotiated settlement.[20] Very few disputes were brought before the panels in the 1960s, and no panels were set up between 1963 and 1970, as Contracting Parties resorted to consultation to resolve disputes, or to working groups when issues were more contentious (ITC Report, 1985). Some Contracting Parties, *e.g.*, Japan, avoided legalism in procedure, as it was thought that strict interpretation of the Agreement would interfere with domestic programmes that were established to manage international trade (Trebilcock, Howse, and Eliason, 2012).

One of the weaknesses of the dispute settlement under the GATT 1947 was the requirement for a positive consensus in the GATT Council to refer a dispute to a panel, *i.e.*, when there was no objection from any of the contracting parties, including the party against whom the dispute was being brought for the referral. Again, the same principle of positive consensus was to be followed for the adoption of any panel report and for authorisation of any countermeasures that the claimant may wish to bring against the respondent (WTO, 2004). This consensus-based conciliatory method clearly favoured the interests of the powerful GATT contracting parties, and either delayed or prevented the implementation of any panel reports.[21] Following the Kennedy Round of negotiations (1964–67), the dispute settlement procedures were progressively codified and supplemented by a number of decisions and understandings adopted by GATT Contracting Parties (Petersmann, 1997).[22] In November 1962 the Panel established a legalistic approach in dispute settlement in *Uruguayan Recourse to Article XXIII*.[23] It was Uruguay's case that benefits accruing to it under the Agreement had been nullified or impaired as a direct result of 576 listed trade restrictions in 15 industrialised countries, which effectively affected Uruguayan exports. The panel set out the presumption of nullification or impairment of benefits when a GATT violation was found, which was a departure from the established principles of State responsibility in public international law (PIL). Under the principles of PIL, the structure of Article XXIII would have required the complainant, *i.e.*, Uruguay, to demonstrate the existence of such nullification or impairment of benefits as pleaded (Lacarte-Muró and Castro, 2004). The Panel in the case interpreted Article XXIII:1 in a manner which reinforced the strength of the legal obligations under the GATT:

> [i]n cases where there is a clear infringement of the provisions of the General Agreement, or in other words, where measures are applied in conflict with the provisions of GATT . . . the action would, *prima facie*, constitute a case of nullification or impairment and would *ipso facto* require consideration of whether the circumstances are serious enough to justify the authorization of suspension of concessions or obligations.[24]

This finding established a definite practice in dispute settlement; where *prima facie* inconsistency was demonstrated, there was a presumption of nullification or impairment of benefits, with the burden of proving otherwise shifting on to the respondent.[25] The trend continued in the case of *US – Superfund*, where the panel went on to hold that "the presumption had in practice operated as an irrefutable presumption".[26]

In 1966, certain special procedures were introduced in 1966 for the resolution of disputes between developing and developed countries. These procedures included a time limit of two months for a supervised negotiation by the GATT director-general, and where the negotiations failed the director-general, upon request by either party, could refer the matter to the GATT Council (Kufuor, 1997). Although improvements were made to the procedure in 1989, it was still possible for a party to prevent the establishment of a panel.[27] After agreeing to establish a panel, it was still possible for a party to prolong the implementation of any agreement regarding a panel's terms of reference or the selection of panellists.[28] Further, GATT did not guarantee any monitoring of the offending party's actions unless the injured party petitioned the Council to do so. The lack of a clear legal framework to administer dispute resolution and for the enforcement of any panel reports rendered the GATT system weak and unreliable. With an increased focus on the issue of treaty violations, the procedures were to become more legalistic than before and gradually acquired some of the characteristics of arbitration.

The power-oriented mode of dispute settlement was to change during the 1970s with a shift in the US trade policy, which recognised the benefits of drafting enforceable rules and procedures through a binding form of dispute resolution, as opposed to threats of unilateral trade retaliation (Lichtenbaum, 1998). The US sought to use the Tokyo Round of negotiations to elaborate and strengthen the panel procedures to achieve a degree of predictability in the outcome of disputes. This move towards a more judicialised, binding dispute settlement process resulted in the 1979 Tokyo Round 'Framework Agreement' on dispute resolution, which codified existing GATT dispute settlement practices.[29] During the 1980s, due to the ongoing Uruguay Round of negotiations, there were a number of non-compliance with dispute settlement rulings, besides experiencing delays in the establishment of panels (Petersmann, 1997). Against that backdrop, the key GATT contracting states, including the US and the European Community (EC), pushed for the overhaul of the GATT dispute settlement system (Bello and Holmer, 1994).

In 1984, an independent study group comprising seven eminent individuals was constituted by the GATT director-general to study possible reform to international trade, which resulted in the Leutwiler Report in 1985.[30] As regards the GATT dispute settlement procedure, the Leutwiler Report recommended the following – a commitment on the part of the GATT Panels to speed up the proceedings; a greater competence and professionalism of panellists; creation of a roster of non-governmental experts for GATT Panels; a more liberal policy regarding the initiation of panel proceedings; a greater publicity with respect to compliance/non-compliance of GATT Panel decisions; and importantly, an enhanced monitoring capability for the GATT (Leutwiler Report, 1985). Although the popular view would be for one to assume that GATT dispute system was prone to abuse by the stronger party to a dispute, contracting parties mostly refrained from blocking consensus decisions and allowed for disputes to proceed, even when they were to be to their detriment (WTO, 2004).[31] Hudec notes that Contracting Parties to GATT behaved as if a compulsory third party adjudication was agreed upon, although none whatsoever existed (Hudec, 1993).[32]

The GATT framework, as a whole, reflected the theories of international trade prevailing at the time of Bretton Woods Conference, which although broader than the traditional conception of international economic order and relations, remained devoid of an appropriate enforcement mechanism in the dispute settlement process. The non-binding nature of the GATT framework was premised on the realist theory of international law and a reflection of the belief that it is the state, and not individuals, that are subject to international law (Bruno, 1997). This position allowed for the GATT to be subject to politically based considerations of state self-interest – where state hegemony was at play, as opposed to being built on the foundations of rule of law and fair play. At the Uruguay Round of negotiations, much of the focus related to the reform of the GATT as an institution; ministerial participation; surveillance of trade policies; and dispute settlement. The developing countries that participated in the preparatory meetings to the Uruguay Round of negotiations were very particular that the GATT dispute settlement was completely reformed.[33] While Hong Kong suggested the formation of a new dispute settlement body to assist the council, Australia put forth the suggestion that parties to a dispute should be prohibited from voting on council decisions to approve a panel decision. The Uruguay Round Preparatory Committee recognised the existing power asymmetry amongst the contracting parties and the urgent need for the legal protection of the rights of less advantaged countries in the enforcement of obligations within the system (Islam, 2014). The mood amongst the contracting parties was in favour of a complete overhaul of the GATT dispute settlement with a clear set of rules.

The Ministerial Declaration of 15 September 1986, signed in 1986 at Punta del Este, set the negotiating objectives as regards the dispute settlement in the following lines:

> to ensure prompt and effective resolution of disputes to the benefit of all contracting parties, negotiations shall aim to improve and strengthen the rules and the procedures of the dispute settlement process, while recognizing the contribution that would be made by more effective and enforceable GATT rules and disciplines. Negotiations shall include the development of adequate arrangements for overseeing and monitoring of the procedures that would facilitate compliance with adopted recommendations.
>
> (GATT, 1986)

In 1988 the US passed the *US Trade and Competitiveness Act 1988*, which effectively extended section 301 of the *US Trade Act 1974*[34] and authorised the US trade secretary to *unilaterally* impose trade sanctions on countries which the US considered was in violation of the GATT obligations. The US defended its position by arguing that the existing GATT dispute system was consensus based and weak, and it was impossible to defend its interests. A ministerial meeting was held in Montreal in December 1988 to review the progress of the Uruguay Round and to make use of any early accomplishments. The report from the Montreal Ministerial Meeting – referred to as the Montreal Rules – came to be adopted in April 1989 by the CONTRACTING PARTIES (GATT, 1989a), which was to form the basis of the Dispute Settlement Understanding (DSU). In May 1992, the legal drafting group of the Uruguay Round of negotiations produced the final version of the dispute settlement understanding, which was later adopted by the Member States.

The Uruguay Round of negotiations produced a tapestry of covered agreements, including a rules-based dispute settlement system, which was a clear departure from the more diplomatically driven dispute settlement order of GATT 1947. Despite the lack of a comprehensive framework for dispute settlement under the GATT, principles and practices evolved over a period of 48 years were codified in decisions and the understandings of the contracting parties to the GATT 1947 (WTO, 2004). In addition, the body of panel reports delivered over the years helped in building a clear jurisprudence on GATT dispute settlement practices. One can argue that the dispute settlement procedures put together under the GATT 1947 worked better than did those of the World Court and some of the other international dispute procedures in vogue. The GATT was to serve as the multilateral trade agreement for the contracting parties until the formation of the WTO in 1995.

3. Dispute Settlement in the WTO

The GATT 1947 was clearly driven by a diplomatic settlement mechanism, whereas the WTO's dispute settlement system is rules based, with the source of law founded on the provisions of the covered agreements of the WTO, and international law. The Marrakesh Agreement Establishing the World Trade Organization (WTO Agreement),[35] which ushered the WTO into existence, provides for a multilateral trade regime with wider operation.[36] The WTO, unlike the GATT, is an organisation on par with the World Bank and the International Monetary Fund (IMF). While the GATT's remit was restricted to trade in goods, the WTO's remit is much wider to include trade in services (GATS),[37] agriculture, trade-related investment (TRIPS),[38] and intellectual property rights (TRIPS).[39] An international institutional structure that provides a platform to forge trade policies would presuppose the existence of rules that are to be complied with, which in turn implies a dispute settlement system.[40] The WTO, being an international institution, needed a strong and reliable enforcement mechanism for the effective implementation of the Agreements that cover the aforementioned commitments. The WTO currently boasts of such a sound dispute settlement system,[41] and the WTO's 'Understanding on the Rules and Procedures Governing the Settlement of Disputes' (DSU) contained in Annex 2 to the WTO Agreement establishes a rules-based and time-bound dispute settlement system.

The DSU is one of the many annexes to the Marrakesh Agreement, where the administration of the disputes is entrusted to the DSB with the participation of all WTO Member States. There is now a broad consensus that the WTO dispute settlement system is the most significant and the most powerful of dispute settlement systems in existence today (WTO, 2004). The WTO preserves and consolidates the body of law and practice that evolved out of the GATT era from 1948 to 1994. The preamble to the WTO Agreement, which facilitated the process, reads as follows:

> Resolved, therefore, to develop an integrated, more viable and durable multilateral trading system encompassing the General Agreement on Tariffs and Trade, the results of

past trade liberalization efforts, and all of the results of the Uruguay Round of Multilateral Trade Negotiations,

Determined to preserve the basic principles and to further the objectives underlying this multilateral trading system.

Likewise, Article XVI:1 of the WTO Agreement provides:

Except as otherwise provided under this Agreement or the Multilateral Trade Agreements, the WTO shall be guided by the decisions, procedures and customary practices followed by the Contracting Parties to GATT 1947.

The decision to enshrine the results of the past trade liberalisation accomplished under the GATT 1947 was designed to provide continuity, stability, and predictability in the multilateral trading system. As a result, the GATT 1994 contains the text of the GATT 1947, which was integrated into the WTO Agreement, together with all amendments, decisions, practices, *etc.*[42] Additionally, Article 3.1 of the DSU asserts the application of GATT 1947 Articles XXII and XXIII. Through the prior process, the jurisprudence of the GATT 1947 (from 1948 to 1994) was integrated and carried forward into the WTO's DSU, thereby ensuring continuity. The WTO dispute settlement is doubtlessly a result of over 40 years of experience gained in the GATT era. The coverage of the DSU is extensive, as it encompasses all disputes that arise in the course of performing trade under the covered agreements of the WTO. The WTO director-general Renato Ruggiero made the following comments in the Special Report of 30 September 1996:

One success that stands out above all the rest is the strengthening of the dispute settlement mechanism. This is the heart of the WTO system. Not only has it proved credible and effective in dealing with disputes, it has helped resolve a significant number at consultation stage. Furthermore, developing countries have become major users of the system, as sign of their confidence in it which was not so apparent under the old system.

4. Theoretical/Legal Framework and Jurisdiction of the DSU

The WTO legal system has come to represent the triumph of the international trade 'legalists' in the running debate with trade 'pragmatists' on the issue of how international trade dispute resolution should be structured (Shell, 1995).[43] The dispute settlement of the WTO, as it stands today, is a testament to the modification of the neoliberal view of multilateral trading order that was created in the post-World War II era under the GATT 1947.

4.1 Theoretical/Legal Framework

The DSU is a detailed set of rules with 27 Articles and spread over 143 paragraphs. As the WTO is a multilateral trading system, built on the foundations of an intergovernmental agreement, the mechanism is 'self-enforcing', *i.e.*, the parties to the agreement determine if there had been a violation of the agreement.[44] In self-enforcing agreements, (i) each party decides unilaterally if they are better off bringing the agreement to an end or to continue performing under the agreement; (ii) each party decides to continue to abide by the agreement – if and only when the expected present value of the benefits from continuing exceeds the current benefit from stopping; and (iii) no third party intervenes to enforce the agreement, to determine whether there has been a violation, to assess damages, or to impose penalties. Under the aforementioned, if one party violates the terms of the agreement, the only recourse of the other party is to terminate the agreement (Telser, 1980). If a violation of a commitment to an agreement by country A appears to reduce market access of country B, and if country A and country B were not able to resolve their differences on their own, then country B can only raise a dispute by making a formal 'request for consultation'. The self-regulating nature of a Member's decision to raise a dispute is encapsulated in Article 3(3) of the DSU, which provides as follows:

> The prompt settlement of situations in which a Member considers that any benefits accruing to it directly or indirectly under the covered agreements are being impaired by measures taken by another Member is essential to the effective functioning of the WTO and the maintenance of a proper balance between the rights and obligations of Members.[45]

The Appellate Body in *Peru – Agricultural Products* noted:

> Members enjoy discretion in deciding whether to bring a case, and are thus expected to be "largely self-regulating" in deciding whether any such action would be "fruitful". The "largely self-regulating" nature of a Member's decision to bring a dispute is "borne out by Article 3.3", which provides that the prompt settlement of situations in which a Member, in its own judgement, considers that a benefit accruing to it under the covered agreements is being impaired by a measure taken by another Member is essential to the effective functioning of the WTO.[46]

The WTO dispute settlement is decentralised, and Member States *ex officio* cannot initiate disputes. There is no supranational authority assigned with powers to initiate complaints against WTO Member States, and disputes can only be launched at the initiative of a WTO Member States (Mavroidis, 2007; Hoekman and Kostecki, 2009). Also, retaliation can be exercised by a Member Country or Countries that have been injured by the adoption of policies that violate a prior agreement of the WTO. The previous discussion, obviously, raises a fundamental question – *is a dispute settlement body essential for the WTO?* A number of arguments can be posited to justify the establishment of the DSB, and some are identified as follows:

i   A well-constituted dispute settlement system within an international trade framework affords a guarantee of protection to developing country and least developed country participants by minimising the role of power in the distribution and enforcement of legal rights and duties (Vázquez and Jackson, 2002).

ii   It reduces the prevalence of unilateral retaliation through the creation of a presumption that an action by one Member Country to change the negotiated terms of an agreement will result in compensation (Hoekman and Kostecki, 2009).

iii   There will often be legitimate uncertainty if a certain policy measure violates a negotiated agreement of the WTO, leading to legitimate need for interpretation in a specific context, and needing the DSB to interpret the provisions (Hoekman and Kostecki, 2009).[47]

iv   By interpreting the provisions of an agreement of the WTO, the DSB effectively reduces the uncertainty surrounding a particular measure and thereby helps reduce the use of unilateral retaliation against perceived violations of an agreement (Hoekman and Kostecki, 2009).[48]

v   The DSB, importantly, plays the key role of specifying an agreed-upon procedure for adjudication (Horn and Mavroidis, 2006), thereby guaranteeing clarity and predictability.

One can conclude with conviction that the DSU is fundamental for the smooth operation of the multilateral trading order established under the WTO and has emerged as an indispensable part of the WTO since its creation.

4.2 Jurisdiction: Exclusive Forum for Adjudication

Article 2 of the DSU establishes the DSB within the WTO. The General Council of the WTO also functions as the DSB, and Article IV(3) of the WTO Agreement highlights this responsibility as follows:[49]

> The General Council shall convene as appropriate to discharge the responsibilities of the Dispute Settlement Body provided for in the Dispute Settlement Understanding. The Dispute Settlement Body may have its own chairperson and shall establish such rules of procedure as it deems necessary for the fulfilment of those responsibilities.

Article 2(1) outlines the administration of the dispute settlement system and reads as follows:

> The Dispute Settlement Body is hereby established to administer these rules and procedures and, except as otherwise provided in a covered agreement, the consultation and dispute settlement provisions of the covered agreements. Accordingly, the DSB shall have the authority to establish panels, adopt panel and Appellate Body reports, maintain surveillance of implementation of rulings and recommendations, and authorize suspension of concessions and other obligations under the covered agreements. With respect to disputes arising under a covered agreement which is a Plurilateral Trade Agreement, the term "Member" as used herein shall refer only to those Members that are parties to the relevant Plurilateral Trade Agreement. Where the DSB administers the dispute settlement provisions of a Plurilateral Trade Agreement, only those Members that are parties to that Agreement may participate in decisions or actions taken by the DSB with respect to that dispute.

Accordingly, Article 2(1) creates the authority of the DSB as follows:

i   To establish dispute settlement panels;[50]
ii   To adopt panel and Appellate Body reports;
iii To maintain surveillance of implementation of rulings and recommendations; and
iv   To authorise the suspension of concessions and other obligations under the covered agreements.

Article 2(3), to facilitate the aforementioned authority, sanctions the DSB to meet "as often as necessary to carry out its function", which permits, if necessary, to exceed the monthly meetings upon request by a Member State. The principal objective of the WTO dispute settlement system remains the swift settlement of disputes brought before the DSB by the Member States. This principle is contained in Article 3(3) of the DSU, which runs as follows:

> The prompt settlement of situations in which a Member considers that any benefits accruing to it directly or indirectly under the covered agreements are being impaired

by measures taken by another Member is essential to the effective functioning of the WTO and the maintenance of a proper balance between the rights and obligations of Members.[51]

Article 3(2) of the DSU lays down the basis of the dispute settlement process as to preserve and clarify the rights and obligations of the Member States as laid out under the covered agreements. Article 3(2) confers compulsory jurisdiction on the DSB for the purposes of resolving disputes arising out of the covered agreements, and states:

> The dispute settlement system of the WTO is a central element in providing security and predictability to the multilateral trading system. The Members recognize that it serves to preserve the rights and obligations of Members under the covered agreements, and to clarify the existing provisions of those agreements in accordance with customary rules of interpretation of public international law. Recommendations and rulings of the DSB cannot add to or diminish the rights and obligations provided in the covered agreements.

In *US – Section 301 Trade Act* the Panel observed:

> [o]f all WTO disciplines, the DSU is one of the most important instruments to protect the security and predictability of the multilateral trading system and through it that of the market-place and its different operators.[52]

The panel also noted that the security and predictability referred to were that of the multilateral trading system, which comprises the Member States as well as the individual economic operators.[53]

The DSB operates on a negative consensus principle, which is the opposite of the GATT, where decisions were taken through positive consensus. The DSB serves as the forum for discussion of matters relating to disputes. This means the party (or parties) that claims that there had been a breach will have to raise a dispute. The provisions of the DSU also make clear that the parties may not take any *unilateral* action against another Member State for any alleged trade violation but follow the *multilateral* procedures laid down under the DSU to pursue any potential claim arising from the agreements of the WTO.

Article 23.1 of the DSU states:

> When Members seek the redress of a violation of obligations or other nullification or impairment of benefits under the covered agreements or an impediment to the attainment of any objective of the covered agreements, they shall have recourse to, and abide by, the rules and procedures of this Understanding.

In *US – Certain EC Products*, the Appellate Body interpreted the obligation arising under Article 23.1 in the following manner:

> Article 23.1 of the DSU imposes a general obligation on Members to redress a violation of obligations or other nullification or impairment of benefits under the covered agreements only by recourse to the rules and procedures of the DSU, and not through unilateral action. Subparagraphs (a), (b) and (c) of Article 23.2 articulate specific and clearly-defined forms of prohibited unilateral action contrary to Article 23.1 of the

DSU. There is a close relationship between the obligations set out in paragraphs 1 and 2 of Article 23. They all concern the obligation of Members of the WTO not to have recourse to unilateral action.[54]

In *Canada – Continued Suspension* the Appellate Body noted:

> Article 23 restricts WTO Members' conduct in two respects. First, Article 23.1 establishes the WTO dispute settlement system as the exclusive forum for the resolution of such disputes and requires adherence to the rules of the DSU. Secondly, Article 23.2 prohibits certain unilateral action by a WTO Member.[55]

Article 23.2(a) further enjoins that a Member State may not make a *unilateral* determination that a violation of WTO has occurred and proceed with initiating retaliatory measures *unilaterally* without recourse to the DSU's dispute settlement mechanism.[56] Article 23.2(a) of the DSU reads as follows:

> not make a determination to the effect that a violation has occurred, that benefits have been nullified or impaired or that the attainment of any objective of the covered agreements has been impeded, except through recourse to dispute settlement in accordance with the rules and procedures of this Understanding, and shall make any such determination consistent with the findings contained in the panel or Appellate Body report adopted by the DSB or an arbitration award rendered under this Understanding.

The Panel in *EC – Commercial Vessels* observed that Article 23.2(a) of the DSU served a dual purpose, *viz.*, by ensuring (i) that WTO Members seek redress of any violations of the WTO Agreement through recourse to the DSU procedures – thereby avoid unilateral action, and (ii) that WTO Members will exclusively resort to DSU procedures while seeking redress for any violations and not resort to the dispute settlement procedures of other fora.[57] There is a clear prohibition against unilateral determination of violation by Member States, as any such action would seriously compromise a Member State's negotiated rights and obligations under the various WTO agreements (WTO, 2017).

5. Recourse to WTO Dispute Settlement

The DSU has exclusivity to adjudicate upon any disputes that may arise between the Member States with regard to the agreements of the WTO. Under the scheme, when countries sign up to the membership of the WTO, they also agree to submit to the exclusive jurisdiction of the WTO's dispute settlement mechanism. This also results in all Member Countries enjoying a guaranteed access to the dispute settlement system. In simple terms, recourse to the WTO dispute settlement is exclusively to its Member States. The Appellate Body in the *US – Shrimp* case unequivocally noted the exclusive nature of access to the WTO's dispute settlement system as follows:

> It may be well to stress at the outset that access to the dispute settlement process of the WTO is limited to Members of the WTO. This access is not available, under the WTO Agreement and the covered agreements as they currently exist, to individuals or international organizations, whether governmental or non-governmental. Only Members may become parties to a dispute of which a panel may be seized, and only Members "having

a substantial interest in a matter before a panel" may become third parties in the proceedings before that panel. Thus, under the DSU, only Members who are parties to a dispute, or who have notified their interest in becoming third parties in such a dispute to the DSB, have a legal right to make submissions to, and have a legal right to have those submissions considered by, a panel.[58]

As mentioned earlier, the dispute settlement system is both government-to-government and self-governing and is open only to those Member States of the WTO. The Appellate Body report in *US – Shrimp* case, besides confirming the prior point, also notes that it will be open to those third parties (Member States) who have registered their interests and have a legal right to make submissions and be considered. As per Article 4.11 of the DSU, any Member State other than a consulting Member State, having a 'substantial trade interest' in the consultations, can be allowed to participate in the consultation after notifying both the consulting Member States and the DSB. This provision to allow third party Member State participation is subject to the consulting Member State agreeing the requesting Member State's 'substantial trade interest' as being credible.

Under Article 10 of the DSU, any Member State having a 'substantial interest' in a proceeding before a panel can be made a third party to the proceedings, after notifying its interest in a timely manner to the DSB. Under Article 17.4 of the DSU, a Member State who was a third party before a panel proceeding may be considered as a third party when the same matter proceeds to the next stage, *i.e.*, before the Appellate Body. Nevertheless, this does not entitle a third party to initiate any proceedings before the DSB. It is worthwhile noting that the proliferation of the Regional Trade Agreements (RTAs) and Preferential Trade Agreements (PTAs) has to some degree encroached upon the jurisdiction of the DSB, as the rulings in one forum spill over to the other (WTO, 2017).[59] While Article XXIV(5) of the GATT permits the formation of RTAs amongst Member States,[60] the RTAs themselves provide for their own dispute settlement mechanism.[61]

Special and Additional Rules

- Article 1.2 and Appendix 2 of the DSU;
- Article 11.2 of the SPS Agreement;
- Articles 2.14, 2.21, 4.4, 5.2, 5.4, 5.6, 6.9, 6.10, 6.11, and 8.1 through 8.12 of the Agreement on Textiles and Clothing;
- Articles 14.2 through 14.4 and Annex 2 of the TBT Agreement;
- Articles 17.4 through 17.7 of the Anti-Dumping Agreement;
- Articles 19.3 through 19.5, Annex II.2(f), 3, 9, and 21 of the Customs Valuation Agreement;
- Articles 4.2 through 4.12, 6.6, 7.2 through 7.10, 8.5, footnote 35, 24.4, 27.7, and Annex V of the SCM Agreement;
- Articles XXII:3 and XXIII:3 of the GATS and Article 4 of the Annex on Financial Services and the Annex on Air Transport Services within that Agreement; and
- Articles 1 through 5 of the Decision on Certain Dispute Settlement Procedures for the GATS.

5.1 Legal Basis of Dispute

The foundation of dispute settlement is traceable to Articles XXII and XXIII of the GATT, upon which much of the dispute settlement provisions were built. There are also a number of specific rules and procedures referred to as "special and additional rules and procedures" on dispute settlement to be found in the covered agreements of the WTO. In *Guatemala – Cement I* the Appellate Body noted that the special rules were "designed to deal with the particularities of dispute settlement relating to obligations arising under a specific covered agreement" and that "in specific circumstance where a provision of the DSU and a special or additional provision of another covered agreement are mutually inconsistent that the special or additional provision may be read to prevail over the provision of the DSU".[62]

The DSU provides to the Member States a single, comprehensive dispute settlement mechanism to cover all disputes arising under the covered agreements of the multilateral trading system.[63] The legal basis for a Member State to invoke the provisions of the dispute settlement system are to be found in the DSU and the covered agreements of the WTO. The relevant passage of Article 1(1) of the DSU lays down the legal basis for the stipulations as follows:

> The rules and procedures of this Understanding shall apply to disputes brought pursuant to the consultation and dispute settlement provisions of the agreements listed in Appendix 1 to this Understanding (referred to in this Understanding as the "covered agreements").

As per Article 1(1) the cause of action for bringing forth a dispute before the WTO is to be found in the 'covered agreements' of the WTO, which is identified in Appendix 1 of the DSU. The wording of Article 1(1) presupposes that the parties to the dispute had exhausted the consultation process prior to raising a dispute. One can conclude that the legal grounds for raising any disputes are to be found in the 'covered agreements' which also contain the rights and obligations of the WTO Member States.

List of WTO Agreements With Relevant Provisions

- Articles XXII and XXIII of GATT 1994;
- Article 19 of the Agreement on Agriculture;
- Article 11 of the Agreement on the Application of Sanitary and Phytosanitary Measures;
- Article 8.10 of the Agreement on Textiles and Clothing;
- Article 14 of the Agreement on Technical Barriers to Trade;
- Article 8 of the Agreement on Trade-Related Investment Measures;
- Article 17 of the Agreement on Implementation of Article VI of GATT 1994 (referred to as Anti-Dumping Agreement);
- Article 19 of the Agreement on Implementation of Article VII of GATT 1994 (referred to as Customs Valuation Agreement);
- Articles 7 and 8 of the Agreement on Pre-Shipment Inspection;
- Articles 7 and 8 of the Agreement on Rules of Origin;
- Article 6 of the Agreement on Import Licensing Procedures;
- Articles 4 and 30 of the Agreement on Subsidies and Countervailing Measures;
- Article 14 of the Agreement on Safeguards;
- Articles XXII and XXIII of the General Agreement on Trade in Services; and
- Article 64 of the Agreement on Trade-Related Aspects of Intellectual Property Rights.

Article 1(2) of the DSU states that the special or additional rules and procedures *shall prevail* over the DSU rules and procedures to the extent that there is a 'difference' between them. In *Guatemala – Cement I* the Appellate Body rendered as follows:

> [I]f there is no "difference", then the rules and procedures of the DSU apply together with the special or additional provisions of the covered agreement. In our view, it is only where the provisions of the DSU and the special or additional rules and procedures of a covered agreement cannot be read as complementing each other that the special or additional provisions are to prevail.[64]

The special and additional rules in covered agreements combine with the generally applicable rules and procedures of the DSU "to form a comprehensive, integrated dispute settlement system for the *WTO Agreement*".[65]

5.2 Categories of Claims

The main Articles that deal with the circumstances when a Member State may approach the dispute settlement are XXII and XXII of the GATT. Article XXII(1)(a) to (c) of the GATT identifies the circumstances where a Member State is entitled to seek legal remedy before dispute settlement for a remedy, and Article XXIII(1) specifies the conditions under which a Member State may approach the dispute settlement system and reads as follows:

1 If any contracting party should consider that any benefit accruing to it directly or indirectly under this Agreement is being nullified or impaired or that the attainment of any objective of the Agreement is being impeded as the result of

   (a) the failure of another contracting party to carry out its obligations under this Agreement, or
   (b) the application by another contracting party of any measure, whether or not it conflicts with the provisions of this Agreement, or
   (c) the existence of any other situation, the contracting party may, with a view to the satisfactory adjustment of the matter, make written representations or proposals to the other contracting party or parties which it considers to be concerned. Any contracting party thus approached shall give sympathetic consideration to the representations or proposals made to it.

Article XXIII(1) under subparagraphs (a), (b), and (c) identifies three possible grounds for raising a complaint before the WTO dispute settlement system, *viz.*, violation complaint under subparagraph (a); non-violation complaint under subparagraph (b); and situation complaint under subparagraph (c).

5.2.1 Violation Complaints

The most common form of complaints before the DSB is the violation complaint. Article XXIII(1) under subparagraph (a) outlines a violation complaint. The complaining Member State is required to demonstrate the nullification or impairment of a benefit accruing to them as a direct result of the failure of another Member State to adhere to their obligations under GATT 1994 and other covered agreements. Under Article 3.8 of the DSU, it is presumed that nullification or impairment exists when a violation, or breach, is established,[66] and this presumption is captured as follows:

> In cases where there is an infringement of the obligations assumed under a covered agreement, the action is considered *prima facie* to constitute a case of nullification or impairment. This means that there is normally a presumption that a breach of the rules has an adverse impact on other Members parties to that covered agreement, and in such cases, it shall be up to the Member against whom the complaint has been brought to rebut the charge.

The Appellate Body in *EC – Bananas III (Article 21.5 – Ecuador II)* noted that Article 3.8 "establishes a legal presumption that a breach of WTO rules constitutes nullification or impairment . . . in clear and unambiguous terms".[67] The Appellate Body in *US – Wool Shirts and Blouses* confirmed that this presumption does not extend to the question of *whether there is* such a violation.[68] The Appellate Body also noted that the complaining Member State was to provide detailed submission for invoking Article XXIII, and thereby shifting the burden of proof on to the respondent Member State to prove how its actions had not nullified or impaired the complainant's benefits accruing to it under the GATT.[69]

5.2.2 Non-Violation Complaints

Article XXIII(1)(b) allows a Member State to bring a claim on the grounds that a certain measure nullifies a pre-existing concession, although no specific rules are violated. The reason behind the incorporation of a 'non-violation' provision is that it is unlikely that a multilateral international trade agreement can possibly encapsulate all the rights and obligations the Member States negotiated and agreed upon during the negotiations. It is very much possible for a Member State to take measures that fully comply with the provisions of a covered agreement, but yet invalidate one of its objectives or an obligation contained in the agreement, thereby prejudicing the trade commitments between two Member States. The US, in such instances, uses unilateral measures to defend its commercial interests.[70] It can be argued that a non-violation complaint is important for the functioning of the system.

Importantly, the procedure envisaged here vindicates the reasonable expectations of the Member States as regards the benefits obtained through reciprocal trade concessions brought about through negotiations. The principles underpinning the non-violation complaints dates back to the GATT era and was maintained and carried forward during the Uruguay Round of negotiations. Its rationale applies to the GATS Agreement and to some degree to the TRIPS Agreement. The burden of proof in such complaints is on the complaining Member State, which is required under Article 26.1 of the DSU[71] to justify the action by detailing the benefits that are nullified or impaired and the measures that are responsible for causing such nullification or impairment and by demonstrating a causal relationship between the measure and the nullification or impairment.[72] Commentators have extensively discussed the remedy of non-violation complaints under the aforementioned article in the years following the formation of the WTO.[73] The Panel report in *EC – Oilseeds I* summarised the rationale for having a non-violation remedy in the GATT, as follows:

> The idea underlying [the provisions of Article XXIII:1(b)] is that the improved competitive opportunities that can legitimately be expected from a tariff concession can be frustrated not only by measures proscribed by the General Agreement but also by measures consistent with that Agreement. In order to encourage contracting parties to make tariff

concessions they must therefore be given a right of redress when a reciprocal concession is impaired by another contracting party as a result of the application of any measure, whether or not it conflicts with the General Agreement.[74]

The Panel was making the previous observation while dealing with legal subsidy schemes granted by the European Community.[75] The Appellate Body stated in *EC – Asbestos* observed:

> the ['non-violation' nullification or impairment] remedy . . . should be approached with caution and should remain an exceptional remedy.[76]

Importantly, where such non-violation complaints are proven, the responded Member State is not obliged to withdraw the measure in question, and it is for the Panel or the Appellate Body to recommend to make 'mutually satisfactory adjustments' to the member concerned, with the possibility for a compensation to be paid to redress any damages. One can safely state that the non-violation complaint mechanism has almost become redundant due to good faith protection in treaty application and interpretation (Cottier and Schefer, 1997; Roessler, 1997) and due to the broad extension of multilateral trade order to include domestic policies (Roessler, 1997; Verhoosel, 2002).

5.2.3 Situation Complaints

Article XXIII(1)(c) of GATT outlines the scope of situation complaints as follows:

> If any contracting party should consider that any benefit accruing to it directly or indirectly under this Agreement is being nullified or impaired or that the attainment of any objective of the Agreement is being impeded as the result of (c) the existence of any other situation.

This is a situation where a Member State may seek to bring a complaint for nullification or impairment of a negotiated benefit not captured under violation or non-violation options. The negotiating history behind Article XXIII(1)(c) of GATT indicates that situation complaints were intended to be used in situations of macroeconomic emergencies, such as high unemployment, balance-of-payment difficulties, and collapse of the price of a commodity. The proviso clearly means that the situation relied on is other than those referred to in subparagraphs (a) and (b) of Article XXIII(1). Article 26.2(a), which deals with situation complaints, makes it clear that the complaining party must "present a detailed justification in support of any argument" as regards the complaint lodged, and that the procedures of the DSU will apply to situation complaints up to the stage where panel reports are circulated to Member States. The significance of the provisions of Article 26.2 as regards situation complaints are twofold, *viz.*, (i) no reverse consensus with respect to the adoption of the report concerned and (ii) an implicit exclusion of an appeal against a panel report based on a situation complaint, which effectively precludes an Appellate Body review of the legal criteria found by a panel. Situation complaints brought during the GATT era did not result in a panel ruling.[77] Likewise, there had never been an adjudication for a situation complaint in the WTO era.

6. The DSB and Stages of the Dispute Settlement Process

As mentioned earlier, the General Council acts as the DSB and derives its authority to do so from Article IV(3) of the WTO Agreement.[78] Article 2.1 establishes and empowers the

DSB to administer the "rules and procedures and, except as otherwise provided in a covered agreement, the consultation and dispute settlement provisions of the covered agreements". Under the powers vested, the DSB has "the authority to establish Panels, adopt panel and Appellate Body reports, maintain surveillance of implementation of rulings and recommendations, and authorize suspension of concessions and other obligations under the covered agreements". For our purposes, the process of dispute settlement at the WTO can be categorised under four distinctively separate stages as follows:

i Consultations;
ii Panel proceedings;
iii Appellate review proceedings; and
iv Implementation and enforcement of Panel and Appellate Body recommendations and rulings.

Do the DSB's organs constitute an international adjudicative organ? As the Panels and the Appellate Body sit *in par* with other international adjudicative bodies, the answer is in the affirmative (Gourgourini, 2016; Sacerdoti, 2006).[79] Notably, the Panels and the Appellate Body consider themselves as international courts, treating interstate trade disputes brought before them as international legal disputes (Gourgourini, 2016). Also, the rulings of the Panels and Appellate Body establish international law obligations upon the losing Member States of the WTO, requiring them to bring the measure in question in conformity with WTO laws, with any refusal to do so leading to trade retaliations. The WTO Panels and the Appellate Body consider themselves as international courts, which position, for instance, was confirmed by the Appellate Body in the *US – Wool Shirts and Blouses* case and by the Panels in the *US – DRAMS* case and *China – Intellectual Property Rights* case.[80]

6.1 Consultation

There is a clear preference for an agreed solution brought about by negotiations between the parties to the dispute, as opposed to solutions resulting from adjudication. In this regard, Article 3(7) of the DSU states as follows:

> The aim of the dispute settlement mechanism is to secure a positive solution to a dispute. A solution mutually acceptable to the parties to a dispute and consistent with the covered agreements is clearly to be preferred.

While the DSB seeks to clarify the scope of the rights and obligations of the Member States (as well as upholding them), the primary objective of the system is not to make rulings or to develop jurisprudence, but to settle disputes – preferably through mutually agreed solutions (WTO, 2017).[81] With this view in mind all disputes brought before the WTO's dispute settlement system go through a process of consultation. Under the scheme envisaged, there are two phases to go through before a Member State could bring a dispute before the DSU. Firstly, by seeking consultation – which is designed as a *bilateral* exercise between the complainant and respondent. Here, the complainant is required to outline the nature and subject matter of the complaint/dispute sought to be raised, to the WTO.[82] It is only possible for another WTO Member to join as a co-complainant if the defendant accepts the request. The relevant passage of Article 4.11 of the DSU reads as follows:

Whenever a Member other than the consulting Members considers that it has a substantial trade interest in consultations being held pursuant to paragraph 1 of Article XXII of GATT 1994 . . . such Member may notify the consulting Members and the DSB, within 10 days after the date of the circulation of the request for consultations under said Article, of its desire to be joined in the consultations. Such Member shall be joined in the consultations, provided that the Member to which the request for consultations was addressed agrees that the claim of substantial interest is well-founded.

In the event the consultation phase does not yield a solution, the Member State/complainant may seek the establishment of a panel to adjudicate the dispute. Although the consultation process may not stand out as a compelling phase of the dispute settlement process, it is accorded an equal status as the panel and appellate stages, as the objective of the DSU is to find a mutually acceptable solution to the dispute as opposed to adjudication. Each dispute settlement proceeding invariably begins with a consultation between the parties, *i.e.*, the Member States to the dispute with the objective of arriving at a mutually agreed solution. This fundamental principle of the dispute settlement mechanism is well captured in Article 3.7 of the DSU, the relevant passage of which reads as follows:

> The aim of the dispute settlement mechanism is to secure a positive solution to a dispute. A solution mutually acceptable to the parties to a dispute and consistent with the covered agreements is clearly to be preferred.

Questions have been raised as to the effectiveness of the consultation process and if the procedures established by the DSU are adequate to achieve the goals. Schuchhardt notes that statistical information available provides some measure of the effectiveness of the consultation process (Schuchhardt, 2005). Yet another question that can be raised is whether a request for consultation is capable of limiting the scope of a subsequent panel request, and thereby the Panel's terms of reference. The WTO Panels had given a liberal interpretation for making a consultation request under Article 4.4 DSU. The Appellate Body in *Brazil – Aircraft* held:

> Articles 4 and 6 of the DSU . . . set forth a process by which a complaining party must request consultations, and consultations must be held, before a matter may be referred to the DSB for the establishment of a panel.[83]

The Panel in *US – Poultry (China)* noted as follows:

> Given the relationship between the consultations request and the panel request, the shared language in Article 4 and Article 6.2 of the DSU, the similar purposes of the two requests, *i.e.* to delimit the scope of the dispute, and the need to interpret both provisions in a harmonious way, we find the Appellate Body reasoning pertinent for the analysis of the consistency of consultations requests with the obligations of Article 4.4 of the DSU as well.[84]

The Appellate Body in *Argentina – Import Measures* noted that the requirements that apply to a consultation request under Article 4.4 of the DSU were not the same as a panel request under Article 6.2, and noted as follows:

> while a consultations request must identify the "measure at issue", a panel request must identify the "specific measure at issue". This difference in the language between

Articles 4.4 and 6.2 makes it clear that, in identifying the measure at issue, greater specificity is required in a panel request than in a consultations request.[85]

The Appellate Body, after having examined the language of Articles 4.4 and 6.2 of the DSU, then concluded as follows:

> Considering that consultations facilitate the exchange of information among the parties to allow them to either reach a mutually agreed solution or refine the contours of the dispute, the measures and claims identified in a panel request may constitute a natural evolution of the consultations process. Thus, there is no need for a "precise and exact identity" between the measures identified in the consultations request and the specific measure identified in the panel request, provided that the latter does not expand the scope of the dispute or change its essence. The determination of whether the identification of the "specific measure at issue" in the panel request expanded the scope or changed the essence of the dispute must be made on a case-by-case basis.[86]

It is also to be noted here that about 40 percent of the cases don't go past the consultations stage (WTO, 2017), as consultations permit the parties (Member States) to the dispute to formally assess their strengths and weaknesses and their chances of success and reach a mutually agreed solution.[87]

6.1.1 Nature and General Features of the Consultation Phase

The consultation phase is viewed as a powerful tool as it provides the requesting party Member State to seek the establishment of a panel, if no response is forthcoming from the defending Member State within 10 or 30 days. A request for consultations also provides the Member State seeking consultations the opportunity to attract the interest of other Member States (the entire WTO membership) with an interest in the outcome of the dispute, any non-governmental organisations, organizations, *etc.*, which could see a quick settlement of the dispute at hand.

The consultations are not monitored by the DSB and are self-managed by the concerned Member States,[88] and as a result could see a more powerful country exerting its influence on a much smaller country to shape the outcome of the process.[89] That said, the negotiation is an essential part of any dispute settlement, where parties would seek to influence any outcome. The litigation strategies adopted by the developed Member States, such as the EU and the US, seem to undermine the consultation process and its objectives, as they tend to consult only when faced with a complaint from a Member State of their own size and importance (Schuchhardt, 2005). The same countries, when faced with a smaller adversary, consider the consultation process as a mere preliminary stage before the commencement of litigation. In short, there is an effort to engage in consultation when the stakes are high, and not otherwise. What is missing in the prior scenarios is the good faith effort on the part of the Member States to reach a quick settlement through consultations, which is the most conciliatory form of settling a dispute.

In recent years, the consultation phase has become more legalized than before, with written rules and panel decisions making the process increasingly detailed. As mentioned earlier, the GATT adopted a power-oriented diplomacy instead of a rule-based approach to dispute settlement. Schuchhardt argues that the consultation phase of the dispute settlement process, being a negotiations-based process, is a residue of the power-oriented approach of the GATT era (Schuchhardt, 2005).

It is to be borne in mind that the prior consultation principle enshrined in international customary law (the *opinion juris*), includes any international trade disputes amongst nation states. As discussed in earlier chapters, the law of the WTO is subjected to these principles. On the obligation of the nation states to consult, the International ICJ in the *North Sea Continental Shelf Cases*[90] noted as follows:

> the parties are under an obligation to enter into negotiations with a view to arriving at an agreement and not merely to go through a formal process of negotiation as a sort of prior condition for the application of a certain method of delimitation in the absence of agreement; they are under an obligation so to conduct themselves that the negotiations are meaningful, which will not be the case when either of them insists upon its own position without contemplating any modification of it.

Commentators take differing views, with some opining that the prior consultation principle seeks the avoidance of prejudice to other states (Sohn, 1983), and others taking the position that although desirable, there is no general obligation on states to engage in any consultations to resolve disputes (Rogoff, 1994). On the strength of commentaries on international dispute settlement[91] and WTO jurisprudence, the author of this book is more inclined to take the view that in economic relations, which includes international trade disputes, there is an implicit obligation on the WTO Member State to engage in intergovernmental consultation before the launch of any disputes. One can advance the statement that a Member State has a right to request consultation, and there is a duty to consult when requested for.

6.1.2 Failure to Consult and Period of Consultation

Consultations are the first (and the least expensive) means of providing relief to a Member State under the DSB. Requesting consultations is viewed as a right, and in response there is a duty to consult if disputes are to be settled amicably following the international law edicts. On the point of failure to consult, the Panel in *Brazil – Desiccated Coconut* case observed as follows:

> Compliance with the fundamental obligation of WTO Members to enter into consultations where a request is made under the DSU is vital to the operation of the dispute settlement system . . . In our view, these provisions [DSU, Articles 4.6 and 4.2] make clear that Members' duty to consult is absolute, and is not susceptible to the prior imposition of any terms and conditions by a Member.[92]

One can conclude from the foregoing that to consult is an absolute duty, and a failure by a Member State to respond to a request for consultations can be considered a violation of the right of the Member State seeking such consultations. In the event a request for consultation is not responded to, the party requesting such consultations after the expiry of 60 days from such request can proceed to seek the establishment of a panel.[93] This move invariably brings the dispute within the ambit of the rules-based system established under the DSB. While there is a minimum requirement of 60 days for consultations, Article 4.8 of the DSU provides for a shorter timeframe in the event there is a need for urgent action, and reads as follows:

> In cases of urgency, including those which concern perishable goods, Members shall enter into consultations within a period of no more than 10 days after the date of receipt of the request. If the consultations have failed to settle the dispute within a period of

20 days after the date of receipt of the request, the complaining party may request the establishment of a panel.

Article 4.8 does not define cases of urgency, besides not outlining how to hold consultations within ten days of the request and how a Member State could seek the establishment of a panel after 20 days. The language employed in Article 4.8 is clear, in that it stipulates that Members 'shall' enter into consultations within ten days, and in the event the consultations fail to resolve the issue, the complaining party may request establishment of a Panel within 20 days. Article 4.9 DSU requires parties, Panels, and the Appellate Body to "accelerate the proceedings to the greatest extent possible". Most consultation requests that had been brought forward had related to perishable goods.[94]

6.1.3 Plurilateral and Private Consultations

The two options available for Member States seeking consultations are to either choose a consultations under Article XXII of the GATT 1994 – which is plurilateral in nature, or under Article XXIII(1) of the GATT 1994 – which is private consultations, where third parties are excluded. In short, it is up to the Member State seeking the consultations to determine the nature of consultations.[95] It is noted that most consultation requests are made under Article XXII for plurilateral consultations. Where consultation requests are made under Article XXIII(1), the consultations are conducted in private excluding any third parties.[96] Where a request for consultations has been processed under Article XXII(1) (or under a corresponding provision in a covered agreement), it is permissible for another Member State to seek to join the consultations on the grounds that it has a "substantial trade interest".[97] A Member State who is not a party to the consultations may be interested in the outcome of any consultations, as it may have a trade interest in the ongoing consultation process. Such a Member State can request to join such consultations if it can be demonstrated that they have a "substantial trade interest" in the matter being discussed, provided such consultation has been called for under Article XXII:1 of the GATT, Article XXII:1 of the GATS or a corresponding provision of any other covered agreements.[98]

6.2 Panel: Request, Terms of Reference, and Establishment

From the foregoing, one can safely conclude that in the event of failure to reach an agreed settlement through consultations within 60 days, the complaining Member State may seek in writing the establishment of a Panel under Article 6.1 of the DSU, which is through negative consensus.[99] As there are no permanent panellists in the WTO, it must be composed *ad hoc* for each dispute and is dissolved once the set task is accomplished. The Panels are composed of three qualified governmental or non-governmental individuals, and exceptionally of five individuals.[100] The complaining Member State and the defending Member State have a period of 20 days to agree on the panellists, failing which a panel will be chosen and appointed by the director-general of the WTO.[101] Importantly, citizens belonging to the Member States to the dispute in question, and citizens of the same customs union or common market, are not eligible to serve on a panel concerned with the dispute.[102] The Panel, when established, will commence the second phase of the dispute settlement process, and is considered *multilateral*.

The Panels normally have a 'standard' term of reference to examine dispute brought before it in the light of the relevant provisions of the law as contained under the covered agreements, which can be modified if the parties to the dispute agree otherwise within 20 days.[103] Article 7.1 of the DSU reads as follows:

> To examine, in the light of the relevant provisions in (name of the covered agreement(s) cited by the parties to the dispute), the matter referred to the DSB by (name of party) in document . . . and to make such findings as will assist the DSB in making the recommendations or in giving the rulings provided for in that/those agreement(s).

The Panel's terms of reference are restricted to the 'matter' referred to the DSB by the claimant/complaining Member State. Hence, the issues before the Panel are largely determined by the complaining Member State's request for the formation of a panel to rule over a certain matter (Pescatore, 1997; Lichtenbaum, 1998). One can safely conclude that a Panel is precluded from considering issues beyond what is identified in the brief of the complaining Member State. This argument is further strengthened by the wording of Article 6.2 which requires that Panel requests

> identify the specific measures at issue and provide a brief summary of the legal basis of the complaint sufficient to present the problem clearly. In case the applicant requests the establishment of a panel with other than standard terms of reference, the written request shall include the proposed text of special terms of reference.

Article 6.2 requires that the party seeking the establishment of a Panel to state (i) if "consultations were held" prior to approaching the DSB, (ii) a brief summary of legal basis of the claim, (iii) the key elements, such as the specific measures at issue, and (iv) a summary of the legal basis of claim sufficient to present the problem clearly.[104] Article 6.2 provides as follows:

> The request for the establishment of a panel shall be made in writing. It shall indicate whether consultations were held, identify the specific measures at issue and provide a brief summary of the legal basis of the complaint sufficient to present the problem clearly. In case the applicant requests the establishment of a panel with other than standard terms of reference, the written request shall include the proposed text of special terms of reference.

The Appellate Body in the *Brazil – Desiccated Coconut* case noted as follows:

> A panel's terms of reference are important for two reasons. First, terms of reference fulfil an important due process objective – they give the parties and third parties sufficient information concerning the claims at issue in the dispute in order to allow them an opportunity to respond to the complainant's case. Second, they establish the jurisdiction of the panel by defining the precise claims at issue in the dispute.[105]

Likewise, the Appellate Body in *US – Carbon Steel*, reiterating the view expressed in *Brazil – Desiccated Coconut*, emphasised that the terms of reference "define the scope of the dispute".[106] Moreover, "pursuant to Article 7 of the DSU, a panel's terms of reference are governed by the panel request, unless the parties agree otherwise".[107] This view was also echoed by the Panel in its report in *Australia – Apples*, where it noted, "a Panel's mandate or terms of reference are determined by the request for the establishment of the Panel".[108]

The Appellate Body in *Korea – Dairy* noted as follows:

> Article 6.2 demands only a summary – and it may be a brief one – of the legal basis of the complaint; but the summary must, in any event, be one that is "sufficient to present the problem clearly". It is not enough, in other words, that "the legal basis of the complaint" is summarily identified; the identification must "present the problem clearly".[109]

The Appellate Body also observed that the complainant, when requesting the establishment of a panel, is required to present the legal basis of the claim with sufficient clarity – without the need to present a detailed set of arguments,[110] besides stating clearly the specific measures at issue.[111] Once adopted, the terms of reference are not to be changed during the subsistence of the dispute process.[112] In *China – Raw Materials*, it was China's contention that the claimants[113] had not presented their claims clearly, which infringed Article 6.2 of the DSU. The Panel at first instance held that although the specifics were unclear in the terms of reference, they did not lead to infringing Article 6.2 of the DSU, as later submissions of the complainant rectified the shortcoming. On appeal by China, the findings of the Panel were reversed by the Appellate Body, which held that the defects arising from non-compliance to Article 6.2 in the terms of reference could not be cured by later submissions, as this would prejudice the right of the respondent in constructing their defence.[114]

A Panel request, whilst stating the legal basis of the complaint, cannot merely refer to a covered agreement in general or resort to standard phrases, such as "including but not necessarily limited to".[115] Likewise, Panels are to exercise of *judicial economy* while considering a complaint, and they are not required to examine each and every one of the legal claims that a complainant puts forward.[116] The Appellate Body in *US – Wool Shirts and Blouses* ruled that Panels are to address those claims that are required to be addressed to resolve the matter at hand.[117] A panel while exercising judicial economy is to state so explicitly for the benefit of the parties to the dispute.[118] In *Australia – Salmon*, the Appellate Body observed that a panel has to address

> those claims on which a finding is necessary in order to enable the DSB to make sufficiently precise recommendations and rulings so as to allow for prompt compliance by a Member with those recommendations and rulings "in order to ensure effective resolution of disputes to the benefit of all Members".[119]

Similarly, the Appellate Body in *EC – Fasteners (China)* rejected China's contention that the panel was wrong not to address one of its key arguments concerning a claim, and observed as follows:

> a panel has the discretion "to address only those arguments it deems necessary to resolve a particular claim" and "the fact that a particular argument relating to that claim is not specifically addressed in the 'Findings' section of a panel report will not, in and of itself, lead to the conclusion that that panel has failed to make the 'objective assessment of the matter before it' required by Article 11 of the DSU".[120]

Article 10 of the DSU deals with the rights of third parties (intervenors) to the disputes raised before the DSB, with Article 10.2, in particular, stating as follows:

> Any Member having a substantial interest in a matter before a panel and having notified its interest to the DSB (referred to in this Understanding as a "third party") shall have an opportunity to be heard by the panel and to make written submissions to the panel.

These submissions shall also be given to the parties to the dispute and shall be reflected in the panel report.

A reading of the previous provision makes one conclude that any Member State that has a substantial interest in the proceedings before the DSB is considered a 'third party'. While the DSU recognises the participation of third parties to disputes, the rights granted are limited to three legal rights.[121] The three legal rights granted to third parties are (i) the opportunity to be heard by the panel,[122] following a written invitation by the Panel, (ii) the right to "make written submissions to the panel" during the proceedings,[123] and (iii) the right to receive the submissions of the parties to the dispute.[124] Following request from the third parties, and after consultation with the Member States/parties to the dispute, the Panel may exercise its discretion and grant "enhanced third party rights" (WTO, 2017).[125] In the *EC – Hormones* case both Canada and the US participated in each other's Panel proceeding as third parties.[126]

Although the provisions of the DSU allow for hearing third parties, the panel report will not include any conclusions and recommendations with respect of third parties, as third parties can always raise a dispute against the respondent under Article 10.4 of the DSU.

6.3 Multiple Complaints and Joint Panels

More often, the interests of more than two Member States are brought in question in the disputes before the DSB. Any measure adopted by a government to regulate trade could affect more than one Member State at a given point in time. This in turn could likely be questioned by more than one Member State who may question the alleged breach of a WTO law, and/or the impairment of benefits accruing under the covered agreements. Article 10.2 of the DSU, in such cases, permits the establishment of a single Panel to consider the disputes,[127] and Article 11 DSU grants such third parties that have an interest in a dispute to be heard by the Panel. Interestingly, the WTO Member States have, at times, resorted to a 'wait-and-watch' approach to see if another Member State raises a claim and secures the withdrawal of the measure under question, rather than raise the issue on their own before the DSB (WTO, 2017). The logic behind this approach is that if the measure under question is withdrawn, the benefits accruing from therein will be applicable to all Member States, as opposed to the one(s) that brought the matter before the DSB. The other approach is to participate as a third party in a dispute that is brought before the DSB by another Member State, which offers the advantage of receiving all legal submissions of the disputing Member States, besides being heard by the panels. Yet another approach is to seek the establishment of a panel – either in parallel or jointly – along with the other complaints.

Article 9 of the DSU provides for the establishment of a Panel when more than one Member State seeks to raise a dispute arising from the same matter at issue. The approach envisaged under Article 9 is aimed at avoiding both multiplicity of proceedings and contradictory outcomes from multiple proceedings arising out of the same issues at hand, and to ensure consistency in any findings handed down by the Panels. Under Article 9.1 a single panel is to be established, considering the rights of all Member States concerned,[128] and under Article 9.3 where more than one panel were to be established to deal with the complaint, the same persons are to serve as panellists to the greatest extent possible.[129] In some cases, the Member States to the dispute had requested the DSB to establish joint panels.[130]

6.3.1 The Panel: Time Scales and Working Procedures

Following its establishment, the Panel operates to a strict time scale. As per Article 12.8, the time scale to complete the Panel process is set at six months – from the date of the composition and terms of reference of the panel have been agreed upon until the date the final report is issued to the parties.[131] In the event the Panel is of the view that it may not complete its enquiry and submit its report within the timeframe prescribed, it is obliged to inform the DSB in writing of its reasons and present a revised timeframe for filing its report. The standard timeframes set for conducting the Panel proceedings are often exceeded in practice. A panel process, from the establishment of panel to the delivery of the panel report, lasts up to 456 days (15 months).[132] The delays are brought about due to a combination of factors, *viz.*, the complexities of the dispute, the availability of experts and time taken to consult experts, scheduling of meetings, *etc.*[133] Following the delays experienced in *EC – Approval and Marketing of Biotech Products*, the chair of the Panel flagged up the issue in a letter addressed to the chair of DSB as follows:

> With the circulation of its Reports, the Panel is completing more than two and a half years of legal proceedings. This is an unusually long period of time for WTO panel proceedings, considering also that Article 3.3 of the DSU stresses the importance of the prompt settlement of disputes. But the number of claims and products involved in this case was unprecedented and the record before the Panel immense. An estimated 7–8 work years of professional Secretariat staff time (not including translation and support staff time) have gone into the preparation of these Reports, not counting the time invested by the Panellists. This quite simply means that panels are unable to complete proceedings concerning such disputes within the 6–9 month timeframe laid down in Article 12.9 of the DSU, without additional resources being made available to the Secretariat for this purpose.[134]

The Panel, which sets the dates and deadlines for the various stages of the proceedings, is guided by the *Working Procedures* set out in Appendix 3 of the DSU (which has evolved over time). The timetables normally include deadlines for written submissions (for both the complainant and the respondent), responses to preliminary rulings, responses to comments on responses, effective summaries, *etc.* (WTO, 2017).[135] Although transparency is one of the key pillars of the trade negotiations at the WTO, the same does not apply to proceedings before the Panel, as the *Working Procedures* enumerated in Appendix 3 of the DSU requires that Panels meet in closed sessions.[136]

After hearing the arguments from the parties to the dispute, the Panel proceeds to make an objective assessment of the matter (both questions of fact and law),[137] while preparing its report. For any objective assessment, a panel is to base its findings on the basis of the evidence on record.[138] The Appellate Body in *US – Continued Zeroing* noted that objective assessment of the facts of the case

> requires a panel to consider evidence before it in its totality, which includes consideration of submitted evidence in relation to other evidence.[139]

When a Panel disregards or distorts the evidence presented, it will not be viewed as an error of judgment, but rather as an "egregious error", and the Appellate Body in *EC – Hormones*, observed thus:

> A claim that a panel disregarded or distorted the evidence submitted to it is, in effect, a claim that the panel, to a greater or lesser degree, denied the party submitting the evidence fundamental fairness . . . or due process of law.[140]

The Panel is, hence, required to consider all the evidence presented before it by the parties to the dispute, assess their credibility, determine their evidentiary value, and base its factual findings on a proper appreciation.[141] Article 11 of the DSU requires that Panels make an objective assessment of the facts of the case and the applicability and conformity of the measure with the relevant covered agreements,[142] which is linked to ensure due process in its proceedings.[143] Whilst reviewing decisions taken by national authorities of the Member States, the objective assessment does not mandate a *de novo* review (a total repetition of the findings of fact of the national authority) or a total deference to domestic authorities (simple acceptance of their decisions).[144]

The Panel works as a collegial body, bringing in expertise (lawyers, economists, *etc.*) from within the WTO Secretariat depending on the subject matter of the dispute.[145] Besides, the Expert Review Groups (ERGs), which work under the authority of the Panels, function as a provider of technical and scientific expertise to Panel members, whenever the need arises.[146] In addition, the Panel may request an advisory report in writing from an Expert Review Group.[147] Also, the Panel's deliberations are to be confidential, with the report to be drafted in the absence of the parties to the dispute. According to Articles 3.2 and 19.2 of the DSU, the Panel's mandate is to apply the law (WTO law) as it stands and not to make new law in the course of handing down reports.[148]

6.3.2 Burden of Proof

The concept of burden of proof is generally understood to be that part of the law of evidence (be it judicial or quasi-judicial) dealing with the fundamental question, which of the disputing parties is to bear the burden of proving a claim, assertion, or defence before a judicial body. In terms of WTO disputes and following from the earlier broad definition, the Member State bringing a dispute to the DSB will be obliged to prove their claims, and likewise, the Member State asserting that it is entitled to an exception is bound to prove the same. Standard of proof, on the other hand, refers to that degree of proof that is required in a particular case, or in other words how much evidence would be required to satisfy the court, or adjudicator, to prove that the party has met their burden (Cook, 2012; Kaul, Schieler, and Wolf, 2016).

Specific rules on the burden of proof in proceedings before the DSB is not contained in any particular provision of the DSU. Hence, Panels and the Appellate Body have relied on general principles of law along with that of the prevalent practices in other international/domestic tribunals to develop evidentiary rules (WTO, 2017).[149] Some commentators hold the view that burden of proof encompasses two questions, *viz.*, (i) which party to the dispute has the burden of persuasion that the conduct under challenge was illegal and (ii) which party to the dispute has the duty to put forward the legal arguments and factual evidence.[150] While Article 11 of the DSU imposes a duty to make an 'objective assessment', it does not refer to the allocation of burden of proof in proceedings before the DSB (Marceau, 2002). This particular issue arose for consideration in *US – Wool Shirts and Blouses*, where India argued that the burden of proof was on the United States, the respondent in the case, to prove that US restrictions on shirts and blouses from India were not contrary to the safeguard provisions contained in the WTO Agreement on Textiles and Clothing. Disagreeing with India, the Appellate Body allocated the burden of proof by applying general principles of law.

> In addressing this issue, we find it difficult, indeed, to see how any system of judicial settlement could work if it incorporated the proposition that the mere assertion of a

claim might amount to proof. It is, thus, hardly surprising that various international tribunals, including the International Court of Justice, have generally and consistently accepted and applied the rule that the party who asserts a fact, whether the claimant or the respondent, is responsible for providing proof thereof. Also, it is a generally accepted canon of evidence in civil law, common law and, in fact, most jurisdictions, that the burden of proof rests upon the party, whether complaining or defending, who asserts the affirmative of a particular claim or defence. If that party adduces evidence sufficient to raise a presumption that what is claimed is true, the burden then shifts to the other party, who will fail unless it adduces sufficient evidence to rebut the presumption.[151]

The aforementioned ruling of the Appellate Body on burden of proof in *US – Wool Shirts and Blouses* has been consistently applied by panels, Appellate Body, and arbitrators alike and can now be considered the norm in WTO dispute settlement proceedings. Following from the decision, one can conclude that the burden of proof in WTO dispute settlement proceedings is on the party (the complainant or the respondent) that puts forth the claim or the defence. With regard to SPS Agreement, though, the Appellate Body in *EC – Hormones* clarified the position as follows:

> The initial burden lies on the complaining party, which must establish a *prima facie* case of inconsistency with a particular provision of the SPS Agreement on the part of the defending party, or more precisely, of its SPS measure or measures complained about. When that *prima facie* case is made, the burden of proof moves to the defending party, which must in turn counter or refute the claimed inconsistency.
>
> . . . It is also well to remember that a *prima facie* case is one which, in the absence of effective refutation by the defending party, requires a panel, as a matter of law, to rule in favour of the complaining party presenting the *prima facie* case.[152]

The Appellate Body in *Japan – Apples* held that the party bearing the burden of proof is to present evidence sufficient to make a *prima facie* case.[153] The Appellate Body in *EC – Hormones* defined a *prima facie* case as one where a Panel,

> in the absence of effective refutation by the defending party . . . as a matter of law, to rule in favour of the complainant presenting the *prima facie* case.[154]

In *US – Section 301 Trade Act*, the Appellate Body summarised the burden of proof in the following manner:

> In accordance with this jurisprudence, both parties agreed that it is for the EC, as the complaining party, to present arguments and evidence sufficient to establish a *prima facie* case in respect of the various elements of its claims regarding the inconsistency of Sections 301–310 with US obligations under the WTO. Once the EC has done so, it is for the US to rebut that *prima facie* case. Since, in this case, both parties have submitted extensive facts and arguments in respect of the EC claims, our task will essentially be to balance all evidence on record and decide whether the EC, as party bearing the original burden of proof, has convinced us of the validity of its claims. In case of uncertainty, *i.e.* in case all the evidence and arguments remain in equipoise, we have to give the benefit of the doubt to the US as defending party.[155]

From the foregoing, the task of the Panel can be identified as one of evaluating and balancing the relevant evidence presented before it, to determine whether the party putting forward a claim has discharged its burden of proof. In the same case, the Appellate Body also made the following observation on the rules on burden of proof:

> the party that alleges a specific fact . . . has the burden to prove it. In other words, it has to establish a *prima facie* case that the fact exists. . . . this *prima facie* case will stand unless sufficiently rebutted by the other party.[156]

The Appellate Body in *EC – Tariff Preferences* noted that the responsibility of the parties to the dispute is not one of providing the Panel with the legal interpretation, but one of adducing "sufficient evidence to substantiate its assertion".[157] In other words, the burden of interpreting the rule or law is not on the parties to the dispute, as that is the responsibility of the Panel. The Appellate Body in *US – Carbon Steel*, while discussing the kind of evidence a complainant is to present, observed as follows:

> [A] responding Member's law will be treated as WTO-consistent until proven otherwise. The party asserting that another party's municipal law, as such, is inconsistent with relevant treaty obligations bears the burden of introducing evidence as to the scope and meaning of such law to substantiate that assertion. . . . The nature and extent of the evidence required to satisfy the burden of proof will vary from case to case.[158]

The DSB's approach to burden of proof is not without criticism, as some commentators opine that the Appellate Body's concepts and terminology on the claimant's burden of proof are disturbingly ambiguous, besides being misleading (Barceló III, 2009). There is an ongoing debate amongst commentators on the shifting of burden of proof before the dispute settlement system (understood as the *burden persuasion*), and if that burden shifts from one party to the other during the course of the dispute proceedings before the WTO (Pauwelyn, 1998; Taniguchi, 2008; Unterhalter, 2009; Barceló III, 2009; Pfitzer and Sabune, 2009).

6.3.3 Panel Report

Upon completion of the arguments, and after the scrutiny of the documentary evidence before it, the Panel reaches a conclusion. The Panel then submits a section of its report – the descriptive part – to the Member States, who are parties to the dispute before it, inviting any comments.[159] Upon receipt of the comments on the descriptive part, the Panel then prepares an interim report, with findings of fact and legal conclusions. When the interim report is released, the parties to the dispute can seek an audience with the Panel for further discussion. The Panel issues a final report to the DSB, after considering any comments from the parties and following the interim review process.[160]

Under Article 12.7 of the DSU, a Panel is required to submit a written report to the DSB setting out (i) the findings of fact; (ii) the relevant provisions of any covered agreements applicable to the case; and (iii) the rationale behind the findings and recommendations the Panel makes.[161] The Appellate Body in *Mexico – Corn Syrup (Article 21.5 – US)* observed that under Article 12.7 the Panel is to provide a basic rationale for its findings, which in effect sets a 'minimum standard' that panels must adopt to support their findings and recommendations, and that Article 12.7 also furthers the objective of promoting security and predictability in the multilateral trading system as contained in Article 3.2 of the DSU.[162] In *Argentina –*

Footwear (EC), the Panel report was challenged by Argentina for lack of basic rationale. The Appellate Body, rejecting the appeal, observed as follows:

> Although Argentina may not agree with the rationale provided by the Panel, and we do not ourselves agree with all of its reasoning, we have no doubt that the Panel set out, in its Report, a "basic rationale" consistent with the requirements of Article 12.7 of the DSU.[163]

When developing country Member States are involved in a dispute before the DSB, the Panel report must state clearly how it had taken into account such factors of special or differential treatment that the developing country Member State has invoked before it. The Panel report in *India – Quantitative Restrictions* is a clear example of such a case, where the Panel referred to the aforementioned requirement and observed as follows:

> In this instance, we have noted that Article XVIII:B as a whole, on which our analysis throughout this section is based, embodies the principle of special and differential treatment in relation to measures taken for balance-of-payments purposes. This entire part G therefore reflects our consideration of relevant provisions on special and differential treatment, as does Section VII of our report (suggestions for implementation).[164]

The DSB has 60 days from the submission of the report to adopt it, barring a consensus against such adoption.[165] In the event the Panel concludes that the measure under challenge is inconsistent with a covered agreement, the report will also contain recommendations to the respondent to bring the challenged measure into conformity with the agreement.[166] If the dispute before the DSB related to a non-violation complaint,[167] then the goal of the Panel is "not the withdrawal of the measure concerned, but rather achieving a mutually satisfactory adjustment, usually by means of compensation".[168] The Panel, in such cases, would normally recommend that the respondent make a 'satisfactory adjustment' which is agreeable to the parties.[169] The report is translated into other WTO languages not used in the proceedings[170] and circulated to all Member States of the WTO. Once adopted, a Panel's recommendations and findings gain legal force. In contrast, the suggestions that a Panel may make for the implementation of the recommendations are not binding.[171] As discussed earlier, a single Panel may be established to hear multiple complaints, wherever possible.[172] In cases where a single panel is established to hear multiple complaints, any party to the proceedings may request a separate report from the Panel.[173] Only in a few instances have Panels issued separate reports for each complaint.[174] In some cases, Panels have issued a combination of joint and separate reports,[175] and a single document with separate report for each complaint.[176]

6.4 The Appellate Body

6.4.1 Historical Background

At the time of launching the Uruguay Round of trade negotiations, the GATT contracting parties were aware that an enhanced dispute settlement procedure was an absolute necessity to forge a more sophisticated multilateral trading system. The GATT's dispute settlement mechanism had major drawbacks and shortcomings, including the lack of a clear mechanism to challenge the report/findings of a Panel. From the complainant's perspective, the major shortcoming of the GATT dispute settlement was the ability of the losing party to block the adoption of a panel report. On the other hand, for the respondent, the shortcoming was the lack of scope to subject the panel report to an appellate review. A suggestion made during the later stages of the Uruguay Round of negotiations was the idea of a discrete appellate review stage (GATT, 1989a).[177] The idea of a standing appeals body was mooted for the first time in September 1989, during a discussion on the procedures for adopting panel reports (GATT, 1989b), and Mexico – one of the negotiating countries – put forward a broad proposal for constituting an appellate body in the following terms:

> 12. The purpose of establishing an appellate body is to compensate for the virtually automatic adoption of panel reports, by allowing parties to a dispute the opportunity to have reports reviewed in their entirety by a body specialized in GATT matters: in other words, by a body whose membership and permanent nature ensure that the final conclusions and recommendations are free from any doubt or error of interpretation concerning GATT rules and disciplines.
>
> 13. The appellate body would be available to all contracting parties. However, this remedy should not be used as just another procedure in dispute settlement. Parties to a dispute which so request must present their case in writing, indicating their grounds for considering that the panel report being appealed is unsound and the specific points they wish to have reviewed by the appellate body. In addition, all appeal applications must be accompanied by a formal declaration reiterating that the applicant will accept the final outcome of the appeal.
>
> (GATT, 1990)[178]

Some of the participating countries expressed their concern about the creation of an appellate review stage, as they feared an increase to the duration of any trade litigation, as well as the dispute settlement proceedings becoming complex. To avoid any complexity, they suggested a structured process, where appeals could only be preferred in extraordinary cases and cannot be utilized to extend litigation (Donaldson, 2005).[179] The 'Draft Final Act Embodying the Results of the Uruguay Round of Multilateral Trade Negotiations' addressed dispute settlement, and in particular draft Article 15 of Section S dealt with appellate review.[180] The remit of subcommittees established at the time of adoption of the DSU and the WTO Agreement included addressing issues related to the Appellate Body.[181] The dispute settlement system of the WTO was strengthened through the establishment of the Appellate Body, whose membership does not change with each case. In sum, the Appellate Body remains the legacy of the Uruguay Round and has contributed enormously to the stability and functionality of the WTO.

The DSU, which was created during the Uruguay Round, is a part of the grand bargain, through which it was agreed by the contracting Member States that (i) the GATT would be replaced by the WTO, (ii) the jurisdiction of the WTO would extend beyond trade in goods, (iii) Member States would reject the unilateral enforcement of their rights, and (iv) the dispute settlement system would be reformed to include an appellate review, making it more efficient and more consistent in its rulings (VanGrasstek, 2013). The prior objectives are incorporated under Articles 17 to 23 of the DSU, which not only establish the Appellate Body, but also the so-called negative consensus rule for the adoption of panel and Appellate Body reports. Importantly, the provisions authorise retaliation, which makes it impossible for the respondent to block a decision handed down by a Panel or the Appellate

Body. With the creation of the Appellate Body, the WTO became the first international organisation to introduce a binding appellate process within its dispute settlement system.

6.4.2 Appellate Body: Nature and Composition

Pursuant to Article 17.6 of the DSU, the Appellate Body is vested with the authority to review "issues of law covered in the panel report and legal interpretations developed by the panel".[182]

The provision for an appellate review, contained in Article 17 of the DSU, deals with the structure, function, and procedure of the Appellate Body.[183] Article 17 provides for a standing Appellate Body, as opposed to the *ad hoc* nature of the Panel's composition. This aspect is well captured in Article 17.1, which reads as follows:

> A standing Appellate Body shall be established by the DSB. The Appellate Body shall hear appeals from panel cases. It shall be composed of seven persons, three of whom shall serve on any one case. Persons serving on the Appellate Body shall serve in rotation. Such rotation shall be determined in the *Working Procedures* of the Appellate Body.

Article 17.4 of the DSU identifies the parties that may appeal are identifies as follows:

> Only parties to the dispute, not third parties, may appeal a panel report. Third parties which have notified the DSB of a substantial interest in the matter pursuant to paragraph 2 of Article 10 may make written submissions to, and be given an opportunity to be heard by, the Appellate Body.

Under the provision, the parties to the disputes (excluding third party participants) have the opportunity to appeal against a panel report before the Appellate Body. The other provisions, besides Article 17 that deals with appeals, are Articles 1, 3, 16.4, 18, and 19 of the DSU. Pursuant to Article 17, the Appellate Body is entitled to adopt its own *Working Procedures* for Appellate Review in consultation with the chairperson of the DSB and the director-general of the WTO. Drafted by the seven original Appellate Body members, the *Working Procedures* came into force in February 1996 and has been used on a number of occasions.[184] While Article 17.6 of the DSU vests the Appellate Body to review "issues of law covered in the panel report and legal interpretations developed by the panel", Article 17.13 further empowers the Appellate Body to "uphold, modify or reverse the legal findings and conclusions" of a Panel under challenge.

Under Article 17.1 of the DSU, a standing Appellate Body is to be established by the DSB, composed of seven judges, or 'Members' of the Appellate Body.[185] Unlike the Panels, which are *ad hoc*, the Appellate Body is permanent and is likened to that of an international tribunal, with a clear set of rules for conducting its affairs. The requisite qualifications for a member of the Appellate Body are outlined in Article 17.3 as follows:

> The Appellate Body shall comprise persons of recognized authority, with demonstrated expertise in law, international trade and the subject-matter of the covered agreements generally. They shall be unaffiliated with any government.

"Demonstrated expertise in law" in a member of the Appellate Body has been identified as the ability to resolve "issues of law covered in the panel report and legal interpretations developed by the panel".[186]

Recognising the requirement of a balance in the representation of the membership of the WTO, Article 17.3 stipulates that the membership of the Appellate body "shall be broadly representative" of the membership in the WTO. The DSB in 1995 noted, "factors such as different geographical areas, levels of development, and legal systems shall be duly taken into account"[187] while making any appointments. The DSB appoints Appellate Body members by consensus,[188] for a term of four years in office, which can be extended for a further term.[189] The appointment of Members are staggered to ensure that not all Members commence and complete their terms at the same time,[190] which also ensures that there is a mix of both experienced and newer Members in the Appellate Body. While Article 17.3 requires that Appellate Body members are not affiliated with any government, the 'Duties and Responsibilities' laid out under *Working Procedures* require that Members shall neither accept any employment nor pursue any professional activity that is inconsistent with their duties and responsibilities.[191]

The Rules also state that a Member shall exercise their office without accepting or seeking instructions from any international, governmental, or non-governmental organisation or from private sources.[192] In this regard, the *Rules of Conduct*, which applies to the settlement of disputes before the DSB, provides that Appellate Body members "shall be independent and impartial, shall avoid direct or indirect conflicts of interest and shall respect the confidentiality of proceedings".[193] The provision clearly sets the bar high by stating that the individual who occupies the position is totally independent and unbiased. Under the *Rules of Conduct*, Members are to disclose any interest that could likely affect or give rise to any doubts about the Member's independence and impartial nature.[194] The Member States of the WTO are invited to nominate individuals to serve on the Appellate Body, which will be considered by the DSB for appointment.[195] The procedure for appointment of Members begins with the selection committee at the DSB putting forward its recommendations at a meeting of the DSB, which the Member States then agree through consensus.

During the Uruguay Round of negotiations, it was felt that it would be sensible to require Appellate Body members to serve on a part-time basis, as the workload contemplated was very small in comparison to the number of appeals preferred against panel decisions since the creation of the Appellate Body in 1995. The appeal process before the WTO has turned out to be much more complex than originally envisaged at the Uruguay Round of negotiations, and as a result requires the members of the Appellate Body to spend more time to go through voluminous paperwork.[196] As per Article 17.3 of the DSU, the Appellate Body members are required to be "available at all times and on short notice". The high volume of appeals, the short period for appealing against a Panel report, and with the DSB not having a say on the number of appeals that could be filed, the engagement of a member of the Appellate Body is anything but part-time (Hughes, 2009). As a result, there are calls from the Member States to consider a change in the status of appointment of Appellate Body members to full-time. A full-time appointment would allow for the Appellate Body members to devote more time to discussions on legal issues and prepare for complex legal matters (Hughes, 2009).[197] Since the creation of the WTO, the Appellate Body had always included a member from Europe and the US,[198] as well as from Egypt and Japan (Hughes, 2009). Barring complaints from the US of an anti-US sentiment on the part of the Appellate Body,[199] there had been no criticism of political bias against the Appellate Body (Hughes, 2009).

6.5 Appellate Review

6.5.1 Structure, Scope, and Timeframe

The chairperson of the Appellate Body is one of its Members, who is elected by the Appellate Body to serve for a term of one year.[200] The chairperson of the Appellate Body is responsible for the overall business, which includes supervisory functions and other responsibilities that may come to be entrusted to them.[201] The chairperson represents the Appellate Body in all communications with the representatives of other organs of the WTO.[202] As per Article 17.1 of the DSU, and Rule 6(1) of the *Working Procedures*, the Appellate Body hears and decides appeals in divisions, comprising three Members each, and does not sit as a full court to hear appeals.[203] The divisions of the Appellate Body are chosen on a rotational basis and at random regardless of the Member's nationality.[204] There had been calls for increasing the number of the Appellate Body membership on the grounds that the seven-member Appellate Body is small for the size of an international adjudication circle.[205] Some commentators hold the view that it is that small size of the membership which gives the Appellate Body its strength, and it is not to be considered a weakness, as it facilitates collegiality, besides free and frank exchange of views amongst the membership (Ehlermann, 2002).[206] The *Working Procedures*, in order to draw on the collective expertise of all members of the Appellate Body, require that the division responsible for deciding an appeal exchanges views with the other Members on the issues raised by the appeal.[207]

Although the decisions on the appeal are reached by consensus, in the event a decision cannot be reached by consensus, the *Working Procedures* provide for the matter at issue to be decided by majority vote.[208] Individual members of the Appellate Body, pursuant to Article 17.11 of the DSU, may express separate opinions in the report anonymously.[209] In the event a member of the Appellate Body is unable to continue to discharge their duties in a division, another Member chosen at random will replace them.[210] In terms of administrative support, the Appellate Body receives the most "appropriate administrative and legal support as it requires" from the Appellate Body Secretariat,[211] which is independent and is "administratively separate" from the WTO Secretariat.[212]

The appeal process before the DSB consists of various stages and can be broadly summarized as follows: (a) presentation of written arguments – consisting of the Notice(s) of Appeal and the written submissions of the participants to the appeal; (b) presentation of oral arguments of the participants to the appeal – presented at an oral hearing before a division of three Appellate Body members; and (c) discussions, deliberations, and drafting of the appeal decision by the Appellate Body (Donaldson, 2005). The timeframe for an appeal is normally set at 60 days, which begins from the day after a Notice of Appeal is lodged and concludes on the day the Appellate Body report is circulated to the Member States of the WTO, and not to exceed 90 days, in any event. The timeframe set under Article 17.5 of the DSU can be extended if "the Appellate Body considers that it cannot provide its report within 60 days". The Article, in such an event, also requires that the Appellate Body

> shall inform the DSB in writing of the reasons for the delay together with an estimate of the period within which it will submit its report. In no case shall the proceedings exceed 90 days.

However, in practice, the Appellate Body has in a majority of cases taken more than 60 days to complete the review process. The longest Appellate Body review proceedings to date have been those in *Russia – Commercial Vehicles*, which lasted for 395 days; *US – Large Civil Aircraft (2nd complaint)*, which lasted for 346 days; and *EC and Certain Member States – Large Civil Aircraft*, which lasted for 301 days.[213] The shortest Appellate Body review proceedings to date was in *India – Autos*, which lasted for 47 days. The average time taken for completing the appellate review stands at 125 days. As a result of the delays experienced, the Appellate Body had come under repeated criticism from the United States and Japan. That said, all Member States recognise that the heavy workload of the Appellate Body, and the increasing complexity of the issues raised, renders it impossible for the Appellate Body to meet the deadline prescribed under Article 17.5 for completing the appellate review.[214]

Under the *Working Procedures*, the Member States that participate in the appeals procedure are designated as 'appellants', 'other appellants', 'appellees', 'participants', or 'third participants' according to their role in the appeal.[215] Under the *Working Procedures* all Member States taking part in the Appellate Body proceedings are referred to as 'participants'. The particular participant that challenges the findings of a Panel report through the appeals process is called the 'appellant', and the participant responding to an appeal is called the 'appellee'. The participant that prefers a cross-appeal from the Panel findings is called an 'other appellant'. Those Member States choosing to participate in the appeal proceedings as interested third parties are referred to as 'third participants'.[216]

As mentioned earlier the scope of any appeal is restricted to those question of law, as provided for under Article 17.6 of the DSU. The Appellate Body in *EC – Hormones*, while making a distinction between factual and legal findings of panels, clearly held that factual findings were not the subject of appellate review, and observed as follows:

> Under Article 17.6 of the DSU, appellate review is limited to appeals on questions of law covered in a panel report and legal interpretations developed by the panel. Findings of fact, as distinguished from legal interpretations or legal conclusions, by a panel are, in principle, not subject to review by the Appellate Body.[217]

On the complex issue of distinguishing the findings of fact and law, and if and when they could be subjected to an appellate review, the Appellate Body further noted that findings that involved the application of a legal rule to a specific fact or a set of facts are findings on issues of law and would fall within the scope of appellate review and observed as follows:

> [t]he consistency or inconsistency of a given fact or set of facts with the requirements of a given treaty provision is . . . a legal characterization issue. It is a legal question.[218]

The findings in *EC – Hormones* had been relied on in several subsequent decisions, when similar questions arose for consideration.[219] Besides the 'questions of law', the Appellate Body also reviewed the treatment by the panel of the factual record, and certain of its findings of fact under Article 11 of the DSU, to determine if the panel had made an objective assessment of the facts before it.[220] In the same case the Appellate Body also held that a decision by the Panel to exclude evidence on the basis of non-relevancy is reviewable for error of law.[221] As a result, certain factual findings of a Panel's report could be subjected to appellate review, if and when the grounds of appeal allege that the findings were inconsistent with Article 11 of the DSU. The Appellate Body in *India – Patents (US)* held that a Panel's interpretation of a Member State's municipal law to determine whether that law conforms with the provisions of a required agreement is also reviewable.[222] In *Philippines – Distilled Spirits*, the Appellate Body ruled as follows:

> For a claim under Article 11 to succeed, the Appellate Body must be satisfied that the panel has exceeded its authority as initial trier of facts, which requires it to provide "reasoned and adequate explanations and coherent reasoning", base its finding on a sufficient evidentiary basis, and treat evidence with "even-handedness".[223]

Whereas in *EC – Fasteners (China)*, the Appellate Body ruled as follows:

> when alleging that a panel ignored a piece of evidence, the mere fact that a panel did not explicitly refer to that evidence in its reasoning is insufficient to support a claim of violation under Article 11. Rather, a participant must explain why such evidence is so material to its case that the panel's failure explicitly to address and rely upon the evidence has a bearing on the objectivity of the panel's factual assessment.[224]

The decision of the Appellate Body in *EC – Fasteners (China)* established that not all contraventions of Article 11 of the DSU are appealable. In *US – Steel Safeguards*, the Appellate Body noted that a challenge under Article 11 of the DSU is not be "made lightly, or merely as a subsidiary argument".[225] The Appellate Body in *EC and Certain Member States – Large Civil Aircraft*, observed as follows:

> we recognize that it is often difficult to distinguish clearly between issues that are purely legal or purely factual, or are mixed issues of law and fact. . . . An appellant may thus feel safer putting forward both a claim that the Panel erred in the application of the law to the facts and a claim that the panel failed to make an objective assessment of the facts under Article 11 of the DSU.[226]

It is also to be borne in mind that the threshold set at the appellate stage for a finding that a panel erred in its duty to make an objective assessment of the facts is much higher than the threshold for a finding that the panel erred in its application of the law to the facts.[227]

6.5.2 Review of New Issues, and Receipt of New Evidence and Arguments

As regards review of new issues at the appellate stage, the Appellate Body in *EC – Tube or Pipe Fittings* rejected the European Communities' argument that a particular issue was not properly before the Appellate Body, observing that the issue was identified during the Panel proceedings.[228] Likewise, in *US – Offset Act (Byrd Amendment)*, the question before the Appellate Body was if it had the authority to entertain and consider new facts at the appellate review stage. The Appellate Body, while holding that it did not have the authority, observed as follows:

> Article 17.6 is clear in limiting our jurisdiction to issues of law covered in panel reports and legal interpretations developed by panels. We have no authority to consider new facts on appeal. The fact that the documents are "available on the public record" does not excuse us from the limitations imposed by Article 17.6. We note that the other participants have not had an opportunity to comment on those documents and, in order to do so, may feel required to adduce yet more evidence. We would also be precluded from considering such evidence.[229]

In *US – Softwood Lumber V*, Canada requested that the United States be directed to submit certain documents to the Appellate Body for consideration. While declining the request to receive fresh evidence, the Appellate Body declined the request as it would constitute reception of new factual evidence and thus fell outside the scope of Article 17.6.[230]

In *Canada – Aircraft*, Brazil sought to introduce 'new arguments' at the appellate stage, which were not forwarded earlier before the Panel. The Appellate Body, while finding that it was beyond the scope of the appellate stage to adduce new arguments that were not presented before the Panel, observed as follows:

> In principle, new arguments are not *per se* excluded from the scope of appellate review, simply because they are new. However, for us to rule on Brazil's new argument, we would have to solicit, receive and review new facts that were not before the Panel, and were not considered by it. In our view, Article 17.6 of the DSU manifestly precludes us from engaging in any such enterprise.[231]

The Appellate Body in *US – FSC* declined to address a 'new argument' forwarded by the United States regarding double taxation under the last sentence of footnote 59 of the SCM Agreement, as it considered the new argument did not involve either an "issue of law covered in the panel report" or "legal interpretations developed by the panel".[232] Similarly, the Appellate Body in *EC – Export Subsidies on Sugar* held that ruling on the 'new argument' at issue would require soliciting, receiving, and reviewing new facts that were not available before the Panel.[233]

As mentioned earlier, all Panel reports were appealed in the first two years of the WTO dispute settlement system, with the exception of *Japan – Film*. As noted by Van den Bossche and Zdouc, the high rate of appeal is not down to the quality of the panel reports but more due to the fact that appealing an unfavourable panel report is a rational decision for a losing party to take; and that an appeal (whether successful or not) will allow the appellant, found to have acted inconsistently with WTO law, to delay the implementation of the panel decision appealed against (Van den Bossche and Zdouc, 2017).

6.5.3 Scope and Remit of the Appellate Review Process

As mentioned earlier, the Appellate Body under Article 17.13 of the DSU has the powers to "uphold, modify or reverse the legal findings and conclusions of the panel". However, the Appellate Body does not have the powers to remand a case back to the panel for fresh consideration (Petersmann, 1997). The Appellate Body, in the absence of a proper remand mechanism, has developed its own technique to complete the Panel's analysis in certain circumstances, *i.e.*, while dealing with appeals where the panel had failed to address a claim or had applied a different legal interpretation to the facts of the case, the Appellate Body had proceeded to reverse or modify the panel's legal interpretation (Yanovich and Voon, 2006).[234] Nevertheless, the Appellate Body, in a number of cases, has gone beyond the mandate of Article 17.13 and has "completed the legal analysis" of the Panel (Van den Bossche and Zdouc, 2017). Such a need may arise for the Appellate Body where the panel, in its exercise of judicial economy, had not addressed certain claims of inconsistency. In such instances, the Appellate Body may either leave the dispute unresolved or proceed to complete the legal analysis which the Panel had not carried out (Van den Bossche and Zdouc, 2017). The Appellate Body in *Canada – Periodicals* noted that it would be inconsiderate not to complete the legal analysis, and observed as follows:

> We believe the Appellate Body can, and should, complete the analysis of Article III:2 of the GATT 1994 in this case by examining the measure with reference to its consistency with the second sentence of Article III:2, provided that there is a sufficient basis in the Panel Report to allow us to do so.[235]

It should be borne in mind that it may not be possible for the Appellate Body to complete the legal analysis in all instances.[236] the Appellate Body will not complete the legal analysis if the completion is not necessary to resolve the dispute.[237] Also, the Appellate Body, in certain circumstances, may declare a panel's findings moot and of no legal consequence, rather than "upholding, modifying or reversing" the Panel's findings. For instance, the Appellate Body in *Brazil – Aircraft (Article 21.5 – Canada)* observed as follows:

> As Brazil has failed to prove one of the elements necessary to prove that payments made under the revised PROEX are justified by item (k), we do not believe it is necessary to examine the issue of whether export subsidies under the revised PROEX are "the payment [by governments] of all or part of the costs incurred by exporters or financial institutions in obtaining credits" within the meaning of the first paragraph of item (k). Therefore, we do not address the Article 21.5 Panel's findings on this issue. These findings of the Article 21.5 Panel are moot, and, thus, of no legal effect.[238]

In *US – Cotton Yarn*, one of the grounds of appeal by the United States was the Panel's interpretation that Article 6.4 of the Agreement on Textiles and Clothing required attribution to all Members the imports from whom cause serious damage or actual threat thereof. The Appellate Body on a proper consideration of the Article 17.13 held as follows:

> our findings resolve the dispute as defined by Pakistan's claims before the Panel. We, therefore, do not rule on the issue of whether Article 6.4 requires attribution to all Members the imports from whom cause serious damage or actual threat thereof. In these circumstances, the Panel's interpretation on this question is of no legal effect.[239]

7. Other Features of the WTO Dispute Settlement

7.1 Amicus Curiae *Briefs Before the Dispute Settlement*

The WTO's decision to entertainment *amicus curiae* briefs has been a controversial issue and has divided the opinion amongst the Member States and legal scholars alike. The practice of *amicus curiae* (friend of the court) was developed in the English law legal system, as an apparatus to be used in circumstances where it is felt that the parties to the dispute may not themselves be able to assist the court in resolving the dispute (Krislov, 1963).[240] The practice has entered the legal domain of dispute settlement before international bodies.[241] The nature of the WTO's dispute settlement mechanism is essentially an intergovernmental system. Nevertheless, the agreements of the WTO, unlike that of the GATT, commits the Member State to a host of agreements that extend deeply into the inner workings of the State, all under a single undertaking. The level of commitment that the WTO requires of its Member States affects an individual in all walks of life. Responding to the aforementioned, the NGOs have demanded increased access to the WTO's processes, including that of the dispute settlement system, and have requested the right to submit *amicus curiae* briefs before the Panels and Appellate Body (Marceau and Stilwell, 2001).

Under the WTO's dispute settlement system, Article 13 of the DSU regulates the panel's right to seek information. Article 13.1 of the DSU states, a "panel shall have the right to seek information and technical advice from any individual or body which it deems appropriate". Article 13.2, on the other hand, states, a panel "may seek information from any relevant source and may consult experts to obtain their opinion on certain aspects of the matter".

However, both the DSU and the *Working Procedures* are silent on the issue of unsolicited *amicus curiae* briefs, which remains a controversial issue. Unsolicited *amicus curiae* briefs have been submitted to panels in *US – Gasoline* but were not considered by the Panel, following practices from the GATT era.[242]

The turning point for reception of *amicus curiae* briefs came with the *US – Shrimp* case.[243] Two sets of *amicus curiae* briefs were forwarded by NGOs to the Panel,[244] on the premise that Article 13 DSU permitted for such submissions, which was rejected by the Panel on the ground that it was not 'sought', but allowed them to be attached to parties' submissions. The Panel was of the view that *amicus curiae* briefs could only be submitted at the Panel's own request and declared that "[a]ccepting non-requested information from nongovernmental sources would be, in our opinion, incompatible with the provisions of the DSU as currently applied".[245]

Although the Panel rejected the *amicus curiae* briefs, it permitted the parties to use any material presented in the *amicus curiae* briefs to support any of their own arguments in the case. The United States did make use of the opportunity to use three materials submitted by NGOs. On appeal, the Appellate Body overturned the Panel's ruling, and observed as follows:

> authority to seek information is not properly equated with a prohibition on accepting information which has been submitted without having been requested by a panel. A panel has the discretionary authority either to accept and consider or to reject information and advice submitted to it, whether requested by a panel or not.[246]

The Appellate Body also found:

> [t]he thrust of Articles 12 and 13, taken together, is that the DSU accords to a panel . . . ample and extensive authority to undertake and to control the process by which it informs itself both of the relevant facts of the dispute and of the legal norms and principles applicable to such facts.[247]

In *US – Shrimp* the Appellate Body concluded that Panels have the authority to accept and consider *amicus curiae* briefs. The Appellate Body also accepted the direct submission of an *amicus curiae* brief, which was an updated version of the material relied on by the United States before the Panel. Following the decision, the Appellate Body had considered a number of *amicus curiae* briefs and has since identified two different methods for the submission of the briefs.[248] The Appellate Body noted that an *amicus curiae* brief may be submitted either to a Panel or to the Appellate Body with the consent of a participating WTO Member State,[249] and that *amicus curiae* briefs may be submitted directly to a panel following Article 13.1 of the DSU, and likewise to the Appellate Body following Article 17.9 of the DSU.

The Appellate Body in *EC – Asbestos* established a set of procedures for reception of *amicus curiae* briefs.[250] It remains the discretion of the Panels and the Appellate Body whether to accept or reject an *amicus curiae* brief. Based on the ruling in *EC – Asbestos*, Panels have proceeded to accept and consider *amicus curiae* briefs. For instance, in *US – Tuna II (Mexico)*, the panel considered the information contained in the *amicus curiae* brief submitted by the *Humane Society International* and *American University's Washington College of Law*.[251] In several other disputes the Panels refused to either accept or consider *amicus curiae* briefs.[252]

While the Appellate Body did not offer a clear explanation of the legal basis for accepting any *amicus curiae* brief in the *US – Shrimp* case, it rectified this deficiency, to some degree, in *US – Lead and Bismuth II*. The Appellate Body in *US – Lead and Bismuth II* observed that nothing in the DSU or in the *Working Procedures* allowed or prohibited the acceptance and consideration of *amicus curiae* briefs. It held, however, that Article 17.9 of the DSU, which provided for the Appellate Body to draw up its own *Working Procedures*, reflected a "broad authority to adopt procedural rules which do not conflict with any rules and procedures in the DSU or the covered agreements",[253] thereby presenting the legal basis for accepting *amicus curiae* briefs. While recognising that non-Members of the WTO did not have a legal right to make submissions to or to be heard by the Appellate Body, or a legal duty on the part of the Appellate Body to accept or consider *amicus curiae* briefs from non-Members of the WTO, the Appellate Body concluded as follows:

> We are of the opinion that we have the legal authority under the DSU to accept and consider *amicus curiae* briefs in an appeal in which we find it pertinent and useful to do so. In this appeal, we have not found it necessary to take the two *amicus curiae* briefs filed into account in rendering our decision.[254]

The Appellate Body, following Article 17.9 of the DSU and Rule 16(1) of the *Working Procedures*, can at its discretion agree to accept *amicus curiae* briefs.[255] In *EC – Sardines*, the Appellate Body, while accepting a part of an *amicus curiae* brief submitted by the Government of Morocco, proceeded to reject an *amicus curiae* brief submitted by a private party as being unhelpful.[256]

The special meeting of the General Council held in November 2000 exposed the deep divisions amongst the WTO Member States opposing the ruling of the Appellate Body and the United States, which supported the ruling.[257] Because of the need to put in place a clear set of rules for the reception of *amicus curiae* briefs, further consultations were called for on the content of such rules. The chair of the General Council noted as follows:

> [I]n light of the views expressed and in the absence of clear rules, he believed that the Appellate Body should exercise extreme caution in future cases until Members had considered what rules were needed.[258]

Some Member States had argued that the issue of *amicus curiae* briefs is not procedural but substantive and, thus, an issue to be regulated by WTO Members alone, and that the Appellate Body has significant discretion to adopt procedural rules, but not substantive rules. This leaves us with the question of how properly to distinguish between procedural and substantive issues. Irrespective of classification of admission of *amicus curiae* briefs as procedural or substantive, the issue that remains to be resolved is who, if at all, is responsible for the creation of rules, if existing rules do not have suitable provisions to deal with the issue – WTO Member States or the Appellate Body? In this regard Chile was critical of the Appellate Body's decision in *EC – Sardines*, on the grounds that it was largely based on the premise that "anything that was not prohibited was permitted", and proceeded to put forward the argument that all WTO Agreements had been negotiated amongst the Member States, and that they were

> the result of compromises and represented a balance of rights and obligations which the parties had specifically laid down in the text. This was why it was not possible to read between the lines and necessarily impose new rights and obligations. They provided the system with certainty and predictability. In the final analysis, what should prevail was the principle that only what was allowed in the Agreements would be permitted.[259]

There is also the fear that lobbyists backed by developed Member States could use the apparatus of *amicus curiae* to further their case in disputes before the WTO's dispute settlement system. Developing country Member States have been critical of the Appellate Body for entertaining *amicus curiae* briefs. Their opposition is based on the premise that the WTO is an international agreement amongst the Member States, and it is outside the scope of its operations to permit entities who are not parties to the WTO agreement to influence adjudicative interpretations and the outcomes of any decisions taken. Around the time of the General Council meeting, their main reasons for opposing the *amicus curiae* briefs were that such practices would bend the dispute settlement proceedings heavily in favour of Member States with more legal resources; and that the *amicus curiae* briefs could be exploited by well-funded NGOs – who were opposed to the policies of developing country Member States – and could influence the outcome of disputes.

Contrary to beliefs held by some Member States, *amicus curiae* briefs have not flooded the WTO dispute settlement system.[260] Some commentators have even argued that not all *amicus curiae* briefs that are received are considered in the deliberation and decision-making of the WTO Panels and Appellate Body, raising the question of whether to consider an *amicus curiae* brief is shaped by the dispute settlement system's political and legal constraints (Squatrito, 2018). Developing country Member States, such as India and the African Groups, advocate prohibiting *amicus curiae* briefs, while developed country Member States, such as the EU, the US, *etc.*, are for the continued reception of *amicus curiae* briefs.

7.2 Other Entities of the Dispute Settlement

There are a number of bodies and entities involved in the WTO that are available for Member States to resolve trade disputes, other than the Panels and the Appellate Body. These could be identified as follows:

1. The chair of the DSB;
2. The WTO director-general;
3. Arbitrators under Articles 21.3, 22.6, and 25 of the DSU;
4. Experts under Articles 13.1 and 13.2 of the DSU;
5. Expert Review Groups under Article 13.2 and Appendix 4 to the DSU;
6. Technical Expert Groups under Article 14.3 of and Annex 2 to the TBT Agreement;
7. The Permanent Group of Experts under Article 4.5 of the SCM Agreement; and
8. The Facilitator under Annex V.4 to the SCM Agreement.

The arbitrators, experts, and expert groups, which directly participate in panel or Appellate Body proceedings, are subject to para. IV(1) of the *Rules of Conduct*.

8. Implementation and Compliance Review

Unlike domestic laws, most international bodies rely more upon extralegal sanctions for compliance, as they lack a central authority to enforce their decisions. Treaty-based international dispute settlement bodies seldom have the enforcing mechanism, and even in instances where such enabling provisions are found in the treaty, the decision to avail them is based more on political economy. Of all the multilateral treaty regimes, the WTO's implementation and enforcement mechanism is unprecedented, as it is founded on the most detailed rules-based system. In effect, through the DSB, the WTO seeks to establish a 'delicate middle ground' in the dispute settlement mechanism between criminalizing the conduct of Member States and permitting a Member State to violate any Agreement at liberty (Shoyer, Solovy, and Koff, 2005). Although the contracting parties to the GATT 1947 had the competence to pursue enforcement of rulings handed down by the Panels, it was used very sparingly (Davey, 1987). During the GATT era, the US frequently used 'Section 301' of its Trade Act 1974 to enforce any GATT rulings. Article 22 of the DSU was introduced as an integral part of the dispute settlement mechanism and as an effective enforcement mechanism.[261] As one commentator notes, when a panel under the DSB delivers "a ruling adverse to a member, there is no prospect of incarceration, injunctive relief, damages for harm inflicted or police enforcement. . . . Rather, the WTO . . . relies upon voluntary compliance" (Bello, 1996).

It is extremely difficult for a Member State to be excused for its non-compliance with a ruling adopted and published by the WTO, especially in an international legal system where the observance of the law heavily depends on extralegal pressures (Shoyer, Solovy, and Koff, 2005). Pursuant to Article 17.14, a report when adopted becomes a binding decision and is to be accepted unconditionally by the parties to the dispute. Prompt compliance of any recommendations or ruling of the DSB ensures "effective resolution of disputes to the benefit of all Members".[262] The final stage before the DSB is the implementation and enforcement of recommendations and rulings of the panel and/or the Appellate Body. Under all circumstances, prompt compliance is highly desirable, as it brings a closure to the dispute. The Member State concerned must inform the DSB of its intentions to promptly bring its measures into compliance with its WTO obligations, through the adoption of the panel and/or Appellate Body report.[263] In the scheme envisaged under the WTO's DSB, no compensation is payable for the economic consequences for the 'contravention' of the WTO Agreement,[264] but it is left to be worked out by the parties bilaterally, or through arbitration.

8.1 'Extension' Under Article 21.3 DSU

While Article 21.1 of the DSU requires prompt compliance of the recommendations and rulings of the DSB,[265] Article 21.4 of the DSB sets the maximum period for implementation as 15 months, and a period not exceeding 18 months in exceptional circumstances.[266] In the event, if it becomes 'impracticable' for a Member State to comply with the recommendations and rulings of the DSB immediately – which may often be the case – the Member State concerned may, pursuant to Article 21.3 of the DSU, seek an extension of a 'reasonable period' of time to comply with the rulings and recommendations.[267] In *US – Zeroing (Japan) (Article 21.5 – Japan)*, the Appellate Body held that while the requirement was immediate compliance, Article 21.3 countenanced the Member State concerned being given a reasonable period of time to comply, and noted as follows:

> An important consideration is that the reasonable period of time is not determined by the implementing Member itself. Instead, the reasonable period of time may be proposed by the implementing Member and approved by the DSB, mutually agreed by the parties, or determined through binding arbitration. This confirms that the reasonable period of time is a limited exemption from the obligation to comply immediately.[268]

In *EC – Hormones (Article 21.3(c)) (Arbitration)*, reasonable period of time was described as the "shortest period possible within the legal system of the (implementing) Member".[269] In a majority of cases, the parties to the dispute agree on the length of the 'reasonable period of time', ranging anywhere between four months and 24 months (Van den Bossche and Zdouc, 2017). Although parties reach agreement within a reasonable period, there are instances where such an agreement is not reached. Article 21.3(c) of the DSU permits the original complainant to refer the matter to arbitration, in the event the parties are not able to reach any agreement within 90 days of the adoption of the recommendations and rulings. Where the parties are not able to agree on an arbitrator within ten days, the director-general of the WTO shall appoint an arbitrator after consulting the parties.[270] The arbitrator to be appointed could be either an individual or a group,[271] and going by the practice prevailing at the DSB, the arbitrator is normally a serving or former member of the Appellate Body.

The remit of arbitration under Article 21.3(c) is the determination of (i) the 'reasonable period of time' for the implementation of the report and recommendations from the date of adoption of the Panel or Appellate Body report, and (ii) when the report and recommendations are to be implemented, and not how they are to be implemented.[272] The guideline envisaged under Article 21.3(c) is that the time to implement the report and recommendations should not exceed 15 months from the date of adoption of a Panel or Appellate Body report.[273] In *EC – Hormones*, the Arbitrator viewed the 15-month period as "a guideline for the arbitrator, and not a rule", and that the 15-month period as "the outer limit in the usual case".[274] The Arbitrator also noted that his mandate was to determine the 'reasonable period of time' within which to complete the implementation, and not to suggesting means of implementation.[275] Similarly, the Arbitrator in *EC – Chicken Cuts (Article 21.3(c))* stressed that his mandate was limited to determining the reasonable period of time and that their task was therefore focused on the 'when' and not the 'what'.[276] However, recent jurisprudence recognises that the remit of the Arbitrator also includes considering the modalities of possible implementation in determining a 'reasonable period of time'.[277]

The Arbitration under 21.3(c) consider several factors to determine the 'reasonable period of time', such as (i) whether compliance will require legislative procedures as opposed to administrative means, as recourse to the former would require more length of time,[278] and (ii) whether new statutes will be required, or a repeal of an existing statute will suffice for the implementation of the reward and recommendations.[279] If the Member State concerned is a developing country, the Arbitrator, pursuant to Article 21.2, will consider granting a longer 'reasonable period of time' for the implementation,[280] and if both parties to the dispute are developing countries, then the said status may not be accounted for.[281] The arbitration award from the Article 21.3(c) proceedings is not adopted by the DSB but posted on the WTO's website. The DSB, following from Article 21.6 of the DSU, is to "keep under surveillance the implementation of adopted recommendations or rulings",[282] and any Member State may raise the issue of improper implementation before the DSB at any point in time.[283] If there are disagreements on the issue of compliance, the dispute will, pursuant to Article 21.5, be referred to the compliance Panel.

> Where there is disagreement as to the existence or consistency with a covered agreement of measures taken to comply with the recommendations and rulings such dispute shall be decided through recourse to these dispute settlement procedures, including wherever possible resort to the original panel.[284]

8.2 Compliance Review Under Article 21.5 DSU

Where in the course of adopting the recommendations of the Panel modifications carried out by the respondent Member State do not meet the expectations of the complaining Member State, Article 21.5 envisages recourse to the compliance panel. Article 21.5 of the DSU seeks to eliminate unilateral determination if the Member State concerned conformed to the

DSB's ruling, by providing for an ongoing multilateral control. The relevant part of Article 21.5 reads as follows:

> Where there is disagreement as to the existence or consistency with a covered agreement of measures taken to comply with the recommendations and rulings such dispute shall be decided through recourse to these dispute settlement procedures, including wherever possible resort to the original panel.

Article 23 DSU outlines the rationale for the establishment of a compliance mechanism, as the mitigation of any trade disputes through initiating procedures laid down under Article 21.5 of the DSU. Importantly, there is no limit to the number of times a Member State could seek recourse under Article 21.5 to determine if the respondent Member State had complied with the rulings and recommendations of the Panel. The mandate of the compliance Panel was addressed by the Appellate Body in *Canada – Aircraft (Article 21.5 – Brazil)*, where the measures taken by Canada constituted 'compliance' for the purposes of Article 21.1 of the DSU was in question. The Appellate Body disagreed with the Panel's reasoning that the scope of Article 21.5 was limited to the issue of whether the respondent Member State had implemented the recommendations of the DSB, and went on to observe as follows:

> [I]n carrying out its review under Article 21.5 of the DSU, a panel is not confined to examining the "measures taken to comply" from the perspective of the claims, arguments and factual circumstances that related to the measure that was the subject of the original proceedings. . . . Article 21.5 proceedings involve, in principle, not the original measure, but rather a new and different measure which was not before the original panel. In addition, the relevant facts bearing upon the "measure taken to comply" may be different from the relevant facts relating to the measure at issue in the original proceedings. . . . Indeed, the utility of the review envisaged under Article 21.5 of the DSU would be seriously undermined if a panel were restricted to examining the new measure from the perspective of the claims, arguments and factual circumstances that related to the original measure, because an Article 21.5 panel would then be unable to examine fully the "consistency with a covered agreement of the measures taken to comply", as required by Article 21.5 of the DSU.[285]

The Appellate Body in *US – Softwood Lumber IV (Article 21.5 – Canada)*, while noting the three key differences between the function and scope of Article 21.5 and the regular Panel proceedings, observed that Article 21.5 proceedings "should not allow circumvention by Members by allowing them to comply through one measure, while, at the same time, negating compliance through another".[286] The Panel in *US – Softwood Lumber VI (Article 21.5 – Canada)* noted that the role of a Panel in a proceedings brought under Article 21.5 was to evaluate the challenged measure to determine its consistency with the respondent Member's obligations under the relevant WTO agreements.[287] The Appellate Body in *EC – Bed Linen (Article 21.5 – India)* observed as follows:

> new claims, arguments, and factual circumstances different from those raised in the original proceedings [may be raised], because a "measure taken to comply" may be inconsistent with WTO obligations in ways different from the original measure . . . [A]n Article 21.5 panel could not properly carry out its mandate to assess whether a "measure taken to comply" is fully consistent with WTO obligations if it were precluded from examining claims additional to, and different from, the claims raised in the original proceedings.[288]

In *US – Gambling (Article 21.5 – Antigua and Barbuda)*, the United States sought to re-examine before the 'compliance' panel the WTO consistency of its original measure "based on new evidence and arguments not previously available to the Panel or the Appellate Body". The Panel declining the request noted that a complainant cannot use a compliance Panel to renew or expand its challenge to the original measure and made clear that the respondent's original defence cannot be relitigated in an Article 21.5 proceeding on the basis of new arguments or evidence.[289] It is worth noting that Article 21.5 'compliance' panel and Appellate Body reports become legally binding on the parties after adoption by the DSB, and are adopted by the DSB by reverse consensus within 30 days after circulation.

8.3 Remedies Under Article 22 DSU

Article 22.1 of the DSU envisages a 'temporary option' where the Member State fails to comply with the recommendations and rulings of the DSB, through a mutually agreed compensation scheme, or the suspension of concessions, or other obligations by the complaining Member State and the defending Member State. In other words, when the losing Member State is not able to agree on a 'mutually agreed solution', the successful Member State could resort to the next measure, *viz.*, seek "authorization from the DSB to suspend the application to the Member concerned of concessions or other obligations under the covered agreements".[290] It is noted that the compensation envisaged here is voluntary and transitional, and the suspension of concessions is a more temporary enforcement measure rebalance the pre-existing balance of rights and obligations.[291] The suspension of concessions – referred to as 'retaliation', draws more attention, as they are imposed unilaterally in line with international standards and with a view to bring about closure of the dispute. Both remedies envisaged under Article 22.1 are far less than what the complaining Member State would have sought for in the complaint, *i.e.*, the complete performance of the commitments undertaken under the WTO Agreement in question. Articles 22 and 23 of the DSU require prior authorisation by the DSB of any suspension of concessions, or other obligations. However, the level of suspension imposed must be equivalent to the nullification or impairment suffered as a result of non-compliance with DSB recommendations or rulings,[292] and such suspensions are temporary and are to be stopped when the measures in question are removed (Alvarez-Jiménez, 2011).[293]

Retaliatory measures result in increasing the duties for certain goods that originate from the non-complying Member State. Importantly, countermeasures taken are to be in the same trade sector of the covered agreement. Nonetheless, the DSB *may* authorise any countermeasures across trade sectors, or under another agreement, if the Member State seeking such authorisation is able to meet the requirements and conditions set out in Article 22.3 for cross-retaliations are met.[294] If in the event the concerned party objects to any countermeasures, the matter will be referred to an Arbitrator[295] to decide on the appropriate level of countermeasures to be imposed. However, only in a handful cases had Member States requested authorization to retaliate pursuant to Article 22.2 of the DSU.[296] However, it is to be noted that Parties to the dispute also cross-retaliate in certain instances. If action under Article 22.3(a) is found impracticable, the suspension contemplated can be imposed on a different sector but covered by the same agreement.[297] In *EC – Bananas III (Ecuador) (Article 22.6 – EC)*, the Arbitrators held that the term 'practicable' connoted 'availability' and 'sustainability', and observed as follows:

> the thrust of this criterion empowers the party seeking suspension to ensure that the impact of that suspension is strong and has the desired result, namely to induce

compliance by the Member which fails to bring WTO-inconsistent measures into compliance with DSB rulings within a reasonable period of time.[298]

When such action under Article 22.3(b) is ineffective, the complaining Member State may seek to enforce the suspended concessions under another agreement (Spadano, 2008; Abbott, 2009).[299] Article 22.3(d) identifies two issues to consider while seeking to suspend concessions, *viz.*, the trade in the sector or under the agreement under which nullification or impairment has been occasioned, and the broader economic consequences of the suspensions of concessions. In this regard, the Arbitrator on *US – Gambling (Article 22.6 – US)* observed as follows:

> The determination, which relates to "circumstances", is of necessity an assessment to be made on a case-by-case basis, and that the circumstances that are relevant may vary from case to case. We note however, that these circumstances should be serious "enough", which suggests that it is only when the circumstances reach a certain degree or level of importance, that they can be considered to be serious enough.[300]

9. Developing Countries and the WTO Dispute Settlement

The WTO's 'rules-based' dispute settlement system is hailed as the most advanced of its kind in comparison to other international institutions. While it is widely understood that the WTO's dispute settlement mechanism facilitates the enforcement of previously negotiated trade concessions, the Member States – in particular developing country Member States – do not effectively utilise the facility (Evans and Shaffer, 2010). This position has changed in the past over a decade, as some of the key developing country Member States have increasingly used the WTO's dispute settlement mechanism. The Sutherland Report from 2004 noted as follows:

> Of course, the major trading powers continue to act either as complainant or respondent in a very large number of cases. Given their large amount of trade with an even greater number of markets, it could hardly be otherwise. Yet, developing countries – even some of the poorest (when given the legal assistance now available to them) – are increasingly taking on the most powerful. That is how it should be.[301]

Member States of the WTO are broadly classified as 'developed countries', 'developing countries', and 'least developed countries'. While there is no clear definition available under the WTO laws regarding classification,[302] it is widely used in WTO legal texts and in the various documentations of the WTO.[303] Member States of the WTO self-declare as one or the other, depending on their economic and socio-economic conditions and from a more strategic perspective. Bohanes and Garza note that the analysis of developing country participation in the WTO dispute settlement presents a "fascinating kaleidoscope" of factors, and also a deep-seated concern regarding "effective access" to justice for all WTO Member States (Bohanes and Garza, 2012).[304] Commentators also note that a lack of participation or utilisation of the WTO dispute settlement system is attributable to the lack of legal resources/capacity to engage in a highly complex legal battle (Busch, Reinhardt, and Shaffer, 2008).[305] But within WTO's membership there are states classified as 'developing' who are fully capable of defending their interests, such as Brazil, China, and India, as they have relatively high aggregate trading stakes in the system (Shaffer, 2009).[306]

Developing country Member States have in some instances used the WTO dispute settlement system to bring cases against developed country Member States and met with success,[307] but that is not to say it happens frequently. In a few instances, developing country Member States have brought complaints against other developing country Member States,[308] but worryingly, there had been no complaints brought forward from an African country Member State before the DSB so far.[309] The first least developed country Member State to use the WTO dispute settlement system was Bangladesh, against India.[310] In sharp contrast, the US and the EU between them have been complainants in over 41 percent of all the complaints brought before the DSB. This brings us to the question of whether the WTO has taken steps to make the dispute settlement mechanism more accessible to developing countries and least developed countries.

9.1 Special and Differential Treatment

Recognising the difficulties faced by developing country and least developed country Member States, the DSU encourages the WTO Member States to accord special treatment to them at each stage of the dispute settlement proceedings. Article 24.1 of the DSU requires Member States to "exercise due restraint" where the disputes involve a least developed country Member State.[311] For developing country Member States, the DSU provides for a more flexible timeframe, besides also providing the use of an accelerated procedure designed for their needs that overrides DSU rules. It will also be noted that Appendix 2 of the DSU lists a number of special and additional rules and procedures to be found in covered agreements.

9.2 Special Rules for Developing Country Member States

Pursuant to Article 4.10 of the DSU, if the issue raised at the consultations concerns the interests of a developing country Member State, the parties may agree to extend the consultations period.[312] In the event the parties are unable to arrive at a solution during such extended period, the chairperson of the DSB is authorised to extend the consultation phase further.[313] At the Panel stage, if one of the parties to the complaint is a developing country Member State, the Panel upon request by the developing country Member State will include one panellist from a developing country Member State.[314] If the respondent to the proceedings is a developing country Member State, the Panel is required to accord sufficient time to formulate and present its arguments, without disrupting the overall time period allowed for the panel proceedings.[315] Where developing country Member States request the special and differential treatment, the Panel report shall clearly state how such provisions are considered.[316] Pursuant to Article 21.2 of the DSU, it is essential that particular attention is paid to matters affecting the interests of developing country Member States at the implementation stage. Article 21.2 had been applied in arbitration proceedings arising under Article 21.3(c) of the DSU, to determine the reasonable period of time needed to implement the rulings and recommendations from the reports.[317]

The arbitrator in *Indonesia – Autos (Article 21.3(c))* took into account both Indonesia's status as a developing country and its then prevailing economic conditions while determining the 'reasonable period of time' under Article 21.3(c) of the DSU. The arbitrator noted that it was a developing country which was in a "dire economic and financial situation", and that as a result would give the 'full weight' to the mandate of Article 21.2 of the DSU.[318] Similarly, the arbitrator in *Chile – Alcoholic Beverages (Article 21.3(c))* observed that Article 21.2 "usefully enjoins, *inter alia*, an arbitrator functioning under Article 21.3(c) to be generally mindful of the great difficulties that a developing country Member may, in a particular case, face as it proceeds to implement the recommendations and rulings of the DSB".[319] Furthermore, the DSB is to consider what further action it might take that would be more appropriate for the circumstances of the case.[320] Pursuant to Article 21.8, the DSB is required to consider not only the trade coverage of the measure under challenge, but also its impact on the economy of the developing country Member State in question.[321]

9.3 Special Rules, Decision of 5 April 1966

Under the Decision of 5 April 1966, the director-general is authorised to use his good offices to conduct consultations upon the request of the developing country Member State, with a view to facilitating a solution to the dispute. In the event no amicable solution is identified within two months, the director-general, on the request of one of the parties, will submit a report of his action, paving the way for the DSB to establish a panel with the approval of the parties. Article 3.12 of the DSU permits a developing country Member State that brings a complaint against a developed country Member State to invoke the accelerated provisions of the Decision of 5 April 1966 of the GATT. The right contained in Article 3.12 is discretionary, and an alternative to the provisions contained in Articles 4, 5, 6, and 12 of the DSU. Article 3.12 was first invoked in March 2007, when Colombia brought a complaint against the EC's introduction of new 'tariff-only' regime for bananas, where the good offices of the director-general assisted the parties to read a mutually agreed solution to settle the dispute.[322] The rare use of the accelerated procedure by developing country Member States could be down to the increasing complexity of subject matter in dispute and also the judicialisation of the dispute settlement system (WTO, 2017).

9.4 Special Rules for Least Developed Country Member States

While the special and differential treatment provisions discussed previously extend to least developed country members, the DSU has established additional rules applicable exclusively to such members. Article 24 of the DSU, which deals with special procedures involving least developed country Member States, states that in a dispute where a least developed country member is involved, "particular consideration shall be given to the special situation" of that Member State.[323] Member States are to exercise due restraint while raising complaints against a least developed country Member State, while seeking compensation for any nullification or impairment, and while seeking authorisation to suspend the application of concessions.[324] As mentioned earlier, the participation of least developed countries had been absent, barring an instance where Bangladesh brought forward a complaint which was resolved at the consultations stage. In *US – Upland Cotton*, Benin and Chad (two least developed countries) participated as third parties, which factor was noted by the Panel and particular consideration was given to the two countries in accordance with Article 24.1 of the DSU.[325] In disputes involving least developed country Member States, where consultations had not be fruitful, the director-general (or the chairperson) of the DSB on request by one of the parties shall offer their good offices, conciliation, and mediation to facilitate the settlement of the dispute before establishment of a Panel.[326]

9.5 Legal Assistance for Developing Country Member States

This section is focused on the legal assistance available to developing country Member States.

Regardless of the status of a Member State, the WTO Secretariat provides assistance to all members, in respect of dispute settlement, and also such additional legal advice and assistance to developing country Member States. The assistance from the Secretariat is aimed at developing country Member States, as they in most cases do not have the specialised legal expertise to participate in the WTO dispute settlement procedures –as both complainant and respondent. The Secretariat, upon request, makes available a qualified legal expert from the WTO technical cooperation services to such a Member State to help them fully participate in any proceedings, but yet with continued impartiality of the Secretariat.[327] In this regard, the Appellate Body *EC – Bananas III* observed as follows:

> that representation by counsel of a government's own choice may well be a matter of particular significance – especially for developing-country Members – to enable them to participate fully in dispute settlement proceedings.[328]

Legal assistance for developing country Member States is given by the Geneva-based Advisory Centre on WTO Law (ACWL). The ACWL is an intergovernmental organisation, which is independent of the WTO and functions essentially as a law firm specialising in WTO law, besides providing training courses and seminars. Between 2001 to 2019, the ACWL provided support in almost 50 WTO dispute settlement proceedings. ACWL's legal services fall broadly under two categories, *viz.*, (i) providing assistance in WTO dispute settlement proceedings – which includes drafting and participating in oral pleadings, and (ii) providing assistance on matters not subject to dispute settlement proceedings, which is free of charge (WTO, 2017). In 2016, the director-general of the WTO, Robert Azevêdo, talking about the contribution of the ACWL, noted, "ACWL has already provided 2,100 legal opinions. The rate today is about 200 opinions per year. . . . it is an indispensable part of the multilateral system today, even though it is not in the WTO". The WTO Secretariat has also, since 1995, provided legal assistance to every developing country member that has sought such assistance, besides also conducting technical cooperation activities and special training courses on dispute settlement system.[329]

10. Summary

The DSB is indeed a unique mechanism of the WTO, which has come to be recognised as, if not the best, one of the best dispute settlement systems currently existing in international law for state-state commercial disputes. What started out an effort to address one of the downsides of the GATT – the lack of a coherent dispute settlement mechanism – evolved into a two-tier rules-based dispute settlement mechanism during the Uruguay Round of negotiations. It ranks as one of the greatest achievements of the Uruguay Round of negotiations, other than the expansion of the remit of the WTO to include trade in services and recognition of IP rights with the multilateral trading system. The DSB's contribution to the success of the WTO's work is unquestionable and to be lauded. Its approach of settling disputes as opposed to delivering judgements has helped in finding solutions to the disputes before it and has rendered the system more predictable and reliable.

The system, which is modelled partly on arbitration and partly on adjudication, has facilitated the jurisprudence of the WTO to develop swiftly. The time-bound nature of the process has provided assurance to the Member States, besides giving them the space to find solutions outside the DSB's procedures. Following any report, most Member States modify their practices that are found to be in violation of any WTO laws, and rulings are adopted and implemented without much delay. Although the DSB has been operational since 1995 and is rules based, we are yet to see Member States from the sub-Saharan African approach the DSB for any redressal. Barring the current impasse at the DSB, brought about by blocking of any new appointments to the Appellate Body membership, there have been no scandals.

Notes

1 The Anglo-Hanse dispute (fourteenth to seventeenth centuries), the Anglo-French trade wars (seventeenth to nineteenth centuries), and Anglo-Dutch rivalry for East India trade (seventeenth century), to name a few trade wars.
2 Article 2.3 of the UN Charter reads as follows: "All Members shall settle their international disputes by peaceful means in such a manner that international peace and security, and justice, are not endangered."
   Article 33.1, Chapter VI, of the UN Charter reads as follows: "The parties to any dispute, the continuance of which is likely to endanger the maintenance of international peace and security, shall, first of all, seek a solution by negotiation, enquiry, mediation, conciliation, arbitration, judicial settlement, resort to regional agencies or arrangements, or other peaceful means of their own choice."
3 Commentators have described the WTO dispute settlement system as the 'jewel in the crown' of the WTO, and some have described it as the 'backbone of the multilateral trading system'. See Bernauer, Elsig, and Pauwelyn (2012) and Moore (2000).
4 The average tariffs around the time were situated in a range between 20 and 30 percent. See WTO (2007).
5 The negotiations on the ITO were not as swift or fruitful as that of the GATT. Towards the end of 1947 it became apparent to the contracting parties that the ITO Charter could take more time to conclude. Although the GATT was to be attached to the ITO, the parties, nevertheless, decided to bring GATT into force, with the result that the parties started trading under the framework provided by the GATT. See Jackson (1998). See also chapter 1 for a discussion on the creation of the GATT.
6 Chapter VIII of the Havana Charter, entitled 'Settlement of Differences', provided for a detailed dispute settlement process, encapsulated in seven articles. Importantly, it included detailed provisions for consultation and arbitration (Article 93), reference to the Executive Board (Article 94), reference to the Conference (Article 95), and reference to the International Court of Justice for advisory opinion (Article 96).
7 Articles 92 to 97 of the Havana Charter contained similar provisions to Articles XXII and XXIII of the GATT, with the possibility of having recourse to the ICJ for an advisory opinion.
8 Article XXIX:

   (1) The contracting parties undertake to observe to the fullest extent of their executive authority the general principles of Chapters I to VI inclusive and of Chapter IX of the Havana Charter pending their acceptance of it in accordance with their constitutional procedures.
   (2) Part II of this Agreement shall be suspended on the day on which the Havana Charter enters into force.
   (3) If by September 30, 1949, the Havana Charter has not entered into force, the contracting parties shall meet before December 31, 1949, to agree whether this Agreement shall be amended, supplemented or maintained.

9 The author notes that to wait for the ITO to be formed and become operational would have been too costly, as there were fears that the tariff concessions agreed upon would come into public domain and traders would act upon them and disrupt the world trade.
10 The GATT negotiations were an extension of the ITO Preparatory Committee sessions, where the same representatives from various contracting parties attended with the same committee chairperson, Dana Wilgress of Canada. See Hudec (1990).
11 The first complaint to be lodged before the GATT was by The Netherlands against Cuba, with the question if the MFN obligation (Article I of the GATT) applied to consular taxes. Upon receipt of the complaint, the matter was referred to the chairperson, who ruled in the affirmative. See Palmeter and Mavroidis (2004).

12 Article XXII (2) reads as follows: "The CONTRACTING PARTIES may, at the request of a contracting party, consult with any contracting party or parties in respect of any matter for which it has not been possible to find a satisfactory solution through consultation under paragraph 1."
13 Article XXIII (1) reads as follows: "the contracting party may, with a view to satisfactory adjustment of the matter, make written representations or proposals to the other contracting party or parties which it considers to be concerned. Any contracting party thus approached shall give sympathetic consideration to the representations or proposals made to it."
   Article XXIII (2) reads as follows: *'If no satisfactory adjustment is effected between the contracting parties concerned within a reasonable time, or if the difficulty is of the type described in paragraph 1 (c) of this Article, the matter may be referred to the CONTRACTING PARTIES. The CONTRACTING PARTIES shall promptly investigate any matter so referred to them and shall make appropriate recommendations to the contracting parties which they consider to be concerned, or give a ruling on the matter, as appropriate.'*
14 Article XXIII (2) reads as follows: "The CONTRACTING PARTIES may consult with contracting parties, with the Economic and Social Council of the United Nations and with any appropriate inter-governmental organization in cases where they consider such consultation necessary."
15 Petersmann (1997) notes that in view of the detailed dispute settlement procedure contained in the Havana Charter and the temporary nature of the GATT 1947 for purposes of tariff negotiations, no detailed provisions for dispute settlement were envisaged. It is to be borne in mind that the original intention was for GATT to be placed within the institutional setting of the ITO.
16 In the history of the GATT, this provision was never made use of by the Contracting Parties.
17 Jackson notes that the phrase 'nullification or impairment' was unfortunately ambiguous, connoting a 'power' or 'negotiation' oriented approach to the dispute, and that it was neither sufficient nor necessary to find a 'breach of obligation' under this language, although later practice made doing so important. See Jackson (1998). See the early case of *Subsidy on Ammonium Sulphate*, 3 April 1950, GATT BISD (Vol II) at 188 (1952), where the phrase 'nullification or impairment' was interpreted to include actions by a Contracting Party which harmed the trade of another, and which 'could not reasonably have been anticipated' by the other at the time it negotiated for a concession. This led to the introduction of the concept of 'reasonable expectations'. See also *Duty on Sardines* case [31 October 1952, GATT BISD (1st Supp.) at 53 (1953)]. The aforementioned cases endorsed the view that the GATT should be construed to protect 'reasonable expectations' of the Contracting Parties.
18 Working parties, a common feature of the GATT/ITO negotiations, were introduced around 1955, at the behest of Director-General Eric Wyndham-White. Jackson argues that this practice ushered in a change in GATT dispute settlement with the approach shifting from a 'negotiating' atmosphere of multilateral diplomacy to that of a more 'arbitral' or 'judicial' procedure designed to impartially arrive at the truth. See Jackson (1998a).
19 For the first time, on 14 October 1952, a panel was composed to examine the complaints brought by Denmark and Norway against the *Family Allowances* system of Belgium. This panel was composed of representatives of six Contracting Parties, but excluding the states involved in the dispute. For the first time in GATT, neither the complainant nor the respondent was included in the body deciding the matter at issue.
20 Interestingly, the panellists under the GATT system were junior to middle-level trade diplomats, or retired trade diplomats with no prior legal training. They were clearly not experts in international trade law, or jurists of any kind, and were expected to take advice from the GATT legal Secretariat.
21 Commentators also note that the advantage the powerful countries (developed countries) enjoyed allowed them to avoid liability for the breach of any obligations through the threat of retaliation or withdrawal of concessions in other sectors. See Islam (2012).
22 For instance, the following reports were adopted by the GATT Contracting Parties: (i) The Decision of 5 April 1966 on Procedures under Article XXIII applying to disputes between developing and developed contracting parties (BISD 14S/18); (ii) The Understanding on Notification, Consultation, Dispute Settlement and Surveillance, adopted on 28 November 1979 (BISD 26S/210); (iii) The Decision on Dispute Settlement, contained in the Ministerial Declaration of 29 November 1982 (BISD 29S/13); and (iv) The Decision on Dispute Settlement of 30 November 1984 (BISD 31S/9).
23 See Panel Report, *Uruguayan Recourse to Article XXIII*, L/1923, adopted on 16 November 1962, 11S/95, 99–100.
24 *Ibid.*, para. 15.

25 Despite the aforementioned finding, the case failed to produce any significant reduction in the barriers for Uruguay. Also, the panel only issued a series of recommendations calling for the removal of only those GATT violations admitted by some of the respondents to the proceedings. See Babu (2012). Uruguay was to later on comment that the lesson to be drawn from the case was that GATT law did not protect developing countries. See Hudec (2011).
26 See Panel Report, *United States – Taxes on Petroleum and Certain Imported Substances*, adopted on 17 June 1987, L/617, GATT BISD (34S/136).
27 See The Decision of 12 April 1989 on *Improvements to the GATT Dispute Settlement Rules and Procedures* (BISD 36S/61;63) para. F(a).
28 *Ibid.*, para. F(b) and F(c). The 1989 improvements provided for standard terms of reference and for automatic appointment of panellists.
29 See The Understanding Regarding Notification, Consultation, Dispute Settlement and Surveillance (28 November 1979), GATT (BISD 26S/210; 212) para. 10 (request for panels to be dealt with "in accordance with standard practice", *i.e.*, by consensus decision-making).
30 The study group, named after its chairperson Fritz Leutwiler, produced a detailed report in 1985 entitled 'Trade Policies for a Better Future – Proposals for Action', which contained 15 key recommendations to improve the trading system.
31 It is to be noted that the respondents in such instances allowed for the disputes to proceed as they had a long-term systematic interest and knew that such use of veto could be counter-productive. See WTO (2004).
32 Hudec's study also demonstrated that between 1947 and 1992, panels were always established (with the exception of one), and the losing party in approximately 90 percent of the cases eventually accepted the results and conceded the adoption of an adverse panel report.
33 Analysing the available data from 1948 and 1989, Hudec concludes that the GATT dispute settlement system was "more responsive to the interests of the strong than to the interests of the weak . . . While the goal of every legal system is, or should be, to reduce the impact of power inequalities, legal systems never accomplish that goal overnight (nor, alas, completely)". See Hudec (1993).
34 A new set of provisions, *viz.*, 'Super 301' and 'Special 301', were introduced under the *Trade and Competitiveness Act 1988*.
35 The Marrakesh Agreement Establishing the World Trade Organization was signed by 124 nations during the final session of the Trade Negotiations Committee Ministerial level held at Marrakesh, Morocco, on 15 April 1994.
36 Four annexes are attached to the WTO Agreement, containing the substance of the organisation. Annex 1 has three subparts, forming the core. Annex 1A contains the 13 agreements covering goods. Annex 2 contains the DSU, Annex 3 contains the Trade Policy Review Mechanism, and Annex 4 contains the text of two plurilateral agreements, *viz.*, *Agreement on Trade in Civil Aircraft* and *Agreement on Government Procurement*. See also chapter 2.
37 General Agreement on Trade in Services 1994 (GATS).
38 Agreement on Trade-Related Investment Measures 1994 (TRIMS).
39 Agreement on Trade-Related Aspects of Intellectual Property Rights 1994 (TRIPS).
40 The international institute perceived here is one that supports the goal of a global 'market', which is aimed at increasing the welfare of the world's population. Accordingly, a market of such proportions can only work when it is founded on a strong institutional framework, which has been alluded to by leading economists such as Coase (1988) and Stiglitz (2002).
41 One of the points of discussion at the Uruguay Round of negotiations was whether a 'negotiation approach' towards dispute resolution would be superior to that of a 'rule-oriented, legalistic approach'. See Jackson (1997).
42 Footer notes that this practice of incorporating law and practice from an earlier treaty was not a novel method and was followed by the European Communities, where an *acquis communautaire* was used during each successive enlargement of the European Communities to ensure that new Member States accepted the original treaties and their political objectives, without reservation. See Footer (1997).
43 Pragmatists support non-binding methods of dispute resolution on the belief that such systems provide the best means of coping with power relationships between countries, and that a diplomatic approach to dispute resolution renders trade politically sustainable. See Shell (1995) for a discussion on the legalist's position *vis-à-vis* the regime management model, the efficient market model, and the trade stakeholders model.

44 In *EC – Bananas III* the Appellate Body held, "a Member has broad discretion in deciding whether to bring a case against another Member under the DSU" and "a Member is expected to be largely self-regulating in deciding whether any such action would be 'fruitful'". See Appellate Body Report, *EC – Bananas III*, para. 135.
45 The Appellate Body in *EC – Bananas III* observed, "[t]he language of Article XXIII:1 of the GATT 1994 and of Article 3.7 of the DSU suggests, furthermore, that a Member is expected to be largely self-regulating in deciding whether any such action would be 'fruitful'". See Appellate Body Report, *EC – Bananas III*, para. 135.
46 See Appellate Body Report, *Peru – Agricultural Products*, para. 5.18.
47 The body of case law developed on similar instances can be used, leading one to the inevitable question of if 'judicial precedence' plays a key role in the WTO's dispute settlement system.
48 Economists note that WTO is an 'incomplete contract', as the scheme presented does not clearly specify what is permitted of governments, but rather contains a few specific, unambiguous disciplines. See Hoekman and Kostecki (2009).
49 The General Council of the WTO is composed of representatives of all Member States of the WTO. Besides discharging the responsibility of the DSB, the General Council also discharges the responsibility of the Trade Policy Review Body (TPRB).
50 Following from the signing of the Montreal Rules 1989, panels are established automatically, unless there is a consensus to the contrary.
51 See Appellate Body Report, *US – Upland Cotton (Article 21.5 – Brazil)*, in para. 246, where the principle of 'prompt settlement of disputes' is referred to. See also Appellate Body Report, *US – Zeroing (Japan) (Article 21.5 – Japan)*, para. 122.
52 See Panel Report, *US – Section 301 Trade Act*, para. 7.75. See also Appellate Body Report, *US – Stainless Steel (Mexico)*, paras. 160–161.
53 See Panel Report, *US – Section 301 Trade Act*, para. 7.76.
54 See *US – Certain EC Products*, para. 111.
55 See Appellate Body Report, *Canada – Continued Suspension*, para. 371.
56 *Ibid.*
57 See Panel Report, *EC – Commercial Vessels*, paras. 7.196, 7.198, 7.200. Mavroidis notes that Article 23.2(a) eliminates the theoretical possibility of submitting trade-related matters to the ICJ completely. See Mavroidis (2007).
58 See Appellate Body Report, *US – Shrimp*, para. 101. See also Appellate Body Report, *India – Quantitative Restrictions*, paras. 84–88, 92, 95, 109.
59 See Panel Report *Mexico – Taxes on Soft Drinks*, paras. 40–57, where Mexico requested that the Panel decide, as a preliminary matter, to decline to exercise jurisdiction "in favour of an Arbitral Panel under Chapter Twenty of the North American Free Trade Agreement (NAFTA)", which was inconsistent with the dispute settlement under the DSB. See also Appellate Body Report, *Peru – Agricultural Products*, paras. 5.15–5.28 and 5.81–5.117; and *Argentina – Poultry Anti-Dumping Duties*, paras. 7.17–7.42.
60 This right is subject to the Member States fulfilling the conditions set out in Article XXIV:5(a)–(c).
61 This gives rise to issues of overlap of jurisdiction/norms in dispute settlement as between the tribunals of RTAs and the WTO, as to where a potential claim could be lodged. For a detailed discussion on overlapping jurisdictions, see Kwak and Marceau (2003); Chase, Yanovich, Crawford, and Ugaz (2013); and Marceau (2015).
62 See Appellate Body Report, *Guatemala – Cement I*, para. 66.
63 *Ibid.*, para. 64.
64 *Ibid.*, para. 65.
65 *Ibid.*
66 This presumption was developed under GATT jurisprudence. See Panel Report, *Uruguayan Recourse to Article XXIII*, L/1923–11S/95 (15 November 1962) (adopted on 16 November 1962) para. 15. The Panel, while considering the provisions on 'nullification or impairment', took the view that where measures applied by a contracting party were in conflict with the provisions of the GATT, a *prima facie* case of nullification or impairment had arisen.
67 See Appellate Body Reports, *EC – Bananas III (Article 21.5 – Ecuador II)*, and *EC – Bananas III*, footnote 400. See also Appellate Body Report, *US – Offset Act (Byrd Amendment)*, para. 300–4. For a contra view, see Davies (2010).

Note: In WTO jurisprudence, there had been no successful rebuttal of this presumption. See Appellate Body Report *EC – Bananas III*, paras. 252 and 253, endorsing the view expressed by the

Panel in *United States – Taxes on Petroleum and Certain Imported Substances* BISD 34S/136 (adopted 17 June 1987), para. 5.1.9.
68 See Appellate Body Report, *US – Wool Shirts and Blouses*, at pp. 334 and 335.
69 *Ibid.*
70 The US uses unilateral trade actions to defend their commercial interests by invoking section 301 of the Trade Act of 1974 (as amended), against alleged unfair trading practices of partner countries.
71 Article 26.1 of the DSU requires that the complainant "present a detailed justification in support of any complaint relating to a measure which does not conflict with the relevant covered agreement". Importantly, Article 26.1 also covers non-violation complaints other than those falling under the category of 'nullification or impairment of a benefit'.
72 The Panels in both *Japan – Film* and *EC – Asbestos* noted that a causal relationship was to be established by the complainant. See Panel Reports *Japan – Film*; *EC – Asbestos*. Commentators, on the other hand, have criticised the three conditions established for a successful non-violation complaint as being rather vague. See Matsushita, Shoenbaum, Mavroidis, and Hahn (2015).
73 See Cho (1998); Cottier and Schefer (1997); Kim (2006); Verhoosel (2002); Staiger and Sykes (2013).
74 See Panel Report *EC – Oilseeds I*, para. 144.
75 A total of 14 non-violation complaints were brought during the GATT era and were all based on the ground that a subsidy paid subsequent to a negotiated concession nullified the benefits accruing to it through the measures taken by the responded. In the WTO era fewer than ten non-violation complaints were lodged, but with no success. Importantly, all disputes with non-violation complaints also contained a violation complaint in them. See, for instance, Panel Report, *Korea – Procurement*; Appellate Body Reports, *US – Gasoline*; *US – Offset Act (Byrd Amendment)*; *China – Auto Parts*.
76 See Appellate Body Report, *EC – Asbestos*, para. 186.
77 The only exception being a request by the EC against Japan in 1982 for consultation on the '*Japanese Way of Life*' case. The efforts of the EC did not, however, result in the establishment of a panel.
78 The DSB has its own chairperson and its own set of rules and procedures from that of the General Council of the WTO.
79 It is now accepted by most commentators that the WTO Panels and Appellate Body are part of the family of international courts and tribunals.
80 See Appellate Body report, *US – Wool Shirts and Blouses*, p. 14. Here, the Appellate Body noted that WTO adjudication was another "system of judicial settlement alongside other international courts and tribunals such as the ICJ". See Panel reports, *US – DRAMS*; *China – Intellectual Property Rights*.
81 See Articles 3.3, 3.6, 3.7, and 4 of the DSU.
82 Mavroidis notes that few disputes are of a purely bilateral nature, and that other Member States may be interested in the interpretation of the rules and may wish to join in the legal action. See Mavroidis (2007).
83 Appellate Body Report, *Brazil – Aircraft*, para. 131.
84 See Panel Report, *US – Poultry (China)*, para. 7.34. While arriving at the aforementioned conclusion, the Panel referred to the findings of the Appellate Body in *Korea – Dairy*, paras. 124–127, and Appellate Body Report, *US – Carbon Steel*, para. 127.
85 See Appellate Body Reports, *Argentina – Import Measures*, paras. 5.5 to 5.16; *Mexico – Anti-Dumping Measures on Rice*, para. 138.
86 See Appellate Body Reports, *Argentina – Import Measures*, para. 5.16. See also Appellate Body Reports *US – Upland Cotton*, para. 293; *US – Shrimp (Thailand)/US – Customs Bond Directive*, para. 295 and 296.
87 See Appellate Body Reports, *Argentina – Import Measures*, para. 5.10, and *Mexico – Corn Syrup (Article 21.5 – US)*, para. 54.
88 The drafters of the DSU did not envisage outside interference during the consultation stage of the dispute settlement process. Besides, the negotiations between parties is more diplomatic, with no clear paper trail, and as a result not subject to a panel review.
89 For instance, a developed country Member State could threaten the suspension of development aid if a developing country were not agreeable to a settlement during consultations.
90 See *North Sea Continental Shelf Cases* [1969] ICJ 3, 47–48, para. 85(a).

91 See *Fisheries Jurisdiction Case* [1974] ICJ 3, 32; United Nations (1992).
92 See Panel Report, *Brazil – Desiccated Coconut*, para. 287.
93 Schuchhardt takes the view that the when a Member State is deprived of the opportunity to settle a dispute at the consultations, it drives the Member State concerned to the next stage, *viz*., seeking the establishment of a panel, which appears to bring the right to consultations somewhat closer to that of a substantive right. See Schuchhardt (2005).
94 See, for instance, *Korea – Measures Concerning the Testing and Inspection of Agricultural Products*, where the US, on 4 April 1995, requested consultations with Korea, which concerned testing and inspection requirements with respect to the importation of certain agricultural products from the US into Korea (WT/DS3/1) (1995); *United States – Anti-Dumping Investigation Regarding Imports of Fresh or Chilled Tomatoes from Mexico*, where a request for consultations was made by Mexico in relation to the anti-dumping investigation undertaken by the US, with respect to the importation of fresh or chilled tomatoes from Mexico (WT/DS49/1) (1996). The case was settled three months later, when Mexico and the US reached a suspension agreement. See *Federal Register* (61) 56617 [A-201–820] (1 November 1996). See also *Peru – Tax Treatment on Certain Imported Products*, where Chile made a request for consultations for import tax treatment of fresh fruit, vegetables, fish, milk, tea, and other natural products (WT/DS255/1) (2002). As the consultations were not successful, Chile requested the setting up of a panel in June 2002 (WT/DS255/3).
95 Article XXII(1) postulates a broad requirement to "accord sympathetic consideration to" and to "afford adequate opportunity" for consultations. In contrast, Article XXIII(1) deals with consultations where complaints have been lodged – on the grounds of nullification or impairment, or the impediment of the attainment of any objective of the Agreement – and states that the Member State against whom the complaint is directed shall "give sympathetic consideration to the representations".
96 See, for example, Request for Consultations by the EC, *Korea – Laws, Regulations and Practices in the Telecommunications Procurement Sector*, WT/DS40/1 (1996) – mutually agreed solution notified on 29 October 1997; Request for Consultations by India, *Turkey – Restrictions on Imports of Textiles and Clothing Products*, WT/DS34/1 (1996). Although the complaint proceeded to the next stages – both Panel and Appellate Body, the parties notified the DSB of a 'mutually acceptable solution' on 6 July 2001 (WT/DS34/14) (19 July 2001).
97 In the *EC – Bananas* case, the Appellate Body briefly examined Article 4.11 DSU and observed that in order to be eligible to join multiple consultations, a Member State should have a "substantial trade interest", and went on to hold that the US had a such an interest. See Appellate Body Report, *EC – Bananas III*.
98 See Article 4.11 of the DSU.
99 Interestingly, under GATT 1947, it was possible for the respondent to block the panel's establishment in the first DSB meeting. Under the WTO rules, Article 6.1 of the DSU states that the DSB which receives the request for setting up a panel "may decide by consensus not to establish a panel". However, it is highly unlikely that a negative consensus could be achieved at the DSB, which means that the complainant is guaranteed that a panel will be established.
100 See Article 8.1 DSU. Also, the WTO Secretariat maintains a list of experts (both governmental and non-governmental individuals) from which panellists may be drawn. See Article 8.4 DSU. When the Secretariat proposes such qualified individuals as panellists, the parties may not oppose such proposals except for compelling reasons.
101 See Article 8.7 DSU. Only in rare cases do the respondents request the director-general to compose the Panel. See, for instance, *Canada – Wheat Exports and Grain Imports* and *Australia – Tobacco Plain Packaging*, where the director-general was requested to compose the Panel.
102 See Article 8.7 DSU.
103 See Article 7 in general and Article 7.1 of the DSU in particular on the terms of reference of Panels.
104 See Appellate Body Reports, *Guatemala – Cement I*, paras. 72 and 76; *EC – Bananas III*, para. 141.
105 See Appellate Body Report, *Brazil – Desiccated Coconut*, para. 186.
106 See Appellate Body Report, *US – Carbon Steel*, para. 126.
107 *Ibid*., at para. 124. See also Appellate Body Report, *Argentina – Import Measures*, para. 5.1.
108 See Panel Report, *Australia – Apples*, para. 2.244.
109 Appellate Body Report, *Korea – Dairy*, at para. 120.
110 *Ibid*., at para. 123.

111 See Appellate Body Report *EC – Computer Equipment*, para. 65. Here, the Appellate Body noted, "measures within the meaning of Article 6.2 of the DSU are not only measures of general application, *i.e.*, normative rules, but also can be the application of tariffs by customs authorities". See also Panel Report, *Argentina – Footwear (EC)*, para. 8.35; and Appellate Body Report, *EC – Chicken Cuts*, paras. 163–169.
112 See Appellate Body Report *Australia – Apples*.
113 See Appellate Body Reports, *China – Raw Materials*. The claimants in the case were the US, EU, and Mexico, who had requested consultations with China with respect to China's restraints on the export from its territory of various forms of raw material.
114 *Ibid.*, para. 234. See Appellate Body Report, *EC and Certain Member States – Large Civil Aircraft*, para. 642. See also, Matsushita (2012), who argues that the ruling of the Appellate Body in the *China – Rare Earths* case may be too rigid, as it could potentially deprive the settlement process of the WTO of its flexibility.
115 See Appellate Body Report, *India – Patents (US)*, paras. 89–90.
116 Judicial economy is the principle of administrative process where an adjudicating body is required to deal only with issues that are necessary for the disposal of the dispute in question, and not addressing other issues raised by the parties.
117 See Appellate Body Report, *US – Wool Shirts and Blouses*, p. 340.
118 See Appellate Body Report, *US – Gambling*, paras. 343–344. See also Panel Report, *Argentina – Preserved Peaches*, paras. 7.141–7.142.
119 See Appellate Body Report, *Australia – Salmon*, para. 223. See also the Appellate Body Reports, *Japan – Agricultural Products II*, para. 111; *US – Wheat Gluten*, para. 183; and *US – Lamb*, para. 194. See Appellate Body Report, *EC – Export Subsidies on Sugar*, paras. 334–335, where it was ruled that the Panel had exercised false judicial economy, constituting a breach of Article 11 of the DSU.
120 See Appellate Body Report, *EC – Fasteners (China)*, para. 511. See Appellate Body Report, *Dominican Republic – Import and Sale of Cigarettes*, para. 125.
121 See Appellate Body Report, *US – Shrimp*, para. 101.
122 See Articles 10.2 and 11 of the DSU, and the *Working Procedures* for Panels, set out in DSU Appendix 3.
123 See Article 10.2 DSU. In practice, Panels normally fix a deadline for third parties to make their written submissions, which is normally set at one or two weeks after the respondent's written submission.
124 See Appellate Body Report, *US – FSC (Article 21.5 – EC)*, para. 245, where it was clarified, "third parties must be given all of the submissions that have been made by the parties to the Panel up to the first meeting of the Panel, irrespective of the number of such submissions which are made, including any rebuttal submissions filed in advance of the first meeting". See also Panel Reports, *Canada – Wheat Exports and Grain Imports*, para. 6.6; *Australia – Salmon (Article 21.5 – Canada)*, paras. 7.5–7.6; and *US – Upland Cotton*, para. 3.
125 The Panel, using their discretion, can decide whether to grant such enhanced rights and the extent of such rights. See Appellate Body Reports, *EC – Hormones*, para. 154; *US – 1916 Act*, para. 150; and Panel Reports, *EC – Export Subsidies on Sugar*, para. 2.3; *Canada – Feed-In Tariff Program/Canada – Renewable Energy*, para. 1.11; and *US – COOL (Article 21.5 – Canada/Article 21.5 – Mexico)*, paras. 1.15–1.16.
126 In the *EC – Hormones* case there were parallel proceedings brought by both Canada and the US against the EC. The members of the Panels proceeded to hold a joint meeting of the two Panels, permitting Canada to access information presented by the US, and *vice versa*. On appeal, EC objected to such procedures adopted by the Panels, which according to the EC exceeded the rights granted to third parties in the WTO proceeding. The Appellate Body noted that the procedures adopted by the Panels were related to 'economy of effort' in a situation of parallel proceedings concerning the same matter. See Appellate Body Reports, *EC – Hormones*, paras. 153–154.
127 Article 10.2 of the DSU reads as follows: "Any Member having a substantial interest in a matter before a panel and having notified its interest to the DSB (referred to in this Understanding as a 'third party') shall have an opportunity to be heard by the panel and to make written submissions to the panel. These submissions shall also be given to the parties to the dispute and shall be reflected in the panel report."
128 See, for instance, Panel Reports, *US – Gasoline*; *Indonesia – Autos*; *US – Shrimp*; *Canada – Autos*; *Chile – Alcoholic Beverages*; *India – Autos*; *US – Offset Act (Byrd Amendment)*; *US – Steel Safeguards*; *China – Rare Earths*; and *Australia – Tobacco Plain Packaging*.

129 See, for instance, Panel Reports *EC – Hormones (US)* and *EC – Hormones (Canada)*; *India – Patents (US)* and *India – Patents (EC)*; *US – Shrimp (Thailand)* and *US – Customs Bond Directive*; *India – Additional Import Duties*; *Canada – Renewable Energy* and *Canada – Feed-in Tariff Programme*; and *China – HP-SSST (Japan)/China – HP-SSST (European Union)*.
130 See, for instance, Panel Reports *US – Shrimp*; *US – Offset Act (Byrd Amendment)*; *US – Steel Safeguards*; and *EC – Bananas III*.
131 Where it is demonstrated by the parties that there is an urgency around the matter (*e.g.*, disputes relating to perishable goods), and in matters relating to subsidies under the SCM Agreement, the time is shortened. See Article 12.8 of the DSU and Article 4 of the SCM Agreement.
132 In reality these times vary, as panel timings are significantly different from the prescribed timeframe.
133 In *US – Large Civil Aircraft (2nd Complaint)*, Panel proceedings lasted for 61 months; in *EC and Certain Member States – Large Civil Aircraft*, Panel proceedings lasted for 59.2 months; in *EC – Approval and Marketing of Biotech Products*, Panel proceedings lasted for 36.9 months; and in *US/Canada – Continued Suspension*, Panel proceedings lasted for 37.3 months.
134 See Communication from the Chair of the Panel, *EC – Approval and Marketing of Biotech Products*, WT/DS291/32, WT/DS292/26, and WT/DS293/26, dated 29 September 2006, para. 1.
135 Where arguments are submitted in languages other than English, the deadline is likely to be extended for translation purposes. See, for instance, *EC – Asbestos* (conducted in French); *Dominican Republic – Safeguard Measures* (conducted in Spanish); *Peru – Agricultural Products* (conducted in Spanish); *Colombia – Textiles* (conducted in Spanish); and *Argentina – Financial Services* (conducted in Spanish).
136 This procedure appears to be changing in recent times, as Panels have opened hearings (either fully or partially) at the request of the parties to the proceedings. See WTO (2017).
137 Article 11 of the DSU, a Panel "should make objective assessment of the matter before it, including objective assessment of the facts of the case and the applicability of and conformity with the relevant covered agreements".
138 See Appellate Body Reports, *US – Continued Zeroing*, para. 338; *EC – Fasteners (China)*, para. 441; and *US – Upland Cotton (Article 21.5 – Brazil)*, para. 292.
139 See Appellate Body Report, *US – Continued Zeroing*, para. 331.
140 See Appellate Body Report, *EC – Hormones*, para. 133.
141 See Appellate Body Reports, *Brazil – Retreaded Tyres*, para. 185, and *EC and Certain Member States – Large Scale Civil Aircraft*, para. 1317. See also Appellate Body Report, *US – Countervailing and Anti-Dumping Measures (China)*, paras. 4.174–4.209, where it was held that the Panel acted inconsistently with Article 11 of the DSU while addressing China's claims under Article 12.7 of the SCM Agreement.
142 See Appellate Body Report, *Chile – Price Band System*, para. 172.
143 See Appellate Body Report, *US – Continued Suspension/Canada – Continued Suspension*, para. 482, where it was held that the Panel failed to comply with its duties as enumerated under Article 11 of the DSU.
144 See Appellate Body Report, *EC – Hormones*, para. 117.
145 It is normal for the Legal Affairs Division of the WTO to staff all cases, with the exception of matters dealing with anti-dumping measures, subsidies, and countervailing measures or safeguards, which are staffed by lawyers from the Rules Division. See WTO (2017).
146 The ERGs reports are only advisory in nature. See DSU Appendix 4, para. 6.
147 *Ibid.*
148 Article 3.2 of the DSU enumerates, "Recommendations and rulings of the DSB cannot add to or diminish the rights and obligations provided in the covered agreements." Likewise, Article 19.2 of the DSU states, "In accordance with paragraph 2 of Article 3, in their findings and recommendations, the panels and Appellate Body cannot add to or diminish the rights and obligations provided in the covered agreements."
149 Pauwelyn takes the position that a major source of confusion before the WTO dispute settlement lies in the "terminology used to express these rules and in the often overlooked distinction between burden of proof and the presentation and evaluation of evidence". See Pauwelyn (1998), p. 228.
150 See Matsushita, Shoenbaum, Mavroidis, and Hahn (2015).
151 See Appellate Body Report, *US – Wool Shirts and Blouses*, p. 14. See also Bartels (2001).

152 See Appellate Body Report, *EC – Hormones*, paras. 98 and 104. See also *US – Gambling*, where the Appellate Body ruled on establishing a *prima facie* case based on "evidence and legal argument", paras. 140–141.
153 See Appellate Body Report, *Japan – Apples*, para. 157.
154 See Appellate Body Report, *EC – Hormones*, para. 104.
155 See Appellate Body Report, *US – Section 301 Trade Act*, para. 7.14.
156 *Ibid.*, para. 7.15.
157 See Appellate Body Report, *EC – Tariff Preferences*, para. 7.14. See also Appellate Body Report, *India – Quantitative Restrictions*, para. 136.
158 See Appellate Body Report, *US – Carbon Steel*, para. 157.
159 See Article 15.1 of the DSU. The descriptive part normally comprises an introduction, factual details of the dispute, the parties' requests for findings, and the summary of legal arguments submitted to the Panel.
160 Interim report was introduced by the DSU with the objective of improving the quality of panel reports. See Article 16.1 of the DSU.
161 See Article 12.7 of the DSU.
162 See Appellate Body Report, *Mexico – Corn Syrup (Article 21.5 US)*, paras. 106–107.
163 See Appellate Body Report, *Argentina – Footwear (EC)*, para. 149.
164 See Panel Report, *India – Quantitative Restrictions*, para. 5.157.
165 See Article 16.4 of the DSU. Panels are known to make every effort to reach decisions through consensus. Where it is found impossible for a decision to be reached through consensus, decisions are taken by a majority vote.
166 See Article 19.1 of the DSU, first sentence.
167 See Article 26.1(b) of the DSU.
168 See Appellate Body Report, *India – Patents (US)*, para. 41. This finding of the Appellate Body is found codified in Article 26.1(b) of the DSU.
169 One of the modes of adjustment, which is widely practised at the WTO, is for the respondent to compensate the complainant with alternative trade opportunities to compensate for the nullified or impaired benefit.
170 Currently, the languages used before the WTO are English, French, and Spanish.
171 See Appellate Body Report, *EC – Bananas III (Ecuador) (Article 21.5 – Ecuador II)/EC – Bananas III (US) (Article 21.5 – US)*, paras. 321–326.
172 See Article 9.1 of the DSU.
173 See Article 9.2 of the DSU.
174 For instance, in the following cases the Panels issued separate reports for each complainant: *EC – Trademarks and Geographical Indications*; *EC – Export Subsidies on Sugar*; and *EC – Chicken Cuts*, *US – Shrimp (Thailand)*, and *US – Customs Bond Directive*.
175 For instance, in *EC – Bananas III*, the Panel issued four separate panel reports in the following order – a joint report for Guatemala and Honduras, and three separate reports for Ecuador, Mexico, and the US.
176 For instance, in *EC – Approval and Marketing and Biotech Products*; *US – Steel Safeguards*; *EC – IT Products*; *Canada – Renewable Energy/Canada – Feed-in-Tariff*; *US – COOL (Article 21.5 – Mexico)*.
177 Interestingly, an appellate review procedure did not feature either in the December 1988 midterm review or in the Contracting Parties' Decision of 12 April 1989.
178 The proposal from Mexico also included set timeframes for the appellate body to submit its recommendations, finality of the appellate process, the composition of the appellate body, *etc.*
179 It was assumed at the time of drafting of the DSU that any appellate review process would only come to be invoked rarely, for instance when a party to the decision sought to overturn the decision of the Panel which was patently wrong. This was not to be the case, as all the Panel reports handed down in the first two years of the WTO were invariably appealed.
180 This particular draft article resembles Article 17 of the DSU, dealing with appellate review.
181 See minutes of the Meeting of the Preparatory Committee for the World Trade Organization, PC/M/1 (29 April 1994).
182 See Article 17.6 of the DSU. See also Appellate Body Report, *US – Stainless Steel (Mexico)*, where the Appellate Body elaborated on the role of the WTO dispute settlement system.
183 Figures from 1 December 2017 show that this feature had been used for over 66 percent against panel reports.

184 See Article 17.9 of the DSU dealing with *Working Procedures* of Appellate Review. The Appellate Body used the *Working Procedures* in *EC and Certain Member States – Large Civil Aircraft*, paras. 17–19, for adopting special procedures for the protection of BCI; in *EC – Asbestos*, para. 52, for the purpose of adopting a special procedure to deal with potential *amicus curiae* briefs; and in *China – HP-SSST (Japan) / China – HP-SSST (European Union)*, para. 1.24, for the purpose of consolidating two appeals.
185 The Recommendations by the Preparatory Committee for the WTO, which elaborated upon many of the criteria identified in Article 17 of the DSU. See 'Establishment of the Appellate Body' WT/DSB/1 (19 June 1995).
186 *Ibid.*, para. 5. DSB recognized that in the process of selecting Members to serve on the Appellate Body, issues arise as their "expertise, representative balance, impartiality, conditions of employment, and the selection procedures to be used". The DSB also noted that the success of the WTO depended on the "proper composition of the Appellate Body" and hence individuals of "the highest calibre should serve on it". See para. 4.
187 *Ibid.*, para. 6. See also Minutes of the DSB Meetings of 31 May 1995, WT/DSB/M/5, p. 12, where the chairperson of the DSB noted that there was a view amongst the delegates that the strength of the Appellate Body rested "in its diversity of representation reflecting: (i) regional, developed and developing country balance; (ii) adequate representation from regions and countries who were active participants in the trading system including smaller as well as larger countries; (iii) different legal systems, on grounds that the credibility and authority of the Appellate Body had [to] be acceptable to all."
188 See Article 2.4 of the DSU.
189 See Article 17.2 of the DSU. To view a list of past and currently serving members of the Appellate Body, see www.wto.org/english/tratop_e/dispu_e/ab_members_descrp_e.htm (accessed 3 August 2021). Also to be noted is that the DSB has always reappointed members willing to serve a second term.
190 Although the seven original Appellate Body members were appointed at the same time, the first terms of three of the original seven expired after only two years.
191 See Rule 2(2) of the *Working Procedures* for Appellate Review.
192 See Rule 2(3) of the *Working Procedures* for Appellate Review.
193 See Para. II(1) of the Rules of Conduct for the Understanding on Rules and Procedures Governing the Settlement of Disputes (hereinafter 'Rules of Conduct'). See also Para. IV(1), which states that the Rules shall apply to each person serving "(a) on a panel; (b) on the Standing Appellate Body; (c) as an arbitrator pursuant to the provisions mentioned in Annex '1a'; or (d) as an expert participating in the dispute settlement mechanism pursuant to the provisions mentioned in Annex '1b'".
194 See Paras. III(1), VI(4)(b), and VI(5) of the Rules of Conduct.
195 It is the practice that Member States usually nominate eminent individuals from their own state. However, in 1995, Canada nominated Mr Julio Lacarte-Muró, a career diplomat from Uruguay, to serve on the Appellate Body. It is to be noted that Mr Julio Lacarte-Muró participated in all eight rounds of the Multilateral Trade Negotiations under the GATT.
196 Some appeals require analysing complex issues, involving multiple parties, and at times extensive technical data and evidence by the Members, before delivering their lengthy reports. Appellate Body reports are anywhere between 100 and 300 pages long.
197 The Appellate Body members spent a considerable amount of time to go through the *EC – Approval and Marketing of Biotech Products* case – which was both fact-heavy and complicated, with the Panel report running close to 900 pages – in anticipation of an appeal from the Panel's findings.
198 Hughes also puts for the argument that such a practice is expected and given the volume of trade flows and the dispute settlement activities of the two Member States, it can serve the system well.
199 A study conducted by the US Government Accounting Office in 2003 found that the WTO rulings had been consistent, in that it ruled for and against the US and other Member States in the same ratios. See GAO (2003).
200 See Rule 5 of the *Working Procedures* for Appellate Review.
201 *Ibid.*
202 *Ibid.*
203 The divisions are appointed in rotation, which is confidential and known only to the Appellate Body members.

204 The nationality of an Appellate Body member is irrelevant, which means they could preside over an appeal to which their country of origin is a party.
205 The ICJ sits as a bench of 15 plus and *ad hoc* judges if one of the parties is not represented on the Court. The Law of the Sea Tribunal has 21 judges plus *ad hoc* members from time to time. Although it is possible for the ICJ and the Law of the Sea Tribunal to sit in smaller chambers, this is exceptional.
206 The author, who served as Member on the Appellate Body from 1995 to 2001, notes that a larger bench would make decision-making a cumbersome process, with deliberations becoming more structured and formalised.
207 Besides their meetings to exchange views on a pending appeal, the members of the Appellate Body meet regularly to discuss matters of policy, practice, and procedure. See Rules 4(1) and 4(3) of the *Working Procedures*.
208 See Rule 3 of the *Working Procedures*.
209 Although expressing separate opinions in Appellate Body reports are a rare occurrence, some of the instances where individual Members expressed their separate opinions can be found in the following reports: *EC – Asbestos*; *US – Upland Cotton*; *US – Continued Zeroing*; *US – Zeroing (Article 21.5 – EC)*; and *EC and Certain Member States – Large Civil Aircraft*. For the separate opinion in *US – Large Civil Aircraft (2nd complaint)*, see footnotes 1118, 1130, and 1153.
210 In *US – Softwood Lumber IV* and *US – Offset Act (Byrd Amendment)*, Mr Arumugamangalam V. Ganesan, one of the members of the Appellate Body, had to step down for 'serious personal reasons' and was replaced by Mr Giorgio Sacerdoti. See Appellate Body Report, *US – Softwood Lumber IV*, para. 10, and Appellate Body Report, *US – Offset Act (Byrd Amendment)*, para. 8.
211 See Article 17.7 of the DSU.
212 See 'Establishment of the Appellate Body' WT/DSB/1, para. 17 (19 June 1995).
213 The lengthy duration of the appellate review process invariably had a knock-on effect on other appellate review proceedings before the DSB. For instance, seven of the ten proceedings in 2011 and 2012 took longer than 90 days, as a result of the long running case in *US – Large Civil Aircraft (2nd complaint)* (Van den Bossche and Zdouc, 2017).
214 See Dispute Settlement Body, *Minutes of Meeting held on 23 July 2012*, WT/DSB/M/320, dated 28 September 2012, paras. 97–109.
215 See Rule 1 of the *Working Procedures*.
216 *Ibid*.
217 See Appellate Body Report *EC – Hormones*, para. 132, where the Appellate Body found that the Panel's findings on whether international standards had been adopted by the Codex Alimentarius Commission were findings on issues of fact and not law, and therefore not subject to an appellate review.
218 *Ibid*. See also Appellate Body Report *EC – Bananas III*, para. 239.
219 See, for instance, Appellate Body reports in *US – Softwood Lumber V*, para. 163, and *US – Anti-Dumping Measures on Oil Country Tubular Goods*, para. 195, where the Appellate Body held that qualitative assessment of facts against legal requirement was subject to appellate review, as they were legal characterization of facts. See also Appellate Body reports in *US – Section 211 Appropriations Act*, para. 105–106, relying on Appellate Body Report, *India – Patents (US)*, paras. 65–66 and 68.
220 See Article 11 of the DSU, which requires that "a panel should make an objective assessment of the matter before it, including an objective assessment of the facts of the case and the applicability of and conformity with the relevant covered agreements, and make such other findings as will assist the DSB in making the recommendations or in giving the rulings provided for in the covered agreements".
221 See Appellate Body Report, *EC – Hormones*, para. 143.
222 See Appellate Body Report, *India – Patents (US)*, para. 68.
223 See Appellate Body Report, *Philippines – Distilled Spirits*, para. 235.
224 See Appellate Body Report, *EC – Fasteners (China)*, para. 442.
225 See Appellate Body Report, *US – Steel Safeguards*, para. 498.
226 See Appellate Body Report, *EC and Certain Member States – Large Civil Aircraft*, para. 872. See also Appellate Body Report, *US – Carbon Steel*, para. 142, where it was established that the Appellate Body will not 'interfere lightly' with a Panel's findings.
227 See Appellate Body Reports, *China – GOES*, para. 183, and *EC and Certain Member States – Large Civil Aircraft*, para. 872.

228 See Appellate Body Report, *EC – Tube or Pipe Fittings*, paras. 183–184.
229 See Appellate Body Report, *US – Offset Act (Byrd Amendment)*, para. 222.
230 See Appellate Body Report, *US – Softwood Lumber V*, para. 9.
231 See Appellate Body Report, *Canada – Aircraft*, para. 211.
232 See Appellate Body Report, *US – FSC*, para. 103.
233 See Appellate Body Report, *EC – Export Subsidies on Sugar*, paras. 240–242.
234 The authors note that the success of the Appellate Body is its willingness to 'complete the analysis' of the first instance decision-makers, or Panels, in appropriate circumstances, but not in all, as in some cases the significant issues of the dispute remained unsolved. See Appellate Body Reports, *US – Zeroing (EC)*, paras. 263(c)(ii), 263g(ii); *US – Softwood Lumber VI (Article 21.5 – Canada)*, paras. 162(c), 163.
235 See Appellate Body Report, *Canada – Periodicals*, para. 469.
236 See Appellate Body Reports, *Australia – Salmon*, para. 118, and *EC – Export Subsidies on Sugar*, para. 340, where the Appellate Body did not complete the analysis due to non-availability of sufficient factual findings.
237 See Appellate Body Report, *US – Steel Safeguards*, para. 430.
238 See Appellate Body Reports, *Brazil – Aircraft (Article 21.5 – Canada)*, para. 78, and *US – Certain EC Products*, paras. 89–90.
239 See Appellate Body Report, *US – Cotton Yarn*, para. 127.
240 Krislov notes that the practice was known in Roman law. At common law, the function of the *amicus curiae* law was one of oral 'shepardizing', or the bringing up of cases not known to the judge.
241 *Amicus curiae* or *amici curiae* (used in plural) briefs are accepted before the ICJ, International Criminal Court, the International Criminal Tribunal for the Former Yugoslavia (ICTY), the International Criminal Tribunal for Rwanda (ICTR), the Special Court of Sierra Leone (SCSL), and the WTO dispute settlement system.
242 See Panel Reports in *US – Gasoline* and in *US – Hormones*.
243 The *US – Shrimp* case is also referred to as the *US – Shrimp-Turtle* case.
244 A joint *amicus curiae* brief was submitted by the *Center for International Environmental Law*; *Center for Marine Conservation*; *The Environmental Foundation Ltd*; *The Philippine Ecological Network*; and *Red Nacional de Accion Ecologia*, and another brief by the *World Wide Fund for Nature, International*, and the *Foundation for International Environmental Law and Development*.
245 See Panel Report, *US – Shrimp*, para. 7.8.
246 See Appellate Body Report, *US – Shrimp*, paras. 108–110.
247 *Ibid.*, para. 106.
248 See Appellate Body Reports, *Canada – Aircraft*, para. 203, and *EC – Sardines*, paras. 156–157.
249 See Appellate Body Report, *US – Hot-Rolled Steel*, para. 362. Here, the Appellate Body invoked Article 17.9 of the DSU, reasoning that it had authority to adopt its own *Working Procedures*.
250 See Appellate Body Report, *EC – Asbestos*, paras. 51–52. This procedure requires that the person submitting the *amicus curiae* brief also submits a summary contained in 20 pages, without repeating the arguments from the brief.
251 See Panel Report in *US – Tuna II (Mexico)*, where the Panel noted that it deemed it appropriate to refer to the information in its findings to the extent that one of the parties had cited or referred to the brief during the panel proceedings.
252 See Panel Reports in *EC – Bed Linen*, para. 6.1, footnote 10; *EC – Export Subsidies on Sugar*, paras. 2.20 and 7.76–7.85; *EC – Approval and Marketing of Biotech Products*, paras. 7.10–7.11; and *US – Zeroing (EC)*, para. 1.7.
253 See Appellate Body Report, *US – Lead and Bismuth II*, para. 39.
254 *Ibid.*, para. 42.
255 *Ibid.*, footnote 33. Although not directly referred to in the body of the judgement, reference is made to Rule 16(1) of the *Working Procedures*, in footnote 33 as follows: "In addition, Rule 16(1) of the *Working Procedures* allows a division hearing an appeal to develop an appropriate procedure in certain specified circumstances where a procedural question arises that is not covered by the *Working Procedures*."
256 See Appellate Body Report, *EC – Sardines*, paras. 153–170.
257 The United States took the view that it was permitted to receive *amicus curiae* briefs under the Appellate Body's general powers as well as under the DSU. Meanwhile, similar views were

expressed by New Zealand and Switzerland; Japan and the European Communities took the position that this might only be appropriate in certain circumstances. The vast majority of Members, including Egypt, India, Malaysia, and Pakistan, were opposed to the acceptance of *amicus curiae* briefs by panels and the Appellate Body.

258 See Dispute Settlement Body, General Council, *Minutes of Meeting from* 22 November 2000, WT/GC/M/60 (23 January 2001), para. 120.
259 Dispute Settlement Body, *Minutes of Meeting from* 23 October 2002, WT/DSB/M/134 (29 January 2003), para. 43. Mexico also expressed a similar sentiment at the same meeting, see para. 48.
260 As of August 2021, a total of 58 *amicus curiae* briefs have been submitted in 16 Appellate Body proceedings.
261 In the Uruguay Round of negotiations, Article 22 was introduced as an enforcement mechanism to placate the US demands for effectiveness of the dispute settlement system.
262 See Article 21.1 of the DSU.
263 See Articles 3.7 and 21.3 of the DSU. Prompt compliance would mean prompt or immediate withdrawal or modification of the WTO-inconsistent measure that was in question in the dispute before the DSB.
264 In common law, the remedy for breach of a contractual term would be to put the innocent party in the position they would be, if the contract were to be performed.
265 See Article 21.1 of the DSU.
266 See Article 21.4 of the DSU.
267 See Articles 21.3(a), (b), and (c) of the DSU.
268 See Appellate Body Report in *US – Zeroing (Japan) (Article 21.5 – Japan)*, para. 157.
269 See Arbitration Award, *EU – Hormones (Article 21.3(c)) (Arbitration)*, para. 26.
270 See footnote 12 to Article 21.3(c) of the DSU.
271 See footnote 13 to Article 21.3(c) of the DSU.
272 See Arbitration award *US – Offset Act (Byrd Amendment) (Article 21.3(c))* (Arbitration), para. 53.
273 See Article 21.3(c) of the DSU.
274 See Arbitration award, *EC – Hormones (Article 21.3(c))*, para. 25. See also Arbitration award, *US – Offset Act (Byrd amendment) (Article 21.3(c))*, para. 25.
275 See Arbitration award, *EC – Hormones (Article 21.3(c))*, para. 38. See also Arbitration awards, *US – Offset Act (Byrd amendment) (Article 21.3(c))*, para. 48, and *Chile – Price Band System (Article 21.3(c))*, para. 32.
276 See Arbitration award, *EC – Chicken Cuts (Article 21.3(c))*, para. 49.
277 See Arbitration award, *US – Hot-Rolled Steel (Article 21.3(c))*, para. 253.
278 See Arbitration awards, *Canada – Pharmaceutical Patents (Article 21.3(c))*, para. 49, and *US – Offset Act (Byrd amendment) (Article 21.3(c))*, para. 70.
279 See Arbitration awards, *Canada – Pharmaceutical Patents (Article 21.3(c))*, para. 49, and *US – Stainless Steel (Article 21.3(c))*, para. 59.
280 See Arbitration awards, *Chile – Alcoholic Beverage (Article 21.3(c))*, para. 45, and *Indonesia – Autos (Article 21.3(c))*, para. 24.
281 See Arbitration awards, *Chile – Price Band System (Article 21.3(c))*, para. 56.
282 See Article 21.6 of the DSU.
283 The US, at the DSB meeting in August 2012, presented its 118th status report on its implementation of the recommendations and rulings from the case *US – Section 211 Appropriations Act*. At this meeting, the EU (the complainants in the case), along with other Member States, Angola, Argentina, Bolivia, Brazil, Chile, China, Cuba, Dominican Republic, Ecuador, Mexico, Nicaragua, Venezuela, and Vietnam expressed serious concerns about the US's failure to implement the rulings and recommendations from the case which was adopted by the DSB as early as in February 2002. See Status Report by the United States, *US – Section 211 Appropriations Act*.
284 See Article 21.5 of the DSU.
285 See Appellate Body Report, *Canada – Aircraft (Article 21.5 – Brazil)*, paras. 40–42. See also Appellate Body Report, *Mexico – Corn Syrup (Article 21.5 – US)*, paras. 78 and 80.
286 See Appellate Body report, *US – Softwood Lumber IV (Article 21.5 – Canada)*, para. 72.
287 See Panel report, *US – Softwood Lumber VI (Article 21.5 – Canada)*, para. 7.12.
288 See Appellate Body report, *EC – Bed Linen (Article 21.5 – India)*, para. 79.
289 See Panel report, *US – Gambling (Article 21.5 – Antigua and Barbuda)*, paras. 6.12–6.22.

290 See Article 22.2 of the DSU. In *US – Section 110(5) Copyright Act*, pending Panel proceedings, the complaining Member State (EC) and the respondent Member State (US) reached an agreement before the running for a period of three years, pursuant to which the US paid US$3.3 million to the EC. See Arbitration Report, *US – Upland Cotton* para. 4.279, where the US agreed to fund US$147.3 million per year for technical assistance to Brazil's cotton sector, as a temporary financial compensation. See also Appellate Body Report *Japan – Alcoholic Beverages II*.

291 See Article 22.1 of the DSU. See Appellate Body Report *EC – Banana III (US)*, para. 6.3, where the Appellate Body observed that the purpose of a countermeasure is to induce compliance. See Arbitration report *US – Upland Cotton*, para. 4.112, where it was observed, "'Inducing compliance' appears rather to be the common purpose of retaliation measures in the WTO dispute."

292 See Article 22.4 of the DSU. See Arbitration award *EC – Bananas III (US) (Article 22.6 – EC)*, para. 4.1.

293 See Article 22.8 of the DSU.

294 See Article 22.3 of the DSU.

295 Normally, it will be referred to a Member from the original Panel that presided over the original complaint.

296 Pursuant to DSU Art. 22.6, authorisation was granted by the DSB to retaliate in the following instances: *EC Bananas III*; *EC – Hormones*; *Brazil – Aircraft*; *US – FSC*; *US – 1916 Act*; *Canada – Aircraft Credits and Guarantees*; *US – Offset Act*; *US – Upland Cotton*; and *US – Gambling*. Detailed statistical data on authorisation is available at www.worldtradelaw.net/databases/suspensionawards.php (accessed 3 August 2021).

297 See Article 22.3(b) of the DSU.

298 See Arbitration award *EC – Bananas III (Ecuador) (Article 22.6 – EC)*, paras. 70–73.

299 See Article 22.3(c) of the DSU. Cross-retaliation, as this is called, has been (at the time of writing) authorized in three cases: Arbitration Award *EC – Bananas III (Ecuador) (Article 22.6 – EC)*, para. 68; Arbitration Award *US – Gambling (Article 22.6 – US)*; and Arbitration Award *US – Upland Cotton (Article 22.6 – US)*.

300 See Arbitration Award *US – Gambling (Article 22.6 – US)*, para. 4.108. See also Arbitration Award *US – Upland Cotton (Article 22.6 – US)*, paras. 5.65–5.66, 5.70–5.71, and 5.77–5.90.

301 Sutherland Report, para. 222.

302 Article XVIII:1 of the GATT contains a broad definition/description of a developing country as one whose economy "can only support low standards of living and [is] in the early stages of development". As regards least developed countries, Article XI:2 of the Marrakesh Agreement accepts the UN's designation of a least developed country.

303 It is to be noted that different methodologies have been used by scholars in their studies to determine the status of a country. For instance, the GDP of the concerned state, or membership of the state in other international organisations, is used as a reference point to determine a nation's status. It could also be understood to include newly industrialised countries, emerging economies, frontier markets – a country that is more developed than a least developed country, and least developed countries. The World Bank classifies countries as 'high income', 'upper middle income', 'lower middle income', and 'low income.' For the purposes of the current study countries are classified as *developed*, *developing*, and *least developed*, which is based on WTO documentation.

304 The authors identify a number of factors that potentially hinder or hold back the developing countries from utilising the WTO's dispute settlement mechanism, *e.g.*, duration and complexity of WTO proceedings, domestic government trade policy, a lack of retaliatory power, and fear of political consequences.

305 It is also argued that the downside to greater legalism (rules oriented) of the WTO's dispute settlement mechanism is its complexity, which also potentially leads to increased transactional costs of settling disputes.

306 The more a Member State trades multilaterally through the WTO, the greater will be its aggregate stakes in the system, and so will be its incentive to defend its trading rights.

307 See, for instance, *US – Gambling*, where Antigua and Barbuda brought a complaint against the US, and *US – Underwear*, where Costa Rica brought a complaint against the US.

308 See, for instance, *Turkey – Textiles*, where India brought a complaint against Turkey; *Chile – Price Band System*, where Argentina brought a complaint against Chile; *Thailand – Cigarettes (Philippines)*, where Philippines brought a complaint against Thailand; and *Dominican Republic – Safeguard Measures*, where Costa Rica, El Salvador, Guatemala, and Honduras brought a complaint against the

Dominican Republic. In 2016, Turkey brought a complaint against Morocco (*Morocco – Hot-Rolled Steel (Turkey)*) which was decided in October 2018.
309 The African states have been participated as third party participants in two important cases, *viz.*, *US – Upland Cotton*, where Benin and Chad supported Brazil's complaints, and in *EC – Export Subsidies on Sugar*, where seven African states supported the EC as respondent.
310 See Request for Consultations by Bangladesh, *India – Anti-Dumping Measure on Batteries from Bangladesh*. This complaint did not proceed beyond the consultation phase, as the parties reported a mutually satisfactory solution to the complaint.
311 Interestingly there had never been a complaint against a least developed country Member State before the DSB.
312 See Article 4.10 DSU.
313 See Article 12.10 DSU.
314 See Article 8.10 DSU.
315 See Article 12.10 DSU. See Panel report, *India – Quantitative Restrictions*, para. 5.10, where India was granted additional time (ten-day period) to prepare for its first written submission pursuant to Article 12.10. See also Panel reports, *Turkey – Rice*, paras. 7.304–7.305; *EC – Bananas III (Article 21.5 – Ecuador II)*, paras. 2.73–2.76 and 7.505–7.508; *Philippines – Distilled Spirits*, paras. 7.189–7.195; *Dominican Republic – Safeguard Measures*, paras. 7.442–7.444; *Argentina – Import Measures*, paras. 6.9–6.10; *Peru – Agricultural Products*, paras. 7.529–7.531; *Colombia – Textiles*, paras. 7.601–7.606; and *India – Solar Cells*, fn. 6 to para. 1.7.
316 See Article 12.11 of the DSU. For instance, Panel Reports, *India – Quantitative Restrictions*, para. 5.157; *US – Offset Act (Byrd Amendment)*, para. 7.87; *Mexico – Telecoms*, para. 8.3; *Turkey – Rice*, paras. 7.302–7.305; *EC – Bananas (Article 21.5 – United States)*, para. 7.722; *Philippines – Distilled Spirits*, paras. 7.189–7.195; *Dominican Republic – Safeguard Measures*, paras. 7.442–7.444; *Argentina – Import Measures*, paras. 6.9–6.10; *Peru – Agricultural Products*, paras. 7.529–7.531; and *Colombia – Textiles*, paras. 7.601–7.606.
317 See . . . Award of the Arbitrator, *Indonesia – Autos (Article 21.3(c))*, para. 24. Award of the Arbitrator, *Chile – Alcoholic Beverages (Article 21.3(c))*, para. 45. Award of the Arbitrator, *Chile – Price Band System (Article 21.3(c))*, paras. 55–56. See also, for instance, Awards of the Arbitrator, *US – Offset Act (Byrd Amendment)*, para. 81; *EC – Tariff Preferences (Article 21.3(c))*, para. 59; *US – Gambling (Article 21.3(c))*, paras. 59–61; *US – Oil Country Tubular Goods Sunset Reviews (Article 21.3(c))*, para. 52; *EC – Export Subsidies on Sugar (Article 21.3(c))*, para. 99; *EC – Chicken Cuts (Article 21.3(c))*, paras. 81–82; *Colombia – Ports of Entry (Article 21.3(c))*, paras. 104–107; *US – COOL (Article 21.3(c))*, para. 71; *Peru – Agricultural Products (Article 21.3(c))*, para. 3.43; and *Colombia – Textiles (Article 21.3(c))*, para. 3.60.
318 See Award of the Arbitrator, *Indonesia – Autos (Article 21.3(c))*, para. 24.
319 See Award of the Arbitrator, *Chile – Alcoholic Beverages (Article 21.3(c))*, para. 45.
320 See Article 21.7 of the DSU.
321 See Arbitration Award, *EC – Bananas III (Ecuador) (Article 22.6)*, para. 136.
322 See Request for Consultations by Colombia, *European Communities – Regime for the Importation of Bananas*, WT/DS361/1.
323 See Article 24.1 of the DSU.
324 *Ibid*.
325 See Panel Report, *US – Upland Cotton*, para. 7.54. See also Panel Report, *US – Upland Cotton (Article 21.5 – Brazil)*, para. 8.29, and Appellate Body Report, *US – Upland Cotton*, para. 512.
326 See Article 24.1 of the DSU.
327 See Article 27.2 of the DSU.
328 See Appellate Body Report, *EC – Bananas III*, para. 12.
329 See Article 27.2 of the DSU.

Bibliography

Abbott, Frederick M. 'Cross Retaliation in TRIPS: Options for Developing Countries,' *ICTSD Program on Dispute Settlement and Legal Aspects of International Trade, Issue Paper 8* (2009).
Alvarez-Jiménez, Alberto. 'Mutually Agreed Solutions under the WTO Dispute Settlement Understanding: An Analytical Framework after the Softwood Lumber Arbitration,' *World Trade Review* Vol 10, No 3 (2011) 343–374.

Babu, Rajesh. *Remedies under the WTO Legal System* (Martin Nijhoff Publishers, 2012).

Barceló III, John J. 'Burden of Proof, Prima Facie Case and Presumption in WTO Dispute Settlement,' *Cornell International Law Journal* Vol 42 (2009) 23.

Bartels, Lorand. 'Applicable Law in WTO Dispute Settlement Proceedings,' *Journal of World Trade* Vol 35, No 3 (2001) 499–519.

Bello, Judith H. 'The WTO Dispute Settlement Understanding: Less Is More,' *The American Journal of International Law* Vol 90, No 3 (1996) 416–418.

Bello, Judith H. and Alan F. Holmer. 'US Trade Law and Policy Series No 24: Dispute Resolution in the New World Trade Organization: Concerns and Net Benefits,' *The International Lawyer* Vol 28, No 4 (1994) 1095–1104.

Bernauer, Thomas, Manfred Elsig and Joost Pauwelyn. 'Dispute Settlement Mechanism: Analysis and Problem,' in Daunton, Martin, Amrita Narlikar and Robert M. Stern (eds.) *The Oxford Handbook on the World Trade Organization* (Oxford University Press, 2012) 485–506.

Bhala, Raj. *Modern GATT Law* Vol 1 (Sweet & Maxwell, 2013).

Bhala, Raj. *Modern GATT Law* Vol 2 (Sweet & Maxwell, 2013).

Bohanes, Jan and Fernanda Garza. 'Going Beyond Stereotypes: Participation of Developing Countries in WTO Dispute Settlement,' *Trade Law and Development* Vol 4, No 1 (2012) 45–124.

Bown, Chad P. *Self-Enforcing Trade: Developing Countries and WTO Dispute Settlement* (Brooking Institute Press, 2009).

Bruno, Roberto. 'Access of Private Parties to International Dispute Settlement: A Comparative Analysis,' LLM thesis (unpublished), Harvard University (1997).

Busch Marc L. and Eric Reinhardt. 'The Evolution of GATT/WTO Dispute Settlement,' *Trade Policy Research* Vol 143 (2003).

Busch Marc L., Eric Reinhardt and Gregory Shaffer. 'Does Legal Capacity Matter? Explaining Patterns of Protectionism in the Shadow of WTO Litigation,' *Issue Paper, International Centre for Trade and Sustainable Development, Geneva, Switzerland* (2008).

Chase, Claude, Alan Yanovich, Jo-Ann Crawford and Pamela Ugaz. 'Mapping of Dispute Settlement Mechanism in Regional Trade Agreements: Innovative or Variations on a Theme,' *WTO Staff Working Paper, No ERSD-2013–07* (2013).

Cho, Sung-Joon. 'GATT Non-Violation Issues in the WTO Framework: Are They the Achilles' Heel of the Dispute Settlement Process?,' *Harvard International Law Review* Vol 39 (1998) 311.

Coase, Ronald H. *The Firm, the Market and the Law* (University of Chicago Press, 1988).

Cook, Graham. 'Defining Standard of Proof in WTO Dispute Settlement Proceedings: Jurists' Prudence and Jurisprudence,' *Journal of International Trade & Arbitration Law* Vol 1, No 2 (2012) 50–61.

Cottier, Thomas and Kristina Nadakavukaren Schefer. 'Non-Violation Complaints in WTO/GATT Dispute Settlement: Past, Present and Future,' in Petersmann, Ernst-Ulrich (ed.) *International Trade Law and the GATT/WTO Dispute Settlement System* (Kluwer Law International, 1997).

Davey, William J. 'Dispute Settlement in GATT,' *Fordham International Law Journal* Vol 11, No 1 (1987) 51–109.

Davies, Arwel. 'The DSU Article 3.8 Presumption That an Infringement Constitutes a *Prima Facie* Case of Nullification or Impairment: When Does It Operate and Why?,' *Journal of International Economic Law* Vol 13, No 1 (2010) 181–204.

Donaldson, Victoria. 'The Appellate Body: Institutional and Procedural Aspects,' in Macrory Patrick F.J., Arthur E. Appleton and Michael G. Plummer (eds.) *The WTO: Legal, Economic and Political Analysis* Vol 1 (Springer, 2005) 1277–1340.

Ehlermann, Claus-Dieter. 'Six Years on the Bench of the "World Trade Court": Some Personal Experiences as a Member of the Appellate Body of the World Trade Organization,' *Journal of World Trade* Vol 36, No 4 (2002) 605–639.

Evans, David and Gregory C. Shaffer. 'Introduction,' in Shaffer, Gregory C. and Ricardo Meléndez-Ortiz (eds.) *Dispute Settlement at the WTO: The Developing Country Experience* (Cambridge University Press, 2010).

Footer, Mary E. 'The Role of Consensus in GATT/WTO Decision-Making,' *Northwestern Journal of International Law & Business* Vol 17 (1997) 653–680.

GAO. *World Trade Organization: Standard of Review and Impact of Trade Remedy Rulings, Report to the Ranking Minority Member, Committee on Finance, US Senate* (GAO-03–824, July 2003) <www.gao.gov/new.items/d03824.pdf> (accessed 3 April 2019).
GATT. 'Ministerial Declaration on the Uruguay Round,' (GATT Doc. No. MIN 86/6) (20 September 1986).
GATT. 'Improvements to the GATT Dispute Settlement Rules and Procedures,' (GATT Doc BISD 36S/61) (12 April 1989a).
GATT. 'Negotiating Group on Dispute Settlement,' (MTN.GNG/NG13/16) (13 November 1989b).
GATT. 'Proposal by Mexico,' *Negotiating Group on Dispute Settlement*, (MTN.GNG/NG13/W/42) (12 July 1990).
Gourgourini, Anastasios. *Equity and Equitable Principles in the World Trade Organization: Addressing Conflicts and Overlaps between the WTO and Other Regimes* (Routledge, 2016).
Hillman, Jennifer. 'Conflicts between Dispute Settlement Mechanisms in Regional Trade Agreements and the WTO: What Should the WTO Do?,' *Cornell International Law Journal* Vol 42 (2009) 193–208.
Hoekman, Bernard M. and Michel M. Kostecki. *The Political Economy of the World Trading System: The WTO and Beyond* (Oxford University Press, 2009).
Horne, Henrik and Petros C. Mavroidis. 'A Survey of the Literature on the WTO Dispute Settlement System,' *IFN Working Paper, No. 684* (2006).
Hudec, Robert E. *The GATT Legal System and World Trade Diplomacy* (Butterworths Legal Publishers, 1990).
Hudec, Robert E. *Enforcing International Trade Law: Evolution of the Modern GATT Legal System* (Butterworths Legal Publishing, 1993).
Hudec, Robert E. *Developing Countries in the GATT Legal System* (Cambridge University Press, 2011).
Hughes, Valerie. 'The Institutional Dimensions,' in Bethlehem, Daniel, Donald McRae, Rodney Neufeld and Isabelle Van Damme (eds.) *The Oxford Handbook of International Trade Law* (Oxford University Press, 2009).
Islam, M. Rafiqul. *International Trade Law of the WTO* (Oxford University Press, 2012).
Islam, M. Rafiqul. 'The WTO Dispute Settlement System and Underlying Motivating Factors for Adjudication,' in Klein, Natalie (ed.) *Litigating International Law Disputes: Weighing the Options* (Cambridge University Press, 2014) 375–400.
ITC Report, 'Review of the Effectiveness of Trade Dispute Settlement Under the GATT and the Tokyo Round Agreements,' International Trade Commission Publication No 1793 (1985).
Jackson, John Howard. 'The Jurisprudence of International Trade: The Disc Case in GATT,' *The American Journal of International Law* Vol 72, No 4 (1978) 747–781.
Jackson, John Howard. *The World Trading System: Law and Policy of International Economic Relations* (MIT Press, 1997).
Jackson, John Howard. 'Dispute Settlement and the WTO: Emerging Problems,' *Journal of International Economic Law* Vol 1, No 3 (1998a) 329–351.
Jackson, John Howard. *The World Trade Organization: Constitution and Jurisprudence* (Royal Institute of International Affairs, 1998) 15–16.
Kaul, Ashok, Manuel Schieler and Michael Wolf. 'Standard of Proof in WTO Dispute Settlement Proceedings: An Applied Statistical Perspective,' *The Theory and Practice of Legislation* Vol 4, No 2 (2016) 303–316.
Kennedy, Kevin C. 'The GATT-WTO System at Fifty,' *Wisconsin International Law Journal* (1997) 421–528.
Kim, Dae-Won. *Non-Violation Complaint in WTO Law: Theory and Practice* (Peter Lang Publishers, 2006).
Koul, Autar Krishen. *Guide to the WTO and GATT: Economics, Law and Politics* (Springer International, 2018).
Krislov, Samuel. 'The Amicus Curiae Brief: From Friendship to Advocacy,' *Yale Law Journal* Vol 72 (1963).
Kufuor, Kofi Oteng. 'From GATT to the WTO: The Developing Countries and the Reform of the Procedures for the Settlement of International Trade Disputes,' *Journal of World Trade* Vol 31, No 5 (1997) 117–145.

Kwak, Kyung and Gabrielle Marceau. 'Overlaps and Conflicts of Jurisdiction between the World Trade Organization and Regional Trade Agreements,' *Canadian Year Book of International Law* Vol 41 (2003) 83–152.

Lacarte-Muró, Julio. and Fernando Piérola Castro. 'Comparing the WTO and GATT Dispute Settlement Mechanisms: What Was Accomplished in the Uruguay Round?,' in Grandos, Jamie (ed.) *Inter-Governmental Trade Dispute Settlement: Multilateral and Regional Approaches* (Cameron May, 2004) 31–60.

Laidhold, Michael. 'Private Party Access to the WTO: Do Recent Developments in International Trade Dispute Resolution Really Give Private Organizations a Voice in the WTO,' *The Transnational Lawyer* Vol 12 (1999) 427–450.

Leutwiler Report. *General Agreement on Tariffs and Trade: Report of Eminent Persons on Problems Facing the International Trade System, Reprinted in* 24 I.L.M. 716 (1985).

Lichtenbaum, Peter. 'Procedural Issues in WTO Dispute Resolution,' *Michigan Journal of International Law* Vol 19 (1998) 1195–1274.

Limenta, Michelle. *WTO Retaliation: Effectiveness and Purposes* (Hart Publishing, 2017).

Marceau, Gabrielle and Matthew Stilwell. 'Practical Suggestions for *Amicus Curiae* Briefs Before WTO Adjudicating Bodies,' *Journal of International Economic Law* Vol 4, No 1 (2001) 155–187.

Marceau, Gabrielle. 'WTO Dispute Settlement and Human Rights,' *European Journal of International Law* Vol 13, No 4 (2002) 753–814.

Marceau, Gabrielle. 'The Primacy of WTO Dispute Settlement System,' *Questions of International Law* Vol 23 (2015) 3–13.

Matsushita, Mitsuo. 'A Note on the Appellate Body Report in the Chinese Minerals Export Restrictions Case,' *Trade, Law and Development* Vol 4, No 2 (2012) 400–420.

Matsushita, Mitsuo, Thomas J. Shoenbaum, Petros C. Mavroidis and Michael Hahn. *The World Trade Organization: Law, Practice, and Policy* (Oxford University Press, 2015).

Mavroidis, Petros C. *Trade in Goods* (Oxford University Press, 2007).

Mavroidis, Petros C. *Trade in Goods* (Oxford University Press, 2013).

Moore, Michael. 'WTO's Unique System of Settling Disputes Nears 200 Cases in 2000,' *PRESS/180 Geneva: World Trade Organization* (2000).

Palmeter, David and Petros C. Mavroidis. *Dispute Settlement in the World Trade Organization: Practice and Procedure* (Cambridge University Press, 2004).

Panizzon, Marion. *Good Faith in the Jurisprudence of the WTO: The Protection of Legitimate Expectations, Good Faith Interpretation and Fair Dispute Settlement* (Hart Publishing, 2006).

Pauwelyn, Joost. 'Evidence, Proof and Persuasion in WTO Dispute Settlement: Who Bears the Burden?,' *Journal of International Economic Law* Vol 1 (1998) 227–258.

Pauwelyn, Joost. *Conflict of Norms in Public International Law: How WTO Law Relates to Other Rules of International Law* (Cambridge, 2003).

Pescatore, Pierre. 'Drafting and Analyzing Decisions on Dispute Settlement,' in Pescatore, Pierre, William J. Davey and Andreas Lowenfeld (eds.) *Handbook of WTO/GATT Dispute Settlement* (Transnational Publishers, 1997).

Petersmann, Ernst-Ulrich. *The GATT/WTO Dispute Settlement System: International Law, International Organizations and Dispute Settlement* (Kluwer Law International, 1997).

Pfitzer, James Headen and Sheila Sabune. 'Burden of Proof in WTO Dispute Settlement: Contemplating Preponderance of the Evidence,' *ICTSD Issue Paper No. 9* (2009).

Roessler, Frieder. 'The Concept of Nullification and Impairment in the Legal System of the World Trade Organization,' in Petersmann, Ernst-Ulrich (ed.) *International Trade Law and the GATT/WTO Dispute Settlement System*, Studies in Transnational Economic Law Vol 11 (Kluwer Law International, 1997) 125–142.

Rogoff, Martin A. 'The Obligation to Negotiate in International Law: Rules and Realities,' *Michigan Journal of International Law* Vol 16, No 1 (1994) 141–185.

Sacerdoti, Giorgio. 'The Dispute Settlement System of the WTO in Action: A Perspective on the First Ten Years,' in Sacerdoti, Giorgio, Alan Yanovich and Jan Bohanes (eds.) *The WTO at Ten: The Contribution of the Dispute Settlement System* (Cambridge University Press, 2006) 35–57.

Schuchhardt, Christian. 'Consultations,' in Macrory Patrick F.J., Arthur E. Appleton and Michael G. Plummer (eds.) *The WTO: Legal, Economic and Political Analysis* Vol 1 (Springer, 2005) 1197–1232.

Shell, G. Richard. 'Trade Legalism and International Relations Theory: An Analysis of the World Trade Organization,' *Duke Law Journal* Vol 44, No 5 (1995) 829–927.

Shaffer, Gregory C. 'Developing Country Use of the WTO Dispute Settlement System: Why It Matters, the Barriers Posed,' in Hartigan, James C. (ed.) *Trade Disputes and the Dispute Settlement Understanding of the WTO: An Interdisciplinary Assessment* (Emerald Group Publishing, 2009) 167–190.

Shoyer, Andrew W., Eric M. Solovy and Alexander W. Koff. 'Implementation and Enforcement of Dispute Settlement Decisions,' in Macrory Patrick F.J., Arthur E. Appleton and Michael G. Plummer (eds.) *The WTO: Legal, Economic and Political Analysis* Vol 1 (Springer, 2005) 1341–1369.

Sohn, Louis B. 'The Future of Dispute Settlement,' in MacDonald, R St. J. and Douglas M. Johnston (eds.) *The Structure and Process of International Law* (Martin Nijhoff, 1983).

Spadano, Lucas Eduardo F.A. 'Cross-Agreement Retaliation in the WTO Dispute Settlement System: An Important Enforcement Mechanism for Developing Countries?,' *World Trade Review* Vol 7, No 3 (2008) 511–545.

Squatrito, Theresa. 'Amicus Curiae Briefs in the WTO DSM: Good or Bad News for Non-State Actor Involvement?,' *World Trade Review* Vol 17, No 1 (2018) 1–25.

Staiger, Robert W. and Alan O. Sykes. 'Non-Violations,' *Journal of International Economic Law* Vol 16, No 4 (2013) 741–775.

Stiglitz, Joseph E. *Globalization and Its Discontent* (Norton, 2002).

Stoll, Peter-Tobias and Frank Schorkopf. *WTO: World Economic Order, World Trade Law* (Martin Nijhoff Publishers, 2006).

Taniguchi, Yasuhei. 'Understanding the Concept of Prima Facie Proof in WTO Dispute Settlement,' in Janow, Merit E., Victoria Donaldson and Alan Yanovich (eds.) *The WTO: Governance, Dispute Settlement & Developing Countries* (Juris Publishing, 2008) 553–572.

Telser, Lester G. 'A Theory of Self-Enforcing Agreements,' *The Journal of Business* (1980) 27–44.

Trachtman, Joel P. 'The Domain of WTO Dispute Resolution,' *Harvard International Law Journal* Vol 40, No 2 (1999) 333–377.

Trebilcock, Michael, Robert Howse and Antonia Eliason. *The Regulation of International Trade* (Routledge, 2012).

Truman, Harry S. 'Address on Foreign Economic Policy,' Speech Delivered at Baylor University, Texas (6 March 1947) <www.trumanlibrary.gov/library/public-papers/52/address-foreign-economic-policy-delivered-baylor-university> (accessed 2 August 2018).

United Nations. *Handbook of Peaceful Settlement of Disputes between States* (United Nations, 1992).

Unterhalter, David. 'Allocating the Burden of Proof in WTO Dispute Settlement Proceedings,' *Cornell International Law Journal* Vol 42 (2009) 209–221.

Van den Bossche, Peter and Werner Zdouc. *The Law and Policy of the World Trade Organization: Text, Cases and Material* (Cambridge University Press, 2017).

VanGrasstek, Craig. *The History and Future of the World Trade Organization* (WTO, 2013).

Vázquez, Carlos M. and John Howard Jackson. 'Some Reflections on Compliance with WTO Dispute Settlement Decisions,' *Law & Policy in International Business* Vol 33 (2002) 555–567.

Verhoosel, Gaëtan. *National Treatment and WTO Dispute Settlement: Adjudicating the Boundaries of Regulatory Autonomy* (Hart Publishing, 2002).

Wilkinson, Rorden. *Multilateralism and the World Trade Organisation: The Architecture and Extension of International Trade Regulation* (Routledge, 2000).

World Trade Organization. *A Handbook on the WTO Dispute Settlement System* (Cambridge University Press, 2004).

World Trade Organization. *World Trade Report: Six Decades of Multilateral Cooperation, What Have We Learnt?* (WTO, 2007).

World Trade Organization. *The Legal Texts: The Results of the Uruguay Round of Multilateral Trade Negotiations* (Cambridge University Press, 2010).

World Trade Organization. *A Handbook on the WTO Dispute Settlement System* (Cambridge University Press, 2017).

WTO, Sutherland, Peter, Jagdish Bhagwati, Kwesi Botchwey, Niall W.A. Fitzgerald, Koichi Hamada, John H. Jackson, Celso Lafer and Thierry de Montbrial. 'The Future of the WTO: Addressing Institutional Challenges in the New Millennium,' Report of the Consultative Board to the Director-General Supachai Panitchpakdi (WTO, 2004).

Yanovich, Alan and Tania Voon. 'Completing the Analysis in Two Appeals: The Practice and Its Limitations,' *Journal of International Economic Law* Vol 9, No 4 (2006) 933–950.

4 Non-Discrimination

Most-Favoured Nation Treatment

Learning Objectives	138
1. Introduction	139
2. The Most-Favoured Nation Obligation Under GATT	139
2.1 MFN Treatment Obligation: Origins	139
2.2 Nature of MFN Treatment Obligation: Article I:1	141
2.3 Interpretation of MFN Obligation: Likeness	144
2.3.1 Likeness Under the GATT Era	145
2.3.2 Likeness Under the WTO Era	146
2.4 MFN Obligation and Special and Differential Treatment	147
2.4.1 Special and Differential Treatment Under GATT	147
2.4.2 Special and Differential Treatment Under GATT 1994	149
2.4.3 Additional Preferential Treatment *Vis-à-vis* Enabling Clause	151
2.5 Exception to MFN: Regional Integration, Quotas, and Waivers	152
2.5.1 Regional Integration (GATT Article XXIV)	152
2.5.2 Quotas	152
2.5.3 Waivers	153
3. The Most-Favoured Nation Obligation Under GATS	153
3.1 Nature of the MFN Treatment Obligation: Article II:1 of GATS	154
3.1.1 Measures Covered Under Article II:1	155
3.2 'Like' Service and 'Like' Service Suppliers	156
3.2.1 Treatment 'No Less Favourable'	157
3.3 Derogation From MFN Obligation Under GATS	159
4. Summary	160

Learning Objectives

This chapter aims to help students understand:

1. The principles of non-discrimination, the origins of the MFN clause, and the nature of the MFN treatment obligation;
2. The interpretation of MFN obligation and the concept of 'likeness' in the GATT era and the WTO era;
3. The MFN obligation and special and differential treatment under GATT and GATT 1994;
4. The exceptions to MFN obligation and MFN obligations under the GATS Agreement; and
5. The derogation from MFN treatment under GATS.

DOI: 10.4324/9780367028183-5

1. Introduction

One of the core principles embedded in the rule book of the WTO is non-discrimination. This is necessitated as discriminatory treatment in international trade relations is bound to distort any trade performed under the multilateral trading system, besides breeding distrust and resentment amongst trading nations. The success of the WTO is predicated on its democratic origins, where non-discrimination as a fundamental principle is espoused. Each rule of the WTO is negotiated by Member States and ratified by the respective parliaments of such states. Member States are treated equally, whether they are big or small, big economies or small economies – the same rules apply to everyone, and the elimination of any discriminatory treatment is considered a core value of the WTO. The non-discrimination principle underpins the equal rights of the Member States and is found in the WTO agreements in all three Annex 1 Agreements.[1]

It will be a useful exercise to first determine what will be considered discriminatory, and how to determine if there is discrimination in practice. The two fundamental elements of discrimination are an intent to discriminate and the effect, or impact, of such discrimination. For our purposes, *i.e.*, international trade, discrimination is likely to occur on the import sector, where similarities are present in both imported and domestically produced goods – *e.g.*, a certain measure may treat domestically produced spirits better than imported spirits. Under one theory, intent is the key to identifying discrimination, where intent refers to the motive or purpose behind the measures introduced and identified as discriminative behaviour. The other factor to be considered is the effect, *i.e.*, whether a measure has a discriminatory effect against imports (Lester, Mercurio, and Davies, 2018).[2] The two categories of discrimination are *de jure* and *de facto* discrimination. When the discrimination is apparent on the face of the measure introduced, it is classified as *de jure*,[3] and when the measure introduced distinguishes between different products based on their physical attributes, it is classified as *de facto* (Lester, Mercurio, and Davies, 2018).[4] The non-discrimination principle consists of two major components, *viz.*, the most-favoured nation (MFN) treatment and the national treatment (NT) obligations.

MFN and NT obligations demand harmonization, *per se*, towards universal norms, but were designed to permit countries to maintain their own policy space and to set their own standards and priorities, as long as all economic actors, both foreign and domestic, are treated equally (Moore, 2005). It should be stressed here that non-discrimination had provided the foundation for the expansion of the global trade in the post-WWII era, commencing with GATT 1947 and progressively introducing new sectors with the creation of the WTO. In the jurisprudential study of the WTO disciplines, the NT obligation receives more attention than the MFN obligation as discrimination against trading partners occurs more frequently than discrimination among trading partners, giving rise to trade disputes (Lester, Mercurio, and Davies, 2018). The two components of the non-discrimination principle, *i.e.*, the MFN and NT obligations, are taken up for discussion respectively in the current chapter and the ensuing chapter.

2. The Most-Favoured Nation Obligation Under GATT

2.1 MFN Treatment Obligation: Origins

The phrase 'most-favoured' seems to imply a 'special favourable treatment' for a particular country, but in reality, the concept is one of equal treatment. Under GATT, the MFN treatment obligation requires each Member State to accord to every other Member State the 'most favourable' treatment which it grants to any country with regards to imports and exports of products (Jackson, 1995). The MFN principles are traceable to the eleventh century, where the northern Italian city of Mantua obtained from the Holy Roman Emperor, Henry III, the guarantee that it would always benefit from all privileges granted by the Emperor to 'whatsoever other town' (Hudec, 1998). The term 'most-favoured nation', as such, first appears in the seventeenth century, and it is fair to say that it is one of the oldest legal obligations in trade practice amongst nations. When trade grew in the fifteenth and sixteenth centuries, MFN-type treaty clauses came to be used by European nations, who sought to develop a network of trading relationship.[5] The introduction of the MFN provision was to link commercial treaties through time and between states, and the provision was initially applied to concessions granted only to particular states, which gradually came to be applied to concessions granted to all countries (Long, 1973). Jackson notes that it is likely that MFN clauses were used as 'short-hand' means to include trade obligations in new treaties, thereby avoiding an arduous detail of those obligations (Jackson, 1969).

Two approaches were taken towards the grant of MFN treatment, *viz.*, (i) unconditional MFN – where no conditions were placed for the grant of concessions to other countries, in that any tariff concessions made to country A for a particular trade agreement would similarly apply to all other countries as well, and (ii) conditional MFN – where tariff concessions were granted on condition that the other country offered compensation in the form of their own concessions.

The Treaty of Amity and Commerce signed on 6 February 1778 between the US and France included a conditional MFN clause (Malloy, 1910; Long, 1973).[6] Similarly, the Treaty of Commerce between Great Britain and France signed in Paris on 23 January 1860, known as the Cobden Treaty, contained an unconditional MFN clause (Ustor, 1968; Long, 1973). The unconditional MFN obligation was prevalent during the eighteenth century, but conditional MFN obligations became more widespread in the early nineteenth century. Interestingly, the unconditional MFN obligation was to make a comeback in the second part of the nineteenth century (Davey and Pauwelyn, 2002). While the US practice during the nineteenth century could be classified as conditional MFN, in contrast the UK, and much of European nations' practice, fell within the category of unconditional MFN (Ustor, 1968). Some commentators take the view that although the US formally adhered to a conditional MFN policy for close to 150 years, it engaged in negligible discrimination, with a few exceptions, and maintained a single column tariff, so that the practice was *de facto* non-discriminatory (Kelly Jr., 1963).[7]

The economic relationship between the US and the European states in the nineteenth century largely dictated the way the MFN principles were interpreted by the two blocs. But with the outbreak of World War I their relationship changed dramatically, and so did the way the MFN principles were perceived. As discussed in earlier chapters, the European states formed trade alliances in the lead-up to World War I, which was considered as one of the causes for the outbreak of the war. This particular trade policy was discussed in the 1920s and 1930s during the League of Nations economic and financial conferences, which led to the European states introducing MFN clauses in the bilateral trade agreements once more (Lester, Mercurio, and Davies, 2018).[8] The League of Nations devoted a substantial amount of time to the promotion of the MFN clause, and at one point even sought to codify the clause, and later went on to prepare a series of reports and studies on the MFN principles, including the legal language for a recommended MFN clause (Hyder, 1968). Likewise, in the 1920s the US changed its trade policy to reflect its broader export interests, offering complete and continuous non-discriminatory treatment and thereby reducing discrimination against US exports (Long, 1973). The Tariff Act of 1922, which was implemented in 1923, gave the authority to the US to offer unconditional MFN treatment to trade partners. Unlike the European states, the US was a much stronger economic power in the post-World War I era, as a major creditor to war debts totalling $12.5 billion (Offner, 1986). The US Reciprocal Trade Agreement of 1934 also contained an unconditional MFN clause, which served as the blueprint for the GATT.

During the ITO negotiations, the US argued that the MFN provision in the trade agreement was "absolutely fundamental".[9] Russell Long notes that the US exports in 1948, at the beginning of the GATT era, were $13 billion, which rose to $45 billion in 1970, and argues that one of the key factors for the steep increase in exports was down to adherence of the MFN principle (Long, 1973). The International Law Commission (ILC) attempted to draft a set of rules on the MFN clause in general, the draft of which defined MFN in the following terms:

> treatment accorded by the granting State to the beneficiary State or to persons or things in a determined relationship with that State, no less favourable than treatment extended by the granting State to a third State or to persons or things in the same relationship with that third State.
>
> (ILC Yearbook, 1978)[10]

The operation of the MFN clause presupposes a relationship of a minimum of three States – a granting State (State X), a beneficiary State (State Y), and a third State (State Z) – where State X enters into an agreement (containing obligations and concessions) with State Y, to extend benefits that are already granted to State Z through incorporation (Schill, 2009; Wolfrum, 2008).[11] The consequence of an MFN clause in the treaty between State X and State Y is that State Y can rely on all such benefits that State X grants to State Z. The treaty between States X and Z does not modify the relationship between States X and Y, and the MFN clause does not break with the *inter partes* effect of international treaties (Schill, 2009).[12]

2.2 Nature of MFN Treatment Obligation: Article I:1

The MFN clause, along with the national treatment obligation, came to be considered a cornerstone of the GATT and a pillar of the WTO.[13] In pure economic terms, application of MFN treatment obligation would ensure a country's imports come from the most efficient international supplier and protect bilateral concessions. The justification for the MFN principle is premised on economic theory that views markets as the most efficient engines for creating global welfare (Schwartz and Sykes, 1998). Through the MFN treatment, an existing bilateral relationship becomes multilateralised through the extension of concessions.[14] The MFN treatment obligation has a variety of other benefits, both economic and political, to the multilateral trading system. MFN treatment (i) eliminates distortions in production patterns; (ii) can result in broader trade liberalisation, as tariff cuts are offered to all countries; (iii) can simplify trade negotiations; (iv) can lead to more straightforward and transparent customs policies, as rules of origin may not be relevant; and (v) treats all nations equally, thereby reducing international tensions and increasing more secure trade (Lester, Mercurio, and Davies, 2018). The justification for the introduction of MFN clause is economic, as the MFN obligation provides a multiplier effect, which assures that advantages accorded to one Member State is extended to all Member States of the multilateral trading system (Matsushita, Shoenbaum, Mavroidis, and Hahn, 2017), thereby reducing the overall negotiating costs. With the aforementioned traits, the MFN obligation stabilises the multilateral trading system and increases the efficiency of the world economy.

On the other side of the MFN principle spectrum is the risk of free-riding and the costs associated with it in practice. Commentators have highlighted the potential costs of free-riding on the bargaining outcomes of others, due to the externality that MFN creates across bargaining pairs (Caplin and Krishna, 1988). It is argued that costs of both direct negotiations and the reducing tariffs fall on the negotiation countries, while benefits accrue to all countries with MFN status, and that the ability to free-ride can prevent governments from reaching the efficiency frontier (Caplin and Krishna, 1988).[15] Assessing the free-riding argument, Ludema and Mayda argue that only the largest exporters of a particular product will take part in negotiations with an importer for tariff concessions, and that there is strong evidence of free-rider effect of the MFN clause for US tariffs (Ludema and Mayda, 2006).

It is equally argued that the MFN free-riding syndrome can be suppressed through reciprocity, *viz.*, bilateral liberalisation, thereby casting doubts on the relevance of a free-rider argument to the GATT/WTO system (Bagwell and Staiger, 2002). The MFN obligation as enshrined in the WTO's legal framework is largely unconditional, with a few exceptions. In the post-Uruguay Round of negotiations, the MFN treatment obligation has suffered a setback due to the proliferation of Regional Trade Agreements (RTAs), which has the effect of rendering the MFN obligation under the WTO a dead letter.[16] Observing the situation of the proliferation of RTAs, the Southerland Report noted as follows:

> [N]early five decades after the founding of the GATT, MFN is no longer the rule; it is almost the exception. Certainly, much trade between the major economies is still conducted on an MFN basis. However, what has been termed the "spaghetti bowl" of customs unions, common markets, regional and bilateral free trade areas, preferences and an endless assortment of miscellaneous trade deals has almost reached the point where MFN treatment is exceptional treatment.[17]

A substantial volume of international trade is now being diverted away from the multilateral trading system and performed through RTAs, and especially through mega-RTAs. This, in effect, undermines the MFN obligation as well as the very foundations of the multilateral trading system. A detailed discussion of RTAs is carried out in chapter 15.

The MFN treatment principle is expressed in Article I of the GATT as follows:

> With respect to customs duties and charges of any kind imposed on or in connection with importation or exportation or imposed on the international transfer of payments for imports or exports, and with respect to the method of levying such duties and charges, and with respect to all rules and formalities in connection with importation and exportation, and with respect to all matters referred to in paragraphs 2 and 4 of Article III, any advantage, favour, privilege or immunity granted by any [Member] to any product originating in or destined for any other country shall be accorded immediately and unconditionally to the like product originating in or destined for the territories of all other [Members].[18]

The phrase "matters referred to in paragraphs 2 and 4 of Article III" occurring in Article I:1 was inserted during the Geneva session of the Preparatory Committee in 1947, on the back of a US proposal, with a view "to extend the grant of most-favoured-nation treatment to all matters dealt with in [these paragraphs] regardless of whether national treatment is provided for in respect of such matters" (UN Economic and Social Council, 1947). The MFN clause found in the Article I of the GATT is multilateral, and unconditional in nature, as opposed to the clauses found in the earlier eras, which were primarily bilateral and largely conditional in nature. Article II of the GATT repeats the MFN obligation with regard to tariff bindings, where each contracting party is to "accord to the commerce of the other contracting parties treatment no less favourable than that provided for" in its schedule of concessions.[19] The other provisions contained within GATT, relating to the MFN obligation, are Article III:7 (on local content requirement); Article V (on freedom of transit); Article IX:1 (on marks of origin); Article XIII:1 (on the non-discriminatory administration of quantitative restrictions); and Article XVII (on State trading enterprises). An MFN-like obligation is to be found in Article XX of the GATT 1994, and in the *Chapeau* of this 'general exceptions' provision.

The MFN principles are followed up in Article 2.3 of the SPS Agreement; Article 2.1 of the TBT Agreement (with regard to goods); Article II of GATS Agreement (with regard to services); and Article 4 of the TRIPS Agreement (with regard to intellectual property rights). However, the scope and nature of the MFN obligation across the prior agreements vary. The Appellate Body in *Canada – Autos* noted that the GATT 1994 contained several 'MFN-type' clauses dealing with varied matters, other than Article I:1.[20] One will observe that the MFN or MFN-type clauses found in other GATT agreements demonstrate the universal character of the MFN principle of non-discrimination in WTO law.[21] The generalisation of MFN obligation, over time, has rendered the MFN concept into a principle of non-discrimination and equal treatment. This section of the chapter, however, takes up for discussion of the MFN treatment obligations as contained in Article I:1 of the GATT 1994 and Article II:1 of the GATS.

Article I:1 of the GATT is a trade restrictive measure, which applies to both border measures and internal regulations. Border measures are referred to in Article I as "customs duties and charges of any kind imposed on or in connection with importation or exportation.... formalities in connection with importation and exportation",[22] and internal measures are referred to as "all matters referred to in paragraphs 2 and 4 of Article III", which are beyond the border, and applied to goods once they have legally entered the market. In short, it covers payments restrictions, as well as all internal measures covered by paragraphs 2 and 4 of Article III. Article I:1 applies to bound and unbound tariffs[23] and to both exportation and importation. Article I:1 identifies four categories of exchange concessions for the application of the MFN principle obligation, which is as follows:

i   To customs duties and charges of any kind imposed on the export and import of goods, including the international transfer of payments for import and export purposes;
ii To the methods of levying such duties and charges;
iii To the rules and formalities of import and export; and
iv To all matters referred to in paras. 2 and 4 of Article III regarding internal taxation.

As border measures have been largely succeeded by internal tax and regulatory measures in recent times, the functionality of MFN treatment has shifted away from border measures and tariffs to internal measures (Diebold, 2010). Article I:1, which adopts an obligatory language, covers *de jure*, as well as *de facto*, discrimination. For instance, Member State B imposes a customs duty of 15 percent on cars from Member State C, while imposing a customs duty of 23 percent on cars originating from Member State D, the imposition of 23 percent customs duty on Member State D will be viewed as *de jure* discrimination. When such measures of discrimination appear on the face not to discriminate, but in fact do discriminate, it will be considered *de facto* discrimination. Both 'origin-based' measures and measures that are factually discriminatory (although appearing to be 'origin-neutral') fall under *de facto* discrimination (Bhala, 2013). The Appellate Body in *Canada – Autos*, while reviewing the Panel's finding on Canadian import duty exemptions on motor vehicles originating from certain countries,[24] found that the prohibition of discrimination under Article I:1 will include both *de jure* and *de facto* discrimination:

> [T]he words of Article I:1 do not restrict its scope only to cases in which the failure to accord an "advantage" to like products of all other Members appears on the face of the measure, or can be demonstrated on the basis of the words of the measure. . . . Article I:1 does not cover only "in law", or *de jure*, discrimination. As several GATT Panel reports confirmed, Article I:1 covers also "in fact", or *de facto*, discrimination. Like the Panel, we cannot accept Canada's argument that Article I:1 does not apply to measures which, on their face, are "origin-neutral".[25]

The panel in *Canada – Pharmaceutical Patents* noted:

> [D]*e facto* discrimination is a general term describing the legal conclusion that an ostensibly neutral measure transgresses a non-discrimination norm because its actual effect is to impose differentially disadvantageous consequences on certain parties, and because those differential effects are found to be wrong or unjustifiable.[26]

2.3 Interpretation of MFN Obligation: Likeness

The theoretical justification behind the principle of the MFN treatment obligation contained in Article I:1 is to ensure all WTO Member States' equality of opportunity to import from, or to export to, other WTO Member States. The MFN obligation prohibits a Member State from discriminating between other countries, or in other words requires Member States to accord the same advantage granted to a product originating in or destined for any other country immediately and unconditionally to the 'like products' originating in or destined for all other Member States.[27] When a government measure draws a distinction as between two products, as opposed to country of origin of the products, it gives rise to the question of 'like products', where one product receives an enhanced treatment to the other. This could lead to the Member State, whose products received a below par treatment, to complain that its products are not accorded the same treatment that 'like products' from other Member State received, which was in violation of Article I:1 of the GATT. In such an event, the key question for consideration will be *if the two products at issue are 'like'*.

It should be borne in mind that the purpose of the MFN obligation as contained in Article I:1 is to protect the equality of competitive opportunities for the Member State within the multilateral trading system, where the determination of 'likeness' leads to the determination of competitive relationships between different products in question (Matsushita, Shoenbaum, Mavroidis, and Hahn, 2017).[28] One can also conclude that Member States may lawfully treat 'unlike' products differently. Although common traits may assist in determining if the products in question are 'like', the same may not aid in deciding the legal issues at hand. That said, the term 'like product' occurs well over a dozen times in the GATT, which does not contain a legal definition of the term, as it is to be understood within the context and purpose of its usage. In the absence of a clear definition, most GATT and WTO Panels looked to the 1970 report of a Working Party on Border Taxes for guidance. Interestingly, it was noted in the report that the term caused uncertainty and was to be interpreted on a case-by-case basis (Working Party Report, 1970). The report went on to note:

> the interpretation of the term should be examined on a case-by-case basis. This would allow a fair assessment in each case of the different elements that constitute a "similar" product. Some criteria were suggested for determining, on a case-by-case basis, whether a product is "similar": the product's end-uses in a given market; consumers' tastes and habits, which change from country to country; the product's properties, nature and quality.[29]

However, commenting on the aforementioned practice of the Panels from the GATT era, Hudec notes that the criteria listed in the report were only suggestions from some members of the Working Party, and even at that the "suggestions are merely reported by the Working Party, but in no way officially recommended by it", and suggests that the value of the quotations from the report are more to legitimise the step-by-step approach to be taken (Hudec, 2002). Given the previously stated position, a study of the jurisprudence of the GATT and the WTO eras on the term 'like products' as occurring in Article I:1 of the GATT would help gain a clearer understanding of the term in the context of the MFN principle.

2.3.1 Likeness Under the GATT Era

Panels during the GATT era generally took the view that any benefit accorded to a Member State, which was not made available to another Member State, as an 'advantage', and fell within GATT Article I:1.[30] For instance, in *Belgian Family Allowances (Allocations Familiales)*, Belgium was imposing a special charge on the purchases made by public agencies of Danish and Norwegian imports and not on purchases made from four other countries. On a complaint, the GATT Panel ruled that Belgium's family allowance levy was in violation of Article I:1, and directed the amendment of the relevant Belgian legislation which "introduced a discrimination between countries having a given system of family allowances and those which had a different system or no system at all, and made the granting of the exemption dependent on certain conditions".[31] Commentators note that, with a view to avoid triggering the MFN obligation, contracting states were tempted to make fine product distinctions in their national tariff classifications (Hudec, 1991; Diebold, 2010). One instance of such an attempt to make product distinction comes from the 1904 German trade measure allowing tariff concessions to Switzerland for "[l]arge dappled mountain cattle reared at a spot at least 300 meters above sea level and having at least one month's grazing each year at a spot at least 800 meters above sea level".[32] Under the WTO's non-discrimination principles, the measure will be considered a clear violation of the MFN principle obligation.

Under the GATT era most cases on Article I:1 turned on the question if similar products originating from different countries and subject to different tariffs could qualify as 'like' under Article I:1 (Diebold, 2010). For instance, in *Germany – Sardines* the German tariff scheme which differentiated between three types of sardines, *viz.*, pilchard, herring, and sprat, was under scrutiny. With regard to tariff rates pilchard was favoured over herring and sprat, which affected Norway as an exporter of herring and sprat in comparison to Portugal, which was exporting pilchard at that time. The Panel was inclined to qualify the three types of sardines as 'alike', relying predominantly on different tariff classifications, and found that there was no violation of Article I GATT.[33] The Panel in *Spain – Unroasted Coffee* took a different approach, where it also considered marketplace factors besides the physical characteristics and tariff classifications while determining likeness.[34] Spain had proceeded to subdivide the imported unroasted coffee into five categories with different tariff rates, which resulted in higher tariffs being levied for coffee exported from Brazil than from coffee exported from Spain's former colonies. The Panel, while considering the different types of unroasted coffee as 'like products', took the position that differences arising from geographical factors, cultivation methods, processing of the beans, and the genetic factor did not permit for imposing different tariff treatment.[35] The Panel also noted that Spain had not bound its tariffs under the GATT for unroasted coffee and ruled that Article I:1 equally applied to bound and unbound tariff items.[36] Hudec notes that the key legal impact of the case had been the general support that it gave to the idea that panels can overlook fine distinctions when they analyse the 'likeness' of two products (Hudec, 2002).

In *Australia – Ammonium Sulphate*, where domestic Australia's consumption subsidy on imported fertilizer was at issue, the Panel, while proceeding to determine 'likeness' between two types of fertilizers, noted that Article I does not distinguish between 'like products' and 'directly competitive or substitutable products', and declined to examine the competitive relationship of the two products in question, *viz.*, fertilizers.[37] In *EEC – Animal Feed Proteins*, the Panel was required to analyse whether all products used in adding protein to animal feeds should be considered as 'like products'. After considering the different tariff classifications, the physical differences relating to varying protein content and different vegetable, animal, and synthetic origins of the products in question, the Panel reached the conclusion that the products were 'unlike'.[38] The Panels under the erstwhile GATT regime adopted a narrow and yet objective interpretation of Article I with regards to 'like' products (Diebold, 2010).

Yet another case to be decided during the GATT era was the *Japan Alcoholics Beverages I* case,[39] where the Panel in 1987 ruled that standard distilled spirit classifications were 'like products', *viz.*, gin, vodka, whiskey, and grape brandy, as well as classic liqueurs, still wine, and sparkling wine. To reach its conclusions the Panel relied on the criteria listed in the Working Party Report from 1970, and the definition applied in *Spain – Unroasted Coffee*, where it was held that minor differences in taste, colour, and other properties would not affect the 'likeness' of products.

2.3.2 Likeness Under the WTO Era

McRae notes that the creation of an Appellate Body in the WTO provided an opportunity to interpret and clarify Article I:1 of the GATT (McRae, 2012). To determine if a measure affecting trade in goods is consistent with the MFN treatment obligation, Article I:1 envisages a four-stage test, namely

i   Whether the measure in question is covered by Article I:1;
ii Whether that measure in question grants an 'advantage';
iii Whether the products concerned are 'like products'; and
iv Whether the 'advantage' has been accorded 'immediately and unconditionally' to all like products concerned, irrespective of their origin or destination.[40]

The Appellate Body in *Canada – Autos*, while emphasizing the breadth of the obligation contained in Article I:1 of the GATT, noted that the provision clearly prohibited discrimination between like products originating in, or destined for, different countries.[41] In *US – Section 211 Appropriation Act*, the Appellate Body observed that the MFN obligation is "central and essential to assuring the success of a global rules-based system for trade in goods".[42] With regards to the non-discrimination obligation, the Appellate Body in *EC – Bananas III* had the following to say:

> The essence of the non-discrimination obligations is that like products should be treated equally, irrespective of their origin. As no participant disputes that all bananas are like products, the non-discrimination provisions apply to all imports of bananas, irrespective of whether and how a Member categorizes or subdivides these imports for administrative or other reasons.[43]

As noted by the Appellate Body in *EC – Seal Products*, the national treatment obligation prohibits discriminatory treatment of lawfully "imported products *vis-à-vis* like domestic products",[44] and the MFN obligation limits the right of Member States to discriminate "between and among like products of different origins".[45] The Appellate Body in *EC – Seal Products* explained that Articles I:1 and III:4 of the GATT 1994 are "concerned, fundamentally, with prohibiting discriminatory measures by requiring . . . equality of competitive opportunities", and thus do not "require a demonstration of the actual trade effects of a specific measure".[46] Both the Appellate Body and the Panels in their reports have repeatedly stressed that the purpose of GATT Article III is to provide equal competitive conditions for like imported products in relation to domestic products.[47] In short, restrictions are imposed under Article I:1 and other MFN clauses on a Member States' freedom to take unilateral measures, *i.e.*, favouring a friendly Member State over another Member State, unless it can be demonstrated that such treatment falls within the exception of Article XXIV.

The Appellate Body in *Japan – Alcoholic Beverages II* described the concept of 'likeness' as relative, and noted as follows:

> The concept of 'likeness' is a relative one that evokes the image of an accordion. The accordion of 'likeness' stretches and squeezes in different places as different provisions of the WTO Agreement are applied. The width of the accordion in any one of those places must be determined by the particular provision in which the term 'like' is encountered as well as by the context and the circumstances that prevail in any given case to which that provision may apply.[48]

In the aforementioned instance, the Appellate Body had cleverly used the imagery of an 'accordion' to characterize the concept of 'like products' and stressed the need for a case-by-case approach while determining there was an alleged discrimination leading to a violation of the MFN obligation by a Member State. In *Philippines – Distilled Spirits* the Appellate Body noted that in order to establish "the nature and extent of a competitive relationship between and among the products" in a 'like product' analysis, four elements are to be established, *viz.*, (i) the end uses of the product in question in a given market; (ii) the consumers' tastes and habits – that vary from country to country; (iii) the properties, nature, and quality of the product in question; and (iv) the tariff classification.[49] To determine 'likeness' the Appellate Body took into account internal regulatory regime of a product.[50]

2.4 MFN Obligation and Special and Differential Treatment

2.4.1 Special and Differential Treatment Under GATT

The origins of the special and differential (S&D) treatment for developing countries, or the 'Enabling Clause', can be traced to the GATT era, when developing countries sought to progressively acquire preferential treatment right (Kofele-Kale, 1987; Hudec, 1992). During the Havana negotiations, there was no formal recognition of developing countries as a formal group or of their special needs (Michalopoulos, 2000). When pre-independent India was presented with the US *Suggested Charter*[51] during the Havana negotiations, there was a clear opposition to the MFN obligation, and it was further felt by India that (i) the instrument clearly did not address the asymmetries across the participating countries and also (ii) did not take into account the development needs of the weaker players, and as a result was not equipped to deal with the countries at different stages of development (Irwin, Mavroidis, and Sykes, 2008).[52] Likewise, under the GATT 1947, the developing countries participated on an essentially equal basis with their developed country counterparts, with the need to justify recourse to any non-tariff barriers. A core principle of the original GATT agreement was that the rights and obligations applied uniformly to all contracting parties. The developing countries were critical of the organising principles of the GATT (developed in the immediate aftermath of World War II), as they found them to be inadequate to deal with the trade problems of the multilateral GATT. Although no specific provision designed to facilitate developing countries existed in the GATT at the time of its creation, a draft charter of the ITO did contain an enabling provision which contemplated the use of protective measures by the contracting parties for the establishment, development, or reconstruction of particular industries or branches of agriculture contrary to their obligations, provided they obtained the permission of the other contracting parties (Michalopoulos, 2000).[53]

One of the central principles of the GATT that came up for criticism from the developing countries was the MFN obligation, which required reciprocal non-discrimination in international trade relations. It was argued by the developing countries that the reciprocal tariff concessions, or MFN obligation, imposed a crushing burden which demanded "disproportionate sacrifices" in relation to those expected of developed industrialised countries, which made it impossible for developing countries to compete with producers in industrialised countries (Kofele-Kale, 1987). Importantly, from the 1960s the membership of the developing countries started to increase in the GATT.[54] The developing countries were concerned that an increase in income and output could only be achieved through increased industrialisation, and that liberal trade policies could not possibly promote industrialisation and development in their respective jurisdictions and could potentially stymie the development of infant industries due to the then prevailing patterns of international trade (Michalopoulos, 2000). The developing countries shifted their trade policy to include the promotion of industrialisation through import substitution and the use of trade controls in response to actual or potential balance-of-payment difficulties.

The request for an S&D treatment for developing countries were premised on the arguments that (i) developing countries are inherently disadvantaged in their participation in international trade, and consequently any multilateral agreement where they participate alongside developed countries must take into account this fundamental weakness while factoring in their rights and responsibilities; (ii) the trade policies that helped maximise sustainable development in developing countries are different from those in developed economies, and hence the same trade policy disciplines applied to developed countries should not apply to developing countries; and (iii) it is in the best interest of developed countries to assist developing countries in their fuller integration and participation in the international trading system (Michalopoulos, 2000).

In 1964, the developing countries succeeded in establishing a rival UN organisation, *viz.*, the United Nations Conference on Trade and Development (UNCTAD), to pursue their international trade agenda.[55] UNCTAD was primarily created to provide a forum for the developing countries to discuss the problems encountered in relation to their trade and economic development.⁵⁶ The agenda of UNCTAD in the 1960s and 1970s included the establishment of a system of preferences for developing country exports of manufactures in developed country markets and the stabilisation of commodity trade. The creation of the new organisation posed a credible threat of the developing countries breaking away from the GATT and take the foreign trade business away to UNCTAD (Hudec, 1992). In 1968 the developing countries succeeded in formulating the Generalised System of Preferences (GSP)⁵⁷ under UNCTAD. Under this scheme the exports and imports of certain agricultural goods from the developing countries entered duty-free or at reduced rates into the developed countries.⁵⁸ In 1971 a GATT waiver from MFN obligations was granted to the developing countries initially for a period of ten years (GATT, 1972), allowing developing country contracting parties to grant preferences amongst themselves. The commitments were to later on take the shape of UN declarations in 1974, *viz.*, the Declaration of New International Economic Order and the Charter of Economic Rights and Duties of States.

In both the Kennedy and Tokyo Rounds of negotiations, the developing countries placed much emphasis on negotiating specific concessions and commitments, which eventually resulted in the adoption of the Decision of 28 November 1979, *i.e.*, the 'Enabling Clause' of 1979 (GATT, 1980). The Enabling Clause established the principles of differential and more favourable treatment, reciprocity, and the fuller participation of developing countries (GATT, 1980).⁵⁹ The Enabling Clause reproduces the non-reciprocity idea, first embedded in GATT Article XXXVI.8, and encapsulates deviation from the MFN rate in favour of goods originating in developing countries. The Enabling Clause may be expressed in both tariffs and non-tariffs. The Enabling Clause provides for a stronger legal foundation for special and differential treatment of developing countries within the rules of the multilateral trading system, and in particular transformed the ten-year waivers for the GSP among developing countries into permanent waivers. The Enabling Clause became the framework document for trade and development in the GATT, establishing the legal basis for the S&D regime. In short, the Enabling Clause was a summation of the efforts made since 1954 by the developing countries to address some of their concerns within the GATT trading system.

In the lead-up to the Uruguay Round of negotiations, the developed countries took the position that if the imposition of import substitution policies had not succeeded in reversing the marginalisation from the multilateral trading system, it was time to limit the scope of the S&D treatment (Kessie, 2007). For the developing countries, it was a negotiating objective to accept a dilution of S&D treatment in exchange for better market access and a better rules-based system. Many developing countries were encouraged by the performances of Chile, South Korea, Singapore, and China and convinced that the way to gain benefits from the multilateral trading system if developed countries were to abolish barriers to their trade (Kessie, 2007). As a result, in the Uruguay Round of negotiations, the reciprocity component of the S&D was transformed. Under the single-undertaking approach, the principle of non-reciprocity was curtailed, as prospective WTO members were required to agree to all WTO disciplines (Garcia, 2004). This approach shifted away from the permanent lower level of obligations for developing countries towards a more limited non-reciprocity of implementation, where an additional period of time was granted to adjust to the burdens of WTO obligations (Garcia, 2004). Thus, the bargain space available for the developing countries came to be narrowed down.

2.4.2 Special and Differential Treatment Under GATT 1994

The GATT Decision on Differential and More Favourable Treatment, Reciprocity and Fuller Participation of Developing Countries 1979, or 'Enabling Clause', plays an important role in granting exception to the MFN treatment obligation of Article I:1 of the GATT 1994. The Appellate Body in *EC – Tariff Preferences* held that the 'Enabling Clause' is one of the "other decisions of the CONTRACTING PARTIES" within the meaning of para. 1(b)(iv) of Annex 1A incorporating the GATT 1994 into the WTO Agreement,[60] and that it is an integral part of the GATT 1994.[61] Under the GATT 1994 the developing countries may be accorded S&D treatment as an important exception to the MFN and Article I:1, which is captured in the paragraph 1 of the 'Enabling Clause' as follows:

> Notwithstanding the provisions of Article I of the General Agreement, [Members] may accord differential and more favourable treatment to developing countries, without according such treatment to other [Members].

The Appellate Body in *EC – Tariff Preferences*, while addressing the relationship between Article I:1 of the GATT 1994 and the 'Enabling Clause' in the context of the complaint against the EC's GSP scheme, which was primarily aimed at compensating WTO members adopting active policies against drug production and trafficking, ruled that the 'Enabling Clause' operated as an exception to Article I:1 of the GATT 1994, allowing positive discrimination in favour of developing countries. The Appellate Body upheld the Panel's characterisation of the 'Enabling Clause' as an exception to Article I:1, and stated that such a characterisation does not affect the importance of the policy objectives of the 'Enabling Clause':

> By using the word "notwithstanding", paragraph 1 of the Enabling Clause permits Members to provide "differential and more favourable treatment" to developing countries "in spite of" the MFN obligation of Article I:1. Such treatment would otherwise be inconsistent with Article I:1 because that treatment is not extended to all Members of the WTO "immediately and unconditionally". Paragraph 1 thus excepts Members from complying with the obligation contained in Article I:1 for the purpose of providing differential and more favourable treatment to developing countries, provided that such treatment is in accordance with the conditions set out in the Enabling Clause. As such, the Enabling Clause operates as an "exception" to Article I:1.[62]

Earlier, the EC had argued that the 'Enabling Clause', although reflecting the fundamental objective of assisting developing country Member States, is not an exception to Article I:1, but operated "side-by-side and on equal level" with Article I:1. Disagreeing with the EC's position, the Appellate Body ruled as follows:

> characterising the Enabling Clause as an exception, in our view, does not undermine the importance of the Enabling Clause within the overall framework of the covered agreements and as a "positive effort" to enhance economic development of developing-country Members. Nor does it "discourag[e]" developed countries from adopting measures in favour of developing countries under the Enabling Clause.[63]

The Appellate Body in *EC – Tariff Preferences*, after a careful examination of the text and context of footnote 3 to paragraph 2(a) of the Enabling Clause and the object and purpose of the WTO Agreement and the Enabling Clause, concluded as follows:

> the term "non-discriminatory" in footnote 3 does not prohibit developed-country Members from granting different tariffs to products originating in different GSP beneficiaries,

provided that such differential tariff treatment meets the remaining conditions in the Enabling Clause. In granting such differential tariff treatment, however, preference-granting countries are required, by virtue of the term "non-discriminatory", to ensure that identical treatment is available to all similarly situated GSP beneficiaries, that is, to all GSP beneficiaries that have the "development, financial and trade needs" to which the treatment in question is intended to respond.[64]

2.4.3 Additional Preferential Treatment Vis-à-vis Enabling Clause

The Enabling Clause distinguishes between developing countries and least developed countries (LDCs) by permitting the latter (a subgroup of the former) for additional preferences under paragraph 2(d). One of the questions raised in *EC – Tariff Preferences* was the grant of additional preferential treatment to certain developing countries to the exclusion of others. This question arose as EC's GSP under Council Regulation No 2501/2001 provided for five preferential arrangements. Also, the Enabling Clause contained different General Arrangements – under paragraph 2(a) for developing countries and paragraph 2(d) for least developed countries. Earlier, the Panel had concluded that the EC's Drug Arrangements were inconsistent with paragraph 2(a) of the Enabling Clause and with the requirement of non-discrimination in footnote 3 thereto,[65] and that the term "non-discriminatory" in footnote 3 required that identical tariff preferences under GSP schemes are to be provided to all developing countries without differentiation.[66]

Hence, on appeal, the key legal issue before the Appellate Body was whether the EC measures relating to the Drug Arrangements were consistent with paragraph 2(a) of the Enabling Clause and with the requirement of non-discrimination in footnote 3 thereto. The Appellate Body, while reversing the finding of the panel, concluded as follows:

> the term "non-discriminatory" in footnote 3 does not prohibit developed-country Members from granting different tariffs to products originating in different GSP beneficiaries, provided that such differential tariff treatment meets the remaining conditions in the Enabling Clause. In granting such differential tariff treatment, however, preference-granting countries are required, by virtue of the term "non-discriminatory", to ensure that identical treatment is available to all similarly situated GSP beneficiaries, that is, to all GSP beneficiaries that have the "development, financial and trade needs" to which the treatment in question is intended to respond.[67]

The Appellate Body, although reversing the findings of the Panel, still proceeded to uphold the Panel's conclusions that the European Communities "failed to demonstrate that the Drug Arrangements are justified under paragraph 2(a) of the Enabling Clause". From the Appellate Body Report in *EC – Tariff Preferences*, one can conclude that the 'Enabling Clause' (i) permits developed Member States to support their developing trading partners (Member States) according to their varying needs, and thus justifies the differences in their treatment, provided that the relevant tariff preferences respond positively to a particular "development, financial or trade need" and are made available on the basis of an objective standard to "all beneficiaries that share that need";[68] (ii) permits the grant of enhanced market access to products from developing country Member States by developed country Member States, thereby extending beyond the access granted to like products from developed countries;[69] (iii) permits developed country Member States to provide "differential and more favourable treatment" to developing country Member States in spite of the

MFN treatment obligation of Article I:1, which normally requires that such treatment be extended to all Members "immediately and unconditionally"; (iv) permits a developed country Member State to grant additional preferential tariff treatment to a chosen developing country Member State over another developing country Member State, as long as additional preferential tariff treatment is available to all similarly situated developing country Member States; and (v) encourages the developed country Member States to deviate from Article I:1 in the pursuit of "differential and more favourable treatment" for developing country Member States.[70]

2.5 Exception to MFN: Regional Integration, Quotas, and Waivers

2.5.1 Regional Integration (GATT Article XXIV)

GATT Article XXIV permits the establishment of customs unions and Free Trade Agreements to facilitate trade amongst countries within a particular region, while still maintaining trade barriers with non-participating countries that fall outside the region. This measure was put in place to encourage the development of special relationship/closer relationship and forge regional development. The provision has witnessed the creation of numerous Free Trade Agreements (FTAs); Regional Trade Agreements, and Preferential Trade Agreements, and in more recent times the emergence of mega-RTAs, which appears to cut across oceans. Of the three types of agreements mentioned, PTAs, which accords 'preferential treatment' to the parties/countries concerned (to the exclusion of other countries), could only be considered legal if they meet the requirements set out under GATT Article XXIV and GATS Article V. The proliferation of RTAs[71] in recent times had witnessed the diversion of a major volume of the trade performed through the multilateral trading system. This, and other issues relating to the RTAs, will be discussed in chapter 15.

2.5.2 Quotas

Quotas are only exceptionally permitted and subject to MFN obligation. The Appellate Body in *EC – Bananas III* dealt with issues relating to banana tariff rate quota (TRQ) 'activity function' rules, under which the requirements for TRQ allocation to importers differed depending on the origin of the bananas so imported. In the case, the EC had two separate import regimes for bananas, *viz*., for the African, Caribbean, and Pacific (ACP) countries and another one for the bananas imported from rest of the world, and argued that GATT Article I:1 applied individually to the two import regimes. Rejecting the case of the EC, the Appellate Body ruled that the non-discrimination obligation applied to the market for a particular product and observed as follows:

> Non-discrimination obligations apply to all imports of like products, except when these obligations are specifically waived or are otherwise not applicable as a result of the operation of specific provisions of the GATT 1994, such as Article XXIV. In the present case, the non-discrimination obligations of the GATT 1994, specifically Articles I:1 and XIII, apply fully to all imported bananas irrespective of their origin, except to the extent that these obligations are waived by the Lomé Waiver. We, therefore, uphold the findings of the Panel that the non-discrimination provisions of the GATT 1994, specifically, Articles I:1 and XIII, apply to the relevant EC regulations, irrespective if there is one or more "separate regimes" for the importation of bananas.[72]

Where quotas are granted Member States that experience balance-of-payment problems, GATT Article XIV provides exceptions, permitting discriminatory administration of quotas. However, in such cases Article XIV is to be read alongside GATT Articles XII and XVII Section B, which authorise quotas for balance-of-payment reasons as exceptions to GATT Article XI:1.[73]

2.5.3 Waivers

The Waiver Decision on Preferential Tariff Treatment for Least Developed Countries made in 1999 (1999 LDC Waiver) allows developing country Member States to grant special preferences to LDC Member States under certain conditions until 30 June 2019. The Waiver Decision permits for the practice of preferential tariff treatment "provided on a generalized, non-reciprocal and non-discriminatory basis" (WTO, 1999). The original Waiver Decision (WTO, 1999), which was to expire on 30 June 2009, was extended by the General Council up to 30 June 2019 (WTO, 2009). The Council for Trade in Goods, which met on 14 June 2019, granted a further extension for the 'waiver' until 30 June 2029, due to the "particular vulnerability of the least developed countries and the special structural difficulties they face in the global economy" (WTO, 2019). As a result, developed country Member States are permitted until 2029 "to provide such treatment to least developed countries on a 'non-discriminatory basis' under the 1999 LDC Waiver". Besides the LDC Waiver, the WTO Ministerial Conference in December 2011 adopted a waiver to facilitate both developing and developed country Member States to accord preferential treatment to service and service suppliers from LDCs (WTO, 2011). As no Member States had made use of the waiver since its adoption in 2011, the Bali Ministerial Conference in 2013, recognising the need to strengthen the domestic service capacity of LDCs, instructed Member States to give effect to the waiver so granted in 2011 (WTO, 2013).

3. The Most-Favoured Nation Obligation Under GATS

As mentioned elsewhere, GATT 1947 did not include trade in services, as it was deemed impossible at the time of concluding the agreement. It is to be borne in mind MFN was a key feature of GATT 1994, which was carried forward to the GATT 1994. In the first draft of the GATS (December 1990), different approaches were taken to the incorporation of MFN clause, *viz.*, (i) a general commitment, where any favourable treatment accorded to one GATS Member State was automatically extended to every GATS Member State when GATS entered into force; (ii) extending favourable treatment to all GATS Member States on only new measures, *i.e.*, those negotiated after entry into force of the GATS Agreement; and (iii) a complete abolition of the MFN treatment clause (Wolfrum, 2008). The US put forth the most liberal proposal that MFN should apply to all signatories and national treatment to general binding obligation. This position of the US was to change dramatically, as the negotiations evolved, as the US backtracked from its original 'open borders' rhetoric (Trebilcock, Howse, and Eliason, 2013).[74]

Following a breakdown in negotiations in 1990, a different approach was adopted, resulting in a more limited scope of GATS. The need for an annex establishing the exceptions to MFN arose due to concerns expressed by some participating Member States that unconditional MFN rule would allow competitor firms located in Member States with relatively restrictive policies to benefit from maintaining protected markets while exploiting less restrictive export markets. This move resulted in over 60 participating Member States submitting MFN exemptions in 1994, which prominently included audiovisual services, financial services, and transportation services, *i.e.*, road, rail, maritime, and air (Hoekman and Kostecki, 2009).

3.1 Nature of the MFN Treatment Obligation: Article II:1 of GATS

The unconditional general obligation under GATS is the MFN treatment obligation principle. As in the case of GATT, the core principle of GATS remains the MFN treatment obligation. The non-discrimination principles contained in Article I:1 of GATT apply to products and to producers, whereas the non-discrimination principles contained in Article II:1 of GATS cover services, and to persons/entities that provide the service, giving rise to several systemic and interpretive questions (Diebold, 2010). Early on, during the Uruguay Round of negotiations, participating Member States had pointed out that GATT rules on non-discrimination were "set up for products, not for producers (or activities), and it was therefore difficult to see how it could be applied to services, the imports of which were not covered by customs duties at the border as was the case with trade in goods" (MTN, 1987). It is to be noted here that GATT and GATS were not negotiated simultaneously, and as a result there are overlaps between the two instruments. Given GATS Agreement's broad modal coverage which also extends to the movement of factors, *i.e.*, capital and labour, the scope for MFN inconsistencies is far wider in services trade than in merchandise trade (Adlung and Carzaniga, 2009). This issue was touched upon by the Appellate Body in *Canada – Periodicals*, where it noted that GATT 1994 and GATS co-exist, and that one does not override the other.[75]

The MFN obligations contained in GATS was given effect even before the WTO Member States were prepared to eliminate discriminatory measures in the services trade, resulting in the difficult task of striking a balance between the creation of multilateral disciplines as well as accommodating discriminatory trade practices (Mattoo, 2002). The MFN treatment obligation, as contained in Article II:1 of GATS, is applicable to any measure under the Agreement that affects trade in services in any sector, irrespective of whether specific commitments have been made in a Member State's Schedule. This is only subject to any exceptions that the Member States might have sought at the time of acceptance of the Agreement about market access, national treatment, and additional commitments. Article II:1 of GATS reads as follows:

> With respect to any measure covered by this Agreement, each Member shall accord immediately and unconditionally to services and service suppliers of any other Member treatment no less favourable than that it accords to like services and service suppliers of any other country.

Article II:1, which prohibits discrimination of 'like' services and service suppliers between different Member States, is well complemented by a number of other MFN or MFN-like provisions contained in the GATS, *viz.*, (i) Article VII (concerning the recognition of education or experience obtained); (ii) Article VIII (concerning the monopolies and exclusive service suppliers); (iii) Article X (concerning the future rules on emergency safeguard measures); (vi) Article XII (concerning the balance-of-payments measures); (v) Article XIV of the GATS – in particular the *Chapeau* of this 'general exceptions' provision, which contains an MFN-like obligation; (vi) Article XXI (concerning the modification of schedules); (vii) Article 5(a) of GATS Annex on Telecommunications; and (viii) Preamble to GATS Understanding on Commitments in Financial Services. The focus of the study in this section will predominantly be on the remit of MFN obligations as contained in Article II:1.

3.1.1 Measures Covered Under Article II:1

The MFN obligation imposed by Article II on each Member State is immediate, unconditional, and automatic to any other WTO member a treatment that is no less favourable than the treatment they accord to like services and like service suppliers from any other country – whether a Member State or not. The Panel in *EC – Bananas III* had earlier noted that the MFN obligation under Article II:1 applied to all service sectors and suppliers irrespective of whether specific commitments had been undertaken by the Member States:

> [T]his provision constitutes a general obligation which is, in principle, applicable across the board by all Members to all services sectors, not only in sectors or subsectors where specific commitments have been undertaken. Any exception to this general obligation would have to be provided for explicitly in accordance with the terms of the GATS.[76]

The objective of MFN treatment obligation is to guarantee that all WTO Member States have equal opportunity to supply like services, regardless of the origin of the services and the service suppliers. Article I defines the scope of the GATS Agreement as to encompass "measures by members affecting trade in services", which reveals that trade in services include cross-border supply, supply of service through consumption abroad, and commercial presence of natural persons. The two expressions occurring in Article I that needs scrutiny are 'measures' and 'services'. For the GATS Agreement to apply to a measure, it should be initiated (i) by a Member State and (ii) affect trade in services. 'Measure' is defined in Article XXVIII(a) of GATS for the purposes of the Agreement as "any measure by a Member, whether in the form of a law, regulation, rule, procedure, decision, administrative action, or any other form". "Measures by Members" is defined in Article I:3(a) of GATS as meaning "measures taken by: (i) central, regional, or local governments and authorities; and (ii) by non-governmental bodies are also 'measures by Members' when they are taken in the exercise of powers delegated by central, regional or local governments or authorities." Hence, "measure by a Member" for the purposes of Article II:1 can be laws introduced by a national parliament, or a delegated legislation, or rules adopted by professional associations authorised by the government.

The Appellate Body in *Canada – Autos* clarified that the logic of Article I:1, in relation to the rest of GATS, requires the determination if a measure is covered by GATS before proceeding to assess the consistency of that measure with any substantive obligation of the GATS Agreement. The Appellate Body observed as follows:

> Article II:1 of the GATS states expressly that it applies only to "any measure covered by this Agreement". This explicit reference to the scope of the GATS confirms that the measure at issue must be found to be a measure "affecting trade in services" within the meaning of Article I:1, and thus covered by the GATS, before any further examination of consistency with Article II can logically be made . . .
>
> . . .
> [W]e believe that at least two key legal issues must be examined to determine whether a measure is one "affecting trade in services": first, whether there is "trade in services" in the sense of Article I:2; and, second, whether the measure in issue "affects" such trade in services within the meaning of Article I:1.[77]

The Appellate Body in *Canada – Autos* rejected the notion that a panel could directly determine whether a measure was 'affecting' trade in services under Article I:1, simply by examining whether the measure violated Article II or Article XVII of GATS. The Appellate Body espoused the view that the analysis of Article II should begin with a threshold determination under Article I that the measure was covered by GATS,[78] which in turn required the existence of 'trade in services' in of the four modes of supply and the measure that would affect such trade,[79] followed by the determination of the treatment by one Member State of 'services and service suppliers' of any other Member State, *etc*. The Appellate Body noted that a panel ought to examine the effect of the measure on the relevant services as 'services', or upon the service suppliers in their capacity as service suppliers.[80] One can safely say that the domain of the MFN treatment obligation under Article II GATS is concerned with both measures affecting products *per se* and the measures affecting service and service suppliers.

Although Article II:1 of the GATS does not explicitly state that it applies to *de facto* discrimination, the Appellate Body in *EC – Bananas III* held that the MFN treatment obligation contained in Article II:1 of the GATS applied to both *de jure* and *de facto* discrimination. The European Communities (EC) argued that as it was not explicitly stated in Article II:1, the MFN obligation did not apply to *de facto* discrimination. The Appellate Body, disagreeing with the argument, ruled as follows:

> [t]he obligation imposed by Article II is unqualified. The ordinary meaning of this provision does not exclude *de facto* discrimination. Moreover, if Article II was not applicable to *de facto* discrimination, it would not be difficult – and, indeed, it would be a good deal easier in the case of trade in services, than in the case of trade in goods – to devise discriminatory measures aimed at circumventing the basic purpose of that Article.[81]

3.2 'Like' Service and 'Like' Service Suppliers

To establish if the MFN obligation under GATS has been satisfied one needs to first establish the 'likeness' of the service, before proceeding to establish the 'likeness' of the supplier of such service.[82] The concept of 'like services and service suppliers' applied in GATS has to date only received a limited attention in WTO jurisprudence. For instance, the Panels in *EC – Bananas III*, *Canada – Autos*, and *China – Publications and Audiovisual Products* only marginally touched upon the issue of 'likeness' in GATS. The Panels had merely stated that to the extent that service providers offer like services, they are like service suppliers. In *China – Electronic Payments Service*, the Panel took a more detailed approach to the topic by observing:

> We agree that the fact that service suppliers provide like services may in some cases raise a presumption that they are "like" service suppliers. However, we consider that, in the specific circumstances of other cases, a separate inquiry into the "likeness" of the suppliers may be called for. For this reason, we consider that "like service suppliers" determinations should be made on a case-by-case basis.[83]

Some commentators take the position that the 'like services and service suppliers' concept lacks a doctrinal analysis comparable to the one related to GATT 'like products' (Diebold, 2010).[84] Both the nature of the service transactions and the idiosyncrasies of the GATS legal framework complicate the 'like services and service suppliers' concept when compared with the 'like product' concept occurring in GATT. Firstly, service transactions are intangible and as a result incomparable with trade goods, which are tangible by nature. Diebold notes that there is no internationally recognised nomenclature that exists for service transactions, and some services are highly individualised – with different supply methods, while some are standardised, making a clear nomenclature improbable (Diebold, 2010). Also, the services trade (cross-border) is based on four delivery methods, with one of them requiring either the supplier or the consumer to relocate.

The Appellate Body in *Canada – Autos* laid down the approach to proceed with when examining the consistency of a measure with regards to Article II:1; after determining whether the measure under examination affects trade in services, one should make "factual findings as to treatment of wholesale trade services and service suppliers of motor vehicles of different Members commercially present" and, finally, apply Article II:1 to these facts in the following steps:

> The wording of this provision suggests that analysis of the consistency of a measure with Article II:1 should proceed in several steps. First, as we have seen, a threshold determination must be made under Article I:1 that the measure is covered by the GATS. This determination requires that there be "trade in services" in one of the four modes of supply, and that there be also a measure which "affects" this trade in services. We have already held that the Panel failed to undertake this analysis.
>
> If the threshold determination is that the measure is covered by the GATS, appraisal of the consistency of the measure with the requirements of Article II:1 is the next step. The text of Article II:1 requires, in essence, that treatment by one Member of "services and services suppliers" of any other Member be compared with treatment of "like" services and service suppliers of "any other country". Based on these core legal elements, the Panel should first have rendered its interpretation of Article II:1. It should then have made factual findings as to treatment of wholesale trade services and service suppliers of motor vehicles of different Members commercially present in Canada. Finally, the Panel should have applied its interpretation of Article II:1 to the facts as it found them.[85]

3.2.1 Treatment 'No Less Favourable'

Article II:1 of GATS imposes an obligation on Member States to accord unconditionally and automatically to services and service suppliers of any given Member State 'treatment no less favourable' than the treatment it accords to 'like services and service suppliers' of any other country – *whether a Member State or not*. The term "no less favourable" occurring in Article II was borrowed from the national treatment clause in Article III GATT 1947. No guidance is provided in Article II as to the meaning of the concept of 'treatment no less favourable'. As mentioned earlier in this chapter, Article XVII of the Agreement on the national treatment obligation contains guidance on the meaning of the concept of 'treatment no less favourable', and Article XVII:3 reads as follows:

> Formally identical or formally different treatment shall be considered to be less favourable if it modifies the conditions of competition in favour of services or service suppliers of the Member compared to the like services or service suppliers of any other Member.

Regardless of the terminology, the objective of the clause remains the same, *viz.*, to protect against any discriminatory treatment (Wolfrum, 2008). The Panel in *EC – Bananas III* opined, "if the standard of 'no less favourable treatment' as occurring in Article II were to be interpreted narrowly", that could lead mostly to "the frustration of the objective behind

Article II which is to prohibit discrimination between like services and service suppliers of other Members".[86] The Appellate Body, while not agreeing with the reasoning of the Panel, reached the same conclusion on the issue of applicability of Article II of GATS to *de facto* discrimination:

> The GATS negotiators chose to use different language in Article II and Article XVII of the GATS in expressing the obligation to provide "treatment no less favourable". The question naturally arises: if the GATS negotiators intended that "treatment no less favourable" should have exactly the same meaning in Articles II and XVII of the GATS, why did they not repeat paragraphs 2 and 3 of Article XVII in Article II? . . . The question here is the meaning of "treatment no less favourable" with respect to the MFN obligation in Article II of the GATS. There is more than one way of writing a *de facto* non-discrimination provision. Article XVII of the GATS is merely one of many provisions in the WTO Agreement that require the obligation of providing "treatment no less favourable". The possibility that the two Articles may not have exactly the same meaning does not imply that the intention of the drafters of the GATS was that a *de jure*, or formal, standard should apply in Article II of the GATS. . . . The obligation imposed by Article II is unqualified. The ordinary meaning of this provision does not exclude *de facto* discrimination . . .
>
> For these reasons, we conclude that "treatment no less favourable" in Article II:1 of the GATS should be interpreted to include *de facto*, as well as *de jure*, discrimination. We should make it clear that we do not limit our conclusion to this case. We have some difficulty in understanding why the Panel stated that its interpretation of Article II of the GATS applied "*in casu*".[87]

The Appellate Body in *Argentina – Financial Services*, commenting and concurring with the views expressed in *EC – Bananas III* on the term 'treatment no less favourable' as occurring in Article II:1 and Article XVII of the GATS, observed as follows:

> the elaboration on the meaning of the term "treatment no less favourable" contained in Article XVII, and in particular in Article XVII:3, should also be pertinent context to the meaning of the same term in Article II:1.
>
> We note that, in *EC – Bananas III*, the Appellate Body . . . based its findings under both provisions on the same notion of "less favourable treatment". . . . The Appellate Body's findings indicate that, on substance, the concept of "treatment no less favourable" under both the most-favoured-nation and national treatment provisions of the GATS is focused on a measure's modification of the conditions of competition. This legal standard does not contemplate a separate and additional inquiry into the regulatory objective of, or the regulatory concerns underlying, the contested measure. Indeed, in prior disputes, the fact that a measure modified the conditions of competition to the detriment of services or service suppliers of any other Member was, in itself, sufficient for a finding of less favourable treatment under Articles II:1 and XVII of the GATS.[88]

The Appellate Body elaborated that its interpretation of the legal standard of 'treatment no less favourable' was also supported by the structure of the GATS, and that

> [u]nder this structure, Members can utilize certain flexibilities, available to them uniquely under the GATS, when undertaking their GATS commitments, and their

obligations are qualified by exceptions or other derogations contained in the GATS and its Annexes.[89]

The Appellate Body described its interpretation of the relevant provisions as follows:

> Article II:1 and XVII of the GATS chimes with the Appellate Body's interpretation of the most-favoured-nation and national treatment obligations in the context of the GATT 1994.[90]

3.3 Derogation From MFN Obligation Under GATS

The GATS Agreement provides for exemptions from the MFN treatment obligation. Two categories of MFN exemptions are contemplated, *viz.*, (i) individual exemptions which a Member State may list in accordance with Article II:2 and the Annex on Article II exemptions and (ii) cases where MFN obligation does not apply by virtue of certain GATS provisions, which are Article II:3 (Preferential Treatment for Trade in Frontier Areas), Article V (Economic Integration), Article XIII (Government Procurement), Article XIV and XIV *bis* (General and Security Exceptions), as well as exceptions specified in certain sectoral annexes, in particular paragraph 2.1 of the Financial Services Annex (Prudential Carveout). During the Uruguay Round of negotiations, where GATS was negotiated and finalised, many participating Member States contemplated avoiding individual MFN exemptions altogether. The formula that emerged at the end of the negotiations allowed Member States to submit their exemptions before the entry into force of the WTO Agreement, which is to be found in Annex on Article II.[91]

Article II:2 only covers measures in existence before the entry into force of the WTO Agreement, and it should be noted that Article II exemptions are more tailored to the original WTO Member States. The Annex contains the list of MFN exempted measures a Member State had opted for – over 400 exempted measures have been listed by Member States, which primarily fall under (i) audiovisual, (ii) bilateral investment treaties, (iii) financial and business services, (iv) maritime transport, and (v) measures regarding the presence of natural persons.[92] Member States, in accordance with Article II:2, may maintain measures that are inconsistent with Article II:1, provided such measures meet the conditions set out in Annex on Article II. Importantly, the list of exemption submitted by a Member State is not necessarily limited to existing measures that it seeks to exempt, but can include future measures constituting exemptions to MFN, provided they are identified clearly. Interestingly, paragraph 6 of the Annex on Article II exemptions requires that the exemptions, in principle, are not to exceed ten years and should be subject to negotiation in subsequent trade rounds. However, many Member States continue to apply the exemptions listed beyond the ten-year period mentioned in paragraph 6, by relying on the language of the provision. This obviously presents problems, as the language of paragraph 6 does not obligate a Member State to end the measures after ten years, but only imposes a duty to negotiate.[93]

Article II:2 permits exemptions from MFN obligations, but not from the obligations set out in Articles XVI and XVII, which relate to grant of market access and national treatment in accordance with the Member's schedule of commitments. Article II:2 also states that new exemptions can only be added pursuant to GATS Article IX:3, under which all exemptions granted for a period of more than five years are reviewed by the Council for Trade in Services.

Where the Council were to conclude that the conditions that prevailed justifying the need for such exemption were no longer applicable, the Member State would be required to accord MFN treatment in respect of the measure in question.[94] If three-fourths of the Member States deem the exemptions to be appropriate, the Council will exempt a Member State from the ordinary obligations of the WTO Agreement in exceptional circumstances. Under the scheme envisaged in Article II:3, measures in place granting advantages to adjacent countries are not subject to the MFN treatment obligation of Article II:1.[95]

4. Summary

A study of the MFN obligations under both the GATT and GATS Agreement demonstrates that the obligations are complex, yet strict in their application. One of the fundamental features highlighted is that the MFN obligation is all-encompassing and to be extended unconditionally. Also to be noted is the fact that the RTAs have encroached upon the policy space of the MFN obligations, and in more recent times the mega-RTAs are redefining the justification for the creation of an RTA. This, and other issues surrounding the creation of RTAs, will be discussed in more detail in chapter 15.

Notes

1. Annex 1 Agreements are the General Agreement on Tariffs and Trade (GATT), General Agreement on Trade in Services (GATS), and Agreement on Trade-Related Aspects of Intellectual Property Rights (TRIPS).
2. The authors also note that the use of 'intent' as a factor in GATT non-discrimination standards has been hotly contested.
3. For instance, where it is stated, "imported cars will be subjected to a levy of 25% sales tax, and domestically produced cars will be subjected to a levy of 15% sales tax". Here, the discrimination is clearly stated in the measure introduced, resulting in all imported cars being subjected to a higher tax.
4. For instance, where the measure imposes a variable tax rate on alcoholic beverages – higher tax is levied where the alcohol content is higher.
5. Wide use of the MFN clause also coincided with the decline of mercantilism. See Long (1973).
6. The Treaty of Amity and Commerce was also the first instance where the conditional MFN clause was used in international trade agreements, and the first time the conditional MFN clause was introduced in a treaty between European states was in 1810 between the UK and Portugal. See Long (1973).
7. The author also notes that the US abandoned the conditional MFN policy unilaterally in 1923 and embarked on a programme of negotiated reciprocal unconditional MFN agreements with major trading nations.
8. The US, in the post-World War I era, moved from being a strong advocate of conditional MFN to that of an avid proponent of the unconditional MFN clause. The reason for the departure was to avoid the frequent controversies between the US and the European states. See Ustor (1968).
9. The draft ITO Charter put forth by the US included an MFN provision and was later on introduced as Article I of GATT. See Jackson (1969).
10. It should, however, be noted that the ILC's deliberations did not result in any form of codification. The International Law Commission, in its 67th session convened in 2015, noted, "MFN clause remain unchanged in character from the time the 1978 draft article were concluded. The core provisions of the 1978 draft articles continue to be the basis for the interpretation and application of MFN clauses today. However, they do not provide answers to all the interpretive issues that can arise with MFN clauses." See ILC (2015).
11. The meaning of the MFN clause has been qualified as drafting by reference.
12. See the judgement of the ICJ in *Anglo-Iranian Oil Company* case, *Anglo-Iranian Oil Company, United Kingdom v Iran* [1952] ICJ Report 93, at p. 109, where it was observed, "It is this [*i.e.*, the basic] treaty which established the juridical link between the [beneficiary State] and a third-party treaty

and confers upon that State the rights enjoyed by the third party. A third-party treaty, independent of and isolated from the basic treaty, cannot produce any legal effect as between the [beneficiary State] and [the granting State]: it is *res inter alios acta*."

13 See Appellate Body Reports, *EC – Tariff Preferences*, para. 101; *Canada – Autos*, para. 69.
14 See Appellate Body Report, *Canada – Autos*, para. 84.
15 The authors can be credited for creating a model for studying the free-rider problem of the MFN clause.
16 RTAs do not conform to the MFN treatment obligation of the WTO. In the WTO era over 500 RTAs have been notified.
17 See Southerland Report (WTO, 2004), para. 60. The expression "spaghetti bowl effect" was coined by Prof Jagdish Bhagwati in 1995, in his paper entitled 'US Trade Policy: The Infatuation with Free Trade Agreements', to refer to the effect produced by the multiplication of free-trade agreements, which supplants WTO multilateral trade.
18 The words 'contracting parties' as appearing in GATT 1947 is substituted with the words 'Member' and 'Members' in the text of Article I presented previously. It will be recalled that GATT 1947 was used as a stand-alone treaty to enter into trade agreements, as the ITO did not come into existence as expected. Member Countries of the GATT 1947 were referred to as 'contracting parties', as opposed to members, in the treaty in the absence of an organisational infrastructure. Long describes Article I as a "direct descendant of the bilateral trade agreements" between the US and other countries. See Long (1973).
19 Where under Article I "advantages" are to be accorded "immediately and unconditionally", under Article II, the treatment that is "no less favourable" is to be provided to other contracting parties (Member States).
20 See Appellate Body Report, *Canada – Autos*, para. 82.
21 *Ibid.*
22 The terminology "[c]ustoms duties and charges of any kind" occurring in Article I refers to tariffs.
23 See Panel Report, *Spain – Unroasted Coffee*, para. 4.3.
24 Under the measure introduced, there were no restrictions, as such, on the origin of the motor vehicles that were eligible for this exemption. Nevertheless, the manufacturers only imported their own make of motor vehicle and from other related companies. This resulted in only motor vehicles originating in a small number of countries benefitting *de facto* from the exemption provided.
25 See Appellate Body Report, *Canada – Autos*, para. 78.
26 See Panel Report, *Canada – Pharmaceuticals*, para. 7.101. It should be noted that the issue before the Panel in this case was the NT obligation under Article III:4 of the GATT and not the MFN treatment obligation under Article I:1 of the GATT.
27 See Appellate Body Report, *EC – Bananas III*, paras. 190–191.
28 See Appellate Body Reports, *Philippines – Distilled Spirits*, para. 170, and *EC – Asbestos*, para. 99.
29 See Working Party Report (1970), para. 18. See also the Appellate Body Report, *Japan Alcoholics Beverages II*, paras. 113 and 114.
30 See also Panel Reports in *EEC – Imports of Beef* and *US – MFN Footwear* and Chairperson's Report in *India – Tax Rebates on Exports*. However, in *US – MFN Footwear*, the need for a specific 'like product' determination was rendered unnecessary due to statutory provisions that required adverse treatment of all products from countries that did not carry the MFN status.
31 See Panel Report, *Belgian Family Allowances*, para. 3.
32 In the working paper on the most-favoured-nation clause in the law of treaties, submitted by Special Rapporteur Mr Endre Ustor, on 19 June 1968, the example of the 'Swiss Cow' case of an unduly specialized tariff was cited under the heading 'Violations of the Clause'. A tariff classification based on such an extraneous consideration as the place where the cows are raised is clearly designed to discriminate in favour of a particular country. See Ustor (1968).
33 See Panel Report in *Germany – Sardines*, paras. 12–13. The Panel, nevertheless, struck down the German measure by upholding Norway's non-violation complaint pursuant to Article XXIII GATT, as negotiations between Norway and Germany had created 'reasonable expectations' of equal treatment.
34 See Panel Report, *Spain – Unroasted Coffee*, para. 4.7. See also Panel Report, *Japan – SPF Dimension Lumber*, paras. 5.10–5.13. The Panel narrowed down the interpretation of 'likeness' in Article I GATT, where the likeness of spruce-pine-fir (SPF) from Canada and the hemlock-fir from the US was treated differently by Japan.
35 Interestingly, a blend of the various types of coffee beans was sold to consumers, with each blend assembled to meet consumer taste. The Panel, relying on the fact that coffee was always sold in a

blended form, held that it was impossible to distinguish between the various types of coffee in the blend. In this case, Brazil lobbied the support of other developing countries, and when the Panel report was close to adoption, 22 developing countries rose to speak in favour of the report.
36 It is to be noted that MFN obligation would be relevant where the tariff is set lower than the bound duty rate, for example where a tariff is set at a lower rate than the bound duty rate in the schedule of concessions under Article II GATT for a particular Member State, and the same lower tariff rate will be required to be extended to all WTO Member States.
37 See Panel Report, *Australia – Ammonium Sulphate*, para. 8. The Panel found the two products to be 'unlike', as Australia, like some other countries, listed the two products in different tariff classifications subject to different tariff rates.
38 See Panel Report, *EEC – Animal Feed Proteins*, para. 4.2.
39 See Panel Report, *Japan – Alcoholic Beverages I*, paras. 5.5–5.16.
40 See Panel Report, *Indonesia – Autos*, para. 14.138, where the Panel set a three-stage test, as opposed to a four-stage test. Here the Panel chose to merge the first and second questions into one.
41 See Appellate Body Report, *Canada – Autos*, para. 84, where the Appellate Body observed that it was following the earlier GATT jurisprudence, where the provisions were applied to both *de jure* and *de facto* discrimination.
42 See Appellate Body Report, *US – Section 211 Appropriation Act*, para. 297.
43 See Appellate Body Report, *EC – Bananas III*, para. 190. The disputed related to the import regime of bananas, where bananas imported into European Communities from Latin American countries were treated less favourably than those imported from the former European Colonies (ACP bananas).
44 See Appellate Body Report, *EC – Seal Products*, para. 5.79.
45 *Ibid*.
46 *Ibid.*, para. 5.82. The legal issues in the appeal centred on the applicable standard for establishing discrimination contrary to GATT Articles I:1 and III:4, in comparison to discrimination contrary to TBT Article 2.1. However, the decision of the Appellate Body came to be criticised by the US on other grounds. See Conconi and Voon (2016) for a discussion of the Appellate Body's report.
47 See Appellate Body Reports, *Japan – Alcoholic Beverages*, paras. 109–110; *Korea – Alcoholic Beverages*, para. 119.
48 See Appellate Body Report, *Japan – Alcoholic Beverages II*, para. 21. The poet laureatus referred here was the distinguished Philippine jurist Florentino P. Feliciano.
49 See Appellate Body Report, *Philippines – Distilled Spirits*, para. 120. While the first three criteria were identified in the report of the Working Party, the Appellate Body in *Japan – Alcoholic Beverages II* (paras. 21–22) added the fourth criteria.
50 See Appellate Body Report, *Philippines – Distilled Spirits*, para. 128.
51 The *Suggested Charter* was prepared by the US administration in consultation with the UK.
52 It was India's position that developing countries with limited financial resources and infrastructure would not be able to protect their infant industries, which would be possible for developed countries through domestic subsidies. Further, India sought clarification on whether the proposed institution would permit it to pursue a policy of industrialisation, and if the non-discrimination obligation embedded in the *Suggested Charter* would help it achieve the income necessary to finance its policy choices. See Irwin, Mavroidis, and Sykes (2008).
53 This provision was later introduced as an amendment to the GATT in 1948.
54 The membership of the GATT grew in the 1960s, through the admission of newly independent states. At the beginning of the 1970s, GATT had a membership of 77 contracting parties, with 52 developing countries. In 1991 the membership stood at 102, with 79 developing countries. It is also to be noted that decolonisation and growth of developmental economics played an important role in newly independent states seeking membership of the GATT.
55 The foundations of UNCTAD took shape based on concerns raised by developing countries over the increasing presence of MNCs and importantly the surrounding disparity between developed nations and developing nations in the international markets.
56 At UNCTAD, the developing countries argued that in order to promote exports of manufactured goods from developing countries, it was essential to offer special tariff concessions to such exports.
57 The GSP is a list of products for which tariff preferences are accorded, mostly by developed countries, in favour of goods originating in developing countries.
58 It can be said that a key achievement of UNCTAD was to conceive and implement the GSP.

59 The Enabling Clause provided for (i) the preferential market access of developing countries to developed country markets on a non-reciprocal, non-discriminatory basis; (ii) 'more favourable' treatment for developing countries in other GATT rules dealing with non-tariff barriers; (iii) the introduction of preferential trade regimes between developing countries; and (iv) the special treatment of least developed countries in the context of specific measures for developing countries.
60 See Appellate Body Report, *EC – Tariff Preferences*, para. 90 and fn. 192.
61 *Ibid.*, para. 90.
62 *Ibid.*
63 *Ibid.*, para. 95.
64 *Ibid.*, para. 173.
65 See Panel Report, *EC – Tariff Preferences*, para. 7.177.
66 *Ibid.*, paras. 7.161 and 7.176.
67 See Appellate Body Report, *EC – Tariff Preferences*, para. 173.
68 *Ibid.*, paras. 162–164.
69 *Ibid.*, para. 106.
70 *Ibid.*, para. 111. It is to be noted that preferential tariff treatment is accorded to imports from developing country Member States through the GSP schemes established by the developed country Member States. The Sutherland Report, nevertheless, is critical of the GSPs in practice. See Sutherland Report, paras. 88–102.
71 The acronyms – FTAs, RTAs, and PTAs – are used interchangeably. In most instances the acronym RTA is used fluidly to refer to all three.
72 See Appellate Body Report, *EC – Bananas III*, para. 191.
73 Since the 1970s the practice of invoking GATT Article XIV is in decline, with Member States receiving support from the IMF to correct balance-of-payment problems.
74 This was in principle due to the US providers becoming concerned that they may have to compete with foreign providers in their own backyard.
75 See Appellate Body Report, *Canada – Periodicals*, para. 19, where the Appellate Body noted, "the ordinary meaning of the texts of GATT 1994 and GATS as well as Article II:2 of the WTO Agreement, taken together, indicate that obligations under GATT 1994 and GATS can co-exist and that one does not override the other." See also Panel Report, *EU – Energy Package*, para. 7.374.
76 See Panel Report, *EC – Bananas III*, para. 7.298.
77 See Appellate Body Report, *Canada – Autos*, paras. 152 and 155.
78 *Ibid.*, paras. 152 and 170.
79 *Ibid.*
80 *Ibid.*, paras. 164–166.
81 See Appellate Body Report, *EC – Bananas III*, para. 233. See also Appellate Body Report, *Argentina – Financial Services*, para. 6.105.
82 *Ibid.*
83 See Panel Report, *China – Electronic Payments Service*, para. 7.705.
84 The author proposes a new methodology for the legal analysis of non-discrimination which is not based on firm legal elements or conditions, but on soft factors.
85 See Appellate Body Report, *Canada – Autos*, paras. 170–171. See also Panel Report, *EU – Energy Package*, paras. 7.227 and 7.404.
86 See Panel Report, *EC – Bananas III*, para. 7.303.
87 See Appellate Body Report, *EC – Bananas III*, paras. 233–234.
88 See Appellate Body Report, *Argentina – Financial Services*, paras. 6.105–6.106.
89 *Ibid.*, para. 6.112.
90 *Ibid.*, para. 6.119, referring to Appellate Body Reports *EC – Seal Products*, paras. 5.87–5.88, 5.90, and 5.101.
91 For the original Member States, it was until 1 January 1995. For those Member States that acceded to the WTO later, exemptions from MFN obligations under Article II:1 of the GATS were negotiated as part of the accession process.
92 The Member States are to provide five types of information, *viz.*, (i) description of the sector or sectors sought to be exempted; (ii) description of the measure, indicating the reasons; (iii) the country or countries to which the measure applies; (iv) the intended duration of the exemption; and (v) the conditions creating the need for the exemption.
93 On a strict interpretation of the provision, the exemptions presented by the original Member States of the WTO, the ten-year period expired on 1 January 2005.

94 Interestingly, the reviews that took place in 2010–2011 did not result in any revision of the listed MFN exemptions. This led to Hong Kong making the comment, "most, if not all, MFN exemptions that had been listed, persisted".
95 For instance, taxi services are established between Geneva, Switzerland, and neighbouring France. It is also to be borne in mind that France is part of the EU, whereas Switzerland is not.

Bibliography

Adlung, Rudolf and Antonia Carzaniga. 'MFN Exemptions under the General Agreement on Trade in Services: Grandfathers Striving for Immortality?,' *Journal of International Economic law* Vol 12, No 2 (2009) 1–36.

Bagwell, Kyle and Robert W. Staiger. *The Economics of the World Trading System* (MIT Press, 2002).

Bhagwati, Jagdish. 'US Trade Policy: The Infatuation with Free Trade Agreements' Columbia Discussion Paper Series No 726 (1995).

Bhala, Raj. *Modern GATT Law: A Treatise on the Law and Political Economy of the General Agreement on Tariffs and Trade and Other World Trade Agreements* Vol 1 (Sweet & Maxwell, 2013).

Caplin, Andrew and Kala Krishna. 'Tariffs and the Most-Favoured-Nation Clause: A Game Theoretic Approach,' *Seoul Journal of Economics* Vol 1 (1988) 267–289.

Choi, Won-Mog. *Like Products' in International Trade Law: Towards a Consistent GATT/WTO Jurisprudence* (Cambridge University Press, 2003).

Conconi, Paola and Tania Voon. 'EC Seal Products: The Tension Between Public Morals and International Trade Agreements,' *World Trade Law Review* Vol 15, No 2 (2016) 211–234.

Cossy, Mireille. 'Determining "Likeness" under the GATS: Squaring the Circle?,' *World Trade Organization Economic Research and Statistics Division Staff Working Paper ERSD-2006–08* (2006).

Cossy, Mireille. 'Some Thoughts on the Concept of "Likeness" in the GATS,' in Panizzon, Marion, Nicole Phol and Pierre Sauvé (eds.) *GATS and the Regulation of International Trade in Services* (Cambridge University Press, 2008) 327–357.

Coutain, Bryan. 'The Unconditional Most-Favoured-Nation Clause and the Maintenance of the Liberal Trade Regime in the Postwar 1870s,' *International Organization* Vol 63, No 1 (2009) 139–175.

Davey, William J. and Joost Pauwelyn. 'MFN Unconditionality: A Legal Analysis of the Concept in View of Its Evolution in the GATT/WTO Jurisprudence with Particular Reference to the Issue of "Like Product",' in Cottier, Thomas and Petros C. Mavroidis (eds.) *Regulatory Barriers and the Principle of Non-Discrimination in World Trade Law* (University of Michigan Press, 2002) 13–50.

Diebold, Nicholas F. 'Non-Discrimination and the Pillars of International Economic Law: Comparative Analysis and Building Coherency,' *IILJ Emerging Scholars Paper 18* (2010).

GATT. BISD 18th Supplement, Geneva (1972).

GATT. Document L/4903, dated 28 November 1979, BISD 26S/203.

GATT. BISD 26th Supplement, Geneva (1980).

Garcia, Frank J. 'Beyond Special and Differential Treatment,' *Boston College International & Comparative Law Review* Vol 27, No 2 (2004) 291–317.

Hoekman, Bernard. 'The WTO: Functions and Basic Principles,' in Hoekman, Bernard, Aaditya Mattoo and Philip English (eds.) *Development, Trade, and the WTO* (World Bank Publication, 2002) 41–49.

Hoekman, Bernard, Constantine Michalopoulos and Alan Winters. 'More Favourable and Differential Treatment of Developing Countries: Toward a New Approach in the World Trade Organization,' *The World Bank* (2003).

Hoekman, Bernard M. and Michel M. Kostecki. *The Political Economy of the World Trading System: The WTO and Beyond* (Oxford University Press, 2009).

Hudec, Robert E. 'Tiger, Tiger in the House: A Critical Evaluation of the Case against Discriminatory Trade Measures,' in Petersmann, Ernst-Ulrich and Meinhard Hilf (eds.) *The New GATT Round of Multilateral Trade Negotiations: Legal and Economic Problems* (Kluwer, 1991) 165–212.

Hudec, Robert E. 'GATT and the Developing Countries,' *Columbia Business Law Review* Vol 67, No 1 (1992) 67–77.

Hudec, Robert E. 'GATT/WTO Constraints on National Regulation: Requiem for an "Aims and Effect" Test,' *International Lawyer* Vol 32 (1998) 619–649.

Hudec, Robert E. '"Like Product": The Differences in Meaning in GATT Articles I and III,' in Cottier, Thomas and Petros C. Mavroidis (eds.) *Regulatory Barriers and the Principle of Non-Discrimination in World Trade Law* (The University of Michigan Press, 2002) 101–124.

Hyder, Khursid Hasan. *Equality of Treatment and Trade Discrimination in International Law* (Martin Nijhoff Publishing, 1968).

International Law Commission. 'Report of the International Law Commission on the Work of Its Thirtieth Session,' (Doc/A/33/10) *ILC Yearbook*, Vol 2, Part 2 (1978) 16–23.

International Law Commission. 'Report of the International Law Commission,' Sixty-Seventh Session (Doc/A/70/10) (2015).

Irwin, Douglas A., Petros C. Mavroidis and Alan O. Sykes. *The Genesis of the GATT* (Cambridge University Press, 2008).

Islam, M. Rafiqul. *International Trade Law of the WTO* (Oxford University Press, 2006).

Jackson, John Howard. *World Trade and the Law of GATT: A Legal Analysis of the General Agreement on Tariffs and Trade* (The Michie Company, 1969).

Jackson, John Howard. *The World Trading System: Law and Policy of International Economic Relations* (MIT Press, 1995).

Jackson, John Howard. *The World Trading System: Law and Policy of International Economic Relations* (MIT Press, 2000).

Kelly Jr., William B. 'Antecedents of United States Commercial Policy, 1922–1934,' in Kelly Jr., William B. (ed.) *Studies in United States Commercial Policy* (University of North Carolina Press, 1963) 58–59.

Kessie, Edwini. 'The Legal Status of Special and Differential Treatment Provisions under the WTO Agreements,' in Bermann, George A. and Petros C. Mavroidis (eds.) *WTO Law and Developing Countries* (Cambridge University Press, 2007) 12–35.

Kofele-Kale, Ndiva. 'The Principle of Preferential Treatment in the Law of GATT: Toward Achieving the Objective of an Equitable World Trading System,' *California Western International Law Journal* Vol 18, No 2 (1987) 291–333.

Lester, Simon, Bryan Mercurio and Arwel Davies. *World Trade Law: Text, Materials and Commentary* (Hart Publishing, 2018).

Long, Russell B. 'The Most-Favoured-Nation Provision,' Committee on Finance United States Senate. *Executive Branch GATT Study No. 9* (1973).

Ludema, Rodney D. and Anna Maria Mayda. 'Do Countries Free Ride on MFN?,' *CEPR Discussion Paper DP5160* (2006) 1–58.

Malloy, William M. *Treaties, Conventions, International Acts, Protocols and Agreements between the United States of America and Other Powers, 1776–1909* Vol 1 (Washington: Government Printing Office, 1910) 468–479.

Maruyama, Warren H. 'Preferential Trade Arrangements and the Erosion of the WTO's MFN Principle,' *Stanford Journal of International Law* Vol 46 (2010) 177.

Matsushita, Mitsuo, Thomas J. Shoenbaum, Petros C. Mavroidis and Michael Hahn. *The World Trade Organization: Law, Practice, and Policy* (Oxford University Press, 2017).

Mattoo, Aditya. 'MFN and GATS,' in Cottier, Thomas and Petros C. Mavroidis (eds.) *Regulatory Barriers and the Principle of Non-Discrimination in World Trade Law* (The University of Michigan Press, 2002).

Mavroidis, Petros C. '"Like Product": Some Thoughts at the Positive and Normative Level,' in Cottier, Thomas and Petros C. Mavroidis (eds.) *Regulatory Barriers and the Principle of Non-Discrimination in World Trade Law* (The University of Michigan Press, 2002).

Mavroidis, Petros C. *Trade in Goods* (Oxford University Press, 2007).

Mavroidis, Petros C. *Trade in Goods* (Oxford University Press, 2013).

McRae, Donald. 'MFN in the GATT and the WTO,' *Asian Journal of WTO and International Health Policy* Vol 7, No 1 (2012) 1–23.

Michalopoulos, Constantine. 'The Role of Special and Differential Treatment for Developing Countries in GATT and the World Trade Organization,' *The World Bank* (2000).

Mitchell, Andrew D. and Tania Voon. 'Operationalizing Special and Differential Treatment in the World Trade Organization: Game Over?,' *Global Governance* Vol 15 (2009) 343–357.

Moore, Mike. 'The Democratic Roots of the World Trade Organization,' in Macrory Patrick F.J., Arthur E. Appleton and Michael G. Plummer (eds.) *The WTO: Legal, Economic and Political Analysis* Vol 1 (Springer, 2005) 39–50.

Multilateral Trade Negotiations. Note on the Meeting of 15–17 September 1987, MTN.GNS/10 (15 October 1987).

Offner, Arnold A. *The Origins of the Second World War: American Foreign Policy and World Politics, 1917–1941* (Krieger Publishing, 1986).

Page, Sheila and Peter Kleen. 'Special and Differential Treatment of Developing Countries in the World Trade Organization,' *EGDI Secretariat, Ministry for Foreign Affairs* (2005).

Schill, Stephan W. *The Multilateralization of International Investment Law* (Cambridge University Press, 2009).

Schwartz, Warren F. and Alan O. Sykes. 'The Economics of the Most Favoured Nation Clause,' in Bhandari, Jagdeep S. and Alan O. Sykes (eds.) *Economic Dimensions in International Law: Comparative and Empirical Perspectives* (Cambridge University Press, 1998) 43–79.

Trebilcock, Michael, Robert Howse and Antonia Eliason. *The Regulation of International Trade* (Routledge, 2013).

UN Economic and Social Council, Second Session of the Preparatory Committee of the United Nations Conference on Trade and Employment (E/PC/W/146) (30 May 1947).

Ustor, Endre. 'The Most-Favoured-Nation Clause in the Law of Treaties,' Working Paper (A/CN.4/L.127), *Yearbook of the International Law Commission* Vol 2 (1968), 165 <www.legal-tools.org/doc/c0b34e/pdf/> (accessed 18 May 2019).

Van den Bossche, Peter and Werner Zdouc. *The Law and Policy of the World Trade Organization* (Cambridge University Press, 2017).

Wolfrum, Rüdiger. 'Article II GATS,' in Wolfrum, Rüdiger, Peter-Tobias Stoll and Clemens Feinäugle (eds.) *Max Plank Commentaries on World Trade Law: WTO-Trade in Services* Vol 6 (Martin Nijhoff Publishers, 2008) 71–91.

Working Party Report. Border Tax Adjustments, BISD 18S/97, para. 18 (adopted on 2 December 1970).

World Trade Organization. General Council, Waiver Decision on Preferential Tariff Treatment for Least-Developed Countries, WT/L/759 (29 May 2009).

World Trade Organization. *The Legal Texts: The Results of the Uruguay Round of Multilateral Trade Negotiations* (Cambridge University Press, 2010).

World Trade Organization. Ministerial Decision, Preferential Treatment to Services and Services Suppliers of Least-Developed Countries, WT/L/847 (17 December 2011).

World Trade Organization. Ministerial Decision, Operationalization of the Waiver Concerning Preferential Treatment of Services and Service Suppliers of Least-Developed Countries, WT/L/918 (7 December 2013).

World Trade Organization. Council for Trade in Goods, Waiver Decision on Preferential Tariff Treatment for Least-Developed Countries, G/C/W/764 (14 June 2019).

World Trade Organization. General Council, Waiver Decision on Preferential Tariff Treatment for Least-Developed Countries, WT/L/304 (15 June 1999).

World Trade Organization. Guidelines for the Scheduling of Specific Commitments under the General Agreement on Trade in Services (GATS), S/L/92 (28 March 2001).

WTO, Sutherland, Peter, Jagdish Bhagwati, Kwesi Botchwey, Niall W.A. Fitzgerald, Koichi Hamada, John H. Jackson, Celso Lafer and Thierry de Montbrial. 'The Future of the WTO: Addressing Institutional Challenges in the New Millennium,' Report of the Consultative Board to the Director-General Supachai Panitchpakdi (WTO, 2004).

5 Non-Discrimination
National Treatment

Learning Objectives	167
1. Introduction	168
2. Origins and Rationale for National Treatment	168
3. National Treatment Provisions of GATT	170
3.1 Article III: Objectives	170
3.2 Direct and Indirect; *De Jure* and *De Facto* Discrimination	172
3.3 Article III:2, First Sentence: Fiscal Measures	172
3.3.1 Article III:2 Like Products	173
3.3.2 Article III:2 Taxed 'In Excess Of'	174
3.3.3 The 'Aims and Effects' Test	174
3.4 Article III:2, Second Sentence	175
3.4.1 Directly Competitive or Substitutable	176
3.4.2 Not Similarly Taxed	177
3.4.3 Applied so as to Afford Protection	177
3.5 Regulatory Measures – Article III:4	178
3.5.1 Law, Regulation, or Requirement Affecting the Internal Sale . . .	178
3.5.2 Domestic Product Needs to Be 'Like' . . .	180
3.5.3 Afforded Less Favourable Treatment . . .	180
4. National Treatment Obligation Under GATS	182
4.1 National Treatment Obligation – Article XVII:1	183
4.2 Violation of National Treatment Obligation	185
4.2.1 Undertaking of Specific Commitments	185
4.2.2 Measures Affecting Trade in Services	186
4.2.3 Like Services and Service Suppliers	186
4.2.4 Treatment No Less Favourable	188
5. Summary	191

Learning Objectives

This chapter aims to help students understand:

1. The origins and rationale for national treatment (NT);
2. The NT provisions of GATT; objectives of Article III of GATT;
3. Direct and indirect discrimination; *de jure* and *de facto* discrimination;
4. Article III:2 of GATT first sentence and second sentence;

DOI: 10.4324/9780367028183-6

5   Article III:4 of GATT – regulatory measures; NT obligations under the GATS Agreement; violation of NT obligations; and
6   Withdrawal and modification of commitments.

1. Introduction

The GATT, which was developed in the immediate aftermath of World War II, was built on the principle of non-discrimination. As mentioned in chapter 4, the GATT was founded on the principles of unconditional most-favoured nation (MFN) and national treatment (NT) obligations, which together form the cornerstone of non-discrimination in the multilateral trading system. NT obligations, along with MFN obligations, demand harmonization, *per se*, towards universal norms, but were designed to permit countries to maintain their own policy space, to set their own standards and priorities. NT obligation is a discipline on internal policies of WTO Member States, whereby imported products are not treated any less favourably than domestically made products in the importing Member State's domestic market. This means, *e.g.*, foreign products (a good, a service, a service provider, an intellectual property right, *etc.*) must be accorded the same treatment that a domestically produced product enjoys in a Member State.

One of the most contentious obligations of the GATT, NT impacts several internal regulations, government measures, and to some degree the national sovereignty of a Member State. Unlike MFN violations, NT violations are much more common and hence likely to cause strain in trading relations amongst Member States, potentially giving rise to trade disputes. The NT obligation, with regards to trade in goods, is contained in Articles III:2 and III:4 of the GATT 1994. Likewise, Article XVII:1 of GATS deals with the NT obligation for measures affecting trade in services. The NT obligation is also found contained in TBT and SPS agreements and the TRIPS Agreement. In this part we will be looking at the NT obligations arising under GATT and GATS, *i.e.*, in relation to goods and services.

2. Origins and Rationale for National Treatment

Though closely connected, theoretically, the origins of NT as a principle of international trade agreements are different from those of MFN principles. The origins of NT principles are traceable to Hebrew laws, before appearing in agreements between Italian city states in the eleventh century (Hart, 1987) and later in the twelfth century in commercial treaties between England and the continental states and among the German city states (Trebilcock, 2013). To gain a clear understanding of the important position NT holds within negotiated trade agreements and the key role it plays in ensuring the smooth operation of multilateral trading, it is helpful to look to the origins of NT in the negotiating history of the GATT. The first NT provisions were put together by the Drafting Committee in early 1947, which was set up by the Preparatory Committee,[1] as a groundwork for the ITO.[2] The work of one of the subcommittees formed during this phase, *viz.*, Committee II, is important for our discussion, as under its aegis the first draft GATT articles, including the NT provision, were prepared (Grossman, Horn, and Mavroidis, 2012). The delegates from six different countries acting as *rapporteurs* participated in the drafting process, with the US proposal (*Suggested Charter*) serving as the basis.[3] The NT provision included in the *Suggested Charter* was the first multilateral attempt to introduce NT-type of provisions in a treaty.[4] The NT draft finalised during the London Conference of 1947 and entered into force on 1 January 1948 was later revised during the Havana Conference in 1948.

At the beginning, the *raison d'être* for the London Conference was the negotiation/drafting of the ITO, and not the GATT. This position was to later change, with the decision to disassociate the drafting of the GATT from the drafting of the ITO, which presented the negotiators the opportunity to work exclusively on the provisions of the GATT. Also, the ambit of the GATT was not fully agreed at the London Conference (Grossman, Horn, and Mavroidis, 2012). Incidentally, the NT obligation was identified as a key element of the GATT discussions and worked on its detail. The negotiators at an early point realised that the tariff concession created by binding GATT commitments to ease trade barriers could be easily undermined by subjecting imported goods to discriminatory treatment once they clear customs and enter the domestic market (Chow and Schoenbaum, 2017). The primary aim of the negotiators was to look for ways of introducing provisions that would outlaw disguised restrictions of trade through internal taxes that had the effect of bestowing an advantage on domestic production. On the recommendations of the UK delegation the term 'indirectly' was introduced into the draft NT provision, to ensure that any domestic measure introduced by the contracting parties to provide a home advantage was put to the test by the NT discipline (Grossman, Horn, and Mavroidis, 2012). There was consensus amongst the delegates that government procurement should not be subject to the NT obligation. The UK, supported by New Zealand, requested the removal of films from being subjected to NT discipline, as it would fall within the ambit of cultural and commercial considerations. The UK's proposal came to be agreed upon by all attendees of the London Conference.

Although the negotiators had a clear idea of what they want to see in NT provision, the provision drafted during the London Conference was the same as the current discipline contained under Article III.1 of the GATT. The text of the NT provision drafted during the London Conference referred to 'similar' or 'identical' products while referring to the treatment of non-fiscal instruments. The draft also prohibited the use of taxes, to afford protection, but without reference to either 'similar' or 'identical' products (ECOSOC, 1946). Also, at the London Conference there was a general dissatisfaction with the choice of the term 'similar' found in Article 15, as it was thought to be too obscure (ECOSOC, 1946). At the New York (Lake Success) Conference, Article 15 of the London draft underwent changes, including to the term 'similar' which was replaced by 'like'. At the Geneva Conference, the remit of the NT provision was redrafted to exclude subsidies and government procurement, and the current Article III.8 started emerging. When the delegates met again at the Cuba Conference in 1948, the GATT had entered into force. Although the primary objective of the conference was to discuss the draft of the ITO, some important GATT decisions were also discussed, including the NT provision, which underwent substantial redrafting, providing clarity and ending the negotiation on NT obligations (Grossman, Horn, and Mavroidis, 2012). Article III of the GATT was born.

The two conclusions that one could arrive at by studying the negotiating records of the NT provision are as follows: (i) the NT provision was created primarily as an anti-circumvention device – to prevent 'concession erosion' and to safeguard the value of tariff concessions exchanged between trading partner, and (ii) the NT obligation was meant to cover all domestic instruments, which with the exception of a few were explicitly exempted from coverage in the body of the provision, whether of fiscal or non-fiscal nature (Grossman, Horn, and Mavroidis, 2012). It should be borne in mind that the GATT, as a framework for multilateral trade, did not contain any general right to market access between contracting parties, but rather only envisaged the progressive reduction and eventual removal of tariffs and other border measures between them.

3. National Treatment Provisions of GATT

3.1 Article III: Objectives

The national treatment obligation is enshrined in Article III of the GATT under three operative provisions. Article III requires that Member States do not afford protection to domestic production instruments. In short, this obligation requires that once imported products have entered the region after due payment of tariffs (customs, *etc.*), they are not subjected to any further tariffs/charges that their domestic counterparts are subjected to. This obligation is put in place to ensure that no domestic regulation or fiscal policy could adversely alter the conditions of competition in a domestic market between like imported products and domestic products. The relevant provisions of Article III, which is appropriately entitled as 'National Treatment on Internal Taxation and Regulation', are presented as follows:

1. The [Members] recognize that internal taxes and other internal charges, and laws, regulations and requirements affecting the internal sale, offering for sale, purchase, transportation, distribution or use of products, and internal quantitative regulations requiring the mixture, processing or use of products in specified amounts or proportions, should not be applied to imported or domestic products so as to afford protection to domestic production.
2. The products of the territory of any [Member] imported into the territory of any other [Member] shall not be subject, directly or indirectly, to internal taxes or other internal charges of any kind in excess of those applied, directly or indirectly, to like domestic products. Moreover, no [Member] shall otherwise apply internal taxes or other internal charges to imported or domestic products in a manner contrary to the principles set forth in paragraph 1.
3. ...
4. The products of the territory of any [Member] imported into the territory of any other [Member] shall be accorded treatment no less favourable than that accorded to like products of national origin in respect of all laws, regulations and requirements affecting their internal sale, offering for sale, purchase, transportation, distribution or use.[5]

Article III:1 deals with the application of NT principles, while establishing non-protectionism as the key concept. The language of Article III:1 captures the true purport of the NT principle contained in the provision, *i.e.*, the avoidance of any protectionist measures on imported goods.[6] Article III:2, on the other hand, extends the NT principles to internal tax measures.[7] In simple terms, Article III:2 stipulates that Member States 'shall' not apply a higher standard on imported goods than those applied to domestically produced like products. Article III:4 applies to domestic public policies other than taxation, subsidies, and government procurement.[8] The interpretive note to Article III:2 reads as follows:

A tax conforming to the requirements of the first sentence of paragraph 2 would be considered to be inconsistent with the provisions of the second sentence only in cases where competition was involved between, on the one hand, the taxed product and, on the other hand, a directly competitive or substitutable product which was not similarly taxed.

From a reading of the aforementioned provisions of Article III:1 and III:2 along with the interpretive note, one can conclude that Article III:2 identifies two distinctive set of obligations and presents (i) rules where the products in question are 'like' and (ii) rules for products that are 'directly competitive or substitutable'. Article III:4's remit, although equally as intrinsic as Article III:2, only sets out one set of obligation, *viz.*, requiring that Member States 'shall' accord imported products treatment 'no less favourable' than accorded to 'like products' of domestic origin. The objective of the NT provision is the avoidance of protectionism in the application of internal measures.[9] Discussing the purpose of Article III, the Panel in *Japan – Alcoholic Beverages II* noted as follows:

> one of the main purposes of Article III is to guarantee that WTO Members will not undermine through internal measures their commitment under Article II.[10]

The Appellate Body in *Japan – Alcoholic Beverages II*, while explaining (and emphasising) the purpose of Article III, observed as follows:

> The broad and fundamental purpose of Article III is to avoid protectionism in the application of internal tax and regulatory measures. More specifically, the purpose of Article III "is to ensure that internal measures 'not be applied to imported or domestic products so as to afford protection to domestic production'".[11] Toward this end, Article III obliges Members of the WTO to provide equality of competitive conditions for imported products in relation to domestic products.[12] "[T]he intention of the drafters of the Agreement was clearly to treat the imported products in the same way as the like domestic products once they had been cleared through customs. Otherwise indirect protection could be given".[13][14]

Similarly, the Appellate Body in *Canada – Periodicals* observed in the following lines:

> The fundamental purpose of Article III of the GATT 1994 is to ensure equality of competitive conditions between imported and like domestic products.[15]

Unlike Articles II and XI of GATT, Article III applies only to internal measures and not to border measures. In *India – Autos*, the panel noted on the relationship between Article III and Article XI of the GATT 1994:

> [I]t . . . cannot be excluded *a priori* that different aspects of a measure may affect the competitive opportunities of imports in different ways, making them fall within the scope either of Article III (where competitive opportunities on the domestic market are affected) or of Article XI (where the opportunities for importation itself, *i.e.* entering the market, are affected), or even that there may be, in perhaps exceptional circumstances, a potential for overlap between the two provisions, as was suggested in the case of state trading.[16]

Article III will come into play, even where products are barred at the border on consumer safety/public health concerns, which may also apply to domestically produced goods. Although the product in question may have not entered the customs territory of the importing country, Article III will be pressed into service to determine the consistency of the import ban.[17]

In sum, Article III fosters a broad protection mechanism against (i) measures favouring domestic products and (ii) measures discriminating like imported products which could be introduced by the importing countries. As noted by the Panel in *Italy – Agricultural Machinery* – and oft quoted by both Panels and by Appellate Body subsequently – Article III "obliges Members of the WTO to provide equality of competitive conditions for imported products in relation to domestic products".[18] This mechanism allows for the protection of the expectations of the Member States "as to the competitive relationship between products and those of the other contracting parties". Nevertheless, some commentators note, the ambiguity arising from the use of the phrase 'directly or indirectly' occurring in Article III:2 has the potential to be interpreted in a number of ways – either narrowing or broadening the remit of Article III:2 (Mavroidis, 2007).

3.2 Direct and Indirect; De Jure and De Facto Discrimination

The Panel in *Italy – Agricultural Machinery* noted that domestic laws, regulations, and fiscal policy are not to adversely modify the surrounding circumstances of competition as between like imported and domestic products in the domestic market.[19] The broad wording of Article III means that it "obliges Members of the WTO to provide equality of competitive conditions for imported products in relation to domestic products",[20] which facilitates protecting the "expectations of the contracting parties as to the competitive relationship between their products and those of the other contracting parties".[21] In essence, Article III safeguards "the predictability needed to plan future trade"[22] and captures both actual and potential[23] and direct and indirect discriminatory measures. Most importantly, Article III also captures both *de jure* (in law) and *de facto* (in fact) discriminatory measures that disproportionally affect foreign goods.[24]

The jurisprudence from *Korea – Various Measures on Beef* presents a good example of *de jure* discriminatory measures, which can be subjected to the NT obligations as contained in Article III.[25] The measure under challenge involved the sale of beef under an 'origin-based' dual retail distribution system, where imported beef was to be sold in specialist stores dealing exclusively in imported beef. Similarly, the case in *Japan – Alcoholic Beverages II* can be identified as an example of *de facto* discriminatory measures.[26] Here, the measure under challenge was the tax regime which contemplated the levy of a higher tax on whisky, brandy, and vodka in comparison to shochu (a domestic spirit), which came to be viewed as being discriminatory against imported alcoholic beverages.

3.3 Article III:2, First Sentence: Fiscal Measures

Article III:2 provides the NT rules for internal tax measures. As noted earlier, Article III:2 obligates the Member States to apply internal taxes on a non-discriminatory basis to both domestic and like imported products originating from other Member States.[27] The wording of Article III:2 makes it clear that it does not apply to "goods destined for importation" but rather to "imported goods" – in other words, the NT scheme contained in Article III does not apply to tariffs but to "imported goods" that have entered a fiscal territory. For the purposes of Article III, "imported goods" mean "a good that has been cleared by customs, meaning that pertinent customs duties and other levies have been paid for".[28]

At the outset, Article III:1 informs Article III:2,[29] first sentence, by recognising that imported products are not to be taxed more than the domestically produced products, with a view to give protection to domestic industry.[30] The first sentence of Article III:2

establishes the standard – in the event where the imported goods are like – by stating that imported goods "shall not be subject, directly or indirectly, to internal taxes or other charges of any kind in excess of those applied, directly or indirectly, to like domestic products". Article III:2's first sentence gives rise to two key provisions, *viz.*, are the imported products in question 'like' the domestic product, and are the taxes that have been imposed on such like imported products 'in excess of' those applied to the like domestic products? Article III:2 clearly refers to taxes and charges but yet does not contain a closed list of measures covered. This raises the question, *does Article III:2 cover all internal taxes*? The Panel in *Argentina – Hides and Leather*, while referring to the findings of the Appellate Body in *Canada – Periodicals*, noted as follows:

> Article III:2, first sentence, is not concerned with taxes or changes as such or the policy purposes Members pursue with them, but with their economic impact on the competitive opportunities of imported and like domestic products.[31]

3.3.1 Article III:2 Like Products

The 'like products' standard is premised on the comparability of similar products – imported and domestic – in question. To determine if an imported product has been discriminated against and will set in motion Article III:2, there must be a comparable similar domestic product in existence. Article III:2, first sentence, requires that the products in question are 'like'. The investigation into whether the products in question are 'like' is triggered when the government of the importing country imposes a higher tax (or other charges, or levies) on the imported product in comparison to the similarly placed domestic products.

The issue of 'likeness' was discussed in *Japan – Alcoholic Beverages II*, where the Appellate Body was called upon to examine the Panel's finding of inconsistency of the Japanese Liquor Tax Law with Article III:2. As mentioned earlier, the crucial issue before the Appellate Body was to determine if various alcoholic beverages – whisky, brandy, and vodka – were 'like' shochu (traditional Japanese alcoholic beverage), which was allegedly receiving favourable tax treatment from the Japanese government. The Appellate Body upheld the Panel's finding that vodka and shochu were 'like'. In the words of the Appellate Body,

> [T]he words of the first sentence [of Article III:2] require an examination of the conformity of an internal tax measure with Article III by determining, first, whether the taxed imported and domestic products are "like" and, second, whether the taxes applied to the imported products are "in excess of" those applied to the like domestic products.[32]

For GATT Article III:2, sentence 1, to apply, it is necessary that (i) the imported and domestic products are like products and (ii) the imported products are taxed 'in excess of' the like domestic products. While analysing what factors were to be taken into consideration in deciding if two products in question were 'like' products, the Appellate Body agreed with the practice established under GATT 1947[33] for determining the likeness of products, *i.e.*, on a case-by-case basis.[34] In essence, the Appellate Body referred to the three criteria established by the Working Party on *Border Tax Adjustments* to determine 'likeness', *viz.*, (i) the product's end use in a given market, (ii) consumer tastes and habits in a given market, and (iii) the product's properties, nature, and quality[35] – which all point in the direction of economic competitiveness of the product in a given market.³⁶ The Appellate Body made the general observation on the issue of 'likeness', comparing it to that of an accordion, as follows:

> The criteria in *Border Tax Adjustments* should be examined, but there can be no one precise and absolute definition of what is "like". The concept of "likeness" is a relative one that evokes the image of an accordion. The accordion of "likeness" stretches and squeezes in different places as different provisions of the WTO Agreement are applied. The width of the accordion in any one of those places must be determined by the particular provision in which the term "like" is encountered as well as by the context and the circumstances that prevail in any given case to which that provision may apply. We believe that, in Article III:2, first sentence of the GATT 1994, the accordion of "likeness" is meant to be narrowly squeezed.³⁷

The Appellate Body has also made clear that the range of 'like products' coming under Article III:2, sentence 1, is meant to be narrower than the range of products contemplated under other provisions of the GATT 1994.³⁸ This difference in interpretation arises due to the differences in the policy goals attached to Article III:2 and Article III:4.

The Panel in *Thailand – Cigarettes (Philippines)* found that it was not necessary to engage in a 'like product' analysis comparing all domestic and imported cigarettes across all price ranges.³⁹ Similarly, the Panel in *Philippines – Distilled Spirits* recalled the Appellate Body's holding in *Mexico – Taxes on Soft Drinks* that a 'likeness' analysis should focus on the physical qualities and characteristics of the final product rather than those of raw materials.⁴⁰ The Appellate Body in *Philippines – Distilled Spirits* noted that the determination of 'likeness' is "fundamentally, a determination about the nature and the extent of a competitive relationship between and among imported and domestic products".⁴¹ This approach of the WTO to 'like' products only takes into account the product *per se* and largely overlooks the process and production methods (PPM) used to produce the product in question.⁴² Commentators have criticised this position, as it is not a "value judgment of the political, social, or eco-compatible environment in which production takes place" (Conrad, 2011; Matsushita, Shoenbaum, Mavroidis, and Hahn, 2017; Van den Bossche and Zdouc, 2017).⁴³

3.3.2 Article III:2 Taxed 'In Excess Of'

The second element to be considered in Article III:2, first sentence, is whether the imported products in question are taxed 'in excess of' the like domestic products. If it is established, following an investigation, that the imported 'like product' has been taxed 'in excess of' those applied to the like domestic product, then the measure will be deemed inconsistent with Article III:2, first sentence. In *Japan – Alcoholic Beverages II*, the Appellate Body, while upholding the finding (and the reasoning) of the Panel that the tax on vodka was 'in excess of' that on shochu, noted that "even the smallest amount of 'excess' is too much"⁴⁴ and will constitute a violation of the Article III:2, first sentence, even if the margin were to be *de minimis*.⁴⁵ Here, the Appellate Body ruled that the prohibition of such taxes falling under Article III:3, first sentence, was not conditional on a "trade effects test".

3.3.3 The 'Aims and Effects' Test

The GATT Panels in the early part of the 1990s developed the 'aims and effects' test to determine if there was a violation in terms of Article III:2. In *US – Malt Beverages*, Canada challenged the decision of the US to tax certain imported alcoholic beverages. A particular measure that was challenged was the Mississippi wine tax which imposed a lower tax on wines produced using a certain variety of grape. The GATT Panel developed the 'aims and effects' test, with an effort to launch a new definition of 'like product' as used in Article III. The GATT Panel in *US – Taxes on Automobiles* embarked on a similar attempt to define the 'likeness' of the product through the 'aims and effects' test.[46] Here, the Panel based the rationale for their rulings on the policy statement contained in Article III:1, which states that internal taxes and internal regulatory measures should not be used "to afford protection to domestic production", as opposed to an investigation of the likeness of the products (imported and domestic) in question. Applying that policy, the GATT Panels ruled that 'like product' was to be defined in terms of two questions, *viz*., whether the product distinction in question had the 'aim' of protecting domestic industry, and the question whether that product distinction had the 'effect' of protecting the domestic industry.[47] The 'aims and effects' approach adopted by the GATT Panels to interpret 'like product' as found under Article III was rejected by the WTO Panel in *Japan – Alcoholic Beverages II* for lack of textual basis.[48] While upholding the decision of the Panel to reject the 'aims and effects' test, the Appellate Body made the following observation:

> Article III:2, first sentence does not refer specifically to Article III:1. There is no specific invocation in this first sentence of the general principle in Article III:1 that admonishes Members of the WTO not to apply measures "so as to afford protection". This omission must have some meaning. We believe the meaning is simply that the presence of a protective application need not be established separately from the specific requirements that are included in the first sentence in order to show that a tax measure is inconsistent with the general principle set out in the first sentence. However, this does not mean that the general principle of Article III:1 does not apply to this sentence. To the contrary, we believe the first sentence of Article III:2 is, in effect, an application of this general principle. . . . If the imported and domestic products are "like products", and if the taxes applied to the imported products are "in excess of" those applied to the domestic like products, then the measure is inconsistent with Article III:2, first sentence.[49]

The Appellate Body also noted that that such an approach – the 'aims and effects' test – was contrary to the text of Article III:2, and suggested that dispute settlement panels should return to the more traditional definitions in terms of 'likeness'.[50]

3.4 Article III:2, Second Sentence

Article III:2, second sentence, reads as follows:

> Moreover, no contracting party shall otherwise apply internal taxes or other internal charges to imported or domestic products in a manner contrary to the principles set forth in paragraph 1.

The interpretive note on Article III:2, second sentence, reads as follows:

> A tax conforming to the requirements of the first sentence of paragraph 2 would be considered to be inconsistent with the provisions of the second sentence only in cases where competition was involved between, on the one hand, the taxed product and,

on the other hand, *a directly competitive or substitutable product which was not similarly taxed* [emphasis added].

This clearly establishes a standard where the products are "directly competitive or substitutable". Interestingly, Article III:2, second sentence, refers back to Article III:1, requiring that internal taxes and charges "should not be applied to imported or domestic products so as to afford protection to domestic production". As noted earlier, the interpretive note clarifies the position by stating that this obligation only arises when "competition was involved between, on the one hand, the taxed product and, on the other hand, a directly competitive or substitutable product which was not similarly taxed".

The Appellate Body in *Japan – Alcoholic Beverages II* defined the legal status of Interpretative Note *Ad* Article III:2 and its relevance for the interpretation of Article III:2 as follows:

> Article III:2, second sentence, and the accompanying *Ad* Article have equivalent legal status in that both are treaty language which was negotiated and agreed at the same time. The *Ad* Article does not replace or modify the language contained in Article III:2, second sentence, but, in fact, clarifies its meaning. Accordingly, the language of the second sentence and the *Ad* Article must be read together in order to give them their proper meaning.[51]

To determine whether an internal tax measure was inconsistent with Article III:2, sentence 2, the Appellate Body in *Japan – Alcoholic Beverages II* developed the three-tier test, which requires addressing three separate issues, *viz*., (i) whether the imported and domestic products are 'directly competitive or substitutable products', that are in competition with each other, (ii) whether the directly competitive or substitutable imported and domestic products are "not similarly taxed", and (iii) whether the dissimilar taxation of the directly competitive or substitutable imported and domestic products is "applied . . . so as to afford protection to domestic production".[52] Where the competitive relationship is to perfect substitutability, Article III:2 limits state interference favouring the domestic like products to eschew unwanted consequences. The three-tier test requires that the appropriate ranges of 'directly competitive or substitutable products' are made on a case-by-case basis.[53]

3.4.1 Directly Competitive or Substitutable

The Appellate Body in *Japan – Alcoholic Beverages II* ruled that the first step under Article III:2, second sentence, is the determination of 'directly competitive or substitutable products', which is to be established on a case-by-case basis, taking into account all the relevant facts. Case law of the WTO has established that the term 'competitive or directly substitutable products' is a broader concept than 'likeness', used in sentence 1.[54] Applying the criterion of elasticity of substitution between products, the Panel in *Japan – Alcoholic Beverages II* held that shochu was not like but directly competitive with "whiskey, brandy, gin, genever, rum and liqueurs".[55] The test to determine if a product is 'directly competitive or substitutable' is by applying the *Border Tax Adjustment* criteria, as laid down by the Appellate Body in *Japan – Alcoholic Beverages II*.

The Appellate Body in *Korea – Alcoholic Beverages* noted that as competition is a dynamic and evolving process, the concept of 'directly competitive or substitutable', "is not to be analysed exclusively by reference to current consumer preferences".[56] The Appellate Body in *Philippines – Distilled Spirits* observed that one has to consider what customers would choose, if only were they not inhibited by such state measures to get familiar with the full range of choices on offer.[57]

3.4.2 Not Similarly Taxed

The second step in the test under Article III:2, sentence 2, is to determine if the products in question are similarly taxed. The Appellate Body in *Japan – Alcoholic Beverages II* observed that the phrase 'not similarly taxed' does not mean the same thing as the phrase 'in excess of' in Article III:2, first sentence. As mentioned earlier, for purposes of Article III:2, sentence 1, even the slightest variations in tax on imported products from domestic products will be considered as being in 'excess'. In contrast, Article III:2, sentence 2, requires a slightly less stringent application, as Member State's obligation is limited to 'similarly tax' the competing products.[58] The Appellate Body in *Japan – Alcoholic Beverages II* noted that to be deemed 'not similarly taxed', the amount of differential taxation must be more than *de minimis*,[59] and the process of determination if a particular differential taxation is *de minimis* is to be done on a case-by-case basis.

3.4.3 Applied so as to Afford Protection

The third leg of the enquiry commences when it is established that 'directly competitive or substitutable products' are 'not similarly taxed'. Once gone past that threshold, the enquiry should continue with establishing whether taxation was applied "so as to afford protection to domestic production". According to the Appellate Body in *Japan – Alcoholic Beverages II*, an examination of whether dissimilar taxation was "applied so as to afford protection" requires a detailed and objective analysis of the measure in question relating to the domestic and imported products in question. The Appellate Body in *Japan – Alcoholic Beverages II* held that the criterion 'so as to afford protection' needs to be established pursuant to GATT Article III:2, sentence 2, as a consequence of that specific linkage to paragraph 1.[60] According to the Appellate Body, this

> third inquiry under Article III:2, second sentence, must determine whether "directly competitive or substitutable products" are "not similarly taxed" in a way that affords protection. This is not an issue of intent. It is not necessary for a panel to sort through the many reasons legislators and regulators often have for what they do and weigh the relative significance of those reasons to establish legislative or regulatory intent. . . . It is irrelevant that protectionism was not an intended objective if the particular tax measure in question is nevertheless, to echo Article III:1, "applied to imported or domestic products so as to afford protection to domestic production." This is an issue of how the measure in question is applied. . . .
>
> Although it is true that the aim of a measure may not be easily ascertained, nevertheless its protective application can most often be discerned from the design, the architecture, and the revealing structure of a measure. The very magnitude of the dissimilar taxation in a particular case may be evidence of such a protective application, as the Panel rightly concluded in this case. Most often, there will be other factors to be considered as well. In conducting this inquiry, panels should give full consideration to all the relevant facts and all the relevant circumstances in any given case.[61]

The test developed the Appellate Body in *Japan – Alcoholic Beverages II* has since been followed by panels and been modified by the Appellate Body in subsequent cases. For instance, the Appellate

Body in *Canada – Periodicals* observed that imported 'split-run' periodicals and the Canadian 'non-split-run' periodicals were 'directly competitive or substitutable' products in the same segment of the Canadian periodicals market, and found that the objective behind the 'design' and 'structure' of excise tax regime was clearly "to afford protection to the production of Canadian periodicals".[62] However, the Appellate Body in *Chile – Alcoholic Beverages* found Chile's tax regime as not being compatible with its commitments under the GATT, by analysis of the 'objective' purpose of the measure under challenge, as revealed by its 'design', 'architecture', and 'structure'.[63] The Appellate Body went on to uphold the Panel's finding that the dissimilar taxation was applied "so as to afford protection to domestic production", which rendered the measure inconsistent with Article III:2, second sentence.[64] One can see that the approach of the Appellate Body in *Canada – Periodicals* was subjective, as opposed to being objective, as laid down in *Japan – Alcoholic Beverages II*. There are differences in the standards under Article III:2, sentence 1 and sentence 2. The first sentence requires a strict standard where the products in question are 'like', and even a *de minimis* difference in taxes will constitute violation of the provision. In contrast, under the second sentence, the difference in taxes must be greater, with the requirement that the 'objective' purpose of the measure taken was to afford protection to domestic products.

3.5 Regulatory Measures – Article III:4

Article III:4 of the GATT covers regulatory measures, *viz.*, laws and regulations, other than taxes and charges. Article III:4 prohibits discrimination through measures that affect the internal sale, offering for sale, purchase, transportation, distribution, or use of the imported products. The three-pronged test to determine if the internal regulation is consistent with the provisions of Article III:4 requires one to examine,

i   If the measure at issue is a 'law, regulation, or requirement' that is covered under Article III:4;
ii If the imported and domestic products are 'like products'; and
iii If the imported products are accorded a 'less favourable treatment'.

This means the complainant who alleges a violation of NT need only show that the 'measure' in question (laws, regulations – government involvement) alters the competitive landscape in favour of the domestic product and need not venture to demonstrate that such measures had actually affected the trade flows. Importantly, an investigation into an alleged violation of Article III:4 does not require a consideration of whether a measure "afford[s] protection to domestic production".[65]

3.5.1 Law, Regulation, or Requirement Affecting the Internal Sale . . .

One of the earliest jurisprudences on the subject comes from the GATT Panel report in *Italian Agricultural Machinery* case, where in response to a complaint from the UK the Panel examined an Italian law providing special credit terms to farmers for the purchase of agricultural machinery, conditional on the purchase of machinery produced in Italy. The GATT Panel observed as follows:

> The selection of the word "affecting" would imply, in the opinion of the Panel, that the drafters of the Article intended to cover in paragraph 4 not only the laws and regulations

which directly governed the conditions of sale or purchase but also any laws or regulations which might adversely modify the conditions of competition between the domestic and imported products on the internal market.[66]

The GATT Panel interpreted the scope of the application of Article III:4 broadly to include measures that could potentially modify the condition of the market. This broad interpretation of the term 'affecting' by the GATT Panel was sustained by the Appellate Body in *US – FSC (Article 21.5)*.[67]

Both GATT and WTO jurisprudence equate "all laws, regulations and requirements" appearing in Article III.4 of the GATT to the term "measure" used in Article XXIII.1b and Article XI of the GATT. Commentators have put forth the argument that although private measures are not covered under Article III:4,[68] if it can be proven, pursuant to general rules of public international law on State Responsibility, that such private conduct is attributable to a Member State, then such measures will come within the ambit of Article III:4 (Matsushita, Shoenbaum, Mavroidis, and Hahn, 2017).[69] The Appellate Body in *Korea – Various Measures on Beef* laid down the three elements of violation of Article III:4 as follows:

> For a violation of Article III:4 to be established, three elements must be satisfied: that the imported and domestic products at issue are "like products"; that the measure at issue is a "law, regulation, or requirement affecting their internal sale, offering for sale, purchase, transportation, distribution, or use"; and that the imported products are accorded "less favourable" treatment than that accorded to like domestic products.[70]

Likewise, the term 'affecting' was interpreted by the Panel in *Canada – Autos* to cover laws and regulations that directly administer the conditions of sale or purchase, besides any laws or regulations which could adversely modify the conditions of competition between domestic and imported products.[71] This interpretation confers a very 'broad scope of application' to the term.[72] The Panel in *US – Renewable Energy*, while considering less favourable treatment, found, "that evidence showing that the measure may have had minimal or no market effects in recent years" would not be sufficient to rebut a *prima facie* case showing that non-local products, including imported products, are treated less favourably than like local products.[73] The Panel found that India's assertion that a tax incentive for the use of domestic ingredients was not sufficient in the absence of more details as to how the "tax incentive modifies the conditions of competition with respect to the final product, is not sufficient to establish the existence of less favourable treatment", to establish the existence of less favourable treatment.[74]

The Appellate Body in *China – Auto Parts* held that imposing "additional administrative procedure" on imported products with a view to encourage domestic manufacturers to utilise domestic products as "affecting" the imported products, although the objective of measure was not intended at regulating the sale.[75] In *EC – Banana III*, the Appellate Body, while considering if the EC's allocation method of tariff quota for bananas was inconsistent with Article III:4, observed as follows:

> a determination of whether there has been a violation of Article III:4 does not require a separate consideration of whether a measure "afford[s] protection to domestic production".[76]

3.5.2 Domestic Product Needs to Be 'Like' . . .

The second obvious stage of the inquiry is to establish if the imported product and the domestic product are 'like'. Similar to Article I:1 and III:2, first sentence, the non-discrimination obligation of Article III:4 applies to 'like products'. The Appellate Body in *EC – Asbestos* noted that the concept of 'like products' occurring in Article III:4 was also used in Article III:2, first sentence. Earlier, the Appellate Body in *Japan – Alcoholic Beverages II* had held that the scope of 'like products' was to be construed 'narrowly' in that provision.[77] Making a distinction between the terms 'like products' occurring in Article III:2 and III:4, the Appellate Body observed as follows:

> In construing Article III:4, the same interpretive considerations do not arise, because the "general principle" articulated in Article III:1 is expressed in Article III:4, not through two distinct obligations, as in the two sentences in Article III:2, but instead through a single obligation that applies solely to "like products". Therefore, the harmony that we have attributed to the two sentences of Article III:2 need not and, indeed, cannot be replicated in interpreting Article III:4. Thus, we conclude that, given the textual difference between Articles III:2 and III:4, the "accordion" of "likeness" stretches in a different way in Article III:4.[78]

In short, the Appellate body found the scope of 'likeness' in Article III:4 to be broader than that found in Article III:2, first sentence.[79] The market-based economic approach advocated by the Appellate Body in *Japan – Alcoholics II* was later rejected in *EC – Asbestos*. In *EC – Asbestos*, Canada sought to challenge a French ban on asbestos in construction materials,[80] arguing that the asbestos it exported was a 'like product' to substitute products used in construction, and as a result deserved 'no less favourable treatment' under the NT standards contained in Article III:4. The Appellate Body in *EC – Asbestos* observed that Article III:4 wold have to be read in light of the overall objective of the NT provision, as contained in Article III:1:

> [A]lthough this "general principle" is not explicitly invoked in Article III:4, nevertheless, it "informs" that provision. Therefore, the term "like product" in Article III:4 must be interpreted to give proper scope and meaning to this principle. In short, there must be consonance between the objective pursued by Article III, as enunciated in the "general principle" articulated in Article III:1, and the interpretation of the specific expression of this principle in the text of Article III:4. This interpretation must, therefore, reflect that, in endeavouring to ensure "equality of competitive conditions", the "general principle" in Article III seeks to prevent Members from applying internal taxes and regulations in a manner which affects the competitive relationship, in the marketplace, between the domestic and imported products involved, "so as to afford protection to domestic production".[81]

From the aforementioned, it is clear that the Appellate Body considered Article III:1 as stating the general purpose that breathes life into Article III as a whole generally.

3.5.3 Afforded Less Favourable Treatment . . .

The third stage of the inquiry relates to the question if the measure under challenge guarantees a 'treatment no less favourable' to the domestic product. The GATT Panel in *US – Section*

337 observed that the words 'treatment no less favourable' occurring in Article III:4 call for 'effective equality of opportunities' for imported products.[82] Both GATT and WTO jurisprudence demonstrates that Panels have consistently interpreted 'treatment no less favourable' in a similar vein.[83] If a measure diminishes the 'effective equality of opportunities for imported products', then the measure will be considered inconsistent with the NT obligation arising under Article III.4.[84] At this stage of the enquiry, it is important to bear in mind that the NT provision is premised on an agenda of anti-protectionism. The purpose of Article III:4 is about competitive opportunities, as opposed to actual trade flows. Hence, to prove a violation of Article III:4, it is necessary to examine if the measure at issue modifies the conditions of competition in the relevant market to the detriment of imported products.[85] It is for the Member State that mounts the challenge to demonstrate that the measure at issue accords 'less favourable treatment'. This was well captured by the Appellate Body in *EC – Asbestos* case, where it was observed as follows:

> A complaining Member must still establish that the measure accords to the group of "like" imported products "less favourable treatment" than it accords to the group of "like" domestic products.[86]

In sum, Article III:4 dictates that foreign products are not treated worse than 'like' domestic products. In contrast in *EC – Asbestos* the challenge was based on the premise that the measure in question *de facto* resulted in 'less favourable treatment' of the imported product. The Appellate Body held that the term 'less favourable treatment' appearing in Article III:4 reiterated the principle contained in Article III:1, *i.e.*, that the WTO Member States are not to use domestic measures to grant protection to domestically produced goods, and observed as follows:

> The term "less favourable treatment" expresses the general principle, in Article III:1, that internal regulations "should not be applied . . . so as to afford protection to domestic production." If there is "less favourable treatment" of the group of "like" imported products, there is, conversely, "protection" of the group of "like" domestic products. However, a Member may draw distinctions between products which have been found to be "like," without, for this reason alone, according to the group of "like" imported products "less favourable treatment" than that accorded to the group of "like" domestic products.[87]

In contrast, in *Korea – Various Measures on Beef*, the measure at issue concerned the 'dual retail system' introduced for marketing beef. The Korean law under challenge restricted the sale of imported beef in designated shops, thereby introducing a dual retail outlet for the sale of beef – one for imported beef and another for domestically produced beef. When sold in supermarkets, the imported beef and domestically produced beef were displayed separately. Where sold by retailers, the imported beef was required to be displayed with a clear sign reading 'Specialized Imported Beef Store'. In the Appellate Body's opinion, although the formal separation of the imported and domestically produced product was not a violation, the separate retail distribution for the two products "modified the conditions of competition in the Korean beef market to the disadvantage of imported product".[88] The 'reduction of competitive opportunity' led to the Appellate Body finding that the measure did not meet the requirements of Article III:4.[89] The Appellate Body explained the three elements of a violation of Article III:4 as follows:

> For a violation of Article III:4 to be established, three elements must be satisfied: that the imported and domestic products at issue are "like products"; that the measure at issue

is a "law, regulation, or requirement affecting their internal sale, offering for sale, purchase, transportation, distribution, or use"; and that the imported products are accorded "less favourable" treatment than that accorded to like domestic products.[90]

In the Appellate Body's opinion, different treatment alone of imported products does not necessarily constitute less favourable treatment, and likewise the absence of formal difference in treatment does not necessarily mean that there is no less favourable treatment.[91]

In the *Dominican Republic – Import and Sale of Cigarettes* case, the measure imposed by the Dominican Republic required that all cigarette packets marketed in the Dominican Republic have a stamp affixed to them. Although applied in a formal manner to both domestic and imported cigarettes, the measure (i) modified the conditions of competition in the marketplace to the detriment of imported products, (ii) imposed additional processes and costs on imported cigarettes, and (iii) presented the imported cigarettes to the consumer in a less appealing manner.[92] The Appellate Body, while upholding the findings of Panel, noted as follows:

> Nor do we accept Honduras' argument that the bond requirement accords "less favourable treatment" to imported cigarettes because, as the sales of domestic cigarettes are greater than those of imported cigarettes on the Dominican Republic market, the per-unit cost of the bond requirement for imported cigarettes is higher than for domestic products. The Appellate Body indicated in *Korea – Various Measures on Beef* that imported products are treated less favourably than like products if a measure modifies the conditions of competition in the relevant market to the detriment of imported products. However, the existence of a detrimental effect on a given imported product resulting from a measure does not necessarily imply that this measure accords less favourable treatment to imports if the detrimental effect is explained by factors or circumstances unrelated to the foreign origin of the product, such as the market share of the importer in this case. In this specific case, the mere demonstration that the per-unit cost of the bond requirement for imported cigarettes was higher than for some domestic cigarettes during a particular period is not, in our view, sufficient to establish "less favourable treatment" under Article III:4 of the GATT 1994. Indeed, the difference between the per-unit costs of the bond requirement alleged by Honduras is explained by the fact that the importer of Honduran cigarettes has a smaller market share than two domestic producers . . . In this case, the difference between the per-unit costs of the bond requirement alleged by Honduras does not depend on the foreign origin of the imported cigarettes.[93]

The key takeaways from the prior case laws on Article III:4 are that (i) there must be a undisputable relationship between the measure in question and its "adverse impact on competitive opportunities for imported versus like domestic products",[94] (ii) a measure will be considered as giving rise to 'treatment less favourable' if it modifies the conditions of competition in the relevant market to the disadvantage of the imported products, and (iii) a complainant under Article III:4 carries a high burden of proof to demonstrate 'less favourable conditions of competition'.[95]

4. National Treatment Obligation Under GATS

The NT obligation contained in Article XVII:1 of GATS is different from the NT obligations contained in Article III of GATT. Article XVII:1 of the GATS, dealing with NT obligations, reads as follows:

> In the sectors inscribed in its Schedule, and subject to any conditions and qualifications set out therein, each Member shall accord to services and service suppliers of any other Member, in respect of all measures affecting the supply of services, treatment no less favourable than that it accords to its own like services and service suppliers.

The primary purpose of the provision is the prohibition of discriminatory treatment against foreign services and service suppliers to the advantage of domestic service suppliers. A reading of the aforementioned provision also makes clear that its remit is narrow, covering only matters affecting trade in services. This position was clearly stated by the Panel in *China – Electronic Payment Services*, where it was observed that the scope of the national treatment obligation under Article XVII extends generally to all measures affecting the supply of services.[95]

4.1 National Treatment Obligation – Article XVII:1

The key feature of NT obligation is its complicated relationship with market access. Unlike trade in goods, where market access and NT obligations are clear, the NT obligations with regards to trade in services is somewhat blurred. While the GATT does not clearly identify market access, the same is not true with GATS, as it is clearly identified and set forth in Article XVI. While Article XVI:1 obligates Member States to accord market access treatment based on its Services Schedule, Article XVI:2 identifies the limitations on such commitments. The four modes of supply determine the scheduling of specific commitments and is identified in Part I of the GATS as follows: (i) cross-border supply, (ii) consumption abroad, (iii) commercial presence, and (iv) temporary entry of natural persons.[97] The relevant parts of Article XVI read as follows:

1 With respect to market access through the modes of supply identified in Article I, each Member shall accord services and service suppliers of any other Member treatment no less [favourable] than that provided for under the terms, limitations and conditions agreed and specified in its Schedule.
2 In sectors where market-access commitments are undertaken, the measures which a Member shall not maintain or adopt either on the basis of a regional subdivision or on the basis of its entire territory, unless otherwise specified in its Schedule, are defined as . . .

The Panel in *US – Gambling* clarified the function of Article XVI and observed that paragraph 1 did not contain restrictions on market access beyond those listed in paragraph 2 in the following manner:

> The ordinary meaning of the words, the context of Article XVI, as well as the object and purpose of the GATS confirm that the restrictions on market access that are covered by Article XVI are only those listed in paragraph 2 of this Article.[98]

As per Article XVII, once Member States make their NT commitments, they are obliged not to apply discriminatory measures to benefit domestic services and service providers. The key obligation under Article XVII is that a Member State is to not modify the conditions of the competition in favour of its own service sector, once a commitment has been made. Article XVII reads as follows:

1 In the sectors inscribed in its Schedule, and subject to any conditions and qualifications set out therein, each Member shall accord to services and service suppliers of any other

Member, in respect of all measures affecting the supply of services, treatment no less favourable than that it accords to its own like services and service suppliers [footnote omitted].
2   A Member may meet the requirement of paragraph 1 by according to services and service suppliers of any other Member, either formally identical treatment or formally different treatment to that it accords to its own like services and service suppliers.
3   Formally identical or formally different treatment shall be considered to be less favourable if it modifies the conditions of competition in favour of services or service suppliers of the Member compared to like services or service suppliers of any other Member.

Under GATS the key objective of the NT obligation is to ensure "equal competitive opportunities for like services of other Members".[99] The NT obligations under Article XVII:1 apply generally to all measures affecting the supply of services with regards to explicit commitment to grant 'national treatment' made by WTO Member States in their Services Schedule with regards to specific sectors.[100] This commitment under the Services Schedule is still subject to 'any conditions and qualifications' set out in Article XXVII. Service sectors not included in a Member's Services Schedule is exempt from any NT obligations arising under Article XVII. Hence, it is arguable that a Member State may resort to discriminatory measures against those services and service suppliers of another Member State in sectors not identified in their Services Schedule, without violating the NT obligations embodied in GATS Article XVII (Wang, 2012).

During the Uruguay Round of negotiations, the developing country representatives took the position that NT was an objective to be attained gradually, sector by sector, and dependent on the coverage, and was only subject to the final framework agreement (Group of Negotiations on Services, 1989).[101] This reservation on NT obligation was put forth by developing countries during the Uruguay Round of negotiations, as they wanted to protect specific domestic services and service suppliers (Wang, 2012). Not surprisingly, many developing country Member States have made NT commitments only to a restricted number of services sectors. That said, even when NT commitments are made, they are usually accompanied by extensive constraints. The Member States limit their commitments through the imposition of conditions and qualifications. For instances, a Member State may impose restrictions on foreign providers by

i   Requiring details of the nationality or residency of service suppliers;
ii   Requiring the investment of a certain amount of assets in local currency;
iii   Requiring the purchase of land by foreign service suppliers;
iv   Granting special subsidy or tax privileges exclusively to domestic service suppliers; and
v   Applying differential capital requirements and special operational limits to operations of foreign service suppliers.

While Article XVII does not provide an exhaustive list of measures inconsistent with NT obligations, paragraph 2 makes clear that limitations on national treatment cover cases of both *de jure* and *de facto* discrimination. On limitations, the Scheduling Guidelines from 2001 note:

[t]he national treatment standard does not require formally identical treatment of domestic and foreign suppliers; formally different measures can result in effective equality of treatment; conversely, formally identical measures can in some cases result in

less favourable treatment of foreign suppliers (*de facto* discrimination). Thus, it should be borne in mind that limitations on national treatment cover both, *de facto* and *de jure* discriminations.[102]

Further, the Scheduling Guidelines present the following as an example of *de facto* discriminatory measure:

> A measure [which] stipulates that prior residency is required for the issuing of a licence to supply a service. Although the measure does not formally distinguish service suppliers on the basis of national origin, it *de facto* offers less favourable treatment to foreign service suppliers because they are less likely to be able to meet a prior residency requirement than like service suppliers of national origin.[103]

4.2 Violation of National Treatment Obligation

In order to determine a Member State's NT commitments as regards services, it is necessary to examine closely the concerned Member State's commitments, conditions, qualifications, and limitations set out in its Services Schedule. The Panel in *EC – Bananas III* established a three-part test to determine violation of Article XVII,[104] which was later confirmed on appeal by the Appellate Body.[105] As per the analysis, to successfully demonstrate a violation of NT commitment under Article XVII, the claimant has to demonstrate the following elements, *viz.*,

i   Whether the Member State in question has undertaken a specific commitment in a relevant sector and a mode of supply;
ii Whether the measure adopted by the Member State affects the supply of services in that sector and/or mode of supply;
iii Whether the foreign and domestic services providers are 'like services and services suppliers'; and
iv Whether the foreign services and service suppliers are accorded a 'treatment no less favourable'.[106]

The approach and test taken here by the Panel and the Appellate Body are akin to their approaches taken in analysing consistency of Article III of GATT and of Article 2.1 Technical Barriers to Trade (TBT). A very similar approach was adopted by the Panel in *China – Publications and Audiovisual Products*,[107] while analysing the consistency with Article XII:1.

4.2.1 Undertaking of Specific Commitments

As stated earlier, the NT obligations contained in Article XII:1 apply only when sector-specific commitments have been made by a Member State. Hence, the first port of call in the investigation will be to establish if an NT commitment has been made by a Member State with regards to a service sector in its Services Schedule. The issue before the Panel in *China – Publications and Audiovisual Products* was if China had made NT commitments with regards to the distribution of sound recordings through electronic means. It was China's argument that such commitments made covered only distribution of sound recordings in physical form and did not extend to distribution through electronic medium. The Panel found that China's commitment in the entry 'Sound recording distribution services' extended to the distribution of content through electronic means.[108] The Appellate, while affirming the findings of the Panel, observed as follows:

> [T]he terms used in China's GATS Schedule ("sound recording" and "distribution") are sufficiently generic that what they apply to may change over time. . . . We further note that interpreting the terms of GATS specific commitments based on the notion that the ordinary meaning to be attributed to those terms can only be the meaning that they had at the time the Schedule was concluded would mean that very similar or identically worded commitments could be given different meanings, content, and coverage depending on the date of their adoption or the date of a Member's accession to the treaty. Such interpretation would undermine the predictability, security, and clarity of GATS specific commitments, which are undertaken through successive rounds of negotiations, and which must be interpreted in accordance with customary rules of interpretation of public international law.[109]

4.2.2 Measures Affecting Trade in Services

The second element of the test, *viz.*, "if the measure accords like foreign services suppliers a treatment less favourable to the domestic services", is broad and includes measures by both the central government authorities and regional governments as well. The Appellate Body in *Canada – Autos* noted that the intention of the drafters of the GATS Agreement were to give a broad meaning to the term 'affecting trade in services', and the word 'affecting' echoed their intent.[110] The Appellate Body clarified the position further by noting:

> we believe that at least two key legal issues must be examined to determine whether a measure is one "affecting trade in services": first, whether there is "trade in services" in the sense of Article I:2; and, second, whether the measure in issue "affects" such trade in services within the meaning of Article I:1.[111]

The Panel in *China – Publications and Audiovisual Products* took a similar position to the Appellate Body in *Canada – Autos* and observed that the measures at issue 'affect' the supply of reading materials distribution services for the purpose of Article XVII:1.[112]

4.2.3 Like Services and Service Suppliers

The third element of the examination revolves around the question of whether the foreign and domestic services and service suppliers are 'like services and service suppliers'. It is to be pointed out here that the GATS Agreement does not define 'like services and service suppliers'. In this regard, the Panels and Appellate Body have relied on the 'likeness' jurisprudence from Article III GATT. The first instance where a Panel was required to interpret 'likeness' in Article XVII was *EC – Bananas III*, where the Panel arrived at the conclusion that foreign and domestic services and suppliers were like, and observed as follows:

> [T]he nature and the characteristics of wholesale transactions as such, as well as of each of the different subordinated services mentioned in the headnote to section 6 of the CPC, are "like" when supplied in connection with wholesale services, irrespective of whether these services are supplied with respect to bananas of EC and traditional ACP origin, on the one hand, or with respect to bananas of third-country or non-traditional

ACP origin, on the other. Indeed, it seems that each of the different service activities taken individually is virtually the same and can only be distinguished by referring to the origin of the bananas in respect of which the service activity is being performed. Similarly, in our view, to the extent that entities provide these like services, they are like service suppliers.[113]

This view of the Panel was later upheld by the Appellate Body and was also subsequently endorsed by the panel in *Canada – Autos*. The Appellate Body in *Argentina – Financial Services* clarified that one must take into account both service and service suppliers while determining 'likeness' under Articles II:1 and XVII:1 of the GATS,[114] and observed as follows:

> The assessment of likeness of services should not be undertaken in isolation from considerations relating to the service suppliers, and, conversely, the assessment of likeness of service suppliers should not be undertaken in isolation from considerations relating to the likeness of the services they provide. We see the phrase 'like services and service suppliers' as an integrated element for the likeness analysis under Articles II:1 and XVII:1, respectively. Accordingly, separate findings with respect to the 'likeness' of services, on the one hand, and the 'likeness' of service suppliers, on the other hand, are not required.[115]

In *China – Electronic Payment Services*, the panel noted that the dictionary definition of 'like' was having "the same characteristics or qualities as some other person or thing; of approximately identical shape, size, *etc.*, with something else; similar".[116] The Panel also ruled that an examination of 'likeness' under Article XVII:1 should "take into account the particular circumstances of each case" or "should be made on a case-by-case basis".[117] The Panel in *China – Publications and Audiovisual Products* concluded that when origin is the key factor on which a measure was challenged as presenting a difference in treatment between domestic service suppliers and foreign suppliers, the 'like service supplier' is met. The Panel also found that the difference of treatment was "not exclusively linked to the origin of service suppliers, but to other factors", and as a result engaged in a more detailed analysis of the likeness issue,[118] and noted as follows:

> In approaching this matter, we do not assume that without further analysis we may simply transpose to trade in services the criteria or analytical framework used to determine "likeness" in the context of the multilateral agreements on trade in goods. We recognize important dissimilarities between the two areas of trade – notably the intangible nature of services, their supply through four different modes, and possible differences in how trade in services is conducted and regulated.[119]

The Panel, while considering the ordinary meaning of the term 'like' and as well the context of the phrase 'like services', observed, "Article XVII seeks to ensure equal competitive opportunities for like services of other Members" and that "like services are services that are in a competitive relationship with each other (or would be if they were allowed to be supplied in a particular market)".[120] The Panel noted as follows:

> Furthermore, we note that Article XVII is applicable to all services,[121] in any sector, and that services – which are intangible – may be provided through any of the four modes of supply. As well, Article XVII refers to "like services and service suppliers". In the light of this complexity, "like services and service suppliers" analyses should in our view take into account the

particular circumstances of each case. In other words, we consider that determinations of "like services", and "like service suppliers", should be made on a case-by-case basis.[122]

In the light of the above, we consider that a likeness determination should be based on arguments and evidence that pertain to the competitive relationship of the services being compared. As in goods cases where a panel assesses whether a particular product is a "like product", the determination must be made on the basis of the evidence as a whole. If it is determined that the services in question in a particular case are essentially or generally the same in competitive terms, those services would, in our view, be "like" for purposes of Article XVII.[123,124]

The Appellate Body in *Argentina – Financial Services* ruled the following criteria as being relevant for determining 'likeness' under the GATS:

the characteristics of services and service suppliers or consumers' preferences in respect of services and service suppliers may be relevant for determining "likeness" under the GATS. We note that, in this vein, the panel in *EC – Bananas III* considered the "nature and the characteristics" of the service transactions at issue, which may be seen as an adaptation of the original criterion in *Border Tax Adjustments* – namely, properties, nature and quality. Furthermore, with respect to the criterion of tariff classification, the classification and description of services under, for instance, the UN Central Product Classification (CPC) could be relevant. The panel in *China – Electronic Payment Services* undertook another such adaptation in considering evidence that the service suppliers at issue "describe[d] their business scope in very similar terms", and that this suggested that "these suppliers compete[d] with each other in the same business sector". This may be seen as adaptations of the criteria of "properties, nature and quality", "end-use", and/or "consumer preferences". As in the context of trade in goods, however, we equally consider that the criteria for analysing "likeness" of services and service suppliers are simply analytical tools to assist in the task of examining the relevant evidence, and that they are neither a treaty-mandated nor a closed list of criteria that will determine the legal characterization of services and service suppliers as "like".[125]

It should stressed that the aforementioned criteria are "simply analytical tools to assist in the task of examining the relevant evidence" and are neither a treaty-mandated nor a closed list of criteria.[126] In sum, the available jurisprudence indicate that an examination of 'likeness' under Article XVII:1 should be based on arguments and evidence pertaining to the competitive relationship of the services that are being compared and the evidence as a whole.[127]

4.2.4 Treatment No Less Favourable

The third element of the examination revolves around the question of whether the foreign services and service suppliers are accorded treatment no less favourable than 'like' domestic services and service suppliers. Article XVII GATS deals with the conditions of competition which favours services or service suppliers of the Member State concerned, compared to like services or service suppliers of any other Member State. Paragraphs 2 and 3 of Article XVII clarify the requirement of 'treatment no less favourable' as contained in paragraph 1 and reads as follows:

2   A Member may meet the requirement of paragraph 1 by according to services and service suppliers of any other Member, either formally identical treatment or formally different treatment to that it accords to its own like services and service suppliers.

3   Formally identical or formally different treatment shall be considered to be less favourable if it modifies the conditions of competition in favour of services or service suppliers of the Member compared to like services or service suppliers of any other Member.

A Member State is likely to be in breach of the NT commitment if, while granting formally identical treatment to service suppliers, it modifies the conditions of competition in favour of the domestic services or service suppliers. The Panel in *China – Publications and Audiovisual Products*, while discussing whether a formal prohibition on supply of certain services by a foreign service supplier would constitute 'no less favourable treatment' as specified in Article XVII:3, held as follows:

> In our view, a measure that prohibits foreign service suppliers from supplying a range of services that may, subject to satisfying certain conditions, be supplied by the like domestic supplier cannot constitute treatment "no less favourable", since it deprives the foreign service supplier of any opportunity to compete with like domestic suppliers. In terms of paragraph 3 of Article XVII, such treatment modifies conditions of competition in the most radical way, by eliminating all competition by the foreign service supplier with respect to the service at issue.[128]

The Panel, drawing upon jurisprudence developed under GATT 1994, discussed the burden of proof on the issue of 'less favourable' treatment and noted that different treatment can be accorded to foreign services or foreign service suppliers, "as long as that treatment does not modify conditions of competition in favour of like domestic services or service suppliers".[129] The Panel considered the observation made by the Appellate Body in *US – FSC (Article 21.5 – EC)*, where it was held as follows:

> The examination of whether a measure involves "less favourable treatment" of imported products within the meaning of Article III:4 of the GATT 1994 must be grounded in close scrutiny of the "fundamental thrust and effect of the measure itself". This examination cannot be rest on simple assertion, but must be founded on a careful analysis of the contested measure and of its implications in the marketplace. At the same time, however, the examination need not be based on the actual effects of the contested measure in the marketplace.[130]

Both the Panel and the Appellate Body in *EC – Bananas III* ruled the imbalance in allocated trading rights as 'treatment less favourable'. In the Panel's view the allocation of the 30 percent quota constituted less favourable treatment. The Appellate Body agreed with the finding and observed as follows:

> We concur, therefore, with the Panel's conclusion that "the allocation to Category B operators of 30 per cent of the licenses allowing for the importation of third-country and non-traditional ACP bananas at in-quota tariff rates creates less favourable conditions of competition for like service suppliers of Complainants' origin and is therefore inconsistent with the requirement of Article XVII of GATS". We also concur with the Panel's conclusion that the allocation to Category B operators of 30 per cent of the licenses for importing third-country and non-traditional ACP bananas at in-quota tariff rates is inconsistent with the requirements of Article II of the GATS.[131]

In *China – Electronic Payment Services*, the Panel noted that Article XVII:3 of the GATS provides valuable clarification regarding the concept of 'less favourable treatment' and observed:

> [Article XVII:3] states that formally identical or different treatment is deemed less favourable "if it modifies the conditions of competition in favour of services or service suppliers of the Member compared to like services or service suppliers of any other Member". We deduce from this that, subject to all other Article XVII conditions being fulfilled, formally identical or different treatment of service suppliers of another Member constitutes a breach of Article XVII:1 if and only if such treatment modifies the conditions of competition to their detriment.[132]

One can conclude from the observation that a Member State may not be in breach of the NT obligations if the formally different treatment to foreign and domestic services or service suppliers does not modify the conditions of competition in favour of the domestic services and service suppliers. The Panel adopted a two-step methodology by first determining (i) if the measure at issue provided different treatment as between domestic services and service suppliers and like services and service suppliers from other Member States, and (ii) if such different treatment resulted in 'less favourable treatment',[133] before concluding that it did amount to 'less favourable treatment'.[134]

The Appellate Body in *Argentina – Financial Services* set out its understanding of the terms 'treatment no less favourable' as occurring in Article II:1 and XVII of GATS and observed, "like Article II of the GATS, Article XVII of the GATS refers not only to 'like services' but also to 'like service suppliers'".[135] With regards Article XVII, the Appellate Body observed:

> Examining the text of these provisions, we note that the second and third paragraph of Article XVII elaborate on the meaning of a Member's obligation to grant "treatment no less favourable" pursuant to Article XVII:1. Specifically, Article XVII:2 recognizes that a Member may meet this requirement by according to services and service suppliers "either formally identical treatment or formally different treatment". Article XVII:3 stipulates that "[f]ormally identical or formally different treatment shall be considered to be less favourable if it modifies the conditions of competition in favour of services or service suppliers of the Member compared to like services or service suppliers of any other Member." In our view, while Article XVII:3 refers to the modification of conditions of competition in favour of domestic services or service suppliers, the legal standard set out in Article XVII:3 calls for an examination of whether a measure modifies the conditions of competition to the detriment of services or service suppliers of any other Member. Less favourable treatment of foreign services or service suppliers and more favourable treatment of like domestic services or service suppliers are flip-sides of the same coin.[136]

The Appellate Body duly noted that it was through the flexibilities and exceptions that the GATS Agreement sought to strike a balance between a Member State's obligations (commitments under the Agreement) and its right to pursue national policy objectives,[137] and observed as follows:

> This balance, too, reinforces the established legal standard for "treatment no less favourable" under the non-discrimination provisions of the GATS, that is, whether a measure

modifies the conditions of competition to the detriment of like services or service suppliers of any other Member. Where a measure is inconsistent with the non-discrimination provisions, regulatory aspects or concerns that could potentially justify such a measure are more appropriately addressed in the context of the relevant exceptions. Addressing them in the context of the non-discrimination provisions would upset the existing balance under the GATS.[138]

The key takeaways from an analysis of the Panel and Appellate Body reports demonstrate that an enquiry into 'treatment no less favourable' as occurring in Article XVII is subjective enquiry and will have to take into consideration (i) conditions of competition which favours services or service suppliers of the Member State concerned; (ii) that a Member State may likely be in breach of the its NT obligations, if while granting formally identical treatment to service suppliers, modifies the conditions of competition in favour of the domestic services or service suppliers; and (iii) a Member State may not be in breach of the NT obligations if its formally different treatment of foreign and domestic services or service suppliers does not modify the conditions of competition in favour of the domestic services and service suppliers.

5. Summary

The multilateral trading system is strongly predicated on the non-discrimination principles. The NT obligation, together with the MFN obligation, serves a major purpose in the delivery of the non-discrimination principle. One will note that the NT obligations arising under Article III of the GATT and Article XVII:1 of the GATS Agreement are different. The NT obligation under the GATT is far wider as it covers trade in goods, and the NT obligation under GATS is far narrower as it only covers those measures where Member States have undertaken to grant national treatment. As discussed, the NT obligation is aimed at achieving the objective of protectionist measures being adopted by Member States in their regulatory measures and internal tax regime. As the jurisprudence demonstrates, the NT obligation is largely achieved in practice, through the checks and balances that are in place.

Notes

1 The Preparatory Committee was established by the United Nations (UN) Economic and Social Council (ECOSOC), following from a proposal for an International Conference on Trade and Employment at its first session on 18 February 1946. The Preparatory Committee was charged with the task of drafting a convention for international trade. See Irwin, Mavroidis, and Sykes (2008).
2 As mentioned in chapter 1, the ITO never came into existence, due to lack of support from the US Congress for a world governing body for international trade. Nevertheless, the GATT 1947, which was to provide the legal framework for the ITO, was utilised by the participating countries (contracting countries) to enter into trade agreements using the GATT as the 'rule book' to carry on trading until the entry into force of the WTO in 1995. Interestingly, even before the decision of the US Congress was known, the participating countries had started trading under the GATT terms.
3 John Leddy, a US State Department official, assumed the key responsibility during the GATT drafting process. See Irwin, Mavroidis, and Sykes (2008). As far as the subcommittee dealing with NT was concerned, delegates from all countries were invited to participate.
4 It is to be noted that this was not the first NT provision, in general. The following treaties drawn up by the US, prior to the GATT 1947, did boast an NT clause: the US Tariff Act of 1930 and the bilateral agreements concluded between the US and Canada (1938), the US and Mexico (1942), and the US and Uruguay (1942).

5   The remaining part of Article III deals with the application and the non-application of the NT obligations to particular measures, such as (i) local content requirements (paragraph 5); (ii) government procurement (paragraph 8(a)); (iii) subsidies to domestic producers (paragraph 8(b)); (iv) internal maximum price control measures (paragraph 9); and (v) screen quotas for cinematograph films (*i.e.*, movies) (paragraph 10).
6   See Appellate Body Report, *Japan – Alcoholic Beverages II*, p. 16.
7   Taxation is covered under Article III:2.
8   Subsidies and government procurement are exempted by Article III:8.
9   The individual paragraphs of Article III are to be read in conjunction with the Note *Ad* Article III, as contained in Annex I and entitled 'Notes and Supplementary Provisions', of the GATT 1994. This is important, especially with regard to the obligation under Article III:2, second sentence. The Note *Ad* Article III clarifies the scope of the measures (internal and border measures) as applicable to Article III.
10 See Panel Report, *Japan – Alcoholic Beverages II*, para. 6.13.
11 (Footnote original) Panel Report, *US – Section 337*, para. 5.10.
12 (Footnote original) Panel Reports, *US – Superfund*, para. 5.1.9, and *Japan – Alcoholic Beverages II*, para. 5.5(b).
13 (Footnote original) Panel Report, *Italy – Agricultural Machinery*, para. 11.
14 See Appellate Body Report, *Japan – Alcoholic Beverages II*, p. 16.
15 See Appellate Body Report, *Canada – Periodicals*, para. 18.
16 See Panel Report, *India – Autos*, para. 7.224.
17 See Panel Report, *Canada – FIRA*, para. 5.14.
18 See Panel Report, *Italy – Agricultural Machinery*, para. 11.
19 See GATT Panel Report, *Italy – Agricultural Machinery*, para. 12. The Panel, while holding Italian law providing for low-interest loans for purchasers of Italian-made tractors, noted that the objective of Article III:4 was "to provide equal conditions of competition once goods had been cleared through customs".
20 See Appellate Body Report *Japan – Alcoholic Beverages II*, paras. 16–17; see also GATT Panel Report *US – Superfund*, para. 5.2.2.
21 See Article III:9 of the GATT.
22 See GATT Panel Report, *US – Superfund*, para. 5.2.2.
23 See Panel Report, *Canada – Autos*, para. 10.80. The Panel noted that the word "affecting" occurring in Article III:4 had been interpreted in such a way to cover both laws and regulations that "directly govern the conditions of sale and purchase" and "any laws or regulations which might adversely modify the conditions of competition between domestic and imported products".
24 See under MFN obligation for a discussion of *de jure* and *de facto* discrimination in chapter 4.
25 See both Panel and Appellate Body Reports, *Korea – Various Measures on Beef*, for a discussion on *de jure* discrimination.
26 See Appellate Body Report, *Japan – Alcoholic Beverages II*.
27 See Panel Report, *Indonesia – Autos*, paras. 14.121–14.122. The Panel found that the National Car Program's tax provisions violated Article III:2, as imported vehicles and domestic vehicles with the same end use were taxed differently.
28 See Appellate Body Reports, *China – Auto Parts*, paras. 161–163 and 165, and *India – Additional Import Duties*, para. 153.
29 See Appellate Body Report, *Japan – Alcoholic Beverages II*, pp. 17–18, where it was held that Article III:1 was there to lay down the principles and objectives of NT, and not an operative provision.
30 See Appellate Body Report, *Japan – Alcoholic Beverages II*, pp. 17–18, where the relationship between paragraph 1 and the remainder of Article III was established. The Appellate Body invoking the principle of effective treaty interpretation found that Article III:1 constitutes part of the context for Article III:2. Later, the Appellate body had the occasion to further refine this position in *Korea – Alcoholic Beverages* and *Chile – Alcoholic Beverages*.
31 See Panel Report, *Argentina – Hides and Leather*, para. 11.182.
32 See Appellate Body Report, *Japan – Alcoholic Beverages II*, pp. 18–19.
33 The Report of the Working Party on *Border Tax Adjustments* (BISD 18S/97) adopted by the CONTRACTING PARTIES in 1970 sets out the basic approach for interpreting 'like or similar products' generally in the various provisions of the GATT 1947, and reads as follows: "[T]he interpretation of the term should be examined on a case-by-case basis. This would allow a fair

assessment in each case of the different elements that constitute a 'similar' product. Some criteria were suggested for determining, on a case-by-case basis, whether a product is 'similar': the product's end-uses in a given market; consumers' tastes and habits, which change from country to country; the product's properties, nature and quality."

34 See Appellate Body Report, *Japan – Alcoholic Beverages II*, p. 20. See also Panel Report, *Indonesia – Autos*, para. 14.109, where the Panel relied on this finding of the Appellate Body in *Japan – Alcoholic Beverages II*.
35 See Appellate Body Report, *Philippines – Distilled Spirits*, para. 119, referring to *EC – Asbestos*, para. 99, where the Appellate Body noted, "a determination of 'likeness' under Article III:4 is, fundamentally, a determination about the nature and extent of a competitive relationship between and among products."
36 See Appellate Body Report, *Japan – Alcoholic Beverages II*, pp. 20–22.
37 *Ibid.*, p. 21.
38 *Ibid.*, where the Appellate Body noted, "in Article III:2, first sentence of the GATT 1994, the accordion of 'likeness' is meant to be narrowly squeezed."
39 See Panel Report, *Thailand – Cigarettes (Philippines)*, paras. 7.425–7.451, where it was concluded, based on an analysis of the physical quality and characteristics, end uses, tariff classification, *etc.*, that domestic and imported cigarettes that were within the same price segments were 'like products'.
40 See Panel Report, *Philippines – Distilled Spirits*, paras. 7.34–7.37.
41 See Appellate Body Report, *Philippines – Distilled Spirits*, para. 170.
42 See Appellate Body Reports, *US – Tuna II* and *US – Shrimp*.
43 It is to be noted that GATT only targets those state measures of production that have an immediate impact on commerce, and not otherwise. Matsushita *et al.* also argue that consumers may find certain PPMs relevant enough when they make their choices – for instance they may look for meat which is *kosher* or *halal* – as they may care about social and other conditions of workers in the manufacturing process.
44 See Appellate Body Report, *Japan – Alcoholic Beverages II*, pp. 18–19.
45 *Ibid.*, p. 23. See also Appellate Body Report, *Thailand – Cigarettes (Philippines)*, para. 116, where it was held that Thailand did levy tax on imported cigarettes taxes in excess of those applied to domestic cigarettes.
46 The report was delivered on 11 October 1994 but was not adopted.
47 See GATT Panel Reports in *US – Malt Beverages* (1993) and *US – Taxes on Automobiles* (1994).
48 See Panel Report, *Japan – Alcoholic Beverages II*, para. 6.15.
49 See Appellate Body Report, *Japan – Alcoholic Beverages II*, pp. 18–19.
50 *Ibid.*
51 See Appellate Body Report, *Japan – Alcoholic Beverages II*, p. 24. See also Panel Reports, in *Korea – Alcoholic Beverages* (footnote 346) and *Chile – Alcoholic Beverages* (footnote 349), where the Panels refer to this finding of the Appellate Body.
52 See Appellate Body Report, *Japan – Alcoholic Beverages II*, p. 24.
53 *Ibid.*, p. 25.
54 See Appellate Body Report, *Korea – Alcoholic Beverages*, para. 118, where it was ruled that the term 'like products' should be considered as a subset of 'competitive or substitutable product'. It is pertinent to note here that the term 'competitive or directly substitutable products' has not received enough interpretive coverage by drafters of the GATT.
55 See Appellate Body Report, *Japan – Alcoholic Beverages II*, p. 24. To determine the elasticity of substitution, the Panel relied on the conclusions of the 1987 *Japan – Alcoholic Beverages* case, where it was held that both white and brown spirits were directly 'competitive or substitutable products' to shochu. Likewise, the Appellate Body in *Canada – Periodicals*, pp. 19, 25, and 28, noted that ArticleIII:2, second sentence, was broader.
56 See Appellate Body Report, *Korea – Alcoholic Beverages*, paras. 114–115.
57 See Appellate Body Report, *Philippines – Distilled Spirit*, para. 226.
58 See Appellate Body Reports, *Japan – Alcoholic Beverages II*, p. 27; *Canada – Periodicals*, pp. 28–29; and *Chile – Alcoholic Beverages*, para. 49.
59 See Appellate Body Report, *Japan – Alcoholic Beverages II*, p. 27.
60 *Ibid.*, pp. 19–23.
61 See Appellate Body Report, *Japan – Alcoholic Beverages II*, pp. 27–29.

62 See Appellate Body Report, *Canada – Periodicals*, paras. 30–32.
63 See Appellate Body Report, *Chile – Alcoholic Beverages*, paras. 61–72. See also Appellate Body Report, *Korea – Alcoholic Beverages*, para. 137.
64 See Appellate Body Report, *Chile – Alcoholic Beverages*, para. 76.
65 See Appellate Body Report, *EC – Bananas III*, para. 216.
66 GATT Panel Report, *Italian Agricultural Machinery*, para. 12.
67 See Appellate Body Report, *US – FSC (Article 21.5 – EC)*, para. 210. See also Appellate Body Report, *China – Auto Parts*, para. 194.
68 The text of the *Draft Articles on Responsibility of States for International Wrongful Acts 2001* was adopted by the International Law Commission in 2001. Article 8 of the Draft Articles entitled 'Conduct Directed or Controlled by a State' reads as follows: "The conduct of a person or group of persons shall be considered an act of a State under international law if the person or group of persons is in fact acting on the instructions of, or under the direction or control of, that State in carrying out the conduct."
69 See, for instance, the Panel Reports, *Turkey – Rice*, paras. 7.217–7.225; *Canada – Autos*, para. 10.107; *Canada – Periodicals*, para. 5.33.
70 See Appellate Body Report, *Korea – Various Measures on Beef*, para. 133. See also Panel Report, *EU – Energy Package*, para. 7.519.
71 See Panel Report, *Canada – Autos*, paras. 10.80 and 10.84–10.85; see also Panel Report, *India – Autos*, paras. 7.195–7.198, 7.304–7.307, and 7.313–7.315. See also the following instances where regulations were viewed as modifying the conditions of competition between imported and domestic products: Panel Report, *Brazil – Retreated Tyres*, para. 7.433, where a regulation imposing the disposal of ten used tyres as a condition for importing one retreated tyre; Panel Report, *China – Publications and Audiovisual Products*, para. 7.1595, regulation subjecting imported electronic sound recordings to content review regimes; Panel Report, *Thailand – Cigarettes (Philippines)*, para. 7.665, regulation subjecting resellers of imported cigarettes to unfavourable administrative requirements related to VAT; Panel Report, *Canada – Wheat Exports and Grain Imports*, para. 6.331, regulation resulting in higher railway transportation costs for imported grain; Panel Report, *Dominican Republic – Import and Sale of Cigarettes*, paras. 7.170–7.171, regulation requiring that imported cigarettes cannot leave the bonded warehouse unless the tax stamps are affixed to each packet in the presence of a tax inspector; and Panel Report, *Turkey – Rice*, para. 7.219, requiring the purchase of rice from domestic producers in order to receive authorization to import rice at preferential tariff levels.
72 See Appellate Body Reports, *US – FSC*, paras. 208–210; *US – FSC (Article 21.5 – EC)*, para. 210.
73 See Panel Report, *US – Renewable Energy*, para. 7.265.
74 *Ibid.*, para. 7.271.
75 See Appellate Body Report, *China – Auto Parts FSC*, paras. 194–195.
76 See Appellate Body Report, *EC – Bananas III*, para. 216.
77 See Appellate Body Report, *EC – Asbestos* (2001), para. 93. In its judgment, the Appellate Body made reference to its Reports in *Japan – Alcoholic Beverages II*, p. 112–113, and *Canada – Periodicals*, p. 473.
78 See Appellate Body Report *EC – Asbestos*, para. 96.
79 *Ibid.*, para. 95.
80 It is widely known that asbestos is a deadly carcinogen. Here, France's ban of the asbestos applied without discrimination to both imported and domestically produced asbestos.
81 *Ibid.*, para. 98.
82 See GATT Panel Report, *US – Section 337*, para. 5.11.
83 See, for instance, Panel Reports, *Canada – Provincial Liquor Boards (US)*, paras. 5.12–5.14 and 5.30–5.31; *US – Malt Beverages*, para. 5.30; *US – Gasoline*, para. 6.10; *EC – Bananas III*, paras. 7.179–7.180; and *Japan – Film*, para. 10.379.
84 See GATT Panel Report, *US – Section 337*, para. 5.11.
85 See Appellate Body Reports *Korea – Various Measures on Beef*, paras. 137, 144, 149, 150, and 151; *Dominican Republic – Cigarettes*, para. 96; and *US – FSC (Article 21.5 – EC)*, para. 221.
86 See Appellate Body Report, *EC – Asbestos*, para. 100.
87 *Ibid.*
88 See Appellate Body Report, *Korea – Various Measures on Beef*, para. 144.
89 *Ibid.*, paras. 147–148.
90 *Ibid.*, para. 133. See Panel Report, *EU – Energy Package*, para. 7.519.

Non-Discrimination: National Treatment   195

91 See also Panel Reports, *US – Section 337 Tariff Act*, para. 5.11, and *US – Gasoline*, para. 6.25.
92 See Panel Report, *Dominican Republic – Import and Sale of Cigarettes*, para. 7.197.
93 See Appellate Body Report, *Dominican Republic – Import and Sale of Cigarettes*, para. 96.
94 See Appellate Body Report, *Thailand – Cigarettes*, para. 134.
95 See Panel Report, *Japan – Film*, paras. 6.79–6.81. Here, the US failed to demonstrate its case that over 20 government measures had the combined effect of granting a less favourable treatment to imported film (US manufactured) and nullified and impaired the benefits that US producers ought to have obtained.
96 See Panel Report, *China – Electronic Payment Services*, para. 7.652.
97 With respect to each of these modes of supply, the Member States have made a horizontal commitment – stretching across all sectors, specific commitments with regards to a particular sector, or none whatsoever.
98 See Panel Reports *US – Gambling*, para. 6.318. See also paras. 6.298–6.299.
99 See Panel Report *China – Electronic Payment Services*, para. 7.700.
100 *Ibid.*, para. 7.652.
101 Peru represented, "national treatment could be interpreted as an objective to be attained in the short, medium and long-term, sector by sector, activity by activity, depending on the coverage and the commitments deriving from the final framework agreement". This view of Peru was endorsed by Mexico and also found favour with some of the other leading developing countries.
102 Scheduling Guidelines 2001, note 25, para. 13.
103 *Ibid.*
104 See Panel Report, *EC – Bananas III*, paras. 7.314, 7.357, and 7.375.
105 See Appellate Body Report, *EC – Bananas III*, paras. 241 and 244.
106 See Panel Report, *EC – Bananas III*, para. 7.314. See also Panel Report, *EC – Bananas III (Article 21.5 – Ecuador)*, para. 6.100.
107 See Panel Report, *China – Publications and Audiovisual Products*, para. 7.942.
108 See Panel Report, *China – Publications and Audiovisual Products*, para. 7.1203.
109 See Appellate Body Report, *China – Publications and Audiovisual Products*, paras. 396 and 397.
110 See Appellate Body Report, *EC – Bananas III*, paras. 396 and 397.
111 See Appellate Body Report, *Canada – Autos*, para. 155.
112 See Panel Report, *China – Publications and Audiovisual Products*, para. 7.971.
113 See Panel Report, *EC – Bananas III*, para. 7.322.
114 See Appellate Body Report, *Argentina – Financial Services*, para. 6.29.
115 *Ibid.*
116 See Panel Report, *China – Electronic Payment Services*, para. 7.699.
117 *Ibid.*, para. 7.701.
118 See Panel Report, *China – Publications and Audiovisual Products*, para. 7.697.
119 *Ibid.*, para. 7.698.
120 *Ibid.*, para. 7.700.
121 (Footnote original) Except for services supplied in the exercise of governmental authority. See Article I:3(b) of the GATS.
122 (Footnote original) For a similar view with regard to 'like products' determinations in the context of Article III of GATT 1994, see Appellate Body Reports, *EC – Asbestos*, para. 101; and *Japan – Alcoholic Beverages II*, DSR 1996:I, 97, at p. 113.
123 (Footnote original) It is important to note that even if relevant services are determined to be 'like' and a measure of a Member is found to result in less favourable treatment of 'like' services of another Member, it may still be possible to justify that measure under one of the general exceptions set out in Article XIV of the GATS.
124 See Panel Report, *China – Publications and Audiovisual Products*, paras. 7.701–7.702.
125 See Appellate Body Report, *Argentina – Financial Services*, para. 6.31.
126 *Ibid.*
127 See Panel Report, *China – Electronic Payment Services*, para. 7.702.
128 See Panel Report, *China – Publications and Audiovisual Products*, para. 7.979.
129 *Ibid.*, para. 7.1130.
130 See Appellate Body Report, *US – FSC (Article 21.5 – EC)*, para. 215.
131 See Appellate Body Report, *EC – Bananas III*, para. 244.
132 See Panel Report, *China – Electronic Payment Services*, para. 7.687.

133 *Ibid.*, para.7.689.
134 *Ibid.*, paras. 7.712, 7.714, 7.725, and 7.736.
135 See Appellate Body Report, *Argentina – Financial Services*, para. 7.493.
136 *Ibid.*, para. 7.744.
137 *Ibid.*, para. 6.114.
138 *Ibid.*, para. 6.115.

Bibliography

Chow, Daniel C.K. and Thomas J. Schoenbaum. *International Trade Law: Problems, Cases, and Materials* (Aspen Publishers, 2017).

Conrad, Christiane R. *Process and Production Methods (PPM) in WTO Law, Interfacing Trade and Social Goals* (Cambridge University Press, 2011).

Grossman, Gene M., Henrik Horn and Petros C. Mavroidis. 'The Legal and Economic Principles of World Trade Law: National Treatment,' *IFN Working Paper, No. 917* (2012).

Group of Negotiations on Services. 'Note on the Meeting of 17–21 July 1989,' (MTN.GNS/24) (28 August 1989).

Hart, Michael M. 'The Mercantilist's Lament: National Treatment and Modern Trade Negotiations,' *Journal of World Trade Law* Vol 21, No 6 (1987) 37–61.

Horn, Henrik. 'National Treatment in the GATT,' *IFN Working Paper, No. 657, Research Institute of Industrial Economics* (2006).

Irwin, Douglas A., Petros C. Mavroidis and Alan O. Sykes. *The Genesis of the GATT* (Cambridge University Press, 2008).

Jackson, John H. 'National Treatment Obligations and Non-Tariff Barriers,' *Michigan Journal of International Law* Vol 10 (1989) 207–224.

Kennedy, Kevin. 'GATT 1994,' in Macrory, Patrick F.J., Arthur E. Appleton and Michael G. Plummer (eds.) *The WTO: Legal, Economic and Political Analysis* Vol 1 (Springer, 2005) 89–186.

Lester, Simon, Bryan Mercurio and Arwel Davies. *World Trade Law: Text, Materials and Commentary* (Hart Publishing, 2018).

Matsushita, Mitsuo, Thomas J. Shoenbaum, Petros C. Mavroidis and Michael Hahn. *The World Trade Organization: Law, Practice, and Policy* (Oxford University Press, 2017).

Mavroidis, Petros C. '"Like Products": Some Thoughts at the Positive and Normative Level,' in Cottier, Thomas and Petros C. Mavroidis (eds.) *Regulatory Barriers and the Principle of Non-Discrimination in World Trade Law* (The University of Michigan Press, 2002) 125–135.

Mavroidis, Petros C. *Trade in Goods* (Oxford University Press, 2007).

Mavroidis, Petros C. *Trade in Goods* (Oxford University Press, 2013).

Melgar, Beatriz Huarte. *The Transit of Goods in Public International Law* (Brill Nijhoff and Hotei Publishing, 2015).

Regan, D.H. 'Regulatory Purpose in GATT Article III, TBT Article 2.1, the Subsidies Agreement, and Elsewhere: *Hic et Ubique*,' in Calster, Van Geert and Denise Prévost (eds.) *Research Handbook on Environment, Health and the WTO* (Edward Elgar Publishing, 2013).

Trebilcock, Michael, Robert Howse and Antonia Eliason. *The Regulation of International Trade* (Routledge, 2013).

United Nations Economic and Social Council (ECOSOC). 'Preparatory Committee of the International Conference on Trade and Employment, Report of the Technical Sub-Committee,' (E/PC/T/C.II/54) (28 November 1946).

Van den Bossche, Peter and Werner Zdouc. *The Law and Policy of the World Trade Organization* (Cambridge University Press, 2017).

Wang, Wei. 'On the Relationship between Market Access and National Treatment under the GATS,' *The International Lawyer* Vol 46, No 4 (2012) 1045–1065.

WTO. *Guidelines for the Scheduling of Specific Commitments under the General Agreement on Trade in Services*, adopted by the Council for Trade in Services on 23 March 2001, S/L/92, dated 28 March 2001.

Part II
General Exceptions, Non-Tariff Barriers, Subsidies, CVDs, and AD Measures

6 General Exceptions Under GATT

Learning Objectives	199
1. Introduction	200
2. General Exceptions Under GATT 1994	200
2.1 Drafting History and the *Chapeau* to Article XX	201
2.2 Article XX of GATT: Remit, Nature, and Function	203
2.3 Two-Tier Test Under Article XX and Burden of Proof	205
2.4 Particular Exceptions Under Article XX: (a), (b), (d), (g)	206
2.4.1 Exceptions Under Article XX(a): Public Morals	207
2.4.2 Exceptions Under Article XX(b): Protection of Human, Animal, or Plant Life or Health	210
2.4.2.1 The First Element: Design and Structure	211
2.4.2.2 The Second Element: 'Necessity'	212
2.4.2.3 Burden of Proof	214
2.4.3 Exceptions Under Article XX(d): Secure Compliance With Laws or Regulations	215
2.4.3.1 The First Element: Design	216
2.4.3.2 The Second Element: Secure Compliance	217
2.4.3.3 The Third Element: Necessity	219
2.4.4 Exceptions Under Article XX(g): Conservation of Exhaustible Natural Resources	220
2.4.4.1 The First Element: 'Conservation of Exhaustible Natural Resources'	221
2.4.4.2 The Second Element: 'Relating To'	223
2.4.4.3 The Third Element: 'Made Effective in Conjunction With'	225
2.4.5 Exceptions Under Article XX(j): Acquisition or Distribution of Products in Short Supply	227
2.4.6 Exceptions Under Article XX(e) and XX(f)	229
3. Summary	229

Learning Objectives

This chapter aims to help students understand:

1. The general exceptions under GATT 1994; the drafting history and the *Chapeau* to Article XX of GATT;
2. The two-tier test under Article XX of GATT;

DOI: 10.4324/9780367028183-8

3   The particular exceptions under Article XX of GATT;
4   Exceptions under public morals; protection of human, animal, or plant life or health;
5   Exceptions under secure compliance with laws or regulations; for the conservation of exhaustible natural resources; and
6   Exceptions under Acquisition or Distribution of Products in Short Supply.

1. Introduction

The GATT, which promotes trade in goods amongst the Member States through the multilateral trading system, also contains several 'general exceptions' under Article XX. These exceptions are to facilitate the governments of the Member States to pursue their other policy goals. These exceptions, which operate only in limited circumstances, permit Member States to pursue policy goals, which would otherwise be considered in violation of the GATT obligations. It is well documented that both exceptions and barriers (tariff and non-tariff) limit and/or hinder trade. The key reason behind the creation of the provisions is that all Member States are sovereign nations with specific domestic agendas which are unique to the socio-economic conditions prevalent within their jurisdictions. In the process of achieving domestic policy goals, it is likely that the governments of the Member States will impose measures/pass legislation that are potentially inconsistent with the WTO obligations.

Tariff barriers demonstrably lead to protectionism, whereas exceptions to trade obligations function as legitimate vehicles to achieve core social values and goals. Some of these goals include the national security initiative, economic development, promotion of public health initiatives, environmental policy measures, measures to create employment opportunities, and protection of consumer rights. Since trade is interlinked with civil society issues, the WTO has accordingly factored in exceptions in the fabric of its legal framework, starting with the GATT. The Sutherland Report (WTO, 2004) appropriately observed the situation as follows:

> Neither the WTO nor the GATT was ever an unrestrained free trade charter. In fact, both were and are intended to provide a structured and functionally effective way to harness the value of open trade to principle and fairness. In so doing they offer the security and predictability of market access advantages that are sought by traders and investors. But the rules provide checks and balances including mechanisms that reflect political realism as well as free trade doctrine. It is not that the WTO disallows market protection, only that it sets some strict disciplines under which governments may choose to respond to special interests.

This chapter focuses on studying some of the key exceptions to trade in goods contained in the GATT and trade in services contained in the GATS Agreement, *viz.*, general exceptions and security exceptions. The exceptions discussed in this chapter permit Member States to either go for a complete divergence of GATT or GATS obligations or for specific deviations. Such deviations are again defined by their duration, *i.e.*, indefinite or temporary. The exception with regards to the formation of RTAs is covered in chapter 15.

2. General Exceptions Under GATT 1994

Several exception clauses are contained in the various agreements of the WTO, but all obligations arising under GATT are subject to the closed set of ten exceptions contained in

Article XX. Article XX of GATT contains a list of government measures ranging from public morals to production restrictions and classified as general exceptions to some of the WTO obligations. Paragraphs (a) to (j) of Article XX contain these exceptions. Parts of Article XX with the provisions that are relevant for our discussions are presented as follows:

> Subject to the requirement that such measures are not applied in a manner which would constitute a means of arbitrary or unjustifiable discrimination between countries where the same conditions prevail, or a disguised restriction on international trade, nothing in this Agreement shall be construed to prevent the adoption or enforcement by any contracting party of measures:
>
> (a) necessary to protect public morals;
> (b) necessary to protect human, animal or plant life or health;
> (c) ...
> (d) necessary to secure compliance with laws or regulations which are not inconsistent with the provisions of this Agreement, including those relating to customs enforcement, the enforcement of monopolies operated under paragraph 4 of Article II and Article XVII, the protection of patents, trademarks and copyrights, and the prevention of deceptive practices;
> (e) relating to the products of prison labour;
> (f) imposed for the protection of national treasures of artistic, historic or archaeological value;
> (g) relating to the conservation of exhaustible natural resources if such measures are made effective in conjunction with restrictions on domestic production or consumption;
> (h) ...
> (i) ...
> (j) measures essential to the acquisition or distribution of products in general or local short supply.[1]

The most frequently invoked paragraphs of Article XX in the disputes brought before the WTO's dispute settlement mechanism are paragraphs (b) and (g), which permit restrictions on imports to promote environmental interests, *i.e.*, sanitary and phytosanitary (SPS) measures and the protection of natural resources.

2.1 Drafting History and the Chapeau to Article XX

As discussed in earlier chapters, the draft charter for establishing the ITO was negotiated from 1946 to 1948. One of the key outcomes of the negotiations was the multilateral treaty of GATT. While the ITO, for reasons discussed earlier, did not come to fruition, the GATT served as the template for carrying on the multilateral trade that was envisaged as the prime objective. One of the architects of Article XX, the UK, wanted to include a provision which would in future operate exclusively as 'exception' to import and export restrictions, and not to internal measures (UN, 1946).[2] In the 1946 London and 1947 Geneva Preparatory Conferences, "no effort was made to develop a coherent theoretical basis unifying the items on Article XX" (Bhala, 2013).[3] The urgency to finalise a list and self-interest motivated the drafters, more than anything, to come up with a closed list of exceptions. As Professor Jackson notes, "the tendency of the drafting sessions [of both Articles XX and XXI], as was the case for other articles, was to add to the list of general exceptions in order to meet the particular conditions existing in specific countries" (Jackson, 1969). Article XX had largely remained the same since its creation in the 1940s, with the exception of an amendment that was carried out to paragraph (j) in 1955, the short supply exception (Jackson, 1969).

The framework of Article XX constitutes a conditional exception to GATT obligations. Accordingly, the *Chapeau*[4] to Article XX limits a Member State's ability to pursue any remedies before the Dispute Settlement Body under the listed policies. The *Chapeau* contains a formulative element subjecting a Member State's measures not to be applied in a manner that would be construed as arbitrary or unjustifiable discrimination between Member States. This means that the Member State, not stopping with satisfying the requirement of the paragraphs of Article XX, will have to prove that such measure (i) will not constitute an arbitrary or unjustifiable discrimination between the Member States where the same conditions prevail, or (ii) will constitute a camouflaged restriction on international trade. The Member State also carries the burden of proof to demonstrate that such measures sought to be introduced come under Article XX exception. This operation of the *Chapeau*, in forbidding both arbitrary and unjustifiable discrimination between 'countries' without qualification, appears to have the same sphere of application as GATT Articles I and III (Schoenbaum, 1997).

In the GATT era there were only two instances where the Panel applied the *Chapeau*, *viz.*, *US – Restrictions on Imports of Tuna Products* (1982) and *US – Imports of Certain Automotive Spring Assemblies* (1983).[5] In the aforementioned cases, the Panels examined first whether the measures at issue fell within one of the paragraphs in Article XX. As most complaints lodged did not go past this stage, the *Chapeau* was not pressed into service in the enquiries (WTO Secretariat, 1998).[6] However, in the WTO era, the Appellate Body 'discovered' the *Chapeau* (Schoenbaum, 1997), which was then effectively used in two prominent cases, *viz.*, *US – Gasoline* and *US – Shrimp*. The *US – Gasoline* case concerned the legality of the reformulated and conventional gasoline programs established under the Clean Air Act 1963 (amended in 1990). Under the Gasoline Rule, only gasoline of a specified cleanliness (reformulated gasoline) was permitted to be sold to consumers in the areas experiencing high levels of pollution.[7] In contrast, in other parts of the country, only gasoline no dirtier than that sold in the base year of 1990 (conventional gasoline) could be sold. To pursue the measure, various methods were employed to calculate separate baselines for domestic refiners, foreign refiners, and importers.

The measure was challenged first by Venezuela and later by Brazil as well, where it was argued that the measure introduced by the US was not covered by Article XX and was also in clear violation of Articles I and III of the GATT[8] and Article 2 of the TBT Agreement. The Panel found that the measure was inconsistent with Article III of GATT and could not be justified under paragraphs (b), (c), or (g) of Article XX. On appeal, the Appellate Body found that the measure failed to meet the requirements of the *Chapeau*. The Appellate Body in *US – Gasoline* interpreted the basic function of the *Chapeau* as "to prevent abuse of the exceptions of Article XX", and observed as follows:

> The *Chapeau* is animated by the principle that while the exceptions of Article XX may be invoked as a matter of legal right, they should not be so applied as to frustrate or defeat the legal obligations of the holder of the right under the substantive rules of the General Agreement. If those exceptions are not to be abused or misused, in other words, the measures falling within the particular exceptions must be applied reasonably, with due regard both to the legal duties of the party claiming the exception and the legal rights of the other parties concerned.[9]

The Appellate Body in *US – Shrimp* provided a guidance on the role of the *Chapeau*, where it characterised the task of interpreting the *Chapeau* as

> the delicate one of locating and marking out a line of equilibrium between the right of a Member to invoke an exception under Article XX and the rights of the other Members under varying substantive provisions . . . of GATT 1994.[10]

The Appellate Body also noted that the line of equilibrium should ensure that

> neither of the competing rights will cancel out the other and thereby distort and nullify or impair the balance of rights and obligations constructed by the Members themselves in that Agreement.[11]

The Appellate Body's ruling in the *US – Shrimp* case is considered a landmark decision, signalling a departure from earlier decision-making of the GATT era, as the rhetoric is more favourable to the environment, thereby offering some hope for greater environmental protection in the years to come (Pyatt, 1999). Other commentators though have articulated scepticism, as the Appellate Body, by concluding that the US applied its law contrary to the conditions outlined in the *Chapeau*, had "unduly privileged trade considerations", showing little understanding of how environmental policy works (Gaines, 2001).[12] It is no surprise that both free trade advocates and passionate environmentalists have also expressed their reservations about the WTO's approach on the bearing of environmental measures on trade.[13]

The special report of the WTO from 1999 notes that the key to successful interplay between trade and the environment is "to strengthen the mechanisms and institutions for multilateral environmental cooperation" (Nordström and Vaughan, 1999). Although the report does not make any specific reference to Article XX, or to the *Chapeau* for that matter, one can make a connection to the aspirations in the report to the objectives and wordings of the Article. Reading the *Chapeau* to Article XX in the light of the prior observation in the WTO report urges one to strike a balance between trade and environment and help take us closer to the goals set out.[14] Regardless, one can observe that within the economic framework of multilateral trade, the *Chapeau* poses a more critical question pertaining to trade-environment policy to the Members of the WTO, by presenting conditional exception to trade obligations.[15]

2.2 Article XX of GATT: Remit, Nature, and Function

The exceptions contained in Article XX are legal exceptions to the obligations assumed by the Member States under the GATT, which aspect is not explicitly stated in the Article. As mentioned in the WTO special report from 1999, it is to allow "countries to sidestep the normal trading rules if necessary, to protect human, animal or plant life or health" (Nordström and Vaughan, 1999). In *US – Gasoline* the Appellate Body while discussing the preambular language of Article XX, made the comment:

> '[T]he chapeau says that "nothing in this Agreement shall be construed to prevent the adoption or enforcement by any contracting party of measures . . . " The exceptions listed in Article XX thus relate to all of the obligations under the General Agreement: the national treatment obligation and the most-favoured-nation obligation, of course, but others as well.'[16]

Earlier, in *US – Section 337* Tariff Act (1989), the Panel whilst discussing the nature and function of the Article XX, noted as follows:

> *Article XX(d) . . . provides for a limited and conditional exception from obligations under other provisions.*[17]

Thus, measures that satisfy the conditions set out in Article XX are permitted, even if such measures are found to be inconsistent with other provisions of the GATT 1994. The Appellate Body in *US – Shrimp* while examining the GATT-consistency of the import ban on shrimp and shrimp products from exporting nations not certified by US, observed as follows:

> '[C]onditioning access to a Member's domestic market on whether exporting Members comply with, or adopt, a policy or policies unilaterally prescribed by the importing Member may, to some degree, be a common aspect of measures falling within the scope of one or another of the exceptions (a) to (j) of Article XX. Paragraphs (a) to (j) comprise measures that are recognized as exceptions to substantive obligations established in the GATT 1994, because the domestic policies embodied in such measures have been recognized as important and legitimate in character. It is not necessary to assume that requiring from exporting countries compliance with, or adoption of, certain policies (although covered in principle by one or another of the exceptions) prescribed by the importing country, renders a measure *a priori* incapable of justification under Article XX. Such an interpretation renders most, if not all, of the specific exceptions of Article XX inutile, a result abhorrent to the principles of interpretation we are bound to apply.'[18]

As regards the measures to be analysed under Article XX, the Appellate Body in *EC – Seal Products* had the following to say:

> '*We begin by noting that the general exceptions of Article XX apply to "measures" that are to be analysed under the subparagraphs and chapeau, not to any inconsistency with the GATT 1994 that might arise from such measures. In US – Gasoline, the Appellate Body clarified that it is not a panel's legal conclusions of GATT-inconsistency that must be justified under Article XX, but rather the provisions of a measure that are infringing the GATT 1994. Similarly, in Thailand – Cigarettes (Philippines), the Appellate Body observed that the analysis of the Article XX(d) defence in that case should focus on the "differences in the regulation of imports and of like domestic products" giving rise to the finding of less favourable treatment under Article III:4. Thus, the aspects of a measure to be justified under the subparagraphs of Article XX are those that give rise to the finding of inconsistency under the GATT 1994.*'[19]

The exceptions found in Article XX are limited and subject to meeting the conditions. Whilst it is possible to argue that exceptions are to be interpreted narrowly, the Appellate Body has not embraced this approach (Van den Bossche and Zdouc, 2017). For instance, the Appellate Body in *US – Gasoline*, took the approach of interpreting the exceptions on a case-by-case basis, giving credence to the words used by the Member States when introducing the measures in question, seeking to strike a balance:

> ' The relationship between the affirmative commitments set out in, *e.g.* Articles I, III and XI, and the policies and interests embodied in the "General Exceptions" listed in Article XX, can be given meaning within the framework of the General Agreement and its object and purpose by a treaty interpreter only on a case-to-case basis, by careful scrutiny

of the factual and legal context in a given dispute, without disregarding the words actually used by the WTO Members themselves to express their intent and purpose.'[20]

The Appellate Body, while interpreting the *Chapeau* describing the purpose of Article XX as a balance of rights and duties, observed as follows:

> '[A] balance must be struck between the right of a Member to invoke an exception under Article XX and the duty of that same Member to respect the treaty rights of the other Members.
> . . . . .
> The task of interpreting and applying the chapeau is, hence, essentially the delicate one of locating and marking out a line of equilibrium between the right of a Member to invoke an exception under Article XX and the rights of the other Members under varying substantive provisions (e.g., Article XI) of the GATT 1994, so that neither of the competing rights will cancel out the other and thereby distort and nullify or impair the balance of rights and obligations constructed by the Members themselves in that Agreement. The location of the line of equilibrium, as expressed in the chapeau, is not fixed and unchanging; the line moves as the kind and the shape of the measures at stake vary and as the facts making up specific cases differ.[21]

From the foregoing observations of the Appellate Body, it is clear that Article XX is to be construed as a balancing provision, and not to be interpreted narrowly, as in the case of provisions which provide for exceptions to the general rule. Commentators note that (i) where measures introduced by Member States were found to be inconsistent with Article XX by the DSB, such measures were subsequently modified as per directions of the DSB and were not challenged any further, and that (ii) many measures that were otherwise GATT-inconsistent and introduced by the Member States with a view to promote societal values, have gone unchallenged as they meet the requirements of Article XX. (Van den Bossche and Zdouc, 2017). This position, in the commentators' opinion, is not an indication that Article XX only plays a marginal role in permitting WTO Members to implement measures that are otherwise GATT-inconsistent to protect societal values.

2.3 Two-Tier Test Under Article XX and Burden of Proof

Pursuant to Article XX, the two-tier test seeks to investigate if a measure introduced by a Member State, which is otherwise inconsistent with GATT obligations, can be justified. This requires that the measure at issue, which is found to be inconsistent with another provision of the GATT, is first evaluated to determine whether it fits within one of the paragraphs of Article XX.[22] The two-tier test relies on the Vienna Convention on the Law Treaties to interpret the language of Article XX, which uses different terms in respect of different categories.[23] The Appellate Body established the two-tier approach as WTO Members have been invoking Article XX frequently to justify measures which are otherwise GATT-inconsistent.[24] The Appellate Body in *US – Gasoline* presented the two-tier test under Article XX in the following manner:

> In order that the justifying protection of Article XX may be extended to it, the measure at issue must not only come under one or another of the particular exceptions – paragraphs (a) to (j) – listed under Article XX; it must also satisfy the requirements imposed by the opening clauses of Article XX. The analysis is, in other words, two-tiered: first, provisional justification by reason of characterization of the measure under XX(g); second, further appraisal of the same measure under the introductory clauses of Article XX.[25]

Likewise, the Appellate Body in *US – Shrimp* while reviewing the Panel's findings concerning an import ban on shrimp and shrimp products harvested by foreign vessels, presented the justification for the two-tier test as follows:

> *The sequence of steps indicated above in the analysis of a claim of justification under Article XX reflects, not inadvertence or random choice, but rather the fundamental structure and logic of Article XX . . .*
>
> *The task of interpreting the chapeau so as to prevent the abuse or misuse of the specific exemptions provided for in Article XX is rendered very difficult, if indeed it remains possible at all, where the interpreter (like the Panel in this case) has not first identified and examined the specific exception threatened with abuse. The standards established in the chapeau are, moreover, necessarily broad in scope and reach: the prohibition of the application of a measure "in a manner which would constitute a means of arbitrary or unjustifiable discrimination between countries where the same conditions prevail" or "a disguised restriction on international trade." When applied in a particular case, the actual contours and contents of these standards will vary as the kind of measure under examination varies.'*[26]

From the above, it can be concluded that in order for GATT-inconsistent measure to be justified under Article XX, it must meet two requirements, *viz*.,

i   the requirements of one of the exceptions listed under paragraphs (a)–(j); and
ii the requirements of the *Chapeau* of Article XX.

The Appellate Body in *Brazil – Retreaded Tyres*, reiterated that examination of a measure under Article XX is two-tiered, *i.e.*, a panel is to first scrutinise whether a measure falls under one of the exceptions listed in the various subparagraphs of Article XX, followed by an examination if the measure in question satisfies the requirements of the *Chapeau* to Article XX.[27] As noted earlier, disputes relating to environmental fall within paragraphs (b) and (g). Paragraph (g) is the preferred route, as the 'relating to' test is perceived as a being easier to satisfy in comparison to the 'necessary to' test applied to justify a measure under paragraph (b). Interestingly protection of humans does not seem to fall under (g), but under (b), which makes it a not-so-easy measure to justify (Morrison and Nielsen, 2013; Appleton, 1999).

As regards the burden of proof, the GATT practice had been to place the burden of proof on the Member State invoking Article XX exception to justify such measures.[28] The Appellate Body in *US – Gasoline*, distinguished between the burden of proof under the individual paragraphs of Article XX on the one hand, and under the *Chapeau* of Article XX on the other as follows:

> *'The burden of demonstrating that a measure provisionally justified as being within one of the exceptions set out in the individual paragraphs of Article XX does not, in its application, constitute abuse of such exception under the chapeau, rests on the party invoking the exception. That is, of necessity, a heavier task than that involved in showing that an exception, such as Article XX(g), encompasses the measure at issue.'*[29]

2.4 Particular Exceptions Under Article XX: (a), (b), (d), (g)

As stated earlier in this chapter, Article XX sets out specific policy goals that may be used by Member States for deviating from specific commitments made under GATT. These exceptions are found contained in paragraphs (a) to (j) The exceptions under paragraphs (b), (d) and (g) have been more frequently invoked than the exception under para. (a).

2.4.1 Exceptions Under Article XX(a): Public Morals

In the first ITO Charter drafted by the US in 1945, the public morality exception of Article XX was mentioned and later incorporated into the final text of GATT 1947 (Charnovitz, 1998). Article XX(a) permits trade restrictions that are "necessary to protect public morals", covering policies that address a range of behaviour, including measures restricting the import or use of pornography, drugs, *etc.*[30] Although very broad in its application, Article XX(a) did not find any application until recently, as Member States did not attempt to invoke the provision to justify a trade restriction based on public morals. The term 'public morals' encompasses a very wide range of perceptions, which includes within its ambit cultural, social, and ethical connotations which are normally rooted in the regional or national context. Article XX(a) is akin to GATS Article XIV(a), which presents exception for measures that are "necessary to protect public morals or to maintain public order".

The first dispute referred to the DSB was *China – Publications and Audiovisual Products*, where the US challenged trade restrictions introduced by China on trading and distribution of publications and audiovisual products in China.[31] Restrictions included those on publications, including books, newspapers, periodicals, and electronic publications, and those on audiovisual materials (audio and videocassettes, video compact discs, digital video discs), sound recordings, and films for theatrical release. The measures introduced permitted China to review content of the imported publications and audiovisual products and to choose the importation entities. The measures also allowed for censor of any material that was deemed 'offensive' to China's public morals. China justified the measure under Article XX(a) as being necessary to protect public morals.

The measures were challenged by the US, on the grounds that (i) there was complete failure on the part of China to afford national treatment to the imported products, (ii) such measures violated the responsibilities imposed under China's Accession Protocol and Working Party Report that enumerates the trading rights commitments of China, and (iii) China has violated such commitments by permitting only state-owned Chinese enterprise to import such products and refusing to permit any foreign enterprises or foreign individuals to import the products. Meanwhile, it was argued by China that measures were clearly designed to protect the public morals of the country. The Panel, engaged directly with analysing the public moral exception by carrying out a two-tiered test to determine (i) if such measures introduced were designed to protect public morals and 'necessary' to protect such public 'morals' as claimed, and (ii) whether the measures introduced by China complied with the requirements the *Chapeau* to Article XX. To carry out its analysis, the Panel followed the 'public morals' definition as laid down in *US – Gambling* and the legal framework laid down collectively in *US – Gambling* and *Korea – Various Measures on Beef* relating to Article XX(b).

Earlier, the Panel in *US – Gambling* stated that the meaning of 'public morals' and 'public order' varied depending on a range of factors, and that a Member had the right to determine the appropriate level of protection:

> We are well aware that there may be sensitivities associated with the interpretation of the terms "public morals" and "public order" in the context of Article XIV. In the Panel's view, the content of these concepts for Members can vary in time and space, depending upon a range of factors, including prevailing social, cultural, ethical and religious values. Further, the Appellate Body has stated on several occasions that Members, in applying similar societal concepts, have the right to determine the level of protection

that they consider appropriate. Although these Appellate Body statements were made in the context of Article XX of the GATT 1994, it is our view that such statements are also valid with respect to the protection of public morals and public order under Article XVI of the GATS. More particularly, Members should be given some scope to define and apply for themselves the concepts of "public morals" and "public order" in their respective territories, according to their own systems and scales of values.[32]

Following a detailed analysis, the Panel in *China – Publications and Audiovisual Products* found a number of Chinese measures to be inconsistent with certain trading rights provisions in China's Accession Protocol,[33] that the measures violated China's national treatment and market access obligations under Articles XVII and XVI of GATS respectively, besides also violating China's national treatment obligation under Article III:4 GATT. The Panel had the occasion to develop the limited WTO jurisprudence on China's Accession Protocol and GATS, besides also clarifying the distinction between goods and services in respect of audiovisual products.[34] On appeal, the Appellate Body upheld the Panel's findings that China had not demonstrated that the relevant provisions were 'necessary' to protect public morals, and that, as a result, China had not established that the measures challenged were justified under Article XX(a).[35]

The Appellate Body in *Colombia – Textiles* ruled that (i) an analysis under Article XX(a) proceeds in two steps, (ii) the measure under challenge must be 'designed' to protect public morals, and (iii) such measure must be 'necessary' for the protection of public morals. As regards the 'design' of the measure, there must be a relationship between an otherwise GATT-inconsistent measure and the protection of public morals.

In *EC – Seal Products*, the EU had introduced the 'EU Seal Regime' which prohibited the importation and introduction on the EU market of seal products, except in circumstances where they were to have been procured through hunts carried out by Inuit communities (IC interests) and other indigenous communities, had been derived from hunts conducted for the purposes of marine resource management (MRM interests), or had been imported for the personal use of travellers. Here, the EU invoked Article XX(a), contending that the measures at issue were adopted in response to public moral concerns within the EU with regards to animal welfare, and the welfare of seals, in particular. The Panel in *EC – Seal Products* found that EU's concerns regarding animal welfare and in particular the welfare of seals were justified, and they fell within the scope of the concept of 'public morals' under Article XX(a) of the GATT 1994.[36]

Norway, appealing against the Panel's decision, argued that the protection of the IC interests and the promotion of the MRM interests were also objectives followed by the EU Seal Regime. The Appellate Body upheld the decision of the Panel that the 'principal' objective of the EU Seal Regime was to address public concerns on seal welfare, and that such measures accommodated IC and other interests in order to mitigate the impact of the Regime on those interests.[37] On the question of burden of proof arising under Article XX(a), the Appellate Body in *EC – Seal Products*[38] had this to say:

> the burden of proving that a measure is "necessary to protect public morals" within the meaning of Article XX(a) resides with the responding party, although a complaining party must identify any alternative measures that, in its view, the responding party should have taken.[39]

In *Colombia – Textiles*, Colombia had introduced a compound tariff on imports of certain textiles, apparel, and footwear on the grounds that they were found inconsistent with Article

II:1(a) and II:1(b) first sentence of GATT 1994. Colombia took recourse to Article XX(a) to justify the imposition of such compound tariff for the items. It was argued by Colombia that the measure was a key weapon to combat money laundering, drug trafficking, and other such criminal activities within its territory, and the introduction of the compound tariff was necessary to protect public morals in Colombia. The panel in *Colombia – Textiles* ruled that the measures in question were not 'designed' to counter money laundering and hence not 'designed' to protect public morals as claimed. On appeal, the decision was reversed by the Appellate Body.

In *Colombia – Textiles*, the Appellate Body held that an Article XX(a) analysis must proceed in two steps. Firstly, the measure in question must be 'designed' to protect public morals, and secondly, the measure must be 'necessary' to protect such public morals. The Appellate Body noted that with regards to the 'design' of the measure, there must be a relationship between an otherwise GATT-inconsistent measure and the protection of public morals, *i.e.*, the measure must 'not be incapable' of protecting public morals, and observed as follows:

> In order to establish whether a measure is justified under Article XX(a), the analysis proceeds in two steps. First, the measure must be "designed" to protect public morals. Second, the measure must be "necessary" to protect such public morals.
>
> With respect to the analysis of the "design" of the measure, the phrase "to protect public morals" calls for an initial, threshold examination in order to determine whether there is a relationship between an otherwise GATT-inconsistent measure and the protection of public morals.[40]

The Appellate Body also noted that the second step of the enquiry may not be necessary, in the event the measure under challenge is incapable of protecting public morals and not 'designed' to protect public morals.[41] The Appellate Body also ruled that the issue of 'necessity' at issue under Article XX(a) required a more thorough and "holistic analysis of the relationship between the inconsistent measure and the protection of public morals",[42] which required "weighing and balancing" of a series of factors, *viz.*, the values at stake, the contribution (if any) of the measure at issue to the identified objectives, and the trade restrictiveness of the measure.[43] The Appellate Body also took into consideration the 'trade restrictiveness' of the measure challenged, and noted that whilst assessing this issue, "a panel must seek to assess the degree of a measure's trade restrictiveness, rather than merely ascertaining whether or not the measure involves some restriction on trade".[44]

The Appellate Body in *Colombia – Textiles* found that the measure at issue was 'designed' to protect public morals in Colombia within the meaning of Article XX(a):

> Our prior examination of Colombia's claim of error revealed that, when several findings by the Panel are read together, it is clear from its analysis that the compound tariff is not incapable of combating money laundering, such that there is a relationship between that measure and the protection of public morals. Indeed, we understand the Panel to have recognized that at least some goods priced at or below the thresholds could be imported into Colombia at artificially low prices for money laundering purposes, and would thus be subject to the disincentive created by the higher specific duties that apply to these goods.
>
> Therefore, on the basis of the Panel's findings, we find that the measure at issue is "designed" to protect public morals in Colombia within the meaning of Article XX(a) of the GATT 1994.[45]

Accordingly, the Appellate Body concluded that the compound tariff introduced by Colombia was capable of combating money laundering, that there was a relationship between the measure at issue and the protection of public morals, and concluded that measure under challenge was indeed 'designed' to protect public morals, and that the Panel ought not to have concluded its scrutiny at the 'design' stage, but should have proceeded to the next stage of the analysis, *viz.*, the 'necessity' element.[46]

The Panel in *Brazil – Taxation*, found that the measure at issue was 'designed' to protect public morals:

> The Panel recalls that the standard adopted by the Appellate Body for determining whether a measure is "designed" to achieve a particular objective is whether that measure "is not incapable" of contributing to that objective. The Panel further recalls the Appellate Body's instructions that "[i]n order to determine whether such a relationship exists, a panel must examine evidence regarding the design of the measure at issue, including its content, structure, and expected operation". Furthermore, the Appellate Body explained that it does "not see the examination of the 'design' of the measure as a particularly demanding step."
>
> . . .
>
> The Panel therefore finds that, notwithstanding its significant reservations regarding the design, structure, and expected operation, Brazil demonstrated that the measure is not incapable of contributing to the objective of bridging the digital divide and promoting social inclusion. In light of its finding above that these objectives have been shown to be "public moral" objectives within the meaning of Article XX(a) of the GATT 1994, the Panel consequently finds that Brazil has demonstrated that the measure is designed to protect public morals within the meaning of Article XX(a).[47]

The Kingdom of Saudi Arabia had invoked Article XX(a) to prohibit importation of the Holy Quran; alcoholic beverages and intoxicants of all kinds; all types of machines and accessories for gambling; live swine and meat products, *etc.* into its territory (WTO, 2005). Likewise, Article XX(a) had also been invoked by Bangladesh to ban the importation of horror comics, and maps and charts that do not conform to the ones published by the Department of Survey, Government of the People's Republic of Bangladesh (WTO, 2006). Although used sparingly until recently, Article XX(a) is very broad in its application and has given rise to the question if it is indeed a 'self-judging clause' that could be exploited by Member States to circumvent their commitments under the multilateral agreements. That said, Article XX(a) does deserve more attention as it has great potential to include human rights concerns within its ambit (Eres, 2004; Wenzel, 2011; Harris and Moon, 2015; Boutilier, 2017).

2.4.2 Exceptions Under Article XX(b): Protection of Human, Animal, or Plant Life or Health

Article XX(b) covers measures that are aimed at protecting human, animal, and plant life and health. The paragraph sets out a two-tier standard to determine if a measure under challenge is justified under Article XX exemption, with the enquiry seeking to establish the 'necessity' requirement. Due to its remit, Article XX(b) overlaps with some of the provisions of the TBT and SPS Agreements. As noted by the Panel in *US – Gasoline*, to bring a GATT-inconsistent measure within the ambit of Article XX(b), a Member State is required to demonstrate that the

(1) policy in respect of the measures for which the provision was invoked fell within the range of policies designed to protect human, animal or plant life or health;
(2) that the inconsistent measures for which the exception was being invoked were necessary to fulfil the policy objective; and
(3) that the measures were applied in conformity with the requirements of the introductory clause of Article XX.[48]

In *EC – Tariff Preferences*, the Panel followed a similar approach to the Panels in *US – Gasoline* and *EC – Asbestos* and ruled as follows:

> In EC – Asbestos, the panel followed the same approach as used in *US – Gasoline*: "We must first establish whether the policy in respect of the measure for which the provisions of Article XX(b) were invoked falls within the range of policies designed to protect human life or health".
>
> Following this jurisprudence, the Panel considers that, in order to determine whether the Drug Arrangements are justified under Article XX(b), the Panel needs to examine: (i) whether the policy reflected in the measure falls within the range of policies designed to achieve the objective of or, put differently, or whether the policy objective is for the purpose of, "protect[ing] human . . . life or health". In other words, whether the measure is one designed to achieve that health policy objective; (ii) whether the measure is "necessary" to achieve said objective; and (iii) whether the measure is applied in a manner consistent with the *Chapeau* of Article XX.[49]

2.4.2.1 THE FIRST ELEMENT: DESIGN AND STRUCTURE

The Appellate Body in *Brazil – Retreaded Tyres* concluded that Article XX(b) "illustrates the tensions that may exist between, on the one hand, international trade and, on the other hand, public health and environmental concerns".[50] The Panels have consistently applied a three-part test to establish if a GATT-inconsistent measure will be permissible within the ambit of Article XX(b). The first step of the enquiry is to examine the design and structure of the measure in question to establish if the policy objectives sought to be furthered.

The Panel in *EC – Tariff Preferences* analysed the design and the structure of the European Communities' (EC) Generalised System of Preferences Programme (GSP Regulation) to establish if the policy objective of the EC's Drug Arrangements was the protection of human life or health. Under the scheme, the granting of the preferences was secured to the existence of problems relating to drug production, and trafficking in specific countries. Finding no references to the stated policy objective of protection of human life and health in the GSP Regulation, and in violation of the MFN obligation arising under Article I:1, the Panel ruled as follows:

> Examining the design and structure of Council Regulation 2501/2001 and the Explanatory Memorandum of the Commission, the Panel finds nothing in either of these documents relating to a policy objective of protecting the health of European Communities citizens. The only objectives set out in the Council Regulation (in the second preambular paragraph) are "the objectives of development policy, in particular the eradication of poverty and the promotion of sustainable development in the developing countries". The Explanatory Memorandum states that "[t]hese objectives are to favour sustainable

development, so as to improve the conditions under which the beneficiary countries are combatting drug production and trafficking" . . .

From an examination of the whole design and structure of this Regulation, the Panel finds nothing linking the preferences to the protection of human life or health in the European Communities.[51]

Article XX(b) covers public health policy measures as well as environmental policy measures. Over the years, the Panels and Appellate Body have had the opportunity to consider a range of policy objectives where the Member States had invoked Article XX(b) to introduce an otherwise GATT-inconsistent measure, including measures introduced (i) to see a reduction in smoking of cigarettes (*Thailand – Cigarettes*), (ii) to reduce risk produced by the build-up of waste tyres (*Brazil – Retreaded Tyres*), (iii) to reduce pollution (*US – Gasoline*), and (vi) to protect dolphins (*US – Tuna II (Mexico)*; *EC – Seal Products*).

In *Brazil – Retreaded Tyres*, Brazil had argued that the measure introduced an import ban on retreaded tyres on the premise that an accumulation of waste tyres created a major risk for the following reasons: (i) they presented the perfect breeding ground for disease-carrying mosquitoes, (ii) which were then spread through the interstate transportation of the waste tyres, and (iii) they also posed health risk to animals. The Panel observed that the party invoking Article XX(b) with regard to environmental policy measures was obliged to establish the existence of both risks to 'the environment' generally, and more specifically of risks to animal or plant life or health.[52] The Panel, accepting Brazil's argument, ruled that the policy objective of

reducing exposure to the risks to human, animal or plant life or health arising from the accumulation of waste tyres falls within the range of policies covered by Article XX(b).[53]

In *China – Raw Materials*, China had argued that its restrictions of certain raw materials were necessitated as part of a wide-ranging environmental protection framework "whose objectives are pollution reduction for the protection of health of the Chinese population".[54] Challenging China's position, the EU, the US, and Mexico contended that the export restrictions were just a "*post hoc* rationalization" created by China exclusively for the purpose of the dispute, and were not designed to address any health risk.[55] The Panel ruled that China failed to demonstrate that the export restrictions under challenge were introduced as part of a "a comprehensive programme" to tackle pollution.[56] In *EC – Seal Products*, a dispute arising under Article XX(a), the Appellate Body held that a panel is required to consider, but not be bound by, the objectives behind the introduction of the measure in question. Elaborating on the proposition, the Appellate Body noted that a Panel while considering such objectives should also take into account "the texts of statutes, legislative history and other evidence regarding the structure and operation" of the measure under challenge.[57]

2.4.2.2 THE SECOND ELEMENT: 'NECESSITY'

The second element of the enquiry, *i.e.*, 'necessary', is critical, as this term qualifies three major exceptions contained in Article XX, *viz.*, paragraph (a) necessary to protect public morals; paragraph (b) necessary to protect human, animal, or plant life or health; and paragraph (d) necessary to secure compliance with laws or regulations. Panels, under the GATT era, resorted to interpreting the term 'necessary' as occurring in Article XX in a strict manner. In *US – Section 337 of the Tariff Act of 1930*, which was the first dispute where the meaning of the term 'necessary' arose for interpretation, the Panel ruled that

It was clear to the Panel that a contracting party cannot justify a measure . . . as "necessary" in terms of Article XX(d) if an alternative measure which it could reasonably be expected to employ and which is not inconsistent with other GATT provisions is available to it. By the same token, in cases where a measure consistent with other GATT provisions is not reasonably available, a contracting party is bound to use, among the measures reasonably available to it, that which entails the least degree of inconsistency with other GATT provisions.[58]

It will be noted that the Panel in *US – Section 337 of the Tariff Act of 1930* developed the test in the context of Article XX(d), which was subsequently applied by the Panel in *Thailand – Cigarettes* to a dispute involving Article XX(b). A strict view of what is 'necessary' adopted by the GATT Panel appears inconsistent with the aims and objectives of Article XX. Implementing the previous interpretation 'necessary' will mean that Article XX(b) can be invoked to protect human health only if they are considered 'necessary', whereas Article XX(g) could be invoked to conserve natural resources without the measure being 'necessary'. In short, a strict interpretation of 'necessary' will require a higher standard to protect human health than to protect resources (Chow and Schoenbaum, 2017).

This approach to the interpretation of the term 'necessary' became unsustainable under the WTO era, as it required a very high threshold. The Appellate Body laid down that an enquiry if a measure was 'necessary' had a broader remit, requiring an analysis of all relevant factors.[59] The Appellate Body in *Brazil – Retreaded Tyres*, while confirming the findings of the Panel, explained that a 'necessity' assessment was required under Article XX(b), which entails an analysis of all relevant factors and observed as follows:

> [I]n order to determine whether a measure is "necessary" within the meaning of Article XX(b) of the GATT 1994, a panel must consider the relevant factors, particularly the importance of the interests or values at stake, the extent of the contribution to the achievement of the measure's objective, and its trade restrictiveness. If this analysis yields a preliminary conclusion that the measure is necessary, this result must be confirmed by comparing the measure with possible alternatives, which may be less trade restrictive while providing an equivalent contribution to the achievement of the objective. This comparison should be carried out in the light of the importance of the interests or values at stake. It is through this process that a panel determines whether a measure is necessary.[60]

The Appellate Body also observed that the weighing and balancing exercise is a 'holistic operation' which involved laying all the variables of the equation together and evaluating them in relation to each other after having examined them individually, in order to reach an overall judgement.[61] Earlier, the Panel in *US – Gasoline*, while addressing the 'necessity' requirement of the measure under scrutiny under Article XX(b), observed,

> it was not the necessity of the policy goal that was to be examined, but whether or not it was necessary that imported gasoline be effectively prevented from benefiting from as favourable sales conditions as were afforded by an individual baseline tied to the producer of a product.[62]

On appeal, the Appellate Body did not address the Panel's findings on paragraph (b).

Earlier, the Appellate Body in *EC – Asbestos*, while deciding if a French ban on asbestos and asbestos products was inconsistent with Article III:4 of the GATT,[63] had the occasion to consider the 'necessary' test with regards to Article XX(b). The Appellate Body delivered four key findings in relation to Article XX(b), which is of importance to our discussion. Earlier, the Panel had ruled that the French measure in question was justified as evidence presented demonstrated that handling of chrysotile asbestos constituted a health risk, and that the measure under challenge was 'necessary'. On appeal, the Appellate Body carried out a thorough investigation of the issue, applying the 'necessity test' it had developed in the *Korea – Beef* case, which related to exemptions under Article XX(d).

In the Appellate Body's view, (i) where it is demonstrated that the measure challenged contributes and promotes the stated societal value pursued by the measures, the concerned measure may be considered to be 'necessary';[64] (ii) in determining whether a proposed alternative measure is 'reasonably available', several factors must be taken into account, including the continued exposure to the identified risk if the measure were not implemented and the difficulty of implementation of an alternative measure; (iii) it is for the WTO Member State concerned to determine the level of protection of health or the environment they consider appropriate,[65] and it is not open for other Member States to challenge the preferred level of protection, or decide what is appropriate; and that (iv) to justify a measure under Article XX(b), a responsible Member State may act in good faith, relying on such available scientific resources, which at that time may represent a divergent, but qualified and respected, opinion.[66]

In *Brazil – Retreaded Tyres*, the Appellate Body ruled that the measure challenged should be capable of material contributions and not merely a minimal or insignificant contribution to the stated objectives; and that it should be demonstrable that such measure (i) has resulted in material contribution, or (ii) is most suitable to produce a material contribution.[67] However, in *EC – Seal Products*, with regards to the 'necessity' requirement under Article XX(a), the Appellate Body clarified that in *Brazil – Retreaded Tyres* it did

> not set out a generally applicable standard requiring the use of a pre-determined threshold of "material" contribution in analysing the necessity of a measure under Article XX of the GATT 1994.[68]

The Appellate Body had also ruled on the 'necessity' requirement in disputes involving Article XX(a) of the GATT and Article 2.2 of the TBT Agreement, which is of relevance here. While deciding on the 'necessity' requirement under Article XX(a) in *EC – Seal Products*, the Appellate Body held, "in most cases, a panel must then compare the challenged measure and possible alternative measures that achieve the same level of protection while being less trade restrictive".[69] While referring to its ruling in *US – Tuna II (Mexico)*, where the issue of 'necessity' under Article 2.2 of the TBT Agreement arose for consideration, the Appellate Body noted that a comparison of alternative measures may be embarked upon, only when the measure challenged is not trade restrictive or makes little contribution in achieving the stated objectives pursued.[70] In *US – COOL (Article 21.5 – Canada and Mexico)*, where the 'necessity' requirement under Article XX(d) of the GATT and Article 2.2 of the TBT Agreement were at issue, the Appellate Body ruled that the particular manner of sequencing the steps of the necessity analysis in Article 2.2 of the TBT Agreement was adaptable, and may be tailored to the specific claims, measures, facts, and arguments at issue in a given case.[71]

2.4.2.3 BURDEN OF PROOF

As regards proving the existence of a reasonable alternative measure, the Appellate Body in *Brazil – Retreaded Tyres* held that the burden of proof is on the party challenging the measure in question. While holding so, the Appellate Body relied on its earlier finding in *US – Gambling*,[72] and observed as follows:

> It rests upon the complaining Member to identify possible alternatives to the measure at issue that the responding Member could have taken. As the Appellate Body indicated in *US – Gambling*, while the responding Member must show that a measure is necessary, it does not have to "show, in the first instance, that there are no reasonably available alternatives to achieve its objectives".[73]

2.4.3 Exceptions Under Article XX(d): Secure Compliance With Laws or Regulations

A Member State may, under Article XX(d), be permitted to take such measures that are necessary to secure compliance with laws relating to customs enforcement, the protection of intellectual property rights, and the prevention of deceptive practices. A measure purporting to be under Article XX(d) may be justified if it is

> necessary to secure compliance with laws or regulations which are not inconsistent with the provisions of this Agreement, including those relating to customs enforcement, the enforcement of monopolies operated under paragraph 4 of Article II and Article XVII, the protection of patents, trade marks and copyrights, and the prevention of deceptive practices.

Article XX(d) has a broad scope, as it is non-exhaustive and covers all measures necessary to secure compliance with (GATT-consistent) laws or regulations. The provision provides an indicative list – customs enforcement, enforcement of monopolies, protection of patents, trademarks and copyrights, and the prevention of deceptive practices – and permits Member States to pursue a wide range of objectives. Article XX(d) establishes the legal standard to justify otherwise GATT-inconsistent measures.

One of the earliest and leading cases on Article XX(d) is the Panel report in *US – Section 337 of the Tariff Act of 1930*.[74] Section 337 of the Tariff Act of 1930 was challenged as being violative of the national treatment obligation under Article III:4 GATT as it treated imported products less favourably than the like domestic products. It was argued by the US that Section 337 was 'necessary' to enforce US patent laws over infringing imports. While rejecting the case of the US, the Panel ruled that Section 337 procedure for resolving US patent law violation cannot be justified as 'necessary' within the meaning of Article XX(d) so as to permit an exemption to the national treatment obligation arising under Article III:4 of the GATT.[75]

The Appellate Body in *Korea – Various Measures on Beef* examined the term 'necessary to secure compliance' under Article XX(d) and provided a number of clarifications. The dispute in this case arose under the sale of beef under an 'origin-based' dual retail distribution system introduced by South Korea, where imported beef was to be sold in specialist stores dealing exclusively in imported beef. The measure under challenge introduced a dual retail outlet for the sale of beef – one for imported beef, and another for domestically produced beef – where the imported beef and domestically produced beef were displayed separately. It was Korea's case that the 'origin-based' dual retail system was designed to secure compliance with a consumer protection law, and thus, although in violation of Article III:4, was justified under Article XX(d). The Appellate Body, while noting that the measure "modified the conditions of competition in the Korean beef market to the disadvantage of imported product",[76] went on to set forth the two elements required to justify a measure under Article XX(d):

> For a measure, otherwise inconsistent with GATT 1994, to be justified provisionally under paragraph (d) of Article XX, two elements must be shown. First, the measure must be one designed to "secure compliance" with laws or regulations that are not themselves inconsistent with some provision of the GATT 1994. Second, the measure must be "necessary" to secure such compliance. A Member who invokes Article XX(d) as a justification has the burden of demonstrating that these two requirements are met.[77]

The Appellate Body in *Thailand – Cigarettes (Philippines)* held that the Member State raising a defence under Article XX(d) has to prove three key elements, *viz.*, (i) that the measure under challenge secures compliance with 'laws or regulations' that are themselves consistent with the GATT 1994; (ii) that the measure under challenge is 'necessary' to secure such compliance; and (iii) that the measure under challenge meets the requirements set out in the *Chapeau* of Article XX:

> A Member will successfully discharge that burden and establish its Article XX(d) defence upon demonstration of three key elements, namely: (i) that the measure at issue secures compliance with "laws or regulations" that are themselves consistent with the GATT 1994; (ii) that the measure at issue is "necessary" to secure such compliance; and (iii) that the measure at issue meets the requirements set out in the *Chapeau* of Article XX. Furthermore, when Article XX(d) is invoked to justify an inconsistency with Article III:4, what must be shown to be "necessary" is the treatment giving rise to the finding of less favourable treatment. Thus, when less favourable treatment is found based on differences in the regulation of imports and of like domestic products, the analysis of an Article XX(d) defence should focus on whether those regulatory differences are "necessary" to secure compliance with "laws or regulations" that are not GATT-inconsistent.[78]

A defence of Article XX(d) may not be successful where the defending Member State is unable to identify and elaborate on the content of the rules supposedly embodied in the instrument relied upon.[79]

2.4.3.1 THE FIRST ELEMENT: DESIGN

The first element, as mentioned earlier, is the determination of whether the measure under challenge is 'designed' to secure compliance with certain laws and regulation. Panels had earlier ruled that the expression 'secure compliance' meant "to enforce obligations under laws and obligations".[80] In *EEC – Parts and Components*, the panel observed that Article XX(d) does not refer to the objectives of laws or regulations, but only to laws or regulations, and that the provision only covered measures designed to secure compliance with laws or regulations and not with their objectives.[81]

The Appellate Body in *India – Solar Cells* noted that the concept of 'laws and regulations' is broader and may include rules in respect of which the Member State concerned seeks to 'secure compliance', for example, through the imposition of 'penalties or sanction', and that greater the normativity of the instruments of the domestic legal system, the more likely they are to be 'laws or regulations' under Article XX(d). The Appellate Body made the following observation:

In assessing whether a rule falls within the scope of "laws or regulations" under Article XX(d), a panel should consider the degree to which an instrument containing the alleged rule is normative in nature. It is therefore relevant for a panel to examine whether a rule is legally enforceable, as this may demonstrate the extent to which it sets out a rule of conduct or course of action that is to be observed within the domestic legal system of a Member. It also may be relevant for a panel to examine whether the instrument provides for penalties or sanctions to be applied in situations of non-compliance.[82]

The Appellate Body in *India – Solar Cells* also noted that 'laws and regulations' within the meaning of Article XX(d) could be a specific provision of a single domestic instrument, or could be a given rule, obligation, or requirement by reference to, or derived from, several complementary instruments. Following from its ruling in *Argentina – Financial Services*, the Appellate Body observed as follows:

> In certain cases, a respondent may be able to identify a specific provision of a single domestic instrument that contains a given rule, obligation, or requirement with which it seeks "to secure compliance" for purposes of Article XX(d). However, it is also possible to envisage situations where a respondent seeks to identify a given rule, obligation, or requirement by reference to, or deriving from, several elements or parts of one or more instruments under its domestic legal system. . . . Indeed, we do not see anything in the text of Article XX(d) that would exclude, from the scope of "laws or regulations", rules, obligations, or requirements that are not contained in a single domestic instrument or a provision thereof. In a given domestic legal system, several elements of one or more instruments may function together to set out a rule of conduct or course of action. In such a scenario, in order to understand properly the content, substance, and normativity of a given rule, a panel may be required to examine together the different elements of one or more instruments identified by a respondent. Of course, insofar as a respondent seeks to rely on a rule deriving from several instruments or parts thereof, it would still bear the burden of establishing that the instruments or the parts that it identifies actually set out the alleged rule.[83]

The Appellate Body in *Mexico – Taxes on Soft Drinks* considered the term 'laws or regulations' as appearing in Article XX(d) and ruled that it meant "rules that form part of the domestic legal system of a WTO Member", that it could include international rules incorporated into or having direct effect within the domestic legal system of a WTO Member. The Appellate Body also ruled that when the terms 'laws or regulations' are used by a Member State while invoking Article XX(d), they do not include obligations of another WTO Member State under an international agreement.[84]

2.4.3.2 THE SECOND ELEMENT: SECURE COMPLIANCE

The second element of the enquiry relates to the law or regulation, with which compliance is sought to be secured, being consistent with GATT rules. The second element is linked to the first and the third elements of the enquiry. Although this part of the enquiry appears to be straightforward on the face of it, there is one issue that is still to be resolved, *viz.*, the evidence that needs to be offered by the defending party to show that the law is consistent. The question is, should there be detailed enquiry based on arguments presented by both parties on the issue of consistency of the measure with regards to WTO provisions, or does it suffice if the defending party declares that there is no evidence to prove that the measure under challenge is inconsistent with any WTO provisions? In the past, this question had been dealt with very briefly by the Panels.[85]

The Panel in *Colombia – Textiles* held that 'to secure compliance' meant to enforce obligations rather than to ensure the attainment of the objectives of laws and regulations.[86] In this respect, a much needed clarification was provided by the Appellate Body in *Colombia – Textiles*, which concluded that as the measure at issue was 'designed' to secure compliance with Colombia's anti-money laundering legislation, the panel ought not have brought to an end its Article XX(d) analysis at the 'design' element, but proceeded to the 'necessity' element of the analysis, so as not to prevent the respondent from presenting crucial aspects of their defence relating to the 'necessity' of the measure at issue.[87] The Appellate Body also noted that a Panel must "examine the relationship between the measure and securing compliance with relevant provisions of laws or regulations that are not GATT-inconsistent".[88]

With regard to the second element of the analysis under Article XX(d), the Appellate Body in *India – Solar Cells* noted:

> An examination of a defence under Article XX(d) thus includes an initial, threshold examination of the relationship between the challenged measure and the "laws or regulations" that are not GATT-inconsistent so as to determine whether the former is designed "to secure compliance" with specific rules, obligations, or requirements under the relevant provisions of such "laws or regulations". If the assessment of the design of a measure, including its content, structure, and expected operation, reveals that the measure is "incapable" of securing compliance with specific rules, obligations, or requirements under the relevant provisions of such "laws or regulations" that are not GATT-inconsistent, then the measure cannot be justified under Article XX(d), and this would be the end of the inquiry.[89]

The Appellate Body in *Mexico – Taxes on Soft Drinks* held that a measure can be said to be designed 'to secure compliance' even if the measure cannot be guaranteed to achieve its result with absolute certainty, and that the 'use of coercion' was not a necessary component of a measure 'designed to secure compliance'.

> In our view, a measure can be said to be designed "to secure compliance" even if the measure cannot be guaranteed to achieve its result with absolute certainty.[90] Nor do we consider that the "use of coercion" is a necessary component of a measure designed "to secure compliance". Rather, Article XX(d) requires that the design of the measure contribute "to secur[ing] compliance with laws or regulations which are not inconsistent with the provisions of" the GATT 1994.[91]

In *India – Solar Cells*, the Appellate Body ruled that the terms 'laws or regulations' in the context of the phrase 'to secure compliance with laws or regulations' in Article XX(d) is to be understood as the "rules of conduct and principles governing behaviour or practice that form part of the domestic legal system of a Member State".[92] The Appellate Body in *India – Solar Cells*, also observed:

> An assessment of whether a given international instrument or rule forms part of the domestic legal system of a Member must be carried out on a case-by-case basis, in light of the nature of the instrument or rule and the subject matter of the law at issue, and

taking into account the functioning of the domestic legal system of the Member in question.[93]

Going by the prior two pronouncements of the Appellate Body, one can safely conclude that the rules that form part of the domestic legal system of a Member include "rules deriving from international agreements that have been incorporated into the domestic legal system of a WTO Member or have direct effect according to that WTO Member's legal system".[94] Importantly, any measure that fails a test on the second element is likely to fail under the 'necessity' test under the third element.[95]

2.4.3.3 THE THIRD ELEMENT: NECESSITY

The third element of the enquiry is to prove 'necessity' for the introduction of the measure in question. The Appellate Body in *Korea – Various Measures on Beef* introduced the 'necessity' requirement into the Article XX(d) enquiry, and developed the 'weighing and balancing' test involving three specific factors and the availability of alternative measures. Upholding the decision of the Panel, the Appellate Body in *Korea – Various Measures on Beef* concluded that Korea does not require a 'dual retail system' for imported beef and domestically produced beef, and any fraud it sought to eliminate in the retail market could be carried following the normal fraud prevention methods, and thus the measure under challenge was not 'necessary' under Article XX(d). The Appellate Body in its report interpreted the term 'necessity' as understood in the enquiry as follows:

> As used in Article XX(d), the term "necessary" refers, in our view, to a range of degrees of necessity. At one end of this continuum lies "necessary" understood as "indispensable"; at the other end, is "necessary" taken to mean as "making a contribution to". We consider that a "necessary" measure is, in this continuum, located significantly closer to the pole of "indispensable" than to the opposite pole of simply "making a contribution to".[96]

With regards to evaluating a measure as being necessary, and weighing and balancing various factors of each case, the Appellate Body concluded as follows:

> [t]here are other aspects of the enforcement measure to be considered in evaluating that measure as "necessary". One is the extent to which the measure contributes to the realization of the end pursued, the securing of compliance with the law or regulation at issue. The greater the contribution, the more easily a measure might be considered to be "necessary". Another aspect is the extent to which the compliance measure produces restrictive effects on international commerce, that is, in respect of a measure inconsistent with Article III:4, restrictive effects on imported goods. A measure with a relatively slight impact upon imported products might more easily be considered as "necessary" than a measure with intense or broader restrictive effects.
>
> In sum, determination of whether a measure, which is not "indispensable", may nevertheless be "necessary" within the contemplation of Article XX(d), involves in every case a process of weighing and balancing a series of factors which prominently include the contribution made by the compliance measure to the enforcement of the law or regulation at issue, the importance of the common interests or values protected by that law or regulation, and the accompanying impact of the law or regulation on imports or exports.[97]

When determining if a measure were 'necessary' under an Article XX(d) analysis, the Appellate Body in *India – Solar Cells* noted as follows:

> [A] determination of whether a measure is "necessary" entails a more in-depth and holistic examination of the relationship between the inconsistent measure and the relevant laws or regulations. This involves, in each case, a process of "weighing and balancing" a series of factors, including: the extent to which the measure sought to be justified contributes to the realization of the end pursued (*i.e.*, securing compliance with specific rules, obligations, or requirements under the relevant provisions of "laws or regulations" that are not GATT-inconsistent); the relative importance of the societal interest or value that the "law or regulation" is intended to protect; and the trade-restrictiveness of the challenged measure. In most cases, a comparison between the challenged measure and reasonably available alternative measures should then be undertaken.[98]

It should be noted the 'necessity' requirement is dealt with and clarified in cases falling under Articles XX(a) and XX(b).[99] It is worth noting that the 'necessity' requirement as applied to Article XX(d) and interpreted by the Appellate Body in *Korea – Various Measures on Beef* has been followed by the Panels.[100] Also, the Appellate Body's ruling in *Korea – Various Measures on Beef* on the 'necessity' element of Article XX(d) formed the basis of the Appellate Body's later rulings on the 'necessity' requirement of Article XIV(a) of the GATS,[101] Article XX(b) of the GATT 1994,[102] Article XX(a) of the GATT 1994,[103] and Article XIV(c) of the GATS.[104]

2.4.4 Exceptions Under Article XX(g): Conservation of Exhaustible Natural Resources

Article XX(g) concerns measures "relating to the conservation of exhaustible natural resources if such measures are made effective in conjunction with restrictions on domestic production or consumption". Article XX(g) addresses measures introduced by Member States that deviate from core GATT rules for the purposes of protecting the environment, which is akin to Article XX(b). But yet, Article XX(g), although written narrowly, is to be construed broadly to include 'conservation of exhaustible natural resources'. The Appellate Body has given the provision a wide interpretation to include clean air and sea turtles as natural resources. As noted by the Appellate Body in *US – Shrimp* and reiterated in *EC – Tariff Preferences*, the WTO Member States retained Article XX(g) from the GATT 1947 without any modification after the conclusion of the Uruguay Round, while being "fully aware of the importance and legitimacy of environmental protection as a goal of national and international policy".[105] The Appellate Body also made an important observation regarding the protection of the environment and the Preamble to the WTO Agreement, and about the economic development of the developing country Member States as follows:

> It is well-established that Article XX(g) is an exception in relation to which the responding party bears the burden of proof. Thus, by authorizing in Article XX(g) measures for environmental conservation, an important objective referred to in the Preamble to the WTO Agreement, Members implicitly recognized that the implementation of such measures would not be discouraged simply because Article XX(g) constitutes a defence to otherwise WTO-inconsistent measures. Likewise, characterizing the Enabling Clause as an exception, in our view, does not undermine the importance of the Enabling Clause within the overall framework of the covered agreements and as a "positive effort" to enhance economic development of developing-country Members. Nor does

it "discourag[e]" developed countries from adopting measures in favour of developing countries under the Enabling Clause.[106]

The first case to come before the WTO was *US – Gasoline*. As discussed earlier in section 2.1, this case concerned the legality of the reformulated and conventional gasoline programs established by the US under the Clean Air Act 1963 (Amended in 1990) to improve air quality in some of the most polluted regions of the country.[107] Venezuela and Brazil, challenging the measure, argued that the measure at issue was GATT-inconsistent, not covered by Article XX exceptions, besides being in clear violation of Articles I and III of the GATT[108] and Article 2 of the TBT Agreement. The US, on the other hand, contented that the measure was justified under Article XX, and clean air was an exhaustible resource within Article XX(g).[109] The Panel ruled the measure under challenge could be justified under Article XX(g), as clean air was a resource which could be depleted, and observed as follows:

> [C]lean air was a resource (it had value) and it was natural. It could be depleted. The fact that the depleted resource was defined with respect to its qualities was not, for the Panel, decisive. Likewise, the fact that a resource was renewable could not be an objection. A past panel had accepted that renewable stocks of salmon could constitute an exhaustible natural resource. Accordingly, the panel found that a policy to reduce the depletion of clean air was a policy to conserve a natural resource within the meaning of Article XX(g).[110]

Importantly, for our discussions, this finding of the Panel was not appealed.[111] Any measure which has been introduced under Article XX(g) and is investigated will be required to meet a three-tier legal standard, that (i) the measure relates to the 'conservation of exhaustible natural resources'; (ii) the measure 'relates to' the conservation of exhaustible natural resources; and (iii) the measure was 'made effective in conjunction with' restrictions on domestic production or consumption.

2.4.4.1 THE FIRST ELEMENT: 'CONSERVATION OF EXHAUSTIBLE NATURAL RESOURCES'

As regards the first element of the analysis under Article XX(g) where the party is to demonstrate that the measure under investigation relates to the 'conservation of exhaustible natural resources', the Appellate Body in *US – Shrimp* addressed the meaning of the term 'exhaustible natural resources' and advocated the need for a dynamic rather than a static interpretation of the term 'exhaustible'. The Appellate Body also noted the need of interpreting the term 'exhaustible' in the light of "contemporary concerns of the community of nations about the protection and conservation of the environment", and observed as follows:

> Textually, Article XX(g) is not limited to the conservation of "mineral" or "non-living" natural resources. The complainants' principal argument is rooted in the notion that "living" natural resources are "renewable" and therefore cannot be "exhaustible" natural resources. We do not believe that "exhaustible" natural resources and "renewable" natural resources are mutually exclusive. One lesson that modern biological sciences teach us is that living species, though in principle, capable of reproduction and, in that sense, "renewable", are in certain circumstances indeed susceptible of depletion, exhaustion and extinction, frequently because of human activities. Living resources are just as "finite" as petroleum, iron ore and other non-living resources.[112]

The words of Article XX(g), "exhaustible natural resources", were actually crafted more than 50 years ago. They must be read by a treaty interpreter in the light of contemporary concerns of the community of nations about the protection and conservation of the environment. While Article XX was not modified in the Uruguay Round, the preamble attached to the WTO Agreement shows that the signatories to that Agreement were, in 1994, fully aware of the importance and legitimacy of environmental protection as a goal of national and international policy. The preamble of the WTO Agreement – which informs not only the GATT 1994, but also the other covered agreements – explicitly acknowledges "the objective of sustainable development".

. . .

From the perspective embodied in the preamble of the WTO Agreement, we note that the generic term "natural resources" in Article XX(g) is not "static" in its content or reference but is rather "by definition, evolutionary".[113] It is, therefore, pertinent to note that modern international conventions and declarations make frequent references to natural resources as embracing both living and non-living resources.[114]

. . .

Given the recent acknowledgement by the international community of the importance of concerted bilateral or multilateral action to protect living natural resources, and recalling the explicit recognition by WTO Members of the objective of sustainable development in the preamble of the WTO Agreement, we believe it is too late in the day to suppose that Article XX(g) of the GATT 1994 may be read as referring only to the conservation of exhaustible mineral or other non-living natural resources.[115] Moreover, two adopted GATT 1947 panel reports previously found fish to be an "exhaustible natural resource" within the meaning of Article XX(g). We hold that, in line with the principle of effectiveness in treaty interpretation, measures to conserve exhaustible natural resources, whether living or non-living, may fall within Article XX(g).[116]

In *China – Raw Materials*, the Appellate Body held that the word 'conservation' meant "the preservation of the environment, especially of natural resources".[117] The Appellate Body in *China – Rare Earths*, recognising that the generic term 'natural resources' in Article XX(g) is not 'static' in its content or reference but is 'by definition evolutionary', observed:

The word "conservation", in turn, means "the preservation of the environment, especially of natural resources". It seems to us that, for the purposes of Article XX(g), the precise contours of the word "conservation" can only be fully understood in the context of the exhaustible natural resource at issue in a given dispute. For example, "conservation" in the context of an exhaustible mineral resource may entail preservation through a reduction in the pace of its extraction, or by stopping its extraction altogether. In respect of the "conservation" of a living natural resource, such as a species facing the threat of extinction, the word may encompass not only limiting or halting the activities creating the danger of extinction, but also facilitating the replenishment of that endangered species.[118,119]

Earlier, the Panel in *China – Rare Earths* had observed that international law principles relating to sovereignty of Member States over their natural resources, and their sustainable development pursuant to Article 31.3(c) of the *Vienna Convention on the Law of Treaties*, must be taken into account when interpreting the term 'conservation'.[120] Agreeing with China, the Panel noted that the term 'conservation' as used in paragraph (g) is not limited to the "mere preservation of natural resources", and that resource-rich WTO Member States are therefore entitled under the multilateral agreement

> to design conservation policies that meet their development needs, determine how much of a resource should be exploited today and how much should be preserved for the future, including for use by future generations, in a manner consistent with their sustainable development needs and their international obligations.[121]

While recognising a sovereign Member State's right to adopt conservation programmes, the Panel noted that such rights do not confer the "right to control the international markets in which extracted products are bought and sold"[122] nor such right "permit the exercise of boundless discretion such that WTO Members may adopt GATT-inconsistent measures as they see fit".[123] As regards the meaning of the term 'conservation' as occurring in Article XX(g) was concerned, the panel in *China – Rare Earths* noted that it must strike an appropriate balance between trade liberalisation, sovereignty over natural resources, and the right to sustainable development. It is to be pointed out here that the wide interpretation of the term 'conservation' by the panel was not appealed, but nevertheless, the Appellate Body made the following note:

> It seems to us that, for the purposes of Article XX(g), the precise contours of the word "conservation" can only be fully understood in the context of the exhaustible natural resource at issue in a given dispute. For example, "conservation" in the context of an exhaustible mineral resource may entail preservation through a reduction in the pace of its extraction, or by stopping its extraction altogether. In respect of the "conservation" of a living natural resource, such as a species facing the threat of extinction, the word may encompass not only limiting or halting the activities creating the danger of extinction, but also facilitating the replenishment of that endangered species.[124]

2.4.4.2 THE SECOND ELEMENT: 'RELATING TO'

In regard to the second element, *i.e.*, 'relating to', the Appellate Body in *US – Gasoline*[125] ruled that the *measure itself*, as a whole, is to be examined, rather than examine the discriminatory aspect of the measure to establish its relationship to the policy goal identified, and noted as follows:

> One problem with the reasoning in that paragraph is that the Panel asked itself whether the "less favourable treatment" of imported gasoline was "primarily aimed at" the conservation of natural resources, rather than whether the "measure", *i.e.* the baseline establishment rules, were "primarily aimed at" conservation of clean air. In our view, the Panel here was in error in referring to its legal conclusion on Article III:4 instead of the measure in issue. The result of this analysis is to turn Article XX on its head. Obviously, there had to be a finding that the measure provided "less favourable treatment" under Article III:4 before the Panel examined the "General Exceptions" contained in Article XX. That, however, is a conclusion of law. The *Chapeau* of Article XX makes it clear that it is the "measures" which are to be examined under Article XX(g), and not the legal finding of "less favourable treatment."[126]

However, some commentators have expressed their reservations about the approach taken by the Appellate Body in applying a broad brush stroke here, as in their view it could permit

Member States to bury a "multitude of discriminatory provisions in a measure and still be covered" under Article XX(g) (Lester, Mercurio, and Davies, 2018). In *US – Gasoline*, the Appellate Body proceeded to deliberate if the 'baseline establishment rules' were 'primarily aimed at' the conservation of natural resources, *i.e.*, clean air, as claimed by the US for the purposes of Article XX(g). The Appellate Body, while ruling that the 'baseline establishment rules' were indeed aimed at the conservation of the natural resources, and that there was evidence of substantial relationship between the measure in question and the policy, observed as follows:

> The baseline establishment rules, taken as a whole (that is, the provisions relating to establishment of baselines for domestic refiners, along with the provisions relating to baselines for blenders and importers of gasoline), need to be related to the "non-degradation" requirements set out elsewhere in the Gasoline Rule. Those provisions can scarcely be understood if scrutinized strictly by themselves, totally divorced from other sections of the Gasoline Rule which certainly constitute part of the context of these provisions. The baseline establishment rules, whether individual or statutory, were designed to permit scrutiny and monitoring of the level of compliance of refiners, importers and blenders with the "non-degradation" requirements. Without baselines of some kind, such scrutiny would not be possible and the Gasoline Rule's objective of stabilizing and preventing further deterioration of the level of air pollution prevailing in 1990, would be substantially frustrated. The relationship between the baseline establishment rules and the "non-degradation" requirements of the Gasoline Rule is not negated by the inconsistency, found by the Panel, of the baseline establishment rules with the terms of Article III:4. We consider that, given that substantial relationship, the baseline establishment rules cannot be regarded as merely incidentally or inadvertently aimed at the conservation of clean air in the United States for the purposes of Article XX(g).[127]

US – Shrimp was the second dispute to be brought before the WTO under Article XX(g) GATT. Here, the US Senate in 1989, banned shrimp imports from a select list of countries, subject to the respective governments demonstrating that they had a similar programme as the US had for shrimp trawlers. The measure under challenge was indeed an extension of the standards set by the domestic US laws from 1987 to imported products.[128] By 1995, through court rulings, the import ban on shrimps was extended worldwide, and in 1996 the US State Department formulated new rules to reflect the decisions of the courts. The Appellate Body held that Article XX(g) was not limited to the conservation of 'mineral' or 'non-living' natural resources, and that sea turtles were a 'natural resource' and that they were exhaustible. The Appellate Body ruled that the measure under challenge was made effective in conjunction with restrictions on domestic production or consumption, and that having met all three elements of Article XX(g), the measure was justified.

It was held by the Appellate Body that Article XX(g) assessment required 'a close and real' relationship between the measure under challenge and the policy objective identified, *i.e.*, conservation of an exhaustible natural resource, by the Member State concerned. The Appellate Body in *China – Raw Materials* observed that for a measure to fall within the ambit of Article XX(g), it must relate "to the conservation of exhaustible natural resources", and that for a measure to relate to conservation in the sense of Article XX(g), there must be "a close and genuine relationship of ends and means".[129] Likewise, the Panel in *China – Rare*

Earths, where China's export quotas on rare earths (tungsten and molybdenum) were under scrutiny, the panel ruled that China's export quotas did not 'relate to' conservation and were not 'made effective in conjunction with' domestic restrictions pursuant to Article XX(g). The panel also noted that and that the evaluation of whether a measure 'relates to' conservation must focus on the 'design and structure' of that measure, and that it does not require an evaluation of the actual effects of the concerned measure.[130]

2.4.4.3 THE THIRD ELEMENT: 'MADE EFFECTIVE IN CONJUNCTION WITH'

The third element in the analysis of a measure introduced under Article XX(g) is whether the measure under challenge is 'made effective in conjunction with' restriction on domestic production or consumption. In *US – Gasoline*, the Appellate Body described the phrase 'measure made effective in conjunction with' as a requirement of even-handedness in the imposition of restrictions' and observed as follows:

> Viewed in this light, the ordinary or natural meaning of "made effective" when used in connection with a measure – a governmental act or regulation – may be seen to refer to such measure being "operative", as "in force", or as having "come into effect." Similarly, the phrase "in conjunction with" may be read quite plainly as "together with" or "jointly with." Taken together, the second clause of Article XX(g) appears to us to refer to governmental measures like the baseline establishment rules being promulgated or brought into effect together with restrictions on domestic production or consumption of natural resources. Put in a slightly different manner, we believe that the clause "if such measures are made effective in conjunction with restrictions on domestic product[ion] or consumption" is appropriately read as a requirement that the measures concerned impose restrictions, not just in respect of imported gasoline but also with respect to domestic gasoline. The clause is a requirement of even-handedness in the imposition of restrictions, in the name of conservation, upon the production or consumption of exhaustible natural resources.[131]

In the Appellate Body's opinion, the "requirement of even-handedness" embodied in Article XX(g) did not amount to a requirement of "identity of treatment", and the provision only required that imported and domestic products are treated in an 'even-handed' manner. In this regard, the Appellate Body in *US – Gasoline* stated as follows:

> There is, of course, no textual basis for requiring identical treatment of domestic and imported products. Indeed, where there is identity of treatment – constituting real, not merely formal, equality of treatment – it is difficult to see how inconsistency with Article III:4 would have arisen in the first place. On the other hand, if no restrictions on domestically-produced like products are imposed at all, and all limitations are placed upon imported products alone, the measure cannot be accepted as primarily or even substantially designed for implementing conservationist goals. The measure would simply be naked discrimination for protecting locally-produced goods.[132]

Thus, by applying the 'even-handedness' requirement to the baseline establishment rules to the measure under challenge in *US – Gasoline*, the Appellate Body found that "restrictions on the consumption or depletion of clean air by regulating the domestic production of 'dirty' gasoline" were established "jointly with corresponding restrictions with respect to imported gasoline".¹³³ Citing its own finding in *US – Gasoline* that the phrase "if such measures are made effective in conjunction with restrictions on domestic product or consumption" in Article XX(g) was a 'requirement of even-handedness', the Appellate Body in *US – Shrimp* held that the measure at issue introduced by the US was justified under Article XX(g), and noted that the US through imposing 'restrictions on domestic production' has met the 'even-handedness' requirement of the third element of the Article XX(g) analysis.¹³⁴ The Appellate Body in *China – Rare Earths* observed as follows:

> [t]he term "even-handedness" was used in *US – Gasoline* as a synonym or shorthand reference for the requirement in Article XX(g) that restrictions be imposed not only on international trade but also on domestic consumption or production. As we see it, "even-handedness" is not a separate requirement to be fulfilled in addition to the conditions expressly set out in subparagraph (g). Rather, and in keeping with the Appellate Body report in *US – Gasoline*, the terms of Article XX(g) themselves embody a requirement of even-handedness in the imposition of restrictions.¹³⁵

In *China – Rare Earths*, the Appellate Body held that to comply with the 'made effective in conjunction with' clause in Article XX(g), the Member concerned must impose a 'real' restriction on domestic production or consumption that reinforces and complements the restriction on international trade.

> The second clause of Article XX(g) requires that the GATT-inconsistent conservation measure be "made effective in conjunction with restrictions on domestic production or consumption". Accordingly, Article XX(g) requires that, when international trade is restricted, restrictions be imposed also on domestic production or consumption. The Appellate Body has described a "restriction" as "[a] thing which restricts someone or something, a limitation on action, a limiting condition or regulation".¹³⁶

The Appellate Body in *China – Rare Earths* found that the panel had erred to the extent that it found that the burden of conservation must be evenly distributed, and observed as follows. The Appellate Body also noted, however, that

> we consider that the clause "made effective in conjunction with restrictions on domestic production or consumption" requires that, when GATT-inconsistent measures are in place, effective restrictions must also be imposed on domestic production or consumption. Just as GATT-inconsistent measures impose limitations on international trade, domestic restrictions must impose limitations on domestic production or consumption. Such restrictions must be "real" rather than existing merely "on the books", particularly in circumstances where domestic consumption accounts for a major part of the exhaustible natural resources to be conserved. Moreover, such restrictions on domestic production or consumption must reinforce and complement the restriction on international trade. However, we have also clarified that Article XX(g) does not require a Member seeking to justify its measure to establish that its regulatory regime achieves an even distribution of the burden of conservation. Accordingly, we find that the Panel erred to the extent that it found that the burden of conservation must be evenly distributed, for example, between foreign consumers, on the one hand, and domestic producers or consumers, on the other hand.¹³⁷

2.4.5 Exceptions Under Article XX(j): Acquisition or Distribution of Products in Short Supply

Article XX(j) exception is designed to allow for Member States to introduce measures that are "essential to the acquisition or distribution of products in general or local short supply". The first case to appear before the WTO's Dispute Settlement Body was *India – Solar Cells*, where the Appellate Body considered whether the analytical framework for 'design' and 'necessity' elements as contemplated under Article XX(d) to be relevant *mutatis mutandis* to Article XX(j). The dispute concerned the Domestic Content Requirement (DCR) measure imposed by India with regards to solar cells and modules on solar power producers who sold electricity to government agencies. When challenged, India, invoking Article XX(j), argued that the measure was 'essential to the acquisition or distribution of products in short supply' within the meaning of Article XX(j). It was India's case that (i) the objective of the measure under challenge was to facilitate access of Indian solar power producers to a continuous and affordable supply of the solar cells and modules needed to generate solar power, and that (ii) India considered it necessary to have adequate reserve of domestic manufacturing capacity for solar cells and modules in the event of a disruption in supply of electricity from foreign solar cells and modules.

Rejecting India's arguments, the panel found the DCR measures under challenge to be inconsistent with Article III:4 of the GATT 1994, and Article 2.1 of the TRIMs Agreement. On appeal by India, the Appellate Body confirmed the findings of the Panel, and held that to successfully bring an otherwise GATT-inconsistent measure within the ambit of Article XX(j), a Member State need to establish that (i) the measure is 'designed' to address the acquisition or distribution of products in general or local short supply, and (ii) the measure is 'essential' to address the acquisition or distribution of such products. While handing down the aforementioned ruling, the Appellate Body observed as follows:

> The analytical framework for the "design" and "necessity" elements of the analysis contemplated under Article XX(d) is relevant *mutatis mutandis* also under Article XX(j). As with Article XX(d), the examination of a defence under Article XX(j) would appear to include an initial, threshold examination of the "design" of the measure at issue, including its content, structure, and expected operation. In the case of Article XX(j), the responding party must identify the relationship between the measure and "the acquisition or distribution of products in general or local short supply", whereas, in the case of Article XX(d), a panel must examine the relationship between the measure and "securing compliance" with relevant provisions of laws or regulations that are not GATT-inconsistent.[138] If the assessment of the design of a measure, including its content, structure, and expected operation, reveals that the measure is "incapable", in the case of Article XX(j), of addressing "the acquisition or distribution of products in general or local short supply", or, in the case of Article XX(d), "secur[ing] compliance with [relevant provisions of] laws or regulations that are not inconsistent" with the GATT 1994, there is no relationship that meets the requirements of the "design" element. In either situation, further analysis with regard to whether the measure is "necessary" or "essential" would not be required. This is because there can be no justification under Article XX(j) for a measure that is not "designed" to address the "acquisition or distribution of products in general or local short supply", just as there can be no justification under Article XX(d) for a measure that is not "designed" to secure compliance with relevant provisions of laws or regulations that are not GATT-inconsistent.[139]

The Appellate Body in *India – Solar Cells* ruled that

> Article XX(j) of the GATT 1994 reflects a balance of different considerations to be taken into account when assessing whether products are "in general or local short supply".[140]

The key issue, both before the Panel and the Appellate Body, was whether a dearth of domestic manufacturing capacity for solar cells would amount to a situation of 'general or local short supply'. In determining the question, the Appellate Body observed that a Panel should examine

> the extent to which a particular product is "available" for purchase in a particular geographical area or market, and whether this is sufficient to meet demand in the relevant area or market. This analysis may, in appropriate cases, take into account not only the level of domestic production of a particular product and the nature of the products that are alleged to be "in general or local short supply", but also such factors as the relevant product and geographical market, potential price fluctuations in the relevant market, the purchasing power of foreign and domestic consumers, and the role that foreign and domestic producers play in a particular market, including the extent to which domestic producers sell their production abroad. Due regard should be given to the total quantity of imports that may be "available" to meet demand in a particular geographical area or market. It may thus be relevant to consider the extent to which international supply of a product is stable and accessible, by examining factors such as the distance between a particular geographical area or market and production sites, as well as the reliability of local or transnational supply chains.[141]

The Appellate Body further noted:

> Whether and which factors are relevant will necessarily depend on the particularities of each case. Just as there may be factors that have a bearing on "availability" of imports in a particular case, it is also possible that, despite the existence of manufacturing capacity, domestic products are not "available" in all parts of a particular country, or are not "available" in sufficient quantities to meet demand. In all cases, the responding party has the burden of demonstrating that the quantity of "available" supply from both domestic and international sources in the relevant geographical market is insufficient to meet demand.[142]

From the Appellate Body's findings, it is clear that the key factor in determining the question is 'availability' of the quantity necessary for consumption, which does not purely hinge on the absence of domestic manufacturing capacity, but also the quantity of 'available' supply from international sources. As it was earlier found by the Panel that solar panels were not in short supply locally within the meaning of Article XX(j), the Appellate Body did not seek to establish if the DCR measures satisfied the nexus requirement of being essential. Under the circumstances, the Appellate Body noted as follows:

> [t]he analytical framework for the "design" and "necessity" elements of the analysis contemplated under Article XX(d) is relevant *mutatis mutandis* also under Article XX(j).[143]

Commenting on the term 'essential', the Appellate Body then noted that the term is defined as '[a]bsolutely indispensable or necessary'.

The participants in the present case disagree as to whether the term "essential" in Article XX(j) introduces a more stringent legal threshold than the necessity analysis under Article XX(d). The Appellate Body has explained in this regard that, in a continuum ranging from "indispensable" to "making a contribution to", a "necessary" measure is "located significantly closer to the pole of 'indispensable' than to the opposite pole of simply 'making a contribution to'". The word "essential" in turn is defined as "[a]bsolutely indispensable or necessary". The plain meaning of the term thus suggests that this word is located at least as close to the "indispensable" end of the continuum as the word "necessary".[144]

The Appellate Body also rules that the term 'essential' as occurring in Article XX(j) involved the same 'weighing and balancing' exercise as the 'necessary' standard occurring in other paragraphs of Article XX.

> Having said this, we recall that a "necessity" analysis under Article XX(d) involves a process of "weighing and balancing" a series of factors. We consider that the same process of weighing and balancing is relevant in assessing whether a measure is "essential" within the meaning of Article XX(j). In particular, we consider it relevant to assess the extent to which the measure sought to be justified contributes to: "the acquisition or distribution of products in general or local short supply"; the relative importance of the societal interests or values that the measure is intended to protect; and the trade-restrictiveness of the challenged measure. In most cases, a comparison between the challenged measure and reasonably available alternative measures should then be undertaken.[145]

2.4.6 Exceptions Under Article XX(e) and XX(f)

Article XX(e) concerns measures 'relating to' the products emerging from prison labour. There is currently no case law currently available under provision, as it is yet to be used by any Member State. A Member State can successfully use Article XX(e) to ban the importation of goods if they can demonstrate that such goods were manufactured by prisoners. Commentators have theorized that it is possible to invoke Article XX(d) if "products of prison labour" could be interpreted to include products produced in conditions of slave labour, or conditions contrary to the most fundamental labour standards (Marceau, 2009). Insofar as Article XX(f) relates to measures "imposed for the protection of national treasures of artistic, historic or archaeological value'". This provision permits Member States to implement otherwise GATT-inconsistent measures with a view to protect national treasures. As in Article XX(e), no case laws are currently available.

3. Summary

The general exceptions contained under Article XX facilitate the governments of the Member States to pursue some of their policy goals which may be in violation of the GATT obligations. The exceptions provided for in the GATT as trade liberalisation, market access commitments, and non-discrimination rules could contradict policies and measures geared towards the promotion and protection of public health, economic development and national security, employment, consumer safety, and the environment. The wide-ranging exceptions contained under Article XX permits Member States, under specific conditions, to introduce legislation or measures that protect societal values and interests over that of market access commitments, trade liberalisation, and non-discrimination. It is to be noted, however, that the jurisprudence on this subject is still evolving, and we are yet to witness a ruling from the Appellate Body on whether it is permissible or justified for a Member State, under Article XX of the GATT 1994 or Article XIV of the GATS, to introduce measures that are aimed at protecting societal value or interest outside its territorial jurisdiction of the Member taking the measure.

Notes

1. Paragraph (c) deals with trade in gold and silver, paragraph (h) deals with obligations under international commodities agreements, and paragraph (i) deals with restrictions on exports of domestic materials that are necessary to ensure essential quantities of material for domestic processing industry.
2. The UK representative, to prevent any exploitation of exceptions, proposed, "[t]he undertakings in Chapter IV of this Charter relating to import and export restrictions shall not be construed to prevent the adoption or enforcement by any member of measures for the following purposes, provided that they are not applied in such a manner as to constitute a means of arbitrary discrimination between countries where the same conditions prevail, or a disguised restriction of international trade."
3. Prof Bhala compares the list of exceptions contained in Article XX to a 'laundry list', as it resembles an image of an assortment of clothes that happened to be worn over a week's time.
4. *Chapeau* is defined as a 'top hat' in normal parlance.
5. Although frequently cited, the *Chapeau* was rarely applied by the Panel during the GATT era, as the Panel developed the practice of first examining whether the measures challenged came under any of the paragraphs of the Article XX. As most measures did not go past this stage, the Panel did not envisage the need to apply the *Chapeau*.
6. Until the *US – Gasoline* case, no complaints went past this stage of the enquiry.
7. Pursuant to Section 211(K)(2)-(3), of the Clean Air Act, with regard to reformulated gasoline following standards applied: "The oxygen content must not be less than 2.0 percent by weight, the benzene content must not exceed 1.0 percent by volume and the gasoline must be free of heavy metals, including lead or manganese. The performance specifications of the CAA require a 15 percent reduction in the emissions of both volatile organic compounds ('VOCs') and toxic air pollutants ('toxics') and no increase in emissions of nitrogen oxides ('NOx')".
8. Venezuela and Brazil argued that the rule in question (i) granted unfair advantages to certain third countries and was a violation of the MFN obligation and (ii) was also inconsistent with Article III:4 GATT, as it accorded less favourable treatment to imported gasoline than to gasoline from US refineries.
9. See Appellate Body Report, *US – Gasoline*, p. 22.
10. See Appellate Body Report, *US – Shrimp*, para. 159.
11. *Ibid*.
12. In the *US – Shrimp* case, the Appellate Body had ruled that unilateral trade measures undermined the multilateral trading system, and the same was not justified under the *Chapeau* to Article XX. The Appellate Body took the position that the US laws were "rigid and unbending" and sought to be imposed without due regard for the conditions prevalent in the exporting countries.
13. Also, developing countries view unilateral environmental measures as disguised trade barriers with a protectionist agenda.
14. The WTO report notes that trade has had a negative effect on the environment, *i.e.*, a degradation of the environment, which includes deforestation, losses to biodiversity, global warming, *etc*.
15. Aspects relating to the trade and environment are discussed in more detail in chapter 16 of this book.
16. See Appellate Body Report, *US – Gasoline*, p. 24.
17. See Panel Report, *US – Section 337 Tariff Act*, para. 5.9.
18. See Appellate Body Report, *US – Shrimp*, para. 121.
19. See Appellate Body Report, *EC – Seal Products*, para. 5.185.
20. See Appellate Body Report, *US – Gasoline*, p. 18.

21 See Appellate Body Report, *US – Shrimp*, paras. 156 and 159.
22 See chapter 11 of this volume for a discussion on the two-tier test under Article XIV GATS.
23 It will be noted that Article XX uses 'necessary' in paragraphs (a), (b) and (d); 'essential' in paragraph (j); 'relating to' in paragraphs (c), (e) and (g); 'for the protection of' in paragraph (f); 'in pursuance of' in paragraph (h); and 'involving' in paragraph (i). See Appellate Body Report, *US – Gasoline*, p. 17.
24 As of 19 May 2015, Member States have relied on Article XX, to justify measures that are otherwise GATT consistent. These measures account for 81 percent of all quantitative restrictions (or, 593 measures) and had been notified to the WTO. For 311 of 593 quantitative restrictions, Member States had relied on Article XX(b).
25 See Appellate Body Report, *US – Gasoline*, p. 22.
26 See Appellate Body Report, *US – Shrimp*, paras. 119 and 120.
27 See Appellate Body Report, *Brazil – Retreaded Tyres*, para. 139.
28 See chapter 11 of this volume for a discussion on burden of proof under Article XIV GATS.
29 See Appellate Body Report, *US – Gasoline*, p. 22.
30 It could also potentially include human rights abroad.
31 This was the third complaint against China since its accession to the WTO in 2001.
32 See Panel Report *US – Gambling*, para. 6.461. The Appellate Body in *US – Gambling*, confirming the ruling of the Panel, summarized its findings and left the definition of 'public morals' and 'public order' and their application to particular measures in relation to gambling untouched. It is worth noting that the Panels in *China – Publications and Audiovisual Products* and *EC – Seal Products* and *Colombia – Textiles* have all adopted the interpretation given to the term 'public morals' in the context of Article XIV(a) of the GATS by the panel in *US – Gambling*.
33 China's obligations under paras. 1.2 and 5.1 of the China's Accession Protocol and paras. 83(b) and 84(a) of the China's Accession Working Party Report to grant the right to trade.
34 The Panel also concluded that several provisions of the Chinese measures under challenge breached China's obligation, under para. 1.2 of China's Accession Protocol and para. 84(b) of China's Accession Working Party Report, to grant in a non-discriminatory manner the right to trade.
35 The Appellate Body further observed that by virtue of the introductory clause of para. 5.1 of China's Accession Protocol, China could, in this dispute, invoke Art. XX(a) to justify provisions found to be inconsistent with China's trading rights commitments under its Accession Protocol and Working Party Report, and that the Panel did not err in respect of the other challenged elements of its analysis under Art. XX(a).
36 See Panel Report, *EC – Seal Products*, para. 7.410.
37 See Appellate Body Report, *EC – Seal Products*, paras. 5.145–5.146.
38 The Appellate Body was recalling its finding in *US – Gambling*, paras. 309–311, where it had noted that a responding party need not identify the universe of "less trade restrictive alternative measures" and then show that none of those measures achieves the desired objective, and that the WTO agreements do not contemplate such an impracticable and impossible burden.
39 See Appellate Body Report, *EC – Seal Products*, para. 5.169.
40 See Appellate Body Report, *Colombia – Textiles*, paras. 5.67–5.68.
41 *Ibid.*, para. 6.21.
42 *Ibid.*, paras. 6.21 and 6.30.
43 In the Appellate Body's view, the analysis of the 'necessity' was a far more demanding component than that of the examination of 'design' of the measure. The Appellate Body also emphasised that the weighing and balancing exercise was a 'holistic' operation. See Appellate Body Report, *Colombia – Textiles*, para. 5.75.
44 See Appellate Body Report, *Colombia – Textiles*, para. 6.26.
45 *Ibid.*, paras. 5.99–5.100.
46 *Ibid.*, paras. 6.42–6.45 and 6.51.
47 See Panel Report, *Brazil – Taxation*, paras. 7.570–7.583.
48 See Panel Report, *US – Gasoline*, para. 6.20. It is pertinent to note that this particular finding of the Panel was not reviewed by the Appellate Body. See also Panel Reports, *EC – Asbestos*, para. 8.184, and *China – Raw Materials*, paras. 7.479–7.480.
49 See Panel Reports, *EC – Tariff Preferences*, paras. 7.198–7.199.
50 See Appellate Body Report, *Brazil – Retreaded Tyres*, para. 210.

51 See Panel Reports, *EC – Tariff Preferences*, paras. 7.201–7.202.
52 See Panel Report, *Brazil – Retreaded Tyres*, para. 7.46.
53 *Ibid.*, para. 7.102.
54 See Panel Report, *China – Raw Materials*, para. 7.498.
55 *Ibid.*
56 *Ibid.*, para. 7.516.
57 See Appellate Body Report, *EC – Seal Products*, para. 5.144.
58 See Panel Report, *US – Section 337 of the Tariff Act of 1930*, para. 5.26.
59 The existence of 'alternative measures' as identified by GATT-era Panel interpretations is still relevant in the examination of 'necessity' element in the WTO era, but only as one of the aspects in the examination.
60 See Appellate Body Report, *Brazil – Retreaded Tyres*, para. 178.
61 *Ibid.*, para. 182.
62 See Panel Report, *US – Gasoline*, para. 6.22.
63 Canada claimed that the measure in question (Decree No. 96–1133) also violated Article XI of the GATT, Articles 2.1, 2.2, 2.4, and 2.8 of the TBT Agreement, besides also nullifying or impairing benefits under GATT Article XXIII:1(b).
64 See Appellate Body Report, *EC – Asbestos*, para. 172. See also Appellate Body Report, *Brazil – Retreaded Tyres*, para. 150, where it was suggested in this regard that the more restrictive the impact of the measure under challenge on international trade, the more difficult it is to consider that measure as being 'necessary'.
65 See Appellate Body Report, *EC – Asbestos*, para. 168. See Panel Report, *Brazil – Retreaded Tyres*, para. 7.108.
66 See Appellate Body Report, *EC – Asbestos*, para. 177–178.
67 See Appellate Body Report, *Brazil – Retreaded Tyres*, para. 151.
68 See Appellate Body Report, *EC – Seal Products*, para. 5.213.
69 *Ibid.*, para. 5.169. See also Appellate Body Report, *Colombia – Textiles*, para. 5.74.
70 See Appellate Body Report, *EC – Seal Products*, para. 5.169, referring to Appellate Body Report, *US – Tuna II (Mexico)*, para. 322 and fn. 647 in para. 322.
71 See Appellate Body Report, *US – COOL (Article 21.5 – Canada and Mexico)*, para. 5.205.
72 See Appellate Body Report, *US – Gambling*, paras. 309–311, where the enquiry into 'necessity' requirement arose under Article XIV(a) of the GATS.
73 See Appellate Body Report, *Brazil – Retreaded Tyres*, para. 156.
74 See Panel Report, *US – Section 337 of the Tariff Act of 1930*.
75 *Ibid.*, para. 5.35.
76 See Appellate Body Report, *Korea – Various Measures on Beef*, para. 144.
77 See Appellate Body Report, *Korea – Various Measures on Beef*, para. 157. See also Panel Report, *US – Gasoline*, para. 6.31; and Appellate Body Report, *Colombia – Textiles*, para. 6.72.
78 See Appellate Body Report, *Thailand – Cigarettes (Philippines)*, para. 177.
79 See Panel Report, *Indonesia – Import Licensing Regime*, para. 7.853, where the Panel noted that Indonesia had merely "listed those laws and regulations without identifying the specific rules", and that as a result it was not possible to proceed any further with Article XX(d) analysis.
80 See Panel Reports, *Canada – Wheat*, para. 6.248; *Canada – Periodicals*, para. 5.9.
81 See Panel Reports, *EEC – Parts and Components*, paras. 5.16–5.17.
82 See Appellate Body Report, *India – Solar Cells*, para. 5.109.
83 See Appellate Body Report, *India – Solar Cells*, para. 5.111.
84 See Appellate Body Report, *Mexico – Taxes on Soft Drinks*, para. 69.
85 See Panel Reports, *Korea – Various Measures on Beef*, para. 655; *Argentina – Hides and Leather*, paras. 11.297–11.298; *Dominican Republic – Cigarettes*, paras. 7.210–7.211.
86 See Panel Report, *Colombia – Textiles*, para. 7.538.
87 See Appellate Body Report, *Colombia – Textiles*, paras. 6.81–6.85 and 6.89.
88 *Ibid.*, para. 6.67.
89 See Appellate Body Report, *India – Solar Cells*, para. 5.58.
90 (Footnote original) The European Communities notes, "even within the domestic legal order of WTO Members, enforcement of laws and regulations may not simply be taken for granted, but may depend on numerous factors" (European Communities' third participant's submission, para. 28).
91 See Appellate Body Reports, *Mexico – Taxes on Soft Drinks*, paras. 75 and 77. See also Appellate Body Report, *India – Solar Cells*, para. 5.108.

92 See Appellate Body Report, *India – Solar Cells*, para. 5.106.
93 *Ibid.*, para. 5.140.
94 See Appellate Body Reports, *Mexico – Taxes on Soft Drinks*, para. 79; Appellate Body Report, *India – Solar Cells*, para. 5.140.
95 See Appellate Body Report, *Argentina – Financial Services*, para. 6.203.
96 See Appellate Body Report, *Korea – Various Measures on Beef*, para. 161.
97 *Ibid.*, paras. 163–164.
98 See Appellate Body Report, *India – Solar Cells*, para. 5.59.
99 See Appellate Body Reports, *Brazil – Retreaded Tyres*, para. 156; *EC – Seal Products*, para. 5.169, and *Colombia – Textiles*, para. 5.142.
100 See Panels Reports in *Canada – Wheat Exports and Grain Imports*, paras. 6.222–6.248; *Colombia – Ports of Entry*, paras. 7.545–7.619; and *Colombia – Textiles*, paras. 7.520–7.536.
101 See Appellate Body Report, *US – Gambling*.
102 See Appellate Body Report, *Brazil – Retreaded Tyres*.
103 See Appellate Body Report, *EC – Seal Products*.
104 See Appellate Body Report, *Argentina – Financial Services*.
105 See Appellate Body Report, *EC – Tariff Preferences*, para. 95.
106 *Ibid.*
107 See footnote 7 supra.
108 See footnote 8 supra.
109 The US argued that clean air, streams, lakes, forests, and crops were all natural resources that could be exhausted through air pollution, and that measures to contain such air pollution are to be considered as measures to conserve exhaustible natural resources coming within the meaning of Article XX(g).
110 See Panel Report, *US – Gasoline*, para. 6.37.
111 On appeal, the Appellate Body found that the measure under challenge failed to meet the requirements of the *Chapeau*. See Appellate Body Report, *US – Gasoline*, p. 22.
112 (Footnote original) We note, for example, that the World Commission on Environment and Development stated: "The planet's species are under stress. There is growing scientific consensus that species are disappearing at rates never before witnessed on the planet." World Commission on Environment and Development, *Our Common Future* (Oxford University Press, 1987), p. 13.
113 (Footnote original) See *Namibia (Legal Consequences) Advisory Opinion* (1971) I.C.J. Rep., p. 31. The International Court of Justice stated that where concepts embodied in a treaty are "by definition, evolutionary", their "interpretation cannot remain unaffected by the subsequent development of law . . . Moreover, an international instrument has to be interpreted and applied within the framework of the entire legal system prevailing at the time of the interpretation." See also *Aegean Sea Continental Shelf Case*, (1978) I.C.J. Rep., p. 3; Jennings and Watts (eds.), *Oppenheim's International Law*, 9th ed., Vol I (Longman's, 1992), p. 1282 and E. Jimenez de Arechaga, "International Law in the Past Third of a Century", (1978-I) 159 *Recueil des Cours* 1, p. 49.
114 Following this sentence, the Appellate Body refers to 1982 United Nations Convention on the Law of the Sea, done at Montego Bay, 10 December 1982, UN Doc. A/CONF.62/122; 21 International Legal Materials 1261, Arts. 56, 61, and 62; Agenda 21, adopted by the United Nations Conference on Environment and Development, 14 June 1992, UN Doc. A/CONF. 151/26/Rev.1.
115 (Footnote original) Furthermore, the drafting history does not demonstrate an intent on the part of the framers of the GATT 1947 to exclude "living" natural resources from the scope of application of Article XX(g).
116 See Appellate Body Report, *US – Shrimp*, paras. 128–131. See Panel Report, *US – Tuna II (Mexico) Article 21.5*, para. 7.521, where the Panel noted and agreed with the common view of the parties that dolphins were an 'exhaustible natural resource.'
117 See Appellate Body Report, *China – Raw Materials*, para. 355.
118 (Footnote original) We note that the Panel engaged in an extensive discussion of the scope of the word "conservation" in Article XX(g), ultimately finding that this word has a "rather broad meaning". We also note that the Panel's interpretation of the word "conservation" in Article XX(g) is not appealed. Consequently, we neither endorse nor reject the Panel's statements in this regard. See Panel Report, *China – Rare Earths*, paras. 7.252–7.277.
119 See Appellate Body Report, *China – Rare Earths*, para. 5.89.
120 See Panel Reports, *China – Rare Earths*, paras. 7.262–7.263; *China – Raw Materials*, para. 7.381.

121 See Panel Report, *China – Rare Earths*, paras. 7.266–7.267.
122 *Ibid.*, para. 7.268.
123 *Ibid.*, para. 7.269.
124 See Appellate Body Report, *China – Rare Earths*, para. 5.89.
125 As referred to earlier, the *US – Gasoline* case was the first dispute to be brought before the WTO under Article XX(g) GATT.
126 See Appellate Body Report, *US – Gasoline*, p. 16.
127 See Appellate Body Report, *US – Gasoline*, p. 19.
128 Earlier, in 1987, the US introduced regulation requiring domestic shrimp trawlers to use turtle excluder devices (TEDs) in trawling nets, which allowed the captured sea turtles and other unintended objects to escape, while retaining the shrimp caught. This regulation applied in designated areas where sea turtles were present.
129 See Appellate Body Report, *China – Raw Materials*, para. 355.
130 See Appellate Body Report, *China – Rare Earths*, paras. 7.290 and 7.379.
131 See Appellate Body Report, *US – Gasoline*, p. 20.
132 *Ibid.*, p. 21.
133 *Ibid.*
134 See Appellate Body Report, *US – Shrimp*, pp. 144–145.
135 See Appellate Body Report, *China – Rare Earths*, para. 5.124.
136 *Ibid.*, para. 5.93.
137 *Ibid.*, para. 5.136.
138 (Footnote original) See Appellate Body Report, *Colombia – Textiles*, para. 5.126. The Appellate Body has remarked that the objectives of, or the common interests or values protected by, the relevant law or regulation may assist in elucidating the content of specific rules, obligations, or requirements in such law or regulation. (Appellate Body Report, *Colombia – Textiles*, fn 272 to para. 5.126 (referring to Appellate Body Report, *Argentina – Financial Services*, fn 495 to para. 6.203)).
139 See Appellate Body Report, *India – Solar Cells*, para. 5.60. It is to be noted that the dispute also involved questions relating to Article XX(d), and government procurement derogation under Article III:8(a) of GATT 1994.
140 *Ibid.*, para. 5.89.
141 *Ibid.*
142 *Ibid.*
143 *Ibid.*, para. 5.60.
144 *Ibid.*, para. 5.62.
145 *Ibid.*, para. 5.63.

Bibliography

Appleton, Arthur E. 'Shrimp/Turtle: Untangling the Nets,' *Journal of International Economic Law* Vol 2, No 3 (1999) 477–496.

Bhala, Raj. *Modern GATT Law: A Treatise on the Law and Political Economy of the General Agreement on Tariffs and Trade and Other World Trade Organization Agreements* Vol 2 (Sweet & Maxwell Publishers, 2013).

Boutilier, Misha. 'From Seal Welfare to Human Rights, Can Unilateral Sanctions in Response to Mass Atrocity Crimes Be Justified under the Article XX(A) Public Morals Exception Clause?,' *University of Toronto Faculty of Law Review* Vol 75, No 2 (2017) 101–128.

Charnovitz, Steve. 'The Moral Exception in Trade Policy,' *Virginia Journal of International Law* Vol 38, No 4 (1998) 689–746.

Chow, Daniel C.K. and Thomas J. Schoenbaum. *International Trade Law: Problems, Cases, and Materials* (Wolters Kluwer Law & Business, 2017).

Eres, Tatjana. 'The Limits of GATT Article XX: A Back Door for Human Rights,' *Georgetown Journal of International Law* Vol 35 (2004) 597–635.

Gaines, Sanford. 'The WTO's Reading of the GATT Article XX Chapeau: A Disguised Restriction on Environmental Measures,' *University of Pennsylvania Journal of International Economic Law* Vol 22, No 4 (2001) 739–862.

Ghei, Nita. 'Evaluating the WTO's Two Step Test for Environmental Measures under Article XX,' *Colorado Journal of International Environmental Law & Policy* Vol 18, No 1 (2007) 117–150.

Harris, Rachel and Gillian Moon. 'GATT Article XX and Human Rights: What Do We Know from the First 2 Years?,' *Melbourne Journal of International Law* Vol 16 (2015) 1–52.

Jackson, John H. *World Trade and the Law of GATT: A Legal Analysis of the General Agreement on Tariffs and Trade* (The Michie Company, 1969).

Lester, Simon, Bryan Mercurio and Arwel Davies. *World Trade Law: Text, Materials and Commentary* (Hart Publishing, 2018).

Marceau, Gabrielle Zoe. 'Trade and Labour,' in Bethlehem, Daniel, Donald McRae, Rodney Neufeld and Isabelle Van Damme (eds.) *The Oxford Handbook of International Trade Law* (Oxford University Press, 2009) 549–552.

Matsushita, Mitsuo, Thomas J. Shoenbaum, Petros C. Mavroidis and Michael Hahn. *The World Trade Organization: Law, Practice, and Policy* (Oxford University Press, 2017).

Moran, Niall. 'The First Twenty Cases Under GATT Article XX: Tuna or Shrimp Dear?,' in Andinolfi, Giovanna, Freya Baetens, José Caiado, Angela Lupone and Anna G. Micara (eds.) *International Economic Law: Contemporary Issues* (Springer, 2017) 3–21.

Morrison, Peter and Laura Nielsen. 'Trade, Environment and Animal Welfare: Conditioning Trade in Goods and Services on Conduct in Another Country?,' in Calster, Geert Van and Denise Prévost (eds.) *Research Handbook on Environment, Health and the WTO* (Edward Elgar Publishing, 2013).

Nordström, Håkan and Scott Vaughan. 'Trade and the Environment,' *World Trade Organization, Special Studies, No 4* (1999).

Pyatt, Suzanne. 'The WTO Sea Turtle Decision,' *Ecology Law Quarterly* Vol 25 (1999) 815–838.

Schoenbaum, Thomas J. 'International Trade and Protection of the Environment: The Continuing Search for Reconciliation,' *American Journal of International Law* Vol 91, No 2 (1997) 268–313.

Trebilcock, Michael, Robert Howse and Antonia Eliason. *The Regulation of International Trade* (Routledge, 2013).

United Nations. 'Preparatory Committee of the International Conference on Trade and Employment,' Economic and Social Council (E/PC/T/C.II/50) (13 November 1946).

Urakami, Kenichiro. 'Unsolved Problems and Implications for the Chapeau of GATT Article XX After the *Reformulated Gasoline Case*,' in Weiss, Edith Brown, John H. Jackson and Nathalie Bernasconi-Osterwalder (eds.) *Reconciling Environment and Trade* (Martin Nijhoff Publishers, 2008) 171–188.

Van den Bossche, Peter and Werner Zdouc. *The Law and Policy of the World Trade Organization* (Cambridge University Press, 2017).

Wenzel, Nicola. 'Article XX Lit. a GATT,' in Wolfrum, Rüdiger, Peter-Tobias Stoll and Holger Hestermeyer (eds.) *WTO-Trade in Goods* (Martinus Nijhoff Publishers, 2011) 479–485.

Wolfrum, Rüdiger, Peter-Tobias Stoll and Holger Hestermeyer (eds.). *WTO-Trade in Goods* (Martin Nijhoff Publishers, 2011).

WTO. 'Report of the Working Party on the Accession of the Kingdom of Saudi Arabia to the World Trade Organization,' WT/ACC/SAU/61, Annex F, List of Banned Products (1 November 2005).

WTO Secretariat. GATT/WTO Dispute Settlement Practice Relating to Article XX, Paragraph (b), (d), and (g) of GATT (WT/CTE/W/53/Rev.1) (26 October 1998).

WTO Secretariat. 'Trade Policy Review: Bangladesh,' WT/TPR/S/168, Appendix, Table AIII.3 (9 August 2006).

WTO, Sutherland, Peter, Jagdish Bhagwati, Kwesi Botchwey, Niall W.A. Fitzgerald, Koichi Hamada, John H. Jackson, Celso Lafer and Thierry de Montbrial. 'The Future of the WTO: Addressing Institutional Challenges in the New Millennium,' Report of the Consultative Board to the Director-General Supachai Panitchpakdi (WTO, 2004).

7 Tariff and Non-Tariff Barriers

Learning Objectives	236
1. Introduction	237
2. Tariffs and Customs Rules: The Political Economy	238
2.1 GATT/WTO Tariff Negotiations	238
2.2 Negotiations and Reduction of Customs Duties	238
2.2.1 Tariff Negotiations and Article XXVIII *bis*	238
2.2.2 Protection of Tariff Concessions: ODCs	240
2.3 The Schedules of Concession and Classification of Goods	244
2.4 Types of Customs Duties/Tariffs	245
2.4.1 *Ad Valorem* and Non-*Ad Valorem* Tariffs	245
2.4.2 Tariffs: Bound, Applied, and TRQ	246
2.5 The DSB's Interpretation of Schedules of Commitments	247
3. Customs Duties and Other Charges on Exports	250
3.1 Export Duties: History and Political Economy	250
3.2 Rules on Export Duties	251
3.3 Debates and the Proposal for Change	253
4. Non-Tariff Barriers/Measures: NTBs	254
4.1 The Political Economy of NTBs: GATT and WTO	254
4.2 Quantitative Restrictions: Rules and Types	255
4.2.1 The Scope of 'Restriction'	257
4.2.2 Quantifying the Limiting Effect of the Measure at Issue	259
4.2.3 *De Facto* Prohibitions or Restrictions	259
4.3 Exceptions to Article XI:1	260
5. Customs-Related NTBs	261
5.1 Agreement on Customs Valuation	261
5.2 Agreement on Import Licensing Procedures	263
5.3 Agreement on Pre-Shipment Inspection	264
5.4 Agreement on Rules of Origin	265
6. Summary	266

Learning Objectives

This chapter aims to help students understand:

1   Tariff and non-tariff barriers;

DOI: 10.4324/9780367028183-9

2   Tariffs and customs rules; GATT/WTO tariff negotiations; schedule of concessions and classification of goods;
3   Types of customs duties/tariffs; the interpretation of schedule of commitments;
4   Customs duties and other charges on exports; rules on export duties;
5   Non-tariff barriers; quantitative restrictions – rules and types; and
6   Customs related non-tariff barriers; agreements on customs valuation, import licensing procedures, pre-shipment inspection, and rules of origin.

1. Introduction

Barriers define a Member State's territory over which it has sovereign control. As a result, when goods are sought to be imported into a country's commerce, it is required to go past these 'barriers', attracting customs duties, tariffs, or taxes. On the one hand it is impossible to perceive international trade without access to overseas markets, and on the other hand there can be no international trade without the prospect of tariffs on imported goods. Simply put, customs duties on imported merchandise are called tariffs, which provide revenue for the importing country.[1] Tariffs are a 'classic market access barrier' which had stood the test of time. Customs duties are referred to as 'border measures', as they are imposed at the border. The entry of 'foreign goods' into a 'domestic market' can be restricted through two types of barriers, *viz.*, tariff barriers and non-tariff barriers. Likewise, export restrictions can be placed on goods that are sought to be exported out of a sovereign state. While tariff barriers are border measures, non-tariff barriers are internal measures, *i.e.*, which are imposed on the imported goods once they go past customs. Tariff barriers are often used as a protectionist measure to safeguard domestic producers and their markets. Tariff barriers play an important role for trade in goods, but only a minimal role when it comes to trade in services. The determination to forge a new world order for international trade in the post-WWII era called for a regime founded on non-discrimination and prohibition of quantitative restrictions and a commitment to reducing trade barriers and opening markets. The GATT 1947, the precursor to the WTO, introduced multilateral tariff negations amongst the CONTRACTING PARTIES to reduce tariffs and help the flow of trade.

The multilateral trade, which is administered by the WTO, prescribes rules on market access by Member States and imposes restrictions on the use of tariffs and quotas. The GATT and WTO rules do not prohibit tariffs but only seek to regulate state measures, *i.e.*, measures taken by Member States with regards to their market access in the form of duties and tariffs. Article II of the GATT sets out the legal regime for tariffs, Articles XI and XIII of the GATT with regard to quotas, and Article XXVIII *bis* provides for multilateral tariff negotiations. The WTO regulations on tariffs kick in, following a Member State's submission of their Schedule of Concessions, binding their tariffs on selected products.[2] A Member State's commitment to binding tariffs is normally made at the time it becomes a Member of the WTO, or during negotiations. Tariffs have been described as the GATT's border protection 'of choice'.[3] In contrast, quotas don't enjoy the same status as tariffs, as they are generally prohibited.[4] An escalation in tariff does not bar the entry of imported merchandise into a domestic market, but only increases the price of the product in the imported country. In contrast, quotas can bar the entry of an import and thereby eliminate any competition. Reduction in tariffs and in the use of quotas multilaterally had led to trade liberalisation and witnessed an exponential growth in international trade.

2. Tariffs and Customs Rules: The Political Economy

2.1 GATT/WTO Tariff Negotiations

Member States seek the relaxation of market access barriers through the negotiation (and renegotiation) of tariffs. At the heart of multilateral negotiations sits the cornerstone of reciprocity, which is the exchange of tariff concessions by Member States. The Preamble to the WTO Agreement states that the WTO Member States will seek to achieve the identified goals of higher standards of living, full employment, growth, and economic development through

> reciprocal and mutually advantageous arrangements directed to the substantial reduction of tariffs and other barriers to trade.

This process of tariff negotiation amongst Member States has been facilitated by the WTO, and earlier by the GATT, to achieve the best possible outcomes. Tariff negotiations are carried out through 'major' rounds, where Member States agree to reduce tariffs – or bind themselves to imposing a lower tariff – on the items taken up for negotiation. Tariff negotiations lead to reduction in both tariffs and non-tariff barriers. While developed country Member States have agreed to bind 99 percent of their tariffs, developing country Member States have committed to bind 73 percent of their tariffs. These figures demonstrate that Member States benefit the most from bound tariff rates. What is also evident is that tariffs, or customs duties, are not *per se* prohibited but are limited to the extent that the Member States have bound themselves to. It has been forecast that through the Doha Round of negotiations, the developing country Member States are set to benefit more than developed country Member States (Hufbauer, Schott, and Wong, 2010).

2.2 Negotiations and Reduction of Customs Duties

2.2.1 Tariff Negotiations and Article XXVIII bis

Article XXVIII *bis* of the GATT governs the tariff negotiating rounds amongst the Contracting Parties (under GATT) and Member States (under WTO). Article XXVIII *bis* is built on the premise that customs duties/tariffs pose a major hurdle for the seamless flow of multilateral trade, and hence the need and necessity for the Member States to engage in negotiation to reduce tariffs on goods and services. Article XXVIII *bis* concerns the modification of tariff schedules and bears the authority to call for tariff negotiations amongst Member States (Bhala, 2013). Article XXVIII *bis* establishes reciprocity as the cornerstone of multilateral trade negotiations. As mentioned in earlier chapters, a total of eight rounds of tariff conferences/trade negotiations were convened between 1947 and 1994 under GATT 1947. The negotiating rounds were as follows: the Geneva Tariff Conference (1947), the Annecy Tariff Conference (1949), the Torquay Tariff Conference (1950–1951), the Geneva Tariff Conference (1956), the Geneva Tariff Conference (1960–1961), also known as the Dillon Round, the Kennedy Round (1964–1967), the Tokyo Round (1973–1979) and the Uruguay Round (1986–1994).[5]

The provisions of Article II, in conjunction with technical rules in Article XXVIII, provided the basis for successive rounds of GATT tariff negotiations.[6] Professor Hoda observes that prior to the introduction of Article XXVIII *bis*, the tariff negotiations were held intermittently on an *ad hoc* basis, although there was no requirement to do so on a multilateral basis under GATT 1947 (Hoda, 2018). During the Review Session of 1954–1955, an agreement was reached in the Review Working Party on 'Schedules and Customs Administration' to add Article XXVIII *bis* to the GATT Agreement (GATT, 1955). Article XXVIII *bis* was added to the GATT in 1957 and came into effect on 7 October 1957. The *ad hoc* negotiating rounds that took place between 1947 and before the passing of Article XXVIII *bis* in 1957 were called under the authority of Article 17 of the *Charter for an International Trade Organization* (ITO Charter), which never came to fruition (Dam, 1970).[7] While Article XXVIII *bis* resembles closely Article 17 of the ITO Charter, it also carries features which were absent in Article 17 of the ITO Charter, *viz.*, special and differential treatment in paragraph 3(b) (Bhala, 2013). The GATT Preamble together with Article XXVIII *bis* provide for the framework for a multilateral tariff negotiation to both reduce tariffs and bind tariff concessions.

As noted by the Working Party in its report, the participation of CONTRACTING PARTIES (Member States, in the case of WTO) in tariff negotiations was optional.[8] The requirement that CONTRACTING PARTIES to GATT 1947 should have a schedule of concessions and commitments to both GATT 1994 and GATS 1994 meant that the participation during the Uruguay Round of negotiations was obligatory (Hoda, 2018). Paragraph 1 of Article XXVIII *bis* reads as follows:

> The contracting parties recognize that customs duties often constitute serious obstacles to trade; thus negotiations on a reciprocal and mutually advantageous basis, directed to the substantial reduction of the general level of tariffs and other charges on imports and exports and in particular to the reduction of such high tariffs as discourage the importation even of minimum quantities, and conducted with due regard to the objectives of this Agreement and the varying needs of individual contracting parties, are of great importance to the expansion of international trade. The CONTRACTING PARTIES may therefore sponsor such negotiations from time to time.

The first round of negotiations to be held following the introduction of Article XXVIII *bis* was the Dillon Round, which enabled CONTRACTING PARTIES to the GATT to timetable future rounds of negotiations "on a reciprocal and mutually advantageous basis". Up until the conclusion of the Dillon Round of negotiations (1964–1967), the methodology adopted by the CONTRACTING PARTIES to tariff reduction was a selective product-by-product approach, where parties submitted 'request lists' which included the type of concessions they sought on specific merchandise and tariffs. This was based on the 'principal supplier rule' where, generally, only the principal suppliers made requests on products to the countries (principal importers) from which concessions were sought. Correspondingly, countries preparing request lists also prepared offer lists, specifying the merchandise/sectors where they were willing to make concessions. The product-by-product negotiations substantially constrain the range of products with respect to which active negotiations may occur, thereby restricting the coverage of any resulting tariff reductions (Trebilcock, 2013). Also, through product-by-product negotiations, small exporting (and importing) countries may come to be frozen out of the negotiating process, as they may not be the principal suppliers of any products and may not be able to provide concessions that other countries find valuable (Trebilcock, 2013).

The aforementioned approach was to change in the Kennedy and Tokyo Rounds of negotiations, where CONTRACTING PARTIES conducted negotiations using a tariff-cutting formula, replacing the product-by-product negotiations approach.[9] This formula was again to be replaced in the Uruguay Round (1986–1994), as the negotiating parties were permitted to apply a method of their choice to reduce tariffs, as long as the reduction arrived at matched the overall reduction of one-third of the duties achieved in the Tokyo Round of negotiations. The method was appropriately named the 'Uruguay Round Approach' and required an average percentage reduction in tariffs over a period of time (years); a minimum tariff cut on each good; and the flexibility for minor reductions on individual goods (Bhala, 2013).[10] The same methodology was also used in negotiating the Agreement on Agriculture.

Article XXVIII *bis* is flexible in permitting Member States to agree mutually on negotiating procedures on a product-by-product basis. Reciprocity is established as the cornerstone of the multilateral negotiation remains, and Article XXVIII:2(b) *bis* recognises the importance of party participation. Unfortunately, the term 'reciprocity' is not defined anywhere in the GATT. Prof Hoda notes:

> [t]here is no provision on the manner in which reciprocity is to be measured and even the rules of the various [multilateral trade] rounds of negotiations did not spell out any guidelines on the issue. The understanding has always been that governments participating in negotiations should retain complete freedom to adopt ay method for evaluating the concessions.
>
> (Hoda, 2018)

Article XXVIII:3 *bis* lays down the rule that negotiations 'shall be conducted' by affording adequate opportunity to take into account the needs of individual contracting parties and individual industries; the needs of less-developed countries for a more flexible use of tariff protection to assist their economic development; and all other relevant circumstances related to the contracting parties. The institutionalisation of Article XXVIII *bis* towards reciprocal tariff negotiations reflects the expectations of the Member States that binding of tariff rates will become the starting point for a "downward spiral leading to a lower tariff rates" (Jackson, 1969; Matsushita, Shoenbaum, and Mavroidis, 2017). Recently produced statistics demonstrate that the average import tariff rate amongst developed country Member States is close to 3 percent.

In December 1996, the WTO Ministerial Declaration on Trade in Information Technology Products (ITA)[11] was agreed upon and can be viewed as an example of tariff negotiations in the WTO era. With a view to creating market access opportunities, the participating Member States agreed to eliminate customs and other duties within the meaning of Article II:1(b) for certain categories of information technology products on an MFN basis. The implementation of the agreed elimination of duties was, however, contingent on Member States representing approximately 90 percent of world trade in IT products acceding to the ITA. At the Nairobi Ministerial Conference in December 2015, over 50 members concluded the expansion of ITA, which covered an additional 201 products valued at over $1.3 trillion per year.

2.2.2 *Protection of Tariff Concessions: ODCs*

Article II reflects the fundamental purpose of the GATT, which, in the words of the Appellate Body, is "to preserve the value of tariff concessions negotiated by a Member with its trading partners, and bound in that Member's Schedule".[12] The Schedules of Concessions outlined in Article II is another core principle of the GATT with regards to a Member State's commitment to bind its tariffs. Article II:1(b)–(c) of the GATT presents the framework of a Member State's basic obligations under their Schedules. Article II:1(a) stipulates, "[e]ach Member shall accord to the commerce of the other Members treatment no less favourable than that provided for in the appropriate Part of the appropriate schedules annexed to this Agreement". Article II:1(a) requires Member States to commit to offering treatment not less than the one promised in their Schedules, *i.e.*, not to deviate from the promised bound tariffs under the schedules. Likewise, Article II:1(b) postulates that Member States must exempt the products of other contracting parties from "ordinary customs duties in excess of those set forth and provided" in their Schedules;[13] and exempt such products "from all other duties or charges of any kind imposed on or in connection with the importation in excess of those imposed on the date of" the GATT. Article II:1(b), first sentence, is specific to customs duties, as it requires a Member State's customs duties to not exceed what is set forth in their Schedules. In *Argentina – Textiles and Apparel*, the question before the Appellate Body was if the duties levied by Argentina was consistent with Article II:1(b). The Appellate Body described the second provision as the regulation of a specific kind of practice and noted that it

> will always be inconsistent with the [general prohibition against according treatment less favourable to imports than that provided for in a Member's schedule, contained in] paragraph a: that is the application of ordinary customs duties in excess of those provided for in the schedule.[14]

The Appellate Body held that the application of a type of duty different from the type committed to in a Member State's Schedule was inconsistent with Article II:1(b), first sentence, "to the extent that it resulted in ordinary customs duties being levied in excess of those provided for" in a Member State's Schedule.[15]

There is consensus that 'other duties and charges' (ODCs),[16] similar to ordinary customs duties (OCDs),[17] are border measures and are a form of tariff barrier. The Uruguay Round's Understanding on the Interpretation of Article II.1(b) presents clarity for the phrase 'other duties and charges' in the second sentence of GATT ArticleII:1(b). Paragraph to the Understanding on Article II:1(b) requires that Member States in their schedules record 'other duties and charges' on goods with tariffs that they have committed to bind. The 'Understanding' in paragraph 1 stipulates that the date when 'other duties or charges' are bound for the purposes of Article II is 15 April 1994. Similarly, at each succeeding renegotiation of a tariff concession, or the negotiation of a new concession, the applicable date for the tariff item under negotiation shall be the date of incorporation of the new concession in the schedule. The Understanding on Article II:1(b) provides in paragraph 4 as follows:

> [w]here a tariff item has previously been the subject of a concession, the level of "other duties or charges" recorded in the appropriate Schedule shall not be higher than the level obtaining at the time of the first incorporation of the concession in that Schedule.

The phrase 'other duties and charges'[18] is acknowledged to include import surcharges, revenue duties, special import taxes, economic development taxes, and import or security deposits.[19] Paragraph 4 indicates that Member States are eligible to challenge ODCs for a period of three years after the date of entry into force of the WTO Agreement, or the date of deposit with the director-general of the WTO of the instrument incorporating a schedule in question into the GATT 1994. Further, paragraph 5 acknowledges that ODCs may still be found to violate the GATT, although they are certified at the end of a negotiating round by the WTO Membership. The Panel in *Dominican Republic – Import and Sale of Cigarettes* analysed the definition of an 'other duty or charge' and observed as follows:

> Although there is no definition of what constitutes an "other duty or charge" in the GATT 1994 and in the "Understanding on the Interpretation of Article II:1(b) of the General Agreement on Tariffs and Trade 1994", the ordinary meanings of Article II:1(b) and Article II:2 make it clear that any fee or charge that is in connection with importation and that is not an ordinary customs duty, nor a tax or duty as listed under Article II:2 (internal tax, anti-dumping duty, countervailing duty, fees or charges commensurate with the cost of services rendered) would qualify for a measure as an "other duties or charges" under Article II:1(b).
>
> The *travaux préparatoires* concerning the Understanding confirm such interpretation. The Secretariat note on "Article II:1(b): OF THE GENERAL AGREEMENT" stated:
>
> > 4 The definition of ODCs falling under the purview of Article II:1(b) can only be done by exclusion – *i.e.* by reference to those categories of ODC not covered by it. It would be impossible, and logically fallacious, to draw up an exhaustive list of ODCs which do fall under the purview of Article II:1(b), since it is always possible for governments to invent new charges. Indeed, an attempt to provide an exhaustive list would create the false impression that charges omitted from it, or newly invented, were exempt from the II:1(b) obligation.[20]

The Appellate Body Report in *India – Additional Import Duties* observed:

> the duties and charges covered by the second sentence of Article II:1(b) are "defined in relation to" duties covered by the first sentence of Article II:1(b), such that ODCs encompass only duties and charges that are not [ordinary customs duties].[21]

The Panel in *Dominican Republic – Safeguards* interpreted the terms 'other duties or charges' by reference to the meaning of 'ordinary customs duties', and recalling prior jurisprudence:

> The use of the expression "all other duties or charges of any kind imposed on or in connection with the importation" in Article II:1(b), second sentence, suggests that the prohibition covers any duty or charge of any kind on or in connection with the importation that is not an ordinary customs duty. In other words, the category of other duties or charges under Article II:1(b), second sentence, is a residual one covering all duties or charges on or in connection with the importation that are not ordinary customs duties and which are not expressly provided for in Article II:2 of the GATT 1994.
>
> In its report in *Chile – Price Band System*, the Appellate Body made it clear that what determines whether "a duty imposed on an import at the border" constitutes an ordinary customs duty is not the form which that duty takes. Nor is the fact that the duty is calculated on the basis of exogenous factors, such as the interests of consumers or of domestic producers. The Appellate Body also explained that a Member may periodically change the rate at which it applies an "ordinary customs duty", provided it remains below the rate bound in the Member's schedule. . . .
>
> All in all, using a meaning that seeks to reconcile the texts of the GATT 1994 in the various official languages, we could conclude that the expression "ordinary customs duties" in Article II:1(b) of the GATT 1994 refers to duties collected at the border which

constitute "customs duties" in the strict sense of the term (*stricto sensu*) and that this expression does not cover possible extraordinary or exceptional duties collected in customs. This would be compatible with the object and purpose of the GATT 1994 which, as the Appellate Body said in *Chile – Price Band System*, seeks to ensure that the application of customs duties gives rise to transparent and predictable market access conditions and does not impede the transmission of international price developments to the domestic market of the importing country. To reach a conclusion in this respect, the Panel must consider the design and structure of the measures concerned.[22]

The Appellate Body in *India – Additional Import Duties*, while considering if certain border charges were inconsistent with Article II:1(b) or whether they correlated with internal taxes and were sheltered by Article II:2(a), observed, "Article II:2(a), subject to the conditions stated therein, exempts a charge from the coverage of Article II:1(b). The participants agree that, if a charge satisfies the conditions of Article II:2(a), it would not result in a violation of Article II:1(b)".[23]

The phrase "subject to the terms, conditions or qualifications set forth in that Schedule" as occurring in Article II:1(b) suggests a wider connotation for permitted concessions. In *EC – Bananas III*, addressing the question as to whether the allocation of tariff quotas as inscribed in a Schedule was inconsistent with GATT Article XIII, the Appellate Body addressed the legal status of tariff concessions. The Appellate Body held that the ordinary meaning of the term 'concessions' indicates that "a Member may yield rights and grant benefits, but it cannot diminish its obligations".[24] The Appellate Body in *EC – Poultry*, while rejecting Brazil's argument that the MFN principle in Articles I and XIII of the GATT 1994 does not necessarily apply to tariff-rate quotas resulting from compensation negotiations under Article XXVIII of the GATT 1994, confirmed its finding in *EC – Bananas III* (as noted earlier).[25] The Appellate Body in its ruling also referred to paragraph 3 of the Marrakesh Protocol, which reads as follows:

> The implementation of the concessions and commitments contained in the schedules annexed to this Protocol shall, upon request, be subject to multilateral examination by the Members. This would be without prejudice to the rights and obligations of Members under Agreements in Annex 1A of the WTO Agreement.

The Appellate Body in *India – Additional Import Duties* observed, "charges that are justified under Article II:2(a) are not in breach of Article II:1(b)".[26] Following an examination of the text of Article II:2(a), the Appellate Body found as follows:

> In our view, these two concepts – "equivalence" and "consistency with Article III:2" – cannot be interpreted in isolation from each other; they impart meaning to each other and need to be interpreted harmoniously. . . . Determining whether a charge is imposed consistently with Article III:2 necessarily involves a comparison of a border charge with an internal tax in order to determine whether one is "in excess of" the other. . . .
>
> . . . as we see it, the reference in Article II:2(a) to consistency with Article III:2 suggests that the concept of equivalence includes elements of "effect" and "amount" that necessarily imply a quantitative comparison.
>
> . . .
>
> We therefore consider that whether a charge is imposed "in excess of" a corresponding internal tax is an integral part of the analysis in determining whether the charge is justified under Article II:2(a). Contrary to what the Panel suggests, a complaining party

is not required to file an independent claim of violation of Article III:2 if it wishes to challenge the consistency of a border charge with Article III:2.[27]

In sum, the Appellate Body in *India – Additional Import Duties* ruled that the term 'equivalent' required both a qualitative and quantitative assessment, which is "not limited to the relative function of a charge and an internal tax" and includes "quantitative considerations relating to their effect and amount".[28]

2.3 The Schedules of Concession and Classification of Goods

Unlike under the GATT, the WTO requires all Member States to submit a schedule. Every Member State of the WTO is required to submit its bound tariffs as a document, which is referred to as 'Schedules of Concessions'. The scheduled tariff rates which a Member State submits is a binding promise, or an *erga omnes* obligation[29] to other Member States of the WTO, and forms part of the GATT. The schedules comprise four parts, covering the following tariff items:

- Part I deals with MFN concessions, which is in turn divided into two sections, addressing agriculture products and non-agriculture products.
- Part II deals with preferential concessions, which are tariffs relating to certain trade arrangements listed in GATT Article I.
- Part III contains a Member State's concessions on non-tariff measures (NTMs).
- Part IV deals with specific commitments on domestic support and export subsidies on agricultural products.

The customs classification is addressed at the WTO, albeit indirectly through the system of harmonised tariff classifications. The Schedules of Concessions, which is overseen by the World Customs Organization (WCO), is often referred to as the tariff schedule and contains the list of products by category that a Member State has bound itself to. The Schedules normally contain the maximum tariffs the Member State may apply, and not the minimum or the actual tariff that will be applied. Hence, the imposition of customs duties requires the determination of the appropriate customs classification of the imported goods.[30]

The Harmonized Commodity Description and Coding System, which is referred to as the Harmonised System (HS), is used by the Member States in their Schedules of Concessions. The HS – considered the common language amongst negotiators – was developed by the WCO[31] and is a multipurpose international product nomenclature and provides a common vocabulary. One of the key reasons to have a harmonised system is the transaction cost, as the same good may not be expressed in identical terms in different jurisdictions. Hence, clarity through a common language on what is specifically being referred to during negotiations is essential. The HS is annexed to form an integral part of the International Convention on the Harmonized Commodity Description and Coding System (HS Convention) and replaces the Brussels Convention on Nomenclature for the Classification of Goods in Customs Tariffs of 1950.[32] The HS which entered into force on 1 January 1988 is used for customs tariffs and for collection of international trade statistics by over 200 countries and economies, and over 98 percent of the merchandise in international trade is classified in terms of the HS.[33] The HS is used for definitions of product coverage for some of the covered WTO agreements and comprises about 5,000 commodity groups. It eliminates any misunderstandings in communications about products amongst Member States and also reduces transaction costs.

As outlined in the preamble to the HS Convention, the main objective of the system is to (i) facilitate international trade; (ii) it is also used for the imposition of internal taxes, economic research, and analysis and (iii) for the monitoring of controlled goods, such as endangered species, hazardous waste, and ozone-depleting substances.[34] The WCO publishes an official interpretation of the HS, which is given in Explanatory Notes. The HS is amended by the WCO every four to six years, to keep it updated, a process which poses considerable challenges for the WTO and its Member States. While the HS is administered within the WCO, the adaptation of WTO schedules to HS changes (which is more of an administrative nature) takes place within the WTO, as it is relevant for the interpretation of the schedules.[35] The HS has, without a doubt, become the common language for both negotiators and appliers of tariff schedules.[36] One can see that the HS is relevant to the performance of international trade and to various international institutions that facilitate trade, and is of significant importance to the WTO as the primary forum for the conduct of multilateral trade.

Article 10 of the HS Convention encourages negotiations to settle any disputes arising from the application of the HS Convention as between Contracting Parties concerning the interpretation or application of the Convention. In the event the parties fail to settle a dispute through negotiation, disputes are to be referred to the HS Committee. Where the HS Committee is unable to settle the dispute, the matter is raised before the WCO Council. Where disputes arise between importers (traders) and the customs authority on classification, it is to be resolved through the domestic courts, or tribunals. The Schedules of Commitments for goods and other WTO agreements, including Agricultural Agreement and the ITA, all apply the HS to refer to their products covered. All WTO Member States base their national tariffs on HS nomenclature, as well as their schedules based on HS (Van den Bossche and Zdouc, 2017; Feichtner, 2010).[37] The HS invariably reduces transactional costs for Member States, as negotiators are able to refer to an HS position for specific product lines (Feichtner, 2010). The HS was adopted for the Uruguay Round of tariff negotiations, and the WTO Member States agreed to finalise the results, or the outcome, of the ongoing non-agricultural market access negotiations under the Doha Round following the HS nomenclature.

2.4 Types of Customs Duties/Tariffs

2.4.1 Ad Valorem *and Non-*Ad Valorem *Tariffs*

Although not defined in the GATT Agreement, tariffs occupy the centre of most discussions and negotiations. The term tariffs can indicate both the product-specific rate or a Member State's laws and regulations which are the basis for customs administration.[38] The term tariffs includes both an import and an export tariff. While the former is charged when a particular good arrives at the border before entering the country of importation, the latter is charged when the particular good leaves the country of its production.[39] Although tariffs can be defined as tax, the wording and structure of the GATT make clear that it is not a tax for the purposes of Article III:2, but is rather addressed by Article II, treating tariffs as border measures, imposed whilst crossing the border of a sovereign state (Matsushita, Shoenbaum, Mavroidis, and Hahn 2017). As mentioned earlier, the two types of barriers are tariff barriers and non-tariff barriers. The Preamble to the GATT refers to tariffs as follows:

> Improvement of interstate economic relations is to be brought about by "entering into reciprocal and mutually advantageous arrangements directed to the substantial reduction of tariffs and other barriers to trade".

Customs duties are used synonymously with tariffs in the WTO agreements, and are broadly classified as *ad valorem* or non-*ad valorem* duties. An *ad valorem* duty is based on the value of the good, *e.g.*, a 10 percent *ad valorem* customs duty on the value of an imported mobile phone. If the mobile phone were to be valued at £850, the *ad valorem* customs duty would be £85. The key advantage of having an *ad valorem* duty on goods is that the liability to pay duty varies according to the rise and fall of the price of the imported good. In contrast, a non-*ad valorem* duty could be specific, compound, mixed customs (also called alternative), or technical duty. Specific duty is based on the physical characteristics of the goods, which are expressed in weight, volume, or surface area, *e.g.*, customs duty of 25 pence per kilogram of rice,[40] requiring the precise measurement to calculate the duty to be imposed. Unlike, *ad valorem* duties, specific duties do not self-regulate to inflation or deflation, which feature is viewed as a vulnerability.

A compound duty, on the other hand, is based on the value and the characteristics of the good combined – an *ad valorem* together with a specific component, which is a hybrid.[41] Mixed duties are expressed as specific or *ad valorem* and are dependent on which of the two earns the most revenue.[42] Technical duties are based on 'product specific' technical factors related to the content, such as alcohol content and sugar content. In *Argentina – Textiles and Apparel*, the Appellate Body ruled that a Member State could move from imposing one type of import duty to another, provided it did not exceed the negotiated level of protection.[43] Of all the aforementioned identified duties, *ad valorem* duties are commonplace and preferable, as they are more transparent than other forms of duties and easier to assess. Although the GATT does not mandate the use of *ad valorem* duties over specific duties, it does encourage the use of *ad valorem* with the caveat that such use does not lead to a higher level of protection (Bhala, 2013).

2.4.2 Tariffs: Bound, Applied, and TRQ

A bound tariff is a particular commitment made by WTO Member States, and it is the maximum MFN tariff applied to a commodity. As referred to earlier, Member States during the negotiation rounds make commitments agreeing for bound tariff rates in their Schedules of Concessions. Bound tariff is the level of protection a Member State has agreed *not to exceed*, which allows for flexibility to increase or decrease tariffs (on a non-discriminatory basis) within the parameters of the commitment made. In short, a bound tariff indicates the upper ceiling of the tariff the particular Member State has agreed to bind itself to with regards to a merchandise. This binding of tariffs on specific products, or lines, reduces the ability of a Member State to increase tariffs, and thereby makes international trade more predictable. There had been proposals for increased binding coverage of the merchandise by developing and least developed country Member States. However, such an increased binding coverage would likely reduce flexibility and raise the extent of obligations in future rounds of tariff negotiations.

An applied, or actual, tariff refers to the rate a WTO Member State actually imposes on imports into the country. Both bound and applied tariffs are not defined under Articles II and XXVIII *bis* of the GATT.[44] In practice, a number of developing country Member States keep their bound rate to the maximum and impose actual tariffs well below the bound commitments (Bhala, 2013). An importing developing country Member State could develop strategies to allow for a gradual increase in the tariffs within its commitment, thereby facilitating a phased opening of their market. If in the event a Member State were to put up its applied tariffs above its bound level, the measure at issue is open for challenge before the

DSB. In some cases, Member States that are affected by such measures can seek compensation in the form of higher tariffs of their own. Aggrieved Member States may also choose to retaliate by increasing their tariffs on merchandise, or product lines of special interest, to exporters in the Member States breaching the tariff commitment.

A tariff rate quota, or TRQ, is a quota for a volume of imports at a particular tariff rate. TRQs are two-level tariffs, which were introduced following the Uruguay Round Agreement on Agriculture (URAA) to expedite market access of commodities which were previously subject to non-tariff protection (Skully, 2001; De Gorter and Kliauga, 2006).[45] Under TRQs a limited volume of imports is permitted at the lower 'in-quota' tariff and all subsequent imports are charged the higher 'out-of-quota' tariff (OECD, 2005; De Gorter and Kliauga, 2006). At first glance the TRQs appear to be the same as 'absolute quotas', but they differ significantly, in that imports can exceed TRQ level but a higher, over-quota tariff is applied on the excess (Skully, 2001).[46] TRQs were primarily introduced to guarantee minimum levels of market access through minimum access quotas, and at the same time to safeguard current levels of access through 'current access quotas'. In this regard, the URAA played a key role in the institutionalisation of TRQs and supported the liberalisation of formerly protected markets.

2.5 The DSB's Interpretation of Schedules of Commitments

The WTO Panels and the Appellate are required, as per Article 3.2 of the DSU, to interpret the covered agreements "in accordance with the customary rules of interpretation of public international law".[47] This provision of the DSU refers to Articles 31 to 33 of the Vienna Convention on the Law of Treaties (VCLT).[48] Any reference to 'customary rules of interpretation' throws the door open for the possibility of applicable rules diverging from those codified in the VCLT (Peat, 2019). The Appellate Body had in a few instances applied the principle of effectiveness or *effet utile*,[49] while interpreting the provisions of the covered agreements.[50] The principle of effectiveness, or *effet utile*, was developed in the courts of the EU and is widely used by the Court of Justice of the European Union (CJEU) as an interpretive tool.[51]

The Appellate Body has largely presented an image of stability and predictability that is characteristic of an international dispute settlement body that strictly adheres to the codified principles of treaty interpretation as found in the VCLT (Van Damme, 2010).[52] While the interpretation of the covered agreements is done following the 'customary rule of interpretation of public international law', the same may not be true as regards the interpretation of the Schedules of Commitments of Member States. Some commentators have opined that Schedules of Commitments must be interpreted differently from multilateral treaties, as they are not multilateral treaties *per se*, and argue that their 'hybrid character' justifies a different approach requiring an emphasis on the intention of the Member State that drafted the Schedules (Van Damme, 2007).[53]

Although Schedules of Commitments are documents that present a detailed list of trade concessions that a Member State has negotiated with their trade partners, once submitted to the WTO, they become a part of the WTO agreements (WTO Secretariat, 2009).[54] Article II:7 of the GATT 1994 makes the Schedules an 'integral part' of Part I of the GATT, which otherwise contains only two articles, *viz.*, Article I (MFN) and Article II (Schedules).[55] The consequence of making the Schedules an 'integral part' of the agreements is that it leads to every line in the WTO Schedules getting interwoven into the whole fabric of the WTO Agreement (WTO Secretariat, 2009). The Appellate Body in *EC – Computer Equipment* observed, "the fact that members' Schedules are an integral part of the GATT 1994 indicates that, while each Schedule represents the tariff commitments made by one member, they represent a common agreement among all members".[56]

Commentators opine that this position has led to Panels and Appellate Bodies to consider Schedules of Commitments as treaties for purposes of interpretation, applying Articles 31 and 33 of VCLT without a proper evaluation of their legal status (Peat, 2019).[57] One of the arguments presented is that there is a clear distinction in the negotiations leading to the formation of treaties (both bilateral and multilateral) and that of a negotiation leading to a Member State firming up its Schedules of Commitments. Article XXX of the GATT stipulates, "amendments to the provisions of Part I of this Agreement or to the provisions of Article XXIX of this Article shall become effective upon acceptance by all the contracting parties", which by extension includes the Schedules contained in Part I. The requirement under Article XXX that changes to schedules can only be carried through a unanimous agreement is a higher 'hurdle' than one identified to carry out other changes, which could be adopted with only a two-thirds majority of members (WTO Secretariat, 2009). In effect, this means that not a single line of any of the Schedules of the Member States may be changed (or introduced) without the approval of all of the members.

The justification of integration of Schedules into the WTO agreements stem from the fact that the Schedules record the market access terms of the contract formed by the WTO, which leads to Member States interpreting and enforcing the Schedules as that of the WTO Agreement (WTO Secretariat, 2009). As discussed in earlier chapters, the multilateral trading system administered by the WTO is based on a reciprocal exchange of rights and obligations among Member States. By acceding to the WTO, the Member States have the opportunity to access the markets of other Member States, and in return provide access to their own markets for others, besides abiding by the rules of the WTO. This in effect is a multilateral contract, which records the terms of an exchange of rights and obligations among all of the Member States and binds each of the parties to abide by its terms (WTO Secretariat, 2009). Another consequence of the Schedules being an 'integral part' of the Agreement is that failure to abide by the obligations arising from the Schedules will be perceived as a violation and can be challenged before the DSB by way of a dispute.

As the Schedules are viewed as being an 'integral part' of the WTO agreements, Member States are to interpret the Schedules in the same manner as they interpret the agreements. Yet another consequence of the 'integral' status of the Schedules is that any changes made are registered with the UN Secretariat, in accordance with Article 102 of the UN Charter,[58] treating them as any other internal treaty or agreement.

The Appellate Body in *EC – Computer Equipment* sought to clarify the position by ruling that Scheduled Concessions are to be interpreted as forming an 'integral part' of the agreement:

> The purpose of treaty interpretation under Article 31 of the Vienna Convention is to ascertain the common intentions of the parties. These common intentions cannot be ascertained on the basis of the subjective and unilaterally determined "expectations" of one of the parties to a treaty. Tariff concessions provided for in a member's Schedule – the interpretation of which is at issue here – are reciprocal and result from a mutually advantageous negotiation between importing and exporting members. A Schedule is made an integral part of the GATT 1994 by Article II:7 of the GATT 1994. Therefore, the concessions provided for in that Schedule are part of the terms of the treaty. As such, the only rules which may be applied in interpreting the meaning of a concession are the general rules of treaty interpretation set out in the Vienna Convention.[59]

Van Damme puts forth the argument that if the characteristic of a treaty rests on the foundation of 'meeting of minds' of state parties, then Schedules of Commitments are a *sui generis* category that is distinguished by "a distinct qualifying unilateral characteristic" (Van Damme, 2007).

One of the key legal issues in *EC – Chicken Cuts* involved the interpretation of the heading 02.10 of the EC Schedules of Commitments, covering salted meat. Heading 02.10 of the EC Schedules of Commitments covered "Meat and edible offal, salted, in brine, dried, or smoked; edible flours, and meals of meat or meat offal". The question before the Panel (and later on before the Appellate Body) was if 'salted' occurring in 02.10 meant that if the meat was salted for the purpose of long-term preservation, then the products at issue did not fall under heading 02.10 and were not being afforded less favourable treatment. Earlier, the Panel had ruled that the Schedules of Commitments of Member States "must be considered treaty language", as the schedules are an integral part of the GATT 1994 through the operation of Article II:7.[60] The Panel observed that Articles 31 and 32 of the VCLT "comprise[d] the legal framework within which this interpretive exercise must take place".[61] The decision of the Panel was challenged before the Appellate Body.

The Appellate Body disagreed with the Panel's finding that EC classification could qualify as subsequent practice under Article 31(3)(b).[62] The Appellate Body, while ruling on the interpretation of the heading 02.10 of the EC Schedules of Commitments in *EC – Chicken Cuts*, espoused a broad understanding of the circumstances surrounding treaty conclusions, as they could potentially include any 'event, act, or instrument', and observed as follows:

> not only if it has actually influenced a specific aspect of the treaty text in the sense of a relationship of cause and effect; it may also qualify as a "circumstance of the conclusion" when it helps to discern what the common intentions of the parties were at the time of conclusion with respect to the treaty or specific provision . . . not only "multilateral" sources, but also "unilateral" acts, instruments, or statements of individual negotiating parties may be useful in ascertaining "the reality of the situation which the parties wishes to regulate by means of the treaty" and, ultimately, for discerning the common intentions of the parties.[63]

Importantly, the Appellate Body ruled that a WTO Member State's domestic legislation, as well as any judgments rendered by their domestic courts, could be of relevance to the interpretation of their respective Schedules of Commitments, insofar as those are relevant circumstances of conclusion within the meaning of Article 32 of the VCLT.[64] Similarly, in *Mexico – Telecoms*, the question before the Panel was if Mexico's proposed measures to liberalise telecommunications services was limited to domestic 'interconnections', or was to extend to cross-border services. Mexico argued that the terms 'interconnections' and 'links' referred to domestic connections, and not for 'cross-supply' falling under Mode 1 provision of GATS commitments. Here, the Panel was required to interpret the provisions of the Telecommunications Reference Paper, which formed an integral part of Mexico's Schedules of Commitments under the GATS Agreement.[65] The Panel resorted to domestic law to establish if a special meaning should be attributed to a term under Article 31(4) of the VCLT,[66] and noted:

> Interconnection is, however, a term which may be given a "special meaning", according to Article 31.4 of the Vienna Convention, "if it is established that the parties so established". Since the provision is a technical one that appears in a specialized service sector, we are

entitled to examine what "special meaning" it may have in the telecommunications context, and whether the "linking" referred to in Section 2.1 is circumscribed by that special meaning.[67]

In the Panel's view the term 'interconnection' was used by Mexico in the domestic context to mean interconnection between domestic networks, as well as between domestic and overseas networks.[68] In, both *EC – Chicken Cuts* and *Mexico – Telecoms*, the Appellate Body and the Panel respectively sought to look to domestic laws of the Member States in the interpretation of the provisions of the covered agreements. This has led commentators to question why was there a reference to domestic law by the Panel in *Mexico – Telecoms* under Article 31(4) and not under Article 32, as in the case of *EC – Chicken Cuts* (Peat, 2019). What is demonstrated, though, is that domestic law may be relevant for interpretation carried out under the rubric of Article 31 VCLT.[69] Peat takes the position that *Mexico – Telecoms*, unlike *EC – Chicken Cuts*, illustrates "how domestic law might be used to preclude an interpretation posited by one party" (Peat, 2019).

3. Customs Duties and Other Charges on Exports

3.1 Export Duties: History and Political Economy

Similar to customs duties and charges on imports, Member States impose duties and charges on exports. Customs duties, or charges on exports, are in essence a form of tax that is levied on a product that is exiting a jurisdiction, before being transported to another jurisdiction. Some of the European nations discontinued the practice of levying export duties in the nineteenth century.[70] Export duties are treated correspondingly to import tariffs in Articles II and XXVII of the GATT, which, unlike export subsidies, are not prohibited. In essence, export duties are legal and can be negotiated over and bound like tariffs. As export duties are infrequently used in practice, the need for an explicit negotiation strategy has not arisen at the highest level. From a political economy perspective, where there is an environment of general equilibrium, an export tax will have the same effect on the economy and welfare of a nation as that of an equivalent import tariff (Ederington and Ruta, 2016).

One of the earliest observations and recommendations (also criticism) of export duties is to be found in the interim report of the US Special Committee on Relaxation of Trade Barriers from 1943. The interim report, while identifying the reasons for imposition of export duties in various jurisdictions,[71] recommended either the regulation or the abolition of certain objectionable export taxes. However, the report also identified certain export taxes as not to be regarded as objectionable, *viz*., those export taxes imposed for revenue purposes; export taxes imposed following from international agreements; export taxes imposed pursuant to conditions of famine or severe domestic shortage in the exporting country, *etc*. (Report of US Special Committee, 1943). It is pertinent to refer to the position taken by US during the GATT negotiations, which was the complete abolishment of export taxes (Irwin, Mavroidis, and Sykes, 2008).[72] This stance of the US, to a certain extent, indicates that export taxes were an important trade policy concern in the pre-GATT era to at least some of the major trading countries (Staiger, 2012). The GATT Agreement, which was reached in the aftermath of WWII, prohibited only export quantitative restrictions, but not export duties.

In the GATT era, the precursor to the WTO, the primary focus was on developing methods to improve market access for foreign exporters and reduce import tariffs (considered as a key barrier to trade). This approach was developed due to historical circumstances, *viz.*, the firm belief that the unchecked increase in import tariffs triggered by the financial crisis of the 1930s played a major role in pushing countries into the disaster of World War II (Ehring and Chianale, 2012). As referred to in earlier chapters, the GATT was conceived as part of the ITO (which did not come to fruition), and to "ensure that the agreed tariff reductions were not diluted or undercut by other trade measures, the GATT incorporated many of the commercial policy provisions of the draft ITO Charter" (World Trade Report, 2012). Commencing from 1968, the GATT Secretariat categorised export duties as a 'non-tariff measure' in the Non-Tariff Measure Inventory.

In the WTO era, Member States are free to impose export taxes, which are treated symmetrically with import tariffs and may be bound (Bagwel, Staiger, and Sykes, 2013). The reason most Member States refrain from using export taxes is likely due to undesirable political economy effects such as redistribution of income away from politically organised producers (Ederington and Ruta, 2016). Not until very recently were export taxes perceived as a category in their own right. The trade effects produced by the imposition of export taxes make it much more similar to import tariffs than to other non-tariff barriers (Espa, 2015). Instead, it is viewed more as another category of export restriction. In current practice some Member States do impose export duties, as they rely on them as a source of revenue.[73]

Member States have used export taxes for various reasons, and some of the product ranges subject to export duties are from fishery, forestry, mineral and metal, leather and hide and skin, and agriculture. For instance, export taxes are used in the food production sector, as a means to insulate the domestic market from high and rising world food prices (Giordani, Rocha, and Ruta, 2014), and in the natural resources sector, to lower the domestic price of the resource as a form of subsidy to the downstream sector (Latina, Piermartini, and Ruta, 2011). Imposing export duties on rare minerals on the one hand can advantage domestic downstream industries,[74] but on the other hand it can disadvantage foreign downstream industries due to higher world prices. For instance, export duties on agricultural products could be used by a Member State to safeguard domestic supply of food products at affordable prices. Russia, during its WTO accessions, explaining the reasons for its export duties, stated as follows:

> [I]n 1998 export duties had been imposed on raw materials and semi-finished goods, mainly for fiscal purposes, and now ranged from 3 to 50 per cent, with a few exceptions where higher export duties were applied. In very few cases (oil seeds, raw hides and skins), export duties had been imposed to ensure greater availability of raw materials for the domestic industry. Export duties on non-ferrous and ferrous metals waste and scrap (and those in the guise of other products, *e.g.* used axle-boxes) had been imposed to address problems of environmental protection.[75]

Commentators also posit the argument that a lack of agreed rules at the multilateral level is a problem, as export tariffs contribute to the volatility of food and natural resource prices in international markets, which in turn trigger policy response from trading partners (Ruta and Venebles, 2012; Giordani, Rocha, and Ruta, 2014).

3.2 Rules on Export Duties

There is no prohibition on export duties on goods traded under GATT 1994, or for that matter under any other provision of the WTO rules. Interestingly, the Schedule of Concessions contained in Article II of the GATT only concerns import duties and charges with regards to imports, and with export duties, and there is no Article II equivalent for export tariffs within the GATT. It is arguable that the drafters of the GATT did consider the potential for trade distortion arising out of both imports and exports, as the GATT MFN provision in Article I:1 applies "with respect to customs duties and charges of any kind imposed on or in connection with importation or exportation" (Crosby, 2008). Mavroidis takes the position that the negotiators knew full well about the "economics of equivalence between export taxes and import duties". But, as Qin notes, the current regime of the WTO with regards to export restraints represent two extremes, *viz.*, the "near complete freedom to levy export duties" that is enjoyed by most Member States[76] and the harsh obligations foisted on acceding Member States[77] which prohibit the use of export duties (Qin, 2016). This position demonstrates that it is possible to negotiate export duties on an *ad hoc* basis during accession of a Member State.[78]

Although the WTO rules do not currently discipline the Member States' application of export taxes, they do hinder exports of commodities. Nevertheless, certain general GATT obligations also apply to export duties, not just import duties. For instance, if a Member State were to impose export duty on a particular variety of coffee that is being exported to another Member State, it must then impose the same export duty on all 'like products' exported to all other Member States. See for example Article I:1 of GATT 1994, which set out the MFN treatment obligation.[79] GATT Article XXVIII *bis* states unequivocally that both import tariffs and export tariffs can be negotiated, and the relevant part reads as follows:

> thus negotiations on a reciprocal and mutually advantageous basis, directed to the substantial reduction of the general level of tariffs and other charges *on imports and exports*[80] and in particular to the reduction of such high tariffs as discourage the importation even of minimum quantities, and conducted with due regard to the objectives of this Agreement and the varying needs of individual contracting parties, are of great importance to the expansion of international trade.

GATT Article II:1(a) reads as follows:

> Each contracting party shall accord to the commerce of the other contracting parties treatment no less favourable than that provided for in the appropriate Part of the appropriate Schedule annexed to this Agreement.

It is debateable if the language used in Article II:1(a) referring to 'the commerce of the other contracting parties' is to be understood to apply to both imports and exports, and accordingly providing coverage for bindings on duties on exports. Nonetheless, Article II:1(b), first sentence, only refers to importation of products and does not cover exports. Likewise, Article II:1(b), second sentence, deals with other duties and charges, which clearly does not cover export duties. As referred to earlier, WTO accession protocols do impose obligations on new Member States (countries who had joined post-1995) as regards export duties are concerned.[81]

In *China – Raw Materials*, the US, Mexico, and the EU challenged various restrictions imposed by China on a range of raw mineral exports, including export duties. The question that arose for consideration before the Panel was if China's export duties on various minerals[82] were inconsistent with paragraph 11.3 of China's Accession Protocol. The panel found that China's levy of export duty was inconsistent with paragraph 11.3 of its Accession Protocol.[83] The ruling has been criticised in some quarters, as on the one hand the WTO Agreement does not require its Member States to limit the use of export duties,[84] and on the other hand China and a few other Member States[85] are bound by very strict obligations on export duties (Qin, 2016). The issue of imposition of export duties by China in contravention with paragraph 11.3 of its Accession Protocol arose once again in *China – Rare Earths*. The Panel, following from its earlier decision in *China – Raw Materials*, found that China's levy of export duties on rare earths such as tungsten and molybdenum were inconsistent with paragraph 11.3 of its Accession Protocol.[86] Also, Mongolia, Saudi Arabia, Ukraine, and Vietnam, *etc.*, have committed to eliminating at least some export taxes in their accession negotiations. Although a founding Member State, Australia, in Part I, Section 2, of its Goods Schedule, provides in the 'Notes' column with regard to 11 tariff lines that "there shall be no export duty on this product".

3.3 Debates and the Proposal for Change

As referred to earlier, Articles II:1(b) and (c) only envisage imports and not export duties. This clearly highlights a lack of legal framework within the GATT to negotiate export duties. However, commentators argue that despite a lack of formal legal framework, nothing in law precludes WTO Member States from negotiating export duty commitments in accordance with Article XXVIII *bis* GATT using a scheduling and binding procedure *à la* Article II:1(b) GATT (Espa, 2015; Matsushita, 2011; Crosby, 2008; Ehring and Chianale, 2012). Commentators have argued that export duty commitments are enforceable inasmuch as WTO Members list such commitments in their GATT schedules of concessions (Matsushita, 2011; Ehring and Chianale, 2012). It is debatable if Article II:1(b) can accommodate both imports and exports, due to its language. Nevertheless, Matsushita argues that export duty concessions are enforceable through Article II:1(b) GATT itself, as the language of Article II:1(b)

> is merely indicative of the fact that the negotiators of the GATT 1947 were preoccupied with the elimination and reduction of import tariffs, and . . . cannot be interpreted to necessarily imply that their intention was to exclude export duties altogether from the scope of Article II:1 (b).
>
> (Matsushita, 2011)

The EU, during the Doha Round of negotiations, has proposed the creation of specific WTO rules on export taxes. Originally presented in 2006, the EU proposal aims to fully reflect "the importance of establishing balanced and proportionate WTO rules for Members' use of export taxes" (WTO, 2008). The key elements of the proposal are threefold, *viz.*,

i Confirmation and operationalisation of basic GATT disciplines to apply to those situations where WTO Members use export taxes for industrial or trade policy purposes with negative effects on other WTO Members and especially on developing countries.[87]
ii Incorporation of additional flexibility for small developing country Members and least-developed country Members to maintain or introduce export taxes in other situations, *i.e.*, over and beyond what would be allowed through the strict application of GATT rules to export taxes.
iii Limitation of the GATT disciplines for export taxes to non-agricultural products in recognition of the mandate for NAMA[88] (WTO, 2008).

The EU proposal is viewed more as a

> workable compromise in the area of export taxes between those many countries affected by the "beggar thy neighbour" measures adopted by a few major suppliers and other large economies, and the use of export taxes by small economies, which includes the majority of developing countries.
>
> (WTO, 2008)

However, this proposal of the EU does not have sufficient support from the Member States to be given effect to.

4. Non-Tariff Barriers/Measures: NTBs

Both tariffs and non-tariff barriers present restrictions to the multilateral trade. Although 'non-tariff barrier/measures' (NTBs)[89] are one of the major causes for trade distortions, they are not defined anywhere in the WTO agreements. The term can be interpreted to include all measures and actions imposed by governments of Member States, as well as sponsored actions or omissions that impact trade flows.[90] The GATT (and a number of RTAs) refer to export duties as non-tariff measures, and likewise the 'Indicative List of Notifiable Measures' annexed to the Decision on Notification Procedures adopted at the conclusion of the Uruguay Round places 'export taxes' in the category of non-tariff measures (Kazeki, 2005). NTBs, which comprise an extremely diverse set of policy measures, can be divided into three categories, *viz.*, (i) NTBs imposed on imports (port-quotas, import prohibitions, import licensing, *etc.*), (ii) NTBs imposed on exports (export taxes, export subsidies, export quotas, export prohibitions, and voluntary export restraints), and (iii) NTBs imposed internally in the domestic economy (Staiger, 2012).[91] The first two categories are applied at the border.

4.1 The Political Economy of NTBs: GATT and WTO

In the earlier part of this chapter we studied the GATT/WTO rules relating to tariffs, and how tariffs were negotiated during the GATT and WTO eras. Trade agreements dating back to the GATT era were primarily concerned with the potential for policy substitution,[92] and as a result, treated any non-tariff barriers/non-tariff measures as imperfect substitutes for tariff barriers (Ederington and Ruta, 2016). In the GATT era tariffs were chosen over quantitative restrictions as the lawful means of regulating imports and exports, and focus remained on the gradual reduction of the level of both import and export tariffs through periodic negotiations. This approach was taken because both the GATT and the WTO sought to concentrate the use of trade barriers into a single measure, *i.e.*, tariffs, to provide the much-required transparency and predictability to traders. GATT's approach towards NTBs was minimalist, or was a 'shallow integration' approach in general (Staiger, 2012). This is understandable, as the GATT was formed to serve as a negotiating forum for a tariff-binding exercise amongst contracting parties.

Although both tariff measures and NTBs impact trade, NTBs are separated from import tariffs, as it is import tariffs alone that are the policy measure with which negotiated market access commitments are made. NTBs are known to affect both trade in goods and trade in services. Staiger raises a fundamental question, whether the GATT/WTO's asymmetric treatment of tariff and NTBs are warranted on economic grounds (Staiger, 2012). Doubtlessly, the answer to this question is complex, as the primary objective of the multilateral trading system is the facilitation of trade through the negotiated trade agreements and trade policies which is premised on the economic development, or trade development, of the contracting parties. NTBs are applied both at the border and behind the border. GATT contains numerous provisions that are designed to induce 'tariffication' of import-protective measures which are aimed at avoiding alternative forms of import protection for tariffs, *i.e.*, border NTBs (Staiger, 2012).[93] On the export side GATT was permissive, but required that all domestic taxes, charges, and regulations satisfied the non-discrimination rules, *i.e.*, the national treatment obligations. To further strengthen this position, GATT also included a second line of defence, which is to be found in the so-called non-violation or nullification-or-impairment provision of the GATT (Hudec, 1990; Staiger, 2012).

The WTO's approach extends the minimalist approach established under the GATT. But with regards to border NTBs we witness the tightening of the obligations in comparison to the GATT (OECD, 2005).[94] As observed by the Panel in *Turkey – Textiles*, the participants of the Uruguay Round, recognising the detrimental effects of NTBs (applied to imports and exports) and the need to favour more tariff-based measures, devised mechanisms to phase out quantitative restrictions in the sectors of agriculture and textiles and clothing.[95] For instance, the Understanding on Balance-of-Payments Provisions,[96] the Agreement on Safeguards,[97] the Agreement on Agriculture[98] and the Agreement on Textiles and Clothing all address the issue of quantitative restrictions either by advocating avoidance of imposition of quantitative restrictions or by imposing a complete ban. Likewise, the WTO Subsidies and Countervailing Measures (SCM) Agreement strengthens significantly the prohibition against export subsidies. Similar to border NTBs, the WTO's approach to behind-the-border NTBs also represents a significant tightening of obligations. For instance, the WTO Technical Barriers to Trade (TBT) and Sanitary and Phytosanitary Measures (SPS) agreements represent a significant strengthening of the non-discrimination/national treatment obligations principles (Staiger, 2012).

4.2 Quantitative Restrictions: Rules and Types

Quantitative restrictions fall within the category of NTBs to trade in goods and not services. In this part of the chapter, we take up for study the rules relating to quantitative restrictions within the multilateral trading system. One of the most important of the GATT 1947 commitments is the Article XI commitment to eliminate quantitative restrictions on imports and exports, which prohibits quantitative restrictions. Quantitative restrictions lack the transparency of customs duties, and also, by creating an artificial short supply, they prevent the law of supply and demand from determining the price at which domestic and imported goods should be sold (Kennedy, 2005). GATT Article XI:1, which is entitled 'General Elimination of Quantitative Restrictions', states as follows:

> No prohibitions or restrictions other than duties, taxes or other charges, whether made effective through quotas, import or export licences or other measures, shall be instituted or maintained by any contracting party on the importation of any product of the territory of any other contracting party or on the exportation or sale for export of any product destined for the territory of any other contracting party.

A reading of Article XI:1 makes clear that quantitative restrictions are prohibited on both exports and imports and regardless of whether such restrictions are being applied through quotas, import and export licences, or any other measures that prohibit or restrict trade other than duties, taxes, and other charges.[99] The Panel in *Turkey – Textiles* highlighted the significance of the XI in the GATT framework and noted:

> The prohibition against quantitative restrictions is a reflection that tariffs are GATT's border protection "of choice". Quantitative restrictions impose absolute limits on imports, while tariffs do not. In contrast to MFN tariffs which permit the most efficient competitor to supply imports, quantitative restrictions usually have a trade distorting effect, their allocation can be problematic and their administration may not be transparent.

The powers of the Member States to take measures at the border, which may have the effect of influencing the trade flow, is restricted by Article XI. Importantly, Article XI does not address so-called internal measures, which apply to products after they have legally entered the market.[100] As per the decision taken before the Council for Trade in Goods in 1995, all Member States are required to notify the Council of all, or any, quantitative restrictions that are in force, including all modifications, as soon as possible, but not later than six months after the provision's entry into force (WTO, 1995, 2012a).[101]

Quantitative restrictions could be classified broadly as (i) those prohibiting an importation or exportation of a product; (ii) those imposing an import or export quota, where restrictions are placed on the quantity imported or exported; (iii) import and export licensing; and (iv) other quantitative restrictions not covered within the aforementioned categories. The prohibition imposed on quantitative restrictions under Article XI:1 is broad, in that it covers quotas and other measures (which is undefined) regardless of the way they are enforced – either through customs regulation[102] or through state-trading companies.[103] From a reading of Article XI:1, it clearly indicates that 'other measures' can refer to any regulation designed to impede imports or exports. Hence, the prohibition contained under Article XI:1 will cover export quotas and minimum export price requirements,[104] data collection and monitoring requirements,[105] discretionary non-automatic licensing systems,[106] minimum import price requirements,[107] prohibiting importation of copyrighted works not manufactured domestically,[108] requiring security deposits,[109] prohibiting imports not produced in a certain way,[110] trade balancing requirements,[111] and restrictions on ports of entry.[112]

In *Japan – Semi-Conductors*, the Panel observed that the wording of Article XI:1 is comprehensive and noted, "it applied to all measures instituted or maintained by a contracting party prohibiting or restricting the importation, exportation or sale for export of products other than measures that take the form of duties, taxes or other charges". In *Argentina – Financial Services*, the Panel distinguished by ruling that one of the measures in question was 'fiscal in nature' and would not come within the ambit of Article XI:1 of the GATT.[113] The Appellate Body in *Argentina – Import Measures* clarified that the scope of Article XI:1 was not unfettered and observed as follows:

> [W]hile the term "or other measures" suggests a broad coverage, the scope of application of Article XI:1 of the GATT 1994 is not unfettered. Article XI:1 itself explicitly excludes "duties, taxes and other charges" from its scope of application. Article XI:2 of the GATT 1994 further restricts the scope of application of Article XI:1 by providing that the provisions of Article XI:1 shall not extend to the areas listed in Article XI:2.[114]

The panel in *Dominican Republic – Import and Sale of Cigarettes* clarified that Article XI:1 would not cover all "measures affecting the opportunities for entering the market" but "only those measures that constitute a prohibition or a restriction on the importation of products, *i.e.* those measures which affect the opportunities for importation itself".[115] The Appellate Body in *China – Raw Materials*, while upholding the findings of the Panel that the minimum price requirement on exporters of raw materials[116] amounted to quantitative restriction on exports and was inconsistent with Article XI:1, observed:

> [t]he use of the word "quantitative" in the title of Article XI of the GATT 1994 informs the interpretation of the words "restriction" and "prohibition" in Article XI:1, suggesting that the coverage of Article XI includes those prohibitions and restrictions that limit the quantity or amount of a product being imported or exported.[117]

In *Argentina – Import Measures*, the Appellate Body further clarified that Article XI does "not cover simply any restriction or prohibition" but that it refers to prohibitions or restrictions "on the importation . . . or on the exportation or sale for export", and it ruled that "not every condition or burden placed on importation or exportation will be inconsistent with Article XI, but only those that are limiting, that is, those that limit the importation or exportation of products".[118]

4.2.1 *The Scope of 'Restriction'*

With regards to the term 'restriction' occurring in Article XI:1, the Panel in *India – Quantitative Restrictions* set out the broad scope of the concept of restriction as follows:

> [T]he text of Article XI:1 is very broad in scope, providing for a general ban on import or export restrictions or prohibitions "other than duties, taxes or other charges". As was noted by the panel in *Japan – Trade in Semi-Conductors*, the wording of Article XI:1 is comprehensive: it applies "to all measures instituted or maintained by a [Member] prohibiting or restricting the importation, exportation, or sale for export of products other than measures that take the form of duties, taxes or other charges." The scope of the term "restriction" is also broad, as seen in its ordinary meaning, which is "a limitation on action, a limiting condition or regulation".[119]

The broad scope of application of Article XI:1 was also confirmed by the Panel in *India – Autos*. One of the questions arising for consideration before the Panel was "whether Article XI can be considered to cover situations where products are technically allowed into the market without an express formal quantitative restriction, but are only allowed under certain conditions which make the importation more onerous than if the condition had not existed", and thereby generating a disincentive to import.[120] The panel responded to this question as follows:

> On a plain reading, it is clear that a "restriction" need not be a blanket prohibition or a precise numerical limit. Indeed, the term "restriction" cannot mean merely "prohibitions" on importation, since Article XI:1 expressly covers both "prohibition or restriction". Furthermore, the Panel considers that the expression "limiting condition" used by the *India – Quantitative Restrictions* panel to define the term "restriction" and which this Panel endorses, is helpful in identifying the scope of the notion in the context of the facts before it. That phrase suggests the need to identify not merely a condition placed on importation, but a condition that is limiting, *i.e.* that has a limiting effect. In the context of Article XI, that limiting effect must be on importation itself.[121]

Similarly, in *China – Raw Materials*, the Appellate Body ruled that the term 'restriction' occurring in Article XI:1 refers to "something that has a limiting effect"; that the use of the term 'quantitative' in the title of the provision informs the interpretation of the words 'restriction' and 'prohibition' in Article XI:1 and XI:2; and it suggests that Article XI covers those prohibitions and restrictions that have a limiting effect on the quantity or amount of a product being imported or exported.[122] Article XI:1, unlike other provisions of the GATT, refers to measures that restrict imports or exports, irrespective of the legal status of the measure. In *Japan – Semi-Conductors*, the panel ruled that the "wording indicated clearly that any measure instituted or maintained by a contracting party which restricted the exportation or sale for export of products was covered by this provision, irrespective of the legal status of the measure",[123] and as a result the measures introduced by the Government of Japan, which operated to exert pressure on the private sector restricting the export of certain semi-conductors at prices below company-specific costs, were 'restrictions' within the meaning of Article XI:1.[124]

This approach clearly indicates that Article XI:1 seeks to protect conditions of competition, as such restrictive measures and quotas will be considered illegal.[125] In *Colombia – Ports of Entry*, the Panel found that "restrictions on ports of entry limit the competitive opportunities for subject textiles, apparel and footwear arriving from Panama" and concluded that "the ports of entry measures has a limiting effect on imports" constituting a restriction on importation within the meaning of Article XI:1, and therefore inconsistent with Article XI:1.[126] It therefore follows that a complaining party need only demonstrate to a Panel that the imposition of quota had restrictive effect, depriving market access. In this regard, the Panel in *India – Autos* observed as follows:

> The question of whether this form of measure can appropriately be described as a restriction on importation turns on the issue of whether Article XI can be considered to cover situations where products are technically allowed into the market without an express formal quantitative restriction, but are only allowed under certain conditions which make the importation more onerous than if the condition had not existed, thus generating a disincentive to import.

As per the aforementioned ruling, in a dispute, the complaining Member State need not demonstrate that the measure in question, which is challenged as being incompatible with Article XI, has had an adverse impact. The Panel in *Brazil – Retreaded Tyres*, while considering if the fines imposed on imported retreaded tyres were restrictive, observed as follows:

> In the present case, we note that the fines as a whole, including that on marketing, have the effect of penalizing the act of "importing" retreaded tyres by subjecting retreaded tyres already imported and existing in the Brazilian internal market to the prohibitively expensive rate of fines. To that extent, we consider that the fact that the fines are not administered at the border does not alter their nature as a restriction on importation within the meaning of Article XI:1.[127]

The panel in *EC – Oilseeds I* (1990) ruled that quantitative restrictions, which do not actually restrict or impede trade, are nonetheless prohibited under Article XI:1:

> [T]he Contracting Parties have consistently interpreted the basic provisions of the General Agreement on restrictive trade measures as provisions establishing conditions of competition. Thus they decided that an import quota constitutes an import restriction within the meaning of Article XI:1 whether or not it actually impeded imports.[128]

4.2.2 Quantifying the Limiting Effect of the Measure at Issue

The Appellate Body in *Argentina – Import Measures*, referring to its findings in *China – Raw Materials*, ruled that the limiting effects of a measure under issue need not be quantified and can be demonstrated through the design, architecture, and revealing structure of the measure:

> [I]n our view, not every condition or burden placed on importation or exportation will be inconsistent with Article XI, but only those that are limiting, that is, those that limit the importation or exportation of products.[129] Moreover, this limitation need not be demonstrated by quantifying the effects of the measure at issue; rather, such limiting effects can be demonstrated through the design, architecture, and revealing structure of the measure at issue considered in its relevant context.[130]

The Panel in *Indonesia – Import Licensing Regimes*, while referring to the Appellate Body's findings in *Argentina – Import Measures* that quantifying the limiting effects of the measures at issue is not required under Article XI:1, noted that a Panel may nevertheless use statistical data as evidence to inform its overall examination of whether a measure has a limiting effect.[131] The panel in *Colombia – Ports of Entry*, taking a slightly different approach, observed:

> [T]o the extent Panama were able to demonstrate a violation of Article XI:1 based on the measure's design, structure, and architecture, the Panel is of the view that it would not be necessary to consider trade volumes or a causal link between the measure and its effects on trade volumes.[132]

4.2.3 De Facto *Prohibitions or Restrictions*

The scope of quantitative restrictions in Article XI:1 prohibits both *de jure* and *de facto* quantitative restrictions. Any measures introduced by a Member State and having that effect will come within the ambit of Article XI:1. In *Argentina – Hides and Leather*, the European Communities argued that Argentina's measure violated Article XI:1 by authorising the presence of domestic tanners' representatives in the customs inspection procedures for hides destined for export operations, and thus imposing *de facto* restrictions on exports of hides. The Panel ruled as follows:

> There can be no doubt, in our view, that the disciplines of Article XI:1 extend to restrictions of a *de facto* nature. It is also readily apparent that Resolution 2235, if indeed it makes effective a restriction, fits in the broad residual category, specifically mentioned in Article XI:1, of "other measures".[133]

The Panel was also required in *Argentina – Hides and Leather* to determine whether the presence of representatives of the domestic hide tanning industry in the Argentine customs inspection procedures for hides destined for export was an export restriction. The Panel found that evidence presented with regards to trade effects carried weight, but the complaining party was required to demonstrate how the measure at issue causes or contributes to a low level of exports, and in the Panel's view

> in the context of an alleged *de facto* restriction and where, as here, there are possibly multiple restrictions, it is necessary for a complaining party to establish a causal

link between the contested measure and the low level of exports. In our view, whatever else it may involve, a demonstration of causation must consist of a persuasive explanation of precisely how the measure at issue causes or contributes to the low level of exports.[134]

4.3 Exceptions to Article XI:1

The drafters of the GATT included a list of exceptions to the quantitative restrictions to the list of obligations contained in Article XI:1. The fundamental distinction "underlying the different legal treatment between tariffs (even prohibitive tariffs) and quantitative restrictions had been a recurrent theme in the drafting of Article XI (at the time Article 20 of the ITO)".[135] The phrase used in the US proposed Charter of 1946 was "conditions of distress". It was explained by the US representative that the phrase did not mean "economic distress but referred to shortages of crops, *etc.*, in cases such as famine" (UN Doc, 1946). With reference to the term 'critical', it was agreed in the discussions (both at Geneva and again at Havana) that the Australian export prohibitions on merino sheep (post-drought shortage of sheep) were covered by paragraph 2(a) (UN Doc, 1947).

These exceptions to Article XI:1 are found in Article XI:2(a)–(c),[136] where paragraph (a) 'temporarily' exempts the application of Article XI:1 to 'export prohibitions or restrictions' to foodstuffs, or other similarly essential products, to 'prevent or relieve' critical shortages of that product;[137] paragraph (b), permits WTO members to apply import or export restrictions necessary to administer grading and classification standards in international trade;[138] and paragraph (c) permits WTO Member States to apply import restrictions on agricultural or fisheries product that are necessary for the enforcement of any governmental measures that (1) restrict the marketing or production of the 'like' domestic product (or a directly substitutable product if there is no substantial production of the like product); (2) remove a temporary surplus of a like domestic product (or a directly substitutable product if there is no substantial production of the like product) by making the surplus available to certain groups of domestic consumers free of charge or at prices below the current market level; or (3) restrict production of any animal product that is directly dependent on the imported commodity, if the domestic production of that commodity is relatively negligible.[139] Jackson notes that the exceptions found in paragraphs (a) and (c) reflect the proposals made by the US in its 1946 draft charter (Jackson, 1969). It will be noted that Article XI:2(c) only permits the restriction of imports, following a public notification with details of the total quantity restricted.

In *China – Raw Materials*, the Panel found that "the burden is on the respondent . . . to demonstrate that the conditions of Article XI:2(a) are met in order to demonstrate that no inconsistency arises under Article XI:1".[140] While the Panel found that refractory-grade bauxite was 'essential' to China on the basis of its importance in steel production,[141] it found that the export restriction on this product (which was in place since 2000), was not 'temporarily applied',[142] and that it did not agree that China 'currently' faced a 'critical shortage' of refractory bauxite.[143] The Appellate Body in *China – Raw Materials* found that the phrase 'temporarily applied' (in the context of Article XI:2(a)) describes a measure applied for a limited time, a measure 'taken to bridge a passing need', and observed as follows:

> First, we note that the term "temporarily" in Article XI:2(a) of the GATT 1994 is employed as an adverb to qualify the term "applied". The word "temporary" is defined as "[l]asting or meant to last for a limited time only; not permanent; made or arranged

to supply a passing need". Thus, when employed in connection with the word "applied", it describes a measure applied for a limited time, a measure taken to bridge a "passing need". As we see it, the definitional element of "supply[ing] a passing need" suggests that Article XI:2(a) refers to measures that are applied in the interim.[144]

The Appellate Body in *China – Raw Materials* concluded that the term 'export prohibition' occurring in Article XI:2 excludes 'duties, taxes, or other charges':

> Turning to the phrase "[e]xport prohibitions or restrictions" in Article XI:2(a), we note that the words "prohibition" and "restriction" in that subparagraph are both qualified by the word "export". Thus, Article XI:2(a) covers any measure prohibiting or restricting the exportation of certain goods. Accordingly, we understand the words "prohibitions or restrictions" to refer to the same types of measures in both paragraph 1 and subparagraph 2(a), with the difference that subparagraph 2(a) is limited to prohibitions or restrictions on exportation, while paragraph 1 also covers measures relating to importation. We further note that "duties, taxes, or other charges" are excluded from the scope of Article XI:1. Thus, by virtue of the link between Article XI:1 and Article XI:2, the term "restrictions" in Article XI:2(a) also excludes "duties, taxes, or other charges". Hence, if a restriction does not fall within the scope of Article XI:1, then Article XI:2 will also not apply to it.[145]

Apart from the specific exceptions mentioned in Article XI:2 to the prohibition of quantitative restrictions, other exceptions contained in GATT are as follows: (i) Articles XII (allowing restrictions to safeguard balance of payments; (ii) Article XX (General Exceptions), and (iii) Article XXI (Security Exceptions). One should, along with the aforementioned, also consider the Escape Clause (GATT Article XIX) as justification for possible non-conforming measures.

5. Customs-Related NTBs

One of the important types of NTBs to trade in goods are customs formalities and procedures, which is, in other words, an 'administrative barrier' to trade. Depending on their nature and extent, customs-related NTBs can constitute a nuisance to traders or act as an outright barrier to trade. Member States may levy customs fees and charges to either increase revenue or use them as a means to protect their domestic markets.[146] Determining customs fees for a particular good requires the appropriate classification,[147] valuation (going by the invoice price), and the origin of the good. These issues are covered in various agreements of the WTO.

5.1 Agreement on Customs Valuation

The general principles for determining the dutiable value of imported goods have been at the forefront of international negotiations from the early part of the twentieth century. The starting point for a harmonised customs valuation was set out in Article VII of GATT 1947.[148] The provision in Article VII allowed the original GATT Contracting Parties the flexibilities in defining the value of imported goods, and permitted some countries by the Protocol of Provisional Application of GATT 1947 to continue applying inconsistent valuation methods. In 1950, 13 European states developed the Brussels Definition of Value (BDV), which sought to achieve greater harmonisation of the valuation practice, which envisaged the determination of imported merchandise on the basis of the "price of the merchandise" or the price the "merchandise would fetch" if sold in an open market (Rege, 2002). Although the BDV received over 100 signatories, leading nations such the US, Canada, Australia, and New Zealand refused to be persuaded to join the scheme.

However, during the preparatory phase of the Tokyo Round of negotiations, the EU agreed to make a fundamental change in its valuation systems by opting "for a positive approach" instead of the "notional approach of the BDV". The EU argued that the new proposals were based on features of the United States' valuation system (Rege, 2002). The Tokyo Round of negotiations, which took place between 1973 and 1979, witnessed the participation of 99 countries, and a key objective of the negotiating round was the reduction of non-tariff distortions to international trade. Also, customs valuation was identified as a non-tariff barrier on the priority list for negotiation (Forrester and Odarda, 2005). It is important to note that GATT Article VII continues to be in force in the WTO era. Depending on the way goods are valued, tariff values can become uneven, and this aspect is addressed by GATT Article VII(a), which reads as follows:

> The value for customs purposes of imported merchandise should be based on the actual value of the imported merchandise on which duty is assessed, or of like merchandise, and should not be based on the value of merchandise of national origin or on arbitrary or fictitious values.

In the GATT era, considerable negotiating time was devoted to the reduction of non-tariff distortions to trade and the development of a customs valuation, during both the Tokyo and the Uruguay Round of negotiations. Significant breakthrough was achieved in the Tokyo Round of Negotiations in 1979, where the Agreement on Implementation of Article VII of the GATT (or the Customs Valuation Code) was adopted.[149] Again, during the Uruguay Round of negotiations, the Agreement on Implementation of Article VII of the General Agreement on Tariffs and Trade 1994 (Customs Valuation Agreement) was agreed.[150]

The Customs Valuation Agreement (CVA) requires Member States to implement a valuation system that is "fair, neutral and uniform (Article 22.1)",[151] and avoid the use of arbitrary or fictitious values. The provisions of the CVA apply only to the valuation of imported goods for the purpose of determining the *ad valorem* duties. Under Article 8, the CVA requires Member States to determine the customs value of imported goods on the basis of the price paid, or payable for export to the country of importation, to include certain payments made by buyers, such as cost of packaging and containers, assists, royalties, and licence fees. As per the scheme envisaged under Article 1 of the CVA, goods are to be assessed at their transaction value. Where the transaction value cannot be determined, due to a lack of sale (no sale, no invoice), or where such transaction value is not acceptable for the importing state as the customs value, due to the price being distorted as a result of conditions identified in Article 1,[152] the CVA limits the discretion available to customs in deciding on the dutiable value and requires that such value be arrived at following the five general principles of valuation to determine the dutiable value in sequential order.[153]

  i Article 2: Value of identical goods sold for export to the same country of importation – the customs value is determined on the basis of the transaction value of previously imported identical goods;

ii   Article 3: Value of similar goods sold for export to the same country of importation – here, the customs value is determined on the basis of the transaction value of previously imported similar goods;
iii   Article 5: Deductive value calculated on the basis of the unit price at which identical or similar imported goods are sold in the domestic market, less applicable deductions for costs incurred within the country of import – the unit price of goods sold in the domestic market within a period of 90 days of importation has to be taken into account;[154]
iv   Article 6: Constructed value computed on the basis of cost of production, *i.e.*, value of the materials and fabrication, in addition to an amount for profits and general expenses;
v   Article 7: Where value cannot be determined under any of the aforementioned approaches, other reasonable methods ('fallback') that rely on information available in the country of importation may be used.[155]

Article 7.2(a) of the CVA clearly eliminates valuation misuses introduced under the American Selling Price mechanism introduced by the US before 1979. While Article 8.2 of CVA permits the use of the Incoterm CIF for customs valuation purpose, countries such as Canada, Japan, and the US continue to use the Incoterm FOB (free on board) for customs purposes, resulting in lower US tariff charges than those levied by other countries under identical tariff rates.

5.2 Agreement on Import Licensing Procedures

The Agreement on Import Licensing Procedures (AILP) is one of the least controversial of all the Uruguay Round agreements. The AILP differs very little from the Import Licensing Code formulated during the Tokyo Round agreement, with the exception of a few changes intended to fine-tune the procedures for import licensing programs. The AILP, unlike the Import Licensing Code, is binding on all Member States of the WTO. The AILP's objectives are to simplify and minimise the administrative procedures to ensure their fair and equitable application to obtain import licences and to ensure that the procedures are not a hindrance to imports. The AILP has eight articles and is designed to minimise the undesirable consequences of GATT-compatible import licensing. Article 1 of the AILP defines import licensing as

> administrative procedure used for the operation of importing licensing regimes requiring the submission of an application or other documentation (other than that required for customs purposes) to the relevant administrative body as a prior condition for importation into the customs territory of the importing Member.

Two basic types of import licensing envisaged are *automatic* licensing and *non-automatic* licensing. Automatic licensing is primarily used for compiling trade statistics, and approval is granted almost in all cases on application. Non-automatic licensing, in contrast, is a means to regulate imports, by requiring applicants to comply with specific criteria. Non-automatic licensing, although it can be used for both economic and non-economic regulatory goals, is used mostly for economic reasons. In more recent times, non-automatic licences have come to be used in connection with TRQs.[156] The AILP's simplified provisions aim to reduce discrimination or administrative discretion in the application of both kinds of licensing. In the event of conflict between the provisions of the AILP and the GATT, the provisions of the AILP are to prevail in GATT Article X:3(a), as it "deals specifically, and in detail, with the administration of import licensing procedure".[157]

Article 1.3 requires import licensing procedures to be "applied neutrally and administered in a fair and equitable manner".[158] As transparency is one of the key features of AILP, Article 1.4(a) requires prior publication of all rules together with relevant information concerning procedures for the submission of applications for the grant of licences, whenever practicable, 21 days prior to the effective date of the requirement and never later than the effective date.[159] AIPL requires that applicant traders are to be allowed a reasonable period of time to submit licence applications. As per Articles 1.5 and 1.6, application and renewal procedures are to be made simple. Article 1.7 requires that applications are not to be refused for "minor documentation errors" and that penalties imposed for omissions should not be excessive and be only for the purposes of warning. While Article 2.1 provides a set of rules for 'automatic' licences, Article 3.1 outlines a comprehensive procedure for non-automatic licences.

5.3 Agreement on Pre-Shipment Inspection

The Agreement on Pre-Shipment Inspection (API) is designed to ensure that pre-shipment inspection (PSI) is carried out in a fair and non-discriminatory way. Alongside the AILP, the API is one of the least controversial of the Uruguay Round agreements. The PSI programs, when first introduced, were designed for foreign exchange purposes and initially introduced in the Democratic Republic of Congo (Zaire) in 1965.[160] In international trade, PSI plays a key role, where private companies (PSI entities) are engaged to verify the quality, quantity, price (including currency exchange rates), and customs classification of the goods to be exported in the territory of the exporting country. This is followed by a Report of Findings, which is then acted upon by the user, or a Clean Report of Findings.

The practice of engaging a PSI entity is commonplace, as governments now require their importers to engage private inspectors to verify price, quality, and other characteristics of goods in the country of origin. PSI is used primarily to avoid misclassification, over-invoicing or under-invoicing (as the case may be), and under-collection of tariffs by stateside customs officials. With this, there is a real fear that PSI has become an NTB. Originally promoted by the developed countries, it gained support from PSI user countries during the Uruguay Round, resulting in a form of Agreement.

The Preamble to the API, while recognising the developing countries' need to have recourse to PSI for as long as they need, also lays down rules requiring user governments to ensure that the PSI entities operate in a non-discriminatory fashion and also protect any confidential business information that is shared with them. The API, under Article 1.1, determines the minimum standard for all government-mandated PSI activities. Article 1.2 defines 'user Members' as those members that have contracted or mandated PSI activities, and notes that it will be those user Members who will be bound by the terms of the API. Article 1.4 defines the PSI entity as "any entity contracted or mandated by a Member to carry out preshipment inspection activities". Article 2 details the obligations of the user Members, and Article 2.1 requires that "preshipment inspection activities are carried out in a non-discriminatory manner, and that the procedures and criteria employed in the conduct of these activities are objective and applied on an equal basis to all exporters affected by such activities".

Article 2.20(b), dealing with price verification, requires that price comparison is to be undertaken only where "the prices of identical or similar goods offered for export from the same country of exportation at or about the same time, under competitive and comparable conditions of sale, in conformity with customary commercial practices and not of any applicable standard discounts". Under the scheme presented,

i PSI activities are to be carried out in a non-discriminatory manner – Article 2.1;
ii PSI inspections are to be performed in accordance with standards agreed between seller and buyers – Article 2.4;
iii PSI activities are to be carried out in a transparent manner – Articles 2.5 to 2.8;
iv Confidential information shall be respected – Articles 2.9 to 2.13;
v Conflict of interests are to be avoided – Article 2.14;
vi PSI activities are to be conducted without reasonable delay – Article 3;
vii Any disputes arising from the PSI operations shall be referred to an independent review procedure – Article 4; and
viii In the event such review procedure is unsuccessful, the matter may, at the behest of either party, be referred to the Independent Entity administered by the WTO – Articles 4(e) and (h).

5.4 Agreement on Rules of Origin

In an ideal world and a completely open economy, 'rules of origin' may not find a place in international trade. The use of 'rules of origin' entirely depends on the purpose for which the origin is determined, *viz.*, for imposition of customs duties; anti-dumping or countervailing duties; administering country specific tariff quotas, *etc.* The 'rules of origin' assist in implementing differential trade policies, *e.g.*, higher tariff rates for imports from developed country Member States than from least developed country Member States, and also for applying trade remedy measures.[161] Also, in modern day production, which uses value chains – where activities are coordinated across geographies, different components of a finished product come from different countries.

Member States use different rules to determine the country of origin of imported goods and also have different sets of preferential origin rules. Simply put, 'rules of origin' exist due to discriminatory restrictions on international trade. As globalisation has not fully levelled the playing field, the origin of a product determines the tariff rate and other border measures, and 'rules of origin' remain relevant for that reason. It is worth noting that the GATT 1947 did not have a set of rules to determine the origin of imported goods. During the Uruguay Round of negotiations, the consensus on the need for a multilateral framework on 'rules of origin' resulted in the Agreement on Rules of Origin, which is part of Annex 1A to the WTO Agreement. Article IX of the GATT permits Member States to have their own laws on marks of origin, which are not to be discriminatory.[162]

The WTO Agreement on Rules of Origin (ROO), which was drafted in conjunction with the WCO, does not seek to impose a set of rules on the Member States, but tolerates regulatory diversity in this respect.[163] Article 2(d) reads as follows:

> Until the work programme for the harmonization of rules of origin set out in Part IV is completed, Members shall ensure that:
> . . .
>
> (d) the rules of origin that they apply to imports and exports are not more stringent than the rules of origin they apply to determine whether or not a good is domestic and shall not discriminate between other Members, irrespective of the affiliation of the manufacturers of the good concerned.

The ROO contains four parts and two annexes and differentiates between non-preferential rules of origin and preferential rules of origin. Article 1.1 establishes that Parts I to IV apply exclusively to non-preferential origin rules, while Article 1.2 establishes that the ROO covers all rules of origin used in non-preferential commercial policy instruments. It is to be noted that most of the disciplines set out in the ROO concern non-preferential rules of origin. Some disciplines for preferential rules of origin are contained in Annex II. The WTO dispute settlement procedures will apply to any rule of origin disputes falling under ROO.[164] As per Article 9, the primary objective of ROO is to harmonise non-preferential rules of origin. Once the harmonisation process is complete, all Member States will be applying one set of non-preferential rules of origin for all purposes. During the transition period, *i.e.*, until the Harmonization Work Programme is completed, the Member States are required to administer rules of origin following the provisions contained in Article 2(a)–(k) of the ROO. The provisions of Article 2(a)–(k) enshrine the principles of non-discrimination and transparency.[165]

The multilateral disciplines covered under Article 2(a)–(k) and applicable during the transition period are detailed and include (i) transparency requirement – the rules applied are to be precise and unambiguous; (ii) prohibition on using rules of origin to pursue trade objectives; (iii) rules of origin applied shall not themselves create restrictive, distorting, or disruptive effects on international trade; (iv) national treatment requirement – rules of origin applied are not to be more stringent than the rules of origin the parties applied to determine whether or not a particular good is domestic; (v) MFN requirement – that rules of origin shall not discriminate between other Member States irrespective of the affiliation of the manufacturers of the good concerned; (vi) requirement that rules of origin shall be administered in a consistent, uniform, impartial, and reasonable manner; (vii) a requirement that rules of origin are based on positive standard, rather than state what does not confer origin (a negative standard); (viii) requirement to publish laws, regulations, judicial decisions, *etc.*, relating to rules of origin; (ix) requirements regarding the issuance of assessments of origin (no later than 150 days after the request) and the validity of the assessments (in principle, three years); (x) prohibition on the retroactive application of new or amended rules of origin; (xi) requirement that any administrative action taken relating to the determination of origin is reviewable promptly by an independent authority; and (xii) requirement to respect and treat all information provided for application of rules purposes as strictly confidential and not to disclose it without the specific permission of the person providing such information.[166]

6. Summary

International trade is premised on gaining access to markets for good and services in other countries. The multilateral trading system seeks to achieve this objective through negotiated market access commitments. Yet, these negotiated commitments on market access for goods and services can be hindered in numerous ways, *i.e.*, through both tariff and non-tariff barriers, which comprise customs and other duties on imports and export duties. It is well documented that tariff barriers have been significantly scaled down through tariff negotiations under the auspices of the GATT, but this has not stopped non-tariff barriers from becoming a true barrier. Not stopping with trade in goods, non-tariff barriers also affect trade in services. Other non-tariff barriers, such as lack of transparency, customs formalities and procedures, and government procurement laws and practices all pose serious hindrances to gaining access to markets for goods and services.

Notes

1 Customs duties still remain as one of the key sources of revenue in developing countries.
2 Tariffs are then multilateralised through the MFN principle to extend to all Member States.

3 See Panel Report, *Turkey – Textiles*, para. 9.63.
4 See Appellate Body Report, *India – Additional Import Duties*, para. 159, where tariffs are categorised as "the preferred trade policy instrument, whereas quantitative restrictions are in principle prohibited".
5 For a detailed discussion and review of the negotiating rounds of the GATT 1947, see Hoda (2018).
6 Most developing countries did not participate in the negotiations as they did not have a schedule of binding tariffs.
7 See chapter 2 for a discussion on the failed efforts taken by the developed nations for the creation of ITO in the immediate aftermath of WWII.
8 The Report of the Working Party notes, "[t]he article would impose no new obligations on contracting parties. Each contracting party would retain the right to decide whether or not to engage in negotiations or to participate in a tariff conference."
9 For a detailed review of the Kennedy Round, see Norwood (1969).
10 Interestingly, the 'single rate' system which is less complex than the 'Uruguay Round Approach' is used in Regional Trade Agreement (RTA) negotiations.
11 See Panel Report, *EC – IT Products*, paras. 7.372–7.384, where the legal status of the Information Technology Agreement (ITA) among the WTO agreements has been discussed in detail.
12 See Appellate Body Report, *Argentina – Textiles and Apparel*, para. 47.
13 See Appellate Body Report, *Chile – Price Band System*, para. 277.
14 See Appellate Body Report, *Argentina – Textiles and Apparel*, paras. 45 and 55.
15 *Ibid.*, paras. 47 and 53–55.
16 See Appellate Body Report, *China – Auto Parts*, para. 141, where it was held that to determine if a charge were internal or a border measure involved the examination of all three types of charges, *i.e.*, ODCs under first sentence of Article II:1(b); OCDs and charges under the second sentence of Article II:1(b); and internal charges and taxes under Article III:2.
17 See Appellate Body Report, *India – Additional Import Duties*, para. 157.
18 Matsushita *et al.* refer to ODCs as the 'unruly sibling' of customs duties. See Matsushita, Schoenbaum, Mavroidis and Hahn (2017).
19 See Appellate Body Report, *Argentina – Footwear*, para. 55, where the Appellate Body invalidated a 'statistical tax' as violative of Article II:1(b). See also Appellate Body Report *India – Additional Import Duties*, para. 159.
20 See Panel Report, *Dominican Republic – Import and Sale of Cigarettes*, paras. 7.113–114.
21 See Appellate Body Report, *India – Additional Import Duties*, para. 151.
22 See Panel Report, *Dominican Republic – Safeguards*, paras. 7.79–7.85.
23 See Appellate Body Report, *India – Additional Import Duties*, para. 153.
24 See Appellate Body Report, *EC – Bananas*, paras. 154–158.
25 See Appellate Body Report, *EC – Poultry*, para. 98.
26 See Appellate Body Report, *India – Additional Import Duties*, fn. 320.
27 *Ibid.*, paras. 170, 172, and 180.
28 *Ibid.*, paras. 175.
29 The concept of *erga omnes* obligation in international law refers to specific obligations that states have towards the international community as a whole. See the Barcelona Traction case (Belgium v Spain, 1962–1970), where the ICJ drew a distinction between *erga omnes* obligations, *i.e.*, the obligations that a State has towards the international community as a whole and in whose protection all states have a legal interest, and the obligations of a state *vis-à-vis* another state.
30 See Appellate Body Reports, *EC – Computer Equipment* and *EC – Chicken Cuts*.
31 The HS was established by the Customs Cooperation Council, which is now the WCO.
32 The Brussels Convention replaced the so-called Geneva Nomenclature of 1937.
33 The WCO Members are not required to become parties to the HS Convention. Also, as per Article 11(c) of the HS Convention, parties to the HS Convention are not required to be Members of the WCO.
34 For a more detailed discussion, see Feichtner (2010).
35 See Appellate Body Reports, *EC – Chicken Cuts* and *China – Auto Parts*.
36 See Appellate Body Report, *EC – Chicken Cuts*, para. 198.
37 Despite the fact that not all WTO Member States are parties to the HS Convention, all WTO Member States base their schedules on HS.

38 For instance, EU's Common Customs Tariff (CCT).
39 Export tariffs, or export duties, have remained largely unbound. Also, several RTAs specifically exclude export duties. See, for instance, Article 314, NAFTA. Note: Article II:1(b) is only concerned with importation and not with exports.
40 A specific tariff also includes weight, length, volume (litres), or numbers (pieces, dozens, *etc.*) of a particular good.
41 See Appellate Body Report, *Colombia – Textiles*, para. 1.3. Here, the measure under challenge involved a compound tariff, with an *ad valorem* component of 10 percent together with a specific component of US$1.75/pair, US$3/kg, US$5/kg, or US$5/pair depending on the product concerned and its declared f.o.b. price.
42 For instance, Indian customs duties on certain rayon fabrics are either 15 percent *ad valorem*, or Rs. 87 per square meter, whichever is higher.
43 See Appellate Body Report, *Argentina – Textiles and Apparel*, paras. 44–55.
44 Articles II:1 (b)–(c) refer to 'ordinary customs duties' and does not contain the term 'bound' duty in the text. Article XXVIII:2(a) *bis* uses the term 'binding'. See Bhala (2013) for a detailed discussion.
45 The Uruguay Round of Agreement on Agriculture (URAA) created over 1,300 TRQs for agricultural products, which replaced quantitative restrictions.
46 TRQs have four components, *viz.*, an in-quota tariff, a quota defining the maximum volume of imports charged the in-quota tariff, an over-quota tariff, and a method of quota administration. See Skully (2001) for details.
47 For instance, Article 17(6)(ii) of the Anti-Dumping Agreement reads as follows:
    the panel shall interpret the relevant provisions of the Agreement in accordance with customary rules of interpretation of public international law. Where the panel finds that a relevant provision of the Agreement admits of more than one permissible interpretation, the panel shall find the authorities' measure to be in conformity with the Agreement if it rests upon one of those permissible interpretations.
48 See, for instance, Appellate Body Reports, *US – Gasoline*, p. 17; *Japan – Alcoholic Beverages II*, p. 10; *India – Patent (US)*, para. 46.
49 As a tool of interpretation, *effet utile* assists in extending the meaning of the wording outside the boundaries of its literal sense. However, this principle was not included in the VCLT, as the drafters apprehended that it would open the door to a strong teleological interpretation. Article 31 of the VCLT states, "[a] treaty shall be interpreted in good faith in accordance with the ordinary meaning", and an *effet utile* assisted interpretation could possibly lead to unwritten powers being read into treaties. See, for instance, *Interpretation of Peace Treaties with Bulgaria, Hungary and Romania (Advisory Opinion, Second Phase)* [1950] ICJ Rep 228 f, where the ICJ did reluctantly express elements of *effet utile*.
50 See Appellate Body Report, *US – Offset Act (Byrd Amendment)*, para. 271.
51 Šadl describes the principle of *effet utile* as "a rhetorical instrument used to persuade Member States to accept judicial doctrines and the ensuing powers of the Court without having to compromise the coherence and continuity of law in the process", and Pickard considers it as being "distinct from the 'object and purpose' standard in that it is an extension of the teleological approach of the Vienna Convention", and expresses the view that the approach taken by *effet utile* and the VCLT complement each other. See Šadl (2015), p. 21 and Pickard (2017), p. 11.
52 Van Damme notes that adherence to the provisions of the Vienna Convention was "instrumental in justifying and making acceptable [the AB's] early choice to function as a court and thus to build its judicial identity." See Van Damme (2010), p. 606.
53 The author adopts the phrase "multilateral acts of special character" to describe the Schedules of Commitments, which is the language used in the dissenting opinion by Judge Alvarez in *Anglo-Iranian Oil Co* case (Jurisdiction) [1952] ICJ Reports 93.
54 The publication of the WTO Secretariat goes on to state, "the Schedules are part of the Agreement and have the same legal status as any of the WTO agreements, such as the General Agreement on Tariffs and Trade (GATT) and the General Agreement on Trade in Services (GATS)." See WTO Secretariat (2009).
55 Similarly, Article XX:3 of the GATS reads, "Schedules of specific commitments shall be annexed to this Agreement and shall form an integral part thereof."
56 See Appellate Body Report, *EC – Computer Equipment*, para. 109.

57 *Ibid.*; See also Appellate Body Reports, *EC – Poultry*, paras. 82–83, and *EC – Chicken Cuts*, paras. 148 and 175.
58 Article 102 of the UN Charter reads as follows: "Every treaty and every international agreement entered into by any Member of the United Nations after the present Charter comes into force shall as soon as possible be registered with the Secretariat and published by it."
59 See Appellate Body Report, *EC – Computer Equipment*, para. 84.
60 See Panel Report, *EC – Chicken Cuts*, para. 7.87.
61 *Ibid.*, para. 7.88.
62 See Appellate Body Report, *EC – Chicken Cuts*, para. 272.
63 *Ibid.*, para. 289.
64 *Ibid.*, paras. 308–309.
65 Interestingly, the Telecommunications Reference Paper was negotiated by WTO Member States and outlined the principles of competition regulation in the telecoms sector.
66 Article 31(4) of the VCLT reads as follows: "A special meaning shall be given to a term if it is established that the parties so intended."
67 See Panel Report, *Mexico – Telecoms*, para. 7.108.
68 *Ibid.*, para. 7.110.
69 See Appellate Body Report, *US – FSC (Article 21.5)*, paras. 141–142, fn. 121.
70 England abolished all export duties in 1842, France in 1857, and Prussia in 1865.
71 The report identifies both export taxes and quantitative restrictions on exports and presents the examples of Latin American countries, where export taxes were imposed on coffee for revenue purposes, and Mexico, where export taxes were imposed for revenue purposes.
72 Also, the US Constitution prohibits the levy of taxes on exports. The US Constitutional provision, *i.e.*, Export Clause, contained in Article I, § 9, cl 5 provides, "[no] Tax or duty shall be laid on Articles exported from any State". Although historical and drafted in the eighteenth century, the Export Clause found a new lease of life in the twenty-first century. See Jensen (2003) for an analysis of the Export Clause of the US Constitution.
73 Member States exporting raw materials and agricultural products widely impose export duties. Some Member States consider export duties as 'indirect subsidies' to domestic downstream industries.
74 The domestic downstream industries will access the good at a lower price.
75 See Report of the Working Party (2011), para. 623. During the negotiations, Russia had indicated that over the last few years (before the WTO accession process), the overall number of its products subject to export duties were reduced from 1,200 to 310 tariff lines.
76 This, in the author's view, renders the WTO discipline on export restrictions ineffective.
77 China, for instance, was made to agree to legally binding commitments with regards to export taxes when it acceded to the WTO on 11 December 2001.
78 For instance, during the accession of Ukraine to the WTO, where Ukraine undertook to reduce its export duties, which was noted in the Report of the Working Party on the Accession of Ukraine § 240 as follows: "The representative of Ukraine confirmed that . . . Ukraine would reduce export duties in accordance with the binding schedule contained in Table 20(b). He also confirmed that as regards these products, Ukraine would not increase export duties, nor apply other measures having an equivalent effect, unless justified under the exceptions of GATT 1994."
79 See Articles VII, VIII, and XVII of the GATT.
80 Emphasis added.
81 See note 76.
82 The minerals in question were bauxite, coke, fluorspar, magnesium, manganese, silicon metal, zinc, and yellow phosphorus.
83 See Panel Report, *China – Raw Materials*, paras. 7.77, 7.81, 7.89, 7.93, 7.98, and 7.101 with regards to various minerals.
84 This aspect renders the WTO's general discipline on export restrictions ineffective. See Qin (2016).
85 The Member States identified here are developing countries, who became Members much later than 1995 when the WTO was founded. Also, the obligations contained in the Accession Protocol are considered non-negotiable and not susceptible to change.
86 See Panel Report, *China – Rare Earth*, para. 7.48.
87 This is keeping in line with core objectives of the WTO and GATT, and to prevent 'beggar thy neighbour' practices. Also, the proposal builds upon existing GATT rules on export duties and

charges, *inter alia* GATT Articles I, VII, VIII, and XVII, as well as incorporates other key elements of the GATT *acquis*.

88 Agricultural products are excluded where export taxes are currently in force in many developing countries.
89 Non-tariff barriers are also sometimes referred to as non-tariff measures. For the purposes of consistency, the acronym NTB has been used throughout this book to refer to non-tariff barriers/measures.
90 Measures identified do not include ordinary customs duties and other duties and charges on imports and exports.
91 For a detailed analysis of various types of NTBs, see OECD (2005).
92 As tariffs are bound, countries tend to respond through the introduction of alternate, secondary trade barriers.
93 See Panel Report, *Turkey – Textiles*, para. 9.63, where the Panel noted that prohibition against quantitative restrictions was a reflection that tariffs are GATT's border protection 'of choice', and that they impose absolute limits on imports.
94 *Ibid.*, para. 9.64, where the Panel noted that the GATT contracting parties "over many years failed to respect completely" the obligation not to impose quantitative restrictions.
95 *Ibid.*, para. 9.65.
96 Paragraphs 2 and 3 of the Understanding provides that the Member States should seek to avoid the imposition of new quantitative restrictions for balance-of-payments purposes.
97 The Agreement on Safeguards evidences a preference for the use of tariffs, and Article 6 provides that provisional safeguard measures "should take the form of tariff increases", and Article 11 prohibits the use of voluntary export restraints.
98 Under the Agreement on Agriculture, quantitative restrictions other than NTBs were prohibited. The Member States had to proceed to a 'tariffication' exercise to transform quantitative restrictions into tariff-based measures. This was despite the fact that contracting parties, for over 48 years, had been relying a great deal on import restrictions and other NTBs.
99 See Panel Report, *India – Quantitative Restrictions*, paras. 5.122–5.144.
100 See GATT Panel Report, *Canada – FIRA*.
101 Such notifications received from the Member States are to contain the following comprehensive details, *viz.*, a general description of the restriction imposed; the type of restriction imposed; the relevant tariff line code; a detailed product description; the WTO justification for the measure concerned; the domestic legal basis for the restriction imposed; information on the administration of the restriction imposed; and, wherever relevant, an explanation of the modification of a previously notified restriction. The WTO Secretariat maintains a database of quantitative restrictions notified by Member States, to which Member States and the general public may consult.
102 See Panel Report, *Canada – Periodicals*, paras. 5.4–5.5.
103 See generally Panel Report, *Canada – Provincial Liquor Boards (US)*.
104 See Panel Reports, *Japan – Semi-Conductors* and *China – Raw Materials*, paras. 7.172–7.175 – an example for minimum export price systems.
105 See Panel Report, *Japan – Semi-Conductors*.
106 See Panel Reports, *India – Quantitative Restrictions*, para. 5.122 and *China – Raw Materials*, para. 7.918.
107 See Panel Reports, *EEC – Minimum Import Prices*, para. 4.14 – an example for minimum import price systems.
108 See Panel Report, *US – Manufacturing Clause*, para. 34.
109 See Panel Report, *EEC – Minimum Import Prices*, para. 4.14.
110 See Panel Report, *US – Shrimp*, para. 7.17.
111 See Panel Report, *India – Autos*, para. 5.233.
112 See Panel Report, *Colombia – Ports of Entry*, para. 7.275.
113 See Panel Report, *Argentina – Financial Services*, paras. 7.1067–7.1069.
114 See Appellate Body Report, *Argentina – Import Measures*, paras. 5.219–5.220.
115 See Panel Report, *Dominican Republic – Import and Sale of Cigarettes*, para. 7.261.
116 The raw materials in question were bauxite, coke, fluorspar, magnesium, silicon carbide, yellow phosphorus, and zinc. See Panel Report *China – Raw Materials*, para. 8.20.
117 See Appellate Body Report, *China – Raw Materials*, para. 320.
118 See Appellate Body Report, *Argentina – Import Measures*, para. 5.217.

119 See Panel Report, *India – Quantitative Restrictions*, para. 5.129.
120 See Panel Report, *India – Autos*, para. 7.269.
121 *Ibid.*, para. 7.270.
122 See Appellate Body Report, *China – Raw Materials*, paras. 319–320.
123 See GATT Panel Report, *Japan – Semi-Conductors*, para. 106.
124 *Ibid.*, paras. 104–117.
125 See GATT Panel Report, *EC – Oilseeds I*.
126 See Panel Report, *Colombia – Ports of Entry*, para. 7.275.
127 See Panel Report, *Brazil – Retreaded Tyres*, para. 7.372.
128 See Panel Report, *EC – Oilseeds I*, para. 150. See also Panel Report, *EEC – Minimum Import Prices*, para. 4.1, where it was held that that automatic import licensing does not constitute a restriction of the type coming within the ambit of Article XI:1.
129 (Footnote original) We note that our understanding of Article XI:1 of the GATT 1994 is supported by two provisions of the Import Licensing Agreement that suggest that certain import licensing procedures may result in some burden without themselves having trade restrictive effects on imports. Footnote 4 of the Import Licensing Agreement provides that "import licensing procedures requiring a security which have no restrictive effects on imports are to be considered as falling within the scope of [Article 2]", which deals with automatic import licensing. In addition, Article 3.2 of the Import Licensing Agreement provides that, while "[n]onautomatic licensing shall not have trade restrictive . . . effects on imports additional to those caused by the imposition of the restriction", such procedures "shall be no more administratively burdensome than absolutely necessary to administer the measure."
130 See Appellate Body Report, *Argentina – Import Measures*, para. 5.217. See also Panel Report, *EU – Energy Package*, paras. 7.974–7.975.
131 See Panel Report, *Indonesia – Import Licensing Regimes*, para. 7.50.
132 See Panel Report, *Colombia – Ports of Entry*, para. 7.252.
133 See Panel Report, *Argentina – Hides and Leather*, para. 11.17.
134 See Panel Report, *Argentina – Hides and Leather*, para. 11.21.
135 See Panel Report, *EC – Bananas*, para. 56.
136 Professor Bhala notes that that this was achieved following the heated debate that took place in London, which resulted in the London Compromise. See Bhala (2013).
137 See Panel Report, *China – Raw Materials*, paras. 7.238–7.353.
138 See GATT Panel Report, *Canada – Herring and Salmon*, para. 4.2.
139 See GATT Panel Report, *Canada – Ice Cream Yoghurt*, para. 62.
140 See Panel Report, *China – Raw Materials*, para. 7.213.
141 *Ibid.*, para. 7.351.
142 *Ibid.*, para. 7.346.
143 *Ibid.*, para. 7.351.
144 See Appellate Body Report, *China – Raw Materials*, para. 323.
145 *Ibid.*, para. 321.
146 Customs fees and charges belong to a broader group of non-tariff barriers commonly referred to as "para-tariff measures". The Dictionary of Trade Policy Terms (Goode, 2020), states that para-tariff is "sometimes used for charges levied on imports instead of, or in addition to, tariffs. These can consist of service fees, additional import surcharges or other fees levied on imported products inside the market".
147 See generally Appellate Body Report, *EC – Chicken Cuts*, where the question of classification of 'salted' chicken under 02.10 of the EC Schedules of Commitments arose for consideration.
148 This provision, nevertheless, allowed GATT's Contracting Parties substantial flexibility in defining the value of imported goods.
149 However, not all GATT Contracting Parties joined the Customs Valuation Code, and as of 31 December 1993, the Customs Valuation Code was only signed by 34 countries from the GATT era. The Tokyo Round Codes were not core GATT obligations applicable to all GATT contracting parties, but rather were stand-alone legal instruments negotiated under GATT auspices and existing side by side, but not fully integrated into GATT. See Bhala and Kennedy (1998).
150 Agreement on Implementation of Article VII of the General Agreement on Tariffs and Trade 1994 (Customs Valuation Agreement) is an integral part of the WTO Agreement, *i.e.*, Article II:2 of the WTO Agreement. See also Appellate Body Report, *Colombia – Textiles*, para. 5.38, where

it was noted that the "general valuation principles" set out in Article VII of the GATT 1994 are further elaborated in the Customs Valuation Agreement.
151 The Preamble to the CVA recalls "the need for a fair, uniform and neutral system for the valuation of the goods for customs purposes that precludes the use of arbitrary or fictitious customs value".
152 See Panel Report, *Thailand – Cigarettes (Philippines)*, paras. 7.134–7.223.
153 See Panel Report, *Colombia – Ports of Entry*, paras. 7.61–7.153.
154 See Panel Report, *Thailand – Cigarettes (Philippines)*, paras. 7.333–7.362.
155 The 'fallback' methods should be consistent with GATT Article VII and with the provisions of the Customs Valuation agreement. See Rege (2002) for a discussion on Customs Valuation Agreement.
156 See Appellate Body Report, *EC – Bananas III*, para. 195, where it was ruled that import licensing procedures for TRQs are within the scope of the AILP.
157 *Ibid.*, para. 204.
158 See Appellate Body Report, *EC – Bananas III*, para. 197 *etc.*, where it was ruled that the requirements of Article 1.3 concern the application and administration of the licensing rules rather than the rules as such. See also Panel Report, *EC – Poultry*, para. 254.
159 See Panel Report, *EC – Poultry*, para. 246, where the Panel rejected Brazil's claim that frequent changes to the licensing rules and procedures regarding poultry TRQ had made it difficult for governments and traders to become familiar with the rules, contrary to the provisions of Article 1.4, 3.3, 3.5(b), 3.5(c), and 3.5(d).
160 It was aimed at avoiding capital flight by both importers and exporters.
161 Rules of origin also come in implementing trade policies outside the WTO framework, *i.e.*, when applying low or zero tariff on imports from PTA partners.
162 GATT Article IX:4.
163 The ROO does not seek to harmonise but only commences the process of harmonisation of the laws and procedures on rules of origin.
164 See Panel Report, *US – Textiles Rules of Origin*, paras. 6.190 et seq. and para. 6.271 et seq., where India challenged two US 'rule of origin' requirements applicable to textiles and apparel under ss. 334 and 405 of the Uruguay Round Agreements Act. The rules required that a yard of fibre to be produced in the exporting country for that country to be considered the country of origin. The Panel ruled that India failed to prove any inconsistency between the US rules of origin and the WTO ROO.
165 ROO Article 2.
166 Although contained in Article 2(a)–(k), these principles resonate with the principles contained in Articles I, III, and X of the GATT 1994.

Bibliography

Bagwel, Kyle, Robert W. Staiger and Alan O. Sykes. 'Border Instruments,' in Horn, Henrick and Petros C. Mavroidis (eds.) *Legal and Economic Principles of World Trade Law* (Cambridge University Press, 2013) 68–204.

Bhala, Raj. *Modern GATT Law: A Treatise on the Law and Political Economy of the General Agreement on Tariffs and Trade and Other World Trade Organization Agreements* Vol 1 (Sweet & Maxwell Publishers, 2013).

Bhala, Raj and Kevin John Kennedy. *World Trade Law: The GATT-WTO System, Regional Arrangements, and US Law* (Lexis Law Publishing, 1998).

Chow, Daniel C.K. and Thomas J. Schoenbaum. *International Trade Law: Problems, Cases, and Materials* (Wolters Kluwer Law & Business, 2017).

Crosby, Daniel. 'WTO Legal Status and Evolving Practice of Export Taxes,' *Bridges* Vol 12, No 5 (2008).

Dam, Kenneth E. *The GATT* (The University of Chicago Press, 1970) 57–58.

De Gorter, Harry and Erika Kliauga. 'Reducing Tariffs versus Expanding Tariff Rate Quotas,' in Anderson, Kym and Will Martin (eds.) *Agricultural Trade Reform and the Doha Development Agenda* (Palgrave Macmillan Publishing and the World Bank, 2006) 117–160.

Ederington, Josh and Michele Ruta. 'Nontariff Measures and the World Trading System,' in Bagwell, Kyle and Staiger (eds.) *Handbook of Commercial Policy 1, Part B* (Elsevier Publication, 2016) 211–277.

Ehring, Lothar and Gian Franco Chianale. 'Export Restrictions in the Field of Energy,' in Selivanova, Y. (ed.) *Regulation of Energy in International Trade Law: WTO, NAFTA and Energy Charter* (Kluwer Law International, 2012).

Espa, Ilaria. *Export Restrictions on Critical Minerals and Metals: Testing the Adequacy of WTO Disciplines* (Cambridge University Press, 2015).

Fabbricotti, Alberta. 'Article XXVIII *bis*,' in Wolfrum, Rüdiger, Peter-Tobias Stoll and Holger Hestermeyer (eds.) *WTO-Trade in Goods* (Martin Nijhoff Publishers, 2011).

Feichtner, Isabel. 'The Administration of the Vocabulary of International Trade: The Adaptation of WTO Schedules to Changes in the Harmonized System,' in Bogdandy, Armin von, Rüdiger Wolfrum, Jochen von Bernstorff Philipp Dann and Matthias Goldmann (eds.) *The Exercise of Public Authority by International Institutions: Advancing International Institutional Law* (Springer International, 2010) 439–474.

Forrester, Ian and Omar E. Odarda. 'The Agreement on Customs Valuation,' in Macrory, Patrick F.J., Arthur E. Appleton and Michael G. Plummer (eds.) *The WTO: Legal, Economic and Political Analysis* Vol 1 (Springer, 2005) 531–572.

GATT Review Working Party II Report. 'Schedules and Customs Administration,' GATT document L/329, BISD 3S/205 (26 February 1955).

Giordani, Paola, Nadia Rocha and Michele Ruta. 'Food Prices and the Multiplier Effect of Trade Policy,' *IMF Working Paper, WP14/182* (2014).

Goode, Walter. *Dictionary of Trade Policy Terms* (Cambridge University Press, 2020).

Harris, Rachel and Gillian Moon. 'GATT Article XX and Human Rights: What Do We Know from the First 2 Years?,' *Melbourne Journal of International Law* Vol 16 (2015) 1–52.

Hoda, Anwarul. *Tariff Negotiations and Renegotiations under the GATT and the WTO: Procedures and Practices* (Cambridge University Press, 2018).

Hudec, Robert E. *The GATT Legal System and World Trade Diplomacy* (Butterworths Legal Publishers, 1990).

Hufbauer, Gary Clyde, Jeffrey J. Schott and Woan Foong Wong. *Figuring Out the Doha Round* Vol 91 (Columbia University Press, 2010).

Irwin, Douglas A., Petros C. Mavroidis and Alan O. Sykes. *The Genesis of the GATT* (Cambridge University Press, 2008).

Jensen, Erik M. 'The Export Clause,' *Florida Tax Review* Vol 6, No 1 (2003) 1–75.

Kazeki, Jun. 'Export Duties,' in *Looking beyond Tariffs: The Role of Non-Tariff Barriers in World Trade*, OECD Trade Policy Studies (OECD Publishing, 2005) 177–199.

Kennedy, Kevin. 'GATT 1994,' in Macrory, Patrick F.J., Arthur E. Appleton and Michael G. Plummer (eds.) *The WTO: Legal, Economic and Political Analysis* Vol 1 (Springer, 2005) 89–186.

Jackson, John H. *World Trade and the Law of GATT: A Legal Analysis of the General Agreement on Tariffs and Trade* (The Michie Company, 1969).

Latina, Joelle, Roberta Piermartini and Michele Ruta. 'Natural Resources and Non-Cooperative Trade Policy,' *WTO Staff Working Paper* (2011).

Lester, Simon, Bryan Mercurio and Arwel Davies. *World Trade Law: Text, Materials and Commentary* (Hart Publishing, 2018).

Lowenfeld, Andreas F. *International Economic Law* (Oxford University Press, 2008).

Martin, Will and Kym Martin. 'Export Restrictions and Price Insulation during Commodity Price Booms,' *World Bank Policy Research Working Paper 5645* (2011).

Matsushita, Mitsuo. 'Export Control of Natural Resources: WTO Panel Ruling on the Chinese Export Restrictions of Natural Resources,' *Trade Law and Development* Vol 3, No 2 (2011) 267–295.

Matsushita, Mitsuo, Thomas J. Shoenbaum, Petros C. Mavroidis and Michael Hahn. *The World Trade Organization: Law, Practice, and Policy* (Oxford University Press, 2017).

Norwood, Bernard. 'The Kennedy Round: A Try at Linear Trade Negotiations,' *The Journal of Law and Economics* Vol 12, No 2 (1969) 297–319.

OECD. *Looking beyond Tariffs: The Role of Non-Tariff Barriers in World Trade*, OECD Trade Policy Studies (OECD Publishing, 2005).

Peat, Daniel. 'Interpretation of Schedules of Commitments in the WTO,' in *Comparative Reasoning in International Courts and Tribunals* (Cambridge University Press, 2019) 83–106.

Pickard, Duncan. 'Judicial Interpretation at the European Court of Justice as a Feature of Supranational Law,' *European Union Law Working Papers, No. 20* (2017).

Qin, Julia Ya. 'Reforming WTO Discipline on Export Duties: Sovereign Over Natural Resources, Economic Development and Environmental Protection,' in Matsushita, Mitsuo and Thomas J. Schoenbaum (eds.) *Emerging Issues in Sustainable Development: International Trade Law and Policy Relating to Natural Resources, Energy, and the Environment* (Springer, 2016) 139–182.

Rege, Vinod. 'Customs Valuation and Customs Reform,' in Hoekman, Bernard, Aaditya Mattoo and Philip English (eds.) *Development, Trade, and the WTO* (World Bank Publication, 2002) 128–138.

Report of the US Special Committee on Relaxation of Trade Barriers (8 December 1943, International Trade Files, Lot File 57D-284).

Report of the Working Party on the Accession of Russia, WT/ACC/RUS/70 (17 November 2011).

Ruta, Michele and Anthony J. Venebles. 'International Trade in Natural Resources: Practice and Policy,' *Annual Review of Resource Economics* Vol 4, No 1 (2012) 331–352.

Šadl, Urška. 'The Role of *Effet Utile* in Preserving the Continuity and Authority of European Union Law: Evidence from the Citation Web of the Pre-Accession Case Law of the Court of Justice of the EU,' *European Journal of Legal Studies* Vol 8, No 1 (2015) 18–45.

Santana, Roy and Lee Ann Jackson. 'Identifying Non-Tariff Barriers: Evolution of Multilateral Instruments and Evidence from the Disputes (1948–2011),' *World Trade Review* Vol 11, No 3 (2012) 462–478.

Skully, David W. 'Liberalizing Tariff-Rate Quotas,' in Burfisher, Mary (ed.) *Agricultural Policy Reform in the WTO-the Road Ahead*, Economic Research Services/USDA (AgEcon Publishers, 2001) 59–67.

Staiger, Robert W. 'Non-Tariff Measures and the WTO,' *WTO Staff Working Paper, No. ERSD-2012–01* (2012).

Sutherland, Peter, Jagdish Bhagwati, Kwesi Botchwey, Niall W.A. Fitzgerald, Koichi Hamada, John H. Jackson, Celso Lafer and Thierry de Montbrial. 'The Future of the WTO: Addressing Institutional Challenges in the New Millennium,' Report of the Consultative Board to the Director-General Supachai Panitchpakdi (WTO, 2004).

Trebilcock, Michael, Robert Howse and Antonia Eliason. *The Regulation of International Trade* (Routledge, 2013).

Van Damme, Isabelle. 'The Interpretation of Schedules of Commitments,' *Journal of World Trade* Vol 41, No 1 (2007) 1–52.

Van Damme, Isabelle. 'Treaty Interpretation by the WTO Appellate Body,' *The European Journal of International Law* Vol 21, No 3 (2010) 605–648.

Van den Bossche, Peter and Werner Zdouc. *The Law and Policy of the World Trade Organization* (Cambridge University Press, 2017).

UN Economic and Social Council. Preparatory Committee of The International Conference On Trade and Employment, UN Doc. EPCT/C.II/36 (31 October 1946) <www.wto.org/gatt_docs/English/SULPDF/90210244.PDF> (accessed 10 May 2020).

UN Economic and Social Council. Second Session of the Preparatory Committee of the United Nations Conference of Trade and Employment, UN Doc. EPCT/A/PV/40(1) (15 August 1947) <www.wto.org/gatt_docs/English/SULPDF/90240203.PDF> (accessed 10 May 2020).

WTO. Decision of the Council for Trade in Goods, WTO Doc. G/L/59 (10 January 1996), Decision on Notification Procedures for Quantitative Restrictions, adopted on 1 December 1995.

WTO. 'Market Access: Unfinished Business: Post Uruguay Round Inventory and Issues,' *WTO Special Studies, No 6* (2001).

WTO. 'Market Access for Non-Agricultural Products, Revised Submission on Export Taxes,' TN/MA/W/101 (17 January 2008).

WTO. Decision of the Council for Trade in Goods, WTO Doc. G/L/59 Rev. 1 (3 July 2012a), Decision on Notification Procedures for Quantitative Restrictions, adopted on 27 June 2012.

WTO. World Trade Report 2012: Trade and Public Policies: A Closer Look at Non-Tariff Measures in the 21st Century (WTO, 2012b).

WTO Secretariat. *A Handbook on Reading WTO Goods and Services Schedules* (Cambridge University Press, 2009).

8 Economic Emergency Measures

Learning Objectives		275
1.	Introduction	276
2.	The Political Economy of Safeguards	277
3.	The Safeguard Regime Under GATT/WTO	278
	3.1 Formation of Safeguard Measures in the GATT and WTO	278
	3.2 Uruguay Round and Beyond	279
4.	Article XIX GATT and the Safeguard Agreement	280
	4.1 Safeguard Agreement	280
	4.1.1 Investigation and Provisional Application	282
	4.1.2 Increased Imports and 'Unforeseen Development'	283
	4.1.3 Determination of Injury	284
	4.1.3.1 Serious Injury and Threat of Serious Injury	285
	4.1.3.2 Factors to Be Considered	286
	4.1.3.3 Identifying the Relevant Domestic Industry	287
	4.1.3.4 Causation and Non-Attribution	288
5.	Special Safeguard Measures Under WTO Agreements	289
	5.1 Special Safeguard Measures Under Agreement on Agriculture	290
	5.2 Emergency Safeguard Measures Under GATS	291
6.	Balance-of-Payments Measures	292
	6.1 Political Economy of BOP Measures and the GATT	292
	6.2 Balance-of-Payments Measures Under GATT 1994	294
	6.2.1 Nature and Scope of Balance-of-Payments Measures	294
	6.3 Balance-of-Payments Measures Under GATS	298
7.	Summary	299

Learning Objectives

This chapter aims to help students understand:

1. Safeguard measures; political economy of safeguard measures;
2. Safeguard measures under GATT and the WTO; the formation of safeguard measures in the GATT and WTO;
3. Article XIX of the GATT and the Safeguard Agreement; investigation and provisional application;
4. Determination of injury under the Agreement, serious injury and threat of serious injury; factors to be considered in the investigation;

DOI: 10.4324/9780367028183-10

276 *General Exceptions, Non-Tariff Barriers*

5   Identifying the relevant domestic industry; causation and non-attribution;
6   Special safeguard measures under WTO agreements; and
7   Balance-of-payments measures.

1. Introduction

Other than general exception and security exceptions, which were discussed in earlier chapters, the WTO also provides for economic emergency exceptions. These come in the shape of safeguard measures and balance-of-payments measures. The safeguard measures contained in GATT 1994 and the Agreement on Safeguards are the most frequently invoked provisions within the multilateral framework. Such measures are invoked to protect the domestic industries from economic harm caused by an unprecedented surge in imports.[1] For maintaining the stability of the multilateral trading system, it is imperative that the Member States are bound by their negotiated concessions for imports. Although safeguard measures run contrary to trade liberalisation, they are yet recognised as necessary for providing a 'breathing space' for the protected domestic industry and to improve their competitiveness (Hahn, 2005). The rationale behind safeguard measures is that multilateral trade with the bound tariffs may expose domestic industries to an unprecedented surge in imports and competition that could potentially lead to serious injury. There is, therefore, a need for measures that permit *ex post* adjustment of levels of binding built into the multilateral trade mechanism. The safeguard measures could take the shape of temporary tariffs, quotas, TRQs, or other measures. It is no exaggeration to state that all international trade agreements do contain safeguard provisions and exceptions, which permit governments in certain circumstances to derogate from their obligations. The justification for this is to be found in the Preamble to the Agreement on Safeguards (SGA), which refers to the "importance of structural adjustment".

Safeguard measures are unilateral by nature and are introduced to provide additional protection, albeit temporary, to the domestic industry of a Member State. The safeguard measures, along with anti-dumping and countervailing duties (both discussed in later chapters of this book), form part of the suite of trade remedies available to the Member States. Unlike anti-dumping duties (AD), which seek to offset unfair pricing by foreign exporters, and counter vailing duties (CVD), which seek to level the playing field between foreign government-subsidised exporters and domestic producers, safeguard measures provide a shield to domestic manufacturers, albeit temporarily, from foreign competitors. Also, unlike AD measures, which are country specific, safeguard measures are non-discriminatory. Safeguard measures, alongside AD and CVD, are classified as trade remedies. Although considered a contingent trade protection measure, safeguards are *per se* not considered a retaliatory measure for unfair trade practices, as they are employed to restrict legally and fairly traded imports from causing any harm to domestic industries, *i.e.*, decrease in local production and in price. The Appellate Body in *US – Line Pipe* had the opportunity to clarify this position with the following observation:

> they are remedies that are imposed in the form of import restrictions in the absence of any allegation of an unfair trade practice. In this, safeguard measures differ from, for example, anti-dumping duties and countervailing duties to counter subsidies, which are both measures taken in response to unfair trade practices. If the conditions for their imposition are fulfilled, safeguard measures may thus be imposed on the

"fair trade" of other WTO Members and, by restricting their imports, will prevent those WTO Members from enjoying the full benefit of trade concessions under the WTO Agreement.[2]

2. The Political Economy of Safeguards

One of the primary outcomes of trade liberalisation is an increase in trade flow. Increase in imports, resulting from trade concessions, can cause a momentous strain on the competing domestic industry leading to unemployment. The economic effect may not stop with unemployment in the particular domestic sector, but may go beyond that, *i.e.*, on related industries. Prof Lee notes that economic difficulties often transform into social and political turmoil (Lee, 2014). The economic justifications for the safeguards policy are twofold, *viz.*, safeguard measures do not require allegations of unfair trade practice (AD measures), as their justification rests on injury due to unforeseen surges of fairly traded imports; and safeguards are designed to protect a domestic industry from all imports, irrespective of their source (Bown and Crowley, 2003). Yet, it is not guaranteed that such safeguard measures will induce the shielded domestic industries to make necessary adjustments, an argument which is strengthened by the instance of the US steel industry that received continued protection but failed to make any structural changes (Lee, 2014). There is also the case of the US automobile industry, which faced a decline in the 1980s due to reliable and efficient Japanese imports but was able to rebound in the 1990s through effecting changes. The justification of safeguard measures from a purely economic perspective is controversial (Sykes, 2006). Prof Lee fires a salvo of caution, reminding that not all industries can be made competitive against imports by way of protection.

From a political economy perspective, safeguard measures are the policy of choice to shield any domestic industry that could potentially face hardship from imports. The arguments for protection are based on the premise that governments have distributional concerns when they draft tariff policies. Here, the safeguard measures introduced seek not only to protect the industry but also to prevent job losses. When safeguards are understood by trade negotiators that they are only a temporary measure and can be relaxed, they could facilitate the granting of trade concessions. There is an assumption that governments choose policies to maximise a weighted social welfare function, with the weights reflecting the ability of interest groups to organise and lobby the government (Grossman and Helpman, 1994). Beshkar and Bond note that in the political economy models the two key prerequisites to invoke the safeguard measures, *viz.*, surge in imports and injury to domestic industries, are absent (Beshkar and Bond, 2016). Sykes, on the other hand, argues that the prior two requirements are included in the agreement on safeguard measures as they mirror the conditions under which political pressures for protection are likely to rise (Sykes, 1991, 2006).

Three political economy reasons for imposing safeguard measures can be put into three categories, *viz.*, firstly the notion that safeguard measures afford a political 'safety valve' for protectionist measures – this allows for safeguard measures to be introduced as an administrative process avoiding legislative perusal; secondly safeguard measures facilitate deviation from trade commitments when the political pressure to do so is intense; and thirdly safeguard measures may be useful as they reduce the risk of trade concessions where there is political uncertainty (Sykes, 2006). A study through the lens of social welfare function model demonstrates the reason that political pressure rises when industries suffer losses in an import-competing sector, which in turn triggers protectionist pressure from the firms. The escape clauses provide a means for dealing with such pressure. Beshkar and Bond observe that political economy models present a "promising avenue" for understanding some features of the escape clause (Beshkar and Bond, 2016). Although they serve as a 'safety valve' against harmful effects of free trade and enable liberalisation of trade, safeguard measures could also become the cause for trade distortions (Das, 2005). As postulated by Sykes, safeguards allow the negotiators/politicians to go the extra mile in trade liberalisation, more than they would have been able to because of domestic pressure (Sykes, 2003).

Functioning as an insurance mechanism, safeguards permit governments to develop policies, taking calculated risks, purse a longer-term free trade strategy, and provide a transition period for domestic industries that are faced with competition as a direct result of trade liberalisation. This transition phase also allows governments to carry out economic changes at the appropriate levels ('macro' or 'micro') to ready the firms to compete with competition. Commentators take the view that the key reason for inclusion of safeguards in trade agreements is that it provides the contracting parties with the flexibility *ex post*, which, besides providing insurance to the governments, also encourages cooperation in the negotiation phase (Hoekman and Kostecki, 2009).

3. The Safeguard Regime Under GATT/WTO

Article XIX GATT, entitled 'Emergency Action on Imports of Particular Products', regulates safeguard measures. As mentioned earlier, Article XIX GATT and the SGA allow Member States in certain circumstances to suspend binding commitments with regards to imports, if it is considered harmful to the domestic industry. From the very beginning of the GATT era, it was foreseen that Contracting Parties may be constrained to relieve themselves from the obligations of tariff commitments. Article XIX was designed to provide a fallback option for cases where particular domestic industries were affected due to trade liberalisation. The argument was that the unintended outcome of the trade concessions was that it led to a serious influx of imports, leading to an increase in competition in the domestic industry, job losses, and injury to the particular domestic sector as a whole. This position justified the affected Contracting Party to suspend equivalent trade concessions. Hence, drafters of the GATT included Article XIX as a mechanism allowing for temporary withdrawal of concessions with regard to tariffs.[3] In the WTO era, in addition to Article XIX, the SGA brings about clarity on the mechanism of safeguard measures.

3.1 Formation of Safeguard Measures in the GATT and WTO

The proposals put forth by the US in 1945 during the GATT negotiations included the creation of an international trade organisation, *i.e.*, the ITO, tariffs, quantitative trade restrictions, subsidies, *etc*. The proposals also included a consideration for the use of an 'escape' or 'safeguard' clause to allow for temporary deviation from tariff commitments. The proposal ran as follows:

> 3. *Emergency action*. Commitments with regard to tariffs should permit countries to take temporary action to prevent sudden and widespread injury to the producers concerned. Undertakings for reducing tariffs should therefore contain an escape clause to cover such contingencies.
>
> (US Department of State, 1945)

Although the US proposal did not have specific wordings, it captured the mood of the US on the impact of tariff commitments with regard to its own domestic producers.

To some extent it also implied the boundaries of US tolerance to tariff commitments (Piérola, 2014).[4] The origin of the US's proposal of an 'escape clause' is traceable to Article XI of the US Reciprocal Trade Agreement of 1942 with Mexico (Lee, 2014).[5] In the International Conference on Trade and Employment 1946, the US followed up its proposal with the *Suggested Charter for an International Trade Organisation of the United Nations*, which contained the first proposed multilateral safeguard clause in Article 29, entitled 'Emergency Action on Imports of Particular Products'. This was to be discussed at the Preparatory Committee during its first session. The US, in 1947, presented a draft GATT document, where the escape clause featured as Article XVI, which was to later become Article XVIII.[6] This provision was further modified, when the GATT was concluded in 1947. As discussed in earlier chapters, the ITO did not come to fruition and instead the GATT entered into force on 1 January 1948.[7]

The escape clause, *i.e.*, Article XIX of the GATT, was used by numerous Contracting States, such as the US, Australia, Canada, and the EC, to afford protection to a range of 'injured' industries (Sampson, 1987).[8] During the 1970s, the GATT Contracting Parties had increasingly applied a range of 'grey area measures' (bilateral voluntary export restraints, orderly marketing agreements, *etc.*) to limit imports of steel, automobiles, and electronic equipment. As these measures were not subject to multilateral discipline of the GATT, their legality under the GATT was questionable. In the GATT Ministerial Meeting 1982, the need to put in place an "improved and more efficient safeguard system" was felt, and the intention was incorporated in the Declaration that followed (GATT Ministerial Declaration, 1982).[9] In the GATT Ministerial Meeting 1986, which took place in Punta del Este, a Ministerial Declaration was made, where it was agreed that safeguards should be based on the basic principles of the General Agreement (GATT); contain the elements of transparency, including the concept of serious injury or threat thereof, temporary nature, compensation and retaliation, consultation, multilateral surveillance, and dispute settlement; clarify and reinforce the disciplines of the General Agreement (GATT); and apply to all Contracting Parties (Ministerial Declaration, 1986).

3.2 Uruguay Round and Beyond

During the Uruguay Round of negotiations, the SGA was negotiated, which became one of the multilateral agreements on trade in goods and is contained in Annex 1A of the WTO Agreement. The objective at the Uruguay Round of negotiations was to bring together the various forms of safeguard actions prevalent within the GATT framework, which is well captured in the Preamble to SGA, which states, "the need to clarify and reinforce the disciplines of the GATT 1994, and especially those of Article XIX (Emergency Action on Imports of Particular Products), to re-establish multilateral control over safeguards and eliminate measures that escape such control".[10] To begin with, the SGA gave shape to the escape clause, which was drafted into the GATT 1947. The Punta del Este Ministerial Declaration served as the template to develop the SA during the Uruguay Round of negotiations.[11] In its own words, the SGA, which explicitly applies equally to all Members, aims to (i) clarify and reinforce GATT disciplines, particularly those of Article XIX; (ii) re-establish multilateral control over safeguards and eliminate measures that escape such control; and (iii) encourage structural adjustment on the part of industries adversely affected by increased imports, thereby enhancing competition in international markets. In Professor Jackson's view, the SGA is one of the substantial achievements of the Uruguay Round of negotiations, "a heroic statement of principle" (Jackson, 1997).

4. Article XIX GATT and the Safeguard Agreement

Article XIX GATT permits a WTO Member State to suspend its trade concessions and deviate from WTO obligations through the imposition of safeguard measures, if the following are met, *viz.*, an increase in imports; injury or threat to domestic industry; and a causal link between the surge in imports and the injury sustained by the domestic industry. Article XIX:1(a) contains the basis framework and reads as follows:

> If, as a result of unforeseen developments and of the effect of the obligations incurred by a contracting party under this Agreement, including tariff concessions, any product is being imported into the territory of that contracting party in such increased quantities and under such conditions as to cause or threaten serious injury to domestic producers in that territory of like or directly competitive products, the contracting party shall be free, in respect of such product, and to the extent and for such time as may be necessary to prevent or remedy such injury, to suspend the obligation in whole or in part or to withdraw or modify the concession.

4.1 Safeguard Agreement

Article XIX GATT, although lacking in detail for its application, contains the necessary principles and foundations for justification of safeguard measures and for the creation of the SGA in the WTO era. The SGA, which builds on the foundation of Article XIX, clarifies and enhances Article XIX through adding further disciplines, introducing increased transparency, and prohibiting the use of alternative safeguard measures other than those identified in the Agreement. Accordingly, the SGA outlines the conditions for lawful imposition of a safeguard measure; its lawful application; the procedure to follow; the obligation to maintain an equivalent level of concessions; and last but not least the elimination of grey area measures. The constraints placed on the use of safeguards under the SGA are that (a) the safeguard measure is applied to an imported product, regardless of its origin, unless it falls under an exception; (b) such safeguard measure may not exceed a duration of four years, and is to be progressively liberalised during the period of application; and (c) the Member State seeking to implement safeguards must give notice to the other Member State concerned, allowing for an opportunity for consultation. The SGA and Article XIX apply cumulatively, which had been emphasised by the Appellate Body in *Korea – Dairy*.

In *Korea – Dairy*, the Appellate Body proceeded to examine the relationship between Article XIX of the GATT 1994 and the Agreement on Safeguards in light of Article II of the WTO Agreement, and Articles 1 and 11.1(a) of the Agreement on Safeguards. The Appellate body concluded that any safeguard measure imposed after the entry into force of the WTO Agreement must comply with the provisions of both Article XIX and the Agreement on Safeguards:

> The specific relationship between Article XIX of the GATT 1994 and the Agreement on Safeguards within the WTO Agreement is set forth in Articles 1 and 11.1(a) of the Agreement on Safeguards:
> . . .
> Article 1 states that the purpose of the Agreement on Safeguards is to establish "rules for the application of safeguard measures which shall be understood to mean those measures provided for in Article XIX of GATT 1994." . . . The ordinary meaning of

the language in Article 11.1(a) – "unless such action conforms with the provisions of that Article applied in accordance with this Agreement" – is that any safeguard action must conform with the provisions of Article XIX of the GATT 1994 as well as with the provisions of the Agreement on Safeguards. Thus, any safeguard measure[12] imposed after the entry into force of the WTO Agreement must comply with the provisions of both the Agreement on Safeguards and Article XIX of the GATT 1994.[13]

Article 1 of the SGA "establishes rules for the application of safeguard measures which shall be understood to mean those measures provided for in Article XIX of GATT". Article 11.1(a) of the SGA clearly prohibits any Member States from applying safeguard measures on import of particular products, unless such measures conform to the provisions of GATT 1994 Article XIX applied in accordance with the SGA. The Panel in *Argentina – Footwear (EC)* had found that "safeguard investigations and safeguard measures imposed after the entry into force of the WTO agreements which meet the requirements of the new Agreement on Safeguards satisfy the requirements of Article XIX of GATT".[14] Some of the early cases on the WTO safeguards regime brought into sharp focus this key issue of the relationship between Article XIX and the SGA in the context of the 'unforeseen developments' requirement.[15]

The Appellate Body in *Argentina – Footwear (EC)*, while reversing the aforementioned finding of the Panel, noted that Articles 1 and 11.1(a) of the SGA described the precise nature of the relationship between Article XIX of GATT 1994 and the SGA within the WTO Agreement. Accordingly, it observed as follows:

> We see nothing in the language of either Article 1 or Article 11.1(a) of the Agreement on Safeguards that suggests an intention by the Uruguay Round negotiators to subsume the requirements of Article XIX of the GATT 1994 within the Agreement on Safeguards and thus to render those requirements no longer applicable Article 1 states that the purpose of the Agreement on Safeguards is to establish "rules for the application of safeguard measures which shall be understood to mean those measures provided for in Article XIX of GATT 1994." . . . This suggests that Article XIX continues in full force and effect, and, in fact, establishes certain prerequisites for the imposition of safeguard measures. . . . Neither of these provisions states that any safeguard action taken after the entry into force of the WTO Agreement need only conform with the provisions of the Agreement on Safeguards.[16]
>
> . . .
>
> Thus, we are obliged to apply the provisions of Article 2.1 of the Agreement on Safeguards and Article XIX:1(a) of the GATT 1994 cumulatively, in order to give meaning, by giving legal effect, to all the applicable provisions relating to safeguard measures.[17]

The Appellate Body in *US – Lamb* reiterated the conclusions arrived at by the Appellate Body in *Argentina – Footwear (EC)* and in *Korea – Dairy* on the relationship between the SGA and GATT Article XIX and observed, "Articles 1 and 11.1(a) of the Agreement on Safeguards express the full and continuing applicability of Article XIX of the GATT 1994, which no longer stands in isolation, but has been clarified and reinforced by the Agreement on Safeguards".[18] The Appellate Body reiterated that view in *US – Steel Safeguards*, by observing that Article XIX of the GATT and the SGA must be read as an "inseparable package of rights and disciplines".[19] Although the 'unforeseen developments' requirement finds a place in Article XIX:1(a), it is not replicated in the SGA. The conclusion one arrives at from the aforementioned is that the 'unforeseen development' requirement of Article XIX must still be met despite being absent in the SGA.

4.1.1 Investigation and Provisional Application

Article 3, which is the 'due process' provision of the SGA, requires that a Member State carry out an investigation prior to the imposition of any safeguard measures. As per Article 3.1, safeguard measures can only be applied following a national investigation. The key elements of Article 3.1 are transparency and procedural fairness, which obligates the investigating authority of a Member State (i) to issue a reasonable public notice of the investigation to all interested parties; (ii) to provide all interested parties – exporters, importers, *etc.* – with the opportunity to present evidence and their views on the proposed application of safeguard measures, including whether such measures sought to be imposed will be justified on public interest; and (iii) to publish a report setting of such findings and any conclusions reached on all issues of fact and law. These reports have been subjected to intense scrutiny by both the Panels and the Appellate Body when challenged.

The Panel in *Korea – Dairy Products* held that Korea's investigation was not adequate since it failed to include the necessary reasoning for its finding of serious injury in its final investigation report.[20] The Panel refused to accept the explanations that there was a mid-investigation report, as they were not included in the final investigation report.[21] In short, the Panel considered the investigation report as final and refused to accept any explanations from Korea outside the final report.[22] However, it is to be noted that a Member State will still be permitted to supplement their reasoning found in the investigation report at a later stage (Lee, 2014). In *US – Steel Products*, where there was a multiplicity of investigation report, the Panel observed that a national authority's report may be produced in parts as long as it was coherent and presented a clear explanation and met the requirements of Article XIX and the SGA.[23] The Appellate Body in *US – Wheat Gluten*, while considering the meaning, nature, and focus of the investigation, noted that a delay of even a few weeks violates this requirement.[24]

Article 3.1 also requires that the Member State concerned notifies the Committee on Safeguards of its commencement of investigation. Article 13 establishes the Committee on Safeguards. Pursuant to Article 12, Member States that seek to initiate an investigation or decide to implement a safeguard measure are to notify the Committee on Safeguards. Further, Article 12.2 requires that the Committee must be provided with "all pertinent information" relating to the aforementioned decisions, enclosing evidence of the "serious injury or threat thereof caused by increased imports". Following Article 12.3 applications and extensions of safeguard measures are to be preceded by "consultations with those Members having a substantial interest as exporters of the product concerned". Under Article 13.1(b) of the SGA, the WTO Committee on Safeguards is "to find, upon request of an affected Member, whether or not the procedural requirements of this Agreement have been complied with in connection with a safeguard measure and report its findings to the Council for Trade in Goods". The primary objective of the consultation process remains, affording the Member States concerned the opportunity to exchange with a view on the safeguard measures proposed and to reach a satisfactory settlement.

Pursuant to Article 6, Member States may impose provisional safeguard measures in "critical circumstances where delay would cause damage which it would be difficult to repair", provided the Member State concerned first makes a preliminary determination that there is "clear evidence that increased imports have caused or are threatening to cause serious injury". Provisional safeguard measures, which take the form of tariff increases, are to be administered for a maximum period of 200 days, and the said period will be included in the total period of the safeguard measure.[25] As noted earlier, safeguard measures are only temporary in nature. In this regard Article 7.1 reads as follows:

> A Member shall apply safeguard measures only for such period of time as may be necessary to prevent or remedy serious injury and to facilitate adjustment. The period shall not exceed four years, unless it is extended under paragraph 2.

The provision establishes that the application of a definitive safeguard measure must not exceed four years. Under Article 7.4 a safeguard measure exceeding one year must be progressively liberalised,[26] and if such measures exceed three years, the Member State concerned must carry out a mid-term review to establish whether the measures still meet the requirements. In the event the measures do not meet the requirements, they are to be withdrawn.

4.1.2 Increased Imports and 'Unforeseen Development'

Pursuant to Article XIX:1(a) GATT, the Member State seeking to impose safeguards must demonstrate that the imports in question are increasing, so as to cause or threaten to cause serious injury, due to 'unforeseen developments' and GATT obligations. On the other hand, Article 2.1 of SGA indicates that safeguard measures may be imposed when a "product is being imported into its territory in such increased quantities, absolute or relative to domestic production, and under such conditions as to cause or threaten to cause serious injury to the domestic industry". The Panel in *Argentina – Footwear (EC)*, acknowledging that both parties had referred to data on both the quantity and the value of imports, observed:

> The Agreement is clear that it is the data on import quantities . . . in absolute terms and relative to (the quantity of) domestic production that are relevant in this context, in that the Agreement refers to imports "in such increased quantities" . . . Therefore, our evaluation will focus on the data on import quantities.[27]

There is no formal recital to be found in either the GATT or the SGA clarifying the relationship between Article XIX and the SGA.[28] In *Korea – Dairy*, the Panel ruled that Article XIX:1 was still generally applicable, and no conflict existed between the provisions of Article XIX:1 and Article 2.1 of the SGA.[29] The Panel, however, rejected the argument that the 'unforeseen developments' clause created any legal obligation. On appeal, the Appellate Body concurred with the Panel's findings that both the SGA and Article XIX applied to the application of safeguards but did not consider the 'unforeseen developments' clause as being merely explanatory. Importantly, the Appellate Body did not find the clause as "establishing independent conditions for the application of a safeguard measure, additional to the condition set forth in the second clause of that paragraph".[30] While Article 2.1 sets forth the conditions of the application of a safeguard measures, Article 4.2 sets forth the operational requirements for determining whether the conditions in Article 2.1 exist.[31] The Appellate Body in *Argentina – Footwear (EC)* ruled that 'unforeseen developments' modifies the phrase "being imported into the territory of that contracting party in such increased quantities and under such conditions as to cause or threaten serious injury to domestic producers in that territory".[32] The Appellate Body emphasised the notion that not any increase is sufficient, but "that the increase in imports must have been recent enough, sudden enough, sharp enough, and significant enough, both quantitatively and qualitatively, to cause or threaten to cause 'serious injury'".[33]

In *Argentina – Footwear (EC)*, the Appellate Body interpreted the meaning of the phrase "as a result of unforeseen developments" (although not included in the SGA), to mean 'unexpected' developments which led to a product being imported in such increased quantities and under such conditions as to cause or threaten to cause serious injury to domestic producers must have been 'unexpected', as opposed to 'unforeseeable'.[34] The Appellate Body also observed that "of the effect of the obligations incurred by a Member under this Agreement, including tariff concessions" meant that "it must be demonstrated, as a matter of fact, that the importing Member has incurred obligations under the GATT 1994, including tariff concessions".[35] The phrase "in such increased quantities", according to the Appellate Body, required the increase to be "recent enough, sudden enough, sharp enough and significant enough, both quantitatively and qualitatively, to cause or threaten to cause 'serious injury'".[36]

The Appellate Body in *US – Lamb* noted, "the demonstration . . . must also feature in the same report of the competent authorities",[37] and also added that "it follows that the published report of the competent authorities, under that Article, must contain a 'finding' or 'reasoned conclusion' on 'unforeseen developments'".[38] The Appellate Body had repeatedly stressed that the national authorities are required to demonstrate unforeseen developments before applying a safeguard measure.[39] The Appellate Body also ruled that it is not sufficient for the national authorities to merely describe certain new developments.[40] The Panel in *Argentina – Preserved Peaches* ruled that the national authorities were also to demonstrate "as a matter of fact the existence of unforeseen developments as required by Article XIX:1(a) of GATT 1994".[41] The Appellate Body in *US – Steel Safeguards* notes that the competent authority must provide a 'reasoned and adequate explanation' of how the facts support its determination for those prerequisites, including 'unforeseen developments' under ArticleXIX:1(a).[42] While rejecting the arguments presented by US, the Appellate Body held that to determine the increase in imports, an investigating authority cannot take a simple end point to end point analysis, as such a comparison could easily be manipulated, leading to a wrong outcome.[43]

One of the few cases that has been repeatedly cited as a reference point for establishing the existence of 'unforeseen developments' is the report of the Working Party in *US – Fur Felts Hat* from 1951 (often referred to as the *Hatters Fur* case),[44] which related to the withdrawal of a concession by the US on women's fur hats and hat bodies.[45] One can safely argue that the Working Party's interpretation of 'unforeseen developments' was liberal, as it set the threshold for invoking a safeguard measure very low. According to the Panel on *Korea – Dairy*, "although the Working Party considered that this phrase (as a result of unforeseen developments) contained a criterion to be respected, it rendered satisfaction of this criterion automatic, since it would not be reasonable to expect a contracting party to foresee that imports would cause serious injury to its domestic industry".[46] Although the Appellate Body in *Korea – Dairy* came to a contrary conclusion to the Panel, siding with the conclusion arrived at in the *Hatters' Case* by the Working Party, it did not comment on the Panel's analysis of the case.[47] It is to be borne in mind that a safeguard measure is an emergency measure, and an 'unforeseen developments' requirement is not to be invoked lightly, as such a practice is highly likely to undermine the predictability of the rules-based multilateral trading order of the WTO.

4.1.3 Determination of Injury

Any Member State seeking to impose safeguard measures must determine the serious injury or threat to serious injury that could potentially befall the domestic industry. The determination of serious injury or threat of injury is contained in Article 4 of the SGA and constitutes an important phase in the investigative process for introducing safeguard measures. Article 4.1 contains a sequence of definitions in relation to the assessment of serious injury.

4.1.3.1 SERIOUS INJURY AND THREAT OF SERIOUS INJURY

Article 4.1(a) defines "serious injury" as a "a significant overall impairment in the position of a domestic industry". Article 4.1(b) defines "threat of serious injury" as "serious injury that is clearly imminent, in accordance with the provisions of paragraph 2". Unlike in the AD Agreement and the SCM Agreement, where specific factors are identified that need to be considered while determining injury, the SGA does not include such factors. The Appellate Body in *US – Lamb* outlined its understanding of the terms in the following manner:

> The standard of "serious injury" set forth in Article 4.1(a) is, on its face, very high. Indeed, in *United States – Wheat Gluten Safeguard*, we referred to this standard as "exacting". Further, in this respect, we note that the word "injury" is qualified by the adjective "serious", which, in our view, underscores the extent and degree of "significant overall impairment" that the domestic industry must be suffering, or must be about to suffer, for the standard to be met.
>
> . . .
>
> [I]n making a determination on . . . the existence of "serious injury" . . . panels must always be mindful of the very high standard of injury implied by these terms.[48]

The Appellate Body in *US – Lamb* contrasted the notion of 'serious injury' as found in the SGA to the concept of 'material injury' contained in the Anti-Dumping Agreement and the Subsidies and Countervailing Measures (SCM) Agreement.

> We are fortified in our view that the standard of "serious injury" in the Agreement on Safeguards is a very high one when we contrast this standard with the standard of "material injury" envisaged under the Anti-Dumping Agreement, the Agreement on Subsidies and Countervailing Measures (the "SCM Agreement") and the GATT 1994. We believe that the word "serious" connotes a much higher standard of injury than the word "material".[49] Moreover, we submit that it accords with the object and purpose of the Agreement on Safeguards that the injury standard for the application of a safeguard measure should be higher than the injury standard for anti-dumping or countervailing measures.[50]

In *Argentina – Footwear (EC)*, the Appellate Body stated that there must be a "significant overall impairment" of the situation regarding the domestic industry in question.[51] This connotes that there should be an overall deterioration of the domestic industry coupled with an increase in the market share of the imports in question. The injury to a domestic industry that is considered for the purposes of imposing a safeguard measure is much greater than the 'material injury' that is considered while imposing an AD or a CVD. As mentioned earlier, the safeguard measures are introduced to provide a shield to domestic manufacturers, albeit temporarily, from foreign imports, whereas ADs are imposed to offset unfair pricing by foreign exporters, and CVDs are introduced to level the playing field between foreign government-subsidised exporters and domestic producers. Hence, the serious injury standard is brought in to strike a balance between the need to provide a much-needed relief to the domestic industry from imports and the consumers who look for affordable imports.

Safeguard measures can be imposed by Member States if there is a 'threat of serious injury' to the domestic industry concerned. Article 4.1(b) enunciates that the threat of serious injury should be understood to mean serious injury that is clearly imminent, and that a determination of the existence of a threat of serious injury must be based on facts and not merely allegation, conjecture, or remote possibility.[52] In other words, such a threat is to be actual and not imagined. The Appellate Body in *US – Lamb* interpreted the phrase 'clearly imminent' to mean that the domestic industry was on the brink of suffering serious injury. In the words of the Appellate Body, "[t]he word 'imminent' relates to the moment in time when the 'threat' is likely to materialize. The use of this word implies that the anticipated 'serious injury' must be on the very verge of occurring".[53] As regards 'threat of serious injury', the Appellate Body interpreted the phrase to mean that there must be "a high degree of likelihood that the anticipated serious injury will materialize in the very near future".[54] A Member State seeking to impose a safeguard measure is obligated under Articles 3.1 and 4.2(c) to examine the condition of its domestic industry and provide a reasoned conclusion of its injury assessment. As noted by the Appellate Body in *US – Line Pipe*, there may exist a "rising continuum of an injurious condition of a domestic that ascends from a 'threat of serious injury' up to 'serious injury'".[55]

4.1.3.2 FACTORS TO BE CONSIDERED

Following from Article 4.2(a) of the SGA, competent national authorities are required to evaluate 'all relevant factors' of an objective and quantifiable nature that have a bearing on the situation of the particular domestic industry. Article 4.2(a) also lists the relevant factors to be considered as the "rate and amount of the increase in imports of the product concerned in absolute and relative terms, the share of the domestic market taken by increased imports, and changes in the level of sales, production, productivity, capacity utilization, profits and losses, and employment". In *US – Wheat Gluten*, the Appellate Body, while reversing the interpretation of the Panel, ruled that a national authority must evaluate all factors listed in Article 4.2(a), besides the ones raised by the parties.[56] The Appellate Body also noted:

> The use of the word "all" in the phrase "all relevant factors" in Article 4.2(a) indicates that the effects of any factor may be relevant to the competent authorities' determination, irrespective of whether the particular factor relates to imports specifically or to the domestic industry more generally. This conclusion is borne out by the list of factors which Article 4.2(a) stipulates are, "in particular", relevant to the determination. This list includes factors that relate both to imports specifically and to the overall situation of the domestic industry more generally.[57]

The Appellate Body in *Argentina – Footwear (EC)* agreed with the Panel's interpretation that Article 4.2(a) of the Agreement on Safeguards requires a demonstration that the competent authorities evaluated, at a minimum, each of the factors listed in Article 4.2(a) as well as all other factors that are relevant to the situation of the industry concerned.[58] The Appellate Body in *US – Wheat Gluten* recognised that the competent national authorities may not have the relevant data pertaining to all domestic producers, but regardless, such data must be sufficiently representative to present a true picture of the domestic industry.[59] In the *Ukraine – Passenger Cars* case, the competent national authorities investigating the issue did not provide a clear assessment of increase in imports, with the explanation that such information had been treated confidential at the request of the domestic industry. The Panel found that the authorities failed to properly evaluate the likely development of imports and observed as follows:

> We express no opinion as to whether a conclusion that imports were likely to continue to increase relative to domestic production (or in absolute terms) could have been made in the present case. Even if such a conclusion could have been drawn, it is not sufficient for the competent authorities to have merely noted the percentage of the relative increase without explaining what inferences were drawn from it with regard to the likely development of imports in the imminent future. As the Appellate Body has pointed out, "[a] panel must not be left to wonder why a safeguard measure has been applied".
>
> Therefore, we find that the competent authorities have failed to properly evaluate and give a reasoned explanation of, the likely development of imports, either in absolute terms or relative to domestic production, and their likely effect on the situation of the domestic industry in the very near future.[60]

As noted by the Appellate Body, authorities are not required to demonstrate that each listed injury factor is deteriorating but, rather, they must reach a conclusion considering the evidence as a whole.[61] However, not all factors need to show a downward trend, as the issue here is whether there is a 'significant overall impairment' of the domestic industry or threat thereof.[62]

4.1.3.3 IDENTIFYING THE RELEVANT DOMESTIC INDUSTRY

Article 4.1(c) of the SGA defines 'domestic industry' as follows:

> in determining injury or threat thereof, a "domestic industry" shall be understood to mean the producers as a whole of the like or directly competitive products operating within the territory of a Member, or those whose collective output of the like or directly competitive products constitutes a major proportion of the total domestic production of those products.

Under Article 2.1 of the SGA, safeguard measures may be applied to protect the relevant 'domestic industry' once it is determined through investigation that there is a serious injury or threat thereof to a 'domestic industry'.

In *US – Lamb*, the question of what fell within the definition of 'domestic industry' had to be decided. Here, the US, while imposing a safeguard measure on imports of lamb meat, had claimed that domestic producers of lamb meat included growers and feeders of live lambs, as there was a continuity in the line of production, besides a commonality of economic interests amongst both producers of the raw meat and the producers of the end product. While it appears difficult not to disagree with the findings of the domestic investigating authority, the Appellate Body ruled that there was no basis for this consideration in the SGA, and further, there was also no basis for the related consideration that there was a "continuous line of production from the raw to the processed product" as claimed by the US.[63] The Appellate Body proceeded to explain the appropriate methodology for identifying the domestic industry in the following words:

> According to the clear and express wording of the text of Article 4.1(c), the term "domestic industry" extends solely to the "producers . . . of the like or directly competitive

products". The definition, therefore, focuses exclusively on the producers of a very specific group of products. Producers of products that are not "like or directly competitive products" do not, according to the text of the treaty, form part of the domestic industry.[64]

The Appellate Body also expressed scepticism that the degree of integration of production process with an industry should have any bearing on the determination of the domestic industry.[65]

4.1.3.4 CAUSATION AND NON-ATTRIBUTION

Causation plays an important role in trade remedy laws, covering the investigative part of any AD, CVD, and safeguard measures. The law, as it stands, requires a causal link between 'increased quantities' of the imported product and the serious injury or threat thereof. Sykes notes that the requirement to establish a causal link between the two, *i.e.*, 'increased quantities' and 'serious injury or threat thereof', is perhaps one of the most difficult and problematic issues posed by the SGA (Sykes, 2006).[66] Article 4.2(b) of the SGA provides as follows:

> The determination referred to in subparagraph (a) shall not be made unless this investigation demonstrates, on the basis of objective evidence, the existence of the causal link between increased imports of the product concerned and serious injury or threat thereof. When factors other than increased imports are causing injury to the domestic industry at the same time, such injury shall not be attributed to increased imports.[67]

WTO jurisprudence highlights two legal requirements for causation under Article 4.2(b) of the SGA, *viz.*, (i) causal link between increased imports of the product concerned and serious injury or threat thereof, and (ii) injury caused by factors other than increased imports must not be attributed to increased imports – referred to as the non-attribution element.[68] It should be stressed here that the non-attribution requirement cannot be easily satisfied through assertions but is to be met through a reasoned and adequate explanation of how the factors causing injury and those not causing injury are distinguished.[69] Article 4.2(b) does not require the Member States to draw a causal link between 'unforeseen developments' or GATT obligations and injury. It is imperative that the national authorities that conduct the investigation examine thoroughly and establish if increased imports are causing or threatening to cause serious injury. The analysis of causation by national authorities often falls short of expectations, and in most instances are challenged before the WTO Panel.

The Appellate Body in *US – Wheat Gluten* established that there needs to exist a "genuine and substantial relationship of cause and effect" between increased imports and any serious injury to the domestic industry or threat thereof, and that the contribution by increased imports must be sufficiently clear so as to establish the existence of 'the causal link' required.[70] Here, the Appellate Body was laying down the law that national authorities are to unequivocally establish that injury caused by factors other than increased imports is not attributed to increased imports.

In *US – Wheat Gluten*, the Appellate Body also reversed the findings of the Panel that the imports in and of themselves must have caused serious injury, and ruled that it was not necessary to show that increased imports alone were capable of causing serious injury, and observed as follows:

> [T]he need to distinguish between the facts caused by increased imports and the facts caused by other factors does not necessarily imply . . . that increased imports on their

own must be capable of causing serious injury nor that injury caused by other factors must be excluded from the determination of serious injury.[71]

The language of Article 4.2(b) suggests that 'the causal link' between increased imports and serious injury may exist, despite 'other factors' contributing 'at the same time' to the situation of the domestic industry.[72] The Appellate Body in *US – Lamb* concluded that Article 4.2(b) required a 'demonstration' of the 'existence' of causal link, which was to be based on 'objective data'.[73] The Appellate Body, in the course of substantiating its findings, also reviewed the relationship between Article 2.1 and Article 4.2 of the SGA and concluded that the competent authorities should determine whether the increase in imports, not alone, but in conjunction with the other relevant factors, causes serious injury. What one gathers from the foregoing is that the existence of the 'causal link' is not sufficient in itself, and the causal link must be sufficiently strong to demonstrate the 'genuine and substantial relationship of cause and effect' indicated. The Appellate Body in *US – Lamb* clarified:

> [t]he primary objective of the process we described in *United States – Wheat Gluten Safeguard* is, of course, to determine whether there is "a genuine and substantial relationship of cause and effect" between increased imports and serious injury or threat thereof.[74]

The SGA does not clearly provide for a methodology to be adopted by national investigating authorities for the purposes of establishing the causal link and injury, as these are left for the Member States to determine using domestic laws. Member States adopt a methodology often referred to as the 'correlation' or 'coincidence' approach, where national authorities seek to determine correlation between increased imports and injury to domestic industry, *i.e.*, falling profits, employment levels, *etc.* to establish causation. In *Argentina – Footwear (EC)*, the Panel observed:

> it is the relationship between the movements in imports (volume and market share) and the movements in injury factors that must be central to a causation analysis and determination . . . [I]f causation is present, an increase in imports normally should coincide with a decline in the relevant injury factors. While such a coincidence by itself cannot prove causation (because, *inter alia*, Article 3 requires an explanation – *i.e.*, "findings and reasoned conclusions"), its absence would create serious doubts as to the existence of a causal link, and would require a very compelling analysis of why causation still is present.[75]

The aforementioned observation of the Panel had come under criticism, as it appears to almost combine correlation and causation.[76] As discussed earlier, the task of the national authority is distinguishing the factors that bring about the injury to the domestic industry.[77] The Appellate Body in *US – Line Pipe*, while reiterating the prior interpretation and relying on *US – Hot-Rolled Steel from Japan*,[78] added that the national authorities must distinguish the injurious effects of the increased imports from the injurious effects of the other factors, which is akin to the standard developed for AD Agreement.[79]

5. Special Safeguard Measures Under WTO Agreements

Special safeguard measure provisions are embedded in other agreements of the WTO, which resemble some of the provisions of the SGA. These provisions allow Member States to impose unilateral import restrictions, which are not in line with AD and CVD. These import restrictions are to be found in the Agreement on Agriculture; the GATS; and the Understanding on Balance of Payments; *etc.* Safeguard measures are applied to goods that are subjected to the GATT 1994 with a view to protecting a domestic industry; the measures contained in specific agreements will only apply to a limited range of products covered in the specific agreements and for general economic requirements of the importing Member State, *viz.*, securing balance of payments, rather than for the protection of a domestic industry.

5.1 Special Safeguard Measures Under Agreement on Agriculture

It is well documented that the agriculture sector has a long history of protection, since the days of the GATT, where the EU/EC and the US lent support to their agriculture sector through heavy subsidies. Under the Agreement on Agriculture (AoA), the Special Safeguard Measure (SSG) provisions are only available to those Member States that have converted an existing market access restriction into tariffs and to agricultural products that have been 'tariffied', been labelled in the schedule as 'SSG', and considered sensitive.[80] SSGs are part and parcel of the AoA and can be classified as falling under the category where safeguards are introduced to provide protection to domestic industry from any injury arising from imports. Article 6 of AoA allows for the application of SSGs on certain agricultural products, in the form of additional duties on the products identified. Also, under the provisions of AoA, the need to demonstrate injury to domestic injury, *i.e.*, agricultural sector, for the purposes of imposing SSG does not arise.

Article 5 of the AoA, which is captioned 'Special Safeguard Measures', establishes the conditions under which a Member State may be permitted to impose SSG measures. In *Chile – Price Band System (Article 21.5 – Argentina)*, the Appellate Body elucidated the provisions objectives and observed as follows:

> One circumstance in which a qualifying Member may be authorized to adopt a special safeguard is when the price of imports of a relevant agricultural product falls below a specified trigger price. However, pursuant to Article 5, a special safeguard can be imposed only on those agricultural products for which measures within the meaning of footnote 1 were converted into ordinary customs duties and for which a Member has reserved in its Schedule of Concessions a right to resort to these safeguards.[81]

Further, Article 5 also outlines the rules the duration of such SSG measures, attaching transparency requirements. Article 5 provides for a volume trigger and a price trigger. Articles 5.1(a), 5.1(b), and 5.1(c) of the AoA contain provisions for invoking SSG measures.[82] Articles 5.1(a) and 5.1(c) permit the imposition of SSG measures in the event there is an increase in the volume of imports of an agricultural product during any year exceeding a specific trigger level as set out in paragraph 4.[83] Article 5.1(b), on the other hand, permits the imposition of SSG measures in the event the import price of such product, as determined on the basis of its c.i.f. import price of the shipment, falls below a trigger price which is equal to the average 1986 to 1988 reference price for the product.[84] In *EC – Poultry*, the Appellate Body held that the import price to be considered against the trigger price was merely the c.i.f. price and that it did not include ordinary customs duties payable on imports.[85]

Article 5.4 contains the method of calculating the trigger levels, which is based on market access opportunities.[86] Article 5.5 contains the method of calculating the additional duty based on the c.i.f. import price. Any additional duties levied are to be calculated following the formulae found in the aforementioned provisions, which is established according to a sliding scale schedule set out in Article 5.4. In *EC – Poultry*, the Appellate Body, the EC had applied SSG on out-of-quota imports of poultry, which was in Brazil's view contravened Article 5.1(b). According to Brazil, the trigger price was to be based on the c.i.f. import price together with the bound duty. The Appellate Body, while addressing the application of price-based SSG, held that under Article 5.5 of the AoA, the comparison of the c.i.f. price with the trigger price could only be on a shipment-by-shipment basis and found the practice of the EC determining the import price on the basis of a fixed standard 'representative price' as impermissible.[87] Commentators view the approach taken here by the Appellate Body as being restrictive, and as "an attempt to curtail an otherwise very generous justification to depart from trade liberalization in agricultural goods" (Matsushita, Shoenbaum, and Mavroidis (2017).

With regards to the relationship of Article 5 with other Articles of the AoA, the Appellate Body in *Chile – Price Band System* identified Article 5 as an exception to the obligations that Article 4.2 imposes to all WTO Member States. The Appellate Body referred to Article 5.1 as an illustration that the phrase "have been required to be converted" in Article 4.2 is broader in scope than the phrase "have been converted" in Article 5.1 and observed as follows:

> the existence of a market access exemption in the form of a special safeguard provision under Article 5 implies that Article 4.2 should not be interpreted in a way that permits Members to maintain measures that a Member would not be permitted to maintain but for Article 5, and, much less, measures that are even more trade-distorting than special safeguards. In particular, if Article 4.2 were interpreted in a way that allowed Members to maintain measures that operate in a way similar to a special safeguard within the meaning of Article 5 – but without respecting the conditions set out in that provision for invoking such measures – it would be difficult to see how proper meaning and effect could be given to those conditions set forth in Article 5.[88]

During the Doha Round of negotiations, developing country Member States had raised the issue of new Special Safeguard Mechanisms (SSM) to raise tariffs on agricultural products temporarily above bindings, which was in response to import increases and price falls. The draft SSM aims at establishing a modality for use by developing country Member States. However, there was no broad consensus on the purpose of SSM, and the divisions of the SSM were even blamed for the breakdown in the Doha Round talks in 2008. Nevertheless, in 2015, at the Nairobi Ministerial Conference, WTO Member States agreed to continue with the negotiations and declared, "[t]he developing country Members will have the right to have recourse to a special safeguard mechanism (SSM)" (WTO Ministerial Conference, 2015).

5.2 Emergency Safeguard Measures Under GATS

With regards to trade in services, the GATS Agreement provides for multilateral negotiations on Emergency Safeguard Measures (ESM). Interestingly, the GATS Agreement does not contain a definition of ESM but is understood as a temporary measure which can be invoked to deviate from specific commitments, in the event a surge in service imports poses the threat of serious injury to like providers of services from the domestic sector.

The first sentence of Article X.1 of GATS reads as follows:

> There shall be multilateral negotiations on the question of emergency safeguard measures based on the principle of non-discrimination.

This does not, however, require Member States to introduce ESM. The possibility of imposing ESM to service imports gives the opportunity to Member States that experience an unprecedented surge in service imports causing injury to domestic service suppliers the authority to deviate from legally binding GATS commitments. But that said, the Member States are still to agree on a clear consensus with regards to the question of ESM, although it is over two decades since GATS was finalised as a covered agreement of the WTO. The negotiating history of and the wordings of Article X indicate that the necessity of the ESM should be considered by Members, but they may not adopt the ESM in the end (Lee, 2014). Although a number of developing country Member States from ASEAN have indicated a clear interest in ESMs, it still remains a discussion point (Lee, 2014). Member States are divided on the benefits of ESM, with some expressing disagreement with the concept and others arguing that for a successful completion of the negotiation under GATS Article X is a precondition for further liberalisation of trade in services.[89] Most OECD country Member States and some developing country Member States are sceptical about the benefits of ESM, as they fear that ESM will likely weaken the stability of scheduling commitments under GATS. Member States that support ESM take the position that the availability of safeguards is necessary in the event of a spike in service imports to convince domestic providers to accept the undertaking of access commitments in services (Annual Report, 2011, 2012). Neither position has helped move the discussions forward.

6. Balance-of-Payments Measures

The term 'balance of payments' (BOP) refers to a summary statement of all economic transactions between the residents of one country and the rest of the world, covering a given period, and includes purchases and sales of goods, services, gifts, government transactions, and capital movements. A country's BOP is made up of two principal components, *viz.*, its financial account/capital account, which registers the net result of public and private international investment flowing in and out of the country, and its current account, which characterises the country's overall balance on goods and services, along with net income such as interests and dividends and net transfer payments (Lowenfeld, 2008). From the aforementioned one will observe that a country's BOP is where its trade and finance flows converge, capturing the relationship between a given economy to the international marketplace. It is well known that an increase in international trade activities brought about by globalisation has also brought about interdependence of national economies, and this in turn has implications for the BOP of a country.

A BOP problem occurs when a country witnesses a steep drop in demand for its currency such that it creates a downward pressure on its currency value, and the resulting depreciation destabilises market transactions and renders citizens unable to purchase everyday necessities (Thomas, 2000). Where an imbalance of payments arises, and a Member State is unable to meet its payments for imports with its foreign currency earnings from export sales without selling gold for foreign currency, it will be constrained to borrow from the IMF.[90] A country can limit the outflow of money through the simple methodology of imposing trade restrictive measures on imports into the country. During the GATT era, BOP measures were resorted to frequently. Any safeguard measures taken by Member States in this regard seek not to protect a specific domestic industry but to resolve serious BOP problems through imposing temporary import restrictions.

6.1 Political Economy of BOP Measures and the GATT

The gold standard,[91] or sterling standard, that prevailed earlier was dominated by Britain, which established and maintained the rules.[92] In the years leading to the outbreak of World

War I, the major Western nations, *i.e.*, the UK, France, Germany, and the US, had tied their currency to gold. This arrangement allowed for the exchange rates among the franc, the mark, the pound, and the dollar to remain fixed (Lowenfeld, 2008). The gold standard was implemented in a hierarchical fashion with the countries of the periphery at the bottom,[93] the core countries above, and Britain at the peak (Igwe, 2018).[94] With the operation of the gold standard, most major countries were able to fix the value of gold to their currencies and maintain a gold reserve. When World War I broke out in 1914, there was disarray with the gold standard, as countries took unilateral measures to stabilise BOP. As there was no international legal regime to oversee the gold standard arrangements, the system collapsed almost overnight at the start of World War I (Lowenfeld, 2008).

In May 1925, Britain with US support succeeded to reinstate the gold standard mechanism, which saw 40 other countries joining the system within a year. But this was not to last, as the system collapsed spectacularly in 1931 (Igwe, 2018). The fixed exchange gold standard mechanism came to be replaced by a floating exchange rate mechanism. Efforts to install a more stable and reliable international monetary system had to wait for the post-World War II era, as there was no international institution to oversee a workable mechanism. This experience from the fragmented monetary system during the 'interwar' period validated the need for an institutional framework that would allow countries to follow policies aimed at domestic objectives without having to export their problems (Aliber, 2011). As Lowenfeld notes, prior to the close of World War II, there was no international legal regime to govern the conduct of states with respect to monetary affairs (Lowenfeld, 2008).

The Bretton Woods Conference of 1944,[95] which drew the plans for the creation of the IMF, the World Bank, and the ITO, also had the ambition of a post-war monetary restructuring to replace gold as the medium of exchange with the US dollar. The US and the UK took the initiative to put forth a treaty called the Articles of Agreement of the International Monetary Fund, *i.e.*, the Bretton Woods Agreement, which had a set of rules to be followed by its Member States when they intervened in the currency market. The system envisaged a method of fixed exchange rates tied to the gold standard.[96] Under this system, each country was required to hold an adequate quantity of gold reserves to back the quantity of its currency in circulation. If a temporary imbalance of payments were to arise,[97] the country that was in financial crisis could reach out to international credits to avert serious economic collapse. The system was based on the US dollar and was also referred to as the 'dollar standard' or 'adjustable peg system' with fixed exchange rate as the underlying principle of monetary stability (Igwe, 2018).[98] Under the arrangements, the IMF was to hold a pool of Member Countries' currencies as well as the currencies of other Member Countries,[99] as it clearly had a central role in managing BOP measures at the transition to a flexible exchange rate system. Some commentators refer to the Bretton Woods System as a diluted form of gold exchange standard (Dam, 1982).

The foundation of the GATT was built on the premise that domestic industries are to be protected only through bound tariffs, which was applied on a non-discriminatory basis. The GATT included a general presumption against the use of quantitative restrictions as it could nullify the positive effects of tariffs. However, the BOP situation was considered as something that justified an exception to the presumption (Anjaria, 1987). During the GATT years countries lowered tariff and non-tariff barriers and avoided all but a strictly temporary use of BOP restrictions, and in contrast, the developing countries traditionally maintained high tariff and non-tariff barriers (Anjaria, 1987).[100] The GATT 1947 had a single BOP provision in Article XII. Following the review session in 1954–1955, two more BOP provisions were introduced in Articles XVIII and XVIII:B. During the 1954–1955 review session, much time was devoted by the Contracting Parties to amending paragraph 3 of Article XII. The US inflation rate began to accelerate in 1968/1969, and in 1971 the US dollar was devalued due to the misalignment of currency values.[101] In 1973, the Bretton Woods system collapsed, leading to the adoption of floating exchange rates among the developed countries, under which trade restrictions for BOP were no longer used by Member States.

6.2 Balance-of-Payments Measures Under GATT 1994

The rules on BOP measures are to be found in Articles XII, XIII, XIV, XV, and XVIII:B of the GATT 1994. Article XII of GATT 1994 permits Member States to impose unilateral import restrictions to secure the necessary levels of BOP measures, and the Understanding on Balance-of-Payments Provisions of the GATT 1994 (Understanding on BOP Provisions) amplifies the provisions of GATT Article XII. Further, Article XVIII:B provides for dealing with the BOP difficulties associated with economic development, and Article XV requires Member States to consult with and seek cooperation of the IMF and pursue a coordinated policy with regard to their international reserves, BOP, and foreign exchange arrangements. The framework presented in the aforementioned rules permit Member States to adopt measures – that are otherwise GATT inconsistent – to safeguard their financial position and to protect their BOP.

The first paragraph of Article XII of the GATT 1994, entitled 'Restrictions to Safeguard the Balance of Payments', reads as follows:

> Notwithstanding the provisions of paragraph 1 of Article XI, any [Member], in order to safeguard its external financial position and its balance of payments, may restrict the quantity or value of merchandise permitted to be imported, subject to the provisions of the following paragraphs of this Article.

One may note that under the provision, the purpose of a Member State's BOP measure is "to safeguard its external financial position and its balance of payments". Similarly, under Article XVIII:B, the purpose of a developing country Member State's BOP measure is "to safeguard its external financial position" with the addition, "to ensure a level of reserves adequate for the implementation of its programme of economic development". Also, Article XVIII of the GATT 1994, entitled 'Governmental Assistance to Economic Development', provides in paragraph 4(a) as follows:

> [A Member], the economy of which can only support low standards of living and is in the early stages of development, shall be free to deviate temporarily from the provisions of the other Articles of this Agreement, as provided in Sections A, B and C of this Article.

6.2.1 Nature and Scope of Balance-of-Payments Measures

The key requirements for BOP trade restrictions are encapsulated in Article XII and Article XVIII, Section B, which is reserved for use by developing countries. The prior provisions only permit the use of quantitative restrictions to address BOP problems. It is to be noted that the GATT neither excludes, nor explicitly requires, a Member State experiencing BOP problems to adopt macro-economic policies lessening demand. On the other hand, Articles XII:3(a) and XII:3(d) provide that countries should implement domestic policies that expand, rather than contract, international trade. Paragraph 2 of the Understanding on BOP Provisions states as follows:

> Members confirm their commitment to give preference to those measures which have the least disruptive effect on trade. Such measures (referred to in this Understanding as "price-based measures") shall be understood to include import surcharges, import deposit requirements or other equivalent trade measures with an impact on the price of imported goods. It is understood that, notwithstanding the provisions of Article II, price-based measures taken for balance-of-payments purposes may be applied by a Member in excess of the duties inscribed in the Schedule of that Member.

The Understanding on BOP commits WTO Member States to give preference to price-based BOP measures. As noted earlier, under Article XII, quantitative restrictions were the only form of BOP measures allowed. In contrast, paragraph 3 of the Understanding on BOP Provisions reads as follows:

> Members shall seek to avoid the imposition of new quantitative restrictions for balance-of-payments purposes unless, because of a critical balance-of-payments situation, price-based measures cannot arrest a sharp deterioration in the external payments position.

This means, any quantitative restriction applied by a Member State as a BOP measure is accompanied by explanation as to why price-based measures are not an adequate instrument to deal with the BOP situation. This also means BOP measures may only be applied when strict requirements are met. Importantly, BOP measures are not to exceed what is necessary to address a BOP problem faced by a Member State. Article XII:2(a) states that BOP measures adopted by a Member State:

> shall not exceed those necessary: (i) to forestall the imminent threat of, or to stop, a serious decline in its monetary reserves, or (ii), in the case of a [Member] with very low monetary reserves, to achieve a reasonable rate of increase in its reserves.

Article XVIII:9, on the other hand, requires that BOP measures adopted by a developing country Member State:

> shall not exceed those necessary: (a) to forestall the threat of, or to stop, a serious decline in its monetary reserves, or (b) in the case of a [Member] with inadequate monetary reserves, to achieve a reasonable rate of increase in its reserves.

In *India – Quantitative Restrictions*, the Panel elaborated the function of Article XVIII:B within the GATT framework.[102] The Panel in particular distinguished the conditions for taking BOP measures under Article XVIII from those applicable under Article XII of GATT and considered paragraphs 2, 4(a), 8, and 11 of Article XVIII:

> It is clear from these provisions that Article XVIII, which allows developing countries to maintain, under certain conditions, temporary import restrictions for balance-of-payments purposes, is premised on the assumption that it "may be necessary" for them to adopt such measures in order to implement economic development programmes. It allows them to "deviate temporarily from the provisions of the other Articles" of GATT

1994, as provided for in, *inter alia*, Section B. These provisions reflect an acknowledgement of the specific needs of developing countries in relation to measures taken for balance-of-payments purposes. Article XVIII:B of GATT 1994 thus embodies the special and differential treatment foreseen for developing countries with regard to such measures. In our analysis, we take due account of these provisions. In particular, the conditions for taking balance-of-payments measures under Article XVIII are clearly distinct from the conditions applicable to developed countries under Article XII of GATT 1994.[103]

We also find that while Article XVIII:2 foresees the possibility that it "may" be "necessary" for developing countries to take restrictions for balance-of-payments purposes, such measures might not always be required. These restrictions must be adopted within specific conditions "as provided in" Section B of Article XVIII. The specific conditions to be respected for the institution and maintenance of such measures include Article XVIII:9, which specifies the circumstances under which such measures may be instituted and maintained, and Article XVIII:11 which sets out the requirements for progressive relaxation and elimination of balance-of-payments measures.[104]

Developing country Member States may also implement BOP measures to preclude a threat of a serious decline in monetary reserves. Note, this right is not available to other Member States. The determination of what constitutes a "serious decline of monetary reserves" or "an imminent threat thereof", or what constitutes very low or inadequate monetary reserves, is left to the IMF to establish. In *India – Quantitative Restrictions*, it was reported by the IMF that India's reserves were US$25.1 billion as of 21 November 1997, and that US$16 billion was an adequate level of reserves at that date. Hence, in the IMF opinion, India did not face a serious decline of its monetary reserves or a threat thereof.[105]

It is also to be noted that the Understanding on BOP Provisions prohibits a combination of price-based measures and quantitative restrictions on the same product. As mentioned earlier, some developing country Member States do continue to follow the practice of employing trade restrictions for BOP.[106] For instance, Ukraine and Ecuador, both developing country Member States, imposed trade restrictions for BOP commitments in 2009 and again in 2015. In February 2015, Ukraine introduced a temporary import surcharge of 5 to 10 percent on most imports, due to exceptional conditions affecting its BOP, which was duly notified to the Committee on Balance of Payment Restrictions of the WTO (Committee on BOP Restrictions, March 2015).[107] Unfortunately, Member States could not reach an agreement on the WTO consistency of the import surcharge levied by Ukraine during several rounds of consultations in 2015. Eventually in February 2016, Ukraine announced before the WTO Committee on Balance-of-Payments Restrictions that it had entirely dismantled its import surcharge.

In Ecuador's case, temporary tariff surcharges were introduced for a period of 15 months due to "highly unfavourable economic climate prevailing in the country and its impact on the balance of payments" (Committee on BOP Restrictions, April 2015).[108] The tariff surcharge imposed by Ecuador ranged from 5 to 45 percent, with the highest tariff surcharge of 45 percent reserved for final consumer goods (Committee on BOP Restrictions, April 2015). Unfortunately, while several Member States were able to relate to Ecuador's plight regarding its BOP, Member States were unable to reach an agreement if the surcharge imposed by Ecuador was WTO consistent. In May 2016, Ecuador was once again constrained to extend the tariff surcharge due its continuing "unfavourable economic climate", brought about by the devastating earthquake that affected the coastal regions of the country in April 2016 (Committee on BOP Restrictions, May 2016). Ecuador phased out the surcharge in

2017. Importantly, Articles XII:2(b) and XVIII:11 require the Member State applying such trade restrictions to progressively ease them with any improvement in the BOP conditions. The second sentence of Article XVIII:11 reads as follows:

> It shall progressively relax any restrictions applied under this Section as conditions improve, maintaining them only to the extent necessary under the terms of paragraph 9 of this Article and shall eliminate them when conditions no longer justify such maintenance.[109]

In *India – Quantitative Restrictions*, India argued that it had the right to maintain BOP measures until the BOP Committee or the General Council advised it to modify these measures under Article XVIII:12, or for that matter, established a time period for their removal under paragraph 13 of the BOP Understanding. The Panel disagreeing held that

> [t]he obligation of Article XVIII:11 is not conditioned on any BOP Committee or General Council decision. If we were to interpret Article XVIII:11 to be so conditioned, we would be adding terms to Article XVIII:11 that it does not contain.
>
> Moreover, the obligation in Article XVIII:11 requires action by the individual Member . . . In light of the unqualified nature of the Article XVIII:11 obligation, it would be inconsistent with the principle *pacta sunt servanda* to conclude that a WTO Member has a right to maintain balance-of-payments measures, even if unjustified under Article XVIII:B, in the absence of a Committee or General Council decision in respect thereof. Thus, we find that India does not have a right to maintain its balance-of-payments measures until the General Council advises it to modify them under Article XVIII:12 or establishes a time-period for their removal under paragraph 13 of the 1994 Understanding.[110]

The Appellate Body in *India – Quantitative Restrictions*, citing its statement in *US – Wool Shirts and Blouses*,[111] agreed with the Panel that it is for the responding party to demonstrate that the complaining party violated its obligation not to require the responding party to change its development policy:

> We consider that the invocation of the proviso to Article XVIII:11 does not give rise to a burden of proof issue insofar as it relates to the interpretation of what policies may constitute a "development policy" within the meaning of the proviso. However, we do not exclude the possibility that a situation might arise in which an assertion regarding development policy does involve a burden of proof issue. Assuming that the complaining party has successfully established a *prima facie* case of inconsistency with Article XVIII:11 and the *Ad* Note, the responding party may, in its defence, either rebut the evidence adduced in support of the inconsistency or invoke the proviso. In the latter case, it would have to demonstrate that the complaining party violated its obligation not to require the responding party to change its development policy. This is an assertion with respect to which the responding party must bear the burden of proof. We, therefore, agree with the Panel that the burden of proof with respect to the proviso is on India.[112]

In sum, the use of BOP measures and notifications to the BOP Committee have in recent years declined.

6.3 Balance-of-Payments Measures Under GATS

It is well documented that the BOP provisions in the GATT were one of the issues to which much time was devoted during the Uruguay Round of negotiations. The GATT provisions in turn have influenced the BOP provisions occurring in GATS which deals with BOP situations arising from external financial difficulties. Incidentally, Article XII of GATS follows the same principles, terms and conditions, and procedural requirements contained in GATT for the invoking the BOP safeguard provisions. Article XII of the GATS Agreement entitles Member States to restrict trade in services to safeguard their external financial position and BOP, provided certain conditions are met. Article XII is entitled 'Restrictions to Safeguard the Balance of Payments', and Article XII:1 reads as follows:

> In the event of serious balance-of-payments and external financial difficulties or threat thereof, a Member may adopt or maintain restrictions on trade in services on which it has undertaken specific commitments, including on payments or transfers for transactions related to such commitments. It is recognized that particular pressures on the balance of payments of a Member in the process of economic development or economic transition may necessitate the use of restrictions to ensure, *inter alia*, the maintenance of a level of financial reserves adequate for the implementation of its programme of economic development or economic transition.

While the first sentence of the Article provides for BOP measures to be taken by a Member State to offset such "financial difficulties or threat thereof" arising from trade in services, the second sentence recognises the necessity for a Member State – which is in the process of economic development – the use of restrictions to maintain a certain level of financial reserves for the implementation of its economic development programmes. The second sentence permits developing country Member States and economies in transition additional flexibility in the use of services trade. Where a Member State experiences serious BOP and external difficulties or a threat thereof, it may impose BOP measures to restrict trade in services which may be GATS inconsistent. Article XII:2, however, imposes certain conditions, *i.e.*, such BOP measures (i) shall not discriminate among Member States; (ii) shall be consistent with the Articles of Agreement of the IMF; (iii) shall avoid unnecessary damage to the commercial, economic, and financial interests of any other Member State; (iv) shall not exceed those necessary to deal with the circumstances described in Article XII:1; and (v) shall be temporary and phased out progressively as the situation described in Article XII:1 improves.

Pursuant to Article XII:4, any BOP measure that restricts trade in services, or any changes thereto, shall be promptly notified to the General Council. Article XII:5(a), on the other hand, requires Member States adopting a BOP measure to consult with the BOP Committee promptly. The Ministerial Conference on BOP measures restricting trade in services carries out periodic consultations, the procedures of which are identical to the procedures laid down in GATT 1994. Article XII:5(d) requires that such consultations with the BOP Committee address the compliance of any restrictions with Article XII:2, and in particular the progressive phasing out of restrictions in accordance with Article XII:2(e). In all consultations with the Ministerial Conference on BOP measures, the statistical findings of the IMF relating to foreign exchange, monetary reserves, and BOP shall be accepted.

7. Summary

Economic emergency measures are referred to as safeguard measures, which temporarily restrict imports, allowing the domestic industry of the importing Member State to make necessary adjustments. Member States tend to introduce safeguard measures, albeit for a limited time, in the form of customs duties which tend to exceed the tariff bindings. The introduction of safeguard measures is justified if they meet three requirements, *viz.*, (i) the requirement of increased imports – must be recent, sudden, and significant; (ii) the requirement of serious injury or threat thereof – with a significant overall impairment to the domestic industry; and (iii) the requirement of causation – serious injury is imminent.

Notes

1 The types of economic harm that are identified here are a decreased production in the domestic industry concerned coupled with lower prices, which in turn leads to unemployment.
2 See Appellate Body Report, *US – Line Pipe*, para. 80.
3 Commentators do query the place of Article XIX and the Agreement on Safeguards within the multilateral trade landscape administered by the WTO. See Sykes (2003).
4 At that time, the US had formidable experience in the area of trade treaties, as it had formulated 32 bilateral trade agreements between 1934 and 1945. The author observes that the rationale of the suggested escape clause was consistent with the provisions of the trade agreements concluded by the US with other nations under the US Reciprocal Trade Agreements Act 1934.
5 A general escape provision was contained in the trade agreement signed between Argentina and the US in October 1941. See Karvis (1954).
6 In February 1947, President Truman issued an executive order which made it mandatory for all US trade agreements negotiated under the US Reciprocal Trade Agreements Act 1934 to contain an escape clause. The US Trade Agreements Extension Act 1951 made the inclusion of an escape clause in new trade agreements a statutory requirement.
7 See chapters 1 and 2 for a discussion on the demise of the ITO due to the failure of the US Congress to endorse its creation, and how the GATT 'rulebook' became the template to conduct multilateral trade amongst the Contracting Parties.
8 Between 1950 and 1986, Article XIX of the GATT was invoked 132 times in all – 28 times by the US, 19 times by the EC, 22 times by Canada, 38 times by Australia, and 25 times by other GATT signatories.
9 The relevant part of the Ministerial Declaration read as follows: "The CONTRACTING PARTIES decide: 1. That, having regard to the objectives and disciplines of the General Agreement, there is need for an improved and more efficient safeguard system which provides for greater predictability and clarity and also greater security and equity for both importing and exporting countries, so as to preserve the results of trade liberalization and avoid the proliferation of restrictive measures."
10 Also, the first sentence of Article 11.1(b) of the SGA reads as follows: "Furthermore, a Member shall not seek, take or maintain any voluntary export restraints, orderly marketing arrangements, or any other similar measures on the export or the import side."
11 It is also noted that the SGA reflects the essence of the US law, *i.e.*, Section 201 of the Trade Act 1974 on the matter. See Matsushita, Shoenbaum, and Mavroidis (2017).
12 (Footnote original) With the exception of special safeguard measures taken pursuant to Article 5 of the Agreement on Agriculture or Article 6 of the Agreement on Textiles and Clothing.
13 See Appellate Body Report, *Korea – Dairy*, paras. 76–77. See also Appellate Body Report, *Argentina – Footwear (EC)*, para. 84.
14 See Panel Report, *Argentina – Footwear (EC)*, para. 8.69.
15 See Panel Reports, *US – Line Pipe*, paras. 7.293–7.300; *US – Lamb*, paras. 7.32–7.45; *Korea – Dairy*, paras. 7.33–7.48; *Argentina – Footwear (EC)*, paras. 8.47–8.69. See also Appellate Body Reports, *US – Lamb*, paras. 65–76; *Korea – Dairy*, paras. 68–77; *Argentina – Footwear (EC)*, paras. 76–84.
16 See Appellate Body Report, *Argentina – Footwear (EC)*, para. 84.
17 *Ibid.*, para. 89.

18 See Appellate Body Report, *US – Lamb*, para. 70.
19 See Appellate Body Report, *US – Steel Safeguards*, paras. 275–279. See also Panel Report, *Argentina – Preserved Peaches*, para. 7.12.
20 See Panel Report, *Korea – Dairy*, paras. 7.58–7.59.
21 *Ibid.*, para. 7.69.
22 *Ibid.*, para. 7.76.
23 See Panel Report, *US – Steel Products*, para. 10.50.
24 See Appellate Body Report, *US – Wheat Gluten*, paras. 108–112.
25 See Article 6, SGA.
26 See Panel Report, *Ukraine – Passenger Cars*, para. 7.365.
27 See Panel Report, *Argentina – Footwear (EC)*, para. 8.152.
28 While Article 1 of the SGA states that the Agreement provides rules for the application of safeguard measures "provided for in Article XIX of GATT 1994", it does not clarify the legal relationship between Article XIX and the SGA.
29 See Panel Report, *Korea – Dairy*, para. 7.39.
30 See Appellate Body Report, *Korea – Dairy*, para. 85. See also Appellate Body Report, *Argentina – Footwear (EC)*, para. 92.
31 *Ibid.*, para. 8.140.
32 See Appellate Body report, *Argentina – Footwear (EC)*, para. 92.
33 See Appellate Body Report, *Argentina – Footwear (EC)*, paras. 129–131.
34 *Ibid.*, para. 91. See also Appellate Body Report, *Korea – Dairy*, para. 84.
35 See Appellate Body Report, *Argentina – Footwear (EC)*, para. 91.
36 *Ibid.*, para. 131.
37 See Appellate Body Report, *US – Lamb*, para. 72.
38 *Ibid.*, para. 76.
39 See Appellate Body reports, *US – Lamb*, para. 72 (holding that unforeseen developments must be demonstrated "before the safeguard measure is applied"); *Argentina – Footwear (EC)*, para. 81 (holding that unforeseen developments "must be demonstrated as a matter of fact"); and *Korea – Dairy*, para. 75 (holding that unforeseen developments "must be demonstrated as a matter of fact").
40 See Appellate Body report, *US – Lamb*, para. 73.
41 See Panel Report, *Argentina – Preserved Peaches*, para. 7.35.
42 See Appellate Body Report, *US – Steel Safeguards*, para. 279.
43 *Ibid.*, paras. 353–356.
44 See the Report of the Intersessional Working Party in *US – Fur Felts Hat*, para. 12 (as quoted in Panel Report, *US – Lamb*, para. 7.23).
45 The *Hatters Fur* case ruled that the damaging effect on the domestic industry of such change should be unforeseen. The US argued that due to a substantial increase in imports of women's fur felt hats, which caused severe injury to the domestic producers, it was constrained to withdraw the tariff concessions made earlier and restore the level of protection that was available previously to domestic producers. Czechoslovakia challenged the measure under Article XIX, and the Working Party ruled that the changes amounted to 'unforeseen developments' and found in favour of the US.
46 See Panel Report, *Korea – Dairy*, para. 7.46, fn. 425.
47 See Appellate Body Report, *Korea – Dairy*, para. 89. See also Appellate Body Report, *Argentina – Footwear (EC)*, para. 96.
48 See Appellate Body Report, *US – Lamb*, paras. 124 and 126.
49 (Footnote original) We find support for our view that the standard of "serious injury" is higher than "material injury" in the French and Spanish texts of the relevant agreements, where the equivalent terms are, respectively, *dommage grave* and *dommage important*; and *daño grave* and *daño importante*.
50 See Appellate Body Report, *US – Lamb*, para. 124.
51 See Appellate Body Report, *Argentina – Footwear (EC)*, para. 139.
52 See Panel Report, *US – Lamb*, paras. 7.192–7.194.
53 See Appellate Body Report, *US – Lamb*, para. 125.
54 *Ibid.*, para. 136.
55 See Appellate Body Report, *US – Line Pipe*, para. 170.
56 See Appellate Body Report, *US – Wheat Gluten*, paras. 55–56.
57 See Appellate Body Report, *US – Wheat Gluten*, para. 72.

58 See Appellate Body Report, *Argentina – Footwear (EC)*, para. 136.
59 See Appellate Body Report, *US – Wheat Gluten*, para. 57.
60 See Panel Report, *Ukraine – Passenger Cars*, para. 57.
61 See Appellate Body Report, *US – Wheat Gluten*, paras. 55–56.
62 See Appellate Body report, *Argentina – Footwear (EC)*, para. 139; Panel report, *US – Wheat Gluten*, para. 1.85.
63 See Appellate Body Report, *US – Lamb*, para. 77.
64 *Ibid.*, para. 84.
65 *Ibid.*, para. 94.
66 Sykes argues that 'injury' is never caused solely by increased imports, and it is inevitably that some 'other factor' is the underlying cause of both the injury and the increase in import quantities. Sykes also posits the argument that, from an economic perspective "increased quantities of imports do not 'cause' injury or threat even as an intermediate step in the causal chain – they arise simultaneously with injury or threat". See Sykes (2006) 158.
67 Sykes notes that the treaty text was borrowed from the deficient standard of causation under US law and is fundamentally deficient.
68 See Appellate Body Report, *US – Line Pipe*, para. 208.
69 *Ibid.*, paras. 209–14; Appellate Body reports, *US – Lamb*, para. 179, and *US – Wheat Gluten*, para. 70.
70 See Appellate Body Report, *US – Wheat Gluten*, para. 69.
71 *Ibid.*, para. 70.
72 *Ibid.*, para. 67.
73 See Appellate Body Report, *US – Lamb*, para. 130.
74 *Ibid.*, para. 179.
75 See Panel Report, *Argentina – Footwear (EC)*, paras. 8.237–8.238.
76 Interestingly, this observation of the Panel was approved by the Appellate Body. See Appellate Body Report, *Argentina – Footwear (EC)*, para. 144.
77 See Appellate Body report, *US – Wheat Gluten*, para. 68.
78 See Appellate Body report, *US – Hot-Rolled Steel from Japan*, paras. 222 and 223.
79 See Appellate Body report, *US – Line Pipe*. paras. 212–217.
80 As of 30 June 2020, 39 Member States have currently reserved the right to use a combined total of 6,156 special safeguards on agricultural products. It is to be noted that Switzerland-Liechtenstein has reserved the most aggressive use of the SSG with 961 products.
81 See Appellate Body Report, *Chile – Price Band System (Article 21.5 – Argentina)*, para. 173.
82 Under the scheme envisaged, concurrent application of subparagraphs (a) and (b) is not permitted.
83 As per Article 5.4, any special safeguard measures of this nature will expire by the end of the given year during which it has been imposed and "may only be levied at a level which shall not exceed one third of the level of the ordinary customs duty in effect in the year in which the action is taken".
84 As per the original footnote to the Article 5.1(b), the reference price will be the average c.i.f. unit value of the product concerned.
85 See Appellate Body Report, *EC – Poultry*, paras. 144–146.
86 Market access opportunities are volume based and defined as percentages of the corresponding domestic consumption taken by imports during the preceding three years.
87 *Ibid.*, paras. 170.
88 See Appellate Body Report, *Chile – Price Band System*, para. 217.
89 Malaysia's revised offer on ESM states it is "conditional upon the outcome of the negotiations stipulated by the GATS, particularly on Art. X (ESM)".
90 The IMF, one of the key international institutions alongside the World Bank, is a crucial source for borrowing funds to correct BOP difficulties for developing countries. For instance, India borrowed $2.3 billion US dollars in 1991, and Thailand borrowed $3.9 billion US dollars in 1997 from the IMF to address their BOP crises.
91 The gold standard experienced its peak between 1870 and 1914, as almost all major trading nations set gold as their monetary base, and by 1978 silver was demonetised by all European countries.
92 Britain was able to influence global monetary policies during that time, as sterling was used internationally and was connected to the financial markets in London.
93 Countries at the periphery were mostly colonies, which came under the direct rule of the colonial powers.

94 The author notes that under the hierarchical structure of gold standard, whenever London raised its bank rate, capital was drawn from the countries on the next tier, and eventually from "the colonies, protectorates and countries with undeveloped financial markets which lacked the power to neutralise this movement".
95 With the participation of 44 nationals, the United Nation Monetary and Financial Conference was held at Bretton Woods, New Hampshire.
96 John Maynard Keynes, one of the architects of the Bretton Woods arrangements, went one step further and proposed a global bank, which he named the International Clearing Union. Under his proposal, the bank was to have its own currency, called 'bancor', which was exchangeable with any national currency at fixed rates of exchange. Using the 'bancor', one was able to measure a country's trade deficit or trade surplus.
97 Where a country is not able to meet payments for imports from its foreign currency earnings (through its exports) without selling its gold reserves for foreign currency.
98 The author notes that as the US held most of the currency and gold bullion reserves accumulated during the gold standard period, and due to the dominance of the US economy – both in terms of productivity and output – the US dollar was chosen over gold.
99 The pool primarily consisted of US dollar, the British pound, and the French franc.
100 The author also notes that developing country tariff schedules were often largely 'unbound' with the space for a unilateral raise at times, and that Chile and Mexico were exceptions as they maintained bound tariff schedules of 35 and 50 percent respectively.
101 The US incurred a cumulative payments deficit of $40 billion in 1969, 1970, and 1971. The other countries – as a group – had a $40 billion payments surplus. This led to a very rapid expansion in their money supplies. See Aliber (2011).
102 This finding of the Panel was not addressed by the Appellate Body.
103 (Footnote original) In particular, the conditions to be met for the institution of balance-of-payments measures are different in Article XVIII:9 and Article XII, and an *Ad* Note which applies to the conditions for progressive relaxation and elimination of restrictions under Article XVIII:11 has no analogue in Article XII.
104 See Panel Report *India – Quantitative Restrictions*, paras. 5.155–5.156.
105 *Ibid.*, paras. 5.174 and 5.177. In this case, the panel based its conclusions largely on the findings of the IMF.
106 Developing country Member States, such as India and Nigeria who were regular users of BOP measures, have long given up on the practice.
107 The reason identified by Ukraine as 'exceptional circumstances' stemmed from a combination of increased barriers to its export to traditional markets, unfavourable market prices for its major exports, anti-terrorist operations in eastern Ukraine, and the annexation of Crimea by Russia, a dramatic devaluation of its currency, as well as the destabilisation of its banking system and the outflow of investments.
108 Ecuador, as justification for its action, contended that the fall in the international prices of oil and other commodities, the decline in remittances (from Ecuadorian residents abroad), and the appreciation of the US dollar (the legal tender in Ecuador) all contributed to an "highly unfavourable economic climate".
109 *Ad* Article XVIII notes as follows: "The second sentence in paragraph 11 shall not be interpreted to mean that a contracting party is required to relax or remove restrictions if such relaxation or removal would thereupon produce conditions justifying the intensification or institution, respectively, of restrictions under paragraph 9 of Article XVIII."
110 See Panel Report *India – Quantitative Restrictions*, paras. 5.79–5.80.
111 See Appellate Body Report *US – Wool Shirts and Blouses*, p. 14.
112 See Appellate Body Report *India – Quantitative Restrictions*, para. 136.

Bibliography

Aliber, Robert Z. *The New International Money Game* (Palgrave Macmillan Publishing, 2011).
Anjaria, Shailendra J. 'Balance of Payments and Related Issues in the Uruguay Round of Trade Negotiations,' *The World Bank Economic Review* Vol 1, No 4 (1987) 669–688.
Annual Report of the Working Party on GATS Rules to the Council for Trade in Services 2011 (S/WPGR/22) (10 November 2011).

Annual Report of the Working Party on GATS Rules to the Council for Trade in Services 2012 (S/WPGR/23) (29 November 2012).

Bagwel, Kyle, Robert W. Staiger and Alan O. Sykes. 'Border Instruments,' in Horn, Henrick and Petros C. Mavroidis (eds.) *Legal and Economic Principles of World Trade Law* (Cambridge University Press, 2013) 68–204.

Beshkar, Mostafa and Eric W. Bond. 'The Escape Clause in Trade Agreements,' in Bagwell, Kyle and Staiger (eds.) *Handbook of Commercial Policy* Vol 1 Part B (North-Holland Publications, 2016) 69–106.

Bhala, Raj. *Modern GATT Law: A Treatise on the Law and Political Economy of the General Agreement on Tariffs and Trade and Other World Trade Organization Agreements* Vol 1 (Sweet & Maxwell Publishers, 2013).

Bown, Chad P. and Meredith A. Crowley. 'Safeguards in the World Trade Organization,' *The Kluwer Companion to the World Trade Organization* (Kluwer Law, 2003).

Chow, Daniel C.K. and Thomas J. Schoenbaum. *International Trade Law: Problems, Cases, and Materials* (Wolters Kluwer Law & Business, 2017).

Committee on Balance-of-Payments Restrictions. *Notification under Paragraph 9 of the Understanding on the Balance-of-Payments Provisions of the General Agreement on Tariffs and Trade 1994, Communication from Ukraine*, WT/BOP/N/78, dated 21 January 2015. See ibid. See also WT/BOP/N/78/Add.1, dated 31 March 2015.

Committee on Balance-of-Payments Restrictions. *Notification under Paragraph 9 of the Understanding on the Balance-of-Payments Provisions of the General Agreement on Tariffs and Trade 1994, Communication from Ecuador*, WT/BOP/N/79, dated 7 April 2015, para. 1.

Committee on Balance-of-Payments Restrictions. *Notification under Paragraph 9 of the Understanding on the Balance-of-Payments Provisions of the General Agreement on Tariffs and Trade 1994, Communication from Ecuador, Addendum*, WT/BOP/N/82, dated 10 May 2016.

Dam, Kenneth W. *The Rules of the Game: Reform and Evolution in the International Monetary System* (University of Chicago Press, 1982).

Das, Susanta S. 'Evolution and Political Economy of Trade Protectionism: Antidumping and Safeguard Measures,' *IIMB Management Review* (2005) 51–65.

Eglin, Richard. 'Surveillance of Balance-of-Payments Measures in the GATT,' *World Economy* Vol 10, No 1 (1987) 1–26.

GATT. Thirty-Eighth Session at Ministerial Level Ministerial Declaration (29 November 1982).

GATT. Punta del Este Ministerial Declaration (20 September 1986).

Grossman, Gene M. and Elhanan Helpman. 'Protection for Sale,' *The American Economic Review* Vol 84, No 4 (1994) 833–850.

Grote, Rainer. 'Article XII GATS,' in Wolfrum, Rüdiger, Peter-Tobias Stoll and Clemens Feinäugle (eds.) *WTO: Trade in Services* (Martin Nijhoff Publishers, 2008).

Hahn, Michael J. 'Balancing or Bending? Unilateral Reactions to Safeguard Measures,' *Journal of World Trade* Vol 39, No 2 (2005) 301–326.

Hoekman, Bernard M. and Michel K. Kostecki. *The Political Economy of the World Trading System: The WTO and Beyond* (Oxford University Press, 2009).

Igwe, Isaac O.C. 'History of the International Economy: The Bretton Woods System and Its Impact on the Economic Development of Developing Countries,' *Athens Journal of Law* Vol 4, No 2 (2018) 105–126.

Jackson, John H. *World Trade and the Law of GATT: A Legal Analysis of the General Agreement on Tariffs and Trade* (The Michie Company, 1969).

Jackson, John H. *The World Trading System* (MIT Press, 1997).

Kravis, Irving B. 'The Trade Agreements Escape Clause,' *American Economic Review* Vol 44, No 3 (1954) 319–338.

Lee, Yong-Shik. *Safeguard Measures in World Trade: The Legal Analysis* (Edward Elgar Publishing, 2014).

Lester, Simon, Bryan Mercurio and Arwel Davies. *World Trade Law: Text, Materials and Commentary* (Hart Publishing, 2018).

Lowenfeld, Andreas F. *International Economic Law* (Oxford University Press, 2008).

Matsushita, Mitsuo, Thomas J. Shoenbaum, Petros C. Mavroidis and Michael Hahn. *The World Trade Organization: Law, Practice, and Policy* (Oxford University Press, 2017).

Mavroidis, Petros C., Patrick A. Messerlin and Jasper M. Wauters. *The Law and Economics of Contingent Protection in the WTO* (Edward Elgar Publishing, 2008).

Pauwelyn, Joost. 'The Puzzle of WTO Safeguards and Regional Trade Agreements,' *Journal of International Economic Law* Vol 7, No 1 (2004) 109–142.

Piérola, Fernando. *The Challenge of Safeguards in the WTO* (Cambridge University Press, 2014).

Qin, Julia Ya. 'Reforming WTO DIscipine on Export Duties: Sovereignty Over Natural Resources, Economic Development and Environmental Protection,' in Matsushita, Mitsuo and Thomas J. Schoenbaum (eds.) *Emerging Issues in Sustainable Development: International Trade Law and Policy Relating to Natural Resources, Energy, and the Environment* (Springer, 2016) 139–182.

Rai, Sheela. *Recognition and Regulation of Safeguard Measures under GATT/WTO* (Routledge Publishing, 2013).

Sampson, Gary. 'Safeguards,' in Finger Michael J. and Andrzej Olechowski (eds.) *The Uruguay Round: A Handbook on the Multilateral Trade Negotiations* (World Bank, 1987) 143.

Sykes, Alan O. 'Protectionism as a Safeguard: A Positive Analysis of the GATT Escape Clause with Normative Speculations,' *The University of Chicago Law Review* Vol 58 (1991) 255–305.

Sykes, Alan O. 'The Safeguards Mess: A Critique of WTO Jurisprudence,' *World Trade Review* Vol 2, No 3 (2003) 261–295.

Sykes, Alan O. *The WTO Agreement on Safeguards: A Commentary* (Oxford University Press, 2006).

Thomas, Chantal. 'Balance-of-Payments Crises in the Developing World: Balancing Trade, Finance and Development in the New Economic Order,' *American University of International Law Review* Vol 15, No 6 (2000) 1249–1278.

Trebilcock, Michael, Robert Howse and Antonia Eliason. *The Regulation of International Trade* (Routledge, 2013).

US Department of State. *Proposals for Expansion of World Trade and Employment* (November 1945).

Van den Bossche, Peter and Werner Zdouc. *The Law and Policy of the World Trade Organization* (Cambridge University Press, 2017).

WTO Ministerial Conference. Ministerial Decision of 19 December 2015 on the Special Safeguard Mechanism (SSM) for Developing Countries (WT/MIN(15)/43) (21 December 2015).

WTO, Sutherland, Peter, Jagdish Bhagwati, Kwesi Botchwey, Niall W.A. Fitzgerald, Koichi Hamada, John H. Jackson, Celso Lafer and Thierry de Montbrial. 'The Future of the WTO: Addressing Institutional Challenges in the New Millennium,' Report of the Consultative Board to the Director-General Supachai Panitchpakdi (WTO, 2004).

Yoo, Ji Yeong. 'Restructuring GATT Balance-of-Payments Safeguard in the WTO System,' *Journal of World Trade* Vol 53, No 4 (2019) 528–623.

9 Subsidies and Countervailing Measures

Learning Objectives	306
1. Introduction	306
1.1 Political Economy of Subsidies and Subsidised Trade	307
1.2 The Concept of Subsidy	308
1.2.1 Financial Contribution	309
1.2.1.1 Direct Transfer of Funds	311
1.2.1.2 Foregone or Not Collected Revenue	313
1.2.1.3 Purchase of Goods or Provision of Goods and Services	316
1.2.2 Benefit Conferred	317
1.2.3 Specificity of the Subsidy	320
1.2.4 'Government or Public Body'	323
2. Regulation of Specific Subsidies Under the SCM Agreement	325
2.1 Prohibited Subsidies	325
2.1.1 Export Subsidies	326
2.1.2 Import Substitution Subsidies	330
2.2 Actionable Subsidies	331
2.2.1 Causing Injury to Domestic Industry	332
2.2.1.1 Like Products	332
2.2.1.2 Domestic Industry	333
2.2.1.3 Injury	333
2.2.1.4 Causation	337
2.2.2 Subsidies Causing Nullification, Impairment, or Prejudice	337
2.2.3 Market Definition	339
2.2.4 Displacement and Impediment to Imports	341
2.2.5 Causation and Article 6.3	342
2.2.5.1 Causation, the 'But for' Approach	344
2.3 Actionable Subsidies and Special Remedies	346
2.4 Non-Actionable Subsidies	348
3. Imposition of Countervailing Duties	348
3.1 Procedures for Investigation and Imposition of CVDs	349
3.2 Conduct of CVD Investigation	351
3.2.1 Concluding the Investigation	354
3.3 Imposition and Collection of CVDs	355
3.3.1 Duration and Review of CVDs	357
3.3.1.1 Administrative Review	357

DOI: 10.4324/9780367028183-11

		3.3.1.2 Sunset Review	359
		3.3.1.3 Judicial Review	360
		3.3.2 Institutional and Procedural Provisions	361
4.	Special and Differential Treatment for Developing Country Member States		361
5.	Subsidies Provisions in Other WTO Agreements		362
	5.1 Agreement on Agriculture		362
	5.2 GATT		365
	5.3 TRIMs Agreement		365
6.	Summary		366

Learning Objectives

This chapter aims to help students understand:

1. Subsidies and countervailing measures; the concept of subsidy; the SCM Agreement;
2. The regulation of specific subsidies under the SCM Agreement;
3. Prohibited subsidies; actionable subsidies; subsidies that cause nullification, impairment, or prejudice;
4. Causation; the 'but for' test; causation and Article 6.3;
5. Actionable subsidies and special remedies; non-actionable subsidies;
6. Imposition of countervailing duties (CVDs); procedures for investigating and imposition of CVDs; collection of CVDs;
7. Duration and review of CVDs; and
8. Special rules for developing country Member States; subsidies provisions in other WTO agreements.

1. Introduction

A contentious area of international trade practice, subsidies have come to occupy an important position within WTO jurisprudence. Subsidies and CVDs have a long history, dating back to the early part of the twentieth century, and are used by major trading nations as a protective measure. All developed and developing country Member States engage in the practice of supporting their domestic industries through subsidies, which are factored into governmental policies. There are also other non-economic reasons for the government of a Member State to subsidise and promote a particular domestic industry, or sector. Unlike tariffs and quotas, which have the effect of putting the prices up for the consumers, subsidies bring prices down and the demand up. In sharp contrast to tariffs and quotas, which are paid for by consumers, subsidies are paid for by the government from taxpayers' money. Subsidies are shaped and used by governments to promote important economic and social policy measures, and it will not be an exaggeration to state that subsidies are ubiquitous in a modern market economy.

Subsidies are different from infrastructure spending, and at a domestic level they affect decisions on resource allocation and income distribution, besides affecting structural and sectoral adjustment. When such subsidies used by Member State 'B' cause or threaten to cause material injury to the domestic industry of Member State 'A', then Member State 'A' is authorised to impose countervailing duties (CVDs) on the subsidised products. In many cases, the ultimate beneficiaries of any subsidised products may not actually be the recipients of the subsidies, but other players, *i.e.*, downstream firms exploiting such subsidised materials in their own production.[1] Agricultural subsidies, which continue to be granted by both developed and developing country Member States and help in the production and export of agricultural products, have been a cause for concern as well as being the subject of litigation. At the international level, disputes regarding subsidies in 'strategic economic sectors' have drawn much attention.[2]

While subsidies provide assistance domestically, they do raise concerns for other Member States, as they can be used as a protectionist tool and cause trade distortions, *i.e.*, bring down the cost of manufacturing, and the cost of the product *per se*. Through the grant of subsidies to import-competing industries, a Member State will most likely undermine its market access commitments. Also, any subsidies granted to competing exporters in third countries will likely divert trade away from a Member State that had relied on negotiated market access. This does give rise to the perception that any government subsidy confers an undue advantage on the private firm concerned. This may not entirely be true, as the government's act of granting subsidy may be founded on legitimate grounds. For instance, government subsidies provide benefits to private entities, who are in turn engaged to deliver public education, build highways, hospitals, and railways, fund R&D, provide fire and security services, *etc*.[3] Though the WTO laws do not prohibit subsidies, they impose restrictions to ensure that the subsidies used by one Member State do not have 'adverse effects' on the trade practices of another WTO Member State. Towards this end, the WTO legal framework provides for a set of rules on subsidisation and CVDs.

1.1 Political Economy of Subsidies and Subsidised Trade

Though tariffs and quotas were the instruments of choice for trading nations to protect domestic producers, subsidies emerged in the early 1900s as another option, gradually taking root as an alternative form of protection. The GATT, in its infancy, was more concerned with the reduction of tariffs, as it was the most frequently used instrument of protection. When tariffs became less of a problem, concern about subsidies grew as they were fast replacing tariffs as an alternative form of protection. During the ITO negotiations, which was driven by the US and the UK, the US advocated the phasing out of domestic (agricultural) subsidies and preserving export subsidies, while the UK argued for the opposite (Irwin, Mavroidis, and Sykes, 2008). In the end a compromise was reached, whereby the *Suggested Charter* contained provisions prohibiting export subsidies and procedural requirements on all trade-affecting subsidies. The efforts taken in the GATT era to discipline the use of subsidies were weak, and the GATT 1947 was very lenient towards the use of subsidies by the Contracting Parties. This also meant CVDs were increasingly used despite restrictions on their use under the GATT. Article XVI only required a notification to other Contracting Parties (upon request) of the subsidies used that were considered encouraging exports or reducing imports.[4] Also, the multilateral disciplines under Article VI and XVI of GATT 1947 permitted Contracting Parties to take domestic action against injurious subsidies and impose CVDs.

Around the time of the Tokyo Round of negotiations, the use of subsidies and CVDs was widespread and became a contentious issue, bringing into focus the need for established procedures for the use of both. The US, the chief user of CVDs, argued for the establishment of procedures for the use of subsidies, while some countries argued for disciplining CVDs. As the then director-general of the GATT observed, the issue of subsidies and CVDs became "one of the most difficult, sensitive and important of the Tokyo Round of negotiations. Production and export subsidies have had a growing and distorting influence on international trade, often protecting inefficient production at the expense of competitive industries" (GATT, 1979). The Tokyo Round of negotiations resulted in the 1979 Subsidies Code, with disciplines for both subsidies and CVDs. The Subsidies Code established a compromise between the US, which demanded more stringent rules on subsidies for non-primary products, and the EU and other countries, which were keen on disciplining the extensive use of CVDs by the US during the 1970s (Croome, 1999). While expanding the obligations of the GATT Article VI on the use of CVDs, the Code also dealt with the discipline on the grant of subsidies that might affect international trade.

Although the 1979 Subsidies Code prohibited the use of export subsidies, such prohibition did not include export subsidies for primary products, *viz.*, agricultural products. The Code imposed looser disciplines on the developing countries, as they were exempt from the use of export subsidies. The Code also dealt with the use of CVDs and when they are justified, besides also providing for consultations and resort to dispute settlement. The Code sought to strike a delicate balance between granting relief to domestic producers who had experienced losses (or a dip in profits) due to subsidised imports and preventing CVDs becoming an unwarranted barrier to trade (Croome, 1999). Some commentators hold the view that the Subsidies Code was ambivalent, as on the one hand subsidies were recognised as being a useful tool to promote important objectives of social and economic policy, and on the other hand identified subsidies as capable of causing an adverse effect to the interests of other signatory nations (Rubini, 2004). The US, to its chagrin, felt that (i) the Code did not go far enough in limiting subsidies, and (ii) the dispute settlement procedure didn't operate to its liking. It was also generally felt by other Contracting Parties that CVD rules were not successful in checking the excessive use of CVDs by the US on their exports. Most frustratingly, the Code did not define important concepts, such as 'subsidy', 'serious prejudice', and 'material injury', leading to differing interpretations by the Contracting Parties. Although the Code was intended to strengthen the rules in Articles VI and XVI of the GATT 1947 by going into greater detail on their application, it had little by way of disciplining the use of subsidies, and as a result, fewer countries came forward to sign on to the Code.

The 1985 GATT Secretariat Report stated that increasing use of subsidies and abuse of CVDs had resulted in the failure of the world economy, and that the 1979 Subsidies code had proven inadequate (Leutwiler Report, 1985). Consequently, the Ministerial Declaration on the Uruguay Round of negotiations included a mandate to improve of the subsidies and CVDs that affect international trade (GATT Ministerial Declaration, 1986). The Uruguay Round of negotiations had a clear mandate to improve the subsidies and CVD disciplines to eliminate distortions to trade (Clarke and Horlick, 2005). The first 18 months of the Uruguay Round of negotiations on subsidies was spent on reviewing Articles VI and XVI and of the 1979 code (Croome, 1999). One area where good progress was made during the Uruguay Round of negotiations was on reaching an agreement on subsidies and CVDs. The Dunkel Draft[5] which was published in 1991 contained the results of the Uruguay Round of negotiations. In 1994 the final text of the Agreement on Subsidies and Countervailing Measures (SCM) was adopted. It is to be noted that the final text of the SCM differs very little from the Dunkel text of 1991.

1.2 The Concept of Subsidy

The SCM Agreement, which was adopted during the Uruguay Round of multilateral trade negotiations, forms an integral part of to the WTO Agreement and is contained in Annex 1A. Unlike the Subsidies Code 1979, the SCM Agreement is binding on all Member States of the WTO. The SCM Agreement enlarges the international discipline on subsidies and

CVDs. Importantly, the SCM Agreement removes the earlier practice under the 1979 Subsidies Code which permitted the Contracting Parties to choose to bring the dispute either under Article VI or Article XVI of the GATT 1947, or under the Subsidies Code 1979.[6] The rules contained in Articles VI and XVI of the GATT 1994 cover subsidies and subsidised trade. The SCM establishes a set of guidance and standards for the conduct of CVD investigations and sets out rules that are to be adhered to for disputes involving subsidies before the DSB. The SCM Agreement contains a definition of the term 'subsidy', which serves both to identify subsidies and to determine what specific practices are actionable.[7]

In *Brazil – Desiccated Coconut*, the Appellate Body observed that the "SCM Agreement contains a set of rights and obligations that go well beyond merely applying and interpreting Articles VI, XVI and XXIII of the GATT 1947".[8] In *US – Carbon Steel*, the Appellate Body observed, "the main object and purpose of the SCM Agreement is to increase and improve GATT disciplines relating to the use of both subsidies and countervailing measures".[9] In *Brazil – Aircraft*, the Panel considered that the object and purpose of the SCM Agreement is to impose multilateral disciplines on subsidies that distort international trade and noted that it was for this reason that "the SCM Agreement prohibits two categories of subsidies – subsidies contingent upon exportation and upon the use of domestic over imported goods – that are specifically designed to affect trade".[10] Similarly, the Panel in *Canada – Aircraft* observed that the object and purpose of the SCM Agreement could be summarised "as the establishment of multilateral disciplines 'on the premise that some forms of government intervention distort international trade, [or] have the potential to distort [international trade]'".[11]

Although subsidy is a frequently used term in both economics and WTO disciplines, no fixed definition of the concept was available prior to the advent of the SCM Agreement. One can also add that there is no consensus on the precise effect of subsidies in the sphere of trade, for that matter. The major issue with defining subsidies relates to the concept of subsidies, and they may not all relate to governments conferring benefits on private firms or individuals. Prior to the entry into force of the SCM Agreement, various categories of state intervention were regarded as subsidies. Subsidy can refer to any government intervention (monetary support) to private enterprises which could potentially distort trade,[12] by lowering the price of goods or services at a price below what a private entity would otherwise have to pay for it (Sykes, 2005). As it is the transfer of money from the government to a private firm or actor, a subsidy can be considered an antonym to a tax which is normally collected by the government (WTO, 2006). As noted by Sykes, there is a drawback in defining subsidies in terms of benefits, as this will also require taking into account the costs imposed by government on the same private actors in the form of taxes or regulations (Sykes, 2003).

1.2.1 Financial Contribution

For the first time since the founding of a multilateral trade agreement under the GATT 1947, followed by the WTO in 1995, a detailed definition of subsidy is provided; it is contained in Article 1 of the SCM Agreement. Article 1 of the SCM Agreement is entitled 'Definition of Subsidy' and states the conditions under which a subsidy is deemed to exist. The SCM Agreement classifies the disciplines of subsidies according to three different categories, *i.e.*, prohibited, actionable, and non-actionable. Article 1 defines the concept of subsidy as a financial contribution (something of economic value) by a government or public body conferring a benefit. Subsidy, as defined under the SCM Agreement, is premised on two key elements, *viz.*, 'financial contribution' from a government and 'benefit' to the recipient.

Article 1 of the SCM Agreement distinguishes between a financial contribution being made[13] and some form of income or price support taking place.[14] The Appellate Body in *US – Carbon Steel (India)* observed, "Article 1.1 of the SCM Agreement stipulates that a 'subsidy' shall be deemed to exist if there is a 'financial contribution by a government or any public body' and 'a benefit is thereby conferred'".[15] In *Brazil – Aircraft*, the Appellate Body distinguished between a financial contribution and benefit in the following lines: "a 'financial contribution' and a 'benefit' [are] two separate legal elements in Article 1.1 of the SCM Agreement, which together determine whether a subsidy exists".[16] The Appellate Body in *US – Softwood Lumber IV*, referring to the two distinct elements of 'financial contribution' and 'benefits', observed as follows:

> The concept of subsidy defined in Article 1 of the SCM Agreement captures situations in which something of economic value is transferred by a government to the advantage of a recipient. A subsidy is deemed to exist where two distinct elements are present.[17] First, there must be a financial contribution by a government, or income or price support. Secondly, any financial contribution, or income or price support, must confer a benefit.[18]

Article 1 goes on to highlight three different types of direct financial contributions by the government, which are as follows:

i A direct transfer of funds by a government to producers or consumers (*e.g.*, grants, loans, equity infusions), direct transfer of funds are liabilities (*e.g.*, loans, guarantees);
ii A government waives revenue that is otherwise due (*e.g.*, fiscal incentives such as tax credits);
iii A government provides goods or services other than general infrastructure, or purchases goods.

The list contained in Article 1 is exhaustive,[19] and the three types of financial contributions identified therein have been broadly interpreted by the Appellate Body and Panels alike. The Panel in *US – Large Civil Aircraft (2nd complaint)* observed, "Article 1.1(a)(1) is a definitional provision that sets forth an exhaustive, closed list (' . . . *i.e.* where . . . ') of the types of transactions that constitute financial contributions under the SCM Agreement".[20] The negotiating history of Article 1 demonstrates that the inclusion of 'financial contribution' in the text of the provision was meant to guarantee that not all government measures that confer benefits would be considered as a subsidy.[21] The Appellate Body in *US – Large Civil Aircraft (2nd complaint)*, while presenting its analysis of the general structure of Article 1.1, shared the observation of the Panel and noted as follows:

> Article 1.1(a)(1) defines and identifies the government conduct that constitutes a financial contribution for purposes of the SCM Agreement. Subparagraphs (i)–(iv) exhaust the types of government conduct deemed to constitute a financial contribution. This is because the introductory *Chapeau* to the subparagraphs states that "there is a financial contribution by a government . . ., *i.e.* where:". Some of the categories of conduct – for instance those specified in subparagraphs (i) and (ii) – are described in general terms with illustrative examples that provide an indication of the common features that characterize the conduct referred to more generally. Article 1.1(a)(1), however, does not explicitly spell out the intended relationship between the constituent subparagraphs. Finally, the subparagraphs focus primarily on the action taken by the government or a public body.[22]

In *US – Softwood Lumber IV*, the Appellate Body determined the term 'financial contribution' in the following manner:[23]

> An evaluation of the existence of a financial contribution involves consideration of the nature of the transaction through which something of economic value is transferred by a government. A wide range of transactions falls within the meaning of "financial contribution" in Article 1.1(a)(1). According to paragraphs (i) and (ii) of Article 1.1(a)(1), a financial contribution may be made through a direct transfer of funds by a government, or the forgoing of government revenue that is otherwise due. Paragraph (iii) of Article 1.1(a)(1) recognizes that, in addition to such monetary contributions, a contribution having financial value can also be made in kind through governments providing goods or services, or through government purchases. Paragraph (iv) of Article 1.1(a)(1) recognizes that paragraphs (i)–(iii) could be circumvented by a government making payments to a funding mechanism or through entrusting or directing a private body to make a financial contribution. It accordingly specifies that these kinds of actions are financial contributions as well.[24]

Although the three types of financial contributions identified in Article 1 are mutually exclusive, it is possible, however, for a transaction to fall under more than one type.[25] The Appellate Body in *Canada – Renewable Energy*, while referring to its ruling in *US – Large Civil Aircraft (2nd Complaint)*, provided guidance on legal characterisation of a transaction under Article 1.1(a)(1) and observed as follows:

> When determining the proper legal characterization of a measure under Article 1.1(a)(1) of the SCM Agreement, a panel must assess whether the measure may fall within any of the types of financial contributions set out in that provision. In doing so, a panel should scrutinize the measure both as to its design and operation and identify its principal characteristics. Having done so, the transaction may naturally fit into one of the types of financial contributions listed in Article 1.1(a)(1). However, transactions may be complex and multifaceted. This may mean that different aspects of the same transaction may fall under different types of financial contribution. It may also be the case that the characterization exercise does not permit the identification of a single category of financial contribution and, in that situation, as described in the *US – Large Civil Aircraft (2nd complaint)* Appellate Body report, a transaction may fall under more than one type of financial contribution. We note, however, that the fact that a transaction may fall under more than one type of financial contribution does not mean that the types of financial contributions set out in Article 1.1(a)(1) are the same or that the distinct legal concepts set out in this provision would become redundant, as the Panel suggests. We further observe that, in *US – Large Civil Aircraft (2nd complaint)*, the Appellate Body did not address the question of whether, in the situation described above, a panel is under an obligation to make findings that a transaction falls under more than one subparagraph of Article 1.1(a)(1).[26]

1.2.1.1 DIRECT TRANSFER OF FUNDS

Article 1.1(a)1(i) identifies the first type of financial contribution as "a government practice [that] involves a direct transfer of funds" – which could take the form of grants, loans, and equity infusion, or "potential direct transfer of funds or liabilities" – which could take the form of loan guarantees. The Appellate Body in *US – Large Civil Aircraft (2nd complaint)* stated, a "direct transfer of funds" in subparagraph (i) captures "conduct on the part of the government by which money, financial resources, and/or financial claims are made available to a recipient".[27] Further, the Appellate Body elaborated on the examples in subparagraph (i) as follows:

> It is clear from the examples in subparagraph (i) that a direct transfer of funds will normally involve financing by the government to the recipient. In some instances, as in the case of grants, the conveyance of funds will not involve a reciprocal obligation on the part of the recipient. In other cases, such as loans and equity infusions, the recipient assumes obligations to the government in exchange for the funds provided. Thus, the provision of funding may amount to a donation or may involve reciprocal rights and obligations.[28]

The words "potential direct transfers of funds or liabilities (*e.g.*, loan guarantees)" establishes a broad scope for the interpretation of the concept of 'direct transfer of funds'. Article 1.1(a)1(i) covers any variation of state support that is capable of increasing the financial capability of the beneficiary, which could be similar to or equivalent to the ones expressly listed under the provision. The Appellate Body, while upholding the findings of the Panel in *Japan – DRAMS (Korea)*, reasoned that the meaning of 'funds' includes not only money, but also financial resources and other financial claims more generally, and observed as follows:

> We observe that the words "grants, loans, and equity infusion" are preceded by the abbreviation "*e.g.*", which indicates that grants, loans, and equity infusion are cited examples of transactions falling within the scope of Article 1.1(a)(1)(i). This shows that transactions that are similar to those expressly listed are also covered by the provision [and include:] Debt forgiveness, which extinguishes the claims of a creditor, is a form of performance by which the borrower is taken to have repaid the loan to the lender. The extension of a loan maturity enables the borrower to enjoy the benefit of the loan for an extended period of time. An interest rate reduction lowers the debt servicing burden of the borrower. In all of these cases, the financial position of the borrower is improved and therefore there is a direct transfer of funds within the meaning of Article 1.1(a)(1)(i).[29]

The Appellate Body in *US – Large Civil Aircraft (2nd complaint)* also noted that that certain measures, joint ventures arrangements, had sufficient features in common with one of the examples in subparagraph (i), *i.e.*, equity infusions, to indicate that the measures fell within the concept of 'direct transfers of funds' in Article 1.1(a)(1)(i) and observed as follows:

> Like equity investors, NASA and the USDOD provide funding. This funding is provided in the expectation of some kind of return. In the case of NASA and USDOD funding to Boeing, the return is not financial, but rather takes the form of scientific and technical information, discoveries, and data expected to result from the research performed. Again, like equity investors, NASA and the USDOD have no certainty at the time they commit the funding that the research will be successful. Success will depend on whether any inventions are discovered and the usefulness of the data collected, as well as the scientific and technical information produced. NASA's and the USDOD's risks are limited to the amount of money they contribute and the opportunity cost of the other support they provide to the project, much like an equity investor. And like some equity investors, NASA and the USDOD contribute to the project by providing access to facilities, equipment, and employees.

Similar to the prior findings of the Appellate Body in *Japan – DRAMS*, the Panel in *EC and Certain Member States – Large Civil Aircraft* concluded that a share transfer involved a 'direct transfer of funds' within the meaning of Article 1.1(a)(1)(i).[30]

1.2.1.2 FOREGONE OR NOT COLLECTED REVENUE

Article 1.1(a)1(ii) identifies the second type of financial contribution as the waiver of government revenue payable – which could be either foregone or not collected, *e.g.*, fiscal incentives such as tax credits. Forgoing the collection of government revenue – a negative action – can be viewed as falling under this category, as the government is waiving revenue that is lawfully due to it from a private entity who then benefits from such waiver. In simple terms this form of financial contribution can be equated to partial non-enforcement of tax laws – tax holidays – to assist the recovery of a struggling enterprise. The waiver of tax envisaged here includes internal taxes – both direct and indirect taxes, and also import duties, *i.e.*, tariffs. However, the tax waiver envisaged under the provisions of Article 1.1(a)1(ii) does not include rebates of indirect taxes and import duties upon exportation, as they are explicitly excluded from the subsidy definition and the SCM Agreement in Footnote 1 of the SCM Agreement.[31] This was clearly laid down by the Appellate Body in *US – FSC*, where the EC challenged a US measure exempting income of certain US economic operators, *i.e.*, Foreign Sales Corporations (FSC), generated outside of the US jurisdiction.[32]

The Appellate Body in *US – FSC* ruled that in establishing if revenue 'otherwise due' has been foregone by the government, a comparison must be made between the revenue actually raised and the revenue that would have been raised 'otherwise'. The Panel and the Appellate Body agreed that the basis of comparison in determining what would otherwise have been due "must be the tax rules applied by the Member in question".[33] The Appellate Body in *US – FSC (Article 21.5 – EC)* clarified that there may be situations where it is possible to apply a 'but for' test, namely where the measure at issue is an 'exception' to a 'general' rule of taxation.[34] The Appellate Body ruled that, in situations where a Panel is required to identify the 'general' rule of taxation, it should

> seek to compare the fiscal treatment of legitimately comparable income to determine whether the contested measure involves the foregoing of revenue which is "otherwise due", in relation to the income in question . . . [T]he normative benchmark for determining whether revenue foregone is otherwise due must allow a comparison of the fiscal treatment of comparable income, in the hands of taxpayers in similar situations.[35]

In *EC and Certain Member States – Large Civil Aircraft*, the debt in question was 9.4 billion Deutschmark owed by Deutsche Airbus to the German government.[36] The Panel in *EC and Certain Member States – Large Civil Aircraft* held that a settlement of government-held debt was essentially the transfer to the debtor of the government's financial claims against that debtor, which resulted in the cancellation of the debt. The Panel also rejected the claim of the EU, which was based on the premise that only a debt due could be forgiven as it constituted a fund, as opposed to an amount that is only payable after a certain period.[37] It also came to light that a part of the 'launch aid' committed by the Air Member States to finance the A380 had not been paid out yet. The Panel did not classify such funds, which remained undisbursed, as a credit line but as a direct transfer of funds, treating them as a loan.[38]

The Panel in *US – Large Civil Aircraft (2nd complaint)* found that certain measures taken involved a foregoing of revenue which would be otherwise due within the meaning of Article

1.1(a)(1)(ii). Recalling the Appellate Body's guidance in *US – FSC* and *US – FSC (Article 21.5 – EC)*, the Panel summarised as follows:

> Therefore, the Appellate Body's analysis suggests that where it is possible to identify a general rule of taxation applied by the Member in question, a "but for" test can be applied. In other situations, the challenged taxation measure should be compared to the treatment applied to comparable income, for taxpayers in comparable circumstances in the jurisdiction in issue.[39]

It should be borne in mind that there is no common tax policy across all the Member States of the multilateral trading system. Also, the WTO cannot impose one, as it does not possess such authority. It is very likely that a transaction could be taxed twice over in the global value chain for reasons of nationality of the operator or place where the transaction happens. Most developed country Member States and a number of developing country Member States have entered into double taxation agreements to avoid the practice of double taxation. Can this practice of the Member States be considered as 'financial contribution' for the purposes of Article 1.1(a)(1)(ii)? While it is possible to interpret the practice as 'financial contribution', one may have to take a closer look at Footnote 59 of Annex 1 of the SCM Agreement before concluding so. Footnote 59 to Annex 1 of the SCM Agreement reads as follows:

> [p]aragraph (e) [of the Annex I] is not intended to limit a Member from taking measures to avoid the double taxation of foreign-source income earned by its enterprises or the enterprises of another Member.

Going by the provision, the answer to the previous question is that such agreements entered into between Member States and intended to avoid double taxation cannot be understood to be an export subsidy for the purposes of the SCM Agreement (Matsushita, Shoenbaum, Mavroidis, and Hahn, 2017). The Appellate Body in *US – FSC (Article 21.5 – EC)* dealt with the aforementioned aspect, providing the legal test to distinguish between what is permissible and what is not.[40] The Appellate Body in *US – FSC (Article 21.5 – EC)* noted that Member States have the authority to determine their rules of taxation, provided they comply with WTO obligations. The Appellate Body upheld the Panel's findings that footnote 59 does not require Members to adopt particular legal standards to define when income is foreign-source for the purposes of their double taxation-avoidance measures and noted that footnote 59 does not give Members an unlimited discretion to avoid double taxation of 'foreign-source income' through the grant of export subsidies. Accordingly, for the Appellate Body, the term 'foreign-source income', as used in footnote 59, cannot be interpreted solely by reference to the rules of the Member State taking the measure to avoid double taxation of foreign-source income. The Appellate Body ruled as follows:

> [F]ootnote 59 does not give Members an unfettered discretion to avoid double taxation of "foreign-source income" through the grant of export subsidies. As the fifth sentence of footnote 59 to the SCM Agreement constitutes an exception to the prohibition on export subsidies, great care must be taken in defining its scope. If footnote 59 were interpreted to allow a Member to grant a fiscal preference for any income that a Member chooses to regard as foreign source, that reading would seriously undermine the prohibition on export subsidies in the SCM Agreement. That would allow Members, relying on whatever source rules they adopt, to grant fiscal export subsidies for income

that may not actually be susceptible of being taxed in two jurisdictions. Accordingly, the term "foreign-source income", as used in footnote 59 cannot be interpreted by reference solely to the rules of the Member taking the measure to avoid double taxation of foreign-source income.[41]

In *US – FSC*, the Appellate Body considered that Member States have a discretion to avoid double taxation:

> [I]t is "implicit" in the requirement to use the arm's length principle that Members of the WTO are not obliged to tax foreign-source income, and also that Members may tax such income less than they tax domestic-source income. We would add that, even in the absence of footnote 59, Members of the WTO are not obliged, by WTO rules, to tax any categories of income, whether foreign- or domestic-source income. The United States argues that, since there is no requirement to tax export related foreign-source income, a government cannot be said to have "foregone" revenue if it elects not to tax that income. It seems to us that, taken to its logical conclusion, this argument by the United States would mean that there could never be a foregoing of revenue "otherwise due" because, in principle, under WTO law generally, no revenues are ever due and no revenue would, in this view, ever be "foregone". That cannot be the appropriate implication to draw from the requirement to use the arm's length principle.[42]

The Appellate Body in *US – Large Civil Aircraft (2nd complaint)* warned about the "the limitations inherent in identifying and comparing a general rule of taxation" and observed:

> For instance . . . it could be misleading to identify a benchmark within a domestic tax regime solely by reference to historical tax rates. By that measure, the fact that commercial aircraft and component manufacturers were previously subject to higher tax rates would not in itself be determinative of what the benchmark is at the time of the challenge. . . .
>
> We have also noted that it could be misleading to compare rates applicable to a general category of income with rates applicable to a subcategory of that income, without considering whether the scope of the "exceptions" undermines the existence of a "general rule".[43]

The Panel in *EC and Certain Member States – Large Civil Aircraft* concluded that the relinquishment of a government-held debt may also constitute a 'direct transfer of funds' within the meaning of Article 1.1(a)(1)(i), and observed as follows:

> If we conclude that the financial contribution confers a "benefit" on Deutsche Airbus, then it may be that the subsidy in question could be described as "debt forgiveness" in an amount equal to the amount of benefit found to have been conferred. However, the first issue for us to determine is whether the 1998 debt settlement constitutes one of the forms of financial contribution set forth in Article 1.1(a)(1). We conclude that the 1998 debt settlement constitutes a financial contribution in the form of a "direct transfer of funds" within the meaning of Article 1.1(a)(1)(i) of the SCM Agreement. We note that, in *Japan – DRAMS*, the Appellate Body interpreted the term "funds" in Article 1.1(a)(1)(i) broadly, as encompassing not only "money" but also "financial resources and other financial claims more generally." Debt owed to the government is an asset held by the

government consisting of certain financial claims (*i.e.*, rights to payment of money or equivalents) that the government has against a debtor. A settlement of government-held debt essentially involves the transfer to the debtor of the government's financial claims against that debtor, resulting in the cancellation of the debt. We therefore regard a settlement of debt as a "direct transfer of funds" by a government, and thus a "financial contribution" within the meaning of Article 1.1(a)(1)(i) of the SCM Agreement.[44]

1.2.1.3 PURCHASE OF GOODS OR PROVISION OF GOODS AND SERVICES

The third form of financial contribution contemplated in Article 1.1(a)(1)(iii) of the SCM Agreement is the provision of goods or services by the government. Subparagraph (iii) of Article 1.1(a)(1) contemplates two distinct types of transactions, *viz.*, where a government "provides goods or services other than general infrastructure" and situations in which the government "purchases goods" from an enterprise.[45] In one of the long-running disputes between the US and Canada, *i.e.*, the complex *US – Softwood Lumber IV* dispute, the US alleged that the Canadian lumber industry was heavily and unfairly subsidised by the government, and that unlike in the US where stumpage fee (price charged to harvest timber) is fixed through a competitive marketplace, in Canada they were set administratively.[46] The US argued that the Canadian lumber production is heavily subsidised, giving them an unfair advantage in the US market, and that they can be subject to CVDs.[47] The Appellate Body in *US – Softwood Lumber IV*, after noting, "[a]n evaluation of the existence of a financial contribution involves consideration of the nature of the transaction through which something of economic value is transferred by a government",[48] explained that Article 1.1(a)(1)(iii) foresaw two types of transaction, and explained the scope of the Article as follows:

> As such, the Article contemplates two distinct types of transaction. The first is where a government provides goods or services other than general infrastructure. Such transactions have the potential to lower artificially the cost of producing a product by providing, to an enterprise, inputs having a financial value. The second type of transaction falling within Article 1.1(a)(1)(iii) is where a government purchases goods from an enterprise. This type of transaction has the potential to increase artificially the revenues gained from selling the product.[49]

Earlier, the Panel in *US – Softwood Lumber III* had discussed the reason for holding the Canadian stumpage programme as constituting a financial contribution falling under Article 1:

> In Article 1.1(a)(1)(iii) SCM Agreement, "goods" is used in the context of "goods or services other than general infrastructure" . . . In our view, the sentence "goods or services other than general infrastructure" refers to a very broad spectrum of things a government may provide. The fact that the only exception provided for in subparagraph (iii) is general infrastructure reinforces our view concerning the unqualified meaning of the term goods as used in this provision . . .
>
> . . . Canada refers to certain provisions which contain the term "imported goods", and concludes on that basis that wherever the term "goods" is used in the Agreement, it refers to products which are capable of being imported and traded across borders. We find no basis for such a conclusion in the text of the SCM Agreement. Although "goods" in Article 1.1(a)(1)(iii) SCM Agreement certainly includes tradable products, there is

no reason to limit its meaning to only such products, particularly where the immediate context in which the term is used does not suggest such a limitation. In particular, this provision states that when the government provides "goods or services", this constitutes a financial contribution. The "goods" in question are not imported or exported, simply provided by the government, and nothing suggests therefore that the goods in question need to be tradeable products with a potential or actual tariff line. Goods in this context are distinguished from services, and in our view the two cover the full spectrum of in-kind transfers the government may undertake by providing resources to an enterprise. Our view is reinforced by the fact that there is only one exception among all possible goods and services that could be provided by the government – general infrastructure – which is explicitly defined as not constituting a financial contribution. We thus find that there is no basis in the text of the SCM Agreement to conclude that "goods" in Article 1.1 is limited to products with an actual or potential tariff line.[50]

The Appellate Body in *US – Softwood Lumber IV* endorsed a wider interpretation of the terms 'goods' and 'provision' where 'goods' include 'property or possession' – where immovable property is considered as goods.[51] The Appellate Body also upheld the Panel's finding that nothing in the text of Article 1.1(a)(1)(iii), its context, or the object and purpose of the SCM Agreement supported the conclusion that standing timber is not covered by the term "goods" in Article 1.1(a)(1)(iii).[52] Likewise, in *Canada – Renewable Energy*, the Appellate Body engaged in a broad interpretation of 'good' in the context to include electricity.[53]

Apart from the three categories of direct financial contributions from the government discussed earlier, a fourth category is covered under 1.1(a)1(iv) which identifies financial contribution provided indirectly by a government or a public body where it makes payments to a funding mechanism, or where a government or a public body entrusts or directs a private body to carry out one or more of the functions illustrated in (i) to (iii). Despite the detailed categorisation, Article 1.1, as such, does not impose any obligation on WTO Members with respect to the subsidies it defines.

1.2.2 Benefit Conferred

As discussed earlier, any financial contribution (or income, or price support) from a government to a private entity can be considered a subsidy for the purposes of Article 1.1(b) of the SCM Agreement only when the financial contribution in question confers a benefit to the recipient. If the financial contribution has made the recipient 'better off' than what they would have otherwise been, then such a contribution will be viewed as a subsidy for the purposes of Article 1.1(b). The Appellate Body in *US – Large Civil Aircraft (2nd complaint)* observed that in order to determine a 'benefit' under Article 1.1(b) of the SCM Agreement, one needs to establish whether the financial contribution has made the recipient 'better off' than what they would otherwise have been, without that contribution.[54] To determine a 'benefit' some form of comparison is to be made, and hence the Appellate Body developed the 'marketplace test' providing the basis for comparison. The Appellate Body in *Canada – Aircraft*, observed:

> the marketplace provides an appropriate basis for comparison in determining whether a "benefit" has been "conferred", because the trade-distorting potential of a "financial contribution" can be identified by determining whether the recipient has received a "financial contribution" on terms more favourable than those available to the recipient in the market.[55]

However, to demonstrate a benefit, the examination needs to be carried out from the recipient's perspective and not from the conferring authority's perspective, as not all 'financial contribution' can confer a 'benefit'. This aspect 'benefit' analysis was highlighted by the Panel in *EC – Countervailing Measures on DRAM Chips* as follows:

> [I]f the financial contribution is not provided by the government (or directed or entrusted by the government), it is of no concern to us. If the financial contribution is provided (or directed or entrusted) by the government but still does not confer an advantage over what was available on the market, there is no need to discipline such government behaviour which lacks a trade distorting potential.[56]

It is essential that the complainant, in order to establish that the recipient derived a benefit, demonstrate that the recipient obtained an advantage, which they would not have in the marketplace. In this regard the Appellate Body in *Canada – Aircraft*, while noting that the focus of the enquiry under Article 1.1(b) should be on the recipient and not on the granting authority, observed as follows:

> A "benefit" does not exist in the abstract, but must be received and enjoyed by a beneficiary or a recipient. Logically, a "benefit" can be said to arise only if a person, natural or legal, or a group of persons, has in fact received something. The term "benefit", therefore, implies that there must be a recipient. This provides textual support for the view that the focus of the inquiry under Article 1.1(b) of the SCM Agreement should be on the recipient and not on the granting authority. The ordinary meaning of the word "confer", as used in Article 1.1(b), bears this out. "Confer" means, *inter alia*, "give", "grant" or "bestow". The use of the past participle "conferred" in the passive form, in conjunction with the word "thereby", naturally calls for an inquiry into what was conferred on the recipient. Accordingly, we believe that Canada's argument that "cost to government" is one way of conceiving of "benefit" is at odds with the ordinary meaning of Article 1.1(b), which focuses on the recipient and not on the government providing the "financial contribution".[57]

The words of the Appellate Body highlight the issue with 'recipients' and beneficiaries, *i.e.*, on the face of it the financial contribution may appear to 'benefit' a particular entity, but the ultimate beneficiary of the financial contribution may be another entity. As noted by the Appellate Body in *US – Softwood Lumber IV*, "[w]here subsidy is conferred on input products, and countervailing duty is imposed on processed products, the initial recipient of the subsidy and the producer of the eventually countervailed product, may not be the same".[58] In practice, one would encounter such situations where entity A is made to buy property from entity B – which is downstream; or entity A selling products to entity B at a reduced price – which is downstream.

While determining if the financial contribution resulted in conferring any 'benefits' under Article 1.1(b), both the Panels and the Appellate Body have gained contextual guidance from Article 14 of the SCM Agreement, which primarily provides guidelines which apply for the purposes of Part V of the SCM Agreement, relating to CVD investigations.[59] The Appellate Body in *Canada – Aircraft* expressed the view that Article 14 constitutes a relevant context for the interpretation of 'benefit' in Article 1.1(b).[60] As mentioned earlier, the Appellate Body, while holding that benefit must be established through the determination of whether the financial contribution makes the recipient better off *vis-à-vis* the market than it would have been absent that financial contribution, also noted, "Article 14, which we have said is relevant context in interpreting Article 1.1(b), supports our view that the marketplace is an appropriate basis for comparison".[61]

In *US – Carbon Steel (India)*, the Appellate Body while discussing the relationship between Article 1.1(b) and Article 14, made the following observation:

> The term "benefit" appears in Article 1.1(b), as well as Article 14, of the SCM Agreement. While the former provision is concerned with the existence of a "benefit", the latter provision is, in the context of Part V of the SCM Agreement, concerned with the calculation of its amount. The determination of the mere existence, as opposed to the amount, of benefit conferred by a financial contribution does not, however, call for different interpretations of the term "benefit". Indeed, the explicit textual reference to Article 1.1 in the *Chapeau* of Article 14 indicates that "benefit" is used in the same sense in Article 14 as it is in Article 1.1.[62]

Article 14(b) requires for a comparison to be made of the "amount that the firm receiving the loan pays on the government loan" with "the amount the firm would pay on a comparable commercial loan which the firm could actually obtain on in the market". In *EC – Large Civil Aircraft*, the Appellate Body relied on Article 14(b) of the SCM Agreement to rule that the comparison between government loans and market prices has to be performed as though both were obtained at the same time,[63] *i.e.*, the comparable commercial loan that would have been available to the recipient at the time it received the government loan.[64] Applying Article 14(b), the Appellate Body noted:

> A panel relying on Article 14(b) would thus examine whether there is a difference between the amount that the recipient pays on the government loan and the amount the recipient would pay on a on a comparable commercial loan, which the recipient could have actually obtained on the market.[65] There is a benefit – and therefore a subsidy – where the amount that the recipient pays on the government loan is less than what the recipient would have paid on a comparable commercial loan that the recipient could have obtained on the market. There is no benefit – and therefore no subsidy – if what the recipient pays on the government loan is equal to or higher than what it would have paid on a comparable commercial loan. The amount the recipient would have paid on a commercial loan is a function of the size of the loan, the interest rate, the duration, and other relevant terms of the transaction. The participants agreed at the oral hearing that Article 14(b) of the SCM Agreement provides useful guidance for purposes of the assessment of whether the LA/MSF measures confer a benefit.[66]

While applying Article 14(d), the Appellate Body in *US – Carbon Steel (India)*, observed that "prevailing market conditions in the country of provision" are the standard for calculating the adequacy of remuneration, as they describe the generally accepted characteristics of an area of economic activity in which the forces of supply and demand interact to determine market prices.[67] The Appellate Body also noted that an assessment of 'prevailing market conditions', within the meaning of Article 14(d), necessarily involves an analysis of the market generally, rather than isolated transactions in that market. It is only through such an analysis that a conclusion can be drawn as to the conditions that are 'prevailing' in the market in the country of provision. Moreover, 'prevailing market conditions' cannot be assessed solely from the perspective of the providers of the relevant good in question. This would be in tension with the proposition that a government-provided financial contribution confers a benefit if the "'financial contribution' makes the recipient 'better off' than it would otherwise have been, absent that contribution".[68]

It is now well settled, following the ruling of the Appellate Body in *Canada – Aircraft*, that there can be no 'benefit' to the recipient unless 'financial contribution' makes the recipient 'better off' than it would otherwise have been, absent that contribution.[69] Concerning the meaning of 'benefits' as occurring in Article 1.1(b) of the SCM Agreement, the issue of the issue of 'extinction' or 'duration' of benefit have come up for consideration before the Appellate Body. The Appellate Body in *US – Countervailing Measures on Certain EC Products* observed, "[p]rivatizations at arm's length and for fair market value may result in extinguishing the benefit" and "there is a rebuttable presumption that a benefit ceases to exist after such a privatization".[70] The Appellate Body also stressed that such determination, however, depended on the facts of each case whether a 'benefit' derived from pre-privatisation financial contributions is extinguished following privatisation at arm's length and for fair market value.[71]

The case in *EC and Certain Member States – Large Civil Aircraft* once again gave rise to the issue of 'extinction' of benefit, where the sales transactions did not amount to a full privatisation of a previously state-owned company. The issue for consideration before the Appellate Body was, how long does a financial contribution benefit the recipient? Reversing the Panel's findings and recognising that a subsidy has a shelf-life, the Appellate Body observed as follows:

> [It] may come to an end, either through the removal of the financial contribution and/or the expiration of the benefit . . . where it is so argued, a panel must assess whether there are "intervening events" that occurred after the grant of the subsidy that may affect the projected value of the subsidy as determined under the *ex ante* analysis. Such events may be relevant to an adverse effects analysis because they may affect the link that a complaining party is seeking to establish between the subsidy and its alleged effects.[72]

1.2.3 *Specificity of the Subsidy*

Having established what is subsidy and how government financial contributions to private entities could constitute subsidy if it gives rise to a benefit, we move on to 'specificity' of the subsidy covered under Article 2 of the SCM Agreement. As noted in the *World Trade Report*, subsidies are likely to distort trade if they are 'specific', as their relative price effect will be greater (WTO, 2006). Pursuant to Article 2, a subsidy will only fall under the discipline of the SCM Agreement if they are specific. Article 1.2 states that a subsidy shall only be subject to provisions of Parts II (prohibited subsidies), III (actionable subsidies), or V (countervailing measures) if it is specific, as defined in Article 2. As a result, any subsidy that is not 'specific' will not be regulated as prohibited or actionable under the SCM Agreement. The objective of such a classification is to distinguish between government financial contribution for the state economy (*e.g.*, spending on schools and universities, hospitals, transportation, *etc.*), which are part of welfare programmes, and subsidies to private entities that have the effect of distorting trade.

Article 2 of the SCM Agreement elaborates the concept of specificity and lays down the rules on when specificity ensues, identifying three principal categories of subsidies. Articles 2.1(a) to (c) outline the three categories where specificity exists. Under Article 2.1, specificity can be *de jure*, as in subparagraphs (a) and (b), or *de facto*, as in subparagraph (c). (i) Article 2.1(a) grant of subsidies in relation to industry specificity – where the government limits access to subsidies to a particular group, industry, or group of industries;[73] (ii) Article 2.1(b) grant of subsidies with regional specificity – where the government targets manufacturers in certain regions of the state;[74] and (iii) Article 2.1(c) prohibited subsidies – where the government targets export goods or goods using domestic inputs for subsidisation.[75] In the following cases, the Appellate Body had the occasion to interpret Article 2 of the SCM Agreement in detail: *US – Anti-Dumping and Countervailing Duties (China)*; *EC and Certain Member States – Large Civil Aircraft*; *US – Large Civil Aircraft (2nd complaint)*; *US – Carbon Steel (India)*; and *US – Countervailing Measures (China)*.

The Appellate Body in *US – Anti-Dumping and Countervailing Duties (China)*, provided general guidance and observed that Article 2 is characterised by a two-tier structure, *i.e.*, the *Chapeau* of Article 2.1 and the scenarios outlined in Article 2.1(a) to (c).[76] The Appellate Body observed that the *Chapeau* of Article 2.1 frames the central inquiry as to whether a subsidy is specific to 'certain enterprises'. While interpreting Article 2 in general, its subparagraphs, and the relationship between its subparagraphs, the Appellate Body observed that the principles set out in subparagraphs (a) through (c) 'shall apply', and that the use of the term 'principles', instead of 'rules' denotes that subparagraphs (a) through (c) are to be "considered within an analytical framework that recognises and accords appropriate weight to each principal".[77] The Appellate Body observed that 'enterprise' may be defined as a 'business firm, a company', whereas 'industry' could signify a "particular form or branch of productive labour; a trade, a manufacture".[78] The panel in *US – Upland Cotton* opined that "an industry, or group of 'industries' may be generally referred to by the type of products they produce", but that "the breadth of this concept of 'industry' may depend on several factors in a given case".[79] Agreeing with the opinion of the Panel, the Appellate Body in *US – Anti-Dumping and Countervailing Duties (China)* noted:

> The above suggests that the term "certain enterprises" refers to a single enterprise or industry or a class of enterprises or industries that are known and particularized. We . . . agree . . . with the panel in *US – Upland Cotton* that any determination of whether a number of enterprises or industries constitute "certain enterprises" can only be made on a case-by-case basis.[80]

The Appellate Body in *US – Countervailing Measures (China)* observed that the objective of the enquiry under Article 2.1 "is to determine whether the subsidy that was found to exist pursuant to Article 1.1 is specific", and in particular, "the analysis of specificity focuses on the question of whether access to subsidy is limited to a particular class of recipients".[81] The Panel in *US – Anti-Dumping and Countervailing Duties (China)* observed that the specificity requirement is not about existence of the subsidy, but rather about the access thereto.[82] As mentioned earlier, specificity under Article 2.1(a) and (b) can be *de jure* and *de facto* under Article 2.1(c). In *US – Countervailing Measures (China) (Article 21.5 – China)*, the Appellate Body stated, "the specificity inquiry under Article 2 . . . involves a consideration of whether there is a limitation on access to the relevant subsidy" and, despite the appearance of non-specificity under Article 2.1(a) and (b), the investigating authority may consider whether the subsidy is *de facto* specific.[83]

The Appellate Body in *US – Large Civil Aircraft (2nd complaint) (2012)* observed that Article 2.1(a) referred to limitations on access to "a subsidy", that although the use of the term in the singular might suggest a limited conception, more specific for the recipient, other context occurring in Article 2.1 suggests a potentially broader framework within which specificity is to be examined.[84] The Appellate Body observed that, though the subsidy is the starting point for an enquiry to establish specificity under Article 2.1(a), the scope of the inquiry should include an examination of the legislation pursuant to which the granting authority operates, or the express acts of the granting authority.[85]

Article 2.1(c) of the SCM Agreement deals with the third principle for determining specificity, where subsidies are *de facto* specific. In the context of examining if a measure under issue was *de facto* specific under 2.1(c), the Appellate Body in *US – Countervailing Measure (China)* elaborated as follows:

> [I]n a situation where the evidence suggests that a subsidy is not *de jure* specific because the conditions set out in subparagraph (b) are satisfied, subparagraph (c) of Article 2.1 clarifies that the specificity inquiry does not necessarily end at that point because, "notwithstanding any appearance of non-specificity" resulting from the application of Article 2.1(a) and (b), a subsidy may nevertheless be found to be "in fact" specific.[86]

Article 2.1(c) of the SCM Agreement lists the following factors as being germane in determining if a subsidy is *de facto* specific: (i) the use of a subsidy programme by a limited number of certain enterprises; (ii) the predominant use of a subsidy programme by certain enterprises; (iii) the granting of disproportionately large subsidies to certain enterprises; and (iv) the manner in which discretion has been exercised by the granting authority in the decision to grant a subsidy.[87] Noting that Article 2.1(c) identifies the factors that investigating authorities and Panel should consider while determining if a subsidy were specific, the Appellate Body in *US – Carbon Steel (India)* observed as follows:

> while *de jure* and *de facto* analyses are both focused on whether a subsidy is specific, they do so from somewhat different perspectives. While a *de jure* analysis examines concrete evidence relating to explicit limitations on access, a *de facto* analysis focuses on indicia of the allocation or use of a subsidy that support a finding of specificity.[88]

Regarding the first factor listed in Article 2.1(c), *i.e.*, use of a subsidy programme by a limited number of certain enterprises, the Appellate Body noted that the said factor was focused on a quantitative assessment of the entities that actually use a subsidy programme and, in particular, on whether such use is shared by a "limited number of certain enterprises".[89] In regards to the third factor, *i.e.*, "granting of disproportionately large amounts of subsidies to certain enterprises", the Appellate Body stated that it is not necessary to establish specificity on the basis of discrimination in favour of 'certain enterprises' against a broader category of other, similarly situated entities.[90]

Article 2.2 states that where a subsidy is 'limited to certain enterprises' within a "designated geographical region within the jurisdiction of a granting authority", such subsidy will be considered specific.[91] The question whether such subsidy granted by a regional authority should be limited to the subset of enterprise within that region to fall within Article 2.2 was addressed by the Panel in *EC and Certain Member States – Large Civil Aircraft*. The Panel, while observing that Article 2.2 was not "particularly clearly drafted", ruled that it "is properly understood to provide that a subsidy available in a designated region within the territory of the granting authority is specific, even if it is available to all enterprises in that designated region".[92] The Appellate Body in *US – Washing Machines*, while upholding the findings of the Panel concluded that (i) the term 'certain enterprises' in Article 2.2 is not limited to entities with legal personality, but also encompasses sub-units or constituent parts of a company – including its branch offices and the facilities through which it conducts manufacturing operations – that may or may not possess distinct legal personality; (ii) the 'designation' of a region for the purposes of Article 2.2 need not be affirmative or explicit, but may also be carried out by exclusion or implication, provided that the region in question is clearly discernible from the text, design, structure, and operation of the subsidy at issue; and that (iii) the concept of 'geographical region' in Article 2.2 does not depend on the territorial size of the area covered by a subsidy.[93]

1.2.4 'Government or Public Body'

The provision of a 'subsidy' is premised on financial support/contributions made by a government, or a public body within the jurisdiction of a Member State. The SCM Agreement refers to government and public body collectively as 'government', which factor is well captured by Article 1.1(a)(1). Further, as per Article 1.1(a)(1)(iv), any financial contribution given by a private body will only qualify as subsidy when such private body is entrusted or directed by the government. The notion of 'public body' came to be discussed by the Appellate Body in *US – Anti-Dumping and Countervailing Duties (China)*, where China challenged the conduct of the underlying investigations on definitive anti-dumping and CVDs carried out by the US authorities, as being inconsistent with the provisions of the GATT,[94] the SCM Agreement,[95] the Anti-Dumping Agreement,[96] and the Protocol on the Accession of the People's Republic of China.[97] The Appellate Body pointed out that "being vested with governmental authority is the key feature of a public body" and that a public body "must be an entity that possesses, exercises or is vested with government authority".[98]

The Appellate Body in *US – Anti-Dumping and Countervailing Duties (China)*, while reversing the Panel's finding that the term 'public body' in Article 1.1(a)(1) of the SCM Agreement means "any entity controlled by a government", ruled that the term 'public body' in the context of Article 1.1(a)(1) of the SCM Agreement covers only those entities that possesses, exercise or are vested with governmental authority.

> We see the concept of "public body" as sharing certain attributes with the concept of "government". A public body within the meaning of Article 1.1.(a)(1) of the SCM Agreement must be an entity that possesses, exercises or is vested with governmental authority. Yet, just as no two governments are exactly alike, the precise contours and characteristics of a public body are bound to differ from entity to entity, State to State, and case to case. Panels or investigating authorities confronted with the question of whether conduct falling within the scope of Article 1.1.(a)(1) is that of a public body will be in a position to answer that question only by conducting a proper evaluation of the core features of the entity concerned, and its relationship with government in the narrow sense.
>
> In some cases, such as when a statute or other legal instrument expressly vests authority in the entity concerned, determining that such entity is a public body may be a straightforward exercise. In others, the picture may be more mixed, and the challenge more complex. The same entity may possess certain features suggesting it is a public body, and others that suggest that it is a private body.[99] We do not, for example, consider that the absence of an express statutory delegation of authority necessarily precludes a determination that a particular entity is a public body. What matters is whether an entity is vested with authority to exercise governmental functions, rather than how that is achieved. . . . It follows, in our view, that evidence that a government exercises meaningful control over an entity and its conduct may serve, in certain circumstances, as evidence that the relevant entity possesses governmental authority and exercises such authority in the performance of governmental functions.[100]

While arriving at that conclusion, the Appellate Body took into consideration (i) the existence of commonalities between the terms, 'government' *stricto sensu* and 'public body' in Article 1;[101] (ii) the definition of the word 'government' as the continuous exercise of authority over subjects, authoritative direction, or regulation and control;[102] (iii) the definition of the word 'private';[103] (iv) the notions of 'entrustment', 'direction', and 'which would normally be vested in the government' in Article 1.1(a)(1)(iv);[104] and (v) the International Law Commission's Articles on Responsibility of States for Internationally Wrongful Acts, *via* Article 31(3)(c) of the Vienna Convention.[105]

In *US – Countervailing Measures (China)*, the Appellate Body observed that there is "a single legal standard that defines the term 'government' under the SCM Agreement". The Appellate Body also clarified that this term, as defined in Article 1.1(a)(1) of the SCM Agreement, "encompasses both the government in the 'narrow sense' and 'any public body within the territory of a Member'".[106] In *Korea – Commercial Vessels*, it was the case of the EU[107] that the Export-Import Bank of Korea (KEXIM) was a public body, as it was formed and operated on the basis of a public statute giving the Government of Korea (GOK) control over its decision-making. The Panel agreed with the EU that KEXIM was a public body because it was controlled by the Korean government (or other public bodies), and observed as follows:

> [A]n entity will constitute a "public body" if it is controlled by the government (or other public bodies). If an entity is controlled by the government (or other public bodies), then any action by that entity is attributable to the government, and should therefore fall within the scope of Article 1.1(a)(1) of the SCM Agreement.[108]

The Appellate Body in *US – Carbon Steel (India)*, while recalling its findings made in *US – Anti-Dumping and Countervailing Duties (China)* that mere ownership or control over an entity by a government was not sufficient to establish that the entity is a public body, observed as follows:

> In determining whether or not a specific entity is a public body, it may be relevant to consider "whether the functions or conduct are of a kind that are ordinarily classified as governmental in the legal order of the relevant Member." The . . . classification and functions of entities within WTO Members generally may also bear on the question of what features are normally exhibited by public bodies.[109]

The Appellate Body, while not agreeing with India's argument that an entity must have the power to regulate, control, or supervise individuals or otherwise restrain conduct of others in order to be a public body, observed as follows:

> Although certain entities that are found to constitute public bodies may possess the power to regulate, we do not see why an entity would necessarily have to possess this characteristic in order to be found to be vested with governmental authority or exercising a governmental function and therefore to constitute a public body.[110]

Considering the fact that the investigation is a complex exercise,[111] the Appellate Body in *US – Anti-Dumping and Countervailing Duties (China)* urged Panels and investigating authorities "to engage in a careful evaluation of the entity in question to identify its common features and relationship with government in the narrow sense, having regard, in particular, to whether the entity exercises authority on behalf of the government".[112] By applying the rules handed down by the Appellate Body, one can summarise that the act of determining whether a particular entity is a 'public body' is a fact-specific exercise.

2. Regulation of Specific Subsidies Under the SCM Agreement

The earlier sections of this chapter discussed how pursuant to Article 1.1 of the SCM Agreement, a subsidy exists if two distinctive elements are present, *viz.*, a financial contribution by a government[113] and a benefit thereby conferred to the recipient. Further, Article 1.2 states that for a subsidy to be subject to the legal framework envisaged under the SCM Agreement and countervailable, it must also be specific. The SCM Agreement not only identifies and defines subsidies, but also identifies protectionist subsidies and the steps to rein them in. In this section the regulation of specific subsidies under the SCM Agreement is taken up for discussion, where the traffic light system is used to categorise subsidies. Under this system, the subsidies are categorised as 'prohibited subsidies', 'actionable subsidies', and 'non-actionable subsidies'. The three categories are clearly distinguished under the provisions of the SCM Agreement.[114] Under the SCM Agreement, 'prohibited subsidies' are covered under Article 3, 'actionable subsidies' are covered in Article 5, and 'non-actionable' subsidies are included under Article 8 – albeit on a provisional basis.

2.1 Prohibited Subsidies

Prohibited subsidies, which are classified as 'red light subsidies', are banned and are addressed in Part II of the SCM Agreement. Article 3.1 of the SCM Agreement reads as follows:

> Except as provided in the Agreement on Agriculture, the following subsidies, within the meaning of Article 1, shall be prohibited:
>
> a) subsidies contingent, in law or in fact,[115] whether solely or as one of several other conditions, upon export performance, including those illustrated in Annex I;[116]
> b) subsidies contingent, whether solely or as one of several other conditions, upon the use of domestic over imported goods.

Article 3.1 identifies two prohibited subsidies, *viz.*, export subsidies and import substitution subsidies. It is to be noted that Article 3.1 creates an exception to agricultural export subsidies that are in conformity with the Agreement on Agriculture. The Appellate Body in *US – Upland Cotton* rejected the US's argument that Article 3.1(b) is inapplicable to Step 2 payments to domestic users, since such payments were consistent with the US's domestic support reduction commitments under the Agreement on Agriculture.[117] In finding that Article 3.1(b) of the SCM Agreement is applicable to agricultural products, the Appellate Body examined the relevant provisions of the Agreement on Agriculture to determine whether they contained specific provisions that deal with subsidies contingent upon the use of domestic over imported goods in light of the introductory language in Article 3 of the SCM Agreement.[118] In looking at the introductory phrase, the Appellate Body agreed with the Panel that Article 3.1(b) of the SCM Agreement can be read together with provisions of the Agreement on Agriculture pertaining to domestic support coherently and consistently that gives effective meaning to the relevant terms of both agreements.[119]

Article 3.2 provides that Member States "shall neither grant nor maintain" subsidies that are mentioned in paragraph 1. Export subsidies and import substitution subsidies are prohibited, as they have the effect of distorting trade and cause such adverse effects to other Member States. It is no exaggeration to say that export subsidies are incompatible with fair, undistorted trade as envisaged under the multilateral trading body. Similarly, import substitution subsidies limit foreign companies' access to a Member State's domestic market. Under the SCM Agreement rules, unlike actionable subsidies, prohibited subsidies do not require any demonstration of actual adverse effects, as they require only the establishment of the elements of the particular subsidy to qualify as 'prohibited'.

On the role of Article 3 of the SCM Agreement, the Appellate Body in *US – Tax Incentives* clarified that the "granting of subsidies is not, in and of itself, prohibited under the SCM Agreement; nor does the granting of subsidies constitute, without more, an inconsistency with that Agreement".[120] Further, the Appellate Body observed as follows:

> Only subsidies contingent upon export performance within the meaning of Article 3.1(a) (commonly referred to as export subsidies), or contingent upon the use of domestic over imported goods within the meaning of Article 3.1(b) (commonly referred to as import substitution subsidies), are prohibited per se under Article 3 of the SCM Agreement. In any event, subsidies, if specific, are disciplined under Part III of the SCM Agreement, but a complaining Member must demonstrate the existence of adverse effects under Article 5 of that Agreement.[121]

2.1.1 Export Subsidies

An export subsidy creates a difference in the price at which a particular good is traded. For instance, the price of the good will be lower on the world market than its price on the domestic market of the exporting country. As noted by Krugman, Obstfeld, and Melitz, export subsidies provide an incentive to export, and as a result, exporters will be more competitive in their export markets (Krugman, Obstfeld, and Melitz, 2018). Pursuant to Article 3 of the SCM Agreement, for a prohibited export subsidy to exist, first there should be a financial contribution by a government, resulting in the conferment of a benefit, and (ii) that subsidy is contingent upon export performance ('export contingency').[122] The Panel in *Canada – Aircraft Credits and Guarantees* found that to prove the existence of an export subsidy within the meaning of Article 3.1(a), a Member State must "establish (i) the existence of a subsidy within the meaning of Article 1 of the SCM and (ii) contingency of that subsidy upon export performance".[123] Annex I of the SCM Agreement offers a non-exhaustive list of prohibited export subsidies falling under 12 categories, which are:

a direct subsidies contingent upon export performance;
b currency retention schemes, involving a bonus on exports;
c domestic/internal transport and freight charges on export shipments, provided or mandated by governments, on terms more favourable than for domestic shipments;
d the provision of imported or domestic products or services for use in the production of exported goods, on terms or conditions more favourable than for provision of like or directly competitive products or services for use in the production of goods for domestic consumption;
e The full or partial exemption remission, or deferral specifically related to exports, of direct taxes or social welfare charges;
f The allowance of special deductions directly related to exports or export performance, over and above those granted in respect to production for domestic consumption;

g   The exemption or remission, in respect of the production and distribution of exported products, of indirect taxes in excess of those levied in respect of the production and distribution of like products when sold for domestic consumption;

h   The exemption, remission, or deferral of prior-stage cumulative indirect taxes on goods or services used in the production of exported products;

i   The remission or drawback of import charges in excess of those levied on imported inputs that are consumed in the production of the exported product (making normal allowance for waste);

j   The provision by governments (or special institutions controlled by governments) of export credit guarantee or insurance programmes;

k   The grant by governments (or special institutions controlled by and/or acting under the authority of governments) of export credits at rates below those which they actually have to pay for the funds so employed (or would have to pay if they borrowed on international capital markets in order to obtain funds of the same maturity and other credit terms and denominated in the same currency as the export credit), or the payment by them of all or part of the costs incurred by exporters or financial institutions in obtaining credits, insofar as they are used to secure a material advantage in the field of export credit terms.

   Provided, however, that if a Member is a party to an international undertaking on official export credits to which at least 12 original Members to this Agreement are parties as of 1 January 1979 (or a successor undertaking which has been adopted by those original Members), or if in practice a Member applies the interest rates provisions of the relevant undertaking, an export credit practice which is in conformity with those provisions shall not be considered an export subsidy prohibited by this Agreement.

Under Article 3.1(a), it is imperative for a complainant to clearly demonstrate the existence of a subsidy and also to demonstrate that such subsidy is 'contingent' on exportation. The meaning of 'contingent' as contained in Article 3.1(a) is "conditional" or "dependent for its existence on something else".[124] This effectively prevents governments that may seek to circumvent the provision under Article 3 by associating subsidies to export performance without providing for it in their domestic laws. Following from Footnote 4 of the SCM Agreement, a subsidy is contingent *de facto* upon export performance:

> [w]hen the facts demonstrate that the granting of a subsidy, without having been made legally contingent upon export performance, is in fact tied to actual or anticipated exportation or export earnings. The mere fact that a subsidy is granted to enterprises which export shall not for that reason alone be considered to be an export subsidy within the meaning of this provision.

There is sufficient jurisprudential guidance from the Appellate Body on the meaning of the expressions found in Article 3.1(a). In *US – FSC (Article 21.5 – EC)*, the Appellate Body ruled that for a subsidy to be an export subsidy, "the grant of the subsidy must be conditional or dependent upon export performance".[125] The SCM Agreement provides that 'contingency' could be present both *de jure* and *de facto*. The Appellate Body also addressed the distinction between *de jure* and a *de facto* export subsidy with reference to the wording of a particular measure, and made the following observation:

> In our view, a subsidy is contingent "in law" upon export performance when the existence of that condition can be demonstrated on the basis of the very words of the

relevant legislation, regulation or other legal instrument constituting the measure. The simplest, and hence, perhaps, the uncommon, case is one in which the condition of exportation is set out expressly, in so many words, on the face of the law, regulation or other legal instrument. We believe, however, that a subsidy is also properly held to be *de jure* export contingent where the condition to export is clearly, though implicitly, in the instrument comprising the measure. Thus, for a subsidy to be *de jure* export contingent, the underlying legal instrument does not always have to provide *expressis verbis* that the subsidy is available only upon fulfillment of the condition of export performance. Such conditionality can also be derived by necessary implication from the words actually used in the measure.[126]

The SCM Agreement clearly prohibits *de facto* export contingency, which functions as a mechanism against Member States who seek to circumvention core principles by linking benefits to exports without clearly stating in the law that this has indeed been the case. In *Canada – Autos*, the Appellate Body clarified the position of law by ruling that subsidies which were not *de jure* contingent but were *de facto* contingent upon the use of domestic goods over imported goods were also prohibited, although Article 3.1(b) does not explicitly provide so.[127] The Appellate Body in *US – Upland Cotton* highlighted that a "relationship of conditionality or dependence", namely that the granting of a subsidy should be "tied to" the export performance, was at the "very heart" of the legal standard found in Article 3.1(a) of the SCM Agreement.[128] The Appellate Body in *Canada – Aircraft* discussed the standard of proof required to establish the existence of a *de jure* or a *de facto* export subsidy, and observed that the establishing the latter was a more onerous task:

> In our view, the legal standard expressed by the word "contingent" is the same for both *de jure* and *de facto* contingency. There is a difference, however, in what evidence may be employed to prove that a subsidy is export contingent. *De jure* export contingency is demonstrated on the basis of the words of the relevant legislation, regulation or legal instrument. Proving *de facto* export contingency is a much more difficult task. There is no single legal document which will demonstrate, on its face, that a subsidy is "contingent . . . in fact . . . upon export performance." Instead, the existence of this relationship of contingency, between the subsidy and the export performance, must be inferred from the total configuration of the facts constituting and surrounding the granting of the subsidy, none of which on its own is likely to be decisive in any given case . . .
>
> . . .
>
> We note that satisfaction of the standard for determining *de facto* export contingency set out in footnote 4 requires proof of three different substantive elements: first, "the granting of a subsidy"; second, "is . . . tied to . . ."; and third, "actual or anticipated exportation or export earnings".[129]

In the *Airbus* case report,[130] the Appellate Body developed the jurisprudence on the standard of *de facto* export contingency with regards to Article 3.1(b) of the SCM Agreement. The Appellate Body while explaining that the contingency "must be inferred from the total configuration" noted that this could include factors such as "(i) the design and structure of the measure granting the subsidy; (ii) the modalities of operation set out in such a measure; and (iii) the relevant factual circumstances surrounding the granting of the subsidy that provide the context for understanding the measure's design, structure, and modalities of operation".[131] The Appellate Body established:

Where the evidence shows, all other things being equal, that the granting of the subsidy provides an incentive to skew anticipated sales towards exports, in comparison with the historical performance of the recipient or the hypothetical performance of a profit-maximizing firm in the absence of the subsidy, this would be an indication that the granting of the subsidy is in fact tied to anticipated exportation within the meaning of Article 3.1(a) and footnote 4 of the SCM Agreement.[132]

In the *Airbus* case, the Appellate Body further elaborated that the standard to determine if the granting of a subsidy is an objective standard, which is to be "established on the basis of the total configuration of facts constituting and surrounding the granting of the subsidy, including the design, structure, and modalities of operation of the measure granting the subsidy".[133] The Appellate Body clearly rejected the argument that a "standard that requires anticipated exportation to be the reason for the granting of the subsidy",[134] and went on to observe that the standard for *de facto* export contingency is not met "by showing that anticipated exportation is the reason for granting the subsidy" or by showing "the subjective motivation of the granting government to promote the future export performance of the recipient".[135] The Appellate Body stated its reasoning in the following words:

> [W]e consider that the standard for *de facto* export contingency under Article 3.1(a) and footnote 4 of the SCM Agreement would be met when the subsidy is granted so as to provide an incentive to the recipient to export in a way that is not simply reflective of the conditions of supply and demand in the domestic and export markets undistorted by the granting of the subsidy.[136]

The Appellate Body in the *Airbus* case established the 'export inducement test' for determining whether a subsidy is *de facto* contingent upon export performance as follows:

> The existence of *de facto* export contingency, as set out above, "must be inferred from the total configuration of the facts constituting and surrounding the granting of the subsidy", which may include the following factors: (i) the design and structure of the measure granting the subsidy; (ii) the modalities of operation set out in such a measure; and (iii) the relevant factual circumstances surrounding the granting of the subsidy that provide the context for understanding the measure's design, structure, and modalities of operation.[137]

The Appellate Body noted that an export subsidy is present where the anticipated export/domestic sales ratio is higher than the one derived from historical or hypothetical sales.[138] The Appellate Body, based on the aforementioned findings and observation, summarised its test for *de facto* export contingency as follows:

> We find that the [*de facto*] conditionality between the granting of a subsidy and anticipated exportation can be established where the granting of the subsidy is geared to induce the promotion of future export performance of the recipient. The standard for *de facto* export contingency under Article 3.1(a) and footnote 4 of the SCM Agreement would be met when the subsidy is granted so as to provide an incentive to the recipient to export in a way that is not simply reflective of the conditions of supply and demand in the domestic and export markets undistorted by the granting of the subsidy.[139]

It is worth noting here that the Appellate Body in the *Airbus* case was unable to reach a conclusion as to whether the measures at issue, *i.e.*, 'Launch Aid/Member State Financing' subsidies, amounted to prohibited export subsidies, as the panel's factual findings and facts on record did not provide a sufficient basis to do so. With regards to *de jure* export subsidy, the measure in place is manifestly contingent on export performance. In *Canada – Aircraft*, the Appellate Body ruled that "[d]*e jure* export contingency is demonstrated on the basis of the words of the relevant legislation, regulation or legal instrument. Proving *de facto* export contingency is a much more difficult task".[140]

Whilst examining the facts to determine if a *de facto* export contingency existed, the Panel in *Australia – Automotive Leather II* held that the language of footnote 4 of the SCM Agreement required it "to examine all the facts concerning the grant or maintenance of the challenged subsidy", emphasizing that the Panel was not precluded from considering any particular fact, and that the specific facts to be considered will vary on a case-by-case basis.[141] The Panel drew a chronological limit to the broad standard of factual analysis, while observing that "the pertinent consideration is the facts at the time the conditions for the grant payments were established, and not possible subsequent developments".[142]

In *Canada – Aircraft*, the Panel confirmed[143] the broad and case-by-case approach to the factual analysis of the Panel in *Australia – Automotive Leather II*. The Panel also stressed that no factual considerations should automatically prevail over others, and pointed out that its finding that "a broad range of facts could be relevant in this context does not mean that the *de facto* export contingency standard is easily met", that footnote 4 of the SCM Agreement requires that the facts must "demonstrate" *de facto* export contingency, and that "*de facto* export contingency must be demonstrable on the basis of the factual evidence adduced".[144] The Appellate Body in *Canada – Aircraft* agreed with the Panel that the fact that a subsidy is granted to enterprises which export may be considered in a determination whether or not a subsidy is *de facto* export contingent, but that this does not mean that export-orientation alone can necessarily be determinative.[145] Consequently, it is for the complainant Member State to demonstrate that the State measure under challenge distorts the market conditions and hence categorised as illegal export subsidy.

2.1.2 Import Substitution Subsidies

Described as the domestic content subsidy (or local content subsidy) in Article 3.1, import subsidies are the second category of prohibited subsidies. Article 3.1(b) of the SCM Agreement reads as follows:

> Except as provided in the Agreement on Agriculture, the following subsidies, within the meaning of Article 1, shall be prohibited: . . . (b) subsidies contingent, whether solely or as one of several other conditions, upon the use of domestic over imported goods.

As laid down in Article 3.1(b) of the SCM Agreement, import substitution subsidies are subsidies contingent upon the use of domestic over imported goods. In *Canada – Renewable Energy*, the Appellate Body noted that Article 3.1(b) of the SCM Agreement "regulates so-called import-substitution subsidies, which are one of only two kinds of subsidies prohibited under the SCM Agreement".[146] The Appellate Body in *Canada – Autos*, citing the report from *Canada – Aircraft*,[147] noted that contingency "in law" is demonstrated like export subsidies pursuant to Article 3.1(a) "on the basis of the words of the relevant legislation, regulation or other legal instrument".[148] In *Canada – Autos*, the Appellate Body observed:

the phrase "contingent . . . upon the use of domestic over imported goods" is not conclusive as to whether Article 3.1(b) covers both subsidies contingent "in law" and subsidies contingent "in fact" upon the use of domestic over imported goods.[149]

In the Appellate Body's opinion, although the words "in law or in fact" are absent from Article 3.1(b), it does not mean that Article 3.1(b) extends to *de jure* contingency only.[150] Accordingly, the Appellate Body ruled that it believed that

> a finding that Article 3.1(b) extends only to contingency "in law" upon the use of domestic over imported goods would be contrary to the object and purpose of the SCM Agreement because it would make circumvention of obligations by Members too easy.[151]

The Panel in *US – Upland Cotton* ruled that the subsidies under challenge, *viz.*, section 1207(a) of the FSRI Act of 2002, which provided for user marketing payments to domestic users, is a subsidy contingent upon the use of domestic over imported goods, that it was inconsistent with Article 3.1(b) of the SCM Agreement, and was consequently also inconsistent with Article 3.2 of the SCM Agreement.[152]

2.2 Actionable Subsidies

The SCM Agreement, in Part III, addresses actionable subsidies, or 'yellow light subsidies' as they are otherwise referred to. The term 'actionable' is used here to mean that under the aforementioned provision subsidies are *per se* prohibited and that a challenge can be launched to prove the adverse trade effects of a subsidy. If in the event the complainant Member State is able to demonstrate the adverse trade effects of the subsidy challenged, then such subsidy will be in violation the SCM Agreement. In essence, actionable means presenting sufficient grounds for a legal action to be brought. Going by that explanation, all subsidies – even non-prohibited subsidies – are in theory actionable.[153] Lending support, the *Chapeau* of Article 5 of the SCM Agreement provides:

> No Member should cause, through the use of any subsidy referred to in paragraphs 1 and 2 of Article 1, adverse effects to the interests of other Members.

Article 5 of the SCM Agreement which set out the trade effects, reads as follows:

> No Member should cause, through the use of any subsidy referred to in paragraphs 1 and 2 of Article 1, adverse effects to the interests of other Members, *i.e.*:
>
> (a) injury to the domestic industry of another Member;
> (b) nullification or impairment of benefits accruing directly or indirectly to other Members under GATT 1994 in particular the benefits of concessions bound under Article II of GATT 1994;
> (c) serious prejudice to the interests of another Member.[154]

It is clear from a reading of Article 5 that the provisions identify three different types of 'adverse effects' caused by the use of subsidies on the Member States. Each of the three types will be analysed.

2.2.1 Causing Injury to Domestic Industry

The first category of actionable subsidy is contained in Article 5(a), which is identified as capable of causing "injury to the domestic industry of another Member". Footnote 11 to Article 5 clarifies that the term "injury to the domestic industry" is used in the same way as in the same sense as it is used in Part V, *i.e.*, same as in the context of CVD procedures. Footnote 45 to Article 15 of the SCM Agreement provides as follows:

> "injury" shall, unless otherwise specified, be taken to mean material injury to a domestic industry, threat of material injury to a domestic industry or material retardation of the establishment of such an industry and shall be interpreted in accordance with the provisions of this Article.

Footnote 45 clearly identifies 3 types of injury, which are as follows:

i   Injury to the domestic industry of another Member State;
ii Threat of material injury to a domestic industry; and
iii Material retardation of the establishment of such an industry.

The US in *EC and Certain Member States – Large Civil Aircraft* argued that the subsidies at issue caused injury to its domestic industry within the meaning of Article 5(a). The Panel adopted the two-step approach used in CVD investigations, *viz.*, (a) asserting the presence of material injury;[155] and, if this were to be proven, then (b) establishing that subsidised imports are causing that material injury.[156] The Panel explained that it would interpret 'injury to the domestic industry' in Article 5(a) harmoniously with the provisions of Article 15 governing countervailing duty investigations and observed as follows:

> we consider that a consistent interpretation of the concept of "injury to the domestic industry" requires us to examine, in considering causation, the effects of subsidized imports as set forth in Articles 15.2 and 15.4 in our analysis of material injury under Article 5(a). Any other conclusion would, we believe, inappropriately establish a different legal standard and obligations for analysis of injury in the context of Part III from that developed under Part V of the SCM Agreement, which in our view would be contrary to footnote 11.
>
> . . .
>
> Since in this case we are essentially fulfilling the role that would be taken by the investigating authority in a countervailing or anti-dumping duty investigation, this means that we must base our examination and determination with respect to injury on positive evidence and an objective examination of the various injury elements as required by the more specific provisions of Article 15.[157]

2.2.1.1 LIKE PRODUCTS

Footnote 46 to Article 15 of the SCM Agreement defines like product as the following:

> a product which is identical, *i.e.* alike in all respects to the product under consideration, or in the absence of such a product, another product which, although not alike in all respects, has characteristics closely resembling those of the product under consideration.

The definition applies throughout the SCM Agreement and is not restricted to the determination of material injury, and also applies in the context of the serious prejudice determination of Article 6 of the SCM Agreement. The definition of 'like products' found in footnote 46 is similar to the 'like product' definitions in the context of MFN and NT principles. Although the interpretation of 'likeness' is somewhat narrower in the context of Article 5 of the SCM Agreement,[158] a very similar approach is taken to determine 'likeness' under both the SCM Agreement and under the Articles I:1, III:2 and III:4 of the GATT. The Panel in *Indonesia – Autos*, while noting that the SCM Agreement, where relevant to the like products analysis, does not preclude considering criteria other than physical characteristics,[159] ruled as follows:

> Although we are required in this dispute to interpret the term "like product" in conformity with the specific definition provided in the SCM Agreement, we believe that useful guidance can nevertheless be derived from prior analysis of "like product" issues under other provisions of the WTO Agreement.[160]

2.2.1.2 DOMESTIC INDUSTRY

Article 16.1 of the SCM Agreement defines domestic industry as follows:

> For the purposes of this Agreement, the term "domestic industry" shall, except as provided in paragraph 2, be interpreted as referring to the domestic producers as a whole of the like products or to those of them whose collective output of the products constitutes a major proportion of the total domestic production of those products.

This definition of 'domestic industry' is comparable to the concept of 'domestic industry' found in the Anti-Dumping Agreement.[161] The two exception to the definition found in the SCM Agreement are (i) domestic producers related to the exporters or importers and importers of such subsidised product,[162] and (ii) in exceptional cases the producers within a region in a Member's territory may be treated as a separate industry in a competitive market, thus constituting a 'domestic industry'.[163]

2.2.1.3 INJURY

As identified earlier in 2.2.1, injury to domestic industry under the SCM Agreement falls under three major areas. Articles 15.1 to 15.6 of the SCM Agreement lay down the rules on injury, which operate as the central requirement for the imposition of countervailing measures. To justify the imposition of such measures, it should be demonstrated that the injury sustained to the domestic industry of the importing Member State producing the like product was caused by the imports.[164] Footnote 45 of the SCM Agreement – which is appended to Article 15 – clarifies that under the Agreement,

> the term "injury" shall, unless otherwise specified, be taken to mean material injury to a domestic industry, threat of material injury to a domestic industry or material retardation of the establishment of such an industry and shall be interpreted in accordance with the provisions of this Article.

Under the SCM Agreement, a Member State, instead of undertaking a unilateral remedy (akin to CVD procedure), can resort to the dispute settlement system seeking a multilateral remedy by demonstrating 'injury' to their domestic industry. The provisions of Article 15 envisage a logical progression of the 'injury' enquiry. The injury is to be proved objectively – firstly, through the analysis of the volume of the subsidised imports and the effect of the subsidised imports on prices in the importing Member State's domestic market, and secondly the impact of such imports on the domestic producers and their products.[165] In *China – GOES*, the Appellate Body considered the requirements of Article 15.2 of the SCM Agreement and the identical requirements arising under Article 3.2 of the Anti-Dumping Agreement. The Appellate Body ruled that Article 3 of the Anti-Dumping Agreement and Article 15 of the SCM Agreement provide an "investigating authority with the relevant framework and disciplines for conducting an injury and causation analysis" and that "these provisions contemplate a logical progression of enquiry leading to an investigating authority's ultimate injury and causation determination".[166] The Appellate Body went on to hold that Article 15.2 of the SCM Agreement contemplates an enquiry into the relationship between subsidised imports and domestic prices in order to establish if the subsidised/dumped imports has led to the affecting the domestic prices of the like product.[167]

In *US – Carbon Steel (India)*, the Appellate Body noted that Article 15.1 of the SCM Agreement is an overarching provision which sets out a Member State's "fundamental substantive obligations in the context of a determination of injury and informing the more detailed obligations in the subsequent paragraphs of Article 15 concerning the determination of injury by an investigating authority".[168] With regards to the volume of the subsidised imports, Article 15.2 provides that the authorities are to consider whether there has been a significant increase in their quantities – either in absolute terms or relative to production or consumption in the importing country. In *US – Countervailing Duty Investigation on DRAMS*, the Panel detailed the three different ways in which an investigating authority may comply with the requirement to consider whether there has been a significant increase in subsidized imports, as follows:

> First, the investigating authority may consider whether there has been a significant increase in the volume of subsidized imports in absolute terms. Second, the investigating authority may consider whether there has been a significant increase in the volume of subsidized imports relative to domestic production. Third, the investigating authority may consider whether there has been a significant increase in the volume of subsidized imports relative to domestic consumption. Article 15.2 provides that "[n]o one or several of these factors can necessarily give decisive guidance".[169]

The Panel in *US – Countervailing Duty Investigation on DRAMS* also noted that the language of Article 15.2 confers considerable latitude on an investigating authority, and that the Article also permitted the investigating authority to consider a significant increase, either in absolute terms or relative to production or consumption.[170] The investigating authority is also required to establish if there had been any significant price undercutting by the subsidised imports, or whether these imports otherwise depress or suppress prices to a significant degree.[171] When examining the second element under Article 15.1 – the subsequent impact of the imports on the domestic producers of such products – Article 15.4 mandates that such examination include an evaluation of all relevant economic factors and indices having a bearing on the state of the industry. The factors listed in Article 15.4 include (i) an actual and potential decline in the output, sales, market share, profits, productivity, return on investments, or utilisation of capacity; (ii) factors affecting domestic prices; and (iii) actual and potential negative effects on cash flow, inventories, employment, wages, growth, or the ability to raise capital or investments. Article 15.4 contemplates that a clear understanding of the impact of subsidised imports be derived on the basis of such examination. In *China – GOES*, the Appellate Body, while comparing the requirements under Article 3.4 of the Anti-Dumping Agreement and Article 15.4 of the SCM Agreement, observed as follows:

> We recall that Articles 3.4 and 15.4 thus do not merely require an examination of the state of the domestic industry, but contemplate that an investigating authority must derive an understanding of the impact of subject imports on the basis of such an examination. Consequently, Articles 3.4 and 15.4 are concerned with the relationship between subject imports and the state of the domestic industry, and this relationship is analytically akin to the type of link contemplated by the term "the effect of" under Articles 3.2 and 15.2. In other words, Articles 3.4 and 15.4 require an examination of the explanatory force of subject imports for the state of the domestic industry. In our view, such an interpretation does not duplicate the relevant obligations in Articles 3.5 and 15.5. As noted, the inquiry set forth in Articles 3.2 and 15.2, and the examination required under Articles 3.4 and 15.4, are necessary in order to answer the ultimate question in Articles 3.5 and 15.5 as to whether subject imports are causing injury to the domestic industry. The outcomes of these inquiries form the basis for the overall causation analysis contemplated in Articles 3.5 and 15.5. Thus, similar to the consideration under Articles 3.2 and 15.2, the examination under Articles 3.4 and 15.4 contributes to, rather than duplicates, the overall determination required under Articles 3.5 and 15.5.[172]

It should be pointed out that the list provided in Article 15.4 is not exhaustive, and as a result other relevant factors are to be considered by the investigating authority. The concept of 'injury' to domestic injury, as envisaged in the SCM Agreement, includes 'material injury' and 'threat to material injury'. Pursuant to Article 15.7, the determination of the 'threat to material injury' is to be based on facts and not merely on allegations, conjecture, or remote possibility. Also, under Article 15.7, the change in circumstances that create a situation in which subsidy would cause injury must be clearly foreseen and imminent. As per Article 15.7, the factors that are to be considered to determine the existence of a 'threat of material injury' are as follows:

i   Nature of the subsidy or subsidies in question and the trade effects likely to arise therefrom;
ii A significant rate of increase of subsidised imports into the domestic market indicating the likelihood of substantially increased importation;
iii Sufficient freely disposable, or an imminent, substantial increase in the capacity of the exporter indicating the likelihood of substantially increased subsidised exports to the importing Member's market, taking into account the availability of other export markets to absorb any additional exports;
iv Whether imports are entering at prices that will have a significant depressing or suppressing effect on domestic prices and would likely increase demand for further imports; and
v   Inventories of the product being investigated.[173]

The aforementioned listed factors are all to be considered while carrying out an investigation under Article 15.7.[174] One would observe that Article 15 of the SCM Agreement is at once substantive in laying down the criteria for the determination of injury, prescriptive of what a Member State may or may not do in its investigative process, and at the same time procedural insofar as the formalities to be observed and factors to be considered by the investigating authority. The last sentence of Article 15.7 notes that the factors identified under 15.7(i)-(v) by itself may not necessarily give decisive guidance, hence, the totality of the factors considered must lead to the conclusion that further subsidised exports are imminent and that, unless protective action is taken, material injury would occur.[175]

Also, Article 15.8 requires 'special care' when considering and deciding on situations of 'threat of material injury' from subsidised imports. The Panel in *US – Softwood Lumber VI* had the occasion to examine the meaning of the requirement under Article 15.8, and opined that "a degree of attention over and above that required of investigating authorities in all anti-dumping and countervailing duty injury cases is required in the context of cases involving threat of material injury".[176] Article 15.3 contemplates a situation where anti-subsidy investigations are to be carried out on imports originating from more than one country and provides for an approach where subsidies are assessed cumulatively to establish injury.[177] It should also be borne in mind that a cumulative assessment could only be carried out when the amount of subsidisation is more than *de minimis* – more than or equal to 1 percent *ad valorem* (as defined in paragraph Article 11.9); the volume of the imports of each country is not negligible; and the cumulative assessment of the effects of the imports is appropriate in light of the conditions of competition between products imported from different countries and the conditions of competition between the imported products and the like domestic products. The Appellate Body in *US – Carbon Steel (India)* observed as follows:

> The central element of Article 15.3 is the provision that "investigating authorities may cumulatively assess" the effects of "such imports". The term "such imports" refers to the first clause of Article 15.3, which describes a situation "[w]here imports of a product from more than one country are simultaneously subject to countervailing duty investigations". The last clause of Article15.3 stipulates the conditions that must be fulfilled in order for such cumulative assessment to be permitted. In particular, investigating authorities may engage in such cumulative assessment only if: "(a) the amount of subsidization established in relation to the imports from each country is more than *de minimis* and the volume of imports from each country is not negligible"; and "(b) a cumulative assessment of the effects of the imports is appropriate in the light of the conditions of competition between the imported products and the like domestic product".
>
> Article 15.3 refers to imports "simultaneously subject to countervailing duty investigations". The provision that investigating authorities may, if the conditions set out in the last clause of Article 15.3 are fulfilled, cumulatively assess the effects of "such" imports thus requires that the imports be "subject to countervailing duty investigations". Conversely, the effects of imports other than such subsidized imports must not be incorporated in a cumulative assessment pursuant to Article 15.3. The text is clear in stipulating that being subject to countervailing duty investigations is a prerequisite for the cumulative assessment of the effects of imports under Article 15.3.[178]

Article 15.4 requires an investigating authority to determine the impact of subsidised imports on the domestic industry,

> including actual and potential decline in output, sales, market share, profits, productivity, return on investments, or utilization of capacity; factors affecting domestic prices; actual and potential negative effects on cash flow, inventories, employment, wages,

growth, ability to raise capital or investments and, in the case of agriculture, whether there has been an increased burden on government support programmes.[179]

Following Article 15.5, it is to be demonstrated how subsidised imports – as per paragraphs 2 and 4 – cause injury within the meaning of the SCM Agreement. Relevant factors to consider will include, *inter alia*, the volumes and prices of non-subsidised imports of the product in question, contraction in demand or changes in the patterns of consumption, trade restrictive practices of and competition between the foreign and domestic producers, developments in technology, and the export performance and productivity of the domestic industry.

In *US – Countervailing Duty Investigation on DRAMS*, the Panel concluded that the evidence presented by Korea, with respect to particular companies that may have had access to capital markets, was insufficient to overturn the ITC's determination. The Panel noted that the last sentence of Article 15.4 makes it clear that no single economic factor necessarily gives decisive guidance on the issue.[180] Also, in *EC – Countervailing Measures on DRAM Chips*, the Panel noted that Article 15.4 requires an objective examination and evaluation of all relevant factors having a bearing on the state of the industry, based on positive evidence.[181]

2.2.1.4 CAUSATION

Pursuant to Article 15.5 of the SCM Agreement demonstration of a causal relationship between the subsidised imports and the injury to the domestic industry of the importing country shall be based on an examination of all relevant evidence before the authorities. As noted by the Appellate Body in *Japan – DRAMS (Korea)*, the first sentence of Article 15.5 requires that the investigating authority demonstrate that the "subsidized imports are, through the effects of subsidies, causing injury" to the domestic industry; the second sentence emphasises that the demonstration of the causal relationship between the subsidised imports and the injury shall be based on all relevant evidence before the investigating authority; and in both sentences, the subject to which the phrase "are causing injury" applies, or in respect of which "a causal relationship" is to be established, is "the subsidized imports".[182]

Factors other than subsidised imports are likely to cause injury to the domestic industry. The factors may include (i) the volumes and prices of non-subsidised imports of the product in question; (ii) a contraction in demand or changes in the patterns of consumption; (iii) trade restrictive practices of, and competition between, the foreign and domestic producers; (iv) developments in technology; and (v) the export performance and productivity of the domestic industry. The Appellate Body in *Japan – DRAMS (Korea)*, while addressing the extent of an investigating authority's remit in considering other causal events, observed as follows:

> [T]he "non-attribution" provisions contained in the third sentence of Article 15.5 already address adequately the concern that the injurious effects of any known factors other than subsidized imports are not attributed to the subsidized imports. This ensures that injuries that may have been caused by other known factors are not attributed to the subsidized imports.[183]

2.2.2 *Subsidies Causing Nullification, Impairment, or Prejudice*

Pursuant to Article 5(b) of the SCM Agreement, when subsidised imports cause the nullification or impairment of benefits accruing directly or indirectly to other Member States under the GATT 1994, they are *per se* actionable. According to footnote 12 to paragraph (b), the term 'nullification or impairment' is used in the SCM Agreement in the same sense as it is used in the application of Article XXIII of the GATT 1994. To constitute a 'nullification of impairment', it is sufficient to demonstrate a violation under the GATT.[184] Pursuant to Article 5(c) of the SCM Agreement, Member States are not to cause any 'serious prejudice' to the interests of another Member States through the use of any subsidies. Footnote 13 to paragraph (c) affirms that the term "serious prejudice to the interests of another Member" is used in the SCM Agreement in the same sense as it is used in paragraph 1 of Article XVI of GATT 1994, and that it includes threat of serious prejudice.[185]

Article 6 of the SCM Agreement is the key provision to look to and invoke where a Member State seeks to challenge a subsidy on the grounds that it causes 'serious prejudice' to its interests. Article 6.1 lists the following instances as constituting 'serious prejudice', *viz.*, (a) the total *ad valorem* subsidisation of a product exceeding 5 percent (footnote omitted); (b) subsidies to cover operating losses sustained by an industry; (c) subsidies to cover operating losses sustained by an enterprise, other than one-time measures which are non-recurrent and cannot be repeated for that enterprise and which are given merely to provide time for the development of long-term solutions and to avoid acute social problems; and (d) direct forgiveness of debt, *i.e.*, forgiveness of government-held debt, and grants to cover debt repayment (footnote omitted). Importantly, Article 6.1 lapsed on 31 December 1999 as mandated by Article 31 of the SCM Agreement and does not have legal force. As a result, one will have to turn to Article 6.3 of the SCM Agreement for guidance.

The focus of a 'serious prejudice' claim under Article 6.3 of the SCM Agreement is different from a countervailing duty investigation.[186] Article 6.3 deals with the effects of subsidisation giving rise to 'serious prejudice'. As per Article 6.3 of the SCM Agreement,

> Serious prejudice in the sense of paragraph (c) of Article 5 may arise in any case where one or several of the following apply:
>
> (a) the effect of the subsidy is to displace or impede the imports of a like product of another Member into the market of the subsidizing Member;
> (b) the effect of the subsidy is to displace or impede the exports of a like product of another Member from a third country market;
> (c) the effect of the subsidy is a significant price undercutting by the subsidized product as compared with the price of a like product of another Member in the same market or significant price suppression, price depression or lost sales in the same market;
> (d) the effect of the subsidy is an increase in the world market share of the subsidizing Member in a particular subsidized primary product or commodity as compared to the average share it had during the previous period of three years and this increase follows a consistent trend over a period when subsidies have been granted.

Upon the complaining Member State demonstrating that a subsidy has any of the aforementioned effects, a 'serious prejudice' may be found to exist. Pursuant to Article 6.2, if the subsidising Member State can demonstrate that such subsidies do not cause any of the effects identified in Article 6.3, then such subsidies will not be considered to cause serious prejudice. 'Serious prejudice' and 'injury' to a particular domestic industry are distinctively different concepts. In *Korea – Commercial Vessels*, the panel observed that the concept of serious prejudice is different from injury and explained that serious injury did not relate to the condition of a particular domestic industry within the territory of a Member, but more to do with the negative effects on a Member State's trade interests in respect of a product caused by another Member State's subsidisation such as lost import or export volume or market share in respect of a given product, adverse price effects, or some combination thereof, in variously defined markets.[187]

Concerning the nature of 'serious prejudice', the Panel in *Korea – Commercial Vessels* noted that this notion is also informed by another provision, *i.e.*, Article 6.2, which established the basis upon which the now-expired presumption of serious prejudice in Article 6.1 could be rebutted, and observed as follows:

> Article 6.2 provided that the subsidizer could rebut the presumption (in the sense that "serious prejudice shall not be found") by demonstrating that the subsidy in question had not resulted in any of the effects enumerated in Article 6.3 (displacement or impedance, price undercutting, price suppression/depression, lost sales). We thus view Article 6.2 as defining by implication the situations listed in Article 6.3 to be in themselves serious prejudice.

Articles 5(c) and 6.3 of the SCM Agreement refer to 'serious prejudice'. In *US – Upland Cotton (Article 21.5 – Brazil)*, the question before the Panel was whether a finding of 'significant price suppression' under Article 6.3(c) would constitute 'serious prejudice' under Article 5(c) of the SCM Agreement. In answering the question, the panel ruled as follows:

> Article 6.3(c) of the SCM Agreement provides that "serious prejudice in the sense of paragraph (c) of Article 5 may arise in any case where one or several of the following apply". The Panel considers that this phrase must be interpreted to mean that "the situations listed in Article 6.3(a)–(d) in themselves constitute serious Prejudice". As a consequence, a finding of significant price suppression under Article 6.3(c) of the SCM Agreement is a sufficient basis for a finding of serious prejudice within the meaning of Article 5(c) of the SCM Agreement.[188]

While assessing if there is 'serious prejudice' within the meaning of Articles 5(c) and 6 of the SCM Agreement, it is necessary to establish (i) what the relevant 'geographical market' and 'product market' is; (ii) whether there is 'displacement' or 'impedance' of imports or exports; (iii) whether there is 'price undercutting', 'price suppression', 'price depression', or 'lost sales'; (iv) whether the price undercutting, price suppression, price depression, or lost sales are 'significant'; (v) whether there is an 'increase in world market share'; (vi) whether there is 'threat of serious prejudice'; and/or (vii) whether the market phenomena referred to previously are 'the effect of' the challenged subsidies (*i.e.* causal link and non-attribution).

2.2.3 Market Definition

Article 6.3 of the SCM deals essentially with substantial damage caused to the export opportunities of a WTO Member State on third country markets. Article 6.3(c) sets out the effect of subsidy as (i) significant price undercutting arising from subsidised product as compared with the price of a like product of another Member State in the same market; (ii) significant price suppression; (iii) price depression; and (iv) lost sales in the same market. This necessarily depends on the definition of market and pertinent market. Article 6.3(c) does not impose any geographical limitation on the scope of the relevant market, other than the qualification that such price undercutting, price suppression, and price depression is in the same market. The Appellate Body in *US – Upland Cotton* held that the phrase 'in the same market' as appearing in subparagraph (c) of Article 6.3 applies to all four situations covered by this provision, *i.e.*, significant price undercutting, significant price suppression, and price depression as well as lost sales,[189] and went on to observe as follows:

> contrasts with the other paragraphs of Article 6.3: paragraph (a) restricts the relevant market to "the market of the subsidizing Member"; paragraph (b) restricts the relevant market to "a third country market"; and paragraph (d) refers specifically to the "world market share" . . . [T]his difference may indicate that the drafters did not intend to confine, *a priori*, the market examined under Article 6.3(c) to any particular area. Thus, the ordinary meaning of the word "market" in Article 6.3(c), when read in the context of the other paragraphs of Article 6.3, neither requires nor excludes the possibility of a national market or a world market.[190]

Earlier, the Panel in *US – Upland Cotton* defined the term 'market' as "a place . . . with a demand for a commodity or service"; "a geographical area of demand for commodities or services"; "the area of economic activity in which buyers and sellers come together and the forces of supply and demand affect prices".[191] The Appellate Body in *US – Upland Cotton* noted that this "does not, of itself, impose any limitation on the 'geographical area' that makes up any given market. Nor does it indicate that a 'world market' cannot exist for a given product" or that the "degree to which a market is limited by geography will depend on the product itself and its ability to be traded across distances".[192] With those observations, the Appellate Body ruled as follows:

> [t]wo products would be in the same market if they were engaged in actual or potential competition in that market. Thus, two products may be "in the same market" even if they are not necessarily sold at the same time and in the same place or country . . . The scope of the "market", for determining the area of competition between two products, may depend on several factors such as the nature of the product, the homogeneity of the conditions of competition, and transport costs. This market for a particular product could well be a "world market". However, we agree with the Panel that the fact that a world market exists for one product does not necessarily mean that such a market exists for every product. Thus the determination of the relevant market under Article 6.3(c) of the SCM Agreement depends on the subsidized product in question. If a world market exists for the product in question, Article 6.3(c) does not exclude the possibility of this "world market" being the "same market" for the purposes of a significant price suppression analysis under that Article.[193]

Having explained that the mere fact a world market exists for one product does not necessarily mean that such a world market exists for every product, the Appellate Body noted that there is no *per se* geographical limitation of a market under Article 6.3(c) and observed as follows:

> It is for the complaining party to identify the market where it alleges significant price suppression and to establish that that market exists. In doing so, it is for the complaining party to establish that the subsidized product and its product are in actual or potential competition in that alleged market. If that market is established to be a "world market", it cannot be said, for that reason alone, that the two products are not in the "same market" within the meaning of Article 6.3(c).[194]

In *EC and Certain Member States – Large Civil Aircraft*, the Appellate Body found that pursuant to Articles 6.3(a) and (b), an assessment of the competitive relationship between products in the market is required to establish "whether such products form part of the same market" and "whether and to what extent one product may displace another".[195] The Appellate Body acknowledged that a complaining Member State may identify a subsidised product and the like product by reference to footnote 46, and that "the products thereby identified must be analyzed under the discipline of the product market so as to be able to determine whether displacement is occurring".[196] In making these observations, the Appellate Body was guided by the fundamental economic proposition that "[a] market comprises only those products that exercise competitive constraint on each other. This is the case when the relevant products are substitutable". The Appellate Body also noted that factors such as physical characteristics, end uses, and consumer preferences may assist in concluding whether two products are in the same market; they should not be treated as the exclusive factors in deciding whether those products are sufficiently substitutable so as to create competitive constraints on each other.[197] The Appellate Body explained:

> Demand-side substitutability – that is, when two products are considered substitutable by consumers – is an indispensable, but not the only relevant, criterion to consider when assessing whether two products are in a single market. Rather, a consideration of substitutability on the supply side may also be required. For example, evidence on whether a supplier can switch its production at limited or prohibitive cost from one product to another in a short period of time may also inform the question of whether two products are in a single market.[198]

In *US – Large Civil Aircraft (2nd complaint)*, the Appellate Body recalled the findings made in *EC and Certain Member States – Large Civil Aircraft* and summarized the geographic dimension of a market as follows:

> In principle, the manner in which the geographic dimension of a market is determined will depend on a number of factors: in some cases, the geographic market may extend to cover the entire country concerned; in others, an analysis of the conditions of competition for sales of the product in question may provide an appropriate foundation for a finding that a geographic market exists within that area, for example, a region. There may also be cases where the geographic dimension of a particular market exceeds national boundaries or could be the world market.[199]

2.2.4 Displacement and Impediment to Imports

As per Article 6.3(a) and (b) of the SCM Agreement, serious prejudice arises when the effect of the subsidy is "to displace or impede the imports of a like product of another Member" either with regard to the importation into the market of the subsidising member or with regard to the importation into a third country market.[200] The Appellate Body in *EC and Certain Member States – Large Civil Aircraft*, while considering the meaning of the terms 'displace' and 'impede', observed that the term displacement connoted that there is a "substitution effect between the subsidized product and the like product of the complaining Member",[201] which in the Appellate Body's view led to displacement and the "imports of a like product of the complaining Member are substituted by a subsidized product in the market of the subsidizing Member".[202] In contrast, according to the Appellate Body, the term 'impede' in

Article 6.3 connotes a broader array of situations than the term 'displace', and referred to situations wherein the exports or imports of the like product of the complaining Member would have likely expanded had they not been blocked by the subsidised product.²⁰³ In the Appellate Body's view it was difficult at times to "draw a clear demarcation between the concepts of displacement and impedance".²⁰⁴

In *EC and Certain Member States – Large Civil Aircraft*, the Appellate Body also had the occasion to consider the relevant product market to be examined for the purpose of displacement and impedance under Article 6.3(a) and 6.3(b). The Appellate Body went on to rule that subject to the surrounding circumstances of each case, the nature of the product at issue, and the supply and demand factors, the product market was likely to vary. The Appellate Body noted as follows:

> In other cases, an assessment . . . may reveal the existence of multiple product markets in which particular products of the complaining Member compete with particular subsidized products of the respondent. However, it is important to note that whether or not a broad or narrow range of products benefit from subsidization says little about whether all these products compete in the same market. Indeed, products benefiting from subsidies may compete in very different markets.²⁰⁵

In the Appellate Body's view, for the assessment of displacement and impedance there was "both a geographic and product market component assessment".²⁰⁶ The Appellate Body explained that the method through which the geographic dimension of a market is determined is largely dependent on a number of factors:

> [I]n some cases, the geographic market may extend to cover the entire country concerned; in others, an analysis of the conditions of competition for sales of the product in question may provide an appropriate foundation for a finding that a geographic market exists within that area, for example, a region. There may also be cases where the geographic dimension of a particular market exceeds national boundaries or could be the world market.²⁰⁷

2.2.5 Causation and Article 6.3

Establishing a substantial and genuine 'causal link' is essential in determining if the subsidies under scrutiny have resulted in causing serious prejudice within the meaning of Article 6.3 of the SCM Agreement to the importing Member State. The Appellate Body in *US – Upland Cotton* held that although Article 6.3(c) does not use the word cause, an enquiry into whether the "effect of the subsidy is . . . significant price suppression" requires the establishment of a causal link.²⁰⁸ The Appellate Body observed that the causal link analysis must establish a 'genuine and substantial relationship of cause and effect' between the subsidies and the alleged market phenomenon identified in Article 6.3(c), and that the particular market phenomena alleged under Article 6.3(c) must result from a chain of causation that is linked to the impugned subsidy.²⁰⁹ Under Article 6.3, it is the effect of the subsidy, rather than the subsidised product (which is the case under Article 15.5), that must cause the market phenomena.²¹⁰ In *US – Upland Cotton (Article 21.5 – Brazil)*, the Appellate Body observed as follows:

> [w]hile the term "cause" focuses on the factors that may trigger a certain event, the term "effect of" focuses on the results of that event. The effect – price suppression – must result from a chain of causation that is linked to the impugned subsidy.²¹¹

In the Appellate Body's esteemed opinion, to satisfy the causation requirement under Articles 5(c) and 6.3, it must be demonstrated that there is a 'genuine and substantial relationship of cause and effect' between the subsidies and the alleged market phenomenon. To this effect, in *EC and Certain Member States – Large Civil Aircraft*, the Appellate Body – citing its own decisions in *US – Upland Cotton* and *US – Upland Cotton (Article 21.5 – Brazil)*[212] – observed that 'genuine and substantial relationship of cause and effect' standard applies in respect of all of the forms of serious prejudice under Article 6.3 of the SCM Agreement.[213] The Appellate Body also noted:

> The language of subparagraphs (a) and (b) of Article 6.3 of the SCM Agreement expresses the causation requirement in very similar terms to those used in subparagraph (c). Under subparagraphs (a) and (b), displacement or impedance must be shown to be "the effect of the subsidy". We see no reason why the standard for causation and non-attribution should be different under subparagraphs (a) and (b) than under subparagraph (c), and the participants and third participants have not suggested that a different standard applies.[214]

The standard was further set out in detail by the Appellate Body in *US – Large Civil Aircraft (2nd Complaint)*, as follows:

> The Appellate Body has consistently articulated the causal link required as "a genuine and substantial relationship of cause and effect." [footnote omitted] In other words, the subsidies must contribute, in a "genuine" [footnote omitted] and "substantial" [footnote omitted] way, to producing or bringing about one or more of the effects, or market phenomena, enumerated in Article 6.3.[215]

In *US – Large Civil Aircraft (2nd Complaint)*, the Appellate Body also observed that a determination of whether the causal link in question meets the requisite standard of a 'genuine and substantial' causal relationship is a 'fact-intensive exercise'[216] that should take into account other causal factors, and observed:

> a panel must seek to understand the interactions between the subsidy at issue and the various other causal factors, and make an assessment of their connections to, as well as the relative importance of the subsidy and of the other factors in bringing about, the relevant effects. In order to find that the subsidy is a genuine and substantial cause, a panel need not determine it to be the sole cause of that effect, or even that it is the only substantial cause of that effect. A panel must, however, take care to ensure that it does not attribute the effects of those other causal factors to the subsidies at issue, and that the other causal factors do not dilute the causal link between those subsidies and the alleged adverse effects such that it is not possible to characterize that link as a genuine and substantial relationship of cause and effect.[217]

The Appellate Body has adopted a holistic approach as the preferred methodology for the analysis of the causal link, which was well captured in *US – Upland Cotton*.[218] The panel in *US – Upland Cotton (Article 21.5 – Brazil)* had adopted a 'unitary approach' to establish if there was price suppression in the world market for upland cotton; if this price suppression was significant; and if a causal relationship existed between the significant price suppression and the subsidies under challenge. On appeal, the Appellate Body, alluding to its own observation in *US – Upland Cotton*, observed:

> [t]he Panel's "unitary analysis", at least in respect of identifying price suppression and its causes, has a sound conceptual foundation.[219]

The Appellate Body, while endorsing the 'unitary approach' adopted by the Panel in its analysis of whether significant price suppression was the effect of the challenged subsidies, made the following observation:

> [i]n undertaking a unitary analysis, the Panel considered both quantitative and qualitative elements in its assessment. It made a quantitative assessment of significance by evaluating the magnitude of the subsidies, the gap between United States upland cotton producers' revenues and costs of production, the United States' share of world production and exports, and the economic simulations; and it made a qualitative assessment by evaluating the structure, design, and operation of the subsidies.[220]

2.2.5.1 CAUSATION, THE 'BUT FOR' APPROACH

Article 6.3(c) implies a 'but for' approach to causation in respect of price suppression/price depression. The Appellate Body in *US – Upland Cotton (Article 21.5 – Brazil)* and in *EC and Certain Member States – Large Civil Aircraft* identified one of the possible approaches to establishing causation was to identify what might have occurred 'but for' the imposition of the subsidies under challenge.[221] The 'but for' test, or 'counterfactual' analysis, requires comparing both the actual market situation and the market situation that would have existed in the absence of the subsidies under issue. In the Appellate Body's view, a 'counterfactual' analysis is part of a causation analysis in instances where price suppression and impedance are to be ascertained.[222] In *US – Upland Cotton (Article 21.5 – Brazil)*, the Appellate Body observed:

> [o]ne way to undertake the analysis is to use economic modelling or other quantitative techniques. These techniques can be used to estimate whether there are higher levels of production resulting from the subsidies and, in turn, the price effects of that production. Economic modelling and other quantitative techniques provide a framework to analyse the relationship between subsidies, other factors, and price movements.[223]

The Appellate Body, while recognising the importance of economic modelling in a legal analysis of Article 6.3 of the SCM Agreement, has also pointed to the limits of such an analysis. The Appellate Body in *US – Upland Cotton (Article 21.5 – Brazil)* explained that a 'but for' test may be "too undemanding" if the subsidy "is necessary but not sufficient to bring about" a market phenomenon, and "too rigorous if it required the subsidy to be the only cause", and that the 'but for' test should determine that there is 'genuine and substantial relationship of cause and effect'.[224] The Appellate Body in *EC and Certain Member States – Large Civil Aircraft*, explained how a 'counterfactual' analysis is a useful tool in the hands of an adjudicator to isolate and properly identify the effects of the subsidies under challenge:

> In general terms, the counterfactual analysis entails comparing the actual market situation that is before the adjudicator with the market situation that would have existed in the absence of the challenged subsidies. This requires the adjudicator to undertake a modelling

exercise as to what the market would look like in the absence of the subsidies. Such an exercise is a necessary part of the counterfactual approach. As with other factual assessments, panels clearly have a margin of discretion in conducting the counterfactual analysis.[225]

Earlier, the Panel in *Korea – Commercial Vessels* observed that Article 6.3(c) provides in relevant part that "the effect of the subsidy is . . . significant price suppression [or] price depression . . . in the same market", and that "there must be a causal relationship between the subsidy and the significant price suppression or price depression".[226] The Panel having recalled that "the text of Article 6.3(c) implies a 'but for' approach to causation in respect of price suppression/price depression", concluded as follows:

> Looking at a counterfactual situation, *i.e.*, trying to determine what prices would have been in the absence of the subsidy, seems to us the most logical and straightforward way to answer this question.[227]
>
> . . .
>
> The question to be answered in respect of the affirmative link between subsidies and prices is, in the case of alleged price depression, whether in the absence of the subsidies prices for ships would not have declined, or would have declined by less than was in fact the case. For price suppression, the question would be whether, in the absence of the subsidies, ship prices would have increased, or would have increased by more than was in fact the case.[228]

Likewise, in *US – Upland Cotton (Article 21.5 – Brazil)*, the Panel, adopting a very similar 'but for' approach to establishing causation, determined whether, but for the relevant subsidies, the world market price for upland cotton "would have increased [significantly], or would have increased by [significantly] more than was in fact the case".[229] This approach of the Panel was endorsed by the Appellate Body, which observed as follows:

> The Panel's choice of a "but for" approach . . . is consistent with the definition of price suppression endorsed by the Appellate Body in the original proceedings, insofar as the counterfactual determination of whether price suppression exists cannot be separated from the analysis of the effects of the subsidies.[230]

The Appellate Body in *EC and Certain Member States – Large Civil Aircraft*, while reiterating the 'genuine and substantial relationship of cause and effect' applied in respect of all of the forms of serious prejudice under Article 6.3, had this to say about the 'but for' test:

> In some circumstances, a determination that the market phenomena captured by Article 6.3 of the SCM Agreement would not have occurred "but for" the challenged subsidies will suffice to establish causation. This is because, in some circumstances, the "but for" analysis will show that the subsidy is both a necessary cause of the market phenomenon and a substantial cause. It is not required that the "but for" analysis establish that the challenged subsidies are a sufficient cause of the market phenomenon provided that it shows a genuine and substantial relationship of cause and effect. However, there are circumstances in which a "but for" approach does not suffice. For example, where a necessary cause is too remote and other intervening causes substantially account for the market phenomenon. This example underscores the importance of carrying out a proper non-attribution analysis.

> . . . As we noted above, a "but for" test is one possible approach to the assessment of causation. Nevertheless, in applying a "but for" test, a panel must ensure that the assessment demonstrates that the subsidies are a "genuine and substantial" cause of the particular market situation that is alleged. Thus, the Panel in this case should have clearly indicated that, in applying a "but for" standard, it would seek to establish whether there was a "genuine and substantial relationship of cause and effect"[231] between the challenged subsidies and the displacement and lost sales. Furthermore, it should have indicated that, in doing so, it would also ensure that the effects of other factors were not improperly attributed to the challenged subsidies.[232]

However, the Appellate Body in *US – Large Civil Aircraft (2nd Complaint)* noted that a "panel is not required to identify and explore every possible hypothetical market scenario, especially where the parties themselves have not elaborated upon, or substantiated the likelihood of, such possible scenarios".[233] Part V and Articles 5 and 6.3 of the SCM Agreement do not share the same language on causation and non-attribution. Unlike Articles 5 and 6.3, the language in Part V is more elaborate and precise, for the purpose for which it was drafted.[234] In *US – Upland Cotton (2005)*, the Appellate Body that the absence of such express non-attribution requirements in Part III suggests:

> [a] panel has a certain degree of discretion in selecting an appropriate methodology for determining whether the "effect" of a subsidy is significant price suppression under Article 6.3(c).[235]

The Appellate Body, while noting that it is necessary to ensure that the effects of other factors on prices are not improperly attributed to the challenged subsidies,[236] observed that it did not find fault with the Panel's approach of

> examin[ing] whether or not "the effect of the subsidy" is the significant price suppression which [it had] found to exist in the same world market [and separately] consider[ing] the role of other alleged causal factors in the record before [it] which may affect [the] analysis of the causal link between the United States subsidies and the significant price suppression.[237]

Also, in *US – Large Civil Aircraft (2nd complaint)*, the Appellate Body recognised the need for a non-attribution analysis, noting that a panel will often be confronted with multiple factors that may have contributed, to varying degrees, to the adverse effect:

> [a]s part of its assessment of the causal nexus between the subsidy at issue and the effect(s) that it is alleged to have had, a panel must seek to understand the interactions between the subsidy at issue and the various other causal factors, and make an assessment of their connections to, as well as the relative importance of the subsidy and of the other factors in bringing about, the relevant effects . . . A panel must, however, take care to ensure that it does not attribute the effects of those other causal factors to the subsidies at issue, and that the other causal factors do not dilute the causal link between those subsidies and the alleged adverse effects such that it is not possible to characterize that link as a genuine and substantial relationship of cause and effect.[238]

2.3 Actionable Subsidies and Special Remedies

Special and additional rules are set out in Article 7 of the SCM Agreement in regard to actionable subsidies that cause adverse effects pursuant to Article 5. These multilateral remedies identified allow for the challenge of such subsidies through the dispute settlement track, as an alternative to resorting to CVDs under Part V of the SCM Agreement. Remedies available for actionable subsidies differ from the remedies available for prohibited subsidies. The Appellate Body in *US – Upland Cotton (Article 21.5 – Brazil)* noted, "special or additional rules and procedures on dispute settlement contained in the covered agreements that are identified in Article 1.2 and Appendix 2 of the DSU, which prevail over the general DSU rules and procedures to the extent that there is a difference between them".[239] The entries in Articles 7.2 to 7.10 provide additional rules or procedures, which in some cases facilitate an accelerated procedure in comparison to the normal DSU rules.

Article 7.2 encapsulates the provisions for request for consultation. Following from Article 7.2 of the SCM Agreement, a Member State may request consultations and may proceed to initiate Panel procedure, provided it is able to demonstrate that (a) the existence and nature of the subsidy in question, and (b) the injury caused to the domestic industry, or (c) the nullification or impairment, or (d) serious prejudice[240] is caused to the interests of the Member State requesting consultations. The Panel in *US – Upland Cotton* determined that Article 7.2 calls for qualitative and, to a degree, quantitative analysis of the existence and nature of the subsidy in question, and any serious prejudice caused therefrom.[241] While Article 7.3 provides for consultation, Article 7.8 provides for the "removal of adverse effects or withdrawal of subsidy" pursuant to the adoption of a Panel's or an Appellate Body's report. Pursuant to Article 7.8 the Member State granting or maintaining such subsidy (i) shall take appropriate steps to remove the adverse effects of such subsidy or (ii) shall withdraw the subsidy. The Appellate Body in *US – Upland Cotton* noted that Article 7.8 provides:

> [w]here it has been determined that "any subsidy has resulted in adverse effects to the interests of another Member", the subsidizing Member must "take appropriate steps to remove the adverse effects or . . . withdraw the subsidy". The use of the word "resulted" suggests that there could be a time-lag between the payment of a subsidy and any consequential adverse effects. If expired measures underlying past payments could not be challenged in WTO dispute settlement proceedings, it would be difficult to seek a remedy for such adverse effects. Further – in contrast to Articles 3.7 and 19.1 of the DSU – the remedies under Article 7.8 of the SCM Agreement for adverse effects of a subsidy are (i) the withdrawal of the subsidy or (ii) the removal of adverse effects. Removal of adverse effects through actions other than the withdrawal of a subsidy could not occur if the expiration of a measure would automatically exclude it from a panel's terms of reference.[242]

Emphasising a Member State's obligation to withdraw such subsidy or remove adverse effects under Article 7.8, the Appellate Body held in *US – Upland Cotton (Article 21.5 – Brazil)* as follows:

> Article 7.8 is one of the "special or additional rules and procedures on dispute settlement contained in the covered agreements" . . . which prevail over the general DSU rules and procedures to the extent that there is a difference between them. As we see it, Article 7.8 specifies the actions that the respondent Member must take when a subsidy granted or maintained by that Member is found to have resulted in adverse effects to the interests of another Member . . . Pursuant to Article 7.8, the implementing Member has two options to come into compliance. The implementing Member: (i) shall take appropriate steps to remove the adverse effects; or (ii) shall withdraw the subsidy. The use of the terms "shall take" and "shall withdraw" indicate that compliance with Article 7.8 of the SCM Agreement will usually involve some action by the respondent Member.

This affirmative action would be directed at effecting the withdrawal of the subsidy or the removal of its adverse effects. A Member would normally not be able to abstain from taking any action on the assumption that the subsidy will expire or that the adverse effects of the subsidy will dissipate on their own.[243]

Pursuant to Article 7.8 of the SCM Agreement, an implementing Member State has the choice between either removing the adverse effects or withdrawing the subsidy under challenge. The Appellate Body in *US – Upland Cotton (Article 21.5 – Brazil)* noted that the availability of the choice to the implementing Members State was "arguably a consequence of the fact that actionable subsidies are not prohibited *per se*; rather, they are actionable to the extent they cause adverse effects".[244] However, the Appellate Body emphasised that because the implementing Member State may choose to remove the adverse effects, rather than withdraw the subsidy, it "[c]annot be read as allowing a Member to continue to cause adverse effects by maintaining the subsidies that were found to have resulted in adverse effects".[245]

Article 7.9 requires the subsidising Member to withdraw the subsidy under challenge or remove adverse effects within six months from the adoption of the report by the DSB. Pursuant to Article 7.9, the aggrieved Member State can initiate countermeasures against a non-complying Member State. Any countermeasures taken by an aggrieved Member State are to be commensurate with the degree and nature of the adverse effects of the subsidies granted.

2.4 *Non-Actionable Subsidies*

Besides prohibited subsidies and actionable subsidies, a third category of subsidies is identified in Part IV of the SCM Agreement, *viz*., non-actionable subsidies. Having lapsed on 31 December 1999, the provisions of the SCM Agreement do not apply. The non-actionable subsidies, while they were still in force, included certain specific subsidies listed in Article 8.2 of the SCM Agreement, *viz*., regional subsidies, environmental subsidies, research and development subsidies, and subsidies for disadvantaged regions within the territory of a Member State.

3. Imposition of Countervailing Duties

Member States can impose countervailing duties, pursuant to Articles 10 and 32.1 of the SCM Agreement, against both actionable and prohibited subsidies. CVDs can be unilaterally imposed on the subsidised imports that cause domestic injury, provided the Member State concerned is able to demonstrate through a properly carried out investigation by a domestic investigating authority following the procedures contained in Part V of the SCM Agreement. Article 11 of the SCM Agreement deals with the initiation of CVDs and any subsequent investigations.[246] The Panel in *US – Carbon Steel* observed that the purpose of the provisions on initiation of investigation as laid out Article 11 is to avoid any unjustified disruptions to international trade on the basis of allegations and claims that are manifestly incorrect.[247] As per Article 11.2, an application under paragraph 1 must include evidence of the existence of

i   A subsidy, and, if possible, its amount (Articles 1, 2, and 14 of the SCM);
ii Injury within the meaning of Article VI of GATT 1994, and as interpreted by the SCM Agreement[248] (Article 15 of the SCM); and
iii A causal link between the subsidized imports and the alleged injury.

Both footnote 36 of the SCM Agreement and Article VI of the GATT 1994 define CVDs. Article 15.1 of the SCM Agreement reads as follows:

> [a] determination of injury for purposes of Article VI of GATT 1994 shall be based on positive evidence and involve an objective examination of both (a) the volume of the subsidized imports and the effect of the subsidized imports on prices in the domestic market for like products and (b) the consequent impact of these imports on the domestic producers of such products.

Article VI of the GATT provides as follows:

> a special duty levied for the purpose of offsetting . . . any subsidy bestowed, directly, or indirectly, upon the manufacture, production or export of any merchandise.

As regards CVDs, Article 10 of the SCM Agreement provides as follows:

> Members shall take all necessary steps to ensure that the imposition of a countervailing duty on any product of the territory of any Member imported into the territory of another Member is in accordance with the provisions of Article VI of GATT 1994 and the terms of this Agreement. Countervailing duties may only be imposed pursuant to investigations initiated and conducted in accordance with the provisions of this Agreement and the Agreement on Agriculture.

3.1 Procedures for Investigation and Imposition of CVDs

As a prerequisite to initiate an investigation, Article 11.1 provides that such investigation "shall be initiated upon a written application by or on behalf of the domestic industry". The SCM Agreement lays out a comprehensive procedural for the initiation and conduct of a CVD to be carried out by competent domestic authorities of the Member State seeking to impose the CVDs on subsidised imports. Articles 11.1 to 11.5, 11.7, and 11.9 clearly set out the framework for a domestic industry to initiate a CVD investigation and the review of the application by the domestic investigating authority. The primary objectives of the requirements set out in Articles 11 to 13 of the SCM Agreement are similar to those found in the anti-dumping investigation found in the provisions of the AD Agreement,[249] *viz.*, to ensure that (i) the investigations are conducted in a transparent manner; (ii) all interested parties have the opportunity to defend their interests; and (iii) the investigating authorities adequately explain the basis for their determinations.

Upon receipt of the application, *i.e.*, a written complaint from the complaining home industry that the subsidised import has an injurious effect, the domestic investigating authority (IA) is to scrutinise if the application/complaint satisfies the requirements of Article 11.2 of the SCM Agreement. As mentioned in the earlier section, Article 11.2 requires that an application under paragraph 1 must include evidence of the existence of (i) a subsidy, and, if possible, its amount (Articles 1, 2, and 14 of the SCM); (ii) injury within the meaning of Article VI of GATT 1994, and as interpreted by the SCM Agreement (Article 15 of the SCM); and (iii) a causal link between the subsidized imports and the alleged injury. As per Article 11.2, the application/complaint should also contain the following:

i   The identity of the applicant and a description of the volume and value of the domestic production of the like product by the applicant;

ii A complete description of the allegedly subsidized product, the names of the country or countries of origin or export in question, the identity of each known exporter or foreign producer, and a list of known persons importing the product in question;
iii Evidence with regard to the existence, amount, and nature of the subsidy in question; and
iv Evidence that the alleged injury to a domestic industry is caused by subsidised imports through the effects of the subsidies; this evidence includes information on the evolution of the volume of the allegedly subsidised imports, the effect of these imports on prices of the like product in the domestic market, and the consequent impact of the imports on the domestic industry, as demonstrated by relevant factors and indices having a bearing on the state of the domestic industry, such as those listed in paragraphs 2 and 4 of Article 15.

As regards substantiating the allegations made in the application, the *chapeau* of Article 11.2 encapsulates two conflicting principles. On the one hand, Article 11.2 states, "simple assertion, unsubstantiated by relevant evidence, cannot be considered to meet the requirements by this paragraph", yet on the other hand, it acknowledges, "the application shall contain such information as is reasonably available to the applicant". Article 11.3 of the SCM Agreement requires the IA to establish if there is "sufficient evidence" to "justify initiation of an investigation". The Panel in *China – GOES*, while addressing the relationship between Articles 11.2 and 11.3 of the SCM Agreement, noted that Article 11.2 sets "the evidence that must be included in an application for initiation submitted to an investigating authority by or on behalf of a domestic industry", and Article 11.3 requires an investigating authority to review the accuracy and adequacy of the evidence in order to determine whether it is 'sufficient' to 'justify initiation of an investigation'.[250]

This aspect was discussed by the Panel in in *China – GOES*, where it observed that adequate evidence, providing a sufficient indication of the existence of these elements, is required under Article 11.3.[251] The Panel held that the same standard of sufficient evidence applies "regardless of whether the evidence relates to the existence of a financial contribution, benefit or specificity".[252] The Panel also noted that, in making the determination of whether there is sufficient evidence for initiation of an investigation,

> [T]he investigating authority is balancing two competing interests, namely the interest of the domestic industry "in securing the initiation of an investigation" and the interest of respondents in ensuring that "investigations are not initiated on the basis of frivolous or unfounded suits".[253]

The Panel in *China – GOES* found that the appropriate standard of review applicable under Article 11.3 is the same as that of the analogous provision under the Anti-Dumping Agreement, as adopted by the panel in *US – Softwood Lumber V*:

> A panel should determine "whether an unbiased and objective investigating authority would have found that the application contained sufficient information to justify initiation of the investigation". The Panel agrees with the parties that its role is not to conduct a de novo review of the accuracy and adequacy of the evidence to arrive at its own conclusion regarding whether the evidence in the application was sufficient to justify initiation.[254]

When applications from the domestic manufacturers are received, an investigation will not be launched automatically. Besides meeting the aforementioned requirements, such applications should be coming from domestic manufacturers whose collective output exceeds 50 percent of the total production of the 'like product'. It is also to be pointed out that an investigation shall not be launched in the event applications are backed by domestic manufacturers whose collective output is less than 25 percent of the total production of the like product domestically.

Under Article 11.4, the IA is required not required to examine the motives of the domestic producers that come forward to support an investigation. In *US – Offset Act (Byrd Amendment)*, the Appellate Body explained as follows:

> The use of the terms "expressing support" and "expressly supporting" clarify that Article . . . 11.4 require[s] only that authorities "determine" that support has been "expressed" by a sufficient number of domestic producers. Thus . . . "examination" of the "degree" of support, and not the "nature" of support is required. In other words, it is the "quantity", rather than the "quality", of support that is the issue.[255]

Pursuant to Article 11.6, in exceptional cases, the IA may initiate such CVD investigation without having received any written application by or on behalf of a domestic industry. However, Article 11.6 cautions that such proceedings initiated by the Member State can only proceed if they have sufficient evidence of the existence of a subsidy, injury, and causal link, as described under paragraph 2,[256] and in special circumstances.[257] The procedure envisaged in Article 11.6 to vest authority in the government of the Member State concerned to initiate investigation is aimed at reducing the time lost waiting for all producers of 'like products' to come together and raise a complaint. An investigation following from an application under paragraph will be terminated if there is no sufficient evidence of either subsidisation or injury to justify proceeding with the investigation.[258] Likewise, there will be an immediate termination where the amount of a subsidy is *de minimis*, or where the volume of subsidized imports, actual or potential, or the injury, is negligible.[259] In *US – Carbon Steel*, the Appellate Body while examining the nature of the *de minimis* rule made the following observation:

> To us, there is nothing in Article 11.9 to suggest that its *de minimis* standard was intended to create a special category of "non-injurious" subsidization, or that it reflects a concept that subsidization at less than a *de minimis* threshold can never cause injury. For us, the *de minimis* standard in Article 11.9 does no more than lay down an agreed rule that if *de minimis* subsidization is found to exist in an original investigation, authorities are obliged to terminate their investigation, with the result that no countervailing duty can be imposed in such cases.[260]

3.2 Conduct of CVD Investigation

Following the decision to initiate investigation, a public notice of the investigation is to be issued as per Article 22 of the SCM Agreement.[261] Following from Article 13, the IA must invite the subsidising Member State for consultations, which are to continue throughout the investigation.[262] Article 12 of the SCM Agreement lays down the procedural framework for carrying out an investigation, which enshrines the principles of procedural due process and the evidentiary rules applicable for any investigation that may be initiated.[263] Pursuant to Article 12.1, all interested Member States and all interested parties in a CVD investigation shall be given notice of the information required by authorities and provide ample opportunity to present in writing all evidence which they consider relevant. All material particulars, including the application, are to be made available to the known exporters of the subsidised products, the exporting Member State, as well as to any other interested parties.[264] Also, Member States and interested parties must be given at least 30 days to reply to the questionnaire they receive from the investigating authorities.[265]

The procedures laid down clearly envisage transparency, fairness, and due process in the conduct of investigation.[266] The Appellate Body in *Mexico – Anti-Dumping Measures on Rice* observed that the 30-day period must be afforded to all exporters and foreign producers receiving a questionnaire, to be counted from the date of receipt of the questionnaire.[267] The IA is not to deviate from the timeline of 30 days, and must strictly adhere to the same.[268] Pursuant to Article 12.10, the IA is to afford opportunities for industrial users of the product under investigation, and for representative consumer organisations in cases where the product is commonly sold at the retail level, to provide necessary information.

Pursuant to Article 12.3, the investigating authorities are to make all relevant information that is not confidential available to all interested Member States and interested parties. Article 12.4, on the other hand, provides that any information that is in nature confidential,[269] or which is provided on a confidential basis by parties to an investigation shall, where good cause is shown, be treated as such by the IA, and that such confidential information will only be disclosed with the clear permission of the party submitting it. Following from Article 12.5, the IA, during the pendency of the investigation, must satisfy themselves as to the accuracy of the information supplied by interested Member States, or interested parties upon which their findings are based. Article 12.7 provides for situations where Member States or interested parties decline to engage with such investigation and refuse to provide information within a reasonable period, thereby impeding the investigation. Article 12.7, in such circumstances, authorises the AI to take such decisions on the basis of the 'best information available'. Article 12.7 of the SCM Agreement reads as follows:

> In cases in which any interested Member or interested party refuses access to, or otherwise does not provide, necessary information within a reasonable period or significantly impedes the investigation, preliminary and final determinations, affirmative or negative, may be made on the basis of the facts available.

In *EC – Countervailing Measures on DRAM Chips*, the Panel noted that Article 12.7 also identifies the circumstances in which investigating authorities may overcome a lack of information, by using 'facts' which are otherwise 'available' to the investigating authority:

> Article 12.7 thus allows an authority to make determinations on the basis of the facts available in case certain necessary information is not provided within a reasonable period, or if access to such information is refused, or in case an interested party or interested Member significantly impedes the investigation. Article 12.7 thus enables an authority to continue with the investigation and make determinations based on the facts that are available in case the information necessary to make such determinations is not provided by the interested parties, or, for example, verification of the accuracy of the information submitted is not allowed by an interested party, thereby significantly impeding the investigation. In other words, Article 12.7 identifies the circumstances in which investigating authorities may overcome a lack of information, in the response of the interested parties, by using "facts" which are otherwise "available" to the investigating authority.[270]

In *EC – Countervailing Measures on DRAM Chips*, the Panel considered the use of information from secondary sources, such as press reports for the purposes of making a subsidy determination in the context of Article 12.7, by an IA, and concluded as follows:

> [t]he weighing of the information and the evidence before it, is part of the discretionary authority of the investigating authority . . . There is no rule in the SCM Agreement that stops the investigating authority from taking into account information from all sources, including press reports.[271]

In *Mexico – Anti-Dumping Measures on Rice*, the Appellate Body clarified that using facts accessible to carry out the investigation serves the purpose of replacing information that is absent, and noting the textual differences in the provisions between the SCM Agreement and the AD Agreement made the following observation:

> Like Article 6.8 of the Anti-Dumping Agreement, Article 12.7 of the SCM Agreement permits an investigating authority, under certain circumstances, to fill in gaps in the information necessary to arrive at a conclusion as to subsidization (or dumping) and injury. As in the Anti-Dumping Agreement, Article 12.7 prescribes the information that may be used for such purposes as the "facts available". Unlike the Anti-Dumping Agreement, the SCM Agreement does not expressly set out in an annex the conditions for determining precisely which "facts" might be "available" for an agency to use when a respondent fails to provide necessary information. This does not mean, however, that no such conditions exist in the SCM Agreement.[272]

The Appellate Body further noted:

> Article 12.7 is intended to ensure that the failure of an interested party to provide necessary information does not hinder an agency's investigation. Thus, the provision permits the use of facts on record solely for the purpose of replacing information that may be missing, in order to arrive at an accurate subsidization or injury determination.
>
> In view of the above, we understand that recourse to facts available does not permit an investigating authority to use any information in whatever way it chooses. First, such recourse is not a licence to rely on only part of the evidence provided. To the extent possible, an investigating authority using the "facts available" in a countervailing duty investigation must take into account all the substantiated facts provided by an interested party, even if those facts may not constitute the complete information requested of that party. Secondly, the "facts available" to the agency are generally limited to those that may reasonably replace the information that an interested party failed to provide. In certain circumstances, this may include information from secondary sources.[273]

Similarly, in *US – Carbon Steel (India)*, the Appellate Body clarified the parameters for recourse to facts available and held that the process of identifying the 'facts available' should be limited to identifying replacements for the 'necessary information' that is missing from the record,[274] and that the 'facts available' are those facts that are in the possession of the investigating authority and on its written record.[275] The Appellate Body in *US – Supercalendered Paper*, while upholding the finding of the panel that the conduct of the USDOC (the IA in the case) was inconsistent with Article 12.7, held

> [t]he USDOC uses "facts available", on the basis of a failure to provide "necessary information", without taking any additional steps to clarify the nature of the unreported assistance and whether the missing information is "necessary" under Article 12.7 of the SCM Agreement. The United States refers to the panel's view in *EC – Countervailing Measures on DRAM Chips* that information is "necessary" if an investigating authority reasonably consider[s]' it so. We consider, however, that the use of "reasonably" by the panel itself indicates that an investigating authority is not entirely unconstrained in its identification of "necessary information". Indeed, in our view, the investigating authority must make a reasonable assessment based on evidence and cannot simply infer, without further clarification, that the missing information is "necessary" within the meaning of Article 12.7.[276]

The Appellate Body in *US – Carbon Steel (India)*, while modifying the Panel's finding, held that Article 12.7 requires an investigating authority to use 'facts available' that reasonably replace the missing 'necessary information', with a view to arriving at an accurate determination, which calls for a process of evaluation of available evidence, the extent and nature of which depends on the particular circumstances of a given case.[277] In *US – Anti-Dumping Methodologies (China)*, the Appellate Body, while considering the similarities in the texts of the SCM Agreement and AD Agreement with regards to the powers of the IA to receive information, observed as follows:

> [g]iven the similarities between the text of Article 12.7 of the Agreement in Subsidies and Countervailing Measures (SCM Agreement) and Article 6.8 of the Anti-Dumping Agreement and that both provisions permit an investigating authority, under certain circumstances, to fill in gaps in the information necessary to arrive at a conclusion as to dumping or subsidization and injury . . . the interpretation of Article 12.7 of the SCM Agreement developed by the Appellate Body in *Mexico – Anti-Dumping Measures on Rice* and *US – Carbon Steel (India)* is relevant to the understanding of the legal standard applied under Article 6.8 and paragraph 7 of Annex II to the Anti-Dumping Agreement.[278]

More recently, in *US – Pipes and Tubes (Turkey)*, the Panel stated that recourse to Article 12.7 is "for the purpose of replacing necessary information that may be missing, to allow the investigating authority to make an accurate subsidization determination" and should not be "to punish non-cooperating parties by intentionally drawing an adverse inference. The use of inferences to select adverse facts to punish non-cooperating parties would result in an inaccurate subsidization determination".[279]

Before a final decision is arrived at, the IA is to inform all interested Member States and interested parties of the essential facts under consideration which form the basis for the decision whether to apply definitive measures, and such disclosure shall take place in sufficient time for the parties to defend their interests. According to the Appellate Body in *China – GOES*, the essential facts that an IA should convey, as per Article 12.8, "are those that are required to understand the basis for . . . the decision whether or not to apply definitive measures"[280] and those that ensure the ability of interest parties to defend their interests.[281] As per Article 11.11, any investigation should be concluded within one year of its commencement and in no case should it exceed 18 months.

3.2.1 Concluding the Investigation

Article 32 of the SCM sets out that no specific action against a subsidy of another Member can be taken except in accordance with the provisions of GATT 1994, as interpreted by the SCM

Agreement. Pursuant to Article 32.1, read in conjunction with Article 10, CVDs may only be imposed in accordance with the provisions of Part V of the SCM Agreement and Article VI of GATT 1994, taken together. In the event of conflicts between the provisions of Article VI and the provisions of SCM Agreement, the provisions of the latter will prevail.[282] Together, the GATT and SCM Agreement three remedies concerning CVD investigations, *viz.*,

i   Direct countermeasures taken through the WTO dispute settlement system;
ii A provisional imposition of CVDs – Article 17 of the SCM Agreement;[283]
iii Price undertakings – Article 18 of the SCM Agreement;[284] and
iv A definitive imposition of CVDs – Article 19 of the SCM Agreement.[285]

In *US – Offset Act (Byrd Amendment)*, the Appellate Body expressed the view that Article 32 of the SCM Agreement prohibited Member States from applying 'specific measures' 'against' subsidies, which are not covered by one of the last three categories. The Appellate Body, while holding that the US legislation introduced 'specific measures' 'against' subsidisation, observed:

> Because the CDSOA [the pertinent US legislation] has an adverse bearing on, and, more specifically, is designed and structured so that it dissuades . . . the practice of subsidization, and because it creates an incentive to terminate such practices, the CDSOA is undoubtedly an action "against" dumping or a subsidy, within the meaning of Article 18.1 of the Anti-Dumping Agreement and of Article 32.1 of the SCM Agreement.[286]

In *EC – Commercial Vessels*, the Panel considered whether the TDM Regulation, as submitted by Korea, was a specific action against a subsidy, and whether the measure was 'specific' action and 'against' a subsidy.[287] The Panel, while examining the notion of 'specific' action, recalled the Appellate Body's findings in the *US – 1916 Act* case, and in *US – Offset Act (Byrd Amendment)*, relating to Article 8.1 of the AD Agreement and Article 32.1 of the SCM Agreement, and if the TDM was inextricably linked to, or had a strong correlation with, the constituent elements of a subsidy.[288]

In the event the IA determines that the investigations were inconclusive, *i.e.*, the conditions laid out in the SCM Agreement have not been met, it may lead to a negotiated understanding between the parties concerned, provided the Member State that initiated the investigation and the other parties prefer such a conclusion.[289] In practice this appears to be the preferred choice amongst the Member States, as the parties stand to benefit from a much speedier conclusion to the proceedings. As mentioned earlier, the IA is authorised to apply provisional CVDs before conclusion of the investigation, provided such measures are justified and "necessary to prevent injury being caused during the investigation",[290] and "shall be limited to as short a period as possible, not exceeding four months".[291]

3.3 Imposition and Collection of CVDs

Article 19 of the SCM Agreement presents the scheme on the imposition and collection of CVDs in an original investigation, in contrast to reviews pursuant to Article 21 of the SCM Agreement. Article 19.1 allows Member States to impose definitive CVDs only upon a final determination that (i) a countervailable subsidy exists and that (ii) through the effects of such subsidies, the subsidised imports cause, or threaten to cause, injury to the domestic industry. The text of Article 19 of the SCM Agreement largely parallels the text of Article 9 of the AD Agreement.

Article 19.2 captures the objective of imposition of CVDs, which is to reverse the negative effects of subsidised imports on the domestic industries of the importing Member State. Article 19.2 states:

> It is desirable that the imposition should be permissive in the territory of all Members, that the duty should be less than the total amount of the subsidy if such lesser duty would be adequate to remove the injury to the domestic industry, and that procedures should be established which would allow the authorities concerned to take due account of representations made by domestic interested parties whose interests might be adversely affected by the imposition of a countervailing duty [footnote omitted].

A closer reading of Article 19.2 reveals that 'it is desirable' that the imposition of CVDs should be permissive – not mandatory (less trade-affecting); to apply the lesser duty, *i.e.*, imposing a CVD that is less than the amount of subsidy, and in the event the lesser amount is found adequate to eliminate the injury caused to the domestic industry. On the other hand, Article 19.4 prohibits the levy of CVDs in excess of the amount of the subsidy that is found to exist, and reads as follows:

> No countervailing duty shall be levied on any imported product in excess of the amount of the subsidy found to exist, calculated in terms of subsidization per unit of the subsidized and exported product [footnote omitted].

As the 'lesser duty rule' is desirable and not mandatory, WTO Member States tend to impose higher duties. Article VI:3 of GATT 1994, which is concomitant to Article 19.4 of the SCM Agreement, sets the maximum level of CVD at "an amount equal to the estimated bounty or subsidy determined to have been granted, directly or indirectly, on the manufacture, production or export of such product". Also, Article VI:3, *inter alia*, sets out that Members shall take all necessary steps to ensure that the imposition of a CVD is in accordance with Article VI of GATT 1994.[292] The question before the Appellate Body in *US – Washing Machines* was whether the subsidies received were tied to the investigated product or attributed also to products not under investigation. Reversing the finding of the Panel, the Appellate Body ruled that the USDOC (i) improperly attributed certain Korean subsidies to all of Samsung's products, as opposed to tying those subsidies to Samsung's digital appliances only, and (ii) incorrectly attributed certain Korean subsidies to Samsung's production in Korea only, as opposed to Samsung's production worldwide, which all resulted in the levy of CVDs in excess of the subsidisation margin.

The Appellate Body in *US – Washing Machines* also ruled that the Panel, while reviewing the 'tying' findings of the IA, erroneously conflated the concept of 'recipient of the benefit' under Article 1.1(b) of the SCM Agreement with the concept of 'subsidized product' under Article 19.4 of the SCM Agreement and Article VI:3 of the GATT 1994.[293] The issue before the Appellate Body in *Japan – DRAMS (Korea)* was whether CVDs can be imposed where the subsidies were non-recurring, and the investigations indicated that the subsidy will no longer exist at the time of imposition. The Appellate Body held that CVDs cannot be imposed in such cases and found that such CVDs would be in excess of the amount of the subsidy found to exist and, therefore, contrary to the provisions of Article 19.4.[294] Also, agreeing with the Panel, the Appellate Body held that 'found to exist' had to be given its literal meaning, *i.e.*, subsidisation was taking place at the time of the imposition.[295]

Also, Article 19.4 requires an IA to establish the precise amount of subsidy to the imported products under investigation. In short, Article 19.4 "places a quantitative ceiling on the amount of a countervailing duty which may not exceed the amount of subsidization".[296] In *China – Broiler*, there was disagreement as to the correct per unit subsidisation rate, and it was argued by the complainant that the IA had improperly calculated the amount of subsidisation per unit, by including a subsidy that benefitted the production of non-subject merchandise. Relying on the relevant jurisprudence from both Article 19.4 of the SCM Agreement and Article VI:3 of the GATT 1994, the Panel explained that the investigating authority "was obligated to accurately determine the per unit subsidy amount and not impose countervailing duties exceeding that amount".[297] The Panel in *US – Supercalendered Paper* stated, in relation to determining the amount of subsidisation, that

> [t]here may be circumstances where it is reasonable for an investigating authority to proceed as if the totality of subsidized inputs produced by an entity are used in the production of a finished product, without necessarily proving that this is the case. However, this will not be the case in circumstances where record evidence indicates that only a very small amount of the subsidized input produced by an entity is in fact used in the production of the finished product.[298]

3.3.1 Duration and Review of CVDs

Pursuant to Article 21.1, the CVDs imposed will only remain in force as long as to the extent necessary to counteract the injurious subsidisation:

> A countervailing duty shall remain in force only as long as and to the extent necessary to counteract subsidization which is causing injury.

In *US – Carbon Steel*, the Appellate Body held that it considered Article 21.1 of the SCM Agreement as

> a general rule that, after the imposition of a countervailing duty, the continued application of that duty is subject to certain disciplines. These disciplines relate to the duration of the countervailing duty ("only as long as . . . necessary"), its magnitude ("only . . . to the extent necessary"), and its purpose ("to counteract subsidization which is causing injury"). Thus, the general rule of Article 21.1 underlines the requirement for periodic review of countervailing duties and highlights the factors that must inform such reviews.[299]

The 'general rule' referred to by the Appellate Body is triggered through two types of review process, *viz.*, (i) the sunset review and (ii) the administrative review. While Article 21.1 sets out the general rule on the continued application of the CVDs, Articles 21.2 and 21.3 present specific scenarios necessitating the review of the decisions taken pursuant to Article 21.1.

3.3.1.1 ADMINISTRATIVE REVIEW

Article 21.2 provides for an administrative review mechanism during the five-year lifespan of a CVD and is also referred to as the 'changed circumstances review'. The review process under Article 21.2 can be initiated either upon request from an interested party any time after the imposition of the CVD or *ex officio* by the IA provided a reasonable time had lapsed since the imposition of the CVD. The objective of the review is to ensure that Member States comply with Article 21.1. The Article 21.2 review process scrutinises the need for the continued imposition of the CVD. As per Article 21.2, an interested party requesting a review is to submit positive information substantiating the need for a review. Pursuant to Article 21.2, while carrying out an administrative review, the IA is to investigate

i   Whether the continued imposition of duty is necessary to offset subsidisation; or
ii   Whether the injury would be likely to recur if the duty in place were removed; or
iii Whether subsidisation resulting in damage will continue/recur, assuming that the duties in place were to be removed.

The Appellate Body in *US – Carbon Steel* took the position that the submission of positive evidence from an interested person is a threshold issue in an administrative review to initiate the process, which is not the same in an *ex officio* initiation of review, and made the following observation:

> We note that Article 21.2 sets down an explicit evidentiary standard for requests by interested parties for a review under that provision. In order to trigger the authorities' obligation to conduct a review, such requests must, *inter alia*, include "positive information substantiating the need for review". Article 21.2 does not, on its face, apply this same standard to the initiation by authorities "on their own initiative" of a review carried out under that provision. Thus, Article 21.2 contemplates that, for reviews carried out pursuant to that provision, the self-initiation by the authorities of a review is not governed by the same standards that apply to initiation upon request by other parties.[300]

Article 21.2 calls for retrospective, present, and prospective analyses of the imposed CVDs, as it relates to the necessity of the CVDs, as well as taking stock of the impact of the CVD to its imposition. Such a review is also forward facing as it looks to the future consequences of the continued imposition and thus differs significantly from a review under Article 21.3. In *US – Carbon Steel (India)*, the Appellate Body, drawing the distinction between Articles 21.2 and 21.3, found as follows:

> Article 21.2 mandates authorities to "review the need for the continued imposition of the duty" and, in particular, to examine "whether the continued imposition of the duty is necessary to offset subsidization". Article 21.2 also gives investigating authorities the power to determine "whether the injury would be likely to continue or recur if the duty were removed or varied, or both". Hence, Article 21.2 appears to call for a present and retrospective analysis as it relates to the necessity and impact of the duty prior to and during the administrative review, as well as a prospective analysis focusing on the likely future consequences of the maintenance, changing, or removal of the duty. This differs in scope from a review under Article 21.3, which is an exclusively prospective analysis that focuses on the future consequences of the removal of the duty. Both provisions, however, bear a similar prospective focus. To the extent that the prospective focus of a review under Article 21.2 is similar to that under Article 21.3, this would suggest that the requirements set out in Article 11 of the SCM Agreement would not apply to administrative reviews conducted pursuant to Article 21.2 of the SCM Agreement.[301]

Concerning the determination an investigating authority must make in an Article 21.2 review, the Appellate Body in *US – Lead and Bismuth II* noted:

> On the basis of its assessment of the information presented to it by interested parties, as well as of other evidence before it relating to the period of review, the investigating authority must determine whether there is a continuing need for the application of countervailing duties. The investigating authority is not free to ignore such information. If it were free to ignore this information, the review mechanism under Article 21.2 would have no purpose.[302]

On the question of the existence of a 'benefit' in an Article 21.2 review, the Appellate Body in *US – Lead and Bismuth II* rejected the view that, in the context of an administrative review under Article 21.2, an IA must always establish the existence of a 'benefit' during the period of review in the same way as an IA must establish a 'benefit' in an original investigation. The Appellate Body held as follows in *US – Lead and Bismuth II*:

> We believe that it is important to distinguish between the original investigation leading to the imposition of countervailing duties and the administrative review. In an original investigation, the investigating authority must establish that all conditions set out in the SCM Agreement for the imposition of countervailing duties are fulfilled. In an administrative review, however, the investigating authority must address those issues which have been raised before it by the interested parties or, in the case of an investigation conducted on its own initiative, those issues which warranted the examination.[303]

Article 21.2 imposes the IA with the obligation to take into account in a review "positive information substantiating the need for a review". In the Appellate Body's view, such information may relate to developments with respect to the subsidy, privatisation at arm's length and for fair market value, or some other information.[304] The Appellate Body hence draws a distinction between the original investigation which is concerned with the initial imposition of a countervailing duty and the review procedure of Article 21.2.[305] Following from such review, if the IA were to reach a conclusion that continued imposition of CVD is no longer necessary, it shall be terminated immediately.[306] If the IA were to conclude that the CVD should remain in place, then it will continue to apply but at a reduced level.

3.3.1.2 SUNSET REVIEW

Article 21.3 provides for the 'sunset review', imposing a limit on the continued imposition of the CVDs. Pursuant to first sentence of Article 21.3, the sunset review must be initiated before the end of the five-year period, and pursuant to second sentence of Article 21.3, CVDs may remain in force pending the outcome of the sunset review. Under the provisions, all CVDs must be terminated five years after their imposition or latest review, unless the Member State concerned has conducted a review. The Appellate Body in *US – Carbon Steel* underpinned the significance of such review and observed that the Member State "does not conduct a sunset review, or, having conducted such a review, it does not make such a positive determination, the duties must be terminated".[307]

The Appellate Body in *US – Carbon Steel*, while observing that the SCM Agreement does not prohibit the automatic self-initiation of sunset reviews by investigating authorities, clarified that there is no indication in the framework of Article 21.3 that the IA's ability to self-initiate a sunset review is conditional upon compliance with evidentiary standards in Article 11, and that no other evidentiary standard is required for the self-initiation of a sunset review under Article 21.3.

> [O]ur review of the context of Article 21.3 of the SCM Agreement reveals no indication that the ability of authorities to self-initiate a sunset review under that provision is conditioned on compliance with the evidentiary standards set forth in Article 11 of the SCM Agreement relating to initiation of investigations. Nor do we consider that any other evidentiary standard is prescribed for the self-initiation of a sunset review under Article 21.3.[308]

As per Article 21.3, where the IA has 'determined' that the expiry of the CVD will likely lead to continuation or recurrence of injurious subsidisation, the duty will not be terminated. In *US – Carbon Steel*, the Appellate Body, while explaining the different objectives of Article 21.2 and Article 21.3 (discussed in the earlier section), noted that the objective of Article 21.3 "is not, *per se*, to conduct a review, but rather to terminate a countervailing duty unless a specific determination is made in a review".[309] The Appellate Body further noted the differing scope of Articles 21.3 and 21.4, rules on collection of evidence, and conduct of investigation as follows:

> As we have noted earlier, the fourth paragraph of Article 21 explicitly applies to Article 21.3 reviews the detailed rules set out in Article 12 of the SCM Agreement regarding evidence and procedure in the conduct of investigations. However, the rules on evidence and procedure contained in Article 12 do not relate to the initiation of such investigations. Rather, the rules relating to evidence needed to initiate an investigation are set out in Article 11, which is not referred to in Article 21.4. The fact that the rules in Article 11 governing such matters are not incorporated by reference into Article 21.3 suggests that they are not, *ipso facto*, applicable to sunset reviews.

Pursuant to Article 21.4, all sunset reviews shall be carried out expeditiously and shall normally be concluded within 12 months of the date of initiation of the review.

3.3.1.3 JUDICIAL REVIEW

Pursuant to any affirmative decision to impose CVDs, an IA is to issue

> a public notice of the imposition of provisional measures shall set forth, or otherwise make available through a separate report, sufficiently detailed explanations for the preliminary determinations on the existence of a subsidy and injury and shall refer to the matters of fact and law which have led to arguments being accepted or rejected. Such a notice or report shall, due regard being paid to the requirement for the protection of confidential information.[310]

Article 22.4 also requires such notice to contain the following particulars:

i   The names of the suppliers or, when this is impracticable, the supplying countries involved;
ii A description of the product which is sufficient for customs purposes;

iii The amount of subsidy established and the basis on which the existence of a subsidy has been determined;
iv Considerations relevant to the injury determination as set out in Article 15; and
v The main reasons leading to the determination.

Pursuant to Article 23, Member States that have national legislation on CVDs

> shall maintain judicial, arbitral or administrative tribunals or procedures for the purpose, *inter alia*, of the prompt review of administrative actions relating to final determinations and reviews of determinations within the meaning of Article 21. Such tribunals or procedures shall be independent of the authorities responsible for the determination or review in question, and shall provide all interested parties who participated in the administrative proceeding and are directly and individually affected by the administrative actions with access to review.

The text of Article 23 of the SCM Agreement largely parallels the text of Article 13 of the AD Agreement.

3.3.2 Institutional and Procedural Provisions

Parts VI and VII of the SCM Agreement are designed to oversee the implementation of the SCM Agreement. Article 24 of the SCM Agreement establishes the WTO Committee on Subsidies and Countervailing Measures, in which all members of the WTO are represented. The Committee is a subsidiary body of the Council for Trade in Goods and is tasked with establishing a permanent group of experts (PGE).[311] The purpose and functions of the Committee can be summarised and are (i) the receipt and review of notifications, (ii) the supervision of the application and implementation of the ASCM Agreement, and (iii) to serve as a forum for consultations and discussions on subsidy issues (Wolfrum, 2008).

Article 25 obligates Member States to notify to the Committee

i About subsidies, covered by Article 1 and 2 of the SCM Agreement (Article 25.1);
ii About preliminary and final actions taken with regard to CVDs (paragraph 11) (Article 25.11); and
iii About the competent authorities (Article 25.12), as well as the domestic procedures governing the initiation and conduct of countervailing duty investigations (paragraph 12).

Pursuant to Article 25, all Member States are required to notify all specific subsidies by 30 June of each year. In *Brazil – Aircraft*, the Appellate Body noted, "Article 25 aims to promote transparency by requiring Members to notify their subsidies, without prejudging the legal status of those subsidies".[312]

4. Special and Differential Treatment for Developing Country Member States

The SCM Agreement, recognising that subsidies could play a crucial role in the economic development programmes of developing and least developed country Member States, establishes preferential rules.[313] Preferential rules for developing and least developed country Member States are contained in Article 27. As per Article 27.2, the prohibition on export subsidies contained in Article 3.1(a) of the SCM Agreement does not apply to developing country Member States, as referred to in Annex VII. Article 27 provides for

i   Exemption from the prohibition of granting export subsidies (Articles 27.2, 27.4, 27.5, 27.6, 27.7, and 27.14);
ii   Exemption from the prohibition of granting import substitution subsidies (Article 27.3);
iii Non-application of the presumption of serious prejudice as contained in Article 6.1 (Article 27.8);
iv   Remedies under Article 7 against actionable subsidies granted by a developing country Member are only available under more limited circumstances than against non-developing Members (Articles 27.9 and 27.13); and
v   Developing country Members benefit from higher *de minimis* thresholds in terms of subsidisation and import shares (Articles 27.10, 27.11, 27.12, and 27.15).

Article 27.10 of the SCM Agreement provides that any CVD investigation of a product originating in a developing country Member shall be terminated as soon as the IA determine that (i) the overall level of subsidies granted to the product in question does not exceed 2 percent *ad valorem* or (2) the volume of the subsidised imports represents less than 4 percent of the total imports of the like product of the importing Member.

5. Subsidies Provisions in Other WTO Agreements

Apart from the rules on subsidies contained in the SCM Agreement, additional rules are to be found in other WTO agreements. Presented next are brief overviews of the additional rules contained in Agreement on Agriculture, the GATT, and the TRIMs Agreement.

5.1 Agreement on Agriculture

For over 2.5 billion people, agriculture remains the primary source of livelihood. With the majority of them living in the developing world and with distributional inequalities in access to food, agricultural subsidies in developed countries remain contentious. Government agricultural policies play a significant role in production and consumption patterns. Hence, one of the most contentious issues in international trade is agricultural subsidies. During the Uruguay Round of negotiations, as well as during the Doha Development Round, agricultural subsidies featured as one of the central issues. Agricultural subsidies (both export and domestic) are crucial for the agricultural policies that are shaped by interest groups in a number of developed country Member States. These agricultural subsidies affect both trade interests and economic development of a number of developing country Member States. Subsidies paid to farmers in developed countries suppress the price of the product in the world market, which in turn severely affects the livelihood of millions of small farmers living in developing countries.

The US policy to subsidise its cotton farmers[314] has been long criticised and was also the subject of a successful challenge from Brazil in *US – Upland Cotton*.[315] To avert a retaliatory action by Brazil on its interests, the US concluded a settlement with Brazil agreeing to pay Brazil and continues to subsidise its cotton farmers. The Agreement on Agriculture (AoA) establishes special rules on agricultural subsidies, which shall prevail over the rules of the SCM Agreement in the event of conflict. Article 21.1 of the AoA states:

The provisions of the GATT 1994 and of other Multilateral Trade Agreements in Annex 1A to the WTO Agreement shall apply subject to the provisions of this Agreement.[316]

The AoA establishes subsidy commitment schedules, akin to tariff schedules for goods. Where a Member State has made a commitment in the schedule for a particular product, it agrees not to provide more than the committed amount of subsidies, and where a Member State has made no commitment, no subsidies are permitted for that product. The approach taken by the AoA and the SCM Agreement differs considerably. The primary focus of the SCM Agreement is on the trade-distorting effects of subsidies, whereas it is not the focus of the AoA. Export subsidies, which are prohibited under Article 3 of the SCM Agreement, also apply to agricultural export subsidies except as provided otherwise in the Agreement on Agriculture. Article 3.1, which defines the relationship between the SCM Agreement and the AoA, prohibits export and import substitution subsidies "[e]xcept as provided in the Agreement on Agriculture".

The AoA does not contain a definition of a subsidy, and the SCM Agreement's definition applies to agricultural subsidies as well. However, Article 1(e) of the AoA defines export subsidies as "subsidies contingent upon export, including the export subsidies listed in Article 9", which is similar to the SCM Agreement. The Panel in *US – FSC* ruled that Article 1 of the SCM Agreement is "highly relevant context for the interpretation of the word 'subsidy' within the meaning the Agreement on Agriculture". The Panel considered that a subsidy within the meaning of the SCM Agreement is also a subsidy within the meaning of the AoA unless the contrary is to be inferred from the AoA.[317] The Appellate Body in *US – FSC* found that the AoA and the SCM Agreement employ the same language to define 'export subsidies', and concluded that it is correct to apply the interpretation of export contingency adopted under the SCM Agreement to the interpretation of export contingency under the Agreement on Agriculture.

> We turn next to the requirement that "export subsidies" under Article 1(e) of the Agreement on Agriculture be "contingent upon export performance". We see no reason, and none has been pointed out to us, to read the requirement of "contingent upon export performance" in the Agreement on Agriculture differently from the same requirement imposed by the SCM Agreement. The two Agreements use precisely the same words to define "export subsidies". Although there are differences between the export subsidy disciplines established under the two Agreements, those differences do not, in our view, affect the common substantive requirement relating to export contingency. Therefore, we think it appropriate to apply the interpretation of export contingency that we have adopted under the SCM Agreement to the interpretation of export contingency under the Agreement on Agriculture.[318]

The Appellate Body in *US – Upland Cotton* noted that the introductory phrase "except as provided in the Agreement on Agriculture" applies to both paragraphs (a) and (b) of paragraph 1 of Article 3, which deal with both export subsidies and import substitution subsidies, respectively.[319] Where there is a conflict, the special rules provided under AoA prevail over the provisions of the SCM. The key provision dealing with the relationship between the SCM Agreement and the AoA is Article 21.1 states:

> The provisions of GATT 1994 and of other Multilateral Trade Agreements in Annex 1A to the WTO Agreement shall apply subject to the provisions of this [Agriculture] Agreement.[320]

The Panel in *US – Upland Cotton* described three situations in which Article 21.1 could apply so that the AoA would prevail over the prohibition on import substitution subsidies in Article 3.1(b) of the SCM Agreement.

> where, for example, the domestic support provisions of the Agreement on Agriculture would prevail in the event that an explicit carve-out or exemption from the disciplines in Article 3.1(b) of the SCM Agreement existed in the text of the Agreement on Agriculture. Another situation would be where it would be impossible for a Member to comply with its domestic support obligations under the Agreement on Agriculture and the Article 3.1(b) prohibition simultaneously. Another situation might be where there is an explicit authorization in the text of the Agreement on Agriculture that would authorize a measure that, in the absence of such an express authorization, would be prohibited by Article 3.1(b) of the SCM Agreement.[321]

The finding of the Panel in *US – Upland Cotton* was upheld by the Appellate Body, which observed, "Article 21.1 could apply in the three situations described by the Panel".[322] The Appellate Body, citing its report in *EC – Banana III*, ruled that Article 21.1 could also apply where the Agreement on Agriculture contained "specific provisions dealing specifically with the same matter" as the provision of another multilateral trade agreement in Annex 1A cited by the United States, namely Article 3.1(b) of the SCM Agreement.[323] Pursuant to Part III of the SCM Agreement, any domestic subsidies to agriculture are to be within the Agriculture Agreement domestic support commitments and also not cause 'adverse effects'.

Unlike the SCM Agreement, which permits Member States to impose CVDs on subsidised imports that cause injury to their domestic producers, the AoA under Article 3 instead establishes upper limits on the number of trade-distorting subsidies. As export subsidies are concerned, the agricultural subsidies that violate Article 3.1(a) of the SCM Agreement would likely not violate the AoA if they are within that agreement's commitment levels for specific products (Bartels, 2016).

Pursuant to Article 9.1 of the AoA, Member States have agreed to subject all export subsidies, identified in paragraphs (a) to (f), to reduction commitments. The subsidies identified in paragraphs (a) to (f) constitute a broader prohibition, as they are more detailed than the subsidy definition of Article 1 of the SCM Agreement and the language of Article 3.1(a) of the SCM Agreement. Pursuant to the first clause in Article 3.3, the Member States "shall not provide export subsidies listed in paragraph 1 of Article 9 in respect of the agricultural products or groups of products specified in Section II of Part IV of its Schedule in excess of the budgetary outlay and quantity commitment levels specified therein".[324] Under the second clause in Article 3.3, the Member States "shall not provide such subsidies in respect of any agricultural product not specified in that Section of its Schedule".[325]

The types of export subsidies covered by the commitment in Article 9.1(a) to (f) are (a) direct export subsidies by governments or their agencies contingent on export performance (including payments-in-kind); (b) sales of non-commercial stocks of agricultural products by the government for export at prices lower than comparable prices for such goods on the domestic market; (c) payments on export of agricultural products financed by virtue of governmental action, whether or not a charge on the public account is involved; (d) subsidies to reduce costs of marketing goods for exports of agricultural goods; (e) internal transport subsidies applying to export shipments, provided or mandated by the government, on terms more favourable than for domestic shipments;[326] and (f) subsidies on agricultural products contingent on their incorporation into exported products.

Article 10.1 of the AoA further provides that export subsidies not listed in Article 9.1 shall not be applied such that a Member State's export subsidy commitments are circumvented, or threatened to be circumvented, and further non-commercial transactions shall not be used to circumvent such commitments. This provides a broader scope for export subsidy. In the Nairobi Ministerial Conference, a decision was reached to fully eliminate any form of agricultural export subsidies, which aimed at ensuring that Member States do not resort to trade-distorting export subsidies and thereby create a level playing field for agriculture exporters (Nairobi Ministerial Conference, 2015). While the developed country Member States were required to eliminate their remaining scheduled export subsidy entitlements (barring a handful of agricultural products) as of the date of adoption of the Ministerial Decision, the developing country Member States were required to eliminate their export subsidy entitlement by the end of 2018, with the exception of specific items.

5.2 GATT

Subsidy rules are also contained in the GATT. Following from Article XVI:1 of the GATT, granting or maintaining any form of subsidy that operates "directly or indirectly to increase exports of any product from, or to reduce imports of any product" into a Member State's territory is required to be notified to Contracting Parties in writing. Article XV:1, second sentence, provides for consultations where "it is determined that serious prejudice to the interests of any other Member is caused or threatened by any such subsidisation". The Panel in *US – Upland Cotton* found that because the term 'serious prejudice' is used in Articles 5(c) and 6.3(c) of the SCM Agreement 'in the same sense' as in Article XVI:1 of GATT 1994, its findings of 'serious prejudice' under SCM Articles 5(c) and 6.3(c) would also be conclusive for a finding of 'serious prejudice' under GATT Article XVI:1.[327]

Further, Article XVI:3 states that Member States "should seek to avoid the use of subsidies on the export of primary products" and, if in the event they are granted, "such subsidy shall not be applied in a manner which results in that contracting party having more than an equitable share of world export trade in that product". The Panel in *US – Upland Cotton* found that the text of Article XVI:3 indicates that "the provision is limited to 'export subsidies' and does not address rights and obligations of Members relating to other types of subsidies"[328] and that it did "not believe that it is appropriate to apply a separate or different definition of 'export subsidies' under Article XVI:3 than that which is now applicable for the purposes of Articles 3.3, 8, 9, 10 and 1(e) of the *Agreement on Agriculture* and Article 3.1(a) of the SCM Agreement".[329] Based on the ordinary meaning of the text of Article XVI:3 read in its context and in light of the object and purpose of the Agreement on Agriculture and the SCM Agreement, and also taking into account the drafting history of the Tokyo Round Subsidies Code, the Panel found that "Article XVI:3 applies only to export subsidies as that term is now defined in the Agreement on Agriculture and the SCM Agreement".[330]

5.3 TRIMs Agreement

The Agreement on Trade-Related Investment Measures (TRIMs) in its Annex contains an illustrative list, where examples of measures that violate GATT Articles III:4 and XI:1 are provided for. This includes measures "compliance with which is necessary to obtain an advantage" requiring actions such as the purchase of goods. Hence, the use of such subsidies will be deemed to be in violation of the aforementioned provisions, as they provide an 'advantage'.[331]

6. Summary

Subsidies and CVDs have come to occupy an important position within the WTO legal framework, and there is now rich jurisprudence on the subject. Both developing and developed country Member States alike engage in the practice of supporting their domestic industries through subsidies, which are normally factored into their governmental policies. The two sectors that are often the recipients of subsidies are the agricultural sector and a selection of industries, and they are a cause for concern. When the grant of a subsidy causes or threatens to cause material injury, the Member States are authorised to impose countervailing duties on the subsidised products. Clear rules are provided under WTO laws with respect to both subsidies and CVDs. The SCM Agreement distinguishes between prohibited subsidies and actionable subsidies, establishes a detailed set of guidance and standards for the conduct of CVD investigations, and sets out rules that are to be adhered to for disputes involving subsidies before the DSB.

Notes

1. Although targeted at specific projects, the benefits of subsidies can in some cases reach an unintended beneficiary. A well-designed subsidy is more likely to reach the intended and actual beneficiaries.
2. The EU and the US have been entangled in a marathon dispute in respect of subsidies granted to their respective civil aircraft industries.
3. In Member States, such as the US, national defence services benefit private firms which in turn reduce risk and lower the cost of capital. See Sykes (2003). Though engaging private operators has raised questions on 'accountability' in conflict zones, the US continues with the practice.
4. Article XVI of GATT 1947 was limited to paragraph 1 of Article XVI of GATT 1994. All Contracting Parties were bound by this obligation. For a discussion on the preparatory work on subsidy disciplines during the GATT, see Jackson (1969).
5. The Dunkel Draft, published in 1991, was named after Mr Arthur Dunkel, the former director-general of the GATT between 1980 and 1993. Mr Dunkel launched and successfully steered the Uruguay Round of multilateral trade negotiations.
6. This, in effect, allowed Contracting Parties to 'forum shop'. See Appellate Body Report, *Brazil – Desiccated Coconut*, p. 12, where Brazil had imposed CVDs on imports from Philippines, based on investigation initiated before the entry into force of the WTO in 1995. The Appellate Body upheld the finding of the Panel that (i) the subsidy rules in the GATT cannot apply independently of the SCM Agreement, and (ii) non-application of the SCM Agreement rendered the subsidy rules in the GATT non-applicable. Further, the Appellate Body held that Articles I, II, and VI of the GATT did not apply to the Brazilian CVD measures at issue as they were based on an investigation initiated prior to 1 January 1995, *i.e.*, the date that the WTO Agreement came into effect for Brazil.
7. It is to be noted that both the GATT 1947 and the Subsidies Code from 1979 did not contain a definition of 'subsidy'.
8. See Appellate Body Report, *Brazil – Desiccated Coconut*, p. 181.
9. See Appellate Body Report, *US – Carbon Steel*, para. 73. The Appellate Body made the observation, despite the SCM Agreement not having a preamble to it or an explicit indication of its objective and purpose.
10. See Panel Report, *Brazil – Aircraft*, para. 7.26.
11. See Panel Report, *Canada – Aircraft*, para. 9.119.
12. Subsidies can be offered through other means, and Member States can provide their own definitions for subsidies in their laws relating to countervailing duty.
13. Article 1.1(a)(1).
14. Article 1.1(a)(2).
15. See Appellate Body Report, *US – Carbon Steel*, para. 4.8.
16. See Appellate Body Report, *Brazil – Aircraft*, para. 157. See also Panel Report, *US – Export Restraints*, para. 8.20.

17 (Footnote original) Appellate Body Report, *Brazil – Aircraft*, para. 157.
18 See Appellate Body Report in *US – Softwood Lumber IV*, para. 51.
19 See Appellate Body Report, *US – Large Civil Aircraft (2nd Complaint)*, para. 613.
20 See Panel Report, *US – Large Civil Aircraft (2nd Complaint)*, para. 7.955.
21 See Panel Report, *US – Export Restraints*, paras. 8.64 and 8.73.
22 See Appellate Body Report, *US – Large Civil Aircraft (2nd Complaint)*, para. 614.
23 See Appellate Body Report, *US – Softwood Lumber IV*, para. 52.
24 (Footnote original) We note, however, that not all government measures capable of conferring benefits would necessarily fall within Article 1.1(a). If that were the case, there would be no need for Article 1.1(a), because all government measures conferring benefits, *per se*, would be subsidies. In this regard, we find informative the discussion of the negotiating history of the SCM Agreement contained in the panel report in *US – Export Restraints*, which was not appealed. That panel, at paragraph 8.65 of the panel report, said the "negotiating history demonstrates . . . that the requirement of a financial contribution from the outset was intended by its proponents precisely to ensure that not all government measures that conferred benefits could be deemed to be subsidies." This point was extensively discussed during the negotiations, with many participants consistently maintaining that only government actions constituting financial contributions should be subject to the multilateral rules on subsidies and countervailing measures.
25 See Appellate Body Report, *Canada – Renewable Energy*, paras. 5.120–5.121.
26 *Ibid.*, para. 5.120. quoting Appellate Body Reports in *China – Auto Parts*, para. 171, and *US – Large Civil Aircraft (2nd complaint)*, para. 586.
27 See Appellate Body Report, *US – Large Civil Aircraft (2nd complaint)*, para. 614.
28 *Ibid.*, para. 617.
29 See Appellate Body Report, *Japan – DRAMS (Korea)*, para. 251. See also Appellate Body Report, *US – Large Civil Aircraft (2nd complaint)*, para. 614.
30 See Panel Report, *EC and Certain Member States – Large Civil Aircraft*, para. 7.1291.
31 Footnote 1 of the SCM Agreement reads as follows: "In accordance with the provisions of Article XVI of GATT 1994 (Note to Article XVI) and the provisions of Annexes I through III of this Agreement, the exemption of an exported product from duties or taxes borne by the like product when destined for domestic consumption, or the remission of such duties or taxes in amounts not in excess of those which have accrued, shall not be deemed to be a subsidy."
32 See Appellate Body Report, *US – FSC*, para. 93.
33 *Ibid.*, para. 91.
34 See Appellate Body Report, *US – FSC*, para. 91. Earlier, the Panel had applied the 'but for' test to establish if revenue had been forgone that was 'otherwise due'. See Panel Report, *US – FSC*, para. 7.45.
35 See Appellate Body Report, *US – FSC (Article 21.5 – EC)*, paras. 91 and 98.
36 The debt in question consisted of (i) launch aid for the A300/A310 and A330/A340 programmes, (ii) a loan underwriting the costs of producing the A320, and (iii) additional German government loans extended to Deutsche Airbus in the 1980s and early 1990s, which had their origin in the 1989 restructuring of Airbus.
37 See Panel Report, *EC and Certain Member States – Large Civil Aircraft*, paras. 7.1316–7.1318.
38 *Ibid.*, 7.378–7.379. This finding of the Panel was not appealed against.
39 See Panel Report, *US – Large Civil Aircraft (2nd complaint)*, para. 7.120.
40 See Appellate Body Report, *US – FSC*, para. 93.
41 See Appellate Body Report, *US – FSC (Article 21.5 – EC)*, para. 140.
42 See Appellate Body Report, *US – FSC*, para. 98.
43 See Appellate Body Report, *US – Large Civil Aircraft (2nd complaint)*, paras. 823 and 824.
44 See Panel Report, *EC and Certain Member States – Large Civil Aircraft*, para. 7.1318.
45 See Appellate Body Report *US – Large Civil Aircraft (2nd complaint)*, para. 618.
46 While US softwood is grown on private land, the Canadian softwood is primarily grown on federally/provincially owned property known as 'Crown lands'. Lumber producers in Canada pay a stumpage fee to harvest softwood lumber from 'Crown lands'. See Panel Report, *US – Softwood Lumber III*, para. 7.14.
47 Softwood lumber is the building block of the US housing industry. Figures from 2003 – at the peak of the softwood lumber dispute – the two-way US-Canada trade amounted to $441.5 billion, of which about $7.5 billion was made up of Canadian softwood lumber exports. Overall, the US remains the largest wood product export destination for British Columbia.

48 See Appellate Body Report, *US – Softwood Lumber IV*, para. 52.
49 *Ibid.*, para. 53.
50 See Panel Report, *US – Softwood Lumber III*, paras. 7.23 and 7.28. This view of the Panel was later confirmed by the Appellate Body in *US – Softwood Lumber IV*, para. 53.
51 See Appellate Body Report, *US – Softwood Lumber IV*, paras. 58–67. Here, the Appellate Body observed that the goods are not required to be tradeable.
52 *Ibid.*, paras. 58–59.
53 See Appellate Body Report, *Canada – Renewable Energy*, para. 5.124.
54 See Appellate Body Report, *US – Large Civil Aircraft (2nd complaint)*, paras. 635–636, 662, and 690.
55 See Appellate Body Report, *Canada – Aircraft*, para. 157.
56 See Panel Report, *EC – Countervailing Measures on DRAM Chips*, para. 7.212.
57 See Appellate Body Report, *Canada – Aircraft*, para. 154.
58 See Appellate Body Report, *US – Softwood Lumber IV*, paras. 143.
59 *Ibid.*, paras. 155 and 158.
60 *Ibid.*, para.155. See also Appellate Body Reports, *EC and Certain Member States – Large Civil Aircraft*, paras. 972–975; *Canada – Renewable Energy*, para. 5.163.
61 See Appellate Body Report *Canada – Aircraft*, paras. 158. See also Appellate Body Report, *Canada – Renewable Energy*, para. 5.163.
62 See Appellate Body Report, *US – Carbon Steel (India)*, paras. 4.122, 4.124, and 4.126.
63 See Appellate Body Report, *EC – Large Civil Aircraft*, paras. 835–838.
64 *Ibid.*, para. 835.
65 (Footnote original) Article 14(b) of the SCM Agreement says that the comparison should be to a comparable commercial loan that the recipient "could actually obtain on the market." This suggests that where the recipient could not have obtained a commercial loan, then the granting of a loan by the government would be deemed to confer a benefit irrespective of the terms of that loan. As the European Union underscored at the oral hearing, the United States did not argue before the Panel that Airbus would have been unable to obtain a commercial loan. Instead, the United States premised its case on Airbus having to pay less for the LA/MSF than it would have paid for a commercial loan.
66 See Appellate Body Report, *EC – Large Civil Aircraft*, para. 834.
67 See Appellate Body Report, *US – Carbon Steel (India)*, para. 4.243.
68 *Ibid.*, para. 4.245.
69 See Appellate Body Report, *Canada – Aircraft*, para. 157.
70 See Appellate Body Report, *US – Countervailing Measures on Certain EC Products*, para. 152.
71 *Ibid.*
72 See Appellate Body Report, *EC and Certain Member States – Large Civil Aircraft*, para. 709.
73 See Article 2.1(a) of the SCM Agreement.
74 See Article 2.1(b) of the SCM Agreement.
75 See Article 2.1(c) of the SCM Agreement.
76 See Appellate Body Report, *US – Anti-Dumping and Countervailing Duties (China)*, para. 366.
77 *Ibid.*
78 *Ibid.*
79 See Panel Report, *US – Upland Cotton*, para. 7.1142.
80 See Appellate Body Report, *US – Anti-Dumping and Countervailing Duties (China)*, para. 373.
81 See Appellate Body Report, *US – Countervailing Measures (China)*, para. 4.169.
82 See Panel Report, *US – Anti-Dumping and Countervailing Duties (China)*, para. 9.22.
83 See Appellate Body Report, *US – Countervailing Measures (China) (Article 21.5 – China)*, para. 5.228.
84 See Appellate Body Report, *US – Large Civil Aircraft (2nd complaint)*, para. 749.
85 *Ibid.*, para. 750.
86 See Appellate Body Report, *US – Countervailing Measures (China)*, para. 4.121.
87 (Footnote original) In this regard, in particular, information on the frequency with which applications for a subsidy are refused or approved and the reasons for such decisions shall be considered.
88 See Appellate Body Report, *US – Carbon Steel (India)*, para. 4.373.
89 *Ibid.*, 4.374.
90 *Ibid.*, 4.390.
91 See Article 2.2 SCM Agreement.
92 See Panel Report, *EC and Certain Member States – Large Civil Aircraft*, para. 7.1223. See also Panel Report, *US – Anti-Dumping and Countervailing Duties (China)*, para. 9.135, where a similar conclusion was reached.

93 See Appellate Body Report, *US – Washing Machines*, para. 5.240.
94 Articles I and VI of the GATT 1994.
95 Articles 1, 2, 10, 12, 13, 14, 19, and 32 of the SCM Agreement.
96 Articles 1, 2, 6, 9, and 18 of the Anti-Dumping Agreement.
97 Article 15 of the Protocol on the Accession of the People's Republic of China (the Protocol of Accession).
98 See Appellate Body Report, *US – Anti-Dumping and Countervailing Duties (China)*, paras. 310 and 317.
99 (Footnote original) In this context, we note that the panel in *US – Countervailing Duty Investigation on DRAMS* commented, with respect to certain entities, that the USDOC had treated as "private bodies", that, "[d]epending on the circumstances", the evidence "might well have justified treatment of such creditors as public bodies." (Panel Report, *US – Countervailing Duty Investigation on DRAMS*, footnote 29 to para. 7.8) While we do not agree with that panel's implication that the particular evidence to which it referred – evidence of government ownership – could be decisive, we do consider that the statement illustrates that the analysis of whether the conduct of a particular entity is conduct of the government or a public body or conduct of a private body is indeed multi-faceted and that an entity may display characteristics pointing into different directions.
100 See Appellate Body Report, *US – Anti-Dumping and Countervailing Duties (China)*, paras. 317–318.
101 *Ibid.*, para. 288.
102 See Appellate Body Report, *Canada – Dairy*, para. 97, where it was observed that the quintessence of government is that it enjoys the effective power to regulate, control, or supervise individuals and/or restrain their conduct through the exercise of lawful authority.
103 See Appellate Body Report, *US – Anti-Dumping and Countervailing Duties (China)*, paras. 292 and 293.
104 *Ibid.*, para. 294.
105 *Ibid.*, para. 304.
106 See Appellate Body Report, *US – Countervailing Measures (China)*, para. 4.42. See also Appellate Body Report, *US – Anti-Dumping and Countervailing Duties (China)*, para. 286.
107 EU and EC are used interchangeably to denote the European Communities.
108 See Panel Report, *Korea – Commercial Measures (China)*, para. 7.50.
109 See Appellate Body Report, *US – Carbon Steel (India)*, para. 4.9 (referring to Appellate Body Report, *US – Anti-Dumping and Countervailing Duties (China)*, para. 297).
110 See Appellate Body Report, *US – Carbon Steel (India)*, para. 4.17 (referring to Appellate Body Report, *US – Anti-Dumping and Countervailing Duties (China)*, para. 318).
111 See Appellate Body Report, *US – Anti-Dumping and Countervailing Duties (China)*, para. 345.
112 *Ibid.*, para. 319.
113 Or some form of income or price support, as contained in Article XVI GATT.
114 From 1 January 2000, under the category of 'non-actionable subsidies', only non-specific subsidies are listed, to which the SCM Agreement does not apply.
115 (Footnote original) This standard is met when the facts demonstrate that the granting of a subsidy, without having been made legally contingent upon export performance, is in fact tied to actual or anticipated exportation or export earnings. The mere fact that a subsidy is granted to enterprises which export shall not for that reason alone be considered to be an export subsidy within the meaning of this provision.
116 (Footnote original) Measures referred to in Annex I as not constituting export subsidies shall not be prohibited under this or any other provision of this Agreement.
117 See Appellate Body Report, *US – Upland Cotton*, para. 552. The US had argued that if US cotton users could claim the subsidy regardless of the origin of the cotton, the benefit to producers would 'evaporate' and the subsidy to cotton producers would become a simple input subsidy for textile mills.
118 *Ibid.*, paras. 530–533.
119 *Ibid.*, para. 549.
120 See Appellate Body Report, *US – Tax Incentives*, para. 5.6 (referring to Appellate Body Report, *Canada – Aircraft (Article 21.5 – Brazil)*, para. 47).
121 *Ibid.*
122 See Panel Report, *Brazil – Aircraft (Article 21.5 – Canada II)*, para. 5.19.
123 See Panel Report, *Canada – Aircraft Credits and Guarantees*, para. 7.16.
124 See Appellate Body Report, *Canada – Aircraft*, para. 166. See also Panel Report, *Australia – Automotive Leather II*, para. 9.55.
125 See Appellate Body Report, *US – FSC (Article 21.5 – EC)*, para. 111.
126 See Appellate Body Report, *Canada – Autos*, para. 100.

127 *Ibid.*, paras. 139–143.
128 See Appellate Body Report, *US – Upland Cotton*, para. 572.
129 See Appellate Body Report, *Canada – Aircraft*, paras. 167 and 169.
130 See Appellate Body Report, *EC and Certain Member States – Large Civil Aircraft*.
131 See Appellate Body Report, *EC and Certain Member States – Large Civil Aircraft*, paras. 1046–1047.
132 *Ibid.*
133 *Ibid.*, para. 1050.
134 *Ibid.*, para. 1063.
135 *Ibid.*, para. 1064.
136 *Ibid.*, para. 1045.
137 *Ibid.*, para. 1046.
138 *Ibid.*, para. 1047.
139 *Ibid.*, para. 1102.
140 See Appellate Body Report, *Canada – Aircraft*, para. 167.
141 See Panel Report, *Australia – Automotive Leather II*, paras. 9.56–9.57.
142 *Ibid.*, para. 9.70.
143 This finding of the Panel was confirmed by the Appellate Body. See Appellate Body Report, *Canada – Aircraft*, para. 169.
144 See Panel Report, *Canada – Aircraft*, para. 9.337–9.338.
145 See Appellate Body Report, *Canada – Aircraft*, para. 173.
146 See Appellate Body Report, *Canada – Renewable Energy*, para. 5.6.
147 *Ibid.*, para. 167.
148 See Appellate Body Report, *Canada – Autos*, para. 123.
149 *Ibid.*, para. 139.
150 *Ibid.*, para. 141.
151 *Ibid.*, para. 142.
152 See Panel Report, *US – Upland Cotton*, paras. 7.1088 and 7.1097–7.1098. This finding of the Panel was upheld by the Appellate Body on appeal. See Appellate Body Report, *US – Upland Cotton*, para. 552.
153 See Panel Report, *Korea – Upland Cotton*, paras. 7.1088 and 7.1097–7.1098.
154 Footnotes occurring in the text of the Article are omitted.
155 See Panel Report, *EC and Certain Member States – Large Civil Aircraft*, para. 7.2082.
156 *Ibid.*, para. 7.2058.
157 *Ibid.*, paras. 7.2068 and 7.2080.
158 This fact was alluded to by the Panel in *Indonesia – Autos*, paras. 14.170–14.193, where the parallels of the 'like product' concept contained in GATT Articles I:1, III:2, and III:4 and in the 'likeness' contained in Article 5(a) of the SCM Agreement were discussed.
159 See Panel Report, *Indonesia – Autos*, para. 14.173.
160 *Ibid.*, para. 14.174.
161 See Appellate Body Report, *EC – Fasteners (China)*, para. 411.
162 See Article 16.1 of the SCM Agreement.
163 See Article 16.2 of the SCM Agreement.
164 Matsushita *et al.* take the view that Article 15 of the SCM Agreement is more producer-centred, which leaves the interests of consumers to one side. See Matsushita, Shoenbaum, Mavroidis, and Hahn (2017).
165 See Panel Report, *US – Softwood Lumber VI*, para. 7.28, where the Panel referring to the Appellate Body Report in *US – Hot-Rolled Steel*, paras. 192–193, noted the definitions of the Appellate Body with respect to 'positive evidence' and 'objective examination' under the Anti-Dumping Agreement.
166 See Appellate Body Report, *China – GOES*, para. 128.
167 *Ibid.*, paras. 136–137.
168 See Appellate Body Report, *US – Carbon Steel (India)*, para. 4.580.
169 See Panel Report, *US – Countervailing Duty Investigation on DRAMS*, para. 7.223.
170 *Ibid.*, para. 7.307.
171 See Appellate Body Report, *China – GOES*, paras. 136–137.
172 *Ibid.*, para. 149.
173 See Appellate Body Report, *US – Softwood Lumber VI (Article 21.5 – Canada)*, para. 151.

Subsidies and Countervailing Measures   371

174 See Panel Report, *Mexico – Corn Syrup*, para. 7.133. Here, the dispute concerned an identical provision in the Anti-Dumping Agreement, and by analogy can be extended to an investigation under Article 15.7 of the SCM Agreement.
175 See Panel Report, *US – Softwood Lumber VI*, paras. 7.97–7.112. Here the Panel observed that a "threat of injury" determination is made against the backdrop of an evaluation of the condition of the domestic industry in light of the Article 15.4 factors.
176 See Panel Report, *US – Softwood Lumber VI*, para. 7.33. See also Appellate Body Report, *US – Softwood Lumber VI (Article 21.5 – Canada)*, paras. 107 and 109.
177 See Appellate Body Report, *China – GOES*, paras. 136–137.
178 See Appellate Body Report, *US – Carbon Steel (India)*, paras. 4.578–4.579.
179 See Article 15.4 of the SCM Agreement. Note, the list presented in Article 15.4 is not exhaustive.
180 See Panel Report, *US – Countervailing Duty Investigation on DRAMS*, para. 7.301.
181 See Panel Report, *EC – Countervailing Measures on DRAM Chips*, para. 7.356.
182 See Appellate Body Report, *Japan – DRAMS (Korea)*, para. 262.
183 *Ibid.*, para. 267.
184 See Panel Report, *US – Offset Act (Byrd Amendment)*, paras. 7.119–7.120.
185 See Appellate Body Report, *US – Upland Cotton (Article 21.5 – Brazil)*, para. 244.
186 Note, countervailing duties are designed to remedy the effects of subsidisation by a third country on the domestic market of the importing country.
187 See Panel Report, *Korea – Commercial Vessels*, para. 7.578.
188 See Appellate Body Report, *US – Upland Cotton (Article 21.5 – Brazil)*, para. 10.255. See also Panel Report, *Indonesia – Autos*, paras. 14.254–14.255.
189 See Appellate Body Report, *US – Upland Cotton*, para. 400–414.
190 *Ibid.*, para. 406.
191 See Panel Report, *US – Upland Cotton*, para. 7.1236.
192 See Appellate Body Report, *US – Upland Cotton*, para. 405. See also Panel Report, *Korea – Commercial Vessels*, paras. 7.562–7.566.
193 See Appellate Body Report, *US – Upland Cotton*, para. 408.
194 *Ibid.*, para. 409.
195 See Appellate Body Report, *EC and Certain Member States – Large Civil Aircraft*, para. 1119.
196 *Ibid.*
197 *Ibid.*, at para. 1120.
198 *Ibid.*, at para. 1121.
199 See Appellate Body Report, *US – Large Civil Aircraft (2nd complaint)*, para. 1076 (referring to Appellate Body Report, *EC and Certain Member States – Large Civil Aircraft*, para. 1117).
200 See Panel Report *Indonesia – Autos*, para. 14.223.
201 See Appellate Body Report, *EC and Certain Member States – Large Civil Aircraft*, para. 1160.
202 *Ibid.*
203 *Ibid.*, at para. 1161.
204 *Ibid.*, at para. 1162. See also Appellate Body Report, *US – Upland Cotton (Article 21.5 – Brazil)*, for price depression and price suppression under Article 6.3(c) of the SCM Agreement.
205 *Ibid.*, at para. 1123.
206 *Ibid.*, at paras. 1168, and 1119.
207 *Ibid.*, at para. 1117; and Appellate Body Report, *US – Large Civil Aircraft (2nd complaint)*, para. 1076.
208 See Appellate Body Report, *US – Upland Cotton*, paras. 435–238.
209 *Ibid.*
210 See Panel Report, *US – Upland Cotton*, para. 7.1227.
211 See Appellate Body Report, *US – Upland Cotton (Article 21.5 – Brazil)*, para. 372.
212 See Appellate Body Reports, *US – Upland Cotton*, para. 438; *US – Upland Cotton (Article 21.5 – Brazil)*, para. 374.
213 See Appellate Body Report, *EC and Certain Member States – Large Civil Aircraft*, para. 1232.
214 *Ibid.*
215 See Appellate Body Report, *US – Large Civil Aircraft (2nd Complaint)*, para. 913.
216 *Ibid.*, para. 915.
217 *Ibid.*, para. 914. See also Panel Report, *US – Large Civil Aircraft (2nd Complaint) (Article 21.5 – EU)*, para. 9.61.
218 See Appellate Body Report, *US – Upland Cotton*, para. 431.

219 See Appellate Body Report, *US – Upland Cotton (Article 21.5 – Brazil)*, para. 354.
220 *Ibid.*, para. 361.
221 The 'but for' test is used in the common law legal system while seeking to establish factual causation under both tort law and criminal law. The 'but for' test is viewed as one of the weaker ones.
222 See Appellate Body Report, *US – Upland Cotton (Article 21.5 – Brazil)*, paras. 351 and 371.
223 *Ibid.*, para. 356.
224 *Ibid.*, paras. 374 and 375.
225 See Appellate Body Report, *EC and Certain Member States – Large Civil Aircraft*, para. 1110. See also Appellate Body Report, *US – Upland Cotton (Article 21.5 – Brazil)*, para. 357.
226 See Panel Report, *Korea – Commercial Vessel*, para. 7.604.
227 *Ibid.*, para. 7.612.
228 *Ibid.*, para. 7.615.
229 See Panel Report, *US – Upland Cotton (Article 21.5 – Brazil)*, para. 10.49.
230 See Appellate Body Report, *US – Upland Cotton (Article 21.5 – Brazil)*, para. 371.
231 (Original footnote) Appellate Body Report, *US – Upland Cotton (Article 21.5 – Brazil)*, para. 371.
232 See Appellate Body Report, *EC and Certain Member States – Large Civil Aircraft*, paras. 1233–1234.
233 See Appellate Body Report, *US – Large Civil Aircraft (2nd Complaint)*, para. 1020.
234 Article 15.5 of the SCM Agreement relates to the imposition of CVDs requiring an examination of "any known factors other than the subsidized imports which at the same time are injuring the domestic industry".
235 See Appellate Body Report, *US – Upland Cotton*, para. 436.
236 *Ibid.*, para. 437.
237 *Ibid.*
238 See Appellate Body Report, *US – Large Civil Aircraft (2nd Complaint)*, para. 914. See also Appellate Body Reports, *US – Upland Cotton*, para. 437; *US – Upland Cotton (Article 21.5 – Brazil)*, para. 375; *EC and Certain member States – Large Civil Aircraft*, paras. 1232 and 1376.
239 See Appellate Body Report, *US – Upland Cotton (Article 21.5 – Brazil)*, para. 235.
240 (Footnote original) In the event that the request relates to a subsidy deemed to result in serious prejudice in terms of paragraph 1 of Article 6, the available evidence of serious prejudice may be limited to the available evidence as to whether the conditions of paragraph 1 of Article 6 have been met or not.
241 See Panel Report, *US – Upland Cotton*, para. 7.1173.
242 See Appellate Body Report, *US – Upland Cotton*, para. 273.
243 See Appellate Body Report, *US – Upland Cotton (Article 21.5 – Brazil)*, para. 235–236.
244 *Ibid.*
245 *Ibid.*
246 The text of Article 11 of the SCM Agreement is largely similar to the text of Article 5 of the WTO Anti-Dumping Agreement.
247 See Panel Report, *US – Caron Steel*, para. 8.35–8.37.
248 See section 2.2.1.3 for a discussion on 'injury' under Article 15 of the SCM Agreement.
249 The procedural requirements set out in the SCM Agreement are similar to the requirements found in the Anti-Dumping Agreement, which is taken up for discussion in chapter 10.
250 See Panel Report, *China – GOES*, para. 7.49.
251 *Ibid.*, para. 7.55.
252 *Ibid.*, para. 7.60.
253 *Ibid.*, para. 7.54.
254 *Ibid.*, para. 7.51.
255 See Appellate Body Report, *US – Offset Act (Byrd Amendment)*, para. 283.
256 See Panel Report, *US – Caron Steel*, para. 8.34.
257 The SCM Agreement does not define such special circumstances.
258 See Article 11.9 of the SCM Agreement.
259 *Ibid.*
260 See Appellate Body Report, *US – Caron Steel*, para. 83. See also Appellate Body Report, *Mexico – Anti-Dumping Measures on Rice*, para. 305.
261 See Article 22.1 of the SCM Agreement.
262 See Articles 13.1 and 13.2 of the SCM Agreement.

263 See Appellate Body Report, *EC – Pipe Fittings*, para. 138, citing Appellate Body Report, *EC – Bed Linen (Article 21.5 – India)*, para. 136.
264 See Article 12.1.3 of the SCM Agreement.
265 See Article 12.1.1 of the SCM Agreement.
266 See Appellate Body Report, *China – GOES*, para. 240, fn. 390.
267 See Appellate Body Report, *Mexico – Anti-Dumping Measures on Rice*, para. 283.
268 *Ibid.*, para. 280.
269 For instance, such disclosure would be of "significant competitive advantage to a competitor or because its disclosure would have a significantly adverse effect upon a person supplying the information or upon a person from whom the supplier acquired the information". See Article 12.4 SCM Agreement.
270 See Panel Report, *EC – Countervailing Measures on DRAM Chips*, para. 7.245.
271 *Ibid.*, para. 7.249.
272 See Appellate Body Report, *Mexico – Anti-Dumping Measures on Rice*, para. 291.
273 *Ibid.*, paras. 293–294.
274 See Appellate Body Report, *US – Caron Steel*, para. 4.416.
275 *Ibid.*, para. 4.417.
276 See Appellate Body Report, *US – Supercalendered Paper*, para. 5.81.
277 See Appellate Body Report, *US – Caron Steel*, para. 4.435.
278 See Appellate Body Report, *US – Anti-Dumping Methodologies (China)*, para. 5.172, fn. 502.
279 See Panel Report, *US – Pipes and Tubes (Turkey)*, para. 7.190. Note: the US has preferred an appeal, and Turkey has preferred a cross-appeal against the Panel Report.
280 See Appellate Body Report, *China – GOES*, para. 242.
281 *Ibid.*, para. 240.
282 See note to Annex 1A of the Marrakesh Agreement establishing the WTO.
283 Article 17 of the SCM Agreement permits the IA to impose CVD measures pending the conclusion of investigations.
284 The IA may accept an undertaking from either the exporters or the government of the Member State concerned as an alternative to the imposition of the CVDs.
285 Article 19 of the SCM Agreement facilitates the imposition of CVDs in an original investigation, as opposed to reviews pursuant to Article 21 of the SCM Agreement.
286 See Appellate Body Report, *US – Offset Act (Byrd Amendment)*, para. 256.
287 See Panel Report, *EC – Commercial Vessel*, para. 7.92.
288 *Ibid.*, paras. 7.108–7.113.
289 See Article 18 of the SCM Agreement, covering undertakings.
290 See Article 17.1 of the SCM Agreement.
291 See Article 17.4 of the SCM Agreement.
292 See Appellate Body Report, *US – Washing Machines*, para. 5.268.
293 *Ibid.*, para. 5.305.
294 See Appellate Body Report, *Japan – Drams (Korea)*, paras. 205–215.
295 *Ibid.*, para. 210.
296 See Appellate Body Report, *US – Anti-Dumping and Countervailing Duties (China)*, para. 554.
297 See Panel Report, *China – Broiler*, para. 7.258.
298 See Panel Report, *US – Supercalendered Paper*, para. 7.237.
299 See Appellate Body Report, *US – Carbon Steel*, para. 70.
300 *Ibid.*, para. 108.
301 See Appellate Body Report, *US – Carbon Steel (India)*, para. 4.530.
302 See Appellate Body Report, *US – Lead and Bismuth II*, para. 61.
303 *Ibid.*, paras. 62–63.
304 *Ibid.*, paras. 146 and 149.
305 *Ibid.*, para. 146.
306 See Article 21.2 of the SCM Agreement.
307 See Appellate Body Report, *US – Carbon Steel*, para. 63.
308 *Ibid.*, para. 116.
309 *Ibid.*, para. 108.
310 See Article 22.4 of the SCM Agreement.

311 See Article 24.3 of the SCM Agreement.
312 See Appellate Body Report, *Brazil – Aircraft*, para. 149.
313 See Article 27.1 of the SCM Agreement.
314 The US is a major producer of cotton and accounts for 13 percent of world production and 32 percent of world exports. Successive governments have introduced generous subsidy packages for cotton farmers.
315 See Appellate Body Report, *US – Upland Cotton*.
316 *Ibid.*, para. 532.
317 See Panel Report, *US – FSC*, para. 7.150.
318 See Appellate Body Report, *US – FSC*, para. 141.
319 See Appellate Body Report, *US – Upland Cotton*, para. 547.
320 Article 13 of the AoA, for a number of years, was considered more important than Article 21.1, as it provided an exception to the stricter SCM Agreement disciplines. Article 13, referred to as the 'peace clause', provided that until 31 December 2003, certain types of agricultural subsidies were exempt from challenges under the SCM Agreement and the GATT 1994.
321 See Panel Report, *US – FSC*, para. 7.1038.
322 See Appellate Body Report, *US – Upland Cotton*, para. 532.
323 *Ibid.*, para. 533.
324 See Appellate Body Report, *US – FSC*, para. 145.
325 *Ibid.*, para. 146.
326 The use of the word 'including' in Article 1(e) suggests that 'export subsidies' are to be interpreted broadly and indicates that the list of subsidies contained in Article 9 is not exhaustive. See Appellate Body Report, *US – Upland Cotton*, para. 615.
327 See Panel Report, *US – Upland Cotton*, paras. 7.1473–7.1475.
328 *Ibid.*, para. 7.997.
329 *Ibid.*, para. 7.1005.
330 *Ibid.*, para. 7.1016.
331 See Panel Report *Indonesia – Autos*, paras. 14.58–14.92.

Bibliography

Bartels, Lorand. 'The Relationship between the WTO Agreement on Agriculture and the Agreement on Subsidies and Countervailing Measures: An Analysis of Hierarchy Rules in the WTO Legal System,' *Journal of World Trade* Vol 50, No 1 (2016) 7–20.

Chow, Daniel C.K. and Thomas J. Schoenbaum. *International Trade Law: Problems, Cases, and Materials* (Wolters Kluwer Law & Business, 2017).

Clarke, Peggy A. and Gary N. Horlick. 'The Agreement on Subsidies and Countervailing Measures,' in Macrory, Patrick F.J., Arthur E. Appleton and Michael G. Plummer (eds.) *The WTO: Legal, Economic and Political Analysis* Vol 2 (Springer, 2005) 679–734.

Coppens, Dominic. *WTO Disciplines on Subsidies and Countervailing Measures: Balancing Policy Space and Legal Constraints* (Cambridge, 2014).

Croome, John. *Reshaping the World Trading System: A History of the Uruguay Round* (Kluwer Law International, 1999).

GATT. 'Multilateral Negotiations, Statement by GATT Director-General on Tokyo Round,' *International Legal Material* Vol 18 (1979) 553, 569.

GATT. 'Report of Eminent Persons on Problems Facing the International Trade System,' *International Legal Material* Vol 24 (1985) 716, 735. (Leutwiler Report).

GATT. 'Ministerial Declaration on the Uruguay Round of Multilateral Trade Negotiations, Doc. No. MIN.DEC. (20 September 1986),' *International Legal Material* Vol 25 (1986) 1623.

GATT. 'Draft Final Act Embodying the Results of the Uruguay Round of Multilateral Trade Negotiations,' Doc. No. MTN.TNC/W/FA (20 December 1991) (Dunkel Text).

Hoekman, Bernard M. and Michel K. Kostecki. *The Political Economy of the World Trading System: The WTO and Beyond* (Oxford University Press, 2009).

Horlick, Gary N. and Peggy A. Clarke. 'The 1994 WTO Subsidies Agreement,' *World Competition* Vol 17, No 4 (1993) 41–54.

Irwin, Douglas A., Petros C. Mavroidis and Alan O. Sykes. *The Genesis of the GATT* (Cambridge University Press, 2008).

Jackson, John H. *World Trade and the Law of GATT: A Legal Analysis of the General Agreement on Tariffs and Trade* (The Michie Company, 1969).

Krugman, Paul R., Maurice Obstfeld and Marc J. Melitz. *International Economics: Theory and Practice* (Pearson Education, 2018).

Lee, G.M. 'Subsidies and Countervailing Duties,' in Bagwell, Kyle and Robert W. Staiger (eds.) *Handbook of Commercial Policy 1, Part B* (Elsevier Publication, 2016) 163–210.

Lester, Simon. 'The Problem of Subsidies as a Means of Protectionism: Lessons from the WTO *EC-AIRCRAFT* Case,' *Melbourne Journal of International Law* Vol 12, No 2 (2011a) 345–372.

Lester, Simon. 'The Problem of Subsidies as a Means of Protectionism: Lessons from the WTO *ES-Aircraft* Case,' *Melbourne Journal of International Law* Vol 12 (2011b) 1–28.

Lester, Simon, Bryan Mercurio and Arwel Davies. *World Trade Law: Text, Materials and Commentary* (Hart Publishing, 2018).

Lowenfeld, Andreas F. *International Economic Law* (Oxford University Press, 2008).

Matsushita, Mitsuo, Thomas J. Shoenbaum, Petros C. Mavroidis and Michael Hahn. *The World Trade Organization: Law, Practice, and Policy* (Oxford University Press, 2017).

Mavroidis, Petros C., Patrick A. Messerlin and Jasper M. Wauters. *The Law and Economics of Contingent Protection in the WTO* (Edward Elgar Publishing, 2008).

McMahon, Joseph A. 'The Agreement on Agriculture,' in Macrory, Patrick F.J., Arthur E. Appleton and Michael G. Plummer (eds.) *The WTO: Legal, Economic and Political Analysis* Vol 2 (Springer, 2005) 187–229.

Müller, Wolfgang. *WTO Agreement on Subsidies and Countervailing Measures: A Commentary* (Cambridge University Press, 2017).

Nairobi Ministerial Conference. *Ministerial Decision on Export Competition* (WT/MIN(15)/45) (21 December 2015).

Rubini, Luca. 'The International Context of EC State Aid Law and Policy: The Regulation of Subsidies in the WTO,' in Biondi, Andrea, Piet Eeckhout and James Flynn (eds.) *The Law of State Aid in the European Union* (Oxford University Press, 2004) 149–188.

Steenblik, R. 'Subsidy Measurement and Classification: Developing a Common Framework,' in *Environmentally Harmful Subsidies: Policy Issues and Challenges* (OECD, 2003) 101–142.

Sutherland, Peter, Jagdish Bhagwati, Kwesi Botchwey, Niall W.A. Fitzgerald, Koichi Hamada, John H. Jackson, Celso Lafer and Thierry de Montbrial. 'The Future of the WTO: Addressing Institutional Challenges in the New Millennium,' Report of the Consultative Board to the Director-General Supachai Panitchpakdi (WTO, 2004).

Sykes, Alan O. 'The Economics of WTO Rules on Subsidies and Countervailing Measures,' *John M. Olin Programme in Law & Economics, Working Paper No 186* (2003) 1–36.

Sykes, Alan O. 'Subsidies and Countervailing Measures,' in Macrory, Patrick F.J., Arthur E. Appleton and Michael G. Plummer (eds.) *The WTO: Legal, Economic and Political Analysis* Vol 2 (Springer, 2005) 83–107.

Trebilcock, Michael, Robert Howse and Antonia Eliason. *The Regulation of International Trade* (Routledge, 2013).

United States Joint Economic Committee. 'Congress,' in *The Economics of Federal Subsidy Programme, Ninety-Second Congress, First Session, Washington DC* (US Government Printing Office, 1972) 12–39.

Van den Bossche, Peter and Werner Zdouc. *The Law and Policy of the World Trade Organization* (Cambridge University Press, 2017).

Wolfrum, Rüdiger. 'Article 24 SCMA,' in Wolfrum, Rüdiger, Peter-Tobias Stoll and Michael Koebele (eds.) *WTO: Trade Remedies* (Martinus Nijhoff Publishers, 2008).

World Trade Organization. *World Trade Report, 2006: Exploring the Links between Subsidies, Trade and the WTO* (World Trade Organization, 2006).

Wouters, Jan and Dominic Coppens. 'An Overview of the Agreement on Subsidies and Countervailing Measures: Including a Discussion of the Agreement on Agriculture,' in Bagwell, Kyle W., George A. Bermann and Petros C. Mavroidis (eds.) *Law and Economics of Contingent Protection in International Trade* (Cambridge University Press, 2010) 7–83.

10 Dumping and Anti-Dumping Measures

Learning Objectives		378
1.	Introduction	378
2.	WTO Law on Dumping	379
	2.1 History and Political Economy of Dumping	379
	2.2 Dumping: Types and Practice	382
3.	The Anti-Dumping Legal Framework of the WTO	382
	3.1 Article VI of GATT	383
	3.2 The Anti-Dumping Agreement	384
	3.3 Investigation of Dumping	385
	3.3.1 Adequacy of Evidence	386
	3.3.2 Evidence and Due Process	387
	3.4 Determination of Dumping: Normal Value, Export Price	388
	3.4.1 Normal Value, Export Price, and 'Like Product'	389
	3.4.2 Zeroing	393
	3.4.3 Non-Market Economies	397
	3.5 Determination of Injury to Domestic Industry	397
	3.5.1 Domestic Industry	398
	3.5.2 Injury	399
	3.5.3 Material Injury	400
	3.5.4 Threat of Material Injury	403
	3.6 Causation	405
4.	Imposition of Dumping	406
	4.1 Provisional AD Measures	406
	4.2 Price Undertakings	407
	4.3 Imposition and Collection of AD Duties	407
	4.4 Duration and Review of AD Duties	409
	4.5 Anti-Circumvention of AD Duties	410
5.	Institutional and Procedural Requirements of AD Agreement	411
	5.1 Dispute Settlement and Review of AD Measures	411
	5.2 The Committee on Anti-Dumping Practices	413
6.	Special and Differential Treatment for Developing Country Members	413
7.	Summary	414

DOI: 10.4324/9780367028183-12

Learning Objectives

This chapter aims to help students understand:

1. The WTO law on dumping; history and political economy of dumping;
2. Dumping – types and practice; anti-dumping legal framework of the WTO;
3. Article VI of the GATT; Anti-Dumping Agreement;
4. Dumping investigation; determination of dumping; determination of injury to domestic industry; threat of material injury;
5. Imposition of dumping; provisional AD measures; price undertakings; imposition and collection of AD duties;
6. Institutional and procedural requirements of AD Agreement; and
7. Special and differential treatment for developing country Member States.

1. Introduction

Considered as one of the most controversial of subjects, anti-dumping laws have come to occupy an important position in the multilateral trading system. Much literature on the subject has been penned by both economists and lawyers since the days of the GATT. Dumping, which is deemed an 'unfair' trade practice alongside subsidisation, occurs when exporters sell their product on the export market for a price that they charge for the same product on their own home market.[1] While injurious dumping is condemned under the WTO laws, it is not *per se* prohibited. Anti-dumping laws were primarily devised to counter the ill effects, of material injury brought about by 'dumped' goods, upon the competing domestic producer. As in the case of subsidisation and CVDs, the WTO law does contain detailed sets of rules under GATT and the Anti-Dumping Agreement, which permit Member States to take such anti-dumping (AD) measures to offset the harm caused to the domestic industry, if it is proven upon investigation that such dumping has caused injury to the domestic industry. One of the reasons for an increase in the imposition of AD measures over the past 60-odd years is the reduction in tariffs brought about by the GATT, and subsequently by the WTO.

Proponents of free trade often oppose anti-dumping laws, but the issues surrounding AD are contentious and diverse. The opinion on dumping and AD is divided, with some taking the view that AD measures are essential, while others taking the position that such practice imposes a very heavy cost on both the implementing Member State and the affected Member State (Prusa, 2005). Some argue that the resulting sales from dumping are 'unfair', which is facilitated by a 'protected' home market, and that it is only justified that AD measures are imposed on such unfair practices to level the playing field. It is also argued that AD laws conflict "with antitrust laws in a more serious and direct manner" and they facilitate "the formation, maintenance, and enforcement of cartels" (Pierce, 2000).[2] Yet another view on AD is that the differentiation in price between the exporting and importing markets of the Member States is advantageous to global welfare, offering benefits to consumers, and that such practices are not to be penalised. Reasons why politicians support AD laws are that they permit the politicians to appear to support free trade while at the same time preserving their discretion to engage in *ad hoc* protectionism at the bidding of constituencies with political clout (Pierce, 2000).[3] AD measures contend that they guarantee that international trade is competitive and fair. But this rhetoric is far removed from economic reality, as producers in some developed countries, like the US, impose AD measures to thwart foreign competition (Mankiw and Swagel, 2005).[4] With the proliferation of AD and the increase in the incidence of AD actions, it comes as no surprise that the debate surrounding AD has intensified.

2. WTO Law on Dumping

The concepts of dumping and AD have been around for close to a couple of centuries (Viner, 1923a;[5] Mavroidis, Messerlin, and Wauters, 2008),[6] and it was not until the early part of the twentieth century that AD legislation was passed. While the 'import substitution' model of economic development was used as a rhetoric by developing countries to push forward their agenda of protectionism, foreign dumping was developed as a rhetoric by the developed countries to promote their agenda of AD measures. Although the prior arguments try to present AD measures as being a "special measure for a special problem", the history of AD measures only demonstrates that AD was anything but a protection for the home producers from import competition (Finger and Artis, 1993).

Often, the cost of anti-dumping duties to consumers outweighs any gain to the domestic industry receiving protection. Economists, including Professor Bhagwhati, a staunch defender of liberal trade, have defended AD measures as they provide a political safety valve that alleviates pressure for more protectionist action (Bhagwhati, 1988; Finger, 1992). Some commentators, on the other hand, don't see an economic rationale for AD measures, as the very definition of dumping is not based on sound economic foundation, and allows for anti-dumping measures to be used for protectionist ends (Kerr, 2001; Janow and Staiger, 2003).[7] Strategic reasons why AD measures have come to be viewed as the remedy of choice, as opposed to CVDs, are that the (i) injury standards imposed under the AD Agreement, *i.e.*, material injury, are on the face of it easier to satisfy than the 'serious injury' test applied in safeguard cases; (ii) unlike safeguard measures, dumping is considered as unfair trade practice, and hence no compensation or retaliation is required when AD measures are imposed; and (iii) it is easy for an investigating authority (IA) to determine dumping margins (Macrory, 2005).

2.1 History and Political Economy of Dumping

The first country to enact anti-dumping legislation was Canada in 1904, followed by New Zealand in 1905, Australia in 1914, South Africa in 1914, and the US in 1916[8] (Viner, 1923a; Finger, 1992).[9] The Canadian AD legislation empowered the customs authorities to impose dumping duties equal to the margin of goods of a 'class or kind' not produced in Canada being specifically exempted (Dale, 1980). The US AD laws were more an extension of pre-existing antitrust laws, and the first AD legislation was an amendment to its antitrust legislation, *i.e.*, the Clayton Act, which deemed dumping with the intent of 'destroying or injuring' a US industry to be a criminal offence.[10] Also, the procedure was 'automatic' without the need to prove injury to a domestic industry before dumping duties were imposed. The Canadian AD legislation, modified in 1907 and 1921, became the model upon which subsequent national AD legislations were based (Dale, 1980). In 1921, four countries, including Great Britain,[11] the US,[12] Australia, and New Zealand, enacted new and comprehensive AD laws (Viner, 1923a).

Countries that introduced AD legislation felt strongly about dumping, with their views rooted in political economy. Justifying the introduction of AD legislation, then US Assistant Attorney General Samuel Graham stated as follows:

> [G]enerally accepted principles of political economy hold that it is not sound policy for any Government to permit the sale in its country by foreign citizens of material at

> a price below the cost of production at the place produced, for the reason that such a system, in its final analysis and on a sufficient scale, spells bankruptcy.
>
> (Graham, 1916)

At the time of drafting the Havana Charter, there was no attempt to introduce any provision to regulate dumping (being non-state action), as the concern was more towards preventing overzealous enforcement of AD measures.[13] The US proposed a draft AD article, which was based on its own domestic legislation, to be included within the GATT 1947 to provide a basic framework to deal with dumping. Despite its introduction in the GATT 1947, AD as a trade instrument was not pursued seriously, as the bulk of protection was through tariffs, quantitative restrictions, or subsidies (Mavroidis, Messerlin, and Wauters, 2008). The current WTO law on dumping and AD measures is contained in Article VI of the GATT 1994 and in the Anti-Dumping Agreement.[14] Article VI, paragraph 1, condemns export sales of products below the normal value if it

> causes or threatens material injury to an established industry in the territory of a contracting party or materially retards the establishment of a domestic industry.

Also, the US and Canada, using the 'grandfather clause' contained in the Protocol of Provisional Application governing accession of countries to the membership of the GATT, retained their own domestic AD laws to deal with dumping issues. With the language of Article VI being unclear, it was interpreted and applied variously by the Contracting Parties of the GATT (Trebilcock, 2013). In short, the application of Article VI was haphazard, and there was a growing feeling that it was creating new barriers to trade as opposed to providing solutions for predatory dumping. The situation prompted a rethink of AD measures, which led to the drafting of the first AD code in the Kennedy Round of negotiations in 1967. The Agreement on Implementation of Article VI of the GATT (IAA) contained minimal procedural standards for AD cases and a requirement to demonstrate causal link that the dumping in question was the principal cause of the injury.[15] The IAA was optional and provided for the establishment of a Committee on Anti-Dumping Practices.

The IAA formalised during the Tokyo Round of negotiations – referred to as the Anti-Dumping Code – replaced the IAA from 1967. The Anti-Dumping Code, while introducing additional rules on dumping, removed the stringent requirement to demonstrate the causal link in injury determination in AD investigations and replaced it with the requirement that "injuries caused by other factors must not be attributed to the dumped imports".[16] The Anti-Dumping Code also introduced a time-bar for the completion of investigation, as well as a dispute settlement procedure under the auspices of the Committee on Anti-Dumping Practices. The AD practices of Contracting Parties became more prevalent and controversial in the 1980s, especially with developed nations (particularly, the US and the EU) targeting developing nations (*i.e.*, newly industrialised nations) with AD duties. Prior to the 1980s, there were only five major users of AD measures, *viz.*, Australia, Canada, EU, New Zealand, and the US, which were considered 'traditional users' (Lindsey and Ikenson, 2001; Vandenbussche and Zanardi, 2008).[17] During the GATT era, developing nations maintained high tariffs coupled with quotas and restrictive import-licence schemes as a protectionist measure (Lindsey and Ikenson, 2001). There was increased criticism of the Anti-Dumping Code 1979 and AD practices, from mostly developing nations. Several of the actions taken were challenged during the Uruguay Round of negotiations, which was used as a strategy by targeted countries to use dispute settlement as a channel to lend support to some of the stances taken during the negotiations (Hoekman and Kostecki, 2009). The proposal to amend the Anti-Dumping Code was on the agenda of the Uruguay Round of negotiations for a complete overhaul.

The Uruguay Round of negotiations touched upon a number of contentious items on the agenda, including the Anti-Dumping Code. Surprisingly, the Anti-Dumping Code was only a later addition to the agenda in the Uruguay Round of negotiations. The US, and the EU, expressed concerns over the avoidance of AD laws by some producers and advocated a clearer framework to facilitate the use of AD measures, but countries like Japan, Korea, and some of the Scandinavian nations backed the imposition of a stricter AD regime to avoid abuse by protectionists. The WTO Anti-Dumping Agreement (AD Agreement), which emerged as a result of the compromises reached amongst the parties, contains the current substantive rules and legal procedures on AD measures and provides clarification to Article VI of the GATT. The Anti-Dumping Agreement still has its shortcomings, as a number of its provisions remain ambiguous. Some ambiguities of AD practices have been clarified through case law from the jurisprudence of the Dispute Settlement Body, yet some others wait their turn.

Although originally propounded by developed nations, AD is now being used widely in the WTO era by developing country Member States, such as India, Brazil, Peru, Mexico, China, Egypt, Turkey, Indonesia, Taiwan, and Thailand.[18] Interestingly, in the first five years of the WTO, the number of AD measures imposed by new users, *i.e.*, developing country Member States, more than doubled, while the number of measures imposed by traditional users, *i.e.*, developed country Member States, declined by 4.5 percent. This is a significant shift from practices of the GATT era, where the proponents of AD were the developed nations led by the US. The shift in the trend is in part due to developing country Member States lowering their tariffs, having introduced sweeping trade liberalisation,[19] which went on to create pressure from domestic industries for other forms of protection from imports (Lindsey and Ikenson, 2001).

As a tool, AD has come to be effectively used in international trade policy negotiations, practice, and dispute settlement by the developed and developing country Member States of the WTO. Some commentators argue that the WTO's AD regime has become a seductive hard-to-resit protectionist device (Prusa and Skeath, 2002), and that the excessive use of AD only serves to weaken competition (Macrory, 2005).

Outside of the multilateral trading system, AD has featured continuously in the negotiations of free trade/Regional Trade Agreements (RTAs).[20] It is also true that the WTO AD regime has been used as the benchmark to build restrictive AD provisions in the free trade negotiations. In the modern era, where multilateral trade is performed both at the WTO and through various RTAs, AD actions and policies come to define international political-economic interaction amongst the trading nations.[21] Although the Member States agree that the AD Agreement requires changes, they are divided on what changes to agree upon, which has not helped with the creation of a proper agenda to review the current laws on AD. As noted by the chair of the Negotiating Group on Rules in its Report from 2014:

> Further, I am entirely conscious that the Group is far from achieving convergence even on any of the very significantly recalibrated proposals now before it. Indeed, the broader environment has not allowed us to really begin negotiations in earnest on these proposals.
>
> (Report by Chairman, 2015)[22]

2.2 Dumping: Types and Practice

As stated earlier, dumping refers to the practice in which exporters sell their goods in the export market for a lower price than what they charge for the same product on their own home market. The price discrimination definition of 'dumping' from Viner is not only between two or more foreign markets, but also between home and foreign markets (Viner, 1923a).[23] In essence, it is sale below cost, amounting to price discrimination between markets. Sale below cost may arise as a direct result of fierce competition, due to a decline in demand, and through the practice of forward pricing. Sale below cost is where a firm sells their product at less than their cost of production or purchase in order to drive out competitors or to increase market share.[24]

It is also possible to sell a product for a lower price in the export market than in the domestic market, if the wages in the country where it is manufactured are very low.[25] Sale below cost arises due to (i) intense market competition; (ii) decline in demand for the product due to economic factors, such as recession; (iii) forward pricing, which is the predetermined delivery price for goods below cost to increase sales volumes; and (iv) predatory pricing, which is the practice of selling a product below cost to drive out competition with a view to gaining monopoly. Also, competitive pricing may not necessarily cover full costs, and could lead to sale below cost in some instances.

Viner classifies dumping by duration as (i) sporadic, (ii) short-run, or intermittent, and (iii) long-run or continuous dumping (Viner, 1923a). As opposed to sporadic dumping, intermittent or continuous dumping gives rise to concerns in the importing market. If continuous dumping is intended to be predatory, it may produce adverse welfare effects, as it could drive competitors out of business. As regards the WTO's legal framework, dumping is defined in Article VI:1 of the GATT 1994 as the introduction of a product into the commerce of another country at less than its 'normal value'. Article 2.1 of the Anti-dumping Agreement echoes Article VI:1 of the GATT.[26]

3. The Anti-Dumping Legal Framework of the WTO

The primary purpose of an AD investigation is to determine if 'dumping' is occurring and thereby causing injury to the domestic industry of the importing Member State. The AD anti-dumping regime of the WTO is contained in Article VI of GATT 1994 and the Anti-dumping Agreement. In this regard the Appellate Body in *US – 1916 Act* ruled that both Article VI of the GATT 1994 and the AD Agreement must be read together,[27] and further observed as follows:

> Since "an anti- dumping measure" must, according to Article 1 of the Anti-Dumping Agreement, be consistent with Article VI of the GATT 1994 and the provisions of the Anti-Dumping Agreement, it seems to follow that Article VI would apply to "an anti-dumping measure", *i.e.*, a measure against dumping.[28]

As referred to earlier, the WTO laws neither prohibit nor regulate dumping, as prices of products are not determined by the Member States but by private firms/manufacturers. Article VI of the GATT and the AD Agreement contain detailed substantive and procedural framework permitting Member States to take such anti-dumping measures to offset the harm caused by 'dumping' to the domestic industry, provided it is established through investigation by the Member State concerned that such dumping has caused injury to the domestic industry. In essence, if in the event a Member State makes the decision to conduct an AD investigation and apply AD measures, they are to do so following the procedures laid down in Article VI of the GATT and the ADA. Although not required, a number of developed and developing country Member States have enacted domestic legislation to carry out AD investigations and to impose such AD measures pursuant to investigations.

3.1 Article VI of GATT

Article VI of the GATT is the enabling provision with regards to the investigation and imposition of AD measures. The relevant part of the Article VI:1 of the GATT identifies dumping as follows:

> The [Members] recognize that dumping, by which products of one country are introduced into the commerce of another country at less than the normal value of the products, is to be condemned if it causes or threatens material injury to an established industry in the territory of a [Member] or materially retards the establishment of a domestic industry.

Article VI:2 of the GATT, on the other hand, authorises the Member States to take such measures to offset the effects of dumping, and the relevant part of the Article reads as follows:

> In order to offset or prevent dumping, a contracting party may levy on any dumped product an anti-dumping duty not greater in amount than the margin of dumping in respect of such product.

A Member State, before proceeding to impose an AD measure, is required to (i) establish that there is dumping, *i.e.*, the export price of a product in question is lower than the price of that product in the domestic market of the exporting country; (ii) demonstrate that, as a result of dumping, the domestic industry in the importing Member State that produces the 'like' product is suffering injury, or threat thereof, or such dumping materially retards the establishment of a domestic industry; and finally (iii) prove the existence of a 'causal link' between the dumped product and the injury suffered by the domestic industry.

Pursuant to Article VI, and Article VI:2 (read along with the AD Agreement), a Member State's response to dumping is limited to imposition of provisional measures; price undertakings; and the imposition of definitive AD duties. The Appellate Body in *US – 1916 Act*, while addressing the question of whether Member States may choose to impose other types of anti-dumping measures than anti-dumping duties, interpreted Article VI:2 in conjunction with Article 18.1 of the Anti-Dumping Agreement, and ruled as follows:

> Article VI of the GATT 1994 and the Anti-Dumping Agreement apply to "specific action against dumping". Article VI of the GATT 1994, and, in particular, Article VI:2, read in conjunction with the Anti-Dumping Agreement, limit the permissible responses to dumping to definitive anti-dumping duties, provisional measures and price undertakings. Therefore, the 1916 Act is inconsistent with Article VI:2 and the Anti-Dumping Agreement to the extent that it provides for "specific action against dumping" in the form of civil and criminal proceedings and penalties.[29]

The Appellate Body in *US – Offset Act (Byrd Amendment)*, while referring to its findings in *US – 1916 Act*, ruled:

> As CDSOA[30] offset payments are not definitive anti-dumping duties, provisional measures or price undertakings, we conclude, in the light of our finding in *US – 1916 Act*, that the CDSOA is not "in accordance with the provisions of the GATT 1994, as interpreted by" the Anti-Dumping Agreement.[31]

Pursuant to Article VI:6(a), national AD authorities may impose an AD measure if it is established through investigation that dumping causes or threatens material injury to an established domestic industry or materially retards the establishment of a domestic industry.

3.2 The Anti-Dumping Agreement

The AD Agreement[32] encapsulates both substantive provisions and procedures for conducting an AD investigation and for imposing AD measures for a Member State to follow. As Professor Bhala notes, Article VI of the GATT forms the 'seed' for the AD Agreement of 1995 (Bhala, 2013).[33] Article 1 of the AD Agreement, twice in two sentences, expressly incorporates by reference its parent provision, *i.e.*, Article VI of the GATT (Bhala, 2013). The AD Agreement contains elaborate rules for calculating the dumping margins and the factors that are to be taken into account to determine such injury caused. The procedural rules are similar to Part V of the Agreement on Subsidies and Countervailing Measures and provide practical guidelines with an emphasis on the due process to be followed in the investigations and implementation of AD measures. The AD Agreement also establishes a Committee on Anti-dumping Practices functions as a forum for consultation amongst the Member States. On the objectives of the AD Agreement, the Appellate Body in *US – Washing Machines* observed as follows:

> Although the Anti-Dumping Agreement does not contain a preamble expressly setting out its object and purpose, it is apparent from the text of this Agreement that it deals with injurious dumping by allowing Members to take anti-dumping measures to counteract injurious dumping and imposing disciplines on the use of such anti-dumping measures.[34]

The AD Agreement does not qualify dumping as an unfair trade practice *per se*, but rather seeks to regulate and discipline AD investigations and the imposition of AD measures. The AD Agreement requires that all AD actions that a Member State seeks to initiate are consistent with the rules set out in the Agreement therein and shall be preceded by an investigation conducted following the provisions of the AD Agreement. In this regard Article 1 reads as follows:

> An anti-dumping measure shall be applied only under the circumstances provided for in Article VI of GATT 1994 and pursuant to investigations initiated [footnote omitted] and conducted in accordance with the provisions of this Agreement.

The Appellate Body in *US – 1916 Act*, while upholding the panel ruling that the US Anti-Dumping Act 1916 was inconsistent with Article 1 of the AD Agreement, Article VI:1 of the GATT, besides various other provisions of the ADA,[35] ruled that Article 1 of the AD

Agreement, as well as Article 18.1, limits AD measures to those expressly authorised by GATT Article VI and the imposition of definitive AD duties, provisional measures, and price undertakings.[36] The Panel in *US – 1916 Act (EC)*, while referring to the Appellate Body Report in *Argentina – Footwear (EC)*, described the relationship of Article VI of the GATT 1994 to the AD Agreement as an "inseparable package of rights and disciplines" and observed as follows:

> In our opinion, Article VI and the Anti-Dumping Agreement are part of the same treaty or, as the panel and the Appellate Body put it in *Argentina – Footwear (EC)* with respect to Article XIX and the Agreement on Safeguards, an "inseparable package of rights and disciplines". In application of the customary rules of interpretation of international law, we are bound to interpret Article VI of the GATT 1994 as part of the WTO Agreement and the Anti-Dumping Agreement is part of the context of Article VI. This implies that Article VI should not be interpreted in a way that would deprive it or the Anti-Dumping Agreement of meaning. Rather, we should give meaning and legal effect to all the relevant provisions. However, the requirement does not prevent us from making findings in relation to Article VI only, or in relation to specific provisions of the Anti-Dumping Agreement, as required by our terms of reference.[37]

The Panel in *US – 1916 Act (EC)* considered that the first sentence of Article 1 of the Anti-Dumping Agreement confirms the purpose of Article VI as "to define the conditions under which counteracting dumping as such is allowed".[38] In *US – 1916 Act (EC)*, the Panel, while examining the scope of Article VI of the GATT 1994, noted that Article 1 of the AD Agreement

> supports the view that Article VI is about what Members are entitled to do when they counteract dumping within the meaning of Article VI . . . by referring to "anti-dumping measure[s]" which may be applied by Members.[39]

3.3 Investigation of Dumping

It is not a legal requirement under WTO laws to establish a domestic legal and institutional basis for carrying out AD investigations and for the imposition of AD measures. Nevertheless, all developed and developing country Member States have their own domestic laws with well-developed institutional frameworks to carry out AD investigations and for decision-making on imposition of AD measures. Normally, all AD investigations are conducted by officials of one of the following ministerial departments, *viz.*, the Ministry of Trade and Industry, the Ministry of Commerce, or the Ministry of Finance, or by the officials of the Customs Department.

The first port of call for a Member State contemplating the imposition of AD measures on an import is to carry out an AD investigation. A combined reading of Article VI of the GATT 1994 and Article 1 of the AD Agreement reveals that a Member State can only impose any AD measure pursuant to an AD investigation, carried out in accordance with the provisions of the AD Agreement; that the results of the investigations reveal that the imports have been dumped; that such dumping has caused material injury to the domestic industry or that the establishment of a domestic industry is materially retarded; and that there is a clear causal link between the injury sustained by the domestic industry and the dumped imports.

Pursuant to Article 5 of the AD Agreement, national AD authorities may initiate AD investigations. They could either be prompted to initiate investigation upon a petition from a domestic industry[40] or on their own accord in certain special circumstances.[41] Article 5.2 requires that petitions lodged seeking an AD investigation shall include evidence of dumping, material injury, and causation that is available to the petitioner. The domestic industry which is affected by the 'alleged dumping' acts as a party seeking to enforce the law by lodging the application under Article 5 of the AD Agreement. The Panel in *US – Lumber V* ruled that an application lodged pursuant to Article 5 need only include such 'reasonably available information' on relevant matters as the applicant deems necessary to substantiate its allegations of dumping, injury, and causality, and not all information available to the applicant.[42]

To avoid the misuse of the AD investigation, Article 5.4 of the AD Agreement requires that an AD investigation

> shall not be initiated pursuant to paragraph 1 unless the authorities have determined, on the basis of an examination of the degree of support for, or opposition to, the application expressed [footnote omitted] by domestic producers of the like product, that the application has been made by or on behalf of the domestic industry [footnote omitted].

Article 5.4 further provides that a petition will be considered to have been made on behalf of the domestic industry if the petition were to be supported by 50 percent of the total production of the like product produced by that portion of the domestic industry. Under the provisions of Article 5.4, no investigation shall be initiated if the application is supported by less than 25 percent of domestic production.

3.3.1 Adequacy of Evidence

Pursuant to Article 5.3 of the AD Agreement, the authorities are to examine the accuracy and adequacy of the evidence presented to substantiate the application and determine if they justify the initiation of an investigation.

In *Guatemala – Cement II*, Mexico had claimed that Guatemala, in violation of Article 5.2, had initiated the AD investigation without sufficient evidence of dumping having been included in the application. The Panel examining the submissions interpreted Article 5.2 with reference to Article 2, which outlines the elements that describe the existence of dumping. The Panel observed that "evidence on the . . . elements necessary for the imposition of an anti-dumping measure may be inferred into Article 5.3 by way of Article 5.2".[43] The Panel in *Guatemala – Cement II* also noted that "statements of conclusion unsubstantiated by facts do not constitute evidence of the type required by Article 5.2".[44]

The Panel in *Thailand – H-Beams*, while agreeing with the Panel in *Mexico – Corn Syrup*,[45] ruled that Article 5.2 does not impose "any additional requirement that the application contain analysis of the data submitted in support of the application", and that raw material data would constitute "relevant evidence" rather than a "simple assertion" within the meaning of the provision.[46]

Article 5.7 of the AD Agreement requires that evidence of both dumping and injury should be considered simultaneously to determine if an investigation is to be initiated, and thereafter during the course of the investigation.

3.3.2 Evidence and Due Process

Article 6.1 of the AD Agreement requires that all interested parties to an AD investigation are put on notice, affording them ample opportunity to present their representation and evidence in writing, which they consider relevant. The interested parties include exporters, importers, and domestic producers. As per Article 6.1.1, exporters and foreign producers must be given at least 30 days to reply to questionnaires. This provision seeks to render the procedure fair and transparent following the due process requirement and WTO standards. Pursuant to Articles 5.3 and 5.10, the domestic AD authorities are to conduct and conclude their investigation within one year and it may not exceed 18 months. A domestic AD authority, under Article 5.3, is required to satisfy itself that there is sufficient evidence before proceeding to initiate an investigation, and such decisions are to be based on an examination of the adequacy and accuracy of the evidence in the application.

With regards to the requirement of Articles 6.2 and 6.3 of the AD Agreement, the Appellate Body in *US – Oil Country Tubular Goods Sunset Reviews* held that the provisions set out the fundamental due process rights to which interested parties are entitled to in AD investigations and reviews.[47] The Panel in *US – Oil Country Tubular Goods Sunset Review (Article 21.5 – Argentina)* held that although Articles 6.1 and 6.2 "set out the fundamental due process rights", that did not mean that claims raised under those provisions could prevail without showing "the specific instances of violation" of those rights.[48] Although transparent, Article 6.5 requires that the evidence presented is to be kept confidential upon request by the provider of the information.

Article 6.8 permits the authorities to proceed with the investigation on the basis of the available information, where information sought from individuals is not forthcoming. To elaborate, Article 6.8 of the AD Agreement permits the use of 'facts available' for determining dumping by the authorities if an interested party (i) declines access to necessary information; (ii) does not provide necessary information; or (3) expressively impedes the investigation.[49] It should be noted that the 'facts available' approach is a last resort for the authorities. In *US – Hot-Rolled Steel*, the Panel indicated:

> One of the principle elements governing anti-dumping investigations that emerges from the whole of the AD Agreement is the goal of ensuring objective decision-making based on facts. Article 6.8 and Annex II advance that goal by ensuring that even where the investigating authority is unable to obtain the "first best" information as the basis of its decision, it will nonetheless base its decision on facts, albeit perhaps "second-best" facts.[50]

In *Egypt – Steel Rebar*, the Panel noted that Article 6.8 of the AD Agreement addresses the dilemma in which IA may find themselves where the necessary information is not forthcoming, and observed, "that they must base their calculations of normal value and export price on some data", and indicated "Article 6.8 identifies the circumstances in which an [investigating authority] may overcome this lack of necessary information by relying on facts which are otherwise available to the investigating authority".[51] As Article 6.1.1 provides a 30-day period for receiving a reply, the domestic AD authorities are not to make any determinations on 'facts available' solely on the basis the information was provided by the exporter after the deadline for response.

In *US – Hot-Rolled Steel*, the US AD authority concluded that the Japanese exporter was not cooperative in submitting evidence and therefore resorted to a 'facts available' methodology.

On appeal, the Appellate Body reversed the finding and ruled that the US AD authority was wrong. The Appellate Body in *US – Hot-Rolled Steel* concluded that, according to paragraph 3 of Annex II of the AD Agreement, investigating authorities are directed to use information if three, and, in some circumstances, four, conditions are satisfied. The conditions identified are that the information is (i) verifiable, (ii) that it was appropriately submitted so that it can be used in the investigation without undue difficulties, (iii) that it was supplied in a timely fashion, and, where applicable, (iv) supplied in a medium or computer language requested by the authorities. The Appellate Body concluded that, in its view, "if these conditions are met, investigating authorities are not entitled to reject information submitted, when making a determination".[52]

3.4 Determination of Dumping: Normal Value, Export Price

As per Article VI of the GATT 1994, and the AD Agreement, only dumping that causes injury is to be condemned and can be the subject of an AD measure. Following from Article 2.1 of the AD Agreement, to determine if a product is dumped, the domestic AD authority must establish whether there is a difference between the 'export price' and the 'normal value' (domestic price) of the product in question. The Appellate Body in *US – Stainless Steel (Mexico)* observed that Article 2.1 of the AD Agreement defines 'dumping', that the opening phrase of that Article makes it clear that the definition applies "[f]or the purpose of this Agreement", and therefore, "dumping" and "margin of dumping" have the same meaning throughout the AD Agreement.[53]

The margin of dumping is the difference between the export price and the 'normal value' of a product. Dumping is investigated from the importer's perspective to establish if there is dumping and a justification to impose AD measures. Hence, dumping and margins of dumping are concepts that are export-specific and not importer-specific, which is established through various provisions of the AD Agreement.[54] As dumping arises from the pricing behaviour of foreign producers/exporters, the Appellate Body has repeatedly found that the AD Agreement prescribes that dumping determinations are made in respect of each exporter and to a "product under consideration", as dumping is "the result of the pricing behaviour of individual exporters or foreign producers".[55]

The Appellate Body had reiterated that 'dumping' and 'dumping margins' must be determined for the products 'as a whole' and in respect of each known exporter or foreign producer examined.[56] The Appellate Body in *US – Stainless Steel* clarified that a "proper determination as to whether an exporter is dumping or not can only be made on the basis of an examination of the exporter's pricing behaviour as reflected in all its transactions over a period of time".[57] The Appellate Body in *US – 1916 Act* ruled that injury to the domestic industry is not a constituent element of 'dumping', and observed as follows:

> under Article VI:1 of the GATT 1994 and Article 2 of the Anti-Dumping Agreement, neither the intent of the persons engaging in "dumping" nor the injurious effects that "dumping" may have on a Member's domestic industry are constituent elements of "dumping".[58]

Pursuant to Article 2.4.2, first sentence, of the AD Agreement, calculation of the dumping margin shall normally be determined on a comparison of the weighted average 'normal value' with a weighted average of prices of all comparable export transactions (the W-W methodology) or by a comparison of normal value and export prices on a transaction-to-transaction basis (the T-T methodology). Following from Article 2.4.2, the domestic AD authorities are required to use the W-W methodology to establish margins of dumping on the basis of the comparison of "all comparable export transactions". The Appellate Body in *EC – Bed Linen*, while specifically addressing the term 'comparable' used in Article 2.4.2, held that

> the word "comparable" in Article 2.4.2 does not affect, or diminish in any way, he obligation of investigating authorities to establish the existence of margins of dumping on the basis of "a comparison of the weighted average normal value with the weighted average of prices of all comparable export transactions".
>
> The ordinary meaning of the word "comparable" is "able to be compared". "Comparable export transactions" within the meaning of Article 2.4.2 are, therefore, export transactions that are able to be compared . . .
>
> . . . All types or models falling within the scope of a "like" product must necessarily be "comparable", and export transactions involving those types or models must therefore be considered "comparable export transactions" within the meaning of Article 2.4.2.[59]

Under the second sentence of Article 2.4.2, the dumping margins are to be calculated using the weighted average-to-transactions (W-T) comparison methodology rather than the weighted average-to-weighted average (W-W), or the transaction-to-transaction (T-T) methodologies. However, the application of the W-T method by the domestic AD authorities is conditional on two factors, *viz.*, (i) the authorities finding "a pattern of export prices which differ significantly among different purchasers, regions or time periods" (targeted dumping) and (ii) if authorities can explain why, in light of these differences, they cannot use W-W or T-T.[60]

3.4.1 Normal Value, Export Price, and 'Like Product'

Normal value is defined in Article 2.1 of the AD Agreement as "the comparable price, in the ordinary course of trade, for the like product when destined for consumption in the exporting country". This connotes that the 'normal value' is the price of the like product in the home market of the exporter. According to the Appellate Body in *US – Hot-Rolled Steel*, Article 2.1 imposes four conditions on sales transactions which could be used to calculate 'normal value', *viz.*, (i) the sale must be 'in the ordinary course of trade'; (ii) the sale must be of the 'like product'; (iii) the product must be 'destined for consumption in the exporting country'; and (iv) the price must be 'comparable'.[61]

Meeting the first of the four conditions, *i.e.*, sales in the domestic market of the exporting Member State are made 'in the ordinary course of trade', can be complex. A number of situations could be identified which would identify that transactions were not made 'in the ordinary course of trade', *i.e.*, sales to affiliated parties; abnormally high-priced or low-priced sales; or sales below cost. The Appellate Body in *US – Hot-Rolled Steel*, while observing that the AD Agreement does not define 'in the ordinary course of trade', ruled that a sale which is not made 'in the ordinary course of trade' must be excluded by the investigating authorities in the calculation of 'normal value'.[62] The Appellate Body in *US – Hot-Rolled Steel* went on to observe as follows:

> Article 2.1 requires investigating authorities to exclude sales not made "in the ordinary course of trade", from the calculation of normal value, precisely to ensure that normal value is, indeed, the "normal" price of the like product, in the home market of the exporter.[63]

The Appellate Body in *US – Hot-Rolled Steel* found that the AD Agreement affords the WTO Member States discretion to determine how to ensure that normal value is not distorted through the inclusion of sales that are not 'in the ordinary course of trade', that such discretion is not limited, and that it is to be exercised in an even-handed manner.[64] The Appellate Body in *EU – Biodiesel*, when interpreting Article 2.2.1.1, noted that the second condition in the first sentence of Article 2.2.1.1 refers "to whether the records kept by the exporter or producer suitably and sufficiently correspond to or reproduce those costs incurred by the investigated exporter or producer that have a genuine relationship with the production and sale of the specific product under consideration".[65] The Appellate Body also upheld the Panel's finding that the EU contravened the first sentence of Article 2.2.1.1, as it failed to calculate the cost of production of biodiesel on the basis of the records kept by the Argentine producers.[66]

The second condition under Article 2.1 is that the sale transactions must relate to a 'like product'. The AD Agreement in Article 2.6 defines 'like product' to mean "a product which is identical, *i.e.*, alike in all respects to the product under consideration, or in the absence of such a product, another product which, although not alike in all respects, has characteristics closely resembling the product under consideration". The 'like product' definition found in the AD Agreement permits variations, giving domestic AD authorities the discretion for such interpretation. The test of 'identical or closely resembling' found in Article 2.6 is different from the 'like product' test created by the GATT jurisprudence in Articles I and III cases. This leaves the issue of 'like product' in the AD Agreement largely unsettled. The 'like product' issue gains in significance as there are differences in the features of the products which may arise due to their commercial purpose, *viz.*, they may be customised to suit a particular market; or may be customised as a result of an earlier AD measure; or may be sold as a fully assembled product or as a kit in another. Legal certainty in the definition of 'like product' is much desirable to avoid multiplicity of interpretation by domestic AD authorities.

The subject of 'like product' is key to the definition of the domestic industry for standing and injury purposes (see Articles 3 and 4 of the AD Agreement), for identifying the home market or third country sales for use in determining the normal value. As per Article 2.6, for a product to be classified as a 'like product', it does not have to be identical but only similar. This position means that if a product were to be deemed 'like' by a domestic AD authority, such decision would most likely not be overturned by the DSB. The issue of 'like product' arises for consideration where a foreign manufacturer uses components purchased at below cost prices from an unrelated supplier and incorporates them in a product for resale in domestic and export markets. This practise is referred to as 'downstream dumping'. 'Downstream dumping' has not been fully considered by either the GATT or the WTO with regards to dumping margin.

Also, the 'like product' issue may arise when determining the domestic industry, which is interpreted in Article 4 of the AD Agreement as referring to "the domestic producers as a whole of the like products or to those of them whose collective output of the products constitutes a major proportion of the total domestic production of those products". One will have to determine 'domestic industry' on a case-by-case basis. Determination of what constitutes 'domestic industry' will have an impact on dumping margins. Where domestic AD authorities proceed to define the domestic industry broadly, it could lead to a decrease in the dumping margin or even the likelihood of finding dumping.

Pursuant to Article 2.2 of the AD Agreement, it is possible to determine the margin of dumping by comparing the export price with the price of the like product when exported to an 'appropriate third country', provided such third-country price is representative. The aforementioned practice of using 'third country' prices to determine dumping margin is only permissible in the following circumstances, *viz.*, (i) when there are no sales of the like product in the ordinary course of trade in the home country or (ii) where there is a low volume of such sales.

The third condition found in Article 2.1 is that the product must be "destined for consumption in the exporting country", and the fourth condition is that the price must be "comparable". The first sentence of Article 2.4 of the AD Agreement requires that a "fair comparison shall be made between export price and normal value". In making a 'fair comparison' under Article 2.4, the Appellate Body in *US – Hot-Rolled Steel* observed as follows:

> Article 2.4 mandates that due account be taken of "differences which affect price comparability", such as differences in the "levels of trade" at which normal value and the export price are calculated.[67]

The Appellate Body in *EC – Fasteners (Article 21.5 – China)* reiterated that Article 2.4 obligates domestic AD authorities to make a fair comparison between the price of the exported product under investigation and the normal value, and to make due allowance for differences which affect price comparability, and that this comparison "shall be made at the same level of trade, normally at the ex-factory level".[68] The Appellate Body referring to *EC – Fasteners (China)* noted that the last sentence of Article 2.4 provides that the "authorities shall indicate to the parties in question what information is necessary to ensure a fair comparison and shall not impose an unreasonable burden of proof on those parties".[69] The Appellate Body also stressed that the requirements of Article 2.4 of the AD Agreement apply in all investigations, regardless of the methodology used to establish normal value.[70]

In instances where the domestic price in the exporting does not produce an appropriate 'normal value' for the purposes of comparison with the export price, it may render a fair comparison impossible due to the market situation, *i.e.*, where there is no sales of like product or there is a low volume of sales. To deal with such situations, Article 2.2 of the AD Agreement stipulates that an importing Member State, in order to determine an appropriate normal value for comparison with the export price, (i) use a third country price as the normal value or (ii) construct the normal value based on "the cost of production in the country of origin plus a reasonable amount for administrative, selling and general costs and for profits".[71]

The Appellate Body in *EU – Biodiesel*, in agreeing with the Panel's view that Article 2.2 of the AD Agreement and Article VI:1(b)(ii) of the GATT 1994 do not limit the sources of information that a domestic AD authority may use to establish the cost of production in the country of origin, observed as follows:

> We observe that Article 2.2 of the Anti-Dumping Agreement and Article VI:1(b)(ii) of the GATT 1994 do not contain additional words or qualifying language specifying the type of evidence that must be used, or limiting the sources of information or evidence to only those sources inside the country of origin. An investigating authority will naturally look for information on the cost of production "in the country of origin" from sources inside the country. At the same time, these provisions do not preclude the possibility that the authority may also need to look for such information from sources outside the country. The reference to "in the country of origin", however, indicates that, whatever information or evidence is used to determine the "cost of production", it must be apt to or capable of yielding a cost of production in the country of origin. This, in turn,

suggests that information or evidence from outside the country of origin may need to be adapted in order to ensure that it is suitable to determine a "cost of production" "in the country of origin".[72]

In *US – Hot-Rolled Steel*, the US authorities, while calculating the 'normal value', proceeded to discard certain sales by exporters to their affiliates on the grounds that these sales were not 'in the ordinary course of trade'. The authorities then replaced the discarded sales with downstream sales of the product that were transacted between the affiliates and the first independent buyer, which had been made 'in the ordinary course of trade'. This methodology was objected to by Japan, as it was implicit under Article 2.1 that a sales transaction may only be used to calculate 'normal value' if the exporter is the seller. The Appellate Body, while reversing the Panel's findings, concluded that if all four conditions in Article 2.1 are satisfied the identity of the seller of the like product "is not a ground for precluding the use of a downstream sales transaction when calculating normal value", and noted that the identity of the seller may still affect 'normal value' as it may affect comparability, and observed as follows:

> We do not mean to suggest that the identity of the seller is irrelevant in calculating normal value under Article 2.1 of the Anti-Dumping Agreement. However, to ensure that prices are "comparable", the Anti-Dumping Agreement provides a mechanism, in Article 2.4, which allows investigating authorities to take full account of the fact, as appropriate, that a relevant sale was not made by the exporter or producer itself, but was made by another party . . .
>
> . . . the use of downstream sales prices may necessitate the provision of appropriate "allowances", under Article 2.4, which take into account any differences demonstrated to affect price comparability.[73]

In the Appellate Body's view, to determine of dumping, one must in the first instance, engage in a comparison of home market and export prices, and further, only in the circumstances set out in Article 2.2 may an investigating authority consider alternative factors to home market prices, such as costs, when determining normal value.[74] Also, GATT Article VI provides that "allowance shall be made in each case for differences in conditions and terms of sale, for differences in taxation, and for other differences affecting price comparability".

Although essential for determining 'normal value' in the investigation, the AD Agreement does not provide a definition of 'the ordinary course of trade'. The Appellate Body in *US – Hot-Rolled Steel* confirmed that the AD Agreement does not define 'in the ordinary course of trade'.[75] The Appellate Body noted that Article 2.2.1 does provide for a method to determine whether 'sales below cost' are 'in the ordinary course of trade', but yet did not purport to exhaust the range of methods for determining whether sales are 'in the ordinary course of trade'.[76] The Appellate Body also ruled that domestic AD authorities must take into account not only the prices but also the other relevant terms and conditions, *viz.*, volume of the sales transaction and any additional liability or responsibilities, like transport or insurance, that may affect the prices, while determining whether a sales price is higher or lower than the ordinary course price.[77]

Further, in calculating and determining dumping, domestic AD authorities are to terminate the investigation if the difference in the price is less than 2 percent of the export price, *i.e.*, *de minimis*; or the volume of dumped imports, actual or potential, or the injury is negligible.[78] Article 2.4 of the AD Agreement requires that a 'fair comparison' of the export price and the normal value is carried out, with the comparison to be made at the same level of trade, normally at the ex-factory level. The relevant part of Article 2.4 of the AD Agreement provides:

> A fair comparison shall be made between the export price and the normal value. This comparison shall be made at the same level of trade, normally at the ex-factory level, and in respect of sales made at as nearly as possible the same time. Due allowance shall be made in each case, on its merits, for differences which affect price comparability, including differences in conditions and terms of sale, taxation, levels of trade, quantities, physical characteristics, and any other differences which are also demonstrated to affect price comparability.

Article 2.4 of the AD Agreement also contains special rules regarding adjustments, and the relevant part of the Article reads as follows:

> allowance for costs, including duties and taxes, incurred between importation and resale, and profits accruing, should also be made.

3.4.2 Zeroing

Zeroing became one of the most disputed subjects in the history of the WTO. Zeroing was discussed in the Uruguay Round of negotiations, as some Member States calculated dumping margins on the basis of comparing weighted-average normal value to individual export prices. Zeroing, a practice developed by the US in determining the dumping margin in AD cases, had been a contentious issue and widely criticised by commentators. The other user of zeroing, the EU, discontinued the practice following from the Appellate Body's Report in the *EC – Bed Linen* case.[79] Zeroing refers to the practice of replacing the actual amount of dumping calculated for model or sales comparisons that yield negative dumping margins with a value of zero prior to the final calculation of a weighted-average margin of dumping for the product under investigation (Vermulst and Ikenson, 2007). Zeroing, effectively, fails to evaluate all relevant factors having a bearing on the state of the domestic industry and overstates dumping margins by denying the full impact of non-dumped models/export sales on the dumping margin for the product as a whole. As the methodology drops transactions that have negative margins, it has the effect of increasing the overall dumping margins and makes it extremely difficult for a firm to avoid dumping (Bown and Prusa, 2010).[80] Although the AD Agreement did not resolve the issue of zeroing, complaints brought against the chief practitioners of zeroing, *i.e.*, the EU and the US, had resulted in the Appellate Body ruling some forms of the practice as being inconsistent with Article 2.4.2 of the AD Agreement.

In over eight AD disputes where zeroing was a key issue, the US has been criticised for inflating the dumping margins and excluding negative amounts from the calculation, thereby increasing the AD measures. In particular, the EU and the US practices of zeroing have come under both scrutiny and criticism. The Appellate Body in *US – Corrosion-Resistant Steel Sunset Review*, noted that zeroing, besides artificially inflating the dumping margin for the product as a whole, may also turn a negative margin of dumping into a positive margin, introducing an 'inherent bias'.[81] A number of disputes have gone before the Appellate Body, where calculation of margins of dumping under Article 2.4.2 have been called into question. In particular, the practice of 'zeroing' has come under scrutiny in AD disputes.

In the *EC – Bed Linen* case, the EU's action of imposing AD duties on cotton-type bed linen imported from India was under challenge, and the Appellate Body struck down the

EC's practice of 'zeroing' negative dumping margins calculated on a model-by-model basis. The EU had calculated the dumping margin on a comparison of weighted average of export prices and the normal value of each model of the product in question. But while calculating the dumping margin, EU did not take into account the 'negative dumping margin' with regards to certain models, resulting in an inflated dumping margin. India argued that the EU's practice was inconsistent with Article 2.4.2 of the AD Agreement. Both the Panel and the Appellate Body found that the EU practice of zeroing was inconsistent with Article 2.4.2 of the AD Agreement.

The Appellate Body examined the first method under Article 2.4.2 for establishing the existence of margins of dumping, *i.e.*, the comparison of a weighted average normal value with a weighted average of prices of all comparable export transactions. The Appellate Body found the European Communities' (EU) practice of 'zeroing' was inconsistent with the aforementioned method, because the EU by zeroing the negative dumping margins had not taken fully into account the entirety of the prices of some export transactions.[82] While deciding that the term 'comparable' in Article 2.4.2 did not detract from the obligation of investigating authorities to consider all relevant transactions, the Appellate Body in *EC – Bed Linen* referred to Article 2.4 as part of the context of Article 2.4.2:

> Article 2.4 sets forth a general obligation to make a "fair comparison" between export price and normal value. This is a general obligation that, in our view, informs all of Article 2, but applies, in particular, to Article 2.4.2 which is specifically made "subject to the provisions governing fair comparison in [Article 2.4]". Moreover, Article 2.4 sets forth specific obligations to make comparisons at the same level of trade and at, as nearly as possible, the same time. Article 2.4 also requires that "due allowance" be made for differences affecting "price comparability". We note, in particular, that Article 2.4 requires investigating authorities to make due allowance for "differences in . . . physical characteristics".
>
> We note that, while the word "comparable" in Article 2.4.2 relates to the comparability of export transactions, Article 2.4 deals more broadly with a "fair comparison" between export price and normal value and "price comparability". Nevertheless, and with this qualification in mind, we see Article 2.4 as useful context sustaining the conclusions we draw from our analysis of the word "comparable" in Article 2.4.2. In our view, the word "comparable" in Article 2.4.2 relates back to both the general and the specific obligations of the investigating authorities when comparing the export price with the normal value. The European Communities argues on the basis of the "due allowance" required by Article 2.4 for "differences in physical characteristics" that distinctions can be made among different types or models of cotton-type bed linen when determining "comparability". But here again we fail to see how the European Communities can be permitted to see the physical characteristics of cotton-type bed linen in one way for one purpose and in another way for another.[83]

One could see that the *EC – Bed Linen* dispute revolved around the first method for calculating the dumping margin as set out in Article 2.4.2, first sentence, *viz.*, the W-T comparison of normal value and export price and fell within the category identified as 'model zeroing'. From 2002, beginning with the *US – Softwood Lumber V* case, the Appellate Body had repeatedly found the US practice of zeroing inconsistent with WTO practices of determining AD margins.[84] The Appellate Body in *US – Softwood Lumber V*, confirmed its view that an authority is not allowed to practise zeroing when using the weighted-average to weighted-average comparison methodology for calculating the margin of dumping, and observed as follows:

> Zeroing means, in effect, that at least in the case of some export transactions, the export prices are treated as if they were less than what they actually are. Zeroing, therefore, does not take into account the entirety of the prices of some export transactions, namely, the prices of export transactions in those sub-groups in which the weighted average normal value is less than the weighted average export price. Zeroing thus inflates the margin of dumping for the product as a whole.[85]

A similar methodology to 'model zeroing' of margin determination was followed by the US in its AD investigations in the *US – Softwood Lumber V* case. The Appellate Body in *US – Softwood Lumber V* ruled:

> [i]f an investigating authority has chosen to undertake multiple comparisons, the investigating authority necessarily has to take into account the results of all those comparisons in order to establish margins of dumping for the product as a whole under Article 2.4.2.[86]

The Appellate Body affirmed the aforementioned rulings in *US – Zeroing (EC)*, *US – Zeroing (Japan)*, and *US – Stainless Steel (Mexico)* while emphasising:

> there is no justification for "taking into account the 'results' of only some multiple comparisons in the process of calculating margins of dumping, while disregarding other 'results'".[87]

The Appellate Body in *US – Softwood Lumber V (Article 21.5 – Canada)* observed that the term 'fair' is generally understood to connote "impartiality, even-handedness, or lack of bias", and that the use of zeroing was "difficult to reconcile with the[se] notions".[88] The Appellate Body found:

> the use of zeroing under the transaction-to-transaction comparison methodology artificially inflates the magnitude of dumping, resulting in higher margins of dumping and making a positive determination of dumping more likely. This way of calculating cannot be described as impartial, even-handed, or unbiased. For this reason, we do not consider that the calculation of "margins of dumping", on the basis of a transaction-to-transaction comparison that uses zeroing, satisfies the "fair comparison" requirement within the meaning of Article 2.4 of the Anti-Dumping Agreement.[89]

In *US – Washing Machines*, Korea had challenged the consistency of the US AD measures on imports of large residential washers under the AD Agreement, the SCM Agreement, and the GATT 1994. Korea, amongst other grounds, challenged the methodologies adopted by the US Department of Commerce (USDOC) to determine whether to apply the weighted average-to-transaction comparison methodology, and in particular the USDOC's use of zeroing in the context of the W-T comparison methodology. This case is the first challenge to zeroing under second sentence of Article 2.4.2 of the AD Agreement. Under the second sentence of Article 2.4.2, the dumping margins are calculated using the W-T comparison methodology rather than the weighted average-to-weighted average or the transaction-to-transaction methodologies.

The question that arose for consideration in *US – Washing Machines* was whether zeroing under the W-T methodology is contemplated in the second sentence of Article 2.4.2. The text of Article 2.4 of the AD Agreement supports the view that W-W and T-T are the 'normal' methods for establishing the dumping margin, and that W-T is only the 'exceptional' method. As the first two methods are not conditioned on any factual circumstances, they are expected to be used by default. As mentioned earlier, the W-T method is predicated on two factors, *viz.*, (i) authorities finding "a pattern of export prices which differ significantly among different purchasers, regions or time periods" and (ii) if authorities can explain why, in light of these differences, they cannot use W-W or T-T. The Appellate Body in *US – Washing Machines*, upholding the Panel's finding, ruled that the third methodology only applied to the export transactions within the pattern found by the investigating authority pursuant to Article 2.4.2, second sentence, and not to all export transactions and observed as follows:

> For the reasons set out above, we agree with the Panel that: (i) the use of the word "individual" in the second sentence of Article 2.4.2 indicates that the W-T comparison methodology does not involve all export transactions, but only certain export transactions identified individually; and (ii) the "individual export transactions" to which the W-T comparison methodology may be applied are those transactions falling within the relevant "pattern". Accordingly, we read the phrase "individual export Transactions" as referring to the universe of export transactions that justify the use of the W-T comparison methodology, namely, the "pattern transactions". Our interpretation gives meaning and effect to the second sentence of Article 2.4.2, whose function is to allow investigating authorities to identify and address "targeted dumping". It also accords with the object and purpose of the Anti-Dumping Agreement. Although the Anti-Dumping Agreement does not contain a preamble expressly setting out its object and purpose, it is apparent from the text of this Agreement that it deals with injurious dumping by allowing Members to take anti-dumping measures to counteract injurious dumping and imposing disciplines on the use of such anti-dumping measures.[90]

The Appellate Body in *US – Washing Machines*, while observing that the function of the second sentence of Article 2.4.2 is to allow a domestic AD authority to identify and address 'targeted dumping' in specific regions or specific time periods, found:

> by setting to zero "individual export transactions" that yield a negative comparison result, an investigating authority fails to compare all comparable export transactions that form the applicable "universe of export transactions" as required under the second sentence of Article 2.4.2, thus failing to make a "fair comparison" within the meaning of Article 2.4.[91]

The Appellate Body in *US – Washing Machines*, while rejecting the US argument that zeroing is necessary in the application of the exceptional W-T comparison methodology to give effect to the second sentence, observed as follows:

> We have considered above that the *effet utile* of the second sentence in addressing "targeted dumping" is fulfilled once an investigating authority has identified the relevant "pattern" within the meaning of the second sentence of Article 2.4.2 and has established dumping and margins of dumping by applying the W-T comparison methodology exclusively to "pattern transactions". In this respect, we have explained above that

zeroing under the W-T comparison methodology is not required in order for the second sentence of Article 2.4.2 to fulfil its function of allowing an investigating authority to identify and address "targeted dumping".[92]

As regards permissibility of zeroing in periodic reviews, the Appellate Body has ruled that such practice is not acceptable as it is inconsistent with Article 9.3 of the AD Agreement. This position was reiterated by the Appellate Body in *US – Zeroing (EC)*, *US – Zeroing (Japan)*, *US – Stainless Steel (Mexico)*, *US – Continued Zeroing*, and *US – Washing Machines*.[93] Other than periodic reviews, the Appellate Body has also ruled that zeroing in sunset reviews (Article 11.3 AD Agreement) and new shipper reviews (Article 9.5 AD Agreement) is not permissible.

3.4.3 Non-Market Economies

The majority of the Member States of the WTO are market economies, and the AD Agreement proceeds on the basis that exporters and importers within the multilateral trading system operate in a market economy. That said, there are exceptions to this general rule, *i.e.*, some countries may not boast a market economy. For instance, China is a non-market economy (NME). In a situation where an exporter manufactures and sells products in an NME, the AD formulas used to calculate the dumping margins for a market economy will not be applicable. In response to a situation of that nature, the text of Note *Ad* Article VI, paragraph 1:2 provides as follows:

> It is recognized that, in the case of imports from a country which has a complete or substantially complete monopoly of its trade and where all domestic prices are fixed by the State, special difficulties may exist in determining price comparability for the purposes of paragraph 1 and in such cases importing contracting parties may find it necessary to take into account the possibility that a strict comparison with domestic prices in such a country may not always be appropriate.

Similarly, Article 2.7 authorises the Member States to deviate from the Article 2 rules in AD investigations involving imports from NME country Member States. Article 2.7 of the AD Agreements provides as follows:

> This Article is without prejudice to the second Supplementary Provision to paragraph 1 of Article VI in Annex I to GATT 1994.

As prices of products are not determined in NME countries based on market forces, Member States have developed a methodology using 'surrogate' prices and costs from a third country with a market economy. Following from that mentioned earlier, in the case of NME countries, the normal value is established on the basis of the information submitted by a producer in a market-economy third country (surrogate country), which is then compared with the average export price of all the product under investigation imported from the NME country.

3.5 Determination of Injury to Domestic Industry

As discussed in the earlier sections, only dumping that causes or threatens to cause injury to the domestic industry of an importing Member State can be the subject of an AD measure under Article VI of the GATT 1994 and the AD Agreement. If, following an AD investigation by a domestic AD authority, it is determined that dumping exists, the domestic AD authority must establish (i) the existence, or threat, of injury to the domestic industry and (ii) the causal link between dumping and injury.

3.5.1 Domestic Industry

Before we proceed to discuss injury in the AD investigation, it is essential to understand the concept of 'domestic industry'. The concept of 'domestic industry' is relevant both for the application for initiation of an investigation – as applications are filed on behalf of a domestic industry – and for establishing injury. Article 4.1 of the AD Agreement defines domestic industry, and the relevant part reads as follows:

> For the purposes of this Agreement, the term "domestic industry" shall be interpreted as referring to the domestic producers as a whole of the like products or to those of them whose collective output of the products constitutes a major proportion of the total domestic production of those products.

It is clear from the aforementioned that the definition of 'domestic industry' is strongly associated with domestic producers and like products. The definition also provides two exceptions, *viz.*, (i) producers that are related to the exporters or importers or producers that import themselves may be excluded from the domestic industry, and (ii) producers in a regional market may be treated as a separate industry where (a) they sell 'all or almost all' of their production in that market; (b) demand in the market is not supplied to any substantial degree from domestic producers outside the market; and (c) dumped imports are concentrated in that market. The Panel in *Argentina – Poultry Anti-Dumping Duties* rejected the argument that Article 4.1 does not contain an obligation but is merely a definition which, as such, cannot be violated. The Panel ruled:

> Article 4.1 provides that the term "domestic industry" "shall" be interpreted in a specific manner. In our view, this imposes an express obligation on Members to interpret the term "domestic industry" in that specified manner. Thus, if a Member were to interpret the term differently in the context of an anti-dumping investigation, that Member would violate the obligation set forth in Article 4.1.[94]

The Panel in *Argentina – Poultry Anti-Dumping Duties* considered whether the phrase "a major proportion" implies that the "domestic industry" refers to domestic producers whose collective output constitutes the majority, that is, more than 50 percent, of domestic total production. The Panel considered different dictionary definitions and noted that the word 'major' is also defined as 'important, serious, or significant'. The Panel therefore ruled, "an interpretation that defines the domestic industry in terms of domestic producers of an important, serious or significant proportion of total domestic production is permissible".[95] In *EC – Fasteners (China)*, the Appellate Body while interpreting Article 4.1 of the AD Agreement noted:

> [by] using the term "a major proportion", the second method focuses on the question of how much production must be represented by those producers making up the domestic industry when the domestic industry is defined as less than the domestic producers as a whole. In answering this question, Article 4.1 does not stipulate a specific proportion for evaluating whether a certain percentage constitutes "a major proportion".[96]

In *EC – Fasteners (China)*, the Appellate Body noted that the term 'a major proportion'

> [s]hould be properly understood as a relatively high proportion of the total domestic production . . . Indeed, the lower the proportion, the more sensitive an investigating authority will have to be to ensure that the proportion used substantially reflects the total production of the producers as a whole.
>
> . . .
>
> Thus, "a major proportion of the total domestic production" should be determined so as to ensure that the domestic industry defined on this basis is capable of providing ample data that ensure an accurate injury analysis.[97]

The Appellate Body in *EC – Fasteners (China)* found that the EU authorities violated Article 4.1, by defining a domestic industry comprising producers accounting for 27 percent of total estimated EU production of fasteners. In the words of the Appellate Body,

> the Commission selected six producers as part of the sample, obtained relevant information from them, and verified the information on their premises. The Commission then used the information obtained from the sampled producers for its analysis of the "microeconomic" injury factors, but conducted its analysis of the "macroeconomic" injury factors on the basis of information obtained from all of the 45 producers included in the domestic industry definition.[98]

The Appellate Body in *EC – Fasteners (Article 21.5 – China)* stressed that in special market situations, *i.e.*, cases where the domestic industry is fragmented, the domestic IA will have to ensure that "the process used to select domestic producers does not introduce a material risk of distortion and that, therefore, the proportion of total production included in the domestic industry definition is representative of the total domestic industry".[99] The Appellate Body also noted:

> a domestic industry definition based on such a self-selection process that introduces a material risk of distortion to the investigating authority's injury analysis would necessarily render the resulting injury determination inconsistent with the obligation to make an objective injury analysis based on positive evidence as laid down in Article 3.1 of the Anti-Dumping Agreement.[100]

3.5.2 Injury

Article 3 of the AD Agreement deals with the determination of injury, which is one of the important factors alongside establishing a causal link for the imposition of AD measures on the dumped imports. Footnote 9 to Article 3 states that the term 'injury' shall mean (i) material injury to a domestic industry; (ii) threat of material injury to a domestic industry; or (iii) material retardation of the establishment of a domestic industry. The AD Agreement, like in the case of the Agreement on Subsidies and Countervailing Measures (SCM Agreement), requires material injury or threat thereof, rather than serious injury as required under the Agreement on Safeguards. The definition of 'injury' in both agreements is identical.[101] The Appellate Body in *Thailand – H-Beams* explained the relationship between the paragraphs of Article 3 as follows:

> Article 3 as a whole deals with obligations of Members with respect to the determination of injury. Article 3.1 is an overarching provision that sets forth a Member's

fundamental, substantive obligation in this respect. Article 3.1 informs the more detailed obligations in succeeding paragraphs. These obligations concern the determination of the volume of dumped imports, and their effect on prices (Article 3.2), investigations of imports from more than one country (Article 3.3), the impact of dumped imports on the domestic industry (Article 3.4), causality between dumped imports and injury (Article 3.5), the assessment of the domestic production of the like product (Article 3.6), and the determination of the threat of material injury (Articles 3.7 and 3.8). The focus of Article 3 is thus on substantive obligations that a Member must fulfil in making an injury determination.[102]

The Appellate Body's opinion in *China – GOES* ruled that Articles 3.1 to 3.8 of the AD Agreement provides the domestic AD investigating authority with the relevant framework and disciplines for conducting an injury and causation analysis, and that the provisions contained in Article 3 contemplate "a logical progression of inquiry leading to an investigating authority's ultimate injury and causation determination".[103]

3.5.3 Material Injury

As per Article VI of the GATT, and Article 3, footnote 9, of the AD Agreement, before proceeding to impose an AD measure, a Member State must establish material injury, or threat of material injury to its domestic industry, or the material retardation of the establishment of a domestic industry. While both the GATT and the AD Agreement do not define 'material injury', Article 3.1 of the AD Agreement requires that a determination of injury to the domestic industry

> [b]e based on positive evidence and involve an objective examination of both (a) the volume of dumped imports and the effect of the dumped imports on prices in the domestic market for like products, and (b) the consequent impact of these imports on domestic producers of such products.

The domestic AD authority must examine whether there is a significant increase in the quantity of dumped product. Pursuant to Article 3.2, the domestic AD authority must also investigate if the dumped product undercuts the like domestic products, reduces the domestic price, or prevents the domestic price from rising. Article 3.1 sets forth a Member State's substantive obligations in determining injury to the domestic industry.[104] Pursuant to Article 3.1, determination of material injury to a domestic industry shall be based on positive evidence regarding (i) the volume of dumped imports and its effect on the price of like domestic products and (ii) its consequent impact on producers of such domestic products. As laid down by the Appellate Body in *Thailand – H-Beams*, Article 3, as a whole, deals with obligations of Member States with respect to the determination of injury to the domestic industry.[105]

According to the Appellate Body in *Thailand – H-Beams*, the obligations of the domestic AD authorities detailed in Articles 3.2 to 3.8 are as follows: (i) to determine the volume of dumped imports and their effect on prices (Article 3.2); (ii) where investigations involve imports from more than one country, to cumulatively assess the effects of such imports (Article 3.3); (iii) the impact of the dumped imports on the domestic industry shall include an evaluation of all relevant economic factors and indices (Article 3.4); (iv) to demonstrate the causal link between the dumped imports and injury sustained to the domestic industry (Article 3.5); (v) to assess the effect of the dumped imports on the domestic production of like products (Article 3.6); and (vi) to determine the threat of injury to the domestic market and as the determination of AD measures thereof (Articles 3.7 and 3.8).[106] The Panel in *Egypt – Steel Rebar*, confirming the role of Article 3.1, explained the relationship between paragraph 5 and paragraphs 2 and 4 as follows:

> It is clear that Article 3.1 provides overarching general guidance as to the nature of the injury investigation and analysis that must be conducted by an investigating authority. Article 3.5 makes clear, through its cross-references, that Articles 3.2 and 3.4 are the provisions containing the specific guidance of the AD Agreement on the examination of the volume and price effects of the dumped imports, and of the consequent impact of the imports on the domestic industry, respectively.[107]

In *US – Hot-Rolled Steel*, the Appellate Body ruled that the thrust of the domestic AD authorities' obligation under Article 3.1 is premised on the requirement that they base their determination on 'positive evidence' and conduct an 'objective examination'.[108] The Appellate Body also ruled that the term 'positive evidence' related to the quality of the evidence that domestic AD authorities may rely on in making a determination, and that the word 'positive' means that the evidence must be of an affirmative, objective, and verifiable character, and must be credible.[109] The Appellate Body ruled that the requirement that the determination of injury is based on an 'objective examination' covers the entire investigation process, indicating that such examination must conform to the fundamental principles of good faith and fair play, and that such an objective examination requires that the investigation is unbiased.[110]

The Appellate Body in *Mexico – Anti-Dumping Measures on Rice* observed that Articles 3.1 and 3.2 do not prescribe a methodology to be followed by domestic AD authority to conduct an injury analysis; that the AD authority enjoys discretion in adopting a methodology to guide their injury analysis; and that an AD authority that uses a methodology premised on unsubstantiated assumptions does not conduct an examination based on positive evidence.[111] In respect of the first requirement in Article 3.1, *i.e.*, an examination of the volume of dumped imports and the effect of the dumped imports on prices in the domestic market for like products, the injury inquiry is to focus on developments in the domestic market of the importing Member State.

With regard to the volume of the dumped imports, Article 3.2 of the AD Agreement elaborates on the obligations arising under Article 3.1. As per Article 3.2, first sentence, the domestic AD authorities are to consider whether there has been a significant increase in dumped imports, either in absolute terms or relative to production or consumption in the importing Member. As per Article 3.2, first sentence, the domestic AD authorities are directed to study the effect of the dumped imports on prices by considering whether there has been significant price undercutting by the dumped imports as compared with the price of a like product of the importing Member State, or whether the effect of such imports is otherwise to depress domestic prices to a significant degree or prevent domestic price increases, which otherwise would have occurred, to a significant degree. The inquiry contemplated under Article 3.2, second sentence, postulates an inquiry as to the 'effect' of dumped imports on domestic prices, and each inquiry links the dumped imports with the prices of the like domestic products.[112] According to the Appellate Body in *China – GOES*, with respect to significant price undercutting, Article 3.2, second sentence, expressly establishes a link between the price of dumped imports and that of like domestic products, by requiring that a comparison be made between the two.[113]

The Appellate Body in *China – HP-SSST (Japan)/China – HP-SSST (EU)* noted that the price undercutting analysis envisaged under Article 3.2 deals with pricing conduct that continues over time, that an isolated instance of dumped imports being sold at lower prices than domestic like products does not justify an inference that there is price undercutting, and observed as follows:

> Rather, a proper reading of "price undercutting" under Article 3.2 suggests that the inquiry requires a dynamic assessment of price developments and trends in the relationship between the prices of the dumped imports and those of domestic like products over the entire period of investigation (POI). An examination of such developments and trends includes assessing whether import and domestic prices are moving in the same or contrary directions, and whether there has been a sudden and substantial increase in the domestic prices.[114]

In *China – GOES*, the Appellate Body observed that, since Article 3.2 contemplates an inquiry into the relationship between dumped imports and domestic prices, it is not sufficient that a domestic AD authority restricts its consideration to what is happening to domestic prices for purposes of considering significant price depression or suppression, but is required to study domestic prices in conjunction with dumped imports to ascertain whether dumped imports have "explanatory force for the occurrence of" significant depression or suppression of domestic prices.[115]

Article 3.4 elaborates on what factors an investigating authority must consider in relation to the "impact of the dumped imports on the domestic industry", and the relevant part reads as follows:

> The examination of the impact of the dumped imports on the domestic industry concerned shall include an evaluation of all relevant economic factors and indices having a bearing on the state of the industry.

Following from Article 3.4, the domestic AD authorities are given wide scope to consider relevant economic factors and indices affecting the domestic industry. The factors and indices listed in Article 3.4 have been interpreted as being a mandatory minimum and can be identified as follows: (i) an actual or potential decline in sales, profits, output, market share, productivity, return on investments, or utilisation of capacity; (ii) factors affecting the domestic prices; (iii) the magnitude of the margin of dumping; and (iv) actual or potential negative effects on cash flow, inventories, employment, wages, growth, or the ability to raise capital or investments.

The Panel in *EC – Bed Linen* considered whether the list of factors in Article 3.4 is illustrative or mandatory.

> The use of the phrase "shall include" in Article 3.4 strongly suggests to us that the evaluation of the listed factors in that provision is properly interpreted as mandatory in all cases. That is, in our view, the ordinary meaning of the provision is that the examination of the impact of dumped imports must include an evaluation of all the listed factors in Article 3.4.[116]

The Panel in *EC – Bed Linen* also addressed the issue of whether only the four groups of 'factors' represented by the subgroups separated by semicolons in Article 3.4 must be evaluated, or whether each individual factor listed must be considered:

we conclude that each of the fifteen factors listed in Article 3.4 of the AD Agreement must be evaluated by the investigating authorities in each case in examining the impact of the dumped imports on the domestic industry concerned.[117]

The panel in *Korea – Certain Paper* proceeded to clarify as to what was expected of the domestic AD authority in terms of the obligations arising from Article 3.4, and observed as follows:

> the obligation to analyse the mandatory list of fifteen factors under Article 3.4 is not a mere "checklist obligation" consisting of a mechanical exercise to make sure that each listed factor has somehow been addressed by the [investigating authority] . . . This analysis cannot be limited to a mere identification of the "relevance or irrelevance" of each factor, but rather must be based on a thorough evaluation of the state of the industry. The analysis must explain in a satisfactory way why the evaluation of the injury factors set out under Article 3.4 lead[s] to the determination of material injury, including an explanation of why factors which would seem to lead in the other direction do not, overall, undermine the conclusion of material injury.[118]

The Appellate Body in *China – GOES* noted that Article 3.4 does not merely require an examination of the state of the domestic industry, but contemplates that a domestic AD authority must derive an understanding of the impact of the dumped imports on the basis of such an examination.[119] In *China – HP-SSST (EU) / China – HP-SSST (Japan)*, the Appellate Body explained that the rationale behind requiring the domestic AD authority to the examine the relevant economic factors and indices is that it provided a 'meaningful basis' for an analysis of whether the dumped imports, through the effect of dumping, cause injury to the domestic industry, and that depending on the circumstances of the particular case, a domestic AD authority may be required consider the relative market shares of product types with respect to which it has made a finding of price undercutting.[120]

In *China – GOES*, the Appellate Body noted that although pursuant to Article 3.4 a domestic AD authority is required to examine the impact of dumped imports on the domestic industry, it is not, however, required to demonstrate that dumped imports are causing injury to the domestic industry, as the latter analysis is specifically mandated by Article 3.5.[121]

3.5.4 Threat of Material Injury

Article 3.7 of the AD Agreement refers to the determination of the threat of material injury, and states that such determination of material injury shall be based on facts and reads as follows:

> A determination of a threat of material injury shall be based on facts and not merely on allegation, conjecture or remote possibility. The change in circumstances which would create a situation in which the dumping would cause injury must be clearly foreseen and imminent.

Pursuant to Article 3.7, domestic AD authorities, while seeking to determine the existence of a threat of material injury, should consider factors such as the following:

i   A significant rate of increase of dumped imports into the domestic market indicating the likelihood of substantially increased importation;

ii Sufficient freely disposable, or an imminent substantial increase in, capacity of the exporter indicating the likelihood of substantially increased dumped exports to the importing Member's market, taking into account the availability of other export markets to absorb any additional exports;
iii Whether imports are entering at prices that will have a significant depressing or suppressing effect on domestic prices, and would be likely to increase demand for further imports; and
iv Inventories of the product being investigated.

Article 3.7 further notes:

> No one of these factors by itself can necessarily give decisive guidance but the totality of the factors considered must lead to the conclusion that further dumped exports are imminent and that, unless protective action is taken, material injury would occur.

The panel in *US – Softwood Lumber VI*, after observing that the text of Article 3.7 concerning "change of circumstances" is "not a model of clarity",[122] went on to find that Article 3.7 required that some change in circumstances would lead to a situation in which injury would occur:

> [T]he relevant "change in circumstances" referred to in Articles 3.7 and 15.7 is one element to be considered in making a determination of threat of material injury. However, we can find no support for the conclusion that such a change in circumstances must be identified as a single or specific event. Rather, in our view, the change in circumstances that would give rise to a situation in which injury would occur encompasses a single event, or a series of events, or developments in the situation of the industry, and/or concerning the dumped or subsidized imports, which lead to the conclusion that injury which has not yet occurred can be predicted to occur imminently.
> What is critical, however, is that it be clear from the determination that the investigating authority has evaluated how the future will be different from the immediate past, such that the situation of no present material injury will change in the imminent future to a situation of material injury, in the absence of measures.[123]

The panel in *Mexico – Corn Syrup*, while noting that a determination that material injury would occur cannot be made solely on the basis of a consideration of the factors listed in Article 3.7, that nothing in the text or context of Article 3.4 limits consideration of the Article 3.4 factors to cases involving material injury, ruled, "consideration of the Article 3.4 factors in examining the consequent impact of imports is required in a case involving threat of injury in order to make a determination consistent with the requirements of Articles 3.1 and 3.7".[124] On determining the existence of a threat of material injury, the Appellate Body in *Mexico – Corn Syrup (Article 21.5 – US)* ruled:

> the investigating authorities will necessarily have to make assumptions relating to "the occurrence of future events" since such future events "can never be definitively proven by facts". Notwithstanding this intrinsic uncertainty, a "proper establishment" of facts in a determination of threat of material injury must be based on events that, although they have not yet occurred, must be "clearly foreseen and imminent", in accordance with Article 3.7 of the Anti-Dumping Agreement.[125]

3.6 Causation

As per Article 3.5 of the AD Agreement, for there to be a positive determine of dumping, it must be demonstrated that there was a causal link between the dumped imports and the injury sustained to the domestic industry. The relevant part of Article 3.5 of the AD Agreement reads as follows:

> It must be demonstrated that the dumped imports are, through the effects of dumping, as set forth in paragraphs 2 and 4, causing injury within the meaning of this Agreement. The demonstration of a causal relationship between the dumped imports and the injury to the domestic industry shall be based on an examination of all relevant evidence before the authorities. The authorities shall also examine any known factors other than the dumped imports which at the same time are injuring the domestic industry, and the injuries caused by these other factors must not be attributed to the dumped imports.

A reading of Article 3.5 makes it clear that, firstly, the domestic AD authorities are required to establish a causal relationship between the dumped imports and the injury sustained to the domestic industry, and towards this end the AD authorities are to examine all relevant evidence before it. Secondly, while examining evidence, the AD authorities are also required to take into account factors other than the dumped imports which also simultaneously cause injury to the domestic industry. Thirdly, injuries caused by such other factors are not to be ascribed to the dumped imports.

The Appellate Body in *US – Hot-Rolled Steel* laid down the requirements that Article 3.5 imposes on the investigating authorities when performing a causation analysis as follows:

> This provision requires investigating authorities, as part of their causation analysis, first, to examine all "known factors", "other than dumped imports", which are causing injury to the domestic industry "at the same time" as dumped imports. Second, investigating authorities must ensure that injuries which are caused to the domestic industry by known factors, other than dumped imports, are not "attributed to the dumped imports".[126]

The Appellate Body in *China – HP-SSST (EU)/China – HP-SSST (Japan)* ruled that in order to establish causation of present material injury under Article 3.5, the domestic AD authority must determine that the dumped imports have the 'effect' of causing material injury to the domestic industry, and that such a finding cannot be made if the relevant imports are not substitutable for the domestic like products.[127] The Panel in *Thailand – H-Beams* found that the term 'known' factors would include those causal factors that are clearly raised before the domestic AD authority by interested parties in the course of an AD investigation, and that therefore there is no express requirement in Article 3.5 AD that domestic AD authorities 'seek out and examine' in each case on their own initiative the effects of all possible factors other than imports that may be causing injury to the domestic industry.[128]

Also, Article 3.5 establishes a 'non-attribution' requirement, which requires the domestic AD authority to examine other possible causes of the injury that exists, to ensure that the injury to the domestic industry is not more properly attributed to these other causes. The Appellate Body in *US – Hot-Rolled Steel*, while recognising that it may not be easy as a practical matter to separate and distinguish the injurious effects of different causal factors, observed that in order to comply with the 'non-attribution' requirement of Article 3.5, domestic AD authorities must "undertake the process of assessing appropriately, and separating and distinguishing, the injurious effects of dumped imports from those of other known causal factors".[129] In *US – Hot-Rolled Steel*, the Appellate Body delimited the situations where the non-attribution language of Article 3.5 plays a role, and specified that the language contained in the Article applies "solely [to] situations where dumped imports and other known factors are causing injury to the domestic industry at the same time".[130]

The Appellate Body in *US – Hot-Rolled Steel* found support for its interpretation of the non-attribution language of Article 3.5 in its two earlier reports safeguard measures, *viz.*, *US – Wheat Gluten* and *US – Lamb*, where it had interpreted the non-attribution language in Article 4.2(b) of the Agreement on Safeguards in a similar manner.[131] In *China – X-Ray Equipment*, the Panel, while acknowledging that a correlation between dumped imports and injury may support a finding of causation, cautioned against attributing determinative effect to such correlation and observed as follows:

> The Panel acknowledges that an overall correlation between dumped imports and injury to the domestic industry may support a finding of causation. However, such a coincidence analysis is not dispositive of the causation question; causation and correlation are two distinct concepts. In the circumstances of this case, even accepting China's position that the domestic industry experienced injury as the dumped imports entered the market at large volumes and low (albeit increasing) prices, in the Panel's view, the causation question is not resolved by such a general finding of coincidence. Rather, we consider that MOFCOM was required to conduct a more detailed analysis. In our view, MOFCOM's analysis was not adequate, due to its failure to explain why the prices of the domestic scanners could not rise at least to the level of the dumped imports in 2008, in circumstances where MOFCOM found no other causes of injury apart from the dumped imports.
>
> Consequently, the Panel concludes that MOFCOM did not provide a reasoned and adequate explanation regarding how the dumped imports caused price suppression in the domestic industry, particularly in 2008 when the prices of the dumped imports were above those of the domestic industry. For this reason, the Panel is of the view that the MOFCOM did not conduct an objective examination of the evidence and concludes that China acted inconsistently with Articles 3.1 and 3.5 of the Anti-Dumping Agreement.[132]

4. Imposition of Dumping

A domestic AD authority may impose AD measures upon a finding of dumping, injury and causation. The AD Agreement permits the imposition of three types of measures, *viz.*, (i) provisional measures; (ii) price undertakings; and (iii) the imposition of definitive AD measures.

4.1 Provisional AD Measures

The primary objective of provisional AD measures is to safeguard payment of AD duties on goods that are imported during an investigation and to avoid injury that may arise during the period of investigation. With this objective in mind, the Article 7 of the AD Agreement permits the imposition of provisional AD measures in circumstances where (i) an investigation has been initiated following the provisions of Article 5; (ii) a preliminary affirmative determination has been made of dumping and consequent injury to a domestic industry; and (iii) the domestic AD authorities consider such measures necessary to prevent injury being caused during the investigation. Pursuant to Article 7.2 duties may be collected through the imposition of provisional duties, as security – *via* a cash deposit or bond – equal to the estimated amount of the AD measure. As a general rule any provisional AD measures may only be applied for four months. However, following from Article 7.4, such measures may be applied for six months, if requested by exporters representing a significant percentage of the trade in question. The Panel in *China – HP-SSST (Japan) / China – HP-SSST (EU)* found that China violated Article 7.4 by keeping a provisional measure in force for six months.[133]

4.2 Price Undertakings

The AD Agreement, as an alternative to AD measures, permits voluntary price undertakings from exporters. Pursuant to Article 8 of the AD Agreement an exporter subject to an AD investigation may offer a price undertaking to the domestic AD authority to the effect that there would be a revision, *i.e.*, increase, of its price, or cease the alleged dumping to eliminate the dumping margin. The reason for price undertaking is that AD investigations are costly, lengthy, and cumbersome affairs – for the exporters, importers, and the domestic AD authorities – and any swift settlement through the price undertaking mechanism under Article 8 is beneficial to all parties concerned, as it can save time and resources.

Before proceeding to accept any price undertaking from an exporter, the domestic AD authority is to make an affirmative preliminary determination of dumping and injury caused by such dumping. The AD investigation is forthright suspended by the Member State, where the domestic AD authority accepts the price undertaking of the exporter. Where a price undertaking is accepted, the exporter concerned can request, or the AD authorities concerned can decide on their own accord, that the AD investigation be completed.

If the domestic AD authority determines that there is neither injury nor threat thereof to the domestic industry, the price undertaking will have no effect. Pursuant to Article 8.6, the domestic AD authorities can require exporters to provide periodic information on the implementation of the price undertaking and, in the event there is a violation of the terms of the price undertaking, the AD authorities may resume the investigation immediately and impose provisional measures.

4.3 Imposition and Collection of AD Duties

The imposition and collection of AD duties pursuant to an AD investigation is governed by Article 9 of the AD Agreement, providing the rules and necessary procedures. The provisions of Article 9 clearly lay down that any decision to impose an AD duty is left to the discretion of the domestic AD authority, even where all the requirements for imposition of AD measures are met.

Article 9.1 contains the 'lesser duty rule', which states that it is 'desirable' that the imposition be permissive, and that the AD measure be less than the margin if such lesser duty would be adequate to remove the injury to the domestic industry. In *EC – Fasteners (China)*, the Appellate Body observed that the second sentence of Article 9.1 expresses a preference for duties lesser than the margin of dumping, if lesser duties are adequate to remove the injury to the domestic industry, and that to express such a preference, Article 9.1 uses the expression "it is desirable".[134]

Pursuant to Article 9.2, the MFN obligations apply to AD measures, as the Member States are required to collect AD duties on a non-discriminatory basis on all imports from 'all sources' found to be dumped and causing injury. The Appellate Body in *EC – Fasteners*

(China), interpreting Article 9.2 of the AD Agreement as being mandatory,[135] observed as follows:

> The first sentence requires investigating authorities to collect anti-dumping duties in the appropriate amounts in each case and on a non-discriminatory basis on imports from all sources – that is, suppliers – while the second sentence requires investigating authorities to name the supplier or suppliers of the product concerned. We also consider that the exception in the third sentence of Article 9.2 does not allow the imposition of a single country-wide anti-dumping duty in investigations involving NMEs where the imposition of individual duties is alleged to be "ineffective", but is not "impracticable".[136]

Pursuant to Article 9.3, the amount of the AD duty cannot exceed the dumping margin as established under Article 2.[137] The provisions of Article 9.3 establish two set of rules for AD duty calculation and collection, *viz.*, assessed on a retrospective basis and a prospective basis. The retrospective AD assessment contemplates the calculation of dumping margins for a period that has passed already, based on actual export sales within 12 months.[138] In the prospective AD assessment, on the other hand, the dumping margin is calculated based on a specific period, which is then applied to future imports.[139]

In *EU – Biodiesel*, the Appellate Body ruled that the EU's action of assessing and imposing AD duties was inconsistent with Article 9.3, as the duties imposed were in excess of the margin of dumping that should have been established under Article 2.[140] The Appellate body also noted that Article 9.3 lays down the 'margin of dumping' as the ceiling for collection of duties regardless of whether the duties are assessed 'retrospectively' or 'prospectively'.[141]

Domestic AD investigations will feature investigations into imports from multiple foreign producers. As per Article 6.10, domestic AD authorities must 'as a rule' determine an individual margin of dumping for each known exporter or producer concerned of the product under investigation. However, Article 6.10 recognises that individual determination of margins may not be always practical, especially in cases where the number of exporters, producers, importers, or types of products involved is large. Article 6.10, second sentence, notes that in such circumstance, the domestic AD authorities may limit their examination either to a reasonable number of interested parties or products by using samples that are statistically valid based on information available at the time of the selection or to the largest percentage of the volume of the exports from the country in question which can reasonably be investigated. Article 9.4 of the AD Agreement requires that the domestic AD authorities (i) disregard in the weighted average calculation any dumping margins that are *di minimis*, zero, or based on the facts available, and (ii) must calculate an individual margin for any exporter or producer who provides the necessary information during the course of the investigation. The Appellate Body in *US – Hot Rolled Steel* noted:

> Article 9.4 does not prescribe any method that WTO Members must use to establish the "all others" rate that is actually applied to exporters or producers that are not investigated. Rather, Article 9.4 simply identifies a maximum limit, or ceiling, which investigating authorities "shall not exceed" in establishing an "all others" rate.[142]

Pursuant to Article 10.1 of the AD Agreement, both provisional and definitive AD measures shall only be applied as of the date on which the preliminary or final determinations of dumping, injury, and causation enter into force. This requirement means that any retroactive application of AD measures is in principle prohibited. The exception to this rule is found in

Article 10.2, which states that where the imposition of the AD measure is based on a determination of material injury – as opposed to a threat thereof, or material retardation – the duties may be levied retroactively as of the date of imposition of the provisional measures. As per Article 10.3, that where definitive duty is lower than the provisional duties collected, the difference is to be reimbursed or the duty recalculated, as the case may be. Pursuant to Article 10.6, a Member State may apply AD measures retroactively where (i) there is a history of dumping which caused injury or that the importer was, or should have been, aware that the exporter practises injurious dumping, and (ii) the injury is caused by huge quantities of dumped imports in a short time which is likely to seriously undermine any remedial effect of the definitive AD measures (which may be down to a rapid build-up of stocks of the imported product). Article 10.6 permits such retroactive application of final duties to a date not earlier than 90 days prior to the application of provisional measures.

4.4 Duration and Review of AD Duties

As per Article 11.1, an AD duty shall remain in force only as long as is necessary to counteract the dumping that causes injury. Article 11 establishes clear rules with regards to the duration of AD measures and requires that a periodic review be carried out (Article 11.2) for any continuing necessity for the imposition of anti-dumping duties. Describing the requirement of Article 11.1, the Panel in *US – DRAMS* noted that as per the provisions, duties "shall remain in force only as long as and to the extent necessary" to counteract injurious dumping. as "a general necessity requirement".[143] As regards the remit of Article 11, the Appellate Body in *US – Anti-Dumping Measures on Oil Country Tubular Goods* observed as follows:

> Article 11.1 of the Agreement establishes an overarching principle for "duration" and "review" of anti-dumping duties in force . . . This principle applies during the entire life of an anti-dumping duty. If, at any point in time, it is demonstrated that no injury is being caused to the domestic industry by the dumped imports, the rationale for the continuation of the duty would cease.[144]

Article 11.2 prescribes a periodic review of AD measures, and provision is contained in two sentences. The first sentence requires that domestic AD authorities review the need for the continued imposition of AD measures, either on their own initiative or upon request by an interested party submitting information to substantiate the need for a review. This review is to be carried out provided that a reasonable period of time has elapsed since the imposition of the definitive AD measure. The Appellate Body in *Mexico – Anti-Dumping Measures on Rice* found that Article 11.2 conditions the obligation of a review of AD measures on

> (i) the passage of a reasonable period of time since imposition of the definitive duty; and (ii) the submission by the interested party of "positive information" substantiating the need for a review. As the Panel correctly observed, this latter condition may be satisfied in a particular case with information not related to export volumes. Where the conditions in Article 11.2 have been met, the plain words of the provision make it clear that the agency has no discretion to refuse to complete a review, including consideration of whether the duty should be terminated in the light of the results of the review.[145]

Further, Article 11.2, second sentence, requires domestic AD authorities to scrutinise whether the "continued imposition" of the AD measure in question is necessary to offset dumping. In *US – DRAMS*, the panel, while interpreting the second sentence, observed as follows:

> However, the second sentence of Article 11.2 requires an investigating authority to examine whether the "continued imposition" of the duty is necessary to offset dumping. The word "continued" covers a temporal relationship between past and future. In our view, the word "continued" would be redundant if the investigating authority were restricted to considering only whether the duty was necessary to offset present dumping. Thus, the inclusion of the word "continued" signifies that the investigating authority is entitled to examine whether imposition of the duty may be applied henceforth to offset dumping.[146]

Under Article 11.3, referred to as the 'sunset' clause, any AD measure shall be terminated upon the expiry of five years from its imposition, unless it is determined by the domestic AD authorities pursuant to a review that such expiry of the AD measures will likely lead to a continuation or recurrence of dumping and injury. While Article 11.3 seeks to remove AD measures that are no longer required by the domestic industry, in practice it has found little application. In *US – Corrosion-Resistant Steel Sunset Review*, the Appellate Body noted that the determination of the likelihood of recurrence, or continuation of dumping and injury, is a prospective one, and that the domestic AD authorities must undertake a forward-looking analysis and seek to resolve the issue of what would likely happen if the AD measure was to be terminated.[147] The Appellate Body, emphasising the key difference between an original investigation and sunset review, observed as follows:

> In an original anti-dumping investigation, investigating authorities must determine whether dumping exists during the period of investigation. In contrast, in a sunset review of an anti-dumping duty, investigating authorities must determine whether the expiry of the duty that was imposed at the conclusion of an original investigation would be likely to lead to continuation or recurrence of dumping.[148]

The Appellate Body in *US – Corrosion-Resistant Steel Sunset Review* noted the language of Article 11.3 envisages a process combining both investigatory and adjudicatory aspects, and observed as follows:

> The words "review" and "determine" in Article 11.3 suggest that authorities conducting a sunset review must act with an appropriate degree of diligence and arrive at a reasoned conclusion on the basis of information gathered as part of a process of reconsideration and examination.[149]

4.5 Anti-Circumvention of AD Duties

Circumvention is a trade strategy adopted by exporters when an importing Member State applies AD measures. The strategy is based on concealing the origin of the dumped goods by misleading both customs officials in importing Member States and consumers. In practice, exporters alter the goods that are subject to AD measures or move the manufacturing/assembly of the goods – either wholly or partly – from the country of origin to a third country. This practice started to attract attention in the 1980s, with the success of multinational corporations in the Japanese assembly sector, and has since gained notoriety.

Circumvention practice can be brought within four categories, *viz.*, (i) third country circumvention through export of individual parts to a third country, (ii) importing country circumvention through export of individual parts to the country imposing the AD measures, (iii) moving the manufacturing process, either partly or wholly, to the importing country or a third country, and (iv) minor alteration circumvention which consists of exporting products that are an alteration of the goods that are subject to AD measures (Ostoni, 2005).

In essence, circumvention practices, if successful, result in the nullification of AD measures. Anti-circumvention measures contained in the AD Agreement are aimed at preventing exporters that are subject to AD measures from circumventing such duties. Member States employ different methods to counter the problem of circumvention. Originally, AD circumvention provisions were intended to be included in the final version of the AD Agreement (Adamantopoulos and Notaris, 2000), but no such resolution was arrived at in the Uruguay Round of negotiations towards this end.[150] This position clearly indicates that there are is no authority under the current WTO laws to justify anti-circumvention practice. Nevertheless, Member States, such as the US and the EU, do have their own anti-circumvention laws, as part of their domestic AD legislation, to counter the threat of circumvention practices.

5. Institutional and Procedural Requirements of AD Agreement

The AD Agreement contains both procedural and institutional provisions. The relevant provisions of the AD Agreement (i) establish the procedures for Member States to refer matters to the DSU, and (ii) the establishment of the Anti-Dumping Committee (AD Committee).

5.1 Dispute Settlement and Review of AD Measures

Article 17 of the AD Agreement provides for consultation and dispute settlement arising under the Agreement. Pursuant to Article 17.3, where a Member State considers that a benefit accruing – either directly or indirectly – under the AD Agreement is being nullified, or that the achievement of any objective of the Agreement is being impeded by another Member State, can refer the matter to the WTO's Dispute Settlement Body (DSB).

The Appellate Body in *Guatemala – Cement I* rejected the finding by the Panel that the provisions of Article 17 provide for a coherent set of rules for dispute settlement specific to anti-dumping cases, which replace the more general approach of the DSU.[151] The Appellate Body first held that the special or additional rules within the meaning of Article 1.2 shall prevail over the provisions of the DSU only to the extent that there is a difference between the two sets of provisions, and proceeded to hold that Article 17 of the AD Agreement does not replace the more general approach of the DSU.[152] The Appellate Body also observed that (i) Article 17.3 of the AD Agreement provides the legal basis for consultations to be requested by a complaining Member State under the AD Agreement, and as a result it is not listed in Appendix 2 of the DSU, and that (ii) it is the equivalent provision in the Anti-Dumping Agreement to Articles XXII and XXIII of the GATT 1994, which serve as the basis for consultations and dispute settlement under the GATT 1994, under most of the other agreements in Annex 1A of the Marrakesh Agreement.[153]

The Appellate Body in *Guatemala – Cement I*, interpreting Article 17.4 of the AD Agreement, held that a 'matter' that could be referred to the DSB for review only when it falls under any one of the following categories, *viz.*, (i) definitive anti-dumping duty; (ii) acceptance of price undertakings; or (3) provisional measures.[154] Other than the prior three instances, pursuant to Article 17.5, the DSB shall, at the request of a Member State, establish a Panel to examine the matter based upon (i) a written statement of the Member State considering if a benefit accruing to it, directly or indirectly, under the Agreement has been nullified or impaired, and (ii) the facts made available to the domestic AD authorities in conformity with appropriate domestic procedures.

Article 17.6 of the AD Agreement, in examining matters referred to in paragraph 5 provides for two special rules for standard of review in WTO anti-dumping cases and reads as follows:

(i) in its assessment of the facts of the matter, the panel shall determine whether the authorities' establishment of the facts was proper and whether their evaluation of those facts was unbiased and objective. If the establishment of the facts was proper and the evaluation was unbiased and objective, even though the panel might have reached a different conclusion, the evaluation shall not be overturned;

(ii) the panel shall interpret the relevant provisions of the Agreement in accordance with customary rules of interpretation of public international law. Where the panel finds that a relevant provision of the Agreement admits of more than one permissible interpretation, the panel shall find the authorities' measure to be in conformity with the Agreement if it rests upon one of those permissible interpretations.

In *US – Hot-Rolled Steel*, the Appellate Body, while comparing the task of Panels under Article 17.6(i) to their task under Article 11 of the DSU, noted that as per subsection (i), the remit of review by the Panel over the domestic AD authority's decision is simply limited to reviewing the authority's establishment and evaluation of the facts, which is closely aligned to the obligation imposed under Article 11 of the DSU to make an objective assessment of facts.[155] Further, the Appellate Body also noted that the Panel is to assess if the domestic AD authorities' establishment of facts was proper and if the evaluation of those facts by the authorities was unbiased and objective.[156] Similarly, the Appellate Body in *China – HP-SSST (EU)/China – HP-SSST (Japan)* observed as follows:

> It follows from the requirement that the investigating authority provide a "reasoned and adequate" explanation for its conclusions that the entire rationale for the investigating authority's decision must be set out in its report on the determination. This is not to say that the meaning of a determination cannot be explained or buttressed by referring to evidence on the record. Yet, in all instances, it is the explanation provided in the written report of the investigating authorities (and supporting documents) that is to be assessed in order to determine whether the determination was sufficiently explained and reasoned.[157]

Pursuant to subsection (ii) of Article 17.6, the AD Agreement is to be interpreted according to the norms of customary rules of interpretation of public international law, following the Vienna Convention on the Law of Treaties (VCLT). The general principle of international law, now embodied in Article 31.1 of the VCLT, requires that international treaties are to be interpreted in good faith in accordance with the ordinary meaning of the terms of the treaty in their context and in the light of its object and purpose. As noted by Lord McNair, the task of interpreting a treaty is "the duty of giving effect to the expressed intention of the parties, that is, their intention as expressed in the words used by them in the light of the surrounding circumstances" (McNair, 1961, p. 365). Article 17.6(ii), second sentence, permits at least two interpretations of the provisions of the AD Agreement.[158] The Appellate Body in *US – Continued Zeroing* observed as follows:

Article 17.6(ii) contemplates a sequential analysis. The first step requires a panel to apply the customary rules of interpretation to the treaty to see what is yielded by a conscientious application of such rules including those codified in the Vienna Convention. Only after engaging this exercise will a panel be able to determine whether the second sentence of Article 17.6(ii) applies. The structure and logic of Article 17.6(ii) therefore do not permit a panel to determine first whether an interpretation is permissible under the second sentence and then to seek validation of that permissibility by recourse to the first sentence.[159]

A reading of Article 17.6(ii) reveals that it has an inherent contradiction. The Appellate Body in *US – Continued Zeroing* observed that the rules and principles of the Vienna Convention do not contemplate interpretations with mutually contradictory results, and that the purpose of interpretation is therefore to narrow the range of interpretations, not to generate conflicting, competing interpretations.[160]

5.2 The Committee on Anti-Dumping Practices

Pursuant to Article 16, the Committee on Anti-Dumping Practices is established (Anti-Dumping Committee) and to be composed of representatives from each of the Member States. As per the provisions of Article 16.1, the Committee is to meet not less than twice in a year. Under the powers vested, the Committee may set up subsidiary bodies as it finds appropriate,[161] and in carrying out their functions both the Committee and the subsidiary bodies may consult with and seek information from any source.[162] As per Article 16.4, Member States are required to report all preliminary or definitive anti-dumping actions taken in their respective jurisdictions on a semi-annual basis.

The Committee is charged with the responsibility of reviewing Member States' notifications of any changes to their laws and regulations with regards to the AD Agreement and in the administration of such domestic laws and regulations pursuant to Article 18.5.[163] As per Article 18.6, the Committee is to carry out an annual review of the implementation and operation of the AD Agreement and inform the Council for Trade in Goods of such developments.

6. Special and Differential Treatment for Developing Country Members

Article 15 of the AD Agreement recognises that special treatment must be given to developing country Member States while seeking to apply AD measures, and reads as follows:

> It is recognized that special regard must be given by developed country Members to the special situation of developing country Members when considering the application of anti-dumping measures under this Agreement. Possibilities of constructive remedies provided for by this Agreement shall be explored before applying anti-dumping duties where they would affect the essential interests of developing country Members.

Although ambitious, it is practically unenforceable. The Panel in *US – Steel Plate* ruled that there are no specific legal requirements for specific action in the first sentence of Article 15 and that, therefore, "Members cannot be expected to comply with an obligation whose parameters are entirely undefined". In the Panel's view, "the first sentence of Article 15 imposes no specific or general obligation on Members to undertake any particular action".[164] Similarly, in *EC – Tube or Pipe Fittings*, the Panel observed:

> even assuming that the first sentence of Article 15 imposes a general obligation on Members, it clearly contains no operational language delineating the precise extent or nature of that obligation or requiring a developed country Member to undertake any specific action.[165]

While it can be seen that there is no clear obligation arising from Article 15, first sentence, the Panel in the *EC – Bed Linen*, following from Article 15, second sentence, ruled that the EC had violated Article 15 by failing to actively consider the possibility of 'constructive remedies' in the form of price undertakings prior to the imposition of AD measures against a developing country Member State.[166] Rejecting the argument of EC that a 'constructive remedy' might be a decision not to impose AD measures at all, the Panel noted that Article 15 refers to 'remedies' in respect of injurious dumping, that a decision not to impose an AD measure, while clearly within the authority of a Member State under Article 9.1 of the AD Agreement, is not a 'remedy' of any type, constructive or otherwise for injurious dumping, and observed as follows:

> "Remedy" is defined as, *inter alia*, "a means of counteracting or removing something undesirable; redress, relief". "Constructive" is defined as "tending to construct or build up something non-material; contributing helpfully, not destructive". The term "constructive remedies" might consequently be understood as helpful means of counteracting the effect of injurious dumping. However, the term as used in Article 15 is limited to constructive remedies "provided for under this Agreement". . . . In our view, Article 15 refers to "remedies" in respect of injurious dumping.[167]

Dwelling on the phrase "constructive remedies provided for by this Agreement" occurring in Article 15, second sentence, the Appellate Body in *EC – Bed Linen* observed as follows:

> The Agreement provides for the imposition of anti-dumping duties, either in the full amount of the dumping margin, or desirably, in a lesser amount, or the acceptance of price undertakings, as a means of resolving an anti-dumping investigation resulting in a final affirmative determination of dumping, injury, and causal link. Thus, in our view, imposition of a lesser duty, or a price undertaking would constitute "constructive remedies" within the meaning of Article 15. We come to no conclusions as to what other actions might in addition be considered to constitute "constructive remedies" under Article 15, as none have been proposed to us.[168]

The aforementioned legal position as regards Article 15 on 'special and differential treatment' for developing countries makes one wonder if the provision is as effective as it is presented within the AD Agreement. Some commentators opine that much more could be done to improve on actually ensuring 'special and differential treatment' for developing countries in cases relating to the imposition of AD measures on developing country Member States (Adamantopoulos and Notaris, 2000).

7. Summary

Although dumping is not prohibited *per se* by WTO laws, anti-dumping laws act as a restraint on unfair trade practices. One of the most controversial laws of the WTO, anti-dumping laws permit Member States to take appropriate measures to protect their domestic industry from such unfair trade practices which cause injury to their industry. In essence, anti-dumping measures are introduced to counteract dumping. A Member State may, following Article VI of the GATT 1994 and the Anti-Dumping Agreement, impose AD measures subject to meeting three conditions, *viz.*, (i) where dumping exists, (ii) where the domestic industry producing the 'like' product of the importing country suffers injury, and (iii) there is a demonstrable causal link between the dumped imports and the injury sustained by the domestic industry in the importing Member State. Domestic industries lobby their respective governments to impose AD measures on particular products, and on the other hand they face pressure from end users/consumers and foreign producers not to impose any measures. In practice, AD measures are used against and by both developing country and developed country Member States. Commentators have argued that dumping should be dealt with using competition laws, not through anti-dumping laws (Hoekman and Mavroidis, 1996). Some commentators have also suggested the incorporation of competition law principles into WTO laws on anti-dumping (Matsushita, Shoenbaum, Mavroidis, and Hahn, 2017).

Notes

1. Dumping also occurs if the export price of the goods is less than the cost of their production.
2. The author presents the case of US producers of ferrosilicon from 1989, how they as a cartel were successful in using AD legislation – both in the US and the EU – to drive away competition from importers, and that the AD measures only succeeded in creating a US market that was susceptible to effective cartelisation but did not benefit the domestic producers and employees.
3. For instance, during the 1999 Seattle Ministerial Conference, the US opposed negotiations on changes to the AD Agreement. Commentators were of the view that it was a tactical move from the US politicians to oppose changes in order to placate the steel workers for the forthcoming presidential elections and to gain the support from the industry sectors that were traditional users of AD measures. See Adamantopoulos and Notaris (2000).
4. The authors describe anti-dumping as the 'third rail' of US trade policy.
5. The author cites an instance in the seventeenth century, where the Dutch were accused of selling their produce to the Baltic countries at very low prices to see off French competition.
6. The authors note that dumping and anti-dumping "have been part of the bilateral trade treaties and domestic regulations since the progressive market opening of the early 1800s" See Mavroidis, Messerlin, and Wauters (2008, p. 3).
7. Kerr argues that part of an economist's problem with analysing dumping is that it is already defined in international trade law, and as a result much of the work on dumping takes the definition as given.
8. The introduction of AD legislation in the US was in response to the threat of predatory dumping by Germany. The US already had the Sherman Antitrust Act and Section 73 of the Wilson Act 1894, which could have been resorted to in 'dumping situations' (Dale, 1980).
9. Viner notes that Canada, led by the Liberal Party, used anti-dumping laws while facing domestic pressure from steel manufacturers and farmers (the Liberal Party owed its majority to the farmers) to increase import duties to protect the domestic industry from foreign dumping. The discontent gave rise to the rapid growth of an independent farmer's party. See also Finger and Artis (1993).
10. In the WTO era, the Revenue Act of 1916 was ruled inconsistent with Article VI of the GATT and other provisions of the AD Agreement by the AB.
11. The key reason for Britain enacting the Safeguards of Industries Act 1921 was the fear of predatory competition from Germany (Viner, 1923a).
12. The US passed the Anti-dumping Act 1921 due to the shortcomings of the Revenue Act of 1916.
13. Interestingly, the UK advocated the banning AD measures, while arguing that dumping was not harmful.
14. WTO Agreement on Implementation of Article VI GATT is referred to as the Anti-Dumping Agreement.
15. Introduction of procedural formalities in the IAA were necessitated, as GATT Contracting Parties had their own set of rules which were not aligned with Article VI GATT. For instance, the US

AD regime permitted the imposition of provisional measures, and the UK's AD regime permitted the imposition of AD measures without notice on the interested parties.
16 See Article 3(4) of the Anti-Dumping Code 1979. This provision was more in line with the US domestic legislation on the subject.
17 Between 1980 and 1989, about 95 percent of all AD measures were imposed by Australia, Canada, the EU, and the US. Over 1,600 investigations were launched in the 1980s. See Finger and Artis (1993). Between 1980 and 1987, a mere seven investigations were initiated by developing countries. See Lindsey and Ikenson (2001).
18 In 1987, Mexico signed the GATT Anti-Dumping Code and went on to initiate 17 cases that year and ten the following year – with the primary targets being the US and EU steel exporters. Finger and Artis note that the actions were in part as retaliation, to serve as a counter-pressure to serve Mexican exporters facing anti-dumping cases in the US and the EU (Finger and Artis, 1993). In the late 1980s, Mexico, Brazil, and Argentina joined the AD users club, which was until then dominated by the US, EU, Britain, Australia, and New Zealand.
19 The trade liberalisation introduced by the developing countries are 'locked in' as they have been made as 'binding commitments' under WTO agreements.
20 Other than AD, it is IP rights (TRIPS-plus, in particular) that has featured as a contentious issue in the negotiations.
21 Alongside AD policies, IP rights features conspicuously in the political-economic interaction of the nations.
22 In the subsequent meeting, which took place in December 2017, the negotiating group only continued its active programme of work in respect of fisheries but not on the AD Agreement. See Report by Chairman (2017).
23 See also Kerr (2001). Following from an analysis of 'dumping' as contained in Article 2.1 of the AD Agreement, Kerr raises the question of why price discrimination should be viewed as an 'unfair' trade practice.
24 See Article 2.2.1 of the AD Agreement.
25 This practice is referred to as 'social dumping'.
26 See Appellate Body Report, *US – Zeroing (Japan)*, para. 140, where it ruled that both Article 2.1 of the ADA and Article VI:1 of the GATT 1994 were 'definitional provisions' and that they do not impose any independent obligations on the Member States.
27 See Appellate Body Report, *US – 1916 Act*, para. 118.
28 *Ibid.*, para. 120.
29 *Ibid.*, para. 137.
30 CDSOA stands for United States Continued Dumping and Subsidy Offset Act of 2000.
31 See Appellate Body Report, *US – Offset Act (Byrd Amendment)*, para. 265.
32 Agreement on Implementation of Article VI of the General Agreement on Tariffs and Trade 1994. The AD Agreement builds on the IAA Code finalised in the 1979 Tokyo Round of negotiations.
33 Professor Bhala, in his seminal work on GATT, provides a table listing each Article of the AD Agreement to the relevant provisions of Article VI of the GATT.
34 See Appellate Body Report, *US – Washing Machines*, para. 5.52.
35 See Appellate Body Report, *US – 1916 Act*, para. 138.
36 *Ibid.*, para. 137.
37 See Panel Report, *US – 1916 (EC)*, para. 6.97.
38 *Ibid.*, para. 6.114. See also Panel Report, *US – 1916 (Japan)*, para. 6.240.
39 See Panel Report, *US – 1916 (EC)*, para. 6.106.
40 See Article 5.1 of the AD Agreement.
41 See Article 5.6 of the AD Agreement.
42 See Panel Report, *US – Lumber V*, para. 7.54.
43 See Panel Report, *Guatemala – Cement II*, para. 8.35.
44 *Ibid.*, para. 8.53.
45 See Panel Report, *Thailand – H-Beams*, paras. 7.75–7.76.
46 *Ibid.*, para. 7.77.
47 See Appellate Body Report, *US – Oil Country Tubular Goods Sunset Reviews*, para. 241.
48 See Panel Report, *US – Oil Country Tubular Goods Sunset Reviews (Article 21.5 – Argentina)*, para. 7.120.
49 See Panel Report, *Guatemala – Cement II*, paras. 8.243–8.244.

50 See Panel Report, *US – Hot-Rolled Steel*, para. 7.55.
51 See Panel Report, *Egypt – Steel Rebar*, para. 7.146.
52 See Appellate Body Report, *US – Hot-Rolled Steel*, paras. 81. See also Panel Report, *US – Hot-Rolled Steel Plate*, para. 7.55.
53 See Appellate Body Report, *US – Stainless Steel (Mexico)*, para. 96.
54 See Appellate Body Report, *US – Stainless Steel (Mexico)*, paras. 87 and 89, where the Appellate Body relied upon the context found in Articles 2.1, 2.2, 2.3, 5.2(ii), 5.8, 6.1.1, 6.7, 6.10, and 9.5 of the AD Agreement.
55 See Appellate Body Reports, *US – Zeroing (Japan)*, paras. 111–114; *US – Stainless Steel (Mexico)*, para. 89; and *US – Continued Zeroing*, para. 283.
56 See Appellate Body Reports, *US – Zeroing (Japan)*, paras. 113–114; *US – Stainless Steel (Mexico)*, para. 94; *US – Washing Machines*, paras. 5.90–5.98, 5.185–5.187; and *EU – Biodiesel*, para. 6.96.
57 See Appellate Body Reports *US – Stainless Steel (Mexico)*, para. 98. See, however, the Appellate Body Report, *US – Washing Machines*, paras. 5.105–5.106, where it was noted that in cases of "targeted dumping" to certain purchasers, regions or in certain time periods, the applicable "universe of export transactions" is more limited.
58 See Appellate Body Report, *US – 1916 Act*, para. 107.
59 See Appellate Body Report, *EC – Bed Linen*, paras. 56–58.
60 See Appellate Body Reports, *US – Softwood Lumber V (Article 21.5 – Canada)*, para. 97; and *US – Zeroing (Japan)*, para. 123.
61 See Appellate Body Report, *US – Hot-Rolled Steel*, para. 165.
62 *Ibid.*, para. 139.
63 *Ibid.*, para. 140.
64 *Ibid.*, para. 148.
65 See Appellate Body Report, *EU – Biodiesel*, para. 6.26.
66 *Ibid.*, paras. 6.55–6.57.
67 See Appellate Body Report, *US – Hot-Rolled Steel*, para. 167.
68 See Appellate Body Reports, *EC – Fasteners (Article 21.5 – China)*, para. 5.163, and *EU – Biodiesel*, para. 6.87.
69 See Appellate Body Report, *EC – Fasteners (Article 21.5 – China)*, paras. 5.163 and 5.204.
70 *Ibid.*, para. 5.205.
71 The amounts for selling, general and administrative costs (SG&A), and profits shall be based on actual data pertaining to production and sales in the ordinary course of trade of the like product by the exporter or producer under investigation. See Appellate Body Reports, *China – HP-SSST (EU)/China – HP-SSST (Japan)*, para. 5.59, and *EC – Bed Linen*, para. 74.83.
72 See Appellate Body Report, *EU – Biodiesel*, para. 6.70.
73 See Appellate Body Report, *US – Hot-Rolled Steel*, paras. 167 and 168.
74 See Panel Report, *US – Oil Country Tubular Goods Sunset Reviews (Article 21.5 – Argentina)*, para. 7.76.
75 See Appellate Body Report, *US – Hot-Rolled Steel*, para. 139.
76 *Ibid.*, para. 147.
77 *Ibid.*, para. 142.
78 Article 5.8 AD Agreement. The volume of dumped imports is to be regarded as negligible if the volume of the dumped imports from a particular country is found to account for less than 3 percent of imports of the like product.
79 See Appellate Body Report from the *EC – Bed Linen* case.
80 Under the AD Agreement, a government can calculate the difference in price on a transaction-by-transaction basis and then proceed to compute the weighted average of the price differences, where individual export transactions are compared with the individual domestic transactions. The US, instead, used to employ the zeroing practice, instead of the transaction-to-transaction comparisons.
81 See Appellate Body Report, *US – Corrosion-Resistant Steel Sunset Review*, para. 135.
82 See Appellate Body Report, *EC – Bed Linen*, paras. 54–55.
83 *Ibid.*, paras. 59–60.
84 Some of the cases where US 'zeroing' actions came under scrutiny are *US – Orange Juice (Brazil)*; *US – Zeroing (EC)*; *US – Zeroing (Japan)*; and *US – Continued Zeroing*. In 2012, the US Trade Representative announced that the US had reached agreements with the EU and Japan to end the long-drawn disputes over zeroing. For a discussion of US zeroing practices, see Saggi and Wu (2013).

85 See Appellate Body Report, *US – Softwood Lumber V*, paras. 56–58.
86 See Appellate Body Report, *US – Softwood Lumber V*, para. 98.
87 See Appellate Body Reports, *US – Zeroing (EC)*, para. 126; *US – Zeroing (Japan)*, paras. 125–128; and *US – Softwood Lumber V*, para. 98.
88 See Appellate Body Report, *US – Softwood Lumber V (Article 21.5 – Canada)*, paras. 138–142.
89 *Ibid.*, para. 142.
90 See Appellate Body Report, *US – Washing Machines*, para. 5.22.
91 *Ibid.*, paras. 5.177 and 5.180.
92 *Ibid.*, para. 5.181.
93 See Appellate Body Reports, *US – Zeroing (EC)*, para. 164; *US – Zeroing (Japan)*, para. 156; *US – Stainless Steel (Mexico)*, para. 133; *US – Continued Zeroing*, para. 285; and *US – Washing Machines*, paras. 5.188–5.190.
94 See Panel Report, *Argentina – Poultry Anti-Dumping Duties*, para. 7.338.
95 *Ibid.*, para. 7.341.
96 See Appellate Body Report, *EC – Fasteners (China)*, para. 411.
97 *Ibid.*, paras. 412–413.
98 *Ibid.*, para. 429.
99 See Appellate Body Report, *EC – Fasteners (Article 21.5 – China)*, para. 319.
100 *Ibid.*, para. 325.
101 See Article 3, footnote 9 of the AD Agreement, and Article 15, footnote 45 of the SCM Agreement.
102 See Appellate Body Reports, *Thailand – H-Beams*, para. 106. See also the Appellate Body Reports, *China – GOES*, para. 128; *China – HP-SSST (EU)/China – HP-SSST (Japan)*, para. 5.137; and *EU – Biodiesel*, para. 6.124, where the Appellate Body reiterated the aforementioned position.
103 See Appellate Body Report, *China – GOES*, paras. 126–128.
104 The Appellate Body has referred to the provision contained in Article 3.1 as an "overarching provision" which sets forth a Member State's obligation with regards to injury determination to its domestic industry. See Appellate Body Reports, *Thailand – H-Beams*, para. 106; *China – GOES*, para. 126; *China – HP-SSST (EU)/China – HP-SSST (Japan)*, para. 5.137; and *EU – Biodiesel*, para. 6.124.
105 See Appellate Body Report, *Thailand – H-Beams*, para. 106.
106 *Ibid.*
107 See Panel Report, *Egypt – Steel Rebar*, para. 7.102.
108 See Appellate Body Report, *US – Hot-Rolled Steel*, para. 192.
109 *Ibid.* See also Appellate Body Reports, *China – HP-SSST (Japan)/China – HP-SSST (EU)*, para. 5.138.
110 *Ibid.*
111 See Appellate Body Report, *Mexico – Anti-Dumping Measures on Rice*, paras. 204–205. See also Panel Report, *Thailand – H-Beams*, para. 7.137.
112 See Appellate Body Report, *China – GOES*, para. 135.
113 *Ibid.*, para. 136.
114 See Appellate Body Report, *China – HP-SSST (Japan)/China – HP-SSST (EU)*, para. 5.159.
115 See Appellate Body Report, *China – GOES*, para. 136.
116 See Panel Report, *EC – Bed Linen*, para. 6.154. It is to be pointed out that this finding was not specifically addressed by the Appellate Body.
117 *Ibid.*, para. 6.159. See Panel Report, *Thailand – H-Beams*, paras. 7.224–7.225, as upheld by Appellate Body Report, and *Thailand – H-Beams*, para. 125. See also Panel Report, *Argentina – Poultry Anti-Dumping Duties*, para. 7.314.
118 See Panel Report, *Korea – Certain Paper*, para. 7.272.
119 See Appellate Body Report, *China – GOES*, para. 149.
120 See Appellate Body Report, *China – HP-SSST (Japan)/China – HP-SSST (EU)*, para. 5.211.
121 See Appellate Body Report, *China – GOES*, para. 150.
122 See Panel Report, *US – Softwood Lumber VI*, para. 7.53.
123 *Ibid.*, paras. 7.57–7.58.
124 See Panel Report, *Mexico – Corn Syrup*, para. 7.127.
125 See Appellate Body Report, *Mexico – Corn Syrup*, para. 85.
126 See Appellate Body Report, *US – Hot-Rolled Steel*, para. 222.
127 See Appellate Body Report, *China – HP-SSST (Japan)/China – HP-SSST (EU)*, paras. 5.251 and 5.262.

128 See Panel Report, *Thailand – H-Beams*, para. 7.273.
129 See Appellate Body Report, *US – Hot-Rolled Steel*, para. 228.
130 *Ibid.*, para. 223.
131 *Ibid.*, para. 230.
132 See Panel Report, *China – X-Ray Equipment*, paras. 7.247–7.248.
133 See Panel Report, *China – HP-SSST (Japan)/China – HP-SSST (EU)*, para. 7.334.
134 See Appellate Body Report, *EC – Fasteners (China)*, para. 336.
135 *Ibid.*
136 *Ibid.*, para. 354.
137 See Appellate Body Report, *US – Zeroing (Japan)*, para. 162.
138 The US uses the retrospective system of assessing AD duties.
139 The EU uses the prospective system of assessing AD duties.
140 See Appellate Body Report, *EU – Biodiesel*, paras. 6.96–6.97 and 6.104.
141 *Ibid.*
142 See Appellate Body Report, *US – Hot-Rolled Steel*, para. 126.
143 See Panel Report, *US – DRAMS*, para. 6.41.
144 See Appellate Body Report, *US – Anti-Dumping Measures on Oil Country Tubular Goods*, para. 115. See also Appellate Body Report, *US – Stainless Steel (Mexico)*, para. 93.
145 See Appellate Body Report, *Mexico – Anti-Dumping Measures on Rice*, para. 314.
146 See Panel Report, *US – DRAMS*, para. 6.27.
147 See Appellate Body Report *US – Corrosion-Resistant Steel Sunset Review*, para. 105.
148 *Ibid.*, para. 107.
149 *Ibid.*, para. 111.
150 Article 12 of the Dunkel Draft (last draft version of the GATT 1994) stated that under certain circumstances, AD measures could be extended in the case of circumvention.
151 See Appellate Body Report, *Guatemala – Cement I*, para. 58.
152 *Ibid.*, paras. 65–66.
153 *Ibid.*, para. 64.
154 *Ibid.*, para. 79.
155 See Appellate Body Report, *US – Hot-Rolled Steel*, para. 55.
156 *Ibid.*, para. 56.
157 See Appellate Body Report, *China – HP-SSST (EU)/China – HP-SSST (Japan)*, para. 5.255.
158 See Appellate Body Report, *US – Hot-Rolled Steel*, para. 59.
159 See Appellate Body Report, *US – Continued Zeroing*, para. 271.
160 *Ibid.*, para. 273.
161 Article 16.2 of the AD Agreement.
162 Article 16.3 of the AD Agreement.
163 Article 18.5 of the AD Agreement requires each Member State to inform the Committee of any changes in its laws and regulations relevant to the AD Agreement and in the administration of such laws and regulations.
164 See Panel Report, *US – Steel Plate*, para. 7.110. See also Panel Report, *EC – Bed Linen*, paras. 65–69.
165 See also Panel Report, *EC – Tube or Pipe Fittings*, para. 7.68.
166 See Panel Report, *EC – Bed Linen*, paras. 6.233.
167 *Ibid.*, para. 6.228.
168 *Ibid.*, para. 6.229.

Bibliography

Adamantopoulos, Konstantinos and Diego De Notaris. 'The Future of the WTO and the Reform of the Anti-Dumping Agreement: A Legal Perspective,' *Fordham International Law Journal* Vol 24, No 1 (2000) 30–61.

Beseler, Johannes Freidrich and A. Neville Williams. *Anti-Dumping and Anti-Subsidy Law: The European Communities* (Sweet & Maxwell Publishing, 1990).

Bhagwhati, Jagdish N. *Protectionism* (MIT Press, 1988).

Bhala, Raj. *Modern GATT Law: A Treatise on the General Agreement on Tariffs and Trade* Vol 2 (Sweet & Maxwell Publishers, 2013) 703–1054.

Blonigen, Bruce A. and Thomas J. Prusa. 'Dumping and Antidumping Duties,' in Bagwell, Kyle and Robert W. Staiger (eds.) *Handbook of Commercial Policy* (Elsevier Publishing, 2016) 107–160.

Bown, Chad P. and Thomas J. Prusa. 'US Antidumping: Much Ado about Zeroing,' *The World Bank, Policy Research Working Paper 5325* (2010).

Choi, Won-Mog. *'Like Products' in International Law: Towards a Consistent GATT/WTO Jurisprudence* (Oxford University Press, 2003).

Clarke, Peggy A. and Gary N. Horlick. 'Injury Determinations in Antidumping and Countervailing Duty Investigations,' in Macrory, Patrick F.J., Arthur E. Appleton and Michael G. Plummer (eds.) *The WTO: Legal, Economic and Political Analysis* Vol 1 (Springer, 2005) 735–748.

Czako, Judith, Johann Human and Jorge Miranda. *A Handbook on Anti-Dumping Investigations* (Cambridge University Press, 2003).

Dale, Richard. *Anti-Dumping Law in a Liberal Trade Order* (Macmillan Press, 1980).

Finger, Michael J. 'Dumping and Antidumping: The Rhetoric and the Reality of Protection in Industrial Countries,' *The World Bank Research Observer* Vol 7, No 2 (1992) 121–144.

Finger, Michael J. and Nellie T. Artis (eds.). *Antidumping: How It Works and Who Gets Hurt* (University of Michigan Press, 1993).

Graham, Samuel J. 'Letter to the Editor,' *New York Times*, 4 July 1916.

Hoekman, Bernard M. and Michel K. Kostecki. *The Political Economy of the World Trading System: The WTO and Beyond* (Oxford University Press, 2009).

Hoekman, Bernard M. and Petros C. Mavroidis. 'Dumping, Antidumping and Antitrust,' *Journal of World Trade* Vol 30, No 1 (1996) 27–52.

Janow, Merit E. and Robert W. Staiger. 'EC-Bed Linen: European Communities-Anti-Dumping Duties on Imports of Cotton-Type Bed Linen from India,' *World Trade Review* Vol 2, No S1 (2003) 115–139.

Kerr, William A. 'Dumping: One of Those Economic Myths,' *Estey Journal of International Law and Trade Policy* Vol 2, No 2 (2001) 211–220.

Krishna, Raj. 'Antidumping in Law and Practice,' *The World Bank* (1999).

Lee, Yong-Shik. *Reclaiming Development in the World Trading System* Vol 26 (Cambridge University Press, 2016).

Lester, Simon, Bryan Mercurio and Arwel Davies. *World Trade Law: Text, Materials and Commentary* (Hart Publishing, 2018).

Lindsey, Brink and Dan Ikenson. 'Coming Home to Roost: Proliferating Antidumping Laws and the Growing Threat to US Exports,' *Center for Trade Policy Studies, CATO Institute* Vol 14 (2001) 1–32.

Macrory, Patrick F.J. 'The Anti-Dumping Agreement,' in Macrory, Patrick F.J., Arthur E. Appleton and Michael G. Plummer (eds.) *The WTO: Legal, Economic and Political Analysis* Vol 1 (Springer, 2005) 485–530.

Mankiw, Gregory N. and Phillip L. Swagel. 'Antidumping: The Third Rail of Trade Policy,' *Foreign Affairs* Vol 84, No 4 (2005) 107–119.

Matsushita, Mitsuo, Thomas J. Shoenbaum, Petros C. Mavroidis and Michael Hahn. *The World Trade Organization: Law, Practice, and Policy* (Oxford University Press, 2017).

Mavroidis, Petros C., Patrick A. Messerlin and Jasper M. Wauters. *The Law and Economics of Contingent Protection in the WTO* (Edward Elgar Publishing, 2008).

Mavroidis, Petros C. and Thomas J. Prusa. 'Die Another Day: Zeroing in on Targeted Dumping: Did the AB Hit the Mark in US-Washing Machines?,' *World Trade Review* Vol 17, No 2 (2018) 239–264.

McNair, Arnold Duncan. *The Law of Treaties* (Clarendon Press, 1961).

Ostoni, Lucia. 'Anti-Dumping Circumvention in the EU and the US: Is There a Future for Multilateral Provisions under the WTO?,' *Fordham Journal of Corporate & Financial Law* Vol 10, No 2 (2005) 407–438.

Pierce Jr., Richard J. 'Antidumping Law as a Means of Facilitating Cartelization,' *Antitrust Law Journal* Vol 67, No 3 (2000) 725–743.

Prusa, Thomas J. 'The Growing Problem of Antidumping Protection,' in Ito, Takeshi and Andrew K. Rose (eds.) *International Trade in East Asia* (University of Chicago Press, 2005) 329–366.

Prusa, Thomas J. and Susan Skeath. 'Modern Commercial Policy: Managed Trade or Retaliation?,' in Choi, Kwan E. and James C. Hartigan (eds.) *Handbook of International Trade* Vol 2 (Blackwell Publishing, 2002) 358–382.

Report by Chairman. *H.E. Mr. Wayne McCook to the Trade Negotiations Committee*, Negotiating Group on Rules, TN/RL/27 (7 December 2015).

Report by Chairman. *H.E. Mr. Wayne McCook to the Trade Negotiations Committee*, Negotiating Group on Rules, TN/RL/28/Suppl.1 (6 December 2017).

Saggi, Kamal and Mark Wu. 'Yet Another Nail in the Coffin of Zeroing: United States: Anti-Dumping Administrative Reviews and Other Measures Related to Imports of Certain Orange Juice from Brazil,' *World Trade Review* Vol 12, No 2 (2013) 377–408.

Stewart, Terence P. and Amy S. Dwyer. 'Antidumping: Overview of the Agreement,' in Bagwell, Kyle W., George A. Bermann and Petros C. Mavroidis (eds.) *Law and Economics of Contingent Protection in International Trade* (Cambridge University Press, 2010) 197–240.

Trebilcock, Michael, Robert Howse and Antonia Eliason. *The Regulation of International Trade* (Routledge, 2013).

Van den Bossche, Peter and Werner Zdouc. *The Law and Policy of the World Trade Organization* (Cambridge University Press, 2017).

Vandenbussche, Hylke and Maurizio Zanardi. 'What Explains the Proliferation of AD Laws?,' *Economic Policy* Vol 23, No 53 (2008) 94–138.

Vermulst, Edwin and Daniel Ikenson. 'Zeroing under the WTO Anti-Dumping Agreement: Where Do We Stand?,' *Global Trade & Customs Journal* Vol 2, No 6 (2007) 231–242.

Vienna Convention on the Law of Treaties. U.N. Doc. A/Conf. 39/27 (23 May 1969) <www.un.org/law/ilc/texts/treatfra.htm>.

Viner, Jacob. 'The Prevalence of Dumping in International Trade: I,' *Journal of Political Economy* Vol 30, No 5 (1922a) 655–680.

Viner, Jacob. 'The Prevalence of Dumping in International Trade: II,' *Journal of Political Economy* Vol 30, No 6 (1922b) 796–826.

Viner, Jacob. 'Dumping as a Method of Competition in International Trade: I,' *The University Journal of Business* (1922c) 34–53.

Viner, Jacob. 'Dumping as a Method of Competition in International Trade: II,' in *The University Journal of Business* (University of Chicago Press, 1923).

Viner, Jacob. *Dumping: A Problem in International Trade* (University of Chicago Press, 1923a) 182–190.

Zanardi, Maurizio. 'Antidumping: A Problem of International Trade,' *European Journal of Political Economy* Vol 22, No 3 (2006) 591–617.

Part III
GATS, TRIPS, TBT, and SPS Agreements

11 Trade in Services

Learning Objectives		426
1. Introduction		426
1.1 Political Economy of GATS: The Uruguay Round of Negotiations		427
2. Objectives and Obligations of GATS		430
2.1 Scope, Definition, and Services Covered		431
2.2 Modes of Supply		433
2.3 The Relationship Between GATT and GATS		435
3. General Obligations and Disciplines		436
3.1 Most-Favoured Nation (MFN) Treatment Obligation		436
3.2 Transparency Obligations		436
3.3 Domestic Regulation		437
4. Specific Commitments		439
4.1 Market Access Under GATS		440
4.2 National Treatment Under GATS		443
4.2.1 Establishing Violation of NT Under GATS		444
4.2.2 Like Services or Service Suppliers		445
4.2.3 Treatment No Less Favourable		447
4.3 Market Access *Vis-à-vis* National Treatment		448
4.4 Additional Commitments		449
4.5 Withdrawal of Commitments		450
5. General Exceptions Under GATS		450
5.1 Article XIV: The Two-Tier Analysis		452
5.1.1 Article XIV: The Necessity Test		453
5.2 *Chapeau* of Article XIV		454
5.3 Economic Integration Exception (Article IV)		455
5.4 Derogation From MFN Obligations		455
6. Specific Rules for Telecommunications and Financial Services		455
6.1 Telecommunications		455
6.2 Financial Services		458
6.2.1 Prudential Carve-Out		459
6.2.2 Understanding on Commitments in Financial Services		459
7. Security Exceptions Under GATS		460
7.1 Article XIV *bis* of GATS		460
8. Summary		461

DOI: 10.4324/9780367028183-14

Learning Objectives

This chapter aims to help students understand:

1 The WTO laws on trade in services as administered under the GATS Agreement; political economy of GATS;
2 The objectives of GATS Agreement; scope, definition, and services covered; modes of supply; GATT *vis-à-vis* GATS;
3 Obligations under GATS; MFN treatment; transparency;
4 Specific commitments; market access under GATS; NT under GATS;
5 Market access *vis-à-vis* National Treatment; additional commitments; withdrawal of commitments;
6 General exceptions under GATS; Article XIV; the two-tier analysis; the necessity test; derogation from MFN obligation; and
7 Specific rules for telecommunications and financial services; security exceptions under GATS.

1. Introduction

One of the key covered WTO agreements to be negotiated during the Uruguay Round of negotiations was the General Agreement on Trade in Services (GATS). Since its entry into force in 1995, the GATS has come to occupy an increasingly important position in the multilateral service economy. Although trade in services was growing exponentially in the last quarter of the twentieth century,[1] it was not part of the GATT 1947. Trade in services include the movement of goods and people, communication, financial institutions, supply chain management and distribution, hospitality industry sector, insurance, construction, tourism, educational institutions, healthcare institutions, construction industry, and accounting, to name a few important activities, aspects, and players. Importantly, trade in services is intertwined with the movement of goods, capital, direct investment, and skilled labour. The services sector occupies the third position in the economy, following production of raw material and manufacturing. Trade in services forms part of almost all activities carried out in an economy. Services hold the global value chains together to ensure fluidity and to achieve their true purpose.

Technological advances, in both the information and telecommunication sector and the transport industry, in the second half of the twentieth century had expanded manifold the scope of services trade across national borders. By the turn of the twenty-first century, the services industry has come to be the largest sector of the economy in most developed and developing Member States of the WTO. The US, which used to be a powerhouse of manufacturing in the early twentieth century, has turned into a powerhouse of services. Increased automation and growing wages in the developed countries witnessed parts of their manufacturing industry move to developing/newly industrialised countries from the 1970s until the early 1990s. This phenomenon resulted in the developed countries losing their comparative advantage in the production of manufacturing goods globally.

Since the 1980s developing countries, particularly from Asia, have witnessed the highest growth rates for services exports. For instance, the services export from India is over one-third of all its exports. With the introduction of GATS, developing countries experienced a four-fold growth in the business services exports between 1995 and 2005. During this period, the average annual growth rate of business services exports in some of the BRICS countries was as follows – 15 percent for Brazil and China and 25 percent for India (Hoekman and Mattoo, 2009). Almost all economies – developed, developing, and least developed – increasingly rely on the services sector. The EU, the US, the UK, China, and Australia rank among the countries that rely heavily on the service sector. Currently, services in trade comprises over two-thirds of global GDP. IMF data suggests that service imports tripled between 1994 and 2004 (Hoekman and Mattoo, 2009). Services in trade attracts over three-quarters of foreign direct investment (FDI) in developed and developing countries. It creates most new jobs worldwide and also employs the most workers. In 2018, the EU was the world's largest exporter and importer of services, with extra-EU trade in services accounting for 29.7 percent of the total value of trade in goods and services (Eurostat, 2019).

As mentioned before, due to technological advances, it is now possible to accomplish service transaction without the need for the physical presence of the provider or the consumer of the service in the same place. Examples are banking services (both domestic and international) and higher educational programmes.[2] One other aspect that contributed to the expansion of the services industry was the regulatory reform carried out during the 1970s and 1980s which resulted in the liberalisation of markets in telecommunications and transportation (Trebilcock, Howse, and Eliason, 2013). Also, the splintering of services from functions integral to the production of goods, and the practice of outsourcing some of the functionalities to third parties, have created new markets for the services trade. There are also a number of services trades that are not actually recorded, as services trades are inherently more complex to record than merchandise trade. Hence, identifying the individual service components that constitute the full value of a product is a difficult task.[3] Especially, their intangible nature makes them elusive, for both the collection of statistical data and analysis. Merchandise trade is comparatively easier to measure when it crosses borders due to its physical nature, whereas the delivery of services trade is difficult to observe and gauge due to its intangible nature. This shortcoming means some of the services trade may go unnoticed and may not be contained in any data compiled by the WTO.

1.1 Political Economy of GATS: The Uruguay Round of Negotiations

The initiatives of the Contracting Parties under GATT to introduce services trade were isolated events, as they focused on specific issues, such as insurance and transport, within the services industry as opposed to the sector as a whole. With the exception of EC, very few international trade agreements touched upon trade in services prior to the launch of the Uruguay Round of negotiations. Efforts were made by the US in the Tokyo Round of negotiations to bring services within the GATT rules. This move was predictably opposed by developing countries because it was perceived as an attempt to introduce investment into the negotiations. One of the key motivating factors for the US to bring forth services into the GATT was its strength in the services sector, especially in the financial services and telecommunications, considered to be highly knowledge and technology-intensive (Trebilcock, Howse, and Eliason, 2013).

As available statistics were in some cases non-existent, limited or mixed up with trade in goods, no real progress could be made (Footer and George, 2005). The measures taken in the 1984 Session of the GATT Ministerial Council to include services on the trade agenda were fraught with division between developed and developing countries, with the developing countries being opposed to the idea. Eventually an agreement was reached by the GATT Contracting Parties to include services in the negotiations as part of the Ministerial Declaration of the Uruguay Round, adopted at Punta del Este (Ministerial Declaration, 1986) on the condition that any negotiations on trade in services will happen separately from trade in goods and be development oriented. The objective of the negotiations on services was

> To establish a multilateral framework of principles and rules for trade in services, including elaboration of possible disciplines for individual sectors, with a view to expansion of such trade under conditions of transparency and progressive liberalization and as a means of promoting economic growth of all trading partners and the development of developing countries. Such framework shall respect the policy objectives of national laws and regulations applying services and shall take into account the work of relevant international organizations.

Forming part of the Uruguay Round of negotiations relating to services sector were the results of a key study of the OECD made in the early part of the 1980s. Also of relevance to the negotiations was the groundwork carried out by the United Nations Conference on Trade and Development (UNCTAD) in the services sector with focus on developing countries; growth and development of the domestic economy; services in the international trade context, *etc.* (UNCTAD, 1985). The UNCTAD report contained detailed recommendations to its Trade and Development Board concerning any multilateral cooperation framework for development of trade in services.

The inclusion of services in the Uruguay Round of negotiations was down to the proposals of a large number of service companies (mostly from the US) to get trade in services included in the agenda for discussion and negotiation (Hoekman and Kostecki, 2009).[4] In 1980, the total global trade in services had increased steeply from US$358 billion to US$931 billion in 1992 (Hoekman, 1995). The US had categorised the basic principles governing services trade under four heads, *viz.*, national treatment (NT); establishment; non-discrimination; and transparency.[5] The developed countries strongly advocated for the creation of rules to regulate the growing services trade, which included financial services, telecommunications, tourism, travel, and professional services, to name a few (Sutherland, 2000).

In the eyes of the developed countries, the trading system was in dire need of an overhaul to reflect the changes brought about by technological advances made in the areas of telecommunications, broadcasting, financial services industry, transport, and most importantly the emergence of the internet in the last quarter of the twentieth century. It was felt that the then existing arrangements for services was not fit for purpose for managing some of the more dynamic and innovative segments of the economy, and that national governments lacked both entrepreneurial spirit and financial resources to realise the growth potential of services in trade (WTO, 2005). During the same period, regulatory regimes governing legal services, accounting, and other professions were being liberalised and were capable of further expansion. The combination of the previous two factors helped reduce the 'proximity burden' (experienced in traditional supply chains) and strengthened the case for a multilateral agreement on trade in services. Also, the fact that OECD countries and the developing countries in Asia, South America, and parts of sub-Saharan Africa were getting wealthier contributed to the growth in services trade in areas such as telecommunication, tourism, banking, *etc.*

The level of lobbying activity by the private sector in support of an ambitious outcome was visible throughout the negotiations. Many developing countries led by the G10 countries (Argentina, Brazil, Cuba, Egypt, India, Nicaragua, Nigeria, Peru, Tanzania, and Yugoslavia) were opposed to launching any negotiations to include services trade, trade-related aspects of intellectual property, and trade-related investment measures during the Uruguay Round of negotiations. The developing countries resisted any negotiations on services trade and were prepared to take up only negotiations that kept trade in services separate from the GATT framework (Fuchs, 2008). This stance of the developing countries prevented any cross-linkage between negotiations on issues relating to GATT and services trade.

The US and Canada argued in favour of liberalisation of trade in services in general, while continuing to be protectionist in certain services sector such as maritime and air transport (Footer and George, 2005). Due to services trade's potential to boost economic growth, the reduction or elimination of barriers to services trade became a priority for a number of developed countries in the Uruguay Round of negotiations. Liberalisation of services trade includes the reduction of regulatory barriers to market access and discriminatory NT practices across the various modes of supply/delivery of services. Unlike deregulation, liberalisation of services trade seeks to ensure that existing regulations do not discriminate against foreign participation in the market without seeking to reduce the amount of state regulation in a sector.

The service industry representatives were reluctant to go with the idea of unconditional MFN treatment, as the level of market openness varied significantly across countries. The key reason for the resistance was that such a policy would allow countries with restrictive policies to 'free ride' in the market of more open countries, while maintaining their *status quo* (Sauvé, 1995). The developing countries generally favoured a universal coverage for the application of MFN treatment to trade in services, whereas the preference of Latin American and Caribbean nations was more a sectoral approach (Reyna, 1993). Being concerned about the likely dominance of transnational corporations in the services sectors, the developing countries emphasised the need for controls within the framework of any inward FDI and restrictive business practices. Based on the previous arguments, the developing countries opposed a general NT obligation, which position was well supported by the EC (Footer and George, 2005).

In September 1989, the parties to the negotiation agreed to establish a separate agreement on services that would be negotiated without any cross-linkages or ramifications on the negotiations on goods (Reyna, 1993). When the Dunkel Draft was drawn up in 1991,[6] a framework agreement on GATS was nowhere near in sight, as the negotiations on services trade had come to a grinding halt due to difficulties in market access and agricultural subsidies and issues relating to application of MFN exemptions to the services sector (Reyna, 1993). When concluded, the General Agreement on Trade in Services was groundbreaking, as it took a gradualist approach to the WTO Member States making their commitments with regards to specific sectors of trade (Sutherland, 2000). The Uruguay Round of negotiations, which culminated in the founding of the WTO, expanded the scope of multilateral trade and regulated, amongst others, trade in services; trade-related aspects of IP; and trade in agricultural products.

GATS has facilitated the Member States to reform areas such as financial services, telecommunications, tourism, travel, and professional services on a negotiated basis taking into account their national interests. Although the opinion on the contribution of GATS to the actual liberalisation of trade is divided, it remains a fact that GATS indeed contributed to the consolidation of the liberalisation achieved prior to the advent of the WTO (Hoekman, 1995).[7] Since the implementation of the GATS Agreement, a number of developing countries have demonstrated that they do possess some comparative advantage in services trade and have been offering a broad range of services efficiently. Upon completion of the specific sectoral negotiations on telecommunications and financial services in 1998, many developing country Member States were using the GATS framework as a decisive instrument to integrate into the global economy and to reap the benefits of modern communications and access to capital (Sutherland, 2000). It should be mentioned here that the GATS Agreement remains an incomplete contract, as the obligations identified were drafted in an ambiguous manner, and the scope of the Agreement remains unclear (Delimatsis, 2010), although it is over 25 years since its entry into force.

2. Objectives and Obligations of GATS

As identified in the Preamble, the primary objective of the GATS Agreement is to contribute to trade expansion

> under conditions of transparency and progressive liberalization and as a means of promoting the economic growth of all trading partners and the development of developing countries.

As opposed to trade expansion, the Preamble identifies GATS as an instrument to promote growth and development with specific reference to "growth of all trading partners and the development of developing countries". The framework of GATS is in many ways inspired by the GATT, and a number of terms and concepts are replicated from the GATT. The inherent nature of trade in services makes the negotiation of liberalisation a complex process. The GATS Agreement seeks (i) to bring about increased transparency and predictability of relevant rules and regulations relating to trade in services and (ii) to promote progressive liberalisation through successive rounds of negotiations. The promotion of liberalisation facilitates market access and the extension of national treatment to foreign service and service providers across a range of sectors. The Preamble recognises the Member States' right to regulate and introduce such domestic rules to meet national policy objectives, as well as to consider the needs of developing countries.

In *China – Publication and Audiovisual Products*, the Appellate Body, while confirming the Panel's interpretation of the term 'progressive liberalisation' occurring in the preamble, ruled that the term indeed does not lend support to an interpretation that would constrain the scope and coverage of specific commitments that have already been undertaken by Member States and observed:

> The principle of progressive liberalization is reflected in the structure of the GATS, which contemplates that WTO Members undertake specific commitments through successive rounds of multilateral negotiations with a view to liberalizing their services markets incrementally, rather than immediately and completely at the time of the acceptance of the GATS. The scheduling of specific commitments by service sectors and modes of supply represents another manifestation of progressive liberalization. In making specific commitments, Members are not required to liberalize fully the chosen sector, but may limit the coverage to particular subsectors and modes of supply and maintain limitations, conditions, or qualifications on market access and national treatment, provided that they are inscribed in their Schedules. We do not consider, however, that the principle of progressive liberalization lends support to an interpretation that would constrain the scope and coverage of specific commitments that have already been undertaken by Members and by which they are bound.[8]

The key disciplines of the GATS Agreement fall under two categories, *viz.*, the 'general obligations and disciplines' and 'specific commitments'. The general obligations (principles and rules) which apply to all Member States across the board to measures affecting trade in services contain a general most-favoured nation (MFN) obligation, and also a 'good trade governance' obligation which includes basic rules on domestic regulations (transparency). The 'specific commitments' on NT and market access apply to the service activities that are listed in a Member State's schedule. The second aspect reflects the 'positive list approach' to determining the coverage of GATS of a Member State's commitment. The commitments of Member States to the GATS are varied, with developed Member States scheduling 45 percent of their services sector, and in contrast developing countries scheduling 12 percent.

Pursuant to Article XIX, the Member States, in keeping with the objectives of the Agreement, are required to enter into negotiations to achieve liberalisation in services trade, with a view to providing effective market access. Article XX further notes that Member States are to bind the results of such negotiations in their schedule of commitments. As per the dictates of Article II, the schedule of commitments so made is to be implemented on an MFN basis.

2.1 Scope, Definition, and Services Covered

The scope of the GATS Agreement is set out in Article I:1, which stipulates that the Agreement applies to 'measures' taken by Member States affecting trade in services.[9] The GATS Agreement does not define what constitutes a 'service', and Article I:3(b) of GATS only states what the term 'services' includes:

> any service in any sector except services supplied in the exercise of governmental authority.

Article I:2 provides that the measures taken by Member States can be at the central, regional, or local government levels, and will include such non-governmental bodies in the exercise of delegated powers vested on them by central, regional, or local governments or authorities. Article I:2 defines "trade in services" as "the supply of a service" in any one of the four listed "modes of supply" as follows:

> For the purpose of this Agreement, trade in services is defined as the supply of a service:
>
> (a) from the territory of one Member into the territory of any other Member;
> (b) in the territory of one Member to the service consumer of any other Member;
> (c) by a service supplier of one Member, through commercial presence in the territory of any other Member;
> (d) by a service supplier of one Member, through presence of natural persons of a Member in the territory of any other Member.[10]

Article XXVIII defines "measure" to mean "any measure by a Member, whether in the form of a law, regulation, rule, procedure, decision, administrative action, or any other form". As per Article XXVIII(b) of GATS, the "supply of services" includes the production, distribution, marketing, sale, and delivery of a service. All services are covered under the GATS Agreement, with the exception of "services supplied in the exercise of governmental authority" and falling under Article I:3(b),[11] and air traffic pursuant to paragraph 2 of the Annex on Air Transport Services.

Article I:3(c) of the GATS Agreement defines "services supplied in the exercise of governmental authority" as "any service which is supplied neither on a commercial basis, nor in competition with one or more service suppliers". It is to be borne in mind that "services supplied in the course of governmental authority" varies from Member State to Member State, with some Member States including primary health care, transport, education, and mail delivery. With the change in the traditional approach to trade with technical advances, and privatisation, some of the services traditionally associated with a government may fall within the ambit of GATS.

The Appellate Body in *US – Gambling*, while examining and interpreting the specific commitments made by the US in its GATS schedule, noted that a Member State may schedule commitments in respect of any service, and that a particular service cannot fall within two different sectors or subsectors of a Member's Schedule, and observed as follows:

> To us, the structure of GATS necessarily implies two things. First, because the GATS covers all services except those supplied in the exercise of governmental authority, it follows that a Member may schedule a specific commitment in respect of any service. Secondly, because a Member's obligations regarding a particular service depend on the specific commitments that it has made with respect to the sector or subsector within which the service falls, a specific service cannot fall within two different sectors or subsectors. In other words, the sectors and subsectors in a Member's Schedule must be mutually exclusive.[12,13]

The GATS Agreement does not define the term 'services'. The term 'trade in services', although not defined directly, is defined in Article I:2 indirectly with reference to the four modes through which supply of services may occur. One of the definitions proposed during the Uruguay Negotiations reads as follows:

> International trade in services is any service or labour activity across national borders to provide satisfaction to the needs of the recipient or consumer other than the satisfaction provided by physical goods (although they might be incorporated in physical goods), or to furnish an input for a producer of goods and/or services other than physical inputs (although the former might be incorporated in the latter).
>
> (WTO, 1988)

Yet, the definition was only one of the several definitions proposed to gain an understanding of what was being mooted during the negotiations, and hence not conclusive. GATS contains definitions of operative words and phrases such as 'measure', 'person', 'supply of a service', 'sector', *etc.* in Article XXVIII. The more popular definitions of trade in services, which has no legal bearing, is "everything you cannot drop on your foot".[14]

The UN Central Product Classification (CPC) plays an important role in categorisation of services into specific groups and subgroups and has been useful in the implementation of the GATS Agreement. The CPC is a coherent and consistent classification structure for products (both goods and services) that is based on a set of internationally agreed concepts, definitions, principles, and classification rules and promulgated by the UN Statistics Division (UNSD). The CPC coding system is hierarchical and purely decimal, and the classification consists of sections (identified by the first digit), divisions (identified by the first and second digits), groups (identified by the first three digits), classes (identified by the first four digits) and subclasses (identified by all five digits, taken together). Following from that, the codes for the sections range from 0 through 9, and each section may be divided into nine divisions. It is to be noted that the code numbers in the CPC comprises five digits without a separation of any kind between digits and was chosen to avoid possible confusion with code numbers of another UN classification, *viz.*, the Standard International Trade Classification, which also has five-digit codes but uses a point to the right of the third digit.[15] The Appellate Body in *US – Gambling*, emphasising the importance of the classification system, observed:

> [t]he CPC is a detailed, multi-level classification of goods and services. The CPC is exhaustive (all goods and services are covered) and its categories are mutually exclusive (a given good or service may only be classified in one CPC category).[16]

2.2 Modes of Supply

When good are traded internationally, they cross national boundaries. It begins with the goods being part-manufactured in one Member State, moved to another Member State where the manufacturing process is completed through further inputs and export-packaged and ready to be transported to another Member State as a finished product. One will notice that the product in hand has multiple national origins. Trade in services works differently, where the service provider and consumer assume different positions for delivery and consumption. The Appellate Body in *US – Gambling* observed:

> the structure of GATS necessarily . . . covers all services except those supplied in the exercise of governmental authority, it follows that a Member may schedule a specific commitment in respect of any service.[17]

Notes 26–34 of the *Guidelines for Scheduling of Specific Commitments Under the GATS* from 2001 (WTO, 2001)[18] describes the four modes of supply, corresponding to the scope of Article I:2 of GATS. Article I:2 defines trade in services as the supply of a services with four possible modes of delivery, which are as follows:

> Mode 1: Referred to as "cross-border supply", where services are delivered from the territory of one Member State into the territory of any other Member State. Here the service supplier is not present in the territory of the receiver of the supply. The service provided is in some recorded form (written documentation, electronic/digital format, *etc.*) that can be transmitted across borders with the use of telecommunication facilities, internet, *etc*. This mode is the second most important mode of supply. Examples: banking or architectural services transmitted through telecommunication network; medical transcription, where the observations/comments of a medical professional in one Member State is sent as an "audio file" electronically to another Member State to be transcribed and returned as a word file electronically.
> Mode 2: Referred to as "consumption abroad" or "movement of consumers", where services are delivered in the territory of one Member State to the service consumer of any other Member State. This mode presupposes the movement of the consumer to the territory of the supplier – freedom for the Member State's residents to purchase services in the territory of another Member State. This mode is the best for services trade in tourism. Examples: travel, tourism, medical tourism, ship repair, higher education (students) *etc*. In medical tourism, the recipient of the medical treatment travels abroad to receive medical treatment (eye surgery, cosmetic surgery, *etc*.), and post-surgery convalesce in a tourist location. In ship repair, the vessel is "dry docked" to undergo services in a Member State where the ship owner is not a citizen/resident of. Student from Singapore moves to a UK university to enrol in a postgraduate programme of study.

Mode 3: Referred to as "commercial presence", where services are delivered by the service supplier of one Member State, through commercial presence in the territory of any other Member State. Under Art. XXVIII (Definitions), "commercial presence" is defined as follows: "(d) 'commercial presence' means any type of business or professional establishment, including through (i) the constitution, acquisition or maintenance of a juridical person, or (ii) the creation or maintenance of a branch or a representative office, within the territory of a Member for the purpose of supplying a service". One will notice that the definition of "commercial presence" is very broad. In this mode there is proximity between supplier and consumer. This mode is akin to an international agreement to liberalise investment, *i.e.*, opening up the sector to foreign investment. Examples: law firm from Member State "A" establishes an affiliate in Member State "B" offering it services, while also employing staff from Member State "B".

Mode 4: Referred to as "presence of natural person", where services are delivered by a service supplier of one Member State, through presence of natural persons of a Member State in the territory of any other Member State. This mode is least significant across all sectors. the Examples: an industry expert in fintech from Member State "A" delivers guest lectures in Member State "B"; a doctor from Member State "B" has temporarily located to Member State "C" to perform specialist services for a period of time.

Note: Member States may make commitments for specific modes only.

The question before the Panel in *Mexico – Telecoms* revolved around the issue of where the service supplier operated or was present. The two modes of supply, *viz.*, 'cross-border supply' and 'commercial presence', were part of the issue, and the Panel after examining Article I:2(a) of GATS found that the provision does not require that the service supplier must itself operate, or be present, in the territory into which the service is supplied, and noted that Article I:2(a) does not address the service supplier or specify where the service supplier operated from, or is present in some way.[19] The Panel also examined whether the international services supplied by a firm in Mexico fell within the definition of services supplied through commercial presence, and found that there was no territorial requirement contained in paragraph 2(c) other than a commercial presence in the territory of any other Member State:

> The definition of services supplied through a commercial presence makes explicit the location of the service supplier. It provides that a service supplier has a commercial presence – any type of business or professional establishment – in the territory of any other Member. The definition is silent with respect to any other territorial requirement (as in cross-border supply under mode 1) or nationality of the service consumer (as in consumption abroad under mode 2). Supply of a service through commercial presence would therefore not exclude a service that originates in the territory in which a commercial presence is established (such as Mexico), but is delivered into the territory of any other Member (such as the United States).[20]

The Panel in *EC – Bananas III*, defining the scope of the application of GATS, noted:

> The scope of the GATS encompasses any measure of a Member to the extent it affects the supply of a service regardless of whether such measure directly governs the supply of a service or whether it regulates other matters but nevertheless affects trade in services.[21]

The Appellate Body in *EC – Bananas III*, while upholding the finding of the Panel with regard to the question if the measure at issue affected trade in services within the meaning of Article I:1, observed as follows:

> In our view, the use of the term "affecting" reflects the intent of the drafters to give a broad reach to the GATS. The ordinary meaning of the word "affecting" implies a measure that has "an effect on", which indicates a broad scope of application. This interpretation is further reinforced by the conclusions of previous panels that the term "affecting" in the context of Article III of the GATT is wider in scope than such terms as "regulating" or "governing".[22]

The concept of 'measures by Members affecting trade in services' has a broad meaning, and likewise, the concept of 'trade in services' within the meaning of Article I:1 of GATS is wide-ranging. The nationality of the entities, *i.e.*, services supplier and consumer, within the four modes of supply, plays an important role. In this regard, Articles XXVIII(k)–(n) of GATS provide definitions of 'natural persons' and 'juridical persons' to help establish nationality. The issue of nationality gains in significance where services are provided by transnational corporations, operating through subsidiaries in different countries/Member States.[23]

2.3 The Relationship Between GATT and GATS

The GATT's origins lie in the Bretton Woods era from the 1940s, whereas the GATS Agreement's origins are in the Uruguay Round of negotiations in the late 1980s and early 1990s. Both instruments were negotiated and concluded in different eras, under different circumstances with entirely different purposes and objectives. They operate side-by-side in the WTO era, resulting in overlaps. In *Canada – Periodicals*, the Appellate explained that the two agreements are not mutually exclusive, and both could apply:

> [t]he ordinary meaning of the texts of GATT 1994 and GATS as well as Article II:2 of the WTO Agreement, taken together, indicate that obligations under GATT 1994 and GATS can co-exist and that one does not override the other.[24]

In *EC – Bananas III*, the Appellate Body, while confirming the finding of the Panel, observed as follows:

> Given the respective scope of application of the two agreements, they may or may not overlap, depending on the nature of the measures at issue. Certain measures could be found to fall exclusively within the scope of the GATT 1994, when they affect trade in goods as goods. Certain measures could be found to fall exclusively within the scope of the GATS, when they affect the supply of services as services. There is yet a third category of measures that could be found to fall within the scope of both the GATT 1994 and the GATS. These are measures that involve a service relating to a particular good or a service supplied in conjunction with a particular good. In all such cases in this third category, the measure in question could be scrutinized under both the GATT 1994 and the GATS. However, while the same measure could be scrutinized under both agreements, the specific aspects of that measure examined under each agreement could be different. Under the GATT 1994, the focus is on how the measure affects the goods involved. Under the GATS, the focus is on how the measure affects the supply of the service or the service suppliers involved. Whether a certain measure affecting the supply of

a service related to a particular good is scrutinized under the GATT 1994 or the GATS, or both, is a matter that can only be determined on a case-by-case basis.[25]

3. General Obligations and Disciplines

The core obligations of GATS contained in Part II of the Agreement are (i) MFN treatment accorded to all Member States – Article II (similar to GATT), and (ii) transparency of laws regulating services – Article III. GATS also requires Member States to ensure that all measures of general application affecting trade in services are administered reasonably, objectively, and in an impartial manner – Article VI (similar to GATT). The exceptions to various obligations, including general and more specific ones, contained in GATS are discussed in section 7 of this chapter.

3.1 Most-Favoured Nation (MFN) Treatment Obligation

Article II of GATS contains one of the core obligations in GATS, requiring that MFN treatment be accorded to all Member States. Article II, although similar in principle to Article I of GATT (provision on non-discrimination), differs slightly in its wordings, and reads as follows:

> With respect to any measure covered by this Agreement, each Member shall accord immediately and unconditionally to services and service suppliers of any other Member treatment no less favourable than that it accords to like services and service suppliers of any other country.

As Article II of GATS and Article I of GATT are not identical in their wordings, their interpretations are not identical. The obligations contained in Article II of GATS is more akin to the obligations found in Article III:4 of GATT, which is captured in its use of the phrase 'treatment no less favourable'. The operation of Article II MFN clause is wide, in that it applies to any measure by Member States in relation to trade in services occurring in any sector implemented through any of the four modes of supply. The MFN treatment obligation is subject to exceptions, exemptions, and limitations identified elsewhere in different GATS Articles.

See chapter 4 for a detailed discussion of MFN obligation under the GATS Agreement.

3.2 Transparency Obligations

The transparency obligations contained in the Article III GATS, in principle, replicates Article X GATT 1994. Transparency plays an important role in the objective and purpose of GATS, as identified in the Preamble, which states:

> to establish a multilateral framework of principles and rules for trade in services with a view to the expansion of such trade under conditions of transparency and progressive liberalization.

Article III of the GATS obligates the Member States to maintain transparency of laws regulating services. The transparency obligation requires that Member States publish all relevant measures with regards to general application that affect the implementation of the GATS

Agreement. Exchange of information regarding market access, and about relevant domestic rules and regulations (transparency) with foreign services providers, increases predictability and legal certainty and thereby facilitates trade in services. Transparency has even been identified as the "real jewel in the crown" of the WTO – as opposed to the dispute settlement system (Mavroidis and Wolfe, 2015). Article III:1 of GATS reads as follows:

> [e]ach Member shall publish promptly and, except in emergency situations, at the latest by the time of their entry into force, all relevant measures of general application which pertain to or affect the operation of this Agreement. International agreements pertaining to or affecting trade in services to which a Member is a signatory shall also be published.

Article III:3 requires that Member States promptly notify (at least annually) the Council for Trade in Services of the introduction of any new, or any changes to existing, national laws, regulations, or administrative guidelines, which "significantly affect trade in services covered by its specific commitments" under the GATS Agreement. Article III:4 imposes a further obligation on the Member States to respond promptly to requests for specific information on measures of general application, and the relevant part of the Article reads as follows:

> Each Member shall respond promptly to all requests by any other Member for specific information on any of its measures of general application or international agreements within the meaning of paragraph 1. Each Member shall also establish one or more enquiry points to provide specific information to other Members, upon request, on all such matters as well as those subject to the notification requirement in paragraph 3.

Article III *bis* is an exemption to the obligation of transparency contained in Article III, and provides that Member States will not be compelled to disclose confidential information, if such disclosure would impede law enforcement, be contrary to public interest, or prejudice legitimate commercial interests of particular public or private enterprises.[26]

3.3 Domestic Regulation

Article VI of GATS deals with obligations of the Member States in the administration of domestic regulation in relation to services trade, *i.e.*, relationship between national regulators and services providers. Domestic regulation is not defined anywhere in the GATS Agreement.

Most Member States' understanding of the term 'domestic regulation' in the context of Article VI is that only certain types of measures are covered by the mandate in Article VI:4 to develop necessary disciplines on domestic regulation, as opposed to the literal meaning of the term which implies that all regulation introduced by a Member State affecting services trade will be covered by the term (Footer and George, 2005).

Article VI:1 contains the general obligation that Member States are to administer all measures of general application affecting trade in services in a reasonable, objective, and impartial manner. The objective is to ensure the non-arbitrary application and administration of domestic regulation by Member States, which contributes to the consistency and predictability of administrative decisions, which are important for foreign services providers (Delimatsis, 2010). Although limited in scope, Article VI:1 of the GATS is similar to Article X:3(a) of the GATT, which has a wider impact.[27] While transparency obligations are contained in paragraphs 1, 2, 3, and 6, substantive obligations are embodied in paragraphs 4 and 5.

Article VI:4 requires the Council for Trade in Services to develop any necessary disciplines to ensure that measures relating to "qualification requirements and procedures, technical standards and licensing requirements do not constitute unnecessary barriers to trade in services", and states:

> Such disciplines shall aim to ensure that such requirements are, *inter alia*:
>
> (a) based on objective and transparent criteria, such as competence and the ability to supply the service;
> (b) not more burdensome than necessary to ensure the quality of the service;
> (c) in the case of licensing procedures, not in themselves a restriction on the supply of the service.

The Working Party on Professional Services (WPPS) – which was established giving priority to professional services – in its efforts to define the scope of Article VI:4, has presented non-binding guidance notes to distinguish between the various categories and subcategories covered by the Article (WTO, 1996b). The WPPS also produced similar non-binding guidance notes for the accountancy sector (WTO, 1997). The WPPS also developed disciplines on domestic regulation in the accountancy sector in December 1998 (WTO, 1998b). The Working Party on Domestic Regulation (WPDR), which was established by the Council for Trade in Services (CTS), assumed the work of WPPS. The WPPS is charged with the development of meaningful and coherent disciplines on domestic regulation, which would be horizontally applicable (*i.e.*, across services sectors).[28]

The provisions of Article VI seek to restore the balance between the three prongs leading to effective market access – *i.e.*, GATS Articles XVI, XVII, and VI – and establish regulatory disciplines for measures relating to qualification requirement procedures (QRP), licensing requirements and procedures (LRP), and technical standards (TS) (Delimatsis, 2010). During the Uruguay Round, the drafters of GATS failed to agree on the content of an instrument that would allow the minimization of the negative impact on trade of regulatory conduct (Delimatsis, 2010). At the end of the Uruguay Round, negotiators were not successful in concluding the necessary legal framework in four areas of rule-making, *i.e.*, domestic regulation, emergency safeguards, government procurement, and subsidies.

While being developed, the disciplines have the potential to restrict the ability to adopt domestic regulations in the particular area of services. Article VI:4 subparagraph (b) requires that the covered measures not be "more burdensome than necessary to ensure the quality of the service", imposing a high threshold of standard on all domestic services regulation related to the covered measures. Pursuant to Article VI:4, the GATS Agreement seeks to facilitate the establishment of equilibrium between multilateral interest in progressive liberalisation of trade in services and each Member's interest in preserving its regulatory autonomy (Delimatsis, 2010).

While progress on the negotiations on domestic regulation disciples in paragraph 4 have not been positive,[29] one major area where disciplines have been developed following Article VI:4 is accountancy. The following requirement has been established through a Decision of the CTS:

> Members shall ensure that measures not subject to scheduling under Articles XVI or XVII of the GATS, relating to licensing requirements and procedures, technical

standards and qualification requirements and procedures are not prepared, adopted or applied with a view to or with the effect of creating unnecessary barriers to trade in accountancy services. For this purpose, Members shall ensure that such measures are not more trade-restrictive than necessary to fulfil a legitimate objective. Legitimate objectives are, *inter alia*, the protection of consumers (which includes all users of accounting services and the public generally), the quality of the service, professional competence, and the integrity of the profession.

(WTO, 1998c)

The aforementioned decision adopted by the CTS was proposed by the Working Party on Professional Services. By defining which measures are 'necessary', the decision explains that covered measures must not be "more trade restrictive than necessary to fulfil a legitimate objective". Under Articles XIV GATS and XX GATT 1994, the 'necessity requirement' is considered being part of an exception, whereas in the context of Article VI:5 GATS,[30] it is part of an obligation (WTO, 2011). It has been argued that case law concerning the latter type of necessity test is more relevant for the interpretation of the necessity requirement in Article VI:5 GATS (Natens, 2016). The Panel in *Mexico – Telecoms*, summarising the Appellate Body's finding in *Korea – Various Measures on Beef*, observed that in a GATS context:

[T]he term "necessary" can refer to a range of degrees of necessity, depending on the context, and the object and purpose of the provision in which it is used. At one end of this continuum, "necessary" can be understood to mean "indispensable" to achieving a policy goal; at the other end, "necessary" can be taken to mean simply "making a contribution to" a policy goal.[31]

Article VI:5 establishes a standard which is not as stringent as the standard set out in Article VI:4, applying only where commitments have been made and only where the measure "could not reasonably have been expected of that Member at the time the specific commitments in those sectors were made". Pending the creation of new disciplines under paragraph 4, Article VI:5(a) of GATS obligates Member States to refrain from applying licensing and qualification requirements and technical standards that (i) are not based on objective and transparent criteria, such as competence and the ability to supply the service, and (ii) are more burdensome than necessary to ensure the quality of the service. The obligations contained in Article VI:5 only apply to sectors in which specific commitments have been scheduled.

4. Specific Commitments

Specific commitments made by Member States are covered in Part III of the GATS Agreement and fall under three categories, *viz.*, market access, NT, and additional commitment. The extent of specific commitments is a matter of choice for a Member State. GATS Agreement encourages Member States to make specific commitments with respect to market access and NT, *i.e.*, to liberalise their trade in services and guarantee the type of treatment to accord. This approach is keeping with the objective of GATS Agreement, which seeks to establish legally binding commitments from Member States to progressively liberalise services trade. Once a binding commitment is made, Member States are required to abide by them. The GATS Agreement and the GATT differ in their approaches with regards to both market access and NT obligation.

Member States can make their specific commitments, either horizontally – across all services sectors – or specific only to particular sectors. Horizontal commitments are contained in Part I of the commitments schedule, and sector-specific commitments are contained in Part II of the commitments schedule. The Schedule of each Member State is to encompass the details of the commitments *vis-à-vis* the modes of supply of services for market access, NT together with any additional commitments.

4.1 Market Access Under GATS

The relevant provision dealing with market access is Article XVI of GATS. Under GATT, market access is permitted for all goods, whereas under GATS, market access to services does not apply unconditionally but is restricted to those sectors where Member States have made specific commitments in the services schedule and subject to terms, limitations, and conditions set out therein. GATS approach to market access is referred to as the 'bottom-up' approach, which recognises a Member State's right to choose the service sectors that it wishes to open to foreign service providers and exclude by omission.[32] Article XVI:1 of GATS requires Member States to accord services and service suppliers of other Member States treatment "no less favourable than that provided for under the terms, limitations and conditions agreed and specified in its Schedule". The obligation under Article XVI:1 applies only to sectors where the Member States have made commitments and is subject to any scheduled limitations. Footnote 8 to Article XVI:1 extends the scope of Article XVI, by stating that movement of cross-border capital, which is both inward and outward, must be allowed for commitments where it is an essential part of the service (Delimatsis and Molinuevo, 2008). Also, in situations where capital is transferred into its territory (under Mode 3), a Member State must grant market access in the sense of Article XVI (Natens, 2016).

The Appellate Body in *US – Gambling* clarified the function of Article XVI of the GATS as follows:

> Article XVI of the GATS sets out specific obligations for Members that apply insofar as a Member has undertaken "specific market access commitments" in its Schedule. The first paragraph of Article XVI obliges Members to accord services and service suppliers of other Members "no less favourable treatment than that provided for under the terms, limitations and conditions agreed and specified in its Schedule." The second paragraph of Article XVI defines, in six sub-paragraphs, measures that a Member, having undertaken a specific commitment, is not to adopt or maintain, "unless otherwise specified in its Schedule". The first four sub-paragraphs concern quantitative limitations on market access; the fifth sub-paragraph covers measures that restrict or require specific types of legal entity or joint venture through which a service supplier may supply a service; and the sixth sub-paragraph identifies limitations on the participation of foreign capital.[33]

In *US – Gambling*, the Panel found that Article XVI:1 did not contain restrictions on market access beyond those listed in Article XV1:2, and observed:

> The ordinary meaning of the words, the context of Article XVI, as well as the object and purpose of the GATS confirm that the restrictions on market access that are covered by Article XVI are only those listed in paragraph 2 of this Article.[34]

Article XVI:2 of GATS requires that Member States refrain from maintaining or adopting measures which fall into any of the six categories of restrictions mentioned therein:

a Limitations on number of service suppliers;
b Limitations on total value of service transactions or assets;
c Limitations on total number of service operations, or on the total quantity of service output;
d Limitations on the total number of natural persons that may be employed in a particular service sector by a service supplier (numerical quotas);
e Measures that restrict or require specific types of legal entity or joint venture through which services may be supplied; and
f Limitations on the participation of foreign capital or investment.

Referred to as the 'positive list approach', each Member State is required to communicate their schedule of market access commitments, identifying both the sector and the extent to which market access is granted. This communication is to include the extent to which such commitments are made, including "terms, limitations and conditions" that are likely to vary the market access. With the exception of Article XVI:2(e), the measures that are covered by Article XVI are roughly the equivalent to quantitative restrictions in the GATT (Footer and George, 2005). In *China – Electronic Payment Services*, the Panel noted that, while the market access obligation under Article XVI:2 of the GATS "applies to six carefully defined categories of measures of a mainly quantitative nature", the scope of the national treatment obligation under Article XVII extends generally to "all measures affecting the supply of services".[35] The types of measures that limit market access can be brought under three categories,[36] which are (i) measures mentioned in paragraphs (a) to (d) of Article XVI:2 – which identify limitations in the form of quantitative restrictions; (ii) paragraph (e) of Article XVI:2 – which contains limitations on the form of establishment; and (iii) paragraph (f) of Article XVI:2 – which regulates the participation of foreign capital or investment.

The measure at issue in the *US – Gambling* case was the restrictions imposed on the ability of gambling companies to provide 'remote' gambling and betting services, besides also prohibiting such services. In short, it related to *cross-border supply of gambling and betting services*. Earlier, Antigua had requested consultations with the US as regards measures applied by the US,[37] which in Antigua's view affected the cross-border supply of gambling and betting services. Antigua argued that the cumulative effect of the measures introduced by the US through various federal laws barred the cross-border supply of gambling and betting services from another WTO Member State to the US. The US, for its part, argued that the measures introduced, *i.e.*, restrictions on internet gambling, were essential to control organised crime; contain money laundering; and prevent underage gambling and were necessary to protect public morals and to maintain public order within the meaning of GATS Article XIV(a). The Panel ruled that although the measures at issue – the Wire Act, the Travel Act, and the Illegal Gambling Business Act (IGBA) – were designed to protect public morals and to maintain public order, the US failed to demonstrate that the measures introduced were necessary to achieve the goals and that the US was not able to justify that the federal Acts in question were necessary within the meaning of GATS Article XIV(a).[38] The Panel further held that the measures were not justified under the *Chapeau* of Article XIV of the GATS Agreement.

The US appealed the ruling of the Panel, and Antigua cross-appealed. While upholding the Panel's findings that the concerns of the US (which the Wire Act, the Travel Act, and IGBA sought to address) fell within the scope of public morals and public order, the Appellate

Body reversed the Panel's finding that due to the US's refusal to enter into consultations with Antigua, it was precluded from justifying the measures as necessary to protect public morals or to maintain public order. The Appellate Body ruled that for reasons of judicial economy, it was not necessary to determine if the Wire Act, the Travel Act, and the IGBA were measures justified under GATS Article XJV(c); and that the US had demonstrated that the Wire Act, the Travel Act, and the IGBA were necessary to protect public morals and/or maintain public order following from Article XVI(a), but failed to demonstrate that the prohibitions embodied in those measures are applied non-discriminatorily to both foreign and domestic service suppliers of remote betting services, and, as a result, the measures under challenge failed to satisfy the requirements of the *Chapeau* of Article XIV of the GATS Agreement.[39]

The Appellate Body in *US – Gambling* found violations of both Article XVI:2(a) and XVI:2(c) of GATS by the US. As regards XVI:2(a), the Appellate Body's finding was based on the premise that the US measures constituted a limitation on the number of service suppliers through a ban on certain means of delivery that acted as a numerical quota of zero. Similarly, as regards XVI:2(c), the Appellate Body finding was based on the view that the measures introduced by the US had the effect of imposing limitations on the number of service operations, or output, through a ban on certain means of delivery that acts as a zero quota. Interpreting Article XIV:2 of GATS, the Appellate Body in *US – Gambling* observed that the text of Article XVI:2 suggests that a complaining party is required to make its *prima facie* case by first claiming that the responding Member State has undertaken market access commitments in its GATS Schedule; and, second, identify with supporting evidence how the challenged laws constitute impermissible 'limitations' falling within one of the six subparagraphs of Article XVI:2.[40]

One of the areas where difficulty may be encountered is the interpretation of specific terms, as there remain ambiguities in Article XVI:2(a). For example, "numerical quotas" occurring in Article XVI:2(a), and "designated numerical units in the form of quotas" occurring in Article XVI:2(c). The Appellate Body in *US – Gambling* found that "certain ambiguities about the meaning of the provision" in Article XVI:2(a) remain, and opined that it was an appropriate case in which "to have recourse to supplementary means of interpretation".[41] The Appellate Body observed that the use of the words 'number' of suppliers and 'numerical' quotas in this provision suggests a focus on 'quantitative limitations'.[42]

Earlier in the case, the US had argued that the two provisions, *i.e.*, XVI:2(a) and XVI:2(c), covered only measures that actually specify a numeric quantity of service suppliers, or service operations or output, and as a result did not cover the measure at issue. Both the Panel[43] and the Appellate Body rejected this argument.[44] Since the dictionary meaning of the word 'form' was broad, the Appellate Body reasoned that the meaning of the phrase 'in the form of' had to be deduced by reading it together with the four types of limitation which it described.[45] The phrase 'in the form of', read together with the words 'numerical quota', suggested that Article XVI:2(a) could encompass a zero quota:

> The fact that the word "numerical" encompasses things which "have the characteristics of a number" suggests that limitations "in the form of a numerical quota" would encompass limitations which, even if not in themselves a number, have the characteristics of a number. Because zero is quantitative in nature, it can, in our view, be deemed to have the "characteristics of" a number – that is, to be "numerical".[46]

The Appellate Body in *US – Gambling* concluded, "limitations amounting to a zero quota are quantitative limitations and fall within the scope of Article XVI:2(a)".[47] Since the Panel's findings on limitations affecting part of a sector, or part of a mode of supply, were not appealed, the Appellate Body was able to quote and uphold the Panel's combined finding that

> [A] prohibition on one, several or all means of delivery cross-border] is a "limitation on the number of service suppliers in the form of numerical quotas" within the meaning of Article XVI:2(a) because it totally prevents the use by service suppliers of one, several or all means of delivery that are included in mode 1.[48]

4.2 National Treatment Under GATS

The relevant provisions dealing with NT is Article XVII of GATS and is placed in Part III of GATS Agreement. In contrast, the MFN treatment and transparency obligations are placed under Part II of GATS as general obligations. Unlike in GATT, where NT is an obligation, under GATS NT applies only where a specific commitment has been made by a Member State. Article XVII reads as follows:

1. In the sectors inscribed in its Schedule, and subject to any conditions and qualifications set out therein, each Member shall accord to services and service suppliers of any other Member, in respect of all measures affecting the supply of services, treatment no less favourable than that it accords to its own like services and service suppliers [footnote omitted].
2. A Member may meet the requirement of paragraph 1 by according to services and service suppliers of any other Member, either formally identical treatment or formally different treatment to that it accords to its own like services and service suppliers.
3. Formally identical or formally different treatment shall be considered to be less favourable if it modifies the conditions of competition in favour of services or service suppliers of the Member compared to like services or service suppliers of any other Member.

As noted by the Panel in *China – Electronic Payment Services*, the purpose of the NT obligation is to "ensure equal competitive opportunities for like services of other Members".[49] The Panel further observed that while the scope of the market access obligation under Article XVI:2 of the GATS "applies to six carefully defined categories of measures of a mainly quantitative nature", the scope of the NT obligation under Article XVII extends generally to "all measures affecting the supply of services".

NT obligations arising under Article XVII of the GATS Agreement are more complex than under Article III of the GATT, as they involve a fair comparison of the treatment of foreign services and service suppliers to domestic services and service suppliers. Although worded differently from its analogous provision in the GATT Agreement, Article XVII of GATS encapsulates some of the GATT Article III jurisprudence[50] by explicitly stating, (i) "either formally identical treatment or formally different treatment" is covered, and also (ii) its reference to modification of the "conditions of competition". As mentioned earlier, the GATT and the GATS are agreements negotiated and formalised during different eras, towards different ends, with the GATT having a jurisprudence stretching back to the 1950s. The NT obligation under GATS is wider in scope but yet limited in its application to that of the GATT. The NT obligation under the GATS Agreement addresses services and service suppliers, and more particularly to specified sectors and activities, as determined by each Member in its Schedule of specific commitments (Sauvé, 1995). In contrast the NT obligation under the GATT Agreement is concerned with measures affecting products/goods and applies to all imported goods, whether or not they are the subject of a scheduled tariff concession.

The NT obligation arising under Article XVII GATS at once creates both a goal and an obligation. On the one hand Article XVII sets a goal as each round of negotiation is meant to encourage Member States' to make further commitments to NT, and on the other hand it creates an obligation by requiring Member States to accord NT in respect of all measures affecting the supply of services in the sectors committed to in their schedules (Koul, 2018). The major difference between the GATS Agreement and the GATT Agreement is in modes of delivery. As discussed earlier, GATS envisages four modes of delivery of services, whereas the GATT has only one mode of delivery, *i.e.*, cross-border. The examination of a claim of violation of NT obligations arising under GATS to foreign services or services suppliers under different modes of services may become difficult. A Member State could encounter problems, when a comparison of the foreign service or service supplier with various competing domestic services and service suppliers is undertaken to determine whether they are 'like', as the four modes do not apply to services supplied by domestic entities (Lester, 2018).

The Scheduling Guidelines from 2001 provide helpful notes to assist in the preparation of national schedules of specific commitments. The objective of the Scheduling Guidelines is to explain how specific commitments are to be set out in schedules to achieve precision and clarity. The Scheduling Guidelines are not to be considered as legal interpretation of the provisions of the GATS Agreement.[51] As per the paragraph 13 of the 2001 Scheduling Guidelines,

> A Member grants full national treatment in a given sector and mode of supply when it accords in that sector and mode conditions of competition no less favourable to services and service suppliers of another Member than those accorded to its own like service and service suppliers. The national treatment standard does not require formally identical treatment of domestic and foreign suppliers; formally different measures can result in effective equality of treatment; conversely, formally identical measures can in some cases result in less favourable treatment of foreign suppliers (*de facto* discrimination). Thus, it should be borne in mind that limitations on national treatment cover both, *de facto* and *de jure* discriminations.
>
> (WTO, 2001)

Further, paragraph 13 presents examples of scheduling NT limitation to demonstrate the working of the GATS Agreement. The Scheduling Guidelines also contains a list of frequently occurring NT restrictions in Attachment 1. Paragraph 15 of the Guidelines state:

> There is no obligation in the GATS which requires a Member to take measures outside its territorial jurisdiction. It therefore follows that the national treatment obligation in Article XVII does not require a Member to extend such treatment to a service supplier located on the territory of another Member.
>
> (WTO, 2001)

4.2.1 Establishing Violation of NT Under GATS

The three-tier approach developed by the Panel in *EC – Bananas III*,[52] to establish any inconsistency of a particular measure with GATS Article XVII, was upheld and followed by the

Appellate Body.[53] This three-tier test developed by the Panel is akin to the tests applied for analysing GATT Article III and Article 2.1 of the TBT Agreement. In *EC – Bananas III*, it was argued before the Panel that the EC was in violation of its NT obligations under the GATS, as it was treating EC distributors of bananas more favourably than their foreign counterparts. The panel found that the EC's banana imports regime and the licensing procedures for the importation of bananas in were inconsistent with the GATT 1994. The Panel ruled:

> In order to establish a breach of the national treatment obligation of Article XVII, three elements need to be demonstrated: (i) the EC has undertaken a commitment in a relevant sector and mode of supply; (ii) the EC has adopted or applied a measure affecting the supply of services in that sector and/or mode of supply; and (iii) the measure accords service suppliers of any other Member treatment less favourable than that it accords to the EC's own like service suppliers.[54]

The Panel in *China – Publications and Audiovisual Products* ruled against restrictions imposed by China on the importation and distribution of publications, audiovisual home entertainment products, sound recordings, and films for release in cinemas. Further, the panel found that the measures introduced by China violated its commitments under its Protocol of Accession, the GATS Agreement, and the GATT Agreement. The Panel observed that China's inscriptions in the 'Audiovisual Services' sector of its GATS Schedule led to the conclusion that the entry on 'Sound recording distribution services' extended to the distribution of content through electronic means,[55] and that it was only reasonable to deduce that the coverage of the entries in China's Schedule under 'Audiovisual Services' should extend to the distribution in non-physical form of audiovisual products.[56] The Appellate Body upholding the panel's findings observed as follows:

> [T]he terms used in China's GATS Schedule ("sound recording" and "distribution") are sufficiently generic that what they apply to may change over time . . . We further note that interpreting the terms of GATS specific commitments based on the notion that the ordinary meaning to be attributed to those terms can only be the meaning that they had at the time the Schedule was concluded would mean that very similar or identically worded commitments could be given different meanings, content, and coverage depending on the date of their adoption or the date of a Member's accession to the treaty. Such interpretation would undermine the predictability, security, and clarity of GATS specific commitments, which are undertaken through successive rounds of negotiations, and which must be interpreted in accordance with customary rules of interpretation of public international law [footnotes omitted].[57]

4.2.2 Like Services or Service Suppliers

All non-discrimination obligations (including NT and MFN treatment) comprise two principal elements that are comparative in nature, *viz.*, 'less favourable treatment' and 'likeness' (Diebold, 2010). The first element identified will be discussed in the next section. The second element of 'likeness' is an important term found in various WTO documents and has been interpreted by the DSB repeatedly over the years. There is no definition of 'like services or service suppliers' in the GATS Agreement. In order to determine if the service suppliers are 'like', both the Appellate Body and the Panels have looked to their own 'likeness' jurisprudence developed in the context of GATT Article III. While the provisions in the GATT and the GATS are not entirely alike, the jurisprudence does serve as a guideline. GATT Article III:2, first sentence, deals with 'like products' – which is a narrow interpretation of 'likeness' and the second sentence deals with 'directly competitive or substitutable', which is a broad interpretation of 'likeness'. Unfortunately, jurisprudence on the issue whether 'likeness' should be construed narrowly as per GATT Article III:2, first sentence, or in a broad sense as per GATT Article III:2, second sentence, for the purposes of Article XVII of GATS does not exist.

The Appellate Body in *Japan – Alcoholic Beverages II*, using colourful language, explained how the accordion of 'likeness' stretches to apply the different provisions of the WTO Agreement, and observed as follows:

> The concept of "likeness" is a relative one that evokes the image of an accordion. The accordion of "likeness" stretches and squeezes in different places as different provisions of the WTO Agreement are applied. The width of the accordion in any one of those places must be determined by the particular provision in which the term "like" is encountered as well as by the context and the circumstances that prevail in any given case to which that provision may apply.[58]

The aforementioned approach of the Appellate Body postulates the view that 'likeness' depends on the purpose for which the products or the services are compared, which in turn depends on the purpose of the respective non-discrimination clause (Diebold, 2010). In *EC – Bananas III*, the Appellate Body reiterated the general understanding of Article XVII of GATS is the protection of equality of competition between foreign and like domestic products. Therefore, both the characteristics of services and service suppliers that reflect the 'competitive relationship between foreign and domestic services and service suppliers' is be taken into account when determining likeness (Krajewski and Engelke, 2008). The notion of 'like' as occurring in Article III:4 of the GATT and any corresponding case laws are to be considered while establishing likeness for the purposes of Article XVII GATS.

The Panel in *EC – Bananas III*, without going into a detailed discussion, came to the conclusion that foreign and domestic services and suppliers were 'like', observing as follows:

> [T]he nature and the characteristics of wholesale transactions as such, as well as of each of the different subordinated services mentioned in the headnote to section 6 of the CPC, are "like" when supplied in connection with wholesale services, irrespective of whether these services are supplied with respect to bananas of EC and traditional ACP origin, on the one hand, or with respect to bananas of third-country or non-traditional ACP origin, on the other. Indeed, it seems that each of the different service activities taken individually is virtually the same and can only be distinguished by referring to the origin of the bananas in respect of which the service activity is being performed.[59]

The Panel in *EC – Bananas III* further noted that "at least to the extent that entities provide these like services, they are like service suppliers".[60] Similarly in *Canada – Autos*, the Panel observed, "to the extent the service suppliers concerned supply the same services, they should be considered like for the purpose of the case".[61] The previous two observations from the two Panels take the position that service suppliers are 'like' if they supply 'like' services (Zdouc, 2004). The Panel in *China – Electronic Payment Services* noted that the analysis presented by the Panels in the *EC – Bananas III* and *Canada – Autos* cases on the automatic 'likeness of service suppliers', where they provide 'like services', is to be read only as a presumption, and that in the given circumstances of the case, the presumption did not hold.[62] The Panel in *China – Electronic Payment Services* did not accept automatic likeness of the service suppliers if the services are like, and thus distinguishes between the 'likeness of services' and that of 'service suppliers'. This position of the Panel, in terms of regulatory autonomy, creates a leeway for governments to distinguish between different service suppliers who supply a like service (Nicolaïdis and Trachtman, 2000; Natens, 2016).

4.2.3 Treatment No Less Favourable

The first comparative element 'less favourable treatment', as identified in the preceding section, requires a comparison between the treatments accorded to the objects at issue, *viz.*, foreign service provider and a 'like' domestic service provider. WTO jurisprudence has established that conditions of competition as a benchmark for the interpretation and application of 'less favourable treatment'. Pursuant to Article XVII:3 of GATS, which concerns the conditions of competition, states, "different treatment shall be considered to be less favourable if it modifies the conditions of competition". Hence, any measure introduced by the host country that in a way changes the competitive relationship to the detriment of the foreign service or service provider is treatment 'less favourable' and hence in violation of GATS Article XVII:3. On the question if the measure introduced 'modifies' conditions of competition, the Panel in *China – Publications and Audiovisual Products* observed as follows:

> Article XVII:3 . . . states that formally identical or different treatment is deemed less favourable "if it modifies the conditions of competition in favour of services or service suppliers of the Member compared to like services or service suppliers of any other Member". We deduce from this that, subject to all other Article XVII conditions being fulfilled, formally identical or different treatment of service suppliers of another Member constitutes a breach of Article XVII:1 if and only if such treatment modifies the conditions of competition to their detriment.[63]

As regards the 'no less favourable treatment' element of Article XVII, the Panel in *China – Publications and Audiovisual Products* observed as follows:

> This treatment is to be assessed in terms of the "conditions of competition" between like services and services suppliers, as specified in Article XVII:3 of the GATS:
> . . .
> In our view, a measure that prohibits foreign service suppliers from supplying a range of services that may, subject to satisfying certain conditions, be supplied by the like domestic supplier cannot constitute treatment "no less favourable", since it deprives the foreign service supplier of any opportunity to compete with like domestic suppliers. In terms of paragraph 3 of Article XVII, such treatment modifies conditions of competition in the most radical way, by eliminating all competition by the foreign service supplier with respect to the service at issue.[64]

The Panel in *China – Publications and Audiovisual Products*, having found that the measure at issue had the effect of prohibiting foreign service suppliers from wholesaling imported materials in China, while 'like' domestic suppliers were permitted to do so, which factor resulted in modifying the conditions of competition to the detriment of the foreign service supplier, held that such measures constituted 'less favourable' treatment as per Article XVII.[65]

The Appellate Body in *Argentina – Financial Services* set out its understanding of the terms 'treatment no less favourable' in Articles II:1 and XVII of the GATS, and in respect to Article XVII of the GATS observed as follows:

> Examining the text of these provisions, we note that the second and third paragraph of Article XVII elaborate on the meaning of a Member's obligation to grant "treatment no less favourable" pursuant to Article XVII:1. Specifically, Article XVII:2 recognizes that a Member may meet this requirement by according to services and service suppliers "either formally identical treatment or formally different treatment". Article XVII:3 stipulates that "[f]ormally identical or formally different treatment shall be considered to be less favourable if it modifies the conditions of competition in favour of services or service suppliers of the Member compared to like services or service suppliers of any other Member." In our view, while Article XVII:3 refers to the modification of conditions of competition in favour of domestic services or service suppliers, the legal standard set out in Article XVII:3 calls for an examination of whether a measure modifies the conditions of competition to the detriment of services or service suppliers of any other Member. Less favourable treatment of foreign services or service suppliers and more favourable treatment of like domestic services or service suppliers are flip-sides of the same coin.[66]

Commenting on footnote 10 to Article XVII:1, the Appellate Body in *Argentina – Financial Services*, observed as follows:

> Footnote 10 to Article XVII:1 provides further insight as to the meaning of the obligation to accord "treatment no less favourable" under Article XVII:1. Footnote 10 stipulates that specific commitments assumed under Article XVII:1 "shall not be construed to require any Member to compensate for any inherent competitive disadvantages which result from the foreign character of the relevant services or service suppliers". As its text indicates, the "inherent competitive disadvantages" referred to in footnote 10 result from the "foreign character" of the relevant services or service suppliers, rather than from the contested measure adopted by the importing Member. The "inherent competitive disadvantages" under footnote 10, therefore, must be distinguished from the measure's impact on the conditions of competition in the marketplace. By stating that a Member is not required to "compensate for" such "inherent competitive disadvantages", footnote 10 thus makes clear that the national treatment obligation under Article XVII:1 is not about the relative competitive advantages or disadvantages of the services and service suppliers that are not caused by the contested measure. Rather, the standard of "treatment no less favourable" must be based on the impact on the conditions of competition that results from the contested measure.[67]

4.3 *Market Access* Vis-à-vis *National Treatment*

The relationship between NT and market access under GATS is somewhat complicated, as a clear demarcation between the two does not exist. This particular aspect was highlighted during the Uruguay Round of negotiations by the Australian representative who pointed out, "the concepts of market access and national treatment seemed to merge" and "[i]f reservations were allowed on both market access and national treatment, drawing the line between the market access conditions and national treatment conditions might be difficult" (WTO, 1990). Out of the three options put forth by the negotiators, the "equality of competitive opportunities" approach supported by the EU, the US, Canada, and Switzerland was accepted.[68] This meant that NT obligation should go beyond *de jure* discrimination and guarantee equality of competitive opportunities (Wang, 2012). An analysis of violation of *de jure* discrimination is easily identifiable by comparing the treatment of domestic and foreign services or services providers, but establishing a *de facto* discrimination may not be possible.[69]

Commentators are also quick to point out that there exists a problem of overlap between Article XVI and XVII of GATS (Wang, 2012: Muller, 2017). Article XX:2 of GATS provides as follows:

> Measures inconsistent with both Articles XVI and XVII shall be inscribed in the column relating to Article XVI. In this case the inscription will be considered to provide a condition or qualification to Article XVII as well.

This means that any limitations/conditions inscribed in the market access column will also be deemed as limitations/conditions in the NT column. The reason for the overlap is that market access restrictions in the form of limitations or conditions on modes of supply are likely to violate NT for these modes as well. But the GATS Agreement does not clarify as to which measures, or what type of measures, entered in the market access column are also regarded as limitations in the NT column (Wang, 2012).

For the first time, Article XX:2 of the GATS was applied by the Panel in *China – Electronic Payment Services*, where the overlap problem between Articles XVI and XVII was well captured. China in its schedule had made its preferences as follows – for "other financial services" sector it inscribed "Unbound" in mode 1 in the market access column and registered "None" in mode 1 in the NT column. The Panel noted that an analysis of the scope of Articles XVI and XVII leads to an apparent ambiguity in China's inscriptions in mode 1 for market access and NT, and observed as follows:

> [T]he main issue is not an ambiguity over the scope of Article XVI and the scope of Article XVII. The main issue is rather a lack of clarity about the scope of the inscriptions "Unbound" and "None" when applied, in China's Schedule, to measures that conflict with both market access and national treatment obligations. In considering this more specific question, we observe that the basic scheduling rule in Article XX:1 . . . does not determine how a Member should inscribe a limitation in such a case. Instead, we note that a special scheduling rule in Article XX:2 aims to resolve this lack of clarity.[70]

4.4 Additional Commitments

Article XVIII of GATS deals with additional commitments and states that Member States "may negotiate commitments with respect to measures affecting trade in services not subject to scheduling under Articles XVI or XVII, including those regarding qualifications, standards or licensing matters", and that "[s]uch commitments shall be inscribed in a Member's Schedule". In short, Article XVIII permits Member States to make additional commitments which fall outside the scope of Article XVI (market access) and Article XVII (NT) in a particular sector. Article XVIII aims at the progressive liberalisation of trade in services, as in the case of Articles XVI and XVII. The Panel in *US – Gambling* endeavoured to analyse the interrelationship between GATS Articles XVI, XVII, and XVIII and observed as follows:

> [I]f a Member undertakes a full market access or a full national treatment commitment, it must not apply any measure that would be inconsistent with the provisions of those articles. Nonetheless, the drafters seem to have realized that there may be other types of restrictions that would not be covered by the disciplines of Articles XVI and XVII. In other words, there could be restrictions that would not be discriminatory and, therefore, would escape the provisions of Article XVII; nor would they be one of the six types of measures referred to in subparagraphs 2(a) to (f) of Article XVI. Apparently, it was considered that such measures would mainly, but not exclusively, relate to qualifications, standards and licensing matters. At the same time, it appears that it may not have been possible to arrive at a clear definition of the restrictive nature of such measures so that disciplines similar to those of Articles XVI and XVII could be established. It seems, therefore, that it was considered best to simply provide a legal framework for Members to negotiate and schedule specific commitments that they would define, on a case-by-case basis, in relation to any measures that do not fall within the scope of Article XVI or XVII. That framework appears to have been provided in Article XVIII [footnote omitted].[71]

Pursuant to Article XVIII, a number of Member States have proceeded to include the *Reference Paper on Telecommunications* – containing pro-competitive regulatory principles to the telecommunications sector (WTO, 1996a), and *Maritime Model Schedule* (containing additional commitments with regards to 'access and use of port services' and 'multimodal transport') in the GATS schedules. Interestingly, Mexico's implementation with regards to the telecom sector came to be challenged by the US in the *Mexico – Telecoms* case.

4.5 Withdrawal of Commitments

Under the GATS Agreement Member States are required to have a Schedule of Specific Commitments, for both market access and NT together with any additional commitments. Likewise, the GATS also contains a provision to either modify or withdraw any commitments made by a Member States, which is akin to tariff concessions under the GATT. Article XXI of GATS permits a Member State to modify or withdraw its specific commitments by offering some form of compensatory trade liberalisation, and yet without violating its obligations under the Agreement. Article XXI can be invoked any time after the lapse of three years from the date of entry into force of a commitment. Pursuant to Article XXI, a Member State may adjust its commitments to new/changed circumstances or policy considerations, providing scope for flexibility and progressive liberalisation (Nartova, 2008). In 1999, the CTS enacted detailed procedures for the modification of Member States Schedules (CTS, 1999).

5. General Exceptions Under GATS

The general and specific obligations arising under NT and market access commitments of the GATS Agreement are subject to exceptions under certain circumstances. Part II of the GATS lists the exceptions under various heads, which are (i) Article V (Economic Integration), (ii) Article XII (Restrictions to Safeguard the Balance of Payments), (iii) Article XIV

(General Exceptions), and (iv) Article XIV *bis* (Security Exceptions).[72] The GATS Agreement provides the above exception as WTO laws seek to strike a balance between different policy goals of a Member State. This objective is sought to be achieved through general exceptions.

An extensive list of general exceptions under the GATS Agreement is provided in Article XIV, which is the analogous parallel provision to GATT Article XX. Article XIV of GATS reads as follows:

> Subject to the requirement that such measures are not applied in a manner which would constitute a means of arbitrary or unjustifiable discrimination between countries where like conditions prevail, or a disguised restriction on trade in services, nothing in this Agreement shall be construed to prevent the adoption or enforcement by any Member of measures:
>
> (a) necessary to protect public morals or to maintain public order;[73]
> (b) necessary to protect human, animal or plant life or health;
> (c) necessary to secure compliance with laws or regulations which are not inconsistent with the provisions of this Agreement including those relating to:
>
>> (i) the prevention of deceptive and fraudulent practices or to deal with the effects of a default on services contracts;
>> (ii) the protection of the privacy of individuals in relation to the processing and dissemination of personal data and the protection of confidentiality of individual records and accounts;
>> (iii) safety;
>
> (d) inconsistent with Article XVII, provided that the difference in treatment is aimed at ensuring the equitable or effective imposition or collection of direct taxes in respect of services or service suppliers of other Members; [footnotes omitted]
> (e) inconsistent with Article II, provided that the difference in treatment is the result of an agreement on the avoidance of double taxation or provisions on the avoidance of double taxation in any other international agreement or arrangement by which the Member is bound.

These exceptions contained in Article XIV also apply to the obligations related to specific commitments and set out the bases for deviating from the application of the GATS Agreement. Similar in substance to Article XX GATT, Article XIV contains additional general exceptions in relation to the prevention of deceptive practice and protection of privacy. Exceptions vary from Member State to Member State. The provisions of Article XIV GATS and Article XX GATT are strikingly similar, with the *Chapeau* of both provisions being almost identical. The Appellate Body, as a result, has allowed the use of jurisprudence arising under Article XX GATT to interpret the exceptions arising under Article XIV GATS.[74]

The jurisprudence on Article XX GATT is well settled as it has been invoked on a number of occasions, whereas Article XIV has been invoked on far fewer occasions, and notably in the *US – Gambling* case. As discussed in the earlier sections, a number of US federal laws regulating internet gambling, and 'remote' gambling, were challenged by Antigua as being in violation of several GATS provisions. One of the defences raised by the US to the challenge of the federal laws was that they were necessary to protect public morals and to maintain public order – XIV(a), and to secure compliance with WTO-consistent laws – XIV(b). The Appellate Body, while explaining the similarities between Article XX of GATT and Article

XIV of GATS, stated that the latter provision sets out general exceptions under the GATS (services) much in the same way as the former does under the GATT (goods), and made the following observation:

> Article XIV of the GATS sets out the general exceptions from obligations under that Agreement in the same manner as does Article XX of the GATT 1994. Both of these provisions affirm the right of Members to pursue objectives identified in the paragraphs of these provisions even if, in doing so, Members act inconsistently with obligations set out in other provisions of the respective agreements, provided that all of the conditions set out therein are satisfied. Similar language is used in both provisions,[75] notably the term "necessary" and the requirements set out in their respective *Chapeaux*. Accordingly, like the Panel, we find previous decisions under Article XX of the GATT 1994 relevant for our analysis under Article XIV of the GATS.[76,77]

5.1 Article XIV: The Two-Tier Analysis

As referred to earlier, much of the GATT jurisprudence pertaining to Article XX has been used in interpreting the Article XIV GATS. For instance, the two-tier test developed to interpret Article XX in the GATT jurisprudence has been applied to interpret Article XIV of GATS.[78] The Appellate Body in *US – Gambling* stated that Article XIV of the GATS, like Article XX of the GATT 1994, contemplates a "two-tier analysis" of a measure that a Member State seeks to justify under that provision, and observed as follows:

> Article XIV of the GATS, like Article XX of the GATT 1994, contemplates a "two-tier analysis" of a measure that a Member seeks to justify under that provision. A panel should first determine whether the challenged measure falls within the scope of one of the paragraphs of Article XIV. This requires that the challenged measure address the particular interest specified in that paragraph and that there be a sufficient nexus between the measure and the interest protected. The required nexus – or "degree of connection" – between the measure and the interest is specified in the language of the paragraphs themselves, through the use of terms such as "relating to" and "necessary to". Where the challenged measure has been found to fall within one of the paragraphs of Article XIV, a panel should then consider whether that measure satisfies the requirements of the *Chapeau* of Article XIV.[79]

The Panel in *Argentina – Financial Services*, recalling the Appellate Body's findings in *US – Gambling* with regard to the parallels between Article XX of the GATT 1994 and Article XIV of the GATS, ruled as follows:

> The analogy between the two provisions led the Appellate Body in US – Gambling to use in its examination of Article XIV of the GATS the same "two-tier analysis" already used in relation to Article XX of the GATT 1994. Thus, Article XIV of the GATS provides for an analysis in two stages: (i) first, the Panel must determine whether the measure falls within the scope of one of the subparagraphs of Article XIV of the GATS; and (ii) after having found that the measure at issue is justified under one of the subparagraphs of Article XIV of the GATS, the Panel must examine whether this measure satisfies the requirements laid down in the introductory clause or *Chapeau* of Article XIV of the GATS.[80]

While striking textual similarities exist between Article XX of the GATT and Article XIV of the GATS, differences do exist in the two provisions. In terms of the width of provisions Article XIV is narrower than Article XX GATT, as it provides only for five grounds to justify deviations by Member States from GATS obligations, whereas Article XX offers more wider justifications for deviation from GATT obligations. In other words, Article XIV only offers a closed list of exceptions to deviate from GATS obligation which are available for pre-defined purposes.

5.1.1 Article XIV: The Necessity Test

With regard to measures introduced to protect public interests – Article XIV(a) public morals and public order; XIV(b) protecting human, animal, or plant life or health; and XIV(c) to secure compliance with laws or regulations which are not inconsistent with the provisions of this Agreement – may be justified only if they can be proven to be 'necessary' to achieve the policy objective and meet the requirement of the *Chapeau*. Exceptions mentioned in Articles XIV(d) and XIV(e) permit deviations from specific GATS provisions, *viz.*, two non-discrimination provisions of (i) Article II, which contains the general obligation of MFN, and (ii) Article XVII, which contains NT, which is subject a Member State's specific commitment under GATS. A Member State invoking the prior two exceptions are not required to demonstrate 'necessity'.

In *US – Gambling*, the Appellate Body explored the required 'necessity' standards for GATS exceptions. It will be recalled that the measure at issue was banning supply of gambling services, which according to Antigua was in violation of GATS obligations. The US for its part had sought to justify the measures under Articles XIV(a) and XIV(c). The Appellate Body in *US – Gambling* sought to clarify two issues, *viz.*, the scope of 'public morals' and 'public order' exceptions and the application of 'necessity' standards for exceptions. In the Appellate Body's view, the term 'public morals' denoted standards of right and wrong conduct maintained by or on behalf of a community or nation,[81] and that the definition of the term 'order', read in conjunction with footnote 5 to the GATS, suggests that 'public order' refers to the "preservation of the fundamental interests of a society, as reflected in public policy and law".[82] As this finding was not challenged, the Panel's observations stand.

As regards the application of the 'necessity' standards for Article XIV GATS exceptions, the Appellate Body in *US – Gambling* referred to its earlier pronouncements on 'necessity' standards made in relation to Article XX GATT, and observed as follows:

> The Appellate Body has pointed to two factors that, in most cases, will be relevant to a Panel's determination of the "necessity" of a measure, although not necessarily exhaustive of factors that might be considered. One factor is the contribution of the measure to the realization of the ends pursued by it; the other factor is the restrictive impact of the measure on international commerce.
>
> A comparison between the challenged measure and possible alternatives should then be undertaken, and the results of such comparison should be considered in the light of the importance of the interests at issue. It is on the basis of this "weighing and balancing" and comparison of measures, taking into account the interests or values at stake, that a Panel determines whether a measure is "necessary" or, alternatively, whether another, WTO-consistent measure is "reasonably available".
>
> The requirement, under Article XIV(a), that a measure be "necessary" – that is, that there be no "reasonably available", WTO-consistent alternative – reflects the shared

understanding of Members that substantive GATS obligations should not be deviated from lightly. An alternative measure may be found not to be "reasonably available", however, where it is merely theoretical in nature, for instance, where the responding Member is not capable of taking it, or where the measure imposes an undue burden on that Member, such as prohibitive costs or substantial technical difficulties. Moreover, a "reasonably available" alternative measure must be a measure that would preserve for the responding Member its right to achieve its desired level of protection with respect to the objective pursued under paragraph (a) of Article XIV.[83]

The Appellate Body, while noting that the US demonstrated that the measures were justified under Article XIV(a), found that it failed to satisfy the requirement of the *Chapeau* to Article XIV. As a result, the Appellate Body ruled that the US did not demonstrate that the challenged measures "are applied consistently with the requirements of the *Chapeau*".[84] By resorting to a process of weighing and balancing, it is clear from the reasoning of the Appellate Body that it draws from its jurisprudence regarding Article XX GATT. The Appellate Body also found that the original burden of proof was on the Member State raising such defence of 'public morals' and 'public order', that where a *prima facie* case has been made out then the burden of proof shifts back to the complaining party Member State to demonstrate that the use of a less restrictive measure to achieve the stated objective, and that where the complaining party succeeds in so doing the burden then shifts back to the Member State raising the defence.[85]

5.2 Chapeau *of Article XIV*

As seen from the foregoing discussion, it becomes clear that a measure found compatible with the specific requirements of Articles XIV(a)–(e) will still need to comply with the conditions set out in the *Chapeau* of the provision. These conditions ensure that rights exercised to deviate from WTO obligations to achieve such non-economic policy goals are not abused and applied in an arbitrary fashion. As observed by the Panel in *US – Gambling*, due to the similar wordings and functions of the *Chapeaux* of Article XIV GATS and Article XX GATT, the extensive GATT jurisprudence on Article XX is to be applied *mutatis mutandis* for the interpretation of Article XIV.[86]

In *US – Gambling*, the Appellate Body observed that the focus of the *Chapeau* is on the application of a measure already found by the Panel to be inconsistent with its obligations under GATS but falling within one of the paragraphs of Article XIV:9:

> The focus of the *Chapeau*, by its express terms, is on the application of a measure already found by the Panel to be inconsistent with one of the obligations under the GATS but falling within one of the paragraphs of Article XIV. By requiring that the measure be applied in a manner that does not to constitute "arbitrary" or "unjustifiable" discrimination, or a "disguised restriction on trade in services", the *Chapeau* serves to ensure that Members' rights to avail themselves of exceptions are exercised reasonably, so as not to frustrate the rights accorded other Members by the substantive rules of the GATS.[87]

The Panel in *Argentina – Financial Services* noted that the *Chapeau* of Article XIV of the GATS is drafted in terms very similar to the *Chapeau* of Article XX of the GATT 1994:

> We note that the *Chapeau* of Article XIV of the GATS describes in terms very similar to those of Article XX of the GATT 1994 the existence of three types of situation relating

to the application of measures that may give rise to inconsistency with the said *Chapeau*: (i) arbitrary discrimination between countries where like conditions prevail; (ii) unjustifiable discrimination between countries where like conditions prevail; or (iii) a disguised restriction on trade in services. In disputes under Article XX of the GATT 1994, the first two situations (i.e., arbitrary discrimination or unjustifiable discrimination) have often been addressed together. The existence of one of these situations suffices to conclude that a measure cannot be justified under Article XX of the GATT 1994.

Bearing in mind this guidance from the Appellate Body, we shall examine whether the application of the measures in question constitutes "a means of arbitrary or unjustifiable discrimination between countries where like conditions prevail".[88]

5.3 Economic Integration Exception (Article IV)

The Article IV GATS economic integration exception is the equivalent of GATT Article XXIV exception for customs unions and free-trade areas. This aspect is discussed later in chapter 15 on Regional Trade Agreements.

5.4 Derogation From MFN Obligations

See chapter 4 for a detailed discussion on when a Member State is permitted to derogate from its MFN obligation arising under the GATS Agreement.

6. Specific Rules for Telecommunications and Financial Services

Prior to the entry of the GATS Agreement, international telecommunication services were traded bilaterally between nations. Telecommunications is an important means through which information-intensive services (*e.g.*, financial, management consulting, audiovisual, advertisement services, *etc.*) are moved across national borders. In short, it is one of most crucial forms of cross-border supply.

The Uruguay Round provided the most suitable forum for negotiations on liberalisation of telecommunications, as opposed to the International Telecommunication Union (ITU), as it was perceived by the developed countries to be influenced by developing countries (Bronckers and Larouche, 2005).[89] With the advent of GATS in 1995, the telecommunications sector was opened up to a multilateral framework and thereby to a new regime of global competition. The ITU estimated the telecommunications market as worth about US$600 billion in 1996, and cross-border trade in telecommunications exceeded US$100 billion in 1996 (ITU, 1998). Trade in telecommunications is defined by the ITU as sales of telecommunication equipment or services that cross national borders (ITU, 1998).

6.1 Telecommunications

The two important annexes[90] to the GATS Agreement are the Annex on Telecommunications and the Annex on Financial Services. The annexes, pursuant to Article XXIX GATS, are considered an integral part of the GATS Agreement, which is akin to the schedules of specific commitments, which are considered an integral part of the GATS Agreement pursuant to Article XX:3 GATS. Viewing telecommunications as an essential tool for other economic activities and with the objective of liberalisation in the services sector, the Member States concluded the Annex on Telecommunications (AT) during the Uruguay Round of negotiations. The AT establishes specific rules for (basic) telecommunication and extends liberalisation in the sector to include telecommunications infrastructure-based services. Article 1 of AT identifies the objective as

> elaborating upon the provisions of the Agreement with respect to measures affecting access to and use of public telecommunications transport networks and services. Accordingly, this Annex provides notes and supplementary provisions to the Agreement.

This arrangement allows for market access commitments to permit suppliers to own and operate their own networks to provide services. While AT elaborates on the provision of the GATS to measures affecting access to the use of the public telecommunications transport network, it does not extend to cable or broadcast distribution of radio or television programmes. The AT does not require Member States to allow any provision of telecommunications services beyond any commitments they have already made in their schedules of commitment.[91]

Other than the GATS Agreement and AT, rules applicable to telecommunications are also to be found in the Reference Paper (WTO, 1996a) and the Schedule of Specific Commitments. The Reference Paper, which was adopted by the CTS in April 1996, was to be attached to a member's Schedule of Commitments as a 'additional commitment'. The Reference Paper addresses several regulatory concerns, or barriers, for which service providers may seek clarification while attempting to access the network of domestic public telecommunications operators. The purpose of the Reference Paper is primarily (i) to provide the necessary safeguards in domestic law for market access and foreign investment commitments to be effective and (ii) to secure firmly these safeguards in the WTO system and make any failure to implement them challengeable under DSU (Bronckers and Larouche, 2005).

The Reference Paper, modelled on US telecommunications and antitrust laws and practices, incorporates six basic obligations which adopting Member States were required to commit to, *viz.*,

a) To implement such competitive safeguards, including prevention of anti-competitive conduct, a ban on cross-subsidisation, and a ban on the abuse of competitively sensitive information by carriers with market power, through telecommunications-specific laws and regulations, or general antitrust and competition laws.
b) To ensure timely, non-discriminatory, cost-oriented, unbundled, and transparent interconnection between carriers with market power and other carriers through publicly available procedures.
c) To implement anti-competitive practices, and administer universal service obligations in a transparent, non-discriminatory, and competitively neutral manner.
d) To ensure public availability of licensing criteria in a transparent manner.
e) To establish independent regulators, whether a government ministry or an independent commission for the review of decisions.
f) To allocate scarce resources, such as radio spectrum, numbers, and rights of way, in an objective, timely, transparent, and non-discriminatory manner.

(Bressie, Kende, and Williams, 2005)

The *Mexico – Telecoms* dispute concerned a number of legal issues in relation to international long distance telecommunications services. The case was the first dispute relating to the interpretation of GATS rules, as well as that of the Reference Paper to go before the DSB. The US telecoms service provider Sprint and Mexico's largest telecom services provider Telmex (once State owned, and subsequently privatised) had partnered to deliver long-distance services between the US and Mexico. This meant, telecoms providers such as AT&T, MCI, *etc.* could not benefit from Telmex's considerably large network. Telmex, which was once State owned and subsequently privatised, was regulated by Comisión Federal de Telecomunicaciones (COFETEL), the Mexican telecommunications regulatory agency. COFETEL rules conferred on Telmex the authority to fix the rate to be paid by all foreign carriers (AT&T, MCI, *etc.*) terminating calls in Mexico. The rules also required other licensed Mexican concessionaires to charge no less than the fee fixed by Telmex. According to the US, the strategy was more geared towards benefitting the Mexican firms and was in violation of the GATS anti-competitive commitments.

The dispute was referred to the DSB after several failed attempts to settle the issues through bilateral discussions. The US alleged that Mexico had adopted anti-competitive and discriminatory regulatory measures, allowed certain privately established market access barriers, and also failed to take regulatory action in the country's basic and value-added telecommunications sectors. It was argued that such actions of Mexico amounted to a violation of Articles VI, XVI, and XVII of GATS and Mexico's additional commitments under Article XVIII as contained in the Reference Paper inscribed in Mexico's Schedule of Specific Commitments and the GATS Annex on Telecommunications. Some of the provisions of the Reference Paper at issue were Sections 1.1, 2.1, and 2.2.

In the US view, Mexico failed to ensure that Telmex provided interconnection to basic telecommunications suppliers from the US, as per GATS commitments, on a cross-border basis on reasonable terms. The US further argued that, pursuant to Section 1.1 of the Reference Paper, Mexico was obliged to prohibit any horizontal price-fixing cartel led by Telmex.[92] Mexico, on the other hand, argued that it had not made any specific commitments in its GATS schedule to trigger Section 2 of the Reference Paper, and that the Reference Paper interconnections did not extend to telecommunication services that originated abroad. Mexico clearly took the stance that the services in question did not fall within the cross-border classification as enumerated in Article I:2(a) of GATS, as the essential nature of the services was the transmission of customer data. The Panel was left to decide if the obligation to grant interconnection covered only mode 3 (commercial presence) or mode 1 (cross-border) as well.

In *Mexico – Telecoms*, the Panel, largely accepting US methodologies demonstrating that Telmex rates for international interconnection were not cost-oriented, concluded that Mexico was obliged to prohibit any horizontal price-fixing cartel led by Telmex as per Section 1.1 of the Reference Paper.[93] The Panel also ruled that interconnection covers both mode 3 (commercial presence) and mode 1 (cross-border),[94] and found as follows:

> In sum the ordinary meaning, in the heading of Section 2 of Mexico's Reference Paper, of the term "interconnection" – that it does not distinguish between domestic and international interconnection, including through accounting rate regimes – is confirmed by an examination of any "special meaning" that the term "interconnection" may have in telecommunications legislation, or by taking into account potential commercial, contractual or technical differences inherent in international interconnection. We find that any "special meaning" of the term "interconnection" in Section 2 of Mexico's Reference Paper does not justify a restricted interpretation of interconnection, or of the term "linking", which would exclude international interconnection, including accounting rate regimes, from the scope of Section 2 of the Reference Paper.[95]

The Panel further ruled that the services in question were cross-border in nature as the telephone calls originated in the US and terminated in Mexico, irrespective of whether the services were provided by the US supplier itself within Mexican territory. The Panel, referring to Section 5(a) of the Annex, observed as follows:

> Section 5(a) of the Annex states that the obligation to ensure access to and use of public telecommunications transport networks and services shall apply for the benefit of "any service supplier of any other Member" for the supply of "a service included in its schedule". This language does not explicitly exclude suppliers of basic telecommunications services. On the contrary, Section 5(a) speaks of "any" service supplier. It also speaks of a "service included" in a Member's schedule which, in the case of any Member, can, and for many Members does, include basic telecommunications services. We consider this to be a further indication that the Annex is not limited in its application to exclude measures ensuring the access to and use of public telecommunications transport networks and services for the supply of any service, including basic telecommunications services.[96]

The report in *Mexico – Telecoms* is one of the only rulings on the services sector relating to telecommunications, and the findings of the Panel stand, as they were not challenged by either party to the proceeding. Some commentators opine that the Panel's application of the Reference Paper and the GATS provisions to the fact at hand were erroneous (Trebilcock, Howse, and Eliason, 2013).

6.2 Financial Services

The negotiations on both telecommunications and financial services in the immediate aftermath of the Uruguay Round produced a number of instruments, which include the Annex on Financial Services (AFS), Understanding on Commitments in Financial Services, and Decision on Financial Services. Interestingly, the various instruments to deal with a single services sector reflect the incomplete nature of the negotiations on the financial services sector during the Uruguay Round. Financial services, which primarily relate to insurance, banking, and securities services, is a key element of GATS. Along with the AT, the AFS is an integral part of the GATS Agreement. The AFS and Understanding on Commitments in Financial Services contain specific provisions as regards trade in financial services, besides outlining the application of GATS Agreement to financial services.

As the financial sector is the foundation of both national and world economies, besides being the backbone of international trade, it is regulated in more detail. Currently, over 140 countries report trade in financial services, which is more than three times that prevailing in the early 2000s. The AFS concerns the application of the GATS to the financial services sector and does not contain specific liberalisation commitments with regards to financial services. A broad definition of financial services is presented in the AFS to include a wide range of activities.

Paragraph 5(a) of the AFS defines financial services in broad terms as "any services of a financial nature offered by a financial service supplier of a Member", which includes all insurance and insurance-related services and all banking and other financial services, including acceptance of deposits, lending of all types, financial leasing, all payment and money transmission services, issue of credit, stock trading, financial consulting, *etc*. Insurance and insurance-related services include direct insurance, reinsurance, and services auxiliary to insurance, and banking services include a range from 'traditional' banking activities such as acceptance of bank deposits, lending of all types, financial leasing, payments systems and guarantees to trading of negotiable instruments and financial assets, participation in issues of all kind of securities, money broking, asset management, settlement and clearing services for financial assets, and provision and transfer of financial information and data. Also coming within the scope of financial services are other auxiliary financial services, *viz.*, credit reference and analysis, investment and portfolio research and advice, and advice on acquisitions and on corporate restructuring and strategy.

Paragraph 1(b) defines "services supplied in the exercise of governmental authority" and paragraph 5(b) defines "financial service supplier" in broad terms to include not only any natural or juridical person of a member supplying financial services but also any person of a member that "wishes" to supply a financial service. Paragraph 5(c) defines a "public entity" to include a government, a central bank or a monetary authority of a Member State, or a private entity performing those functions.

6.2.1 Prudential Carve-Out

The AFS contains two key provisions, *viz.*, the prudential carve-out and a requirement for specific expertise in dispute settlement, besides provisions for the recognition of such prudential measures. When the Working Group on Financial Services met during the Uruguay Round of negotiations, discussion on financial services included the need for an annex on financial services, and a prudential exception, or 'carve-out'. All the three formal papers[97] submitted during the negotiations contained proposals for a prudential exception. Interestingly, the expression 'prudential carve-out' was used even during the Uruguay Round of negotiations.

Provision on prudential carve-out is contained in paragraph 2 of the AFS, which permits Member States to take "measures for prudential reasons, including for the protection of investors, depositors, and policy holders or persons to whom a fiduciary duty is owed by a financial service supplier, or to ensure the integrity and stability of the financial system". The prudential carve-out enables Member States to take measures that are otherwise inconsistent with the Member State's financial services commitments under the GATS and could be inconsistent with NT, market access commitments, or its MFN obligation. Unlike the general exceptions contained in Article XIV GATS (discussed in section 5), where only measures that are 'necessary' are allowed, carve-out covers both 'necessary' and 'any' prudential measures.

Prudential carve-out seeks to strike a balance between trade values and non-trade values and applies to all four modes of supply in relation to trade in services. The provision ensures that objectives, such as consumer protection and financial stability, can be protected. Although not defined in the AFS, prudential carve-out refers to prudential reason and not prudential regulation. The WTO jurisprudence on prudential carve-out is scarce, with the notable exception of *Argentina – Financial Services*.

6.2.2 Understanding on Commitments in Financial Services

Although included in the Final Act of the Uruguay Round, the Understanding on Commitments in Financial Services (UCFS) is not an integral part of the GATS. UCFS is described in its introductory clauses as an 'alternative approach' to the regulation of specific commitments with regards to financial services under the GATS Agreement. It is to be pointed out that the UCFS does not have legal force and becomes binding when incorporated into a Member States' Schedule of Specific Commitments.

The UCFS was designed as a formula or template for commitments and is a model schedule which is somewhat complex (Key, 2005) and presents an alternative framework for liberalisation of trade in financial services to the one set out in Part III of GATS. The UCFS was drafted by a group of 12 OECD countries, including the EU, the US, Japan, Australia, New Zealand, who were not pleased with the extent of liberalisation in the financial services sector. Most OECD country Member States, using the UCFS, have made broad commitments covering a range of financial services to establish and expand their commercial services. Similar schedule-specific commitments have also been made by developing country Member States as regards financial services.

The UCFS's provisions contain an extensive degree of liberalisation and include a 'standstill obligation', *i.e.*, the obligation of the Member States to include any existing monopoly rights in the financial services sector in their Schedules of Commitments. As regards cross-border trade, Articles 3 and 4 of the UCFS provide for specific commitments from Member States allowing foreign suppliers of financial services to supply services on a cross-border basis and for consumption abroad. Articles 5 and 6, on the other hand, provide for granting financial service suppliers of other Member States the right for commercial presence, and Article 9 requires Member States to permit temporary entry of certain personnel into their territory. Under Article 10, the UCFS requires that Member States strive to remove or to limit any adverse effects on financial service suppliers of any Member State. Article 11 of the UCS requires that the Member States accord access on an NT basis to financial service suppliers of other members to payments and clearing systems operated by public entities, as well as to official funding and refinancing facilities available in the normal course of ordinary business.

7. Security Exceptions Under GATS

7.1 *Article XIV* bis *of GATS*

Similar to security exceptions contained in GATT in Article XXI, Article XIV *bis* of GATS provides exceptions for measures taken for the "protection of essential security interests". Article XIV *bis* is for all relevant purposes virtually identical to Article XXI of the GATT.[98] The rationale behind Article XIV *bis* is to preserve a Member State's freedom to operate in matters relating to national security and defence. The security exceptions under Article XIV *bis* include the disclosure of information that a Member State considers contrary to its national security interests, as well as action that a Member State considers necessary for the protection of its essential security interest (i) relating to the supply of services for the purpose of provisioning of a military establishment; (ii) relating to fissionable or fusionable material or the materials from which they are derived; and (iii) taken in time of war or other emergency in international relations.

As per Article XIV *bis*:1(c), Member States shall not be prevented from undertaking "action in pursuance of . . . obligations under the United Nations Charter for the maintenance of international peace and security". This provision refers to compliance with a Member State's obligations under Chapter VII of the UN Charter should the need arise.[99] Article XIV *bis*:2 contains a transparency provision, under which the Member States are required to inform the Services Council to the fullest extent possible of the measures taken under paragraphs 1(b) and (c). The language used in paragraph 2 is "shall be informed to the fullest extent possible".[100]

Since its introduction, Article XIV *bis* had hardly ever been invoked, meaning there is little or no jurisprudence on security exceptions arising under GATS Agreement. As noted by commentators, the lack of practice may be down to the risk of abuse of the security exceptions (Cottier and Delimatsis, 2008). Considering the sensitive nature of such interests, it is likely that a panel would grant extensive regulatory autonomy to the invoking Member and would only reject manifest misuse of the exceptions (Cottier and Delimatsis, 2008; Natens, 2016). While the language of Article XIV *bis* is considered to be broad, the limited use of the provision indicates that Member States understand the systemic implications of using these security exceptions without restraint (Akande and Williams, 2003; Natens, 2016).

8. Summary

One of the achievements of the Uruguay Round of negotiations was the expansion of remit of the multilateral trading system through the inclusion of the services trade. The GATS Agreement establishes legal parameters for trade in services. Although detailed, there are shortcomings in the Agreement, as the modes of supply are not clearly defined and clarity is needed as regards the core provisions, *e.g.*, the relationship between Article VI and XVII *vis-à-vis* Article XVI. Yet another issue about trade in services is that the continued liberalisation in certain sectors could lead to privatisation and deregulation of government-owned sectors, which could negatively affect certain segments of the society (Lester, Mercurio, and Davies, 2018). The Agreement has been used as a model to build and extend trade in services in RTAs. Since its entry into force, the GATS Agreement, besides the creation of employment in developing country Member States, has facilitated the growth and expansion of global services trade.

Notes

1 Trade in services, measured by its value, has increased at a rate of approximately 7.5 percent per annum since 1980.
2 More recently, during the COVID-19 pandemic in 2020, the internet had even facilitated the conduct of court hearings without the lawyers or witnesses being physically present in the courts.
3 Other aspects that do not permit the full determination of the value is the 'bundling factor' which is used in the industry as a strategy to gain better control over markets and to control consumers.
4 Leading players included financial institutions such as American Express and American International Group, and professional services firms such as Arthur Anderson. See Hoekman and Kostecki (2009).
5 It is to be noted that these are principles which are fundamental to the GATT, as well as the WTO. Under WTO principles both non-discrimination and transparency are viewed as fundamental to ensuring the predictability of the trading system.
6 Dunkel Draft refers to the draft compiled by Arthur Dunkel who served as the director-general of the GATT between 1980 and 1993. When agreement was not reached past the deadlines, Dunkel took the responsibility to compile a draft, which is referred to appropriately as the 'Dunkel Draft' and was tabled in December 1991. The draft, besides compiling the results of negotiations, also provided a well-assessed solution to matters where negotiators failed to reach any agreement. It is to be noted that the Dunkel Draft was eventually accepted with very minor changes and became the foundation for the WTO's agreements.
7 The author takes the view that GATS is a landmark in terms of creating multilateral disciplines in 'virgin territories' but a failure in terms of generating liberalisation, and accordingly awaits negotiation in future rounds of negotiations.
8 See Appellate Body Report, *China – Publications and Audiovisual Products*, para. 394.
9 See Appellate Body Report, *EC – Bananas III*, para. 220, where it was held that the word "affecting" had a "broad scope of application".

10 See section 2.3 for a discussion on modes of services.
11 According to the WTO website, governmental services would include social security schemes, and health and public services such as education, that are supplied neither on a commercial basis nor in competition with other suppliers.
12 (Footnote original) If this were not the case, and a Member scheduled the same service in two different sectors, then the scope of the Member's commitments would not be clear where, for example, it made a full commitment in one of those sectors and a limited, or no, commitment in the other. At the oral hearing in this appeal, both the United States and Antigua agreed that the entries in a Member's Schedule must be mutually exclusive. See also Panel Report, paras. 6.63, 6.101, and 6.119.
13 See Appellate Body Report, *US – Gambling*, para. 180.
14 This is attributed to a discussion that took place between Lori Wallach (from Public Citizen), and the former director-general of the WTO, Mr Pascal Lamy.
15 See Introductory Note to the UN Central Product Classification (CPC), para. 31.
16 See Appellate Body Report, *US – Gambling*, para. 172. See also para. 203, where the Appellate Body spoke about the importance of using a common format and terminology in scheduling.
17 *Ibid.*, para. 180.
18 As mentioned earlier, the GATS Agreement creates two different types of obligations, *viz.*, (i) General Obligations – MFN, Transparency, Domestic Regulations, *etc.*, which apply to all Member States, to include every type of service provided in that State, including legal services; and (ii) Specific Commitments/Obligations – negotiated undertaking particular to each GATS signatory, recorded/listed legal services on 'Schedule of Specific Commitments.' Each WTO Member State's Schedule of Specific Commitments is unique and differs from another Member State.
19 See Panel Report, *Mexico – Telecoms*, para. 7.30.
20 *Ibid.*, para.7.375.
21 See Panel Report, *EC – Bananas III*, para. 7.285.
22 See Appellate Body Report, *EC – Bananas III*, para. 220.
23 See Panel Report, *Canada – Autos*, para. 10.257.
24 See Appellate Body Report, *Canada – Periodicals*, para. 19.
25 See Appellate Body Report, *EC – Bananas III*, para. 221.
26 See Panel Report, *EC – Bananas III*, para. 7.331.
27 Some commentators express the view that case law relating to Article X:3 of GATT can be used in the interpretation of Article VI:1 of GATS. See Krajewski (2008). See also Appellate Body Report, *EC – Bananas III*, para. 231.
28 For a detailed discussion on services negation on the creation of rules on domestic regulation, see Delimatsis (2010). The author puts forth the proposal for a 'necessity test' applicable across the service sectors, arguing that only a 'necessity test' can allow for the elimination of unnecessary barriers to trade in services and regulatory arbitrariness.
29 The negotiations on domestic regulations are part of the Doha Round, which had reached a stalemate. See chapter 17.
30 Similarly, under 2.2 TBT Agreement and 2.2 SPS Agreement.
31 See Panel Report, *Mexico – Telecoms*, para. 7.338.
32 In contrast, RTAs have a 'top-down' approach to market access in trade in services, where all services are included in the agreement unless specifically excluded. See, for example, NAFTA.
33 See Appellate Body Report, *US – Gambling*, para. 214.
34 See Panel Report, *US – Gambling*, para. 6.318. See also 6.298–6.299.
35 See Panel Report, *China – Electrical Payment Services*, para. 7.652.
36 See Appellate Body Report, *US – Gambling*, para. 214.
37 The federal laws through which the measure under challenge was imposed were the Wire Act 1961, the Travel Act 1961, and the Illegal Gambling Business Act (IGBA).
38 The Panel followed the two-tier analysis applied by the Panel in *Korea – Various Measures on Beef* to determine the questions of public morality and public order under GATT Article XX.
39 See Appellate Body Report, *US – Gambling*, para. 299.
40 *Ibid.*, para. 143.
41 *Ibid.*, para. 236.
42 *Ibid.*, para. 125.
43 See Panel Report, *US – Gambling*, paras. 6.326–6.365.

44 See Appellate Body Report, *US – Gambling*, paras. 224–239.
45 *Ibid.*, para. 226.
46 *Ibid.*, para. 227.
47 *Ibid.*, para. 238.
48 See Panel Report, *US – Gambling*, para. 6.335.
49 See Panel Report, *China – Electronic Payment Services*, para. 7.700.
50 Some commentators even opine that the GATS Agreement in this regard has even made connections with the jurisprudence of the EU. See Koul (2018).
51 See Appellate Body Report, *US – Gambling*, paras. 175, 178, and 193, where it was held that the 1993 Scheduling Guidelines was drafted by the Secretariat and not by the parties to the negotiations and could not be accepted as an instrument related to the treaty. Further, the Appellate Body also found that the 2001 Scheduling Guidelines could not constitute subsequent practice within the meaning of Article 31(3)(b) of the Vienna Convention.
52 See Panel Report, *EC – Bananas III*, paras. 7.314, 7.357, and 7.375.
53 See Appellate Body Report, *EC – Bananas III*, paras. 241–244.
54 See Panel Report, *EC – Bananas III*, para. 7.314.
55 See Panel Report, *China – Publications and Audiovisual Products*, para. 7.1203.
56 *Ibid.*, para. 7.1205.
57 See Appellate Body Report, *China – Publications and Audiovisual Products*, paras. 396 and 397.
58 See Appellate Body Report, *Japan – Alcoholic Beverages II*, p. 21.
59 See Panel Report, *EC – Bananas III*, para. 7.322.
60 *Ibid.*, para. 7.346.
61 See Panel Report, *Canada – Autos*, paras. 10.247–10.248.
62 See Panel Report, *China – Electronic Payment Services*, paras. 7.705.
63 See Panel Report, *China – Publications and Audiovisual Products*, para. 7.687.
64 *Ibid.*, paras. 7.978–7.979.
65 *Ibid.*, paras. 7.996.
66 See Appellate Body Report, *Argentina – Financial Services*, para. 6.103.
67 *Ibid.*, para. 6.104.
68 The other two options were (i) the traditional definition of NT to be applied, which is *de jure* NT (supported by Japan and South Korea), and (ii) equivalent treatment.
69 See Wang (2012) and Muller (2017) for a more detailed analysis of the relationship between market access and NT obligation under GATS Agreement.
70 See Panel Report, *China – Electronic Payment Services*, para. 7.656.
71 See Panel Report, *US – Gambling*, paras. 6.311.
72 See section 7 of this chapter for a discussion on security exceptions.
73 This exception may be invoked only where a sufficiently serious threat is posed to the fundamental interests of society.
74 See Appellate Body Report, *US – Gambling*, para. 291.
75 (Footnote original) Notwithstanding the general similarity in language between the two provisions, we note that Article XIV(a) of the GATS expressly enables Members to adopt measures "necessary to protect public morals or to maintain public order", whereas the corresponding exception in the GATT 1994, Article XX(a), speaks of measures "necessary to protect public morals".
76 (Footnote original) In this respect, we observe that this case is not only the first where the Appellate Body is called upon to address the general exceptions provision of the GATS, but also the first under any of the covered agreements where the Appellate Body is requested to address exceptions relating to "public morals".
77 See Appellate Body Report, *US – Gambling*, para. 291.
78 See chapter 6 of this volume for a discussion on two-tier test under Article XX.
79 *Ibid.*, para. 292.
80 See Panel Report, *Argentina – Financial Services*, para. 7.586.
81 See Panel Report, *US – Gambling*, para. 6.465.
82 *Ibid.*, para. 6.467.
83 See Appellate Body Report, *US – Gambling*, paras. 306–308.
84 *Ibid.*, paras. 361–369.
85 *Ibid.*, paras. 309–311. See chapter 6 of this volume for a discussion on burden of proof under Article XX.

86 See Panel Report, *US – Gambling*, para. 6.571.
87 *Ibid.*, paras. 339.
88 See Panel Report, *Argentina – Financial Services*, paras. 7.745–7.746.
89 The authors note that one of the influencing factors leading to the developed countries taking such a stance was ITU's role in discussions on the North-South dialogue and the 'New International Economic Order' in the 1970s, which led them to conclude that deregulation and liberalisation of telecommunication would be better served if it were to be discussed at the Uruguay Round, where the negotiating techniques were more appropriate for such pursuits.
90 The annexes are there to provide "notes and supplementary provisions to the Agreement".
91 See Panel Report, *Mexico – Telecoms*, paras. 7.291 and 7.293.
92 *Ibid.*, para. 7.222.
93 *Ibid.*, paras. 7.234, 7.235, and 7.237.
94 *Ibid.*, paras. 7.108–7.117.
95 *Ibid.*, para. 7.117.
96 *Ibid.*, para. 7.281.
97 The three papers originated from the EC, the SEACEN countries (comprising Indonesia, Korea, Nepal, Malaysia, Myanmar, Philippines, Singapore, Sri Lanka, and Thailand), and the US. For a discussion of the negotiations leading to the incorporation of prudential carve-out, see Marchetti (2011).
98 On the security exception found in Article XXI GATT, see Panel Report, *EC – Tariff Preferences*, para. 7.37; where it was explained that security exceptions do not establish a positive obligation. See also the more recent Panel Report, *Russia – Traffic in Transit*, from 2019.
99 Chapter VII of the UN Charter relates to the actions taken with respect to threats to peace, breaches of the peace, and acts of aggression.
100 The language used in paragraph 2 of Article XIV *bis* is similar to the language used in the decision taken by the GATT Contracting Parties in 1982, which stated that subject to the exception in Article XXI(a), Contracting Parties should be informed to the fullest extent possible of trade measures taken under Article XXI. See GATT (1982).

Bibliography

Akande, Dapo and Sope Williams. 'International Adjudication on National Security Issues: What Role for the WTO?,' *Virginia Journal of International Law* Vol 43 (2003) 365–404.

Bhala, Raj. *Modern GATT Law: A Treatise on the General Agreement on Tariffs and Trade* Vol 2 (Sweet & Maxwell Publishers, 2013) 703–1054.

Bogdandy, Armin von and Joseph Windsor. 'Annex on Financial Services,' in Wolfrum, Rüdiger, Peter-Tobias Stoll and Clemens Feinäugle (eds.) *Max Plank Commentaries on World Trade Law: WTO-Trade in Services* Vol 6 (Martin Nijhoff Publishers, 2008) 618–639.

Bressie, Kent, Michael Kende and Howard Williams. 'Telecommunications Trade Liberalization and the WTO,' *Info: The Journal of Policy, Regulation and Strategy for Telecommunications* Vol 7, No 2 (2005) 3–24.

Bronckers, Marco and Pierre Larouche. 'Telecommunications Services,' in Macrory, Patrick F.J., Arthur E. Appleton and Michael G. Plummer (eds.) *The WTO: Legal, Economic and Political Analysis* Vol 1 (Springer, 2005) 989–1040.

Cottier, Thomas and Panagiotis Delimatsis. 'Article XIV *bis* GATS,' in Wolfrum, Rüdiger, Peter-Tobias Stoll and Clemens Feinäugle (eds.) *Max Plank Commentaries on World Trade Law: WTO-Trade in Services* Vol 6 (Martin Nijhoff Publishers, 2008) 329–348.

Cottier, Thomas, Panagiotis Delimatsis and Nicholas F. Diebol. 'Article XIV GATS,' in Wolfrum, Rüdiger, Peter-Tobias Stoll and Clemens Feinäugle (eds.) *Max Plank Commentaries on World Trade Law: WTO-Trade in Services* Vol 6 (Martin Nijhoff Publishers, 2008) 287–328.

Cowhey, Peter F. and Jonathan D. Aronson. 'Trade in Services: Telecommunications,' in Mattoo, Aaditya, Robert M. Stern and Gianni Zanini (eds.) *A Handbook of International Trade in Services* (Oxford University Press, 2008) 414–436.

CTS, Council for Trade in Services. *Procedures for the Implementation of Article XXI of the General Agreement on Trade in Services (GATS) (Modification of Schedules)*, Adopted by the Council for Trade in Services on 19 July 1999, S/L/80 (29 October 1999).

Delimatsis, Panagiotis. 'Don't Gamble with GATS: The Interaction between Articles VI, XVI, XVII and XVIII GATS in the Light of the *US-Gambling* Case,' *Journal of World Trade* Vol 40, No 6 (2006) 1059–1080.

Delimatsis, Panagiotis. 'Due Process and Good Regulation Embedded in the GATS: Disciplining Regulatory Behaviour in Services through Article VI of the GATS,' *Journal of International Economic Law* Vol 10, No 1 (2007) 13–50.

Delimatsis, Panagiotis. 'Article III GATS,' in Wolfrum, Rüdiger, Peter-Tobias Stoll and Clemens Feinäugle (eds.) *Max Plank Commentaries on World Trade Law: WTO-Trade in Services* Vol 6 (Martin Nijhoff Publishers, 2008) 92–107.

Delimatsis, Panagiotis. 'Concluding the WTO Services Negotiations on Domestic Regulation: Hopes and Fears,' *World Trade Review* Vol 9, No 4 (2010) 643–673.

Delimatsis, Panagiotis. 'Protecting Public Morals in a Digital Age: Revisiting the WTO Rulings on *US-Gambling* and *China-Publications and Audiovisual Products*,' *Journal of International Economic Law* Vol 14 (2011) 257–293.

Delimatsis, Panagiotis and Martín Molinuevo. 'Article XVI GATS,' in Wolfrum, Rüdiger, Peter-Tobias Stoll and Clemens Feinäugle (eds.) *Max Plank Commentaries on World Trade Law: WTO-Trade in Services* Vol 6 (Martin Nijhoff Publishers, 2008) 367–395.

Diebold, Nicholas F. *Non-Discrimination in International Trade in Services: 'Likeness' in WTO/GATS* (Cambridge University Press, 2010).

Drake, William J. and Eli M. Noam. 'Assessing the WTO Agreement on Basic Telecommunications,' in Hufbauer, Gary Clyde and Erika Wada (eds.) *Unfinished Business: Telecommunications after the Uruguay Round* (Institute for International Economics, 1997) 27–62.

Eurostat. 'World Trade in Services,' *Highlights* (July 2019) <https://ec.europa.eu/eurostat/statistics-explained/index.php/World_trade_in_services> (accessed 2 February 2021).

Footer, Mary E. and Carol George. 'The General Agreement on Trade in Services,' in Macrory, Patrick F.J., Arthur E. Appleton and Michael G. Plummer (eds.) *The WTO: Legal, Economic and Political Analysis* Vol 1 (Springer, 2005) 799–953.

Fuchs, Christine. 'GATS Negotiating History,' in Wolfrum, Rüdiger, Peter-Tobias Stoll and Clemens Feinäugle (eds.) *Max Plank Commentaries on World Trade Law: WTO-Trade in Services* Vol 6 (Martin Nijhoff Publishers, 2008) 1–16.

GATT General Agreement on Tariffs and Trade. 'Decision Concerning Article XXI of the General Agreement of November 30, 1982,' (L/5426) (2 December 1982) <www.wto.org/gatt_docs/english/SULPDF/91000212.pdf> (accessed 2 March 2021).

Hodge, James. 'Liberalization of Trade in Services in Developing Countries,' in Hoekman, Bernard M., Aditya Mattoo and Philip English (eds.) *Development, Trade and the WTO: A Handbook* (World Bank Publication, 2002) 221–234.

Hoekman, Bernard M. 'Assessing the General Agreement on Trade in Services,' in Martin, Will and Alan Winters (eds.) *The Uruguay Round and the Developing Economies* (World Bank Publications, 1995) 327–364.

Hoekman, Bernard M. and Michel M. Kostecki. *The Political Economy of the World Trading System* Vol 3 (Oxford University Press, 2009).

Hoekman, Bernard M. and Aaditya Mattoo. 'Services Trade and Growth,' in Marchetti, Juan and Martin Roy (eds.) *Opening Markets for Trade in Services: Countries and Sectors in Bilateral and WTO Negotiations* (Cambridge University Press, 2009).

ITU. 'World Telecommunication Development Report 1996/1997: Trade in Telecommunications,' WTP Forum, Geneva, 16–18 March 1998 <www.itu.int/newsarchive/press/WTPF98/TradeInTelecomsExSum.html> (accessed 23 February 2021).

Kelsey, Jane. *Serving Whose Interests?: The Political Economy of Trade in Services Agreements* (Routledge-Cavendish Publishers, 2008).

Key, Sydney J. 'Financial Services,' in Macrory, Patrick F.J., Arthur E. Appleton and Michael G. Plummer (eds.) *The World Trade Organization: Legal, Economic and Political Analysis* Vol 1 (Springer, 2005) 955–988.

Koul, Autar Krishen. *Guide to the WTO and GATT: Economics, Law and Politics* (Springer, 2018).

Krajewski, Markus. 'Article VI GATS,' in Wolfrum, Rüdiger, Peter-Tobias Stoll and Clemens Feinäugle (eds.) *Max Plank Commentaries on World Trade Law: WTO-Trade in Services* Vol 6 (Martin Nijhoff Publishers, 2008) 165–197.

Krajewski, Markus and Maika Engelke. 'Article XVII GATS,' in Wolfrum, Rüdiger, Peter-Tobias Stoll and Clemens Feinäugle (eds.) *Max Plank Commentaries on World Trade Law: WTO-Trade in Services* Vol 6 (Martin Nijhoff Publishers, 2008) 396–420.

Lester, Simon, Bryan Mercurio and Arwel Davies. *World Trade Law: Text, Materials and Commentary* (Hart Publishing, 2018).

Marchetti, Juan A. 'The GATS Prudential Carve-Out,' in Delimatsis, Panagiotis and Nils Herger (eds.) *Financial Regulation at the Crossroads: Implications for Supervision, Institutional Design and Trade* (Wolters Kluwer Publication, 2011) 279–295.

Marchetti, Juan A. and Petros C. Mavroidis. 'The Genesis of the GATS (General Agreement on Trade in Services),' *The European Journal of International Law* Vol 22, No 3 (2011) 689–721.

Matsushita, Mitsuo, Thomas J. Shoenbaum, Petros C. Mavroidis and Michael Hahn. *The World Trade Organization: Law, Practice, and Policy* (Oxford University Press, 2017).

Mavroidis, Petros C. and Robert Wolfe. 'From Sunshine to a Common Agent: The Evolving Understanding of Transparency in the WTO,' *The Brown Journal of World Affairs* Vol 21, No 2 (2015) 117–129.

Mclarty, Taunya L. 'Liberalized Telecommunications Trade in the WTO: Implications for Universal Service Policy,' *Federal Communications Law Journal* Vol 51, No 1 (1998) 1–59.

'Ministerial Declaration on the Uruguay Round,' Declaration of 20 September 1986 <https://docs.wto.org/gattdocs/q/UR/TNCMIN86/MINDEC.PDF> (accessed on 3 February 2021).

Muller, Gilles. 'Troubled Relationships under the GATS: Tensions between Market Access (Article XVI), National Treatment (Article XVII), and Domestic Regulation (Article VI),' *World Trade Law* Vol 16, No 3 (2017) 449–474.

Nartova, Olga. 'Article XXI GATS,' in Wolfrum, Rüdiger, Peter-Tobias Stoll and Clemens Feinäugle (eds.) *Max Plank Commentaries on World Trade Law: WTO-Trade in Services* Vol 6 (Martin Nijhoff Publishers, 2008) 465–479.

Natens, Bregt. *Regulatory Autonomy and International Trade in Services* (Edward Elgar Publication, 2016).

Nicolaïdis, Kalypso and Joel P. Trachtman. 'From Policed Regulation to Managed Recognition in GATS,' in Sauvé, Pierre and Robert M. Stern (eds.) *GATS 2000: New Directions in Services Trade Liberalization* (Brookings Institution Press, 2000) 241–282.

OECD. 'OECD Balanced Trade Statistics,' *OECD Balanced Trade in Services Database* (2018).

Reyna, Jimmie V. 'Services,' in Stewart, Terence P. (ed.) *The GATT Uruguay Round: A Negotiating History (1986–1992)* Vol 2 (Kluwer Law Publishing, 1993).

Sauvé, Pierre. 'Assessing the General Agreement on Trade in Services: Half-Full or Half-Empty?,' *Journal of World Trade* Vol 29, No 4 (1995) 125–145.

Sutherland, Peter. 'Concluding the Uruguay Round: Creating the New Architecture of Trade for the Global Economy,' *Fordham International Law Journal* Vol 24, No 1 (2000) 15–29.

Trebilcock, Michael, Robert Howse and Antonia Eliason. *The Regulation of International Trade* (Routledge, 2013).

UN Central Product Classification <https://unstats.un.org/unsd/publication/SeriesM/SeriesM_77ver1_1E.pdf> (accessed on 5 February 2021).

'UNCTAD Secretariat, Services and the Development Process,' (42 UN Doc. TD/B/1008/Rev.1) (1985).

Van den Bossche, Peter and Werner Zdouc. *The Law and Policy of the World Trade Organization* (Cambridge University Press, 2017).

Van Grasstek, Craig. *The History and Future of the World Trade Organization* (WTO, 2013).

Wang, Wei. 'On the Relationship between Market Access and National Treatment under GATS,' *The International Lawyer* Vol 46, No 4 (2012) 1045–1065.

Wolfrum, Rüdiger. 'Article II GATS,' in Wolfrum, Rüdiger, Peter-Tobias Stoll and Clemens Feinäugle (eds.) *Max Plank Commentaries on World Trade Law: WTO-Trade in Services* Vol 6 (Martin Nijhoff Publishers, 2008) 71–91.

WTO. 'General Agreement on Trade in Services (GATS); Objectives, Coverage and Disciplines,' <www.wto.org/english/tratop_e/serv_e/gatsqa_e.htm> (accessed 5 February 2021).

WTO. 'Draft Glossary of Terms,' (MTN.GNS/W/43) (8 July 1988) <https://docs.wto.org/gattdocs/q/UR/GNS/W43.PDF> (accessed 5 February 2021).

WTO. 'Multilateral Trade Negotiations, The Uruguay Round,' Working Group on Financial Services Including Insurance: Note on the Meeting of 11–13 June 1990 (MTN.GNS/FIN/1) (5 July 1990).

WTO. Negotiating Group on Basic Telecommunications, *Telecommunication Services: Reference Paper* (24 April 1996a) <www.wto.org/english/tratop_e/serv_e/telecom_e/tel23_e.htm> (accessed 18 February 2021).

WTO. Working Party on Professional Services, 'The Relevance of the Disciplines of the Agreements on Technical Barriers to Trade (TBT) and on Import Licensing Procedure to Art. VI:4 of the GATS,' Note by the Secretariat (WTO Doc. S/WPPS/W/9) (11 September 1996b).

WTO. Working Party on Professional Services, 'Guidelines for Mutual Recognition Agreements or Arrangements in the Accounting Sector,' Revision (WTO Doc. S/WPPS/W/12/Rev.1) (20 May 1997).

WTO. Working Party on Professional Services, 'Disciplines on Domestic Regulation in the Accountancy Sector,' (S/WPPS/W/21) (30 November 1998a).

WTO. Trade in Services, 'Disciplines on Domestic Regulation in the Accountancy Sector,' (S/l/64) (17 December 1998b).

WTO. Council for Trade in Services, 'Decision on Disciplines Relating to the Accountancy Sector,' (S/L/63) (15 December 1998c).

WTO. Trade in Services, 'Guidelines for the Scheduling of Specific Commitments Under the General Agreement on Trade in Services (GATS),' (S/L/92) (28 March 2001).

WTO. *A Handbook on the GATS Agreement* (Cambridge University Press, 2005).

WTO. *The Legal Texts: The Results of the Uruguay Round of Multilateral Trade Negotiations* (Cambridge University Press, 2010).

WTO. Working Party on Domestic Regulation, 'Necessity Tests in the WTO,' Note by the Secretariat, Addendum (S/WPDR/W/27/Add.1) (18 January 2011).

WTO, Sutherland, Peter, Jagdish Bhagwati, Kwesi Botchwey, Niall W.A. Fitzgerald, Koichi Hamada, John H. Jackson, Celso Lafer and Thierry de Montbrial. 'The Future of the WTO: Addressing Institutional Challenges in the New Millennium,' Report of the Consultative Board to the Director-General Supachai Panitchpakdi (WTO, 2004).

Zdouc, Werner. 'WTO Dispute Settlement Practice Relating to the General Agreement on Trade in Services,' in Ortino, Federico and Ernst-Ulrich Petersmann (eds.) *The WTO Dispute Settlement System 1995–2003* (Kluwer Law International, 2004) 381–420.

12 Intellectual Property Rights

Learning Objectives	469
1. Introduction	469
2. Political Economy of TRIPS	470
2.1 Uruguay Round: Forum Shifting From WIPO to GATT	471
3. Intellectual Property Rights: Historical Origins	472
3.1 Economic Theories and Private Rights	472
3.2 Economic Analysis of Intellectual Property Laws	475
4. Objectives and Scope of the TRIPS Agreement	478
4.1 Structure and Basic Principles of the TRIPS Agreement	480
4.1.1 Intellectual Property	481
4.2 TRIPS Agreement and WIPO Conventions	482
4.3 The NT and MFN Treatment Obligations	483
4.4 Exhaustion of Intellectual Property Rights	485
5. Rights Protected Under the TRIPS Agreement	486
5.1 Copyright and Related Rights	486
5.1.1 TRIPS Agreement and the Berne Convention 1971	487
5.1.2 Copyright Protection Under TRIPS	487
5.2 Trademarks	490
5.3 Geographical Indication	496
5.4 Patents	499
5.4.1 Compulsory Licensing	501
5.4.2 TRIPS Flexibilities for Public Health Purposes	504
5.5 Layout Designs of Integrated Circuits	505
6. Enforcement of Intellectual Property Rights	506
6.1 General Principles	506
6.2 Civil and Administrative Procedures and Remedies	506
6.3 Provisional Measures and Border Measures	508
6.4 Criminal Procedures	508
6.5 Acquisition and Maintenance of Intellectual Property Rights	508
7. Institutional Provisions of the TRIPS Agreement	509
7.1 Council for TRIPS	509
7.2 Transparency and Dispute Settlement	509
8. Special Rules for Developing Country and LDC Members	510
8.1 Transitional Periods	510
8.2 Technical Assistance and Transfer of Technology	511
9. Summary	511

Learning Objectives

This chapter aims to help students understand:

1. Intellectual property rights in the WTO; historical origins of IP rights; political economy of the TRIPS Agreement;
2. Objectives and scope of the TRIPS Agreement; structure and basic principles of the TRIPS Agreement; TRIPS and WIPO conventions;
3. NT and MFN treatment obligations; protected rights under the TRIPS Agreement; copyright; trademarks; geographical indications; patents;
4. Compulsory licensing; pharmaceutical patents and access to medicines;
5. Enforcement of IP rights; institutional provisions of the TRIPS Agreement; and
6. Special rules for developing country and LDC Member States;

1. Introduction

The Uruguay Round of negotiations introduced a number of new disciplines into the multilateral trading system that were to be launched in January 1995. One of the most contentious and controversial agreements to emerge out of the Uruguay Round of negotiations was the Agreement on Trade-Related Aspects of Intellectual Property Rights (TRIPS). Considered as the most important instrument in the vision for a global governance of IP rights protection, the TRIPS Agreement is built on the foundations of national and international IP laws of developed market economies. IP rights are abstract and exist only in particular products, yet are characteristic to creative ideas and information. Although viewed as a single set of rights, IP rights comprise a bundle of different types of rights, classified under patents, trademarks, copyright, performer's rights, *etc.* A majority of the IP rights, *i.e.*, patents and copyrights, are held by corporations from developed nations.

It will be recalled that the GATT was founded with the foremost objective of liberalising world trade, *i.e.*, trade in goods, and protection for IP rights was not part of its remit. The TRIPS Agreement, on the other hand, not only introduces a new international IP rights regime as a covered agreement of the WTO, but also incorporates other earlier conventions[1] that afford protection to patents, trademarks, copyrights, performer's rights and other IP rights. The abstract nature of IP rights made it difficult to be integrated into the GATT, as it dealt with private rights of IP rights holders, necessitating a radically different approach to protection of IP rights within the multilateral trading system. Although Article IX:6 of the GATT, which dealt with the protection of distinctive regional or geographical names, was an exception, it did not go into the details of standards of protection and only called for cooperation amongst GATT Contracting Parties on their protection.

The Agreement does not replace existing international IP rights regimes, but rather incorporates them in its scheme of international IP rights protection. The TRIPS Agreement has at its foundation a large body of existing laws, which includes both international conventions and domestic legislation. As opposed to the international conventions that preceded it, the TRIPS Agreement requires all Member States to provide 'minimum' standards of IP protection and also allows Member States to provide for a more extensive protection of IP right if they so wish and a minimum standard of protection from others who may not favour the idea of an extensive protection. The Agreement also contains flexibilities in its implementation, which is particularly aimed at developing country Member States and least developed country (LDC) Member States. Progressive liberalisation, which is a standard feature found in other covered agreements, is absent in TRIPS.

2. Political Economy of TRIPS

The vision for an international IP rights protection was initially conceived and promoted by patent rights–holding transnational corporations from developed countries (US, EU, and Japanese corporations), which had campaigned ceaselessly for the inclusion of an agreement on IP rights in the Uruguay Round of negotiations (Drahos, 2003). The TRIPS Agreement came to be an output of private nodal governance (Drahos, 2003; Weissman, 1996), with the process starting in the 1980s when one of the transnational pharmaceutical corporations took the lead in creating an agenda to include US IP rights protection abroad (Drahos, 2003).[2] It was claimed by US industries, which included pharmaceuticals, chemicals, biotechnology, computer software, entertainment, *etc.*, that they suffered heavy losses from the absence of adequate protection of their intellectual property rights in foreign markets (Adede, 2003).

The US, a developed nation with substantial patent rights holding (besides having high stakes in other IP interests) and a strong advocate of international IP rights protection, led the initiative to introduce IP protection in the GATT negotiations. Commentators have expressed a strong view that some 12 US corporations were primarily responsible for the lobbying that brought the TRIPS Agreement into existence (Sell, 2003; Drahos and Braithwaite, 2002; Matthews, 2002). The arguments from patent-holding transnational corporations (backed by developed nations) were that widespread piracy, counterfeiting, and infringement of other IP rights diminished their chances of market access in developing countries which had lax IP rights protection. It was also argued that as IP rights were linked to technology transfer agreements, it would benefit developing countries in their growth agenda. One industry that particularly engaged in aggressive lobbying campaigns on the need to secure greater patent protection abroad was the pharmaceutical industry. Lobbying campaigns by the pharmaceutical industry included funding academic studies aimed at proclaiming the merits of patent protection (Weissman, 1996). Their arguments were focused on developing countries that had a much shorter period of patent protection to pharmaceuticals than was available in the US and other European countries.

For the US pharmaceutical industry, anything less than an American-style patent protection would constitute stealing by other nations. It sought to persuade US policymakers to coerce Third World/developing countries to introduce restrictive patent laws into their domestic legislation (Kosterlitz, 1993).[3] Following the efforts of the pharmaceutical corporations, the US government in the 1980s started introducing suitable provisions protecting IP rights as an investment activity in the Bilateral Investment Treaty (BIT) program, which it was negotiating with developing countries during that time (Drahos, 2003). The US pharmaceutical industry also achieved moving the traditional international trade policy away from tariffs and related matters and in the direction of strict international IP rights protection (Weissman, 1996).[4]

In 1986, a coalition of 13 major US corporations, including Pfizer, Bristol-Meyers, Merck, and Johnsons & Johnson, to name a few, formed an *ad hoc* committee called Intellectual Property Committee (IPC), with the stated objective of being "dedicated to the negotiation of a comprehensive agreement on intellectual property in the current GATT round of multilateral trade negotiations" (Drahos, 2003; Weissman, 1990). The United States Trade Representative (USTR), in pursuit of a higher IP protection overseas, was empowered by section 301 of the Trade Act of 1974 to take action against foreign governments and use such trade measures as leverage to achieve minimum standards of IP. In 1986, the lobbyists successfully introduced their agenda on international IP rights protection to the GATT under the

Uruguay Round of negotiations. The US Omnibus Trade and Competitiveness Act, passed in 1988, besides providing the tools necessary to participate in the Uruguay Round of negotiations and revising US foreign trade laws, also identified the protection of IP rights as one of the principal priorities of United States trade policy, thereby strengthening US resolve to seek international protection for IP rights at the international level.[5]

2.1 Uruguay Round: Forum Shifting From WIPO to GATT

The World Intellectual Property Organization (WIPO), created in 1967, was seen as the custodian of the key conventions on IP, *viz.*, the Paris Convention 1893 and the Berne Convention 1896. WIPO was also the first international organisation that attempted to address some of the issues relating to international IP rights implementation. In the eyes of patent-holding developed nations, WIPO was incapable of responding effectively to issues relating to intellectual property rights violation, and as a result sought to shift the IP rights agenda away from WIPO (Crump and Druckman, 2012). On the other hand, the developing countries, who had a stronger voice in WIPO, were opposed to altering the WIPO system to strengthen IP rights protection (UNCTAD-ICTSD, 2005).[6] Seeking an expanded international IP rights protection regime, the patent-holding developed countries, including the US, the EC, and Japan, acted fast to shift the global IP rights administration from WIPO to the GATT.

Industry groups from patent-holding developed countries successfully created a coalition of governments that would pursue the objective of moving IP rights regulation from WIPO to the GATT (Stewart, 1993). This tactic adopted by both state and non-state actors is described as 'forum shifting' or 'regime shifting', which allows for rule-making to be relocated to a more favourable forum (Helfer, 2004; Drahos, 2004a; Sell, 2009, 2011).[7] The move for a global IP rights protection mooted by developed countries and led by the US was strongly opposed by developing countries, including Argentina, Brazil, India, and South Africa, amongst others.[8] The developing countries were strongly in favour of a WIPO-led negotiation, as opposed to a revision of international IP rights obligations through the GATT, as the WIPO had traditionally been the forum for such matters (Weissman, 1996).[9] Patent-holding businesses in the US, the EU, and Japan successfully exerted pressure on their respective governments to ensure that IP rights became a global commercial issue and also the focus of attention during the Uruguay Round of GATT negotiations (Sundaram, 2015).

For the developed country negotiators, the body of IP law, both international and domestic laws (from developed nations), became the foundation to proceed with the negotiations. Also, the negotiators from developed nations benefitted from their vast experience of working in the fields of competition policies (Cottier, 2015). According to the industries' own admission, the US position calling for adoption of a US-style patent law was developed largely by the pharmaceutical industry (Weissman, 1996). India, along with similarly placed developing countries like Brazil and Argentina, strongly opposed the proposal on the premise that the GATT mandate did not allow for the discussion of substantive issues on IP, and that it was only WIPO that had the mandate and the institutional competence to discuss such matters (Watal, 2001; Sundaram, 2015).[10]

India's stance, well supported by other developing countries, was that any principle or standard relating to IP rights was to be carefully tested against the needs of developing countries, and that it would be inappropriate to focus the negotiations on the protection of monopoly rights of the owners of IP rights, when almost 99 percent of the patents were owned by industrialised nations (UNCTAD-ICTSD, 2005; Sundaram, 2015).[11] By the end of 1989 and the beginning of 1990, the developing countries were constrained to change their standpoint completely, paving the way for a US-style IP rights protection to be imposed through the GATT, thereby circumventing and undermining the authority of the WIPO. The forum shifting of international IP rights negotiations from WIPO to the GATT was complete. The TRIPS Agreement "remains a controversial but forceful legacy of the Uruguay Round Trade Agreements" (Okediji, 2003).

Besides the imposition of 'minimum' standards of IP protection, TRIPS obligates Member States to make available patents for products and processes without discrimination as to the field of technology[12] and requires the introduction of product patents for chemical and pharmaceutical patents. The TRIPS Agreement effectively globalised standards of protection for patent, trade secrets, and trademark protection – the three areas considered most relevant to the success of chemical and pharmaceutical companies. Many countries, who came to the negotiations under the genuine impression that they were negotiating a ceiling on IP rights, were, all along, indeed only negotiating a floor (Sell, 2003).[13] In the post-WTO era, the developed country Member States have introduced TRIPS-plus provisions into the RTAs, thereby preventing some of the key TRIPS flexibilities from being exercised by developing countries.

3. Intellectual Property Rights: Historical Origins[14]

The inclusion of IP rights within the multilateral trading system was a lengthy and arduous process, as most developing country Member States were opposed to the idea of international IP rights protection put forth by developed nations. Historically, the very notion of IP rights came to be recognised only after economic theories gained strength to reach the houses of Parliament of European powers, where lengthy debates ensued. The drafters, while seeking to introduce a uniform IP rights protection through the TRIPS Agreement, did not engage in any new economic or legal analysis of IP rights to justify the promotion of pre-existing IP rights to the status of universal norms (Reichman, 1995). The TRIPS Agreement is instead, built on the edifice of the Paris Convention 1883 and the Berne Convention 1886. This section traces the economic background of IP rights from its origins in the early part of the seventeenth century in the Statute of Monopolies to its steady and gradual emergence as a private right, in both the common law and the civil law traditions.

3.1 Economic Theories and Private Rights

The foundations of economic theories, deeply entrenched in utilitarianism, present the framework for analysis of the IP rights as currently enshrined in the TRIPS Agreement. Historically, utilitarian theorists strongly supported the creation of IP rights as an appropriate means to foster innovation, while non-utilitarian theorists had looked to the creator's moral rights to have control over their work (Menell, 2000). The recognition of IP rights started with the grant of patent rights with the passing of the Statute of Monopolies of 1623,[15] which also laid down the principle that only a true and first inventor should be granted a monopoly patent. Just over 200 years after the passing of the Statute of Monopolies of 1623, the subject of patent reform was raised once more before the English Parliament, for the reason that the procedure for obtaining a patent was expensive, clumsy, and uncertain (Machlup and Penrose, 1950). This prompted a lengthy debate in England, which was to soon spread to the Continent, where economists too would join in the debate, to create pro-patent and anti-patent lobbies (Machlup and Penrose, 1950).[16] The lobbying and debating produced a number of changes to the laws on patents – both in England and on the Continent – and also witnessed the emergence of economic theories on the subject, with notable ones coming from England and France.

Classical writers in England almost completely fell in line with the traditional principles contained in the Statute of Monopolies of 1623 that justified the grant of temporary monopolies for the exploitation of innovations due to their special character and function, and so being exempt from the prohibition of monopoly. Jurist Jeremy Bentham, regarded as the founder of modern-day utilitarianism, held the view that there was

> one species of privilege certainly very advantageous: the patents which are granted in England for a limited time, for inventions in arts and manufactures. Of all the methods of existing and rewarding industry, this is the least burthensome, and the most exactly proportioned to the merit of the invention.
>
> (Bentham, 1843, p. 533)

He went on to observe, "[t]his privilege has nothing in common with monopolies, which are justly decried" (Bentham, 1843, p. 533).

Adam Smith, recognised as the pioneer of political economy, whilst referring to the risks that a company of merchants undertake and the expenses they incur to establish a new trade, opined that the state should compensate the merchants by granting them

> a monopoly of the trade for a certain number of years . . . [to] recompense them for hazarding a dangerous and expensive experiment, of which the public is afterwards to reap the benefit. A temporary monopoly of this kind may be vindicated upon the same principles upon which a like monopoly of a new machine is granted to its inventor, and that of a new book to its author.[17]

Smith also felt such monopolies for inventions could be defended on the grounds of equity, and as far as extending similar rights to new books was concerned, he argued that such exclusive privilege could be regarded as "an encouragement to the labours of learned men" and being beneficial to the society. Endnote 18. Ibid. Smith clearly supported both patents and copyrights, as he viewed them as a just reward for the inventors and authors.

John Stuart Mill, yet another proponent of utilitarianism, took a similar stance and categorically stated, "the condemnation of monopolies ought not to extend to patents" (Mill, 2004, pp. 271–272). Mill also observed that the originator of an improved process should be allowed to enjoy, for a limited period, "the exclusive privilege of using his own improvement", and that inventors should be both compensated and rewarded. Whereas Michel Chevalier, the French economist, was most emphatic in his opposition of both tariffs and patents, declaring that both "stem from the same doctrine and result in the same abuses" (Chevalier, 1878).[18] The opponents of the privilege and monopoly were able to ideologically link patent protectionism with tariff protectionism and patent monopoly, to argue against monopoly privileges, which was clearly exemplified in the views expressed by Michel Chevalier. On the other hand, the advocates of a strong patent protection were able to separate the idea of patent protection from the monopoly issue and the free trade issue to present the case of patent protection as one of natural law and private property, and of man's right to live by his work (Machlup and Penrose, 1950).[19]

David Hume argued that property has no purpose where there is abundance; it arises, and derives its significance, out of the scarcity of the objects that become appropriated, in a world in which people desire to benefit from their own work and sacrifice (Hume, 1902). According to Hume, systems of justice protect property rights solely on account of their utility. Hume further argued that where the security of property was adequately assured, property owners generally see to it that scarce 'means' are directed to those uses, which within their knowledge and judgment are most productive of what they want. In the eighteenth century, yet another strand of thought emerged, that man has a natural property right in his own ideas. The preamble to the patent laws passed by French Constitutional Assembly in 1791 reads as follows:

> that every novel idea whose realisation or development can become useful to society belongs primarily to him who conceived it, and that it would be a violation of the rights of man in their very essence if an industrial invention were not regarded as the property of its creator.[20]

This preamble captured and encapsulated the spirit of the arguments of the pro-patent economists who favoured the grant of a patent monopoly. The Congress in US was soon to follow suit with the introduction of new patent laws in 1793, which were based on the copyright provisions contained in its Constitution (Fenning, 1929; Donner, 1992). Article I, Section 8, Clause 8 of the United States Constitution expressly vests the US Congress with powers to grant authors and inventors exclusive rights "to their respective Writings and Discoveries" *i.e.*, copyrights and patents, on a utilitarian foundation.[21] Interestingly, the term used is 'discoveries' and not 'inventions'. This clause was referred to as the 'Copyright Clause', 'Patent Clause', and in later years as the 'Intellectual Property Clause'.[22] Although the actual author of the copyright clause is still unknown, most commentators believe that it was either James Madison or Charles C. Pinckney. The International Copyright Act 1891, more popularly referred to as the Chace Act, was passed in the US, extending limited protection to foreign copyright holders from select nations. The passage of the Act brought to an end the long feud between the intellectual establishments in England and the US over international copyright.[23]

In a letter written on 13 August 1813 to the inventor Isaac McPherson, Thomas Jefferson expressed the view that

> [i]f nature has made any one thing less susceptible than all others of exclusive property, it is the action of the thinking power called an idea, which an individual may exclusively possess as long as he keeps it to himself; but the moment it is divulged, it forces itself into the possession of every one, and the receiver cannot dispossess himself of it. Its peculiar character, too, is that no one possesses the less, because every other possesses the whole of it.
> (Jefferson, 1813)

He further added:

> ideas should freely spread from one to another over the globe, for the moral and mutual instruction of man, and improvement of his condition, seems to have been peculiarly and benevolently designed by nature, when she made them, like fire, expansible over all space, without lessening their density in any point, and like the air in which we breathe, move, and have our physical being, incapable of confinement or exclusive appropriation.
> (Jefferson, 1813)

Importantly, Jefferson was not in favour of the argument of the French philosophers that inventors and authors had a 'natural rights' claim to property in their creations, as he was clear in his view that inventions cannot be a subject of property in nature. Jefferson's comments came two decades after the passing of the first US laws on the subject in 1793, and the fact that he was the principal author of the US Declaration of Independence and the third president of the US cannot be ignored.

The economic rationale for protection of IP rights is founded on the premise that unless an invention or a creation is compensated at its full social value, there will be very little incentive to undertake or engage in such activities (Trebilcock, Howse, and Eliason, 2013). The mainstream economics profession has consistently argued that inventors need support and protection from the government for their innovations in order to maintain an incentive for creative inquiry. Patent rights are deliberate creations of statue law, and it is the intention of the legislators that the beneficiary shall be placed in a position to secure an income from the monopoly conferred upon him by placing restrictions on the supply of the information (Plant, 1934). Grant of such rights is intended to stimulate innovation by allowing the rights holder to work his patented product for a definite period of time to recover the investment and also make a profit. Such exclusive rights are designed to empower the rights holder to prevent third parties from unauthorised use of the subject matter.

So, one can assume that the statutes creating and granting patent rights monopolies would not have continued to remain in statute books, in the absence of a widespread expectation of public advantage from their operation. The dissenting traditions have argued that government action of any kind, including the awarding of copyrights and patents, is unnecessary to stimulate such activity (Plant, 1934). The picture that emerges is a debate of polarised views, with one side arguing that ideas should benefit the public, and the other arguing that individuals should benefit from their ideas.

3.2 *Economic Analysis of Intellectual Property Laws*[24]

This section of the chapter seeks to analyse some of the key economic theories to emerge in the twentieth century on the subject of IP rights protection which lay the foundations for the creation of an international IP rights protection regime to come in the form of the TRIPS Agreement under the auspices of the WTO. Currently, as it stands, the principal policy objective of IP laws is the promotion of new and improved works through the recognition and creation of property rights, whether they are in the realms of expressive media, chemicals and pharmaceuticals, technology, or other forms. It will be beneficial for our purposes to present a more contemporary analysis of the economic foundations of IP rights and the justification for the grant of exclusive rights for inventions and other similar intangibles.

There had been a fundamental shift in conventional thinking of trade as goods-oriented, which was brought about as a result of the sheer significance of IP to developed economies (Marcellin, 2016). The modern-day intellectual property rights principles are strongly modelled on the US intellectual property regime, which in turn is severely influenced by the pharmaceutical industry, computing industry, and music and motion picture industries. Today, much of the value of the leading corporate bodies in the world are estimated by their portfolio of intangible assets, which range from the better-defined forms of IP (patents and copyrights) to the least tangible of the intangibles (trade secrets and trademarks) (Menell and Scotchmer, 2007). Calandrillo explains the justification behind the US IP regime as being built on the premise that it is socially desirable to encourage and produce many types of information, whose value to society far exceeds its developmental costs (Calandrillo, 1998). Calandrillo further asserts that most supporters of the US incentive system ignore the exorbitant costs it involves and the restrictions placed upon the availability of information generated by the system.

IP rights generally confer an exclusive right to exploit the protected subject matter, or in other words, confer a right on the titleholder to prevent third parties from using the protected knowledge without authorization (Correa, 2003). Tangible goods which are rivalrous, *i.e.*, when fully consumed by one individual, cannot be accessed by another. Intellectual resources are non-rivalrous, and the consumption by one does not lead to a scarcity. Hence, non-rivalrous goods (*e.g.*, the radio, the internet, *etc.*), which include knowledge,[25] can be made available for public use, usually at low cost and sometimes at no cost (Stiglitz, 1999; David, 1993). But knowledge can be made excludable through actions by its possessor or through legal means – for instance, where a company may prevent its competitors from knowing how a particular manufacturing process operates by tightly controlling access to its physical premises and preventing the disclosure of relevant data by its employees (Correa, 2003).[26] Unlike goods which are tangible and can be appropriated and separated from the commons, knowledge and intellectual products are intangible and not appropriable (Muzaka, 2011). This distinction between rivalrous and non-rivalrous goods have led commentators to question the status given to IP right (Menell, 2007).

As it stands, IP rights are intended to encourage innovation. Some commentators have expressed doubts about the perceived benefit of IP rights, as it is difficult to establish if such rights truly work as an incentive to engage in such pursuits, and on the other hand, IP rights attempt to restrict the use of knowledge in one way or another and pose potential impediments to diffusion and cumulative innovation (Stiglitz, 2008; Menell and Scotchmer, 2007). The number of patents granted in a technologically fast growing world, especially set against the backdrop of a globalised economy, requires a different philosophical basis and a clear set of theories to justify their grant than what was presented in the nineteenth century US and Europe, as the rationale for grant of a monopoly has changed.[27] Until the early part of the 1990s, very little empirical research was done on the impact of economics on public policy in the area of IP rights, especially in comparison to the influence of professional writings in areas such as antitrust and taxation (Besen and Raskind, 1991).

Kitch argues that although good progress was made in the understanding of economics of IP rights in the twentieth century, much still remains to be done.[28] Kitch identifies recurring errors in the literature on the subject matter, and in his view, writers over a period of time have repeatedly analysed IP rights on the assumption that they confer an economic monopoly on the rights holder (Kitch, 2000). Kitch notes that most authors begin with an analysis of IP rights on the presumption that the rights holder of the intellectual property possesses an economic monopoly, *viz.*, a monopoly where the rights holder is protected from competition and able to sell into a market with a downward sloping demand curve. He further argues that characterisation of patents as a monopoly can only be true if the claims cover all of an economically relevant market, *i.e.*, there is no alternative way for competitors to provide the same economic functionality to their customers without infringing the claims. For Kitch, the empirical question if IP rights confer any economic monopoly, although persistently raised in the literature, is not properly addressed, as it is addressed only in passing.

Scotchmer presents a similar, yet more emphatic argument on the point by stating that most innovators "stand on the shoulders of giants, and never more so than in the current evolution of high technologies, where almost all technical progress builds on a foundation provided by earlier innovators" (Scotchmer, 1991). Scotchmer advances the argument that latter-day innovators simply bettered previous technologies, and notes that most economic literature on patenting have proceeded to "study innovations in isolation, without focusing on the externalities or spill-overs that early innovators confer on later innovators. But the cumulative nature of research poses problems for the optimal design of patent law that are not addressed by that perspective". Going by that assertion, one is tempted to conclude that it is mere cumulative research leading to innovation, which in the eye of the law is patentable, resulting in the 'inventor' being rewarded with exclusive patent rights.

Stiglitz, a Nobel Laureate in economics, argues that many of the most important ideas, like the mathematics that underlies the modern computer, the fundamentals behind atomic energy, lasers, *etc.*, are not protected by IP rights and have been used freely by academics and researchers, and that academics disseminate their research findings without charging for them. Stiglitz argues that an IP regime, in contrast, rewards innovators by creating a temporary monopoly power, which allows the rights holder to charge far higher prices than they could possibly charge if there were to be a competition (Stiglitz, 2005). Machlup, in a study carried out on the US patent system, observes that there is a general perception that 'property' and 'monopoly' are one and the same from an economic perspective, and the rights holder of an invention has a 'monopoly' over its use just as the owner of a house has a 'monopoly' of the use of the house, which according to Machlup could encumber economic analysis (Machlup, 1958).[29] The term property, although used frequently in discussions, is indeed complex and highly political besides being in every way legal, as it vests the individual with tangible and intangible rights.

For Landes and Posner, the standard rationale of patent law is that "it is an efficient method of enabling the benefits of research and development to be internalized, thus promoting innovation and technological progress" (Landes and Posner, 2003). The rationale for granting legal protection to inventions is the difficulty that a manufacture may encounter whilst trying to recover his fixed costs of research and development when the product or process that embodies a new invention is readily 'copiable'. But this protection presents a greater danger, as the "inventor will be enabled to charge a higher price than he needs to recover for the fixed costs of his invention, thereby restricting access to the invention more than is necessary" (Landes and Posner, 2003). Landes and Posner assert that a patentee's monopoly mark-up, which is influenced by the degree of protection afforded, bears no direct relation to the fixed costs that the patentee incurred in the creation of the patented product. Landes and Posner also maintain that legislation and policy are for the most part non-excludable public goods,[30] and in contrast IP is an excludable public good. The public-choice theory, seen as the driving force behind policy decisions, had neither succeeded in explaining the forces that brought into being the system of property rights that is fundamental to a capitalist economy nor said anything about the extension of that system to encompass intellectual property (Landes and Posner, 2003).

Posner, in a more recent contribution made to an online blog, expresses concerns that both patent and copyright protection, particularly the former, may be excessive. He argues that the cost of inventing must be comparable to the cost of copying in order to determine the optimal patent protection for an inventor, and that when patent protection is too strongly in favour of the inventor, market efficiency is decreased (Posner, 2012). Posner also avers that pharmaceutical drugs are the "poster child" for patent protection, and that "few other products have the characteristics that make patent protection indispensable to the pharmaceutical industry". The most interesting, if not scathing, comment to come from Posner is with regards to the 20-year duration of the patent protection granted, which in his view confers no real benefit – except to enable the producer to extract licence fees from firms wanting to make a different product that incorporates his invention. Posner concludes the brief with a parting shot that the need for reform of both patent and copyright laws are sufficiently acute to warrant serious attention from the US Congress and the courts (Posner, 2012). According to Posner, the long protection afforded to patents under the current US laws leads to profiteering by the rights holder, which defeats the very basis for the grant of a patent protection.[31]

The modern, or contemporary, perception of IP rights is strongly influenced and shaped by US expansionist economic policies and law making. It has its foundations in utilitarianism and the Lockean model of natural laws, and was also strongly influenced by the common law notions of property rights. This understanding of IP, as propagated by Anglo-Saxon jurisprudence and later by Anglo-American jurisprudence (which, in turn, is influenced by Posnerian economic analysis from the 1970s), has paved the way for a winner-take-all 'wealth maximisation' outlook towards the recognition and grant of IP rights. From the foregoing discussions one can infer that economic theories are yet to produce a convincing and coherent set of principles to justify IP protection for intangible rights. What we witness now is the evolution of IP laws following the school of thought based on "wealth maximisation" (Posner, 1983)[32] and the establishment of an international regime through the WTO, which provides strong IP rights protection. This attitude towards IP rights protection goes way beyond the utilitarian principles expounded by Jeremy Bentham.

One cannot ignore the fact that we live in an information-driven society, where developed economies (and also some developing economies) are strong information producers which naturally support the establishment of strong IP rights protection laws to serve their interests. In that landscape, IP rights policies emerge as essential organisational principles of the knowledge-based economy, since it determines the way in which knowledge relations are structured and governed (Ghafele, 2008).

4. Objectives and Scope of the TRIPS Agreement

In contrast to the GATT 1947, which only recognised rights of the Contracting Parties, the WTO TRIPS Agreement explicitly addresses private rights of IP rights holders/economic operators. As mentioned in the introduction, the Agreement fully incorporates other earlier conventions[33] that afford protection to patents, trademarks, copyrights, performer's rights, and other IP rights. The TRIPS Agreement requires Member States to introduce or maintain a number of domestic legal rules and procedures for the granting, protecting, and enforcing IP rights. These legal rules include obligations such as providing effective procedures for the acquisition, maintenance, and enforcement of IP rights, including "civil judicial procedures concerning the enforcement of any intellectual property right covered by this Agreement"[34] as well as criminal procedures.[35]

Part II of the Agreement extends protection to the following IP rights, *viz*., copyright and related rights; trademarks; geographical indications; industrial designs; patents; lay-out designs (topographies) of integrated circuits; and protection of undisclosed information. The key objectives of the TRIPS Agreement identified in the Preamble capture the contentious nature of the negotiation process leading to the Agreement,[36] and reads as follows:

> to reduce distortions and impediments to international trade . . . taking into account the need to promote effective and adequate protection of intellectual property rights, and to ensure that measures and procedures to enforce intellectual property rights do not themselves become barriers to legitimate trade.

The objectives of the TRIPS Agreement contained in the Preamble are to be read along with Article 7 (Objectives) and Article 8 (Principles) of the Agreement, as they contain a range of general principles and objectives of the Agreement. As a result, they are to be borne in mind while examining the substantive provisions of the TRIPS Agreement.[37] Article 7 of the TRIPS Agreement encapsulates the rationale of the TRIPS Agreement and seeks to strike a balance between (i) protecting and enforcing IP rights and (ii) disseminating technology in a manner conducive to social economic welfare, and it reads as follows:

> The protection and enforcement of intellectual property rights should contribute to the promotion of technological innovation and the transfer and dissemination of technology, to the mutual advantage of producers and users of technological knowledge and in a manner conducive to social and economic welfare, and to a balance of rights and obligations.

Article 8 of the TRIPS Agreement, which contains the key provisions providing for flexibilities in the implementation of the Agreement, seeks to strike a balance between the objective of rewarding creators and protecting public health and public interest. While paragraph 1 permits a Member State to adopt measures necessary to protect public health and promote sectors of vital importance to the country's socio-economic and technological development, paragraph 2 permits the introduction of measures needed to prevent the abuse of IP rights by rights holders. Article 8 does not create exceptions to the TRIPS obligations, but elaborates the socio-economic policies of the Member States, and requiring that such measures taken are still in conformity with the TRIPS Agreement.

The Doha Declaration on the TRIPS Agreement and Public Health (Doha Declaration), 2001 stipulates, "[i]n applying the customary rules of interpretation of public international law, each provision of the TRIPS Agreement shall be read in the light of the object and purpose of the Agreement as expressed, in particular, in its objectives and principles". Since the TRIPS Agreement's implementation in 1995, the remit of the two Articles have featured in a few disputes that had come before the DSB. The dispute in *Canada – Pharmaceutical Patents* arose in relation to the interpretation of Article 30, where a determination of the objectives of Article 7 and 8 were called into question.[38]

In *Canada – Pharmaceutical Patents*, the Canadian patent law stockpiling exception was challenged by the EC as being in violation of the TRIPS Agreement. Canada sought to defend its position by arguing that Articles 7 and 8 of the Agreement called for a liberal interpretation of the three conditions stated in Article 30 of the Agreement, so that governments of the Member States would have the necessary flexibility to adjust patent rights to maintain the desired balance with other important national policies.[39] While not disputing the stated goal of Articles 7 and 8, the EC argued that the two Articles are statements that describe the balancing of goals that had already taken place in negotiating the final texts of the TRIPS Agreement. While striking a compromise between the two positions of the disputing Member States and considering the importance of Article 30 and the extent to which other provisions, such as Article 7 and 8 of the Agreement, are to be considered, the Panel ruled as follows:

> In the Panel's view, Article 30's very existence amounts to a recognition that the definition of patent rights contained in Article 28 would need certain adjustments. On the other hand, the three limiting conditions attached to Article 30 testify strongly that the negotiators of the Agreement did not intend Article 30 to bring about what would be equivalent to a renegotiation of the basic balance of the Agreement. Obviously, the exact scope of Article 30's authority will depend on the specific meaning given to its

limiting conditions. The words of those conditions must be examined with particular care on this point. Both the goals and the limitations stated in Articles 7 and 8.1 must obviously be borne in mind when doing so as well as those of other provisions of the TRIPS Agreement which indicate its object and purposes.[40]

Commentators have been critical of the outcome of the dispute, as in their view the Panel Report takes away a Member State's needed discretion in developing their public policies (Barbosa, Chon, and Moncayo von Hase, 2007; Howse, 2000; Okediji, 2003). Correa points out that the Panel avoided elaboration of the content and implications of Articles 7 and 8.1, despite the specific reference that the parties made thereto in their submission (Correa, 2020). In this regard, the Doha Declaration on the TRIPS Agreement and Public Health affirms the rights of the Member States to fully implement the flexibilities that are provided for in the TRIPS Agreement to protect public health.[41]

The Panel in *Australia – Tobacco Plain Packaging*, while considering the types of reasons that may support the application of special requirements that could encumber the use of trademark within the meaning of Article 20, referred to the remit of Article 8 and made the following observation:

> Article 8.1 . . . makes clear that the provisions of the TRIPS Agreement are not intended to prevent the adoption, by Members, of laws and regulations pursuing certain legitimate objectives, specifically, measures "necessary to protect public health and nutrition" and "promote the public interest in sectors of vital importance to their socio-economic and technological development", provided that such measures are consistent with the provisions of the Agreement.
>
> Article 8 offers, in our view, useful contextual guidance for the interpretation of the term "unjustifiably" in Article 20. Specifically, the principles reflected in Article 8.1 express the intention of drafters of the TRIPS Agreement to preserve the ability for WTO Members to pursue certain legitimate societal interests, at the same time as it confirms their recognition that certain measures adopted by WTO Members for such purposes may have an impact on IP rights, and requires that such measures be "consistent with the provisions of the [TRIPS] Agreement".[42]

4.1 Structure and Basic Principles of the TRIPS Agreement

The TRIPS Agreement is presented in seven parts, with the substantive rules of the Agreement to be implemented by the Member States in their respective jurisdictions contained in Parts I and II. While the enforcement obligations of Member States are to be found in Part III, the provisions relating to securing and maintaining IP rights are contained in Part IV. Dispute settlement rules for the TRIPS Agreement are found in Part V. These rules state that disputes arising out of the obligations set out in the TRIPS Agreement between WTO Member States are subject to the dispute settlement procedures of the WTO. Part VI of the Agreement contains transitional arrangements, and Part VII outlines the institutional materials.

Part I, comprising Articles 1 to 8, contains the basic principles. Article 1.1 of the TRIPS Agreement provides that Member States will "give effect to the provisions" of the Agreement, which restates the obligations of the nation states to perform an international agreement in good faith,[43] and thus integrates international IP protection into the domestic legislation of the Member States. Article 1.1 states that Member States may, but need not, adopt a more extensive protection of IP rights than is required under the agreement, and that Member States "shall be free to determine the appropriate method of implementing the provisions of this Agreement within their own legal system and practice".[44]

In *India – Patents (US)* case, India argued that pursuant to Article 1.1 it was permitted to implement the requirement of establishing the 'mailbox' provision (mechanism for the receipt and preservation of patent applications) in a manner determined appropriate for its requirements, and that as a result the 'mailbox' mechanism that was established was adequate. The Appellate Body, while acknowledging India's freedom to establish an appropriate mechanism, ruled that such a right is not the equivalent of a right to self-certify compliance, and that such a right did not preclude a scrutiny of the measures introduced by India to determine if India has met its obligations under the Agreement.[45] The Panel in *China – Intellectual Property Rights* observed that the overall language of Article 1.1 does not permit Member States to implement a lower standard, but rather set a minimum standard, granting the freedom to determine the appropriate method of implementation of the Agreement.[46]

Prior to the formation of the WTO, the conventions administered by WIPO did not establish a common set of norms for the protection of IP rights, and the signatories were at liberty to adopt a more extensive protections than those mandated by the agreements.[47] Although the second sentence of Article 1.1 states the Member States "shall not be obliged" to implement more extensive protection, a number of RTAs concluded in the post-WTO period require that signatories to the RTAs adopt a TRIPS-plus standard of protection, often resulting in the developing country Member States giving up on their 'TRIPS flexibilities'. This, obviously, raises the question if the Member State making such a demand is in breach of the obligation to perform the TRIPS Agreement in 'good faith'.

4.1.1 Intellectual Property

In the pre-TRIPS era, 'industrial property' connoted patents and trademarks, which was in the domain of business, and author's right, or that of an artist, fell under copyright and related rights. Before the late nineteenth century, the term 'intellectual property' was not in vogue.[48] Article 2 (viii) of the Convention Establishing the World Intellectual Property Organization, which entered into force in 1970, contains a broad definition of 'intellectual property' and reads as follows:

Article 2 (viii) "intellectual property" shall include the rights relating to:

- literary, artistic and scientific works,
- performances of performing artists, phonograms, and broadcasts,
- inventions in all fields of human endeavor,
- scientific discoveries,
- industrial designs,
- trademarks, service marks, and commercial names and designations,
- protection against unfair competition, and all other rights resulting from intellectual activity in the industrial, scientific, literary or artistic fields.

This definition does not define the scope of rights but provides a useful basis for comparison with the provisions of the TRIPS Agreement. Article 1.2 of the TRIPS Agreement does not define 'intellectual property' in clear terms, but instead defines the nature and scope of obligations by referring to the rights granted to categories of IP under Articles 9–39, contained in Sections 1 to 7 of Part II of the Agreement. The rights contained in Articles 9–39 include

(i) copyright and related rights, (ii) trademarks, (iii) geographical indications, (iv) industrial designs and utility models, (v) patents, (vi) layout designs (topographies) of integrated circuits, and (vii) protection of undisclosed information. Article 1.2 seeks to limit the subject matter of IP by defining it with reference to "all categories of intellectual property that are subject of Sections 1 through 7 of Part II". It can be argued that Article 1.2 excludes other categories that are not mentioned in Sections 1 to 7 that have the potential to be categorised as IP from its operation of the Agreement.

US – Section 211 Appropriation Act, where the issue surrounding the case was in relation to trade names, did not fall within the ambit of the TRIPS Agreement but was covered by Article 1.2 of the Paris Convention. The Panel ruled that a textual reading of Article 1.2 establishes an inclusive definition as it uses the words "all categories", which indicates that it is an exhaustive list and that there are no obligations under those Articles in relation to categories of IP not set forth in Article 1.2, *e.g.*, trade names, consistent with Article 31 of the Vienna Convention. The Appellate Body in *US – Section 211 Appropriations Act*, while disagreeing with the Panel's interpretation of Article 1.2, observed as follows:

> The Panel interpreted the phrase "'intellectual property' refers to all categories of intellectual property that are the subject of Sections 1 through 7 of Part II" as if that phrase read "intellectual property means those categories of intellectual property appearing in the titles of Sections 1 through 7 of Part II." To our mind, the Panel's interpretation ignores the plain words of Article 1.2, for it fails to take into account that the phrase "the subject of Sections 1 through 7 of Part II" deals not only with the categories of intellectual property indicated in each section title, but with other subjects as well. For example, in Section 5 of Part II, entitled "Patents", Article 27.3(b) provides that Members have the option of protecting inventions of plant varieties by *sui generis* rights (such as breeder's rights) instead of through patents.[49]

The Appellate Body also noted that the Panel's interpretation of Article 1.2 of TRIPS cannot be reconciled with the plain wording of Article 2.1, as it "explicitly incorporates Article 8 of the Paris Convention (1967) into the TRIPS Agreement".[50]

4.2 TRIPS Agreement and WIPO Conventions

As mentioned earlier, the TRIPS Agreement incorporates substantive provisions of treaties and conventions that were administered and/or negotiated by WIPO. The Preamble to TRIPS seeks to create "a mutually supportive relationship between the WTO and the World Intellectual Property Organization". In essence, the methodology of TRIPS is to align and follow as closely as possible with existing IP conventions and add to or update the framework wherever necessary (Gervais, 2012). As the WIPO-administered IP conventions provided a sound basis for international IP rights protection, it was felt unnecessary to overhaul the international law on IP rights. Instead, the TRIPS Agreement incorporates the WIPO-administered IP conventions within the Scheme of the Agreement through reference, and obligating Member States to conform and apply the rules of the Convention. Article 2 incorporates the material provisions of the Paris Convention (1967 Revision of Stockholm), dealing with industrial property, into the TRIPS Agreement.

Articles 2.1 states Member States shall "comply" with the provisions of the Paris Convention, which require Member States to bring their domestic laws in line with the Paris Convention (Brand, 2009).[51] Article 9, in similar fashion to Article 2.1, requires Member States to comply with the provisions of the Berne Convention (1971 Revision of Paris), dealing with copyrights, and its Appendix thereto. The TRIPS Agreement also requires the Member States to comply with certain other multilateral conventions administered by WIPO. Importantly, the incorporation of WIPO conventions into the TRIPS Agreement means such conventions are subjected to the WTO's dispute settlement process, thereby permitting the provisions to be interpreted by the DSB. TRIPS effectively establishes the WTO's jurisdictional oversight of WIPO-administered IP conventions.

4.3 The NT and MFN Treatment Obligations

Since the entry into force of the Paris Convention and the Berne Convention in the later nineteenth century, NT obligation has been a norm amongst its signatories. The TRIPS Agreement extends the NT and MFN obligations to individuals and businesses in connection with the acquisition, maintenance, and enforcement of IP rights. These NT and MFN obligations are set out in Articles 3 and 4 respectively, and are subject to exceptions already provided in other IP rights conventions.[52] The footnote to Article 3 Trips Agreement reads as follows:

> For the purposes of Articles 3 and 4, "protection" shall include matters affecting the availability, acquisition, scope, maintenance and enforcement of intellectual property rights as well as those matters affecting the use of intellectual property rights specifically addressed in this Agreement.

In *US – Section 211 Appropriations Act*, the EC argued that section 211(a)(2) of the US Omnibus Appropriations Act of 1998 violated the NT obligation in both Article 2(1) of the Paris Convention (1967)[53] and Article 3.1 of the TRIPS Agreement by treating non-US nationals less favourably than US nationals. The Appellate Body in *US – Section 211 Appropriations Act* ruled that the NT obligation is a "fundamental principle" underlying the TRIPS Agreement and found the measure under challenge to be in violation of the NT obligations in Article 2(1) of the Paris Convention and Article 3(1) of the TRIPS Agreement as it treated foreign successors-in-interest to original trademark owners that are non-US nationals less favourably than US nationals.[54]

The Appellate Body, noting that the licensing procedure introduced by the US imposed "additional hurdles" and citing an earlier ruling of the Panel in *US – Section 337*, concluded that "even the possibility that non-US successors-in-interest face two hurdles is inherently less favourable than the undisputed fact that US successors-in-interest face only one".[55] In its ruling, the Appellate Body found subsections 211(a)(2) and 211(b) of the US Omnibus Appropriations Act of 1998 to be "discriminatory" as they sought to apply less favourable treatment to "designated nationals", *i.e.*, Cuban nationals, who were asserting rights relating to certain trademarks,[56] and that the provisions under challenge apply to "original owners" who are Cuban nationals, but not to "original owners" who are US nationals.[57] Accordingly, the Appellate Body concluded that the US was in violation by not according protection to trademarks of businesses confiscated by the Cuban government.

In *EC – Trademarks and Geographical Indications*, the Panel examined an EC Regulation which contained two different sets of procedures for the registration of geographical indications (GIs) for agricultural products and foodstuffs. The Panel found that one set applied to the names of geographical areas located within the European Communities and the other set applied to the names of geographical areas located in third countries outside the European

Communities. The Panel concluded that the second set contained additional conditions on the availability of protection which, in the Panel's view, modified the effective equality of opportunities as regards the protection of IP, and observed as follows:

> The Panel considers that those conditions modify the effective equality of opportunities to obtain protection with respect to intellectual property in two ways. First, GI protection is not available under the Regulation in respect of geographical areas located in third countries which the Commission has not recognized under Article 12(3). The European Communities confirms that the Commission has not recognized any third countries. Second, GI protection under the Regulation may become available if the third country in which the GI is located enters into an international agreement or satisfies the conditions in Article 12(1). Both of those requirements represent a significant "extra hurdle" in obtaining GI protection that does not apply to geographical areas located in the European Communities.[58]

In *EC – Trademarks and Geographical Indications*, the two sets of procedures in the EC Regulation contained differences with regards to the application procedures. The procedures required applications for GIs located in an EC Member State to be filed with the EC Member State's government, and applications for GIs located outside the European Communities were to be filed with the third country government. The Panel found that this modified the effective equality of opportunities as regards the protection of IP.[59]

The MFN provision contained in Article 4 of the TRIPS Agreement states that any advantage, favour, privilege, or immunity granted by a Member State to the nationals of any other country shall be accorded immediately and unconditionally to the nationals of all other Member States. Article 4 is subject to certain exemptions and limitations and applies to 'nationals' as defined in Article 1.3, rather than to 'like products' or 'like services and service suppliers' as found in Article I:1 of the GATT and Article II:1 of the GATS. The MFN treatment is made applicable to 'nationals' as IP rights are intangible and attach to the rights holder rather than the product *per se*. The Appellate Body in *US – Section 211 Appropriations Act*, emphasising the importance MFN treatment obligation for the smooth functioning of the multilateral trading system, observed as follows:

> Like the national treatment obligation, the obligation to provide most-favoured-nation treatment has long been one of the cornerstones of the world trading system. For more than fifty years, the obligation to provide most-favoured-nation treatment in Article I of the GATT 1994 has been both central and essential to assuring the success of a global rules-based system for trade in goods. Unlike the national treatment principle, there is no provision in the Paris Convention (1967) that establishes a most-favoured-nation obligation with respect to rights in trademarks or other industrial property. However, the framers of the TRIPS Agreement decided to extend the most-favoured-nation obligation to the protection of intellectual property rights covered by that Agreement. As a cornerstone of the world trading system, the most-favoured-nation obligation must be accorded the same significance with respect to intellectual property rights under the TRIPS Agreement that it has long been accorded with respect to trade in goods under the GATT. It is, in a word, fundamental.[60]

In *US – Section 211 Appropriations Act*, the Appellate Body applying analogous reasoning to claims under Articles 3.1 and 4 of the TRIPS Agreement ruled that the measure on its face discriminated between the nationals of one other Member State and the nationals of all other countries. The Appellate Body, dismissing the argument that the discrimination could be eliminated through an administrative procedure, observed as follows:

> Cuban nationals that reside in a country that is part of the "authorized trade territory", such as the Member States of the European Communities, can apply to OFAC to be "unblocked". This implies that Cuban nationals that reside in the "authorized trade territory" face an additional administrative procedure that does not apply to non-Cuban foreign nationals who are original owners, because the latter are not "designated nationals". Therefore, as we stated earlier, treatment that is inherently less favourable persists.[61]

Pursuant to Article 4(b), the MFN treatment obligation of the TRIPS Agreement excludes from its coverage the advantages granted in the Rome Convention (1967) and the Berne Convention (1971) on condition of reciprocity. Also, the TRIPS Agreement does not contain a provision similar to Article XXIV of the GATT, and as a result the MFN treatment obligation under the TRIPS Agreement applies to the provisions of FTAs. This means parties entering into an FTA may find TRIPS-plus provisions being the new minimum standard to proceed from in future WTO trade negotiations (Drahos, 2003).

4.4 Exhaustion of Intellectual Property Rights

The entry into force of the TRPS Agreement brought into focus a number of concerns with regards to IP rights practice, *viz*., exhaustion of IP rights, parallel imports, access to medicines, and patent evergreening – to name a few. The one issue that connects almost all of the concerns identified earlier is the exhaustion of IP rights. IP rights exist independently of the product they are incorporated in and also control the use of the product. IP rights are not granted for an indefinite period of time and come to an end at some point, which is referred to as exhaustion of rights. The most common way for exhaustion to occur is, when the rights holder places a product that contains the IP right in the marketplace for sale, where following the first sale,[62] the right to regulate how the product is resold downstream within that internal market is lost. This is referred to as exhaustion of IP rights.

Exhaustion touches upon one of the important aspects attached to IP rights, *i.e*., the right of sale of the product after the first sale or, more precisely, 'resale' of the product. For instance, a legitimately obtained IP protected item, such as a DVD, can be resold by the purchaser to another individual without the need for further authorisation from the rights holder. But this does not affect the core principle of IP right, *viz*., the right to authorise reproduction of the DVD. The theory of exhaustion is premised on the need to maintain a balance between remunerating the IP rights holder for the innovation and that of public interest to consume such innovative products.

The three major theories are national (or domestic) exhaustion theory, regional exhaustion theory, and international exhaustion theory. Under the national exhaustion theory, a rights holder's rights are exhausted with the first sale of the rights-protected product in the territory where they hold the rights. This allows the rights holder to oppose the importation of the IP rights-protected product marketed and sold abroad. National exhaustion favours market segmentation, as well as differential pricing. Under the regional exhaustion theory, with the first sale of the protected product a rights holder's rights are exhausted not only domestically, but also within the whole region. The rights holder may not be able to oppose the importation of the IP rights-protected product marketed and sold within the region.

As regards the international exhaustion theory, an IP rights holder's rights over an IP rights-protected product is exhausted when it is sold for the first time in a market anywhere in the world, paving the way for resale (including export and import) to any territory in the world. A resale could also take place in the country where the IP rights holder have their rights registered/ recognised. Thus, international exhaustion facilitates 'parallel' importation at a lower price, *i.e.*, sales of a legally produced product in a different territorial market. When exhaustion of IP rights is extended to internationally traded goods, it permits parallel imports, or grey market products. Not surprisingly, international exhaustion of IP rights is strongly opposed by developed country Member States.[63] Article 6 of the TRIPS Agreement reads as follows:

> For the purposes of dispute settlement under this Agreement, subject to the provisions of Article 3 and 4, nothing in this Agreement shall be used to address the issue of the exhaustion of intellectual property rights.

A plain reading of Article 6 seems to indicate that international exhaustion of IP rights is outside the scope of the TRIPS Agreement. One will note that Article 6 is simple in its content. During the Uruguay Round of negotiations, the complex issues surrounding exhaustion of IP rights were not gone into in detail by the GATT Contracting Parties, and there was a strong disagreement about the issue of exhaustion. Some developed countries, such as Switzerland and the US, advocated a territorial exhaustion principle, and others, including Australia, Brazil, India, New Zealand, *etc.*, preferred an international exhaustion regime (Gervais, 2012). The compromise reached amongst the negotiators was to leave exhaustion out of the dispute settlement, and hence the second part of the Article 6.

There are differing views on the application of exhaustion of IP rights within the multilateral trading order. Some commentators take the position that the TRIPS Agreement represents a specific agreement among the Member States with regards to all IP rights issues, which allows for the Member States to choose their preferred exhaustion system (Bronckers, 1998).[64] Others maintain the position that the WTO rules impose international exhaustion of IP rights, as both the TRIPS Agreement and the GATT 1994 are relevant. While opinions differ, the Member States at the Doha Ministerial Conference in 2001 reaffirmed that each Member State is free to establish its own regime on exhaustion.[65] Paragraph 5(d) of the Declaration reads as follows:

> The effect of the provisions in the TRIPS Agreement that are relevant to the exhaustion of intellectual property rights is to leave each Member free to establish its own regime for such exhaustion without challenge, subject to the MFN and national treatment provisions of Articles 3 and 4.[66]

5. Rights Protected Under the TRIPS Agreement

5.1 Copyright and Related Rights

Copyright and related rights are dealt with in Section 1 of Part II of the TRIPS Agreement. The Agreement effectively incorporates the relevant provisions of the Berne Convention (1971), which forms the overall framework for multilateral protection.[67] Through the act of incorporation, the TRIPS Agreement subjects the Berne Convention to the DSB and gives teeth to a convention, which was until then difficult to enforce due to a lack of authority to interpret its provisions (Gervais, 2012). During the Uruguay Round of negotiations, reconciling the common law concept of copyright (especially US practices) with that of the continental civil law legal system, which includes neighbouring rights (rights of performers and broadcasters), was a challenge (Cottier, 1991). The negotiations relating to copyrights witnessed a North-North confrontation on a number of issues, which was unlike the negotiations on patents where a strong North-South confrontation raged (Correa, 2020). These differences related to common law and civil law notions of copyright revolving around neighbouring rights. The US, while supporting the general consensus regarding the Berne Convention (1971) being part of the TRIPS Agreement, was opposed to the entitlement based on moral rights. The TRIPS Agreement overall expands the copyright laws by introducing disciplines to protect records, software and electronic data, and related or neighbouring rights for performers and broadcasters.

5.1.1 TRIPS Agreement and the Berne Convention 1971

It was agreed during the Uruguay Round of negotiations that the pre-existing Berne Convention standards for copyright protection was adequate for the most part. Accordingly, as mentioned in section 5.1, the TRIPS Agreement effectively incorporates the key provisions, *i.e.*, Article 1 to 21 of the Berne Convention (1971) into the multilateral trading system. Pursuant to Article 9.1, the TRIPS Agreement requires all Member States to comply with Article 1 to 21 of the Berne Convention and its Appendix, effectively incorporating the Convention into the multilateral trading system. Through incorporation, Article 9.1 subjects the Berne Convention to the DSB's jurisdiction and enforcement mechanism. It is to be noted that while still being administered by WIPO, the Berne Convention lacked any dispute settlement or enforcement mechanism, rendering it almost ineffective. The incorporated provisions of the Berne Convention (1971) are supplemented by the TRIPS Agreement. With regards to copyright protection, the TRIPS Agreement has a so-called Berne-plus regime, adding new standards and interpretations, which are set out in Articles 10–13. The new subject matter relates to computer programs and databases (Articles 10 and 11), and new rights relate to rental rights (Article 11).

5.1.2 Copyright Protection Under TRIPS

The rationale for copyright protection is that the grant of exclusive rights stimulates creation and cultural activities and is considered as the economic backbone of cultural industries. Importantly, copyright protection does not require a formal registration or deposit under the Berne Convention (Article 5(2)), and consequently under the TRIPS Agreement (Article 62.1). A broad definition provided in *Black's Law Dictionary* reads as follows:

> The right to copy; specifically, a property right in an original work of authorship (including literary, musical, dramatic, choreographic, pictorial, graphic, sculptural, and architectural works; motion pictures and other audiovisual works; and sound recordings) fixed in any tangible medium of expression, giving the holder the exclusive right to reproduce, adapt, distribute, perform, and display the work.
>
> (*Black's Law Dictionary*, 2014)

In its narrow sense, copyright relates to the rights of authors relating to literary and artistic output, and in the wider sense includes 'related rights'. Common law legal systems employ the term 'copyright' to include related rights, and civil law legal systems use the term 'neighbouring rights' to connote related rights. The original domain of copyright was literature, art, and other cultural activities forming the core, which has now expanded to include computer programs. As in the case of authors, performers too are protected for their creative work. Interestingly, the TRIPS Agreement does not provide a definition of copyrighted works, and one has to refer to the Berne Convention for guidance, as it is incorporated into the TRIPS Agreement. Turning to the Berne Convention, we note that Article 2.1 contains a non-exhaustive list of protected works, covering "every production in the literary, scientific and artistic domain". Works covered by copyright protection include books, newspapers, other writings; musical compositions; films; photographs; paintings; and architecture.

The question before the Panel in *China – Intellectual Property Rights* was if China's laws which denied copyright protection to works that are subject to censorship or prohibited from publication and dissemination in China was in violation of the TRIPS Agreement, *i.e.*, inconsistent with Article 5(1) of the Berne Convention. The Panel ruled that as Article 9.1 of the TRIPS Agreement incorporates the Berne Convention, that while Article 17 of the Berne Convention allows censorship, Article 5.1 of the Convention requires that copyright be available to such works, and observed as follows:

> [a] government's right to permit, to control, or to prohibit the circulation, presentation, or exhibition of a work may interfere with the exercise of certain rights with respect to a protected work by the copyright owner or a third party authorized by the copyright owner. However, there is no reason to suppose that censorship will eliminate those rights entirely with respect to a particular work.[68]

In *US – Section 110(5) of the US Copyright Act*, the Panel, while examining the consistency of certain provisions of the US Copyright Act with the TRIPS Agreement, addressed the relationship between the TRIPS Agreement and the Berne Convention, and observed as follows:

> Articles 9–13 of Section 1 of Part II of the TRIPS Agreement entitled "Copyright and Related Rights" deal with the substantive standards of copyright protection. Article 9.1 of the TRIPS Agreement obliges WTO Members to comply with Articles 1–21 of the Berne Convention (1971) (with the exception of Article 6bis on moral rights and the rights derived therefrom) and the Appendix thereto . . .
>
> We note that through their incorporation, the substantive rules of the Berne Convention (1971), including the provisions of its Articles 11bis(1)(iii) and 11(1)(ii), have become part of the TRIPS Agreement and as provisions of that Agreement have to be read as applying to WTO Members.[69]

Elaborating further, the Panel in *US – Section 110(5) of the US Copyright Act* clarified the status of the relationship between the TRIPS Agreement and the Berne Convention, besides also noting how the provisions are to be interpreted, and observed as follows:

> In the area of copyright, the Berne Convention and the TRIPS Agreement form the overall framework for multilateral protection. Most WTO Members are also parties to the Berne Convention. We recall that it is a general principle of interpretation to adopt the meaning that reconciles the texts of different treaties and avoids a conflict between them. Accordingly, one should avoid interpreting the TRIPS Agreement to mean something different than the Berne Convention except where this is explicitly provided for. This principle is in conformity with the public international law

presumption against conflicts, which has been applied by WTO panels and the Appellate Body in a number of cases.[70] We believe that our interpretation of the legal status of the minor exceptions doctrine under the TRIPS Agreement is consistent with these general principles.[71]

Article 9 of the TRIPS Agreement effectively assimilates the provisions of Article 2 of the Berne Convention dealing with the range of copyright material to be covered. Article 2(1) identifies seven categories to be accorded with protection, *viz*., (a) literary works, which cover all forms of writings, whether by words or numbers or symbols; (b) dramatico-musical works such as plays, mimes, choreography, operas, and musical comedies; (c) cinematographic works, which include film or videotaped dramatic works and other forms of content fixed in film; (d) works of music with or without words; (e) visual art works in two- and three-dimensional forms, including applied art (for example, this category would include architecture, sculptures, engravings, lithography, maps, plans, and photographic works); (f) derivative works, which include translations, adaptations, and arrangements; (g) compilations and collective works such as encyclopaedias and, more recently, databases.[72] The manner in which copyright protection is provided differs from Member State to Member State.

Article 9.1, second sentence, excludes any rights or obligations in respect of moral rights conferred under Article 6 *bis* of the Berne Convention. Article 9.2 of TRIPS recognises and awards copyright protection to expressions and not to ideas, procedures, methods of operation, or mathematical concepts as such. Article 9.2 may also be interpreted as requiring protection of all qualifying 'expressions' in the context of Article 9.1, thereby widening the scope of copyright works (Gervais, 2012). Ideas are considered forming part of the common good that should be freely shared with all, but the expression thereof can be subject to property rights and protection thereof. The absence of any definition of excluded items under TRIPS has led to much debate about the 'methods of operation' with regards to computer programs.

Article 10 of TRIPS extends remit of copyright protection to two new types of works, *viz*., computer programs and databases.[73] Under Article 10.1 protection is afforded to a computer program as a literary work regardless of its form, whether in source or object code, *i.e.*, whether the code is in a form readable by an individual (source code) or readable by a machine (object code).[74] A computer program can be understood as a set of instructions that is used directly or indirectly in a computer to achieve a certain result. Article 10.1 confirms this position by stating computer programs must be protected as literary works, and Article 10.2 adds, "compilations of data or other material, whether in machine readable or other form", which by reason of their arrangement constitute intellectual creations, shall be protected. Article 10.2 also clarifies that such protection afforded "shall not extend to the data or material itself".

For the first time the TRIPS Agreement introduces rental rights to the authors of their copyrighted work. Article 11 obligates Member States to provide authors (and their successors) of computer programs and cinematographic works the right to authorise, or to prohibit, commercial rental to the public of originals or copies of their copyrighted works. Article 11 establishes an international minimum standard for rental rights in respect of a computer programs and cinematographic works. The rights with regard to cinematographic works are subject to the so-called exception of impairment-test, *i.e.*, if it can be proven that such rental has led to excessive copying of the copyrighted work, which thereby materially impairs the right of reproduction of the author. This obligation does not apply to rentals where the computer program itself is not the object of rental.

Pursuant to Article 12, the minimum term of copyright protection must be not less than 50 years from the end of the calendar year of authorised publication. Under Article 13 of the TRIPS Agreement, a limited exception to copyright protection is provided for "certain special cases which do not conflict with a normal exploitation of the work and do not unreasonably prejudice the legitimate interests of the right holder". Article 13 is often referred to as the three-step test for exception to copyright.[75] The limited exceptions that a Member State may provide under Article 13 fall under two categories, *viz.*, (i) free use, *i.e.*, the use of copyright protected works without the obligation to ask for authorisation and to pay remuneration, and (ii) non-voluntary licences, *i.e.*, allowing the use of protected works without authorisation but with the obligation to pay equitable remuneration to rights holder (Taubman, Wager, and Watal, 2020).

The case in *US – Section 110(5) Copyright Act* involved the issue of the grant of exception to the playing of music in small retail establishments and restaurants under Section 110(5) of the US Copyright Act, as amended by the Fairness in Music Licensing Act, 1998. The EC had contended that section 110(5) of the Copyright Act was in violation of Article 9(1) of the TRIPS Agreement (Articles 11 and 11 *bis* of the Berne Convention). The Panel in *US – Section 110(5) Copyright Act* distinguished the two Berne provisions and observed:

> Regarding the relationship between Articles 11 and 11bis, we note that the rights conferred in Article 11(1)(ii) concern the communication to the public of performances of works in general. Article 11*bis*(1)(iii) is a specific rule conferring exclusive rights concerning the public communication by loudspeaker or any other analogous instrument transmitting, by signs, sounds or images, the broadcast of a work.[76]

The Panel interpreted Article 13 narrowly to incorporate the 'minor exceptions' to the copyright doctrine of the Berne Convention (Articles 11 and 11 *bis*) into the TRIPS Agreement,[77] and established that the TRIPS Article 13 contains three requirements, *viz.*, (i) the limitations or exceptions are confined to certain special cases; (ii) such exceptions do not conflict with the normal exploitation of the work; and (iii) they do not unreasonably prejudice the legitimate interests of the rights holder.[78] Applying the aforementioned exemptions to the case at hand, the Panel ruled that the "homestyle" exemption introduced by the US met the three criteria of Article 13 as they were well defined and limited in scope.[79] Section 110(5)(B) of the US Copyright Act applied to a substantial number of restaurants (over 50 percent) and to 27 percent of retail establishments, and as a result, the exemption did not qualify as special.[80] In the Panel's opinion, the legislation failed all three criteria in relation to the "business exemption" as the scope of potential users was open-ended, covering a potentially large number of facilities.[81]

Since the entry into force of the TRIPS Agreement four more multilateral treaties on the subject of copyright have been adopted, but are yet to be incorporated into the TRIPS Agreement. The newly drawn treaties countenance a higher level of protection copyright than that of TRIPS. The four treaties are (i) the WIPO Copyright Treaty (WTC), (ii) the WIPO Performances and Phonograms Treaty (WPPT),[82] (iii) the Beijing Treaty on Audiovisual Performances 2012, and (iv) the Marrakesh VIP Treaty 2013. While the Beijing Treaty recognises copyright for audiovisual performances and expands the performers' rights,[83] the Marrakesh VIP Treaty establishes exceptions[84] to facilitate the creation of accessible versions of books and other copyrighted material for visually impaired persons.

5.2 Trademarks

A trademark is any sign or a combination of signs that are used to differentiate the goods or services of one business enterprise from another. Goodwill is attached to trademarks as they build reputation through long use and generate economic value. On the one hand the trademark system protects the producers against unfair competition arising from unscrupulous producers seeking to exploit the goodwill of the trademark owner, and on the other hand, trademarks help consumers to identify and differentiate from other similar products their product of their choice.[85] Prior to the entry into force of the TRIPS Agreement, the international law on trademark protection was covered under the Paris Convention 1967 and administered by WIPO. The Paris Convention 1967, although it played an important role in the development of trademark law, did not contain any substantive trademark law provisions. Generally, WIPO-administered IP rights instruments were heavy on registration and light on substantive trademark law and enforcement. In contrast, the WTO-administered TRIPS Agreement is heavy on substantive trademark law and enforcement but very light on registration and administrative issues (Gervais, 2020).[86]

Rights and protection of trademarks are covered under Part II, Section 2, of the TRIPS Agreement comprising Articles 15 to 21. In a marketplace, a distinctive trademark acts as an identifier that rapidly conveys information about the brand, helping the customer to distinguish one product from the other. It is to be pointed out that one of the major reasons for the recalibration of IP rights during the TRIPS negotiations was trademark counterfeiting.[87] Article 15 of the TRIPS Agreement enhances the protection afforded to trademarks under the Paris Convention (1967)[88] and covers both trademarks for goods and trademarks for services.[89] What constitutes a trademark is set out in Article 15.1 of the TRIPS Agreement, and reads as follows:

> Any sign, or any combination of signs, capable of distinguishing the goods or services of one undertaking from those of other undertakings, shall be capable of constituting a trademark. Such signs, in particular words including personal names, letters, numerals, figurative elements and combinations of colours as well as any combination of such signs, shall be eligible for registration as trademarks. Where signs are not inherently capable of distinguishing the relevant goods or services, Members may make registrability depend on distinctiveness acquired through use. Members may require, as a condition of registration, that signs be visually perceptible.[90]

The Appellate Body in *US – Section 211 Appropriations Act* ruled as follows:

> If such signs are capable of distinguishing the goods or services of one undertaking from those of other undertakings, then they become eligible for registration as trademarks. To us, the title of Article 15.1 – "Protectable Subject-Matter" – indicates that Article 15.1 embodies a definition of what can constitute a trademark. WTO Members are obliged under Article 15.1 to ensure that those signs or combinations of signs that meet the distinctiveness criteria set forth in Article 15.1 – and are, thus, capable of constituting a trademark – are eligible for registration as trademarks within their domestic legislation.[91]

In the *US – Section 211 Appropriation Act* case, the subject matter of the dispute revolved around the registration of the trademark 'Havana Club'. A family-owned enterprise in Cuba sold rum under the trademark 'Havana Club', which was registered both in Cuba and the UK. When the revolutionary government led by Fidel Castro came to power in Cuba in 1959, the assets of the family-owned business were confiscated, including the trademarks. The trademark registered in the US would lapse, as the former owners of the trademark did not seek to renew the trademark, nor did the Castro government for that matter, due to political differences. The dispute arose when two rival factions, *viz.*, Pernod Ricard (joint venture with the Cuban government) and Bacardi (joint venture with the Cuban-family owners), sought to enter the US market to sell rum under the tradename 'Havana Club', and the US Congress passed legislation US Omnibus Appropriation Act of 1998, which retroactively invalidated the assignment of the 'Havana Club' trademark.

The US had refused to register the trademark 'Havana Club' on grounds that the party claiming ownership of the mark was not its rightful owner. The EC sought to challenge section 211 of the US Omnibus Appropriations Act, as it effectively prohibited registration and renewal of trademarks and trade names used in connection with a confiscated business or assets by the Cuban government after the revolution, without seeking the consent of the original owner or *bona fide* successor-in-interest. The Appellate Body, upholding such refusal, ruled that it was within US discretion to make determinations regarding the lawful holders of trademarks.

The Appellate Body in *US – Section 211 Appropriations Act*, while rejecting the argument that Member States must register trademarks that meet the requirements of Article 15.1, stressed that the fact a sign falls under the definition of Article 15.1 means that it is capable of registration, and it does not mean a Member State is obligated to register it, and observed as follows:

> This Article states that such signs or combinations of signs "shall be eligible for registration" as trademarks. It does not say that they "shall be registered".
>
> It follows that the wording of Article 15.1 allows WTO Members to set forth in their domestic legislation conditions for the registration of trademarks that do not address the definition of either "protectable subject-matter" or of what constitutes a trademark.
>
> . . .
>
> In our view, Article 15.1 of the TRIPS Agreement limits the right of Members to determine the "conditions" for filing and registration of trademarks under their domestic legislation pursuant to Article 6(1) [of the Paris Convention (1967) as incorporated in the TRIPS Agreement] only as it relates to the distinctiveness requirements enunciated in Article 15.1.[92]

Pursuant to Article 15.2 of the TRIPS Agreement, Member States are permitted to refuse to register a trademark on "other grounds", provided that they do not derogate from the Paris Convention (1967). As noted by the Appellate Body in *US – Section 211 Appropriations Act*, such "other grounds" are "grounds different from those already mentioned in Article 15.1, such as lack of inherent distinctiveness of signs, lack of distinctiveness acquired through use, or lack of visual perceptibility".[93] The Appellate Body in *US – Section 211 Appropriations Act* went on to observe as follows:

> The right of Members under Article 15.2 to deny registration of trademarks on grounds other than the failure to meet the distinctiveness requirements set forth in Article 15.1 implies that Members are not obliged to register any and every sign or combination of signs that meet those distinctiveness requirements.[94]

Member States are at liberty to define in the domestic legislation as to what constitutes the 'other grounds' for denial registration of trademarks, as long as they are not explicitly prohibited by the Paris Convention 1967. On the question of the denial of trademarks on 'other grounds', the Appellate Body noted:

"other grounds" for the denial of registration within the meaning of Article 15.2 of the TRIPS Agreement are not limited to grounds expressly provided for in the exceptions contained in the Paris Convention (1967) or the TRIPS Agreement.[95]

Article 15.4 states, the "nature of the good or services to which a trademark is to be applied shall in no case form an obstacle to registration" of the trademark submitted for registration. The Panel in *Australia – Tobacco Plain Packaging*, while considering the meaning of "registration of the trademark" in Article 15.4, referred to the Appellate Body's clarification of the overall structure and operation of Article 15 in combination with Article 6(1) of the Paris Convention (1967), which provides that each country of the Paris Union has the right to determine the conditions for filing and registration of trademarks in its domestic legislation.[96] The Panel explained the position of law as follows:

> The "considerable discretion" provided by this general rule is limited in Article 15 of the TRIPS Agreement by setting out specific options and limitations regarding the conditions that Members may establish for the registration of trademarks in their national legislation.[97]

The Appellate Body in *US – Section 211 Appropriations Act* found that the TRIPS Agreement does not contain a provision that determines who owns or who does not own a trademark, and observed as follows:

> As we read it, Article 16 confers on the owner of a registered trademark an internationally agreed minimum level of "exclusive rights" that all WTO Members must guarantee in their domestic legislation. These exclusive rights protect the owner against infringement of the registered trademark by unauthorized third parties.
>
> We underscore that Article 16.1 confers these exclusive rights on the "owner" of a registered trademark. As used in this treaty provision, the ordinary meaning of "owner" can be defined as the proprietor or the person who holds the title or dominion of the property constituted by the trademark. We agree with the Panel that this ordinary meaning does not clarify how the ownership of a trademark is to be determined. Also, we agree with the Panel that Article 16.1 does not, in express terms, define how ownership of a registered trademark is to be determined. Article 16.1 confers exclusive rights on the "owner", but Article 16.1 does not tell us who the "owner" is.
>
> [W]e conclude that neither Article 16.1 of the TRIPS Agreement, nor any other provision of either the TRIPS Agreement [or] the Paris Convention (1967), determines who owns or who does not own a trademark.[98]

Article 16 of the TRIPS Agreement states:

> The owner of the registered trademark shall have the exclusive right to prevent all third parties not having the owner's consent from using in the course of trade identical or similar signs for goods or services which are identical or similar to those in respect of which the trademark is registered where such use would result in a likelihood of confusion. In case of the use of an identical sign for identical goods or services, a likelihood of confusion shall be presumed. The rights described above shall not prejudice any existing prior rights, nor shall they affect the possibility of Members making rights available on the basis of use.[99]

The emphasis in Article 16.1 is using the trademark "in the course of trade", and one will observe the Article does not contain any provision on how similarity is to be determined, and it is for a Member State to provide in their domestic laws. Also, the exclusive right to prevent the use of a trademark is only granted where "such use would result in a likelihood of confusion". The panel in *EC – Trademarks and Geographical Indications* scrutinised whether Member States, pursuant to Article 16.1 of the TRIPS Agreement, are required to make available to trademark owners the right to prevent confusing uses of signs, even where the signs are used as GIs, and made the following observation:

> Although each of the Sections in Part II provides for a different category of intellectual property, at times they refer to one another, as certain subject-matter may be eligible for protection by more than one category of intellectual property. This is particularly apparent in the case of trademarks and GIs, both of which are, in general terms, forms of distinctive signs. The potential for overlap is expressly confirmed by Articles 22.3 and 23.2, which provide for the refusal or invalidation of the registration of a trademark which contains or consists of a GI.[100]

The Panel in *EC – Trademarks and Geographical Indications* interpreted the exclusive right which must be conferred under Article 16.1 as a negative right that belongs to the owner of the registered trademark alone to prevent certain uses by "all third parties" not having the owner's consent, subject to certain exceptions:

> The right which must be conferred on the owner of a registered trademark is set out in the first sentence of the text. There are certain limitations on that right which relate to use in the course of trade, the signs, the goods or services for which the signs are used and those with respect to which they are registered and the likelihood of confusion. The ordinary meaning of the text indicates that, basically, this right applies to use in the course of trade of identical or similar signs, on identical or similar goods, where such use would result in a likelihood of confusion. It does not specifically exclude use of signs protected as GIs.
>
> The text of Article 16.1 stipulates that the right for which it provides is an "exclusive" right. This must signify more than the fact that it is a right to "exclude" others, since that notion is already captured in the use of the word "prevent". Rather, it indicates that this right belongs to the owner of the registered trademark alone, who may exercise it to prevent certain uses by "all third parties" not having the owner's consent. The last sentence provides for an exception to that right, which is that it shall not prejudice any existing prior rights. Otherwise, the text of Article 16.1 is unqualified.
>
> Other exceptions to the right under Article 16.1 are provided for in Article 17 and possibly elsewhere in the TRIPS Agreement. However, there is no implied limitation *vis-à-vis* GIs in the text of Article 16.1 on the exclusive right which Members must make available to the owner of a registered trademark. That right may be exercised against a third party not having the owner's consent on the same terms, whether or not the third party uses the sign in accordance with GI protection, subject to any applicable exception.[101]

Article 16.2 of the TRIPS Agreement extends the protection of Article 6 *bis* of the Paris Convention (1967) *mutatis mutandis* to services, and that Member States, in determining whether a trademark is well known, are to take account of the knowledge of the trademark in the relevant sector of the public, including knowledge in the Member State concerned. Similarly, Article 16.3 of the Agreement extends the protection of Article 6 *bis* of the Paris Convention (1967) *mutatis mutandis* to goods or services that are not similar to those in respect of which a trademark is registered, "provided that use of that trademark in relation to those goods or services would indicate a connection between those goods or services and the owner of the registered trademark and provided that the interests of the owner of the registered trademark are likely to be damaged by such use". The knowledge mentioned in Article 16.2 refers to presence of the knowledge in "relevant sector". Likewise, with regards to extension of protection to "well known" trademark on goods or services mentioned in Article 16.3 is aimed at undermining or devaluing the trademark in question.

Pursuant to Article 17, Member States may provide limited exceptions (*e.g.*, fair use of the descriptive terms) to the trademark rights, provided that such exceptions take account of the legitimate interests of the owner of the trademark and of third parties. The provision contemplates two requirements before an exception could be made, *viz.*, (i) the exception is limited, and (ii) the exception should take into account the "legitimate interests of the owner of the trademark and of third parties".[102] The Panel in *EC – Trademarks and Geographical Indications* held:

> The addition of the word "limited" emphasizes that the exception must be narrow and permit only a small diminution of rights. The limited exceptions apply "to the rights conferred by a trademark". They do not apply to the set of all trademarks or all trademark owners.[103]

As regards the second requirement contained in Article 17 of the TRIPS Agreement, the Panel in *EC – Trademarks and Geographical Indications* agreed with the interpretation of the Panel in *Canada – Pharmaceutical Patents*[104] of the term "legitimate interests" of a patent owner and third parties in the context of Article 30 of the TRIPS Agreement.[105]

The term of protection of a trademark is contained in Article 18 of the Agreement. Prior to the entry into force of the TRIPS Agreement, the duration of protection afforded to trademarks amongst the Member States varied. During the TRIPS negotiation, the US put forth a proposal for ten years, with the developing countries suggesting a period of seven years. Pursuant to Article 18 of the TRIPS Agreement, the initial registration of a trademark shall be for a term of no less than seven years, which is to be renewed. While trademarks can be protected for an unlimited period (unlike copyright), Article 18 states that trademarks "shall be renewable indefinitely". However, Article 19.1 permits Member States to make conditions and cancel registration for non-use of the trademark, provided there had been uninterrupted period of at least three years of non-use, unless valid reasons based on the existence of obstacles to such use are shown by the trademark owner. Article 5.C(1) of the Paris Convention provides that "the registration may be cancelled only after a reasonable period". Article 19.1 of the TRIPS Agreement, thus, effectively defines the "reasonable period" contained in the Paris Convention.

Article 20 states that Member States cannot unjustifiably encumber the use of a trademark in the course of trade through special requirements, such as use with another trademark, use in a special form, or use in a manner detrimental to its capability to distinguish the goods or services of one undertaking from those of other undertakings. Prior to the coming into force of the TRIPS Agreement, it was a practice in many developing countries to include requirements concerning the manner in which trademarks could be used (UNCTAD-ICTSD, 2005). Article 20 precludes the imposition of unjustified encumbrances on trademarks. The

Panel in *Australia – Tobacco Plain Packaging*, in considering the meaning of the term "unjustifiably", first sought the ordinary meaning of that term in its context:

> In Article 20, the term "unjustifiably" qualifies the verb "encumbered". The above definitions therefore suggest that the term "unjustifiably", as used in Article 20, connotes a situation where the use of a trademark is encumbered by special requirements in a manner that lacks a justification or reason that is sufficient to support the resulting encumbrance.[106]

The Appellate Body in *Australia – Tobacco Plain Packaging* held that the term "unjustifiably" "suggests the degree of rationalization that needs to be provided for imposing encumbrances on the use of a trademark by special requirements under Article 20".[107] The Appellate Body upheld the Panel's interpretation that a determination of whether the use of a trademark in the course of trade is being 'unjustifiably' encumbered by special requirements could involve a consideration of (a) the nature and extent of encumbrances resulting from special requirements, (b) the reasons for the imposition of special requirements, and (c) a demonstration of how the reasons for the imposition of special requirements support the resulting encumbrances.[108] However, the Appellate Body sought to clarify its findings by noting:

> [W]hile an inquiry under Article 20 could include the consideration of the abovementioned factors, the degree of discretion vested in Members under Article 20 does not call for a rigid and exact set of considerations that are relevant for the examination of whether the use of a trademark is unjustifiably encumbered by special requirements.[109]

Under Article 21, Member States are at liberty to determine conditions on the licensing and assignment of trademarks but are yet prohibited from compulsory licensing of trademarks. Article 21 also provides that the owner of a registered trademark shall have the right to assign the trademark with or without the transfer of the business to which the trademark belongs.

5.3 Geographical Indication

The protection for GI remains one of the most contentious issues surrounding the TRIPS Agreement. In the mid-1970s, the term 'geographical indication' was used for the first time in the WIPO negotiations. Geographical indications (GIs) became commonplace within the IP circles with the entry of the TRIPS Agreement in 1995.[110] At common law the doctrine of 'passing off', which was based on protection against the tort of unfair competition, was used to protect merchants against deceptive geographic claims.[111] In contrast, in civil law jurisdictions, the 'appellation of origin' was used to protect against false claims of geographic origin. A key demand put forth by the European negotiators during the Uruguay Round of negotiations was the protection of GIs.[112] Section 3 of Part VII of the TRIPS Agreement covers four key topics, *viz.*, (a) protection for GIs, (b) GIs and trademarks, (c) additional protection of GIs for wines and spirits, and (d) review of section 3.

GIs indicates the causal link between a product and its place of origin, which is subject only to environmental factors and traditional production methods. Prior to the advent of the TRIPS Agreement, a patchwork of legal regimes regulated origin marking, affording protection to such signs against exploitation by third parties. Currently there are numerous GIs registered with WIPO.[113] Pursuant to Article 22, all Member States are required to create a legal system of protection for GIs where the reputation or quality of a good is 'essentially attributable' to its geographical origin. Geographical indications are defined succinctly in Article 22.1, which reads as follows:

> Geographical indications are, for the purposes of this Agreement, indications which identify a good as originating in the territory of a Member, or a region or locality in that territory, where a given quality, reputation or other characteristic of the good is essentially attributable to its geographical origin.[114]

Although the definition renders the eligibility narrower than for trademarks or collective marks, it expands the concept of appellation of origin as contained in the Lisbon Agreement to protect goods which derive a reputation from their place of origin. In order for a GI to be protected under the scheme envisaged in the TRIPS Agreement, it has to be an indication, but not necessarily the name of a geographical place on earth (Blakeney, 2014).[115] The definition under Article 22.1 of TRIPS specifies that the quality, reputation, and/or other characteristics of a product can constitute a sufficient grounds to establish eligibility to be granted a GI, where that quality, reputation, or other characteristic is essentially attributable to its geographical origin. Hence, in order to qualify for GI protection, a party must demonstrate that the product from that geographical areas is different from a similar product which originates elsewhere.

A GI is different from a trademark, as it indicates only the place where the product is produced, whereas a trademark is any sign or combination of signs that are used to differentiate the goods or services of one business enterprise from another. Also, a GI is to be differentiated from geographical origin, such as 'Made in Japan', which states or identifies the place or country where it is manufactured and does not contain any product attributes.

Article 22.2 of the TRIPS Agreement sets out the standard level of protection to be accorded to all products and directs Member States to provide the legal means for interested parties to prevent (a) the use of any means in the designation or presentation of a good that indicates or suggests that the good in question originates in a geographical area other than the true place of origin in a manner, which misleads the public as to the geographical origin of the good; and (b) any use which constitutes an act of unfair competition within the meaning of Article 10 *bis* of the Paris Convention (1967). The two provisions focus on preventing misuse of GIs so as to mislead the public or constitute unfair competition within the meaning of the Paris Convention.

Article 22.3 requires Member States to decline to register, or invalidate the registration of a trademark, *ex officio* if its legislation so permits or at the request of an interested party, which contains or consists of a geographical indication with respect to goods not originating in the territory indicated, if use of the indication in the trademark misleads the public as to the true place of origin. Article 22.3, although relying on the language of "mislead the public" found in Article 22.2(a), does not refer back to Article 22.2(a). As the practical effect of Article 22.3 is affected by Article 24.5, it is to be read with Article 24.5.[116]

Article 23 of the TRIPS Agreement provides a higher, absolute level of protection of goodwill and reputation for wines and spirits, and such protection must be provided even if misuse would not mislead the public. The protection afforded here is much stronger. Article 23.1 requires Member States to provide the legal means for the holder of a GI to prevent the use of the GI identifying wines/spirits, for wines/spirits not originating in the place indicated by the GI in question, even where the true origin of the goods is indicated and the public is not being misled or the geographical indication is used in translation or accompanied by expressions such as 'kind', 'type', 'style', 'imitation', or the like (*e.g.*, 'Champagne-like' or

'Bordeaux-type'). The use of homonymous GIs for wines is dealt with in Article 23.3, where the use is not misleading under Article 22.4. For instance, 'Rioja' wine is produced both in Spain and Argentina.[117] Importantly, this provision is not available for spirits. Under Article 23.3, Member States are to determine the practical conditions under which the homonymous GIs in question will be differentiated from each other and ensure in the process the producers concerned are treated equitably and that consumers are not misled.

Article 24 lays the groundwork for future negotiations aimed at increasing the protection of GIs under afforded under Article 23. Article 24 contains seven exceptions which apply to additional protection for GIs relating to wines and spirits granted under Article 23. In *EC – Trademarks and Geographical Indications (Australia)*, the Panel indicated that Article 24 refers to the protection of individual GIs at the relevant date and not to the system or protection in place.[118] Article 24.1 prohibits the use of the provisions contained in paragraphs 4 through 8 by Member States that refuse to conduct negotiations or conclude bilateral or multilateral agreements.[119] Article 24.3 prohibits Member States from diminishing the protection of GIs that existed prior to the entry into force of the TRIPS Agreement, and Article 24.5 explicitly states that the provisions in the TRIPS Agreement shall not prejudice prior trademark rights that have been acquired in good faith.

The Panel in *Australia – Tobacco Plain Packaging* found that the scope of Article 24.3 is not limited only to those measures that implement the obligation to "provide the legal means for interested parties to prevent" for the use of a geographical indication within the meaning of Article 22.2:

> Article 24.3 appears in Section 3 of Part II of the TRIPS Agreement, entitled "Geographical Indications", which comprises Articles 22–24. By its express terms, the obligation in Article 24.3 relates to the implementation of "this Section". This reference is therefore not limited to measures that implement the specific obligation to "provide the legal means for interested parties to prevent" the use of a GI within the meaning of Article 22.2. Rather, it relates to the implementation of the provisions of Section 3 of Part II as a whole, namely Articles 22 to 24.
>
> . . .
>
> In light of the above, we find that the obligation in Article 24.3 applies to a measure that implements any of the provisions of Section 3 of Part II of the TRIPS Agreement. Accordingly, its application is not limited to measures that implement the obligation to provide the legal means for interested parties to prevent the use of a GI within the meaning of Article 22.2.[120]

Article 24.6 does not require a Member States to provide protection for a GI where it is used as a generic term to describe the product in question. A good example is 'cheddar', which refers to a popular hard cheese in the UK associated with the English village of Cheddar in Somerset in England but is produced in nearly all parts of the world.[121]

Article 24.4 is designed to permit a Member State to maintain the *status quo* that existed prior to the entry into force of the TRIPS Agreement. This allows Member States for the continuous use of a particular GI of another Member State identifying wines or spirits in connection with goods or services by any of its nationals or domiciliaries who have used that GI in a continuous manner with regard to the same or related goods or services in the territory of that Member State either (i) for at least 10 years preceding 15 April 1994 or (ii) in good faith preceding that date. Article 24.5 deals with the relationship between GIs and trademarks that refers to trademarks that are 'similar' to a GI.

Pursuant to Article 24.8, the GIs protected in 'this section' will not in any way prejudice the right of any person to use, in the course of trade, that person's name or the name of that person's predecessor in business, except where such name is used in such a manner as to mislead the public.

In *EC – Trademarks and Geographical Indications*, the Panel interpreted the term "this Section" as a reference to Section 3 of Part II of the TRIPS Agreement:

> Article 24.5 appears in Section 3 of Part II of the TRIPS Agreement. Therefore, the reference to "this Section" is a reference to Section 3.[122]

Following from Article 24.9, the Member States are not obliged to protect GIs which are not or ceased to be protected in their country of origin, or GIs that have fallen into disuse in that country. Paragraph 18 of the Doha Ministerial Declaration provides the mandate (i) for the negotiation of the establishment of a multilateral system of notification and registration of GIs for wines and spirits, and (ii) for the extension of the higher, enhanced level of protection offered through Article 23 to products beyond just wines and spirits. Although to be completed in the Fifth Ministerial Conference in Cancún in 2003, due to disagreements prevailing amongst Member States, no agreement has been reached on such a system to date (Council for TRIPS, 2015).

5.4 Patents

Within the IP system, patent rights are identified as the most dominant right. Patent rights enable the rights holder, or patentee, to exclude all others from making, selling, or using the subject matter of a valid patent right for a specific period of time. This right grants the patent holder the authority to even prevent an independent subsequent discoverer of the same subject matter from making, using, or selling it. The provisions relating to protection of patent rights is set out in Section 5 Part II of the TRIPS Agreement.

One of the most contentious subjects of the Uruguay Round of negotiations was the extended protection sought to be introduced through the TRIPS Agreement. It is no exaggeration to state that the negotiations were dictated by patent-holding developed countries, as they had a much higher stake in global patent rights. The TRIPS negotiation was closely monitored by the pharmaceutical industry, which had taken the first step in the direction of patent protection through their lobbying efforts in the 1980s with the US government to introduce patent protection in the agenda for negotiations in the Uruguay Round (Sundaram, 2018). The negotiations were fraught with North-South divide, with haves and have-nots, *i.e.*, patent-holding developed nations and non-patent-holding (or, holding very little) developing nations. The developing countries strongly opposed product patents for certain fields of innovation, including pharmaceutical patents,[123] as well as to the minimum duration of protection contemplated. In the area of compulsory licensing, the developing countries argued for an obligation to work the patent domestically, which eventually led to the introduction of Article 31 to the TRIPS Agreement.

Patents and inventions are not defined in the TRIPS Agreement. Article 27.1, first sentence, defines patentable subject matter as follows:

> Subject to the provisions of paragraphs 2 and 3, patents shall be available for any inventions, whether products or processes, in all fields of technology, provided that they are new, involve an inventive step and are capable of industrial application.

Pursuant to Article 27.1, first sentence, Member State are required to extend patent protection to all inventions – products and processes – in all fields of technology, for a minimum period of 20 years, if they meet the following requirements: (a) where the invention is new, (b) where it involves an inventive step, and (c) where it is capable of industrial application. Article 27.1, second sentence, prohibits discrimination as regards availability and enjoyment of patent rights based on (i) the place of invention, (ii) the field of technology, and (iii) whether products are imported or locally produced, subject to paragraph 4 of Article 65, paragraph 8, of Article 70, and paragraph 3 of Article 27.

In *Canada – Pharmaceutical Patents*, the EC contended that Canada was in violation of Article 27.1 of the TRIPS Agreement. It was EC's case that under Canadian law patent rights were not enjoyable without discrimination as to the field of technology. The panel did not find a violation of Article 27.1, as the challenged provision of the Canadian law, *i.e.*, Section 55.2(1), was not limited to pharmaceutical products, but was applicable to every product that was subject to marketing approval requirements.[124] The Panel in *Canada – Pharmaceutical Patents*, while analysing the term "without discrimination" in Article 27, advised against using the term "discrimination" whenever "more precise standards are available", given the potentially "infinite complexity" of the term.[125]

Addressing a claim of discrimination in terms of the field of technology, the Panel in *Canada – Pharmaceutical Patents* held that it had ascertained neither *de jure* nor *de facto* discrimination and observed as follows:

> the evidence in record before it did not raise a plausible claim of discrimination under Article 27.1 of the TRIPS Agreement. It was not proved that the legal scope of Section 55.2(1) was limited to pharmaceutical products, as would normally be required to raise a claim of *de jure* discrimination. Likewise, it was not proved that the adverse effects of Section 55.2(1) were limited to the pharmaceutical industry, or that the objective indications of purpose demonstrated a purpose to impose disadvantages on pharmaceutical patents in particular, as is often required to raise a claim of *de facto* discrimination. Having found that the record did not raise any of these basic elements of a discrimination claim, the Panel was able to find that Section 55.2(1) is not inconsistent with Canada's obligations under Article 27.1 of the TRIPS Agreement. Because the record did not present issues requiring any more precise interpretation of the term "discrimination" in Article 27.1, none was made.[126]

Articles 27.2 and 27.3 set out the exception to Article 27.1. Pursuant to Article 27.2, Member States are permitted to exclude certain inventions from patentability. Article 27.2 reads as follows:

> Members may exclude from patentability inventions, the prevention within their territory of the commercial exploitation of which is necessary to protect *ordre public*[127] or morality, including to protect human, animal or plant life or health or to avoid serious prejudice to the environment, provided that such exclusion is not made merely because the exploitation is prohibited by their domestic law.

The first exception identified under Article 27.2 is for inventions that are necessary to protect *ordre public* (public order) or morality, including to protect human, animal, or plant life or health or to avoid serious prejudice to the environment. Pursuant to Article 27.3, Member States may also exclude from patentability (i) diagnostic, therapeutic, and surgical methods for the treatment of humans or animals, and (ii) plants and animals other than micro-organisms, and essentially biological processes for the production of plants or animals other than non-biological and microbiological processes. Referred to as the 'biotechnology clause', Article 27.3(b) addresses one of the most controversial issues covered by the Agreement. It permits Member States to exclude from patentability plant varieties and animals, while at the same time specifically obliging the Member States to protect micro-organisms and certain biotechnological processes.

The rights granted to patent owners, for patent and process, are enumerated in Article 28 of the TRIPS Agreement, and Article 28.1 reads as follows:

> A patent shall confer on its owner the following exclusive rights:
>
> (a) where the subject-matter of a patent is a product, to prevent third parties not having the owner's consent from the acts of: making, using, offering for sale, selling, or importing for these purposes that product;
> (b) where the subject-matter of a patent is a process, to prevent third parties not having the owner's consent from the act of using the process, and from the acts of: using, offering for sale, selling, or importing for these purposes at least the product obtained directly by that process.

Article 28.1 defines the patentee's rights as exclusive. The rights of a patent holder are a negative right, *i.e.*, the right to prevent third parties from doing certain acts relating to the protected invention (*ius excluendi*), rather than a positive right with regard to the patent owner's products or processes. Article 28.1(b), which deals with the protection of a process patent to the product directly obtained by that process, introduces into the TRIPS framework standards established in domestic legislations of developed country Member States, but unknown in most developing country Member States. Pursuant to Article 28.2, patent owners shall have the additional right to assign, or transfer by succession, the patent and to conclude licensing contracts.

Under Article 29, Member States shall require patent applicants to disclose the invention "in a manner sufficiently clear and complete" for a person skilled in the art to be able to carry out the invention. This is a positive obligation for Member States to perform, requiring a patent applicant to physically "disclose the invention". Under Article 29.2, Member States may require the patent applicant to provide information concerning the applicant's foreign applications and grants of patents.

5.4.1 Compulsory Licensing

Articles 30 and 31 of the TRIPS Agreement contain exceptions to the exclusive rights conferred by a patent, *viz.*, limited exceptions and compulsory licences. The limited exceptions to patent rights contained in Article 30 are akin to Article 13 providing for exceptions to copyright, and Article 17 providing for exceptions to trademarks. Article 30 of the TRIPS Agreement states:

> Members may provide limited exceptions to the exclusive rights conferred by a patent, provided that such exceptions do not unreasonably conflict with a normal exploitation of the patent and do not unreasonably prejudice the legitimate interests of the patent owner, taking account of the legitimate interests of third parties.

Article 30 authorises limited exceptions to patent rights for carrying out research, prior user rights, and pre-expiration testing. The reasons that a Member State may invoke Article 30 will largely depend on the policy objectives pursued and the domestic laws of the Member State concerned. The TRIPS Agreement does not attempt to constrain the freedom of Member States to determine the grounds of possible exceptions but establishes the principal conditions for their admissibility.[128] The provision has come to be used, in more recent times, by developing countries to authorise the manufacture of generic drugs.[129]

In *Canada – Pharmaceutical Patents*, the stockpiling exceptions found in Canadian patent laws were challenged by the EC. Canada, relying on Article 30 to justify its measures, argued that the objectives and principles of Articles 7 and 8 of the TRIPS Agreement should inform the interpretation of Article 30. The panel in *Canada – Pharmaceutical Patents*, addressing the basic structure, identified three cumulative conditions to be met to qualify for an exception under Article 30, and observed as follows:

> Article 30 establishes three criteria that must be met in order to qualify for an exception: (1) the exception must be "limited"; (2) the exception must not "unreasonably conflict with normal exploitation of the patent"; (3) the exception must not "unreasonably prejudice the legitimate interests of the patent owner, taking account of the legitimate interests of third parties". The three conditions are cumulative, each being a separate and independent requirement that must be satisfied. Failure to comply with any one of the three conditions results in the Article 30 exception being disallowed.
>
> The three conditions must, of course, be interpreted in relation to each other. Each of the three must be presumed to mean something different from the other two, or else there would be redundancy. Normally, the order of listing can be read to suggest that an exception that complies with the first condition can nevertheless violate the second or third, and that one which complies with the first and second can still violate the third. The syntax of Article 30 supports the conclusion that an exception may be "limited" and yet fail to satisfy one or both of the other two conditions. The ordering further suggests that an exception that does not "unreasonably conflict with normal exploitation" could nonetheless "unreasonably prejudice the legitimate interests of the patent owner".[130]

With regards to the first requirement, the panel gave a narrow interpretation of what 'limited' means in Article 30:

> when the word "limited" is used as part of the phrase "limited exception". The word "exception" by itself connotes a limited derogation, one that does not undercut the body of rules from which it is made. When a treaty uses the term "limited exception", the word "limited" must be given a meaning separate from the limitation implicit in the word "exception" itself. The term "limited exception" must therefore be read to connote a narrow exception – one which makes only a small diminution of the rights in question.[131]

By adopting a narrow interpretation of the word 'limited' occurring in Article 30, the panel in *Canada – Pharmaceutical Patents* focused on the extent of the curtailment and not on the extent of the economic impact thereof. The Panel also noted that the economic impact of the exception must be evaluated under the other conditions of Article 30. With regard to the stockpiling exception, the Panel found that it constituted a substantial curtailment of the exclusive rights to be granted to patent owners under Article 28.1, and as a result was not a 'limited' exception.[132] On the regulatory review exception, the Panel found as follows:

> It is "limited" because of the narrow scope of its curtailment of Article 28.1 rights. As long as the exception is confined to conduct needed to comply with the requirements of the regulatory approval process, the extent of the acts unauthorized by the right holder that are permitted by it will be small and narrowly bounded.[133]

In *Canada – Pharmaceutical Patents*, one of the objections raised by EC was with regard to the "legitimate interests" requirement. The EC argued that patent owners suffer due to delays arising from the requirement to obtain marketing approval of their innovative products, which results in them unable to achieve market exclusivity during the regular patent term, and that they should be able to impose a similar delay in connection with corresponding regulatory requirements for the market entry of competing products.[134] In the Panel's view, the "primary issue was whether the normative basis of that claim rested on a widely recognized policy norm".[135] The Panel concluded that Canada's regulatory review exception fell within the exception arising under Article 30 of the TRIPS Agreement, and as a result was not inconsistent with the provisions of Article 28.1.[136]

Article 31 relates to the 'other use' exception of a patent without authorisation of the rights holder. Footnote 7 of Article 31 defines 'other use' as use "other than that allowed under Article 30". This 'other use' of a patent without the authorisation of the right holder is commonly known as compulsory licensing, although this term is not used in Article 31. Article 31 refers to the situation as

> [w]here the law of a Member allows for other use of the subject-matter of a patent without the authorization of the right holder, including use by the government or third parties authorized by the government.[137]

Article 31 conditions the grant of 'compulsory licence', requiring minimum obligations to be fulfilled. Subsection (b) to the Article permits the granting of a compulsory licence only if "the proposed user has made efforts to obtain authorisation from the right holder on reasonable commercial terms and conditions and that such efforts have not been successful within a reasonable period of time". While mentioning some possible grounds (public commercial use, national emergency, remedying of anti-competitive practices, dependent patents), it does not limit the grounds on which compulsory licences may be granted. Subsection (b), second sentence, notes that this requirement "may be waived by a Member in the case of a national emergency or other circumstances of extreme urgency or in cases of public non-commercial use". Further, subsection (b), third sentence, notes that in "situations of national emergency or other circumstances of extreme urgency, the right holder shall, nevertheless, be notified as soon as reasonably practicable".

Article 31(f) to the Article restricts the issue of a compulsory licence unless it is used "predominantly for the supply of the domestic market of the Member authorizing such use". The wordings contained in subsection (f) implies that Member States must have the means (wherewithal, infrastructure) to produce the product in question, as the use is primarily "for the supply of the domestic market". This provision has been the focus in developing country Member States where access to affordable medicines is still a major problem (Sundaram, 2014; Sundaram, 2018). While Article 31(h) requires that the patent holder must receive "adequate remuneration" based on the "economic value of the authorisation", the text does not present any interpretive guidance for this purpose.

5.4.2 TRIPS Flexibilities for Public Health Purposes

The TRIPS Agreement contains flexibilities . . . which could be utilised for public health purposes by Member States. A number of scholarly articles have been written on the subject of flexibilities contained in the TRIPS Agreement and the WTO's failure to address the problem of the access to medicines in developing and least developed countries. The patent-related flexibilities identified include provision for grant of compulsory licensing, public, non-commercial use of patents (government use), parallel importation, exceptions to patent rights, the exhaustion of rights, provisions relating to patentable subject matter, control of anti-competitive practices, scope of patentability and optional exclusion, exceptions to patent rights, and enforcement.[138]

During the Fourth Session of the WTO Ministerial Conference in Doha, developing country Member States and developed country Member States were engaged in bitter debate over the interpretation and scope of the flexibilities in the TRIPS Agreement and the use of the flexibilities to improve access to essential medicines. Some developing countries feared that the extended IP rights protection granted for pharmaceutical patents under the TRIPS Agreement was likely to increase dependency on multinational pharmaceutical companies and affect the developing countries and LDCs severely, as essential medicines could become even more unaffordable and beyond their reach (Sundaram, 2018). The developing countries were fully aware that the patent-holding developed countries, who advocated a wider global IP rights protection and promoted the TRIPS Agreement, would not be affected by the pharmaceutical patent regime of the Agreement as they could rely on their strong public health care system.

The US and Switzerland (both home to pharmaceutical corporations holding a number of pharmaceutical patents), well supported by other developed countries, took the stance that the only flexibility afforded under the Agreement was its staggered implementation in certain cases. In contrast, the developing countries argued that the TRIPS Agreement did not limit their sovereign powers when addressing domestic health crises, such as HIV/AIDS (Sundaram, 2018). Due to growing pressure from the developing countries, and in particular from the Member States from Africa, the Council for TRIPS held a special session in June 2001 to consider the relationship between IP rights and access to essential medicines under the TRIPS Agreement.

In November 2001, the Ministerial Conference in Doha adopted a Ministerial Declaration on the TRIPS Agreement and Public Health (Ministerial Conference, 2001). In November 2001, the Doha Declaration on TRIPS and Public Health (Doha Declaration) was made, addressing some of the concerns of the developing countries, which also sought to clarify other divergent views held by the Member States on the application and ambit of the TRIPS Agreement. This Declaration reaffirms the flexibilities contained in the TRIPS Agreement and the rights of the Member States to grant compulsory licences, determine the grounds for the grant, determine what constituted a national emergency, and determine the measures to protect public health.

The Declaration expressly states that the TRIPS Agreement does not limit, or restrict, the grounds on which a compulsory licence may be granted by a Member State, while acknowledging the right of Member States to determine when a national emergency or circumstance of extreme urgency exists in their territory. Due to concerns regarding the interpretation of this provision, the Doha Declaration on the TRIPS Agreement and Public Health confirms:

> [e]ach member has the right to grant compulsory licences and the freedom to determine the grounds upon which such licences are granted.[139]

The Doha Declaration in paragraph 5(c) recognises this position and states explicitly that as part of the 'flexibilities' provided in the TRIPS Agreement:

> [e]ach member has the right to determine what constitutes a national emergency or other circumstances of extreme urgency, it being understood that public health crises, including those relating to HIV/AIDS, tuberculosis, malaria and other epidemics, can represent a national emergency or other circumstances of extreme urgency.[140]

The Doha Declaration through paragraph 5(c) clarified the position that 'national emergency' or 'extreme emergency' are not limited to short-term crisis. After nearly two years of negotiations, on 30 August 2003 (General Council, 2003) the General Council finally adopted the Decision on Implementation of paragraph 6 of the Doha Declaration on the TRIPS Agreement and Public Health (the August Decision). The paragraph 6 solution is essentially an interim waiver with regard to the obligations under 31 (f) and (h) of the TRIPS Agreement, which allows for the total quantity of drugs produced under a compulsory licence to be exported. Paragraph 6 of the Doha Declaration reads as follows:

> WTO members with insufficient or no manufacturing capacities in the pharmaceutical sector could face difficulties in making effective use of compulsory licensing under the TRIPS Agreement.

Some developing countries have made constructive use of the TRIPS flexibilities while giving effect to the TRIPS Agreement into their national legislations. Some others have delayed the introduction of product patents into their legislation,[141] and others have used the compulsory licensing provisions to manufacture or procure generic medicines at an affordable price.[142] Yet, the implementation of flexibilities in key pharmaceutical markets like Brazil, India, and South Africa came at a very high price, as transnational pharmaceutical corporations, well supported by developed country Member State participation, were able to mount oppositions and cause delays in the actual implementation (Sundaram, 2018).

Pursuant to Article 31, compulsory licences may be issued to authorise manufacturers of generic medicines to copy a patented drug without consent of the patent holder. Article 31, although granting Member States the right to issue a compulsory licence, is seldom successfully used, as the right is severely limited. In particular, the efforts of the developing country Member States to grant compulsory licences had been extremely difficult and unworkable (Sundaram, 2018).[143] It is to be noted that any implementation of the decision will require carrying out changes to national laws, and also ensuring that countries do not assume TRIPS-plus obligations under bilateral or RTAs (Correa, 2004a).[144] The General Council, on 6 December 2005, adopted the decision to amend the TRIPS Agreement with a view to resolve the conflict with Article 31(f) permanently (General Council, 2005).[145] On 23 January 2017, following the ratification from two-thirds of the Member States, the amendment came into force.

5.5 *Layout Designs of Integrated Circuits*

Integrated circuits referred to as 'chips' are the key component of the computer industry and are incorporated into a number of digital equipment which process data. The TRIPS Agreement affords protection of such layout designs that form part of the integrated circuits. Pursuant to Article 35, Member States are to give IP protection to layout designs (topographies) of integrated circuits (semi-conductor chips).[146] Under Article 38, the term of such protection must be for a period of ten years from the date of filing an application for registration or from the first commercial exploitation anywhere in the world.

6. Enforcement of Intellectual Property Rights

As mentioned earlier, the TRIPS Agreement requires its Member States to maintain minimum standards for IP rights protection and provides for the enforcement of such minimum standards through civil and administrative procedures and remedies, provisional measures, border measures, and criminal procedures. The rules on domestic enforcement of IP rights are contained in Articles 41–61, Part III, of the TRIPS Agreement. As IP rights are private rights, Part III of the Agreement contains procedural rules allowing rights holders to enforce them. Part III of the Agreement applies to all IP rights covered by the Agreement.[147] Some of the provisions establish obligations on the part of the Member States, and a number of other provisions require Member States to vest judicial authorities (or other "competent" or "relevant" authorities) with the authority to take certain actions.[148]

6.1 General Principles

Pursuant to Article 41.1 Member States are to ensure that enforcement procedures "are available under their law so as to permit effective action against any act of infringement of IPRs covered by this Agreement, including expeditious remedies to prevent infringements and remedies which constitute a deterrent to further infringements". The Panel in *China – Intellectual Property Rights* noted that "enforcement procedures", as found in Part III of the TRIPS Agreement, is an extensive concept.[149] It further noted that where a Member State denies copyright protection under its domestic laws in a manner inconsistent with its obligations under the TRIPS Agreement, then the Member States' enforcement measures are not available to a rights holder as mandated under Article 41.1.[150] Article 41.2 requires that procedures concerning the enforcement of IP rights are fair and equitable, and are not be unnecessarily complicated or costly or entail unreasonable time limits or unwarranted delays.

The due process requirements are contained in Articles 42.1–41.4 of the TRIPS Agreement. Article 41.1 requires that the enforcement procedures are applied in a way that avoids the creation of barriers to legitimate trade and to provide for safeguards against their abuse. Article 41 further requires that decisions on the merits of a case are preferably in writing and reasoned and be made available at least to the parties to the proceedings without undue delay. Importantly, Article 41.5 makes it clear that Member States are under no obligation to create special courts for the enforcement of IP rights or allocate resources earmarked for the purpose of IP rights enforcement.

6.2 Civil and Administrative Procedures and Remedies

The basic principles for the conduct of civil and administrative proceedings for the enforcement of IP rights are set out in Articles 42–49 of the Agreement. Being a private right, IP rights are to be enforced by initiating civil procedures at the behest of or by the rights holder.[151] Under Article 42, Member States are required to make available to 'rights holders'[152] civil judicial procedures for the enforcement of any IP right covered by the TRIPS Agreement, which means that the provision of only administrative enforcement procedures is insufficient.

The Appellate Body in *US – Section 211 Appropriation Act*, while holding that the term "right holders" included not only persons who had been established as owners of rights but also persons who claimed to have legal standing to assert rights, observed as follows:

> We agree with the Panel that the term "right holders" as used in Article 42 is not limited to persons who have been established as owners of trademarks. Where the TRIPS Agreement confers rights exclusively on "owners" of a right, it does so in express terms, such as in Article 16.1, which refers to the "owner of a registered trademark". By contrast, the term "right holders" within the meaning of Article 42 also includes persons who claim to have legal standing to assert rights. This interpretation is also borne out by the fourth sentence of Article 42, which refers to "parties". Civil judicial procedures would not be fair and equitable if access to courts were not given to both complainants and defendants who purport to be owners of an intellectual property right.[153]

The Article also establishes the right of the defendants to timely written notice, containing sufficient details, including the basis of any claims made. Article 42 requires that Member States allow parties to be represented by independent legal counsel and have the right of appearance and opportunity to present evidence. The EC in *US – Section 211 Appropriations Act* claimed that Sections 211(a)(2) and 211(b) of the US Appropriations Act contravened the provisions of Article 42 of the TRIPS Agreement, as they expressly denied the rights holder recourse to US courts to enforce the rights targeted by Section 211. The panel, while finding that Section 211(a)(2) was inconsistent with Article 42,[154] observed as follows:

> While Section 211(a)(2) would not appear to prevent a right holder from initiating civil judicial procedures, its wording indicates that the right holder is not entitled to effective procedures as the court is ab initio not permitted to recognize its assertion of rights if the conditions of Section 211(a)(2) are met. In other words, the right holder is effectively prevented from having a chance to substantiate its claim, a chance to which a right holder is clearly entitled under Article 42, because effective civil judicial procedures mean procedures with the possibility of an outcome which is not pre-empted *a priori* by legislation.[155]

When those findings were challenged by the US, the Appellate Body upheld the findings of the Panel and noted:

> the ordinary meaning of the term "make available" suggests that "right holders" are entitled under Article 42 to have access to civil judicial procedures that are effective in bringing about the enforcement of their rights covered by the Agreement . . . The term "right holders" . . . also includes persons who claim to have legal standing to assert rights.[156]

Article 42 requires that procedures established do not impose 'overly burdensome' requirements concerning mandatory personal appearances, and the procedures also provide a means to identify and protect confidential information. The other provisions of the Agreement relating to civil and administrative procedures are contained in Article 43 (production of evidence); Article 44 (preventing the entry of infringing imports into channels of commerce); Article 45 (power to award damages); Article 46 (covering other remedies); Article 47 (covering judicial right of information), Article 48 (the indemnification of the defendant covering); and Article 49 (covering administrative procedures).

6.3 Provisional Measures and Border Measures

While Provisional measures are provided for in Article 50, Articles 51–60 contain rules detailing the measures that Member States should take to prevent the entry of infringing goods into circulation. Article 50 sets forth the minimum requirements to be met by proceedings for provisional measures and establishes the obligation of the Member States to empower judicial authorities to grant provisional measures. Article 50 requires judicial authorities to have the authority to adopt provisional measures *inaudita altera parte* where appropriate, *i.e.*, (i) where any delay is likely to cause irreparable harm to the right holder, or (ii) where there is a demonstrable risk of evidence being destroyed. Article 51 of the TRIPS Agreement addresses procedures to be in place at the border before the entry of any infringing product into free circulation by the customs authority. Articles 52 to 60 of the TRIPS Agreement outlines the rules with regards to the application of the border measures.

6.4 Criminal Procedures

Article 61 of the TRIPS Agreement requires Member States to have in place criminal procedures and provide for criminal penalties for "trademark counterfeiting and copyright piracy on a commercial scale". The criminal procedures and penalties contained in Article 61 contemplate possible remedies, including imprisonment and/or monetary fines "sufficient to provide a deterrent, consistently with the level of penalties applied for crimes of a corresponding gravity"; and in appropriate cases "the seizure, forfeiture and destruction of the infringing goods and of any materials and implements the predominant use of which has been in the commission of the offence". The panel in *China – Intellectual Property Rights* proceeded to clarify several aspects on the scope of Article 61, observing as follows:

> The terms of the obligation in the first sentence of Article 61 of the TRIPS Agreement are that Members shall "provide for criminal procedures and penalties to be applied". That obligation applies to "wilful trademark counterfeiting or copyright piracy on a commercial scale". Within that scope, there are no exceptions. The obligation applies to all acts of wilful trademark counterfeiting or copyright piracy on a commercial scale.[157]

6.5 Acquisition and Maintenance of Intellectual Property Rights

Article 62 is the sole provision contained in Part IV of the TRIPS Agreement and deals with the procedural aspects of the acquisition and maintenance of IP rights. Article 62 safeguards a Member State's right to maintain formalities in their domestic laws (*e.g.*, registration of a trademark or filing of patent) for the acquisition and maintenance of IP rights, but at the same time ensures that such domestic laws do not prevent the effective protection of IP rights and adhere to due process standards. To ensure that procedural formalities are not used unfairly to undermine the grant of IP rights protection, Article 62 identifies the procedures and formalities for the acquisition and maintenance of IP rights.

Accordingly, Article 62.1 requires that Member States are to (i) ensure that the procedures for grant or registration are subject to compliance with the substantive conditions for acquisition of the right, and (ii) permit the granting or registration of the right within a reasonable period of time so as to avoid unwarranted curtailment of the period of protection. Article 62.5 requires that the final administrative decisions on the acquisition or maintenance of IP rights be subject to judicial or quasi-judicial review.

7. Institutional Provisions of the TRIPS Agreement

The TRIPS Agreement provisions relating to institutional and procedural arrangements are contained in Parts V and VII. The provisions are arranged as follows: (i) the Council for TRIPS – Articles 68 and 71; (ii) the transparency requirements – Article 63; (iii) the rules on dispute settlement under the TRIPS Agreement – Article 64; (iv) international cooperation between Members to prevent trade in goods that infringe IP rights – Article 69; and (v) the prohibition on reservations to the provisions of the TRIPS Agreement without the consent of other Member States – Article 72.

7.1 Council for TRIPS

The legal basis for the establishment of the Council is found in Article IV.5 of the WTO Agreement, which stipulates that the Council "shall oversee the functioning" of the TRIPS Agreement. The Council for TRIPS operates under the general guidance of the General Council, and Article 68 of the TRIPS Agreement provides for the Council for TRIPS, where all Member States are represented. The remit of the Council for TRIPS include (i) to monitor the operation of the TRIPS Agreement, and in particular, the compliance of Member States with their obligations under the TRIPS Agreement; (ii) to afford the opportunity for Member States to consult on matters relating to the trade-related aspects of IP rights; and (iii) to carry out any other responsibilities assigned to it by the Member States, and provide any assistance requested by them in the context of dispute settlement procedures.

In carrying out its functions, the TRIPS Council may consult with and seek information from any source it deems appropriate; and was required to establish, within one year of its first meeting, appropriate arrangements for cooperation with WIPO. Accordingly, a cooperative agreement was entered into between the WTO and WIPO in 1995 and came into force on 1 January 1996. The Council for TRIPS had established its own set of rules of procedure, which was approved by the General Council.

7.2 Transparency and Dispute Settlement

The first provision under 'Dispute Settlement and Prevention' relates to the obligation of Member States to maintain transparency in matters relating to IP rights under domestic laws. Pursuant to Article 63, Member States are required to maintain a high level of transparency in their laws and regulations, intergovernmental agreements, final judicial decisions, and administrative rulings of general application, pertaining to the availability, scope, acquisition, enforcement, and prevention of the abuse of IP rights.[158] The Member States are also required to notify such domestic laws to the Council for TRIPS to assist the Council in its review of the operation of the TRIPS Agreement.

The use of the terms "made effective" in Article 63 indicates that the obligation of a Member State to notify arises only after any law has entered into force, and not at a stage where it is still being considered. The primary objective of the transparency obligation is to keep other Member States and private IP right holders informed about possible changes in a Member State's legislation on IP rights to ensure and contribute to a stable and predictable legal environment. Such transparency could also effectively prevent any potential dispute that may arise between Member States.

As mentioned earlier, the TRIPS Agreement is subject to the dispute settlement provisions in the GATT.[159] Article 64.1 states:

> The provisions of Articles XXII and XXIII of GATT 1994 as elaborated and applied by the Dispute Settlement Understanding shall apply to consultations and the settlement of disputes under this Agreement except as otherwise specifically provided herein.

Articles 64.2 and 64.3, however, state that Articles XXIII.1(b) and (c) of the GATT 1994 pertaining to non-violation and situation complaints should not apply for the first five years of the WTO's existence, *i.e.*, between 1995 and 1999. As earlier discussed in chapter 3, Article XXXIII(b) provides that Member States can bring three types of complaints, including non-violation complaints. During the Uruguay Round of negotiations, the developing country Member States opposed the inclusion of non-violation and situation complaints as a cause of action under the TRIPS Agreement. They were apprehensive that the inclusion of such a remedy within the scheme of the TRIPS Agreement will extend the protection afforded under the Agreement beyond the scope originally envisaged.

Although the moratorium under Article 64.2 expired on 1 January 2000, the Doha Ministerial Conference in November 2001, pursuant to Article 64.3, directed the TRIPS Council to continue its examination of the scope and modalities for non-violation and situation complaints and make suitable recommendations to the Ministerial Conference for approval. The moratorium has been extended in successive rounds of Ministerial Conference up until 2017.[160] The Member States have agreed not to initiate any non-violation or situation complaints under the TRIPS Agreement while the TRIPS Council continues to examine the scope and modalities of such complaints falling under non-violation and situation complaints. The next Ministerial Conference has been scheduled to take place in late 2021.[161]

8. Special Rules for Developing Country and LDC Members

Concessions are contained in the TRIPS Agreement for developing and least developed country Member States, as they may not have the necessary regulatory capacity and infrastructure for the enforcement of TRIPS obligations. Hence, the TRIPS Agreement grants revised implementation periods (i) for the implementation of the obligations arising from the Agreement and (ii) for technical cooperation.

8.1 Transitional Periods

Part VI of the TRIPS Agreement contains provisions on transition periods, transfer of technology, and technical cooperation. Member States are granted different deadlines for implementation of the TRIPS Agreement based on their level of economic development. It should be borne in mind that there are no definitions of 'developed countries', 'developing countries', and 'least developed countries' provided within the WTO legal framework. While applying for membership, the Member States take the decision to classify themselves as a developed or developing country.[162] As regards 'least developed countries', the criteria set by the UN is recognised by the WTO (WTO, 2021; UN, 2015, 2021).[163]

Under Article 65.1 of the TRIPS Agreement, all developed countries were provided a one-year implementation period for the implementation of the TRIPS Agreement into domestic laws. Under Article 65.2, developing countries (and transition economies under certain conditions[164]) were granted a transition period of five years, until January 2000.[165] Pursuant to Article 65.4, those developing country Member States which did not provide product patent protection in a specific area of technology (*i.e.*, process patents) were given an extended transition period of up to 1 January 2005 to introduce such protection into their domestic laws. The aforementioned transitional periods granted to developing countries have now come to an end. Article 66.1 of the TRIPS Agreement granted least developed country Member States a transitional period of ten years from the date of entry into force of the TRIPS Agreement, *i.e.*, until 1 January 2006. The least developed country Member States are granted further concessions under TRIPS Agreement under the Doha Declaration on the TRIPS Agreement and Public Health.

The Doha Declaration provides that with regards to pharmaceutical products, the least developed country Member States will not be required to implement the obligations of the TRIPS Agreement regarding patents and the protection of undisclosed information or to enforce these IP rights until 1 January 2016 (Council for TRIPS, 2005). On 6 November 2015, the Council for TRIPS extended the implementation period to 1 January 2011 or until the date when the concerned Member State ceases to be a least developed country, whichever date is earlier (Council for TRIPS, 2015). This date was further extended to 1 July 2021. However, the Council for TRIPS, which met on 29 June 2021, has now extended the transition period to 1 July 2034 for least developed country Members to comply with the TRIPS Agreement. Under the agreed decision, LDC country members shall not be required to apply the provisions of the TRIPS Agreement, other than Articles 3, 4, and 5, until 1 July 2034, or until the date when they cease to be a least developed country, whichever date is earlier (Council for TRIPS, 2021).

8.2 Technical Assistance and Transfer of Technology

Under Article 66.2, developed country Member States are required to provide incentives to enterprises and institutions in their territories for the purpose of promoting and encouraging technology transfer to least developed country Member States "in order to enable them to create a sound and viable technological base". Article 67 seeks to facilitate the implementation of the TRIPS Agreement by requiring developed country Member States to provide, "on request and on mutually agreed terms and conditions, technical and financial cooperation in favour of developing and least-developed country Members". The Article further states that such

> cooperation shall include assistance in the preparation of laws and regulations on the protection and enforcement of IPRs as well as on the prevention of their abuse, and . . . support regarding the establishment or reinforcement of domestic offices and agencies relevant to these matters, including the training of personnel.

The Decision of the Council for TRIPS from 2005 requires further commitments on technical assistance for least developed country Member States to help them prepare in the implementation of the Agreement (Council for TRIPS, 2005).

9. Summary

One of the most controversial agreements to be negotiated during the Uruguay Round of negotiations, the TRIPS Agreement had polarised the Member States into 'haves' and 'have nots', *i.e.*, IP rights holders and IP rights users. Right from the moment IP rights protection was introduced in the agenda of the Uruguay Round of negotiations following the strong lobbying by the IP rights-holding industry sector, the TRIPS Agreement has stirred up controversy. The key reason being that intangible private rights were sought to be protected within the scheme of the multilateral trading system, which was primarily concerned with the facilitation of trade in goods and services. It cannot be denied that the TRIPS Agreement is one of the most innovative of all WTO agreements and reflects the recognition that IP rights protection and international trade are closely connected. Critics still argue that the TRIPS Agreement, while granting extended protection to IP rights, exacerbated the problems associated with access to medicines.

Notes

1. The conventions referred to are the Paris Convention 1893, the Berne Convention 1886, the Rome Convention 1961, and the Washington Treaty 1989.
2. The author identifies the US pharmaceutical corporation Pfizer Inc. as taking the lead in lobbying through its well-established business networks to disseminate the idea of a trade-based approach to IP rights, and later on through interlinking of the networks. The author also identifies the role played by the Advisory Committee on Trade Negotiations (ACTN), which was part of a private sector advisory committee system which was to ensure concordance between official US trade objectives and US commerce, and how the CEO of Pfizer Inc. and chairperson of ACTN, with the help of other like-minded CEOs of leading US corporations, were able to develop a trade and investment agenda to protect US IP rights abroad.
3. Starting in 1985, the United States Trade Representative (USTR) served notice on a number of countries informing them about possible trade sanctions if they were to not bring their domestic patent laws into line with American laws. The USTR, acting under Section 301 of the Trade Act 1974, placed countries which did not provide adequate protection to US IP interests on its "watch lists" and "priority watch lists". The primary targets were large Third World/developing countries like India, Argentina, Brazil, Taiwan, and Thailand, which had begun to develop domestic industries to compete against US pharmaceutical manufacturers in their own markets.
4. US President Reagan, in a message to Congress in February 1986, proposed that a key item for consideration was to seek much greater protection of US IP rights interest in overseas territories.
5. For a discussion on the Omnibus Trade and Competitiveness Act 1988, see Barton and Fisher (1988), and for an analysis on trade and IP rights, see Gadbaw (1989).
6. For a discussion on the role played by the pharmaceutical industry in moving the agenda on IP rights protection from WIPO to the Uruguay Round of negotiations leading to the WTO, see Sundaram (2015).
7. The term 'forum shifting' refers to different dynamics, where an agenda from one forum is moved to another, with a view to achieving an intended outcome. When an agenda is moved between forums, they are subjected to different rules, which enables parties to influence the outcome of a process. Forum shifting also includes pursuing agendas simultaneously in multiple forums.
8. For the role played by India on behalf of the developing countries during the negotiations, see Sundaram (2014).
9. The developing countries were distrustful of GATT, which was largely constructed and dominated by developed, industrialised countries. The developing countries favoured discussing international IP rights protection before a United Nations-affiliated organisation, such as WIPO, where the Third World countries exerted greater influence.
10. A number of developing countries that sought membership of the WTO and entered the Uruguay Round of negotiations were not granting patent monopolies for pharmaceuticals. The Punta del Este mandate made reference to negotiations aiming to clarify the GATT provisions and to the elaboration, as appropriate, of new rules and disciplines, and further to develop a multilateral framework of principles, rules, and disciplines dealing with international trade in counterfeit goods. Many developing countries, rather naively, believed that the goal was to establish a framework to establish a multilateral framework dealing with international trade in counterfeit goods. See UNCTAD (2010).
11. India also stressed that substantive standards on IP rights were more in the realm of socio-economic and technological development, especially in the case of developing countries. It urged that the group focus on restrictive and anti-competitive practices of the owners of IP rights to evolve standards and principles for their elimination and to avoid distortion of trade. See Sundaram (2014).

12 See Article 27.1 of the TRIPS Agreement.
13 Quoting from an interview with Jacques Gorlin, Aanser, IPC, in Washington DC in January 1996.
14 For a detailed analysis, see Sundaram (2015).
15 It is widely accepted that the policy of granting privileges of monopoly under the royal prerogative in England culminated in the Statute of Monopolies of 1623. See Machlup and E Penrose (1950).
16 Select committees of the English Parliament and Royal commissions investigated the operation of the patent system in 1851–1852, in 1862–1865, and again in 1869–1872. Some of the testimonies before the two commissions were so damaging to the reputation of the patent system that leading statesmen in the two houses of Parliament proposed the complete abolition of patent protection. The Patent Bill 1874, although passed in the House Lords, came to be withdrawn in the House of Commons.
17 See Smith (2012) pp. 753–754.
18 Chevalier, Michael. *Les brevets d'inventions dans leurs relations au principe de la liberté, du travail et de l'égalité* (1878) 38. As cited in Machlup and Penrose (1950) p. 9.
19 The authors, writing in 1950, observe that these arguments were still being used in the twentieth century in debates on the issue.
20 One of the main arguments put forth by Stanislas de Bouffle at the time of presenting the bill to the French Constitutional Assembly in 1790 was that a man's property in his ideas was more sacred than his property in things material. As cited by Machlup in his work from 1950. See Machlup (1950).
21 Article I, Section 8, Clause 8 reads as follows: "To promote the Progress of Science and useful Arts, by securing for limited Times to Authors and Inventors the exclusive Rights to their respective Writings and Discoveries." See Donner (1992), who notes that at the time of the Constitutional Convention, 12 of the 13 states had already enacted copyright laws. See also Walterscheid (1994) for a detailed account of the background and origins of the IP clause of the US Constitution.
22 Bugbee notes that the description is misleading as the clause contains no reference to 'property' or to patents and copyrights as such. See Bugbee (1967).
23 Prior to the passing of the Chace Act in 1891, British books (literary works) were widely pirated in the US, robbing British authors of royalty. For an analysis of the Chace Act, see West III (1992).
24 For a detailed analysis, see Sundaram (2015).
25 Stiglitz, while arguing that knowledge is a public good, expresses the view that Thomas Jefferson anticipated the modern concept of public good when he wrote to Isaac McPherson, the inventor in 1813, as follows: "he who receives an idea from me, receives instruction himself without lessening mine; as he who lights his taper at mine, receives light without darkening me." David, on the other hand, argues that Jefferson grasped the essential point that the cost of transmitting useful knowledge in codified form is negligible when compared with the cost of creating it, and that for society's need to encourage the pursuit of ideas, such information should be distributed freely.
26 According to Menell and Scotchmer (2007), knowledge is "non-excludable" in its natural state, even if someone claims to own the knowledge, it is difficult to exclude others from using it. IP laws attempt to solve this problem by legal means, by granting exclusive use of the protected knowledge or creative work to the creator. Through the device of IP, the inventor can control entry and exclude users from the intangible assets.
27 For instance, significant changes have taken place in the legal approach to the grant of patents to software since the late 1970s. When VisiCalc, the first computer spreadsheet programme, was developed in 1979, the US Patent Office, relying upon US Supreme Court case law, took the position that the mathematical algorithms in computer programs were incapable of being protected as a subject matter. This position was to change when the US Supreme Court in the *Diamond v Diehr* case [450 U.S. 175, 185–187 (1981)] held that controlling the execution of a physical process, by running a computer program, did not preclude patentability of the invention as a whole, and found patentable subject matter in a process utilising a computer algorithm.
28 Coase and Calabresi, considered as pioneers in the field of economic analysis of law, were the first to attempt and apply economic analysis in a systematic way to areas of law that did not purport to regulate economic relationships. See Coase (1960) and Calabresi (1961). Coase and Calabresi were followed by the likes of Posner in later years. See Posner (1975).
29 The author also observes that there is some confusion regarding the meaning and object of 'property' and 'property rights', which again is more troublesome to lawyers than to economists, and how quite often the controversial idea of property right in an invention is confused with the non-controversial idea of a property right in a patent. See Machlup (1958).

30 The authors observe, "A person can enjoy the full benefit of the statute, regulation, or other policy in question without having contributed a dime to the collective effort that was necessary to get it promulgated."
31 This strong criticism, coming from Posner, can be extended to the 20-year patent protection granted under the TRIPS Agreement, which was in turn shaped by the US-led developed countries during the Uruguay Round of negotiations.
32 Posner, while noting "wealth maximization" as the guiding principle of common law, argues that the "basic function of law in an economic or wealth-maximization perspective is to alter incentives".
33 The Paris Convention 1893, the Berne Convention 1886, the Rome Convention 1961, and the Washington Treaty 1989.
34 See Article 42 of the TRIPS Agreement.
35 See Article 61 of the TRIPS Agreement.
36 The preamble to the TRIPS Agreement reflects the Uruguay Round mandates of the TRIPS negotiators in the Punta del Este Declaration of 1986 and the mid-term review decision from 1988. See Taubman, Wager, and Watal (2020).
37 See generally, Panel Report, *Australia – Tobacco Plain Packaging*.
38 See generally, Panel Report, *Canada – Pharmaceutical Patents*.
39 *Ibid.*, para. 7.23.
40 *Ibid.*, para. 7.26.
41 The Doha Declaration on the TRIPS Agreement and Public Health is discussed later in this chapter at 5.4.2.
42 See Panel Report, *Australia – Tobacco Plain Packaging*, paras. 7.2403–7.2404.
43 The obligation of nation states, *i.e.*, Member States of the WTO, to perform an international agreement in good faith ('*pacta sunt servanda*') is established in Article 26 of the Vienna Convention on the Law of Treaties.
44 The implementation of the TRIPS Agreement in Member States pursuant to Article 1.1 of the Agreement is subject to the laws of the individual Member States, and dependent on the legal traditions, *i.e.*, monism, dualism, or a variation. Under 'monist' legal traditions, the treaty is considered as part of domestic law without any further action needed to integrate the treaty into national laws (*e.g.*, Argentina, France, *etc.*). In contrast, under the 'dualist' legal traditions, the treaty is not considered as part of the domestic laws and the government takes steps to incorporate all or part of the treaty into national laws (*e.g.*, the UK). In the third category, the treaties may be given direct effect, with the possibility of variations to obligations by the legislature (*e.g.*, the US).
45 See Appellate Body Report, *India – Patents (US)*, paras. 58–60, 64–66, and 70.
46 See Panel Report, *China – Intellectual Property Rights*, paras. 7.513–7.2404.
47 The Berne Convention for Protection of Literary and Artistic Work 1886 established minimum standards of copyright protection, whereas the Paris Convention for the Protection of Industrial Property 1883 did not define the substantive standards of patent protection, leaving the same to the signatories.
48 Jurists Joseph Kohler and Edmond Picard are credited with coining the term 'intellectual property' in the late nineteenth century. See Reichman (1995).
49 See Appellate Body Report, *US – Section 211 Appropriations Act*, para. 335.
50 *Ibid.*, para. 336.
51 The author notes that Article 1.3, which establishes the legal fiction that all Member States are Union parties to the WIPO-administered conventions, supports the proposition.
52 See Articles 3.1, 4.1(a), (b), (c), and (d), and 5 of the TRIPS Agreement.
53 Article 2(1) of the Paris Convention reads as follows: "Nationals of any country of the Union shall, as regards the protection of industrial property, enjoy in all the other countries of the Union the advantages that their respective laws now grant, or may hereafter grant, to nationals; all without prejudice to the rights specially provided for by this Convention. Consequently, they shall have the same protection as the latter, and the same legal remedy against any infringement of their rights, provided that the conditions and formalities imposed upon nationals are complied with."
54 See Appellate Body Report, *US – Section 211 Appropriations Act*, paras. 233–244.
55 *Ibid.*, paras. 261–265.
56 Section 515.305 of Title 31 CFR defines "designated national" as "Cuba and any national thereof including any person who is a specially designated national".

Intellectual Property Rights   515

57 *Ibid.*, paras. 274–281 and 296. See also Panel Report, *Indonesia – Autos*, paras. 14.264–274.
58 See Panel Report, *EC – Trademarks and Geographical Indications*, paras. 7.139 and 7.189, citing the Appellate Body Report, *US – Section 211 Appropriations Act*, para. 268.
59 See Panel Report, *EC – Trademarks and Geographical Indications*, paras. 7.271–7.272.
60 See Appellate Body Report, *US – Section 211 Appropriations Act*, para. 297.
61 *Ibid.*, para. 314.
62 In some jurisdictions, exhaustion of IP rights is referred to as the "first-sale doctrine".
63 Drexl notes that in the absence of international exhaustion, rights holders are able to control the flow of cross-border trade in a desired direction, *i.e.*, towards the most prosperous markets and, consequently, to price discriminate between richer and poorer countries. See Drexl (2016).
64 Bronckers also asserts that only the TRIPS Agreement applies to exhaustion issues given that it is a *lex specialis* agreement, which has absolute precedence over the GATT 1994 in relation to all IP rights issues. Bronckers is of the opinion that Article 6 of the TRIPS Agreement is essentially an 'agreement to disagree'.
65 See Declaration on the TRIPS Agreement and Public Health 2001, para. 5(d).
66 See Doha Ministerial Declaration 2001 for a full declaration.
67 See Panel Report, *US – Section 110(5) Copyright Act*, para. 6.66.
68 See Panel Report, *China – Intellectual Property Rights*, para. 7.132.
69 *Ibid.*, paras. 6.17–6.18.
70 (Footnote original) Appellate Body Report on *Canada – Certain Measures Concerning Periodicals* ("*Canada – Periodicals*"), adopted on 30 July 1997, WT/DS31/AB/R, p. 19. Appellate Body Report on *European Communities – Regime for the Importation, Sale and Distribution of Bananas* ("*EC – Bananas III*"), adopted on 25 September 1997, WT/DS27/AB/R, paragraphs 219–222.
71 See Panel Report, *US – Section 110(5) Copyright Act*, para. 6.66.
72 It is important to bear in mind that the works identified in Article 2(1) of the Berne Convention are only illustrations of the kind of works that qualify as "literary and artistic works". Hence, it is possible to extend copyright protection to works that are not listed in Article 2(1), so long as the work can reasonably qualify as "productions in the literary, scientific and artistic domain".
73 Prior to the entry into force of the TRIPS Agreement, computer programs were able to receive general protection due to a broad interpretation of "literary and artistic works" found Article 2.1 of the Berne Convention.
74 Machine readable form is understood that such form is stored on a computer hard-disk and executed by a computer – object code or machine code.
75 Where the TRIPS Agreement confers a new right not created by Berne, Article 13 applies in a stand-alone capacity as the relevant basis for providing exceptions to those rights. See Correa (2020).
76 See Panel Report, *US – Section 110(5) Copyright Act*, para. 6.25.
77 *Ibid.*, paras. 6.42–6.70.
78 *Ibid.*, paras. 6.87–6.89.
79 *Ibid.*, paras. 6.159, 6.219, and 6.272.
80 *Ibid.*, paras. 6.118. Note: Where music is being played in public, the number of right holders involved are numerous and impracticable for users to seek permission from each of them. Hence, in many countries right holders in musical works authorise so-called collective management organisations (CMOs) to license restaurants, retail outlets, *etc.* to perform their music on their behalf. See Taubman, Wager, and Watal (2020).
81 *Ibid.*, paras. 6.133, 6.211, and 6.266. The Panel ruled that the exemption did not qualify as a "certain special case", that the business exemption embodied in subparagraph (B) of Section 110(5) of the Act conflicted with a normal exploitation of the work; and as a result, did not meet the requirement of the third condition of Article 13 of the TRIPS Agreement.
82 The two WIPO treaties are referred to as the "internet treaties", as they address a number of questions in relation to that of protected materials in cyberspace.
83 The Beijing Treaty, which entered into force on 28 April 2020, grants performers both economic and moral rights in their fixed (such as motion picture) and unfixed (live) audiovisual performances.
84 The Marrakesh VIP Treaty, which entered into force on 30 September 2016, makes the production and international transfer of specially adapted books for individuals with visual impairment easier, and achieves this through establishing a set of limitations and exceptions to traditional copyright laws.

85 Landes and Posner posit the argument that trademarks not only protect the owners of the mark, but also benefit consumers by reducing the search costs of a product. See Landes and Posner (2003).
86 For a discussion on whether the TRIPS Agreement is common law and civil law based, see Gervais (2020).
87 Footnote 14(a) of Article 15 reads as follows: "'counterfeit trademarked goods' shall mean any goods, including packaging, bearing without authorization a trademark which is identical to the trademark validly registered in respect of such goods, or which cannot be distinguished in its essential aspects from such a trademark, and which thereby infringes the rights of the owner of the trademark in question under the law of the country of importation."
88 Article 6 *quinquies* of the Paris Convention requires that Paris Union and WTO Member States protect a foreign registered mark 'as is' in their jurisdiction.
89 Gervais notes that the TRIPS Agreement "is meant to continue painting the international trademark law canvas on which Paris was first inscribed". See Gervais (2020).
90 The Paris Convention (1967) did not contain a definition of trademark. Article 15.1 of the TRIPS Agreement, on the other hand, by defining a trademark limits the ability of WTO Member States to define protectable subject matter and what constitutes a trademark in their domestic legislation.
91 See Appellate Body Report, *US – Section 211 Appropriation Act*, para. 154.
92 *Ibid.*, paras. 155, 156, and 165.
93 *Ibid.*, para. 158.
94 *Ibid.*, para. 159.
95 *Ibid.*, para. 178.
96 See Appellate Body Report, *US – Section 211 Appropriation Act*, para. 132.
97 See Panel Report, *Australia – Tobacco Plain Packaging*, para. 7.1843.
98 See Appellate Body Report, *US – Section 211 Appropriation Act*, paras. 186, 187, and 195.
99 Article 16.1 fills the gap in the Paris Convention by providing minimum rights to trademark owners.
100 See Panel Report, *EC – Trademarks and Geographical Indications (US)*, para. 7.512, and Panel Report, *EC – Trademarks and Geographical Indications (Australia)*, para. 7.516.
101 *Ibid.*, paras. 7.601–7.603, and *ibid.*, paras. 7.601–7.603.
102 *Ibid.*, para. 7.648, and *ibid.*, para. 7.648.
103 *Ibid.*, para. 7.650, and *ibid.*, para. 7.650.
104 See Panel Report, *Canada – Pharmaceutical Patents*, para. 7.69, where it was held that the term, in the context of Article 30 of the TRIPS Agreement, must be defined as a normative claim calling for protection of interests that are "justifiable", in the sense that they are supported by relevant public policies or other social norms.
105 See Panel Report, *EC – Trademarks and Geographical Indications (US)*, para. 7.663, and Panel Report, *EC – Trademarks and Geographical Indications (Australia)*, para. 7.663.
106 See Panel Report, *Australia – Tobacco Plain Packaging*, para. 7.2295.
107 See Appellate Body Report, *Australia – Tobacco Plain Packaging*, para. 6.646.
108 *Ibid.*, para. 6.651.
109 *Ibid.*, footnote 1683.
110 The 1951 Stresa Convention proposed a system for the protection of appellations of origin and designations for cheeses contained in an annex to the Convention. Subsequently, the Lisbon Agreement on the Protection of Appellations of Origin and their International Registration 1958 defined "appellations of origin", and elements of this definition were carried forward into the definition of GIs in the TRIPS Agreement.
111 Under US and UK laws, geographic origin was protected by collective marks and certification marks. For instance, in the UK, Stilton cheese and Harris Tweed (registered in 1909) are protected by certification trademarks. See UNCTAD-ICTSD (2005).
112 The European negotiators proposed a French-style protection, while the US proposed protection of GIs through a certification mark system. The proposal from a group of developing nations comprising Argentina, Brazil, Chile, China, Colombia, Cuba, Egypt, India, Nigeria, Peru, Tanzania, and Uruguay largely relied on unfair competition principles to address the protection of GIs.
113 WIPO data from 2019 reveals that an estimated 55,800 protected GIs are in existence. China is among the top with 7,834 filings, with the EU coming second with 4,794 registrations.
114 Also, the WTO Secretariat has come up with the following useful explanation: "A product's quality, reputation or other characteristics can be determined by where it comes from. Geographical

indications are place names (in some countries also words associated with a place) used to identify products that come from these places and have these characteristics (for example, 'Champagne', 'Tequila' or 'Roquefort')."

115 For example, 'Basmati' is taken to be an indication for a rice variety coming from the Indian subcontinent, although it is not a place name as such.
116 See Panel Report, *EC – Trademarks and Geographical Indications (US)*, para. 7.622, and Panel Report, *EC – Trademarks and Geographical Indications (Australia)*, para. 7.622, where it was noted that Article 22.3 can resolve conflicts between GIs and later trademarks, but not prior trademarks that meet the conditions set out in Article 24.5.
117 While most of the Spanish wines from the Rioja region are produced from Tempranillo, Garnacha tinta, Mazuelo and Graciano, Viura, Malvasia, and Garnacha blanca grapes, the Argentinian wines from La Rioja region are produced using the Torrontés Riojano grapes.
118 See Panel Report, *EC – Trademarks and Geographical Indications (Australia)*, para. 7.633.
119 Commentators note that reference in Article 24.1 to 'individual' GIs emphasises the point that the provision is partly designed to protect the EC practice of seeking bilateral agreements with other countries (Malbon, Lawson, and Davison, 2014).
120 See Panel Report, *Australia – Tobacco Plain Packaging*, paras. 7.2924 and 7.2926.
121 Cheddar cheese is the most popular cheese variety in the UK and the second most popular cheese in the US. Cheddar is produced in Australia, Argentina, Belgium, Canada, Finland, Germany, Ireland, Netherlands, South Africa, Sweden, and the US. Cheddar cheese, *per se*, has no protected designation of origin. However, in 2007, a Protected Designation of Origin, 'West Country Farmhouse Cheddar' was created. Cheddar produced locally in Somerset, Dorset, Devon, and Cornwall, using local ingredients and traditional methods, may use the designation.
122 See Panel Report, *EC – Trademarks and Geographical Indications (US)*, para. 7.606, and Panel Report, *EC – Trademarks and Geographical Indications (Australia)*, para. 7.606.
123 At the time of Uruguay Round of negotiations, nearly 50 countries did not confer patent protection for pharmaceutical products and in some cases for food and beverages, and a number of countries were granting process patents for pharmaceutical products.
124 See Panel Report, *Canada – Pharmaceutical Patents*, para. 7.99.
125 *Ibid.*, paras. 7.94 and 7.98.
126 *Ibid.*, para. 7.105.
127 The French expression "*ordre public*" is found in the text of the European Patent Convention (EPC) and was introduced into the TRIPS Agreement upon a proposal by the EC. By adopting the notion of *ordre public* as opposed to 'public order' or 'public interest', the TRIPS Agreement embraced a narrower standard. See Gervais (2012).
128 During the TRIPS negotiations, some of the negotiating parties (EC, Brazil, Canada, *etc.*) were proposing to develop a non-exhaustive list of specific exceptions.
129 A case in point is India, which successfully invoked Article 30 of the TRIPS Agreement to grant compulsory licence for the manufacture of generic drugs. See Sundaram (2014) and Sundaram (2018).
130 See Panel Report, *Canada – Pharmaceutical Patents*, paras. 7.20–7.21.
131 *Ibid.*, para. 7.30.
132 *Ibid.*, para. 7.36.
133 *Ibid.*, para. 7.45.
134 *Ibid.*, para. 7.74.
135 *Ibid.*, para. 7.77.
136 *Ibid.*, para. 7.84.
137 *Chapeau* of Article 31 of the TRIPS Agreement.
138 See Musungu, Oh, and WTO (2006) and Deere (2009) for a study of the use of flexibilities and the practical difficulties faced by developing countries to promote access to medicines.
139 Paragraph 5(b), Doha Declaration 2001.
140 Paragraph 5(c), Doha Declaration 2001.
141 India, one of the developing countries, has made maximum use of the flexibilities. India was able to delay the entry of the product patent regime into its patent laws, and ably support its generics market which was developed on the back of the process patent regime introduced in the Patent Act of 1970. Besides, in recent years India has also made use of the compulsory licensing provision introduced in TRIPS compliant legislation of 2005. For a detailed account, see Sundaram (2014).

142 Brazil, which introduced the TRIPS-compliant patent laws in its national legislation much earlier than others, was able to use the compulsory license provisions to procure generic medicines at affordable prices for its much-lauded anti-AIDS programme. For a detailed account, see Sundaram (2018).
143 The author presents five case studies from three different continents, capturing the experience of developing country Member States in implementing the TRIPS Agreement and their struggles to gain affordable access to medicines.
144 The author notes that bilateral agreements established by the US with some developing and developed countries (*e.g.*, Australia, the Central American countries, Chile, Jordan, and Morocco) require the protection of data under a *sui generis* regime of data exclusivity for at least five years from the date of the first approval of a pharmaceutical product in the country.
145 This was the first amendment to the TRIPS Agreement since its entry into force on 1 January 1995.
146 Integrated circuits are referred to in the TRIPS Agreement as "layout designs".
147 See Appellate Body Report, *US – Section 211 Appropriation Act*, para. 204.
148 For a detailed discussion, see UNCTAD-ICTSD (2005).
149 See Panel Report, *China – Intellectual Property Rights*, para. 7.179.
150 *Ibid.*, paras. 7.161–7.181.
151 See Panel Report, *China – Intellectual Property Rights*, para. 7.180.
152 Footnote 11 of Article 42 states as follows: "For the purpose of this Part, the term 'right holder' includes federations and associations having legal standing to assert such rights."
153 See Appellate Body Report, *US – Section 211 Appropriation Act*, para. 217.
154 See Panel Report, *US – Section 211 Appropriation Act*, para. 8.162.
155 *Ibid.*, para. 8.100.
156 See Appellate Body Report, *US – Section 211 Appropriation Act*, paras. 215, and 217.
157 See Panel Report, *China – Intellectual Property Rights*, para. 7.516.
158 See Panel Report, *India – Patents (US)*, para. 7.48.
159 *Ibid.*, para. 29.
160 While developing country Member States have been vocal in their opposition of non-violation and situation complaints, developed country Member States such as the US and Switzerland have been in support of such complaints.
161 The 12th Ministerial Conference (MC12) is slated to take place from 30 November to 3 December 2021 in Geneva, Switzerland. The MC12 originally scheduled to take place in 2020 in Nur-Sultan, Kazakhstan, was rescheduled due to the COVID-19 pandemic.
162 For instance, South Africa (one of the founding Member States) entered the Uruguay Round of negotiations as a developed country, under the apartheid regime. When the TRIPS Agreement entered into force, South Africa was a democracy with severe disparities, both economic and social, and nowhere closer to calling itself a developed country Member State. As a developed country Member State, it was required to introduce a TRIPS-compliant domestic legislation within one year, which proved to be an uphill task. For a discussion of the difficulties faced by South Africa in implementing the TRIPS Agreement, see Sundaram (2018).
163 The three criteria studied by the UN to designate a country as 'least developed' are (i) gross national income per capita; (ii) Human Assets Index (HAI); and (iii) Economic Vulnerability Index (EVI).
164 See Article 65.3 of the TRIPS Agreement.
165 The transitional periods found in Article 65 of the TRIP Agreement does not apply to Article 70.8, which requires Member States establish a 'mailbox' provision. See Panel Report, *India – Patents (US)*, para. 7.27, and 7.28. See also Sundaram (2014, 2018).

Bibliography

Adede, Adronico Oduogo. 'Origins and History of the TRIPS Negotiations,' in Bellman, Christopher, Graham Dutfield and Rcardo Meléndez-Oritz (eds.) *Trading in Knowledge: Development Perspectives on TRIPS, Trade and Sustainability* (Earthscan Publishing, 2003) 23–35.

Barbosa, Denis Borges, Margaret Chon and Andrés Moncayo von Hase. 'Slouching towards Development in International Intellectual Property,' *Michigan State Law Review* Vol 1 (2007) 71–141.

Barton, John H. and Bart S. Fisher. 'United States: Omnibus Trade and Competitiveness Act 1988: Title I.' *International Legal Materials* Vol 28, No 1 (1988) 15–120.

Bentham, Jeremy. 'Observation on Parts of the Declaration of Rights, as Proposed by Citizen Sieyes,' in Bowring, John (ed.) *The Works of Jeremy Bentham* Vol 2 (Simpkin, Marshall & Co, London, 1843).

Besen, Stanley M. and Leo J. Raskind. 'An Introduction to the Law and Economics of Intellectual Property,' *The Journal of Economic Perspectives* Vol 5, No 1 (1991) 3–27.

Blakeney, Michael. *The Protection of Geographical Indications: Law and Practice* (Edward Elgar Publication, 2014).

Brand, Oliver. 'Article 2,' in Stoll, Peter-Tobias, Jan Busche and Katrin Arend (eds.) *WTO-Trade Related Aspects of Intellectual Property* (Martinus Nijhoff Publishers, 2009) 95–149.

Bronckers, Marco. 'The Exhaustion of Patent Rights under WTO Law,' *Journal of World Trade* Vol 32, No 5 (1998) 137–159.

Bugbee, Bruce W. *The Genesis of American Patent and Copyright Law* (Public Affairs Press, 1967).

Calabresi, Guido. 'Some Thoughts on Risk Distribution and the Law of Torts,' *Yale Law Journal* Vol 70, No 4 (1961) 499–553.

Calandrillo, Steve P. 'Economic Analysis of Property Rights in Information: Justifications and Problems of Exclusive Rights, Incentives to Generate Information, and the Alternative for a Government-Run Reward System,' *Fordham Intellectual Property Media & Entertainment Law Journal* Vol 9, No 1 (1998) 301–360.

Chevalier, Michel. *Les brevets d'inventions dans leurs relations au principe de la liberté, du travail et de l'égalité* (Librairie Guillaumin et Cie, Paris, 1878).

Coase, Ronald H. 'The Problem of Social Cost,' *Journal of Law & Economics* Vol 56, No 4 (1960) 837–877.

Correa, Carlos M. 'Managing the Provisions of Knowledge: The Design of Intellectual Property Management,' in Kaul, Inge, Pedro Conceição, Katell Le Goulven and Ronald U. Mendoza (eds.) *Providing Global Public Goods: Managing Globalization* (Oxford University Press, 2003) 410–429.

Council for TRIPS. 'Extension of the Transition Period under Article 66.1 for the Least-Developed Country Members, Decision of 29 November 2005,' (IP/C/40) (30 November 2005).

Council for TRIPS. 'Extension of the Transition Period under Article 66.1 for the Least-Developed Country Members for Certain Obligations with Respect to Pharmaceutical Products, Decision of the Council for TRIPS of 6 November 2015,' (IP/C/73) (6 November 2015).

Council for TRIPS. 'Extension of the Transition Period under Article 66.1 for the Least-Developed Country Members for Certain Obligations with Respect to Pharmaceutical Products, Decision of the Council for TRIPS of 29 June 2021,' (IP/C/73) (29 June 2021).

Correa, Carlos M. 'Implementation of the WTO General Council Decision on Paragraph 6 of the Doha Declaration on the TRIPS Agreement and Public Health,' in *Essential Drugs and Medicines Policy* (WHO, 2004a).

Correa, Carlos M. 'Bilateralism in Intellectual Property: Defeating the WTO System for Access to Medicines,' *Case Western Reserve Journal of International Law* Vol 36 (2004b) 79–94.

Correa, Carlos M. *Trade-Related Aspects of Intellectual Property Rights: A Commentary on the TRIPS Agreement* (Oxford University Press, 2020).

Cottier, Thomas. 'The Prospect for Intellectual Property in GATT,' *Common Market Law Review* Vol 28, No 2 (1991) 383–414.

Cottier, Thomas. 'The Agreement on Trade-Related Aspects of Intellectual Property Rights,' in Macrory, Patrick F.J., Arthur E. Appleton and Michael G. Plummer (eds.) *The WTO: Legal, Economic and Political Analysis* Vol 1 (Springer, 2005) 1041–1120.

Cottier, Thomas. 'Working Together towards TRIPS,' in Watal, Jayashree and Antony Taubman (eds.) *The Making of the TRIPS Agreement: Personal Insights from the Uruguay Round Negotiations* (WTO Publication, 2015) 79–94.

Council for TRIPS. 'Multilateral System of Notification and Registration of Geographical Indications for Wines and Spirits,' Report by the Chairman, Ambassador Dacio Castillo (TN/IP/23) (3 December 2015).

Crump, Larry and Daniel Druckman. 'Turning Points in Multilateral Trade Negotiations on Intellectual Property,' *International Negotiation* Vol 17, No 1 (2012) 9–35.

David, Paul A. 'Intellectual Property Institutions and the Panda's Thumb: Patent, Copyrights, and the Trade Secrets in Economic Theory and History,' in Wallerstein, Mitchel B., Mary E. Mogee and Robin A. Schoen (eds.) *Global Dimensions of Intellectual Property Rights in Science and Technology* (National Academy Press, 1993) 20–61.

Deere, Caroline. *The Implementation Game: The Global Politics of Intellectual Property Reform in Developing Countries* (Oxford University Press, 2009).

Demsetz, Harold. 'Toward a Theory of Property Rights,' *American Economic Review* Vol 57 (1967) 347–359.

Donner, Irah. 'The Copyright Clause of the U.S. Constitution: Why Did the Framers Include It with Unanimous Approval,' *The American Journal of Legal History* Vol 36, No 3 (1992) 361–378.

Drahos, Peter. 'Developing Countries and International Intellectual Property Standard-Setting,' *The Journal of World Intellectual Property* Vol 5, No 5 (2002) 765–789.

Drahos, Peter. 'Expanding Intellectual Property's Empire: The Role of FTAs,' *Regulatory Institutions Network, Research School of Social Sciences, Australian National University* (2003) 1–19.

Drahos, Peter. 'Securing the Future of Intellectual Property: Intellectual Property Owners and Their Nodally Coordinated Enforcement Pyramid,' *Case Western Reserve Journal of International Law* Vol 36, No 1 (2004a) 53–77.

Drahos, Peter. 'Intellectual Property and Pharmaceutical Markets: A Nodal Governance Approach,' *Temple Law Review* Vol 77, No 1 (2004b) 401–424.

Drahos, Peter and John Braithwaite. *Information Feudalism: Who Owns the Knowledge Economy?* (Earthscan Publishing, 2002).

Drexl, Joseph. 'The Concept of Trade-Relatedness of Intellectual Property Rights in Times of Post-TRIPS Bilateralism,' in Ullrich, Hanns, Reto M. Milty, Matthias Lamping and Joseph Drexl (eds.) *TRIPS-Plus 20: From Trade Rules to Market Principles* (Springer International, 2016) 53–83.

Edgar, Craig. 'Patenting Nature: GATT on a Hot Tin Roof,' *Washburn Law Journal* Vol 34 (1994) 76–118.

Elfring, Klaus and Katrin Arend. 'General Provisions and Basic Principles,' in Stoll, Peter-Tobias, Jan Busche and Katrin Arend (eds.) *WTO-Trade Related Aspects of Intellectual Property* (Martinus Nijhoff Publishers, 2009) 75–94.

Fenning, Karl. 'The Origin of the Patent and Copyright Clause of the Constitution,' *Journal of Patent Office Society* Vol 11 (1929) 438–445.

Gadbaw, Michael R. 'Intellectual Property and International Trade: Merger or Marriage of Convenience?,' *Vanderbilt Journal of Transnational Law* Vol 22, No 2 (1989) 223–242.

Garner, Bryan A. *Black's Law Dictionary* (Thomson West Publishers, 2004).

Gathii, James Thuo. 'The Legal Status of Doha Declaration on TRIPS and Public Health under the Vienna Convention on the Law of Treaties,' *Harvard Journal of Law & Tech* Vol 15, No 2 (2002) 291–317.

General Council. 'Implementation of Paragraph 6 of the Doha Declaration on the TRIPS Agreement and Public Health,' (WT/L/540) (30 August 2003).

General Council. 'Amendment of the TRIPS Agreement: Decision of the General Council of 6 December 2005,' (WT/L/641) (8 December 2005).

Genovesi, Luis Mariano. 'The TRIPS Agreement and Intellectual Property Rights Exhaustion,' in Correa, Carlos M. (ed.) *Research Handbook on the Protection of Intellectual Property under the WTO Rules* (Edward Elgar Publishing, 2010) 216–225.

Gervais, Daniel. *The TRIPS Agreement: Drafting History and Analysis* (Sweet & Maxwell Publishing, 2012).

Gervais, Daniel. 'A Look at the Trademark Provisions in the TRIPS Agreement,' in Calboli, Irene and Jane C. Ginsburg (eds.) *The Cambridge Handbook of International and Comparative Trademark Law* (Cambridge University Press, 2020) 27–45.

Ghafele, Roya. 'Perceptions of Intellectual Property: A Review,' *MPRA Paper No. 38093* (2008) 1–42.

Helfer, Laurence R. 'Regime Shifting: The TRIPS Agreement and New Dynamics of International Intellectual Property Lawmaking,' *The Yale Journal of International Law* Vol 29, No 1 (2004) 1–83.

Hoekman, Bernard M. and Michel M. Kostecki. *The Political Economy of the World Trading System* Vol 3 (Oxford University Press, 2009).

Howse, Robert. 'The Canadian Generic Medicines Panel: A Dangerous Precedent in Dangerous Times,' *Journal of World Intellectual Property* Vol 3, No 4 (2000) 493–507.

Hume, David. *Enquiries Concerning the Human Understanding and Concerning the Principles of Morals* (Oxford University Press, 1902).

Islam, M. Rafiqul. *International Trade Law of the WTO* (Oxford University Press, 2006).

Jefferson, Thomas. 'To Isaac McPherson Monticello' (13 August 1813) in 'The Letters of Thomas Jefferson 1743–1826,' *American History: From Revolution to Reconstruction and Beyond* <www.let.rug.nl/usa/presidents/thomas-jefferson/letters-of-thomas-jefferson/jefl220.php> (accessed 14 March 2021).

Kitch, Edmund W. 'Elementary and Persistent Errors in the Economic Analysis of Intellectual Property,' *Vanderbilt Law Review* Vol 53, No 6 (2000) 1727–1741.

Kosterlitz, J. 'Rx: Higher Prices,' *National Journal* Vol 25, No 7 (1993) 396–399.

Landes, William M. and Richard A. Posner. *The Economic Structure of Intellectual Property Law* (Harvard University Press, 2003).

Lester, Simon, Bryan Mercurio and Arwel Davies. *World Trade Law: Text, Materials and Commentary* (Hart Publishing, 2018).

Machlup, Fritz. 'An Economic Review of the Patent System,' in *Study of the Subcommittee on Patents, Trademarks, and Copyrights of the Committee on the Judiciary, United States, Senate, Eighty-Fifth Congress, Second Session; Pursuant to S. Res. 236* (US Government Printing Office, 1958).

Machlup, Fritz and Edith Penrose. 'The Patent Controversy in the Nineteenth Century,' *The Journal of Economic History* Vol 10, No 1 (1950) 1–29.

Malbon, Justin, Charles Lawson and Mark Davison. *The WTO Agreement on Trade-Related Aspects of Intellectual Property Rights: A Commentary* (Edward Elgar Publishing, 2014).

Marcellin, Sherry S. *The Political Economy of Pharmaceutical Patent: US Sectional Interests and the African Group at the WTO* (Routledge Publishing, 2016).

Matsushita, Mitsuo, Thomas J. Shoenbaum, Petros C. Mavroidis and Michael Hahn. *The World Trade Organization: Law, Practice, and Policy* (Oxford University Press, 2017).

Matthews, Duncan. *Globalising Intellectual Property Rights* (Routledge, 2002).

Menell, Peter S. 'Intellectual Property: General Theories,' in Bouckaert, Baudewijn and Gerrit De Geest (eds.) *Encyclopedia of Law and Economics: The History and Methodology of Law & Economics* Vol 2 (Edward Elgar Publishing, 2000) 129–188.

Menell, Peter S. 'The Property Rights Movement's Embrace of Intellectual Property: True Love or Doomed Relationship?,' *Ecology Law Quarterly* Vol 34 (2007) 713–754.

Menell, Peter S. and Suzanne Scotchmer. 'Intellectual Property,' in Polinsky, A. Mitchell and Steven Shavell (eds.) *Handbook of Law and Economics* Vol 2 (Elsevier Publishing, 2007) 1473–1570.

Mill, John Stuart. *Principles of Political Economy with Some of Their Applications to Social Philosophy* (Lee and Shepard Publishing, 1872).

Mill, John Stuart. *Principles of Political Economy with Some of Their Applications to Social Philosophy* (Hackett Publishing, 2004).

Ministerial Conference. 'Doha Declaration on TRIPS Agreement and Public Health,' (WT/MIN(01)DEC/2) (20 November 2001).

Musungu, Sisule F., Cecilia Oh and World Health Organization. *The Use of Flexibilities in TRIPS by Developing Countries: Can They Promote Access to Medicines?* (South Centre, 2006).

Muzaka, Valbona. *The Politics of Intellectual Property Rights and Access to Medicines* (Palgrave MacMillan, 2011).

Okediji, Ruth L. 'Public Welfare and the Role of the WTO: Reconsidering the TRIPS Agreement,' *Emory International Law Review* Vol 17 (2003) 819–918.

Plant, Arnold. 'The Economic Theory Concerning Patents for Inventions,' *Economica* Vol 1, No 1 (1934) 30–51.

Posner, Richard A. 'The Economic Approach to Law,' *Texas Law Review* Vol 53 (1975) 757–782.

Posner, Richard A. *The Economics of Justice* (Harvard University Press, 1983) 75–115.

Posner, Richard A. 'Do Patent and Copyright Law Restrict Competition and Creativity Excessively?,' *The Becker-Posner Blog* (30 September 2012) <www.becker-posner-blog.com/2012/09/do-patent-and-copyright-law-restrict-competition-and-creativity-excessively-posner.html> (accessed 16 March 2021).

Rangnekar, Dwijen. 'Geographical Indications: A Review of Proposals at the TRIPS Council: Extending Article 23 to Products Other Than Wines and Spirits,' *Issue Paper No. 4* (ICTSD-UNCTAD, 2003) 1–46.

Reichman, Jerome H. 'Charting the Collapse of the Patent-Copyright Dichotomy: Premises for a Restructured International Intellectual Property System,' *Cardozo Arts and Entertainment Law Journal* Vol 13 (1995) 475–520.

Schuller, Ant. *Handbuch der Gesetze über ausschließende Privilegien auf neue Erfindungen im Gebiete der Industrie, enthaltend den Originaltext des Düßfalls geltenden Gesetze* (Karl Gerold, Vienna, 1843).

Scotchmer, Suzanne. 'Standing on the Shoulders of Giants: Cumulative Research and the Patent Law,' *The Journal of Economic Perspectives* Vol 5, No 1 (1991) 29–41.

Sell, Susan K. *Private Power, Public Law: The Globalization of Intellectual Property Rights* (Cambridge University Press, 2003).

Sell, Susan K. 'Cat and Mouse: Forum-Shifting in the Battle over Intellectual Property Enforcement,' *American Political Science Association Meeting* Vol 3, No 6 (2009).

Sell, Susan K. 'TRIPS Was Never Enough: Vertical Forum Shifting, FTAS, ACTA, and TTP,' *Journal of Intellectual Property* Vol 18, No 2 (2011) 447–478.

Slotboom, Marco M. 'The Exhaustion of Intellectual Property Rights: Different Approaches in EC and WTO Law,' *The Journal of World Intellectual Property Law* Vol 6, No 3 (2003) 421–440.

Smith, Adam. *An Inquiry Into the Nature and Causes of the Wealth of Nations* (W. Statham, and T. Citadell, 1776).

Stewart, Terence P. *The GATT Uruguay Round: A Negotiating History (1986–1992)* Vol 3 (Kluwer Law and Taxation Publishers, 1993).

Stiglitz, Joseph E. 'Knowledge as a Global Public Good,' in Kaul, Inge, Isabelle Grunberg and Marc A. Stern (eds.) *Global Public Goods: International Cooperation in the 21st Century* (Oxford University Press, 1999) 308–325.

Stiglitz, Joseph E. 'Intellectual-Property Rights and Wrongs,' *Project Syndicate* (5 August 2005) <www.project-syndicate.org/commentary/intellectual-property-rights-and-wrongs?barrier=accesspaylog> (accessed 16 March 2021).

Stiglitz, Joseph E. 'Economic Foundations of Intellectual Property Rights,' *Duke Law Journal* Vol 57 (2008) 1693–1724.

Sundaram, Jae. 'India's Trade-Related Aspects of Intellectual Property Rights Compliant Pharmaceutical Patent Laws: What Lessons for India and Other Developing Countries?,' *Information & Communications Technology Law* Vol 23, No 1 (2014) 1–30.

Sundaram, Jae. 'Analysis of TRIPS Agreement and the Justification of International IP Rights Protection in the WTO's Multilateral Trading System, with Particular Reference to Pharmaceutical Patents,' *Information & Communications Technology Law* Vol 24, No 2 (2015) 121–163.

Sundaram, Jae. *Pharmaceutical Patent Protection and World Trade Law: The Unresolved Problem of Access to Medicines* (Routledge Publishing, 2018).

Taubman, Antony, Hannu Wager and Jayashree Watal (eds.). *A Handbook on the TRIPS Agreement* (Cambridge University of Press, 2020).

Trebilcock, Michael, Robert Howse and Antonia Eliason. *The Regulation of International Trade* (Routledge, 2013).

UNCTAD. *Intellectual Property in the World Trade Organization: Turning It into Developing Countries' Real Property* (United Nations Publication, 2010).

UNCTAD-ICTSD. *Resource Book on TRIPS and Development* (Cambridge University Press, 2005).

United Nations, Committee for Development. 'List of Least Developed Countries,' (as of 11 February 2021) <www.un.org/development/desa/dpad/wp-content/uploads/sites/45/publication/ldc_list.pdf> (accessed 18 April 2021).

United Nations, Committee for Development Policy. *Handbook on the Least Developed Country Category: Inclusion, Graduation and Special Support Measures* (United Nation, 2015).

Van den Bossche, Peter and Werner Zdouc. *The Law and Policy of the World Trade Organization* (Cambridge University Press, 2017).

Walterscheid, Edward C. 'To Promote the Progress of Science and Useful Arts: The Background and Origin of the Intellectual Property Clause of the United States Constitution,' *Journal of Intellectual Property Law* Vol 2, No 1 (1994) 1–56.

Watal, Jayashree. *Intellectual Property Rights in the WTO and Developing Countries* (Kluwer Law International, 2001).

Watal, Jayashree and Antony Taubman (eds.). *The Making of the TRIPS Agreement: Personal Insights from the Uruguay Round Negotiations* (WTO Publication, 2015).

Weissman, Robert. 'Patent Plunder: *TRIPing the Third World*,' *Multinational Monitor* Vol 11, No 11 (November 1990).

Weissman, Robert. 'A Long, Strange TRIPS: The Pharmaceutical Industry Drive to Harmonize Global Intellectual Property Rules, and the Remaining WTO Legal Alternatives Available to Third World Countries,' *University of Pennsylvania Journal of International Economic Law* Vol 17, No 4 (1996) 1069–1125.

West III, James L.W. 'The Chace Act and Anglo-American Literary Relations,' *Studies in Bibliography* Vol 45 (1992) 303–311.

WIPO. 'Patent Related Flexibilities in the Multilateral Legal Framework and Their Legislative Implementation at the National and Regional Levels,' *Committee on Development and Intellectual Property, Fifth Session*, WIPO (26–30 April 2010).

WTO. 'Least Developed Countries,' *Understanding the WTO: The Organization* <www.wto.org/english/thewto_e/whatis_e/tif_e/org7_e.htm> (February 2021) (accessed 18 April 2021).

13 Technical Barriers to Trade
TBT Agreement

Learning Objectives	525
1. Introduction: The Role of TBT and SPS Agreements	525
2. Scope and Application of TBT Agreement	526
2.1 Application of TBT Agreement	529
2.1.1 Principal Actors Under the TBT Agreement	529
2.1.2 Temporal Scope of the TBT Agreement	529
2.2 TBT Agreement and Other WTO Agreements	530
2.2.1 The GATT 1994	530
2.2.2 The Agreement on Government Procurement and the SPS Agreement	532
3. Substantive Provisions of the TBT Agreement	532
3.1 MFN and NT Treatment Obligations	533
3.1.1 Technical Regulations	534
3.1.2 Like Products	537
3.1.3 Treatment No Less Favourable	538
3.2 'Least Trade Restrictive'	542
3.2.1 'Legitimate Objective'	543
3.2.2 'Not More Trade Restrictive Than Necessary'	544
3.3 The Obligation to Use International Standards	548
3.3.1 'Existence of Relevant International Standards'	549
3.3.2 International Standards 'As a Basis' for Domestic Standards	550
3.3.3 'Ineffective and Inappropriate International Standards'	551
4. Other Substantive Provisions of the TBT Agreement	552
4.1 Equivalence and Mutual Recognition	552
4.2 Performance Requirements	553
4.3 Transparency and Notification	553
4.4 Special and Differential Treatment	555
5. Institutional Provisions of the TBT Agreement	556
5.1 TBT Committee	557
5.2 Dispute Settlement and TBT Agreement	557
5.3 Technical Assistance	558
6. Summary	558

DOI: 10.4324/9780367028183-16

Learning Objectives

This chapter aims to help students understand:

1 The role of the TBT Agreement; application of the TBT Agreement;
2 The principal actors under the TBT Agreement; temporal scope of the TBT Agreement;
3 Substantive provisions of the TBT Agreement; MFN and NT treatment obligations; technical regulations; like products; treatment no less favourable;
4 Least trade restrictive; legitimate objective; not more trade restrictive than necessary;
5 The obligation to use international standards; international standards as a basis for domestic standards;
6 Other substantive provisions of the TBT Agreement; and
7 Institutional provisions of the TBT Agreement.

1. Introduction: The Role of TBT and SPS Agreements

Technical regulations and standards have existed since time immemorial and help regulate the standard of goods, enhance food safety, improve product compatibility, and establish a common trade language that provides the consumer with the correct information on the standard of the products traded. Governments of Member States apply both mandatory technical regulations and voluntary standards for the purpose of assessing the conformity of goods with standards. The technical regulations and product standards are ubiquitous and to be found in consumer durables (toys, refrigerators, washing machines, *etc.*), cosmetics, medical equipment, meat, cheese, *etc.* and the way in which they are produced and sourced. Technical regulations and standards diminish information asymmetry between producers and consumers and are the tools in the hands of governments to implement economic, social, and health policies that foster development (Villareal, 2018).

The characteristics of product standards can include *design, size, weight, safety, energy and environmental performance, interoperability*, and *material* (also process of production), and may be expressed in *marking, labelling, packaging, testing, inspection and quarantine*, and *information requirements* (WTO, 2005). The technical measures, although introduced for legitimate public regulation purposes of protecting health and safety of the citizens and the environment, operate as 'non-tariff barriers' in their own manner, and are referred to as 'behind-the-border' barriers. Where the technical standards, or product standards, are not intended to serve any genuine regulatory purposes but surreptitiously introduce trade barriers, they will cause additional losses that make them more inefficient than traditional instruments of protection (Sykes, 1999). Technical measures, or policy instruments, can dilute, or in some instances even nullify, the value of tariff bindings and affect trade in unpredictable ways (WTO, 2012). During the GATT era, the Contracting Parties had entered into plurilateral agreements, negotiated and introduced during the Kennedy and Tokyo Rounds, with a view to address some of the non-tariff barriers and extend the cover of the GATT, which only resulted in a fragmentation of the GATT (Marceau and Trachtman, 2014).[1]

There is strong evidence to suggest that the effects of such heterogeneous product standards could potentially constitute barriers to international flow of goods (Fontagné, Orefice,

Piermartini, and Rocha, 2015). As the measures are driven by a variety of considerations and are diverse in character, they have a highly variable trade and welfare effect. The GATT and the WTO have worked successfully over the decades to address the reduction of protectionist measures, *i.e.*, tariffs, quotas, and other forms of border measures, identified as 'tariff barriers', to achieve trade liberalisation. The success of trade liberalisation comes on the back of negotiated reciprocal commitments from Member States to eliminate protectionist tariff barriers. However, in their place, 'behind-the-border' barriers have emerged, with governments using technical regulations and other conformity assessment procedures to protect domestic producers from imports. In practice, there was also an increasing use of multiplicity of standards. Such technical regulations introduced by the Member States are laid down by domestic bodies and may not be in conformity with international standard-setting bodies and pose a major obstacle to international trade.

The Agreement on Technical Barriers to Trade (TBT) and the Agreement on Sanitary and Phytosanitary Measures (SPS) have a shared origin in the Standards Code. The TBT and SPS agreements address 'disguised protectionism' which arises from product regulation and health measures put in place by Member States. The TBT and SPS agreements link international standards and public international law by defining the former as the benchmark for compliance of some of the provisions established in the agreements (Villareal, 2018). The two agreements seek to promote regulatory harmonisation by encouraging Member States to align their domestic rules on TBT and SPS measures which are based on standards set by the relevant international standard-setting bodies. The agreements serve as instruments of trade liberalisation by bringing international standards to heterogeneous product standards. The TBT and SPS agreements are part of the concept of a WTO 'single undertaking', through which a state party to the Marrakesh Agreement Establishing the WTO entered into all of the WTO agreements annexed to it simultaneously, with the exception of plurilateral agreements.[2]

With the introduction of the TBT and SPS agreements from the mid-1990s, there had been a sharp decline in tariff barriers but a significant increase in the notifications made to the WTO Secretariat under the two agreements.[3] This increase in standardisation by Member States reflects consumer demand for safer and higher quality products, rising living standards, technological innovations, the expansion of global economic integration, and the increased concern paid by many governments and non-governmental organisations (NGOs) to social issues and the environment (WTO, 2005). This chapter, i.e., chapter 13 covers the TBT Agreement, and chapter 14 deals with the SPS Agreement.

2. Scope and Application of TBT Agreement

The TBT Agreement establishes rights and obligations for Member States to follow in the use of legal instruments relating to regulatory and standardisation interests. The TBT Agreement is intended to allow WTO Member States to pursue legitimate regulatory and standardisation interests (*e.g.*, to protect human, animal, or plant life or health; to safeguard the environment; or to meet other consumer interests), and at the same time, ensure that such regulations and standards do not become unnecessary obstacles to international trade in goods. The Appellate Body in *US – Clove Cigarettes* observed that the balance set out in the Preamble of the TBT Agreement between

> on the one hand, the desire to avoid creating unnecessary obstacles to international trade and, on the other hand, the recognition of Members' right to regulate, is not, in principle, different from the balance set out in the GATT 1994, where obligations such as national treatment in Article III are qualified by the general exceptions provision of Article XX.[4]

The Preamble to the TBT Agreement sets out the object and purpose of the Agreement by establishing the preference for the use of international standards and conformity assessment procedures. In *US – Clove Cigarettes*, the Appellate Body observed that the Preamble to the Agreement "sheds light on the object and purpose of the Agreement".[5] The recitals of the preamble also establish the important policy objective, by recognising that no Member State should be prevented from taking measures to ensure "the quality of its exports, or protection of human, animal or plant life or health, of the environment . . . at levels it considers appropriate", but subject to the requirement that such regulations, standards, and conformity assessment procedures do not create unnecessary obstacles to international trade.

The TBT Agreement covers two legal instruments and one procedure, *viz.*, 'technical regulations', 'standards', and conformity assessment procedures taken by governments of Member States. The measures to which the TBT Agreement applies are identified in Annex 1, which are as follows:

> Annex 1.1 Technical regulations: Document which lays down product characteristics or their related processes and production methods, including the applicable administrative provisions, with which compliance is mandatory. It may also include or deal exclusively with terminology, symbols, packaging, marking or labelling requirements as they apply to a product, process or production method.
>
> Annex 1.2 Standard: Document approved by a recognized body, that provides, for common and repeated use, rules, guidelines or characteristics for products or related processes and production methods, with which compliance is not mandatory. It may also include or deal exclusively with terminology, symbols, packaging, marking or labelling requirements as they apply to a product, process or production method.
>
> Annex 1.3 Conformity assessment procedures: Any procedure used, directly or indirectly, to determine that relevant requirements in technical regulations or standards are fulfilled.

Technical regulations are mandatory, and can be understood as product regulation, covering physical characteristics, process and production methods, *etc.* and deal with terminology, symbols, packaging, marking, or labelling requirement.[6] Examples of technical regulation are *measures requiring automobile emissions do not exceed a certain level, measures requiring a label to provide information whether toys contain parts that could harm young children, etc.* In contrast, standards are voluntary measures approved by a recognised body, that provide rules, guidelines, or characteristics for products or related processes and production methods.[7] Conformity assessment procedures, on the other hand, help determine whether the requirements of technical regulations and standards have been satisfied. Conformity assessment procedures include *procedures for sampling, testing and inspection, evaluation, verification, and assurance of conformity, registration, etc.* The rules apply specifically to conformity assessment procedures that are contained in Articles 5 to 9 of the TBT Agreement.

The definition of both a 'technical regulation' and a 'standard' refers to a document, which is in turn defined as "something written, inscribed, *etc.*, that furnishes evidence or information upon any subject". In *US – Tuna II (Mexico)*, the Appellate Body observed that the use of the term 'document' could therefore cover a wide range of instruments, or even apply to an array of measures.[8] In *EC – Seal Products*, the Appellate Body specified that the definition in Annex 1.1 implied that only documents "that establish or prescribe something and thus have a certain normative content" were documents for the purposes of the technical regulation.[9] The Appellate Body in *EC – Asbestos* set out a three-pronged criterion to define technical regulations.[10] The Appellate Body in *EC – Sardines*, while referring to its earlier decision in

EC – Asbestos,[11] held that a document must meet three criteria to fall within the definition of 'technical regulation' in the TBT, *viz.*, (i) the product in question must be identified, (ii) the document that applies to the identified product must lay down product characteristics, and (iii) compliance with the stipulations in the document must be mandatory. In its own words, the Appellate Body observed as follows:

> First, the document must apply to an identifiable product or group of products. The identifiable product or group of products need not, however, be expressly identified in the document. Second, the document must lay down one or more characteristics of the product. These product characteristics may be intrinsic, or they may be related to the product. They may be prescribed or imposed in either a positive or a negative form. Third, compliance with the product characteristics must be mandatory. As we stressed in *EC – Asbestos*, these three criteria are derived from the wording of the definition in Annex 1.1.[12]

The three-tier test laid down by the Appellate Body in *EC – Sardines* has been used invariably in all subsequent disputes relating to TBT Agreement.[13] Technical regulations, due to their mandatory nature,[14] have a greater potential to restrict international trade than do standards which are voluntary. As a result, the TBT Agreement rules for technical regulations are detailed and strict. In *US – Tuna II*, the Appellate Body observed that the definition of standard is textually very similar to that of technical regulation.[15] The Appellate Body in *EC – Seal Products* observed that the scope of Annex 1.1 with regard to 'technical regulations' appears to be limited "to those documents that establish or prescribe something and thus have a certain normative content".[16]

Following the ruling in *EC – Asbestos*, four elements are to be satisfied to meet the definition of standard, *viz.*, (i) a standard must provide rules, guidelines, or characteristics for products or related process and production methods (PPMs), (ii) a standard must be approved by a 'recognised body', (iii) a standard must apply to an identifiable product or group of products, and (iv) the compliance with a product must not be mandatory.[17] The Appellate Body in *EC – Asbestos* explained that whether a measure is a 'technical regulation' is a 'threshold issue', as the outcome of the enquiry "determines whether the TBT is applicable" and that if the measure is not a technical regulation, "then it does not fall within the scope of the TBT Agreement".[18]

The provisions of the TBT Agreement are applicable to technical regulations, standards, and conformity assessment procedures relating to (i) products (industrial and agricultural products) and (ii) processes and production methods (PPMs). Intense controversy surrounds the subject matter of PPMs, especially pursuant to the reports in the two *US – Tuna* cases, where a restricted view on the legality of PPM measures was expressed by the Panels. The debate on whether the PPMs to which the TBT Agreement applies include non-product-related processes and production methods (NPR–PPMs) still continues.

The term NPR–PPMs is commonly used to refer to PPMs that do not influence the physical characteristics of a final product that reaches the market. Examples include use of child labour in the production of a product. Although discussed during the Uruguay Round of negotiations, no agreement was reached on the inclusion of technical regulations, standards, or conformity assessment procedures relating to NPR–PPMs in the final draft of the TBT Agreement. Some commentators hold the view that the definitions found in Annex 1 indicate that technical regulations, standards, or conformity assessment procedures relating to NPR–PPMs do not fall within the scope of TBT Agreement (Van den Bossche and Zdouc, 2017), and debate on the issue continues.

2.1 Application of TBT Agreement

2.1.1 Principal Actors Under the TBT Agreement

The principal actors under the TBT Agreement are central government bodies, local government bodies, and non-governmental bodies. In other words, the TBT Agreement is aimed at bodies both governmental and non-governmental involved in the preparation, adoption, and application of technical regulations, standards, and/or conformity assessment procedures. In this regard Annex 1.4 describes international standardising institutions as bodies or systems whose membership is open to at least all Members, whereas Annex 1.5 describes regional standardising institutions as regional bodies or systems whose membership is open to the relevant bodies of only some of the Member States.

Local government bodies are defined under Annex 1.7 as all bodies of government other than central government, such as provinces or municipalities, or any organ subject to the "control of such a government in respect of the activity in question". Annex 1.8 defines non-governmental bodies very broadly as bodies other than central government or local government bodies, having legal authority to enforce a technical regulation.[19]

Article 3 governs the preparation, adoption, and application of technical regulations by local government bodies and non-governmental bodies within the territories of Member States. The objective of Article 3 is the extension of the institutional coverage of the TBT Agreement to local government and non-governmental bodies by obligating the Member States (i) to take "such reasonable measures as may be available to them" to ensure compliance with the TBT Agreement by local government and non-governmental bodies; and (ii) to refrain from taking measures that could encourage actions by these bodies that are inconsistent with the provisions of the TBT Agreement. Article 3.5, second sentence, further provides as follows:

> Members shall formulate and implement positive measures and mechanisms in support of the observance of the provisions of Article 2 by other than central government bodies.

Article 4 of the TBT Agreement requires the central government standardising bodies of the Member States to accept and comply with the 'Code of Good Practice' for 'Preparation, Adoption and Application of Standards' found in Annex 3. The Code of Practice provides a comprehensive legal framework for the day-today operations of standardising bodies, which reiterates or mirrors the solutions found in the TBT Agreement with respect to technical regulations (Koebelle and Lafortune, 2007). The Code of Practice is designed to regulate the use of voluntary standards, and Article 4 details the extent to which Member States are to give effect to the Code in their territories. Article 4 and Annex 3 complement each other. The obligations arising from Article 4 and Annex 3.B are of importance due to the impact of private sector standards on international trade. Instances of private sector standards are to be found in standards adopted by supermarket chains.

2.1.2 Temporal Scope of the TBT Agreement

The temporal scope of the TBT Agreement was decided in the *EC – Sardines* case, where one of the key issues for consideration was whether the TBT Agreement applies to technical regulations by the EC which were already in force on the date of entry into force of the TBT

Agreement, *i.e.*, 1 January 1995. In deciding the issue, the Panel looked to Article 28 of the Vienna Convention on the Law of Treaties (VCLT), which reads as follows:

> Unless a different intention appears from the treaty or is otherwise established, its provisions do not bind a party in relation to any act or fact which took place or any situation which ceased to exist before the date of the entry into force of the treaty with respect to that party.

In the light of that recital, the Panel, and later the Appellate Body,[20] ruled that the TBT Agreement applies to EC technical regulations enacted prior to the establishment of the WTO and had not ceased to exist.

2.2 TBT Agreement and Other WTO Agreements

The General Interpretative Note to Annex 1A of the WTO Agreement provides that, in the event of conflict between a provision of the GATT 1994 and a provision of another Agreement in Annex 1A (including the TBT Agreement), the provisions of the latter will prevail to the extent of the conflict. The TBT Agreement, the SPS Agreement, and the GATT Agreement all address behind-the-border measures which affect international trade. Hence, it is essential to understand the relationship of the TBT Agreement with the GATT and the SPS agreements. Firstly, the relationship between the TBT Agreement and the GATT Agreement is examined, followed by a TBT Agreement and the SPS Agreement.

2.2.1 The GATT 1994

There is the potential for conflict, and overlap, between the covered agreements of the WTO. It could be as a direct result of the complexities of trade measures, or similarities in provisions detailing fundamental obligations of Member States arising under the covered agreements *vis-à-vis* the GATT, or simultaneous application of the agreements. The WTO Agreement, which requires a single undertaking from its Member States, demands cumulative compliance with all covered agreements. In the absence of a negotiated conflict rule in the WTO Agreement defining relationship between its different annexes, the norms are left to be defined by the WTO dispute settlement system through its pronouncements (Chase, 2012). As regards the need to apply the provisions of the WTO agreements harmoniously, the Appellate Body in *Korea – Dairy* observed as follows:

> In the light of interpretive principle of effectiveness, it is the duty of any treaty interpreter to "read all applicable provisions of a treaty in a way that gives meaning to all of them, harmoniously".[21] An important corollary of this principle is that a treaty should be interpreted as a whole, and, in particular, its sections and parts should be read as a whole.[footnote omitted] Article II:2 of the WTO Agreement expressly manifests the intention of the Uruguay Round negotiators that the provisions of the WTO Agreement and the Multilateral Trade Agreements included in its Annexes 1, 2 and 3 must be read as a whole.[22]

Both the GATT 1994 and TBT Agreement form part of Annex 1A to the WTO Agreement. As the rights and obligations arising under the GATT also apply in parallel with the more specific rules in TBT, it is possible for the same measure to be challenged, both under the provisions of the TBT Agreement and under the NT obligations arising under the GATT. The TBT Agreement expands on the pre-existing GATT disciplines, and requires that the two agreements are interpreted in a consistent manner. As noted by the Appellate Body in *US – Clove Cigarettes*, the balance set out in the preamble of the TBT Agreement to avoid creating needless obstacles to international trade and recognition of a Member State's right to regulate, is similar to the balance set out in the GATT 1994, where NT obligations in Article III are qualified by the general exceptions provision of Article XX.[23] The Appellate Body also observed that while interpreting the provisions of the TBT Agreement (Article 2.1, in this case), a Panel should focus on the text of the Article in the context of the TBT Agreement together with the contextual elements, and observed as follows:

> We further note that technical regulations are in principle subject not only to Article 2.1 of the TBT Agreement, but also to the national treatment obligation of Article III:4 of the GATT 1994, as "laws, regulations and requirements affecting the internal sale, offering for sale, purchase, transportation, distribution or use" of products. The very similar formulation of the provisions, and the overlap in their scope of application in respect of technical regulations, confirm that Article III:4 of the GATT 1994 is relevant context for the interpretation of the national treatment obligation of Article 2.1 of the TBT Agreement. We consider that, in interpreting Article 2.1 of the TBT Agreement, a panel should focus on the text of Article 2.1, read in the context of the TBT Agreement, including its preamble, and also consider other contextual elements, such as Article III:4 of the GATT 1994.[24]

In *EC – Asbestos* it was ruled that, where both the GATT 1994 and the TBT Agreement appear to apply to a given measure, a panel was obliged to first examine whether the measure at issue is consistent with the TBT Agreement, as the Agreement deals "specifically, and in detail" with the Technical Barriers to Trade.[25] On appeal, the Appellate Body, while confirming the findings of the Panel concerning the cumulative application of the two agreements, observed as follows:

> We observe that, although the TBT Agreement is intended to "further the objectives of GATT 1994", it does so through a specialized legal regime that applies solely to a limited class of measures. For these measures, the TBT Agreement imposes obligations on Members that seem to be different from, and additional to, the obligations imposed on Members under the GATT 1994.[26]

However, in the event a panel were to find the measure to be consistent with the TBT Agreement, it will still be required to examine whether the measure is also consistent with the GATT 1994. The Appellate Body in *US – Tuna II (Mexico)* was critical of the Panel's decision to exercise judicial economy and not address the claim under GATT 1994, after having considered the claim under Article 2.1 of the TBT Agreement. The Appellate Body noted that the Panel's decision rested upon the assumption that the non-discrimination obligations under the TBT Agreement and the GATT 1994 are substantially the same,[27] and ruled that the Panel after finding that the measure under challenge was not inconsistent with Article 2.1 of the TBT Agreement ought to have addressed the complainant's claims under the GATT 1994.[28]

2.2.2 The Agreement on Government Procurement and the SPS Agreement

The TBT Agreement, pursuant to Article 1.4, is not applicable to government procurement activities, which instead falls under the WTO Agreement on Government Procurement (AGP).[29] Likewise, pursuant to Article 1.5 of the TBT Agreement, its provisions are inapplicable to SPS measures as defined in Annex A of the SPS Agreement. Article 1.5 of the TBT Agreement is complemented by Article 1.4 of the SPS Agreement, which provides that "nothing in this Agreement shall affect the rights of Members under the TBT Agreement with respect to measures not within the scope of this [SPS] Agreement". The SPS measure, in principle, is to be considered as a type of technical barrier to trade adopted in a particular form and for a particular purpose. The SPS Agreement applies to a distinct set of measures, and accordingly, the TBT and the SPS agreements are mutually exclusive. Hence, an SPS measure will be excluded from the scope of application of the TBT Agreement, even if it takes the form of technical regulations, standards, or conformity assessment procedures. Accordingly, the rules of the SPS Agreement constitute a *lex specialis* in relation to the TBT Agreement.

The Panel in *EC – Hormones* referred to Article 1.5 of the TBT Agreement and observed, "since the measures in dispute are sanitary measures, we find that the TBT Agreement is not applicable to this dispute".[30] In *EC – Approval and Marketing of Biotech Products*, a single EC measure was adopted for multiple purposes, which included both SPS and non-SPS-related measures. Canada and Argentina made alternative claims under the TBT Agreement, including Article 2.2, in the event that the measures were found to be covered by the TBT Agreement in addition to, or instead of, the SPS Agreement. The panel observed as follows:

> we consider that to the extent the requirement in the consolidated law is applied for one of the purposes enumerated in Annex A(1), it may be properly viewed as a measure which falls to be assessed under the SPS Agreement; to the extent it is applied for a purpose which is not covered by Annex A(1), it may be viewed as a separate measure which falls to be assessed under a WTO agreement other than the SPS Agreement.[31]

In the Panel's view, Article 1.5 of the TBT Agreement does not exclude from the scope of application of the Agreement a measure covered by the SPS Agreement "to the extent it embodies a non-SPS measure".[32] Further, the Panel found that the measures at issue were SPS measures, and as a result, did not address the claims under the TBT Agreement.[33] In theory, there may be situations where a single measure adopted with multiple purposes by a government falls within the scope of application of both the TBT and the SPS agreements (Kudryavtsev, 2013).

3. Substantive Provisions of the TBT Agreement

The substantive provisions of the TBT Agreement contain a number of principles found in the GATT 1994, *i.e.*, the MFN and NT obligations (arising from non-discrimination), the prevention of unnecessary obstacles to international trade (the necessity test), and the obligation to use international standards. These principles as contained in the TBT Agreement and elaborated by the Appellate Body are analysed in this section of the chapter, in the following order: (i) most-favoured nation (MFN) and national treatment (NT) obligations; (ii) the necessity test; and (iii) the obligation to use international standards.

3.1 MFN and NT Treatment Obligations

Article 2 of the TBT Agreement governs the preparation, adoption, and application of technical regulations and seeks to ensure that such technical regulations do not create barriers to international trade. The principle of non-discrimination, as applied under the GATT, contains two obligations, *viz.*, MFN and NT. The TBT Agreement does not contain an analogous provision to Article XX of the GATT, which would allow a measure to be justified even if it provisionally violated Article III:4 or Article I, but was necessary to achieve certain legitimate objectives. Broadly, Article 2.1 of the TBT Agreement can be analogised to Article III:4 and I:1 of the GATT 1994. Article 2.1 of the TBT Agreement embodies both the MFN and the NT obligations in relation to technical regulations, and reads as follows:

> Members shall ensure that in respect of technical regulations, products imported from the territory of any Member shall be accorded treatment no less favourable than that accorded to like products of national origin and to like products originating in any other country.

The non-discrimination obligation, in respect of the TBT Agreement, requires WTO Member States to ensure that technical regulations, standards, and conformity assessment procedures are not applied to favour domestic products over imported like products, or like products from one Member State over those from another Member State. The MFN and NT obligations with respect to preparation, adoption, and application of standards are contained in paragraph D of Annex 3 of the TBT Agreement (Code of Good Practice), and the operation of conformity assessment procedures are contained in Article 5.1.1 of the TBT Agreement. For instance, requiring testing for the presence of chlorine in the chicken imported from the US, while such a requirement is waived, chicken imported from Canada would constitute a violation of the MFN treatment obligation set out under Article 5.1.1 of the TBT Agreement.

The NT obligation arising under Article 2.1 of the TBT Agreement was for the first time interpreted in *US – Clove Cigarettes*, where the Appellate Body established the test to determine violation of NT obligation under Article 2.1 and held:

> [f]or a violation of the national treatment obligation in Article 2.1 to be established, three elements must be satisfied: (i) the measure at issue must be a technical regulation; (ii) the imported and domestic products at issue must be like products; and (iii) the treatment accorded to imported products must be less favourable than that accorded to like domestic products.[34]

The Appellate Body further noted that the language of the NT obligation arising under Article 2.1 of the TBT Agreement 'closely resembles' the language of Article III:4 of the GATT, and accordingly Article III:4 could be regarded as "relevant context for the interpretation of the national treatment obligation of Article 2.1".[35] The Appellate Body observed:

> the determination of likeness under Article 2.1 of the TBT Agreement, as well as under Article III:4 of the GATT 1994, is a determination about the nature and extent of a competitive relationship between and among the products at issue.[36]

The Appellate Body noted that the competitive relationship between the products under Article 2.1, as well as under GATT Article III:4, is determined through examination of four relevant criteria of 'likeness', *viz.*, (i) product characteristics, (ii) product end use, (iii) consumers' tastes and habits, and (iv) product tariff classification.[37] Following from its decision in *US – Clove Cigarettes*, the Appellate Body has further clarified the NT obligation arising under the TBT Agreement in *US – Tuna II (Mexico)* and *US – COOL*. The Appellate Body also addressed the MFN treatment obligation arising under Article 2.1 in *US – Tuna II (Mexico)*, and observed:

> Article 2.1 of the TBT Agreement consists of three elements that must be demonstrated in order to establish an inconsistency with this provision, namely: (i) that the measure at issue constitutes a "technical regulation" within the meaning of Annex 1.1; (ii) that the imported products must be like the domestic product and the products of other origins; and (iii) that the treatment accorded to imported products must be less favourable than that accorded to like domestic products and like products from other countries.[38]

3.1.1 Technical Regulations

The first element of the test of consistency with the non-discrimination obligations of Article 2.1 of the TBT Agreement relates to the issue of 'technical regulation'. In *US – Clove Cigarettes*, the panel differentiated Article 2.1 of the TBT Agreement from GATT Article III:4 by noting that under the TBT Agreement the NT obligation is restricted to a particular type of measures, *i.e.*, technical regulations, while Article III:4 of the GATT 1994 embodies a larger group of measures, *viz.*, "laws, regulations and requirements affecting their internal sale, offering for sale, purchase, transportation, distribution or use".[39] In *EC – Asbestos*, where it was to determine if the measure under challenge was a technical regulation within the meaning of the TBT Agreement, the Appellate Body ruled that the proper legal character of the measure is to be established by looking at the measure as a whole, which includes both the prohibitive and the permissive elements that are part of it.[40] The Appellate Body elaborated on the first element of the definition of a technical regulation as follows:

> A "technical regulation" must, of course, be applicable to an identifiable product, or group of products. Otherwise, enforcement of the regulation will, in practical terms, be impossible. This consideration also underlies the formal obligation, in Article 2.9.2 of the TBT Agreement, for Members to notify other Members, through the WTO Secretariat, of "the products to be covered" by a proposed "technical regulation". Clearly, compliance with this obligation requires identification of the product coverage of a technical regulation. However, in contrast to what the Panel suggested, this does not mean that a "technical regulation" must apply to "given" products which are actually named, identified or specified in the regulation. Although the TBT Agreement clearly applies to "products" generally, nothing in the text of that Agreement suggests that those products need be named or otherwise expressly identified in a "technical regulation". Moreover, there may be perfectly sound administrative reasons for formulating a "technical regulation" in a way that does not expressly identify products by name, but simply makes them identifiable – for instance, through the "characteristic" that is the subject of regulation.

In *EC – Asbestos*, the Appellate Body stated:

> the heart of the definition of a "technical regulation" is that a "document" must "lay down" – that is, set forth, stipulate or provide – "product characteristics".[41]

The Appellate Body explained that the term "product characteristics" appearing in Annex 1.1 of the TBT Agreement is to be interpreted in accordance with its ordinary meaning and observed as follows:

> The word "characteristic" has a number of synonyms that are helpful in understanding the ordinary meaning of that word, in this context. Thus, the "characteristics" of a product include, in our view, any objectively definable "features", "qualities", "attributes", or other "distinguishing mark" of a product. Such "characteristics" might relate, *inter alia*, to a product's composition, size, shape, colour, texture, hardness, tensile strength, flammability, conductivity, density, or viscosity. In the definition of a "technical regulation" in Annex 1.1, the TBT Agreement itself gives certain examples of "product characteristics" – "terminology, symbols, packaging, marking or labelling requirements". These examples indicate that "product characteristics" include, not only features and qualities intrinsic to the product itself, but also related "characteristics", such as the means of identification, the presentation and the appearance of a product.[42]

The Appellate Body in *EC – Asbestos* observed that a 'technical regulation' lays down product characteristics or their related PPMs with which compliance is mandatory, and that that a 'technical regulation' must "be applicable to an identifiable product, or group of products".[43] Based on the prior three considerations, the Appellate Body ruled that the measure under challenge comprises a 'technical regulation' under the TBT Agreement.[44]

The Appellate Body in *EC – Sardines*, referring to its earlier decision in *EC – Asbestos*, established a three-tier test for determining whether a measure is a 'technical regulation' under the TBT Agreement:

> First, the document must apply to an identifiable product or group of products. The identifiable product or group of products need not, however, be expressly identified in the document. Second, the document must lay down one or more characteristics of the product. These product characteristics may be intrinsic, or they may be related to the product. They may be prescribed or imposed in either a positive or a negative form. Third, compliance with the product characteristics must be mandatory. As we stressed in EC – Asbestos, these three criteria are derived from the wording of the definition in Annex 1.1.[45]

This test established by the Appellate Body has been followed by both panels and the Appellate Body in subsequent cases.[46] As regards the requirement that a document lay down product characteristics with which compliance is 'mandatory', the Appellate Body in *EC – Asbestos*, made the following observations:

> The definition of a "technical regulation" in Annex 1.1 of the TBT Agreement also states that "compliance" with the "product characteristics" laid down in the "document" must be "mandatory". A "technical regulation" must, in other words, regulate the "characteristics" of products in a binding or compulsory fashion.[47]

In *EC – Sardines*, the Appellate Body (and the Panel before that) concluded that the measure at issue set forth product characteristics that were 'mandatory', as the measure at issue stated that the requirements contained therein were "binding in its entirety and directly applicable in all Member States".[48] Similarly, in *US – Tuna II (Mexico)*, the Appellate Body, agreeing with the Panel's conclusion that the US 'dolphin-safe' labelling provisions established "labelling requirements, compliance with which is Mandatory" and therefore constituted a 'technical regulation',[19] and provided general observation on how Panels should asses if a measure constituted a technical regulation, in the light of the three-tier test:

> [A] panel's determination of whether a particular measure constitutes a technical regulation must be made in the light of the characteristics of the measure at issue and the circumstances of the case.... Certain features exhibited by a measure may be common to both technical regulations falling within the scope of Article 2 of the TBT Agreement and, for example, standards falling under Article 4 of that Agreement. Both types of measure could, for instance, contain conditions that must be met in order to use a label. In both cases, those conditions could be "compulsory" or "binding" and "enforceable".... it will be necessary to consider additional characteristics of the measure in order to determine the disciplines to which it is subject under that Agreement. This exercise may involve considering whether the measure consists of a law or a regulation enacted by a WTO Member, whether it prescribes or prohibits particular conduct, whether it sets out specific requirements that constitute the sole means of addressing a particular matter, and the nature of the matter addressed by the measure.[50]

The Appellate Body in *US – Tuna II (Mexico)*, after a close examination of the issues at hand, concluded as follows:

> In this case, we note that the US measure is composed of legislative and regulatory acts of the US federal authorities and includes administrative provisions. In addition, the measure at issue sets out a single and legally mandated definition of a "dolphin-safe" tuna product and disallows the use of other labels on tuna products that do not satisfy this definition. In doing so, the US measure prescribes in a broad and exhaustive manner the conditions that apply for making any assertion on a tuna product as to its "dolphin-safety", regardless of the manner in which that statement is made. As a consequence, the US measure covers the entire field of what "dolphin-safe" means in relation to tuna products. For these reasons, we find that the Panel did not err in characterizing the measure at issue as a "technical regulation" within the meaning of Annex 1.1 to the TBT Agreement.[51]

The Panel in *EC – Seal Products* found that the EU Seal Regime comprised both prohibitive and permissive aspects, *viz.*, (i) a prohibition of all seal products, whether they are made exclusively of seal or contain seal as an input (prohibitive aspect), and (ii) an exception with regard to the import and/or placing on the market of seal products in three situations, namely when they result from IC hunts, MRM hunts, or in the case of Travellers imports (the permissive aspect).[52] The Panel found that the prohibition on seal-containing products under the EU Seal Regime laid down a product characteristic in the negative form, and concluded the EU Seal Regime to be a technical regulation. Disagreeing with the Panel's approach, the Appellate Body ruled that the Panel should have sought to identify the 'integral and essential' aspects of the measure as a whole before reaching a final conclusion as to its legal characterisation.[53]

The concept of 'technical regulation' as occurring in Annex 1.1 has received good jurisprudential coverage, but the same cannot be said about the concept of 'standard' as found in Annex 1.2 of the TBT Agreement, as it has received lesser coverage before DSB. In *EC – Sardines*, the Panel, while assessing whether Codex Stan 94 was a relevant international standard within the meaning of Article 2.4 of the TBT Agreement, observed that international standards are developed by international bodies. The Panel began by analysing whether Codex Stan 94 fell within the scope of the definition of 'standard' provided in Annex 1.2 of the TBT Agreement.[54] Referring to the definition of the term 'standard' in Annex 1.2, the Panel held as follows:

> A standard comes within the definition set out in paragraph 2 of Annex 1 of the TBT Agreement if it provides "for common and repeated use, rules, guidelines or characteristics for products or related processes and production methods"; compliance is not mandatory; and is approved by a "recognized body". We note that the parties are in agreement that Codex Stan 94 is a "standard" and see no reason to disagree with that assessment for the purposes of this dispute. We therefore find that Codex Stan 94 is a standard within the meaning of Annex 1.2 of the TBT Agreement.[55]

The Appellate Body in *EC – Sardines* confirmed the Panel's findings that the definition of a 'standard' in Annex 1.2 does not require approval by consensus for standards adopted by a 'recognized body' of the international standardisation community.[56]

3.1.2 Like Products

Analysis of the second element of the test of consistency within non-discrimination obligation involves determining the 'likeness' of the product at issue. Similar to the non-discrimination obligations arising under the GATT 1994, the non-discrimination obligation arising under Article 2.1 of the TBT Agreement applies only to 'like products'. This relates to the questions (i) whether the imported and domestic products under challenge are 'like' – for the NT obligation, and (ii) if the imported products originating in different Member States are 'like' – for the MFN obligation. The Appellate Body in *US – Clove Cigarettes* observed that the language of the national treatment obligation of Article 2.1 'closely resembles' the language of GATT Article III:4; and, thus, Article III:4 could be regarded as "relevant context for the interpretation of the national treatment obligation of Article 2.1".[57]

The Appellate Body in *US – Clove Cigarettes* endorsed a competition-oriented approach to the determination of the 'like products' analysis under Article 2.1 of the TBT Agreement and rejected the approach based on the regulatory objectives of a technical regulation.[58] Analogous to Article III:4 of the GATT, the competitive relationship between the products under Article 2.1 of the TBT Agreement is determined through the examination of four relevant criteria of 'likeness', *viz.*, (i) product characteristics, (ii) product end use, (iii) consumers' tastes and habits, and (iv) product tariff classification.[59] Adopting the aforementioned approach, the Appellate Body reversed the findings of the Panel that the text and context of the TBT Agreement supported an interpretation of the concept of 'likeness' in Article 2.1 that focused on "the legitimate objectives and purposes of the technical regulation, rather than on the competitive relationship between and among the products".[60]

In the Appellate Body's opinion, "regulatory concerns underlying technical regulations may play a role in the determination of likeness" to the extent they influence the competitive relationship between the products determined according to the criteria of 'likeness'.[61] The Appellate Body, based on the 'likeness' criteria, upheld the Panel's finding that clove cigarettes and menthol cigarettes were 'like products' within the meaning of Article 2.1 of the TBT Agreement.[62] Also, the Appellate Body disagreed with the particular importance that the Panel attached to the health objective of the technical regulation at issue in its assessment of the products' physical characteristics and consumers' tastes and habits.[63] According to the Appellate Body:

> [T]he very concept of "treatment no less favourable", which is expressed in the same words in Article III:4 of the GATT 1994 and in Article 2.1 of the TBT Agreement, informs the determination of likeness, suggesting that likeness is about the "nature and extent of a competitive relationship between and among products". Indeed, the concept of "treatment no less favourable" links the products to the marketplace, because it is only in the marketplace that it can be determined how the measure treats like imported and domestic products.[64]

3.1.3 Treatment No Less Favourable

The third element of the test of consistency with the non-discrimination obligations of Article 2.1 of the TBT Agreement relates to the issue of whether there is 'treatment no less favourable' of the like product at hand. In order to determine if a measure in question is inconsistent with Article 2.1 of the TBT, a Panel ought to examine whether imported products are accorded a 'treatment no less favourable' than the like products imported from other countries – relating to the MFN treatment obligation, or like domestic products – relating to NT obligation. The Appellate Body in *Korea – Various Measures on Beef*, when interpreting the term 'treatment no less favourable' as occurring in Article III:4 of the GATT 1994, held:

> [w]hether or not imported products are treated "less favourably" than like domestic products should be assessed . . . by examining whether a measure modifies the conditions of competition in the relevant market to the detriment of imported products.[65]

Accordingly, the term 'treatment no less favourable' as occurring in Article III:4 of the GATT 1994 clearly prohibits Member States from altering the conditions of competition in the marketplace to the detriment of the imported products *vis-à-vis* the 'like' domestic products. While interpreting the term 'treatment no less favourable' in Article 2.1 of the TBT Agreement, the Appellate body in *US – Clove Cigarettes* referred to its decision in *Korea – Various Measures on Beef*, where it had the occasion to determine the purport of the term 'treatment no less favourable' in Article III:4 of the GATT 1994. The Appellate Body noted that its earlier findings

> in the context of Article III:4 of the GATT 1994 to be instructive in assessing the meaning of "treatment no less favourable," provided that the specific context in which the term appears in Article 2.1 of the TBT Agreement is taken into account.[66]

In answering the question if there was 'less favourable treatment' of the like products, the Appellate Body in *US – Clove Cigarettes* noted:

> the object and purpose of the TBT Agreement is to strike a balance between, on the one hand, the objective of trade liberalization and, on the other hand, Members' right to regulate. This object and purpose therefore suggests that Article 2.1 should not be interpreted as prohibiting any detrimental impact on competitive opportunities for imports in cases where such detrimental impact on imports stems exclusively from legitimate regulatory distinctions.[67]

The Appellate Body in *US – Clove Cigarettes* found that the context, object, and purpose of the TBT Agreement countenance the interpretation of 'treatment no less favourable' requirement of Article 2.1 as prohibiting both *de jure* and *de facto* discrimination against imported products, and at the same time tolerating detrimental impact on competitive opportunities for imports that stems exclusively from legitimate regulatory distinctions.[68] Accordingly, the Appellate Body in *US – Clove Cigarettes* explained the two-tier test that a complaint based on Article 2.1 of the TBT Agreement needs to pass, as follows:

> [W]here the technical regulation at issue does not *de jure* discriminate against imports, the existence of a detrimental impact on competitive opportunities for the group of imported *vis-à-vis* the group of domestic like products is not dispositive of less favourable treatment under Article 2.1. Instead, a panel must further analyze whether the detrimental impact on imports stems exclusively from a legitimate regulatory distinction rather than reflecting discrimination against the group of imported products. In making this determination, a panel must carefully scrutinize the particular circumstances of the case, that is, the design, architecture, revealing structure, operation, and application of the technical regulation at issue, and, in particular, whether that technical regulation is even-handed, in order to determine whether it discriminates against the group of imported products.[69]

After carefully considering all issues at hand, the Appellate Body in *US – Clove Cigarettes* concluded that the US through the introduction of the measure to impose a ban on clove cigarettes treated clove cigarettes from Indonesia 'less favourably' in comparison with like domestic products in violation of Article 2.1 of the TBT Agreement.[70]

As referred to earlier, the TBT Agreement does not contain a general exceptions clause similar to Article XX of the GATT 1994. Nevertheless, the sixth recital of the Preamble[71] to the TBT Agreement recognises the right of Member States to take necessary measures to pursue policy objectives, such as the protection of human, animal, or plant life or health, the protection of the environment, or the prevention of deceptive practices, *etc*. The sixth recital further states that countries should not be prevented from taking such measures

> subject to the requirement that [these measures] are not applied in a manner which would constitute a means of arbitrary or unjustifiable discrimination between countries where the same conditions prevail or a disguised restriction on international trade and are otherwise in accordance with the provisions of this Agreement.

The Appellate Body in *US – Clove Cigarettes* ruled, "the explicit recognition of Members' right to regulate in order to pursue certain legitimate objectives" in the sixth recital "qualifies" the objective of avoiding the creation of unnecessary obstacles to international trade through technical regulations, standards, and conformity assessment procedures.[72] The Appellate Body went on to note that the sixth recital sought to balance the objectives expressed in the preamble was not different from the balance set out in the GATT 1994, and observed as follows:

> The balance set out in the preamble of the TBT Agreement between, on the one hand, the desire to avoid creating unnecessary obstacles to international trade and, on the other hand, the recognition of Members' right to regulate, is not, in principle, different from the balance set out in the GATT 1994, where obligations such as national treatment in Article III are qualified by the general exceptions provision of Article XX.[73]

The Appellate Body in *US – Tuna II (Mexico)* ruled that the sixth recital of the Preamble sheds light on the meaning and ambit of the 'treatment no less favourable' requirement in Article 2.1, and observed as follows:

The sixth recital of the preamble recognizes that a WTO Member may take measures necessary for, *inter alia*, the protection of animal or plant life or health, or for the prevention of deceptive practices, at the levels it considers appropriate, subject to the requirement that such measures "are not applied in a manner which would constitute a means of arbitrary or unjustifiable discrimination" or a "disguised restriction on international trade" and are "otherwise in accordance with the provisions of this Agreement". Although the sixth recital does not explicitly set out a substantive obligation, we consider it nonetheless sheds light on the meaning and ambit of the "treatment no less favourable" requirement in Article 2.1, by making clear, in particular, that technical regulations may pursue legitimate objectives but must not be applied in a manner that would constitute a means of arbitrary or unjustifiable discrimination.[74]

The two-tier test established in *US – Clove Cigarettes* to determine whether a technical regulation accords 'treatment no less favourable' within the meaning of Article 2.1 of the TBT Agreement has been further clarified and built upon by the Appellate Body jurisprudence in *US – Tuna II (Mexico)*, *US – COOL*, *US – Tuna II (Mexico) (Article 21.5)*, and *US – COOL (Article 21.5 – Canada and Mexico)*. In *US – Tuna II (Mexico)*, the Appellate Body noted that the scope, content, and obligations of TBT Article 2.1 are not the same as or even 'substantially the same as' those of GATT Articles III:4 and I:1.[75]

There are similarities in the language used in Article 2.2 of the TBT Agreement and Article XX of the GATT 1994, which were highlighted by the Appellate Body in some of the disputes brought before it in 2012. In interpreting Articles 2.1 and 2.2 of the TBT Agreement, the Appellate Body has used some of the language of the *Chapeau* of GATT Article XX. Besides, the Appellate Body has also used some of the techniques in applying the word 'necessary' in GATT Article XX(a), (b), and (c) to Article 2.2 of the TBT Agreement. However, commentators have opined that the content of TBT Articles 2.1 and 2.2 does not align precisely with the analytical approach adopted by the Appellate Body with respect to the *Chapeau* and subparagraphs respectively of Article XX of the GATT 1994 (Voon, Mitchell, and Gascoigne, 2013).

The Appellate body in *US – Tuna II (Mexico)*, referring to its earlier decisions in *Korea – Various Measures on Beef*[76] and *Thailand – Cigarettes (Philippines)*[77] dealing with 'treatment less favourable' in relation to Articles III:4 and I:1 of the GATT, noted that it considered those findings to be

> instructive in assessing the meaning of the expression "treatment no less favourable", provided that the specific context in which the term appears in 2.1 of the TBT Agreement is taken into account.[78]

As a first step, in order to determine if the measure at issue distorts the conditions of competition to the detriment of imported products, it is essential to establish a genuine relationship between the measure at issue and the detrimental impact on competitive opportunities for imported products.[79] The Appellate Body in *US – COOL* ruled:

> Such an examination must take account of all the relevant features of the market, which may include the particular characteristics of the industry at issue, the relative market shares in a given industry, consumer preferences, and historical trade patterns. That is, a panel must examine the operation of the particular technical regulation at issue in the particular market in which it is applied.[80]

The Appellate Body in *US – COOL*, referring to its earlier decision in *Thailand – Cigarettes (Philippines)*,[81] also noted that a panel may reach its findings on the detrimental impact of such measures on the basis of evidence and arguments discernible from the "design, structure, and expected operation of the measure" instead of relying on evidence of the actual trade effects of that measure at issue.[82]

The second step in the analysis under Article 2.1 to establish 'treatment no less favourable' concerns the question of whether the detrimental impact arises wholly from a legitimate regulatory distinction. In assessing whether the measure at issue was even-handed, the Appellate Body examined if the differences in access to the dolphin-safe label prescribed by the measure were 'calibrated' to the risk that dolphins may be killed or seriously injured when tuna is caught. Rejecting the US arguments that its 'dolphin-safe' labelling provisions were 'calibrated' to the risks to dolphins arising from different fishing methods in different areas of the ocean, the Appellate Body ruled as follows:

> [W]e conclude that the United States has not demonstrated that the difference in labelling conditions for tuna products containing tuna caught by setting on dolphins in the ETP, on the one hand, and for tuna products containing tuna caught by other fishing methods outside the ETP, on the other hand, is "calibrated" to the risks to dolphins arising from different fishing methods in different areas of the ocean. It follows from this that the United States has not demonstrated that the detrimental impact of the US measure on Mexican tuna products stems exclusively from a legitimate regulatory distinction. We note, in particular, that the US measure fully addresses the adverse effects on dolphins resulting from setting on dolphins in the ETP, whereas it does "not address mortality (observed or unobserved) arising from fishing methods other than setting on dolphins outside the ETP". In these circumstances, we are not persuaded that the United States has demonstrated that the measure is even-handed in the relevant respects, even accepting that the fishing technique of setting on dolphins is particularly harmful to dolphins.[83]

In *US – Tuna II (Mexico)*, the Appellate Body ruled that the detrimental impact of the measure at issue (requiring the use of a 'dolphin-safe' label on tuna products) did not arise wholly from a legitimate regulatory distinction due to the lack of even-handedness of the measure in addressing the risks to dolphins.[84] Similarly, in *US – COOL*, the Appellate Body ruled that the Panel's findings provided a sufficient basis for it to determine whether the detrimental impact on Canadian and Mexican livestock stemmed exclusively from a legitimate regulatory distinction. The Appellate Body indicated that the assessment would include an inquiry into whether the COOL measure lacked 'even-handedness' because it was designed or applied in a manner that constituted a means of arbitrary or unjustifiable discrimination, and ruled that one must examine whether the measure at issue

> is designed and applied in an even-handed manner, or whether it lacks even-handedness, for example, because it is designed or applied in a manner that constitutes a means of arbitrary or unjustifiable discrimination, and thus reflects discrimination in violation of Article 2.1 of the TBT Agreement.[85]

In *US – COOL*, the Appellate Body also noted that in order to determine if the detrimental impact arises wholly from a legitimate regulatory distinction, one must scrutinise the particular circumstances of the case, including the design, architecture, revealing structure, operation, and application of the measure at issue.[86] The Appellate Body in *US – COOL (Article 21.5 – Canada and Mexico)* observed:

> if a panel finds that a technical regulation has a *de facto* detrimental impact on competitive opportunities for like imported products, the focus of the inquiry shifts to whether such detrimental impact stems exclusively from legitimate regulatory distinctions. This inquiry probes the legitimacy of regulatory distinctions through careful scrutiny of whether they are designed and applied in an even-handed manner such that they may be considered "legitimate" for the purposes of Article 2.1.[87]

3.2 'Least Trade Restrictive'

Article 2.2 of the TBT Agreement imposes the additional obligation of using measures that are least trade restrictive, and thereby strengthens the ambit of the non-discrimination obligation contained in Article 2.1 of the Agreement. As new types of measures are frequently challenged before the DSB, it is of significant importance to have a definitive definition of 'trade restrictiveness'. Despite its relevance and importance in settling disputes, the WTO agreements do not contain a definition of 'trade restrictiveness' (Voon, 2015).[88]

Article 2.2 of the TBT Agreement requires:

> Members shall ensure that technical regulations are not prepared, adopted or applied with a view to or with the effect of creating unnecessary obligations to international trade. For this purpose, technical regulations shall not be more trade-restrictive than necessary to fulfil a legitimate objective, taking account of the risks non-fulfilment would create. Such legitimate objects are, *inter alia*: national security requirements; the prevention of deceptive practices; protection of human health or safety; animal or plant life or health, or the environment. In assessing such risks, relevant elements of consideration are, *inter alia*: available scientific and technical information, related processing technology or intended end-uses of products.

The scheme of Article 2.2 envisages a two-step analysis, which requires that technical regulations pursue a "legitimate objective" and not be "more trade restrictive than necessary to fulfil a legitimate measure".[89] Therefore the first step in the process of determining the consistency of the measure is to identify the objective of the measure and to establish if the identified objective is legitimate within the meaning of Article 2.2.[90] The second test, *i.e.*, the necessity test, relates to the question of whether the measure at issue is 'trade restrictive'. The Appellate Body in *US – Tuna II (Mexico)* provided the following general guidance to Panels adjudicating claims under Article 2.2 of the TBT Agreement:

> in adjudicating a claim under Article 2.2 of the TBT Agreement, a panel must assess what a Member seeks to achieve by means of a technical regulation. In doing so, it may take into account the texts of statutes, legislative history, and other evidence regarding the structure and operation of the measure. A panel is not bound by a Member's characterization of the objectives it pursues through the measure, but must independently and objectively assess them. Subsequently, the analysis must turn to the question of whether a particular objective is legitimate, pursuant to the parameters set out above.[91]

The Appellate Body in *US – Tuna II (Mexico)* defined 'trade restrictive' to mean "having a limiting effect on trade".[92] The Appellate Body observed that Article 2.2 refers to "unnecessary obstacles" to trade and thus allows for some trade-restrictiveness; more specifically, Article 2.2 stipulates that technical regulations shall not be "more trade restrictive than necessary to fulfil a legitimate objective". Article 2.2 is thus concerned with restrictions on international trade that exceed what is necessary to achieve the degree of contribution that a technical regulation makes to the achievement of a legitimate objective.[93]

Accordingly, the mere fact that a measure is 'trade restrictive' does not make that measure inconsistent with Article 2.2, and that a measure that is not 'trade restrictive' cannot be inconsistent with Article 2.2 of the TBT Agreement.

3.2.1 'Legitimate Objective'

The question of whether the measure at issue fulfils a 'legitimate objective' is the third element of the test of consistency with Article 2.2 of the TBT Agreement. Interpreting 'legitimate objective' requires establishing the objective pursued by the measure under challenge, when a measure fulfils the legitimate objective, and how to establish if a measure has fulfilled the legitimate objective pursued. The Appellate Body in *US – Tuna II (Mexico)* interpreted 'legitimate objective' to mean "an aim or target that is lawful, justifiable, or proper".[94] Article 2.2, third sentence, lists examples of legitimate objectives. But the use of the word '*inter alia*' before listing the examples indicates that it is not a closed list.[95] This obviously raises the question, when and under what conditions can an objective be viewed as being legitimate? As noted by the Appellate Body in *US – Tuna II (Mexico)*,

> objectives expressly listed provide a reference point for which other objectives that may be considered to be legitimate in the sense of Article 2.2 . . . Furthermore, we consider that objectives recognized in the provisions of other covered agreements may provide guidance for, or may inform, the analysis of what might be considered to be a legitimate objective under Article 2.2 of the TBT Agreement.[96]

The Appellate Body in *US – COOL* observed that guidance should also be provided by a comparative analysis of "whether the identified objective is reflected in other provisions of the covered agreements".[97] The Appellate Body, referring to its decision in *US – Tuna II (Mexico)*, noted that the sixth and seventh recitals of the TBT refer to several objectives, which partially overlap with the objectives listed in Article 2.2 TBT.[98] Accordingly, the open-ended list of objectives contained in Article 2.2 permits Member States to pursue legitimate objectives through the use of technical regulations. The Panel in *US – Tuna II (Mexico)* found that the objectives of the measure under challenge, *i.e.*, consumer information and dolphin protection, were legitimate and reasoned as follows:

> Article 2.2 of the TBT Agreement provides a non-exhaustive list of legitimate objectives under this provision.[99] This list includes, as the United States has pointed out, the "prevention of deceptive practices" and the "protection of . . . animal or plant life or health, or the environment". We are satisfied that the objectives of the US dolphin-safe provisions, as described in the previous section, fall within the scope of these two categories of legitimate objectives. The objective of preventing consumers of tuna products from being deceived by false dolphin-safe allegations falls within the broader goal of preventing deceptive practices. Similarly, the protection of dolphins may be understood as intended to protect animal life or health or the environment. In this respect, a measure that aims at the protection of animal life or health need not, in our view, be directed

exclusively to endangered or depleted species or populations, to be legitimate. Article 2.2 refers to "animal life or health" in general terms, and does not require that such protection be tied to a broader conservation objective. We therefore read these terms as allowing Members to pursue policies that aim at also protecting individual animals or species whose sustainability as a group is not threatened.[100]

The finding of the Panel was confirmed by the Appellate Body on appeal. In *US – COOL*, the Appellate Body accepted as legitimate the objective of providing "consumers with information on the countries in which the livestock from which the meat they purchase is produced were born, raised, and slaughtered", while noting that the arguments and evidence submitted by Canada "failed to persuade the Panel that providing consumers with information on origin, as defined under the COOL measure, is not a legitimate objective".[101] The Appellate Body in *US – COOL* observed:

> the provision of information to consumers on origin bears some relation to the objective of prevention of deceptive practices reflected in both Article 2.2 itself and Article XX(d) of the GATT 1994, insofar as consumers could be deceived as to the origin of products if labelling is inaccurate or misleading. In our view, support for the legitimate nature of the objective of providing information to consumers on origin is also found elsewhere in the covered agreements, in particular in Article IX of the GATT 1994.[102]

As regards the question of how to establish the degree of fulfilment of the legitimate objective sought to be pursued by the measure under challenge, the Appellate Body in *US – Tuna II (Mexico)* noted as follows:

> A panel adjudicating a claim under Article 2.2 of the TBT Agreement must seek to ascertain to what degree, or if at all,[103] the challenged technical regulation, as written and applied, actually contributes to the legitimate objective pursued by the Member. The degree of achievement of a particular objective may be discerned from the design, structure, and operation of the technical regulation, as well as from evidence relating to the application of the measure.[104]

3.2.2 'Not More Trade Restrictive Than Necessary'

The question of whether the measure at issue is 'not more trade restrictive than necessary' to fulfil a legitimate objective is the final element of the test of consistency with Article 2.2 of the TBT Agreement. The second sentence in Article 2.2 of the TBT Agreement provides that technical regulations shall not be 'more trade restrictive than necessary' to fulfil a legitimate objective, taking account of the risks non-fulfilment would create. Unlike the necessity test contained in GATT Article XX, Article 2.2 of the TBT Agreement is independent of any substantive obligations. Even where a technical regulation does not discriminate against imported like products, it can still be in violation of Article 2.2 if it is found 'more trade restrictive than necessary' (Du, 2020). A reading of the text of Article 2.2 reveals that what is being tested for 'necessity' is the trade restrictiveness of the measure and not the measure *per se*. As pointed out by the Appellate Body, 'trade restrictiveness' in the context means "having a limiting effect on trade".[105]

The Appellate Body's jurisprudence on the issue of necessity under Article 2.2 is closely aligned with the necessity test developed in connection with the provisions of Article XX(b) of the GATT Agreement and Article XIV(b) of the GATS Agreement. The Appellate Body in *US – Tuna II (Mexico)* set out the necessary test involved in an assessment to determine whether a technical regulation is 'not more trade restrictive than necessary' within the meaning of Article 2.2 as follows:

> In sum, we consider that an assessment of whether a technical regulation is "more trade-restrictive than necessary" within the meaning of Article 2.2 of the TBT Agreement involves an evaluation of a number of factors. A panel should begin by considering factors that include: (i) the degree of contribution made by the measure to the legitimate objective at issue; (ii) the trade-restrictiveness of the measure; and (iii) the nature of the risks at issue and the gravity of consequences that would arise from non-fulfilment of the objective(s) pursued by the Member through the measure. In most cases, a comparison of the challenged measure and possible alternative measures should be undertaken. In particular, it may be relevant for the purpose of this comparison to consider whether the proposed alternative is less trade restrictive, whether it would make an equivalent contribution to the relevant legitimate objective, taking account of the risks non-fulfilment would create, and whether it is reasonably available.[106]

The Appellate Body noted that the use of the term "more . . . than" in the second sentence suggests that a comparative analysis of the challenged and possible alternative measures can serve as a "conceptual tool" to establish the existence of an "unnecessary obstacle to international trade".[107] Hence, a comparative analysis of the challenged and possible alternative measures is to be undertaken to determine if a technical regulation is 'more trade restrictive than necessary'.[108] Following the examination of the importance of comparing the challenged measures with possible alternative measures, the Panel in *Australia – Tobacco Plain Packaging* observed:

> [F]or a proposed alternative measure to form the basis of a determination that the challenged measure is more trade-restrictive than necessary, it would need to cumulatively satisfy all of the elements of the comparative analysis. It would thus need to be demonstrated that a proposed alternative measure would not only be less trade-restrictive than the challenged measures, but also that it would make at least an equivalent contribution to the objective being pursued through the challenged measure, and be "reasonably available" to the Member as an alternative to the challenged measures.[109]

With regards to identifying valid alternative measures, the Panel in *Australia – Tobacco Plain Packaging* observed that a proposed measure may be a valid alternative even if it already exists in some form in the legal system of the responding Member State. In the Panel's view,

> [W]here it exists in the responding Member, albeit in a different form from that proposed by the complainant. In such a case, it is the variation proposed by the complainants as a substitute for the challenged measure that would be the subject of the comparative analysis under Article 2.2 of the TBT Agreement, including of whether that variation of an existing measure would make an equivalent contribution to the objective pursued by the responding Member.[110]

The Panel in *Australia – Tobacco Plain Packaging* emphasised that, in assessing proposed alternative measures, regard must be had to the broader regulatory context in which the challenged measures exist and how the challenged measures work together with other measures to achieve the desired objective.[111] Summarising its discussion on reviewing proposed alternative measures, the Panel reiterated the following guidelines:

> [A] proposed alternative measure need not contribute to the objective to a degree that is identical to the measure at issue, and that a proposed alternative measure may achieve an equivalent degree of contribution in ways different from the technical regulation at issue. However, as discussed above, we do not understand this to imply that, where the concern being addressed is of a multifaceted nature and legitimately involves a multidimensional response, one aspect of a comprehensive strategy could be substituted for another, where they would address different aspects of the problem. In addition, a panel's "margin of appreciation" in assessing equivalence should be informed by the risks that non-fulfilment of the technical regulation's objective would create, the nature of the risks and the gravity of the consequences arising from the non-fulfilment of the technical regulation's objective, the characteristics of the technical regulation at issue as revealed through its design and structure, the nature of the objective pursued, and the nature, quantity and quality of the evidence available.[112]

The Appellate Body in *US – COOL (Article 21.5 – Canada and Mexico)* held that an assessment of whether a technical regulation is more trade restrictive than necessary under Article 2.2 "involves the holistic weighing and balancing of all relevant factors".[113] The Appellate Body further noted that although Article 2.2 does not explicitly prescribe the sequence and order of analysis in carrying out the assessment whether the technical regulation at issue is more trade restrictive than necessary, nonetheless, a certain sequence and order of analysis flow logically from the nature of the examination under Article 2.2.[114] As regards the weighing and balancing of relevant factors, the Appellate Body, referring to its earlier pronouncement in *EC – Seal Products* arising under Article XX of the GATT 1994, observed:

> The weighing and balancing of the relevant factors both in respect of the challenged technical regulation and in the comparison with proposed alternative measures involves a holistic analysis in order to reach an overall conclusion on claims under Article 2.2. A panel should proceed with this weighing and balancing even if a particular factor under Article 2.2 . . . cannot be quantified with precision or can only be assessed in qualitative terms.[115]

The Appellate Body in *US – COOL (Article 21.5 – Canada and Mexico)* ruled that to meet the requirement that an alternative measure makes an equivalent contribution to the 'identified legitimate objective' does not obligate a complainant to demonstrate that its proposed alternative measure achieves a degree of contribution identical to that achieved by the measure at issue. In the words of the Appellate Body, there is "a margin of appreciation in the assessment of whether a proposed alternative measure achieves an equivalent degree of contribution, the contours of which may vary from case to case".[116] The Appellate Body noted:

> The assessment of whether a proposed alternative measure achieves an equivalent degree of contribution should also be made in the light of the characteristics of the technical regulation at issue as revealed through its design and structure, as well as the nature of the objective pursued and the nature, quantity, and quality of the evidence available. We emphasize, in this respect, that a proposed alternative measure may achieve an equivalent degree of contribution in ways different from the technical regulation at issue.[117]

The Appellate Body noted that for the purpose of assessing the equivalence between the contribution of the challenged technical regulation and the proposed alternative measures, "it is the overall degree of contribution that the technical regulation makes to the objective pursued that is relevant, rather than any individual isolated aspect or component of contribution".[118] The Appellate Body also noted that it is likely that

> Some imprecision[s] in assessing the equivalence of the respective degrees of contribution of a technical regulation and a proposed alternative may be inevitable in certain circumstances. However, such imprecision should not, in and of itself, relieve a panel from its duty to assess the equivalence of the respective degrees of contribution. In spite of such imprecision, a panel should proceed with the overall weighing and balancing under Article 2.2.[119]

As regards the obligation to "take account of the risks non-fulfilment would create", the Appellate Body in *US – COOL (Article 21.5 – Canada and Mexico)* opined, "the nature of the risks and the gravity of the consequences that would arise from non-fulfilment would themselves, in the first place, need to be identified".[120] The Appellate Body noted:

> Article 2.2 does not prescribe further a particular methodology for assessing "the risks non-fulfilment would create" or define how they should be "tak[en] account of". However, in the context of Article XX of the GATT 1994, the Appellate Body has recognized that risks may be assessed in either qualitative or quantitative terms. Some kinds of risks might not be susceptible to quantification, and some types of risk assessment methods might not be of assistance in respect of particular kinds of objectives listed in Article XX of the GATT 1994.[121]

Ruling that risks may be assessed in either "qualitative or quantitative terms", the Appellate Body observed as follows:

> In order to take account of "the risks non-fulfilment would create" under Article 2.2 of the TBT Agreement, in some contexts, it might be possible and appropriate to seek to determine separately the nature of the risks, on the one hand, and to quantify the gravity of the consequences that would arise from non-fulfilment, on the other hand. In other contexts, however, it might be difficult, in practice, to determine or quantify those elements separately with precision. In such contexts, it may be more appropriate to conduct a conjunctive analysis of both the nature of the risks and the gravity of the consequences of non-fulfilment, in which "the risks non-fulfilment would create" are assessed in qualitative terms.[122]

In *Australia – Tobacco Plain Packaging*, the Panel, upon examining 'the gravity of the consequences of non-fulfilment', observed:

> [A] Panel's assessment of "the risks non-fulfilment would create" entails, in the first place, identifying the nature and gravity of the "risks non-fulfilment would create", and that this does not entail a comparison of the challenged measures and possible alternative measures, or a consideration of their respective degrees of contribution to the objective. Rather, such identification involves assessing the following two key aspects: the nature of the risks and the gravity of the consequences of non-fulfilment of the objective of the challenged measures.[123]

The requirement that alternative measures are 'reasonably available' was first mentioned in *US – Tuna II (Mexico)*, as a relevant factor to consider in the comparative analysis under Article 2.2 of the TBT Agreement.[124] The Appellate Body in *US – COOL (Article 21.5 – Canada and Mexico)* referred to the jurisprudence under Article XX(a) of the GATT 1994 and Article XIV(a) of the GATS Agreement as the interpretive context to understand the 'reasonably available' under Article 2.2 of the TBT Agreement.[125] The Appellate Body in *US – COOL (Article 21.5 – Canada and Mexico)* observed:

> it is important to keep in mind that such "reasonable availability" pertains to proposed alternative measures that function as "conceptual tool[s]" to assist in assessing whether a technical regulation is more trade restrictive than necessary. Such alternative measures are of a hypothetical nature in the context of the analysis under Article 2.2 because they do not yet exist in the Member in question, or at least not in the particular form proposed by the complainant.[126]

Under Article 2.2 of the TBT Agreement, unlike under Article XX of the GATT 1994, the burden is on the complaining Member State to make a *prima facie* case that a less trade restrictive alternative measure, which also achieves an equivalent contribution to the relevant objective, was reasonably available.[127] The nature and degree of evidence required for a complaining Member State to establish the 'reasonable availability' of a proposed alternative measure as part of a claim under Article 2.2 of the TBT Agreement will necessarily vary from measure to measure and from case to case.[128] The Appellate Body in *US – COOL (Article 21.5 – Canada and Mexico)* also noted that such alternative measures are of a hypothetical nature for purposes of an analysis under Article 2.2, and that the complainant Member State cannot be expected "to provide complete and exhaustive descriptions of the alternative measures they propose".[129] In the words of the Appellate Body:

> It would appear incongruous to expect a complainant, under Article 2.2 of the TBT Agreement, to provide detailed information on how a proposed alternative would be implemented by the respondent in practice, and precise and comprehensive estimates of the cost that such implementation would entail.[130]

Member States are to continually assess whether a technical regulation is more trade restrictive than necessary, as a technical regulation which is found to be 'not more trade restrictive than necessary' within the meaning of Article 2.2 of the TBT Agreement, will not continue to be so.

3.3 The Obligation to Use International Standards

After the Kennedy Round of negotiations, there was an increase in the multiplicity of standards, which viewed as a potential barrier to trade and pointed towards a need to consider harmonisation of standards (Marceau and Trachtman, 2014). Hence disciplines were required to ensure that such standards were not applied by Contracting Parties "so as to afford protection to the domestic production" (GATT, 1971). The process of harmonisation involves the adoption of identical standards by two or more jurisdictions (Hoekman, 2015). Harmonisation of technical regulations has the potential to facilitate trade across borders by creating economics of scale and allowing for more efficient allocation of resources (Du, 2020). There is convincing empirical evidence to demonstrate that harmonisation increases trade flows, and particularly developing countries stand to benefit through the harmonisation of product standards (Du, 2020). Through harmonisation of national technical regulations, the TBT Agreement seeks to reduce the trade restrictive effect of technical barriers to trade. Articles 2.4 to 2.6 of the TBT Agreement deals with international standardisation and harmonisation. Article 2.4 of the mandates the use of international standards by Member States and states:

> Where technical regulations are required and relevant international standards exist or their completion is imminent, Members shall use them, or the relevant parts of them, as a basis for their technical regulations except when such international standards or relevant parts would be an ineffective or inappropriate means for the fulfilment of the legitimate objectives pursued, for instance because of fundamental climatic or geographical factors or fundamental technological problems.

The second part of Article 2.4, however, provides for an exception, or escape clause, to the previous requirement where such international standards will be "ineffective or inappropriate means for the fulfilment of the legitimate objectives pursued". The WTO jurisprudence on the subject provides for a three-tier test to establish consistency of a technical regulation with Article 2.4,[131] *viz*., (i) whether a relevant international standard exists; (ii) whether the aforementioned international standard is "used as a basis" for the technical regulation under challenge; and (iii) whether the relevant international standard is an ineffective or inappropriate means for the fulfilment of the legitimate objectives pursued, taking into account fundamental climatic or geographical factors or fundamental technological problems.[132]

3.3.1 'Existence of Relevant International Standards'

As per Article 2.4 of the TBT Agreement, the first element of the three-tier test of consistency of technical regulation relates to whether a relevant international standard exists or its completion is imminent. Under the TBT Agreement, Member States have the right to take measures necessary to achieve their policy objectives at the levels they consider appropriate. The TBT Agreement does not identify a 'relevant' body for the purposes of implementing Article 2.4 but allows for flexibility to be exercised by a Member State in deciding which international standard that it considers relevant for a given situation (Wijkström and McDaniels, 2013). Although referred to in various provision, the TBT Agreement does not define the concept of 'relevant international standard'.[133]

For the purposes of the TBT Agreement, a standard is international if it is approved by a standardising body. Article 1.4 of Annex 1 defines 'international body or system' as "body or system whose membership is open to the relevant bodies of at least all Members". In a decision made in 2013, the Committee on Technical Barriers to Trade confirmed the position that an international body as envisaged under Article 2.4 of the TBT Agreement should "be open on a non-discriminatory basis to relevant bodies of at least all WTO Members" (WTO, 2013). In *US – Tuna II (Mexico)*, the Appellate Body found:

> it is primarily the characteristics of the entity approving a standard that makes a standard an "international" standard. By contrast, the subject matter of a standard would not appear to be material to the determination of whether the standard is "international".[134]

The Appellate Body in *US – Tuna II (Mexico)* observed that as the definition in Annex 1 to the TBT Agreement prevails over the definitions found in ISO/IEC Guide 2:1991, in order to constitute an "international standard", a standard has to be adopted by an "international standardizing body" for the purposes of the TBT Agreement.[135]

As regards what an international standardising body was, the Appellate Body in *US – Tuna II (Mexico)* sought to distinguish between a 'body' and an 'organisation' and observed as follows:

> With respect to the type of entity approving an "international" standard, the ISO/IEC Guide2:1991 refers to an "organization", whereas Annex 1.2 to the TBT Agreement stipulates that a "standard" is to be approved by a "body". According to the ISO/IEC Guide 2: 1991, a "body" is a "legal or administrative entity that has specific tasks and composition", whereas an "organization" is a "body that is based on the membership of other bodies or individuals and has an established constitution and its own administration" . . .
>
> Annex 1.2 to the TBT Agreement refers to a "body", not to an "organization", and Annex 1.4 defines an "international body or system", but not an "international organization". This suggests that, for the purposes of the TBT Agreement, "international" standards are adopted by "bodies", which may, but need not necessarily, be "organizations".[136]

In order to qualify as a standardizing body, the 'entity' must have demonstrated relevant standardisation activities. In the Appellate Body's opinion *US – Tuna II (Mexico)*, "evidence of recognition by WTO Members as well as evidence of recognition by national standardizing bodies would be relevant" for "recognition" of the international body concerned as a "standards body",[137] and that an "international standardising body" does not need to have "standardisation as its principal function".[138]

In *EC – Sardines*, it was argued that the product covered by the international standard (Codex Stan 94) and the EC's technical regulation differed, and that the international standard was not relevant to EC technical regulation. Neither party disputed that Codex Stan 94 was an international standardisation body. It is relevant to note that the international standard, in this regard, applied to 21 species, whereas the EC technical regulation applied to only one of the species, *i.e.*, *Sardina pilchardus*. The Appellate Body ruled that the international standard was pertinent to the EC Regulation and observed as follows:

> we have already concluded that, although the EC Regulation expressly mentions only *Sardina pilchardus*, it has legal consequences for other fish species that could be sold as preserved sardines, including preserved *Sardinops sagax*. Codex Stan 94 covers 20 fish species in addition to *Sardina pilchardus*. These other species also are legally affected by the exclusion in the EC Regulation. Therefore, we conclude that Codex Stan 94 bears upon, relates to, or is pertinent to the EC Regulation.[139]

While answering the question if approval of standards takes place through consensus, or other methods, the Appellate Body in *EC – Sardines*, while relying upon the explanatory note +sensus by a 'recognized body' of the international standardisation community fell within the definition of a 'standard' in Annex 1.2, and thus were relevant for the purposes of Article 2.4 of the Agreement.[140]

3.3.2 *International Standards 'As a Basis' for Domestic Standards*

Pursuant to Article 2.4 of the TBT Agreement, the second element of the three-tier test of consistency of technical regulation relates to whether the relevant international standard is 'used as a basis' for the technical regulation under challenge. The meaning of the term 'used as a basis' was analysed by the Appellate Body in *EC – Sardines*, which held that an international standard is used 'as a basis for' a technical regulation when it is used as the principal constituent, or fundamental principle for the purpose of enacting the technical regulation.[141] The Appellate Body also noted that there ought to be a 'very strong and very close relationship' between the measure and the standard in order to be able to say that one is 'the basis for' the other,[142] and that, if the technical regulation and the international standard contradict each other, it cannot properly be concluded that the international standard has been used 'as a basis for' the technical regulation.[143]

3.3.3 'Ineffective and Inappropriate International Standards'

The last element of the three-tier test of consistency of technical regulation with Article 2.4 of the TBT Agreement relates to whether the relevant international standard is an ineffective or inappropriate means for the fulfilment of the legitimate objectives pursued. As noted by the Appellate Body in *EC – Hormones*, the purpose of establishing international standards is to promote harmonisation of national product standards on as wide a basis as possible.[144] Under the TBT Agreement, Member States are not required to use an international standard 'as a basis' for regulations if it would not be appropriate or effective for achieving the desired level of protection in respect of the envisaged policy objectives. A Member State can choose to (i) convert the international standard into domestic standards, thereby avoiding the creation of unnecessary barriers to international trade, (ii) use the international standards as a basis for the technical regulation, which will be subject to scrutiny for its consistency, (iii) set its technical regulation with a lower protection level than that of an international standard, or (iv) deviate from the relevant international standard (Du, 2020).

The Appellate Body in in *EC – Sardines* observed that the words 'ineffective means' is a means that does not have the function, or the result, of accomplishing the legitimate objective pursued. Likewise, the terms 'inappropriate means' is a means that is not especially suitable for the fulfilment of the legitimate objective pursued, due to the nature of the standard.[145] The Appellate Body agreed with the Panel that the legitimate objectives referred to in Article 2.4 must be interpreted in the context of Article 2.2, which also in turn refers to 'legitimate objectives' and includes a description of what the nature of some such objectives can be.[146] The Appellate Body, accepting the findings of the Panel that the stated objectives of the EC regulations were market transparency, consumer protection, and fair competition, ruled that the relevant international standard in question, *i.e.*, Codex Stan 94, was both 'effective' and 'appropriate' to achieve the regulatory objectives as it contained labelling regulations to ensure market transparency and reduce consumer confusion in a manner not to mislead consumers, and that the EC's regulation was excessive and too restrictive.[147]

In a finding that was not appealed against, the Panel in *US – COOL* ruled that CODEX STAN 1–1985 did not have the function or capacity to accomplish the legitimate objective sought to be achieved by the measure (consumer information on country of origin of the animal, where it was raised and slaughtered), and was ineffective and inappropriate for the fulfilment of the specific objectives as stated by the US, because it did not "have the function or capacity of accomplishing the objective of providing information to consumers about the countries in which an animal was born, raised and slaughtered".[148] The Panel arrived at that conclusion on the basis that CODEX STAN 1–1985 conferred origin according to the concept of substantial transformation (determining an animal's origin exclusively through where its meat was processed), and therefore it could not achieve the objective of providing information to consumers about the countries in which an animal was born, raised, and slaughtered.[149]

> the Appellate Body in *EC – Sardines* observed that there are conceptual similarities between Article 2.4 of the TBT Agreement and Articles 3.1 and 3.3 of the SPS Agreement,[150] and ruled that the burden of proof to i) demonstrate that the measure under challenge was ineffectiveness or inappropriateness of the relevant international standard, and ii) to demonstrate that the international standard in question is both an effective and an appropriate means to fulfil the legitimate objective is on the complaining Member State.[151]

Article 2.5 of the TBT Agreement determines in detail what behaviour pursuant to TBT Article 2.4 entails:

> A Member preparing, adopting or applying a technical regulation which may have a significant effect on trade of other Members shall, upon the request of another Member, explain the justification for that technical regulation in terms of the provisions of paragraphs 2 to 4. Whenever a technical regulation is prepared, adopted or applied for one of the legitimate objectives explicitly mentioned in paragraph 2, and is in accordance with relevant international standards, it shall be rebuttably presumed not to create an unnecessary obstacle to international trade.

The first sentence of Article 2.5 requires Member States to provide justifications for technical regulations that may have a significant effect on trade relations with other Member States when they are being prepared, adopted, or applied. The first sentence is to be construed as an obligation arising from the requirement to maintain transparency and information sharing, which is part of the objectives being pursued in other provisions of the TBT Agreement.[152] The Appellate Body in *EC – Sardines* observed that Article 2.5 of the TBT Agreement "establishes a compulsory mechanism requiring the supplying of information by the regulating Member".[153] The second sentence of Article 2.5 contains a rebuttable presumption that such technical regulation being adopted in pursuit of legitimate objectives is in accordance with relevant international standards and does not create an unnecessary obstacle to trade.

4. Other Substantive Provisions of the TBT Agreement

The scheme envisaged under the TBT Agreement includes provisions relating to (i) equivalence and mutual recognition (Article 2.7); (ii) performance requirements of product (Article 2.7); (iii) transparency and notifications (Article 2.9); and (iv) special and differential treatment for developing country Member States (Articles 12.1, 12.2, and 12.3).

4.1 Equivalence and Mutual Recognition

Pursuant to Article 2.7 of the TBT Agreement, Member States are required to give positive consideration to accepting as equivalent the technical regulations of other Member States. This recognition is to be accorded, even if these regulations differ from their own, provided they are satisfied that the said regulations adequately fulfil the objectives of their own regulations. This requirement of equivalence and mutual recognition can be viewed as a less trade restrictive means of fulfilling a legitimate objective (Tamiotti, 2007). Member States can enter into such reciprocal mutual recognition agreements (MRAs) whereby the parties mutually accept defined standards of their counterparts as equivalent.[154] Also, pursuant to Article 6.1 of the TBT Agreement, Member States are required to ensure, whenever possible, that results of such procedures by other Member States are accepted even when those procedures differ from their own procedures, provided they are satisfied that those procedures offer an assurance of conformity with applicable technical regulations or standards equivalent to their own.

4.2 Performance Requirements

Pursuant to Article 2.8 of the TBT Agreement, wherever appropriate, Member States are required to specify technical regulations based on product requirements in terms of performance rather than design or descriptive characteristics. The principal objective of this provision is to permit producers to locate the most cost-effective way of fulfilling the requirements contained in a technical regulation. This provision is aimed at the performance of a product, as opposed to the way in which the stated objective is achieved. The Panel in *US – Clove Cigarettes* ruled that the object and purpose of Article 2.8 of the TBT Agreement is to avoid the creation of unnecessary obstacles to trade by requiring that product requirements be laid down in 'functional' terms, wherever appropriate.[155] Also, Annex 3.I of the TBT Agreement requires that wherever appropriate, the standardising body is to specify standards based on product requirements in terms of performance, rather than design or descriptive characteristics.

4.3 Transparency and Notification

As discussed in earlier chapters, transparency is one of the core principles of the WTO, and accordingly has been incorporated in the Article X of the GATT, Article III of the GATS Agreement, Article 63 of the TRIPS Agreement, and Article 7 and Annex B of the SPS Agreement. Similarly, the TBT Agreement incorporates transparency obligations in Articles 2.9 to 2.12. Article 2.9 clearly imposes on all Member States transparency and notification requirements. Pursuant to Article 2.9.2 of the TBT Agreement, Member States are required to notify all Member States, through the Secretariat, of any forthcoming technical regulations. Further, Member States are also required, upon request, to provide a justification for the intended regulatory intervention. Member States are also required to notify other Member States at an early stage of the process, to provide interested parties the opportunity to make comments which can be taken into account while carrying out any amendments.

Article 2.10.1 of the TBT Agreement concerns measures already adopted for urgent reasons (for safety, health, environmental protection, or national security) that have arisen, or threaten to arise, where a Member State may omit the notification requirements enumerated in Article 2.9 of the TBT Agreement. Article 2.11 of the TBT Agreement requires the prompt publication of all adopted technical regulations, or that such technical regulations be made available in such a manner as to enable interested parties in other Member States to become acquainted with them. Article 2.12 of the TBT Agreement provides that except when a technical regulation addresses an urgent problem, that technical regulation may not enter into force immediately after publication. Article 2.12 requires Member States to

> [A]llow a reasonable interval between the publication of technical regulations and their entry into force in order to allow time for producers in exporting Members to adapt their products or methods of production to the requirements of the importing Member.

As regards 'reasonable interval' envisaged in Article 2.12, paragraph 5.2, of the Doha Ministerial Decision on *Implementation-Related Issues and Concerns* of 14 November 2001, provides as follows:

> Subject to the conditions specified in paragraph 12 of Article 2 of the Agreement on Technical Barriers to Trade, the phrase "reasonable interval" shall be understood to mean normally a period of not less than 6 months, except when this would be ineffective in fulfilling the legitimate objectives pursued.

The Appellate Body in *US – Clove Cigarettes* agreed with the Panel that paragraph 5.2 of the Doha Ministerial Decision constitutes a subsequent agreement between the parties, within the meaning of Article 31(3)(a) of the Vienna Convention, and interpreted Article 2.12, taking into account paragraph 5.2 of the Doha Ministerial Declaration as follows:

> Thus, we consider that, taking into account the interpretative clarification provided by paragraph 5.2 of the Doha Ministerial Decision, Article 2.12 of the TBT Agreement establishes a rule that "normally" producers in exporting Members require a period of "not less than 6 months" to adapt their products or production methods to the requirements of an importing Member's technical regulation.[156]

However, the Appellate Body noted that an importing Member State may depart from this obligation if this interval "would be ineffective to fulfil the legitimate objectives pursued" by the technical regulation.[157] As regards the burden of proof under Article 2.12 was concerned, the Appellate Body explained:

> a complaining Member is required to establish a *prima facie* case that the responding Member has failed to allow for a period of at least six months between the publication and the entry into force of the technical regulation at issue. If the complaining Member establishes such a *prima facie* case, the burden rests on the responding Member that has allowed for an interval of less than six months between the publication and the entry into force of its technical regulation to establish either: (i) that the "urgent circumstances" referred to in Article 2.10 of the TBT Agreement surrounded the adoption of the technical regulation at issue; (ii) that producers of the complaining Member could have adapted to the requirements of the technical regulation at issue within the shorter interval that it allowed; or (iii) that a period of "not less than" six months would be ineffective to fulfil the legitimate objectives of its technical regulation.[158]

Annexes 3.L, M, N, and O of the TBT Agreement contains transparency and notification provisions with regard to standards, and Articles 5.6, 5.7, 5.8, and 5.9 of the TBT Agreement contain transparency and notification provisions with regard to standards conformity assessment procedures. Under Article 10 of the TBT Agreement, Member States are required to establish enquiry points, which will answer queries of other Member States and provide relevant documentation with regards to adopted technical regulations, standards, and conformity assessment procedures. Also, a publicly accessible database (Technical

Barriers to Trade Information Management System) of all technical regulations, standards, and conformity assessment procedures is maintained by the WTO Secretariat.

4.4 Special and Differential Treatment

Special and differential treatment of developing country Member States is dealt with under Article 12 of the TBT Agreement. Goods produced for exports are required to comply with a range of technical regulations and standards. While some regulations and standards are aligned with international standards, a vast majority differ from country to country, which impacts the developing countries (Mayeda, 2013). The cost of complying with technical regulations is higher for producers in developing country Member States than it is for domestic producers in importing Member States or for exporters from other Member States (Baller, 2007; Czubala, Shepherd, and Wilson, 2009).

Pursuant to Article 12.1 of the TBT Agreement:

> Members shall provide differential and more favourable treatment to developing country Members to this Agreement, through the following provisions as well as through the relevant provisions of other Articles of this Agreement.

Articles 12.2 and 12.3 require that Member States give particular attention to the developing country Member States' special rights and obligations under TBT and their special development, financial, and trade needs, in particular in implementation of the TBT Agreement, as well as in the preparation and application of technical regulations, standards, and conformity assessment procedures.

The Panel in *EC – Approval and Marketing of Biotech Products* observed, "Article 12.3 requires that in preparing and applying technical regulations, standards and conformity assessment procedures, Members take account of the special needs of developing country Members".[159] That Panel also noted, "Article 12.3 is a specific application of the obligation in Article 12.2 to take account of developing country needs in the implementation of the TBT Agreement at the national level".[160] Pursuant to Article 12.4 of the TBT Agreement, developing country Member States are not expected to use international standards as a basis for their technical regulations or standards, including test methods, which are not appropriate to their development, financial, and trade needs.

Article 12.6 of the TBT Agreement requires that Member States take such reasonable measures "as may be available to them" to ensure that the international standardising bodies, upon the request of developing country Member States, examine the possibility of developing international standards concerning products of special interest to developing country Member States. In accordance with Article 12.8 of the TBT Agreement, a developing country Member State may request the TBT Committee specific, time-limited exceptions (in whole or in part) in the performance of the obligations arising under TBT Agreement.

The Panel in *US – Clove Cigarettes* rejected Indonesia's claim under Article 12.3 on the grounds that Indonesia could not demonstrate that the US did not 'take account of' its special needs as a developing country, *i.e.*, special development, financial, and trade needs when preparing and applying the measures at issue. The Panel began by providing some general observations on the obligation, in Article 12.3, to 'take account of' a developing country's special needs. Referring to the findings of the Panel in *EC – Approval and Marketing of Biotech Products*, it observed as follows:

> We note that there is no jurisprudence examining the nature of the obligation in Article 12.3 of the TBT Agreement to "take account of" the special needs of developing countries. However, the panel in *EC – Approval and Marketing of Biotech Products* examined a claim brought by Argentina under Article 10.1 of the SPS Agreement, which the panel described as the "equivalent provision" to Article 12.3 of the TBT Agreement.
>
> . . .
>
> That panel also found that it is the complaining party that carries the burden of proving that the Member adopting the technical regulation did not "take account of" developing country Members' needs.
>
> We agree with that panel's interpretation of the obligation to "take account of" developing country Members' needs, and we agree with the panel that it is the complaining party, in this case Indonesia, that carries the burden of proof.[161]

The Panel in *US – Clove Cigarettes* also noted:

> to "take account of" the special financial, development and trade needs of a developing country does not necessarily mean that the Member preparing or applying a technical regulation must agree with or accept the developing country's position and desired outcome. In our opinion, the fact that the United States ultimately decided not to exclude clove cigarettes from the scope of the ban in Section 907(a)(1)(A) does not mean that the United States did not take account of Indonesia's special financial, development and trade needs.[162]

The Panel in in *US – COOL* followed a similar an approach to the one taken by the Panel in *EC – Approval and Marketing of Biotech Products*, and observed that in the context of Article 12.3 of the TBT Agreement, the term 'take account of' entails that Members are "obliged to accord active and meaningful consideration to the special development, financial and trade needs of developing country Members". The Panel further elaborated as follows:

> As to what such active and meaningful consideration means in practical terms, we do not read Article 12.3 of the TBT Agreement as prescribing any specific way. In particular, while not excluding it, Article 12.3 does not specifically require WTO Members to actively reach out to developing countries and collect their views on their special needs. Further, we do not interpret the term "take account of" in Article 12.3 of the TBT Agreement as an explicit requirement for Members to document specifically in their legislative process and rule-making process how they actively considered the special development, financial and trade needs of developing country Members. Indeed, the panel in *EC – Approval and Marketing of Biotech Products* held that "it is not sufficient, for the purposes of establishing a claim under Article 10.1 [of the SPS Agreement], to point to the absence in the EC approval legislation of a reference to the needs of developing country Members".

5. Institutional Provisions of the TBT Agreement

The TBT Agreement contains a number of institutional and procedural provisions, covering the TBT Committee, dispute settlement, and technical assistance to developing country Member States.

5.1 TBT Committee

Pursuant to Article 13.1, a Committee on Technical Barriers to Trade (TBT Committee) is established. The TBT Committee is composed of representatives of all WTO Member States and meets when required, but at least once every year. The TBT Committee provides a forum providing the Member States the space for discussions, consultations, and informal dispute resolution where matters relating to the TBT Agreement are involved. The TBT Committee has also served as a forum to discuss 'specific trade concerns' (STCs) relating to proposed draft measures notified to the TBT Committee or the implementation of existing measures.

The TBT Committee gives the Member States the opportunity to review STCs in a multilateral setting and to seek further information and clarification, with a view to working towards resolution of concerns. The number of STCs discussed has increased steadily since the creation of the WTO in 1995 – with four in 1995 to 214 in 2020 (TBT Committee, 2021). The discussions at the TBT Committee are a means of reducing potential trade tensions amongst Member States. The meetings help improve the delegations' understanding of the rationale behind other Member States' regulations, sheds light on details regarding implementation and enforcement, and presents an opportunity for clarification – and for delegations to flag potential problems. The TBT Committee meetings, in some cases, have even facilitated the resolution of trade issues arising between Member States (TBT Committee, 2021). The TBT Committee undertakes both an annual review of the implementation and operation of the TBT Agreement and a triennial review at the end of every three-year period to carry out an in-depth review of the operation of the Agreement.

In the TBT Committee that met in 2020, Member States reviewed a total of 214 STCs, including 57 new concerns (TBT Committee, 2021). The TBT Committee met on 24–26 February 2021 to complete its Ninth Review of the Operation and Implementation of the TBT Agreement. The Member States that met reviewed proposals – spanning 81 STCs – aimed at improving implementation of the TBT Agreement. A number of the new STCs relate to issues on the environment and labelling of electric and electronic equipment, with some concerns touching upon a range of products, including, *inter alia*, cosmetics, medical devices, chemicals, and cryptography products, and relating to how labelling, testing, and certification requirements could be viewed as burdensome or overly complicated (IISD, 2021). The TBT Committee also adopted the 26th Annual Review of the Implementation and Operation of the TBT Agreement. In 2020, the TBT Committee launched 'eAgenda' to enable Member States to submit STCs in real time, with additional transparency (IISD, 2021).

5.2 Dispute Settlement and TBT Agreement

Disputes arising out of any measures introduced under a WTO agreement are to be raised before the DSB pursuant to Article XXII and XXIII of the GATT. Article 14 and Annex 2 of the TBT Agreement contains additional rules and procedures pertaining to disputes arising from the TBT Agreement. Under Articles 14.2, a Panel may, following a request from a party to a dispute, or on its own initiative, establish an expert group to assist in questions of a technical nature.

In *EC – Asbestos*, the Panel, having determined that the case raised scientific or technical issues, decided to consult experts on an individual basis, rather than in the form of a technical expert group, as envisaged under Article 14 and Annex 2 of the TBT Agreement. Responding to an argument put forward by the EC that expert consultations under the TBT

Agreement can only be conducted in the form of technical expert groups, the Panel observed as follows:

> In the present case, Article 14:2 of the TBT Agreement provides that a Panel "may" establish a technical expert group. Like Article 13:2 of the DSU, this text envisages the possibility of establishing a technical expert group and lays down the procedures that would be applicable in the event. Nevertheless, it does not exclusively prescribe the establishment of a technical expert group, and this possibility, in our opinion, is not incompatible with the general authorization given under Article 13 of the DSU to consult with individual experts. The two provisions can be read as complementing each other.
>
> The Panel believes that in this case the consultation of experts on an individual basis is the more appropriate form of consultation, inasmuch as it is the one that will better enable the Panel usefully to gather opinions and information on the scientific or technical issues raised by this dispute. Considering in particular the range of areas of competence that might be required, it is appropriate in this case to gather information and different individual opinions rather than asking for a collective report on the various scientific or technical matters in question.[163]

A similar approach was adopted by the Panel in *EC – Approval and Marketing of Biotech Products*, where it decided to consult with individual scientific experts to obtain their advice on certain scientific and/or technical issues.[164] Article 14.4 of the TBT Agreement provides the dispute settlement provisions enumerated under Article 14 can be invoked in cases where a Member State considers that another Member State has not achieved satisfactory results under Articles 3, 4, 7, 8, and 9, and its trade interests are significantly affected, and that such results shall be equivalent to those as if the body in question were a Member.

5.3 Technical Assistance

Article 11 of the TBT Agreement, in similar terms as Article 12, contains special provisions for developing country Member States. Under Article 11 of the TBT Agreement, a Member State, upon request, is required to advise or provide technical assistance to the requesting Member State, in particular if such request were to come from a developing country Member State. The obligations arising under Article 11 are legally binding requirements. Pursuant to Article 11, Member States are required to grant technical assistance only upon request, and such request may be made to individual Member States, a group of Member States, or to the WTO Membership as a whole. Article 11 primarily assists in establishing institutions or legal frameworks to deal with the preparation of technical regulations and standards, besides the development of conformity assessment procedures. Granting of such technical assistance is subject to "mutually agreed terms and conditions", and a requesting Member State can choose the terms on which the technical assistance is provided. Pursuant to Article 11.8, in providing advice and technical assistance to other Member States, priority is be given to the needs of least developed country Members.

6. Summary

Regulatory measures for trade in goods, which are otherwise viewed as 'Technical Barriers to Trade', are essential for the success of the multilateral trading system. Technical regulations help regulate the standard of goods and product compatibility and establish a common trade language. The technical regulations and product standards which are to be found in consumer durables, meat, cheese, cosmetics, medical equipment, *etc.* provide the consumer with the correct information on the standards of the product that they seek to purchase. The technical regulations diminish information asymmetry between producers and consumers and facilitate the governments to implement economic and health policies. The TBT Agreement applies to technical regulations, standards, and conformity assessment procedures relating to products and PPMs. The Agreement addresses the central government bodies and seeks to promote regulatory harmonisation around international trade.

Notes

1. The authors note that the desire to avoid such fragmentation in the future was one of the factors that led to the introduction of the concept of a WTO 'single undertaking'.
2. See Appellate Body Report, *Korea – Dairy*, para. 74, where it was held, "it is now well established that the WTO Agreement is a 'Single-Undertaking' and therefore all WTO obligations are generally cumulative and Members must comply with all of them simultaneously."
3. The number of technical measures notified to the WTO Secretariat under the TBT Agreement increased from 364 in 1995 to 2,043 in 2020 (WTO, 2021a). Likewise, the annual number of new notifications under the SPS Agreement rose from 189 in 1995 to 1,253 in 2019 (WTO, 2021b).
4. See Appellate Body Report, *US – Clove Cigarettes*, para. 96.
5. *Ibid.*, para. 89.
6. See, Annex 1 'Terms and Their Definitions for the Purpose of This Agreement'.
7. *Ibid.*
8. See Appellate Body Report, *US – Tuna*, para. 185. See also Appellate Body Report, *EC – Seal Products*, para. 5.9.
9. See Appellate Body Report, *EC – Seal Products*, para. 5.10.
10. See Appellate Body Report, *EC – Asbestos*, paras. 66–70.
11. *Ibid.*
12. See Appellate Body Report, *EC – Sardines*, para. 176.
13. See Panel Reports, *EC – Seal Products*, paras. 7.85–7.87; *US – COOL*, paras. 7.147–7.148; *US – Tuna II (Mexico)*, paras. 7.53–7.55; and *US – Clove Cigarettes*, paras. 7.24–7.25. See also Appellate Body Reports, *EC – Seal Products*, paras. 5.21–5.23, and *US – Tuna II (Mexico)*, para. 183.
14. See Appellate Body Reports, *EC – Asbestos*, para. 68; *EC – Sardines*, para. 194; *US – Tuna*, para. 199.
15. See Appellate Body Report, *US – Tuna*, para. 187.
16. See Appellate Body Report, *EC – Seal Products*, para. 5.10.
17. For a discussion of product standards in international trade, see Du (2020).
18. See Appellate Body Report, *EC – Asbestos*, para. 59.
19. Examples of non-governmental bodies are ANSI (American National Standards Institute), CEN (European Committee for Standardization), and ABNT (Associação Brasileira de Normas Técnicas).
20. See Appellate Body Reports, *EC – Sardines*, paras. 206–207. The Appellate Body referred to its earlier decision in *EC – Hormones*, where it dealt with a similar question in relation to the SPS Agreement.
21. See Appellate Body Report, *Argentina – Footwear*, para. 81. See also Appellate Body Reports, *US – Gasoline*, para. 23; *Japan – Alcoholic Beverages*, para. 12; and *India – Patents*, para. 45.
22. See Appellate Body Report, *Korea – Dairy*, para. 81.
23. See Appellate Body Report, *US – Clove Cigarettes*, para. 96.
24. *Ibid.*, para. 100.
25. See Panel Report, *EC – Asbestos*, para. 8.16. See also Appellate Body Report, *EC – Bananas III*, para. 204, and Panel Report, *EC – Sardines*, paras. 7.14–7.19.
26. See Appellate Body Report, *EC – Asbestos*, para. 80.
27. See Appellate Body Report, *US – Tuna II (Mexico)*, para. 405.
28. *Ibid.*, para. 406.

29 Note: the AGP is a plurilateral agreement, where the majority of developing country Member States, as well as a few developed country Member States, are not signatories. Their government procurement activity falls neither under the TBT Agreement nor under the AGP.
30 See Panel Report, *EC – Hormones (Canada)*, para. 8.32, and *EC – Hormones (US)*, para. 8.29.
31 See Panel Report, *EC – Approval and Marketing of Biotech Products*, para. 7.165.
32 *Ibid.*, para. 7.167.
33 *Ibid.*, paras. 7.2524, 7.2528, 7.3412–7.3413, 8.38, 8.42–8.46, 8.53, and 8.57–8.62.
34 See Appellate Body Report, *US – Clove Cigarettes*, para. 87. See also Appellate Body Report, *US – Tuna II (Mexico)*, para. 202.
35 *Ibid.*, paras. 99–100.
36 *Ibid.*, para. 120.
37 *Ibid.*, para. 104.
38 See Appellate Body Report, *US – Tuna II (Mexico)*, para. 202.
39 See Panel Report *US – Clove Cigarettes*, para. 7.76.
40 See Appellate Body Report, *EC – Asbestos*, para. 64.
41 *Ibid.*, para. 67.
42 *Ibid.*
43 *Ibid.*, para. 69.
44 *Ibid.*, para. 75.
45 See Panel Report *EC – Sardines*, para. 176 (referring to Appellate Body Report, *EC – Asbestos*, paras. 66–70.
46 See Panel Reports, *EC – Seal Products*, paras. 7.85–7.87; *US – COOL*, paras. 7.147–7.148; *US – Tuna II (Mexico)*, paras. 7.53–7.55; and *US – Clove Cigarettes*, paras. 7.24–7.25. See also Appellate Body Reports, *EC – Seal Products*, paras. 5.21–5.23; and *US – Tuna II (Mexico)*, para. 183.
47 See Appellate Body Report, *EC – Asbestos*, para. 68.
48 See Appellate Body Report, *EC – Sardines*, para. 194.
49 See Appellate Body Report, *US – Tuna II (Mexico)*, para. 199.
50 *Ibid.*, para. 188.
51 *Ibid.*, para. 199.
52 See Panel Reports, *EC – Seal Products*, paras. 7.54 and 7.105.
53 See Appellate Body Report, *EC – Seal Products*, para. 5.29.
54 See Panel Reports, *EC – Sardines*, para. 7.63.
55 See Panel Reports, *EC – Sardines*, paras. 7.64–7.65.
56 See Appellate Body Report, *EC – Sardines*, para. 227.
57 See Appellate Body Report, *US – Clove Cigarettes*, paras. 99–100.
58 *Ibid.*, paras. 107–120.
59 *Ibid.*, para. 104.
60 *Ibid.*, para. 112.
61 *Ibid.*, para. 120.
62 *Ibid.*
63 *Ibid.*, paras. 107, 112, and 121–160.
64 *Ibid.*, para. 111.
65 See Appellate Body Report, *Korea – Various Measures on Beef*, para. 137.
66 See Appellate Body Report, *US – Clove Cigarettes*, para. 180.
67 *Ibid.*, para. 174.
68 *Ibid.*, para. 175.
69 *Ibid.*, para. 182.
70 *Ibid.*, para. 226.
71 Interestingly, the TBT Agreement does not explicitly contain a 'Preamble'. Nevertheless, the introductory clauses of the TBT Agreement have been referred to as the 'Preamble' by the Appellate Body in its jurisprudence. Under international law such introductory clauses form a Preamble, as they contain the common goals and objectives of the international Convention/ Agreement in general, and in the instant case the introductory clause enshrine the shared principles of the Member States of the WTO.
72 See Appellate Body Report, *US – Clove Cigarettes*, para. 94.
73 *Ibid.*, para. 96.
74 See Appellate Body Report, *US – Tuna II (Mexico)*, para. 213.
75 *Ibid.*, para. 405.

76 See Appellate Body Report, *Korea – Various Measures on Beef*, para. 137.
77 See Appellate Body Report, *Thailand – Cigarettes (Philippines)*, para. 134.
78 See Appellate Body Report, *US – Tuna II (Mexico)*, para. 214. See also Appellate Body Report, *US – Clove Cigarettes*, paras. 180 and 215.
79 See Appellate Body Report, *US – Tuna II (Mexico)*, para. 215.
80 See Appellate Body Report, *US – COOL*, para. 269.
81 See Appellate Body Report, *Thailand – Cigarettes (Philippines)*, para. 130.
82 See Appellate Body Report, *US – COOL*, paras. 269 and 325.
83 See Appellate Body Report, *US – Tuna II (Mexico)*, para. 297.
84 *Ibid.*, para. 298.
85 See Appellate Body Report, *US – COOL*, para. 340.
86 *Ibid.*, para. 271.
87 See Appellate Body Report, *US – COOL (Article 21.5 – Canada and Mexico)*, para. 5.92.
88 In 2011, Australia introduced the 'Tobacco Plain Packaging Act 2011', which bans the use of logos, brand imagery, symbols, other images, colours, and promotional text on tobacco products and tobacco product packaging. This legislation, which is referred to as the 'plain tobacco packaging' law, had been challenged in recent years before the High Court in Australia, an investment challenge under the Hong Kong–Australia Bilateral Investment Treaty, and before the dispute settlement system of the WTO. See Panel Reports, *Australia – Tobacco Plain Packaging (Indonesia)*; *Australia – Tobacco Plain Packaging (Cuba)*; and Appellate Body Reports, *Australia – Tobacco Plain Packaging (Honduras)*; and *Australia – Tobacco Plain Packaging (Dominican Republic)*.
89 See Appellate Body Report, *US – Clove Cigarettes*, para. 7.333.
90 See Appellate Body Report, *US – Tuna II (Mexico)*, para. 314. See also Appellate Body Report, *US – COOL*, paras. 371–372.
91 See Appellate Body Report, *US – Tuna II (Mexico)*, para. 314.
92 See Appellate Body Report, *US – Tuna II (Mexico)*, para. 319.
93 *Ibid.*
94 *Ibid.*, para. 313.
95 *Ibid.*
96 *Ibid.*
97 See Appellate Body Report, *US – COOL*, para. 372.
98 *Ibid.*, para. 372.
99 (Footnote original) Appellate Body Report, *EC – Sardines*, para. 286.
100 See Panel Report, *US – Tuna II (Mexico)*, para. 7.437.
101 See Appellate Body Report, *US – COOL*, para. 453.
102 *Ibid.*, para. 445.
103 (Footnote original) This may involve an assessment of whether the measure at issue is capable of achieving the legitimate objective.
104 See Appellate Body Report, *US – Tuna II (Mexico)*, para. 317.
105 *Ibid.*, para. 319.
106 *Ibid.*, para. 322.
107 *Ibid.*, 320.
108 *Ibid.*, para. 322.
109 See Panel Report, *Australia – Tobacco Plain Packaging*, para. 7.1364.
110 *Ibid.*, para. 7.1682.
111 *Ibid.*, para. 7.1391.
112 *Ibid.*, para. 7.1722.
113 See Appellate Body Report, *COOL (Article 21.5 – Canada and Mexico)*, para. 5.202.
114 *Ibid.*
115 *Ibid.*, para. 5.211.
116 *Ibid.*, para. 5.215.
117 *Ibid.*
118 *Ibid.*, para. 5.216.
119 *Ibid.*
120 *Ibid.*, para. 5.217.
121 *Ibid.*, para. 5.218.
122 *Ibid.*
123 See Panel Report, *Australia – Tobacco Plain Packaging*, para. 7.1321.

124 See Appellate Body Report, *US – Tuna II (Mexico)*, para. 322.
125 See Appellate Body Report, *COOL (Article 21.5 – Canada and Mexico)*, para. 5.330.
126 See Appellate Body Report *COOL (Article 21.5 – Canada and Mexico)*, para. 5.328. See also Appellate Body Report, *US – Tuna II (Mexico)*, para. 320.
127 See Appellate Body Report, *US – Tuna II (Mexico)*, para. 320. See also Appellate Body Report *COOL (Article 21.5 – Canada and Mexico)*, para. 5.337.
128 See Appellate Body Report *COOL (Article 21.5 – Canada and Mexico)*, para. 5.327.
129 *Ibid.*, para. 5.334.
130 *Ibid.*, para. 5.338.
131 See Panel Report, *EC – Sardines*, paras. 7.61–7.139. See also Appellate Body Report, *EC – Sardines*, paras. 217–291, where the Appellate Body adopted the same approach on appeal from the Panel's decision.
132 See Panel Report, *US – Tuna II (Mexico)*, para. 7.627.
133 Articles 2, 5, and 6 and Annex 3 of the TBT Agreement refer to 'relevant international standard'.
134 See Appellate Body Report, *US – Tuna II (Mexico)*, para. 353.
135 *Ibid.*, para. 356.
136 *Ibid.*, para. 356.
137 *Ibid.*, para. 363.
138 *Ibid.*, para. 362.
139 See Appellate Body Report, *EC – Sardines*, para. 232.
140 *Ibid.*, paras. 219–227.
141 See Appellate Body Report, *EC – Sardines*, para. 243.
142 *Ibid.*, para. 245.
143 *Ibid.*, para. 248.
144 See Appellate Body Report, *EC – Hormones*, para. 177. The Appellate Body was ruling on the objective of Article 3 of the SPS Agreement, which by analogy can be extended to the objective of Article 2.4 of the TBT Agreement, which seeks to harmonise technical regulations.
145 See Appellate Body Report, *EC – Sardines*, para. 285.
146 *Ibid.*, para. 286.
147 *Ibid.*, para. 290.
148 See Panel Report, *US – COOL*, paras. 7.734–7.735.
149 *Ibid.*
150 See Appellate Body Report, *EC – Sardines*, para. 274. The Appellate Body noted, the "heart of Article 3.1 of the SPS Agreement is a requirement that Members base their sanitary or phytosanitary measures on international standards, guidelines, or recommendations. Likewise, the heart of Article 2.4 of the TBT Agreement is a requirement that Members use international standards as a basis for their technical regulations."
151 *Ibid.*, para. 275.
152 See Articles 2.9–2.10, 10.1, and 10.3 of the TBT Agreement.
153 *Ibid.*, para. 277.
154 See, for instance, Swiss Federal Law on Technical Barriers to Trade (THG), which permits Swiss manufacturers to have the choice to align their products to the technical requirements of Switzerland or to those of the EU or an EU/EEA Member State. See also Marceau and Trachtman (2014).
155 See Panel Report, *US – Clove Cigarettes*, paras. 7.481–7.482.
156 See Appellate Body Report, *US – Clove Cigarettes*, para. 272.
157 *Ibid.*, para. 275.
158 *Ibid.*, para. 290.
159 See Panel Report, *EC – Approval and Marketing of Biotech Products*, para. 7.47, sub-para. 75.
160 *Ibid.*, para. 7.47, sub-para. 77.
161 See Panel Report, *US – Clove Cigarettes*, paras. 7.631–7.634.
162 *Ibid.*, para. 7.646.
163 See Panel Report, *EC – Asbestos*, paras. 5.18–5.19.
164 See Panel Report, *EC – Approval and Marketing of Biotech Products*, para. 7.18.

Bibliography

Appleton, Arthur E. 'The Agreement on Technical Barriers to Trade,' in Macrory, Patrick F.J., Arthur E. Appleton and Michael G. Plummer (eds.) *The WTO: Legal, Economic and Political Analysis* Vol 1 (Springer, 2005) 371–410.

Appleton, Arthur E. 'National Treatment under the TBT Agreement,' in Sanders, Anslem Kamperman (ed.) *The Principle of National Treatment in International Economic Law* (Edward Elgar Publishing, 2014) 92–124.

Arcuri, Alessandra. 'Global Food Safety Standards: The Evolving Regulatory Epistemology at the Intersection of the SPS Agreement and the Codex Alimentarius Commission,' in Delimatsis, Panagiotis. (ed.) *The Law, Economics and Politics of International Standardization* (Cambridge University Press, 2015) 79–103.

Baller, Silja. 'Trade Effects of Regional Standards Liberalization: A Heterogeneous Firms Approach,' *World Bank Policy Research Working Paper 4124* (2007).

Chase, Claude. 'Norm Conflict between WTO Covered Agreements: Real, Apparent or Avoided?,' *The International and Comparative Law Quarterly* Vol 61, No 4 (2012) 791–821.

Conrad, Christiane R. *Processes and Production Methods (PPMs) in WTO Law: Interfacing Trade & Social Goals* (Cambridge University Press, 2011).

Czubala, Witold, Ben Shepherd and John S. Wilson. 'Help or Hindrance? The Impact of Harmonized Standards on African Exports,' *Journal of African Economies* Vol 18, No 5 (2009) 711–744.

Du, Michael Ming. 'Domestic Regulatory Autonomy under the TBT Agreement: From Non-Discrimination to Harmonization,' *Chinese Journal of International Law* Vol 6, No 2 (2007) 269–306.

Du, Michael Ming. 'Standard of Review under the SPS Agreement after EC-Hormones II,' *International and Comparative Law Quarterly* Vol 59, No 2 (2010) 441–459.

Du, Ming. 'How to Define "Public Morals" in WTO Law? A Critique of *Brazil-Taxation and Charges* Panel Report,' *Global Trade and Customs Journal* Vol 13, No 2 (2018) 69–74.

Du, Ming. *The Regulation of Product Standards in World Trade Law* (Hart Publishing, 2020).

Du, Ming and Fei Deng. 'International Standards as Global Public Goods in the World Trading System,' *Legal Issues of Economic Integration* Vol 43, No 2 (2016) 113–144.

Epps, Tracy. *International Trade and Health Protection: A Critical Assessment of the WTO's SPS Agreement* (Edward Elgar Publishing, 2008).

Fontagné, Lionel, Gianluca Orefice, Roberta Piermartini and Nadia Rocha. 'Product Standards and Margins of Trade: Firm Level Evidence,' *Journal of International Economics* Vol 97, No 1 (2015) 29–44.

GATT Drafting Group on Standards. 'Proposed GATT Code of Conduct for Preventing Technical Barriers to Trade,' Spec(71)143 (30 December 1971).

Hartmann, Stephanie. 'Comparing the National Treatment Obligations of the GATT and the TBT: Lessons Learned from the *EC-Seal Products* Dispute,' *North Carolina Journal of International Law* Vol 40, No 3 (2015) 629–678.

Hoekman, Bernard M. 'Trade Agreements and International Regulatory Cooperation in a Supply Chain World,' *Robert Schuman Centre for Advanced Studies Research Paper No. RSCAS* 4 (2015).

Hoekman, Bernard M. and Michel M. Kostecki. *The Political Economy of the World Trading System* Vol 3 (Oxford University Press, 2009).

Howse, Robert. 'A New Device for Creating International Legal Normativity: The WTO Technical Barriers to Trade Agreement and International Standards,' in Joerges, Christian and Ernst-Ulrich Petersmann (eds.) *Constitutionalism, Multilevel Trade Governance and Social Regulation* (Hart Publishing, 2006) 383–395.

IISD. 'WTO Members Discuss Proposals under Triennial Review of Technical Barriers to Trade Agreements,' *SDG Knowledge Hub* (10 March 2021) <https://sdg.iisd.org/news/wto-members-discuss-proposals-under-triennial-review-of-technical-barriers-to-trade-agreement/> (accessed 20 May 2021).

Islam, M. Rafiqul. *International Trade Law of the WTO* (Oxford University Press, 2006).

Koebelle, Michael and Gordon Lafortune. 'Article 4 and Annex 3 TBT,' in Wolfrum, Rüdiger, Peter-Tobias Stoll and Anja Seibert-Fohr (eds.) *WTO-Technical Barriers and SPS Measures* (Martinus Nijhoff Publishers, 2007) 243–260.

Kudryavtsev, Arkady. 'The TBT Agreement in Context,' in Epps, Tracey and Michael J. Trebilcock (eds.) *Research Handbook on the WTO and Technical Barriers to Trade* (Edward Elgar Publishing, 2013) 17–80.

Laowonsiri, Akawat. 'Application of the Precautionary Principle in the SPS Agreement,' *Max Planck Yearbook of United Nations Law* Vol 14, No 1 (2010) 563–623.

Lester, Simon, Bryan Mercurio and Arwel Davies. *World Trade Law: Text, Materials and Commentary* (Hart Publishing, 2018).

Marceau, Gabrielle and Joel P. Trachtman. 'The Technical Barriers to Trade Agreement, the Sanitary and Phytosanitary Measures Agreement, and the General Agreement on Tariffs and Trade: A Map of the World Trade Organization Law of Domestic Regulations of Goods,' *Journal of World Trade* Vol 48, No 2 (2014) 351–432.

Matsushita, Mitsuo, Thomas J. Shoenbaum, Petros C. Mavroidis and Michael Hahn. *The World Trade Organization: Law, Practice, and Policy* (Oxford University Press, 2017).

Mayeda, Graham. 'The TBT Agreement and Developing Countries,' in Epps, Tracey and Michael J. Trebilcock (eds.) *Research Handbook on the WTO and Technical Barriers to Trade* (Edward Elgar Publishing, 2013) 358–390.

Meltzer, Joshua and Amelia Porges. 'Beyond Discrimination? The WTO Parses the *TBT Agreement* in *US-Clove Cigarettes, US-Tuna II (Mexico)* and *US-COOL*,' *Melbourne Journal of International Law* Vol 14, No 2 (2013) 699–726.

Prévost, Denise. 'National Treatment in the SPS Agreement: A *Sui Generis* Obligation,' in Sanders, Anselm Kamperman (ed.) *The Principle of National Treatment in International Economic Law* (Edward Elgar Publishing, 2014) 125–157.

Prévost, Denise and Peter Van den Bossche. 'The Agreement on the Application of Sanitary and Phytosanitary Measures,' in Macrory, Patrick F.J., Arthur E. Appleton and Michael G. Plummer (eds.) *The WTO: Legal, Economic and Political Analysis* Vol 1 (Springer, 2005) 231–370.

Rigod, Boris. 'The Purpose of the WTO Agreement on the Application of Sanitary and Phytosanitary Measures (SPS),' *The European Journal of International Law* Vol 24, No 2 (2013) 503–532.

Scott, Joanne. *The WTO Agreement on Sanitary and Phytosanitary Measures: A Commentary* (Oxford University Press, 2009).

Sifonios, David. *Environmental Process and Production Methods (PPMs) in WTO Law* (Springer International, 2018).

Stoler, Andrew L. 'TBT and SPS Measures in Practice,' in Chauffour, Jean-Pierre and Jean-Christophe Maur (eds.) *Preferential Trade Agreement Policies for Development: A Handbook* (World Bank Publishing, 2011) 217–233.

Sykes, Alan O. 'Regulatory Protectionism and the Law of International Trade,' *The University of Chicago Law Review* Vol 66, No 1 (1999) 1–46.

Tamiotti, Ludivine. 'Article 2 TBT,' in Wolfrum, Rüdiger, Peter-Tobias Stoll and Anja Seibert-Fohr (eds.) *WTO-Technical Barriers and SPS Measures* (Martinus Nijhoff Publishers, 2007) 210–234.

TBT Committee. *Twenty-Sixth Annual Review of the Implementation and Operation of the TBT Agreement* (G/TBT/45) (18 February 2021).

Trebilcock, Michael, Robert Howse and Antonia Eliason. *The Regulation of International Trade* (Routledge, 2013).

Van den Bossche, Peter and Werner Zdouc. *The Law and Policy of the World Trade Organization* (Cambridge University Press, 2017).

Villareal, Andrea Barrios. *International Standardization and the Agreement on Technical Barriers to Trade* (Cambridge University Press, 2018).

Voon, Tania. 'Exploring the Meaning of Trade-Restrictiveness in the WTO,' *World Trade Review* Vol 14, No 3 (2015) 451–477.

Voon, Tania, Andres Mitchell and Catherine Gascoigne. 'Consumer Information, Consumer Preferences and Product Labels under the TBT Agreement,' in Epps, Tracey and Michael J. Trebilcock (eds.) *Research Handbook on the WTO and Technical Barriers to Trade* (Edward Elgar Publishing, 2013) 454–484.

Wagner, Marcus. 'International Standards,' in Epps, Tracey and Michael J. Trebilcock (eds.) *Research Handbook on the WTO and Technical Barriers to Trade* (Edward Elgar Publishing, 2013) 238–279.

Wijkström, Erik and Devin McDaniels. 'Improving Regulatory Governance: International Standards and the WTO TBT Agreement,' *Journal of World Trade* Vol 47, No 5 (2013) 1013–1046.

Wirth, David A. 'The Role of Science in the Uruguay Round and NAFTA Trade Disciplines,' *Cornell International Law Journal* Vol 27 (1994) 817–860.

WTO. 'Doha Decision on Implementation-Related Issues and Concerns,' Ministerial Conference (WT/MIN(01)/17) (14 November 2001).

WTO. *World Trade Report 2005: Exploring the Links between Trade, Standards and the WTO* (WTO, 2005).

WTO. Technical Barriers to Trade Information Management System (20 January 2021a) <www.tbtims.wto.org> (accessed 24 April 2021).

WTO. Sanitary and Phytosanitary Information Management System (10 February 2021b) <www.spsims.wto.org> (accessed 24 April 2021).

WTO, Committee on Sanitary and Phytosanitary Measures. 'Technical Assistance Typology,' Note by the Secretariat (G/SPS/GEN/206) (18 October 2000).

WTO, Committee on Sanitary and Phytosanitary Measures. 'Decision on the Implementation of Article 4 of the Agreement on the Application of Sanitary and Phytosanitary Measures,' (Revision, G/SPS/19/Rev.2) (23 July 2004).

WTO, Committee on Sanitary and Phytosanitary Measures. 'Guidelines to Further the Practical Implementation of Article 6 of the Agreement on the Application of Sanitary and Phytosanitary Measures,' (G/SPS/48) (16 May 2008).

WTO, Committee on Sanitary and Phytosanitary Measures. 'Decision by the Committee on Procedure to Enhance Transparency of Special and Differential Treatment in Favour of Developing Country Members,' (G/SPS/33/Rev.1) (18 December 2009).

WTO, Committee on Sanitary and Phytosanitary Measures. 'Decision of the Committee on a Procedure to Encourage and Facilitate the Resolution of Specific Sanitary or Phytosanitary Issues Among Members,' (G/SPS/61) (8 September 2014).

WTO, Committee on Sanitary and Phytosanitary Measures. 'Specific Trade Concerns,' Note by the Secretariat, Revision (G/SPS/GEN/204/Rev.15) (24 February 2015).

WTO, Committee on Technical Barriers to Trade. 'Decisions and Recommendations Adopted by the Committee since 1 January 1995,' (WTO Doc. G/TBT/1 Rev.11) (16 December 2013).

WTO. *World Trade Report 2012: Trade and Public Policy: A Closer Look at Non-Tariff Measures in the 21st Century* (WTO, 2012).

14 Technical Barriers to Trade

SPS Agreement

Learning Objectives	567
1. Introduction: The Role of SPS Agreements	567
2. Scope and Application of the SPS Agreement	567
2.1 Measures to Which SPS Agreement Applies	568
2.2 The Temporal Scope of the SPS Agreement	571
2.3 SPS Agreement and Other WTO Agreements	571
2.3.1 The GATT 1994	571
2.3.2 The TBT Agreement	572
3. Substantive Provisions of the SPS Agreement	573
3.1 Basic Principles	573
3.1.1 The Right to Take SPS Measures	573
3.1.2 'Only to the Extent Necessary'	574
3.1.3 Scientific Basis for SPS Measures	574
3.1.4 No Arbitrary or Unjustifiable Discrimination	578
3.2 International Standards and Harmonisation	579
3.3 Obligation to Assess Risk	581
3.3.1 Risk Assessment	581
3.3.2 Based on Risk Assessment	583
3.3.3 Appropriate Level of Protection	584
3.3.4 'Not More Trade Restrictive Than Required'	586
3.4 The Precautionary Principle and SPS Agreement	587
3.4.1 Where SPS Measures Are Adopted as a Precaution	588
3.4.2 Maintaining Provisional SPM Measures Based on Article 5.7	590
4. Other Substantive Provisions of the SPS Agreement	590
4.1 Recognition of Foreign SPS Policy and Measures	591
4.2 Adaptation of Regional Conditions	591
4.3 Control Inspection and Approval Procedures	593
4.4 Transparency and Notifications	594
4.5 Special and Differential Treatment	595
5. Institutional Provisions of the SPS Agreement	596
5.1 SPS Committee	596
5.2 Dispute Settlement	597
5.2.1 Scientific Experts	597
5.2.2 Standard of Review	598
5.3 Technical Assistance	599
6. Summary	600

DOI: 10.4324/9780367028183-17

Learning Objectives

This chapter aims to help students understand:

1 Technical regulations and standards that help regulate the standard of goods;
2 The role of SPS Agreement; application of SPS Agreement;
3 The objectives and temporal scope of the SPS Agreement; SPS Agreement and GATT Agreement; SPS Agreement and TBT Agreement;
4 The substantive provisions of the SPS Agreement; the right to take SPS measures; scientific basis of SPS measures;
5 International standards and harmonisation; obligation to assess risk; appropriate level of protection; not more trade restrictive than required;
6 The Precautionary Principle and the SPS Agreement; other substantive provisions of the SPS Agreement; and
7 Institutional provisions of the SPS Agreement; dispute settlement; the use of scientific experts; standard of review; and technical assistance.

1. Introduction: The Role of SPS Agreements

As mentioned in chapter 13, where we discussed TBT Agreement, technical regulations and standards help regulate the standard of goods, enhance food safety, *etc.* to establish a common trade language to provide the consumer with the correct information on the standard of the products traded. The SPS Agreement, together with the TBT Agreement, address 'disguised protectionism' arising from product regulation and health measures put in place by Member States. The SPS Agreement seeks to promote regulatory harmonisation by encouraging Member States to align their domestic rules on SPS measures which are based on standards set by the relevant international standard-setting bodies. As mentioned earlier, both SPS and TBT agreements serve as instruments of trade liberalisation by bringing international standards to heterogeneous product standards.[1]

2. Scope and Application of the SPS Agreement

As mentioned earlier, the Agreement on the Application of Sanitary and Phytosanitary Measures (SPS Agreement) seeks to promote regulatory harmonisation by encouraging Member States to align their domestic rules on SPS measures which are based on standards set by the relevant international standard-setting bodies. The aim of the SPS Agreement can be identified as that of balancing the legitimate right of Member States to take health protection measures, with the objective of promoting free trade and preventing protectionism.

The SPS Agreement was originally put forth as part of the Agreement on Agriculture and designed to address measures intended for the protection of human, animal, or plant life or health from certain specified risks. Prior to the Uruguay Round of negotiations, such measures were subject to the general requirements of the Standards Code. During the Uruguay Round, the SPS Agreement was negotiated on the premise that domestic SPS measures based on international norms could not only lower transaction costs but also reduce trade conflicts amongst Member States. However, it has been suggested that serious disagreement between the US and the EU over hormone-treated beef was one of the motivating factors for the SPS Agreement and was aimed at preventing the abuse of sanitary and phytosanitary measures as non-tariff barriers to trade (Wirth, 1994).

As mentioned earlier, the TBT and SPS agreements have a shared origin in the Standards Code and are mutually exclusive in their scope. The SPS Agreement is used (i) to ensure food safety and to prevent the spread of disease among animals and plants, and (ii) as a tool to regulate SPS measures being misused for protectionist purposes as non-tariff barriers. SPS measures introduced by Member States can be through the inspection of products; permission to use only certain additives in food; designation of disease-free areas; determination of maximum levels of pesticide residues; import bans; quarantine requirements; *etc*.

The proliferation of such SPS measures can be attributed to the potential risks contained in food and agricultural products;[2] the growth in imports from developing countries whose domestic food-safety infrastructures are often inadequate; increased affluence and consumer awareness of food-related risks; and increased pressure from the agriculture and food industry lobbies in the face of increased competition due to agricultural trade liberalisation (Prévost and Van den Bossche, 2005). Unlike the TBT Agreement, the SPS Agreement begins with a Preamble. Recommendation 1 of the Preamble reaffirms:

> no Member should be prevented from adopting or enforcing measures necessary to protect human, animal or plant life or health, subject to the requirement that these measures are not applied in a manner which would constitute a means of arbitrary or unjustifiable discrimination between Members where the same conditions prevail or a disguised restriction on international trade.

Recommendation 1 clearly refers to the requirement that SPS measures are not to be applied arbitrarily or in a manner that constitutes unjustifiable discrimination.

2.1 Measures to Which SPS Agreement Applies

The SPS Agreement does not cover all measures for the protection of human, animal, or plant life or health, but only a defined set of measures, to the exclusion of TBT. Article 1.1 of the SPS Agreement identifies the scope and application of the Agreement. Pursuant to Article 1.1, the SPS Agreement applies "to all sanitary and phytosanitary measures which may, directly or indirectly, affect international trade".[3] As noted by the Appellate Body, akin to the TBT Agreement,[4] the SPS Agreement applies to all currently applicable state measures covered by the respective agreement.[5] Annex 1 of the SPS Agreement outlines the type of measures that are regulated by the SPS Agreement as follows:

> Sanitary or phytosanitary measures include all relevant laws, decrees, regulations, requirements and procedures including, *inter alia*, end product criteria; processes and production methods; testing, inspection, certification and approval procedures; quarantine treatments including relevant requirements associated with the transport of animals or plants, or with the materials necessary for their survival during transport; provisions on relevant statistical methods, sampling procedures and methods of risk assessment; and packaging and labelling requirements directly related to food safety.

Further, paragraph 1 of Annex A of the SPS Agreement defines an SPS measure as follows:

Any measure applied:

(a) to protect animal or plant life or health within the territory of the Member from risks arising from the entry, establishment or spread of pests, diseases, disease-carrying organisms or disease-causing organisms;
(b) to protect human or animal life or health within the territory of the Member from risks arising from additives, contaminants, toxins or disease-causing organisms in foods, beverages or feedstuffs;
(c) to protect human life or health within the territory of the Member from risks arising from diseases carried by animals, plants or products thereof, or from the entry, establishment or spread of pests; or
(d) to prevent or limit other damage within the territory of the Member from the entry, establishment or spread of pests.

The Panel in *Australia – Apples* noted that Annex A(1) contains the legal definition for the term SPS measure.[6] Whether a measure can be subjected to the SPS Agreement depends on its purpose or goal. To determine whether a particular measure is an SPS measure, an inquiry will have to be undertaken into its purpose or goal. In *EC – Approval and Marketing of Biotech Products* case, the US, Canada, and Argentina raised a complaint against the EC with regards to measures relating to biotech products (*i.e.*, genetically modified organisms or GMOs), which required the determination of whether the contested measures were 'SPS measures' within the meaning of Annex A(1) of the SPS Agreement, quoted earlier. The Panel in *EC – Approval and Marketing of Biotech Products*, while examining whether various EC's actions constituted an SPS measure that would fall under the SPS Agreement, particularly focusing on the definition of SPS measure set out in Annex A(1), explained that in determining whether a measure is an SPS measure, regard must be had to such elements as the purpose of the measure, its legal form, and its nature and observed as follows:

Annex A(1) indicates that for the purposes of determining whether a particular measure constitutes an "SPS measure" regard must be had to such elements as the purpose of the measure, its legal form and its nature. The purpose element is addressed in Annex A(1) (a) through (d) ("any measure applied to"). The form element is referred to in the second paragraph of Annex A(1) ("laws, decrees, regulations"). Finally, the nature of measures qualifying as SPS measures is also addressed in the second paragraph of Annex A(1) ("requirements and procedures, including, *inter alia*, end product criteria; processes and production methods; testing, inspection, certification and approval procedures; [*etc.*]").[7]

The Panel in *US – Poultry (China)* considered that the first part of Annex A(1) refers to the purpose of the measure while the second part provides a list of the types of SPS measures.[8] As ruled by the Appellate Body in *Australia – Apples*, the fundamental element of the definition of 'SPS measure' as set out in Annex A(1) is that such a measure must be one applied to protect at least one of the listed interests or to prevent or limit specified damage,[9] and further held that the purpose of a measure

must be ascertained not only from the objectives of the measure as expressed by the responding party, but also from the text and structure of the relevant measure, its surrounding regulatory context, and the way in which it is designed and applied.[10]

The Panel in *EC – Approval and Marketing of Biotech Products*, while enumerating the purposes stated in subparagraphs (a)–(d) of Annex A(1) very broadly, found that almost all the objectives of the challenged EC approval legislation, as well as those of the EU Member States' bans, fell within the scope of Annex A(1)(a)–(d).[11] The Panel in *Australia – Apples* had a different reading of how two of the elements, *viz*., form and nature, are reflected in the second paragraph of Annex A(1) from that adopted by the Panel in *EC – Approval and Marketing of Biotech Products*, and went on to rule that the ordinary way to read 'laws, decrees, regulations, requirements and procedures' is as an enumeration of five items with the words 'all relevant' qualifying each one of them, and observed:

> the second paragraph of Annex A(1) sets out elements of the definition of SPS measures by providing examples. In fact, the second paragraph starts with the words "Sanitary and phytosanitary measures include". Thus, the items spelt out in the second paragraph do not form a closed list. This is quite different from the closed list of possible purposes of a covered SPS measure under the first paragraph of Annex A(1), in particular its subparagraphs (a)–(d).
>
> Further, the Panel does not consider that the list of examples in the second paragraph of Annex A(1) provides a clear-cut division between the elements of form and nature, the first three items ("laws, decrees, regulations") corresponding to the form, and the latter two ("requirements and procedures") to the nature of SPS measures. Given the placing of the word "and" between the fourth and fifth items, the ordinary way to read "laws, decrees, regulations, requirements and procedures" is as an enumeration of five items, with the words "all relevant" qualifying each one of them.[12]

The panel in *EC – Approval and Marketing of Biotech Products* disagreed with the EC's argument that Annex A of the SPS Agreement was not intended to cover risks to the environment in general. Instead, the panel interpreted 'other damage' in subparagraph (d) to include not only economic damage or damage to property, but also damage to the environment (other than to the life or health of plants or animals) encompassing adverse effects on biodiversity, population dynamics of species, and biogeochemical cycles.[13] The Panel in *EC – Approval and Marketing of Biotech Products*, while addressing the exclusion of environmental measures *per se* from the scope of application of the SPS Agreement, turned to the 1990 Draft Text on Sanitary and Phytosanitary Measures circulated by the chairperson of the Working Group on Sanitary and Phytosanitary Measures. On consideration of the style used in the draft text, the Panel refrained from offering any views on the argument that the removal of bracketed texts in that instance amounts to dismissal of environmental measures from the scope of the SPS Agreement.[14]

The Panel in *US – Poultry (China)*, while referring to the Panel decision in *EC – Approval and Marketing of Biotech Products*,[15] held that in determining whether an act of a member is an SPS measure within the definition in SPS Annex A(1), regard must be had not just to its wording, legal form, and nature, but in particular to its purpose.[16] In *US – Poultry (China)*, the measure under challenge was one introduced by the US that prohibited the use of funds under the relevant bill to establish or implement a rule allowing Chinese poultry products to be imported into the US. The US had introduced the measure due to the high incidence of H5N1 virus in China. As the measure was clearly aimed at protecting human and animal life and health from risks posed by contaminated poultry products from China, although not normally associated with SPS measures, it led the Panel to conclude that the measure fell within the definition of SPS measure as described in the last sentence of Annex A(1).[17] One is inclined to conclude from the foregoing that once it is established that the measure under challenge is directed at achieving one of the purposes enumerated in Annex A(1)(a)–(d) of the SPS Agreement and is of a type covered by the open, illustrative list in the final paragraph of Annex A(1), it falls within the definition of an 'SPS measure'.

2.2 The Temporal Scope of the SPS Agreement

The temporal scope of the SPS Agreement was decided in the *EC – Hormones* case, where the question regarding the application of SPS Agreement to those measures applied prior to the entry into force of the SPS Agreement arose for consideration. The Appellate Body, while holding that the SPS Agreement applied to pre-1995 SPS measures, to the extent they were in force, observed as follows:

> If the negotiators had wanted to exempt the very large group of SPS measures in existence on 1 January 1995 from the disciplines of provisions as important as Articles 5.1 and 5.5, it appears reasonable to us to expect that they would have said so explicitly. Articles 5.1 and 5.5 do not distinguish between SPS measures adopted before 1 January 1995 and measures adopted since; the relevant implication is that they are intended to be applicable to both.[18]

2.3 SPS Agreement and Other WTO Agreements

Both the GATT 1994 and the TBT Agreement contain measures for the protection of human, animal, or plant life or health, which is akin to the SPS Agreement. The reach of the SPS Agreement is hard to fathom, in many respects (Scott, 2009). In certain instances, determining the consistency of a health measure may require the application of three agreements. In this part of the chapter the relationship of the SPS Agreement, the GATT 1994, and the TBT Agreement are examined.

2.3.1 The GATT 1994

The interpretive note to Annex 1A of the WTO Agreement provides:

> in the event of a conflict between the General Agreement on Tariffs and Trade 1994 and a provision of another agreement in Annex 1A of the Agreement establishing the World Trade Organization, the provision of the other agreement shall prevail to the extent of the conflict.

A conflict may arise where the two agreements in question give rise to 'mutually exclusive obligations'. Unlike the TBT Agreement, no relationship of mutual exclusivity exists between the SPS Agreement and the GATT 1994. As held by the Appellate Body in *Korea – Dairy Products*, where obligations laid down in two agreements are not mutually exclusive, these obligations "are generally cumulative and Members must comply with all of them simultaneously".[19] Although a measure may be subject to the SPS as well as to the GATT Agreement,[20] the relationship between the two are somewhat qualified by Article 2.4 of the SPS Agreement, which states:

> Sanitary or phytosanitary measures which conform to the relevant provisions of this Agreement shall be presumed to be in accordance with the obligations of the Members

under the provisions of GATT 1994 which relate to the use of sanitary or phytosanitary measures, in particular the provisions of Article XX(b).

Article 2.4 provides that measures that conform to the SPS Agreement are presumed to be in accordance with the relevant provisions of the GATT 1994, and more specifically with Article XX(b). Although the nature of this presumption is not further elaborated in the SPS Agreement, the Appellate Body in *EC – Hormones* found the presumption to be rebuttable.[21] Should it transpire that the presumption of conformity with the GATT is rebuttable, it would result in a reversal of the burden of proof in the application of the GATT exception.[22] As noted earlier, the WTO is a 'single undertaking' requiring it to be interpreted as a whole, in such a way to give meaning to all its applicable provisions, 'harmoniously'.

2.3.2 The TBT Agreement

The relationship of the SPS Agreement with the TBT Agreement is different to its relationship with the GATT 1994. SPS measures, similar to the TBT Agreement, take the form of technical regulations, standards, and conformity assessment procedures. The TBT Agreement does not apply to SPS measures as identified in Article 1.5 of the TBT Agreement. The SPS and the TBT agreements give rise to mutually exclusive obligation. However, Article 1.4 of the SPS Agreement states:

> Nothing in this Agreement shall affect the rights of Members under the Agreement on Technical Barriers to Trade with respect to measures not within the scope of this Agreement.

It should be noted that a single measure, or requirement, may constitute an SPS measure and a TBT measure. The Panel in *EC – Approval and Marketing of Biotech Products*, responding to the question posed by the EC, "whether a law, or a requirement contained therein, may, if it meets the applicable conditions, be considered to incorporate an SPS measure as well as a distinct measure which falls to be assessed under a WTO agreement other than the SPS Agreement, such as the TBT Agreement" observed as follows:

> to the extent the requirement in the consolidated law is applied for one of the purposes enumerated in Annex A(1), it may be properly viewed as a measure which falls to be assessed under the SPS Agreement; to the extent it is applied for a purpose which is not covered by Annex A(1), it may be viewed as a separate measure which falls to be assessed under a WTO agreement other than the SPS Agreement. It is important to stress, however, that our view is premised on the circumstance that the requirement at issue could be split up into two separate requirements which would be identical to the requirement at issue, and which would have an autonomous *raison d'être*, *i.e.*, a different purpose which would provide an independent basis for imposing the requirement.
>
> ... neither the WTO Agreement nor WTO jurisprudence establishes that a requirement meeting the condition referred to in the previous paragraph may not be deemed to embody two, if not more, distinct measures which fall to be assessed under different WTO agreements. We note that Annex A(1) of the SPS Agreement, which defines the term "SPS measure", refers to "[a]ny measure" and to "requirements". But these references do not imply that a requirement cannot be considered to embody an SPS measure as well as a non-SPS measure.[23]

In short, there is nothing in Article 1.5 of the TBT Agreement to preclude a scenario as envisaged earlier.

3. Substantive Provisions of the SPS Agreement

This section of the chapter discusses the substantive provisions contained in Article 2 of the SPS Agreement, the non-discrimination obligation (Articles 2.3 and 5.5), obligations relating to harmonisation (Article 3), obligations relating to risk assessment (Article 5), provisional SPS measures and precautionary principle (Article 5.7, *etc.*), recognition of equivalence (Article 4), transparency (Article 7), and differential treatment of developing country Member States (Article 14).

3.1 Basic Principles

Article 2 of the SPS Agreement outlines the basic rights and obligations arising under the Agreement that permit the Member States to adopt SPS measures for protecting human, animal, or plant life or health while complying with the requirements set out in Articles 3 to 6 of the agreement. As observed by the Panel in in *US – Poultry (China)*, the 'overarching and encompassing' title of Article 2 being 'Basic Rights and Obligations' leads one to the conclusion that the obligations in Article 2 are to inform all of the SPS Agreement.[24] Article 2.1 of the SPS Agreement, which reflects the underlying aim of the SPS Agreement, reads as follows:

> Members have the right to take sanitary and phytosanitary measures necessary for the protection of human, animal or plant life or health, provided that such measures are not inconsistent with the provisions of this Agreement.

The basic principles contained under Article 2 can be identified as (i) the sovereign right of Member States to take SPS measures (Article 2.1); (ii) the obligation to apply only SPS measures necessary to protect human, animal, or plant life or health (necessity requirement – Article 2.2); (iii) the obligation to apply only SPS measures based on scientific principles and on sufficient scientific evidence (scientific disciplines – Article 2.2); and (iv) the obligation not to adopt or maintain SPS measures that arbitrarily or unjustifiably discriminate or constitute a disguised restriction on trade ('non-discrimination' requirement – Article 2.3).

3.1.1 The Right to Take SPS Measures

The right to adopt SPS measures by a Member State in order to protect human, animal, or plant life or health is a sovereign right and is encapsulated in Article 2.1. Yet, this right is limited and subject to the various obligations indicated in Articles 2.2 and 2.3 of the SPS Agreement. The right of Member States to adopt SPS measures differs significantly from the right of Member States to adopt health measures under GATT rules, as the latter require Member States to justify such measures under the exceptions found in Article XX(b) of the GATT 1994. The burden of proving that a health measure under Article XX(b) of the GATT 1994 squarely rests on the Member State invoking the provision, as it constitutes a quantitative restriction. When a measure under the SPS Agreement is challenged, the burden of proof is on the complaining Member State to demonstrate that the measure under challenge is inconsistent with the provisions of the SPS Agreement.

3.1.2 'Only to the Extent Necessary'

Article 2.2 of the SPS Agreement limits the application of SPS measures by Member States by requiring:

> any sanitary or phytosanitary measure is applied only to the extent necessary to protect human, animal or plant life or health.

As observed by the Appellate Body in *EC – Hormones*, Article 2.2 of the SPS Agreement is a reflection of the "delicate and carefully negotiated balance . . . between the shared, but sometimes competing, interests of promoting international trade and of protecting the life and health of human beings"[25] that underpins and informs the whole SPS Agreement. The Panel in *EC – Approval and Marketing of Biotech Products* listed the requirements within Article 2.2 of the SPS Agreement as follows:

> It is apparent from the text of Article 2.2 that this provision contains three separate requirements: (i) the requirement that SPS measures be applied only to the extent necessary to protect human, animal or plant life or health; (ii) the requirement that SPS measures be based on scientific principles; and (iii) the requirement that SPS measures not be maintained without sufficient scientific evidence.[26]

While there is little or no WTO jurisprudence on the necessity requirement arising under Article 2.2, the more specific requirement 'necessity test' contained in Article 5.6 of the SPS Agreement has been subject to WTO judicial interpretation. The Appellate Body in *Australia – Apples* has suggested that "Article 2.2 and Article 5.6 should be constantly read together".[27] The jurisprudential authority on Article 5.6 suggests that a violation of obligations arising from Article 5.6 may imply a violation of obligations arising from Article 2.2.[28] The panel in *India – Agricultural Products* observed, "a finding that a measure is inconsistent with Article 5.6 may lead to a presumption that the same measure is inconsistent with the obligation in Article 2.2 to ensure that an SPS measure is applied only to the extent necessary to protect human, animal or plant life or health".[29] The Panel went on to rule that the measures introduced by India were inconsistent with Article 5.6 of the SPS Agreement and consequentially inconsistent with Article 2.2 of the SPS Agreement as they were applied beyond the extent necessary to protect human and animal life or health.[30]

3.1.3 Scientific Basis for SPS Measures

The second part of Article 2.2 of the SPS Agreement requires that SPS measures be based on scientific principles and may not be maintained without sufficient scientific evidence, except as provided under Article 5.7. the relevant part of Article 2.2 reads as follows:

> any sanitary or phytosanitary measure . . . is based on scientific principles and is not maintained without sufficient scientific evidence, except as provided for in paragraph 7 of Article 5.

The Panel in *US – Poultry (China)* opined that to maintain a measure with sufficient scientific evidence, the scientific evidence must bear a rational relationship to the measure, be sufficient to demonstrate the extent of the risk which the measure is supposed to address, and be of the kind necessary for a risk assessment.[31] The SPS Agreement introduces scientific principles as the basis against which an SPS measure is to be tested for its consistency with the provisions of the Agreement. Article 5.1 of the SPS Agreement adds to this requirement by stating that SPS measures are to be based on a risk assessment. As observed by the Appellate Body in *EC – Hormones*,

> The requirements of a risk assessment under Article 5.1, as well as of "sufficient scientific evidence" under Article 2.2, are essential for the maintenance of the delicate and carefully negotiated balance in the SPS Agreement between the shared, but sometimes competing, interests of promoting international trade and of protecting the life and health of human beings.[32]

The meaning of the term 'scientific' and 'evidence' as occurring in Article 2.2 was first considered by the Panel in *Japan – Apples*. The Panel explained the significance of the nature of the evidence that ought to be considered when a member is making a determination of what measure to put in place, and observed as follows:

> We consider that . . . we must give full meaning to the term "scientific" and conclude that, in the context of Article 2.2, the evidence to be considered should be evidence gathered through scientific methods, excluding by the same token information not acquired through a scientific method. We further note that scientific evidence may include evidence that a particular risk may occur . . . as well as evidence that a particular requirement may reduce or eliminate that risk . . .
>
> Likewise, the use of the term "evidence" must also be given full significance. Negotiators could have used the term "information", as in Article 5.7, if they considered that any material could be used. By using the term "scientific evidence", Article 2.2 excludes in essence not only insufficiently substantiated information, but also such things as a non-demonstrated hypothesis.
>
> . . .
>
> requiring "scientific evidence" does not limit the field of scientific evidence available to Members to support their measures. "Direct" or "indirect" evidence may be equally considered. The only difference is not one of scientific quality, but one of probative value within the legal meaning of the term, since it is obvious that evidence which does not directly prove a fact might not have as much weight as evidence directly proving it, if it is available.[33]

In *Japan – Agricultural Products II*, the meaning of the term 'sufficient' as occurring in Article 2.2 was considered. The Appellate Body, while observing that 'sufficiency' requires the existence of a sufficient or adequate relationship between two elements between the SPS measure concerned and the scientific evidence,[34] noted that the existence of the word 'sufficient' or the phrase 'maintained without sufficient scientific evidence' in Article 2.2 includes Articles 5.1, 3.3, and 5.7 of the SPS Agreement.[35] On the notion of 'patent insufficiency', the Appellate Body observed as follows:

> We do not agree with Japan's proposition that direct application of Article 2.2 of the SPS Agreement should be limited to situations in which the scientific evidence is "patently" insufficient, and that the issue raised in this dispute should have been dealt with under Article 5.1 of the SPS Agreement. There is nothing in the text of either Articles 2.2 or

5.1, or any other provision of the SPS Agreement, that requires or sanctions such limitation of the scope of Article 2.2.[36]

The Appellate Body in *Japan – Agricultural Products II* established that Article 2.2 requires a 'rational or objective relationship between' the SPS measure and the scientific evidence, *i.e.*, a relationship that is to be determined on a case-by-case basis:

> we agree with the Panel that the obligation in Article 2.2 that an SPS measure not be maintained without sufficient scientific evidence requires that there be a rational or objective relationship between the SPS measure and the scientific evidence. Whether there is a rational relationship between an SPS measure and the scientific evidence is to be determined on a case-by-case basis and will depend upon the particular circumstances of the case, including the characteristics of the measure at issue and the quality and quantity of the scientific evidence.[37]

The Appellate Body in *EC – Hormones* observed that in establishing if sufficient scientific evidence exists, panels ought to bear in mind that

> responsible, representative governments commonly act from perspectives of prudence and precaution where risks of irreversible, *e.g.*, life-terminating, damage to human health are concerned.[38]

In a finding upheld by the Appellate Body, the Panel in *Japan – Apples* ruled that all the individual requirements contained in the measure should be treated cumulatively as the phytosanitary measure at issue in the case, and that a measure as a whole should be considered to be maintained 'without sufficient scientific evidence' if one or more of its elements are not justified by the relevant scientific evidence addressing the risk at issue.[39] Where the risk to life or health is more serious, the 'sufficient scientific evidence' requirement is less stringent. Thus, introducing a 'proportionality criterion' into Article 2.2 of the SPS Agreement, the Panel in *Japan – Apples* ruled that the risk of transmission of fire blight through the importation of apple fruit was negligible,[40] and found that there was a violation of Article 2.2, as the measure at issue was clearly disproportionate to the risk perceived.[41] The Appellate Body in *India – Agricultural Products* held that assessing whether a rational and objective relationship exists between the SPS measure and the scientific evidence involves "an inquiry into evidence adduced by the parties regarding the particular risks that such measure is said to protect against, and to whom the risk is posed (*e.g.*, humans, animals, plants and/or the environment)".[42]

According to Article 2.2 of the SPS Agreement, SPS measures must not be maintained without sufficient scientific evidence, except as provided for under Article 5.7. Where Member States are required to introduce measures to prevent a possible risk, and insufficient scientific evidence exists on the likelihood of the risk, Article 2.2 expressly refers to Article 5.7, which permits for provisional SPS measures to be taken. In *Japan – Agricultural Products II*, the Appellate Body addressed the relationship between the requirement of sufficient scientific evidence under Article 2.2 and Article 5.7 and considered that Article 5.7 operates as a qualified exemption from the obligation under Article 2.2

> [I]t is clear that Article 5.7 of the SPS Agreement, to which Article 2.2 explicitly refers, is part of the context of the latter provision and should be considered in the

interpretation of the obligation not to maintain an SPS measure without sufficient scientific evidence. Article 5.7 allows Members to adopt provisional SPS measures "[i]n cases where relevant scientific evidence is insufficient" and certain other requirements are fulfilled. Article 5.7 operates as a qualified exemption from the obligation under Article 2.2 not to maintain SPS measures without sufficient scientific evidence. An overly broad and flexible interpretation of that obligation would render Article 5.7 meaningless.[43]

However, the Panel in *EC – Approval and Marketing of Biotech Products* applied the Appellate Body's logic from *EC – Tariff Preferences and EC – Hormones*, where the Appellate Body considered the relationship between Articles 3.1 and 3.3 of the SPS Agreement, to rule that Article 5.7 establishes an autonomous right of the importing Member as follows:

> Evaluating the relationship between Article 2.2 and Article 5.7 in the light of the general test provided by the Appellate Body in *EC – Tariff Preferences*, we consider that the relationship in question is one where "one provision [Article 5.7] permits, in certain circumstances, behaviour [namely, the provisional adoption of SPS measures in cases where scientific evidence is insufficient on the basis of available pertinent information] that would otherwise be inconsistent with an obligation in another provision [namely, the obligation in Article 2.2 not to maintain SPS measure without sufficient scientific evidence], [where] one of the two provisions [namely, Article 2.2] refers to the other provision, [and] where one of the provisions [namely, Article 2.2, and in particular the clause 'except as provided for in paragraph 7 of Article 5'] suggests that the obligation [in Article 2.2 not to maintain SPS measure without sufficient scientific evidence] is not applicable" to measures falling within the scope of Article 5.7.
>
> Thus, we find the general test provided by the Appellate Body in *EC – Tariff Preferences* to be applicable, and application of that test leads us to the conclusion that Article 5.7 should be characterized as a right and not an exception from a general obligation under Article 2.2. In other words, we consider that in the same way that "Article 3.1 of the SPS Agreement . . . excludes from its scope of application the kinds of situations covered by Article 3.3 of that Agreement", Article 2.2 excludes from its scope of application the kinds of situations covered by Article 5.7.[44]

In order to successfully claim that an SPS measure is inconsistent with Article 2.2, a complaining Member State may also have to show that the measure does not fall under Article 5.7. The Appellate Body in *US/Canada – Continued Suspension* addressed the relationship between Articles 2.2, 5.1, and 5.7 of the SPS Agreement. The Appellate Body emphasised the requirement common to these articles, that the application of one or another provision depends on the availability of sufficient scientific evidence and ruled that where the "relevant scientific evidence is insufficient to perform a risk assessment, a WTO Member may take a provisional SPS measure on the basis provided in Article 5.7, but that Member must meet the obligations set out in that provision".[45]

The Appellate Body has consistently held that a violation of Articles 5.1 and 5.2 of the SPS Agreement can be presumed to imply a violation of Article 2.2, but the reverse does not hold true, *i.e.*, a violation of Article 2.2 does not imply a violation of Articles 5.1 and 5.2.[46] The Appellate Body in *India – Agricultural Products* stressed that the presumption of inconsistency with Article 2.2 of an SPS measure that violates Articles 5.1 and 5.2 is rebuttable, and observed:

establishing that there exists a rational or objective relationship between the SPS measure and the scientific evidence for purposes of Article 2.2 would, in most cases, be difficult without a Member demonstrating that such a measure is based on an assessment of the risks, as appropriate to the circumstances.[47]

It can be said the in the majority of the cases, a measure that violates Articles 5.1 and 5.2 will also be in violation of Article 2.2.

3.1.4 No Arbitrary or Unjustifiable Discrimination

Article 2.3 of the SPS Agreement encapsulates the fundamental GATT non-discrimination obligations of MF and NT obligations. Article 2.3 reads as follows:

> Members shall ensure that their sanitary and phytosanitary measures do not arbitrarily or unjustifiably discriminate between Members where identical or similar conditions prevail, including between their own territory and that of other Members. Sanitary and phytosanitary measures shall not be applied in a manner which would constitute a disguised restriction on international trade.

In *India – Agricultural Products*, the Panel observed that the language of Article 2.3 of the SPS Agreement bore similarities to that of the *Chapeau* of Article XX of the GATT 1994.[48] The Panel in *Australia – Salmon (Article 21.5 – Canada)* noted that three elements, cumulative in nature, are necessary to find a violation of the first sentence of Article 2.3, which are as follows: (i) the measure discriminates between the territories of Members State other than the Member State imposing the measure, or between the territory of the Member State imposing the measure and that of another Member State; (ii) the discrimination is arbitrary or unjustifiable; and (iii) identical or similar conditions prevail in the territory of the Member States compared.[49] In *India – Agricultural Products*, the Appellate Body further noted, "the three elements identified in the first sentence of Article 2.3 inform each other, such that the analysis of each element cannot be undertaken in strict isolation from the analysis of the other two elements".[50]

While the Panel in *Australia – Salmon (Article 21.5 – Canada)* found no violation of Article 2.3, it also noted that Article 2.3 prohibits not only discrimination of similar products, but also between different products,[51] which differs significantly from the non-discrimination rules of Articles I and III of the GATT 1994, and Article 2.1 of the TBT Agreement that apply only to 'like' or 'directly competitive or substitutable' products. In *India – Agricultural Products*, the Appellate Body found that the burden of demonstrating a *prima facie* case of inconsistency with Article 2.3, first sentence, rests on the complainant raising such a claim. In that regard, the Appellate Body distinguished between Article XX of the GATT 1994 and Article 2.3, first sentence, which "sets out an obligation and is not expressed in the form of an exception".[52]

As regards the formulation of the legal test in Article 2.3, the Appellate Body in *Australia – Salmon* opined that the provision

> takes up obligations similar to those arising under Article I:1 and Article III:4 of the GATT 1994 and incorporates part of the *Chapeau* to Article XX of the GATT 1994. Its fundamental importance in the context of the SPS Agreement is reflected in the first paragraph of the preamble of the SPS Agreement.[53]

The Panel in *US – Poultry (China)* found that discrimination under Article 2.3 could stem from both substantive SPS measures and procedural or information requirements, because the text of Article 2.3 obligates Member States to ensure non-discrimination in 'their SPS measures' without making any distinction between possible types of SPS measures.[54]

3.2 International Standards and Harmonisation[55]

The wide variety of SPS measures which the exporters face in their export market require them to adapt their products to different SPS measures. While these SPS measures reflect consumer preferences, industry interests, *etc.* in the relevant market, they also have a negative effect on market access. Article 3 of the SPS Agreement deals with harmonisation of SPS measures, by requiring the Member States to 'base' their SPS measures 'on international standards, guidelines or recommendations', unless otherwise provided for in the SPS Agreement.[56] In this regard the SPS Agreement and the TBT Agreement are unique amongst WTO agreements, as they require Member States to harmonise their domestic standards to international standards, as well as recognise foreign SPS policy and measures and TBT technical regulations of other Member States. The Appellate Body in *EC – Hormones* held that the object and purpose of Article 3 was to promote the harmonisation of national SPS measures:

> In generalized terms, the object and purpose of Article 3 is to promote the harmonization of the SPS measures of Members on as wide a basis as possible, while recognizing and safeguarding, at the same time, the right and duty of Members to protect the life and health of their people. The ultimate goal of the harmonization of SPS measures is to prevent the use of such measures for arbitrary or unjustifiable discrimination between Members or as a disguised restriction on international trade, without preventing Members from adopting or enforcing measures which are both "necessary to protect" human life or health and "based on scientific principles", and without requiring them to change their appropriate level of protection.[57]

The Appellate Body in *US/Canada – Continued Suspension* recalled the harmonisation objective of the SPS Agreement in the Preamble as furthering the use of harmonised SPS measures between Member States, on the basis of international standards, guidelines, and recommendations developed by the relevant international organisations.[58] The Appellate Body further elaborated that this objective identified in the Preamble is reflected in Article 3 of the SPS Agreement, which encourages the harmonisation of SPS measures on the basis of international standards, while at the same time recognising the WTO Member State's right to determine their appropriate level of protection, subject to Article 3.2 of the Agreement.[59] Due to the various exceptions contained in Article 3 of the SPS Agreement, the Appellate Body tends to leave the binding language of SPS Article 3.1 largely unmentioned, and speaks of 'encouragement of harmonization'.[60]

Pursuant to Article 3.4 and Annex A(3) of the SPS Agreement, three standard-setting bodies are currently recognised by the SPS Agreement as being authoritative, which are (a) the Codex Alimentarius Commission (Codex) for food safety measures,[61] (b) the International Office of Epizootics (OIE) for animal health and zoonoses (now named the World Organisation for Animal Health), and (c) the International Plant Protection Convention Secretariat (IPPC) for plant health.[62] In terms of basing their domestic standards on international standards, Article 3 of the SPS Agreement provides the Member States with three options, *viz.*, (i) base their domestic SPS measures on international standards following Article 3.1; (ii) adapt their domestic SPS measures to international standards following Article 3.2; or (iii) impose SPS measures resulting in a higher level of protection than would be achieved by the relevant international standard in terms of Article 3.3.

Pursuant to Article 3.1, Member States are obliged to base their domestic SPS measures on international standards where they exist, as wide as possible, except as provided for in Article 3.3. The Appellate Body in *US/Canada – Continued Suspension* specified that the 'international standards, guidelines and recommendations' considered in Article 3.1 and 3.2 of the SPS Agreement emphasises the Codex Alimentarius as the relevant standardisation body in matters of food safety.[63] The Appellate Body in *EC – Hormones* observed that 'based on' is a looser standard than 'conform to', that a measure 'based on' international standard is 'founded on' international standard.[64]

In *US – Animals*, the Panel further clarified that a panel's task under Article 3.1 is to determine whether the challenged measures are 'founded' or 'built' upon or 'supported by' the relevant standards, guidelines, or recommendations, such that they serve as a principal constituent or fundamental principle of the measures under challenge.[65] According to the Panel, the term 'based on' "does not require the wholesale adoption of the international standard, guideline or recommendation into the measure of the importing Member" as "this would wipe out any distinction between the scope of coverage of Articles 3.1 and 3.2".[66] The Panel in *India – Agricultural Products* considered if the measures introduced by India prohibiting the import of poultry from countries reporting avian influenza (bird flu) were 'based on' the relevant international standard set out in the Terrestrial Code of the World Organisation for Animal Health (OIE). Noting that the OIE Code did not envisage import prohibition,[67] the Panel concluded that the measures at issue departed from the OIE Code and were therefore not 'based on' the relevant international standard under Article 3.1 of the SPS Agreement.[68]

Under Article 3.2 of the SPS Agreement, SPS measures 'conforming to' international standards 'shall be deemed to be necessary to protect human, animal or plant life or health' and 'presumed to be consistent with' the SPS Agreement and the GATT 1994. The use of the term 'conforming' to indicates that the requirement is more stringent than 'based on' and means that such SPDS measures would embody the international standard completely.[69] The Appellate Body in *US/Canada – Continued Suspension* observed:

> International standards are given a prominent role under the SPS Agreement, particularly in furthering the objective of promoting the harmonization of sanitary and phytosanitary standards between WTO Members. This is to be achieved by encouraging WTO Members to base their SPS measures on international standards, guidelines or recommendations, where they exist. There is a rebuttable presumption that SPS measures that conform to international standards, guidelines or recommendations are "necessary to protect human, animal or plant life or health, and . . . [are] consistent with the relevant provisions of this Agreement and of GATT 1994".[70]

The third option available to Member States under Article 3.3 for aligning with international standards is to impose SPS measures resulting in a higher level of protection than would be achieved by the relevant international standard in terms of Article 3.3, provided there is a scientific justification. In this regard, the Appellate Body in *EC – Hormones* held as follows:

Article 3.3 recognizes the autonomous right of a Member to establish such higher level of protection, provided that that Member complies with certain requirements in promulgating SPS measures to achieve that level.

...

[t]his right of a Member to establish its own level of sanitary protection under Article 3.3 of the SPS Agreement is an autonomous right and not an "exception" from a "general obligation" under Article 3.1.[71]

The Appellate Body in *EC – Hormones* also ruled that the right of a Member State to define its appropriate level of protection is not an absolute or unqualified right.[72] In order to justify such deviation from international standards, pursuant to Article 3.3, (i) a Member State must demonstrate a scientific justification for the SPS measure (defined in the footnote as "a scientific justification if, on the basis of an examination and evaluation of available scientific information in conformity with the relevant provisions of this Agreement") or (ii) the measure introduced must be a result of the level of protection chosen by the Member in accordance with Articles 5.1–5.8 of the SPS Agreement. The Appellate Body in *US/Canada – Continued Suspension* observed that the right of a Member State to adopt an SPS measure under Article 3.3 that results in a higher level of protection "is qualified in that the SPS measure must comply with the other requirements of the SPS Agreement, including the requirement to perform a risk assessment".[73] In principle, Article 3.3 envisages a 'risk assessment' under Article 5.1 to justify deviation from international standards and establish a higher level of protection.

3.3 Obligation to Assess Risk

Article 5.1 of the SPS Agreement necessitates that SPS measures be based on a risk assessment, as appropriate to the circumstances, and Article 5.2 requires that the risk assessment take into account the available scientific evidence. Article 5.1 reads as follows:

Members shall ensure that their sanitary or phytosanitary measures are based on an assessment, as appropriate to the circumstances, of the risks to human, animal or plant life or health, taking into account risk assessment techniques developed by the relevant international organizations.

3.3.1 Risk Assessment

The panel in *EC – Approval and Marketing of Biotech Products* noted that two distinct issues must be addressed to determine whether there is a violation of Article 5.1 of the SPS agreements, *viz.*, (i) whether there is a 'risk assessment' within the meaning of the SPS Agreement and (ii) whether the SPS measure at issue is 'based on' this risk assessment.[74] Although not defined directly in the SPS Agreement, risk is addressed indirectly through the characterisation of 'risk assessment' in the Agreement. The concept of risk assessment is laid out in Annex A(4) of the SPS Agreement as follows:

The evaluation of the likelihood of entry, establishment or spread of a pest or disease within the territory of an importing Member according to the sanitary or phytosanitary measures which might be applied, and of the associated potential biological and economic consequences; or the evaluation of the potential for adverse effects on human or animal health arising from the presence of additives, contaminants, toxins or disease-causing organisms in food, beverages or feedstuffs.

The two types of risk assessment contemplated in Annex A(4) are (a) evaluation of risk associated with pests or diseases and (b) evaluation of risk to human or animal health, which are food-borne arising the from the presence of specified substances in food, beverages, or feedstuffs. As laid down by the Appellate Body in *Australia – Salmon*, the first of the risk assessment is aimed at establishing the spread of a disease, and the associated potential biological and economic consequences, and must comprise three elements, *viz*., (i) identify the disease (or pests) whose entry, establishment, or spread a Member State wants to prevent within its territory, as well as the potential biological and economic consequences associated with the entry, establishment, or spread of such diseases (or pests); (ii) evaluate the likelihood of entry, establishment, or spread of these diseases (or pests), as well as the associated biological and economic consequences; and (iii) evaluate the likelihood of entry, establishment, or spread of these diseases (or pests) according to the SPS measures that might be applied.[75]

As regards the second type of risk assessment, which is associated with food-borne risk, the steps involved are (i) identify the adverse effects on human or animal health (if any) arising from the additive, contaminant, toxin, or disease-causing organism in food/beverages/feedstuffs and, if such adverse health effects exist, (ii) evaluate the potential for such adverse effects to occur.[76] There is a less strict assessment criteria when dealing with risks to human health, *viz*., from food safety issues, than where risks are related to animals or plant pests or diseases (Van den Bossche and Zdouc, 2017). Some general observations that can be made following from the Appellate Body jurisprudence in this regard are that a risk assessment (i) must demonstrate proof of an actual risk, not a mere theoretical speculation;[77] (ii) does not require the risk assessed to be quantified numerically,[78] and may be expressed quantitatively or qualitatively; and (iii) may go beyond controlled laboratory conditions and take account of the actual potential for adverse effects in the "real world where people live and work and die".[79] The Appellate Body has also noted that the risk must be specific to the particular type of risk at issue in the case and not merely show a general risk of harm.[80]

Importantly, pursuant to Article 5.1 of the SPS Agreement, Member States are not obliged to carry out their own risk assessments, but can instead rely on risk assessments carried out by other Member States or an international organisation.[81] The phrase "taking into account risk assessment techniques developed by the relevant international organisations" occurring in Article 5.1 does not impose a condition that a risk assessment must conform to such techniques, or mean that compliance with such techniques alone suffices to show that the risk assessment is consistent with the requirements under the SPS Agreement.[82] The requirement that SPS measures are maintained with sufficient scientific evidence necessitates the use of any new development or evolution of scientific evidence since the completion of the risk assessment, as "this may be an indication that the risk assessment should be reviewed or a new assessment undertaken".[83]

Articles 5.2 and 5.3 detail the conduct of the risk assessment. Article 5.2 of the SPS Agreement lists the factors – both scientific and technical – that Member States are required to consider when assessing risks. The relevant part of Article 5.2 reads as follows:

> Members shall take into account available scientific evidence; relevant processes and production methods; relevant inspection, sampling and testing methods; prevalence of

specific diseases or pests; existence of pest- or disease-free areas; relevant ecological and environmental conditions; and quarantine or other treatment.

Pursuant to Article 5.3, Member States, while assessing the risk concerning animal and plant life or health, are required to take into account the following factors, *viz.*, (i) the potential damage in terms of loss of production or sales in the event of the entry; (ii) the costs of control or eradication in the territory of the importing Member State; and (iii) the relative cost-effectiveness of alternative approaches to limiting risks.

The Panel in *Australia – Salmon* noted that Articles 5.2 and 5.3 only qualify the way in which a risk assessment has to be carried out, not the substantive obligation to base a sanitary measure on a risk assessment.[84] The Appellate Body in *Australia – Apples* observed that Article 5.2 requires a risk assessor to take into account the available scientific evidence, together with other factors. According to the Appellate Body, whether a risk assessor has taken into account the available scientific evidence in accordance with Article 5.2 of the SPS Agreement and whether its risk assessment is a proper risk assessment within the meaning of Article 5.1 and Annex A(4) "must be determined by assessing the relationship between the conclusions of the risk assessor and the relevant available scientific evidence".[85] The Appellate Body in *EC – Hormones* held, "there is nothing to indicate that the listing of factors that may be taken into account in a risk assessment of Article 5.2 was intended to be a closed list".[86] The Appellate Body in *US/Canada – Continued Suspension* observed:

> Where a WTO Member has taken such risks into account, they must be considered by a panel reviewing that Member's risk assessment. Any suggestion that such risks cannot form part of a risk assessment would constitute legal error.[87]

Noting that the risk assessment cannot be entirely isolated from the appropriate level of protection, the Appellate Body in *US/Canada – Continued Suspension* observed as follows:

> The risk assessment cannot be entirely isolated from the appropriate level of protection. There may be circumstances in which the appropriate level of protection chosen by a Member affects the scope or method of the risk assessment. This may be the case where a WTO Member decides not to adopt an SPS measure based on an international standard because it seeks to achieve a higher level of protection. In such a situation, the fact that the WTO Member has chosen to set a higher level of protection may require it to perform certain research as part of its risk assessment that is different from the parameters considered and the research carried out in the risk assessment underlying the international standard.[88]

3.3.2 Based on Risk Assessment

Pursuant to Article 5.1 of the SPS Agreement, SPS measures are to be 'based on' a risk assessment. The Appellate Body in *EC – Hormones* ruled that for an SPS measure to be 'based on' a risk assessment, there must be a 'rational relationship' between the measure and the risk assessment, and the risk assessment must 'reasonably support' the measure.[89] The Panel in *EC – Approval and Marketing of Biotech Products* addressed the question of whether an SPS measure could be considered 'based on' a risk assessment if it reflects a divergent opinion expressed in the risk assessment. The Appellate Body in *EC – Hormones* concluded that in certain circumstances, an SPS measure that reflects a divergent opinion from the risk assessment could still be considered to be 'based on' that risk assessment, and observed as follows:

> Where a given risk assessment sets out a divergent opinion and this opinion comes from qualified and respected sources, it can be reasonably said that an SPS measure which reflects the divergent opinion is "based on" the risk assessment in question inasmuch as the divergent opinion is expressed in that risk assessment. In contrast, where a given risk assessment sets out a single opinion, it cannot be reasonably said that an SPS measure is "based on" that risk assessment if the relevant SPS measure reflects a divergent opinion which is not expressed in the risk assessment in question.

In *US/Canada – Continued Suspension*, the Appellate Body confirmed that the "scientific basis need not reflect the majority view within the scientific community but may reflect divergent or minority views".[90] In *Australia – Apples*, the Appellate Body expressed the view that, if a risk assessor reaches certain conclusions based on its expert judgment, having determined that there is a certain degree of scientific uncertainty, this does not preclude a panel from assessing whether those conclusions are objective and coherent and have a sufficient basis in the available scientific evidence.[91]

3.3.3 Appropriate Level of Protection

In contrast to risk assessment, risk management is the policy-based process of determining the level of protection a country wants to ensure within its territory, and accordingly choosing the measure that will be used to achieve that level of protection envisaged. Risk management takes into account both the scientific results of the risk assessment and other considerations relating to societal values such as consumer preferences, industry interests, relative costs, *etc*. Risk management involves a decision on the 'appropriate level of protection', which is defined in Annex A(5) of the SPS Agreement as follows:

> The level of protection deemed appropriate by the Member establishing a sanitary or phytosanitary measure to protect human, animal or plant life or health within its territory.

In *Australia – Salmon*, the Appellate Body observed, "determination of the level of protection . . . logically precedes and is separate from the establishment or maintenance of the SPS measure",[92] which is but a tool used to implement the chosen policy.[93] It is the prerogative of the Member State seeking to impose the SPS measure to choose the level of protection of human, animal, or plant life or health it will ensure in its territory.[94] The Appellate Body in *Australia – Salmon* noted that a Member State first defines the appropriate level of protection it seeks to apply within its territory, and then chooses the instrument that will be used to achieve the level sought:

> It can be deduced from the provisions of the SPS Agreement that the determination by a Member of the "appropriate level of protection" logically precedes the establishment or decision on maintenance of an "SPS measure". The provisions of the SPS Agreement also clarify the correlation between the "appropriate level of protection" and the "SPS measure".[95]

Articles 5.4 and 5.5 of the SPS Agreement deal with the parameters for the appropriate level of protection. Article 5.4 provides:

Members should, when determining the appropriate level of sanitary or phytosanitary protection, take into account the objective of minimizing negative trade effects.

The obligation under Article 5.4 of the SPS Agreement is to take into account the objective of minimising negative trade effects, while 'determining the appropriate level' of SPS protection. Article 5.5 deals with the appropriate level of protection, and provides in the relevant part as follows:

With the objective of achieving consistency in the application of the concept of appropriate level of sanitary or phytosanitary protection against risks to human life or health, or to animal and plant life or health, each Member shall avoid arbitrary or unjustifiable distinctions in the levels it considers to be appropriate in different situations, if such distinctions result in discrimination or a disguised restriction on international trade.

The Appellate Body in *EC – Hormones* found that three elements must be demonstrated to establish an inconsistency with Article 5.5 of the SPS Agreement:

The first element is that the Member imposing the disputed measure complained of has adopted its own appropriate levels of sanitary protection against risks to human life or health in several different situations. The second element to be shown is that those levels of protection exhibit arbitrary or unjustifiable differences ("distinctions" in the language of Article 5.5) in their treatment of different situations. The last element requires that the arbitrary or unjustifiable differences result in discrimination or a disguised restriction of international trade. We understand the last element to be referring to the measure embodying or implementing a particular level of protection as resulting, in its application, in discrimination, or a disguised restriction on international trade.[96]

The Appellate Body in *EC – Hormones* also observed that the three elements (three-tier test), are cumulative in nature, *i.e.*, all of the elements must be demonstrated to be present if a claim of violation of Article 5.5 is to be sustained. Further, the Appellate Body emphasised that the third element should be demonstrated positively and independently of the second element and observed, the "implementing measure must be shown to be applied in such a manner as to result in discrimination or a disguised restriction on international trade".[97] The Panel in *Australia – Salmon (Article 21.5 – Canada)* found that Australia had not violated Article 5.5 because neither the second nor the third element of Article 5.5 were met.[98]

In *EC – Hormones*, the Appellate Body ruled that to perform the test of 'different situations' referred to in Article 5.5 of the SPS Agreement (as the first element of the three-tier test), comparability must be established across situations, and they must have some common element or elements.[99] In *Australia – Salmon*, the Appellate Body upholding the Panel's finding ruled:

situations can be compared under Article 5.5 if these situations involve either a risk of entry, establishment or spread of the same or a similar disease, or a risk of the same or similar "associated potential biological and economic consequences".[100]

The second element of the three-tier test under Article 5.5 relates to 'arbitrary and unjustifiable distinctions', *i.e.*, determining whether the Member State concerned has set different levels of protection in different situations, and if these arbitrary or unjustifiable differences lead to discrimination or disguised restrictions to trade.[101] With regard to the last element of the Article

5.5 test (whether the arbitrary or unjustifiable differences result in discrimination or a disguised restriction of international trade), the Appellate Body in *EC – Hormones* stated, "whether arbitrary or unjustifiable differences or distinctions in levels of protection established by a Member do in fact result in discrimination or a disguised restriction on international trade must be sought in the circumstances of each individual case".[102] In *Australia – Salmon*, the Appellate Body established a test to determine the third element by means of three 'warning signals',[103] which are (i) substantial difference in the level of protection,[104] (ii) the arbitrary character of the differences in the level of protection, and/or (iii) the violation of SPS Article 5.1.[105] However, the 'warning signals' are not conclusive in their own right, and are to be taken together with other factors to support any finding that arbitrary or unjustifiable distinctions in levels of protection lead to "discrimination or disguised restrictions on trade".[106]

3.3.4 'Not More Trade Restrictive Than Required'

The SPS Agreement also contains rules on the choice of the SPS measure to achieve the envisaged level of protection. In this regard Article 5.6 of the SPS Agreement provides as follows:

> Without prejudice to paragraph 2 of Article 3, when establishing or maintaining sanitary or phytosanitary measures to achieve the appropriate level of sanitary or phytosanitary protection, Members shall ensure that such measures are not more trade-restrictive than required to achieve their appropriate level of sanitary or phytosanitary protection, taking into account technical and economic feasibility.

A footnote to Article 5.6 of the SPS Agreement further specifies as follows:

> For purposes of paragraph 6 of Article 5, a measure is not more trade-restrictive than required unless there is another measure, reasonably available taking into account technical and economic feasibility, that achieves the appropriate level of sanitary or phytosanitary protection and is significantly less restrictive to trade.

In *Australia – Apples*, the Appellate Body identified the general function of Article 5.6 as follows:

> The function of Article 5.6 is to ensure that SPS measures are not more trade restrictive than necessary to achieve a Member's appropriate level of protection. Compliance with this requirement is tested through a comparison of the measure at issue to possible alternative measures. Such alternatives, however, are mere conceptual tools for the purpose of the Article 5.6 analysis. A demonstration that an alternative measure meets the relevant Member's appropriate level of protection, is reasonably available, and is significantly less trade restrictive than the existing measure suffices to prove that the measure at issue is more trade restrictive than necessary. Yet this does not imply that the importing Member must adopt that alternative measure or that the alternative measure is the only option that would achieve the desired level of protection.[107]

As regards the structure of Article 5.6, the Appellate Body in *Australia – Salmon* identified three separate elements that applied cumulatively, and observed as follows:

> We agree with the Panel that Article 5.6 and, in particular, the footnote to this provision, clearly provides a three-pronged test to establish a violation of Article 5.6. As already noted, the three elements of this test under Article 5.6 are that there is an SPS measure which:

(1) is reasonably available taking into account technical and economic feasibility;
(2) achieves the Member's appropriate level of sanitary or phytosanitary protection; and
(3) is significantly less restrictive to trade than the SPS measure contested.

These three elements are cumulative in the sense that, to establish inconsistency with Article 5.6, all of them have to be met. If any of these elements is not fulfilled, the measure in dispute would be consistent with Article 5.6.[108]

It is for the complainant Member State to establish "a *prima facie* case that there is an alternative measure that meets all three elements under Article 5.6".[109] In *Australia – Apples*, the Appellate Body explained that there was an implicit obligation contained in Annex B(3) and Articles 4.2, 5.4, and 5.5 for a Member State to determine their appropriate levels of protection, as follows:

> While there is no obligation to set the appropriate level of protection in quantitative terms, a Member is not free to establish its level with such vagueness or equivocation as to render impossible the application of the relevant disciplines of the SPS Agreement, including the obligation set out in Article 5.6.[110]

In *India – Agricultural Products*, the Appellate Body reiterated that the specification of the appropriate level of protection is "both a prerogative and an obligation of the responding Member", and further stated:

> in the context of WTO dispute settlement proceedings, a responding Member is generally better placed than the complainant to know what objective it has set in terms of the level of SPS protection it wishes to achieve. For these reasons, typically a panel adjudicating a claim under Article 5.6 of the SPS Agreement would be expected to accord weight to the respondent's articulation of its appropriate level of protection.[111]

3.4 The Precautionary Principle and SPS Agreement

The precautionary principle[112] is part of the risk management which allows for imposition of SPS measures on a temporary basis. It will be recalled that Article 2.2 provides that Member States shall not maintain an SPS measure without sufficient scientific evidence, "except as provided for in paragraph 7 of Article 5". Pursuant to Article 5.7, Member States are permitted to provisionally adopt SPS measures in case of scientific uncertainty, on the basis of available pertinent information, including that from the relevant international organisations as well as from SPS measures applied by other Member States. The SPS Agreement seeks to use scientific evidence to base the decision to impose SPS measures, but where this is not possible, *i.e.*, due to a paucity of scientific evidence, a Member State my proceed with precaution to impose SPS measures without waiting for the collection of scientific evidence to assess the risks irrefutably.

The Appellate Body in *EC – Hormones* noted that Article 5.7 does not explicitly refer to the precautionary principles, but only reflects it.[113] The precautionary principle is reflected in Article 5.7 in a restrictive manner and to be applied only provisionally. As pointed out by the Appellate Body in *Japan – Agricultural Products II*:

> Article 5.7 operates as a qualified exemption from the obligation under Article 2.2 not to maintain SPS measures without sufficient scientific evidence. An overly broad and flexible interpretation of that obligation would render Article 5.7 meaningless.[114]

The Appellate Body in *US/Canada – Continued Suspension* clarified the purpose of Article 5.7 by noting that the provision intervenes in cases where a Member State would revise its SPS measure in light of scientific progress but where relevant scientific evidence does not allow performance of an adequate risk assessment.[115] The Appellate Body in *Japan – Agricultural Products II* identified four requirements imposed upon a Member State having recourse to this provision. Further, the Appellate Body noted that these four requirements are cumulative in nature, and observed as follows:

> Article 5.7 of the SPS Agreement sets out four requirements which must be met in order to adopt and maintain a provisional SPS measure. Pursuant to the first sentence of Article 5.7, a Member may provisionally adopt an SPS measure if this measure is:
>
> (1) imposed in respect of a situation where "relevant scientific information is insufficient"; and
> (2) adopted "on the basis of available pertinent information".
>
> Pursuant to the second sentence of Article 5.7, such a provisional measure may not be maintained unless the Member which adopted the measure:
>
> (1) "seek[s] to obtain the additional information necessary for a more objective assessment of risk"; and
> (2) "review[s] the . . . measure accordingly within a reasonable period of time".
>
> These four requirements are clearly cumulative in nature and are equally important for the purpose of determining consistency with this provision. Whenever one of these four requirements is not met, the measure at issue is inconsistent with Article 5.7.[116]

3.4.1 Where SPS Measures Are Adopted as a Precaution

Article 5.7 of the SPS Agreement only allows for the provisional adoption of SPS measures in the absence of sufficient scientific evidence but does not override Articles 5.1 and 5.2. Conformity with Article 5.7 does not serve to release Member States from their risk assessment obligation arising under Article 5.1 (Scott, 2009).[117] As observed by the Appellate Body in *Japan – Agricultural Products II*:

> Article 5.7 operates as a qualified exemption from the obligation under Article 2.2 not to maintain SPS measures without sufficient scientific evidence. An overly broad and flexible interpretation of that obligation would render Article 5.7 meaningless.[118]

The wording in Article 5.7 is 'where relevant scientific evidence is insufficient' implies the existence of scientific evidence, but not sufficient enough. The Appellate Body in *Japan – Apples* observed that 'relevant scientific evidence' will be 'insufficient' within the meaning of Article 5.7 if the body of available scientific evidence does not allow, in quantitative or qualitative terms, the performance of an adequate assessment of risks as required under Article 5.1 and as defined in Annex A to the SPS Agreement.

The first requirement of Article 5.7 is that there must be insufficient scientific evidence. When a Panel reviews a measure claimed by a Member to be provisional, that Panel must assess whether "relevant scientific evidence is insufficient". This evaluation must be carried out, not in the abstract, but in the light of a particular inquiry. . . . "relevant scientific evidence" will be "insufficient" within the meaning of Article 5.7 if the body of available scientific evidence does not allow, in quantitative or qualitative terms, the performance of an adequate assessment of risks as required under Article 5.1 and as defined in Annex A to the SPS Agreement. Thus, the question is not whether there is sufficient evidence of a general nature or whether there is sufficient evidence related to a specific aspect of a phytosanitary problem, or a specific risk.[119]

The relationship of Article 5.7 *vis-à-vis* that of Articles 2.2, 5.1 and 5.2 was clarified by the Appellate Body in *Japan – Apples*, which observed that where science is well settled on an issue, recourse to precaution is unwarranted:

> The application of Article 5.7 is triggered not by the existence of scientific uncertainty, but rather by the insufficiency of scientific evidence. The text of Article 5.7 is clear: it refers to "cases where relevant scientific evidence is insufficient", not to "scientific uncertainty". The two concepts are not interchangeable. Therefore, we are unable to endorse Japan's approach of interpreting Article 5.7 through the prism of "scientific uncertainty".[120]

The 'insufficiency of relevant scientific evidence' arose for consideration in *EC – Approval and Marketing of Biotech Products*, where the EC argued that the bans imposed by some of its Member States on biotech products were provisional in nature and hence fell to be assessed under Article 5.7 and not under Article 5.1. The Panel, examining the argument in light of the first sentence of Article 5.7, found as follows:

> The first sentence follows a classic "if – then" logic: if a certain condition is met (*in casu*, insufficiency of relevant scientific evidence), a particular right is conferred (*in casu*, the right provisionally to adopt an SPS measure based on available pertinent information). Thus, it is clear that Article 5.7 is applicable whenever the relevant condition is met, that is to say, in every case where relevant scientific evidence is insufficient. The provisional adoption of an SPS measure is not a condition for the applicability of Article 5.7. Rather, the provisional adoption of an SPS measure is permitted by the first sentence of Article 5.7.[121]

The Appellate Body in *US/Canada – Continued Suspension* further clarified that the existence of scientific controversy in itself is not sufficient to conclude that the relevant scientific evidence is 'insufficient',[122] as Article 5.1 of the SPS Agreement permits Member States to base their SPS measures on divergent, or minority, views from a qualified and respected source. The Appellate Body further noted that Article 5.7 is concerned with situations where deficiencies in scientific evidence/data do not allow a Member State to arrive at a sufficiently objective conclusion in relation to the risk.[123] The Appellate Body further noted that the mere fact that further scientific investigation is possible does not, by itself, mean that the relevant scientific evidence is insufficient, and that the body of scientific evidence underlying a risk assessment can always be supplemented with additional information by conducting more research or obtaining additional information.[124]

While rejecting the Panel's finding that "there must be a critical mass of new evidence and/or information that calls into question the fundamental precepts of previous knowledge and evidence so as to make relevant, previously sufficient, evidence now insufficient",[125] the Appellate Body in *US/Canada – Continued Suspension*, also observed:

> Limiting the application of Article 5.7 to situations where scientific advances lead to a paradigm shift would be too inflexible an approach. WTO Members should be permitted to take a provisional measure where new evidence from a qualified and respected source puts into question the relationship between the pre-existing body of scientific evidence and the conclusions regarding the risks.[126]

3.4.2 Maintaining Provisional SPM Measures Based on Article 5.7

Article 5.7, second sentence, requires that Member States supplement the factual basis of a provisional SPS measure they chose to take, with "additional information necessary for a more objective assessment of risk", in order for the SPS measure to remain compatible with the science-based approach of the SPS Agreement. According to the Appellate Body, this obligation highlights "the provisional nature of measures adopted pursuant to Article 5.7".[127] In the Appellate Body's view, in the absence of an obligation to improve the insufficient scientific basis,

> the provisional nature of measures taken pursuant to Article 5.7 would lose meaning. The "insufficiency" of the scientific evidence is not a perennial state, but rather a transitory one, which lasts only until such time as the imposing Member procures the additional scientific evidence which allows the performance of a more objective assessment of risk.[128]

As regards the requirement that provisional measures must be adopted on the basis of available pertinent information, the Appellate Body in *US/Canada – Continued Suspension* noted that the rule referred to situations where "there is some evidentiary basis indicating the possible existence of a risk, but not enough to permit the performance of a risk assessment".[129] Article 5.7 of the SPS Agreement obliges Members to seek to obtain the additional information necessary for a more objective risk assessment. The Appellate Body in *Japan – Agricultural Products II* and *US/Canada – Continued Suspension* sought to clarify the requirement by observing that (i) the insufficiency of scientific evidence "is not a perennial state, but a transitory one", and as regards the adoption of the provisional measure, a Member State "must make best efforts to remedy the insufficiency", (ii) Article 5.7 does not specify what actual results must be achieved, and that the obligation is to "seek to obtain" additional information, and (iii) the information sought must be "germane" to conducting a risk assessment within the meaning of Article 5.1.[130]

Article 5.7 of the SPS Agreement requires the review of provisional SPS measures adopted by Member States within a reasonable period of time. Article 5.7 refers to a 'reasonable period of time' to carry out a review, as insufficiency of scientific evidence may persist, justifying an extended period of time to carry out a review. According to the Appellate Body, what constitutes a 'reasonable period of time' depends on the specific circumstances of each case, including the difficulty of obtaining the additional information necessary for the review and the characteristics of the provisional SPS measure.[131]

4. Other Substantive Provisions of the SPS Agreement

The scheme envisaged under the SPS Agreement also includes provisions relating to (i) recognition of foreign SPS policy and measures mutual recognition (Article 4); (ii) adaption to regional conditions (Article 6); (iii) inspection and approval procedures (Article 8; Annex C(1)); (iv) transparency and notification (Article 7; Annex B); and (v) special and differential treatment for developing country Member States (Article 10).

4.1 Recognition of Foreign SPS Policy and Measures

Apart from harmonisation, the SPS Agreement also encourages the concept of equivalence amongst the Member States to avoid trade impediments. As is well known, differing climatic and geographical conditions, consumer preferences, asymmetric technological growth, *etc.* may render harmonisation of SPS measures a difficult goal to achieve amongst the Member States. Article 4.1 requires Member States to accept the SPS measures of other Member States as

> equivalent, even if these measures differ from their own or from those used by other Members trading in the same product, if the exporting Member objectively demonstrates to the importing member that its measures achieve the importing Member's appropriate level of sanitary and phytosanitary protection. For this purpose, reasonable access shall be given, upon request, to the importing Member for inspection, testing, and other relevant procedures.

Article 4.2, on the other hand, encourages Member States to enter into consultation with a view to achieving bilateral and multilateral agreements on the recognition of the equivalence of specified SPS measures. The Panel in *US – Poultry (China)* observed that while the Decision on Equivalence is not binding, it expands on the Member States' own understanding of how Article 4 relates to the rest of the SPS Agreement and how it is to be implemented.[132]

The Appellate Body in *Australia – Salmon* noted that although the SPS Agreement does not explicitly oblige Member States to determine their appropriate level of protection, such an obligation is implicit in several provisions of the Agreement, including Articles 4.1 and 4.2:

> We recognize that the SPS Agreement does not contain an explicit provision which obliges WTO Members to determine the appropriate level of protection. Such an obligation is, however, implicit in several provisions of the SPS Agreement, in particular, in paragraph 3 of Annex B, Article 4.11, Article 5.4 and Article 5.6 of the SPS Agreement.[133]

The SPS Committee had held discussions with the Member States, as problems were encountered in the mutual recognition of SPS measures. These consultations had resulted in the adoption in October 2001 of the 'Decision on Equivalence'. This decision was followed up by the SPS Committee with a work programme which sought to clarify and elaborate on the Decision on Equivalence. This has now been firmed up as the current version of the Decision (WTO, 2004).

4.2 Adaptation of Regional Conditions

Article 6 requires Member States to take the measures 'necessary' to ensure the maintenance of their appropriate level of protection. To ensure the adaptation of SPS measures to regional conditions in order to avoid excessively trade restrictive practices, Article 6 of the SPS Agreement establishes a number of obligations on the Member States, which are contained in three interconnected paragraphs. Article 6.1 reads as follows:

Members shall ensure that their sanitary or phytosanitary measures are adapted to the sanitary or phytosanitary characteristics of the area – whether all of a country, part of a country, or all or parts of several countries – from which the product originated and to which the product is destined. In assessing the sanitary or phytosanitary characteristics of a region, Members shall take into account, *inter alia*, the level of prevalence of specific diseases or pests, the existence of eradication or control programmes, and appropriate criteria or guidelines which may be developed by the relevant international organizations.

Article 6.1 addresses both the areas from which the product originated and to which the product is destined, regardless of the legal status of that territorial Space. Pursuant to Article 6.1 of the SPS Agreement, Member States are to ensure that the measures imposed are adapted to the SPS characteristics of the region of origin as well as the destination of the product. The characteristics identified in Article 6.1 are to be determined with reference to (i) the level of prevalence of diseases or pests; (ii) the existence of eradication or control programmes; and (ii) criteria or guidelines developed by international organisations.

In interpreting Article 6.1, the Appellate Body in *India – Agricultural Products* noted that the relevant areas subject of the adaptation obligation can "vary, and may entail a territory that can be smaller than, the same size as, or bigger than, a country".[134] The Appellate Body further emphasised the continuing nature of the adaptation obligation, "requiring that SPS measures be adjusted over time so as to establish and maintain their continued suitability in respect of the relevant SPS characteristics".[135] According to the Appellate Body:

> [T]he general "adaptation" obligation in Article 6.1 may well encompass both a requirement to adapt appropriately at the time the SPS measure is adopted, as well as a requirement to adapt appropriately if and when relevant SPS characteristics in relevant areas in the territory of the importing or exporting Member change or are shown to warrant an adaptation of a specific SPS measure.[136]

Further, Article 6.2 of the SPS Agreement obligates Member States to recognise the concepts of pest- or disease-free areas and areas of low pest or disease prevalence. The Panel in *India – Agricultural Products* interpreted the meaning of the terms used in Article 6.2 as requiring Member States to recognise "the idea or notion of pest- or disease-free areas and areas of low pest or disease prevalence in the abstract; the obligation under Article 6.2, first sentence, is not linked to specific areas of a given exporting Member".[137] In the Panel's view, the provision did not prescribe any particular manner in which a Member State should recognise the concepts of pest- or disease-free areas and areas of low pest or disease prevalence.[138] The Appellate Body in *India – Agricultural Products* noted that it agreed with the panel's observation that

> SPS measures or regulatory schemes that explicitly foreclose the possibility of recognition of the concepts of pest- or disease-free areas and areas of low pest or disease prevalence cannot, when these concepts are relevant with respect to the diseases addressed by such SPS measures, be found to be consistent with Article 6.2.[139]

As regards the obligation arising under Article 6.3, the Panel in *US – Animals* explained that it required the exporting Member State to

> [P]rovide evidence to the importing Member to objectively demonstrate that its areas are, and are likely to remain, pest- or disease-free or areas of low pest or disease

prevalence. The Member shall also provide reasonable access to the importing Member for inspection, testing and other relevant procedures. As the plain language of Article 6.3 indicates, the exporting Member is not only required to objectively demonstrate that areas within its territory are pest- or disease-free or of low pest or disease prevalence at a given point in time, but also that such areas are "likely to remain" in the same pest- or disease-condition.[140]

In 2008, the SPS Committee adopted non-binding guidelines to facilitate the implementation of Article 6 of the SPS Agreement, which is referred to as the Regionalisation Decision (WTO, 2008).

4.3 Control Inspection and Approval Procedures

Pursuant to Article 8 of the SPS Agreement, Member States are to have in place control, inspection, and approval procedures in order to ensure that SPS requirements are complied with. To this end, the Member States are to observe the provisions contained in Annex C, which in the relevant part reads as follows:

1   Members shall ensure, with respect to any procedure to check and ensure the fulfilment of sanitary or phytosanitary measures, that:

   (a) such procedures are undertaken and completed without undue delay and in no less favourable manner for imported products than for like domestic products;
   (b) the standard processing period of each procedure is published or that the anticipated processing period is communicated to the applicant upon request; when receiving an application, the competent body promptly examines the completeness of the documentation and informs the applicant in a precise and complete manner of all deficiencies; the competent body transmits as soon as possible the results of the procedure in a precise and complete manner to the applicant so that corrective action may be taken if necessary; even when the application has deficiencies, the competent body proceeds as far as practicable with the procedure if the applicant so requests; and that upon request, the applicant is informed of the stage of the procedure, with any delay being explained . . .
   (c) information requirements are limited to what is necessary for appropriate control, inspection and approval procedures, including for approval of the use of additives or for the establishment of tolerances for contaminants in food, beverages or feedstuffs.

Annex C also contains other obligations of the Member States to follow to ensure transparency, procedural and substantive due process, fair and equitable procedures, and administrative reasonableness. In this regard the Panel in *US – Animals*, while rejecting the US argument the procedures covered by Article 8 and Annex C are limited, ruled that Article 8 and Annex C of the SPS Agreement cover a broad range of procedures and exclude procedures aiming at determinations of the disease status of certain geographic regions.[141] As regards the 'without undue delay' requirement of Annex C(1)(a), the Appellate Body ruled in *Australia – Apples* that

> Annex C(1)(a) requires Members to ensure that relevant procedures are undertaken and completed with appropriate dispatch, that is, that they do not involve periods of time

that are unwarranted, or otherwise excessive, disproportionate or unjustifiable. Whether a relevant procedure has been unduly delayed is, therefore, not an assessment that can be done in the abstract, but one which requires a case-by-case analysis as to the reasons for the alleged failure to act with appropriate dispatch, and whether such reasons are justifiable.[142]

The term 'undertaken and completed without undue delay' in Annex C(1)(a) was interpreted by the Panel in *US – Animals* to include undue delay both (i) in the commencement of the procedure and its completion, and (ii) in the intervening process that leads from commencement to completion.[143] The Panel in *US – Poultry (China)* observed that Article 8 and Annex C(1) apply to the procedures dealing with control, inspection, and approval "which are aimed at checking and ensuring the fulfilment of SPS measures".[144] In *EC – Approval and Marketing of Biotech Products*, the Panel found that a failure to observe the provisions of Annex C(1) implies a breach of Article 8.[145]

4.4 Transparency and Notifications

Pursuant to Article 7 of the SPS Agreement, Member States are obliged to notify changes in their SPS measures and to provide relevant information in accordance with the provisions of Annex B of the SPS Agreement. This procedure is to ensure transparency with regards to changes made by Member States to their SPS measures and avoid any barriers to market access. Annex B of the SPS Agreement requires (i) that all adopted SPS regulations (laws, decrees, or ordinances) be published; (ii) the establishment of enquiry points, and (iii) the prior notification of proposed SPS measures that diverge from international standards and allow time for comments/feedback from other Member States.

The Panel in *Japan – Agricultural Products II* set the conditions of application of the publishing requirements under Annex B as follows:

> [I]n our view, for a measure to be subject to the publication requirement in Annex B, three conditions apply: (1) the measure "[has] been adopted"; (2) the measure is a "phytosanitary regulation", namely a phytosanitary measure such as a law, decree or ordinance, which is (3) "applicable generally".[146]

The Appellate Body in *Japan – Agricultural Products II* found that the object and purpose of Annex B(1) is

> "to enable interested Members to become acquainted with" the sanitary and phytosanitary regulations adopted or maintained by other Members and thus to enhance transparency regarding these measures. In our opinion, the scope of application of the publication requirement of paragraph 1 of Annex B should be interpreted in the light of the object and purpose of this provision.[147]

The Appellate Body in *Japan – Agricultural Products II* further opined that the listed instruments were "not exhaustive in nature",[148] due to the function to ensure full transparency for the benefit of affected parties.[149] Prior notification of SPS measures contemplated under Annex B(5) and (7) allows exporters from Member States to either scale back or stop their export of agricultural products and thereby reduce any economic losses which may arise out of the notified SPS measures. The *Chapeau* of Annex B(5) reflects this position by making prior notifications mandatory, if the measure may "have a significant effect on trade of other Members".[150]

The Panel in *Japan – Apples*, while determining whether any changes in a Member State's SPS measures constitute changes that must be notified under Article 7, found that the most important factor to be taken into consideration is whether the changes made affect the conditions of market access for the product concerned, *i.e.*, would the exported product still be permitted to enter the market if they complied with the prescription contained in the previous regulations under the *Chapeau* of Annex B(5).[151]

The Panel in *India – Agricultural Products* held that to meet the requirement in Annex B(5)(b) a Member State has to notify a proposed regulation, as opposed to a regulation that is already in force:

> Annex B(5)(b) concerns the notification of a "proposed" regulation and thus notification must occur at least before that regulation enters into force, so that amendments can still be introduced and comments taken into account. We note that the SPS Committee's Transparency Procedures support our understanding that the notification obligation in Annex B(5)(b) concerns proposed regulations, as it recommends that the notification takes place once a draft of the complete text of a regulation is available.[152]

The Panel in *India – Agricultural Products* noted that India acted inconsistently with the requirements of Annex B, as it had notified the measure to the WTO Secretariat well after the SPS measure under challenge entered into force.[153] The Panel concluded that because India's measures did address health problems that were urgent and did not meet the condition of the *Chapeau* of Annex B(6), the Panel did not need to look into their compatibility with any of the three specific conditions spelled out in subparagraphs (a) through (c) of Annex B(6).[154]

As mentioned earlier, Annex B(3) also provides that Member States are to ensure that one enquiry point exists which is responsible for the provision of answers to all reasonable questions from interested Member States as well as for the provision of relevant documents regarding SPS regulations; control and inspection procedures; risk assessment procedures; and membership and participation of the Member State in international and regional SPS organisations and systems.

4.5 Special and Differential Treatment

Special and differential treatment of developing country Member States is dealt with under Article 10 of the SPS Agreement. Pursuant to Article 10.1 of the SPS Agreement, developed country Member States must "take account of the special needs" of developing and least developed country Member States with regard to the preparation and application of SPS measures. The obligation contained in Article 10.1 is unconditional.

The Panel in *EC – Approval and Marketing of Biotech Products* examined a claim by Argentina that by adopting and applying a general *de facto* moratorium on approvals of applications to place genetically modified organisms on the market, the EC had failed to apply its legislation in a manner which takes account of developing country Member State's needs. The Panel found that the phrase 'take account of' does not prescribe a specific result to be achieved and that merely because a Member State (the EC) did not afford special and differential treatment to a developing country member (*i.e.*, Argentina) does not establish a *prima facie* case that the developed country Member State did not 'take account of' the developing country's needs when it made its decision. The Panel held that a successful claim based on SPS Article

10.1 will require the difficult task of showing that the developed country Member State *a priori* disregarded the special needs of a developing country Member State.[155]

The Panel in *US – Animals* concurred with the Panel's view in *EC – Approval and Marketing of Biotech Products* that Article 10.1 of the SPS Agreement imposes a positive obligation which is subject to dispute settlement and rejected the argument that certain terms of that provision are too vague to be enforceable. According to the Panel, accepting such a proposition could render ineffective "many special and differential treatment provisions throughout the covered agreements, and upset the balance of rights and obligations between developed and developing country Members".[156] The Panel in *US – Animals* further noted that Article 10.1 does not require an importing Member State to automatically grant priority to the developing country Member State's products, in particular in the conduct of a risk assessment procedure.[157]

As regards the term 'special needs of developing country Members' was concerned, the Panel in *US – Animals* interpreted it broadly, "so as to encompass both the needs of developing country Members generally, and the needs of a particular developing country Member".[158] Pursuant to Article 10.2, wherever possible, phased introduction of new SPS measures and longer timeframes are to be accorded for compliance on products of interest to developing country Member States so as to maintain opportunities for their exports. The term used in Article 10.2 is "wherever possible" and does not oblige Member States to grant developing country Member States a longer period for compliance with new SPS measures. The extended period contemplated under Article 10.2 was specified as not less than six months in the 2001 Doha Ministerial Decision on Implementation-Related Issues and Concerns (WTO, 2001).

The SPS Committee, pursuant to Article 10.3, can grant developing country Member States 'time-limited exceptions' from obligations arising under SPS Agreement, to facilitate compliance, while taking into account their financial trade and development needs. Pursuant to Article 10.4 of the SPS Agreement, Member States are to encourage and facilitate the participation of developing countries in the relevant international organisations. In 2009, the SPS Committee adopted the 'Procedure to Enhance Transparency of Special and Differential Treatment in Favour of Developing Country Members'. This procedure requires Member States to allow for at least a 60-day period between the proposal of an SPS measure and its implementation, in order to allow consideration of comments (WTO, 2009).

5. Institutional Provisions of the SPS Agreement

The SPS Agreement contains a number of institutional and procedural provisions relating to the SPS Committee, dispute settlement, and technical assistance to developing country Member States.

5.1 SPS Committee

A Committee on Sanitary and Phytosanitary Measures (SPS Committee) has been established under Article 12.1 of the SPS Agreement. The SPS Committee is composed of representatives of all Member States desirous of participation and carries out the necessary functions to implement the provisions of the SPS Agreement, and to further its objectives, in particular with regards to harmonisation. Pursuant to Article 12.2, the SPS Committee shall encourage and facilitate *ad hoc* consultations or negotiations amongst Member States on specific SPS issues and encourage the use of international standards, guidelines, or recommendations by all Member States. The SPS Committee must meet at least three times a year,[159] as well as when requested. The developing country Member States have raised significantly more concerns relating to SPS measures before the Committee than developed country Member States.

Under Article 12.3, the SPS Committee is required to maintain close contact with the relevant international organisations in the field of SPS protection, especially with the Codex Alimentarius Commission, the International Office Epizootics, and the Secretariat of the International Plat Protection Convention, for purposes of securing the best available scientific and technical advice for the administration of the SPS Agreement and to avoid unnecessary duplication. Pursuant to Article 12.7 of the SPS Agreement, the SPS Committee is required to carry out a review of the operation and implementation of the SPS Agreement, three years after its entry into force, and as and when necessary thereafter. The SPS Committee is a much sought-after forum for discussions, as well as for informal dispute resolution where SPS measures and trade concerns come to be addressed (WTO, 2015).

5.2 Dispute Settlement

The settlement of disputes arising under the SPS Agreement is covered under Article 11 of the SPS Agreement. Article 11.1 of the SPS Agreement provides for the application of Articles XXII and XXIII of the GATT 1994 as elaborated by the DSU to consultations and the settlement of disputes under the SPS Agreement, except as otherwise provided. The much-debated issues with regards to the SPS Agreement are (i) the role of scientific experts who are consulted by Panels and (ii) the standard of review to be applied by Panels when reviewing the SPS consistency of SPS measures imposed by Member States.

5.2.1 Scientific Experts

Article 13 of the DSU authorises Panels to seek technical advice and information from any individual body, consult experts, or request advisory reports. In invariably all disputes arising from the SPS Agreement before the DSB, the assistance of experts has been sought for by the SPS Panels. Article 11.2 of the SPS Agreement states:

> In a dispute under this Agreement involving scientific or technical issues, a Panel should seek advice from experts chosen by the Panel in consultation with the parties to the dispute. To this end, the Panel may, when it deems it appropriate, establish an advisory technical experts group, or consult the relevant international organizations, at the request of either party to the dispute or on its own initiative.

The Appellate Body in *Japan – Agricultural Products II* ruled that Article 11.2 'explicitly instructs' panels in SPS disputes involving scientific and technical issues to seek advice from experts.[160] The Panel in *US/Canada – Continued Suspension* stated that the role of the experts was to act as an 'interface' between the scientific evidence and the Panel, so as to allow it to perform its task as the trier of fact.[161] The Appellate Body in *US/Canada – Continued Suspension* noted that Article 11.2 specifically addresses the consultation of experts in disputes under the SPS Agreement,[162] and that the experts consulted by a panel can significantly influence the decision-making process.[163]

The Appellate Body in *Japan – Agricultural Products II* stressed that the investigative authority of a panel did not stretch so far as to "make the case for a complaining party", and observed as follows:

Article 13 of the DSU and Article 11.2 of the SPS Agreement suggest that Panels have a significant investigative authority. However, this authority cannot be used by a Panel to rule in favour of a complaining party which has not established a *prima facie* case of inconsistency based on specific legal claims asserted by it. A Panel is entitled to seek information and advice from experts and from any other relevant source it chooses, pursuant to Article 13 of the DSU and, in an SPS case, Article 11.2 of the SPS Agreement, to help it to understand and evaluate the evidence submitted and the arguments made by the parties, but not to make the case for a complaining party.[164]

In the context of the Panel's consultation with experts, the Panel in *Australia – Apples* ruled that a Panel is precluded from considering issues that fall outside the terms of reference approved by the DSB.[165] The Appellate Body in *US/Canada – Continued Suspension* observed that Panels are understood to have significant investigative authority under Article 13 of the DSU and Article 11.2 of the SPS Agreement, and broad discretion when exercising this authority.[166]

5.2.2 Standard of Review

As mentioned earlier, the second issue with regards to the settlement of disputes arising under SPS Agreement is the 'standard of review' to be applied by the Panels while reviewing the consistency of SPS measures. The Appellate Body in *Japan – Apples* held that Article 5.1 sets out a key discipline under Article 5, namely, "Members shall ensure that their sanitary or phytosanitary measures are based on an assessment . . . of the risks to human, animal or plant life or health", and that this discipline informs the other provisions of Article 5, including Article 5.7.[167]

The Appellate Body in *US/Canada – Continued Suspension* determined that a Panel reviewing the consistency of an SPS measure with Article 5.1 must determine whether that SPS measure is based on a risk assessment, that the Panel's task is to review the risk assessment, and that the review power of the Panel is not to determine whether the risk assessment undertaken by a Member State is correct but rather to determine whether that risk assessment is supported by coherent reasoning and respectable scientific evidence and is, *i.e.*, objectively justifiable.[168] The Appellate Body in *US/Canada – Continued Suspension* set out four key indicators that must be considered by a Panel when reviewing a Member State's risk assessment, which are

a   Whether the views upon which an SPS measure is based are from qualified and respected sources;
b   Whether the reasoning articulated on the basis of scientific evidence is objective and coherent;
c   Whether the particular conclusions drawn by the Member assessing the risk find sufficient support in the scientific evidence relied upon; and
d   Whether the results of the risk's assessment sufficiently warrant the SPS measure at issue.[169]

The Appellate Body in *Australia – Apples* reiterated the four indicators for evaluating a Member State's risk assessment duties of a panel as set out in *US/Canada – Continued Suspension*.[170] The Appellate Body also noted that the applicable standard of review, set out in Article 11 of the DSU, requires that a Panel reviewing a risk assessment under Article 5.1 of the SPS

Agreement neither undertake a *de novo* review nor give total deference to the risk assessment it reviews.[171] On the role of Panels in reviewing whether an SPS measure is based on a risk assessment, the Panel in *EC – Hormones* observed:

> it is for the European Communities to submit evidence before the Panel that its measures are based on a risk assessment; it is not for the Panel itself to conduct its own risk assessment on the basis of scientific evidence gathered by the Panel or submitted by the parties during the Panel proceedings.[172]

In *US/Canada – Continued Suspension*, the Appellate Body observed that SPS measures can be based on a divergent or minority view rather than mainstream scientific opinion, provided that it "comes from a qualified and respected source" and has "the necessary scientific and methodological rigour to be considered reputable science".[173] In *EC – Approval and Marketing of Biotech Products*, the Panel addressed the question of whether an SPS measure could be considered 'based on' a risk assessment if it reflects a divergent opinion expressed in the risk assessment. The Panel, following the Appellate Body's ruling in *EC – Hormones*, concluded that in certain circumstances an SPS measure that reflects a divergent opinion from the risk assessment could still be considered to be 'based on' that risk assessment:

> Where a given risk assessment sets out a divergent opinion and this opinion comes from qualified and respected sources, it can be reasonably said that an SPS measure which reflects the divergent opinion is "based on" the risk assessment in question inasmuch as the divergent opinion is expressed in that risk assessment. In contrast, where a given risk assessment sets out a single opinion, it cannot be reasonably said that an SPS measure is "based on" that risk assessment if the relevant SPS measure reflects a divergent opinion which is not expressed in the risk assessment in question.[174]

5.3 Technical Assistance

Under Article 9.1 of the SBS Agreement, Member States are to provide 'technical assistance' to other Member States, especially developing country Member States, either bilaterally or through the appropriate international organisations. Technical assistance contemplated under Article 9 includes information and training to enhance understanding of the disciplines of the SPS Agreement, the provision of soft infrastructure (training of technical and scientific personnel and the development of national regulatory frameworks), and hard infrastructure (laboratories, equipment, veterinary services, and the establishment of pest- or disease-free areas) (WTO, 2000).

Article 9.2 contemplates situations where substantial investments are required for an exporting developing country Member State to fulfil the SPS requirements of an importing Member State. In such situations, Article 9.2 obliges the importing Member State to 'consider providing' technical assistance to allow the developing country Member State to maintain or increase its market opportunities for the relevant product. Unlike in the TBT Agreement, where obligations arising under Article 11 are legally binding, the obligations arising under Article 9 of the SPS Agreement are of a 'good practice' or 'best-endeavour' nature and difficult to enforce.

At the Doha Ministerial Conference in 2001, Member States resolved to "provide, to the extent possible, the financial and technical assistance necessary to enable least-developed countries to respond adequately to the introduction of any new [sanitary or phytosanitary] measures which may have significant negative effects on their trade". It was also decided by the Member States to ensure a level of technical assistance necessary to enable least developed Member States to respond to the special problems they face in implementing the Agreement on Sanitary and Phytosanitary Measures (WTO, 2001). Following from the Doha Ministerial Conference, the Standards and Trade Development Facility (STDF) was created in 2004, which has as its goal to assist developing country Member States to establish and implement international SPS standards, provide guidelines and recommendations, and thereby develop the ability to gain and maintain market access. The STDF also has, as part of its vision, sustainable economic growth, poverty reduction, food security, and environmental protection in developing countries.

6. Summary

SPS measures aim to protect human or animal life or health from food-borne risks, or aim at the protection of human, animal, or plant life or health from risks from pests or diseases. While acknowledging the sovereign right of Member States to take SPS measures, the SPS Agreement obligates the Member States to (i) take or maintain only those SPS measures necessary to protect human, animal, or plant life or health; (ii) take or maintain only those SPS measures 'based on' scientific principles and sufficient scientific evidence; and (iii) not adopt or maintain SPS measures that arbitrarily or unjustifiably discriminate or constitute a disguised restriction on trade. As in the case of the TBT Agreement, the SPS Agreement too encourages the harmonisation of SPS measures around international standards.

Notes

1. For a discussion on the role of the SPS and TBT agreements, see the introduction to chapter 13.
2. The risk arises from the increasing use of new technologies in agriculture and food processing such as pesticides, additives, and genetic modification. Some of the disputes involving SPS measures in recent times have revolved around the (i) fear that domestic salmon will be infected with diseases found in foreign salmon; (ii) fear that domestic apples will be infected with diseases found in foreign applies; and (iii) fear that meat is treated with hormones and products are made with or contain genetically modified organisms.
3. See Panel Report, *EC – Hormones*, para. 8.39.
4. See Appellate Body Report, *EC – Sardines*, para. 216.
5. See Appellate Body Report, *EC – Hormones*, para. 128.
6. See Panel Report, *Australia – Apples*, para. 7.116.
7. See Panel Report, *EC – Approval and Marketing of Biotech Products*, para. 7.149.
8. See Panel Report, *US – Poultry (China)*, para. 7.149. See also Panel Report, *Russia – Pigs (EU)*, para. 7.196.
9. See Appellate Body Report, *Australia – Apples*, para. 172.
10. *Ibid.*, para. 173.
11. See Panel Report, *EC – Approval and Marketing of Biotech Products*, para. 7.149.
12. See Panel Report, *Australia – Apples*, paras. 7.144–7.1452. See also Panel Report, *US – Poultry (China)*, paras. 7.99 and 7.100.
13. See Panel Report, *EC – Approval and Marketing of Biotech Products*, paras. 7.198–7.211.
14. *Ibid.*, para. 7.211.
15. *Ibid.*, para. 7.149.
16. See Panel Report, *US – Poultry (China)*, para. 7.94.
17. *Ibid.*, paras. 7.119 and 7.120.
18. See Appellate Body Report, *EC – Hormones*, para. 128.
19. See Appellate Body Report, *Korea – Safeguards*, para. 74.
20. See Panel Report, *US – Poultry (China)*, paras. 7.399 and 7.455.

21 See Appellate Body Report, *EC – Hormones*, para. 128.
22 For a discussion on the issue of presumption under Article 2.4 of the SPS Agreement, see Scott (2009) and Marceau and Trachtman (2014).
23 See Panel Report, *EC – Approval and Marketing of Biotech Products*, para. 7.165.
24 See Panel Report, *US – Poultry (China)*, para. 7.142.
25 See Appellate Body Report, *EC – Hormones*, para. 177.
26 See Panel Report, *EC – Approval and Marketing of Biotech Products*, para. 7.1424.
27 See Appellate Body Report, *Australia – Apples*, para. 339.
28 See Appellate Body Report, *Australia – Salmon*, fn. 166 to para. 213.
29 See Panel Report, *India – Agricultural Products*, para. 7.614.
30 *Ibid.*, para. 7.615.
31 See Panel Report, *US – Poultry (China)*, para. 7.200.
32 See the Appellate Body Report, *EC – Hormones*, para. 177.
33 See Panel Report, *Japan – Apples*, paras. 8.92–8.93 and 8.98.
34 See the Appellate Body Report, *Japan – Agricultural Products II*, para. 73.
35 *Ibid.*, para. 74.
36 *Ibid.*, para. 82.
37 *Ibid.*, para. 84.
38 See Appellate Body Report, *EC – Hormones*, para. 124.
39 See Panel Report, *Japan – Apples*, paras. 8.179–8.180, 8.182, and 8.198.
40 *Ibid.*, para. 8.169.
41 *Ibid.*, paras. 8.169 and 8.198.
42 See Appellate Body Report, *India – Agricultural Products*, para. 5.27.
43 See Appellate Body Report, *Japan – Agricultural Products II*, para. 80.
44 See Panel Report, *EC – Approval and Marketing of Biotech Products*, paras. 7.2968–7.2969.
45 See Appellate Body Report, *US/Canada – Continued Suspension*, para. 674.
46 *Ibid.*, para. 5.23. See also Appellate Body Reports, *Australia – Apples*, para. 340; *Australia – Salmon*, para. 138.
47 See Appellate Body Report, *India – Agricultural Products*, para. 5.29.
48 See Panel Report, *India – Agricultural Products*, para. 7.400.
49 See Appellate Body Report, *Australia – Salmon (Article 21.5 – Canada)*, para. 7.111. See also Panel Reports, *India – Agricultural Products*, para. 7.389; *US – Animals*, para. 7.571; and *Russia – Pigs (EU)*, para. 7.1297.
50 See Appellate Body Report, *India – Agricultural Products*, para. 5.261.
51 See Panel Report, *Australia – Salmon (Article 21.5 – Canada)*, para. 7.112.
52 See Appellate Body Report, *India – Agricultural Products*, para. 5.260. See also Appellate Body Report, *Korea – Radionuclides (Japan)*, para. 5.58.
53 See Appellate Body Report, *Australia – Salmon*, para. 251.
54 See Panel Report, *US – Poultry (China)*, para. 7.147.
55 See section 13.3.3 entitled 'The Obligation to Use International Standards' for the reasons to harmonise and align domestic standards following international standards. See also Marceau and Trachtman (2014).
56 See Appellate Body Report, *EC – Hormones*, paras. 102, 165–166, and 171. The right to deviate from basing the domestic SPS measures on international standards is again conditioned on the requirements of scientific risk assessment in the regulatory process detailed under Article 5 of SPS.
57 *Ibid.*, para. 177.
58 See Appellate Body Report, *US/Canada – Continued Suspension*, para. 690.
59 *Ibid.*
60 *Ibid.*, para. 692. See also Appellate Body Report, *Australia – Apples*, para. 215, referring to Appellate Body Reports in *Japan – Agricultural Products II*, para. 84, *Japan – Apples*, para. 162, and *EC – Hormones*, para. 193.
61 The adoption of both the SPS and the TBT agreements has transformed Codex standards from merely voluntary standards to quasi-binding obligations. See Arcuri (2015) for a discussion on the SPS Agreement and the Codex Alimentarius Commission.
62 In this regard, the SPS Committee is authorised to identify other relevant international standard-setting organisations to the existing list enumerated under Annex A(3) of the SPS Agreement.

63 See Appellate Body Report, *US/Canada – Continued Suspension*, para. 693.
64 See Appellate Body Report, *EC – Hormones*, para. 163.
65 See Panel Report, *US – Animals*, para. 7.233.
66 *Ibid.*, para. 7.239.
67 See Panel Reports, *India – Agricultural Products*, para. 7.253.
68 *Ibid.*, paras. 7.271–7.274.
69 See Appellate Body Report, *EC – Hormones*, paras. 170.
70 See Appellate Body Report, *US/Canada – Continued Suspension*, para. 532.
71 See Appellate Body Report, *EC – Hormones*, paras. 104 and 172.
72 *Ibid.*, para. 173.
73 See Appellate Body Report, *US/Canada – Continued Suspension*, para. 532.
74 See Panel Report, *EC – Approval and Marketing of Biotech Products*, para. 7.3019.
75 See Appellate Body Report, *Australia – Salmon*, para. 121.
76 See Panel Reports, *EC – Hormones (Canada)*, para. 8.101, and *EC – Hormones (US)*, para. 8.98, as modified in Appellate Body Report, *EC – Hormones*, paras. 184–186.
77 See Appellate Body Report, *EC – Hormones*, para. 186. See also Appellate Body Report, *US/Canada – Continued Suspension*, para. 569.
78 See Appellate Body Report, *EC – Hormones*, para. 186; Appellate Body Report, *Australia – Salmon*, para. 124–125; and Appellate Body Report, *US/Canada – Continued Suspension*, para. 569.
79 See Appellate Body Report, *EC – Hormones*, para. 187.
80 *Ibid.*, para. 200.
81 *Ibid.*, para. 190.
82 See Appellate Body Report, *Australia – Apples*, para. 246.
83 See Panel Report, *Japan – Apples*, para. 7.12. See also Panel Report, *EC – Approval and Marketing of Biotech Products*, paras. 7.3033–7.3034.
84 See Panel Report, *Australia – Salmon*, para. 8.57.
85 See Appellate Body Report, *Australia – Apples*, para. 208.
86 See Appellate Body Report, *EC – Hormones*, para. 187. See also Appellate Body Reports, *US/Canada – Continued Suspension*, para. 527, and *Australia – Apples*, para. 207.
87 See Appellate Body Report, *US/Canada – Continued Suspension*, para. 545.
88 *Ibid.*, para. 434.
89 See Appellate Body Report, *EC – Hormones*, paras. 189–194.
90 See Appellate Body Report, *US/Canada – Continued Suspension*, para. 591.
91 See Appellate Body Report, *Australia – Apples*, paras. 236 and 242.
92 See Appellate Body Report, *Australia – Salmon*, para. 203.
93 *Ibid.*, para. 200.
94 *Ibid.*, para. 199. See also Appellate Body Report, *US/Canada – Continued Suspension*, para. 523.
95 See Appellate Body Report, *Australia – Salmon*, para. 201.
96 See Appellate Body Report, *EC – Hormones*, para. 214.
97 *Ibid.*, para. 215. See also Panel Report, *EC – Approval and Marketing of Biotech Products*, para. 7.1415.
98 See Panel Report, *Australia – Salmon (Article 21.5 – Canada)*, paras. 7.86–7.108.
99 See Appellate Body Report, *EC – Hormones*, para. 217.
100 See Appellate Body Report, *Australia – Salmon*, para. 146.
101 See Appellate Body Report, *EC – Hormones*, para. 214. See also Appellate Body Report, *Australia – Salmon*, para. 158.
102 See Appellate Body Report, *EC – Hormones*, para. 240.
103 See Appellate Body Report, *Australia – Salmon*, para. 162.
104 *Ibid.*, para. 164.
105 *Ibid.*, para. 166.
106 *Ibid.*, paras. 162, 164, and 166.
107 See Appellate Body Report, *Australia – Apples*, para. 363.
108 See Appellate Body Report, *Australia – Salmon*, para. 194.
109 See Appellate Body Report, *Japan – Agricultural Products II*, para. 126.
110 See Appellate Body Report, *Australia – Apples*, para. 343.
111 See Appellate Body Report, *India – Agricultural Products*, para. 5.221.
112 See Laowonsiri (2010) for a discussion on the application of precautionary principle in the SPS Agreement. The precautionary principle was pioneered in the German legal system and was later

applied to the field of international environmental law. The author argues that the precautionary principle as a general principle of law subsists in International Health Regulations of the WHO, and Cartagena Protocol on Biosafety, and could be applicable law within the WTO legal system.

113 See Appellate Body Report, *EC – Hormones*, para. 124.
114 See Appellate Body Report, *Japan – Agricultural Products II*, para. 80.
115 See Appellate Body Report, *US/Canada – Continued Suspension*, para. 197.
116 See Appellate Body Report, *Japan – Agricultural Products II*, para. 89. See also Appellate Body Report, *US/Canada – Continued Suspension*, para. 676.
117 The author postulates the argument that conformity with Article 5.7 implies, on the face of it, a time-limited reprieve from the obligation arising from Article 5.1 of the SPS Agreement.
118 See Appellate Body Report, *Japan – Agricultural Products II*, para. 80.
119 See Appellate Body Report, *Japan – Apples*, para. 179.
120 *Ibid.*, para. 184.
121 See Panel Report, *EC – Approval and Marketing of Biotech Products*, para. 7.2939.
122 See Appellate Body Reports, *US/Canada – Continued Suspension*, para. 677.
123 *Ibid.*
124 *Ibid.*, para. 702.
125 *Ibid.*, para. 703.
126 *Ibid.*, para. 703.
127 *Ibid.*, para. 674.
128 *Ibid.*, para. 679.
129 *Ibid.*, para. 678.
130 See Appellate Body Report, *Japan – Agricultural Products II*, para. 92. See also Appellate Body Reports, *US/Canada – Continued Suspension*, para. 679.
131 See Appellate Body Report, *Japan – Agricultural Products II*, para. 93.
132 See Panel Report, *US – Poultry (China)*, para. 7.136.
133 See Appellate Body Report, *Australia – Salmon*, para. 205.
134 See Appellate Body Report, *India – Agricultural Products*, para. 5.132.
135 *Ibid.*
136 *Ibid.*, para. 5.154.
137 See Panel Report, *India – Agricultural Products*, para. 7.695.
138 *Ibid.*, para. 7.698.
139 See Appellate Body Report, *India – Agricultural Products*, para. 5.138.
140 See Panel Report, *US – Animals*, para. 7.649.
141 *Ibid.*, paras. 7.68 and 7.69.
142 See Appellate Body Report, *Australia – Apples*, para. 437.
143 See Panel Report, *US – Animals*, para. 7.112.
144 See Panel Report, *US – Poultry (China)*, para. 7.356.
145 See Panel Report, *EC – Approval and Marketing of Biotech Products*, para. 7.1569.
146 See Panel Report, *Japan – Agricultural Products II*, para. 8.111.
147 See Appellate Body Report, *Japan – Agricultural Products II*, para. 106.
148 *Ibid.*, paras. 105 and 107.
149 *Ibid.*, para. 106.
150 See Panel Report, *Japan – Apples*, para. 8.314.
151 *Ibid.*
152 See Panel Report, *India – Agricultural Products*, para. 7.788.
153 *Ibid.*, para. 7.763.
154 *Ibid.*, para. 7.764.
155 See Panel Report, *EC – Approval and Marketing of Biotech Products*, paras. 7.1620–7.1625.
156 See Panel Report, *US – Animals*, para. 7.690.
157 *Ibid.*, para. 7.704.
158 *Ibid.*, para. 7.692.
159 The TBT Committee, in contrast, need only meet once a year, which signifies the practical need for transparency in the field of agricultural trade.
160 See Appellate Body Report, *Japan – Agricultural Products II*, para. 128.
161 See Panel Reports, *US – Continued Suspension*, para. 6.72; and *Canada – Continued Suspension*, para. 6.67.

162 See Appellate Body Report, *US/Canada – Continued Suspension*, para. 438.
163 *Ibid.*, para. 480.
164 See Appellate Body Report, *Japan – Agricultural Products II*, paras. 126 and 129.
165 See Panel Report, *Australia – Apples*, para. 7.81.
166 See Appellate Body Report, *US/Canada – Continued Suspension*, para. 439.
167 See Appellate Body Report, *Australia – Apples*, para. 179.
168 See Appellate Body Report, *US/Canada – Continued Suspension*, para. 590.
169 *Ibid.*, para. 591.
170 See Appellate Body Report, *Australia – Apples*, paras. 213–214.
171 *Ibid.*, paras. 211–212.
172 See Panel Reports, *EC – Hormones (Canada)*, para. 8.104, and *EC – Hormones (US)*, para. 8.101.
173 See Appellate Body Report, *US/Canada – Continued Suspension*, para. 591.
174 See Panel Report, *EC – Approval and Marketing of Biotech Products*, para. 7.3060. See also Appellate Body Report, *EC – Hormones*, paras. 193–194.

Bibliography

Arcuri, Alessandra. 'Global Food Safety Standards: The Evolving Regulatory Epistemology at the Intersection of the SPS Agreement and the Codex Alimentarius Commission,' in Delimatsis, Panagiotis (ed.) *The Law, Economics and Politics of International Standardization* (Cambridge University Press, 2015) 79–103.

Baller, Silja. 'Trade Effects of Regional Standards Liberalization: A Heterogeneous Firms Approach,' *World Bank Policy Research Working Paper 4124* (2007).

Chase, Claude. 'Norm Conflict between WTO Covered Agreements: Real, Apparent or Avoided?,' *The International and Comparative Law Quarterly* Vol 61, No 4 (2012) 791–821.

Du, Michael Ming. 'Standard of Review under the SPS Agreement after EC-Hormones II,' *International and Comparative Law Quarterly* Vol 59, No 2 (2010) 441–459.

Du, Ming. *The Regulation of Product Standards in World Trade Law* (Hart Publishing, 2020).

Du, Ming and Fei Deng. 'International Standards as Global Public Goods in the World Trading System,' *Legal Issues of Economic Integration* Vol 43, No 2 (2016) 113–144.

Epps, Tracy. *International Trade and Health Protection: A Critical Assessment of the WTO's SPS Agreement* (Edward Elgar Publishing, 2008).

Fontagné, Lionel, Gianluca Orefice, Roberta Piermartini and Nadia Rocha. 'Product Standards and Margins of Trade: Firm Level Evidence,' *Journal of International Economics* Vol 97, No 1 (2015) 29–44.

Hoekman, Bernard M. and Michel M. Kostecki. *The Political Economy of the World Trading System* Vol 3 (Oxford University Press, 2009).

Laowonsiri, Akawat. 'Application of the Precautionary Principle in the SPS Agreement,' *Max Planck Yearbook of United Nations Law* Vol 14, No 1 (2010) 563–623.

Lester, Simon, Bryan Mercurio and Arwel Davies. *World Trade Law: Text, Materials and Commentary* (Hart Publishing, 2018).

Marceau, Gabrielle and Joel P. Trachtman. 'The Technical Barriers to Trade Agreement, the Sanitary and Phytosanitary Measures Agreement, and the General Agreement on Tariffs and Trade: A Map of the World Trade Organization Law of Domestic Regulations of Goods,' *Journal of World Trade* Vol 48, No 2 (2014) 351–432.

Matsushita, Mitsuo, Thomas J. Shoenbaum, Petros C. Mavroidis and Michael Hahn. *The World Trade Organization: Law, Practice, and Policy* (Oxford University Press, 2017).

Prévost, Denise. 'National Treatment in the SPS Agreement: A *Sui Generis* Obligation,' in Sanders, Anslem Kamperman (ed.) *The Principle of National Treatment in International Economic Law* (Edward Elgar Publishing, 2014) 125–157.

Prévost, Denise and Peter Van den Bossche. 'The Agreement on the Application of Sanitary and Phytosanitary Measures,' in Macrory, Patrick F.J., Arthur E. Appleton and Michael G. Plummer (eds.) *The WTO: Legal, Economic and Political Analysis* Vol 1 (Springer, 2005) 231–370.

Rigod, Boris. 'The Purpose of the WTO Agreement on the Application of Sanitary and Phytosanitary Measures (SPS),' *The European Journal of International Law* Vol 24, No 2 (2013) 503–532.

Scott, Joanne. *The WTO Agreement on Sanitary and Phytosanitary Measures: A Commentary* (Oxford University Press, 2009).

Stoler, Andrew L. 'TBT and SPS Measures in Practice,' in Chauffour, Jean-Pierre and Jean-Christophe Maur (eds.) *Preferential Trade Agreement Policies for Development: A Handbook* (World Bank Publishing, 2011) 217–233.

Sykes, Alan O. 'Regulatory Protectionism and the Law of International Trade,' *The University of Chicago Law Review* Vol 66, No 1 (1999) 1–46.

Trebilcock, Michael, Robert Howse and Antonia Eliason. *The Regulation of International Trade* (Routledge, 2013).

Van den Bossche, Peter and Werner Zdouc. *The Law and Policy of the World Trade Organization* (Cambridge University Press, 2017).

Wirth, David A. 'The Role of Science in the Uruguay Round and NAFTA Trade Disciplines,' *Cornell International Law Journal* Vol 27 (1994) 817–860.

WTO. Committee on Sanitary and Phytosanitary Measures, 'Technical Assistance Typology,' Note by the Secretariat (G/SPS/GEN/206) (18 October 2000).

WTO. 'Doha Decision on Implementation-Related Issues and Concerns,' Ministerial Conference (WT/MIN(01)/17) (14 November 2001).

WTO. Committee on Sanitary and Phytosanitary Measures, 'Decision on the Implementation of Article 4 of the Agreement on the Application of Sanitary and Phytosanitary Measures,' (Revision, G/SPS/19/Rev.2) (23 July 2004).

WTO. *World Trade Report 2005: Exploring the Links between Trade, Standards and the WTO* (WTO, 2005).

WTO. Committee on Sanitary and Phytosanitary Measures, 'Guidelines to Further the Practical Implementation of Article 6 of the Agreement on the Application of Sanitary and Phytosanitary Measures,' (G/SPS/48) (16 May 2008).

WTO. Committee on Sanitary and Phytosanitary Measures, 'Decision by the Committee on Procedure to Enhance Transparency of Special and Differential Treatment in Favour of Developing Country Members,' (G/SPS/33/Rev.1) (18 December 2009).

WTO. *World Trade Report 2012: Trade and Public Policy: A Closer Look at Non-Tariff Measures in the 21st Century* (WTO, 2012).

WTO. Committee on Technical Barriers to Trade, 'Decisions and Recommendations Adopted by the Committee since 1 January 1995,' (WTO Doc. G/TBT/1 Rev.11) (16 December 2013).

WTO. Committee on Sanitary and Phytosanitary Measures, 'Decision of the Committee on a Procedure to Encourage and Facilitate the Resolution of Specific Sanitary or Phytosanitary Issues among Members,' (G/SPS/61) (8 September 2014).

WTO. Committee on Sanitary and Phytosanitary Measures, 'Specific Trade Concerns,' Note by the Secretariat, Revision (G/SPS/GEN/204/Rev.15) (24 February 2015).

WTO. Sanitary and Phytosanitary Information Management System (10 February 2021) <www.spsims.wto.org> (accessed 24 April 2021).

Part IV
RTAs, Environment, Human Rights, and Reform of the WTO

15 Regional Trade Agreements

Learning Objectives	609
1. Introduction	609
2. History of RTAs: Regionalism	610
3. Political Economy of RTAs	613
4. Article XXIV of the GATT: Customs Unions and FTA Exceptions	614
4.1 Customs Unions	615
4.1.1 Conditions for the Formation of a Customs Union	618
4.2 Free-Trade Areas	618
4.3 Interim Agreements	619
5. Special Rules for Developing Country Member States	620
6. Obligation to Notify the CRTA	620
7. RTAs and Dispute Settlement at the WTO	621
8. Emergence of Mega-RTAs	624
9. Summary	625

Learning Objectives

This chapter aims to help students understand:

1. Regional Trade Agreements (RTAs); history of RTAs; regionalism;
2. Political economy of RTAs;
3. Article XXIV of the GATT; customs unions and FTA exceptions; formation of customs unions; free-trade areas; and interim agreements;
4. Special rules for developing country Member States;
5. Obligation to notify the CRTA; RTAs and dispute settlement at the WTO; and
6. Emergence of mega-RTAs.

1. Introduction

A discourse on international trade is not complete without mention of Regional Trade Agreements (RTAs), as they are an important feature of the trade policy of all Member States. RTAs are understood to mean "any reciprocal trade agreement between two or more partners, not necessarily belonging to the same region" (WTO, 2021). There had been an exponential growth in the number of RTAs[1] entered into amongst the Member States since the founding of the WTO in 1995. During the GATT era, close to 70 RTAs were concluded between 1948 and 1994, and in contrast, in the WTO era, over 500 RTAs have been

DOI: 10.4324/9780367028183-19

notified.[2] These statistics reveal that the growth of RTAs during the GATT era was gradual, but during the WTO era it has been fourfold, with more to come. Not surprisingly, as of February 2021, all Member States of the WTO are parties to RTAs, and in many cases the Member States are parties to three or more RTAs – although several of them have not been notified to the WTO. Not surprisingly, RTAs regulate more sectors than the multilateral trade performed under the WTO.

The exceptions to MFN treatment obligation contained in Article XXIV of the GATT authorises the creation of FTAs/RTAs and runs counter to the principle considered to be the cornerstone of the multilateral trading system, *viz.*, non-discrimination. This means, a substantial volume of international trade is performed outside the framework of the multilateral trading system. Hence, RTAs have an impact on the welfare of countries as well as on the stability of the WTO. RTAs establish either a customs union or a free-trade area. As early as in the 1950s, Viner in his classic work noted that RTAs have a trade diversion effect (Viner, 2014). The creation of RTAs raises several questions, including if there is a dire need to revisit Article XXIV of the GATT and the purposes for which it was originally introduced into the legal fabric of the GATT (later retained in the WTO), whether Article XXIV of the GATT has outlived its purpose, and whether Article XXIV of the GATT is causing more harm to the institution of the WTO, to name a few.

The different types of RTAs can be identified as follows: (i) preferential agreement (PA) grants each participant preferential access to particular segments of the other participants' markets – the initial Association of Southeast Asian Nations (ASEAN);[3] (ii) a free-trade area (FTA) is marked by the reduction or elimination of trade barriers on most (if not all) products within the arrangement – NAFTA and both ASEAN (since 1992) and the SADC (since 2000); (iii) customs unions (CUs), on the other hand, are trade arrangements in which members eliminate trade barriers on other participants' goods and impose a common external tariff (CET) on imports from third parties; (iv) a common market (CM) is a customs union that is augmented by similar product regulations and the free flow of factors of production among members; and (v) an economic union is a common market whereby members also coordinate fiscal and monetary policies (Bhagwati and Panagariya, 1996; Mansfield and Milner, 2012).

Some of the well-known RTAs are the European Union (EU),[4] the European Free Trade Association (EFTA), the European Economic Area (EEA), the ASEAN (Association of Southeast Asian Nations) Free Trade Area (AFTA), the Comprehensive and Progressive Agreement for Trans-Pacific Partnership (CPTPP),[5] the Southern Common Market (MERCOSUR), the Andean Community, the Common Market of the Caribbean (CARICOM), the Australia–New Zealand Closer Economic Relations Agreement (ANZCERTA), the Regional Comprehensive Economic Partnership (RCEP),[6] the African Continental Free Trade Area (AfCFTA),[7] the Southern African Development Community (SADC), the Economic Community of West African States (ECOWAS), the United States-Mexico-Canada Agreement (USMCA),[8] and the Common Market of Eastern and Southern Africa (COMESA). CPTPP, AfCFTA, and RCEP are identified as mega-RTAs and have the potential to divert a major trade volume away from the multilateral trading system.

2. History of RTAs: Regionalism

Regionalism, as we have come to understand today, indicates certain types of trade agreements which have been entered into between two or more countries. The agreement may involve several signatories, as in the case of the EU (27 signatories); a couple of signatories, as in the case of ANZCERTA (Australia and New Zealand); countries that are in close proximity geographically, as in the case of USMCA or ECOWAS; or countries that are geographically dispersed, as in the case of CPTPP. In some cases, trade policies pursued may define the type of trade agreement entered into, *e.g.*, trade liberalisation, or a narrower agreement covering only select products, *e.g.*, information technology agreement. This understanding of regionalism sits well with the WTO's definition of regionalism.

Historically, regional integration coupled with economic integration were the key motivating factors behind the creation of bilateral and Regional Trade Agreements amongst the key trading nations. There was widespread use of conditional MFN clauses in the late nineteenth century, which resulted in a complex network of trading relationships, where preferential treatment was reserved to those countries deemed to be politically important and countries considered as competitors were discriminated against. The original version of MFN clause became corrupt over time through the concept of reciprocity. When the Great Depression struck in the last quarter of the nineteenth century, key trading nations embraced protectionism and high tariffs. Bismarck was to abandon the German free-trade policy in 1879; in the US, Benjamin Harrison won the presidency on a protectionist ticket in 1888; and France introduced the Méline Tariff in 1892.

In the aftermath of World War I, economic nationalism was gaining ground. The interwar period witnessed the emergence of trading blocs, with Japan, Britain, and Germany withdrawing from the world trading system, and at the same time the US abandoning protectionism and redoubling its commitment to MFN principles (Chase, 2008). In its quest for a global market free of trading blocs, the US gave up on conditional MFN principles and enacted the Reciprocal Trade Agreement Act of 1934 to pursue liberalised bilateral trade agreements. In the post-World War II era, the objective was set as the prevention of a repeat of the destruction brought about by the two world wars. As a result, the GATT 1947 was driven by the desire to create an international economic order which was grounded on a non-discriminatory multilateral trading system. The MFN principle was considered a key building block in the post-World War II architecture and was adopted by the Contracting Parties of the GATT 1947 as the core principle and duly enshrined in Article I.

The GATT 1947 restored the unconditional MFN principle, which in effect was to give away concessions whilst receiving none in return. Commentators argue that the GATT was not fundamentally different in spirit from any of the bilateral PTAs concluded in the late nineteenth century (Cattaneo, 2015). The same GATT Contracting Parties also incorporated Article XXIV within the GATT, as a significant exception to Article I, which permits the creation of customs unions and free-trade agreements. Through Article XXIV, the GATT, besides permitting the creation of RTAs, also granted 'grandfather rights' to existing RTAs.

In the GATT era, the first wave of regionalism started with the creation of the European Coal and Steel Community (ECSC) in 1952. The ECSC placed the French and German steel industries under a common authority, which lessened the likelihood of any serious conflict arising between France and Germany. By picking coal and steel (two main forms of energy), the ECSC Member States were looking to avoid the prospect of a new war on the European continent. The ECSC eventually led to the formation of the European Economic Community (EEC) in 1958. Although the Treaty of Rome did not fully comply with the spirit of Article XXIV, the EC agreement was allowed to pass in the GATT. It had the strong backing of the US, which was desirous of seeing a peaceful Western Europe in the post-World War II era (Bhagwati, 1999; Carpenter, 2008).[9] A decade later, in 1968, moves were under way for the creation of a common external tariff. Around the same time, the EFTA was formed by countries left out of the EC, prominent amongst them being the

UK. Five of the seven EFTA contracting parties, including the UK, were to later become members of the EC.

In the period between 1955 and 1974, a total of 57 trade agreements were concluded, which included efforts by developing countries, who were driven by ideologies rather than trade concessions (Carpenter, 2008). The non-aligned movement under the leadership of India was born during this period. The ASEAN, although originally formed in 1967 for security reasons, was to transform itself into an RTA a decade later, with the inclusion of a trade list. In the 1960s and 1970s, economic integration was promoted through RTAs, coupled with a policy of industrialisation. Interestingly, in 1979, the GATT Contracting Parties agreed upon the 'Enabling Clause', which permits less-developed countries to grant each other preferences that do not meet the criteria specified in Article XXIV.[10] This was again a departure from the core GATT principles.

The mid-1980s witnessed the 'second wave' of regionalism. The EC deepened and widened its sphere by including new members to its fold, which paved the way for a single European Market for goods, services, capital, and labour. This resulted in the birth of the European Union in 1992. The US, which had until then abstained from invoking Article XXIV of the GATT, commenced negotiations on trade agreements, starting with Israel and followed by Canada and Mexico.[11] The conversion of the US to regionalism is considered a major turning point, as it had steadfastly held on to its commitment to multilateralism through the post-war years until up to the 1980s. The US move towards regionalism clearly tilted the "balance of forces at the margin away from multilateralism to regionalism" (Bhagwati, 1999).[12] Also of significance was Mexico's decision to join hands with the US and Canada to form NAFTA, which posed a major challenge to Latin American countries.[13] The year 1986 also saw the launch of the Uruguay Round of negotiations, which would eventually culminate in the founding of the WTO in 1995.[14] In 1991, MERCOSUR was founded under the Enabling Clause with four signatories, *viz.*, Argentina, Brazil, Paraguay, and Uruguay. The 1980s and early 1990s produced some of the key RTAs from the second wave of regionalism, which emerged as a prominent tool for economic cooperation.

The third wave of regionalism was witnessed at the conclusion of the Uruguay Round. As mentioned earlier, numerous RTAs have been forged since the creation of the WTO in 1995, resulting in all Member States becoming parties to one or more RTAs. Unlike the first and second wave of regionalism, the third wave is a surge, where there are North-South and South-South agreements making up to two-thirds of all RTAs. The RTAs in the third wave are no longer from within the same region and are geographically dispersed. The developing country participation in the third wave has been active, and they have often been the *demandeurs* for agreements with the EU and the US. Both smaller and larger agreements have already been signed, and those that are being negotiated make the RTAs regulate trade and investment flows and are to be considered the most important governance instrument (Mansfield and Milner, 2016). The RTAs now appear to help open up markets, and they provide regulatory innovation for participating nations, as only modest results have been produced at the WTO through multilateral negotiations. The MFN clause has been lost in the 'spaghetti bowl' of RTAs.[15]

With the emergence of mega-RTAs, a substantial trade volume is diverted away from the WTO. RTAs now regulate issues ranging from trade in goods and services to investment, IP rights, government procurement, *etc*. The Member States view the RTAs as policy alternative to the WTO, and the surge of the third wave is a clear example of this. In some areas, like IP rights, the RTAs assist patent-holding developed country Member States to protect their IP rights through the introduction of TRIPS-plus provisions.[16]

3. Political Economy of RTAs

The reasons that countries may want to join an RTA varies. Some of the persistent arguments in favour of RTAs is that they result in trade creation, enhanced global efficiency, and optimal allocation of global resources, resulting in economies of scale and specialisation. Both political and economic factors are motivating factors for a country to enter into an RTA. On the other hand, the reason against the formation of RTAs is the argument for multilateralism, *i.e.*, it builds trade liberalisation on the foundations of non-discrimination, and the proliferation of RTAs has led to a criss-crossing of trade preferences and hence to a veritable 'spaghetti bowl', where products sold in key markets are sold on widely varying terms depending on where they are supposed to originate (Bhagwati and Panagariya, 1996).

Ravenhill classifies the political motivational factors as (i) economic cooperation and confidence building, (ii) reward for security partners, (iii) regional economic cooperation over security threats, (iv) a bargaining tool, (v) in the case of LDCs, to gain aid from donor countries, (vi) for locking in reform, (vii) to satisfy domestic political constituencies, and (viii) practical ease in negotiating and implementing agreements (Ravenhill, 2017). Ravenhill identifies the chief economic motivational factors for choosing regionalism over multilateralism as being (i) an enabler for continued protection of sectors that may not survive in a global competition, (ii) a creator of opportunities for 'deeper integration', and (iii) a provider of access to larger markets and increased foreign investment (Ravenhill, 2017).

Political considerations are counted as one of the major factors for concluding RTAs. Although it is not possible to delineate completely the interplay between political and economic motivations, politicians often pursue RTAs for political reasons (Damro, 2006). For instance, the EC in its 'Global Europe' Communication from 2006 acknowledged that it had been largely motivated by political considerations to conclude trade agreements with countries that were candidates for EU membership, with the exception of Mexico, South Africa, and Chile.[17]

The revised EC policy from 2006 restored economics as the chief criterion for any future bilateral agreements, where partners will be selected on the basis of (i) their market potential, *i.e.*, economic size and growth; (ii) their level of protection against EU export interests, *i.e.*, tariffs and non-tariff barriers; and (iii) the state of negotiations with EU competitors to gauge the likely impact of a bilateral agreement with a competitor on EU markets and economy and the risk of erosion of the preferential access to EU markets currently enjoyed by the EU's neighbouring and developing country partners (Cattaneo, 2015).[18] The EU had not put this policy to full use in practice, as various trade agreements concluded by the EU since 2006 have deviated from this rhetoric, and are a combination of both economic and political factors.

A similar approach is taken by the US towards its potential trade partners, with the US General Accounting Office (GAO) listing the factors that determine the selection of potential partners for RTAs as follows: (i) country readiness, (ii) economic/commercial benefit, (iii) benefits to the broader trade liberalisation strategy, (iv) compatibility with US interests, (v) Congressional/private sector support, and (vi) US government resource constraints (USGAO, 2004). Tracing the formation of RTAs during the different eras shows that the motivating factors could be various, *i.e.*, political, economic, for reasons of security, trade policies, *etc.* Mansfield and Milner have stressed the role played by key sectors of the economy, and domestic institutions, besides interest groups, in shaping RTAs (Mansfield and Milner, 2012). A democratically elected government is more prone to entering into RTAs, as they depend on the support of constituents to stay in power and as a result have a greater incentive to conclude trade agreements. This contrasts with autocracies, where a democratic process is absent. For instance, the Dominican Republic concluded no RTAs before becoming a democracy in 1978. Likewise South Korea, prior to becoming a democracy, had signed just one RTA.[19] In a democracy, leaders can be pressurised by interest groups through lobbying for protectionist trade policies. Mansfield and Milner argue that when elections are held during poor economic circumstances, voters may blame incumbents in office for their economic woes and vote them out of power (Mansfield and Milner, 2016).

The motivating factors for both RTAs and multilateral agreements are not too dissimilar. Cattaneo argues that once the free-trade spirit blows over, "whatever instrument is most readily available will be instinctively used" (Cattaneo, 2015, p. 34). Multilateral deals, which are considered the most efficient way to accelerate, will be used sparingly, while RTAs will remain the key instrument for forging international trade policies (Cattaneo, 2015). Mega-RTAs have been concluded in recent years which appear to take a substantial trade volume away from the WTO. Being an outsider to such mega-RTAs is costlier than being a party and compromising on issues such as TRIPS-plus provisions. However, Mansfield and Milner argue that the GATT/WTO global reach may affect the dominance of RTAs in the years to come.

4. Article XXIV of the GATT: Customs Unions and FTA Exceptions

Article XXIV of the GATT provides for 'regional trade exceptions' in addition to 'general and security exceptions' and 'economic emergency exceptions'. As discussed in earlier chapters, one of the cornerstones of the WTO is the MFN principle, which is enshrined in Article I of the GATT Agreement, as well as in Article II of the GATS Agreement.[20] Article XXIV:4 of the GATT contains the general principles on the formation of 'customs unions' and 'free-trade areas', identifying their purpose as bringing about 'closer integration' of the participants. On the other hand, Article XXIV:5 lays down the conditions for the creation of free-trade agreements. Pursuant to Article XXIV:5, for a free-trade area to be GATT consistent, its contracting parties are required to liberalise trade between themselves, and for a customs union to be GATT consistent, its contracting parties are also required to agree on a common trade policy *vis-à-vis* the rest of the WTO Member States.

Article I:1 of the GATT obligates Member States to provide equal treatment to imports of products from all other Member States. Article XXIV is an exception to Article I of the GATT and reads as follows:

> The Members recognize the desirability of increasing freedom of trade by the development, through voluntary agreements, of closer integration between the economies of the countries parties to such agreements. They also recognize that the purpose of a customs union or of a free-trade area should be to facilitate trade between the constituent territories and not to raise barriers to the trade of other contracting parties with such territories.

The *Chapeau* of Article XXIV:5 of the GATT 1994 provides, in relevant part:

> [T]he provisions of this Agreement shall not prevent, as between the territories of [Member States], the formation of a customs union or of a free-trade area or the adoption of an interim agreement necessary for the formation of a customs union or of a free-trade area.

Although the key provision in the *Turkey – Textiles* dispute related to paragraph 5 of Article XXIV, the Appellate Body held that "paragraph 4 of Article XXIV constitutes an important element of the context of the *Chapeau* of paragraph 5".[21] In examining the purport of the *Chapeau* to Article XXIV:5, the Appellate Body in *Turkey – Textiles* observed as follows:

> We read this to mean that the provisions of the GATT 1994 shall not make impossible the formation of a customs union. Thus, the *Chapeau* makes it clear that Article XXIV may, under certain conditions, justify the adoption of a measure which is inconsistent with certain other GATT provisions, and may be invoked as a possible "defence" to a finding of inconsistency.[22]

The Appellate Body in *Turkey – Textiles* indicated the two conditions that a measure otherwise incompatible with WTO law must satisfy to be justified by virtue of Article XXIV:

> First, the party claiming the benefit of this defence must demonstrate that the measure at issue is introduced upon the formation of a customs union that fully meets the requirements of sub-paragraphs 8(a) and 5(a) of Article XXIV. And, second, that party must demonstrate that the formation of that customs union would be prevented if it were not allowed to introduce the measure at issue. Again, both these conditions must be met to have the benefit of the defence under Article XXIV.[23]

The Appellate Body in its report in *Argentina – Footwear (EC)* reiterated the aforementioned findings in *Turkey – Textiles* while examining the Panel's finding that Argentina had violated Article 2 of the Agreement on Safeguards by including imports from all sources in its investigation of 'increased imports' of footwear products into its territory but excluding other MERCOSUR Member States from the application of the safeguard measures.[24]

The two-tier test that emerges from the Appellate Body's Report is that a measure that is otherwise inconsistent with GATT 1994 can be justified provided (i) it is introduced upon the formation of a 'customs union', a 'free-trade area', or such interim agreement that meets the requirements set out in Article XXIV of the GATT 1994, and (ii) that the contracting parties are able to demonstrate that the formation of the customs union will be prevented if the measure were not permitted to be introduced. Regional trade exceptions contained in Article XXIV had been the subject of disputes before the DSB on very few occasions, and not surprisingly the jurisprudence in this area is sparse.[25]

4.1 Customs Unions

Article XXIV:8(a) defines 'customs union' as follows:

> A customs union shall be understood to mean the substitution of a single customs territory for two or more customs territories so that
>
> i   duties and other restrictive regulations of commerce (except, where necessary, those permitted under Articles XI, XII, XIII, XIV, XV and XX) are eliminated with respect to substantially all the trade between the constituent territories of the union or at least with respect to substantially all the trade in products originating in such territories, and

ii . . . substantially the same duties and other regulations of commerce are applied by each of the members of the union to the trade of territories not included in the union.

In order to satisfy the criteria found in Article XXIV:8(a) of the GATT, a customs union comprising constituent territories should establish (i) a standard of trade where duties and restrictive regulations of commerce are eliminated, and (ii) a standard of trade framework for trade of constituent territories with third countries. The Appellate Body in *Turkey – Textiles*, noting that Member States have never reached an agreement on the interpretation of the term 'substantially all' in this provision, and agreeing with the Panel that Article XXIV:8(a)(i) offers 'some flexibility' with regards to liberalising internal trade, observed as follows:

> Sub-paragraph 8(a)(i) of Article XXIV establishes the standard for the internal trade between constituent members in order to satisfy the definition of a "customs union". It requires the constituent members of a customs union to eliminate "duties and other restrictive regulations of commerce" with respect to "substantially all the trade" between them. Neither the GATT CONTRACTING PARTIES nor the WTO Members have ever reached an agreement on the interpretation of the term "substantially" in this provision. It is clear, though, that "substantially all the trade" is not the same as all the trade, and also that "substantially all the trade" is something considerably more than merely some of the trade. We note also that the terms of sub-paragraph 8(a)(i) provide that members of a customs union may maintain, where necessary, in their internal trade, certain restrictive regulations of commerce that are otherwise permitted under Articles XI through XV and under Article XX of the GATT 1994. Thus, we agree with the Panel that the terms of sub-paragraph 8(a)(i) offer "some flexibility" to the constituent members of a customs union when liberalizing their internal trade in accordance with this sub-paragraph. Yet we caution that the degree of "flexibility" that sub-paragraph 8(a)(i) allows is limited by the requirement that "duties and other restrictive regulations of commerce" be "eliminated with respect to substantially all" internal trade.[26]

It is to be noted that there is still some degree of uncertainty as regards what constitutes 'substantially all the trade' as appearing in Article XXIV:8(a)(i), due to a lack of both WTO jurisprudence and consensus amongst the Member States.

The Panel in *Argentina – Footwear (EC)* found that Argentina violated Article 2 of the Agreement on Safeguards by including imports from all sources in its investigation of 'increased imports' of footwear products into its territory but excluding other MERCOSUR Member States from the application of the safeguard measures. The Appellate Body in *Argentina – Footwear (EC)*, reversing the Panel's decision, ruled that footnote 1 to Article 2.1 of the Agreement on Safeguards only applies when a customs union applies a safeguard measure "as a single unit or on behalf of a member State",[27] and further observed that Article XXIV:8(a)(i) did not prohibit the imposition of safeguard measures on other MERCOSUR Member States.[28]

The Panel in *US – Wheat Gluten* found that the US had acted inconsistently with Articles 2.1 and 4.2 of the Agreement on Safeguards by including imports from all sources in its investigation but excluding imports from Canada from the application of the safeguard measures. On appeal, the US raised the ground that the Panel erred in not assessing the legal relevance of footnote 1 to the Safeguards Agreement and Article XXIV of the GATT 1994. The Appellate Body, upholding the Panel's decision, ruled that the issue to be determined was if, as a general principle, a member of a free-trade area can exclude imports from other members of that free-trade area from the application of a safeguard measure, and that the issue can be decided without recourse to Article XXIV or footnote 1 Article 2.1 of the Agreement on Safeguards.[29]

Both Panels and the Appellate Body have dealt with the issue of whether trade remedies can be applied within RTAs, which is referred to as 'parallelism'. The Appellate Body in *Argentina – Footwear (EC)*, *US – Wheat Gluten*, and *US – Lamb* observed that there should be a parallelism between the scope of investigation for a safeguard measure conducted by a Member State and the scope of safeguard which is applied as the result of it.[30]

As regards the standard of trade framework of constituent territories with third countries, Article XXIV:8(a)(ii) of the GATT 1994 requires that the constituent members of a customs union apply 'substantially the same' duties and other regulations of commerce to trade with third countries. The Appellate Body in *Turkey – Textiles* addressed the requirement contained in Article XXIV:8(a)(ii) that constituent members of a customs union apply 'substantially the same' duties and other regulations of commerce to their external trade with third countries, and observed:

> Sub-paragraph 8(a)(ii) establishes the standard for the trade of constituent members with third countries in order to satisfy the definition of a "customs union". It requires the constituent members of a customs union to apply "substantially the same" duties and other regulations of commerce to external trade with third countries. The constituent members of a customs union are thus required to apply a common external trade regime, relating to both duties and other regulations of commerce. However, sub-paragraph 8(a)(ii) does not require each constituent member of a customs union to apply the same duties and other regulations of commerce as other constituent members with respect to trade with third countries; instead, it requires that substantially the same duties and other regulations of commerce shall be applied.[31]

The Appellate Body in *Turkey – Textiles* also noted that the phrase 'substantially the same' in Article XXIV:8(a)(ii) offered a certain degree of 'flexibility' to the constituent members of a customs union in 'the creation of a common commercial policy', but yet cautioned that such flexibility is limited, and observed as follows:

> Here too we would caution that this "flexibility" is limited. It must not be forgotten that the word "substantially" qualifies the words "the same". Therefore, in our view, something closely approximating "sameness" is required by Article XXIV:8(a)(ii). . . . Sub-paragraph 8(a)(ii) requires the constituent members of a customs union to adopt "substantially the same" trade regulations. In our view, "comparable trade regulations having similar effects" do not meet this standard. A higher degree of "sameness" is required by the terms of sub-paragraph 8(a)(ii).[32]

Besides meeting the requirements set in Article XXIV:8(a), a customs union must also meet the requirements set under Article XXIV:5(a), which in relevant part states:

> [W]ith respect to a customs union . . . the duties and other regulations of commerce imposed at the institution of any such union . . . in respect of trade with [Member States] not parties to such union . . . shall not on the whole be higher or more restrictive than the general incidence of the duties and regulations of commerce applicable in the constituent territories prior to the formation of such union . . . as the case may be.

618 RTAs, Environment, Human Rights

The requirement that the duties and other regulations of commerce imposed after the formation of such customs union shall not on the whole be higher or more restrictive than the general incidence of the duties and other regulations of commerce applicable prior to the formation of the customs union has generated controversy in its interpretation. Paragraph 2 of the 1994 Understanding on Article XXIV, which seeks to clarify this requirement, in its relevant part reads as follows:

> The evaluation under paragraph 5(a) of Article XXIV of the general incidence of the duties and other regulations of commerce applicable before and after the formation of a customs union shall in respect of duties and charges be based upon an overall assessment of weighted average tariff rates and of customs duties collected.

Paragraph 2 further adds that such "assessment shall be based on import statistics for a previous representative period to be supplied by the customs union, on a tariff-line basis and in values and quantities, broken down by WTO country of origin".[33] Paragraph 2, recognising the difficulties that may be encountered in quantification and aggregation of regulations of commerce other than duties, provides as follows:

> [F]or the purpose of the overall assessment of the incidence of other regulations of commerce . . . the examination of individual measures, regulations, products covered and trade flows affected may be required.[34]

4.1.1 Conditions for the Formation of a Customs Union

As discussed earlier, the two-tier test for a measure that is otherwise incompatible with GATT 1994 can be justified provided it satisfies two conditions, with the first being that it meets the requirements contained in Articles XXIV:8(a) and XXIV:5(a). The second condition is that the contracting parties are to demonstrate that the formation of the customs union will be prevented if the measure were not permitted to be introduced. In *Turkey – Textiles*, the measures under challenge were quantitative restrictions on textiles and clothing from India, where Turkey argued that in the absence of the such GATT-inconsistent measures, it would have been prevented from forming a customs union with the EC. The Appellate Body, rejecting the argument, ruled as follows:

> As the panel observed, there are other alternatives available to Turkey and the European Communities to prevent any possible diversion of trade, while at the same time meeting the requirements of subparagraph 8(a)(i). For example, Turkey could adopt rules of origin for textile and clothing products that would allow the European Communities to distinguish between those textile and clothing products originating in Turkey, which would enjoy free access to the European Communities under the terms of the customs union, and those textile and clothing products originating in third countries, including India.[35]

4.2 Free-Trade Areas

Article XXIV:8(b) defines 'free-trade area' as follows:

> A free-trade area shall be understood to mean a group of two or more customs territories in which the duties and other restrictive regulations of commerce (except, where

necessary, those permitted under Articles XI, XII, XIII, XIV, XV and XX) are eliminated on substantially all the trade between the constituent territories in products originating in such territories.

It will be noted that the definition of a 'free-trade area' establishes only a standard for the internal trade between constituent members and does not require the establishment of a standard for the trade of constituent members with third countries. As regards the standard for the internal trade between constituent members of a free-trade area, it is akin to the standard for the internal trade between constituent members of a customs union. Hence, much of the jurisprudence discussed under 'customs union' is relevant for a discussion of free-trade areas. Other than meeting the requirement of Article XXIV:8(a), free-trade areas are also subject to Article XXIV:5(b), which in its relevant part reads as follows:

> [W]ith respect to a free-trade area . . . the duties and other regulations of commerce maintained in each of the constituent territories and applicable at the formation of such free-trade area . . . to the trade of [Member States] not included in such area . . . shall not be higher or more restrictive than the corresponding duties and other regulations of commerce existing in the same constituent territories prior to the formation of the free-trade area.

Pursuant to Article XXIV:5(b), free-trade areas require that the duties and other regulations of commerce maintained by a constituent member of a free-trade area to trade with third countries after the formation of the free-trade area must not be higher or more restrictive than the duties and other regulations of commerce maintained by that constituent member before the formation of such free-trade area.

4.3 Interim Agreements

Pursuant to Article XXIV:5(c) of the GATT 1994:

> [A]ny interim agreement referred to in subparagraphs (a) and (b) shall include a plan and schedule for the formation of such a customs union or of such a free-trade area within a reasonable length of time.

Pursuant to Article XXIV:8.5(c), only agreements that have already been implemented are considered 'full' Regional Trade Agreements, and an agreement which only includes an implementation period is merely an 'interim agreement' leading to a Regional Trade Agreement, as it does not meet the definition. What is a 'reasonable period of time' for the formation of a free-trade agreement was not clearly set out under the GATT 1947. Paragraph 3 of the 1994 Understanding on Article XXIV brings about clarity by stating that 'reasonable period of time' should not exceed ten years, except under exceptional circumstances, and where it is thought that the ten-year period may be insufficient, the participating Member States may provide explanation to the Council for Trade in Goods for the need for a longer period.

It should be noted that some discrepancies exist in the terminology referring to interim agreements in the GATT Agreement due to the language used to describe an interim agreement. While the *Chapeau* of Article XXIV:5 refers to "an interim agreement necessary for the formation of a customs union or of a free-trade area", Articles XXIV:5(a) and (b), Article

XXIV:7(a), and paragraphs 1 and 12 of the 1994 Understanding on Article XXIV refer to "an interim agreement leading to the formation of a customs union or free trade area".

5. Special Rules for Developing Country Member States

On 28 November 1979, the Contracting Parties of the GATT adopted the 'Enabling Clause' through the decision entitled 'The Differential and More Favourable Treatment, Reciprocity and Fuller Participation of Developing Countries'. The Enabling Clause, which is the result of the Tokyo Round of negotiations, is considered a milestone as it was the result of a long process of legitimisation of developing countries into an international organisation which was originally created by developed countries. The developing countries, in turn, were to reciprocate by progressively undertaking more trade obligations as their level of development increased.

The Enabling Clause enlarged the possibilities of the preferential treatment of developing countries. It permitted but did not oblige Contracting Parties of the GATT to provide preferential tariff treatment to developing countries, as well as special treatments to least developed countries (LDCs). On the other hand, the Enabling Clause granted developing countries flexible conditions regarding the application GATT rules in relation to RTAs. The relevant part of the Enabling Clause reads as follows:

1. Notwithstanding the provisions of Article I of the General Agreement, [Members] may accord differential and more favourable treatment to developing countries, without according such treatment to other [Member States].
2. The provisions of paragraph 1 apply to the following:

    . . .

    (c) Regional or global arrangements entered into amongst less-developed [Member States] for the mutual reduction or elimination of tariffs and, in accordance with criteria or conditions which may be prescribed by the [Ministerial Conference], for the mutual reduction or elimination of non-tariff measures, on products imported from one another.
3. Any differential and more favourable treatment provided under this clause:

    (a) shall be designed to facilitate and promote the trade of developing countries and not to raise barriers to or create undue difficulties for the trade of any other [Member States].

As the 'Enabling Clause' is part of the GATT 1994, it permits preferential agreements between developing country Member States, departing from the MFN treatment obligation arising under Article I of the GATT. Consequently, developing country Member States that enter into RTAs under the Enabling Clause are required to meet less demanding and less specific conditions than those set out in Article XXIV of the GATT 1994.[36]

6. Obligation to Notify the CRTA

Member States desiring to enter into an RTA are required to notify their intentions to the Council for Trade in Goods, which in turn will transfer such notification over to the WTO Committee on Regional Trade Agreements (CRTA). Article XXIV:7(a) of the GATT requires Member States to 'promptly' notify their participation in Regional Trade Agreements concerning trade in goods. Also, paragraph 4(b) of the Enabling Clause requires the notification of RTAs, where developing countries are participating. In December 2006, the Member States agreed on the Transparency Mechanism for Regional Trade Agreements (WTO, 2006).[37] The General Council in 1996 abolished the GATT Article XXIV working party, replacing it with the CRTA as its successor.

The CRTA is mandated under paragraphs 1(a) and 1(d) of the Decision Establishing the CRTA to examine any free-trade agreements referred to it by the Council for Trade in Goods (under Article XXIV of the GATT 1994) and the Committee on Trade and Development (agreements between developing countries, established under the Enabling Clause).[38] The CRTA is thereafter to present a report to the relevant body for appropriate action and further direct the Committee to "consider the systemic implications of such [RTAs] and regional initiatives for the multilateral trading system".

Under the powers vested, the CRTA is to make recommendations (i) on the reporting requirements for each type of agreement, and (ii) to further develop procedures to facilitate and improve the examination process of agreements. Any decisions taken at the Committee are only by consensus. Article XXIV:7(a) of the GATT requires Member States to "make available to them such information . . . as will enable [the working party] to such reports and recommendations to contracting parties as [the working party] deem appropriate". Further, Article XXIV:7(b), relating to interim agreements, requires that the "parties shall not maintain or put into force, as the case may be, such agreement if they are not prepared to modify it in accordance with these recommendations". This brings us to the RTA Transparency Mechanism, which was only established on a provisional basis. So far, the efforts to transform the Transparency Mechanism into a permanent feature has not met with success. It is not surprising that not all RTAs that have been entered into have been notified to the CRTA by the Member States.

7. RTAs and Dispute Settlement at the WTO

Paragraph 12 of the Understanding on the Interpretation of Article XXIV of the GATT reads as follows:

> The provisions of Articles XXII and XXIII of GATT 1994 as elaborated and applied by the Dispute Settlement Understanding may be invoked with respect to any matters arising from the application of those provisions of Article XXIV relating to customs unions, free-trade areas or interim agreements leading to the formation of a customs union or free-trade area.

Paragraph 12 clearly vests the Panels and Appellate Body with wide powers to review matters arising from the application of Article XXIV of the GATT in relation to customs unions, free-trade areas, or interim agreements. Since the creation of the WTO, no dispute had come before the DSB where a Member State had challenged the consistency of an RTA to Article XXIV of the GATT. Only a handful of Panels have so far been established to examine the consistency of RTAs in relation to WTO rules. Coming against the backdrop of a cumulative notification of over 536 RTAs,[39] it is indeed surprising that there had been no clear review of RTAs by the Panels.

As regards the ambit of judicial review of an RTA by a Panel, the report in *Turkey – Textiles* presents the most comprehensive discussion to date. In *Turkey – Textiles*, India challenged the quantitative restrictions introduced by Turkey on 19 of its textiles and clothing products, arguing that it had suffered damage as a result of Turkey's decision to erect new barriers to its textiles exports, suffering a violation of its MFN rights. Turkey in turn had argued that it was justified to introduce the measures, as it was necessary for the purposes of complying with the terms of the Turkey–EC Association Council adopted decision from 1995, which required Turkey to apply "substantially the same commercial policy as the [European] Community in the textile sector including the agreements or arrangements on trade in textile and clothing", and as the measures under challenge were introduced pursuant to a customs union, they were compliant with Article XXIV of the GATT.

The Panel in *Turkey – Textiles* ruled that WTO adjudicating bodies are fully competent to examine and adjudicate on RTA-related issues, but such examination does not permit an overall assessment regarding the WTO consistency of an RTA, and observed as follows:

> As to the second question of how far-reaching a panel's examination should be of the Regional Trade Agreement underlying the challenged measure, we note that the Committee on Regional Trade Agreements (CRTA) has been established, *inter alia*, to assess the GATT/WTO compatibility of Regional Trade Agreements entered into by Members, a very complex undertaking which involves consideration by the CRTA, from the economic, legal and political perspectives of different Members, of the numerous facets of a Regional Trade Agreement in relation to the provisions of the WTO. It appears to us that the issue regarding the GATT/WTO compatibility of a customs union, as such, is generally a matter for the CRTA since, as noted above, it involves a broad multilateral assessment of any such customs union, i.e., a matter which concerns the WTO membership as a whole.
>
> As to whether panels also have the jurisdiction to assess the overall WTO compatibility of a customs union, we recall that the Appellate Body stated that the terms of reference of panels must refer explicitly to the "measures" to be examined by panels. We consider that Regional Trade Agreements may contain numerous measures, all of which could potentially be examined by panels, before, during or after the CRTA examination, if the requirements laid down in the DSU are met. However, it is arguable that a customs union (or a free-trade area) as a whole would logically not be a "measure" as such, subject to challenge under the DSU.[40]

When appealed against, the Appellate Body took the position that the Member State seeking to justify such measures by invoking Article XXIV of the GATT must explain why their RTA is GATT consistent, and it concluded that the Panels should always have the power to discuss the overall consistency of PTAs with the multilateral rules:

> First, the party claiming the benefit of this defense must demonstrate that the measure at issue is introduced upon the formation of a customs union that fully meets the requirements of sub-paragraph 8(a) and 5(a) of Article XXIV. And second, that party must demonstrate that the formation of that customs union would be prevented if it were not allowed to introduce the measure at issue.
>
> We would expect a panel, when examining such a measure, to require a party to establish that both of these conditions have been fulfilled. It may not always be possible to determine whether the second of the two conditions has been fulfilled without initially determining whether the first condition has been fulfilled.[41]

In the *US – Line Pipe* case, Korea argued that the US was in violation of the MFN treatment obligation as set out in Articles I, XIII:1, and XIX of the GATT and Article 2.2 of the

Safeguards Agreement through its action of excluding Mexico and Canada from the 'line pipe' safeguard measure. Defending its position, the US argued that the differential treatment accorded to the imports from Mexico and Canada, who were both parties to the NAFTA, was justified under the 'limited exception' of Article XXIV of the GATT. The Panel, while considering if the conditions contained in Articles XXIV:5(a) and (c) and XXIV:8(b) were met, ruled that the burden of proof was on the party seeking to rely on the defence of 'limited exception' under Article XXIV to demonstrate compliance with the conditions. One of the key arguments put forth by Korea was that NAFTA was not compliant with Article XXIV:8 as the CRTA was yet to issue a final decision on the free-trade arrangement.

The Panel in *US – Line Pipe* ruled that the burden was on the US to demonstrate consistency of NAFTA with Article XXIV of the GATT.[42] The Panel also ruled that it was on the party carrying the burden of proof to let in evidence to establish a *prima facie* case of the consistency of an RTA with the WTO rules, and observed as follows:

> In our view, the information provided by the United States in these proceedings, the information submitted by the NAFTA parties to the Committee on Regional Trade Agreements ("CRTA") (which the United States has incorporated into its submissions to the Panel by reference), and the absence of effective refutation by Korea, establishes a *prima facie* case that NAFTA is in conformity with Article XXIV:5(b) and (c), and with Article XXIV:8(b).[43]

The Appellate Body in *US – Line Pipe* avoided ruling on whether Article 2.2 of the Agreement on Safeguards "permits a Member to exclude imports originating in member states of a free-trade area from the scope of a safeguard measure". Nevertheless, the Appellate Body asserted that the latter question becomes relevant in two circumstances:

> The question of whether Article XXIV of the GATT 1994 serves as an exception to Article 2.2 of the Agreement on Safeguards becomes relevant in only two possible circumstances. One is when, in the investigation by the competent authorities of a WTO Member, the imports that are exempted from the safeguard measure are not considered in the determination of serious injury. The other is when, in such an investigation, the imports that are exempted from the safeguard measure are considered in the determination of serious injury, and the competent authorities have also established explicitly, through a reasoned and adequate explanation, that imports from sources outside the free-trade area, alone, satisfied the conditions for the application of a safeguard measure, as set out in Article 2.1 and elaborated in Article 4.2.[44]

On a few instances where disputes had reached the Panel stage, it has been argued by Member States that a disputed measure was justified due to the Member State's involvement in an RTA. Most of the debate before the Panel have revolved around three areas, *viz.*, the preliminary question, *i.e.*, competency of WTO Panels to review the consistency of RTAs to WTO rules; the role of RTAs in the interpretative exercise of WTO adjudicators; and in the case of obligational conflict, the approach to be adopted by the WTO adjudicator and the solution that it offers (Zang, 2018). One is prompted to ask the question, why is there so little litigation on the issue of consistency of RTAs with Article XXIV of the GATT before the DSB?

Some commentators trace the attitude of not questioning RTAs back to the GATT era, when Europe initiated its integration programme, and that the first step was the creation of European Coal and Steel Community (ECSC). Mavroidis argues that the ECSC was a blatant violation of the GATT rules, and no one wanted to challenge the European integration process by calling into question the GATT consistency of the ECSC (Mavroidis, 2016).[45] Other arguments that have been put forth are that Member States are risk-averse and don't choose to challenge any RTAs. The simple reason is that most of the Member States are participants in two or more RTAs and will not want to challenge the formation of an RTA for strategic reasons.

8. Emergence of Mega-RTAs

The third wave of regionalism is witnessing the emergence of a new kind of RTAs, *i.e.*, mega-RTAs. Major global economic powers, with the likes of China, the EU, and the US, have been engaged in negotiating mega-RTAs, which can be identified as a new generation of free-trade agreements. Negotiations for another high-profile mega-RTA between the EU and the US, *viz.*, the Transatlantic Trade and Investment Partnership (TTIP), was halted in 2018, when US President Donald Trump withdrew from further negotiations.[46] The mega-RTAs are incorporated through lengthy and complex agreements – at times as many as 1,500 pages. The mega-RTAs primarily focus on market access aiming to eliminating trade barriers to both goods and services, besides also covering TBT and SPS measures and IP rights protection covered under the TRIPS Agreement. The agreements contain a number of 'WTO-plus' provisions, which often lead to developing country Member States embracing far-reaching obligations over and above the benchmarks set under the WTO rules. For instance, RTAs contain TRIPS-plus provisions, which often see developing country Member States give up on some of the guaranteed rights contained in the TRIPS Agreement. That said, RTAs also contain 'WTO-minus' provisions, which tend to relax commitments below the level set by WTO agreements. Stoll notes that mega-RTAs, in particular, contain 'WTO-more' provisions, which often include issues that are not addressed by the WTO rules or taken up for discussion at the WTO (Stoll, 2017).

Bown identifies two major reasons for the emergence of mega-RTAs. The MNCs were keen on developing new types of trade disciplines that were not even on the agenda for discussion at the WTO, and companies that were involved in global supply chains wanted to produce goods that are capable of being certified for multiple jurisdictions. This would require an improved coordination of product regulations which are set independently across different markets and clearly outside the remit of the WTO. Second, the rise of China as a major power had prompted the likes of the US to shift its focus in developing trade times in the Asia-Pacific region (Bown, 2018). One can also add another major reason, *viz.*, the stalling of the multilateral trade talks at the Doha Round of negotiations, which did not allow Member States to negotiate rule changes multilaterally.

The mega-RTAs may not offer a forum to negotiate new, country-specific commitment multilaterally, nor can they offer a rules-based and impartial dispute settlement for its members, but they appear to present the members the opportunity to negotiate trade terms bilaterally and in a much speedier fashion. It is also to be noted that although dispute settlement provisions are contained in RTAs, most formal disputes arising since 1995 between members of the RTAs have been adjudicated at the WTO (Bown, 2018). The emergence of mega-RTAs does raise a host of questions for the multilateral trading system and the WTO, as they add a new dimension to RTAs by envisaging deeper economic integration, which has the potential to divert a major trade, in terms of economic volume, away from the multilateral trading system of the WTO. From being perceived as 'building blocks' for trade liberalisation, during the GATT era, RTAs have come a long way. Mega-RTAs are clearly a different phenomenon, as they seek to build on the benchmark and standards set by the WTO through its multilateral trade negotiations. This feature of mega-RTAs is to be found in 'WTO-plus', 'WTO-more', and 'WTO-minus' provisions of the agreements.

9. Summary

What was originally viewed as a facilitator is now being viewed as a threat to the multilateral trading system. During the GATT era, RTAs were considered as a tool to encourage regional integration. The key motivating factors behind the creation of RTAs were regional integration and economic integration. Political considerations are counted as one of the major factors for concluding RTAs, such as (i) economic cooperation and confidence building, (ii) reward for security partners, (iii) regional economic cooperation over security threats, *etc.* As noted by commentators, it may not be possible to delineate completely the interplay between political and economic motivations, as politicians often pursue RTAs for political reasons (Damro, 2006). We are witnessing mega-RTAs in the third wave, which has a very different effect on the WTO. It has gradually eroded into the business of the multilateral trading system, as it has shifted a substantial amount of trade away from the WTO. The transparency obligation of the WTO is effectively lost due to the emergence of RTAs, as several RTAs are yet to be notified to the WTO. Article XXIV of the GATT raises several questions for its continued presence within the rule book of the WTO.

Notes

1. Throughout this chapter, the term RTAs is used to connote free-trade agreements (FTAs), preferential trade agreements (PTAs), customs unions, and bilateral trade agreements.
2. As of February 2021, the cumulative notification of RTAs in force comes to 536. The UK, for instance, has created over 35 RTAs, since 2020 pursuant to its departure from the EU in 2016. The WTO's Regional Trade Agreement gateway (www.wto.org/english/tratop_e/region_e/region_e.htm) provides a number of statistics in this regard.
3. The initial membership of ASEAN, when it was founded in 1977, comprised Indonesia, Malaysia, Philippines, Singapore, and Thailand.
4. The EU currently comprises 27 European nations. The UK, in 2016, voted to leave the EU, and effectively departed from the Union in January 2021.
5. Also known as TPP11 or TPP-11, the CPTPP is a free-trade agreement between Australia, Brunei, Canada, Chile, Japan, Malaysia, Mexico, New Zealand, Peru, Singapore, and Vietnam. CPTPP has its origins in the Trans-Pacific Partnership Agreement, which was negotiated between Australia, Brunei, Canada, Chile, Japan, Malaysia, Mexico, New Zealand, Peru, Singapore, Vietnam, and the US, and signed in February 2016. The US, under President Donald Trump, withdrew from the TPP in January 2017, and as a result it did not enter into force. The remaining countries negotiated the CPTPP, which substantially contains the provisions of the TPP, and it entered into force in December 2018. CPTPP is also referred to as TPP11 or TPP-11.
6. The RCEP was concluded on 15 November 2020 and has been so far ratified by four of the 15 signatories. The RCEP will enter into force when ratified by at least six of the ten ASEAN and three of the five non-ASEAN signatories.
7. A free-trade agreement amongst 54 of the 55 African Union nations, which was founded in 2018, and became effectively operational in January 2021.
8. The USMCA is a free-trade agreement and economic integration agreement between Canada, Mexico, and the United States, and was formerly known as the North America Free Trade Agreement (NAFTA).
9. The EC excluded an entire sector, *viz.*, agriculture. Bhagwati notes that some of the European nations insisted on retaining discriminatory preferences for 18 former colonies from Arica, which required a waiver of the GATT rules. See Bhagwati (1999), p. 9.
10. The 'Enabling Clause' is discussed in section 5 of this chapter.

11 The North American Free Trade Agreement (NAFTA) between Canada, Mexico, and the US, which came into force on 1 January 1994, was to supersede the Canada-US Trade Agreement. See note 8 on USMCA, which in 2018 replaced NAFTA.
12 Writing in 1999, Bhagwati stated, he suspected that the "'second regionalism' will endure: it shows many signs of strength and few points of vulnerability". See Bhagwati (1999), p. 10.
13 Carpenter notes that NAFTA was a partnership between highly asymmetric partners, with limited or no special treatment for the less-developed partner of the three countries, *viz.*, Mexico. See Carpenter (2008).
14 Carpenter notes that inclusion of services in the Uruguay Round of negotiations was a direct result of the planned deepening of integration in Western Europe. See Carpenter (2008).
15 Bhagwati first used the term 'spaghetti bowl' effect to describe the multiplication of FTAs as a path towards globalisation, as opposed to the globalisation through multilateralism of the WTO.
16 Developing country Member States, on the other hand, feel that they are forced into accepting TRIPS-plus provision, which deprive them of their rights guaranteed under the TRIPS Agreement.
17 This policy, although in line with the EU's neighbourhood and development objectives, did little to serve its central trade interests. See European Commission (2006) and Cattaneo (2015).
18 The 2010 Free Trade Agreement with South Korea is an exception, as it was concluded in accordance with the 'economic' priorities set out by the EC in 2006.
19 South Korea also experienced sustained protestation against its proposed RTA with Chile and with the US.
20 Article II of the GATS Agreement reads as follows: "With respect to any measure covered by this Agreement, each Member shall accord immediately and unconditionally to services and service suppliers of any other Member treatment no less favourable than that it accords to like services and service suppliers of any other country."
21 See Appellate Body Report, *Turkey – Textiles*, para. 56.
22 *Ibid.*, para. 45.
23 *Ibid.*, para. 58.
24 See Appellate Body Report, *Argentina – Footwear (EC)*, para. 109.
25 See the disputes relating to *Turkey – Textiles*; *Canada – Autos*; *US – Line Pipe*; and *Brazil – Retreaded Tyres*.
26 See Appellate Body Report, *Turkey – Textiles*, para. 48.
27 See Appellate Body Report, *Argentina – Footwear (EC)*, paras. 106–108.
28 *Ibid.*, para. 110.
29 *Ibid.*, para. 99.
30 See Matsushita (2005) for a brief discussion on parallelism in safeguard measures.
31 See Appellate Body Report, *Turkey – Textiles*, para. 49.
32 *Ibid.*, para. 50.
33 See Paragraph 2 of the Understanding on Article XXIV.
34 *Ibid.*
35 See Appellate Body Report, *Turkey – Textiles*, para. 62.
36 Some of the RTAs entered into under the Enabling Clause are (i) the Cartagena Agreement Establishing the Andean Community; (ii) the Treaty Establishing the Common Market for Eastern and Southern Africa (COMESA); (iii) the Treaty Establishing the Common Market of the South (MERCOSUR); and (iv) the Common Effective Preferential Tariffs Scheme for the ASEAN Free Trade Area (AFTA).
37 See Transparency Mechanism for Regional Trade Agreements (2006). In this regard, it should be noted that the Doha Round of negotiations on the clarification and improvement of the substantive rules on RTAs have not been successful.
38 The CRTA is also mandated to examine any agreements referred to it by the Council for Trade in Services (CTS) (under Article V of the GATS).
39 As of February 2021, the cumulative notification of RTAs in force comes to 536.
40 See Panel Report, *Turkey – Textiles*, paras. 9.52–9.53.
41 See Appellate Body Report, *Turkey – Textiles*, paras. 58–59.
42 See Panel Report, *US – Line Pipe*, para. 7.142.
43 *Ibid.*, para. 7.144.
44 See Appellate Body Report, *US – Line Pipe*, para. 198.

45 In the author's view not challenging the Article XXIV consistency of the European integration process was the 'original sin', as many more were to follow.
46 The emergence of mega-RTAs is discussed in section 8 of this chapter.

Bibliography

Acharya, Rohini. 'Regional Trade Agreements: Recent Developments,' in Acharya, Rohini (ed.) *Regional Trade Agreements and the Multilateral Trading System* (Cambridge University Press, 2016) 1–18.

Baber, Graeme. *Preferential Trade Agreements and International Law* (Routledge Publishing, 2019).

Bartels, Lorand. 'Interim Agreements under Article XXIV GATT,' *World Trade Review* Vol 8, No 2 (2009) 339–350.

Bhagwati, Jagdish. 'Regionalism and Multilateralism: An Overview,' in Bhagwati, Jagdish, Pravin Krishna and Anand Panagariya (eds.), *Trading Blocs: Alternative Approaches to Analyzing Preferential Trade Agreements* (MIT Press, 1999) 3–32.

Bhagwati, Jagdish and Anand Panagariya (eds.). *The Economics of Preferential Trade Agreements* (AEI Press, 1996).

Bown, Chad P. 'Mega-Regional Trade Agreements and the Future of the WTO,' *Global Policy* Vol 8, No 1 (2018) 107–112.

Carpenter, Theresa. 'A Historical Perspective on Regionalism,' in Baldwin, Richard and Patrick Low (eds.) *Multilateralizing Regionalism* (Cambridge University Press, 2008) 13–27.

Cattaneo, Olivier. 'The Political Economy of PTAs,' in Lester, Simon, Bryan Mercurio and Lorand Bartels (eds.), *Bilateral and Regional Trade Agreements: Commentary and Analysis* Vol 1 (Cambridge University Press, 2015) 28–52.

Chase, Kerry. *Trading Blocs: States, Firms, and Regions in the World Economy* (University of Michigan Press, 2008).

Damro, Chad. 'The Political Economy of Regional Trade Agreements,' in Bartels, Lorand and Federico Ortino (eds.) *Regional Trade Agreements and the WTO Legal System* (Oxford University Press, 2006) 23–42.

European Commission. 'Global Europe: Competing in the World: A Contribution to the EU's Growth and Jobs Strategy,' Communication to the Council, the European Parliament, the European Economic and Social Committee and the Committee of the Regions (COM/2006/0567) (4 October 2006).

Fiorentino, Roberto V., Jo-Ann Crawford and Christelle Toqueboeuf. 'The Landscape of Regional Trade Agreements and the WTO Surveillance,' in Baldwin, Richard and Patrick Low (eds.) *Multilateralizing Regionalism* (Cambridge University Press, 2008) 28–76.

Hoekman, Bernard M. and Michel M. Kostecki. *The Political Economy of the World Trading System: The WTO and Beyond* (Oxford University Press, 2009).

Islam, M. Rafiqul. *International Trade Law of the WTO* (Oxford University Press, 2006).

Lester, Simon, Bryan Mercurio and Arwel Davies. *World Trade Law: Text, Materials and Commentary* (Hart Publishing, 2018).

Lynch, David A. *Trade and Globalization: An Introduction to Regional Trade Agreements* (Rowman & Littlefield Publishers, 2010).

Mansfield, Edward D. and Helen V. Milner. *Votes, Vetoes, and the Political Economy of International Agreements* (Princeton University Press, 2012).

Mansfield, Edward D. and Helen V. Milner. 'The Political Economy of Preferential Trade Agreements,' in Dür, Andreas and Manfred Elsig (eds.) *Trade Cooperation: The Purpose, Design and Effects of Preferential Trade Agreements World Forum* (Cambridge University Press, 2016) 56–81.

Matsushita, Mitsuo. 'Regionalism and the Disciplines of the WTO: Analysis of Some Legal Aspects under Article XXIV of the GATT,' *Asia Pacific Law Review* Vol 13, No 2 (2005) 191–202.

Matsushita, Mitsuo, Thomas J. Shoenbaum, Petros C. Mavroidis and Michael Hahn. *The World Trade Organization: Law, Practice, and Policy* (Oxford University Press, 2017).

Mavroidis, Petros C. *The Regulation of International Trade: GATT* (MIT Press, 2016).

Pauwelyn, Joost. 'The Puzzle of WTO Safeguards and Regional Trade Agreements,' *Journal of International Economic Law* Vol 7, No 1 (2004) 109–142.

Ravenhill, John. *Global Political Economy* (Oxford University Press, 2017).

Stoll, Peter-Tobias. 'Mega-Regionals; Challenges, Opportunities, and Research Questions,' in Rensmann, Tino (ed.) *Mega-Regional Trade Agreements* (Springer International, 2017) 3–24.

Theresa Carpenter. 'A Historical Perspective on Regionalism,' in Baldwin, Richard and Patrick Low (eds.) *Multilateralizing Regionalism* (Cambridge University Press, 2008) 13–27.

Trebilcock, Michael, Robert Howse and Antonia Eliason. *The Regulation of International Trade* (Routledge, 2013).

USGAO. 'International Trade: Intensifying Free Trade Negotiating Agenda Calls for Better Allocation of Staff and Resources,' GAO-04–233 (January 2004) <www.gao.gov/assets/gao-04-233.pdf> (accessed 14 June 2021).

Van den Bossche, Peter and Werner Zdouc. *The Law and Policy of the World Trade Organization* (Cambridge University Press, 2017).

Viner, Jacob. *The Customs Union Issue* (Oxford University Press, 2014).

WTO. General Council, 'Transparency Mechanism for Regional Trade Agreements,' Decision Adopted on 14 December 2006 (WT/L/671) (18 December 2006).

WTO. 'Regional Trade Agreements and the WTO,' (2021) <www.wto.org/english/tratop_e/region_e/scope_rta_e.htm> (accessed 7 June 2021).

Zang, Michelle Q. 'When the Multilateral Meets the Regionals: Regional Trade Agreements at the WTO Dispute Settlement,' *World Trade Review* Vol 18, No 1 (2018) 33–61.

16 Environment, Human Rights, and Trade

Learning Objectives 629
1. Introduction 629
2. GATT, the WTO, and the Environment 631
3. Sustainable Development and the WTO 633
4. Jurisprudence on Environmental Issues 635
    4.1 *US – Tuna I (Mexico)* 635
    4.2 *US – Tuna II (Mexico)* 636
    4.3 *US – Shrimp* 637
    4.4 *EC – Approval and Marketing of Biotech Products* 637
5. RTAs, MEAs, and the Multilateral Trading System 638
6. Trade, Human Rights, and the WTO 640
    6.1 Human Rights Obligations of Member States 642
    6.2 Human Rights *Vis-à-vis* WTO Law 643
    6.3 WTO Agreements and Human Rights 644
        6.3.1 TRIPS Agreement: Private Rights, Human Rights, and Access to Medicines 644
        6.3.2 GATS Agreement: Trade in Services and Right to Work 644
        6.3.3 Human Rights and the DSU 646
7. Summary 648

Learning Objectives

This chapter aims to help students understand:

1. Environment issues and trade;
2. Trade and sustainable development;
3. WTO jurisprudence on environmental issues: *US – Tuna I*; *US – Tuna II*; *US – Shrimp*; and *EU – Approval and Marketing of Biotech Products*;
4. The role of RTAs, MEAs, and environmental issues;
5. Trade, human rights, and the WTO; human rights and the covered agreements;
6. TRIPS Agreement and human rights; GATS Agreement and human rights; and
7. DSU and human rights.

1. Introduction

Issues surrounding international trade and environment are complex and have engaged both policymakers and advocates of environmental protection for decades. Trade and environment policy encompass a multiplicity of issues, including sustainable development, health and safety, human rights, *etc.* Environmental concerns relate to clean air and water, carbon emissions (considered the chief contributor to climate change), protection of endangered species, protection of natural resources, and transportation of hazardous substances, to name a few. Environmental issues were not part of the trade agenda in the post-World War II GATT, as it was completely dominated by economic issues and the need for liberalisation, *i.e.*, tariff reduction. It has been strongly argued by environmentalists since the 1990s that international trade will worsen environment conditions. The topic of the impact of trade on environment dominated the NAFTA debate and emerged as a major concern in the closing stages of the Uruguay Round of negotiations. Alongside environmental concerns, issues such as health and safety, labour rights, and human rights have come to the fore.

The exponential growth in world economy, which is driven by trade, has witnessed environmental degradation through deforestation, losses in biodiversity, overfishing, air pollution, and so on. From the environmentalist's perspective, trade liberalisation is driven by business-oriented international business bureaucrats, who have the desire to create jobs and make profits, which results in unsustainable consumption of natural resources, leading to degradation of the environment and loss of habitat. Environmentalists also argue that trade liberalisation entails market access which often overrides environmental regulations, and that trade restrictions should be available as leverage to promote worldwide environmental protection and reinforce international environmental agreements (Esty, 1994). On the other hand, the advocates of free trade view the environmentalist's agenda with scepticism, as they block foreign producers from entering the markets and reducing the efficiency gains from trade (Esty, 1994). Environmentalists strongly advocate an effective resource management, *i.e.*, sustainable development, as industrialisation driven by international trade has led to the depletion of the earth's mineral wealth.

In the post-WTO era, environmental concerns have gained traction, as trade agreements are no longer limited to tariff reductions and regulatory regimes but are also about sustainable development. They have also found their voice in some of the key decisions handed down by the Appellate Body.[1] Since the Stockholm Intergovernmental Conference in 1972 (UN Conference on Human Environment), multilateral environmental agreements (MEAs) have gained prominence, and several MEAs have been finalised between the Member States.[2] Transboundary environmental problems[3] have been addressed through environmental governance with the use of MEAs. In the WTO era, the Member States have met in other international fora to forge the Paris Agreement, which is the legally binding international treaty on climate change with 196 signatories.[4] The use of MEAs in trade agreement demonstrates the link between trade and the environment and the need for protection of the environment.

WTO has a membership of 164 countries who are committed to doing trade through the rules-based multilateral trading system established in 1995. The WTO with its large membership is viewed as the prime institution to act as the international arbiter on environmental issues by both environmental groups and green-leaning governments. On the other hand, policymakers in developing country Member States are wary of handing over the lead on environmental issues to the WTO, as WTO-approved trade sanctions could be used to enforce environmental norms that are not necessarily shared by all nations (Lester, Mercurio, and Davies, 2018).

International trade policy and the protection of the environment are an integral part of any development agenda and should be supportive of each other. Although the remit of the WTO does not permit the organisation from assuming such wide powers on environmental protection at the international level, the Preamble to the WTO Agreement does refer to the optimal use of the world's resources in accordance with the objective of sustainable development. Doubtlessly, environmental concerns have become a mainstream trade issue.

2. GATT, the WTO, and the Environment

In 1971, the GATT was asked to make its contribution to the Stockholm Intergovernmental Conference by the UN. In response, the GATT established the Group on Environmental Measures and International Trade in 1971 and carried out a study, entitled 'Industrial Pollution Control and International Trade', which focused on the implications of environmental protection policies on international trade. This study was presented to the GATT Contracting Parties for discussion in 1971. The GATT Council of Representatives also agreed to set up a Group on Environmental Measures and International Trade (EMIT), which would be open to all GATT Contracting Parties. EMIT was a standby machinery created by the GATT which would be ready to act, at the request of a contracting party, when the need arose (Nordström and Vaughan, 1999). As it was provided for the group to only convene when requested, a meeting of EMIT did not take place before 1991, when the European Free Trade Association (EFTA) requested one.

During the Uruguay Round, trade-related environmental issues led to modifications to the TBT Agreement, besides also being addressed in the GATS Agreement, the Agreement on Agriculture, the SPS Agreement, and the TRIPS Agreement. At the close of the Uruguay Round, negotiators agreed to establish a Committee on Trade and Environment (CTE) within the newly established multilateral trade body, the WTO.

The primary objective of the WTO is to liberalise trade and provide a forum to its Member States for periodic negotiations to ensure that trade remains fair and predictable in the multilateral trading system. While Member States are to conduct trade following the core principles of transparency and non-discrimination, no clear provisions are contained in the WTO's rules to directly regulate a Member State's actions on issues relating to the preservation and protection of the environment. The Preamble to the Marrakesh Agreement Establishing the World Trade Organization emphasises the need for a balanced approach between the goal of trade expansion through trade in goods and services on the one hand and the need to protect the environment on the other. The first recital of the Preamble to the Marrakesh Agreement reads as follows:

> *Recognizing* that their relations in the field of trade and economic endeavour should be conducted with a view to raising standards of living, ensuring full employment and a large and steadily growing volume of real income and effective demand, and expanding the production of and trade in goods and services, while allowing for the optimal use of the world's resources in accordance with the objective of sustainable development, seeking both to protect and preserve the environment and to enhance the means for doing so in a manner consistent with their respective needs and concerns at different levels of economic development.

The aforementioned recital encapsulates both sustainable development and environmental protection as goals. Although not binding on Member States, the WTO Preamble has been used in the disputes before the DSB to interpret provisions of WTO agreements. In *US – Gasoline*, the Appellate Body emphasised the importance of the Preamble in the context of environmental issues as follows:

> in the preamble to the WTO Agreement and in the Decision on Trade and Environment, there is specific acknowledgement to be found about the importance of coordinating policies on trade and the environment. WTO Members have a large measure of autonomy to determine their own policies on the environment (including its relationship with trade),

their environmental objectives and the environmental legislation they enact and implement. So far as concerns the WTO, that autonomy is circumscribed only by the need to respect the requirements of the General Agreement and the other covered agreements.[5]

The aforementioned recital from the Preamble has been often cited by environmentalists to underpin the WTO's role in preserving the environment while facilitating multilateral trade amongst Member States. Many WTO agreements contain conditional exceptions for environmental measures. Article XX of the GATT 1994 reads as follows:

> Subject to the requirement that such measures are not applied in a manner which would constitute a means of arbitrary or unjustifiable discrimination between countries where the same conditions prevail, or a disguised restriction on international trade, nothing in this Agreement shall be construed to prevent the adoption or enforcement by any contracting party of measures:
>
> . . .
> (b) necessary to protect human, animal or plant life or health;
> . . .
> (g) relating to the conservation of exhaustible natural resources if such measures are made effective in conjunction with restrictions on domestic production or consumption.

Pursuant to Articles XX(b) and XX(c), Member States may adopt policy measures that are necessary to protect human, animal, or plant life or health or to the conservation of exhaustible natural resources respectively but are otherwise inconsistent with GATT disciplines.[6] Lending support, the wording in the *Chapeau* to Article XX states, "nothing in this Agreement shall be construed to prevent the adoption or enforcement" of measures enumerated in Articles XX(a)–(j). Identical exceptions to Article XX of the GATT are also to be found in Article XIV of the GATS Agreement,[7] which affirms:

> Subject to the requirement that such measures are not applied in a manner which would constitute a means of arbitrary or unjustifiable discrimination between countries where like conditions prevail, or a disguised restriction on trade in services, nothing in this Agreement shall be construed to prevent the adoption or enforcement by any Member of measures:
>
> (a) . . .
> (b) necessary to protect human, animal or plant life or health.

Similarly, Article 27.2 of the TRIPS Agreement states, "Members may exclude from patentability inventions, the prevention within their territory of the commercial exploitation of which is necessary . . . to protect human, animal or plant life or health or to avoid serious prejudice to the environment". Article 8.2(c) of the SCM Agreement contains exemptions for certain environmental subsidies, and Article 2.2 of the TBT Agreement states that protection of the environment is a 'legitimate objective' that allows a WTO member to enact high standards of protection. The SPS Agreement, on the other hand, seeks to supplement GATT Article XX(b) by establishing the legal framework that validates government measures passed to protect humans, animals, and plants from diseases, pests, toxins, and other contaminants.

To summarise, (i) the Preamble to the WTO establishes both environment and sustainable development objectives; (ii) Article XX of the GATT establishes environmental grounds for exceptions, provided a number of conditions are met by Member States, besides also defining market access for products, including on environmental criteria; (iii) Article XIV of the GATS Agreement establishes environmental grounds for exceptions, provided a number of conditions are met; (iv) the TBT Agreement establishes rules on measures based on production and process methods (PPMs), which are relevant to environmental standards and labelling, besides also requiring the use of relevant international standards where they exist;[8] and (v) the SPS Agreement establishes that SPS standards introduced by Member States are required to comply with one of three international standards list, or conduct risk assessments to justify more stringent measures.[9]

It is to be pointed out that it may not be legally possible for Member States to meet all of the relevant conditions set out under Article XX of GATT and Article XIV of the GATS Agreement to seek exemptions for such measures on environmental considerations. Environmentalists have hence argued that Member States should not view the aforementioned provisions as a guarantor that environmental actions will not be challenged (Deere Birkbeck, 2021). This could also be a reason for unwillingness on the part of the policymakers and stakeholders in implementing environmental measures at the national level, as they apprehend breaching WTO rules. As a consequence, Member States underreport their environment-related trade measures to the WTO (Deere Birkbeck, 2021).[10]

In 1995, the WTO established the Committee on Trade and Environment, with the remit to make suitable recommendations on "the need for rules to enhance the positive interaction between trade and environment measures for the promotion of sustainable development". The CTE is open to participation by all Member States, yet no decision of significance has been made by the CTE.[11]

3. Sustainable Development and the WTO

Sustainable development, both conceptually and in terms of implementation, has come a long way in international law since the Brundtland Report of 1987, which identified the objective of sustainable development as being "to ensure that it meets the needs of the present without compromising the ability of future generations to meet their own needs" (WCED, 1987, introduction, para. 27). It has gained traction in international circles, due to the social and environmental connotations and economic implications. International law principles have been developed in recent decades in relation to sustainable development. In terms of trade and environment, the principles of sustainable use of natural resources plays an increasingly important role, due to the increased competition for access to natural resources brought about by the 2000s' commodity 'supercycle' (Espa, 2020). There is now a growing awareness of the social costs and environmental impacts linked to natural resources exploitation, from increased levels of price commodity volatility to the resurgence of disputes concerning natural resource protection before different international arenas, including law of the sea, human rights, trade law, and investment law (Espa, 2020).

Sustainable development goals have been developed through international commitments through sustainable production and consumption in order to green trade and trade policy. Greening trade and trade policies are viewed as the way forward to achieve sustainable development. Following the outcomes of the 2012 UN Conference on Sustainable Development (Rio+20), *viz.*, Agenda 2030, the global Sustainable Development Goals (SDGs) were developed by the UN (UN, 2012, 2015). The United Nations in 2015 established the 17

Sustainable Development Goals "To ensure sustainable consumption and production patterns". The SDGs were developed to ensure good use of natural resources, improve energy efficiency, encourage sustainable infrastructure, provide access to basic services, provide green and decent jobs, and ensure a better quality of life for all (UN, 2015).

It is safe to say that the international efforts on sustainable production and consumption (SCP) is contained in the Sustainable Development Goal 12 (SDG 12), which is set out in the UN's 2030 Agenda (UN, 20). The SDGs are directed towards the roots of world poverty by adopting a holistic development approach and specifically address the issue of resource efficiency in a comprehensive fashion. In particular, SDG 12 'Ensure sustainable consumption and production patterns', explicitly mentions "sustainable management and efficient use of natural resources" among its core, cross-cutting targets (United Nations, 2013). Frustratingly, international trade was not systemically integrated into the SDG goals and targets concerned with natural resources use and management, which showcases only a general 'lack of interest' in trade policy and trade-related measures during the SDGs production process and in its resulting working framework (Messerlin, 2017). Commentators note that this lack of engagement is due to the SDGs' regulatory agenda being geared towards the economic dimension of trade and its failure to innovatively account for its environmental dimension (Espa, 2020). As noted by Hoekman,

> The focus in the SDGs is on improving market access for developing countries, including through WTO negotiations and [duty-free and quota-free (DFQF)] treatment for exporters in [least developed countries (LDCs)], and ensuring that developing countries have "policy space" – matters that have long been on the international agenda. . . . The language on trade and trade policy in the various SDGs constitutes "business as usual" – the underlying approach that has been pursued in the UN and the General Agreement on Tariffs and Trade (GATT)/WTO context for decades. The only specific target, that is, to double the global share of LDC exports by 2020, is already included in the Istanbul Programme of Action (United Nations, 2012). There is a mercantilist flavour to how trade is included in the SDGs: the focus is on exports as opposed to trade (imports and exports) and improving governance and the business environment confronting firms in developing countries is underemphasized.
>
> (Hoekman, 2017, p. 43)

SDG 17, which is to 'Strengthen the means of implementation and revitalize the Global Partnership for Sustainable Development', relates to the WTO. This reflects a relatively old-fashioned vision of trade as a means of implementation for sustainable development basically centred on development assistance, policy space, and preferential market access, and only residually are trade-related commitments incorporated into environmentally targeted SDGs (Espa, 2020). In 2002, the International Law Commission identified seven key principles of international law whose consolidation and realisation would be instrumental in pursuing the objective of sustainable development. These principles were first formulated in the 2002 New Delhi Declaration of Principles of International Law Relating to Sustainable Development, and later reaffirmed and elaborated in 2012 in light of subsequent judicial developments (ILA, 2012; Espa, 2020). Although much global trade is performed on a daily basis, the status of the principle of sustainable use of natural resources is yet to be definitively determined.

The International Law Commission had articulated the view that "as a matter of common concern, the sustainable use of all natural resources represents an emerging rule of general customary international law" (ILA, 2012). Also of relevance here is Agenda 21 of the UN Conference on Environment and Development 1992, which in its relevant part reads as follows:

> Environment and trade policies should be mutually supportive. An open multilateral trading system makes possible a more efficient allocation and use of resources and thereby contributes to an increase in production and incomes and to lessening demands on the environment. It thus provides additional resources needed for economic growth ... and improved environmental protection. A sound environment, on the other hand, provides the ecological and other resources needed to sustain growth and underpin continuing expansion of trade.

The WTO, needless to say, is the trading platform through which nation states come to perform multilateral trade. The WTO is a key player in achieving the 2030 Agenda for Sustainable Development and its SDGs, as it plays an important role in the performance of international trade. The WTO reports annually to the UN's High-Level Political Forum (HLPF)[12] on its efforts to achieve trade-specific targets in the SDGs. That said, the aspirations contained in Agenda 21 are yet to take shape in the WTO's policy framework.

4. Jurisprudence on Environmental Issues

The jurisprudence on environmental issues had been brought before the GATT Panels during the 1990s and following the formation of the WTO before the Panels and the Appellate Body with mixed results.

4.1 US – Tuna I (Mexico)

The GATT/WTO jurisprudence dates back to the *US – Tuna I* dispute from the early 1990s. The dispute between Mexico and the US dates back to 1933 when the US increased customs duties on tuna. In response, Mexico retaliated by prohibiting foreign boats from catching tuna within 12 miles of its coastline, and later in 1976 to within 200 miles. In 1980 the US. responding to seizure of its fishing boats in the Mexican exclusive maritime zone, imposed an embargo on Mexican tuna, which was to last until 1986. The US passed the Marine Mammal Protection Act (MMPA) in 1972 to protect marine mammals from serious injury or incidental killing in the course of commercial fishing.[13] This Act was applicable to both domestic and foreign fishing vessels operating in the Eastern Tropical Pacific Ocean (ETP).[14] As a result, countries exporting tuna to the US were required to meet the dolphin protection standards set out in the MMPA. The US also introduced a labelling regime under the Dolphin Protection Consumer Information Act (DPCIA), to be used on tuna products entering the US market as proof that purse seine nets were not used for tuna harvesting.

The US unilaterally banned imports of yellow fin tuna caught using purse seine fishing nets which also killed dolphins.[15] This was challenged by Mexico before a GATT Panel in 1991, on the grounds that such measures imposed by the US were quantitative restrictions on importation under Article XI of the GATT. The US, on the other hand, argued that the measures were internal regulations enforced at the time, or point of importation under Article III:4 and the Note *Ad* Article III of the GATT. The Panel in its report ruled that the MMPA did not regulate tuna products as such but instead prescribed certain fishing techniques to protect dolphins. Rejecting the US argument that the measures imposed under MMPA were eligible to an exception under Article XX GATT, the Panel ruled that the impugned measure was in violation of the prohibition of quantitative trade restrictions under Article XI of the GATT. The Panel observed as follows:

> if the broad interpretation of Article XX(b) suggested by the United States were accepted, each contracting party could unilaterally determine the life or health protection policies from which other contracting parties could not deviate without jeopardizing their rights under the General Agreement. The General Agreement would then no longer constitute a multilateral framework for trade among all contracting parties but would provide legal security only in respect of trade between a limited number of contracting parties with identical internal regulations.

The Panel did not discuss in detail the significance of MEAs in GATT law, nor for that matter domestic environmental policies. The Panel, instead, chose to penalise the US measure which sought to mitigate unnecessary harm caused to marine mammals. In short, it failed to take note of the larger picture of the link between trade and environment and recognise the efforts taken by trade partners to alleviate harm caused to the environment. The EEC and The Netherlands, as 'intermediaries', also challenged the US measures. The Panel followed the same approach as the Panel in the *US – Tuna I* case and ruled that the measure under challenge was in violation of the prohibition of quantitative trade restrictions under Article XI of the GATT. Both Panel reports were unadopted.

4.2 US – Tuna II (Mexico)

With the Panel reports from the earlier disputes relating to tuna harvesting being unadopted, the US and Mexico negotiated the Agreement on the International Dolphin Conservation Program (AIDCP) in 1999 under the auspices of the Inter-American Tropical Tuna Commission (IATTC). The AIDCP's labelling scheme was less stringent than that of the standards set under US DPCIA. Environmentalist (NGOs) challenged the use of AIDCP labelling through court action,[16] on the grounds that it was far less stringent than DPCIA and was not fit for purpose. Following the court ruling in favour of the NGOs, the AIDCP standard was not adopted by the US Department of Commerce, and the US used the DPCIA standards which required tuna product to carry the 'dolphin-safe' labelling.

As a result, Mexico initiated a dispute challenging the DPCIA as being inconsistent with the Articles I:1 and III:4 of the GATT and discriminatory under Articles 2.1, 2.2, and 2.4 of the TBT Agreement. The WTO Panel ruled that Mexican and US tuna should be considered as 'like products', that (i) Mexican tuna was not afforded treatment less favourable in relation to domestic (US) products, as the 'dolphin-safe' labelling did not discriminate tuna products based on the country of origin,[17] (ii) the US measures were more trade restrictive than necessary to achieve the stated objectives and in breach of Article 2.2 of the TBT,[18] and (iii) the AIDCP standard was a relevant international standard.[19] The Panel did not offer any views on Mexico's claim on issues arising under the provisions of the GATT. On appeal, some of the Panel's findings were reversed by the Appellate Body, which held that the impugned measure should be considered a technical regulation,[20] and that the measure was inconsistent with Article 2.1 of the TBT Agreement as it was discriminatory.[21] Interestingly, both the Panel and the Appellate Body in *US – Tuna II (Mexico)* ruled that 'dolphin-safe' labelling under the DPCIA was a technical regulation.

4.3 US – Shrimp

The *US – Shrimp* dispute revolved around the legislation passed by the US to prevent the killing of sea turtles. The Convention on International Trade in Endangered Species of Wild Fauna and Flora (CITES), which is an MEA, acknowledges sea turtles as an endangered species.[22] The US had introduced legislation to prevent the accidental killing of sea turtles.[23] In 1996, the US Department of State determined that all shipments of shrimp and shrimp products entering the US markets were to be accompanied by a declaration attesting that the shrimp or shrimp product in question was harvested under conditions that do not adversely affect sea turtles. The measure included prohibiting the sale of any product, including shrimps, that had been harvested without turtle excluding devices (TED).[24] As the two species – turtles and shrimp – often swim together, TED was seen as an effective mechanism to protect the accidental killing of sea turtles while fishing for shrimp.[25]

The US measure was challenged by a number of exporters of shrimps, *viz.*, Malaysia, Thailand, India, and Pakistan, on the ground that the measure introduced by the US was inconsistent with the GATT as it was unilateral in nature. The Panel ruled that the import ban on shrimp and shrimp products as applied by the US was inconsistent with Article XI:1 of the GATT 1994, and cannot be justified under Article XX of the GATT 1994. On appeal, the Appellate Body reversed the findings, holding that Member States were at liberty to unilaterally regulate the market, provided that they respected the relevant GATT disciplines, *i.e.*, a measure introduced by a Member State cannot be determined to be GATT inconsistent merely on the basis that it was unilaterally defined. In the Appellate Body's own words,

> conditioning access to a Member's domestic market on whether exporting Members comply with, or adopt, a policy or policies unilaterally prescribed by the importing Member may, to some degree, be a common aspect of measures falling within the scope of one or another of the exceptions (a) to (j) of Article XX. Paragraphs (a) to (j) comprise measures that are recognized as exceptions to substantive obligations established in the GATT 1994, because the domestic policies embodied in such measures have been recognized as important and legitimate in character. It is not necessary to assume that requiring from exporting countries compliance with, or adoption of, certain policies (although covered in principle by one or another of the exceptions) prescribed by the importing country, renders a measure *a priori* incapable of justification under Article XX. Such an interpretation renders most, if not all, of the specific exceptions of Article XX inutile, a result abhorrent to the principles of interpretation we are bound to apply.[26]

The Appellate Body ruled that that the extraterritorial application of unilaterally adopted environmental policy measures is justifiable under Article XX of the GATT,[27] but their adoption must be preceded by "serious negotiating efforts".[28] In interpreting the general exceptions under Article XX of the GATT, the Appellate Body relied upon the Preamble to the WTO Agreement. The Appellate Body in *US – Shrimp* have effectively overturned the path taken in *US – Tuna I* and *US – Tuna II*. The Appellate Body's finding in *US – Shrimp* has been consistently followed in subsequent disputes.[29] Following from the aforementioned decision, Member States are at liberty to determine their environmental policies, including becoming signatories to MEAs.

4.4 EC – Approval and Marketing of Biotech Products

The dispute in *EC – Approval and Marketing of Biotech Products* arose at a time when no genetically modified products (GM products) had been approved for marketing or release into the environment in the EU. The EU over the years, starting from 1990, had established horizontal and area-specific rules to regulate the contained use of genetically modified microorganisms and deliberate release into the environment of genetically modified organisms (GMOs) respectively. The complainants, the US, Canada, and Argentina, challenged the EC regulatory controls on GMOs, on the grounds that they were inconsistent with the SPS Agreement, the TBT Agreement, and the GATT, and argued that the EU through its directives established a *de facto* moratorium against imports of GMOs. The EU sought to justify its position by referring to MEAs,[30] which in its view permitted such practice.

At the outset it should be noted that the dispute did not concern the issue of whether biotech products are safe or not. The dispute concerned the alleged EC *de facto* moratorium on the approval of biotech products; EC measures affecting the approval of specific biotech products; and the safeguard measures of six EC Member States. The Panel dismissed the argument, as not all parties to the dispute were signatories to such MEAs and held that the EU applied a general *de facto* moratorium on the approval of biotech products between June 1999 and August 2003, and that the EU had acted inconsistently with its obligations under Annex C(1)(a), first clause, and Article 8 of the SPS Agreement. The Panel observed that following from Article 31(c)(3) of the Vienna Convention on the Law of Treaties, it was not required to consider as a rule of international law treaties that are not applicable between all the parties to the dispute.[31]

In sharp contrast to the *US-Shrimp* case, where the Appellate Body stressed the importance of environmental law in its interpretive exercise, the Panel in *EC – Approval and Marketing of Biotech Products* did not discuss the norms of the Biosafety Protocol.

5. RTAs, MEAs, and the Multilateral Trading System

It is well known that all Member States are parties to RTAs where they conduct trade on a bilateral basis.[32] The EU, the US, and the UK are currently negotiating a number of bilateral trade agreements with both developed and developing country trade partners, where environmental provisions feature prominently. For instance, the proposed Trans-Pacific Partnership Agreement (TPP)[33] was identified as the 'greenest' trade agreement but yet condemned for being an ecological disaster hidden under a 'green' cover (Berger, Brandi, and Bruhn, 2017). There are also RTAs in which developing countries seek to establish bilateral trade agreements with other developing countries.[34]

WTO studies from 2016 reveal that almost 90 percent of 690 RTAs contained at least one environmental provision, besides also containing a range of other environmental provisions/sustainable development provisions with varying legal strength (Monteiro, 2016). A study carried out in 2017 concludes that each RTA contains around 60 different environmental provisions, and that both developed and developing country Member States include them in their RTAs (Berger, Brandi, and Bruhn, 2017). The EU and the US attach significant importance to the preservation of the environment in their RTAs, where EU requires prospective trade partners to adopt climate change policies, and the US for its part introduces environmental provisions enforceable through 'sanction-based' dispute settlement systems (Jinnah and Lindsay, 2016). It is undisputable that international trade and environmental issues are increasingly linked through RTAs in the WTO era, and the environmental provisions contained in RTAs are far more detailed than pursued in the WTO context (WTO, 2011).

Negotiations on environmental issues progress slowly in UN fora, and in contrast during the same period close to 20 new RTAs are finalised with detailed provisions on environmental provisions. Commentators note that environmental provisions found in RTAs are more effective than those provisions contained in environmental agreements themselves in addressing environmental problems (Jinnah and Lindsay, 2016).[35] Environmental issues do not play a marginal role in trade policies anymore, as witnessed by the environmental provisions in RTAs. It was noted earlier[36] that amongst the reasons for a Member State seeking to be a signatory to RTAs is the failure of the Doha Round of negotiations, *i.e.*, the difficulty in reaching multilaterally negotiated trade policies at the WTO, which also include a consensus on environmental issues. Evidence suggests that environmental provisions contained in RTAs are not incorporated to serve as window dressing but are introduced due to domestic electoral pressure from citizens sensitive to environmental concerns (Morin, Dür, and Lechner, 2018).[37]

Environment-related provisions are to be found in the RTAs (i) in the Preamble to the RTAs as sustainable development with broad objectives; (ii) as environmental exceptions arising under Article XX of the GATT and Article XIV(b) of the GATS Agreement; (iii) as specific commitments to comply with domestic environmental laws, to not derogate from environmental laws, effective enforcement of environmental laws, access to remedies for violations of environmental laws; (iv) to reaffirm the importance of MEAs, reference to specific provisions of MEAs, and implementation of MEAs; (v) in core chapters of the RTAs outlining the conditions under which goods and services can cross borders based on environmental considerations; and (v) as environmental cooperation provisions which are to be found in separate chapters dedicated to environment, sustainable development chapters, as side agreements, or in annexes (Deer Birkbeck, 2021). The provisions found in RTAs also specifically focus on climate change, with reference to renewable energy or energy efficiency. The EU, seen as a pioneer in the integration of trade and climate agendas, has included reference to the greenhouse effect as early as 1989 (Berger, Brandi, and Bruhn, 2017). In the WTO era, most EU trade agreements invariably include provisions addressing climate change.

NAFTA, which entered into force in January 1994, had the most detailed and innovative environmental provisions, *i.e.*, 48 provisions, to be found in RTAs.[38] Although the side agreements of NAFTA opened the door for linking environmental policy to trade objectives, it came under criticism as being weak and ineffective.[39] While RTAs come under criticism for moving a substantial volume of trade away from the multilateral order, they incorporate detailed provisions to address some of the environmental concerns of the Member States that are not covered in WTO rules and policies. As mentioned earlier, the provisions of WTO agreements only provide for environmental exceptions outlining conditions whereby domestic environmental measures may contravene GATT rules. RTAs articulate more detailed provisions on environmental issues associated with trade rules than WTO rules do, and are of increasing relevance to global environmental governance.

This brings us to the interplay between RTAs, multilateral environmental agreements (MEAs), and the WTO. One of the important features of the environment-related provisions found in RTAs is that they focus on MEAs, identifying specific commitments on a list of covered MEAs (Monteiro, 2016). The nature of some of the environment-related provisions in RTAs are to reaffirm the importance of MEAs and the rights and obligations established under MEAs. While some of the provisions commit the signatory nations to introduce such environmental laws in order to fulfil the obligations of specific MEAs, others require that parties accede to certain MEAs. There are also instances where environment-related provisions contained in RTAs refer to the role of MEAs under the RTA's consultations and dispute settlement mechanisms (Monteiro, 2016).

As mentioned earlier, MEAs are agreements between States to collaborate on a range of environmental issues, and as such, they are 'soft law'. Hence, they are only required to be considered by contracting parties when taking decisions on environmental issues. MEAs are not part of the WTO legal framework. The CTE, in its very first report from 1996, noted that that international community, *i.e.*, Member States, preferred MEAs for coordinating policy action to "tackle global and transboundary environmental problems cooperatively" (WTO, 1996),[40] and expressed concerns about trade measures applied pursuant to MEAs which had the potential to affect WTO Member States' rights and obligations (WTO, 1996). Member States had put forth a number of proposals before the CTE, which included amongst others:

i   To study the link between the MEAs and the WTO legal framework;
ii   Seeking the modification of Article XX of the GATT (the General Exceptions clause) to ensure effective participation of the trade and the environment communities in each other's meetings;
iii All measures taken under MEAs to be eligible for a waiver, provided they meet specified criteria set out in the headnote to Article XX of the GATT; and
iv   To develop guidelines to provide more predictability over the treatment of certain trade measures applied pursuant to MEAs and allow for the development of mutually supportive trade and environment policies, as envisaged in Agenda 2.

Also, a number of proposals concerned developing a non-binding understanding on the interpretation of Article XX to assist WTO dispute resolution panels while dealing with cases involving MEAs (WTO, 1996). The CTE did not accept any of the aforementioned proposals put forth by the Member States.[41] In 2010, in its special session, the chairperson of the WTO Trade Negotiating Committee (TNC) issued a report summarising the progress in relationship between trade and environment (WTO, 2011). More recently in the March 2021 meeting of the CTE, the Member States discussed the trade-related aspects of the European Green Deal and heard presentations from several developing countries on their national environmental initiatives (IISD, 2021). The CTE was also updated on the developments in MEAs dealing with chemicals and waste, the establishment of InforMEA initiative,[42] which is an ongoing collaboration with the WTO Secretariat to include trade-related measures pursuant to select MEAs.

6. Trade, Human Rights, and the WTO

The post-World War II era gave birth to both the international trade regime – the GATT – and the international human rights regime. Institutionally, this era witnessed the creation of the GATT, the IMF, the World Bank, and the UN.[43] The Universal Declaration of Human Rights (UDHR), adopted within months of the formation of the GATT, encapsulates the following values which are to be found in contemporary human rights framework: universality, dignity, freedom (or liberty), justice, equality (or fairness, including distributive fairness), accountability (of governments), participation, empowerment, and brotherhood (or solidarity) amongst people (UDHR, 1948; Joseph, 2013). In simple terms, the UDHR aims primarily to protect individuals and groups from abusive action by states and state agents. It has its roots in natural rights theories, which evolved beyond their libertarian roots and encompassed worker's rights, welfare rights, rights of women, rights of minorities, and importantly the need for persons to function as members of society rather than as mere individuals (Morsink, 1982). The GATT was formed as a multilateral framework with trade liberalisation set as its goal, to revive a world economy ravaged by war, and to avoid the repeat of the two world wars which blighted humanity. Within the framework of the GATT was the vision to expand trade to raise living standards and increase employment opportunities and income. Both post-World War II phenomena have developed on parallel paths.

The Universal Declaration refers to itself as a "a common standard of achievement for all peoples and all nations, to the end that every individual, and every organ of society" and to strive to promote respect for, and observance of, rights (UDHR, 1948). Both the Universal Declaration and the GATT share a common goal, as they were created to limit a state's scope for making policy decisions that were based on misguided or unjust judgments of the value of human freedom (Dommen, 2002). The WTO was formed in 1995 nearly five decades after the creation of GATT trade regime and the Universal Declaration. The remit of the UN's human rights regime and that of the international trade regime established under the GATT have widened and have become more sophisticated. The UN now has six treaties and several other instruments on human rights with detailed literature and mechanisms for the promotion and protection of human rights (Dommen, 2009). Likewise, the trade regime established under the GATT evolved into the WTO, following several rounds of multilateral trade negotiations. The GATT's jurisdiction and remit used to be confined to trade in goods amongst its Contracting Parties, and it has expanded further under the WTO to include trade in services (covered by GATS) and protection of intellectual property (a private right) under the TRIPS Agreement. The dispute settlement under the GATT was narrow, was based on Article XXIII of the GATT, and was not rules based. The WTO dispute settlement system founded on Article XXIII of the GATT and the detailed rules of the Dispute Settlement Understanding, on the other hand, is far wider in its remit, having a compulsory jurisdiction where the Member States bring disputes on the grounds of violation of WTO rules by other Member States. One can argue that the environment surrounding the formation of the GATT and the WTO are different. But one cannot forget that the WTO's foundations are firmly rooted in the GATT, from which it evolved.

A number of goals of the WTO are aimed at promoting employment, better living standards, *etc.* through trade in both goods and services. The Marrakesh Agreement Establishing the World Trade Organization in its Preamble identifies the objectives as

> to raising standards of living, ensuring full employment and a large and steadily growing volume of real income and effective demand, and expanding the production of and trade in goods and services, while allowing for the optimal use of the world's resources in accordance with the objective of sustainable development.

As mentioned earlier, the Preamble refers to the needs of developing countries and to conduct trade in accordance with the objective of sustainable development. These are non-economic policy goals, and alongside the core principles of non-discrimination in the GATT are akin to the 'balancing principles' contained in human rights treaties (Petersmann, 2005).

In the words of Pascal Lamy, the former director-general of the WTO, the WTO rules are primarily based on human rights, *i.e.*, "individual freedom and responsibility, non-discrimination, rule of law, and welfare through peaceful cooperation among individuals" (Lamy, 2010). As noted by Petersmann, the multilateral trade regime under the WTO promotes (i) freedom by seeking to remove restrictions to trade; (ii) non-discrimination through the MFN and NT obligations; (iii) the rule of law by committing Member States to transparency obligations and an enforceable rules-based international trading system (through the DSB); and (iv) economic efficiency leading to enhanced welfare (Petersmann, 2002). The views expressed by both Lamy and Petersmann seem congruent with the promotion of human rights principles until subjected to greater scrutiny (Joseph, 2013). Given the shared origins and objectives of the two regimes, one might assume that their bodies of law and the legal framework to be mutually supporting and evolving on parallel tracks (Dommen, 2002). As noted by Allmand, both trade law and human rights law, each of which narrows the range of policy options available to states, developed simultaneously but in "splendid isolation" (Allmand, 1999).

6.1 Human Rights Obligations of Member States

Every Member State of the WTO has ratified one or more UN conventions relating to human rights, wherein they have made binding commitments. A number of them were entered into prior to the formation of the WTO in January 1995. The 1966 UN Covenant on Economic, Social and Cultural Human Rights (ICESCR)[44] has 171 state parties as of January 2020, which includes a majority of WTO Member States. The 1989 UN Convention on the Rights of the Child has been ratified by all Member States, with the exception of the US. All Member States have accepted the Universal Declaration of Human Rights (UDHR).

The 1993 Vienna Declaration and Programme of Action was adopted by the World Conference on Human Rights, wherein all UN Member States (also Member States of the WTO) have committed themselves to protect inalienable human rights as part of general international law. All WTO Member States are parties to this declaration. Additionally, a number of states (who are Member States of the WTO) and the EU recognise human rights in their constitutional law as constitutional restraints on government powers.[45] The International Court of Justice (ICJ) has recognised human rights as constituting not only individual rights but also, in case of universally recognised human rights, *erga omnes* obligations of governments based on the UN Charter, human rights treaties, and general international law (Petersmann, 2005).[46] The ICJ has also recognised the applicability of general international law rules to intergovernmental organisations.[47] Likewise, the Court of Justice of the European Union (CJEU) and the European Court of Human Rights (ECHR) have both recognised that general international law and human rights may be binding also on intergovernmental organisations.

The reference in the GATT Preamble for the need to raise living standards and to promote 'sustainable development' implicitly recognise the hierarchal supremacy of 'non-trade public values' and license new 'enlightened' modes of interpretation by GATT Panels and the Appellate Body (Howse and Mutua, 1999). It is also argued that pursuant to Article 103 of the UN Charter[48] (which covers economic, social, and cultural rights, as well as civil and political rights), the text of the GATT Agreement, and all other WTO agreements, should recognise that "human rights are fundamental . . . [over] free trade itself" (Howse and Mutua, 1999). As a result of such acceptance of human rights by WTO Member States through international treaty law, general international law, and in some instances in domestic laws, human rights are relevant for the interpretation and application of the WTO agreements and rules that deal with the

> guarantees of freedom, non-discrimination, rule of law, private property, access to courts, due process of law, and for the numerous WTO exceptions that permit restrictions of freedom of trade so as to protect human, animal or plant life or health, public morals and other 'human rights values'.
>
> (Petersmann, 2005, p. 627)

6.2 Human Rights Vis-à-vis WTO Law

One of the fundamental differences between the regimes of trade and human rights is that the former, administered by the WTO, protects the interest of the parties, *i.e.*, that of the Member States, and the latter seeks to place a boundary on the powers wielded by states and protects the rights of the individual regardless of which country they live in. The WTO laws, through its efforts to facilitate the free movement of goods and services, extends the boundaries of trade operation through negotiated market access, thereby increasing the power of those who are capable of offering trade and marginalising the already marginalised countries or groups of people (Dommen, 2002).[49]

Member States are often lobbied by their respective industries which seek to establish a trade policy that is suitable to grow their businesses. On the other hand, the governments of the Member States are also obliged to protect the most vulnerable amongst their populations. Some of the trade policies that are negotiated at the WTO may push the economically disadvantaged further to the precipice in breach of their human rights. The Member States represent the business interest of its industries at the WTO by raising disputes at the DSB, but the human rights of the marginalised are never raised as a point of issue at the DSB, as Article XXIII of the GATT and the dispute settlement rules do not cover human rights but only trade measures that are in violation of WTO agreements.

The key areas that have raised concerns amongst human rights advocates in relation to the WTO's agreements include the right to health and access to medicines,[50] the right to food, the right to education, women's rights, labour rights, and indigenous peoples' rights. General concerns have also been raised about equity, democracy, and transparency in the WTO legal setup. The Panel in *US – Section 301 Trade Act* emphasised, "it would be entirely wrong to consider that the position of individuals is of no relevance to the GATT/WTO legal matrix . . . indeed one of the primary objects of the GATT/WTO as a whole, is to produce certain market conditions which would allow . . . individual activity to flourish"[51] by protecting the international division of labour against discriminatory trade restrictions and other distortions. The same Panel also emphasised, "(n)either the GATT nor the WTO has so far been interpreted by GATT/WTO institutions as a legal order producing direct effect".[52] This position means the WTO as an international body is not empowered to both create rights and obligations for WTO Member States and direct individual rights for traders, producers, and consumers of goods (Petersmann, 2005).

The UN initiated a broad work programme under the rubric 'Globalization and Its Impact on the Full Enjoyment of All Human Rights' in 1999, which resulted in a series of six reports (UN, 1999). The first of the reports to be released was in 2001, which addressed the TRIPS Agreement and its impact on human health (UN, 2001), followed by reports on agricultural liberalisation and the right to food, liberalisation of trade in services, investment liberalisation, *etc*. The UN human rights bodies increasingly insist that all WTO Members should adopt a 'human rights approach to trade', which

i Sets the promotion and protection of human rights as objectives of trade liberalisation, not exceptions;
ii Examines the effect of trade liberalisation on individuals and seeks to devise trade law and policy to take into account the rights of all individuals, in particular vulnerable individuals and groups;
iii Emphasises the role of states in the process of liberalisation – not only as negotiators of trade law and setters of trade policy, but also as the primary duty bearers of human rights;

iv Seeks consistency between the progressive liberalisation of trade and the progressive realisation of human rights;
v   Requires a constant examination of the impact of trade liberalisation on the enjoyment of human rights; and
vi Promotes international cooperation for the realisation of human rights and freedoms in the context of trade liberalisation (UN, 2002).

6.3 WTO Agreements and Human Rights

The Uruguay Round of negotiations, which culminated in the formation of the WTO, expanded the existing multilateral trading rules under GATT 1947. The international trade regime under the GATT was limited to trade in goods, whereas the trade regime under the WTO was expanded to include trade in services, protection of IP rights, trade in agricultural products, *etc.*[53] The Uruguay Round of negotiations created new global trade rules covering agriculture, textiles and clothing, telecommunications, banking, government procurements, product safety, and food sanitation regulations, amongst others. The Uruguay Round of negotiations also introduced a full-fledged rules-based dispute settlement system within the multilateral trading system to cover disputes that may arise while performing trade under the multilateral trade regime. This necessitated the creation of multilateral agreements, *i.e.*, the General Agreement on Trade in Services Agreements (GATS);[54] the Agreement on Trade-Related Aspects of Intellectual Property Rights (TRIPS);[55] Agreement on Technical Barriers to Trade (TBT);[56] Agreement on the Application of Sanitary and Phytosanitary Measures (SPS);[57] and the Understanding on Rules and Procedures Governing the Settlement of Disputes (DSU), besides other plurilateral agreements. This part of the chapter analyses the possible conflicts between the TRIPS Agreement, the GATS Agreement, and the DSU.

6.3.1 TRIPS Agreement: Private Rights, Human Rights, and Access to Medicines

The TRIPS Agreement, considered as one of the most controversial of trade regimes to emerge out of the Uruguay Round of negotiations, introduced private rights into the multilateral trading system. Although considered as the most important instrument for global governance of IP rights protection, the TRIPS Agreement has come under severe criticism from various commentators. The TRIPS Agreement, considered a legacy of the Uruguay Round of negotiations, remains controversial for various reasons (Okediji, 2003). See chapter 12 for a detailed discussion of the controversial introduction of private rights through the TRIPS Agreement into the multilateral trading system and the problem of access to medicines (considered a human right) brought about by extended protection given to pharmaceutical patents,[58] which also opened up the floodgates by permitting transnational pharmaceutical corporations to sue Member States for non-compliance of WTO laws before national courts.[59]

6.3.2 GATS Agreement: Trade in Services and Right to Work

The GATS Agreement sets out a broad framework for the liberalisation of trade in services, covering all internationally traded services. Services are an essential factor in the production of goods and facilitate growth and economic development. Services can be offered in relation to a wide range of economic activities, such as health care, education, telecommunications, tourism, transport, construction, banking and finance, *etc*. Although numerous agreements and policies drive and shape the liberalisation of trade in services, the role of the GATS Agreement is significant as the first multilateral agreement to set a legal framework for the liberalisation process. The GATS Agreement includes general obligations that apply to all services that come within the scope of GATS for all WTO Member States.

Concerns about GATS's implications for equity, costs, distribution, and availability of services, human development, and the sovereignty of governments in defining and pursuing their national objectives and priorities in the service sector persist. These concerns are predominantly felt in social services, such as healthcare and education, where there are recognised market failures and governments are heavily involved as regulators, providers, and distributors of such services (Chanda, 2002). The UN Report from 2002 notes that liberalisation of trade in services could impact on human rights

> in various ways, depending on a range of issues, not least the type of services being supplied, the mode of service delivery, the development level of the country and its internal infrastructure, the regulatory environment and the level of existing services prior to liberalization.
>
> (UN, 2002)

The report goes on to identify the various ways in which services trade could affect the lives of the citizens living in a developing country Member State, as follows:

i   The establishment of a two-tiered service supply with a corporate segment focused on the healthy and wealthy and an underfinanced public sector focusing on the poor and sick;
ii Brain drain, with better trained medical practitioners and educators being drawn towards the private sector by higher pay scales and better infrastructures;
iii An overemphasis on commercial objectives at the expense of social objectives which might be more focused on the provision of quality health, water, and education services for those that cannot afford them at commercial rates; and
iv An increasingly large and powerful private sector that can threaten the role of the government as the primary duty bearer for human rights by subverting regulatory systems through political pressure or the co-opting of regulators (UN, 2002).

The UN report notes that, to the extent that these phenomena can be linked to the liberalisation of trade in services, regulators need to be conscious of ensuring that liberalisation policies take into account State responsibilities to respect, protect, and fulfil human rights. Although human rights laws do not place obligations on Member States to be the sole provider of essential services, they must nevertheless guarantee the availability, accessibility, acceptability, and adaptability of essential services including their supply, especially to the poor, vulnerable, and marginalised (UN, 2002). Services liberalisation can affect economic growth and trade, besides having an impact on the provision of essential entitlements accepted as human rights such as health care, education, and water (UN, 2002). The report further notes that, given the opportunities and challenges posed by the liberalisation of trade in services to the enjoyment of human rights, it is important to understand the interaction between the rules and disciplines in GATS and the norms and standards of human rights law.

The GATS Agreement identifies trade in services under four modes, *viz.*, (i) Mode 1: cross-border supply, (ii) Mode 2: consumption abroad, (iii) Mode 3: commercial presence, and (iv) Mode 4: presence of natural persons. Article 1(2)(d) of the GATS seeks to liberalise the "supply of a service of one Member through presence of natural persons of a Member in the territory of any other Member". This allows for temporary migration, albeit limited to services occupations. This falls under Mode 4 of the deliverance of service under the GATS Agreement which contemplates migration of labour. Carzaniga notes that as regards temporary labour migration, Mode 4 is of limited value, the GATS Agreement under Article 1:2(d) terminologically reduces the temporary movement of natural persons to a 'mode' of service supply (Carzaniga, 2008). Commentators also note that destination countries of migrants have so far 'lacked the comfort' to use Mode 4 to liberalise the movement of service suppliers on a broader scale and have been particularly hesitant with regard to low skills (Panizzon, 2008). The GATS Agreement makes an 'artificial' distinction between 'foreign' and 'domestic' employment, which leaves unresolved the sensitive issue of whether the Member States intended to liberalise the entry into a host country's labour market (Carzaniga, 2008). Also, the GATS Agreement lacks a regulatory mandate to address the difficult issues associated with labour migration, such as overstays, brain drain, and waste or exploitation, which raises issues of human rights.

One of the arguments from the human rights perspective against an overly commercial interpretation of the GATS Agreement is that the prevailing differences in wealth amongst individuals living in the developed and developing country Member States could lead to a system that will provide for those who have the wherewithal to pay for it. The UN Report warns of a two-tiered "service-supply with a corporate segment focused on the healthy and wealthy and an under-financed public sector focusing on the poor and the sick" (UN, 2002). There is also the argument that the GATS could witness a 'brain drain' where practitioners are naturally drawn to the better pay and conditions of the private sector (Harrison, 2007). There is also the increased risk of the permanent or semi-permanent movement of skilled persons from poorer to richer countries.

6.3.3 Human Rights and the DSU

Member States of the WTO are obliged to bring any disputes arising in relation to the conduct of the multilateral trade before the DSB. WTO jurisprudence states that WTO agreements are to be interpreted in accordance with customary rules of interpretation of public international law, as the GATT and other WTO agreements constitute part of the body of public international law.[60] Interpreting WTO laws according to customary treaty interpretation requires the application of the Vienna Convention on the Interpretation of Treaties, in the light of other rules of international law and subject to *jus cogens*. The argument that the WTO laws are a 'self-contained regime' is unsustainable as the Appellate Body has rejected this argument. In *US – Gasoline*, the Appellate Body observed, the "General Agreement is not to be read in clinical isolation from public international law".[61]

The WTO has produced more judicial pronouncements on international law than any other international law institution since its creation in 1995 (Bacchus, 2015).[62] Bacchus also notes that if there is a line that demarcates international law and WTO law, it is not drawn by the Appellate Body of the WTO, but rather by the Member States themselves. International dispute settlement is a broad concept and is invariably subject to substantive laws of the institution that establishes the process. As one can observe, the remit of the WTO's dispute mechanism is limited to WTO laws. While substantive jurisdiction of the WTO is limited to adjudicating claims arising under the negotiated multilateral and plurilateral agreements, there is "nothing in the WTO treaty to suggest that the applicable law available to [P]anels and the Appellate Body in fulfilling their responsibilities to the members of the WTO is limited to the covered agreements" (Bacchus, 2015, p. 515). Both the Panels and the Appellate Body have ruled that Article 3.2 of the DSU is not intended to limit the sources of law for a WTO Panel to only those rules of general international law that relate to interpretation of treaties.[63]

There are numerous instances where both the Panels and the Appellate Body have used general international law to interpret substantive provisions of the WTO. For example, in *US – Shrimp*, the Appellate Body gave a dynamic reading of Article XX(g) using customary law, while answering the question whether turtles are 'exhaustible natural resources'. The Appellate Body observed that the words of Article XX(g), having been drafted over 50 years ago, "must be read by a treaty interpreter in the light of contemporary concerns of the community of nations about the protection and conservation of the environment".[64] The Appellate Body, relying on the observations made by the ICJ in its advisory opinion,[65] observed that the generic term 'natural resources' as occurring in Article XX(g) is not 'static' in its content but is rather 'by definition, evolutionary',[66] and that "measures to conserve exhaustible natural resources, whether living or non-living, may fall within Article XX(g)".[67]

The questions that follow are, can the Member State use human rights arguments to bring claims before the DSB? Is a Member State precluded from using human rights arguments to defend a position, *i.e.*, non-compliance of obligations arising from WTO agreements? As regards the first question, the answer is straightforward – a claim to be prosecuted successfully must meet the requirement of Article XXIII of the GATT, *i.e.*, a Member State will have to demonstrate that a nullification or impairment of the benefits accruing directly or indirectly under the WTO agreements through a measure introduced or through non-compliance by another Member State. The second question, though, is predicated on human rights laws having direct application in the WTO legal order. There is little or no jurisprudence available to demonstrate that Member States have successfully used human rights consideration to defend their position, *i.e.*, of non-compliance with the provisions of a WTO Agreement, either through commission or omission.[68]

How will the WTO's adjudicatory bodies address an issue before them which carries human rights claims, or arguments to support a complaint, or in defending a complaint? Some legal scholars argue that the WTO panellists are to be sensitive to political decisions taken elsewhere, including in other international organisations and in domestic fora (Howse and Mutua, 1999), while other scholars, inspired by the European integration model, espouse vesting the WTO Panels and Appellate Body with the powers needed to decide more issues than allowed under the WTO's current regime (Petersmann, 1996). Howse and Mutua link the trade regime to human rights through the WTO jurisprudence and advocate the reinterpretation of Article XX exceptions to permit unilateral trade remedies to remedy human rights abuses; reinterpretation of TRIPS rules that require adequate compensation in the compulsory licensing of patents; and reinterpretation of SPS and TBT to give primacy to underlying economic, social, and cultural rights.[69]

Alvarez, responding to some of the arguments presented by Howse and Mutua, argues that Article 103 of the UN Charter is unlikely to play a major role in the settlement of disputes before the WTO. Alvarez further notes that Article 103 does not identify the customary international law obligations that are to be given the privileged status as UN Charter obligations, and as a result the references to 'human rights' in the UN Charter, including those in its Preamble and in Article 55 (urging UN members to 'promote' undefined human rights), would appear to be of little direct use in the WTO context (Alvarez, 2001). Alvarez advocates a cautious approach to Howse and Mutua's suggestion that human rights instruments be embedded within other international organisations, including the ILO, and be routinely applied in radically different contexts by the WTO Appellate Body in trade disputes, as there are rules to be followed for treaty-based remedies, including the principle about *lex specialis* (Alvarez, 2001).

Marceau notes that both the Panels and the Appellate Body are creations of the DSU, which defines and limits their mandate to interpreting WTO laws to determine if a provision of the covered agreements has been violated. As a result, the Panels and Appellate Body are only vested with powers to interpret and apply WTO law, and therefore cannot interpret, let alone reach any legal conclusion of a violation of or compliance with, other treaties or customs. Therefore, claims relating to human rights violations cannot be pursued before the DSB, and Panels and the Appellate Body cannot enforce or give direct effect to human rights provisions between Member States other than pursuant to WTO provisions including the general exceptions (Marceau, 2002). In Marceau's opinion, WTO law must evolve and be interpreted consistently with international law, including human rights law, advocating a "good faith interpretation of the provisions of the WTO, including its exception provisions, which should lead to a reading and application of WTO law consistent with human rights" (Marceau, 2002, p. 753).

7. Summary

It is well documented that exponential growth in global trade leads to environmental degradation, through deforestation, losses in biodiversity, overfishing, air pollution, *etc*. The criticism often aired by the environmentalist is that the business-oriented international business bureaucrats who seek trade liberalisation are driven by the desire to create jobs and make profits and are not concerned about sustainable growth or the environment. Environmental issues were not present in the trade negotiations of the GATT era, as the trade agenda was dominated by economic issues and tariff reductions and liberalisation. Although warned about the adverse effects of unchecked trade expansion, it was not on the agenda at the Uruguay Round of negotiations. Meticulous preparations went into the details of each agreement negotiated and entered into during the Uruguay Round of negotiations in the early 1990s, but environmental issues only emerged as a concern in the closing stages of the negotiations. During the same period, the NAFTA was negotiated between Canada, Mexico, and the US, where environmental issues dominated the debate.

In the WTO era environmental concerns have gained traction, as sustainable development is linked with trade expansion, and the agenda is not limited to tariff reduction. Not satisfied with the lack of space to discuss environmental issues multilaterally, Member States have signed to MEAs to address transboundary environmental problems. This demonstrates the link between trade and the environment and the need for protection of the environment. With its large membership, the WTO is more suited to act as the international arbiter on environmental issues by both environmental groups and green-leaning governments.

The trade regime administered by the WTO protects the interest of the parties/Member States; human rights on the other hand seeks to place a boundary on the powers wielded by states and protects the rights of the individual. With the expansion in global trade/multilateral trade, which has brought about a greater movement of goods and services, the boundaries of trade operations have been extended, which in turn has side-lined the already marginalised countries or groups of people. The linkage between human rights and international trade has also been dominating the debate, as we witness access to affordable medicines (a human right) being denied due to the rollout of the TRIPS Agreement in the WTO era.[70]

Notes

1 See Appellate Body Report, *US – Tuna*, *US – Shrimp*, and *EC – Approval and Marketing of Biotech Products*.
2 MEAs are agreements between States to collaborate on a range of environmental issues. MEAs are non-binding principles, or 'soft law', which are required to be considered by contracting parties when taking decisions on environmental issues.
3 *E.g.*, release of pollutants (industrial waste) into shared resources, such as rivers that flow between countries.
4 Under President Donald Trump, the US withdrew its membership of the Paris Agreement on 1 January 2011. However, under President Joe Biden, the US has renewed US's membership of the Paris Agreement on his first day in office, *i.e.*, 20 January 2021.
5 See Appellate Body Report, *US – Gasoline*, p. 30.
6 *Ibid.*
7 See Appellate Body Report, *US – Gambling*, para. 291. The Appellate Body stated that Article XIV of the GATS Agreement sets out general exceptions under the GATS (services) much in the same way as Article XX of the GATT does under the GATT (goods).
8 See chapter 13 for a discussion on the TBT Agreement.
9 See chapter 14 for a discussion on the SPS Agreement.
10 The author also notes that Member States implement WTO agreements incompletely and do not face any legal consequences, and that they proceed on the basis that the "likelihood a trading partner would indeed request a WTO consultation or launch a formal WTO dispute in regard to a given environmental measure is low".
11 See section 5 of this chapter for further discussion on the role of the CTE.
12 The UN's main means of reviewing the 2030 Agenda for Sustainable Development is through the HLPF, which allows all UN Members and specialised agencies to meet annually to evaluate progress on achieving the SDGs.
13 The Eastern Tropical Pacific Ocean (ETP) is inhabited by dolphins and tuna. Commercial fishermen were in the habit of using purse seine nets to catch tuna which swam beneath schools of dolphins. The use of purse seine nets resulted in trapping the dolphins along with the tuna. According to the Inter-American Tropical Tuna Commission (IATTC), the number of dolphin deaths due to purse seine nets reached 132,000 in 1986.
14 The US did not enforce the MMPA between 1984 and 1990, despite evidence that foreign fleets were exceeding their permitted dolphin mortality rate. The Earth Island Institute, an environmental organisation, brought legal action against the Commerce and Treasury Departments for their failure to enforce the MMPA comparability requirement. At the time of the dispute, the American Tuna Boat Association was the only operator issued with a permit to operate in the region, where the limit was set at 20,500 dolphin kills per annum.
15 The MMPA also regulated intermediary countries that processed the catch *en route* from Mexico before their arrival in the US. The intermediary countries included Costa Rica, Italy, Japan, Spain, and The Netherlands.
16 See the case in *Earth Island Institute v Hogarth* United States Court of Appeals for the Ninth Circuit, 484 F.3d (9th Cir. 2007) 1123.
17 See Panel Report, *US – Tuna II (Mexico)*, para. 7.374.
18 *Ibid.*, paras. 7.629–7.621.
19 *Ibid.*, para. 7.702.
20 See Appellate Body Report, *US – Tuna II (Mexico)*, para. 199.
21 *Ibid.*, para. 299.
22 Due to their migratory nature, sea turtles are threatened in the high seas, and all seven species of turtle are categorised and listed as endangered under CITES. Although categorised as endangered, sea turtles are still harvested in many countries. All species of sea turtles, except the Australian flatback, are listed in Appendices I and II of the 1979 Convention on Migratory Species of Wild Animals (CMS). They also appear as endangered or vulnerable in the IUCN Red List.
23 It is to be noted that all sea turtles found in US waters are listed as endangered or threatened species under the US Endangered Species Act of 1973 (ESA).
24 TED is a grid trapdoor installed inside a trawling net which allows sea turtles to swim out of the trawling net.

25 The incidental capture and drowning of sea turtles by shrimp trawlers are considered the most significant source of mortality of sea turtles.
26 See Appellate Body Report, *US – Shrimp*, para. 121.
27 *Ibid*. paras. 123–124.
28 *Ibid*.
29 See Appellate Body Report, *US – Shrimp (Article 21.5 – Malaysia)*, paras. 137–138.
30 The EU referred to the Cartagena Biosafety Protocol and the 'precautionary principle' as a key defence.
31 See Appellate Body Report, *EC – Approval and Marketing of Biotech Products*, paras. 7.70–7.95.
32 See chapter 15 for a discussion on RTAs.
33 The TPP could not be ratified due to the withdrawal of the US from the agreement in January 2017 under the presidency of Donald Trump. The remaining signatories to the TPP continued with the negotiations to establish the Comprehensive and Progressive Agreement for Trans-Pacific Partnership (CPTPP), which substantially contains the provisions of the TPP. CPTPP is also referred to as TPP11 or TPP-11.
34 The more recent additions to the RTAs are the CPTPP, the AfCFTA, and the RCEP. See chapter 15 for details.
35 The US has long used bilateral trade agreements to pursue its environmental objectives abroad, and the tone of the environmental provisions have intensified over time. See Jinnah and Kennedy (2011).
36 See chapter 15 for a discussion on RTAs.
37 The authors also note that democratic countries that face import competition and countries that care about the environment are more willing to commit to environmental protection in trade agreements than autocracies are.
38 President Bill Clinton, bowing to pressure from both environmental and labour groups, decided not to sign NAFTA unless the side agreements on both labour and environment were also concluded. See Berger, Brandi, and Bruhn (2017).
39 Charnovitz argued that the orientation of the side agreement to NAFTA was premised on the misunderstanding that US and Mexican environmental laws were substantially equivalent. See Charnovitz (1994).
40 The CTE, in this regard, referred to Agenda 21 of the UN Conference on Environment and Development 1992.
41 Some NGOs called for disbanding the CTE at the 1996 Ministerial Conference in Singapore, as there were no concrete recommendations in the CTE's report from 1996.
42 InforMEA is a one-stop portal which not only provides information on MEAs but also offers free online courses on a range of topics including Convention on International Trade in Endangered Species of Wild Fauna and Flora, farmers' rights in the International Treaty on Plant Genetic Resources for Food and Agriculture, and the Basel Convention on the Control of Transboundary Movements of Hazardous Wastes, to name a few. The InforMEA website can be accessed at www.informea.org/en.
43 Technically, the UN was founded on 25 June 1945, when the UN charter was adopted, and before World War II came to end, *i.e.*, on 2 September 1945.
44 As of January 2020, the ICESCR has been signed by 45 parties and ratified by 24, and entered into force on 5 May 2013. The US has not ratified the Convention.
45 See Articles 6.2 and 6.3 of the EU Treaty, which read as follows:

   2 The Union shall accede to the European Convention for the Protection of Human Rights and Fundamental Freedoms. Such accession shall not affect the Union's competences as defined in the Treaties.
   3 Fundamental rights, as guaranteed by the European Convention for the Protection of Human Rights and Fundamental Freedoms and as they result from the constitutional traditions common to the Member States, shall constitute general principles of the Union's law.

46 See the judgment in *Barcelona Traction Light and Power Company Ltd* [1970] ICJ Rep., 32, and *Nicaragua v United Sates of America* [1986] ICJ Rep., 114.
47 See the ICJ Advisory Opinion of 25 March 1951 on *WHO v Egypt*.
48 Article 103 of the UN Charter reads as follows: "In the event of a conflict between the obligations of the Members of the United Nations under the present Charter and their obligations under any other international agreement, their obligations under the present Charter shall prevail."

49 For instance, the DSB is described as a rules-based dispute settlement system which can be accessed by all Member States. Nevertheless, the most active participants before the DSB are either from the developed country Member States or developing country Member States who conduct most of the trade through the multilateral trading system.
50 See chapter 12 for a discussion of access to medicines and the TRIPS Agreement.
51 See Panel Report, *US – Section 301 Trade Act*, para. 7.73.
52 *Ibid.*, para. 7.72.
53 The Uruguay Round of negotiations also produced (i) the Agreement on Agriculture (AoA), containing commitments to reduce support for and protection of the agricultural sector in market access, export subsidies, and domestic support, and (ii) the Agreement on Textiles and Clothing, which aims at reducing barriers to trade in the textiles and clothing industries.
54 See chapter 11 for a discussion on GATS Agreement.
55 See chapter 12 for a discussion on TRIPS Agreement.
56 See chapter 13 for a discussion on TBT Agreement.
57 See chapter 14 for a discussion on SPS Agreement.
58 See Sundaram (2018) on the never-ending problem of access to medicines in developing countries, and how this was exacerbated by the introduction of the TRIPS Agreement. To date, this problem continues to blight the developing country and least developed country Member States.
59 *Ibid*.
60 See, for instance, Appellate Body Reports, *US – Gasoline*, *US – Shrimp*, and *US – Hormone*, where the Vienna Convention was applied to interpret WTO rules. See also chapter 3 for a discussion on dispute settlement at the WTO.
61 See Appellate Body Report, *US – Gasoline*, p. 17. This was also the first appeal to be brought before the Appellate Body of the WTO.
62 The author, James Leonard Bacchus, was a founding member and twice chairperson of the Appellate Body between 1995 and 2003. Before serving as a member of the Appellate Body, Bacchus also served in the US House of Representatives from 1991 to 1995.
63 See Powell (2004) for a discussion on the relationship between WTO and other general international laws.
64 See Appellate Body Report, *US – Shrimp*, para. 129.
65 See *Namibia (Legal Consequences) Advisory Opinion* [1971] ICJ Rep., p. 31, where the ICJ stated that where concepts embodied in a treaty are "by definition, evolutionary", their "interpretation cannot remain unaffected by the subsequent development of law. . . . Moreover, an international instrument has to be interpreted and applied within the framework of the entire legal system prevailing at the time of the interpretation." *Aegean Sea Continental Shelf (Greece v Turkey)* [1978] ICJ Rep., p. 3.
66 See Appellate Body Report, *US – Shrimp*, para. 130.
67 *Ibid.*, para. 131.
68 See Marceau (2002) for a discussion on this issue.
69 See also Alvarez (2001), for a response to Howse and Mutua (1999).
70 See Sundaram (2018) for a discussion on the unresolved problem of access to medicines.

Bibliography

Allmand, Warren. 'Preface,' in Howse, Robert and Makau Mutua, 'Protecting Human Rights in a Global Economy: Challenges for the World Trade Organization,' *Human Rights in Development Online* Vol 6, No 1 (1999) 51–82.

Alvarez, Jose E. 'How *Not* to Link: Institutional Conundrums of an Expanded Trade Regime,' *Widener Law Symposium Journal* Vol 7 (2001) 1–20.

Bacchus, James. 'Not in Clinical Isolation,' in Marceau, Gabrielle (ed.) *A History of Law and Lawyers in the GATT/WTO: The Development of the Rule of Law in the Multilateral Trading System* (Cambridge University Press, 2015) 507–516.

Berger, Axel, Clara Brandi and Dominique Bruhn. 'Environmental Provisions in Trade Agreements: Promises at the Trade and Environment Interface,' *Briefing Paper, No 16/2017, Deutsches Institut für Entwicklungspolitik* (DIE) (2017).

Bown, Chad P. and Rachel McCulloch. 'Environmental Issues,' in Macrory, Patrick F.J., Arthur E. Appleton and Michael G. Plummer (eds.) *The WTO: Legal, Economic and Political Analysis* Vol 3 (Springer, 2005) 137–170.

Carzaniga, Antonio. 'A Warmer Welcome? Access for Natural Persons under PTAs,' in Marchetti, Juan A. and Martin Roy (eds.) *Opening Markets for Trade in Services: Countries and Sectors in Bilateral and WTO Negotiations* (Cambridge University Press, 2008) 475–502.

Chanda, Rupa. 'GATS and Its Implications for Developing Countries: Key Issues and Concerns,' *United Nations Department of Economics and Social Affairs Paper 25* (2002).

Charnovitz, Steve. 'The NAFTA Environmental Side Agreement: Implications for Environmental Cooperation, Trade Policy and American Treaty Making,' *Temple International and Comparative Law Journal* Vol 8 (1994) 257.

Charnovitz, Steve. 'Environment and Health under WTO Dispute Settlement,' *The International Lawyer* (1998) 901–921.

Crowley, Meredith and Robert Howse. '*Tuna-Dolphin II*: A Legal and Economic Analysis of the Appellate Body Report,' *World Trade Review* Vol 13, No 2 (2014) 321–355.

Deere Birkbeck, Carolyn. 'Greening International Trade: Pathways Forward,' *Global Governance Centre and the Forum on Trade, Environment & the SDGs (TESS)* (2021).

Dommen, Caroline. 'Raising HR Concerns in the World Trade Organization: Actors, Processes and Possible Strategies,' *Human Rights Quarterly* Vol 24, No 1 (2002) 1–50.

Dommen, Caroline. 'Safeguarding the Legitimacy of the Multilateral Trading System: The Role of Human Rights Law,' in Abbott, Frederick M., Christine Brining-Kaufmann and Thomas Cottier (eds.) *International Trade and Human Rights: Foundations and Conceptual Issues* (University of Michigan Press, 2009) 121–132.

Espa, Ilaria. 'Natural Resources Management in the Sustainable Development Goals Era,' in Beverelli, Cosimo, Jürgen Kurtz and Damian Raess (eds.) *International Trade, Investment, and the Sustainable Development Goals* (Cambridge University Press, 2020) 76–107.

Esty, Daniel C. *Greening the GATT: Trade, Environment, and the Future* (Institute for International Economics, 1994).

Harrison, James. *The Human Rights Impact of the World Trade Organization* (Hart Publishing, 2007).

Hoekman, Bernard. 'Trade and the Post-2015 Development Agenda,' in Helble, Matthias and Ben Shepherd (eds.), *Win-Win: How International Trade Can Help Meet the Sustainable Development Goals* (Asian Development Bank Institute, 2017) 32–60.

Horn, Henrik and Petros C. Mavroidis. 'Multilateral Environmental Agreements in the WTO: Silence Speaks Volumes,' *International Journal of Economic Theory* Vol 10, No 1 (2014) 147–165.

Howse, Robert and Makau Mutua. 'Protecting Human Rights in a Global Economy: Challenges for the World Trade Organization,' *Human Rights in Development Online* Vol 6, No 1 (1999) 51–82.

Hufbauer, Gary Clyde, Steve Charnovitz and Jisun Kim. *Global Warming and the World Trading System* (Peterson Institute for International Economics, 2009).

Hufbauer, Gary Clyde and Meera Fickling. 'Trade and Environment,' in Narlikar, Amrita, Martin Daunton and Robert M. Stern (eds.) *The Oxford Handbook of the World Trade Organization* (Oxford University Press, 2012) 719–740.

IISD. 'The WTO Committee on Trade and Environment Discusses Efforts to Address Climate Change, Improve Stability,' SDG Knowledge Hub (7 April 2021) <https://sdg.iisd.org/news/wto-committee-on-trade-and-environment-discusses-efforts-to-address-climate-change-improve-sustainability/> (5 July 2021).

ILA (International Law Association). 'New Delhi Declaration of Principles of International Law Relating to Sustainable Development,' (2 April 2002) <www2.ecolex.org/server2neu.php/libcat/docs/LI/MON-070850.pdf> (6 July 2021).

ILA (International Law Association). 'Sofia Guiding Statements on the Judicial Elaboration of the 2002 New Delhi Declaration of Principles of International Law Relating to Sustainable Development,' (ILA Resolution No. 7/2012) (2012).

Jinnah, Sikina and Julia Kennedy. 'A New Era of Trade-Environment Politics: Learning from US Leadership and Its Consequences Abroad,' *Whitehead Journal of International Relations* Vol 12, No 1 (2011) 95–110.

Jinnah, Sikina and Abby Lindsay. 'Diffusion through Issue Linkage: Environmental Norms in US Trade Agreements,' *Global Environmental Politics* Vol 16, No 3 (2016) 41–61.

Joseph, Sarah. *Blame It on the WTO? A Human Rights Critique* (Oxford University Press, 2013).

Lamy, Pascal. 'Towards Shared Responsibility and Greater Coherence: Human Rights, Trade and Macroeconomic Policy,' Speech at the Colloquium on Human Rights in the Global Economy, Co-organized by the International Council on Human Rights and Realizing Rights, Geneva, 13 January (2010) <www.wto.org/english/news_e/sppl_e/sppl146_e.htm> (accessed 19 July 2021).

Leader, Sheldon. 'Trade and Human Rights II,' in Macrory, Patrick F.J., Arthur E. Appleton and Michael G. Plummer (eds.) *The WTO: Legal, Economic and Political Analysis* Vol 2 (Springer, 2005) 663–696.

Lester, Simon, Bryan Mercurio and Arwel Davies. *World Trade Law: Text, Materials and Commentary* (Hart Publishing, 2018).

Marceau, Gabrielle. 'WTO Dispute Settlement and Human Rights,' *European Journal of International Law* Vol 13, No 4 (2002) 753–814.

Matsushita, Mitsuo, Thomas J. Shoenbaum, Petros C. Mavroidis and Michael Hahn. *The World Trade Organization: Law, Practice, and Policy* (Oxford University Press, 2017).

Messerlin, Patrick. 'From MDGs to SDGs: The Role of Trade,' in Helble, Matthias and Ben Shepherd (eds.), *Win-Win: How International Trade Can Help Meet the Sustainable Development Goals* (Asian Development Bank Institute, 2017) 9–31.

Monteiro, José-Antonio. 'Typology of Environment-Related Provisions in Regional Trade Agreements,' *WTO Staff Working Paper, No. ERSD-2016–13* (2016).

Morin, Jean-Frédéric, Andreas Dür and Lisa Lechner. 'Mapping the Trade and Environment Nexus: Insights from a New Dataset,' *Global Environmental Politics* Vol 18, No 1 (2018) 122–139.

Morsink, Jonannes. 'The Philosophy of the Universal Declaration,' *Human Rights Quarterly* Vol 6 (1982) 309–334.

Nordström, Håkan and Scott Vaughan. 'Trade and Environment,' *WTO Special Studies* No 4 (1999).

Okediji, Ruth L. 'Public Welfare and the Role of the WTO: Reconsidering the TRIPS Agreement,' *Emory International Law Review* Vol 17 (2003) 819–918.

Panizzon, Marion. 'How Human Rights Violations Nullify and Impair GATS Commitments,' in Panizzon, Marion, Nicole Pohl and Pierre Sauvé (eds.) *GATS and the Regulation of International Trade in Services* (Cambridge University Press, 2008) 534–560.

Petersmann, Ernst-Ulrich. 'Constitutionalism and International Organizations,' *Journal of International Law and Business* Vol 17, No 1 (1996) 398–469.

Petersmann, Ernst-Ulrich. 'Time for a United Nations "Global Compact" for Integrating Human Rights into the Law of Worldwide Institutions: Lessons from the European Integration,' *European Journal of International Law* Vol 13, No 3 (2002) 621–650.

Petersmann, Ernst-Ulrich. 'Trade and Human Rights I,' in Macrory, Patrick F.J., Arthur E. Appleton and Michael G. Plummer (eds.) *The WTO: Legal, Economic and Political Analysis* Vol 2 (Springer, 2005) 623–653.

Powell, Stephen J. 'The Place of Human Rights Law in World Trade Organization Rules,' *Florida Journal of International Law* Vol 16 (2004) 219–231.

Prévost, Denis. 'Opening Pandora's Box: The Panel's Findings in the *EC-Biotech* Dispute,' *Legal Issues of Economic Integration* Vol 34, No 1 (2007) 67–101.

Shelton, Dinah. 'Protecting Human Rights in a Globalized World,' *Boston College International and Comparative Law Review* Vol 25, No 2 (2002) 273–322.

Sundaram, Jae. *Pharmaceutical Patent Protection and World Trade Law: The Unresolved Problem of Access to Medicines* (Routledge Publishing, 2018).

Tarasofsky, Richard G. 'The WTO Committee on Trade and Environment: Is It Making a Difference?,' *Max Planck Yearbook of United Nations Law Online* Vol 3, No 1 (1999) 471–488.

Trachtman, Joel P. 'WTO Trade and Environment Jurisprudence: Avoiding Environmental Catastrophe,' *Harvard International Law Journal* Vol 58, No 2 (2017) 273–309.

Trebilcock, Michael, Robert Howse and Antonia Eliason. *The Regulation of International Trade* (Routledge, 2013).

United Nations. 'Universal Declaration of Human Rights,' GA Resolution 217 A(III) (UN Doc.A/810) (1948).

United Nations. 'Globalization and Its Impact on the Full Enjoyment of all Human Rights,' (E/CN/4/RES/1999/59) (28 April 1999).

United Nations. 'The Impact of the Agreement on Trade-Related Aspects of Intellectual Property Rights on Human Rights: Report of the High Commissioner,' (E/CN.4/Sub.2/2001/13) (27 June 2001).

United Nations. 'Liberalization of Trade in Services and Human Rights: Report of the High Commissioner,' (E/CN.4/Sub.2/2002/9) (25 June 2002).

United Nations. 'Report of the United Nations Conference on Sustainable Development,' Rio de Janeiro, Brazil, 20–22 June (UN Doc. A/CONF.216/16) (2012).

United Nations. UNEP, 'The 10-Year Framework of Programmes on Sustainable Consumption and Production: Rio+20 Adopts the 10YFP,' (February 2013) <https://sustainabledevelopment.un.org/content/documents/944brochure10yfp.pdf> (accessed 6 July 2021).

United Nations. 'Transforming Our World: The 2030 Agenda for Sustainable Development,' (UN Doc. A/RES/70/1) (25 September 2015).

WCED (World Commission on Environment and Development). *Our Common Future* (Oxford University Press, 1987).

World Trade Organisation. 'Report of the Committee on Trade and Environment,' (WT/CTE/1) (12 November 1996).

World Trade Organisation. 'World Trade Report 2011: The WTO and Preferential Trade Agreements: From Co-Existence to Coherence,' (WTO, 2011).

17 The Case for a Reform of the WTO

Learning Objectives	655
1. Introduction	655
2. The Doha Round: The Failure of Multilateral Negotiations	656
3. WTO Working Practice: Consensus-Driven Decision-Making, SDT	657
4. The Reform of the DSB	658
4.1 Appointment of Appellate Body Members	659
4.2 EU's Solution: The MPIA	659
5. The Pandemic and the WTO's Response	660
6. Summary	661

Learning Objectives

This chapter aims to help students understand:

1 Some of the current issues facing the WTO;
2 The failure of the Doha Round;
3 Reforming the WTO; key areas of reform sought;
4 Reforming the DSB; and
5 Appointment of Appellate Body members.

1. Introduction

The GATT's remit, in the post-World War II era, was trade in goods with the key agenda of liberalisation of trade through tariff reductions. The WTO's remit, in contrast, ushered in a multilateral trade regime with much more to offer than the GATT, by including amongst other things trade in services, trade in agriculture, textiles, and an extended protection regime for IP rights. The WTO, unlike the GATT, has a built-in rules-based dispute settlement system (administered by the DSB) which allows Member States to seek remedies where the undertakings under WTO agreements are transgressed. The dispute settlement system also features an Appellate Body, which was clearly missing in the GATT 1947. The WTO's business model, which is based on consensus, was shaped through several rounds of several negotiations. Under the GATT, Contracting Parties were able to choose the agreement they wanted to embrace, whereas the membership of the WTO required the Member States to sign up to all covered agreements and submit all disputes to the jurisdiction of the DSB. This is referred to as the 'principle of single undertaking', where every item of the negotiation is part of a whole and indivisible package and cannot be agreed separately.

DOI: 10.4324/9780367028183-21

With an expanded remit, the WTO has been largely successful in administering the implementation of the covered agreements, as well as adjudicating numerous disputes brought before the DSB through Panel and Appellate Body rulings. It also successfully concluded agreements on telecommunications, financial services, and information technology products in the late 1990s. That said, the WTO had not been successful in negotiating rules on competition, investment, and transparency in government procurement. The WTO for some time now has been beset with challenges, highlighting the need to modernise and reform its institutions and policies. The reform debate, which has been going on for close to two decades, has focused on the WTO's working practice, which includes the consensus-driven decision-making, member-driven governance model, and use of special and differential treatment (SDT) by developing county Member States; the failure of the multilateral trade negotiations (MTN), *i.e.*, the Doha Development Agenda; among others. The reform debate from recent times had focused on the reform of the DSB and the process of appointment of members to the Appellate Body.

The governance model of the WTO, which is consensus-driven, and that of the appointment of members to the Appellate Body are interconnected. While there are various challenges that confront the WTO today, this chapter takes up for study the following issues, *viz.*, the failure of the Doha Round; working practice; the reform of the DSB; and the missed opportunity during the COVID-19 pandemic to use the organisation to boost global trade in medical products, cooperation on trade in vaccines, issue of IP rights protection to pharmaceutical products, *etc.*

2. The Doha Round: The Failure of Multilateral Negotiations

The Doha Development Agenda, the first round of trade negotiations since the creation of the WTO, was launched in 2001. The Doha Round's agenda was firmed in the Singapore Ministerial Meeting in 1996, which was essentially the unfinished business from the Uruguay Round of negotiations, which culminated in the founding of the WTO in 1995. It is considered the longest running trade round in the history of multilateral trade. All the earlier rounds of multilateral trade negotiations had taken place under the auspices of the GATT, which eventually culminated in the founding of the WTO in 1995. The Doha Round became deadlocked in 2008, and there is no clear indication if the trade round will ever be concluded.

Commentators are quick to point out that since the conclusion of the Uruguay Round of negotiations in 1995 much has changed in the global political economy, and that there was a failure to include issues of intense concern to the agenda from more recent years, such as food security and climate change (Trebilcock, Howse, and Eliason, 2013). For many developing country Member States some of the items on the agenda, such as investment and antitrust, were unacceptable for multilateral negotiations. Many developing country Member States were keen for the perceived imbalances arising from the Uruguay Round – such as the orientation towards neoliberal ideology (privatisation, regulatory reform in services) and restriction of policy space in areas such as IP rights and subsidies – to be corrected in the Doha Round. In contrast, the developed country Member States viewed the objectives of Doha Round as further liberalisation on a neoliberal model, with the addition of disciplines on investment and competition (Trebilcock, Howse, and Eliason, 2013). Some commentators have expressed the view that the Doha Round was a distraction, as it was focusing on minor issues, and the market access agenda that was being negotiated had little economic relevance and did not respond to the challenges posed by increasing global integration (Mattoo and Subramanian, 2008, 2009).[1]

While the business community remained optimistic and lent their support for the Doha Round of negotiations,[2] there remained major differences amongst the Member States in terms of both principle and vision for the negotiations. For many Member States the negotiating agenda was backward-looking, as it prioritised tariffs on manufacturing and agricultural support policies over trade in services and environmental policies to reduce carbon emissions. The Doha Round agenda was disconnected from twenty-first-century priorities, as it did not touch upon policies affecting the digital economy, cross-border data flows, and foreign investment and regulating the behaviour of state-owned or -controlled enterprises (Fiorini, Hoekman, Mavroidis, Nelson, and Wolfe, 2021). Barring one important new agreement (on trade facilitation), *viz.*, on discriminatory trade policies, where little progress was made since the establishment of the organisation in 1995, Member States were not able to conclude anything of significance in the Doha Round of negotiations.

With the launch of the WTO, most of the objectives of the multilateral trade negotiating rounds were met, *viz.*, the possible mutual gains from tariff concession, binding border measures all negotiated on an MFN basis. The political economy and the landscape of international trade had changed significantly since the creation of the WTO, as the Member States had concluded several RTAs, where trade in services, driven by technological advances, has been liberalised.[3] One of the major drivers for the change in the landscape was the rapid economic growth achieved by China and other emerging economies since 1995 and the associated rebalancing of the world economy (Fiorini, Hoekman, Mavroidis, Nelson, and Wolfe, 2021). Also, issues of greater significance were left out from the negotiations, *e.g.*, climate change and trade, and sustainable development.

3. WTO Working Practice: Consensus-Driven Decision-Making, SDT

Some the reasons that impeded progress in the Doha Round of negotiations are attributable to the formulaic approach in the market access negotiations, the single undertaking principle (nothing is agreed until everything is agreed),[4] and consensus (universality), *i.e.*, all WTO Member States are to participate and need to agree to the outcome (Hoekman and Kostecki, 2009).[5] The formulaic approach obviously gave rise to efforts by groups of Member States to obtain exemptions from the full force of the formula, with many developed country Member States seeking to apply a narrow interpretation of tariff-binding principles. Hoekman and Kostecki argue that as opposed to a multilateral approach, a greater reliance on a plurilateral approach could have benefitted the negotiations in Doha, and the principle of 'single undertaking', which was successfully adopted in the Uruguay Round, did not hold water in the Doha Round of negotiations, as the landscape of political economy had changed considerably since (Hoekman and Kostecki, 2009).

As referred to earlier, the consensus-driven working practice of the WTO impeded progress in the Doha Round of negotiations (and continues to impede) and the ability of Member States to address emerging issues in international trade. The consensus approach and the principles and practices of rule-making, carried over from the Uruguay Round of negotiations are obsolete and are not fit for the twenty-first century. The Doha Round fiasco witnessed the Member States shifting some of the rule-making away from the WTO to RTAs – moving from a multilateral forum to a bilateral forum.[6] For instance, at the Buenos Aires Ministerial Conference in 2017, many Member States moved away from negotiations premised on consensus decision-making by launching plurilateral talks among groups of countries, which address measures to support micro, small, and medium-sized enterprises (MSMEs), rules of the game for e-commerce and digital trade, action to facilitate investment, and disciplines on domestic regulation of services (Fiorini, Hoekman, Mavroidis, Nelson, and Wolfe, 2021). This signals a clear departure from the consensus-based/single undertaking paradigm that has been the mantra of the WTO decision-making process (Vickers, Soobramanien, and Enos-Edu, 2019). Some developed country Member States, including Canada, the EU, and the US have identified their reform priorities to improve on the WTO's functioning. Suggestions on the reform of the governance of the WTO have come from various quarters (Warwick Commission, 2007; Bertelsmann Stiftung, 2018).

The consensus has posed problems all along due to the general unwillingness of many developing country Member States to discuss emerging issues. The WTO working practices have also been abused by Member States to impede the day-to-day functioning of WTO bodies. The most notable recent example was the US blocking consensus on the choice of a new director-general in 2020.[7] Similarly, in 2018–2019 the consensus practice was used by the US to block the appointment of members to the Appellate Body, thereby making it non-operational.[8] The consensus practice is useful when seeking to change or modify the substantive rules of the WTO that apply to specific trade-related policies, but the same should not be used as a tool to block Member States that seek to conclude agreements with commitments that bind only signatories (Hoekman and Mavroidis, 2021).

Although consensus practice is an important feature, it should not be applied to matters such as setting the agenda of WTO committee meetings. Hoekman and Mavroidis note that the 'member-driven' mantra has "constrained deliberation in WTO bodies and limited the scope of the Secretariat to provide information and analysis" when assisting Member States develop a common understanding on trade issues. The consensus-based decision-making process has been used by Member States to veto initiatives at the WTO. Yet another shortcoming of consensus is that it has restricted engagement with other key actors in the decision-making process, *viz.*, stakeholders (international business and civic society representatives) and other international organisations and regulatory bodies with relevant knowledge and expertise (Hoekman and Mavroidis, 2021).

This brings us to the invocation of 'special and differential treatment' (SDT) by developing country Member States in the member-driven governance model of the WTO, which has effectively weakened the WTO's function as a venue to address trade tensions and promote cooperation (Hoekman, 2019).[9] Originally introduced as a basic principle in the 1960s, the SDT has lived beyond its shelf life and is no longer acceptable to many developed country Member States. This stems from the fact that Member States can self-determine as developing country, or developed country Member State. Advanced developing country Member States have utilised the SDT to offer less than full reciprocity in trade negotiations and in the application of WTO rules, which leads one to develop a perception that such economies have an unfair competitive advantage (Bertelsmann Stiftung, 2018). Hoekman also argues that insistence on consensus-based operating modalities and SDT for large, successful developing country Member States are no longer viable (Hoekman, 2019). Hoekman and Mavroidis favour reconceptualising the SDT for developing countries as a way forward.

4. The Reform of the DSB

Often referred to as the 'crown jewel' of the WTO, the DSB is by far the most successful state-state international dispute settlement body created in the post-World War II era. The DSB since its establishment in 1995 has adjudicated close to 600 trade disputes brought before it by its Member States. The ICJ, which adjudicates disputes in most areas of international law, has so far addressed 176 disputes since its creation in 1947. Although the jurisdiction of the

WTO is far narrower than the ICJ's, the sheer volume of trade that is conducted through its multilateral platform by Member States gives rise to numerous disputes. The DSB's rules-based approach, which is geared towards finding a solution to disputes as opposed to delivering judgements, encourage litigants (Member States) to seek resolution before it.

4.1 Appointment of Appellate Body Members

One of the strongest critics of the DSB, the US alleges that the Appellate Body has too frequently overstepped its mandate. Over the years, the United States Trade Representative (USTR) has frequently criticised or rejected proposals for the appointment of AB members.[10] US trade diplomats have vetoed the appointment of WTO Appellate Body members on a number of occasions, with reasons ranging from 'bias' to 'unpatriotic'. In December 2019 the Appellate Body ceased operations due to the US refusal under President Trump's administration to agree to appoint new members and reappoint incumbents.[11] The dispute settlement mechanism comprises a two-step process, where Panels hear disputes brought before it by Member States and proceed to deliver their reports. When not adopted, the reports are subject to appeal to the Appellate Body, which is the final arbiter of any trade dispute that comes before the WTO. It is this second stage of the process that was been crippled by the blockage. Some of the criticisms of the US are shared by other Member States.

The demise of the WTO's Appellate Body has indeed created an uncertainty in the rules-based multilateral trading system. The confidence of the Member States has been shaken as no finality or enforceability can be attached to the findings of the Panels, and as a result, a fundamental premise of the legal commitments under WTO treaties is undermined (Bacchus, 2018). One of the top priorities for the WTO is resolving the Appellate Body crisis, as there are a total of 14 appeals pending before the dysfunctional Appellate Body. This raises the question of the status of the associated panel reports (Hoekman and Mavroidis, 2021). While Article 16.4 of the DSU permits appeal of panel reports even if the AB is non-operational, the panel reports will have no legal value unless adopted.

4.2 EU's Solution: The MPIA

The EU, in response to the impasse, has developed an independent arbitration body called the Multi-Party Interim Appeal Arbitration Arrangement (MPIA) in April 2020 (European Commission, 2020). Under the MPIA the general arbitration mechanism in Article 25 of the DSU is used as the basis for an appeal. The MPIA, inspired by a research paper from a group of WTO lawyers, has now been joined by 23 WTO Member States (Lester, 2020). The MPIA, which has a pool of ten arbitrators, commits signatories (complainants or respondents) to either accept a panel report or use the MPIA to appeal the findings through a process that closely resembles the Appellate Body proceedings. All the MPIA arbitrators have extensive experience in the field of trade disputes, with some having served as panellists or in the WTO Secretariat division that assist Panels and the Appellate Body (Lester, 2020). The MPIA, which is open to WTO Member States, ensures that participating Member States will continue to benefit from a functioning two-step dispute settlement system akin to the WTO's DSB, including the availability of an independent and impartial appeal stage.

Due to its limited membership and disputed legality, the MPIA cannot be considered a strong solution. Howse argues that the EU's solution leads to further confusion and uncertainty into the legal order of the WTO, as there is the risk that jurisprudence will be made for some Member States that is not applicable to others (Howse, 2021). It should not be forgotten that the MPIA offers a temporary replacement for the Appellate Review of the DSB and does not replace the Appellate Body *per se*. As Howse notes, the "demise of the WTO Appellate Body and the resulting uncertainty and incoherence in the dispute settlement system do not by any means condemn the WTO to irrelevance or failure" (Howse, 2021).

5. The Pandemic and the WTO's Response

The COVID-19 virus, which was first reported in the Wuhan province of China in January 2000, spread across the globe, regardless of a country's status as a developed, developing, or least developed country Member State. The inaction on the part of the WTO in the early stages of the COVID-19 pandemic constrained many Member States to impose export restriction unilaterally on medical supplies and personal protective equipment (PPE). This negative response on the part of the WTO impeded supply responses by disrupting the global production network. During the pandemic,[12] the Member States missed the opportunity to use the WTO as a coordination mechanism to boost global trade in medical products and cooperate on trade in vaccines (Hoekman and Mavroidis, 2021). Some of the suggestions made on actions that could be taken by Member States is cooperation at a time of crisis to help the world economy recover from the pandemic and prepare for similar eventualities in the future. One of the major criticisms to emerge is the lack of cooperation on trade in vaccines.

Commentators have criticised the Member States for resorting to 'vaccine nationalism' to allocation of medication, arguing that without global coordination countries may bid against each other, thereby driving up the price of vaccines, and that this will have a profound effect on the low- and middle-income countries globally (Bollyky and Bown, 2020). There had also been a complete lack of action to support the operation of global value chains producing and distributing critical supplies amongst the Member States, due to a lack of understanding of the mechanism, which has led to countries applying measures against each other (Fiorini, Hoekman, and Yildirim, 2020). In addition, suggestions had been made for a new basis for reciprocity in medical goods, and the negotiation of a global agreement under the auspices of the WTO to govern the use of trade restrictions during a global public health crisis. The two strands of the proposed agreement would include (i) the elimination of tariffs on an MFN basis on the covered medical goods and medicines and (ii) the elimination of all export limits on any covered medical goods and medicines (Evenett and Winters, 2020).[13]

The trade challenges arising from the COVID-19 pandemic have highlighted both the importance and the limitations of the WTO's role in implementation of WTO disciplines on export restrictions and the more recent trade facilitation agreement. Some Member States adopted trade restrictions paying scant regard to WTO rules, thereby undermining the very public health objectives they were intended to serve by delaying the delivery of critical medical goods to patients in need. In contrast, some Member States have proposed an acceleration in the implementation of existing trade facilitation commitments, while others have embarked on a round of preliminary discussions to explore the possibilities of developing new commitments to encourage freer trade in medical goods (Alben and Brown, 2021).

International trade should have been used as a powerful tool to help contain the pandemic and contribute to the economic recovery. As pointed out by the Ottawa Group proposal, work should start on a Trade and Health Initiative under the auspices of the WTO, as the health crisis requires coordinated global response (Ottawa Group, 2020). The WTO, as the cornerstone of the international trading system, can facilitate the delivery of an effective global response to crisis situations. It is through multilateral solutions that we can be better prepared to fight both the current and any future pandemics. Howse notes the WTO has an "important function as a multilateral forum for deliberation and coordination of responses to trade-related crises and other relevant global developments", and the role does not depend on negotiation of new rules or even enforcement of existing ones through dispute settlement (Howse, 2021).

6. Summary

The WTO is the premier institution through which a major part of world trade is performed today. The WTO is the facilitator of multilateral trade, which is performed under the terms and conditions of the covered agreements. The failure of the Doha Round, if at all, has taught the international community important lessons on the need to review the WTO's consensus-based approach to negotiations. Despite its shortcomings the DSB, which has a compulsory jurisdiction over all disputes arising under the covered agreements, has performed exceptionally well under difficult/testing conditions. In the words of Mavroidis,

> the WTO has a very important mandate anyway which is independent of the success/failure of rounds: discussions in the various committees manage to produce better communication across trading nations, and resolve many disputes as well: a look into the TBT Committee for example, suffices to persuade the observer that dozens of specific trade concerns are being resolved at this level with no need to go to dispute settlement and the ensuing administrative cost for the WTO; through its publications it disseminates information about all issues coming under its purview.
>
> (Mavroidis, 2011)

Notes

1 The authors observe that since the mid-1990s, *i.e.*, since the creation of the WTO, overall trade has flourished, but the multilateral process that governs trade has languished.
2 WTO surveys from 2012 indicated that two-thirds of business leaders thought that the Doha Round could deliver benefits to businesses. See WTO (2013).
3 See chapter 15 for a discussion on RTAs.
4 See Wolfe (2009) for a discussion on how the principle of single undertaking is used as a negotiating technique in the WTO's rule-making process. The author notes that the exact phrase "single undertaking" is used only in the declarations launching the Uruguay Round and Doha Round of negotiations, although this principle dates back to the Dillon Round in the late 1950s and the Kennedy Round in the 1960s.
5 The authors are critical of the practice of the Member States in the Doha Round for reverting to the Tokyo Round practice of relying on a formula approach to determine tariff cuts and reductions in permitted agricultural subsidies.
6 The deadlock in the Doha Round/WTO has induced many Member States to move over to RTAs, which deepens the integration of markets with trade partners. On the other hand, such deepening of market integration risks fragmenting the rules that apply to global value chains.
7 Although approved by all other Member States of the WTO, the US under President Donald Trump was able to block the appointment of Dr Ngozi Okonjo-Iweala as the director-general of the WTO in the autumn of 2020, using the consensus mechanism. President Joe Biden, shortly after assuming office, ended the deadlock by supporting Dr Ngozi Okonjo-Iweala's appointment as the director-general of the WTO.
8 As of August 2021, the deadlock continues.
9 The author identifies both consensus-based decision-making and SDT as the elements that have weakened the WTO's function.
10 Even under the Obama administration, the USTR refused to reappoint or appoint specific judges. Jennifer Hillman, who was Appellate Body member between 2007 and 2011 was refused

reappointment, and the proposed appointment of Prof James Gathii was turned down by the USTR, to cite a few instances.
11 Howse notes that there was no formal executive order or other administrative action of any legal force under the Trump administration on the refusal to entertain new Appellate Body appointments. See Howse (2021).
12 The pandemic is still ongoing when the first draft of this book is being submitted to the publishers, having taken a toll of over 4,250,000 lives.
13 Similar proposals were also put forward by the Ottawa Group in 2020. See Ottawa Group (2020).

Bibliography

Alben, Elissa and Logan Brown. 'Is the WTO in Sync with the Business Community?,' *Global Policy* Vol 12, Supplement 3 (2021) 23–29.

Bacchus, James. 'Might Unmakes Right: The American Assault on the Rule of Law in World Trade,' *CIGI Paper No 173* (2018).

Bertelsmann Stiftung. 'Revitalizing Multilateral Governance at the World Trade Organization,' Report of the High-Level Board of Experts on the Future of Global Trade Governance (2018).

Bollyky, Thomas J. and Chad P. Bown. 'The Tragedy of Vaccine Nationalism: Only Cooperation Can End the Pandemic,' *Foreign Affairs* Vol 99, No 5 (2020) 96–108.

European Commission. 'Interim Appeal Arrangement for WTO Disputes Becomes Effective,' Dispute Settlement, News Archive (30 April 2020) <https://trade.ec.europa.eu/doclib/press/index.cfm?id=2127> (accessed 29 July 2021).

Evenett, Simon J. and L. Alan Winters. 'Preparing for a Second Wave of COVID-19: A Trade Bargain to Secure Supplies of Medical Goods,' *UK Trade Policy Observatory Briefing Paper 40* (2020). <www.globaltradealert.org/reports/52> (accessed 30 July 2021).

Fiorini, Matteo, Bernard Hoekman, Petros C. Mavroidis, Douglas Nelson and Robert Wolfe. 'Stakeholder Preferences and Priorities for the Next WTO Director General,' *Global Policy* Vol 12, Supplement 3 (2021) 13–22.

Fiorini, Matteo, Bernard Hoekman and Aydin Yildirim. 'COVID-19: Expanding Access to Essential Supplies in a Value Chain World,' in Baldwin, R. and S. Evenett (eds.) *COVID-19 and Trade Policy: Why Turning Inward Won't Work* (CEPR Press, 2020) 63–76.

Hoekman, Bernard. 'Urgent and Important: Improving WTO Performance by Revisiting Working Practices,' *Journal of International Trade* Vol 53, No 3 (2019) 373–394.

Hoekman, Bernard M. and Michel M. Kostecki. *The Political Economy of the World Trading System: The WTO and Beyond* (Oxford University Press, 2009).

Hoekman, Bernard and Petros C. Mavroidis. 'Preventing the Bad from Getting Worse: Is It the End of the World (Trade Organization) as We Know It?,' *European University Institute, Robert Schuman Centre for Advanced Studies, Global Governance Programme Working Paper No. RSCAS 2020/06* (2020).

Hoekman, Bernard and Petros C. Mavroidis. 'WTO Reform: Back to the Past to Build the Future,' *Global Policy* Vol 12, Supplement 3 (2021) 5–12.

Howse, Robert. 'Appointment with Destiny: Selecting WTO Judges in the Future,' *Global Policy* Vol 12, Supplement 3 (2021) 71–82.

Jones, Ken. *Reconstructing the World Trade Organization for the 21st Century: An Institutional Approach* (Oxford University Press, 2015).

Koul, Autar Krishen. *Guide to the WTO and GATT: Economics, Law and Politics* (Springer International, 2018).

Lester, Simon. 'Can Interim Appeal Arbitration Preserve the WTO Dispute System?,' Free Trade Bulletin, Cato Institute (1 September 2020) <www.cato.org/free-trade-bulletin/can-interim-appeal-arbitration-preserve-wto-dispute-system?queryID=9f4d8ae439d052d49e824c5837f6dc04> (accessed 29 July 2021).

Mattoo, Aditya and Arvind Subramanian. 'Multilateralism Beyond Doha,' *World Bank Policy Research Working Paper No. 4735* (2008).

Mattoo, Aditya and Arvind Subramanian. 'From Doha to Next Bretton Woods: A New Multilateral Trade Agenda,' *Foreign Affairs* Vol 88, No 1 (2009) 15–26.

Mavroidis, Petros C. 'Right Back to Where We Started From (Or Are We?),' *The Journal of World Investment and Trade* Vol 12, No 4 (2011) 449–456.

Ottawa Group. 'COVID-19 and Beyond: Trade and Health,' Communication from Australia, Brazil, Canada, Chile, the European Union, Japan, Kenya, Republic of Korea, Mexico, New Zealand, Norway, Singapore and Switzerland (WT/GC/223) (24 November 2020).

Trebilcock, Michael, Robert Howse and Antonia Eliason. *The Regulation of International Trade* (Routledge, 2013).

Vickers, Brendan, Teddy Y. Soobramanien and Hilary Enos-Edu. 'Introduction,' in Soobramanien, Teddy Y., Brendan Vickers and Hilary Enos-Edu (eds.) *WTO Reform: Reshaping Global Trade Governance for 21st Century Challenges* (Commonwealth Secretariat, 2019) 1–6.

Warwick Commission. 'The Multilateral Trade Regime: Which Way Forward?,' The Report of the First Warwick Commission (University of Warwick, 2007).

Wolfe, Robert. 'The WTO Single Undertakings as Negotiating Technique and Constitutive Metaphor,' *Journal of International Economic Law* Vol 12, No 4 (2009) 835–858.

World Trade Organization. 'Annual Report 2013,' <www.wto.org/english/res_e/booksp_e/anrep_e/anrep13_e.pdf> (accessed 28 July 2021).

Index

2030 Agenda for Sustainable Development 635

A

absolute advantage, theory (Smith) 11
abus de droit doctrine 50
actionable subsidies (yellow light subsidies) 331–346; domestic industry (definition) 333; domestic industry, injury (causing) 332–337; domestic industry, injury (identification) 333–337; like products 332–333; special remedies 346–348
Adams, John 21
ad hoc protectionism 378–379
adjudication: agreed-upon procedure, DSB role 78; exclusive forum (WTO/DSU) 78–80
ad valorem customs 246
ad valorem duties: basis 246; determination 262
ad valorem tariffs 245–246
Advisory Centre on WTO Law (ACWL) 117
"affecting" term, implication 178–179
affirmative commitments 204–205
African, Caribbean, and Pacific (ACP): bananas, in-quota tariff rates 189; countries 152; origin 186–187, 446
African Continental Free Trade Area (AfCFTA) 610
Agenda for Sustainable Development 635
AGP (Agreement on Government Procurement): amendment 56; SPS Agreement, relationship 532
Agreement Establishing the Multilateral Trade Organization 41
Agreement on Agriculture (AoA) 365; agricultural subsidies rules 362–363; negotiation 240; special safeguard measures 290–291; subsidy commitment schedules establishment 363
Agreement on Government Procurement (AGP): amendment 56; SPS Agreement, relationship 532
Agreement on Import Licensing Procedures (AILP) 263–264
Agreement on Pre-Shipment Inspection (API) 264–265
Agreement on Safeguards (SGA) 276, 278, 385; Article 2.2 ruling, avoidance 623; Article 2, Argentina violation 616; Article XIX GATT 280; creation/usage 280–289; "due process" provision (Article 3) 282; imports increase/"unforeseen development" 283–284; investigation/provisional application 282–283; Preamble 276; Uruguay Round negotiation 279
Agreement on Safeguards (SGA), injury determination 284–289; causation/non-attribution 288–289; domestic industry identification 287–288; factors 286–287; serious injury/threat of serious injury 285–286
Agreement on Sanitary and Phytosanitary Measures (SPS): agreements, role 525–526; approval procedures 593–594; arbitrary/unjustifiable discrimination, absence 578–579; Article 5.7 46; Committee on Sanitary and Phytosanitary Measures (SPS Committee), establishment 596–597; control inspection 593–594; dispute settlement 597–599; foreign SPS policy/measures, recognition 591; harmonisation 579–581; international standards 579–581; "not more trade restrictive than required" 586–587; "only to the extent necessary" 574; other substantive provisions 590–596; precautionary principle, SPS Agreement (relationship) 587–590; protection, appropriate level 584–586; provisional SPS measures, maintenance (Article 5.7 basis) 590; regional conditions, adaptation 591–593; review standard 598–599; risk assessment 581–583; risk assessment, basis 583–584; risk assessment, obligation 581–587; scientific experts, assistance 597–598; special/differential treatment 595–596; technical assistance 599–600; technical barriers to

trade (TBT) 566; transparency/notifications 594–595
Agreement on Sanitary and Phytosanitary Measures (SPS) Agreement 96, 210; Agreement on Government Procurement (relationship) 532; Article 2.3 143; Article 5.7 46; institutional provisions 596–600; role 567; scope/application 567–573; substantive provisions 573–590; substantive provisions, basic principles 573–579; temporal scope 571
Agreement on Sanitary and Phytosanitary Measures (SPS) measures: adoption 588–590; Agreement application 568–571; scientific measures 574–578; taking (right) 573
Agreement on Subsidies and Countervailing Measures (SCM), adoption 308
Agreement on Subsidies and Countervailing Measures (SCM) Agreement, impact 308–309
Agreement on Technical Barriers to Trade (TBT) 524, 644; Agreements, role 525–526; Agreement, WTO Agreements (relationship) 530–532; Annex 1.1 527; Annex 1.2 527, 537, 538; Annex 1.3 527; Annex 1.4 529; Annex 1.5 529; Annex 1.7 529; Annex 1A 530–531; Article 3 529; Article 3.5 529; Article 4 529; Committee on Technical Barriers to Trade (TBT Committee), establishment 557; dispute settlement, TBT Agreement (relationship) 557–558; equivalence/mutual recognition 552–553; "existence of relevant international standards" 549–550; "ineffective and inappropriate international standards" 551–552; international standards, usage (obligation) 548–552; international standards "as a basis" for domestic standards 550–551; "least trade restrictive" 542–548; "legitimate objective" 543–544; like products 537–538; measures 624; MFN treatment obligations, NT treatment obligations (relationship) 533–542; "not more trade restrictive than necessary" 544–548; performance requirements 552; provisions, application 528; special/differential treatment 555–556; technical assistance 558; technical regulations 534–537; transparency/notification 553–555; "treatment no less favourable" 538–542
Agreement on Technical Barriers to Trade (TBT) Agreement 210–211; Annex 3, paragraph D (Code of Good Practice) 533; Annexes 3.L/M/N/O 554–555; application 529–530; Article 1.5, reference 532; Article 1.5, SPS measures (identification) 572; Article 2 536; Article 2.1 537–541, 636; Article 2.1, "treatment no less favourable" requirement 538–539; Article 2.1, violation 541; Article 2.2 214, 542–548; Article 2.4 537, 549–552; Article 2.4, technical regulation consistency (three-tier test) 551; Article 2.5 552; Article 2.6 549; Article 2.7 552; Article 2.8 553; Article 4 536; Article 11 558; Article 12 555–556; Article 12.3 requirement 555; Article 12.6 requirement 555; Article 13.1 557; Article 14.2 558; Article 14.4 558; Articles 2.9–2.12 553–554; institutional provisions 556–558; legally binding obligations 599; other substantive provisions 552–556; preamble, Appellate Body observation 531; principal actors 529; scope/application 526–532; substantive provisions 532–552; temporal scope 529–530

Agreement on Trade-Related Aspects of Intellectual Property Rights (TRIPS) 43, 44, 469, 644; Berne Convention, relationship 488–489; Council for TRIPS 509; intellectual property, rights (inclusion) 481–482; political economy 470–472; technical assistance/technology transfer 511

Agreement on Trade-Related Aspects of Intellectual Property Rights (TRIPS) Agreement 168; amendment 56; Article 1.1 480–481; Article 4, MFN provision 484; Article 6 486; Article 7 479–480; Article 8 479–480; Article 9 489; Article 10 489; Article 11 489; Article 12 489; Article 13 489–490, 501; Article 15.1 491–492; Article 15.2 492–493; Article 16 493–494; Article 17 495, 501; Article 19.1 495; Article 20 495–496; Article 21 496; Article 22 496–497; Article 23 497–499; Article 24 498–499; Article 27 499–501; Article 27.1, Canada violation 500; Article 28 501; Article 30 501–503; Article 31 499, 503; Article 41 506; Article 42 provisions, US Appropriations Act (contravention) 507; Article 45 507; Article 46 507; Article 47 507; Article 48 507; Article 49 507; Article 50 508; Article 61 508; Article 62 508; Article 63 509, 553; Article 64 509, 510; Article 68 509; Article 69 509; Article 72 509; Articles 42–49 506–507; Articles 42.1–41.4, due process requirements 506; Articles 51–60 508; Articles 68–71 509; developing country/LDC members, special rules 510–511; flexibilities 504–505; institutional provisions 509–510; objectives/scope 478–486; Part II, Section 5 499; Part IV, Article 62 508; Part VII, Section 3 topics 496; private rights/human rights/medicine access 644; rights protection 486–506; Section 44 507; Section 211(a)(2) 507; structure/principles 480–482; transitional periods 510–511; transparency/dispute settlement 509–510; WIPO Conventions (relationship) 482–483

Agreement on Trade-Related Investment Measures (TRIMs) 365; rules 362
Agreements on Agriculture 43
AILP (Agreement on Import Licensing Procedures) 263–264
"aims and effects" test, national treatment provisions (GATT) 174–175
Airbus case: "export inducement test," Appellate Body establishment 329; report, Appellate Body jurisprudence (development) 328–329
"alleged dumping" acts 386
American Convention on Human Rights 1969 48
amicus curiae (friend of the court) briefs: apparatus, usage 108–109; developing country Member States advocacy 109; Humane Society International/American University's Washington College of Law, submission 107; pre-dispute settlement 106–109; reception 108
amicus curiae (friend of the court) practice, development 106
Andean Community 610
Annecy Round 38
Annecy Tariff Conference 238
Annex 1A (WTO Agreement part) 42–43
Annex 1B (WTO Agreement part) 43
Annex 1C (WTO Agreement part) 43
Annex 2 (WTO Agreement part) 43
Annex 3 (WTO Agreement part) 43
Annex 4 (WTO Agreement part) 43
Annex on Financial Services (AFS) 458–460
anti-circumvention laws 411
anti-dumping (AD): code, drafting 380; Committee on Anti-Dumping Practices, establishment 413; duties, imposition 393–394, 414; evidence, adequacy 386; evidence/due process 387–388; investigations 323; investigations, Member State suspension 407; investigations, misuse (avoidance) 386; legal framework (WTO) 382–406; "like product" sale 389–393; measures 277, 377–379; measures, "continued imposition" (necessity) 409–410; measures, dispute settlement/review 411–413; measures, retroactive application (prohibition) 408–409; measures, review (obligation) 409; Negotiating Group on Rules 381; non-market economy (NME) 397; proponents, impact 381; provisional AD measures 406–407; zeroing 393–397
Anti-Dumping Agreement (AD Agreement) (ADA) 378, 384–385; Article 1, inconsistency 384–385; Article 2.1 390–392; Article 2.2 390–392; Article 2.2.1.1 interpretation 390; Article 2.4 391–395; Article 2.4.2., dumping margin calculation 388–389; Article 2.6 390; Article 2.7 397; Article 3 399–401; Article 3.4 factors, list 403; Article 3.4 requirements, comparison 335; Article 3.5, interpretation 405; Article 3.5, non-attribution requirement establishment 405–406; Article 4.1 398; Article 5 386; Article 5.4 386; Article 5.7 386; Article 6.1 387; Article 6.8 353, 387; Article 6.10 408; Article 9.1, "lesser duty rule" 407; Article 9.2, Appellate Body interpretation 407–408; Article 9.3 408; Article 11.1 requirements 409; Article 11.2 409–410; Article 11.2 requirements 410; Article 11.3 language, impact 410; Article 15, legal requirements (absence) 413–414; Article 17.4 411–412; Article 17.6 412; Article 17.6(ii), sequential analysis 412–413; Articles 3.7/15.7, "change in circumstances" 404; domestic industry concept 33; institutional/procedural requirements 411–413; "material injury" concept 285; "ordinary course of trade" definition, absence 392; preamble 384; provisions, anti-dumping investigation 349
Anti-Dumping Code 380–381
anti-dumping (AD) duties 276; anti-circumvention 410–411; duration/review 409–410; imposition/collection 407–409
anti-protectionism, agenda 181
antitrust laws 378
API (Agreement on Pre-Shipment Inspection) 264–265
Appellate Body (AB): appeal 185; chairperson, election 101–102; cross-appeal 103; disagreement 112; equilibrium line 203; evidence (exclusion), non-relevancy (basis) 103; jurisprudence 582; jurisprudence, development 328–329; legal authority 108; mandate, overstepping (US accusation) 659; members, appointment 659; members, collective expertise 102; political bias, criticism (absence) 101; proceedings, participants (reference) 102; reports 78; reports, adoption 99–100; reports, circulation 102; *Working Procedures* 100–102, 107–108
Appellate Body (WTO dispute settlement process) 50, 54, 98–101; historical background 98–100; nature/composition 100–101
Appellate review (WTO dispute settlement process) 101–106; new evidence/arguments, receipt 104–105; new issues, review 104–105; process, scope/remit 105–106; structure/scope/timeframe 101–104
Application of Sanitary and Phytosanitary 43
applied tariffs (actual tariffs) 246
arbitrary/unjustifiable discrimination, absence (SPS Agreement) 578–579
Argentina–Financial Services 158, 188, 256; Appellate Body observations 217; prudential carve-out, WTO jurisprudence 459; "treatment no less favourable," Appellate

Body understanding 448; *US–Gambling* Appellate Body findings, usage 452
Argentina–Footwear (EC) 98, 281; Appellate Body observations 281–282; Appellate Body phrase interpretation 284; Appellate Body Report, reference 385; Article 2 violation 616; Panel interpretation, Appellate Body agreement 286–287; Panel observation 289; "significant overall impairment," presence (necessity) 285; "unforeseen developments," impact 283–284
Argentina–Hides and Leather 173; export level, contributions (Panel perspective) 259–260
Argentina–Import Measures 87–88, 256; Appellate Body clarification 257; limiting effects, quantification (nonnecessity) 259
Argentina–Poultry Anti-Dumping Duties 52; argument, Panel rejection 398; "major proportion" phrase, implication 398
Argentina–Textiles and Apparel 241, 246
Aristotle, money use condemnation 4
Articles of Agreement of the International Monetary Fund (Bretton Woods Agreement) 293
Association of Southeast Asian Nations (ASEAN) 292, 610; formation 612
Association of Southeast Asian Nations Free Trade Area (AFTA) 610
Australia–Ammonium Sulphate 146
Australia–Apples 91; Article 5.6, function 586; form/nature, reading (differences) 570; SPS Annex A(1), SPS measure (legal definition) 569; SPS Annex C(1)(a) 593–594
Australia–Automotive Leather II, SCM Agreement language (Panel observation) 330
Australia-New Zealand Closer Economic Relations Agreement (ANZCERTA) 610, 611
Australia–Salmon 92; Article 5.6 structure 586–587; SPS Articles 5.2/5.3, Panel observation 583
Australia–Salmon (Article 21.5–Canada) 578; SPS Article 5.5 violation, absence 585
Australia–Tobacco Plain Packaging: alternative measures, assessment 545–546; challenged measures, comparison (importance) 545; non-fulfilment, consequences 547; Panel observations 480; trademark registration, meaning (consideration) 493; TRIPS Article 24.3 scope, impact 498; "unjustifiably" (word), suggestion 496
"available" term, usage 228

B

balance of payments (BOP) acceptance 298
balance of payments (BOP) measures 292–297; GATS 154, 298; political economy, GATT (relationship) 292–294

balance of payments (BOP) measures, GATT (1994) 294–297; nature/scope 294–297
balance of payments (BOP) problems: addressing, quantitative restrictions (usage) 294–295; occurrence 292
balance of payments (BOP) purposes 98
balance of trade, maintenance 6
"balancing principles" 641
Bali Ministerial Conference 58
Bank of England, gold standards (decline) 12
"baseline establishment rules" 224; "even-handedness" requirement, application 225–226
Beijing Treaty on Audiovisual Performances (2012) 490
Belgian Family Allowances (Allocations Familiales) 145
"benefit" term, beneficiary/recipient receiving/enjoying 318
Bentham, Jeremy 473, 478
Berne Convention (1896) 471
Berne Convention (1971) 485–487; Articles 11/11 *bis* 490; TRIPS Agreement, relationship 488–489
betting services, cross-border supply 441
bias rule 47
Bilateral Investment Treaty (BIT) program 470
bilateral trade agreements: creation 611; MFN principle, usage 37
binding promise 244
biotech products approval, ED *de facto* moratorium 638
bond requirement, per-unit costs (difference) 182
Border Tax Adjustments 173–174, 188; criteria, examination 174, 176
bound tariffs 143, 246–247
brain drain 645
Brazil–Aircraft 87; Appellate Body distinctions 310; Article 25, Appellate Body examination 361; Panel considerations 309
Brazil–Aircraft (Article 21.5 Canada) 106
Brazil–Desiccated Coconut 49, 89, 91; Appellate Body, observation 309
Brazil–Retreaded Tyres 206, 211, 212, 214; Appellate Body burden of proof 214–215; Appellate Body explanation 213; policy objective 212
Brazil–Taxation 210
Bretton Woods Agreement 35; Articles of Agreement of the International Monetary Fund 293; exit 35–37
Bretton Woods Conference 36; international trade theories, prevalence 74
Bretton Woods system, collapse 294
BRICS countries, business services exports (average annual growth rate) 426–427
Brundtland Report 633

Brussels Convention on Nomenclature for the classification of Goods in Customs Tariffs, replacement 244
Brussels Definition of Value (BDV) 261–262
Buenos Aires Ministerial Conference 58
bullionism 5
burden of proof: Appellate Body allocation 95–96; Article XX (GATT) 205–206, 214–215; WTO dispute settlement process 95–97
burden persuasion 97
"but for" approach 344–346

C

Canada–Aircraft 104–105, 330; Appellate Body observation 317; *de jure/de facto* export subsidy, existence (Appellate Body discussion) 328; Panel observation 309; recipient enquiry, focus (Appellate Body ruling) 318; SCM Article 14, meaning 318–319
Canada–Aircraft (Article 21.5–Brazil) 112
Canada–Aircraft Credits and Guarantees, export subsidy (existence) 326
Canada–Autos 143, 144, 146, 155–156, 179, 186; Appellate Body approach 157; Appellate Body observation 330–331; service suppliers, concerns/considerations 446–447
Canada–Continued Suspension 80
Canada–Periodicals 105, 154, 171, 173; agreements, application 435
Canada–Pharmaceutical Patents 144; "limited" (word), Panel interpretation 502–503; Panel interpretation 495; patent law, challenge 479; stockpiling exceptions, EC challenge 502–503; TRIPS Article 27.1 violation 500
Canada–Renewable Energy, transaction (legal characterisation) (Appellate Body guidance) 311
Cancun Ministerial Conference 58
Capital (Marx) 16–17, 19, 20
capitalism: contradictions, demonstration 16–17; theoretical system 9
causation 288–289; establishment, approaches 344
"cause" (Appellate Body observation) 342–343
cause and effect standard, application 343–3434
Central Product Classification (CPC): role 432–433; section 6 186, 188
Chace Act 474
Chapeau: function 202–203; interpretation 203–205; privileged trade considerations 203; requirements, meeting (failure) 202
Chapeau (Article XIV) (GATS) 454–455
Chapeau (Article XX) (GATT) 201–203, 223
Chapeau, viz., US–Restrictions on Imports of Tuna Products 202

Charter of Economic Rights and Duties of States 149
Chevalier, Michel 473
Chile–Alcoholic Beverages 51, 178
Chile–Alcoholic Beverages (Article 21.3(c)) 115–116
Chile–Price Band System 242–243; AoA, Article 5 (relationship) 291; Appellate Body observations 290
China: Accession Protocol 252–253; power, impact 624
China–Auto Parts 179
China–Electronic Payment Services 183, 187, 188, 441; GATS Article XX:2 application 449; NT obligation, purpose 443; service suppliers, automatic likeness (Panel nonacceptance) 447
China–GOES 334, 335, 354; AD Agreement Articles 3.1–3.8, Appellate Body opinion 400; dumped imports, impact examination (AD authority requirement) 403; price undercutting 401; SCM Agreement, Articles 11.2/11.3 relationship 350
China–HP-SSST (Japan/China)–HP-SSST (EU): China violations 407; IA conclusions, "reasoned and adequate" explanation (providing) 412; present material injury, causation (establishment) 405; price undercutting 402–403
China–Intellectual Property Rights 86; copyright protection denial 488; enforcement procedures, concept 506; TRIPS Article 61 clarification 508
China–Publications and Audiovisual Products 156, 185–187, 189; Article XVII:3 statement 447; dispute, referral 207; importation/distribution restrictions imposition, Panel ruling 445; measures, inconsistency 208; "progressive liberalisation," Panel interpretation 430
China–Rare Earths 222–223, 253; Appellate Body observation 226; Panel ruling 224–225
China–Raw Materials 92, 212, 252–253; Appellate Body ruling/observations 222, 224–225; "export prohibition" term (exclusions), Appellate Body decision 261; exports, Appellate Body restrictions 257; respondent burden 260–261; "restriction" (term, occurrence), Appellate Body ruling 258
China–X-Ray Equipment 406
c.i.f. import price, customs duties (noninclusion) 290–291
circulating capital, usage 14
circumvention practice, categories 411
civil/administrative procedures/remedies (intellectual property rights) 506–507
civil society (classical liberalism principle) 21
claims, WTO categories 83–85
classical economics: criticism 17; Marx 16–21; Ricardo 11–16; Smith 9–11

classical economic theory, reconstruction 23
classical economic thought, Keynes (relationship) 22–23
classical liberalism, principles 21
classical theory (international trade theories) 4–5
Classless society, emergence 18–19
Clayton Act 379
Clean Air Act (1963) 202, 221
closed economy, stimulus (impact) 24–25
Code of Good Practice (TBT Agreement, Annex 3) 533
Codex Alimentarius Commission (Codex) 579; emphasis 580
CODEX STAN 1–1985 551–552
Codex Stan 94, relevance 536–537, 550
coercion, minimisation (classical liberalism principle) 21
"coincidence" approach 289
Colombia–Ports of Entry 258–259
Colombia–Textiles 208–209; Appellate Body, finding 209–210; "to secure compliance," meaning 218
Comision Federal de Telecomunicaciones (COFETEL), regulation 457
commercial objectives, overemphasis 645
"commercial presence" 434
commitments (financial services), understanding (GATS) 459–460
commitments schedules, DSB interpretation 247–250
Committee on Anti-Dumping Practices, establishment 413
Committee on Regional Trade Agreements (CRTAs), notification (obligation) 620–621
Committee on Technical Barriers to Trade (TBT Committee), establishment 557
Committee on Trade and Development 621
Committee on Trade and Environment (CTE): Member State proposals 640; WTO establishment 633
commodities, exchangeability 20
commodity-money-commodity (CMC), exchange relationship 19
common agricultural policy (CAP), EEC establishment 38–39
common external tariff (CET) 610; EEC establishment 38–39
common human value (classical liberalism principle) 21
common market (CM) 610
Common Market of Eastern and Southern African (COMESA) 610
Common Market of the Caribbean (CARICOM) 610
Communist Manifesto (Marx) 18
"comparable," term (analysis) 389

comparative advantage: term, usage (absence) 15; theory 14–16; theory, demonstration 15
compensatory trade liberalisation 450
"competitive or directly substitutable products" concept 176–177
complainant/respondent, bilateral exercise 86
complete freedom, principle 9
compliance review (Article 21.5 DSU) 111–113
Comprehensive and Progressive Agreement for Trans-Pacific Partnership (CPTPP) 610, 611
compulsory licensing rules 56
concessions, benefits 331
concession, schedules (WTO) 244–245
"conditions of competition," modification 443
consensus-based operating modalities, insistence 658
consensus-driven decision making (WTO) 657–658
conservation programmes, Member State right (adoption) 223
"conservation" term, understanding 223
"constructive," definition 414
consultation: request, Member State response 89; WTO dispute settlement process 86–90; failure/period 89–90; phase 85–89
consumer deception, prevention 543–544
"consumer preferences" 188
"consumption abroad" 433
"contingency" (presence), SCM Agreement judgment 327–328
"continued imposition" necessity (question) 409–410
"continued" temporal relationship 410
Convention Establishing the World Intellectual Property Organization, Article 2 (viii) 481
Convention on International Trade in Endangered Species of Wild Fauna and Flora (CITES) 637
copyright: common law concept 487; protection, *Black's Law Dictionary* definition 487–488
Corn Model 13–14
"correlation" approach 289
corvée, abolition (physiocrat demand) 8
Council for Services 59
Council for Trade in Goods 59, 153; decision 256; informing 413
Council for Trade in Services (CTS) 59, 450; GATS Article VI:4 requirements 438; Reference Paper adoption 456–457
Council for TRIPS 59, 509
Council Regulation 2501/2001 211–212
counterfactual analysis, usefulness 344–345
countervailing duties (CVDs) 276, 305, 306; abuse, impact 308; administrative review 357–359; duration/review 357–361; GATT 1994 definition 349; imposition 348–361; imposition/collection 355–361;

imposition, objective 356; institutional/procedural provisions 361; investigation 323; investigation, concluding 354–355; investigation, conduct 351–355; investigation/imposition procedures 349–351; judicial review 360–361; sunset review 359–360; unilateral imposition 348; usage (excess), Contracting Parties (impact) 308
country of importation, entry 245
country of provision, "prevailing market conditions" (Appellate Body observation) 319–320
Court of Justice of the European Union (CJEU) 246, 642
covered agreements 95; consultation/dispute settlement provisions 86; dispute settlement 347–348
COVID-19 pandemic 656, 660
cross-border delivery 444
"cross-border supply" 433
cross-border supply, trade in services inclusion 155
customs classification 244
customs duties 250–254; negotiations/reduction 238–244; types 245–250
customs-related NTBs 261–266
customs rules 238–250
customs unions (CUs) 610; definition 615; definition, satisfaction 617
customs unions (GATT Article XXIV) 614, 615–618; formation, conditions 618
customs valuation agreement 261–263
Customs Valuation Agreement 43
Customs Valuation Agreement (CVA), Member State requirements 262

D

Decision on Differential and Most Favourable Treatment, Reciprocity and Fuller Participation of Development Countries (GATT) 149–150
Decision on Notification Procedures, Uruguay Round adoption 254
Declaration of New International Economic Order 149
de facto conditionality, establishment 329
de facto discrimination 139, 158, 184–185; absence 500; establishment, problem 449; national treatment provisions (GATT) 172
de facto export contingency: existence 329; standard, Appellate Body observation 329; standard, meeting (ease) 330
de jure/de facto export subsidy, existence (establishment) 328
de jure discrimination 139, 158, 184–185; absence 500; national treatment provisions (GATT) 172

de jure export contingency, SCM Agreement prohibition 328
delimitation method 89
demandeurs, impact 612
demand-side substitutability, Appellate Body explanation 341
de minimis margin 174
de minimis rule 351
de minimis standard, intention 351
de minimis thresholds 362
derogation, most-favoured nation obligation (GATS) 159–160
"designated nationals," less favourable treatment (application) 483
developed countries, Member States (WTO classification) 114
developed country Member States: benefits 238; "differential and more favourable treatment" development 151–152
developing countries/least developed countries, Enabling Clause distinctions 151–152
developing countries, special and differential (S&D) treatment (origins) 147–148
developing countries, WTO dispute settlement: least developed country member states, special rules 116; member states, legal assistance 116–117; member states, special rules 115–116; special/differential treatment 115; special rules (decision of 5 April 1966) 116; usage 114–117
developing country members: special/differential treatment 413–414; TRIPS Agreement, special rules 510–511
developing-country Members, economic development (enhancement) 150
developing country member states: special/differential treatment 361–362; special rules (RTAs) 620
developing country Member States: *amicus curiae* briefs advocacy 109; timeframe flexibility 115
Dillon Round 37, 238; product-by-product approach 239
diminishing returns, theory 13–14
direct discrimination, national treatment provisions (GATT) 172
direct financial contributions, types 310
"direct transfer of funds," Appellate Body statement 312
"dirty" gasoline, domestic production (regulation) 225–226
discrimination, prohibition 144
dispute, legal basis (WTO) 82–83
dispute settlement: process, consultation phase (negotiations-based process) 88; TBT Agreement, relationship 557–558
dispute settlement (GATT) 71–75; power-oriented mode 73; system, administration 78

dispute settlement (RTAs) 621–624
dispute settlement (SPS) 597–599
dispute settlement (WTO) 56–57, 69, 75–76; process, stages (DSB involvement) 85–106; recourse 80–85
Dispute Settlement Body (DSB): Article 3(3) 78–79; authority, creation 78; Berne Convention, impact 486–487; commitments schedules interpretation 247–250; disputes 656; dispute settlement process (WTO) 85–106; disputes, WTO Preamble (usage) 631–632; *India–Solar Cells* case 227–228; informing, writing (usage) 102; "likeness" interpretation 445–446; negative consensus principle, usage 79; *Rules of Conduct* 101; third party, consideration 93
Dispute Settlement Understanding (DSU) (WTO) 42; Appellate Body members, appointment 659; Article 1(2) 83; Article 3(7) 86; Article 3.3 94; Article 3.7 87; Article 3.8 83–84; Article 4.4 87–88; Article 4.8 90; Article 4.11 86–87; Article 6.2 88, 91; Article 6.4 106; Article 7.1 91; Article 10 92–93; Article 10.4 93; Article 11 93, 103; Article 12.7 98; Article 17.1 100; Article 17.3 100–101; Article 17.6 100; Article 17.13 100, 105, 106; Article 21.2 115–116; Article 21.3(c) 115–116; Article 21.3 DSU, extension 110–111; Article 21.4 110; Article 21.5 106, 111–113; Article 21.5 DSU, compliance review 111–113; Article 21.8 116; Article 22, remedies 113–114; Article 23 113; Article 24 116; basis, formation 75; challenges 456, 542; human rights, relationship 646–648; jurisdiction 76, 78–80; reform 658–660; *Rules of Conduct* 109; theoretical/legal framework 76–78; *Working Procedures* 94
division of labour 10–11
Doha Declaration on the TRIPS Agreement and Public Health (Doha Declaration) 479, 504–505; Decision on Implementation, General Council adoption 505
Doha Development Agenda 656
Doha Development Round, agricultural subsidies (issue) 362
Doha Ministerial Conference 58, 486, 600; technical cooperation 56
Doha Ministerial Decision on Implementation-Related Issues and Concerns 596
Doha Ministerial Decision, paragraph 5.2 554
Doha Ministerial Declaration 55
Doha Round 56, 238, 656–657; breakdown, blame 291; export taxes, WTO rules creation (proposal) 253–254; impeding, WTO (impact) 657–658
Dolphin Protection Consumer Information Act (DPCIA) 635–636

"dolphin-safe" labelling, usage 636
Domestic Content Requirement (DCR) measure (India), dispute 227–228
domestic industry: concept 398–399; concept (Anti-Dumping Agreement) 333; injury 337; SCM Agreement Article 16.1 definition 333
"domestic industry" determination 390
"domestic industry" term, Article 4.1 interpretation 398
"domestic injury," SGA Article 4.1(c) definition 287
domestic legal system, WTO agreements (entrenchment) 55
"domestic marker," "foreign goods" entry 237
domestic production, protection 171, 548–549
domestic regulation (GATS) 437–439
Dominican Republic–Import and Sale of Cigarettes 182, 256–257; Panel analysis 242
Dominican Republic–Safeguards, Panel interpretation 242–243
double taxation, avoidance: discretion 315; measures 314
"downstream dumping" 390
"due allowance" basis 3294
due process 46, 47–49; principle 48; requirements (TRIPS) 506
due process of law, guarantees 642
dumped imports, increase 403
dumped product, domestic industry injury (causal link) 383
dumping 377; "alleged dumping" acts 386; causation 405–407; determination 388–397; domestic industry injury, determination 397–404; "downstream dumping" 390; exporter, price undertaking 407; GATT 1994 Article VI:1 definition 382; history 379–381; identification 383; imposition 406–411; investigation 385–388; normal value (domestic price), export price (difference) 388–397; political economy 379–381; price discrimination definition 382; "specific action" 383; "targeted dumping," addressing 396–397; types/practice 382; unfairness 378; WTO law 379–382
"dumping," "margin of dumping" (meaning agreement) 3288
dumping margins: calculation 388–389; impact 393; negative dumping margins, zeroing 394
Dunkel Draft 308, 429
Dutch East India Company, formation 6

E

Eastern Tropical Pacific Ocean (ETP) 541, 635
EC and Certain Member States–Large Civil Aircraft 321; Appellate Body decision 313; causation, establishment 344; cause and effect, "genuine and substantial relationship" 345–346; cause

and effect standard 343; counterfactual analysis, usefulness 344–345; enterprise, subsidy subset (Panel question) 322–323; government-held debt, relinquishment (Panel observation) 315–316; products/market, competitive relationship (assessment) 341; subsidies argument 332

EC–Approval and Marketing of Biotech Products 94, 577; Argentina claim, Panel examination 595–596; dispute, origin 637–638; EC measure, adoption 532; "insufficiency of relevant scientific evidence," consideration 589; SPS Annex A, disagreement 570; SPS Panel observation 572; TBT Article 12.3 requirements 555

EC–Asbestos 85, 107, 180–181, 211, 527–528; Appellate Body decision 213–214; scientific/technical issues 557–558; TBT Agreement, consistency 531; technical regulation challenge 534; technical regulation, impact 535

EC–Bananas III 84, 117, 147, 152, 156–158, 179, 185, 186, 188, 189; agreements, application (scope) 435–436; Article 21.1 ruling 364; foreign/domestic services/suppliers, "like" (Panel conclusion) 446; GATS application, scope (defining) 434–435; tariff quotas, allocation 243; three-tier approach 444–445

EC–Bananas III (Ecuador) 113–114

EC–Bed Linen: ADA Article 3.4 factors 402–403; ADA Article 15, Panel ruling 414; AD duties, imposition 393–394; Appellate Body Report 393; "comparable" (term analysis) 389; dispute, origin 394–395

EC–Bed Linen (Article 21.5–India) 112

EC–Biotech 46

EC–biotech products (approval/marketing) 637–638

EC–Chicken Cuts 249–250

EC–Chicken Cuts (Article 21.3(c)) 111

EC–Commercial Vessels 80, 355

EC–Computer Equipment 247–248; position, Appellate Body clarification 248–249

EC–Countervailing Measures on DRAM Chips: benefit analysis (Panel observation) 318; information (absence), investigating authorities (impact) 352–353; information, necessity 354

EC–Export Subsidies on Sugar 52, 105

EC–Fasteners 92

EC–Fasteners (Article 21.5–China) 391; domestic IA, impact 399

EC–Fasteners (China) 104; ADA Article 9.2, Appellate Body interpretation 407–408; "major proportion" term, Appellate Body observation 399

EC–Hormones 46, 93–96, 103, 111, 577; Appellate Body observation 575; Article 3.3, Appellate Body observation 580–581; SPS Agreement Article 5.5 inconsistency 585; SPS Agreement temporal scope, decision 571; SPS measure, basis (Appellate Body ruling) 583–584; SPS measure, divergent opinion 599; TBT Agreement Article 1.5, reference 532

EC–Hormones (Article 21.3(c)) 110–111

EC–Large Civil Aircraft, Article 14(b) (Appellate Body usage) 319

EC–Oilseeds I 84; panel ruling 258

economic activity, reduction 17

Economic Community of West African States (ECOWAS) 610, 611

Economic Consequences of the Peace (Keynes) 22, 23

economic emergency measures 275

economic factors 18

Economic Integration (Article V) 159

economic integration exception (Article IV) (GATS) 455

economic model building 13

economics, "quasi-natural-law treatment" 10

economic theories, private rights (relationship) 472–475

economic theory, historical materialism (relationship) 17–19

economic thought (Keynes) 22–25

economy, interrelated social system 10

EC–Poultry 243, 290

EC–Sardines 108, 527–528; "ineffective means," definition 551; product, international standard coverage 550; TBT Agreement, temporal scope decision 529–530; three-tier test, establishment 535

EC–Seal Products 147, 204, 208, 212, 527; EU Seal Regime, prohibitive/permissive aspects 536; GATT 1994 Article XX, impact 546; measure, proof (burden) 208

EC–Tariff Preferences 97, 150–152, 211, 577

EC–Trademarks and Geographical Indications 483–484, 494; "limited" (word), addition 495

EC–Tube or Pipe Fittings 104; ADA Article 15, assumptions 414

Ecuador, trade restrictions 296

EEC–Animal Feed Proteins 146

EEC–Parts and Components 216

effet utile 396–397

Egypt–Steel Rebar: ADA Article 3.1, Panel confirmation 401; ADA Article 6.8 (Panel observation) 387

"Emergency Action on Imports of Particular Products" (Article 29, multilateral safeguard clause) 279

"Emergency Action on Imports of Particular Products" (GATT Article XIX) 278

Emergency Safeguard Measures (ESM) (GATS) 291–292

Enabling Clause 620; GATT Contracting Parties agreement 612; importance 220–221; paragraph 4(b) requirements 620–621
"Enabling Clause" of 1979 149; policy objectives 150
Enabling Clause, preferential treatment usage 151–152
enforcement procedures, concept 506
Engels, Friedrich 16, 18
England's Treasure by Forraign Trade (Mun) 6
English East India Company, formation 6
enhanced third party rights, granting 93
enlightened monarch, principle 9
environment: GATT, relationship 631–633; issues, jurisprudence 635–638; trade, relationship 629; WTO, relationship 631–633
equity investors, funding 312
erga omnes obligation 244
"escape clause," US proposal (origin) 279
Essay on Profits (Essay) (Ricardo) 12
Essay on the Influence of a Low Price of Corn on the Profits of Stock (Ricardo) 12
estoppel 46, 51–53
EU–Biodiesel: AD duties assessment/imposition, inconsistency 408; Article 2.2.1.1 interpretation 390
European Coal and Steel Community (ECSC) 611; creation 623–624
European Community (EC): classification, disagreements 249; Generalised System of Preferences Programme (GSP Regulation) 211; Schedules of Commitments 249
European Community and Certain Member States–Large Civil Aircraft 102, 104
European Community (EC), Drug Arrangements (inconsistency) 151
European Community (EC), participation 39
European Convention for the Protection of Human Rights and Fundamental Freedoms (1950), Article 6 48
European Court of Human Rights (ECHR) 642
European Economic Area (EEA) 610
European Economic Community (EEC) 611; stature, growth 38–39
European Enlightenment 9
European Free Trade Association (EFTA) 610; EMIT meeting 631; formation 611–612
European Market, creation 612
European Union (EU) 610; debt due claim, Panel rejection 313
"even-handedness" requirement, application 225–226
evidence (disregard/distortion), error of judgment (perception) 94–95
evidentiary rules, development 95
exclusive right, Panel interpretation 494
exhaustible natural resources, conservation 221; Article XX(g) exceptions (GATT) 220–226
exhaustion 485–486; international exhaustion theory 486
"existence of relevant international standards" (TBT) 549–550
Expert Review Groups (ERGs), impact 95
Explanatory Memorandum 211–212
Explanatory Notes 245
export duties: levy practice, discontinuation 250; WTO explanations 251
exporter, price undertakings 407k
Export-Import Bank of Korea (KEXIM), GOK decision-making control 324
"export inducement test," Appellate Body establishment 329
export performance 327
export price, normal value/domestic price (difference) 388–397
exports charges 250–254
exports duties: change, debates/proposal 253–254; history/political economy 250–251; rules 251–253
export subsidies 326–330; coverage 364
export taxes: import duties, economics of equivalence 252; WTO rules, creation (proposal) 253–254

F

"facts available," investigating authority usage 353
Fairness in Music Licensing Act (1998) 490
false universalisation, criticism 17
fascism, rise 34
"financial contribution": Appellate Body determination 311; "benefits" distinction 310; recipient, impact 320
financial contribution, subsidies (relationship) 309–317
financial services: commitments (understanding) (GATS) 459–460; prudential carve-out (GATS) 159, 459; specific rules (GATS) 455, 458–460
fixed capital 14
foregone or not collected revenue 313–316
foreign direct investment (FDI), services percentage 427
foreign/domestic consumers, purchasing power 228
foreign/domestic employment, artificial distinction 646
"foreign goods," entry 237
foreign providers, Member State restrictions (imposition) 184
"foreign-source income" term, usage 314–315
foreign SPS policy/measures, recognition 591

674   *Index*

foreign trade 14–16
"forum shifting" 471
forum shifting (WIPO to GATT), Uruguay Round 471–472
forward pricing 382
Foundations of the Critique of Political Economy (Marx) 17
freedom, guarantees 642
free enterprise economy, problems 24
free-riding, risk 142
free-trade agreement, formation 619
Free Trade Agreements (FTAs) 152
free-trade area (FTA) 610; definition 618–619; exceptions (GATT Article XXIV) 614, 615–618
free trade charter, perspective 200
free trade, negotiations 381
French Constitutional Assembly, patent laws (preamble passage) 474
French kingdom, economic policy (criticism) 8
FSRI Act of 2002 331
"funds," Appellate Body ruling 312
funds, direct transfer 311–313

G
gambling services, cross-border supply 441
Gasoline Rule 202, 2243
General Agreement on Tariffs and Trade (GATT): Agreement on Implementation of Article VI (IAA) 380; Agreement on Import Licensing Procedures (AILP) 263–264; Agreement on Pre-Shipment Inspection (API) 264–265; Article I 244, 614; Article I:1 143; Article II 171, 251–252; Article II:1(b) 240–241, 253; Article II:1(c) 240–241; Article III 171; Article III:2 105, 172–173, 175, 180; Article III:2, interpretive note 175–176; Article III:2, third inquiry 177; Article III:4 533–534; Article III:4, violation 181, 227; national treatment obligation, violation 215–216; Article III, violation 221; Article I, violation 221; Article VI 383–385; Article VII 261–262; Article X:3(a) 263–264; Article XI 171; Article XI:1 exceptions 260–261; Article XIX 278; Article XIX:1(a) 283; Article XX 201, 204–205, 261, 533, 637–639; Article XX(a) 210; Article XX(d) 227–229; Article XX(g) 54, 221–222; Article XX *Chapeau* 540; Article XX, *Chapeau* 632; Article XX (a), (b), (d), (g) exceptions 206–229; Article XX(e), exceptions 229; Article XX(f), exceptions 229; Article XX(j): acquisition or distribution of products in short supply, exceptions 227–229; Article XX: burden of proof 205–206; Article XX: Chapeau 201–203; Article XX(g): conservation of exhaustible natural resources (exceptions), conservation of exhaustible natural resources (first element) 221–223; Article XX(g): conservation of exhaustible natural resources, exceptions 220–226; Article XX(g): conservation of exhaustible natural resources (exceptions), "made effective in conjunction with" (third element) 225–226; Article XX(g): conservation of exhaustible natural resources (exceptions), "relating to" (second element) 223–225; Article XXII 90, 557; Article XXII:1 90; Article XXIII 72, 557; Article XXIII.1b 179; Article XXIII: 1, interpretation 73; Article XXIV 152; Article XXIV (customs unions/FTA exceptions) 614–620; Article XXIV (regional integration) 152; Article XXIV:4 614; Article XXIV:5 614–619; Article XXIV:5 *Chapeau* 619–620; Article XXIV:8(a) 615–619; Article XXIV:8(a), requirements (meeting) 617–618; Article XXIV working party, General Council dissolution 621; Article XXIX 248; Article XX(b): protection of human, animal or plant life or health (exceptions) 210–215; Article XX(b): protection of human, animal or plant life or health (exceptions), burden of proof 214–215; Article XX(b): protection of human, animal or plant life or health (exceptions), design/structure element 211–212; Article XX(b): protection of human, animal or plant life or health (exceptions), necessity (second element) 212–214; Article XX(a): public morals (exceptions) 207–210; Article XX: remit/nature/function 203–205; Article XX(d): secure compliance with laws or regulations 215–220; Article XX(d): secure compliance with laws or regulations, design (first element) 216–217; Article XX(d): secure compliance with laws or regulations, necessity (third element) 219–220; Article XX(d): secure compliance with laws or regulations, secure compliance (second element) 217–219; Article XX (a) to (j) 201; Article XX: two-tier test 205–206; Article XXVIII *bis* 237–239, 246–247, 253; Article XXX 248; balance of payments (BOP) measures, political economy 292–294; balance of payments (BOP) measures (GATT 1994), nature/scope 294–297; basis 36; commitments 206–207; commitments, Mode 1 provision 249; Contracting Parties 72; Contracting Parties, behavior 74; Contracting Parties, Enabling Clause agreement 612; Council, matter (referral) 73; Council of Representatives, EMIT setup 631; customs duties 250–254; customs-related NTBs 261–266; customs valuation agreement 261–263; Decision on Differential and Most Favourable Treatment, Reciprocity and Fuller Participation of

Development Countries 149–150; drafting history 201–203; environment, relationship 631–633; evolution 37–42; exceptions 199; exports charges 250–254; exports duties (debates/proposal) 253–254; exports duties (history/political economy) 250–251; exports duties (rules) 251–253; framework, non-binding nature 74; GATS, relationship 435–436; general exceptions (GATT 1994) 200–229; GSP establishment 38; inconsistency 205–206; jurisprudence 390; likeness 145–146; Ministerial Council 427–428; Ministerial Declaration 74; Ministerial Meeting (1982), safeguard system need 279; most-favoured nation (MFN) obligation 139–153; most-favoured nation (MFN) special/differential treatment 147–149; most-favoured nation (MFN) special/differential treatment (1994) 149–151; national treatment provisions 170–182; negotiating history 168; negotiating rounds 37–39; negotiations 37–38; negotiations, Uruguay Round 471; negotiations, US proposals (1945) 278–279; non-discrimination obligations 578; non-tariff barriers (NTBs) measures 254–261; non-tariff barriers (NTBs) measures, *de facto* prohibitions/restrictions 259–260; non-tariff barriers (NTBs) measures, "restriction" (scope) 257–258; non-tariff barriers (NTBs), political economy 254–255; non-tariff barriers (NTBs), quantitative restrictions (rules/types) 255–260; non-violation remedy 84–85; obligations 202; obligations, US violation 74–75; origins 35–37; power-oriented diplomacy adoption 88; Preamble 245; Preamble, reference 642; pre-GATT trade policy concern 250; principles 148; provisions 213; regional integration (Article XXIV) 152; rules, consistency 215, 217–218; rules/disciplines 99; rules of origin, agreement 265–266; rules template, creation 70; safeguard agreement 280–289; safeguard measures, formation 278–279; safeguard regime 278–279; Secretariat Report (1985) 308; subsidy rules, relationship 365; tariff negotiations 238; trade negotiations 39; waiver 149

General Agreement on Tariffs and Trade (GATT), Agreement on Safeguards (SGA) 280–289; imports increase/"unforeseen development" 283–284; injury determination 284–289; injury determination (causation/non-attribution) 288–289; injury determination (domestic industry identification) 287–288; injury determination (factors) 286–287; injury determination (serious injury/threat of serious injury) 285–286; investigation/provisional application 282–283

General Agreement on Tariffs and Trade (GATT) dispute settlement 71–75; mechanism, problems 98–99; overhaul 74; procedure, Leutwiler Report recommendation 74; system, overhaul (US/EC pressure) 73–74

General Agreement on Tariffs and Trade (GATT), GATT 1947 153, 237, 611; Article III 157; Article XI commitment 255; Contracting Parties (concessions/commitments schedule) 239; Protocol of Provisional Application 261–262; termination 42; text integration 76

General Agreement on Tariffs and Trade (GATT), GATT 1994 42, 76, 143, 150, 209, 530–531, 571–572; Article III:4 538; Articles XXII/XXIII, Anti-Dumping Agreement provision 411; Articles XXII/XXIII, provisions 621; Article VI 388; Article VI:1, dumping definition 382; Article VI:3 356–357; Article X:3(a) 48; Article XII 294, 298; Article XII:1 298; Article XII:2 298; Article XX 539; Article XX(b) 573; Article XX, *Chapeau* 578; Article XXIII(1) 90; Article XX, impact 546; balance of payments (BOP) measures 294–297; concessions, benefits 331; GATS, co-existence 154; inconsistency 216; text reconciliation 242–243

General Agreement on Trade in Services (GATS) 43, 75, 290, 426, 644; additional commitments 449–450; Annex on Financial Services (AFS) 458–460; Annex on Telecommunications 154; application, scope (defining) 434–435; Article I:1 435; Article II 614; Article II:1 157–159; Article II:2 159; Article III 436–437; Article IV (economic integration exception) 455; Article V 450–451; Article VI 437–438; Article VI:1 437–438; Article VI:4 438; Article VI:5 439; Article VII 154; Article VIII 154; Article X 154; Article X.1 291–292; Article XII 154, 451; Article XIV 154, 451–452; Article XIV(b) 639; Article XIV, two-tier analysis 452–454; Article XIV (necessity test) 453–454; Article XIV *bis* 460–461; Article XIV *bis*:1(c) 460; Article XIV *Chapeau* 452, 454–455; Article XJV(c) 442; Article XVI 183, 449–450; Article XVI:2(a), impact 442–443; Article XVI:2, restrictions 441; Article XVI, function 440–441; Article XVII 158, 183–184, 189, 449–450; Article XVII:1 168, 182–183; Article XVII:1, NT obligations 184; Article XVII:3 189, 447–448; Article XVIII 449–450; Article XVII, Member State commitment 443; Article XX 451, 453; Article XX:2, application 449; Article XX, "necessity" standards 453–454; balance of payments (BOP) measures 298; Chapeau (Article

676 *Index*

XIV) 454–455; commitments 439–450; commitments, withdrawal 450; definitions 431–433; domestic regulation 437–439; economic integration exception (Article IV) 455; Emergency Safeguard Measures (ESM) 291–292; financial services, commitments (understanding) 459–460; financial services, prudential carve-out 458; financial services, specific rules 455, 458–460; GATT, relationship 435–436; general exceptions 450–455; general obligations/disciplines 436–439; "less favourable treatment" 447; like services 445–447; limited scope 153–154; market access 440–443; market access, national treatment (relationship) 448–449; MFN obligations, derogation 455; modes of supply 433–435; national treatment (NT) 443–448; national treatment (NT) provisions 158; national treatment (NT) violation, establishment 444–445; negotiators, language (differences) 158; objectives/obligations 430–436; political economy 427–430; Preamble to GATS Understanding on Commitments in Financial Services 154–155; scope 431–433; security exceptions 460–461; services coverage 431–433; services definition 431; service suppliers 445–446; telecommunications, specific rules 455–458; trade in services, definition 431; transparency obligations 436–437; treatment no less favourable 447–448; two-tier analysis (Article XIV) 452–454

General Agreement on Trade in Services (GATS) Agreement: Annex on Financial Services (AFS) 455–456, 458–460; Annex on Telecommunications (AT) 45–456; Article I:1, scope 431; Article I:3(c) 431–432; Article XIV(b) 545; Schedules of Commitments (Mexico) 249; trade in services/right to work, relationship 644–646

General Agreement on Trade in Services (GATS) most-favoured nation (MFN) obligation 153–160; treatment obligation 154–156

General Council (WTO): convening, responsibility 78; meetings 58–59

"General Elimination of Quantitative Restrictions" 255

Generalised System of Preferences (GSP): beneficiaries, development/financial/trade needs 151; GATT establishment 38; Regulation, impact 211

Generalised System of Preferences Programme (GSP Regulation) 211

general principles of law, WTO law (relationship) 46–53

General Theory of Employment, Interest and Money (Keynes) 22, 24, 25

genetically modified organisms (GMOs), release 638

Geneva Ministerial Conference 58

Geneva Preparatory Conference 201

Geneva Tariff Conference 238

geographical indications (GIs): differentiation 497; implied limitation, absence 494; protection 496; registration procedures 483–484

"geographical market," relevance 339

Germany, reparation cost (imposition) 23

Germany–Sardines 145

"Globalization and Its Impact on the Full Enjoyment of All Human Rights" 643–644

gold: gold bullion standard, proposal (Ricardo) 12–13; *numéraire* 13

gold standard 12; disarray 293; dominance 292–293; return, Ricardo recommendation 12–13

good faith (*bona fide*) 46, 49–51; principle 50

goods: classification (WTO schedules) 244–245; international flow, barriers 525–526; purchase 316–317

goods/services, provision 316–317

"goods," term (interpretation) 316–317

goodwill, impact 490–491

Government of Korea (GOK), decision-making control 324

Government Procurement 43

Government Procurement (Article XIII) 159

Graham, Samuel 379

Great Depression 25, 34; impact 611; state regulation/market ownership 23

Group on Environmental Measures and International Trade (EMIT), setup 631

Guatemala–Cement I 82; Panel finding, Appellate Body rejection 411

Guatemala–Cement II 52; Mexico claims 386

Guidelines for Scheduling of Specific Commitments Under the GATS, Notes 26–34 433

H

harmonisation (SPS Agreement) 579–581

Harmonised System (HS) 244

harmonization MFN/NT obligation demands 139, 168

Harmonized Commodity Description and Coding System (HS Convention) 244–245

Harrison, Benjamin 611

Hart, H.L.A. 49

Hatters Fur case 284

Havana Charter for International Trade Organization (ITO) 44; adoption 35, 36; international trade rules 71; negotiations 148

"Havana Club" trademarking, US refusal 491–492
Hayek, F.A. 21
Heckscher-Ohlin theory (international trade theories) 5
High-Level Political Forum (HLPF) 635
historical materialism, economic theory (relationship) 17–19
Holy Quran, importation (prohibition) 210
Honduras, argument (acceptance) 182
Hong Kong Ministerial Conference 58
horizontal price-fixing, prohibition 457
human rights: DSU, relationship 646–648; member states obligations 642; trade, relationship 629, 640–648; treaties, "balancing principles" 641; TRIPS Agreement, relationship 644; WTO agreements, relationship 644–648; WTO law, impact 643–644
Hume, David 7, 9–10, 473–474
hydraulic Keynesianism, essence 25

I

Illegal Gambling Business Act (IGBA) 441–442
impairment, subsidies (impact) 337–339
"impede," term (Article 6.3 connotation) 341–342
"imported goods" 172; term, Canada conclusions 316–317
imported products, opportunities 181
importing Member, autonomous right (establishment) 577
importing Member State, AD measures application 410
Import Licensing Procedures 43
imports: displacement/impediment, subsidies (impact) 341–342; injury 282–283, 287; substitution subsidies 330–331; volume, impact 336
import substitution: model 379; subsidies, nongranting/nonmaintaining 325–326
inconsistency, *prima facie* case (establishment) 297
India–Additional Import Duties: Appellate Body observations 243–244; Appellate Body Report 242; border charges, Appellate Body considerations 243
India–Agricultural Products: inconsistency, presumption 577–578; Panel observation 574; SPS Annex B(5)(b) requirement 595; SPS Article 6.1, interpretation 592; SPS measure/scientific evidence, rational/objective relationship 576
India–Autos 52, 102–103, 171; Panel observations 258
India–Patents (US) 49, 103; mailbox provision, establishment 481

India–Quantitative Restrictions 98, 295–296; Appellate Body *US–Wool Shirts and Blouses* statement, usage 297; BOP measures, India maintenance/argument 297; restriction, concept 257; "restriction" term, panel definition 257
India–Solar Cells 216; Appellate Body, Article XX(d) analysis 218; "necessary" term, usage 220; single domestic instrument, provision 217; WTO Dispute Settlement Body case 227–228
"Indicative List of Notifiable Measures" 254
indirect discrimination, national treatment provisions (GATT) 172
"indirectly" term, introduction 169
"individual export transactions" 396
Indonesia–Autos 115–116; SCM Agreement relevance, Panel ruling 333
Indonesia–Import Licensing Regimes 259
"ineffective and inappropriate international standards" (TBT) 551–552
"ineffective means," definition 551
information technology products, trade liberalisation 56
"inherent bias," introduction 393
injury: definition 399–400; determination, Agreement on Safeguards (SGA) 284–289; material injury, definition 400–403; material injury, threat 403–404; types 332
"injury," meaning 333
innovation: encouragement, IP rights (impact) 476; fostering 472–473
Inquiry Into the Nature and Causes of the Wealth of Nations (Smith) 9
intellectual property, Article 2 (viii) definition 481
Intellectual Property Committee (IPC), formation 470–471
intellectual property (IP) laws, economic analysis 475–478
"intellectual property," Panel interpretation 482
intellectual property (IP) rights 38, 45, 75, 468; acquisition/maintenance 508; border measures 508; civil/administrative procedures/remedies 506–507; criminal procedures 508; economics, understanding 476; economic theories, private rights (relationship) 472–475; enforcement 506–508; enforcement principles 506; exhaustion 485–486; global IP rights protection 504; historical origins 472–478; implementation 471; principles, modeling 475–476; protection 469, 470, 478–479, 506; protection, absence 477; protection, economic rationale 475; protection, MFN obligations (extension) 484; provisional measures 508; testing 471–472; WIPO-administered IP rights 491

Inter-American Tropical Tuna Commission (IATTC) 636
"interconnection," special meaning 457
intergovernmental consultation, WTO Member State engagement 89
intergovernmental system 106
interim agreement, definition 619
Interim Commission for the International Trade Organization (ICITO) 36
International Bank for Reconstruction and Development (IBRD) charter, establishment 35
International Bovine Meat Agreement 43
international commerce, restrictive effects 219
International Copyright Act (1891) 474
International Court of Justice (ICJ) 96, 642, 658–659
International Covenant on Civil and Political Rights 1996 (ICCPR) 48
International Dairy Agreement 43
International Dolphin Conservation Program (AIDCP) 636
international exhaustion theory 486
international IP rights regimes, TRIPS Agreement (relationship) 469
international law: principles, ILC identification 634; WTO law, relationship 45–46
International Law Commission (ILC) 141; natural resources, usage (viewpoint) 634–635
international long distance telecommunications services, legal issues 456–457
International Monetary Fund (IMF) 75; borrowing constraints 292
International Monitory Fund (IMF): charter, establishment 35; intention 36
International Office of Epizootics (OIE) 579
International Plant Protection Convention Secretariat (IPPC) 579
international reserves, availability 5
international standards, usage obligation (TBT) 548–552
international standards "as a basis" for domestic standards (TBT) 550–551
international standards, SPS Agreement 579–581
international tensions, reduction 141–142
international trade: business-to-business (B2B) model 4; framework, dispute settlement system (benefits) 77; government trade, mercantilist pressure 6–7; obstacles 533; organisation, Clinton Administration opposition 41; reform, study 73–74; relations, discriminatory treatment (elimination) 54
International Trade Organization (ITO) 70–71, 169, 201; establishment/creation 71, 278
International Trade Organization (ITO) Charter: Article 17 239; draft, commercial policy provisions 251; drafting 207
international trade theories 4–7; classical theory 4–5; Heckscher-Ohlin theory 5; neoclassical theory 5; presence 74
investigating authority (IA): Article 21.2 imposition 359; impact 349; investigation determination 355; provisional measures (imposition), public notice (issuance) 360
invisible hand 10
ISO/IEC Guide2:1991 550
Istanbul Programme of Action 634
Italian Agricultural Machinery case 178–179
Italy–Agricultural Machinery 172

J
Jackson, John H. 41
Japan–Agricultural Products II: investigative authority, Appellate Body examination 597–598; SPS Annex B requirements 594; SPS Article 5.7, function 587–588; SPS Article 5.7, qualified exemption operation 588; "sufficient" (meaning) 575–576
Japan–Alcoholic Beverages II 147, 171–178, 180; "likeness," Appellate Body explanation 446; textual basis, absence 175
Japan Alcoholics Beverages I (case) 146
Japan–Apples 96; measure, individual requirements (presence) 576; "relevant scientific evidence," insufficiency 58–589; "scientific"/"evidence," terms (consideration) 575
Japan–DRAMS (Korea): Appellate Body observation 337; CVD imposition, issue 356; "direct transfer of funds" decision 313; "funds" (Appellate Body ruling) 312; "funds" term, Appellate Body interpretation 315–316
Japanese Liquor Tax Law, inconsistency 173
Japan–Film 105
Jefferson, Thomas 474–475
Joint Panels, multiple WTO complaints (relationship) 93–98
judicial economy, exercise 92
judicial review (CVDs) 360–361
jurisdiction, adjudication (exclusive forum) 78–80
jus cogens 646

K
Kennedy Round 37–39, 238, 510; AD code, drafting 380; negotiations 149, 239; political achievement 39
Keynesian economics 25
Keynesian economic thought 22–25
Keynes, John Maynard 22–25; classical economic thought, relationship 22–23; historical background/writings 22; legacy 25; theories 23–25
King Alfonso X, *Livro de als Legies* 47

Kingdom of Saudi Arabia, Article XX(a) invocation 210
Korea–Alcoholic Beverages 176–177
Korea–Certain Paper, domestic AD authority expectations 403
Korea–Commercial Vessels 324; serious prejudice concept, difference 338–339; subsidy, effect 345
Korea–Dairy 49, 92, 280; Appellate Body observations 281–282; Article XIX:1 applicability 283; effectiveness, interpretive principle 530; Korea investigation, inadequacy 282
Korea–Dairy Products, obligations 571–572
Korea, dual retail system 219
Korea–Various Measures on Beef 172, 179, 181–182, 207, 214–215; Appellate Body decisions, reference 540; Appellate Body "necessity" requirement 219; Appellate Body ruling 220; Panel summarisation 439; "treatment no less favourable," Appellate Body interpretation 538

L
labour, division 10–11
labour theory of value 19
laissez passer et laissez faire (let be and let pass) 8
laissez faire doctrine 10
Lamy, Pascal 45–46, 641
"largely self-regulating," phrase (usage) 77
"laws and regulations" concept (broadness) 216–217
League of Nations 34
least developed country (LDC): aid, gaining 613; developing countries, Enabling Clause distinction 151–152; exporters, treatment 634; Member States, impact 469; member states, WTO dispute settlement special rules 116; members, TRIPS Agreement (special rules) 510–511; special treatments 620
"least trade restrictive" (TBT) 542–548
"legitimate objective" (TBT) 543–544
less-developed countries, needs 240
"lesser duty rule" 356, 407
"less favourable treatment" 179, 181, 447
Leutwiler Report 74, 308
Lex Duodecim Tabularum (Twelve Tablets) 47
liberalism 21
licensing requirements and procedures (LRP) 438
"like" domestic products 181
"like" imported products 181
likeness: concept (*Japan–Alcoholic Beverages II*) 147; issue, analysis 187; MFN obligation interpretation 144–147
likeness (WTO era) 146–147
"likeness": concept 174–175; criteria 537–538; determination 188; DSB interpretation 445

"likeness of services," "service suppliers" (distinction) 447
"like product" 537–538; classification 390; definitions, comparison 333
like products: actionable subsidies 332–333; national treatment provisions (GATT) 173–174; price, impact 339–340; question 144
like products (TBT) 537–538
"like product" sale 389–393
"like products" term, usage 180
like services, national treatment obligation (GATS) 186–188
like services (GATS) 445–447
"like" services 188; treatment 157
"like" services, discrimination (prohibition) 154–155
like "services"/like "service suppliers" (most-favoured nation treatment obligation) 156–159
"like service suppliers" 188, 190
"like," term (usage) 147
"limited exception," phrase (usage) 502
limited government (classical liberalism principle) 21
"limiting condition," *India–Quantitative Restrictions* panel usage 257
limiting effect (quantification), non-tariff barriers (NTBs) 259
Lisbon Agreement 497
litigation strategies, Member States adoption 88
Livro de als Legies (1265) 47
local government bodies, defining 529
Lomé Waiver 152
London Conference 169, 201
Long, Russell 141
Lord Hailsham of St Marylebone 47

M
macro-economic policies, impact 294–295
macroeconomic solutions 24
Madison, James 474
Magna Carta 47
"mailbox" mechanism, establishment 481
"major proportion" phrase, interpretation 398
Manifesto of the Communist Party (Marx/Engels) 16
"margin of dumping," "dumping" (meaning agreement) 388
"margins of dumping" calculation 395
Marine Mammal Protection Act (MMPA) 635–636
marine resource management (MRM): hunts, seal product market 536; interests 208
market: competition, intensity 382; geographical limitation, absence 340; geographic dimension, summarization 341; segmentation, national exhaustion (impact) 485
market access (GATS) 440–443; national treatment, relationship 448–449

"market," Panel definition 340
marketplace (competition conditions), Member States alteration (prohibition) 538
Marrakesh Agreement Establishing the World Trade Organization 53, 526; Annex 1A 411; Annex 3, impact 57; Article IV.1 57–58; Article IV.2 (General Council composition) 58–59; foundations 55; impact 41–42, 75; multilateral trade agreements 42; Preamble, recital 631
Marrakesh VIP Treaty (2013) 490
Marshall, Alfred 22
Marx, Karl 16–21
material injury 379; determination 400–403; threat 403–404
"material injury" concept 285
"material injury," SCM Agreement inclusion 335
McCulloch, J.R. 7
McPherson, Isaac 474
"measure at issue," identification 87–88
"Measures by Members" definition 155
medicines (access), TRIPS Agreement (relationship) 644
mega-RTAs 610; emergence 624–625
Méline Tariff (1892) 611
Member's Services Schedule, service sectors exemption 184
Member States: Agreement violation 109; claim, bringing 84; commitment level, WTO requirements 106; complaints 90; dispute settlement system usage 83; disputes, legal submissions 93; domestic market, access (conditioning) 204; export taxes usage 251; legal resources 109; litigation strategies adoption 88; non-complying Member State, goods origination 113; obligations, national policy objectives (balance) 190–191; rights/obligations, preservation 57, 79; risk assessment, Panel review 598; safeguard measures imposition 286; Schedules of Concessions 244; Special Safeguard Measure (SSG) provisions, availability 290; suspended concessions, enforcement 114; trade practices, "adverse effects" 307; TRIPS-plus provisions, introduction 472; WTO classification 114
member states, human rights obligations 642
mercantilism 5–7; cornerstone 5; criticism 7; proper doctrine, recognition 6–7; protectionism, relationship 6; term, usage 5
Mercier de la Rivière, Pierre-Paul 8
Merkantilismus, usage 5
Mexico–Anti-Dumping Measures in Rice: accessible facts, usage 353; ADA Article 11.2, impact 409–410; ADA Articles 3.1/3.2, methodologies (examination) 401; exporter/foreign producers, 30-day period observation 352; SCM Article 12.7 interpretation 354

Mexico–Corn Syrup (Article 21.5–US) 97; Appellate Body ruling 404
Mexico–Corn Syrup, material injury (occurrence) 404
Mexico–Taxes on Soft Drinks 51, 174; "laws or regulations," Appellate Body considerations 217
Mexico–Telecoms 249–250; international long distance telecommunications services, legal issues 456–457; Panel summarisation 439; service supplier operation/presence 434
micro, small, and medium-sized enterprises (MSMEs), support 657
Mill, James 12
Mill, John Stuart 16, 473
"mineral" resources (conservation), limitation (absence) 221
Ministerial Conference (WTO) 57–58
Ministerial Conference in Doha, Ministerial Declaration adoption 504
Ministerial Declaration (1986) 74
Ministerial Declaration on Trade in Information Technology Products (ITA) 240, 245
"minor documentation errors" 264
mixed duties, expression 246
modes of supply (GATS) 433–435
MOFCOM, analysis (requirement) 406
money: commodity function 20; function (Keynes) 23; laundering, combatting 210; theory of rent, relationship 19–21; use, condemnation (Aristotle) 4; wages, elasticity 25
money-commodity-money (M-C-M) 19
Montreal Ministerial Mid-Term Review Conference, trade policy review mechanism (introduction) 40
most-favoured nation (MFN): basis, negotiations 657; concessions 244; core principle 38; exceptions 152–153; principle 37, 145, 611; principle obligation, application 143; quotas 152–153; regional integration 152–153; requirement 266; unconditional MFN treatment 429; waivers 153
most-favoured nation (MFN) obligation (GATS) 153–160; derogation 45, 159–160; like "services"/like "service suppliers" 156–159; treatment "no less favourable" 157–159; treatment obligation (Article II:1) 154–156; treatment obligation (Article II:1), measures 155–156
most-favoured nation (MFN) obligation (GATT) 139–153; interpretation, likeness 144–147; origins 139–141; special/differential treatment 147–152; special/differential treatment (1994) 149–151
most-favoured nation (MFN) obligations 533; application 407–408; presence 431

Index 681

most-favoured nation (MFN) treatment 138, 139, 436; clause, abolition 153; principle, expression 142
most-favoured nation (MFN) treatment obligation 154, 483–485; Appellate Body, impact 534; importance 484; nature (Article I:1) 141–144; NT treatment obligations, relationship 533–542
"movement of consumers" 433
Multi Fibre Arrangement (MFA), protectionism pattern 40
multilateral agreements, motivating factors 614
multilateral disciplines, creation 154
multilateral environmental agreements (MEAs) 630, 636; implementation 639; RTAs, relationship 638–640
multilateral negotiations, failure 656–657
multilateral trade agreements 42
Multilateral Trade Agreements 3623
Multilateral Trade in Goods 42
multilateral trade order 85
multilateral trade rules, improvement 56
multilateral trading system 149; RTAs, relationship 638–640; vision 36
Multi-Party Interim Appeal Arbitration Arrangement (MPIA), EU solution 659–660
multiple WTO complaints, Joint Panels (relationship) 93–98
multiplier effect, providing 141–142
Mun, Thomas 6
"mutually satisfactory adjustments" 85
mutual recognition agreements (MRAs) 5532

N
Nairobi Ministerial Conference 58, 240, 291, 365
NASA, funding (providing) 312
national gains, centralised state power (usage) 6
national income determination, theory 25
national treatment (NT): market access, relationship 448–449; non-discrimination 167; origins/rationale 168–169; treatment obligations 483–485; treatment obligations, MFN obligations (relationship) 533–542
national treatment (NT) (GATS) 443–446; violation, GATS establishment 444–445
national treatment obligation (GATS) 182–191; Article XVII:1 183–185; like services 186–188; service suppliers 186–188; specific commitments, undertaking 185–186; trade in services, measures (impact) 186; treatment no less favourable 188–191; violation 185–191
national treatment obligation (GATT) 42
national treatment (NT) obligations 139, 533; purpose 443; US Omnibus Appropriations Act violation 483
"National Treatment on Internal Taxation and Regulation" 170

national treatment provisions (GATT) 170–182; afforded less favourable treatment 180–182; "aims and effects" test 174–175; "applied so as to afford protection" 177–178; Article III:2 (first sentence/fiscal measures) 172–175; Article III:2 (like products) 173–174; Article III:2 (second sentence) 175–178; Article III:2 (taxed "in excess of") 174; Article III:4 (regulatory measures) 178–182; Article III: Objectives 170–172; *de jure/de facto* discrimination 172; direct/indirect discrimination 172; directly competitive or substitutable concept 176–177; domestic product needs to be "like" 180; law/regulation/requirement affecting the internal sale 178–179; "not similarly taxed" phrase, usage 177
Natural and Essential Order of Political Societies, The (Mercier de la Rivière) 8
Natural Law, minimum content 49
"natural resources" (generic term) 647
natural resources, conservation 224
Nazism, rise 34
"necessary" term, reference 439
"necessity" analysis 229
necessity test 533
necessity test (Article XIV) (GATS) 453–454
negative consensus principle, usage 79
negative dumping margins, zeroing 394
negotiations: multilateral negotiations, failure 656–657; negotiations-based process 88; tariff negotiations, GATT Article XXVII *bis* (relationship) 238–240; trade negotiations, WTO forum 56; Uruguay Round 39–41, 279, 427–428
neoclassical theory (international trade theories) 5
New Delhi Declaration of Principles of International Law Relating to Sustainable Development 634
Newton, Isaac 10
"no less favourable" treatment (most-favoured nation obligation) 157–159
non-actionable subsidies 348; enforcement 348
non-*ad valorem* tariffs 245–246
Non-Agricultural Market Access (NAMA) mandate, recognition 253
non-attribution 288–289; provisions (SCM Agreement Article 15.5) 337; requirements, ADA Article 3.5 establishment 405–406; requirements, expression (absence) 346
non-complying Member State, goods origination 113
non-discrimination 138; ensuring 579; guarantees 642; national treatment 167; obligation, application 152; principle, components 139; principle, MFN concept (rendering) 143; requirement 151

"non-discriminatory," term (usage) 151
non-fulfilment risks, assessment 547
non-governmental organisations (NGOs) 59
"non-living" resources (conservation), limitation (absence) 221
non-market economy (NME): anti-dumping 397; China qualification 397; involvement 408
non-product-related processes and production methods (NPR-PPMs) 528
non-tariff barriers (NTBs) 54, 236; customs-related NTBs 261–266; *de facto* prohibitions/restrictions 259–260; measures 254–261; political economy 254–255; quantitative restrictions (measure at issue), limiting effect (quantification) 259; quantitative restrictions, "restriction" (scope) 257–258; quantitative restrictions, rules/types 255–260
non-tariff measures (NTMs), Member State concessions 244
non-violation complaints (WTO) 84–85; principles 84
"normal value": calculation, ruling 389; production, absence 391
normal value, definition 389–393
normal value (domestic price), export price (difference) 388–397
North American Free Trade Agreement (NAFTA) 610, 612; debate 630; enforcement 639; GATT Article XXIV:5(b) conformity, *prima facie* case 623
North Sea Continental Shelf cases 89
"not more trade restrictive than necessary" (TBT) 544–548
nullification, subsidies (impact) 337–339

O

"only to the extent necessary" (SPS Agreement) 574
On the Principles of Political Economy and Taxation (Principles) (Ricardo) 12, 15
"ordinary course of trade," AD Agreement definition (absence) 392
ordinary customs duties (OCDs) 241
Organisation for Economic Co-operation and Development (OECD) 292, 428; UCFS usage 460
origin-based dual retail distribution system 215
Other Duties and Charges (ODCs) 240–244
"other duties and charges" (ODCs) 241–242
"other measures" reference 256
Ottawa Group proposal 660–661
outcomes, noncompliance 57
"out-of-quota" tariff 247

P

pacta sund servanda rule/principle 51, 297
pandemic, WTO response 660–661
Panels (WTO dispute settlement process): report 97–98; request/terms of reference/establishment 90–93; time scales/working procedures 93–95
parallelism 617
Paris Convention (1893) 471
Paris Convention (1967) 482, 491, 493; Article 6 *bis* protection 494–495
patent: law, challenge 479; laws, preamble (passage) 474; protection 477–478; rights, granting 472–473
patentee, rights (exclusivity) 501
period of investigation (POI) 402
Peru–Agricultural Products 77
Philippines–Distilled Spirits 103, 147, 174, 176–177
Philosophie Rurale (de Miarbeau) 5
physiocrats, emergence 7–9
Pigou, A.C. 22
Pinckney, Charles C. 474
plurilateral consultations, WTO dispute settlement process 90
political opinions/attitudes, changes 21
"positive information" 409
post hoc rationalization 212
post-World War II trade 34–35
power asymmetry, Uruguay Round Preparatory Committee recognition 74
power-oriented diplomacy, GATT adoption 88
precautionary principle, SPS Agreement (relationship) 587–590
pre-classical theories 7–9
predatory pricing 382
preferential concessions 244
Preferential Trade Agreements (PTAs) 152; consistency 622; impact 81
Preferential Treatment for Trade in Frontier Areas (Article II:3)l 159
pre-GATT trade policy concern 250
prejudice, subsidies (impact) 337–339
Preparatory Committee (1947) 142–143
"presence of natural person" 434
present material injury, causation (establishment) 405
pre-shipment inspection (PSI) 264–265
presumption of freedom (classical liberalism principle) 21
pre-World War II trade 34–35
price-based measures 295
price-specie-flow mechanism, usage 7
price suppression 339–340; subsidy, impact 342–343
"price undercutting" 402
price verification (Article 2.20(b)), requirements 264–265
primacy of individual (classical liberalism principle) 21

prima facie case: establishment 96, 297, 554, 623; rebuttal 179
principle of due process 47–48
principle of good faith 50
principles of law, application 95–96
private consultations, WTO dispute settlement process 90
private enterprises, government intervention/monetary support 309
private property, guarantees 642
private rights: economic theories, relationship 472–475; TRIPS Agreement, relationship 64
procedural due process, governance 47
process and production methods (PPM) 528; usage 174
product: "available" for purchase, consideration 228; demand, decline 382; inventories, investigation 404; market, displacement impedance examination 342; markets, existence (assessment) 342
product-by-product negotiations 239
"product characteristics," term (Appellate Body explanation) 534–535
production: factors, usage 11; theory of capitalist form 20
production and process methods (PPMs), basis 633
productivity, enhancement 11
"product market," relevance 339
products/market, competitive relationship (assessment) 341
PROEX 106
profit: rate, defining 14; redistribution 20
prohibited subsidies (red light subsidies) 325–331
"property"/"monopoly," similarity (perception) 477
property/trade/markets (classical liberalism principle) 21
"Proposals for Expansion of World Trade and Employment" 36
proposed alternative measure, impact 546
protectionism 200; *ad hoc* protectionism 378–379; mercantilism, relationship 6
protectionist measures, trigger 277–278
protectionist tool, usage 307
protection of human, animal, or plant life or health, Article XX(b) exceptions (GATT) 210–215
Protocol of Provisional Application (GATT 1947) 261–262
"Protocol of Provisional Application," usage 37
provisional AD measures 406–407
provisional SPS measures, maintenance (Article 5.7 basis) 590
"provision" term, interpretation 317
prudential carve-out (GATS) 159, 459

"public body": concept, Appellate Body examination 323; entity, relationship 324
"public entity," definition 459
public international law (PIL): interpretation, customary rules 186; principles, impact 732
public morals: Article XX(a) exceptions (GATT) 207–210; protection 209–210
"public morals," meaning 207–208
"public order," meaning 207–208
Punta del Este Declaration 40–41

Q

qualification requirement procedures (QRP) 438
quantitative restrictions, prohibition (Article XI:1) 259
Quesnay, François 7–8
quotas (most-favoured nations) 152–153

R

reading materials distribution services 186
Reciprocal Trade Agreement Act (RTAA) 34, 611
reciprocity, establishment 240
Reference Paper, CTS adoption 456–457
Reference Paper on Telecommunications 450
"regime shifting" 471
Regional Comprehensive Economic Partnership (RCEP) 610
Regionalisation Decision (WTO) 593
regionalism, impact 611–612
Regional Trade Agreements (RTAs) 81, 152, 505, 609; Committee on Regional Trade Agreements (CRTAs), notification (obligation) 620–621; customs unions/FTA exceptions (GATT Article XXIV) 614–620; developing country member states, special rules 620; environmental provisions, presence 638; formation 200; GATT/WTO compatibility, assessment 622; history 610–612; interim agreements 619–620; mega-RTAs, emergence 624–625; motivating factors 614; multilateral environmental agreements (MEAs), relationship 638–640; multilateral trading system, relationship 638–640; negotiations 381; parallelism 617; political economy 613–614; proliferation 142, 613; regionalism 610–612; TRIPS-plus provisions, introduction 472; WTO dispute settlement 621–624
"relevant international standard" concept 549
"remedy," definition 414
rent: exclusion 13; theory of rent, money/surplus value (relationship) 19–21
representative government (classical liberalism principle) 21
Res Judicata 46, 51–53
res judicata principle 52
restriction, concept 257

"restriction" (scope), non-tariff barriers (NTBs) 257–258
"Restrictions to Safeguard the Balance of Payments" (GATT 1994 Article XII) 294, 298
"restriction" term (occurrence), Appellate Body (ruling) 258
revenue, foregone or not collected revenue 313–316
revenue "otherwise due," Appellate Body ruling 313
Revision of the Treaty (Keynes)22
Ricardo, David 7, 11–16, 17, 19–20; proposal, UK Parliament adoption 12–13
"right holders," term (inclusiveness) 507
right to work, GATS Agreement (relationship) 644–646
risk assessment: obligation (SPS Agreement) 581–587; types 582
risk management, decisions (involvement) 584
Rome Convention (1967) 485
Roosevelt, Franklin D. 34
Ruggiero, Renato 76
Rule of Law (classical liberalism principle) 21
rule of law, guarantees 642
rules-based dispute settlement system 70, 75
rules-based Dispute Settlement System, adjudication process 48
rules-based international trading system 641–642
rules of origin, agreement 265–266
Rules of Origin (ROO), draft 265–266
Russia–Commercial Vehicles 102

S
safeguard measures: formation (GATT/WTO) 278–279; imposition, political economy reasons 277–278; Member State usage/imposition 284–289; special safeguard measures (agreement on agriculture) 290–291; special safeguard measures (WTO agreements) 290–292
safeguard regime (GATT/WTO) 278–279
safeguards, political economy 277–278
"sanction-based" dispute settlement systems, usage 638
Sanitary and Phytosanitary Measures (SPS) agreements 255
sanitary or phytosanitary protection 587
Schedule of Concessions (GATT Article II) 251–252
Schedules of Commitments 245, 249
Schedules of Commitments of Member States 247
Scheduling Guidelines (2001), paragraph 13 444
Schmoller, Gustav 6
Scottish Enlightenment 9–10
Seattle Ministerial Conference 58

sector-specific commitments 440
security exceptions (GATS) 460–461
self-enforcing agreements 76–77
self-interested behaviour, channeling 10
self-judging clause 210
"serious injury," Article 4.1(a) definition 285
serious prejudice: concept, difference 338–339; forms, cause and effect standard (application) 343; rebuttal 339
"serious prejudice": cause, absence 338; claim (SCM Agreement Article 6.3) 338
services, growth 428
services supplied: definition 434; governmental authority exercise 459
service suppliers (GATS) 445–447; national treatment obligation 186–188
service transaction, physical presence necessity (absence) 427
SGA (Agreement on Safeguards) 276–284
"shallow integration" approach 254
"significant overall impairment," presence (necessity) 285
simple commodity production 19
Singapore Ministerial Conference 58
single-output model 13
single-undertaking approach 149
situation complaints (WTO) 85
Smith, Adam 5–7, 9–11, 17, 23, 473
Smoot-Hawley Tariff Act (1930) 34
social crisis 18–19
social economic welfare 479
social organisations, importance 18
Southerland Report 142
Southern African Development Community (SADC) 610
Southern Common Market (MERCOSUR) 610, 612; Member States, safeguard measures (imposition) 616
Spain–Unroasted Coffee 145–146
"special and differential treatment" 414
special and differential (S&D) treatment, origins 147–148
special and differential treatment (SDT), WTO (relationship) 657–658
"special favourable treatment" 139–140
Special Safeguard Measure (SSG): issuance 291; provisions, availability 290
Special Safeguard Mechanism (SSM) 291
specificity, concept 320–321
"specific measure at issue," identification 87–88
"specific trade concerns" (STCs) 557
spontaneous order (classical liberalism principle) 21
SPS (Agreement on Sanitary and Phytosanitary Measures) 526; Agreement on Government Procurement (AGP), relationship 532; agreements, role 525–526; approval

Index   685

procedures 593–594; arbitrary/unjustifiable discrimination, absence 578–579; Article 2.3 143; Article 5.7 46; Committee on Sanitary and Phytosanitary Measures (SPS Committee), establishment 596–597; control inspection 593–594; dispute settlement 597–599; foreign SPS policy/measures, recognition 591; harmonisation 579–581; international standards 579–581; measure, legal definition 569; "not more trade restrictive than required" 586–587; "only to the extent necessary" 574; precautionary principle, SPS Agreement (relationship) 587–590; protection, appropriate level 584–586; provisional SPS measures, maintenance (Article 5.7 basis) 590; regional conditions, adaptation 591–593; review standard 598–599; risk assessment 581–583; risk assessment basis 583–584; risk assessment obligation 581–587; scientific experts, assistance 597–598; special/differential treatment 595–596; technical assistance 599–600; technical barriers to trade (TBT) 566; transparency/notifications 594–595

SPS (Agreement on Sanitary and Phytosanitary Measures) Agreement 96, 210; Annex 1 568; Annex A, paragraph 1 568–569; Annex B 591, 594; Annex B(5) *Chapeau* 594–595; Annex C 593; Annex C(1)(a) 593–594; Article 2 573; Article 2.2 574–577; Article 2.3 violation, absence 578–579; Article 2.4 571–572; Article 3 573, 579; Article 3.2 580; Article 3.3 481, 577; Article 4 573, 590; Article 4.11 591; Article 5.1 581–582; Article 5.2 581–583; Article 5.4 584–585, 591; Article 5.5 584–585; Article 5.5, inconsistency 585; Article 5.6 574, 586, 591; Article 5.6, alternative measure (*prima facie* case) 587; Article 5.7 577, 587–590; Article 5.7, application (trigger) 589; Article 5.7, clarification 588; Article 5.7, function 587–588; Article 5.7, qualified exemption operation 588; Article 6 573, 591–592; Article 6.1 592; Article 6.2 592; Article 6.3 592–593; Article 7 573, 591, 594; Article 8 593–594; Article 9.1 599; Article 9.2 599–600; Article 10 591; Article 10.1 556; Article 10.3 596; Article 11.1 597; Article 12.1 596; Article 12.2 596–597; Article 12.3 597; Article 12.7 597; Article 14 573; Articles 4.1/4.2 591; institutional provisions 596–600; other substantive provisions 590–596; role 567; scope/application 567–573; substantive provisions 573–590; basic principles 573–579; temporal scope 571; three-tier test 585–586; WTO agreements, relationship 571–573

SPS (Agreement on Sanitary and Phytosanitary Measures) measures: adoption 588–590; Agreement application 568–571; basis 599; consistency, Panel review 598; coverage 624; harmonisation, Article 3 promotion 579; identification 572; product adaptation 579; proliferation 568; scientific basis 574–578; taking (right) 573

Standards and Trade Development Facility (STDF), creation 600

Statute of International Court of Justice (ICJ): Article 38(l) 43; Article 38(l)(a) 44, 45; Article 38(l)(d) 44

Statute of Monopolies (1623) 472–473

sterling standard, dominance 292–293

Stockholm Intergovernmental Conference (1972) 630

stock market crash (1929) 34

"strategic economic sectors" 307

structural modification, occurrence 18

subsidies: benefits 317–320; causation, "but for" approach 344–346; causation, Article 6.3 (relationship) 342–346; commitment schedules, AoA establishment 363; concept 308–325; export subsidies 326–330; export subsidies, nongranting/nonmaintenance 325–326; financial contribution, relationship 309–317; foregone or not collected revenue 313–316; funds, direct transfer 311–313; goods, purchase 316–317; goods/services, provision 316–317; "government or public body," concept 323–325; granting 329; impact 337–339; import displacement/impediment 341–342; import substitution subsidies 330–331; import substitution subsidies, nongranting/nonmaintaining 325–326; injury types 332; market definition 339–341; Member State challenge 338; non-actionable subsidies 348; nullification/impairment/prejudice, impact 337–339; political economy 307–308; prohibited subsidies (red light subsidies) 325–331; provisions (agreement on agriculture) 362–365; provisions (WTO agreements) 362–365; regulation (SCM Agreement) 325–348; rules, GATT (relationship) 365; specificity 320–323; usage, increase (impact) 308

subsidies, actionable subsidies 331–346; domestic industry (definition) 333; domestic industry injury (causing) 332–337; domestic industry injury (identification) 333–337; like products 332–333; special remedies 346–348

subsidies and countervailing measures (SCM) 305; subsidies regulation (SCM Agreement) 325–348

Subsidies and Countervailing Measures (SCM) 43, 44

Subsidies and Countervailing Measures (SCM) Agreement 255, 285; Annex I, export subsidy

686 *Index*

categories 326–327; Annex VII 362; Article 1.1(a)(1) 323; Article 2.1(a) 321–322; Article 2.1(c) 322; Article 2.2 322–323; Article 3.1 325; Article 3.1(a) 327; Article 3.1(b) 330–331; Article 3.2 325–326; Article 5 338–339; Article 5(a) 332; Article 5(b) 337–338; Article 5(c) 339; Article 5, *Chapeau* 331; Article 5, "likeness" (interpretation) 333; Article 6 338; Article 6.2 338–339; Article 6.3 338–339; Article 6.3, "impede" (connotation) 341–342; Article 6.3(c), market (geographical limitation, absence) 340; Article 7 346–347; Article 7.2, consultation request provisions 347; Article 7.8 347–348; Article 8.2(c) 632; Article 9.1(a)-(f) commitment 364; Article 10 349; Article 11.1 349; Article 11.2 348–349; Article 11.4 351; Article 11.6 351; Article 11.9 351; Article 12 351–352; Article 12.3 352; Article 12.4 352; Article 12.5 352; Article 12.7 352–354; Article 15.1 349; Article 15.2 language, impact 334–335; Article 15.3 336; Article 15.4, investigating authority requirement 336–337; Article 15.4 requirements, comparison 335; Article 15.5, non-attribution provisions 337; Article 15.8, special care requirement 336; Article 15, Footnote 46 332–333; Article 15, substantiveness 335–336; Article 16.1 333; Article 19 355–356; Article 19.2 356; Article 19.4 356–357; Article 21.1 357, 363–364; Article 21.2 357–359; Article 21.3 357, 359–360; Article 22.4 360–361; Article 23 361; Article 24 361; Article 25 361; Article 27 361–362; Article 31 338; Article 32 354–355; Articles 11.2/11.3, relationship 350; Articles 21.2/21.3, distinctions 358; *de facto* contingency prohibition 328; footnote 4 language, Panel observation 330; Footnote 11 332; footnote 36 349; Part III, actionable subsidies 331; Part V 332; product market, displacement impedance examination 342; terms, commonalities 324
Subsidies Code (1979): creation, Tokyo Round (impact) 308; SCM Agreement, contrast 308–309
subsidisation: amount, determination 357; "specific measures against" 355
subsidised imports (impact): determination, Article 15.4 investigating authority requirements 336–337; understanding, derivation 335
subsidised imports, injury causation (demonstration) 337
subsidised trade 307–308
subsidized imports (increase determination), Panel details 334
Suggested Charter 168, 307

Suggested Charter for an International Trade Organisation of the United Nations 279
sunset review (CVDs) 359–360; automatic self-initiation 359–360
suppliers, "likeness" 156
supply modes (GATS) 433–435
surplus value: theory 21; theory of rent, relationship 19–21
surplus (*produit net*), yield 8
Sustainable Development Goal 12 (SDG 12), impact 634
sustainable development, WTO (relationship) 633–635
Sutherland Report (2004) 114, 200
système mercantile, usage 5
"system of natural liberty" 10

T
Tableau Economique (Quesnay) 7
"targeted dumping," addressing 396–397
Tariff Act (1922) 141
Tariff Rate Quota (TRQ) 246–247, 263
tariffs: *ad valorem* tariffs 245–246; applied tariffs (actual tariffs) 246–247; barriers 200, 236, 241; bound tariffs 246–247; changes 170; concessions, allowance 145–146; concessions, protection (ODCs) 240–244; customs rules (political economy) 238–250; negotiations, GATT Article XXVIII *bis* (relationship) 238–240; non-*ad valorem* tariffs 245–246; rates, variation 146; reduction, negotiations 71; schedules 245; tariff-only regime, EC introduction 116; types 245–250; values, unevenness 262
taxed "in excess of," national treatment provisions (GATT) 174–175
TBT (Agreement on Technical Barriers to Trade) 525–526; Agreement, Article 2.2 214; agreements 168, 210
TDM Regulation 355
technical assistance (TRIPS) 511
technical barriers to trade (TBT) 43, 168, 524, 566; agreements, role 525–526; Committee on Technical Barriers to Trade (TBT Committee), establishment 557; dispute settlement, TBT Agreement (relationship) 557–558; "existence of relevant international standards" 549–550; "ineffective and inappropriate international standards" 551–552; international standards, usage (obligation) 548–552; international standards "as a basis" for domestic standards 550–551; "least trade restrictive" 542–548; "legitimate objective" 543–544; like products 537–538; MFN treatment obligations, NT treatment obligations (relationship) 533–542; "not

more trade restrictive than necessary" 544–548; performance requirements 553; special/differential treatment 555–556; SPS Agreement 566; technical assistance 558; technical regulations 534–537; transparency/notification 553–555; "treatment no less favourable" 538–542
Technical Barriers to Trade (TBT) 255
technical barriers to trade (TBT) Agreement 211, 572–573; application 529–530; dispute settlement 557–558; equivalence/mutual recognition 552–553; institutional provisions 556–558; other substantive provisions 552–556; principal actors 529; scope/application 526–532; substantive provisions 532–552; temporal scope 529–530; WTO Agreements, relationship 530–532
Technical Barriers to Trade (TBT), Article 2.1 185
technical cooperation: Doha Ministerial Conference emphasis 56; objectives 55–56
technical measures (policy instruments) 525
"technical regulation": applicability, Appellate Body elaboration 534; concept, occurrence 536–537; definition 534; threshold issue 528
technical regulation (consistency), three-tier test (usage) 551
technical regulation, trade-restrictiveness (assessment) 545
technology transfer (TRIPS) 511
telecommunications: liberalisation, Uruguay Round negotiations 455; specific rules (GATS) 455–458
Telmex, COFETEL regulation 457
"temporarily" term, usage 260–261
Thailand–Cigarettes (Philippines) 174, 212, 540; elements, proving 216
Thailand–H-Beams: ADA Article 3, impact 400; ADA Article 5.2, Panel ruling 386
theory of comparative advantage 14–16; demonstration 15
theory of diminishing returns 13–14
theory of national income determination 25
theory of rent, money/surplus value (relationship) 19–21
theory of surplus value 21
third parties (intervenors), DSU interaction 92
"threat to material injury": subsidised imports, impact ("special care" consideration) 336
"threat to material injury," existence determination 335
three-tier approach, development 444–445
three-tier legal standard 221
three-tier test 176, 445, 550–551, 585–586; establishment 535
Tokyo Round 37, 39, 40, 238, 510, 525; agreements 42, 263; "Framework Agreement" 73; impact 308; negotiations 149, 239–240, 380, 427, 620; negotiations, preparatory phase 262; Subsidies Code, drafting history 365; subsidies/CVD usage, contention 307–308
Tokyo Round of Negotiations 262
Tokyo Round Subsidies Agreement 365
Torquay Tariff Conference 238
"to secure compliance," Appellate Body consideration 218–219
Tract on Monetary Reform (Keynes) 23
trade: administration 71; agreements, WTO implementation/administration 55–56; barriers, usage 254; compensatory trade liberalisation 450; distortion, subsidies (impact) 320; diversion, prevention 618; effects test 174; environment, relationship 629; human rights approach 643–644; human rights, relationship 629, 640–648; liberalisation, success 526; negotiations, WTO forum 56; policy disciplines, application 148; policy review (WTO) 57; post-World War II 34–35; pre-classical theories 7–9; pre-World War II 34–35; Regional Trade Agreements (RTAs) 609; retaliations 86; subsidised trade 307–308; technical barriers 524; WTO, relationship 640–648
Trade Act (1974) 110
Trade and Health Initiative, initiation 660–661
Trade in Civil Aircraft 43
trade in services 426; concept, range 435; definition 431; General Agreement on Trade in Services (GATS) 291–292, 298, 426; General Agreement on Trade in Services (GATS) Agreement, relationship 644–646; impact 155; liberalisation, arguments 429
"trade in services" 155, 157
"trade in services," definition 432
trade liberalisation 54, 56; political economy 37; WTO process 14–15
trademarks 490–496; goodwill, attachment 490–491; protection 495
Trade Negotiating Committee (TNC) 640
Trade Policy Review Mechanism (TPRM) 43; administration 55, 57
Trade-Related Investment Measures (TRIMs) agreement 43, 365
transaction, legal characterisation (Appellate Body guidance) 311
transaction-to-transaction (T-T) comparison methodology 395
transaction-to-transaction (T-T) methodology 389
Transatlantic Trade and Investment Partnership (TTIP) 624
Trans-Pacific Partnership (TPP) 638
transparency obligations (GATS) 436–437

travaux préparatoies 242
Travel Act 441
Treaties of Money, The (Keynes) 24
Treatise of Money, The (Keynes) 22
"treatment no less favourable" 158, 188; Appellate Body interpretation 538–542; requirement, interpretation 538–539
Treatment of Prisoners of War (1949) 48
Treaty of Amity and Commerce 140
Treaty of Commerce between Great Britain and France 140
trigger levels (calculation), market access opportunities (basis) 290
TRIMs (Agreement on Trade-Related Investment Measures) 365
TRIPS (Agreement on Trade-Related Aspects of Intellectual Property Rights) 75, 469
TRIPS (Agreement on Trade-Related Aspects of Intellectual Property Rights) Agreement 168; private rights/human rights/medicine access 644
Truman, Harry 70
Trump, Donald (TTIP withdrawal) 624
Turgot, Anne-Robert-Jacques 8–9, 13
Turkey–Textiles 255, 615; Article XI, significance 256; Article XXIV:8(a)(ii) requirement, Appellate Body consideration 617; India challenges 621–622; "substantially all" phrase, interpretation (issue) 616; WTO adjudicating bodies (impact), Panel ruling 622
turtle excluding devices (TEDs) 637
two-tier analysis, Article XIV (GATS) 452–454
two-tiered service supply, establishment 645–646
two-tier test 618; Article XX (GATT) 205–206

U

Ukraine, import surcharge 296
Ukraine–Passenger Cars 286–287
unbound tariffs 143
UN Central Product Classification (CPC): role 432–433; section 6 188
unconditional MFN treatment 429
Understanding on Balance-of-Payments Provisions of the GATT 1994 (Understanding on Balance of Payments) 290, 294; developing country Member State adoption measures 295; paragraph 3 295; prohibitions 296
Understanding on Commitments in Financial Services (UCFS) 459–460
Understanding on Rules and Procedures Governing Settlement of Disputes (DSU) 43, 44, 55, 644
"unfavourable economic climate," Ecuador continuation 296–297
"unforeseen development," Agreement on Safeguards (SGA) 283–284

"unforeseen development" clause, Panel argument rejection 283–284
unilateral retaliation, prevalence 77
"unitary analysis" (Appellate Body observation) 344
United Nations Charter: Article 55 35, 647–648; Article 103 647–648
United Nations Conference on Environment and Development 635
United Nations Conference on Sustainable Development (Rio+20) 633–634
United Nations Conference on Trade and Development (UNCTAD) 38, 148–149, 428, 471
United Nations Conference on Trade and Employment 35
United Nations Covenant on Economic, Social and Cultural Human Rights (ICESCR) 642
United Nations High-Level Political Forum (HLPF) 635
United Nations, human rights regime (remit) 641
United States: European states, economic relationship 140–141; inflation rate, acceleration 294; open borders rhetoric 153
United States-Mexico-Canada Agreement (USMCA) 610, 611
United States Trade Representative (USTR): criticism/proposal rejection 659; empowerment 470–471
United States–Wheat Gluten Safeguard 285
Universal Declaration on Human Rights (UDHR) 640–641
UN Statistics Division (UNSD) 432
Uruguayan Recourse to Article XXIII 72–73
Uruguay Round (of negotiations) 37, 39–41, 238, 427–430; Anti-Dumping Code discussion 381; closing stages 630; conclusion 220, 612; continuation 73; covered agreements, production 75; discrete appellate review stage, suggestion 99; forum shifting (WIPO to GATT) 471–472; HS Convention adoption 245; imbalances, perception 656; lobbying activity level, visibility 428–429; NT objective, attainment 184; post-Uruguay Round of negotiations 142; progress, review 75; services, inclusion 428; SGA negotiations 279; tariff-cutting formula, usage 239; trade in services, discussion 427; TRIPS Agreement, emergence 644
Uruguay Round Agreement on Agriculture (URAA) 247
Uruguay Round of Multilateral Trade Negotiations, results 76
Uruguay Round Preparatory Committee, power asymmetry recognition 74
Uruguay Round Trade Agreements 472

US–1916 Act: ADA Article 1 consideration 385; anti-dumping measure ruling 382; case, Appellate Body finding 355; domestic industry injury 388

US–Animals: Panel view, concurrence 596; SPS Article 3.1, impact 580; SPS Article 6.3, impact 592–593

US Anti-Dumping Act (1916), inconsistency 384–385

US–Anti-Dumping and Countervailing Duties (China): Appellate Body guidance 321; entity, evaluation 324–325; Panel finding, Appellate Body reversal: 323–324

US Appropriations Act, contravention 507

US/Canada–Continued Suspension 577, 579; Appellate body observation 580; Articles 3.1/3.2, emphasis 580; risk assessment, isolation 583; risk, existence (evidentiary basis) 590; scientific controversy, existence (problem) 589–590; SPS Article 5.7 clarification 588; SPS measures, basis 599

US–Carbon Steel 91, 97; investigation (initiation), provisions (purpose) 348; SCM Agreement, Article 21.1 (Appellate Body decision) 357; sunset reviews, automatic self-initiation 359–360

US–Carbon Steel (India) 321; Appellate Body findings 324; Appellate Body observation 310; Article 1.1(b)/Article 14, relationship 319; Articles 21.2/21.3, distinction 358; country of provision, "prevailing market conditions" (Appellate Body observation) 319–320; Panel finding, modification 354; recourse, parameters (clarification) 353; SCM Agreement, Article 15.1, Appellate Body observation 334; SCM Agreement, Article 15.3, Appellate Body observation 336

US–Certain EC Products 79–80

US–Clove Cigarettes 526–527; Appellate Body competition-oriented approach 537–538; "take account of," meaning 556; TBT Agreement, Article 2.8 (purpose) 553; TBT Agreement context/object/purpose, impact 538–539; TBT Agreement interpretation 533; TBT Agreement preamble, Appellate Body observation 531

US Constitution: Article I, Section 8, Clause 8 474; Fifth Amendment 47

US–Continued Zeroing 94; Article 17.6(ii), sequential analysis 412–413

US–COOL 534, 540; Appellate Body ruling 540–541; consumer information, provision, Appellate Body observation 544; detrimental impact, determination 541–542; guidance, providing 543

US–COOL (Article 21.5–Canada and Mexico) 214, 540; non-fulfilment risks, accounting 547; technical regulation, *de facto* detrimental impact (Appellate Body observation) 542; technical regulation, trade restrictiveness (assessment) 546

US Copyright Act, Section 110(5) 490

US–Corrosion-Resistant Steel Sunset Review: dumping/injury, recurrence/continuation (likelihood) 410; zeroing, impact 393

US–Cotton Yarn 106

US–Countervailing Duty Investigation on DRAMS 334–335; evidence, Korea presentation 337

US–Countervailing Measures 321

US–Countervailing Measures (China) (Article 21.5–China) 321

US Declaration of Independence 475

US Department of Commerce (USDOC): attribution issues 356; weighted average-to-transaction comparison methodology usage, determination 395

USDOD, funding (providing) 312

US–DRAMS 86; ADA Article 11.1 interpretation 410; ADA Article 11.1 requirements 409

"used as a basis" term, meaning 550–551

US–FSC 48, 105; Appellate Body guidance 314; double taxation, avoidance (discretion) 315; revenue "otherwise due," Appellate Body ruling 313; SCM Agreement, Article 1 (Panel ruling) 363

US–FSC (Article 21.5) 179, 327–328

US–FSC (Article 21.5–EC) 189; Appellate Body guidance 314

US–Fur Felts Hat (*Hatters Fur* case) 284

US–Gambling 183, 207; Appellate Body findings 215; GATS Article XIV, Appellate Body statement 452; GATS Article XVI:2(a), ambiguity 442; GATS Article XVI function 440–441; GATS exceptions, "necessity" standards (Appellate Body exploration) 453; service commitments, Member State scheduling 432; WTO case 221; zero quota, limitations 442–443

US–Gambling (Article 21.5–Antigua and Barbuda) 113

US–Gambling (Article 22.6–US) 114

US–Gasoline 45, 54, 107, 202–207, 211–212; Appellate Body observation 646; Appellate Body ruling 225; "necessity" requirement 213

US General Accounting Office (GAO), partner selection 613

US–Hot-Rolled Steel: ADA Article 3.5 requirements 405; ADA Article 9.4, Appellate Body observations 408; Japanese exporter, uncooperativeness (US AD authority conclusion) 387–388; non-attribution language, Appellate Body interpretation 406;

"normal value" calculation 392; objective decision making, ensuring 387; Panels task, Appellate Body comparison 412; sale, IA exclusion 389

US–Hot-Rolled Steel from Japan 289

US–Imports of Certain Automotive Spring Assemblies 202

US–Lamb: Appellate Body clarification 289; Appellate Body observations 281–282; "demonstration" 284

US–Large Civil Aircraft (2nd complaint) 102, 321; Appellate Body observations 321–322, 343; "direct transfer of funds," Appellate Body statement 312; market scenario, identification/exploration requirements 346; Panel observation 310; revenue, foregoing 313–314; taxation identification/comparison, limitations (Appellate Body warning) 315; transaction, legal characterisation (Appellate Body guidance) 311

US–Lead and Bismuth II 107–108; Article 21.2 review 359

US–Line Pipe 289; Agreement on Safeguards Article 2.2 ruling, avoidance 623; Appellate Body observation 276–277; injurious condition, continuum (increase) 286; Korea argument 622–623

US–Malt Beverages 174–175

US–Offset Act (Byrd Amendment) 50; Article 11.4 requirements 351; US 1916 Act findings 384

US–Oil Country Tubular Goods Sunset Reviews 387

US–Oil Country Tubular Goods Sunset Reviews (Article 21.5–Argentina) 387

US Omnibus Appropriations Act (1998) 492; NT obligation violation 483

US–Pipes and Tubes (Turkey), Article 12.7 recourse 354

US–Poultry (China) 87; challenge 570–571; discrimination, presence 579; measure (maintenance), scientific evidence (impact) 574–575; SPS Annex A(1), reference 569

US Reciprocal Trade Agreement (1934) 141

US Reciprocal Trade Agreement of 1942 with Mexico, Article XI 279

US–Renewable Energy 179

US–Section 110(5) of the US Copyright Act 488–489

US–Section 211 Appropriation Act 146–147, 492–493; EC argument 483; MFN treatment obligation, importance (emphasis) 484; "right holders," term (inclusiveness) 507; trade names case 482

US–Section 301 Trade Act 96; Panel opinion 643

US–Section 337 180–181

US–Section 337 of the Tariff Act of 1930 212–213, 215

US–Shrimp 54, 80, 107, 202–203, 206; Appellate Body considerations 20; dispute, jurisprudence 637; WTO dispute 224–225

US–Softwood Lumber 52, 104

US–Softwood Lumber III 316–317

US–Softwood Lumber IV: Appellate Body distinctions 310; dispute, complexity 316; "financial contribution," Appellate Body determination 311; "goods"/"provision" terms, interpretation 317; input products, subsidy (conferring) 318

US–Softwood Lumber IV (Article 21.5–Canada) 112

US–Softwood Lumber V 350; IA comparisons, results 395

US–Softwood Lumber V (Article 21.5–Canada) 395

US–Softwood Lumber VI (Article 21.5–Canada) 112

US–Softwood Lumber VI, Article 15.8 requirements (examination) 336

US Special Committee on Relaxation of Trade Barriers, interim report 250

US–Stainless Steel: Appellate Body ruling 395; exporter dumping determination 388

US–Steel Plate, Panel ruling 413–414

US–Steel Safeguards 104, 281–282; Appellate Body observation 284

US *Suggested Charter* 148

US–Supercalendered Paper 353; subsidisation amount, determination 357

US–Superfund 73

US–Taxes on Automobiles 175

US–Tax Incentives 326

US Trade Act (1974) 74–75

US Trade and Competitiveness Act (1988) 74–75

US–Tuna I (Mexico): dispute 635; jurisprudence 635–636

US–Tuna II (Mexico) 107, 212, 527–528, 540–544; importance 531; international body recognition 550; international standard 549; jurisprudence 636; Panel conclusion, Appellate Body agreement 535–536; "treatment no less favourable" requirement (Article 2.1) 539–540

US–Upland Cotton 116; Article 21.1, application 364; Brazil challenge 362; cause and effect 343–344; export subsidies/import substitution subsidies, issues 363; "market," Panel definition 340; non-attribution requirements, expression (absence) 346; Panel opinion 321; price suppression 342; "relationship of conditionality or dependence" (Appellate Body observation) 328; "unitary analysis" (Appellate Body observation) 344; US argument, Appellate Body rejection 325

US–Upland Cotton (Article 21.5–Brazil): adverse effects, removal 347–348; causation, establishment 344; "cause" (Appellate Body observation) 342–343; cause and effect standard 343; dispute settlement issues 347

US–Washing Machines: Appellate Body conclusion 322–323; Appellate Body observations 384; Korea challenge 395; "tying" findings, review 356; US argument, Appellate Body rejection 396–397; zeroing, Article 2.4.2 contemplation 396

US–Wheat Gluten 282; cause and effect ("genuine and substantial relationship"), existence (need) 288; Panel interpretation, Appellate Body reversal 286, 288–289; safeguard measures 406; US actions, inconsistency 616–617

US–Wool Shirts and Blouses 84, 86, 92, 95; Appellate Body statement, usage 297

US–Zeroing (Japan) (Article 21.5–Japan) 110

US–Zeroing (EC), Appellate Body ruling 395

US–Zeroing (Japan), Appellate Body ruling 395

utilitarianism 473

V

value: labour theory of value 13, 19; surplus value, theory of rent (relationship) 19–21

Vienna Convention on the Laws of Treaties 1969 (VCLT) 45, 49, 59, 205; Article 28 530; Article 31(4) 249–250; Article 31(c)(3) 638; Articles 31–33 247–248; consideration 222–223; trade names, consistency 482; treaty interpretation 248–249

Vienna Convention on the Laws of Treaties 1969 (VCLT)usage 412

Vienna Declaration and Programme of Action, adoption 642

violation complaints (WTO) 83–84

W

Waiver Decision on Preferential Tariff Treatment for Least Developed Countries (1999) 153

waivers (most-favoured nations) 153

wealth maximisation 478

Wealth of Nations (Smith) 5–6

weighted average-to-transaction (W-T) comparison methodology 389; USDOC usage determination 395

weighted average-to-weighted average (W-W) methodology 389

weighted social welfare function, maximisation 277

whole economic system, presentation 13

wholesale transactions, nature/characteristics 186–187

Wire Act 441

Working Group on Financial Services, meeting 459

Working Party on Border Taxes report, usage 145

Working Party on Domestic Regulation (WPDR) 438

Working Party on Professional Services (WPPS), establishment 438

World Bank (WB) 40; charter, establishment 35

World Conference on Human Rights 642

World Customs Organization (WCO) tariff schedule 244

World Intellectual Property Organization (WIPO): Conventions, TRIPS Agreement (relationship) 482–483; creation 471; GI registration 496–497

World Intellectual Property Organization Copyright Treaty (WTC) 490

World Intellectual Property Organization Performances and Phonograms Treaty (WPPT) 490

"world market," nonexistence 340

World Organisation for Animal Health (OIE), Terrestrial Code 580

World Trade Organization (WTO) 33; accessions, export duty explanations 251; adjudication, exclusive forum 78–80; adjudicatory bodies, reaction 647; agreement on agriculture, special safeguard measures 290–291; agreement on agriculture, subsidies provisions 362–365; Agreement on Government Procurement (AGP), SPS Agreement (relationship) 532; Agreement on Textiles and Clothing 95; agreements 244, 632; agreements, obligations (non-compliance) 647; Agreements, TBT Agreement (relationship) 530–532; anti-dumping legal framework 382–406; applied tariff (actual tariff) 246–247; Article 21.3 DSU, extension 110–111; Article 21.5 DSU, compliance review 111–113; Article 22, remedies 113–114; Article XXIII(1) 83–85; bound tariffs 246–247; claims, categories 83–85; commitments schedules, DSB interpretation 247–250; Committee on Safeguards, function 282; concession schedules 244–245; consensus-driven decision making 657–658; countries, accession 56; creation 56; dispute, agreements/provisions 82; dispute, legal basis 82–83; dispute settlement mechanism 106; due process 46, 47–49; dumping law 379–382; economic principles, basis 4; environment, relationship 631–633; establishment, Marrakesh Agreement (impact) 41–42; establishment, proposal 41; estoppel 46, 51–53; functions 55–57; GATT evolution 37–42; General Council, meetings 58–59; General Council, role 78; goals 641; good faith (*bona fide*) 46, 49–51; goods, classification (schedules) 244–245; implementation/ compliance review 109–114; jurisdiction 78–80; jurisdiction, limitation 646–647; jurisprudence 306; legal framework, dumping

692 *Index*

(relationship) 382; legal system, benefits 76; likeness 146–147; mandate 53–59; Member States, GATS (impact) 645; Member State, trade practices ("adverse effects") 307; Ministerial Conference 57–58; Ministerial Declaration on Trade in Information Technology Products (ITA) 240; multilateral negotiations, failure 656–657; Multi-Party Interim Appeal Arbitration Arrangement (MPIA), EU solution 659–660; negotiated agreement, violation 77; non-tariff barriers (NTBs), political economy 254–255; non-violation complaints 84–85; objectives 53–54; origins 35–37; pandemic response 660–661; Preamble 53–54; Preamble, usage 631–632; reform 655; Regionalisation Decision 593; *Res Judicata* 46, 51–53; RTA dispute settlement 621–624; rules, conformity 57; safeguard measures, formation 278–279; safeguard regime 278–279; self-enforcing mechanism 76–77; situation complaints 85; Special Report (30 September 1996) 76; sustainable development 633–635; tariff negotiations 238; Technical Barriers to Trade (TBT) 255; technical cooperation, objectives 55–56; Trade Negotiating Committee (TNC) 640; violation/breach, establishment 84; violation complaints 83–84; working practice 657–658; *Working Procedures*, improvement 56; WTO-minus provisions 624

World Trade Organization (WTO) Agreement 45–46, 281; Annex 1A 243; Annex 1A, interpretive note 571; Annex 1A, Multilateral Trade Agreements 363; Annex 2, "Understanding on the Rules and Procedures Governing the Settlement of Disputes" (DSU) 75; Article IV(3) 78, 85–86; Article XVI:1 76; divisions 42–43; preamble 75–76

World Trade Organization (WTO) agreements: human rights, relationship 644–648; special safeguard measures 290–292; SPS Agreement, relationship 571–573; subsidies provisions 362–365

World Trade Organization (WTO) dispute settlement 56–57, 69, 75–76; Appellate Body 98–101; Appellate Body, historical background 98–100; Appellate Body, nature/composition 100–101; Appellate review 101–106; Appellate review, new evidence/arguments (receipt) 104–105; Appellate review, new issues review 104–105; Appellate review process, scope/remit 105–106; Appellate review, structure/scope/timeframe 101–104; burden of proof 95–97; consultation 86–90; consultation, failure/period 89–90; consultation phase, nature/features 88–89; developing countries, relationship 114–117; developing countries, special/differential treatment 115; Dispute Settlement Understanding (DSU) (WTO) 46–49, 76–80, 110–113; entities 109; features 106–109; joint panels 93–98; multiple complaints 93–98; Panels report 97–98; Panels request/terms of reference/establishment 90–93; Panels time scales/working procedures 93–95; plurilateral/private consultations 90; pre-dispute settlement *Amicus curiae* briefs 106–109; process, stages (DSB involvement) 85–106; recourse 80–85; recourse, special/additional rules 81; system 75

World Trade Organization (WTO) law 42–53; general principles of law, relationship 46–53; human rights, relationship 643–644; international law, relationship 45–46; sources 43–44

World Trade Organization (WTO) trade: agreement implementation/administration 55–56; negotiation forum 56; policy review 57

Y

yellow light subsidies 331–346

Z

zeroing 393–397; impact 393–394; meaning 395

zero quota, limitations 442–443